P9-DZA-382

BELMONT UNIVERSITY LIBRARY

International Directory of
COMPANY
HISTORIES

Ref
HD
2721
D36
v.75

International Directory of

COMPANY

HISTORIES

VOLUME 75

Editor

Jay P. Pederson

ST. JAMES PRESS

An imprint of Thomson Gale, a part of The Thomson Corporation

THOMSON

™

GALE

Detroit • New York • San Francisco • San Diego • New Haven, Conn. • Waterville, Maine • London • Munich

Ws

THOMSON
★
GALE

International Directory of Company Histories, Volume 75
Jay P. Pederson, Editor

Project Editor
Miranda H. Ferrara

Editorial
Virgil Burton, Donna Craft, Louise Gagné,
Peggy Geeseman, Julie Gough, Linda Hall,
Sonya Hill, Keith Jones, Lynn Pearce,
Maureen Puhl, Holly Selden,
Justine Ventimiglia

Imaging and Multimedia
Lezlie Light, Michael Logusz

Manufacturing
Rhonda Dover

Product Manager
Gerald L. Sawchuk

© 2006 Thomson Gale, a part of The Thomson Corporation.

Thomson and Star Logo are trademarks and Gale and St. James Press are registered trademarks used herein under license.

For more information contact
St. James Press
27500 Drake Rd.
Farmington Hills, MI 48331-3535
Or you can visit our Internet site at
http://www.gale.com/stjames

ALL RIGHTS RESERVED
No part of this work covered by the copyright hereon may be reproduced or used in any form or by any means—graphic, electronic, or mechanical, including photocopying, recording, taping, Web distribution, or information storage retrieval systems—without the written permission of the publisher.

For permission to use material from this product, submit your request via Web at http://www.gale-edit.com/permissions, or you may download our Permissions Request form and submit your request by fax or mail to:

Permissions Department
Thomson Gale
27500 Drake Rd.
Farmington Hills, MI 48331-3535
Permissions Hotline:
248-699-8006 or 800-877-4253, ext. 8006
Fax: 248-699-8074 or 800-762-4058

Cover photograph (Michigan Avenue, Chicago) courtesy of Chicago Convention and Tourism Bureau.

While every effort has been made to ensure the reliability of the information presented in this publication, Thomson Gale does not guarantee the accuracy of the data contained herein. Thomson Gale accepts no payment for listing; and inclusion of any organization, agency, institution, publication, service, or individual does not imply endorsement of the editors or publisher. Errors brought to the attention of the publisher and verified to the satisfaction of the publisher will be corrected in future editions.

LIBRARY OF CONGRESS CATALOG NUMBER 89-190943
ISBN: 1-55862-579-8

BRITISH LIBRARY CATALOGUING IN PUBLICATION DATA
International directory of company histories. Vol. 75
I. Jay P. Pederson
33.87409

Printed in the United States of America
10 9 8 7 6 5 4 3 2 1

CONTENTS

PREFACE

The St. James Press series *The International Directory of Company Histories (IDCH)* is intended for reference use by students, business people, librarians, historians, economists, investors, job candidates, and others who seek to learn more about the historical development of the world's most important companies. To date, *IDCH* has covered over 7,650 companies in 75 volumes.

Inclusion Criteria

Most companies chosen for inclusion in *IDCH* have achieved a minimum of US$25 million in annual sales and are leading influences in their industries or geographical locations. Companies may be publicly held, private, or nonprofit. State-owned companies that are important in their industries and that may operate much like public or private companies also are included. Wholly owned subsidiaries and divisions are profiled if they meet the requirements for inclusion. Entries on companies that have had major changes since they were last profiled may be selected for updating.

The *IDCH* series highlights 10% private and nonprofit companies, and features updated entries on approximately 50 companies per volume.

Entry Format

Each entry begins with the company's legal name, the address of its headquarters, its telephone, toll-free, and fax numbers, and its web site. A statement of public, private, state, or parent ownership follows. A company with a legal name in both English and the language of its headquarters country is listed by the English name, with the native-language name in parentheses.

The company's founding or earliest incorporation date, the number of employees, and the most recent available sales figures follow. Sales figures are given in local currencies with equivalents in U.S. dollars. For some private companies, sales figures are estimates and indicated by the abbreviation *est.* The entry lists the exchanges on which a company's stock is traded and its ticker symbol, as well as the company's NAIC codes.

Entries generally contain a *Company Perspectives* box which provides a short summary of the company's mission, goals, and ideals, a *Key Dates* box highlighting milestones in the company's history, lists of *Principal Subsidiaries, Principal Divisions, Principal Operating Units, Principal Competitors,* and articles for *Further Reading.*

American spelling is used throughout *IDCH*, and the word "billion" is used in its U.S. sense of one thousand million.

Sources

Entries have been compiled from publicly accessible sources both in print and on the Internet such as general and academic periodicals, books, annual reports, and material supplied by the companies themselves.

Cumulative Indexes

IDCH contains three indexes: the **Index to Companies**, which provides an alphabetical index to companies discussed in the text as well as to companies profiled, the **Index to Industries**, which allows researchers to locate companies by their principal industry, and the **Geographic Index**, which lists companies alphabetically by the country of their headquarters. The indexes are cumulative and specific instructions for using them are found immediately preceding each index.

Suggestions Welcome

Comments and suggestions from users of *IDCH* on any aspect of the product as well as suggestions for companies to be included or updated are cordially invited. Please write:

The Editor
International Directory of Company Histories
St. James Press
27500 Drake Rd.
Farmington Hills, Michigan 48331-3535

St. James Press does not endorse any of the companies or products mentioned in this series. Companies appearing in the *International Directory of Company Histories* were selected without reference to their wishes and have in no way endorsed their entries.

AB	Aktiebolag (Finland, Sweden)
AB Oy	Aktiebolag Osakeyhtiot (Finland)
A.E.	Anonimos Eteria (Greece)
AG	Aktiengesellschaft (Austria, Germany, Switzerland, Liechtenstein)
A.O.	Anonim Ortaklari/Ortakligi (Turkey)
ApS	Amparteselskab (Denmark)
A.Š.	Anonim Širketi (Turkey)
A/S	Aksjeselskap (Norway); Aktieselskab (Denmark, Sweden)
Ay	Avoinyhtio (Finland)
B.A.	Buttengewone Aansprakeiijkheid (The Netherlands)
Bhd.	Berhad (Malaysia, Brunei)
B.V.	Besloten Vennootschap (Belgium, The Netherlands)
C.A.	Compania Anonima (Ecuador, Venezuela)
C. de R.L.	Compania de Responsabilidad Limitada (Spain)
Co.	Company
Corp.	Corporation
CRL	Companhia a Responsabilidao Limitida (Portugal, Spain)
C.V.	Commanditaire Vennootschap (The Netherlands, Belgium)
G.I.E.	Groupement d'Interet Economique (France)
GmbH	Gesellschaft mit beschraenkter Haftung (Austria, Germany, Switzerland)
Inc.	Incorporated (United States, Canada)
I/S	Interessentselskab (Denmark); Interesentselskap (Norway)
KG/KGaA	Kommanditgesellschaft/Kommanditgesellschaft auf Aktien (Austria, Germany, Switzerland)
KK	Kabushiki Kaisha (Japan)
K/S	Kommanditselskab (Denmark); Kommandittselskap (Norway)
Lda.	Limitada (Spain)
L.L.C.	Limited Liability Company (United States)
Ltd.	Limited (Various)
Ltda.	Limitada (Brazil, Portugal)
Ltee.	Limitee (Canada, France)
mbH	mit beschraenkter Haftung (Austria, Germany)
N.V.	Naamloze Vennootschap (Belgium, The Netherlands)
OAO	Otkrytoe Aktsionernoe Obshchestve (Russia)
OOO	Obschestvo s Ogranichennoi Otvetstvennostiu (Russia)
Oy	Osakeyhtiö (Finland)
PLC	Public Limited Co. (United Kingdom, Ireland)
Pty.	Proprietary (Australia, South Africa, United Kingdom)
S.A.	Société Anonyme (Belgium, France, Greece, Luxembourg, Switzerland, Arab speaking countries); Sociedad Anónima (Latin America [except Brazil], Spain, Mexico); Sociedades Anônimas (Brazil, Portugal)
SAA	Societe Anonyme Arabienne
S.A.R.L.	Sociedade Anonima de Responsabilidade Limitada (Brazil, Portugal); Société à Responsabilité Limitée (France, Belgium, Luxembourg)
S.A.S.	Societá in Accomandita Semplice (Italy); Societe Anonyme Syrienne (Arab speaking countries)
Sdn. Bhd.	Sendirian Berhad (Malaysia)
S.p.A.	Società per Azioni (Italy)
Sp. z.o.o.	Spólka z ograniczona odpowiedzialnoscia (Poland)
S.R.L.	Società a Responsabilità Limitata (Italy); Sociedad de Responsabilidad Limitada (Spain, Mexico, Latin America [except Brazil])
S.R.O.	Spolecnost s Rucenim Omezenym (Czechoslovakia)
Ste.	Societe (France, Belgium, Luxembourg, Switzerland)
VAG	Verein der Arbeitgeber (Austria, Germany)
YK	Yugen Kaisha (Japan)
ZAO	Zakrytoe Aktsionernoe Obshchestve (Russia)

$	United States dollar	ISK	Icelandic krona
£	United Kingdom pound	ITL	Italian lira
¥	Japanese yen	JMD	Jamaican dollar
AED	Emirati dirham	KPW	North Korean won
ARS	Argentine peso	KRW	South Korean won
ATS	Austrian shilling	KWD	Kuwaiti dinar
AUD	Australian dollar	LUF	Luxembourg franc
BEF	Belgian franc	MUR	Mauritian rupee
BHD	Bahraini dinar	MXN	Mexican peso
BRL	Brazilian real	MYR	Malaysian ringgit
CAD	Canadian dollar	NGN	Nigerian naira
CHF	Swiss franc	NLG	Netherlands guilder
CLP	Chilean peso	NOK	Norwegian krone
CNY	Chinese yuan	NZD	New Zealand dollar
COP	Colombian peso	OMR	Omani rial
CZK	Czech koruna	PHP	Philippine peso
DEM	German deutsche mark	PKR	Pakistani rupee
DKK	Danish krone	PLN	Polish zloty
DZD	Algerian dinar	PTE	Portuguese escudo
EEK	Estonian Kroon	RMB	Chinese renminbi
EGP	Egyptian pound	RUB	Russian ruble
ESP	Spanish peseta	SAR	Saudi riyal
EUR	euro	SEK	Swedish krona
FIM	Finnish markka	SGD	Singapore dollar
FRF	French franc	THB	Thai baht
GRD	Greek drachma	TND	Tunisian dinar
HKD	Hong Kong dollar	TRL	Turkish lira
HUF	Hungarian forint	TWD	new Taiwan dollar
IDR	Indonesian rupiah	VEB	Venezuelan bolivar
IEP	Irish pound	VND	Vietnamese dong
ILS	new Israeli shekel	ZAR	South African rand
INR	Indian rupee	ZMK	Zambian kwacha

International Directory of
COMPANY HISTORIES

A. Nelson & Co. Ltd.

Broadheath House
83 Parkside
Wimbledon
London SW19 5LP
United Kingdom
Telephone: +44-20-8780-4200
Fax: +44-20-8780-5871
Web site: http://www.nelsonbach.com

Private Company
Incorporated: 1860
Employees: 163
Sales: £38.1 million ($65 million) (2003)
NAIC: 325411 Medicinal and Botanical Manufacturing

A. Nelson & Co. Ltd., doing business as Nelsons, is the United Kingdom's oldest producer and distributor of homeopathic medicines, and is also a leading producer and distributor of a variety of herbal and alternative medicines and preparations. The Wimbledon-based company markets a full range of homeopathic medicines under the Nelson brand name. These are sold under three main categories: Creams, including topical applications ranging from Calendula to Tea Tree and Rhus Tox, as well as spray-on forms, including the company's Pyrethrum spray; the Nelsons Formulated range, ready-made remedies targeted at specific illnesses and marketed under names such as Candida, Coldenz, Rheumatic, Sootha, Travella, and Teetha; and the Clikpak range, which presents the company's formulations in the form of small tablets and pills. A major segment of A. Nelson & Co. is its production of Bach's Flower Remedies, a system of tinctures created by Dr. Edward Bach in the 1930s, which treated emotional conditions as a cause of illness. A. Nelson also markets a number of other natural preparations, such as Spatone, acquired by the company in 2004. In addition to its production of homeopathic and alternative medicines, Nelsons continues to operate its original pharmacy in London. A. Nelson & Co. is a privately held company controlled by the Wilson family.

U.K. Homeopathic Pioneer in the 19th Century

Homeopathic medicine was developed in the late 18th century by Dr. Samuel Hahnemann of Germany. Appalled by the standard medical practices of the day, which included leeching, blood letting, dangerous purgatives, and toxic "medicines," among other treatments, Hahnemann sought an alternative method for treating patients. A botanist and chemist who also had trained as a physician, Hahnemann eventually left medical practice, and began working as a translator instead. It was while translating medical documents that Hahnemann first found mention that quinine, an effective malaria treatment, was capable of producing similar symptoms in uninfected people.

This information came in large part from Dr. Edward Cullen, of Scotland, who argued that quinine's effectiveness against the disease, and its side-effects in healthy people, were due to its astringent properties. Hahnemann disagreed, pointing out that other substances also had astringent properties, but had no effect on the disease nor caused similar symptoms to develop in the uninfected. Hahnemann instead deduced that quinine's ability to provoke the same symptoms was related to its effectiveness as a cure.

Hahnemann decided to test his theory on himself, taking large doses of quinine, and indeed developed symptoms similar to malaria (although without the associated fever). From this and subsequent tests, called "proving," of the effects of other substances on himself and others, Hahneman developed the notion of "like cures like" that formed the basis of a new medical discipline, homeopathy (from the Greek homeo, or "similar," and pathy, or "suffering"). Hahnemann's idea was not necessarily new. Indeed, mention of related ideas had been found in text dating back thousands of years. Yet Hahnemann, who already enjoyed a certain standing for his work as a chemist, brought a different credibility to the "like cures like" idea.

Hahnemann set out developing a compendium of substances and the symptoms they provoked. As most of these substances were by nature poisonous (innocuous substances did not tend to exhibit quite the same ability to provoke physical symptoms), however, Hahnemann was forced to find ways of diluting the substances. Eventually, he invented a dilution method that in-

Company Perspectives:

Nelsons Philosophy: Nelsons believes passionately in the importance of holistic healthcare and the increasing role that complementary medicine can play in an integrated healthcare system. Our goal is to help people and other living beings enjoy healthier and happier lives through our range of natural products.

volved dissolving substances in water or crushing them into powder, then mixing them in alcohol, and finally diluting the mixture to an extreme, to the point at which the original substance was no longer actually present in the solution. Faced with this conundrum, Hahneman proposed the second basic concept of homeopathy, that the more a substance is diluted, the greater its effectiveness.

Hahnemann, who later moved to Paris, devoted himself to the promulgation of his ideas, writing extensively, both for the medical community and, of importance, for the general public as well. Hahnemann also took in a great many students, whether these were trained medical practitioners or not, who then joined in the effort (some called them disciples) to promote the new medical treatment. The fact that many of Hahnemann's ideas had long been in existence, in one form or another, and even were part of traditional culture, provided an undercurrent of respectability to the new discipline. Hahnemann's stature, and that of his medical ideas, were further enhanced as he developed a clientele including many notable figures of the day.

Meanwhile, Hahnemann continued to develop the basic principles of homeopathy. The third and final of these was based on the concept of ''psora,'' literally a suppressed itch, which Hahnemann felt to exist at the root of all disease. Homeopathic medicine, Hahnemann reasoned, must, therefore, target the patient's psora. As these were said to vary from patient to patient, individualized treatment became a necessary part of homeopathic medicine. Because of the highly spiritual element underlying the concept of psora, this principle was less widely accepted among the growing body of homeopathic practitioners, even in Hahnemann's day. Nonetheless, a ''holistic'' and individualized approach became a consistent part of homeopathic therapies. The idea of a metaphysical component to disease also would play a role in the work of Edward Bach and others.

Given the rather barbaric status of ''mainstream'' medical practice of the day, homeopathic medicine caught on widely in Europe in the early 19th century, and quickly spread to the United States as well. The lack of knowledge in many now basic areas of biology and chemistry, such as the role of bacteria and viruses in the cause of disease (an example of which was the palludium virus, carried by mosquitoes, in the case of malaria), allowed a certain plausibility to homeopathy. By the middle of the 19th century, homeopathy had been introduced in the United Kingdom, which at the time played a central role in the rapid development of modern science.

Efforts were made to ban the practice of homeopathy into the mid-19th century, as its basic principles were called into question. Yet homeopathy's ''gentler'' nature, since a homeo-

pathic treatment in substance consisted of little more than drinking water, contrasted sharply with the far harsher medicines then available. The appeal of nonpainful treatments, coupled with the decidedly spiritual aspects of homeopathy and its apparent ability to effectuate spontaneous healing, proved irresistible to the British public as well.

Hahnemann died in 1843 at the age of 88. By then, homeopathic medicine had taken on a life of its own, developing its own body of literature and professional associations. By the mid-19th century, the first schools of homeopathic medicine also had begun to appear. Hahnemann himself had been responsible for training a large number of students in homeopathy as well, and many others embraced Hahnemann as their spiritual teacher. Among the many students of homeopathy was Ernst Louis Ambrecht, who set up shop as a homeopathic pharmacist in London in 1860. The role of the pharmacist had been disputed by Hahnemann himself, who declared that homeopathic medicines should only be prepared by the treating physician. Yet by the middle of the century, the preparation of homeopathic medicines had become, in large part, the province of pharmacists such as Ambrecht.

Bach Association in the 1930s

Ambrecht later brought his son, Nelson, into the business. Under the younger Ambrecht, the pharmacy became known as A. Nelson & Co. By the early 20th century, the company had become one of the leading producers of homeopathic medicines. By then, however, the practice of homeopathy had lost much of its following; by the 1930s, some were even willing to declare the ''death'' of homeopathy. The development of modern scientific methods, the greater understanding of what are now considered basic medical principles, the creation of new types of more effective and less painful drugs, and other advancements, had cast a large shadow over homeopathy. A large part of homeopathy's decline at the time was also political. As the modern medical community developed in strength and, especially, in empirical proof, efforts were made to negate and discredit other medical methods, which were now considered as ''alternative'' treatments.

Homeopathy had long inspired the development of other alternative medicines and treatments. Among these was a system of so-called ''flower remedies'' developed by Dr. Edward Bach in the late 1920s and early 1930s. Born in 1886, Bach had been trained as a physician at the University College Hospital in London, and had begun working in the field of immunology. This led Bach to an interest in homeopathy, and in 1919, he began working at the Royal London Homeopathic Hospital.

Bach soon developed his own system based on homeopathic thought. In what seems to be a derivation of Hahnemann's identification of psoras, Bach determined that physical health conditions were manifestations of emotional imbalance, and that by treating a patient's negative state of mind, one might influence his or her physical health. By the late 1920s, Bach had completed the first part of his work, that of the creation of a system of ''nosodes,'' that is, groupings of emotional problems, such as uncertainty, over-sensitivity, loneliness, lassitude, and the like. Bach initially developed homeopathic treatments for the nosodes.

Key Dates:

1860: Ernst Louis Ambrecht founds a pharmacy in London and begins producing homeopathic medicines; he is later joined by his son, Nelson, who changes the company name to A. Nelson & Co.

1933: Nelson becomes one of only two distributors of Bach's Flower Remedies.

1991: Nelson reaches agreement to bottle and distribute Bach's Flower Remedies.

1993: Nelson acquires Bach Centre, which becomes Nelsonbach.

1999: Nelson loses the trademark right to the Bach name.

2005: Nelsonbach becomes Nelsons.

According to Bach, patients with similar emotional difficulties, while manifesting quite different physical symptoms, were all treatable by using the treatments from within the same nosode. Yet Bach, brought up in the Birmingham countryside, soon began seeking to develop his own class of treatments based on flowers or, more specifically, based on morning dew collected from the petals of flowers. Bach began his work in 1928, and in 1930 moved to the Oxford countryside in order to devote himself to the development of his "flower remedies."

By 1935, Bach had completed a system of 38 flower remedies, noting the precise location and variety of flowers from the gathered dew. Bach also tested his remedies on himself, considering a substance effective if it produced one of the emotional conditions described by the nosodes. Meanwhile, Bach also developed his own preparation method. Bach ultimately hit on an extremely simple method in large part because, like Hahnemann, he intended for his remedies to be individually prepared by the physician for each patient. Dew collected from flowers was either allowed to dry in the sun, or boiled. The remaining "tincture" (called the Mother Tincture by the later Bach society) was then mixed into brandy or alcohol and "sucussed" (that is, shaken) a specific number of times. As with homeopathic medicines, the tincture was then extremely diluted.

The dilution process, as in the case of homeopathic medicine in general, presented a specific advantage: Very small quantities of raw material were required to produce extremely large quantities of final product. By weight, therefore, homeopathic medicines were among the most valuable substances in the history of mankind. This fact made them ideal candidates for becoming consumer products. Bach himself seemed to recognize this, creating one of the most enduring Bach "remedies," the Rescue Remedy, which contained a mixture of flower essences to be taken in the case of emotional emergency.

Despite the ease of preparation for Bach's Flower Remedies, as they came to be called, Bach, who began promoting his ideas and remedies through a series of writings, recognized that many practitioners and their customers would be interested in purchasing the remedies ready-made. Already by 1933, Bach had reached an agreement with two London-based pharmacists to produce quantities of the remedies. A. Nelson & Co. was to become the most enduring partner for the company. Bach him-

self died at the age of 50 in 1936; the Bach Centre, in Mount Vernon, however, carried on his work, and remained the source of the "Mother Tinctures."

Alternative Interest in the New Century

The late 20th century saw an upsurge in interest in alternative medicines, which coupled a distrust in modern medicine's symptom-specific approach with the rising interest in so-called "new age" religion and philosophies. Homeopathic medicine enjoyed a renewed respectability in the United Kingdom, in part because of the government's acceptance of homeopathic preparations as medicines, which were then introduced as part of the National Health System.

This in turn led to a greater acceptance of other alternative therapies, including Bach's Flower Remedies. By the early 1990s, demand for Bach's Flower Remedies had begun to outpace the Bach Centre's ability to produce, bottle, and distribute the remedies. In 1991, the Bach Centre turned to longtime partner A. Nelson & Co. for help. A partnership was reached in which Nelson took over bottling, distribution, and marketing of the products, while the Bach Centre remained responsible for the Mother Tincture. By 1993, however, the partnership expanded into an outright acquisition by Nelson of the Bach Centre. The new remedy-producing company then took on the new name of Nelsonbach. Meanwhile, Nelson continued its production of homeopathic medicines as well.

In the late 1990s, Nelsonbach faced an effort to break its attempt to control the Bach's Flower Remedies trademark. The attempt proved successful, and in 1999, the British House of Lords affirmed the court's ruling that neither the Bach name nor the term Bach's Flower Remedies could be considered a brand name.

The Bach remedies represented just a small portion of Nelsonbach's revenues, however. The group's homeopathic medicine business continued to grow strongly. The company developed an extended line of homeopathic products and delivery methods, adding cream-based products and targeted formulations, combining several "active" substances, as well as the company's new "Clikpak" packaging.

The Wilson family was now the force behind privately held A. Nelson. In 2005, the family extended its position within its Bach subsidiary as well, when Patrick Wilson, along with a longtime member of the Nelson Co., Peter Warren, were placed in charge of preparation of the Mother Tinctures. As a result, in September 2005, the company changed the subsidiary's name to Nelsons. A. Nelson & Co. remained the United Kingdom's most prominent producer of homeopathic and related treatments into the new century.

Principal Subsidiaries

Bach's Flower Remedies; Nelsons Homeopathic Pharmacy.

Principal Competitors

GNC Corporation; Healing Herbs; Nature's Sunshine Products, Inc.; NBTY, Inc. (NTY).

Further Reading

''A. Nelson Loses Bach Battle,'' *Chemist & Druggist,* October 30, 1999.

''Complementary Medicines: A Testing Problem,'' *Chemist & Druggist,* July 16, 2005, p. 31.

Devlin, Dory, ''Flowers Produce the Essence of Natural Anxiety Relief,'' *Star-Ledger,* July 7, 1998, p. 2.

Hughes, Ivor, ''The Enigma of Dr. Edward Bach and the Flower Remedies,'' *Herbal Data New Zealand,* December 2002.

Lavery, Sheila, ''Flower Remedies,'' *Sunday Times,* March 10, 1996, p. 18.

''Nelson Name Change,'' *Chemist & Druggist,* September 24, 2005, p. 30.

''Nelsons Targets Mums' Natural Feelings,'' *Chemist & Druggist,* March 10, 2001, p. 12.

''Spatone Relaunches Across Europe and US,'' *Marketing,* January 22, 2004, p. 12.

—M.L. Cohen

Abercrombie & Fitch

Abercrombie & Fitch Company

6301 Fitch Path
New Albany, Ohio 43054
U.S.A.
Telephone: (614) 283-6500
Fax: (614) 577-6980
Web site: http://www.abercrombie.com

Public Company
Incorporated: 1904
Employees: 62,150
Sales: $2.02 billion (2005)
Stock Exchanges: New York
Ticker Symbol: ANF
NAIC: 448110 Men's Clothing Stores; 448120 Women's
Clothing Stores; 448130 Children's and Infants'
Clothing Stores

Abercrombie & Fitch Company is a clothing retailer marketed toward young people, from children to young adults. While Abercrombie considers its clothing a "lifestyle brand," others have railed against its often sexually explicit tees and over-the-top marketing campaigns. The company oversees more than 800 stores nationwide, of which about 175 are its children's brand, abercrombie, and 260 are Hollister Company stores. Its latest concept, Ruehl, debuted in Ohio in 2004, appealing to more mature buyers, those in their late 20s and early 30s. Once owned by fashion firm The Limited, Abercrombie gained its independence in 1999 and went public on the New York Stock Exchange under the ticker symbol ANF. Its sales soared to more than $2 billion in 2005.

The Early Years: 1890s to 1910s

Abercrombie & Fitch Company (A&F) was founded in 1892 in New York City by David T. Abercrombie and Ezra H. Fitch. Abercrombie, a former prospector, miner, trapper, and railroad surveyor, originally produced camping equipment in lower Manhattan; Fitch, one of his customers, was a successful lawyer in Kingston, New York, who loved the outdoors. The two men pooled their interests and opened a sporting goods store.

Fitch was the visionary of the two, anticipating a clientele far broader than merely those who camped out in the course of earning a living. The partners proved ill-matched, and both men were hot-tempered. Following the latest of many long and violent arguments, Abercrombie resigned in 1907 to return to manufacturing camping equipment. Retaining the company name, Fitch continued with other partners. In 1909 he mailed out 50,000 copies of a 456-page catalogue. Since they cost a dollar each to produce, the catalogues almost bankrupted the company, but the subsequent flood of orders justified the expense. In 1917 A&F moved into a 12-story building on Madison Avenue at East 45th Street, a location the advertising department described as "Where the Blazed Trail Crosses the Boulevard." It included a luxuriously furnished log cabin that Fitch made his townhouse, with an adjoining casting pool.

By this time A&F's reputation as purveyor to the sporting elite was well established. It had equipped Theodore Roosevelt for an African safari, outfitted polar expeditions led by Roald Amundsen and Admiral Richard Byrd, and provided goods to aviators Charles Lindbergh and Amelia Earhart. Ernest Hemingway was a customer; and every president from Roosevelt to Gerald Ford would buy something from the store.

Growth and Change: 1920s–30s

Fitch retired in 1928, selling his interest in the company to his brother-in-law, James S. Cobb, who became president, and an employee, Otis L. Guernsey, who became vice-president. In his first year at the helm, Cobb acquired a similar New York business, Von Lengerke & Detmold, respected for its European-made sporting guns and fishing tackle, and Von Lengerke & Antoine, the Chicago branch, which became a subsidiary of A&F but continued until 1959 under its own name. In 1930 Cobb bought Griffin & Howe, a gunsmith shop. The merchandise of Von Lengerke & Detmold and Griffin & Howe was added to the Madison Avenue store.

Abercrombie & Fitch was selling outdoor and sporting equipment not only for hunting, fishing, camping, and exploration, but also for skating, polo, golf, and tennis. The store also carried a variety of outdoor clothing, boots, and shoes for men

Company Perspectives:

*Abercrombie & Fitch Company is a leading specialty re-
tailer encompassing four concepts: A&F, abercrombie,
Hollister Company, and Ruehl. The merchandise is sold in
retail stores throughout the United States and through cata-
logs. The company also operates several e-commerce websites for A&F, Abercrombie, and Hollister.*

and women, as well as cameras, pocket cutlery, and indoor
games. In the 1920s A&F became the epicenter of the burgeoning mah-jongg craze and the place in New York to thumb one's
nose at Prohibition by purchasing a hip flask. A&F also opened
a summer-only store in Hyannis, Massachusetts, for the yacht-
ing set. Net sales and income, rising steadily during the decade,
reached a record $6.3 million and $548,000, respectively, in
1929. These figures would not be topped in the next decade.
Sales in the grip of the Great Depression fell to under $2.6
million in fiscal 1933, when a loss of $521,118 was recorded, on
top of a loss of $241,211 the previous year. During this period,
Guernsey's negotiations with the firm's creditors probably
saved it from collapse. Subsequent years were profitable, and in
1938 A&F resumed paying dividends. It also established golf
and shooting schools in the store.

By 1939 A&F was calling itself the "Greatest Sporting
Goods Store in the World." It boasted the world's largest and
most valuable collection of firearms and the widest assortment
of fishing flies obtainable anywhere (15,000 in all) to accompany its array of rods, reels, and other fishing tackle. Riders, dog
fanciers, skiers, and archers all found every conceivable type of
gear. Guns and camping and fishing equipment accounted for
30 percent of the New York store's sales volume in 1938. Sales
of clothing, shoes, and furnishings accounted for 45 percent.
Inventory on hand was valued at about 40 percent of annual
sales, an extremely high ratio that reflected A&F's readiness to
meet its customers' demands. Catalogue mail orders accounted
for about 10 percent of business.

Abercrombie & Fitch at Mid-Century

Net profit during the 1940s was highest in fiscal 1947, when
it reached $682,894, which turned out to be an all-time record.
In 1958 A&F opened a store in San Francisco. Soon thereafter,
it added small winter-only stores in Palm Beach and Sarasota,
Florida, and summer stores in Bayhead, New Jersey, and Southampton, New York. Guernsey, who had succeeded Cobb as
president, explained his firm's mission at this time in frankly
elitist terms: "The Abercrombie & Fitch type does not care
about the cost; he wants the finest quality."

The New York store remained the company's flagship. At
the close of the 1950s the main floor sported heads of buffalo,
caribou, moose, elk, and other big game, stuffed fish of spectacular size, and wastebaskets made from elephants' feet. The store
sold an unmatched variety of contraptions for indoor and outdoor pursuits: one corner held dog and cat items; the basement
was a shooting range; and the mezzanine contained paraphernal-
ia for skindiving, archery, skiing, and lawn games. Floors two

through five were reserved for clothing suitable for any terrain
or climate. Floor six had a picture gallery and bookstore concentrating on sporting themes, and there was a watch repair
facility and the golf school, complete with a resident pro. On the
seventh floor was the gun room with about 700 shotguns and
rifles, constituting the most lavish assemblage of sporting firearms on earth. The eighth floor was devoted to fishing, camping,
and boating, and housed a fishing instructor who gave lessons at
the pool on the roof. He also handled mail and telephone
inquiries on fishing, hunting, and skiing. The fishing section
alone stocked about 48,000 flies and 18,000 lures.

In 1960 Abercrombie's net sales rose to a record $16.5
million, but net profits fell for the fourth straight year to
$185,649. The next year net sales fell below $15.5 million and
net profit dropped again to $124,097. Guernsey's successor as
president, John H. Ewing, saw no cause for alarm, and rejected
the idea of a budget shop or to "splash ads for storewide sales."
He told a *Business Week* interviewer in 1961 that A&F enjoyed
a special niche "by sticking to our knitting; by not trying to be
all things to all people."

Fall from Grace: Mid-1960s to Late 1970s

During the 1960s A&F opened new stores in Colorado, New
Jersey, Florida, and Michigan. It also opened small shops in
other stores. In 1968, a year in which city riots, protests against
the war in Vietnam, and the assassinations of Martin Luther
King and Robert Kennedy seemed to be tearing the country
apart, A&F was finally ready to shake up its way of doing
business by holding a warehouse sale. More than 90,000
bemused customers sifted through the Manhattan store one
summer day for bargains that included pop-up tents bought so
far in the past that no one remembered how to pop them up,
boots made of long-haired goatskin hide, miniature antique
cannons, leather baby elephants, and Yukon dog sleds.

In early 1970 the company initiated another gigantic sale. A
horde of hopefuls turned up to seize such bargains as a 15-foot
inoperative hovercraft for $3 and eight $100 surfboards for $17
each. An offbeat newspaper advertising campaign followed,
featuring a single item, such as hunting shoes, accompanied by
diagrams and copy that overwhelmed the reader with product
information. If these antics indicated a measure of desperation,
it was because A&F had recorded a loss of more than $500,000
in the latest fiscal year. In October 1970 William Humphreys,
the new company president, said the ads would be changed and
sales would cease because the people who showed up were not
A&F's kind of customer.

In the ensuing years, Humphreys, a former Lord & Taylor
executive, concentrated on cutting the company budget, improving inventory control and credit practices, and expanding
into the suburbs. A new A&F store opened in Oak Brook,
Illinois, west of Chicago. To win a broader range of clientele,
the New York store moved its expensive sailboats upstairs from
the main floor, expanded its gift and sportswear lines, added a
discount clothing shop on the tenth floor, and hired new buyers
for women's wear. Nevertheless, the company continued to lose
money under Humphreys and his successor, Hal Haskell, its
chief stockholder.

Key Dates:

1892: Abercrombie & Fitch (A&F) is founded in New York City.
1917: A&F relocates to flagship store on Madison Avenue.
1969: The company runs its first television ad.
1976: A&F files for Chapter 11 bankruptcy protection.
1978: The chain is bought by Oshman's Sporting Goods.
1984: A&F returns to New York City, opening a store at South Street Seaport.
1988: The Limited takes over A&F.
1992: A&F is repositioned toward casual apparel.
1999: A&F becomes an independent company again and launches abercrombie for kids.
2000: The first Hollister Company store opens in Columbus, Ohio.
2002: A&F moves to its new headquarters in New Albany, Ohio.
2004: A&F hires a new president from Gucci and moves into the casual-luxury clothing segment.
2005: The first Ruehl store opens in Columbus, Ohio.

In August 1976, after a year in which the company had lost $1 million, Abercrombie filed for Chapter 11 bankruptcy. When it closed its doors for good in November 1977, postmortems pointed out the obvious: the company had failed to make the transition from supplying fat-cat sportsmen of the old school to the skiers, bikers, and backpackers of the 1970s. One advertising man described management as ''ossified,'' and another said company officers had no faith in television's ability to draw in customers even after its first TV commercials, in 1969, filled the store.

The Oshman Decade: 1978–80s

Oshman's Sporting Goods, a Houston-based chain, bought the Abercrombie & Fitch name, trademark, and mailing list in 1978 and opened a store in 1979 under the A&F name in Beverly Hills, California. With a 52-page catalogue and eclectic merchandise, including exercise machines, Harris-tweed jackets, and $70 pith helmets, the company gained attention by outfitting actor Jack Lemmon for an Alaskan fishing trip and Dodger baseball star Steve Garvey for grouse hunting in Minnesota. A bigger Dallas store opened in 1980, complete with $40,000 elephant guns and an Abercrombie Runabout sports convertible for $20,775.

Abercrombie returned to New York City in 1984, opening in the renovated South Street Seaport area of lower Manhattan. By the end of 1986 the chain had grown to 26 stores, including a second Manhattan outlet in midtown's glitzy Trump Tower. Net sales reached an estimated $40 million in 1985. The Oshman-owned A&F chain stocked relatively few hunting and fishing supplies or exotic items, concentrating on exercise machines, tennis rackets, golf clubs, and other paraphernalia of more contemporary interest, much of it designed exclusively for the chain. Men's and women's clothing departments featured business and casual dress as well as sportswear, and the gift departments offered an array of goods, including gourmet edibles.

An upbeat assessment of the new A&F by *Chain Store Age Executive* in September 1986 was followed by a more skeptical appraisal by *Forbes* six months later, which described the chain's merchandise as a hodgepodge of unrelated items and concluded, ''Sometimes it is better to bury the dead than to try reviving them.'' *Forbes* estimated sales for 1986 at $48 million and profits at ''a so-so $1.5 million.''

In January 1988 The Limited, Inc. acquired 25 of the existing 27 A&F stores from Oshman's for about $45 million in cash. The organization was moved to corporate headquarters in Columbus, Ohio, and the inventory was cleared out. A stronger emphasis was placed on apparel, with 60 to 65 percent of the merchandise men's sportswear and furnishings, 20 to 25 percent women's wear, and the remaining 15 to 20 percent gifts, including grooming products and nature books. ''We can't get caught up in guns and fishing rods,'' the chain's president, Sally Frame-Kasaks, told a *Daily News Record* reporter. Nearly all the goods were mid-priced and bore an A&F label.

Expansion and Independence: 1990s

When Frame-Kasaks left to head Ann Taylor in February 1992, she was succeeded as president of A&F by Michael Jeffries, an executive at Paul Harris Stores. At this time the chain had 36 stores credited with annual sales of about $50 million. From the outset, Jeffries focused on transforming A&F into the retailer of choice for American youth, a demographic said to be growing the fastest during that time. He replaced conservative clothing lines, primarily for men, with high-priced casualwear for both young men and women à la Ralph Lauren.

Soon A&F had a corporate and retail culture all its own, one dedicated to youth, good looks, and fun. Jeffries ensured that the company kept in touch with the demands of young Americans by hiring executives and designers in tune with their preferences in clothing, music, and entertainment. The company also began publishing its own catalogue/magazine, *A&F Quarterly,* featuring its clothing lines as well as articles on pop culture, sex, music, and other teen topics. Photographer Bruce Weber imbued the catalogue and A&F's advertising with an open sexuality, which appealed to target customers but concerned some parents and their legislators. The changes initiated by Jeffries began paying off; sales increased to $85 million in 1992, $111 million in 1993, and $165 million in 1994. There were 67 A&F stores at the end of January 1995, compared to 49 a year earlier. Moreover, the A&F division established new records for merchandise margin rates and profitability for its parent, The Limited, in 1994.

When The Limited spun off Abercrombie in February 1999, headquarters moved from Columbus to nearby Reynoldsburg, Ohio, and Jeffries continued to helm the operation. By this time competition had heated up, particularly from American Eagle Outfitters, which began offering similar merchandise, marketed in a similar manner, and for lower prices. A&F sued American Eagle for violating its trademarks, but the lawsuit was dismissed when a judge determined that clothing style and image were not copyrightable. Amid reports that the company's growth might be slowing, its stock dropped but rebounded again after the 1999 holiday selling-season produced satisfactory results: net sales had reached $1.03 billion for the fiscal year with net income topping $149 million.

Continuing its provocative advertising methods, A&F had issued a Christmas catalogue featuring nude models and overt sexual content in 1999; a predictable outrage ensued and proof of age was required to purchase it thereafter. While A&F continued to have record sales and a loyal following, the company decided to broaden the scope of its clientele by opening a children's and preteen store, abercrombie, in 1999 and planned to launch another chain geared toward West Coast surfer types the following year.

Wider Horizons: 2000s

True to its word, Abercrombie launched its latest "lifestyle brand," Hollister Company, in Columbus, Ohio, in 2000. While the store's theme was surfing and fun in the sun, Hollister carried the same cheeky t-shirts and sexy clothing that had made its sibling famous. Ironically, few realized the new company was a part of the A&F empire and many considered Hollister a rival to A&F. As more stores opened in California, Georgia, Kansas, and New Jersey, buyers bought into Hollister's surf chic, with some believing they were snubbing A&F, and the company's executives laughed all the way to the bank. By the end of the new millennium's first year, Abercrombie had 275 A&F stores, 44 abercrombie stores, five Hollister Company stores, and net sales of over $1.23 billion with net income of over $158 million.

For 2001 A&F continued to roll out its Hollister stores, opening shops across the country for a total of 32 by the end of the year. Both its original A&F stores and the abercrombie kids' stores also grew, with the former occupying 485 mall stores and the latter climbing to 144 shops nationwide. Despite more venues, however, sales began falling mid-year and the company's stock tumbled to under $10 per share, when it had traded as high as $50 two years before.

While the A&F legend for sexually charged advertising and daring or barely there clothes drew in young buyers, the pricing often sent them to buy imitation tees from rivals American Eagle and Aéropostale. Despite some lackluster same-store sales during the year, A&F finished 2001 with net sales of just under $1.4 billion and net income up slightly to $168 million. In the following year as A&F moved to its new headquarters "campus" on 300 wooded acres in New Albany, Ohio, the company was once again courting controversy. This time A&F drew the ire of Asian Americans with a perceived racial slur ("Wong Brothers Laundry Service, two wongs make it white"), parent and advocacy groups for the latest edition of the *A&F Quarterly*, and practically everyone with the introduction of thongs for young girls. Though the company quietly withdrew the suggestive thongs from its abercrombie kids' stores, they remained a staple in its A&F and Hollister locations.

In 2003 A&F managed to anger folks again: this time it was residents of West Virginia, with a t-shirt that read "It's All Relative in West Virginia." The stink went as far as the state's governor, who demanded A&F pull the shirt from store shelves; Jeffries refused. His next battle was a proposed boycott of all A&F labels over the increasingly racy *A&F Quarterly*. This time Jeffries capitulated, shelving the periodical in late 2003. Despite or perhaps because of the continued controversy, sales reached $1.7 billion for fiscal 2003, with net income rising to over $205 million.

By early the next year, Hollister had become the company's fastest growing segment, expanding to 177 shops nationwide and overtaking its younger sibling abercrombie's 170 stores. A&F still operated the lion's share of stores, however, with over 700 shops featuring a seasonal range of clothing from bathing suits and flip flops to its trademark hoodies and racy tees. While retail pundits had considered A&F in a slump for several years due to its same-store sales, Jeffries decided to make over the company's image by channeling one of its founders, Ezra Fitch. The new A&F was a casual luxury clothier, a step up from its previous incarnation, with the launch of the Ezra Fitch line and the arrival of Bob Singer as A&F's new president and chief operating officer. Formerly of the Gucci Group, Singer understood luxury brands and brought considerable panache to A&F's transformation.

Jeffries' gambit worked as A&F sales began climbing across the board in 2004, topping $2 billion with net income reaching more than $216 million. Jeffries also announced the company would introduce another lifestyle brand, one directed to an older clientele. To A&F, "older" was a relative term, meaning post-college buyers in their mid- to late 20s and early 30s. The new concept, called Ruehl, opened its first prototype in Columbus, Ohio, resembling a Greenwich Village brownstone more than a store. A&F planned to build several hundred Ruehl stores over the next few years, while continuing to expand its core brands as well.

By 2005 A&F's image took a few serious hits. The first was the settlement of a lawsuit the previous year amidst complaints of racial discrimination. Though the company admitted no wrongdoing, it did alter its hiring and promotion policies. Next came questions about Jeffries and his compensation packages, including an investigation into A&F's corporate governance in 2005. Jeffries gave up a number of perks and slashed his compensation to appease shareholders, though many believed his rapid concession had more to do with preventing further investigation than anything else. Then came the resignation of President and COO Singer, who left due to disagreements with Jeffries over A&F's international expansion. Singer walked away with a compensation package rumored to be worth more than $13 million, Jeffries offered little comment and concentrated on the company's expansion into Canada and the United Kingdom.

Entering 2006 A&F continued to provoke mainstream America, selling the company's oversexed ideal of casual and luxury clothes to kids, teens, and young adults through its four "lifestyle" brands, A&F, Hollister Company, abercrombie, and Ruehl.

Principal Operating Units

A&F; Abercrombie; Hollister Company; Ruehl.

Principal Competitors

Aéropostale, Inc.; American Eagle Outfitters, Inc.; Gap, Inc.; The Limited, Inc.; The Buckle, Inc.; Urban Outfitters Inc.

Further Reading

"A&F," *Fortune,* July 1939, pp. 124+.

"Abercrombie's Misfire," *Time,* August 23, 1976, p. 55.

Bailey, Lee, "The Abercrombie Effect," *Daily News Record,* September 26, 2005, p. 20.

Berner, Robert, "Flip Flops, Torn Jeans—And Control," *Business Week,* May 30, 2005, p. 68.

——, "No Longer Big Brand on Campus," *Business Week,* September 29, 2003, p. 90.

"Caterer to the Outdoor Man," *Business Week,* December 16, 1961, pp. 84–86, 89.

Derby, Meredith, "Abercrombie's Singer Exiting," *WWD,* August 30, 2005, p. 3.

Frazier, Mya, "Hot Retail Concept: Ruehl," *Advertising Age,* July 11, 2001, p. 12.

Goldstein, Lauren, "The Alpha Teenager," *Fortune,* December 20, 1999, pp. 201+.

Kestout, Brian P., "Fashion Pizazz," *Kiplinger's Personal Finance Magazine,* January 2001, p. 68.

Lockwood, Lisa, "Edgy Ads," *WWD,* January 14, 2000, p. 16.

Marcial, Gene G., "Shoppers Bonanza at the Limited," *Business Week,* September 23, 1996, p. 142.

"Minorities Win Bias Lawsuit," *Jet,* December 6, 2004, p. 36.

Palmieri, Jean E., "A&F Aim: 100 Units; $300M Sales," *Daily News Record,* June 14, 1991, p. 7.

Paris, Ellen, "Endangered Species?," *Forbes,* March 9, 1987, pp. 136–37.

Perman, Stacy, "Fashion Forward: Abercrombie's Beefcake Brigade," *Time,* February 14, 2000.

"Robert Singer," *Chain Store Age,* October 2005, p. 22.

Sayre, Joel, "The Twelve-Story Game Room," *Holiday,* December 1959.

Stringer, Kortney, "A&F Best of Best," *Cleveland Plain Dealer,* June 22, 1999, p. 1C.

Wells, Melanie, "Anticlimax," *Forbes,* March 20, 2000.

Zimbalist, Kristina, "Mike Jeffries: 61, CEO, A&F," *Time,* September 13, 2005, p. 76.

—Robert Halasz
—updates: Mark Swartz; Nelson Rhodes

adidas

adidas Group AG

Adi-Dassler-Strasse 1-2
91074 Herzogenaurach
Germany
Telephone: 49-9132-842471
Fax: 49-9132-843127
Web site: http://www.adidas.com

Public Company
Incorporated: 1949
Employees: 14,254
Sales: EUR 6.48 billion (2004)
Stock Exchanges: Frankfurt
Ticker Symbol: ADDDY
NAIC: 315211 Men's and Boys' Cut and Sew Apparel
Contractors; 315212 Women's, Girls', and Infants'
Cut and Sew Apparel Contractors; 315299 All Other
Cut and Sew Apparel Manufacturing; 339920
Sporting and Athletic Goods Manufacturing; 316211
Rubber and Plastics Footwear Manufacturing; 316219
Other Footwear Manufacturing

Germany-based adidas Group AG, the world's number two sports footwear and apparel company, is going for the gold. In 2005, the company announced that it had reached a merger agreement with Reebok International Inc., the world's number three sports footwear and apparel brand. The resulting company will post revenues of more than $9.5 billion, creating a true rival to the world's dominant brand in the industry, Nike ($12.5 billion in revenues in 2005). The merger also represents adidas's decision to shift its focus more directly onto its core footwear and apparel operations. In October 2005, as part of that effort, the company completed the sale of its Salomon winter sports division, acquired in 1997, to Finland's Amer Sports Corporation. Included in that sale were the company's Mavic bicycle division, and other brands, including Arc'Teryx, Bonfire and Cliché. Nonetheless, adidas has kept its golf equipment, footwear and apparel division, TaylorMade-adidas, as well as its Maxfli line of golf balls, golf clubs, and accessories. A globally operating company, with some 110 subsidiaries worldwide, adidas has targeted China as a key growth market; the company has fought hard to become an official sponsor and

supplier to that country's Olympic Games in 2008. In this way, the company hopes to position itself as the brand of choice as the Chinese market shifts from merely manufacturing the world's sports shoes to becoming the world's largest consumer sports footwear market. adidas remains listed on the Frankfurt Stock Exchange and is led by CEO Herbert Hainer.

Humble Beginnings for the Athletic Shoe: 1920s–40s

adidas emanated from a bitter dispute between two brothers, Rudolph and Adi Dassler, in the small Bavarian mill town of Herzogenaurach. Rudi and Adi were born in 1898 and 1900, respectively, to Christolf and Pauline Dassler. Their hometown of Herzogenaurach was a regional textile manufacturing center at the time, but during the early 1900s most of the mills converted to shoemaking. Adi was trained to be a baker, but those skills offered him little hope of finding a job in the final years of World War I. Instead, the Dassler family started a tiny shoemaking business in the back of Pauline's laundry. Adi began making shoes using materials from old helmets, tires, rucksacks, and other refuse that he could scavenge. Adi's sister cut patterns out of canvas, and the always innovative Adi built a shoe trimmer that was powered by a bicycle.

The company's first shoes were bedroom slippers that sported soles made from used tires. Adi, who had a lifelong love of sports, converted those slippers into unique lightweight gymnastics and soccer shoes with nailed-on cleats. Demand for those shoes allowed the family to build a factory in 1926, when output rose to about 100 pairs per day. Adi's brother and father both quit their jobs to work in the company.

The Dassler family's company received a major boost when their shoes were worn by German athletes in the 1928 Olympics in Amsterdam. Four years later, moreover, athletes clad in Dassler shoes won medals in the Olympics in Los Angeles. Then, in the 1936 Games, the world-renowned American sprinter Jesse Owens raced to victory in Dassler shoes. Owens's shoes featured two widely spaced stripes that wrapped over the ball of the foot, a design that became increasingly commonplace on the feet of athletes around the world.

Demand for Dassler shoes mushroomed during the early 1930s and continued until the start of the German offensive that

Company Perspectives:

The adidas Group strives to be the global leader in the sporting goods industry with sports brands built on a passion for sports and a sporting lifestyle. We are consumer focused. That means we continuously improve the quality, look, feel and image of our products and our organizational structures to match and exceed consumer expectations and to provide them with the highest value. We are innovation and design leaders who seek to help athletes of all skill levels achieve peak performance with every product we bring to the market. We are a global organization that is socially and environmentally responsible, creative and financially rewarding for our employees and shareholders. We are committed to continuously strengthening our brands and products to improve our competitive position and financial performance.

led to World War II. During the war, the Dassler factory was commandeered for the production of boots for German soldiers. Both Adi and Rudi were reportedly members of the Nazi party, but only Rudi was called to service. Adi stayed home and ran the factory. Allied forces occupied the region at the war's end, and American soldiers even moved into the Dassler home. Christolf Dassler died about that time. Adi befriended some of the American soldiers, and made a pair of track shoes for a GI who eventually wore them in the 1946 Olympics.

After the soldiers left, Rudi returned to Herzogenaurach and rejoined his brother. He had spent several years fighting and one year interned in an American prisoner-of-war camp. Just as they had been forced to do after World War I, Adi and Rudi scavenged for shoemaking material to rebuild their business in war-torn Germany. They used army tents for canvas and old American tank materials for soles. They paid their 47 workers with such materials as firewood and yarn.

Sibling Rivalry and the Birth of adidas: Late 1940s

It was only a few years after Rudi's return that an infamous dispute broke out between the two brothers. Although the men kept the impetus for the fight a secret until their deaths, rumors swirled that the battle stemmed from disagreements related to the war. One story indicated that Rudi was upset that Adi had not used his connections with the Allies to get him out of the prison camp during the conflict. Whatever the reason for the feud, Rudi walked away from the family home and business forever in the spring of 1948, intent on starting his own shoe business. He took with him the company's sales force and control of a building that was to become a new factory. Adi kept most of the workforce and the original headquarters offices and factory. From that time forward, the brothers never spoke a word to one another except in court. The businesses that they created represented one of the most intense rivalries in all of Europe.

When they split, Rudi and Adi agreed that neither would be allowed to use the Dassler brand name on their shoes. Rudi named his new company and shoes Ruda, while Adi named his Addas. Shortly thereafter, Adi changed the name to adidas (emphasis on the last syllable) and Rudi, on the advice of an

advertising agency, changed the name of his shoes to Puma. Adi altered the Dassler family trademark of two stripes by adding a third. He also adopted the slogan ''The Best for the Athlete'' as part of his marketing campaign. Rudi chose as his logo a cat's paw in motion.

For many years a signpost in the center of town had two arrows: one pointed to adidas and the other to Puma, which faced adidas on the opposite side of the River Aurach. Each company had its own soccer team, and employees from each company drank different beers. Enrollment at the two elementary schools in town was determined by the factory at which a child's father worked (adidas employees' children attended one school, while Puma employees' children attended the other), and children learned early in their lives to look down on the competing shoe company.

Each shoe company's culture bore the mark of its founder. It may have been for that reason that Adi came to dominate the global athletic shoe industry. Both Rudi and Adi were intelligent and able. Puma eventually became a venerable and established shoe company throughout the global industry. But under Adi Dassler's guiding hand, adidas grew during the mid-1900s to became the undisputed world shoe industry giant. Adi, considered shy but extremely bright, was respected in his village. A natural athlete, inventor, and craftsman, Adi combined his interests to produce a number of breakthrough innovations that catapulted the company to prominence. By the time Dassler died in 1978, in fact, adidas shoes were being worn throughout the world, more than any other sports shoe, by both professional and weekend athletes, and as casual footwear.

An Innovative Leader in Athletic Footwear: 1950s–70s

Adi was credited with numerous inventions during the late 1940s and 1950s, including the first shoes designed for ice and the first multi-studded shoes. adidas is also credited with pioneering the now commonplace practice among athletic shoe manufacturers of selling sports bags and athletic clothing bearing their brand name. Among Adi's most notable early contributions was his improvement of the soccer shoe. Prior to 1957, soccer shoes were designed as they had been for decades, with metal studs mounted in leather. These shoes were heavy, particularly when they got wet. Adi designed a new type of shoe that sported a nylon sole and molded rubber studs. The result was a more lightweight, durable shoe. Introduced in 1957, the revolutionary soccer shoe was eventually copied by other shoe companies, including chief rival Puma.

Another of Adi's pivotal innovations, and the one that helped most to thrust the company into the global limelight, was the screw-studded soccer shoe, which allowed worn cleats to be replaced. The cleats were introduced in 1954 at the World Soccer Championships in Bern, Switzerland. Heavy rains during the first half of an important game turned the soccer field to a muddy mess by half-time. The West German national team members went to their locker room, removed their standard cleats, and installed longer cleats to get a better grip in the field. Adi watched as the West German team captured a 3–2 victory over the favored Hungarians, a triumph that was viewed by the German people as a symbol of their return from the ashes of

Key Dates:

1926: Dassler family builds a factory to make athletic shoes.
1936: American runner Jesse Owens, wearing Dassler shoes, wins a gold medal in the 1936 Olympic Games.
1948: The Dassler brothers part ways, and Adi Dassler starts his own shoe company.
1949: adidas is registered as a company.
1957: adidas introduces a pioneering soccer shoe.
1978: Adi Dassler dies, and control of his company is handed to his family.
1990: French entrepreneur Bernard Tapie buys adidas.
1993: adidas acquires Sports Inc., a U.S. company; Tapie sells adidas to a group of European investors, and Robert Louis-Dreyfus joins adidas as CEO.
1995: adidas goes public.
1997: adidas acquires Salomon Worldwide and is renamed adidas-Salomon AG.
2000: The company restructures in an effort to boost its image as a ''lifestyle'' brand.
2001: First adidas Originals retail stores open in Berlin and Tokyo.
2002: The company acquires Arc'Teryx, a high-end equipment and apparel group based in Vancouver; opens first adidas Originals store in United States.
2003: Cycling division Mavic-adidas Cycling is formed; company fails in attempt to acquire golf ball manufacturer Top Flite.
2005: The company agrees to sell Salomon to Amer Sports in Finland; announces acquisition of Reebok International, to be completed in 2006.

war. Soon after that event, adidas's shipments exploded from about 800 pairs to 2,000 pairs of shoes per day.

Two years later Adi started its successful and longstanding tradition of naming one of its shoes after the Olympics. The shoe introduced at the 1956 Olympics was the Melbourne. The Games were held in that Australian city that year and the shoe was the first to offer multiple studs. Adi's son Horst handled the promotion with a marketing strategy that won accolades abroad. He simply gave the shoes away to Olympic athletes, who wore them for a global audience. Athletes wearing adidas shoes won a whopping 72 medals that year and set 33 records. After that, adidas scored another major marketing coup by signing agreements to supply entire sports teams with footwear, an agreement that ensured that adidas equipment would be worn by many of the world's greatest athletes on both sides of the Iron Curtain. Other shoe and sports equipment companies eventually followed the company's lead, and contracts to supply free equipment to such high-profile athletes became highly competitive.

adidas initiated a number of savvy marketing programs during the 1950s, 1960s, and 1970s, but the Olympics remained the centerpiece of its marketing strategy for several years. In the 1964 Tokyo Games, medals won by adidas-shod competitors amounted to 80 percent of the total, as they captured all but 30 of the medals awarded. At the Montreal Olympics, adidas outfitted all of the winners in hockey, soccer, volleyball, and women's basketball. adidas shoes were worn by athletes who accounted for 83 percent of all medals awarded and a fat 95 percent of the track-and-field gold medals. adidas became virtually dominant in the athletic shoe industry. Aside from its clever marketing and winning designs, moreover, it was considered the quality leader. Indeed, other shoemakers considered adidas superior in machinery, craftsmanship, and materials.

adidas's most lucrative strategic maneuver was its entry into the giant and blossoming U.S. athletic shoe market in the late 1950s. adidas attacked that market at a good time. Its major competitors were manufacturers of canvas sneakers that bore such names as Keds and P.F. Flyers. adidas's high quality, well-designed shoes became explosively popular, first with more serious athletes, but finally with the weekend athlete and casual footwear markets. Puma also made a run in the United States beginning in the 1950s. Its shoes sold relatively well, but ultimately came to be regarded as inferior to adidas in quality. In contrast, by the mid-1970s adidas had become nearly synonymous with quality athletic shoes in the United States.

adidas expanded globally during the 1960s and 1970s, maintaining its dominant position in the world sports shoe industry. By the late 1970s the company was churning out about 200,000 pairs per day and generating well over a half billion dollars in sales annually. (The company was still privately owned, so revenue figures are speculative.) adidas operated 24 factories in 17 countries and was selling a wide range of shoes in more than 150 nations. In addition, the company had moved by that time into diverse product lines including shorts, jerseys, balls and other equipment, track suits, and athletic bags. The company had registered about 800 patents and was producing roughly 150 different styles of shoes. About 90 percent of all Formula 1 drivers, for example, raced in adidas.

Throughout the company's rampant growth, its founder continued to lead and innovate. In 1978 the 77-year-old president introduced what he considered to be his greatest contribution ever to his beloved game of soccer. In recognition of the fact that players spent about 90 percent of their time on the field running rather than kicking the ball, Adi designed an ultralight soccer shoe with a sole resembling a sprint shoe. The shoe also featured an orthopedic footbed, a wider positioning of the studs to give better traction and even a special impregnation treatment designed to counter the weight-increasing effect of the humid Argentinian climate. The shoes were first used in the World Cup in Argentina by almost every team in the competition.

Increased Competition and the Loss of Global Dominance: 1980s and Early 1990s

Adi Dassler died shortly after he introduced his landmark soccer shoe in 1978. He had run the company and its predecessor for about 60 years and built it into the unmitigated giant of the world shoe industry. His death marked the end of an era at the company. Indeed, adidas suffered a string of defeats in the late 1970s and 1980s that severely diminished its role in the world sports shoe industry. The company's loss of dominance was not solely attributable to Dassler's death, however. In fact, the athletic shoe industry became intensely competitive following his death, primarily as a result of aggressive U.S. entrants. The increased competition actually began after the 1972 Olympics in Munich, when a mob of companies decided to hop into the lucrative business. After having the industry mostly to themselves for years, adidas and Puma suddenly found themselves under attack from shoe manufacturers worldwide.

Dassler had carefully arranged a management succession before his death. Family members remained in key management positions, but several professional managers were also brought in to take over key functions including marketing, production, and public relations. Unfortunately, the effort failed to keep the company vibrant. adidas retained its lead in the global athletic shoe market for several years and remained dominant in its core European market into the 1990s. Importantly, though, it was soundly thrashed in the North American market by emerging athletic shoe contenders Nike and Reebok. Those companies launched an almost militant marketing offensive on the North American sports shoe market during the 1980s that caught adidas completely off guard.

adidas, not used to such fierce competition, effectively ceded dominance of that important region. Incredibly, adidas's U.S. sales shrank to a mere $200 million by the end of the decade, while Nike's grew to more than $2.4 billion. By that time, Reebok and Nike together claimed more than 50 percent of the U.S. athletic shoe market, compared to about 3 percent for adidas. The adidas brand name had become a fading memory in the minds of many aging baby boomers, and many younger U.S. buyers were virtually unaware of the brand. "This is a brand that has taken about five bullets to the head," said one observer in *Business Journal-Portland* in February 1993.

adidas managed to maintain its lead in the soccer shoe market and even to keep a healthy 26 percent of the European market for its products. However, the North American market became the core of the global athletic shoe industry, and adidas found itself scrambling to maintain respect worldwide. Moreover, besides increased competition, adidas suffered during the 1980s and early 1990s from relatively weak management. To make matters worse, members of the Dassler family and relatives that still owned adidas began fighting over control of the company. Amid increased competition and family squabbling, adidas's bottom line began to sag. The organization lost about $77 million in 1989 before the family sold the entire organization for only $289 million the following year. The buyer was Frenchman Bernard Tapie, a 47-year-old entrepreneur and politician.

From the beginning, analysts doubted Tapie's ability to turn the ailing company around. A perpetual showman, Tapie purchased the company partly for the attention he would get from the French people for securing ownership of a renowned German institution. Tapie had already gained notoriety as an entrepreneur and as a parliamentary head of the ruling Socialist Party. Tapie's promotional skills did little for adidas. The company continued to lag and Tapie himself became embroiled in political and business scandals. Tapie stepped aside as chief of the company in 1992 and handed the reins to Gilbert Beaux. Tapie also started searching for a buyer for adidas.

Under new management, adidas looked as though it was beginning to turn the corner going into the mid-1990s. Of import was the company's 1993 purchase of U.S.-based Sports Inc., an enterprise that had been founded by Rob Strasser.

Strasser was credited as the marketing genius that had helped to make Nike into the leading U.S. athletic shoe company. Strasser quit Nike in 1987 to form Sports Inc. When adidas bought out his 50-person marketing venture, it named Strasser head of the newly formed adidas America subsidiary. Strasser brought with him another former Nike executive, Peter Moore, with whom he hoped to regain some of adidas's lost glory. "We'll compete from day one," he said in the *Business Journal-Portland* in 1993, "but it won't happen overnight." Tapie finally found a buyer for adidas in 1993. The company was purchased by a group of European investors for $371 million. Unfortunately, Strasser died late in 1993. Moore took over as head of the U.S. subsidiary. adidas expected Moore to lead the company's turnaround on that continent and to help it eventually attain the kind of strength adidas International still exerted in Europe and some other parts of the world.

In 1993 the new owners of adidas hired Robert Louis-Dreyfus, a French businessman, to run the company. Though Louis-Dreyfus was unfamiliar with the athletic shoe business, he had a reputation for revitalizing failing companies; in fact, Louis-Dreyfus was credited with saving London advertising agency Saatchi and Saatchi. After joining adidas, Louis-Dreyfus implemented severe cost-cutting and reorganization strategies and moved production to Asia. He also increased the marketing budget, from 6 percent of sales to 11 percent, to increase brand visibility.

Merged and Emerging in the Mid-2000s

adidas reacted favorably to Louis-Dreyfus's changes, and profits rebounded, reaching DEM 244.9 million in 1995, up from DEM 117.3 million in 1994. The company went public in 1995, and the relatively unathletic Louis-Dreyfus signaled his commitment to adidas and its athletic roots by running in the Boston Marathon. Also that year a new CEO, Steve Wynne, joined adidas's U.S. subsidiary. In 1996 apparel sales rose an impressive 50 percent, and brand visibility was enhanced by adidas's involvement with the 1996 Olympic Games. The company provided gear for about 6,000 competing athletes, representing 33 countries, and the Olympians sporting adidas's equipment won 220 medals.

In a significant move to strengthen its position in the global sporting goods category, adidas acquired French holding company Sport Developpement SCA in late 1997. Sport Developpement owned 38.87 percent of Salomon's shares and 56.12 percent of the voting rights. After sealing the deal with Sport Developpement, adidas acquired the outstanding shares of Salomon in a deal estimated to be worth $1.4 billion. The purchase, which included U.S.-based Taylor Made, manufacturer of premium golf clubs, and the French Mavic, maker of cycling equipment, positioned adidas in the number two position of sporting goods worldwide, behind Nike Inc. but ahead of Reebok International Ltd. Traditionally known as a manufacturer of ski equipment, Salomon had begun to branch out in the mid-1990s to shield itself from the declining winter sports and ski segments. The company placed a greater emphasis on Taylor Made and Mavic and also focused on hiking boots, inline skates, and snowboards. Salomon also changed its name to Salomon Worldwide in mid-1997 to signal its international diversification.

Though industry observers applauded adidas's purchase of Salomon and stated that consolidation within the sporting goods industry, particularly between equipment manufacturers and makers of apparel and shoes, was a growing trend, news of adidas's decision caused the share price to decline nearly 4 percent. Concerns that adidas's earnings would be adversely affected for several years by the debt-financed acquisition made many investors nervous. Still, many felt the adidas and Salomon merger was a positive move. Allan Raphael, president of Raphael, C.R.I. Global LP, said in the *Financial Post,* ''adidas' goal is to be the No. 1 sports equipment company in the world and I think they're going to get there. . . . The key is that adidas' management has a very innovative sense of how to recreate a brand.''

In 1998 adidas-Salomon turned toward the U.S. market while also focusing on integrating Salomon's operations. Though the global sporting goods market experienced flat growth that year, adidas managed to achieve extremely high sales growth. Overall net sales grew 48 percent in 1998 compared to 1997, and the company achieved record high net sales in both footwear and apparel. In the United States, the top market for sporting goods, adidas-Salomon achieved extraordinary growth rates. Net sales in the U.S. market alone rose 71 percent over 1997 results, and the brand's share of the U.S. footwear market reached 12 percent, thanks to the increase in footwear sales of 93 percent. Apparel sales also fared well in the United States, growing 48 percent. Sales in Europe, Asia, and Latin America also rose in 1998.

Despite strong growth rates in 1998, adidas-Salomon was not without difficulties. Integration of Salomon proved to be more time-consuming and challenging than had been anticipated, and the company's share prices fell 24 percent during the year. In addition, though some Asian countries experienced positive sales growth, overall sales in the Asian region fell more than 20 percent. The economic problems in Russia led to poor sales as well. The golf industry faced a difficult year in 1998, and this affected sales of Taylor Made, which declined by 15 percent.

adidas-Salomon concentrated on the positive rather than the negative, and although expecting flat growth during 1999, the year of its 50th anniversary, the company endeavored to improve sales and strengthen operations. The company planned to construct a new world headquarters in Herzogenaurach and thus acquired a 90 percent interest in GEV Grundstücksgesellschaft mbH & Co. KG, a property investment firm that owned the property adidas selected for the building. adidas-Salomon also extended operations globally in the late 1990s, forming a subsidiary, adidas Japan K.K., to handle the distribution of adidas products in Japan, as well as ventures in The Netherlands and Turkey.

In terms of sports, adidas-Salomon had many winners in the late 1990s. adidas was the official sponsor of the 1998 Soccer World Cup, which had extremely high visibility and coverage, and in 1999 the company sponsored the Women's World Cup, which achieved strong popularity. The company also sponsored the New York Yankees baseball team beginning in late 1997. The Yankees won the World Series that season, and adidas-Salomon publicized its partnership with the team through award-winning advertising campaigns. Among the athletes signed by the company were cyclist Jan Ullrich, winner of the Tour de France in 1997 and runner-up in 1998, and National Basketball Association player Kobe Bryant.

adidas made a good effort at integrating the Salomon operations. Faced with increasing competition from the entry of such designer brands as Tommy Hilfiger and Polo Ralph Lauren into the sportswear market, the company began a streamlining effort to boost its own brand position. As part of the streamlining, adidas-Salomon launched a major worldwide restructuring in 2000. Reorganized into three major divisions, including a new high-performance division named Forever Sport, adidas-Salomon abandoned its former divisional separation between its footwear and apparel operations. The restructuring also moved to reduce its previous operational subdivisions targeting individual sports, in an effort to reposition the brand in the general lifestyle market as well.

The move had only mixed results, however, as the Nike brand continued to dominate the global sporting goods market. At the same time, adidas began to lose ground in the United States, where Reebok International had begun its own aggressive push to gain market share. The hoped-for synergies with the Salomon operations failed to manifest themselves; indeed, during the 2000s, the group's focus on adidas's traditional markets left little room for development of the Salomon line, which saw a loss of market share as a result.

Nonetheless, the company launched several attempts at continued expansion in the 2000s. The company relaunched its golf division, combining the Taylor Made and adidas Golf operations into a single Taylor Made-adidas Golf segment, then began an effort to reposition itself as a supplier to the professional and ''serious'' golf segments. Yet the company's efforts to challenge market leader Callaway Golf hit an impasse when the company failed to acquire golf ball manufacturer Top-Flite, which was picked up by Callaway instead.

In 2002, adidas-Salomon acquired Vancouver-based Arc'Teryx Equipment, a maker of high-end technical equipment and apparel. The company also launched an effort to break into the retail market, launching its first adidas Originals retail shops in Berlin and Tokyo in 2001. In 2002, the company brought the retail concept to the United States, going head-to-head against Nike's massively successful Niketown retail format and opening a shop in New York City. The following year, the company streamlined its bicycling division, combining its cycling accessories and apparel operations under a single division, called Mavic-adidas Cycling. In another move to expand its appeal in the general lifestyle sportswear market, the company signed designer Stella McCartney to create a new line of women's running, fitness, and swimming fashions for 2005.

The mid-2000s offered new perspectives to the global sporting goods industry, as new classes of consumers appeared in the vast Indian and Chinese markets. The rush was on to achieve first-entry position in these markets. The potential for growth appeared all the more promising given that Nike, which for years had built its success on the phenomenal appeal of the Michael Jordan franchise, had no clear ''superstar'' backing its line into the mid-2000s. Both adidas-Salomon and Reebok launched an aggressive effort to sign up the world's next generation of sports superstars, in an effort to beat Nike at its own game. By 2003, meanwhile, rumors had begun to spread that adidas and Reebok, number two and three, respectively, had begun to discuss a possible merger. Both companies denied the rumor, however.

adidas also successfully fought for control of the lucrative footwear sponsorship for the upcoming Beijing Olympic Games. In this way, the company hoped to position itself as the brand of choice as Chinese consumers adopted the Western fashion craze for branded sportswear fashions.

In 2005, adidas returned to its history of footwear innovation, launching the world's first ''smart'' shoe, a running shoe with a microprocessor built into its heel. The computerized shoe utilized a sensor to react to surface conditions, measuring shock impact and making minute adjustments to the heel cushioning. The company hoped the new shoe, which could be adapted to the company's high-performance basketball and soccer shoes, and even to its entire range, would become the next revolution in sports technology.

In the meantime, the company was forced to acknowledge that the Salomon winter sports operations no longer fit with its increasing focus on the core adidas-branded sportswear operations. Recognizing that it had not given sufficient attention to the development of the Salomon operations, adidas decided to sell out, and in October 2005 completed the sale of Salomon, together with the Mavic, Arc'Teryx, and Bonfire brands, to Finland's Amer Sports Corporation.

By then, adidas and Reebok had gone public with their merger plans, announcing in May 2005 that they had reached an agreement, in which adidas would acquire Reebok for $3.8 billion. By October 2005, the two companies appeared to have cleared antitrust reviews, and announced their intention to complete the merger by 2006. The combined company created a true rival to Nike, with more than $9.5 billion in total sales, and two strong, internationally recognized brands. The merger also came ahead of the 2006 World Cup, to be held in Germany, which was expected to provide an extra boost to adidas's revenues. The race for global sportswear dominance was not quite finished, however. Following the adidas-Reebok merger, many observers expected Nike to strike back by acquiring longtime adidas arch-rival Puma.

Principal Subsidiaries

adidas America Inc.; adidas-Salomon North America Inc.; adidas-Salomon USA, Inc.; Taylor Made Golf USA; adidas (Canada) Ltd.; Erima Sportbekleidungs GmbH; Salomon GmbH; GEV Grundstücksgesellschaft Herzogenaurach mbH & Co. KG (90%); adidas Sarragan France S.a.r.l.; adidas Espana SA (Spain); adidas Portugal Lda; adidas Sport GmbH (Switzerland); Salomon SA (France); adidas Austria AG; adidas Benelux B.V. (The Netherlands); adidas Belgium N.V.; adidas Budapest Kft. (Hungary); adidas (U.K.) Ltd.; adidas (Ireland) Ltd.; adidas Norge A/S (Norway); adidas Sverige AB (Sweden); adidas Poland Sp.z.o.o.; adidas Ltd. (Russia); adidas de Mexico S.A. de C.V.; adidas do Brasil Ltda. (Brazil); adidas Latin America S.A. (Panama); adidas Corporation de Venezuela, S.A.; adidas Japan K.K.; adidas Hong Kong Ltd.; adidas Singapore Pte Ltd.; adidas Asia/Pacific Ltd. (Hong Kong); adidas (Thailand) Co., Ltd.; adidas Australia Pty Ltd.; adidas New Zealand Pty Ltd.; adidas (South Africa) Pty Ltd.

Principal Competitors

Nike Inc.; Fila Holding S.p.A.; New Balance Corporation; Fortune Brands Inc.; Brunswick Corp.; PUMA AG; Amer Sports Oyj.

Further Reading

Bates, Tom, ''Adidas Names Moore to Replace Strasser,'' *Portland Oregonian,* November 10, 1993.

Buckley, Chris, ''Let the Competition Begin,'' *New York Times*, January 25, 2005, p. C6.

Carofano, Jennifer, and Eric Newman, ''Adidas Advances with Reebok Plans,'' *Footwear News*, October 17, 2005, p. 6.

Carofano, Jennifer, ''A Perfect Union?'' *Footwear News*, September 12, 2005, p. 8.

Carrel, Paul, ''Adidas Shares Soar on Revamp Plan,'' *Reuters English News Service,* January 27, 2000.

Carter, Donna, ''Mutombo's Shoes Take Off Worldwide,'' *Denver Post,* December 18, 1992, p. C1.

Colodny, Mark M., ''Beaux Knows Adidas,'' *Fortune*, December 31, 1990, p. 111.

''Dreyfus Launches Adidas into Foot Race with Nike,'' *Financial Post,* September 17, 1997, p. 13.

Fallon, James, ''Adidas Sold for $370.48 Million,'' *Footwear News,* February 22, 1993, p. 39.

Feitelberg, Rosemary, ''Wynne to Exit Adidas,'' *WWD*, January 13, 2000, p. 16.

Francis, Mike, ''Strasser Headed for Top of Adidas? One of the Founders of Sports Inc. May Become Head of adidas U.S.A.,'' *Portland Oregonian,* February 3, 1993.

Harnischfeger, Uta, ''Flagging Golf Brand Hits Adidas Profits,'' *Financial Times London,* April 13, 1999, p. 28.

Holmes, Stanley, ''The Machine of a New Sole,'' *Business Week*, March 14, 2005, p. 99.

''How Adidas Ran Faster,'' *Management Today*, December 1979, pp. 58–61.

''If the Shoe Fits . . . ,'' *Business Week Online*, August 8, 2005.

Jung, Helen, ''Adidas-Salomon AG Said Monday It Will Sell Its Salomon Group of Ski and Equipment Businesses for About $624 Million,'' *Oregonian*, May 3, 2005.

Manning, Jeff, ''Adidas Slows Impressive Pace As Flat Sales Expected for 1999,'' *Portland Oregonian*, May 21, 1999.

''Adidas, Sports Inc. Join Forces, Strasser Heads U.S. Operation,'' *Business Journal-Portland,* February 8, 1993, p. 1.

Mitchener, Brandon, and Amy Barrett, ''Adidas and Salomon Play by New Rules in $1.4 Billion Deal,'' *Wall Street Journal Europe*, September 17, 1997, p. 1.

Mulligan, Thomas S., ''Adidas to Put U.S. Market in Hands of Ex-Nike Whiz,'' *Los Angeles Times,* February 5, 1993, p. D2.

Silverman, Edward R., ''Foothold in Sneaker War,'' *New York Newsday,* July 8, 1992, p. 31.

Strasser, J.B., and Laurie Becklund, *Swoosh: The Unauthorized Story of Nike and the Men Who Played There,* New York: Harcourt Brace Jovanovich, 1991.

Wallace, Charles P., ''Adidas Back in the Game,'' *Fortune*, August 18, 1997, pp. 176+.

Waxman, Sharon, ''Tapie: The Flashy Frenchman Behind the Adidas Acquisition,'' *Washington Post,* July 22, 1990, p. H1.

—Dave Mote
—updates: Mariko Fujinaka; M.L. Cohen

AgustaWestland N.V.

AgustaWestland Italy
Via Giovanni Agusta, 520
21017 Cascina Costa di Samarate (VA)
Italy
Telephone: +39 0331 229111
Fax: +39 0331 229605
Web site: http://www.agustawestland.com

AgustaWestland UK
Yeovil, Somerset
BA20 2YB
United Kingdom
Telephone: +44 (0) 1935 475222
Fax: +44 (0) 1935 702131
Web site: http://www.agustawestland.com

Wholly Owned Subsidiary of Finmeccanica S.p.A.
Incorporated: 2001
Employees: 8,968
Sales: EUR 2.54 billion (2004)
NAIC: 541710 Research and Development in the
   Physical, Engineering, and Life Sciences; 336411
   Aircraft Manufacturing

AgustaWestland N.V. is one of the world's largest helicopter manufacturers. It produces a wide range of high-performance rotorcraft for civil and military markets. Of 92 helicopters delivered in 2004, 66 went to commercial customers. Formed by combining two leading European helicopter manufacturers, the company has operations in Italy (near Milan), the United Kingdom (near Somerset, England), and the United States (Fort Worth and Philadelphia). A highly modified version of its EH101 Merlin won a U.S. Navy contract to supply helicopters for the president of the United States in 2005.

AgustaWestland N.V. was established in 2000 through a 50–50 joint venture between Italy's Finmeccanica S.p.A. and GKN PLC of the United Kingdom. Both of the companies joined to form AgustaWestland began their helicopter manufacturing by licensing U.S. designs.

Agusta History

Giovanni Agusta built and flew his first aircraft in 1907. This formed the beginnings of his namesake firm, Costruzioni Aeronautiche Giovanni Agusta S.p.A., based in Cascina Costa, near Milan. It originally designed and produced fixed wing aircraft in the 1920s, but became better known for motorcycles, at least until the mid-1950s.

The company began producing Bell Model 47 light helicopters under license in 1952. Agusta's version first flew in 1954; the company would produce more than 1,200 of them in the next 22 years. Agusta went on to build more of Bell's successful designs in the 1960s. These included the Model 204 UH-1 Iroquois and the ubiquitous JetRanger. The company also produced designs from other U.S. manufacturers.

Eventually, the firm acquired the expertise to develop its own prototype, the A101G. This three-engined military transport never saw production, however. A few other early designs reached the prototype stage but were unable to win more than limited orders from the Italian military. These were followed by the innovative A109 Hirundo twin turbine helicopter, which first flew in August 1971. Fast and versatile, it was soon adopted by Italy and Argentina. About a dozen a month were being produced in 1979, three years after its service introduction.

In the late 1970s, Agusta began designing the 15-ton EH101 helicopter with its British partner, Westland. It was first delivered to the Royal Navy in 1997.

In 1983, Agusta introduced the first combat helicopter to be designed and produced entirely in Europe, the A129 Mangusta. In the 1980s, Agusta also was developing the 11-ton NH90 helicopter in conjunction with French, Dutch, and German companies.

Agusta created a joint venture with Bell Helicopter in 1998. The Bell/Agusta Aerospace Company was formed to produce the AB139 and the BA609, a civil variant of the tiltrotor aircraft being developed for the U.S. military.

An updated version of the A109 hit the market to a strong response in 1999. The A119 Koala, introduced in 2000, enjoyed success in the law enforcement market in the Americas and

Company Perspectives:

AgustaWestland's mission is to consolidate and strengthen its position as a global leader in the rotorcraft industry.

AgustaWestland, the Anglo-Italian helicopter company owned by Italy's Finmeccanica, has achieved another year of good results in 2004. The Company is one of the world's leading helicopter manufacturers, with a full range of rotorcraft for every commercial, government and military application and provides an unrivalled capability in training and customer support. AgustaWestland is more than just a helicopter manufacturer; it is a provider of total rotorcraft capability solutions. Although AgustaWestland is proud of its heritage, it recognises the challenge of continuing to delight customers in its mission to strengthen its position as a global leader in the rotorcraft industry.

Asia. Exports accounted for more than 60 percent of sales in 2000, when revenues were more than EUR 930 million.

Westland History

Like Agusta, Westland also started its helicopter program through licensing. Westland was formed from the Petter engine works and had made aircraft at its site in Yeovil, England, since 1915. Its first planes were fabric-clad aircraft built under license from the manufacturers Short, Sopwith, and de Havilland; Westland produced more than 1,100 planes during World War I.

Between the wars Westland pioneered high-altitude flying; a flyover of Mount Everest in a Westland-Houston PV-3 Wapati made international headlines. Work on cabin pressurization was carried on during World War II in developing the Welkin high-altitude interceptor.

Notable aircraft produced for the military in World War II included the Lysander utility craft and the heavily armed, twin-engined Whirlwind interceptor. Westland was one of three companies chosen to produce Spitfires after the Supermarine factory in Southampton was bombed. The company made more than 2,000, including the Seafire naval variant it helped to design.

Westland was early to enter the rotorcraft field, producing Cierva-designed autogyros in 1936. This enterprise was cut short by the impending hostilities. The company built its first helicopter, the Dragonfly, in October 1948. This was a modified version of the Sikorsky S-51. Another Sikorsky-based design, the S-55, was designated the Westland Whirlwind and had a production run of almost 400.

Westland produced 250 models of Agusta's AB47G helicopter in the 1960s. This later became known as the Westland-Agusta-Bell 47G "Sioux." The company began producing its first indigenously designed helicopters after buying the operations of Saunders-Roe (SARO) in 1959. Successful SARO models included the P 531 Scout/Wasp, which saw about 200 built for the British military.

Westland soon acquired other pioneering British firms, including the Fairey Aviation Company and the Bristol Aircraft Company. Bristol's Type 171 Sycamore had been the first helicopter built in postwar Britain. Bristol also produced the United Kingdom's first multi-engine helicopters. Westland Helicopters entered the 1960s as Britain's sole helicopter manufacturer. In 1969, Westland introduced one of its biggest successes, the Sea King, which was a variant of Sikorsky's SH-3D (S-61). It was exported to several navies.

Westland led the Anglo-French partnership that produced the Lynx in collaboration with Aerospatiale (formerly Sud-Aviation) from the mid-1960s to the 1970s. More than 400 were made after it entered service in December 1977. Aerospatiale led the design of the two other helicopters made by the partnership, the Puma and the Gazelle.

After a period of unprecedented success, Westland entered a difficult decade, the 1980s. It lacked capital for developing new designs. It sought other manufacturers to share some of the burden. Westland found one partner in Sikorsky, albeit this was a controversial choice due to its U.S., rather than European, origins. U.K. Defence Secretary Michael Heseltine, who preferred an all-European solution to Westland's difficulties, resigned in January 1986 in what came to be known as the "Westland Affair," which split Margaret Thatcher's cabinet.

Westland teamed with Agusta again to develop the 15-ton EH101 Merlin, a replacement for the Sea King. This was accomplished through the joint venture E.H. Industries Limited. Interestingly, the U.S. firm IBM became the prime contractor on a 1991 Ministry of Defence contract for 44 EH101s configured for the antisubmarine role due to its ability to underwrite the EUR 1.5 billion project.

Westland Group was acquired by the engineering firm GKN PLC in 1994. It was subsequently renamed GKN Westland Helicopters. GKN had owned a stake in Westland for several years, and obtained control of the company after Sikorsky parent United Technology sold its stake. GKN offered considerable financial strength, which allowed Westland to become a prime contractor for major projects, such as a EUR 600 million Merlin HC Mk 3 order for the RAF.

Westland won a EUR 2.2 billion contract to build 67 Apache AH MK.1 helicopters in 1996. These were produced under license from Boeing Company, which was also a subcontractor. By the end of the 1990s, GKN Westland had revenues of about $1 billion.

Forming AgustaWestland in 2000

GKN and Finmeccanica S.p.A., the respective parent companies of Westland and Agusta, officially combined their helicopter operations on January 1, 2001, after more than two years of negotiations. In the deal a new holding company, AgustaWestland N.V., was incorporated in The Netherlands. AgustaWestland was one of the world's largest helicopter manufacturers, with annual revenues exceeding $2 billion and 10,000 employees. It had 6,000 aircraft in service. A major restructuring program was implemented soon after the merger.

In 2003, the company reported more than 100 orders for the AB 139 medium helicopter it was producing in collaboration with Bell Helicopter. Revenues were EUR 2.6 billion ($3.3 billion) in 2003, when the company delivered 118 aircraft, up nearly 20 percent from the previous year. According to *Flight International,* AgustaWestland had a 12 percent share of the

Key Dates:

1907: Giovanni Agusta forms an aircraft firm in Italy.
1948: Westland produces its first helicopter, a modified Sikorsky S-51.
1952: Agusta begins producing Bell helicopters under license.
1983: Agusta's A129 Mangusta is the first all-European combat helicopter.
1986: The "Westland Affair" controversy over the U.S.-led rescue package shakes up the Thatcher cabinet.
1994: Engineering firm GKN PLC acquires Westland Group.
1998: The Bell/Agusta Aerospace Company joint venture is formed to develop the AB139 helicopter and BA609 Tiltrotor.
2000: GKN and Finmeccanica S.p.A. form the Agusta-Westland joint venture.
2004: Finmeccanica acquires GKN's 50 percent holding in AgustaWestland.

global helicopter market, and its constituent companies had delivered a total of 7,500 helicopters.

Finmeccanica bought out GKN's 50 percent holding in AgustaWestland N.V. in 2004 for EUR 1 billion ($1.8 billion). Finmeccanica was shifting its corporate focus to the aerospace and defense market, and was also buying out its avionics joint venture with BAe Systems. Finmeccanica was 32.4 percent owned by the Italian government.

In January 2005, AgustaWestland, part of a team led by Lockheed Martin, won a $6.1 billion U.S. Navy contest to build Marine One, the U.S. president's helicopter (actually 23 helicopters were ordered). This was a controversial honor for a foreign manufacturer; AgustaWestland's three-engined US101 design, a derivative of the EH101, won out over a Sikorsky model since it was more spacious, had been proven in combat, and could be delivered sooner. Bell Helicopter, AgustaWestland's partner in Bell/Agusta Aerospace, was also part of the Lockheed Martin team. The news of the presidential helicopter win unfortunately was followed by layoffs of 640 workers at the U.K. plant due to other contracts winding up. The company had employed 4,000 people there.

The company hoped the prestigious Marine One order would lead to more success with the U.S. military, including a contract to supply up to 141 helicopters for the Air Force's $10 billion Personnel Recovery Vehicle program. Another bid, announced in October 2005, teamed AugustaWestland with L-3 Communications to pitch the twin-engine US139 for the U.S. Army's Light Utility Helicopters requirement to replace the Vietnam era UH-1 Huey. AgustaWestland also was winning large orders in the United Kingdom, including a EUR 1 billion deal for Future Lynx helicopters. The company was in the bidding for other Ministry of Defence requirements.

In a reversal of the company's origins, AgustaWestland was licensing its designs to foreign manufacturers. Denel Aerospace of South Africa was building the A109 light utility helicopter while Japan's Kawasaki Heavy Industries was making EH101s. AgustaWestland formed a joint venture in China to build and sell its A109 helicopter there. The company, which was getting established in Australia, also was promoting its products heavily in the South Pacific. While the world commercial helicopter market was expected to be flat, military demand was growing.

Principal Subsidiaries

Agusta Aerospace Corporation (U.S.A.); Agusta S.p.A. (Italy); AgustaWestland Inc. (U.S.A.); Westland Ltd. (U.K.).

Principal Operating Units

AgustaWestland Italy; AgustaWestland UK; AgustaWestland North America; AgustaWestland - AAC.

Principal Competitors

Bell Helicopter Textron Inc.; Eurocopter S.A.; MD Helicopters Holding, Inc.; Sikorsky Aircraft Corporation.

Further Reading

Boles, Tracey, "Agusta Expects Windfall of Orders After Bush Contract," *Sunday Business* (London), January 30, 2005.

Chambliss, Lauren, "AgustaWestland Has US Partners in Sight," *Evening Standard* (London), June 15, 2001, p. 42.

Cortes, Lorenzo, "AgustaWestland Is Upbeat About American Market, Cites Work with Domestic Producers," *Defense Daily,* March 18, 2003.

Cox, Bob, "Longtime Affiliate Agusta Now Providing Bell Helicopter Products to Make, Sell," *Fort Worth Star-Telegram,* February 8, 2005.

Crocker, Stan, "Whose Chopper Creates More Jobs? That's What the $7 Billion Battle Between Sikorsky and Europe's AgustaWestland to Replace the Marine One Fleet May Come Down To," *Business Week Online,* March 26, 2004.

Harrison, Michael, "Westland in £1.4bn Tie-Up with Agusta," *Independent* (London), July 27, 2000, p. 16.

"Helicopter Firm to Axe 640 Jobs," *Birmingham Post* (England), February 1, 2005, p. 15.

Hodge, Nathan, "Bid to Build on a Rare Victory," *Financial Times* (London), June 13, 2005, p. 4.

Hoyle, Craig, and Graham Warwick, "Talking Italian," *Flight International,* November 2, 2004, p. 48.

Montgomery, Dave, and Bob Cox, "Lockheed-Led Group Wins $6.1 Billion Contract to Build Marine One," *Fort Worth Star-Telegram,* January 28, 2005.

Muradian, Vago, and Neil Baumgardner, "Execs: EH101 Would Become 'American' If Selected for U.S. Service," *Defense Daily International,* June 1, 2001.

O'Brien, Heather, and Lisa Clifford, "AgustaWestland Loses British Pedigree," *Daily Deal,* May 27, 2004.

Polmar, Norman, and Floyd D. Kennedy, Jr., *Military Helicopters of the World: Military Rotary-Wing Aircraft Since 1917,* Annapolis, Md.: Naval Institute Press, c. 1981.

Sutton, Oliver, "Transition to AgustaWestland," *Interavia Business & Technology,* February 2001, p. 22.

Taylor, Michael J.H., and John W.R. Taylor, *Helicopters of the World,* New York: Charles Scribner's Sons, 1978.

Wastnage, Justin, "Focusing on Profit," *Flight International,* August 19, 2003, p. 30.

—Frederick C. Ingram

Alabama National BanCorporation

1927 First Avenue North
Birmingham, Alabama 35203
U.S.A.
Telephone: (205) 583-3600
Toll Free: (888) 583-3200
Fax: (205) 521-9307
Web site: http://www.alabamanational.com

Public Company
Founded: 1986
Employees: 1,492
Total Assets: $5.31 billion (2004)
Stock Exchanges: NASDAQ
Ticker Symbol: ALAB
NAIC: 551111 Offices of Bank Holding Companies; 522110
 Commercial Banking; 522120 Savings Institutions

Alabama National BanCorporation (ANB), a bank holding company, operates ten bank subsidiaries in Alabama, Florida, and Georgia. Through them the company offers full banking services to individuals and businesses. ANB also provides investment services and property and casualty insurance through its subsidiaries. The holding company's expansion was facilitated by relationships formed with smaller community banks.

Building Assets in Alabama: 1981–94

James A. Taylor purchased First National Bank of Ashland in 1981. He formed a bank holding company following the acquisition of three additional banks and served as chairman of the company. Two more banks and one thrift joined the Alabama National BanCorporation fold through 1993, according to *American Banker.*

Two acquisitions completed in the spring of 1994 boosted Alabama National's assets by $100 million. An initial public offering in November 1994 brought in $10 million. The funds were earmarked for long-term debt retirement and acquisitions of other financial institutions.

Plans to merge with another company of equal size were in the works in early spring 1995. Alabama National's CEO, CFO,

and treasurer would step down and sell their stock if the deal went forward. The Shoal Creek based operation made the announcement in April 1995, in the wake of stock activity.

American Banker reported: "William P. Johnson, attorney for the holding company, said it 'made sense' to issue the early announcement, because 'there was some market movement, and we wanted to avoid the risk of some parties' trading with less information than others.' "

Alabama National's stock had risen from $8.75 per share at year-end 1994 to $11.62 per share in early April. Trading had been 16 percent above normal during the negotiating period preceding the announcement. Peoples Bank and Trust of Selma and Community Bank of Blountsville, the two Alabama banks with slightly more assets than Alabama National's $271 million, were considered potential merger partners, according to *American Banker.*

Commenting on Alabama National's performance, Raymond James & Associates Inc. analyst Richard X. Bove told *American Banker,* "Their strategy has been not to run the hottest bank in America, but to piece together low-cost deposits in community banks and build a nice little company ultimately to be acquired." Bove concluded, "They've executed this very admirably."

Unusual Move: 1995–97

Alabama National did merge, but with a bank holding $130 million more in assets. National Bank of Commerce (NBC), based in Birmingham, would become the wholly owned subsidiary of Alabama National. The move allowed the larger bank a less cumbersome entry into the public arena. NBC shareholders would own majority interest in the company and control the board of directors. The two Alabama families owning 80 percent of NBC would hold 50.1 percent of Alabama National after the deal was completed, according to *American Banker.* Alabama National assumed $17.9 million of NBC's debt.

Earlier in 1995, Alabama National lost to NBC in a bid for the control of a $35 million thrift bank. "In trying to acquire new banks, we were butting heads with them," Frank W. Whitehead, Alabama National's CFO, told *American Banker* in

Company Perspectives:

Community Focus—Maintaining the local identities of our community banks provides a better understanding of our customers' needs in ANB's diverse markets. This insight enables us to tailor our product offerings and delivery channels to provide outstanding service to our customers.

June. "They run a bank similar to the way we do, and we just thought it was foolish to be bidding against each other."

In May 1996, Alabama National's founder James A. Taylor resigned and John H. Holcomb III succeeded him as chairman and CEO. Holcomb, who had been president and chief operating officer (COO) of Alabama National, also continued as president and CEO of National Bank of Commerce of Birmingham. Victor E. Nichol, Jr., executive vice-president (EVP) of Alabama National, succeeded Holcomb as president and COO. Nichol, following 23 years with AmSouth Bancorp, joined NBC in 1994 as EVP and CFO.

Alabama National, with $929 million in assets, ranked as the sixth largest bank in its home state in 1997. The holding company increased its presence in the northern part of Alabama through the purchase of First American Bancorp of Decatur, a $223 million asset bank. Alabama National crossed the border in Florida that year. Citizens & Peoples Bank, N.A. opened in Escambia County.

New Territory: 1998–2002

In 1998, Alabama National continued to turn its attention outside of its home state. The company, already holding one office in the Florida Panhandle, purchased a small commercial bank in the hot central Florida market. The commercial bank based in St. Cloud held $50 million in assets.

"Our board of directors wanted the bank to keep its identity and remain a local, community bank," Jack Shoffner, president of Public Bank, told the *Orlando Business Journal*. "That's what really attracted the board to Alabama National—they have seven banking subsidiaries that are run as independent community banks."

Alabama National then looked to the peach state and acquired Georgia State Bank of Mableton. The suburban Atlanta bank held $124 million in assets. Alabama National would also purchase its parent company, Community Financial Corp., for an estimated total of $37.6 million.

In September 1998, Alabama National went forth with its third bank deal of the year, this time in Naples, Florida. The west Florida-based Community Bank held $80 million in assets. As with the earlier deals, this was a stock transaction.

Alabama National entered the insurance business in 1999, when First American Bank purchased Rankin Insurance Inc.

In 2000, Alabama National reported net income of $24.4 million. Its 1.19 percent return on average assets beat the industry's 1 percent benchmark for strong earnings.

Alabama National acquired another central Florida bank in 2001, the $130 million in assets Peoples State Bank of Groveland. The Alabama holding company, now with a network of 11 banks and $2.2 billion in assets, continued to allow acquired banks to hold their names, bank charters, management, and local board of directors, reported Jim Freer for *Orlando Business Journal*.

Alabama National President Richard Murray told Freer: "What made our banks successful was the involvement and local knowledge of senior management and boards of directors." He added, "We try to keep a hands-off approach, unless it is providing back-office help along with technology and products that we have developed within the holding company."

To keep up with larger competitors, Peoples State Bank needed to broaden its services, either through developing them from the ground up, hiring third-party vendors, or merging with another operation. Alabama National offered Peoples access to its securities division, mortgage banking company, and property and casualty insurance businesses. The merger also enabled Peoples to up its loan limit.

Although separate charters increased costs relative to its regulation obligations, Alabama National felt the earnings produced by the independent banks justified the cost. In addition, with its banks operating in and around major cities, but not within them, Alabama National generally did not have to compete head-to-head with SouthTrust, AmSouth, and Colonial Bank for its business customers.

Alabama National's insurance business, operating as ABA Insurance Services Inc., purchased two small agencies, one in Alabama, another in Florida, in the second half of 2002. The operation had expanded in areas served by Alabama National banks, opening offices in nine markets in Alabama, Florida, and Georgia.

As for the bank holding company, assets had climbed to $3.2 billion. Its 11 bank subsidiaries operated a total of 62 branches. The largest bank was Birmingham's National Bank of Commerce.

Relationship-Building Paying Off: 2003–05

Alabama National announced its second and third Florida acquisitions of the year in October 2003. The purchase of Indian River Banking Company of Vero Beach, Florida, would be the biggest deal to date for the holding company. The $520 million Indian River Banking promised to build Alabama National's presence in that high growth region. The transaction was valued at $107 million in stock.

The company also planned to buy Cypress Bankshares Inc. of Palm Coast, Florida, and the acquisition of Millennium Bank in Gainesville had closed in June. The two smaller Florida banks had $110 million and $130 million in assets, respectively. The three purchases boosted Alabama National's holdings in Florida to seven banks with a total of $1.4 billion in assets.

The string of deals were a culmination of "relationship-building" begun in Florida several years earlier, according to John Pandtle, a Raymond James & Associates Inc. analyst quoted in *American Banker*.

Key Dates:

1981: James A. Taylor lays groundwork for Alabama bank holding company.
1995: Alabama National merges with National Bank of Commerce of Birmingham.
1997: Company buys first bank outside of home state.
1999: Company enters insurance business.
2003: Alabama National announces largest acquisition in company history.
2005: Internal consolidation reduces number of bank subsidiaries.

All of the Florida bank acquisitions announced by Alabama National during 2003 were with banks that had relationships with the holding company. "In fact, most of the 12 banks the $3.9 billion-asset company owns were once customers of its bond division," Victor Nichol, Jr., Alabama National's vice-chairman and head of NBC Securities, told *American Banker*.

The investment subsidiary allowed Alabama National to engage in an acquisition strategy that set it apart from most other holding companies acquiring community banks. Few of its competitors for the smaller banks sold bonds or had correspondent banking arrangements, and much larger banks were not interested in purchasing them.

Alabama's relationships laid the groundwork for future purchases in the competitive Florida market and benefited the holding company when it came time to strike a deal.

Jefferson Harralson, an analyst with Keefe, Bruyette & Woods Inc. in New York, told *American Banker* that Alabama National was making banks deals when others could not and bought them at a price lower than average for the Florida community bank market.

Furthermore, Alabama National's investment services income rose 38 percent in 2003 primarily due to an increase in bond sales. The bond business was begun in 1995, when Alabama National hired Victor Nichol, Jr., and eight other traders when AmSouth Bancorp of Birmingham shut down its bond division. Five AmSouth support employees also were hired. Some in the group had worked together for a quarter of a century. The team had relationships with 250 community banks, primarily in Alabama and Florida. Alabama had added more than 100 more banks since that time and expanded in Mississippi, Tennessee, Louisiana, and Georgia, as well, according to *American Banker*. The bond business planned a move into Kentucky and South Carolina.

Peoples State Bank merged with Public Bank in June 2004. In July, Coquina Bank of Ormond Beach, Florida, was acquired. Coquina and Cypress banks, with adjacent markets, merged to form CypressCoquina Bank in August.

NBC Securities' Victor J. Nichol and five others in the investment subsidiary resigned in late 2004. Nichol had been vice-chairman since 2000, had served as president and chief operating officer from 1996 to 2000, and had served on the board of directors since 1995. Six employees remained. The holding company planned to continue operating its correspondent and investment businesses despite the departures.

Alabama National's net income increased 33.1 percent in 2004, rising to $54.6 million from $41.0 million in 2003. During the year the company's market capitalization topped $1 billion for the first time.

In February 2005, National Bank of Commerce and First American Bank subsidiaries merged as First American Bank. The new bank held $2.4 billion in assets and operated in 33 locations in north and central Alabama. In May, First Citizens Banks was to be added to the fold, bringing in more than $100 million in assets.

In March 2005, First Gulf Bank and Citizens & Peoples Bank, N.A. merged as First Gulf Bank, N.A. The $491 million asset bank was headquartered in Pensacola, Florida. The internal mergers would reduce the number of subsidiaries to ten.

Principal Subsidiaries

First American Bank.

Principal Competitors

AmSouth Bancorporation; The Colonial BancGroup, Inc.; Compass Bancshares, Inc.

Further Reading

"Alabama National Plans In-State Deal," *American Banker*, July 29, 1997, p. 25.

Dillon, Paul, "Alabama, Public Tie the Knot: Public Bank Agrees to $14.8M Merger," *Orlando Business Journal*, March 13, 1998, pp. 1+.

Fontana, Dominick, "New Chairman for Alabama National in Merger's Wake," *American Banker*, May 2, 1996, p. 7.

Freer, Jim, "Alabama National Comes to Town," *Orlando Business Journal*, March 16, 2001, p. 18.

"In Brief: Ala. National Deals Expand Agency," *American Banker*, October 16, 2002, p. 9.

Kline, Alan, "In Brief: Buyout Would Expand Ala. National into Ga.," *American Banker*, June 15, 1998, p. 10.

Rhoads, Christopher, "After Trading Surge, Alabama National Reveals Negotiations for Merger of Equals," *American Banker*, April 3, 1995, p. 6.

——, "Curious Wrinkle in $55M Alabama Deal: Buyer to Assume the Smaller Bank's Name," *American Banker*, June 6, 1995, p. 4.

Thompson, Laura K., "Alabama National in Another Fla. Acquisition Deal," *American Banker*, October 24, 2003, p. 4.

——, "Turning Bond Customers into Buyout Candidates," *American Banker*, January 23, 2003, p. 1.

Osuri, Laura Thompson, "Alabama National Consolidating," *American Banker*, November 2, 2004, p. 8.

——, "In Brief: Bond-Unit Defections at Alabama National," *American Banker*, November 18, 2004, p. 27.

Whiteman, Louis, "Alabama National to Buy Fla. Bank for $15M," *American Banker*, September 23, 1998, p. 7.

—Kathleen Peippo

American Reprographics Company

700 North Central Avenue, Suite 550
Glendale, California 91203
U.S.A.
Telephone: (818) 500-0225
Fax: (818) 500-0195
Web site: http://www.e-arc.com

Public Company
Incorporated: 1967 as Micro Device, Inc.
Employees: 3,410
Sales: $443.8 million (2004)
Stock Exchanges: New York
Ticker Symbol: ARP
NAIC: 323122 Prepress Services; 323110 Commercial
Lithographic Printing; 323121 Tradebinding and
Related Work

American Reprographics Company (ARC) is the largest reprographics company in the United States, providing document management services to architectural, engineering, and construction firms, as well as to companies involved in financial services, retail, entertainment, and food and hospitality. Reprographics services generally include digital management and reproduction of construction documents and other graphics-related material. ARC's proprietary "PlanWell" software is an Internet-based solution that enables architects, engineers, and other construction professionals to view plans and submit bids online. ARC sells PlanWell to its customers and licenses the software to independent reprographers. The company also operates "PEiR" (Profit and Education in Reprographics), a program that provides purchasing, technology, and educational material to other reprographers. ARC operates more than 180 reprographic centers in 141 cities in 30 states. The company also operates four service centers in the greater Toronto metropolitan area and one in Mexico City. ARC expands by acquiring small, local reprographics firms, typically retaining management and the name of the firms after they are acquired.

Origins

For more than 30 years, ARC's predecessor led a quiet, unassuming existence, never showing a sign of becoming the aggressive consolidator that later stood atop its industry. The dramatic change in purpose and strategy that transformed a modestly sized, locally oriented business into a national giant came after new owners and new management assumed control over the company. Sathiyamurthy "Mohan" Chandramohan and his childhood friend Kumarakulasingam "Suri" Suriyakumar were the individuals responsible for spearheading the transformation, two Sri Lankan natives who changed the face of the U.S. reprographics industry. Chandramohan came from a background in banking and retail, spending his professional career in Sri Lanka at the Hong Kong and Shanghai Banking Corporation before joining U-Save Auto Parts Stores in 1981, where he rose to the positions of chief operating officer and chief financial officer during a seven-year stay. Suriyakumar's Sri Lankan years were spent at Aitken Spence & Co. Ltd., a conglomerate that ranked as one of the country's five largest corporations. Although Aitken Spence's diverse business activities required Suriyakumar to work in several different capacities, the majority of his time was spent in shipping and freight-forwarding.

Before Chandramohan and Suriyakumar began their assault on the reprographics industry, the company they used to launch their assault operated as one of thousands of small reprographics firms populating the nation. ARC was founded as a sole proprietorship in 1960, beginning as a single storefront in Los Angeles that operated under the name Ford Graphics. In 1967, the company was dissolved and a new corporate structure was established, marking the birth of Micro Device, Inc., which continued to provide reprographics services under the Ford Graphics banner. Over the course of the next 20 years, Micro Device expanded, but not by much, adding another shop by the time Chandramohan joined the company in 1988 as president. Suriyakumar joined his friend the following year, accepting the post of vice-president. Suriyakumar's arrival coincided with the owner's decision to retire, which prompted the two Sri Lankans to acquire the company's assets. Micro Device, with two stores and $9 million in annual revenue in 1989, was much like the type of company Chandramohan and Suriyakumar would spend

Company Perspectives:

Our objective is to continue to strengthen our competitive position as the preferred provider of business-to-business document management, document distribution and logistics, and print-on-demand services.

the next 15 years aggressively acquiring, with each acquisition representing a building block that eventually formed the industry's leader, ARC.

Although Micro Device increased in size by a factor of 75 during the 1990s, the acquisition campaign that delivered such startling growth did not begin immediately after Chandramohan and Suriyakumar acquired the company. Unfortunately for the two new owners, their purchase was completed just before recessive economic conditions settled in, scuttling any plans for expansion and placing a premium on squeezing any profit they could out of the business. The two partners later put a positive spin on their first years in control, claiming that the bleak economic conditions gave them time to learn the reprographics business. Once the economic climate improved, the new owners began to make their first acquisitions, using what Suriyakumar, in a February 2, 2001 interview with the *San Francisco Business Times* called "very creative financing."

Micro Device's acquisitive activity, which intensified later in the decade under the ARC name, was designed to consolidate a highly fragmented industry. According to the International Reprographics Association, the market generated $5 billion in annual revenues, a total collected by roughly 3,000 relatively small reprographics firms. A typical firm employed 20 to 25 workers, generated $1.5 million in annual revenue, and was privately owned, usually by the founders of the firm. Chandramohan and Suriyakumar planned to build on their base in California and create the industry's first nationwide competitor, a company that would serve as an umbrella organization for the scores of small firms dotting the country, giving each member of their family the benefits of operating within a greater whole and access to technology unique to their company. Almost without exception, Chandramohan and Suriyakumar retained the management of each acquired company and kept the name of the firm, cobbling together a collection of locally branded firms that to the unknowing eye appeared to be independent.

ARC Launching an Aggressive Acquisition Campaign in 1997

After establishing a small base of operations with "creative financing," Chandramohan and Suriyakumar turned to traditional bank loans to fund the expansion of their company. The scope of their acquisition campaign widened considerably after they refinanced the company in 1997, a recapitalization effort that involved changing the corporate structure of the company to a California limited liability company, which took the name American Reprographics Holdings, LLC. The change in structure and name coincided with a $15 million investment by TZS Capital, which gave Chandramohan and Suriyakumar the capital to accelerate their acquisition program. After the deal was

completed, Chandramohan and Suriyakumar owned 50 percent of the company, while outside investors owned the other half.

After the investment by TZS, the company began to record strident growth. By 1998, the company's annual revenues had increased to $140 million, a total that leaped to $223 million in 1999 when the company completed 20 separate acquisitions, half the number of acquisitions completed during the 1990s. The supply of capital available for acquisitions received another infusion in February 2000, when the Chicago-based investment firm Code Hennessy & Simmons LLC acquired TZS Capital's 50 percent stake. Code Hennessy, which managed more than $1 billion in investments, provided Chandramohan and Suriyakumar with $82.5 million to continue their buying spree. After completing 20 acquisitions in 1999, they purchased 14 reprographic firms in 2000, including their largest acquisition up to that point, Houston, Texas-based Ridgway's Inc. in September 2000. Ridgway's, which was acquired for $100 million, was the second largest reprographics company in the country with $70 million in annual revenue and 22 locations in the southern and eastern United States.

The acquisition of Ridgway's represented a major step toward national dominance, bringing ARC's closest rival into its network, but the acquisition was an anomaly because of its size. The company's growing national presence was built almost entirely by purchasing reprographics firms with between $3 million and $5 million in annual revenues, companies that were a fraction of Ridgway's' size. "The companies we acquire have a stranglehold on the local market," Suriyakumar explained in a February 2, 2001 interview with the *San Francisco Business Times*. "And they are very strong in that way because we chose companies that have built up customer bases," he added. "What we do is figure out a way to let them operate as separate companies under their current ownership, so that the strong locality does not suffer under the larger corporate identity." A more typical example of the company's acquisition strategy was a firm purchased one month after Suriyakumar spoke with the *San Francisco Business Times*. The company acquired Rhode Island Blueprint, a supplier of reprographics products and services with 17 employees and $3 million in revenues. Rhode Island Blueprint's president and founder, Peter Morn, reacted to the deal in much the same way other owners and operators responded after joining the ARC network. "There won't be any changes to the operation or employees," he said. "Joining ARC opens new competitive technological advantages for us." For Rhode Island Blueprint, as it was for the dozens of firms gathering under the ARC umbrella, it was business as usual after joining the network, but with benefits of being part of a national organization.

By the time Rhode Island Blueprint was acquired, Chandramohan and Suriyakumar were striving to reach $500 million in sales by the end of the year. They fell short of the $500 million mark, and failed to reach the financial goal for the next three years, but the stature of the company was no less impressive. They spent $32.6 million on acquiring 14 reprographics firms in 2001, helping to lift revenues to $420 million. By this point, the firms that were joining the company were benefiting from more than just ARC's financial resources and managerial support. In June 2000, the company launched Plan-Well, the "technological advantage" Peter Morn referred to

Key Dates:

1960: Predecessor Ford Graphics opens a store in Los Angeles.

1967: Micro Device, Inc. is formed to take over the business of Ford Graphics.

1989: Micro Device is acquired by Chandramohan and Suriyakumar.

1997: An investment by TZS Capital touches off an ambitious acquisition campaign for Micro Device, which changes its name to American Reprographics Holdings, LLC.

2000: Code Hennessy & Simmons acquires TZS Capital's stake.

2005: American Reprographics Company completes its initial public offering of stock.

after becoming part of the ARC family. PlanWell was web-based software that offered a ''planroom-to-print'' solution to the firms operating under ARC's control, enabling architects, engineers, and other construction professionals to view plans, submit bids, and purchase reprographics services via the Internet. Initially, PlanWell technology was only available to firms operating under the ARC umbrella, but in 2003 the company began licensing the technology to independent reprographers, the same year the company started PEiR (Profit and Education in Reprographics). PEiR was a trade organization through which the company charged membership fees and provided purchasing, technology, and educational benefits to reprographers.

ARC inched toward the $500 million in annual sales as it entered the mid-2000s, continuing to add reprographics firms to its ever expanding network. After spending $34.4 million for eight reprographers in 2002, the company purchased four firms for $870,000 in 2003 and six firms for $3.7 million in 2004. By the end of 2004, the company had completed 86 acquisitions since 1997, giving it a total of 181 locations in 30 states. As a low-cost way to complement its expansion via acquisitions, the company opened 30 branch offices in 2004 and planned to open 12 more locations in 2005.

Public Debut in 2005

ARC maintained a dominant market position midway through the decade, standing as the only nationally oriented

reprographics company in the country. The company controlled more than five times as many service locations as its closest rival and maintained a presence in eight times as many cities as its nearest competitor. Chandramohan and Suriyakumar decided to sell the company's stalwart position on Wall Street, both as a way to gain access to capital and to allow private investors to cash out on their investment. They filed for an initial public offering (IPO) of stock in December 2004, reorganizing American Reprographics Holdings, LLC as a Delaware corporation named American Reprographics Company in preparation for the IPO. The company completed its IPO in February 2005, raising $174 million. With the proceeds from the stock offering, Chandramohan and Suriyakumar were expected to continue their acquisition campaign and build on their already considerable lead in the industry. In the years ahead, there was every expectation that the ARC organization would factor as the preeminent competitor in the reprographics industry.

Principal Subsidiaries

American Reprographics Company, LLC.

Principal Competitors

Service Point Solutions, S.A.; Thomas Reprographics, Inc.; ABC Imaging, LLC; National Reprographics Inc.

Further Reading

Adams, Brent, ''Former Blue Print Firm Reinvents Itself with New Owner,'' *Indianapolis Business Journal,* March 15, 2004, p. 35.

Berry, Kate, ''Architectural Technology Firm Poised to Benefit from Boom,'' *Los Angeles Business Journal,* June 20, 2005, p. 30.

''Blueprint Maker Keeps Growing,'' *Los Angeles Business Journal,* February 26, 2001, p. 33.

''Blueprint Sales Firm Acquires Cook's,'' *Wisconsin State Journal,* November 5, 2005, p. D12.

''California Company Acquires Rhode Island Blueprint,'' *Providence Business News,* April 9, 2001, p. 16.

Garcia, Shelly, ''One of Valley's Largest Private Companies Files IPO,'' *San Fernando Business Journal,* December 6, 2004, p. 1.

Hopkins, Brent, ''Public Offering on Tap Today,'' *Daily News,* February 4, 2005, p. B1.

Materna, Jessica, ''Print Firm Duplicates Company Philosophy,'' *San Francisco Business Times,* February 2, 2001, p. 21.

Myerhoff, Matt, ''Tale of Two Companies Highlights Different Strategies to Business Growth,'' *Los Angeles Business Journal,* July 18, 2005, p. 19.

—Jeffrey L. Covell

Anderson Trucking Service, Inc.

203 Cooper Avenue North
P.O. 1377
St. Cloud, Minnesota 56302
U.S.A.
Telephone: (320) 255-7400
Toll Free: (800) 328-2307
Fax: (320) 255-7494
Web site: http://www.ats-inc.com

Private Company
Incorporated: 1955
Sales: $422 million (2004 est.)
NAIC: 484121 General Freight Trucking, Long-Distance, Truckload

Anderson Trucking Service, Inc. (ATS), ranked among the top transportation companies in the United States, is a leader in specialized transportation. The company also serves customers in need of wind energy, heavy haul, vans, and pad wrap van transportation. By way of wholly owned subsidiaries and alliances, the Minnesota-based company offers additional shipping solutions, such as international and logistics services. During its anniversary year of 2005, ATS's resources consisted of more than 1,900 tractors and 3,300 trailers, delivering more than 100,000 loads each year.

Roots in the Back Woods: 1920s–40s

Anderson Trucking Service, Inc.'s legacy dates back to a time and place in which horses provided the most reliable pulling power. Elmer Anderson contracted with a timber company to haul logs out of the northeastern Minnesota forest during the early days of the 1920s.

He shifted to a different kind of horsepower in 1922, selling his teams and buying a used truck. In 1926, Anderson fabricated his first semi, using Model T parts, and hauled cattle to stockyards in South St. Paul. That same year, Anderson brokered a transportation relationship with Cold Spring Granite, building a semi to haul 15-ton blocks out of an Isle, Minnesota, quarry to

the railroad right of way. Anderson would also establish a road construction business, a venture grown out of the need to keep roads passable from the quarry to the railway, and car and truck dealerships.

In 1935, Elmer Anderson embarked on transporting finished monuments and building granite, moving into competition with railroad companies. Elmer's son Harold was behind the wheel by then. Three Anderson units provided long-distance service for Cold Spring Granite by 1941.

Harold Anderson enlisted in the Army Air Corps in 1942, eventually flying 29 missions. The end of the war with Germany, in 1945, brought the younger Anderson home to his wife in Isle, Minnesota, and back to his father's trucking enterprise.

Expansion Drive: 1950s–70s

A prolonged illness forced Harold Anderson out from behind the wheel, to a desk in St. Cloud, beginning in 1951. The move would prove pivotal for the family business, with Anderson envisioning and enacting on new ideas.

In 1955, the Andersons gained Granite City Transfer's operating authority, covering trucking in 20 states. The business incorporated as Anderson Trucking Service, Inc. Harold Anderson then convinced competing granite companies in the St. Cloud area to combine their shipments through ATS, thus gaining an advantage against other regional quarries.

In 1957, construction began on a new interstate highway system, a boon for the trucking industry. The purchase of another operating authority in 1958 gave ATS entry into new areas of transport, including heavy machinery and construction equipment, within the states of Minnesota, Wisconsin, and Iowa.

ATS continued to expand its reach geographically and in terms of the materials it was authorized to handle. In 1959, the company set up its first out-of-state terminal, in Illinois, to facilitate its growing operation.

Revenues topped $1 million in 1961. The trucking business now served all 48 contiguous states. Sadly, founder Elmer Anderson died in 1967. A year later, ATS gained an authority to

Company Perspectives:

Behind the trucks and the technology there are always THE PEOPLE OF ATS. Our employees are the real reason ATS is such a spectacular operation. We attract—and keep—the best, working hard to make ATS a place that good talented people want to be. In all honesty we can say that Anderson Trucking Service, Inc. employs the very best transportation professionals in the world today, whether drivers, office people or mechanics. You want to talk competitive advantage? Our success always points back to them.

move iron and steel, marking the beginning of a significant area of business for the company. In 1969, Harold Anderson bought K&W Transportation, serving the Alaskan pipeline. The transaction was separate from his involvement with ATS. Around the same time Anderson established St. Cloud Truck Sales.

In 1971, Harold Anderson acquired the family's ATS shares. His son Rollie joined the company in 1972, bringing in data processing expertise gained in the Air Force.

By the end of the decade, 463 people worked as employees or independent contractors for ATS, hauling a variety of specialized loads.

New Rules of the Road: 1980s–90s

The Surface Transportation Act of 1980 moved the industry toward deregulation, ending operating authorities and producing an explosion of new carriers. ATS responded by ramping up marketing and service and upgrading its fleet. The wave of deregulation put many trucking companies under, but the diversified ATS not only survived, it grew.

In 1983 the company purchased Haupt Contract Carriers, thus establishing a van division. That same year, ATS began operating its own articulated rail cars, a first in the carrier business.

Sureway Transportation Company was established as the ATS Brokerage Division in 1989, the year revenues topped $100 million. The ATS fleet consisted of more than 600 power units and 1,500 trailers.

The early 1990s marked expansion of services to the south: Mexico in 1990 and Puerto Rico in 1992. The 1993 purchase of Iowa-based Warren Transport from Federal Express added 450 tractors and 1,500 trailers to the fleet.

Back home in Minnesota, there was as much grumbling about the business climate as the weather. Minnesota workers' compensation rates, much higher than surrounding states, drove trucking companies to seek creative remedies to cut costs. Some companies began hiring drivers out-of-state through employee leasing operations, allowing them to minimize the risk of paying Minnesota rates to injured drivers. Anderson Trucking, which employed more than 400 drivers, had stopped hiring in its home state during the latter half of the 1980s, shifting hiring and training to hub states of Wisconsin, Indiana, and North Carolina.

In 1999, ATS produced sales in excess of $250 million and had four business divisions.

Harold Anderson, a decorated World War II pilot, reflected on how he had drawn upon his military experience to build the trucking business. "In war, you learn the difference between being a boss and being a leader," Anderson said, according to Sue Halena of the *St. Cloud Times*.

Challenges in the 21st Century: 2000–05

Fuel costs, along with job injuries, ranked high on the list of concerns for trucking firms trying to maintain competitive rates while turning a profit. Diesel fuel climbed from about 97 cents a gallon in January 1999 to $1.47 a gallon in early February 2000. The high cost had forced many independent drivers off the road. ATS had begun levying a fuel surcharge to customers, but the fee covered loaded miles only. The result was pressure on the company's operating margins.

John Hausalden, president of the Minnesota Trucking Association, told the *St. Cloud Times*, "I think it's important to note that the diesel price problem comes at a time when the trucking industry is being attacked by the government." He explained, "The government wants to reduce the number of hours truckers can drive, and there are new stringent emission standards for sulphur in fuel, which drives down the efficiency. It's like a triple whammy for truckers to handle."

In response to customer and internal demand, ATS introduced a more sophisticated Internet site in October 2000; a basic site was launched in 1997. Load tracking, its most popular feature, allowed customers to track shipments and family members to follow their trucker's route.

"The new site also acts as a target marketing campaign in that it enables the company to differentiate itself from transportation competitors, including Warner Transportation, Sioux Falls, S.D., and Trism Inc., Kennesaw, Ga. 'We're constantly looking at ways to respond to customers' and drivers' needs—whatever it takes to make it easier and more profitable to do business with us,' " Larry Weston, e-commerce manager for ATS, told *B to B*. The site had also drawn the interest of potential employees.

Harold Anderson died in November 2001, at the age of 85. "Harold was really considered one of the pillars of the Minnesota trucking industry," the state's Trucking Association's Hausalden said of Anderson. "One of the things that made Harold so respected was that he was willing to share what he knew and was willing to help other trucking companies get better." Corporate revenues, by that time, had reached nearly $300 million.

Two years later, revenues stood at $360 million. While the company was still headquartered in St. Cloud, other offices were located in Indiana, Iowa, California, Texas, North Carolina, Wisconsin, Florida, Montana, and Puerto Rico.

In an effort to bring more drivers aboard, Anderson began offering signing bonuses and higher wages. The driver shortage was related in part to the wage scale, nature of the work, and federal minimum age of 21 for drivers, according to a Novem-

Key Dates:

1922: Elmer Anderson sells his horses and buys a truck.
1926: Anderson forms transportation relationship with Cold Spring Granite.
1942: Son Harold Anderson leaves job as truck driver to enlist in Army.
1951: Illness gives Harold Anderson new perspective.
1955: Family business incorporates as Anderson Trucking Service, Inc. (ATS).
1958: Company attains authorization to begin hauling materials other than granite or stone.
1959: First out-of-state terminal is established.
1961: Gross revenues top $1 million.
1971: Harold Anderson buys family shares of ATS.
1980: Surface Transportation Act marks the beginning of increased competition for trucking industry.
1983: Van division is created with purchase of Haupt Contract Carriers.
1991: Company opens sales office in Mexico.
1992: New division is created to serve Puerto Rican market.
1993: Company purchases Warren Transport.
2000: Total ATS revenues reach more than $275 million.
2005: ATS celebrates 50 years in business.

ber 2004 *St. Paul Pioneer Press* article. Moreover, the nations' manufacturing downturn during the early years of the 21st century had put scores of trucking companies out of business, sending many drivers into other lines of work. The industry also faced new federal hours-of-service rules limiting driving hours.

Anderson Trucking began work on its new $10 million headquarters in May 2005.

Growth of the city of St. Cloud and the company had limited access to the site established 50 years earlier. The new facility would be twice as large as the old, incorporating data and voice systems in compliance with Homeland Security regulations for transportation businesses. Stone from Cold Spring Granite quarries was to be incorporated in the building, a bow to the company's roots.

Principal Subsidiaries

ATS Logistics; ICE International.

Principal Competitors

Crete Carrier; Landstar System, Inc.; Schneider National.

Further Reading

"Anderson Trucking Wins 2nd Straight Safety Award," *St. Cloud Times*, April 15, 2004, p. 1A.

Barbour, Tracy, "Trucking Firm Buys Out Rival: Purchase of K&W Transportation Makes Carlile State's Largest," *Anchorage Daily News*, June 23, 1994, p. 1D.

Bjorhus, Jennifer, "Help Wanted for Long Haul," *St. Paul Pioneer Press*, November 14, 2004, p. 1A.

Freeman, Laurie, "Case Study: Indulging Your Client-Side," *B to B*, June 11, 2001, p. 18.

Halena, Sue, "Anderson Trucking Founder Dies at 85," *St. Cloud Times*, November 29, 2001, p. 1A.

——, "Anderson Trucking Starts Work on I-94 Headquarters," *St. Cloud Times*, May 1, 2005, p. 1E.

——, "Anderson Trucking to Relocate Headquarters," *St. Cloud Times*, August 19, 2004, p. 1A.

——, "War Duty Prepared St. Cloud Entrepreneur," *St. Cloud Times*, May 31, 1999, p. 3A.

McGrath, Dennis J., and Diane Alters, "Trucking Loophole: Firms Escaping Workers' Comp Rates in State," *Star Tribune*," March 3, 1992, p. 1A.

Tan, Michelle, "High Diesel Prices a Drain on Trucking Industry," *St. Cloud Times*, August 3, 2000, p. 1A.

Witham, Tracy, *One Man's Life: The Harold E. Anderson Story*, St. Cloud, Minn.: Anderson Trucking Service, Inc., 1999.

—Kathleen Peippo

Archer Daniels Midland Company

4666 East Faries Parkway
P.O. Box 1470
Decatur, Illinois 62525
U.S.A.
Telephone: (217) 424-5200
Toll Free: (800) 637-5843
Fax: (217) 424-5839
Web site: http://www.admworld.com

Public Company
Incorporated: 1923
Employees: 26,317
Sales: $35.94 billion (2005)
Stock Exchanges: New York
Ticker Symbol: ADM
NAIC: 111419 Other Food Crops Grown Under Cover;
112511 Finfish Farming and Fish Hatcheries; 311119
Other Animal Feed Manufacturing; 311211 Flour
Milling; 311212 Rice Milling; 311213 Malt
Manufacturing; 311221 Wet Corn Milling; 311222
Soybean Processing; 311223 Other Oilseed Processing;
311225 Fats and Oils Refining and Blending; 311312
Cane Sugar Refining; 311320 Chocolate and
Confectionery Manufacturing from Cacao Beans;
311823 Dry Pasta Manufacturing; 311830 Tortilla
Manufacturing; 311999 All Other Miscellaneous Food
Manufacturing; 312140 Distilleries; 325193 Ethyl
Alcohol Manufacturing; 325411 Medicinal and
Botanical Manufacturing; 422510 Grain and Field Bean
Wholesalers; 493130 Farm Product Warehousing and
Storage; 522110 Commercial Banking; 523130
Commodity Contracts Dealing

Archer Daniels Midland Company (ADM) is one of the world's leading processors and distributors of agricultural products for food and animal feed, with additional operations in transportation and storage of such products. Its principal operations process soybeans, corn, and wheat, the three largest crops in the United States. ADM also processes cocoa beans, milo, oats, barley, and peanuts. The company's feed products are sold to farmers, feed dealers, and livestock producers, while its food products are sold to food and beverage manufacturers. Among ADM's better-known products are NutriSoy, a soy protein; Novasoy Isoflavones, an ingredient used in dietary supplements; xanthan gum, a thickening agent used in food products such as salad dressings; citric acid and lactic acid, both used as food additives in food and beverage products to increase their acidity; natural vitamin E; and ethanol, an additive made from corn that is added to gasoline to improve the fuel efficiency of vehicles. AMD operates more than 250 processing plants throughout the world.

Early History

John W. Daniels began crushing flaxseed to make linseed oil in Ohio in 1878, and in 1902 he moved to Minneapolis, Minnesota, to organize the Daniels Linseed Company. The company consisted of a flax crushing plant that made three products: raw linseed oil, boiled linseed oil, and linseed cake or meal. In 1903 George A. Archer joined the firm, and in a few years it became the Archer-Daniels Linseed Company. Archer also brought experience to the firm, as his family had been in the business of crushing flaxseed since the 1830s. Archer and Daniels then hired a young bookkeeper by the name of Samuel Mairs, who eventually became the company's chairperson.

These three men had a common goal of "year-round production at low margins," a goal that continued to direct the company into the 21st century. Archer and Daniels used hydraulic presses to process flaxseed, and their linseed oil was essentially the same as that used by the ancient Egyptians. In the early years, profits were low, but Archer-Daniels Linseed never finished a year in debt. They also grew slowly, buying the stock of the Toledo Seed & Oil Company as well as the Dellwood Elevator Company, a grain elevator firm.

In 1923 the company purchased the Midland Linseed Products Company and then incorporated as the Archer Daniels Midland Company. The 1920s also brought other significant changes. Archer, Daniels, and Mairs began the scientific explo-

Company Perspectives:

Because everything ADM does begins with agriculture, our partnership with the farming community is vital. Farmers are essential to the overall economy, and that's why we work to be essential to them—creating thousands of products from their crops, hundreds of markets for their crops.

ration of methods to alter the chemical structure of linseed oil. This project initiated the company's successful research and development program. Research and development allocations were not commonplace for companies at that time, and the market took note of the company's slogan: "Creating New Values from America's Harvests."

Throughout the 1920s the company made steady purchases of oil processing companies in the Midwest while engaging in other agricultural activities. It built elevators on Minneapolis loading docks to store grain awaiting shipment down the Mississippi to other ports. Then, in 1930, Archer Daniels Midland purchased the Commander-Larabee Company, a major flour miller with plants in Minnesota, Kansas, and Missouri. Commander-Larabee was capable of producing 32,000 barrels per day. The purchase of Commander-Larabee had two additional advantages: it allowed ADM to coordinate its oil byproduct business with Commander-Larabee's feedstuff byproduct business, and the mutual sales effort lowered overhead. During this time, the company also discovered how to extract lecithin from soybean oil, reducing the price of lecithin from ten dollars to one dollar per pound. (Lecithin was widely used as an emulsifier in the food and confectionery industries.) As a result of Archer Daniels Midland's growth strategies and research activities, the company had $22.5 million in assets by 1938.

As a linseed oil manufacturer, Archer Daniels Midland interacted with more than just the food market. The paint product industry used drying oils, namely, linseed, tung, and perilla, in the manufacture of various products to add critical gloss and hardness properties to paint finishes. The demand for drying oil in the paint industry fluctuated widely because it depended heavily on construction, as well as on the availability and price of imported oils, since most oils were imported from the Far East and South America. Sales and profits also fluctuated due to the quality and size of each year's harvest. Despite these challenges and the onset of the Great Depression, the company continued to turn a profit, in part because Archer Daniels Midland had been working to adapt oils to new markets, including soaps, drugs, brake fluids, lubricants, petroleum, and chemicals.

Since Archer Daniels Midland knew the value of its research department, it appropriated 70 percent of its earnings ($1 million to $2 million annually) back into the business for development and expansion. One result was a process whereby the usable fibers (the tow) of flax straw (a waste product up to then) could be used in the manufacture of flax papers. World War II made it impossible for the company to increase its facilities as much as it wished; nevertheless, ADM's capacities grew significantly from 1930 to 1945. From a 1929 processing capacity of 20 million bushels of flaxseed per day, the company could process 36.6 million bushels per day by 1945. Wheat flour capacity went from zero to 30 million bushels per day. Grain storage capacity increased from 7.5 million to 50.4 million bushels per day.

Postwar Growth

The immediate postwar years from 1946 through 1949 showed dramatic growth: sales increased 287 percent, and net income increased 346 percent. In 1949 sales were $277 million, with a $12 million net profit. Archer Daniels Midland was well positioned in several market areas because it supplied basic ingredients to a wide range of industries. The company was the leading U.S. processor of linseed oil, the fourth largest flour miller, and the largest soybean processor. It also served the paint, leather, printing, gasoline, paper, cosmetics, pharmaceuticals, rubber, ceramics, munitions, and insecticides industries.

A conservative management style had consistently safeguarded the company's success. For instance, whenever possible, Archer Daniels Midland hedged its purchases of raw products by sales in the futures markets or by forward sales of the completed products. By the end of fiscal 1949, the company had no bank debt, and it had paid a dividend every year from 1927 onward. All plants were kept at a high state of operating efficiency, using modern, streamlined methods. There had also been a change in the processing level. The company began to put its products through advanced physical processing instead of selling them in a raw or semi-finished state, thereby increasing profit margins. Overall, management estimated that 40 percent of its increase in sales from 1939 to 1949 was due to new products and methods.

Because the company supplied core oils used in foundry industries, the outbreak of the Korean War increased demands on production through the early 1950s. The company was also increasing its outlay for whale oil procurement, which it had begun in the 1930s, and began increasing its production of protein concentrates, marketing them extensively for stock-feeding purposes.

When President Thomas L. Daniels (son of the founder) and Chairperson Samuel Mairs celebrated Archer Daniels Midland's 50th anniversary in 1952, the company was manufacturing over 700 standard products and had extended its operations overseas. More foreign expansion followed in Peru, Mexico, The Netherlands, and Belgium. In these ventures, the company specialized in partnerships with local interests. President Daniels expressed the company's attitude toward foreign involvement in the late 1950s when he said: "ADM looks with particular favor on Western Europe as an area of great chemical producers. . . . All industry there is expanding rapidly, both for local consumption and for export to other parts of the world."

Archer Daniels Midland had weathered the Great Depression and World War II, but ran into trouble during the 1960s. Although it made several grain production and storage purchases in the early 1960s, unstable commodities prices and the company's chemicals operations were causing losses. Net earnings were $75 million in 1963 and then declined to about $60 million in 1964, dropping even further to $50 million the following year. By 1965, the company could not cover its

---

Key Dates:

1878: John W. Daniels begins crushing flaxseed to make linseed oil in Ohio.

1902: Daniels moves to Minneapolis to organize the Daniels Linseed Company.

1903: George A. Archer joins the firm, which is renamed the Archer-Daniels Linseed Company within a few years.

1923: Company purchases the Midland Linseed Products Company, then incorporates as the Archer Daniels Midland Company.

1930: Commander-Larabee Company, a major flour miller, is acquired.

1966: Dwayne O. Andreas purchases a block of stock, gaining seats on the company board and the executive committee.

1970: Andreas is named CEO.

1971: Company purchases Corn Sweeteners, Inc., producer of high-fructose syrups, glutens, oil, and caramel color.

1972: Andreas is elected chairman.

1981: The Columbian Peanut Company is acquired.

1986: Company forms grain marketing joint venture with Growmark.

1996: Company pleads guilty to two counts of fixing prices of lysine and citric acid and pays $100 million in criminal fines.

1997: Company acquires W.R. Grace's cocoa business, marking its entry into that sector; G. Allen Andreas is named CEO.

1998: Three former company executives, including Michael D. Andreas, are convicted by a federal jury of price fixing.

1999: Dwayne Andreas retires as chairman; CEO Allen Andreas is named to the additional post of chairman; Michael Andreas begins serving two-year prison sentence.

2004: Company pays $400 million to resolve allegations it had colluded in fixing prices for high-fructose corn syrup.

2005: Net earnings eclipse $1 billion for the first time.

---

dividend. At this time, John Daniels, president and grandson of one of the founders, and Shreve M. Archer, Jr., a company director, recruited Dwayne O. Andreas to the leadership team. Andreas gradually took control of the company, gaining seats on the board and the executive committee in 1966, rising to CEO in 1970, and becoming chairman in 1972. Andreas revolutionized Archer Daniels Midland.

Mid-1960s Through 1980s: Andreas the "Soybean King"

Andreas's low profile appealed to the company management, as did his background in the production of farm products. One of the first things Andreas did was eliminate a 27-person public relations department. Eschewing the advice of analysts and often declining to talk to reporters, Andreas was a unique executive. His political views were often in opposition to those of the larger business community; for example, he advocated increases in the corporate income tax rate.

Andreas believed that one specific product, soybeans, could do a great deal to turn the company around. Andreas recalled, "I knew that ADM was a dozen years ahead of everyone else in textured vegetable protein research, and I believed that was where important action was going to be." Whereas scientists advocated an almost pure protein product derived from the soybean, Andreas encouraged the development of textured vegetable protein, a 50 percent protein soy product that was far more economical to produce. His increasing power in the company (by 1968 he was chair of the executive committee) made his plans a reality. Andreas described his actions thus: "One of the first things I did was to take the edible soy out of the lab and construct a plant in Decatur (Illinois) to make all the grades of edible soy protein in 1969." He expected to exceed the plant's capacity by 1976. However, by 1973, with doubled production, the plant was already short of demand. Textured vegetable protein was widely used in foodstuffs, and soybean oil later became the number one food and cooking oil in use.

The company also sold its troublesome chemical properties to Ashland Oil & Refining Company for $35 million in 1967. That year, it acquired the Fleischmann Malting Company, which would become a very profitable producer of malts for the food and beverage industry. Andreas proved expert at maintaining a good profit margin on soybeans, too. Two or three cents shaved off costs made large differences on this item, which carried slender profit margins. Andreas's management rules of efficiency and profitability echoed the founders' practices.

With unprofitable operations sold, profitable ones newly acquired, and the increasing success of the soybean, the company entered another major area of operations. In 1971 it purchased Corn Sweeteners, Inc., producer of high-fructose syrups, glutens, oil, and caramel color. Corn Sweeteners brought good returns for Archer Daniels Midland and increased the company's finished-food capabilities.

Throughout the 1970s, the company built textured vegetable protein plants in Europe and South America. In addition, Dwayne Andreas brought several other members of his family into Archer Daniels Midland as the company expanded. (In fact, a 1988 treatment in *Financial World* characterized ADM as the Andreas "family dynasty.") Three Andreas family members became heads of various divisions, although the company continued to retain one Archer and one Daniels in high-ranking positions into the 1990s.

From the net low of $50 million in earnings in 1965, net earnings were near $117 million in 1973. This increase paralleled the upward swing in U.S. soybean production and exports from 700 million bushels per day in 1965 to 1.3 billion in 1973.

That growth continued through the 1970s and into the 1980s. During this time, Archer Daniels Midland had several major subdivisions, the largest of which was the Oilseed Processing Division. In this division, soy products soon outstripped linseed and all others, earning Andreas the nickname "Soybean King." The next largest, the Corn Sweeteners Division, produced ethanol in addition to high-fructose products. In fact, the Decatur,

Illinois, plant was the single largest source of ethanol in the United States. Archer Daniels Midland Milling Company processed the company's grains, and in 1986 the milling division became even larger when ADM entered into a grain marketing joint venture with Growmark Inc., a large Midwestern grain merchandising and river terminal cooperative. The venture was called ADM/Growmark.

Another division, the Columbian Peanut Company, acquired in 1981, produced oil and peanut products, and Archer Daniels Midland was the leading domestic peanut sheller. Gooch Foods, Inc., was the company's market name for a line of pasta products, which increased in demand after the advent of microwave pasta dishes. Other divisions of Archer Daniels Midland included Southern Cotton Oil Company, Fleischmann Malting Company, Inc., American River Transportation Company, Supreme Sugar Company, and the British Arkady Co., Ltd., which was a supplier of specialty products to the bakery industry.

1990s and Beyond

ADM made its first ever foray into consumer food products with the characteristically low-profile launch of its Harvest Burger brand soy-based meat substitute in the early 1990s. The product's reduced fat, calories, and cholesterol attracted American consumers, many of whom sought out the product even before it had advertising support. In 1993 the Pillsbury Company assumed responsibility for supermarket retailing of Harvest Burgers. For the hungry of the world, the soy product was an inexpensive source of protein with a longer shelf life than traditional sources such as meat and milk. As CEO Andreas pointed out in a 1993 interview with *Direct Marketing* magazine, "You can feed 20 times as many people off of an acre of land by raising soy alone, than growing soy and feeding it to an animal and then eating that animal." Andreas called the development of the meatlike soy product "the most important food development of this century."

During the second half of the 1990s, ADM experienced significant growth, with revenues increasing from $12.56 billion to $16.11 billion from 1995 to 1998 before falling to $14.28 billion in 1999. Net earnings declined throughout this period, however, falling from the record level of $795.9 million in 1995 to $266 million in 1999. ADM blamed the declining results of the late 1990s largely on two coinciding phenomena: the Asian economic crisis, which later spread to Russia and Latin America, and record crop harvests. The economic downturn significantly dampened demand for protein and vegetable oils in the affected areas, while at the same time prices for farm commodities fell to their lowest levels in more than a decade.

The squeeze on profit margins led to increasing competition and consolidation in the food industry. Archer Daniels Midland was heavily involved in this consolidation and spent about $4.6 billion in the second half of the 1990s building new plants, expanding existing ones, and making numerous acquisitions. In mid-1997 ADM paid $470 million for the cocoa business of W.R. Grace & Co., thereby entering the chocolate and cocoa industry. The company quickly added six additional cocoa-processing plants purchased from E D & F Main Group PLC for $223 million. ADM organized these operations as its ADM Cocoa Division, which by the end of the 1990s was grinding

450,000 metric tons of cocoa beans per year, about 20 percent of the world crop. Also in 1997 the company acquired Quincy, Illinois-based soybean processor Moorman Manufacturing Co. for $296 million; purchased a 42 percent stake in United Grain Growers of Canada, a firm involved in grain merchandising and other agricultural activities; acquired a 30 percent stake in Minnesota Corn Processors, operator of wet corn milling plants in Minnesota and Nebraska; and spent $258 million for a 22 percent interest in Mexico-based Gruma S.A. de C.V., the world's largest producer and marketer of corn flour and tortillas. During this period ADM also formed a number of joint ventures, including International Malting Company, 40 percent owned by ADM and 60 percent by the LeSaffre Company, which operated barley malting plants in the United States, Australia, Canada, and France; ADM-Riceland Partnership, a 50–50 venture with Riceland Foods Inc., which processed rice and rice products; and a joint venture with Gruma, 40 percent owned by ADM, that operated seven wheat flour mills in Mexico. The most significant divestments during the later 1990s were those of Supreme Sugar and British Arkady.

Many of these deals occurred after G. Allen Andreas, nephew of Dwayne Andreas, was named CEO in April 1997. Allen Andreas's path to the top was cleared following the downfall of Michael D. Andreas, Dwayne's son and heir-apparent, in a highly publicized price-fixing scheme. The scheme first came to light in 1995 when Mark E. Whitacre, a whistleblower for the FBI, was fired by ADM from his position as head of its BioProducts division for allegedly embezzling millions of dollars from the company. Whitacre had been secretly acting as an informant to the FBI, providing the bureau with documentation, including audio- and videotapes, of alleged price-fixing schemes involving three products derived from corn: lysine, high-fructose corn syrup, and citric acid. At the center of the collusion were two top ADM executives: Vice-Chairman Michael Andreas and Terrance S. Wilson, head of the company's Corn Processing division. In late 1996, following guilty pleas by its partners in price fixing (including Ajinomoto Co. and Kyowa Hakko Kogyo, both of Japan), Archer Daniels Midland pleaded guilty to two counts of fixing prices for lysine, a hot-selling livestock feed additive, and for citric acid, and agreed to pay $100 million in fines, by far the largest criminal antitrust settlement in history. By late 1998 the company had paid nearly another $100 million to settle lawsuits brought by customers and investors. Whitacre in 1998 was sentenced to nine years in prison for swindling $9.5 million from ADM; the following year he was sentenced to an additional 20 months for his role in price-fixing at ADM (he had originally been given immunity in the price-fixing case but it was stripped after prosecutors learned of the embezzlement). Wilson retired from ADM in 1996 and Michael Andreas went on an indefinite leave of absence. They both were convicted by a federal jury of price fixing in 1998, and began serving two-year sentences in October 1999. In addition, they were each fined $350,000.

ADM's legal difficulties were far from over. The company faced a number of class-action civil antitrust lawsuits, the largest of which involved purchasers of high-fructose corn syrup—including beverage giants PepsiCo, Inc., and the Coca-Cola Company. The federal government had not pursued the corn-syrup case because, according to federal prosecutor Scott Lassar, "Whitacre wasn't involved in corn syrup; there wasn't anything on tape regarding it," as quoted in the June 19, 2004 edition of the *Chicago Tribune.* PepsiCo, Coca-Cola, and other corn-syrup customers filed their own lawsuit against ADM, extending the company's legal difficulties into the 21st century.

A New Image for the 21st Century

With another lawsuit looming, ADM executives decided it was time to improve the company's tarnished image. In 2001, the company began recasting its image, abandoning its slogan, "Supermarket to the World," which was introduced during the 1970s, and replacing its logo, a symbol of a chemical molecule, first used in 1962. The company adopted the new tagline, "The Nature of What's to Come," and a logo of a green leaf inside a blue diamond, part of a new promotional campaign designed to shift attention from the company's bulk commodity business to a range of nutritional products, such as vegetarian burgers and soy milk, and alternative fuels, including ethanol and biodiesel. Toward this end, the company collaborated with Japan-based Kao Corp. in 2001 to produce a weight-control cooking oil. In early 2003, the oil, marketed as Enova, was introduced in Atlanta and Chicago, the first step of national rollout slated for early 2004. In another example of the "new" ADM and its emphasis on developing new products from natural, renewable resources, the company signed an agreement with Volkswagen AG in early 2004 to produce biodiesel, a combination of vegetable oil and diesel fuel. The partnership represented the first agreement between a major automaker and a major agricultural company in the renewable energy field. In 2005, ADM announced plans to build its first wholly owned biodiesel production facility, a plant expected to be constructed in Velva, North Dakota. The company also strengthened its traditional, bulk commodity business during the first half of the decade, which continued to serve as its mainstay business despite the efforts to promote ADM as more than the "Supermarket to the World." In 2000, the company began constructing five new crushing plants in China. In 2001, a Turkish vegetable oil producer, Doysan Yag Sanayii, was acquired, giving ADM a crushing plant, refinery, and packaging operations, as well as Bolivian vegetable oil producer Sociedad Aceitera del Oriente, S.A. In 2002, the company acquired Minnesota Corn Processors, LLC, a deal that gave the company corn wet-milling plants in Marshall, Minnesota, and Columbus, Nebraska.

ADM's legal difficulties reached what company executives hoped was a conclusion in mid-2004. The fructose lawsuit filed by the private sector was settled for $400 million, an amount the company chose to pay instead of a possible $4.8 billion it would be forced to pay if the plaintiffs prevailed in court. "This essentially settles all the open cases with the potential to be material for us," an AMD spokesperson said in a June 19, 2004 interview with the *Chicago Tribune.* "This was the big one." The settlement payment led to a $103 million loss for the fourth quarter of 2004, but once the one-time expense was incurred ADM demonstrated encouraging financial health. The fourth quarter of 2005 produced $195 million in net earnings, helping the company to surpass $1 billion in net income for the year, a record high. Looking ahead, with its legal problems behind it, the company promised to figure as one of the world's largest agricultural concerns for years to come, as it sought to develop and to deliver "The Nature of What's to Come" to markets throughout the world.

Principal Subsidiaries

ADM Agri-Industries Company (Canada); ADM Europe BV (The Netherlands); ADM Canadian Holdings BV (The Netherlands); ADM Worldwide Holdings LP (Cayman Islands); ADM International Ltd. (U.K.); ADM Ireland Holdings Ltd.; ADM Ringsaskiddy Unlimited Liability Co. (Ireland); ADM German Holdings BV (The Netherlands); ADM European Management Holding GmbH & Co. (Germany); Hickory Point Bank & Trust; ADM Investor Services, Inc.; Archer Financial Services; ADM Investor Services International Limited.

Principal Competitors

Ag Processing Inc; Agribrands International, Inc.; Ajinomoto Co., Inc.; The Andersons, Inc.; Bartlett and Company; Bunge Limited; Cargill, Incorporated; Cenex Harvest States Cooperatives; ConAgra, Inc.; ContiGroup Companies, Inc.; Corn Products International, Inc.; Eridania Beghin-Say; Farmland Industries, Inc.; GROWMARK Inc.; Pioneer Hi-Bred International, Inc.; Riceland Foods, Inc.; The Scoular Company; Southern States Cooperative, Incorporated; Tate & Lyle PLC; Universal Corporation.

Further Reading

"Archer Daniels Midland Launches New Ad Campaign, Slogan, Logo," *Knight Ridder/Tribune Business News,* April 5, 2001.

Brinkman, Paul, "ADM Execs Report to Federal Prison," *Decatur (Ill.) Herald & Review,* October 6, 1999.

——, "ADM Focuses on Ethics in Wake of Price-Fixing Case," *Decatur (Ill.) Herald & Review,* July 11, 1999.

Burton, Thomas M., et al., "Corn Plot: Investigators Suspect a Global Conspiracy in Archer-Daniels Case," *Wall Street Journal,* July 28, 1995, pp. A1+.

Grant, Jeremy, "Ethanol Processing Boom Sows Problems for ADM," *Financial Times,* May 2, 2005, p. 29.

Henkoff, Ronald, "The ADM Tale Gets Even Stranger," *Fortune,* May 13, 1996, pp. 113–14, 116, 118, 120.

——, "Betrayal," *Fortune,* February 3, 1997, pp. 82–85, 87.

Hoak, Amy, "ADM Reaps Healthy Fourth-Quarter Earnings," *Herald & Review,* July 30, 2005.

Howie, Michael, "ADM's Annual Earnings Increase $1B," *Feedstuffs,* August 8, 2005, p. 15.

Kahn, E.J., Jr., *Supermarketer to the World: The Story of Dwayne Andreas, CEO of Archer Daniels Midland,* New York: Warner, 1991, 320 p.

Kilman, Scott, "ADM Ex-Officials Get 2 Years in Jail in Sign of Tougher Antitrust Penalties," *Wall Street Journal,* July 12, 1999, p. A4.

——, "ADM Warns Grain Suppliers to Start Segregating Genetically Altered Crops," *Wall Street Journal,* September 2, 1999, p. A2.

——, "Jury Convicts Ex-Executives in ADM Case," *Wall Street Journal,* September 18, 1998, p. A3.

——, "Mark Whitacre Is Sentenced to 9 Years for Swindling $9.5 Million from ADM," *Wall Street Journal,* March 5, 1998, p. B5.

Kilman, Scott, and Thomas M. Burton, "Three Ex-ADM Executives Are Indicted: Wilson, Michael Andreas, and Informant Whitacre Cited in Antitrust Case," *Wall Street Journal,* December 4, 1996, p. A3.

Kilman, Scott, Bruce Ingersoll, and Jill Abramson, "Risk Averse: How Dwayne Andreas Rules Archer-Daniels by Hedging His Bets," *Wall Street Journal,* October 27, 1995, pp. A1+.

Lieber, James B., *Rats in the Grain: The Dirty Tricks of the "Supermarket to the World," Archer Daniels Midland,* New York: Four Walls Eight Windows, 1999.

Manor, Robert, "Archer Daniels Midland Settles Price-Fixing Charges for $400 Million," *Chicago Tribune,* June 19, 2004.

Melcher, Richard A., "All Roads Lead to ADM," *Business Week,* September 23, 1996, p. 42.

——, "Into the Harsh Glare at Archer Daniels," *Business Week,* October 23, 1995, pp. 34–35.

Melcher, Richard A., Greg Burns, and Douglas Harbrecht, "It Isn't Dwayne's World Anymore," *Business Week,* November 18, 1996, pp. 82, 84.

Miller, James P., "Grain-Processing Giant Plans to Launch 'Fat-Reducing' Vegetable Oil," *Knight Ridder/Tribune Business News,* June 13, 2001.

Neal, Mollie, "Reaping the Rewards of Skillful Marketing While Helping Humanity," *Direct Marketing,* September 1993, pp. 24–26.

Noah, Timothy, "EPA Came Through for Archer Daniels Midland Soon After Andreas's Role at Presidential Dinner," *Wall Street Journal,* July 6, 1994, p. A20.

Sachar, Laura, "Top Seed," *Financial World,* May 3, 1988, pp. 2–28.

Upbin, Bruce, "Vindication," *Forbes,* November 17, 1997, pp. 52 + .

"Volkswagen, Food Giant Invest in Biodiesel," *Waste News,* January 19, 2004, p. 7.

Whitacre, Mark, "My Life As a Corporate Mole for the FBI," *Fortune,* September 4, 1995, pp. 52 + .

—April Dougal Gasbarre
—updates: David E. Salamie; Jeffrey L. Covell

Austal Limited

100 Clarence Beach Road
Henderson, Western Australia 6166
Australia
Telephone: +61 8 9410 1111
Fax: +61 8 9410 2564
Web site: http://www.austal.com

Public Company
Incorporated: 1987 as Austal Ships Pty. Ltd.
Employees: 1,273
Sales: AUD 321.3 million (2005)
Stock Exchanges: Australian
Ticker Symbol: ASB
NAIC: 336611 Ship Building and Repairing; 541710
Research and Development in the Physical,
Engineering, and Life Sciences

Austal Limited is the world's leading manufacturer of high-speed ferries. It also produces a broad line of other vessels, ranging from luxury yachts to military patrol boats. The company has always been primarily an exporter, and a U.S. manufacturing subsidiary set up in 1999 is expected to be a major source of growth. About 70 percent of revenues come from military sales. Austal is touted as a success story for Western Australia, whose shipbuilding tradition goes back decades.

Origins

Austal Limited dates back to the June 1987 founding of Austal Ships Pty. Ltd. by John Rothwell, a boat builder from Fremantle, Australia. The business began with about 40 employees. It bought a second shipyard in 1992.

The firm was based 20 kilometers south of Perth in the Henderson Industrial Area. The West Australia government had designated this space for shipbuilding, which had flourished there in the days of steel-hulled cray (or lobster) boats.

Austal focused on the Asian market at first, and found great and enduring success in China. By 1993 Austal was the world's

leading producer of 40-meter passenger catamarans. Sales were AUD 85 million. During the year, the company introduced gas turbine power as well as its own Ocean Leveller ride control system on two ferries in Hong Kong. Austal soon added large, high-speed vehicle ferries to its lineup.

These could carry automobiles and passengers at 35 to 40 knots, about twice as fast as conventional ferries. They were typically powered by multiple 20-cylinder diesel engines made by MTU of Germany. The 40-meter ferries cost about $5 million each.

China was among its largest markets, acquiring nearly two dozen ferries in the early 1990s, most destined for the busy waterways of the Pearl River Delta. Austal Chairman John Rothwell told the *South China Morning Post* that the key to the company's success in the People's Republic was its ability to customize vessels to the operators' requirements, combined with speed and affordability.

According to *Business Week,* Australian Prime Minister Paul J. Keating wanted to downplay the country's historical ties to the United Kingdom in favor of a role as an integral part of Asia's booming economy. Austal made its first sales to Britain and Japan in 1994.

In 1994 a group of venture capitalists acquired 30 percent of equity for AUD 15 million. Austal was spending AUD 18 million to expand its shipyard, adding space for two more 50-meter vessels and two more 100-meter vessels to its previous capacity of four 50-meter vessels. It also was adding computer-aided design and cutting tools to speed production.

Huge Growth in the Mid-1990s

Employment tripled to 750 from 1993 to 1996, reported the *West Australian,* exhausting the local supply of skilled workers. The company was scrambling to fill vacancies through an intensive four-month training program called TAFE. Austal was one of the largest employers in the west, and its economic impact extended to hundreds of jobs in support businesses.

Australia exported AUD 500 million worth of ferries in 1995. Its success inspired other countries such as Italy and

+--+
| **Company Perspectives:** |
| |
| *Austal's vision and continued focus is to provide customers* |
| *with the perfect solution, designing, constructing and deliv-* |
| *ering vessels that are ideally suited to operational require-* |
| *ments and fully comply with the needs and desires of its* |
| *customers.* |
+--+

Spain to enter the high-speed business, observed *Marine Log.* Austal delivered its first vehicle-passenger ferries to Europe in 1996. By the end of the decade its crafts were operating in Scandinavia, Greece, Turkey, the English Channel, and the Irish Sea. (After years of conquering world markets with its ferries, Austal would finally sell one to a local operator, Kangaroo Island SeaLink, in January 2002.)

According to *Lloyd's List International,* Austal exported nearly AUD 140 million worth of ferries in 1997. The 82-meter Auto Express series was the largest in Austal's product lineup. It had a capacity of 200 automobiles and 800 passengers and could be unloaded and reloaded in 15 minutes.

Public in 1998

In its first ten years, Austal produced about 50 ferries. All of them were exported, according to *Lloyd's List;* more than half went to Chinese operators. The financial crisis in Asia put a damper on its business there.

Austal had a rival in its Tasmanian neighbor, Incat, for leadership of the world's high-speed ferry market. Incat would go into receivership in 2002, however. Other Aussie competitors were South Australia Ships and Advanced Multihull Design. Image Marine, a maker of 40- to 50-meter aluminum vessels, was acquired in July 1998.

The company began delivering ferries to Greece in 1998. The country was an established operator of high-speed ferries and was beginning to replace its fleet, observed *Lloyd's List.* Around this time, Austal introduced a shorter, 48-meter version of the Auto Express to a Caribbean operator. It had a capacity of 329 passengers and ten automobiles. Austal also had begun to design cargo-only vessels.

Austal Ships went public in December 1998, offering 16.6 percent of shares on the Australian Stock Exchange. By this time, Austal had 1,000 employees and sales of about AUD 196 million a year, or 14 percent of the AUD 1.4 billion ($885 million) world market. The name was shortened to Austal Pty. Ltd. a few months before the initial public offering.

The military business was growing fast. Austal won a contract to build eight Bay Class patrol boats for the Australian Customs Service in 1998. Other customers, such as the Royal Australian Navy (RAN), soon followed. The Republic of Yemen ordered ten patrol boats in 2003. In 2004 the company began to produce 14 new 56-foot patrol boats for the RAN over a period of 42 months. As part of the AUD 550 million contact, Defense Maritime Services was hired to service these vessels for 15 years.

Acquiring Oceanfast in 1999

In May 1999 Austal bought Oceanfast Ltd., one of its Hendersonville neighbors, which made a range of vessels including smaller ferries and high-end motor yachts. Oceanfast had a reputation for quality of styling and finish but was undercapitalized. Austal underwrote AUD 8 million in debt as part of the acquisition.

Oceanfast had been formed in 1983 by businessman Don Johnston and John Farrell, who would be its CEO. Sales were AUD 50 million in 1996, when the venture employed 400 people. Oceanfast had teamed up with Austal in the Ferries Australia joint venture to market vessels in the Baltics.

Oceanfast raised AUD 5.5 million in its September 1997 public offering. Turnover slipped to AUD 20 million to AUD 30 million a year, or one boat a year, by the end of the decade but the company was hoping to triple that with a new line of long-range expedition yachts. The first of these was ordered by Australian golf legend Greg Norman, nicknamed "Great White Shark."

Austal looked for growth from the yacht business as a slowing global economy discouraged ferry sales. This was to be an expensive proposition, however. The company lost AUD 18.7 million in the 2002–03 fiscal year, in large part due to cost overruns at the Oceanfast unit, which was losing money on a AUD 70 million luxury craft for Norman and two other boats. Millions in losses at the new U.S. branch were also a factor.

New U.S. Unit in 1999

To court U.S. business, in December 1999 a Mobile, Alabama shipyard had been established in partnership with Bender Shipbuilding & Repair Co. The facility originally employed 180 people.

Austal was able to win a contract from the U.S. military in 2001 in spite of its protectionist tradition. Austal was the Marine Corps' first supplier for the high-speed 101-meter Theater Support Vessel. Based in Japan and dubbed *WestPac Express,* it could carry a battalion of 950 Marines and 550 tons of vehicles.

The U.S. unit also attracted civilian business. Two supply vessels were delivered to Otto Candies LLC in January 2002. Florida's Island Queen Cruises ordered a 34-meter dinner cruise ship. It sold an AUD 6 million, 26-meter passenger ferry to New York's Lighthouse Fast Ferry in the spring of 2002. A year later, it was hired to build an AUD 28 million ($19 million) 50-meter vehicle-passenger ferry for Lake Express LLC of Milwaukee, which was operating a service across Lake Michigan. This was the first high-speed vehicle-passenger ferry in the continental United States.

Trimarans in 2003 and Beyond

The development of a slender, stabilized monohull (trimaran) design opened up new vistas for Austal in both civil and military markets. In June 2003, Spanish company Fred. Olsen, S.A. became the first to order a new 126.7-meter cargo-vehicle-passenger fast ferry, which would be the largest of its kind in the world, with a capacity of 1,350 passengers and 341 vehicles. The AUD 100 million *Benchijigua Express,* which

Key Dates:
1983: Luxury yacht builder Oceanfast Ltd. is launched.
1988: Austal Ships begins operations as a fabricator of aluminum vessels.
1998: Austal goes public.
1999: Austal forms a U.S. venture and acquires Oceanfast.
2004: The first 127-meter trimaran is launched.

was placed into service in the Canary Islands, also would be called the largest aluminum ship ever built upon its launching in September 2004. Its trimaran design would be the basis for a new fast vessel for the U.S. military.

Austal USA was a subcontractor to General Dynamics subsidiary Bath Iron Works on a contract to design a new high-speed surface vessel, the Littoral Combat Ship (LCS), for the U.S. Navy in 2004. Austal USA started a $25 million, 120,000-square-foot expansion in January 2005 and was adding 600 jobs to support LCS work during the design phase.

The LCS project had a potential total value of $14 billion for 57 ships. In October 2005, the Bath team won a $223 million contract to build the first of two vessels. Half of this was designated for Austal USA's construction of the seaframe, making it Austal's largest contract to date.

Austal had 1,200 employees by the end of 2004. Net income was AUD 20.1 million ($13.6 million) on revenues of AUD 310.1 million ($213.9 million).

The company delivered its first Armidale Class patrol boat and 127-meter trimaran to the Royal Australian Navy during the 2004–05 fiscal year. About 70 percent of the company's revenues for the next three years was expected to come from military sales. Total revenues were AUD 321.3 million in 2005.

The company's U.S. facility in Mobile, Alabama, was designed to withstand a Category 4 hurricane, and only suffered minor damage from Katrina in August 2005. The facility was being quadrupled in size to build the LCS.

Austal was signed up to supply two 340-foot ferries to the Hawaii Superferry project beginning in 2006. This was a planned $100 million interisland ferry service.

Principal Subsidiaries

Austal Ships Pty. Ltd.; Oceanfast Pty. Ltd.; Image Marine Pty. Ltd.; Seastate Pty. Ltd.; Oceanfast Properties Pty. Ltd.; Austal Insurance Pte. Ltd. (Singapore); Austal Holdings Inc. (U.S.A.); Austal USA LLC (70%); Oceanfast LLC (U.S.A.); Oceanfast Exclusive Motor Yachts Pty. Ltd.; Austal Ships Sales Pty. Ltd.; Maritima Hesperides SL (Spain); Austal Hull 130 Chartering LLC (U.S.A.).

Principal Competitors

Incat Australia Pty. Ltd.

Further Reading

"Austal Anchors WA Oceanfast Shipbuilding Operations," *Australian Associated Press,* May 31, 1999.

"Austal Breaks into Caribbean Market with Fast Cat Order," *Lloyd's List International,* June 11, 1997.

"Austal Delivery Cements Turkish Links," *Lloyd's List International,* December 8, 1998.

"Austal Hands Over Benchijigua Express," *MarineLog.com,* April 12, 2005.

"Austal Leaves Rivals Behind in Dream Year," *South China Morning Post,* November 23, 1994.

"Australian Fast Cats Consolidate Business Association with China," *Lloyd's List International,* August 20, 1997.

"Australian Shipbuilder Austal Looks for Contracts in the US," *Asia Pulse,* September 13, 1999.

Bell, Stephen, "Australia's Austal Set for US Navy Decision," *Dow Jones International News,* May 11, 2004.

——, "Calmer Waters for Austal," *Dow Jones International News,* August 29, 2003.

Bolt, Cathy, "Austal Predicts Massive US Orders," *Australian Financial Review,* April 8, 2002, p. 16.

——, "Buoyant Shipbuilders Can Push the Boat Out," *Australian Financial Review,* June 13, 2002, p. 7.

——, "High Tide for Austal Yacht," *Australian Financial Review,* May 11, 2000, p. 27.

Burns, Anne, "Skill Shortage Strains Shipyard," *West Australian,* September 13, 1996, p. 4.

Connolly, John, "Oceanfast Shows How to Take Banana Out of Mega Yachts," *Australian Financial Review,* June 6, 1986, p. 44.

Drummond, Mark, "Oceanfast Owners Planning to List the WA Ship Builder," *Sydney Morning Herald,* March 17, 1997, p. 41.

——, "Wind Goes Out of Oceanfast Sales," *Australian Financial Review,* February 19, 1999, p. 3.

Duffy, Evelyn, "Austal Signs Breakthrough Deal with US Marine Corps," *Shipping Times,* July 9, 2001.

Engardio, Pete, and Stephen Hutcheon, "The Newest Player in Asia Is Down Under; After Years of Recession, Australia Is Sharply Boosting Exports to Its Neighbors," *Business Week,* September 5, 1994, p. 21.

"Fast Ferries—Austal Surging On in the Fast Track," *Lloyd's List International,* February 24, 1998.

Hanna, Jim, "New Navy Vessels to Be Built for $500M," *Canberra Times,* August 30, 2003, p. 15.

Kitney, Damon, "Australian Ferries Conquer the Baltic," *Australian Financial Review,* April 4, 1996, p. 22.

Kleyn, Gary, "Austal Rules Out Buying Incat," *WA Business News,* April 4, 2002.

Lampathakis, Paul, "Smooth Sailing for Big Cats," *West Australian,* March 13, 1998, p. 11.

Lyne, Jack, "Austal Adding 600 Alabama Jobs to Build New Navy Ship," *Site Selection,* January 31, 2005.

MacKinnon, Morag, "Tide May Turn for Australia's Austal," *Dow Jones International News,* June 21, 2004.

"$100M Ferry Job Coup for Austal," *Hobart Mercury,* June 21, 2003, p. 28.

Peacock, Sue, "Austal On a Roll As Rival Rides Trough," *West Australian,* February 22, 2002, p. 38.

Pownall, Mark, "Austal Buy-Back Tees Up Partial Float," *West Australian,* July 10, 1998, p. 34.

——, "Investors Fear a Bumpy Ride Over Austal Spec Ship," *West Australian,* June 27, 2000, p. 32.

Prior, Neale, "Oceanfast Plots Change of Tack," *West Australian,* December 1, 1998, p. 48.

"Shark Takes a Bite Out of Austal," *Australian,* September 6, 2003, p. 30.

''Shipbuilder Austal Turns Loss into Profit,'' *Asia Pulse,* August 23, 2004.

Wong Joon San, ''West Australian Ferry Builder Confident of Future of Booming Mainland Business,'' *South China Morning Post,* February 24, 1993, p. 1.

Wright, Peter, ''Teeing Off: Golfing Great Greg Norman Plans to Play a Global Course on His Swift New 87-Foot Oceanfast Sportfisherman,'' *Motor Boating & Sailing,* April 1, 1996, p. 60.

—Frederick C. Ingram

Avalon Correctional Services, Inc.

13401 Railway Drive
Oklahoma City, Oklahoma 73114
U.S.A.
Telephone: (405) 752-8802
Toll Free: (800) 919-9113
Fax: (405) 752-8852
Web site: http://www.avaloncorrections.com

Public Company
Incorporated: 1990 as Southern Corrections Systems, Inc.
Employees: 430
Sales: $27.17 million (2004)
Stock Exchanges: Pink Sheets
Ticker Symbol: CITY
NAIC: 561210 Facilities Support Services

Avalon Correctional Services, Inc. operates 12 prisons and halfway houses in Oklahoma, Texas, and Colorado. The company owns three-fourths of the facilities, which have a total of 2,300 beds. Avalon also runs programs that serve as an alternative to incarceration, including day monitoring, work-release, and weekend sanctions. Founder Don Smith owns controlling interest in the firm and serves as its CEO and chairman.

Beginnings

Avalon Correctional Services was founded in 1985 by Don Smith in Oklahoma City, Oklahoma. Trained as an accountant, Smith had co-owned an oil drilling business that closed in the wake of the early 1980s oil bust, and was looking for work. Noting that the state's prisons were overcrowded, he reasoned that it might be possible for private companies to handle some of the overflow, and in 1985 won a contract to provide halfway house services for 25 drunk-driving offenders. He leased the Carver Center, a 48-bed facility that had once served as a school for handicapped children, to house them.

The dormitory-style facility was set up to help its inhabitants improve their lives while paying their debt to society, and offered counseling for substance abuse and other problems.

Smith's staff also worked with local businesses to find employment for those who needed jobs. When the first group of ''low-risk'' offenders arrived, Smith was shocked to see them appear in shackles and leg irons, but he quickly adapted to the reality of corrections work, and within several years the building had been expanded to 145 beds.

Halfway houses were a growing business, with the typical operating cost of $12.50 per bed per day significantly less than the $21 to $53 per bed for larger, more secure facilities. They were used to house a variety of individuals, ranging from those making the transition from prison, to others allowed to work during the day while incarcerated at night. Such facilities better prepared inmates for their return to society, with recidivism rates of approximately 38 percent reported in Oklahoma, as compared with 41.5 to 46.3 percent for those released directly from prison.

Reverse Merger Creating Avalon Community Services in 1992

Not long after he began operating the Carver Center, Smith also began providing residential care services for mentally ill persons in halfway house-like settings. In 1990 he formally incorporated the company as Southern Corrections Systems, Inc. (SCS). Seeking funds for expansion, in 1992 the firm engineered a reverse merger with Avalon Enterprises, Inc., a publicly traded shell company. It was then renamed Avalon Community Services, Inc., with SCS designated as its sole subsidiary.

In the fall of 1993 the company expanded its scope by signing a seven-year lease to operate 8,500-acre Lake Stanley Draper Park in Oklahoma City. The park's boating and fishing facilities would be repaired and upgraded, and a public swimming beach, campsites, and boat and personal watercraft rental added. At year's end the firm also bought two residential care facilities in Elk City and Norman, Oklahoma, while taking an option to buy another in Oklahoma City. The firm's annual revenues now topped $2 million.

In the summer of 1995 Avalon opened a 255-bed corrections facility in a former warehouse in Tulsa, Oklahoma. The firm had recently won a contract with the state to house 45 inmates there

Company Perspectives:

Our Philosophy: Avalon Correctional Services, Inc. and Southern Corrections Systems, Inc., a wholly owned subsidiary's mission is to operate safe, humane, and secure community correctional facilities, protect the public, and provide offenders with training, education and treatment programs designed to reduce recidivism.

and provide them with substance abuse treatment and employment assistance. Over the next several years more were added.

The company now had plans underway to build a new 60-unit assisted living facility for senior citizens near Oklahoma City. The $2.5 million project was funded by Bank One, which had sold Avalon the 14-acre property. The firm had also recently canceled its money-losing park management contract and installed seven-year company veteran Jerry Sutherland as president, with Don Smith continuing to serve as CEO and chairman.

In October 1995 Avalon's stock began trading on the NAS-DAQ SmallCap Market, moving up from its bulletin board listing. The year 1995 also saw the company win a contract with the State of Nebraska Department of Correctional Services to provide substance abuse treatment in five correctional centers. For the year, the firm reported revenues of $3.1 million and a net loss of $85,000.

In the spring of 1996 an agreement was reached with Kansas City Community Center to operate eight substance abuse treatment programs at correctional centers in Florida. The company also announced that it would buy Diamond Crest Assisted Living Center in Fort Collins, Colorado. Avalon would invest $2.5 million to purchase and renovate the 20,000-square-foot facility, which would be expanded to 60 units.

The summer of 1996 saw Avalon pay $3.7 million for a 144-bed medium security prison in El Paso, Texas. The firm also signed a 15-year contract worth $20 million to operate the prison for the West Texas Community Supervision and Corrections Department.

Focus Narrowing to Corrections in Late 1996

In November Avalon's newly completed Oklahoma City assisted living center opened. Although the company announced plans to open a number of similar facilities, by year's end management had made an abrupt turnaround and decided to abandon all non-correctional operations, in part because the firm's residential care facilities were losing money and experiencing other problems, including the deaths of several patients. The change of plans resulted in a nearly $1 million loss from discontinued operations for the year.

In early 1997 contracts were signed to provide substance abuse services at two prisons in Missouri, and in the fall Avalon made a deal to buy a 150-bed community corrections facility in Tulsa from owner Freedom Ranch. The company also completed a $4.15 million private stock sale during the year.

In March 1998 the firm won a new contract from Oklahoma to build and run an 80-bed medium-security facility for juvenile offenders. It would add $3.6 million to the company's annual revenues. The spring also saw Avalon begin operating a 30-bed halfway house in Fordland, Missouri.

In late June a deal was reached to acquire three juvenile detention facilities from Rebound Programs in Colorado, Utah, and Virginia, plus two others under construction. The stock swap deal was expected to boost the firm's earnings by $9.8 million per year, but it fell through when the state of Utah refused to allow Avalon to run its program, due to the firm's inexperience with juvenile offenders.

In July 1998 a deal was signed with the Texas Department of Criminal Justice to design and build a 200-bed facility to house substance abusers and other prisoners in that state. That same month saw the firm change its name to Avalon Correctional Services, Inc., and in September Rice Sangalis Toole & Wilson invested $15 million to fund further growth. For 1998 Avalon had revenues of $7.7 million and a net loss of $450,000.

Major Expansion in 1999

In February 1999 the company's new Union City Juvenile Detention Center was opened. The 44,000-square-foot, 80-bed facility was the first privately run center of its kind in Oklahoma. It offered education, counseling, and treatment programs to help youthful criminals return to school or begin work upon their release, and was expected to bring Avalon an additional $3.6 million in revenues per year. Soon after opening it was plagued with problems, however, including several escapes and an attack on guards by inmates. The firm subsequently beefed up security at the site.

Early 1999 also saw Avalon cut deals to acquire The Villa at Greeley LLC and Adams Community Corrections Programs, Inc., which provided halfway house, counseling, and alternative sentencing services in Greeley and Denver, Colorado, respectively. In June a 300-bed addition was completed at Avalon's El Paso facility, which had outgrown its 150 beds.

Other new ventures for 1999 included a private pay community corrections offender program in Oklahoma, which provided alternative sentencing options such as day reporting and work release to individuals who agreed to pay the costs of the services themselves. Revenues jumped to $16.8 million for the year, with net income finally in the black at $83,000. The company's employment ranks increased dramatically as well, rising to 470.

In June 2000 Avalon opened the 150-bed Turley Correctional Center in Tulsa. The minimum-security prison for women had been built on the site of the former Freedom Ranch. Growth continued the following year in that city with a new contract to develop a Public Inebriant Alternative Program. It would be located in a vacant 360-bed detention facility that the firm would lease. A total of $1 million was spent on renovations, with the new operation expected to bring in $3 million annually. The facility would later also be used to house private pay and Intermediate Sanction programs.

In June 2001 Avalon named the former head of the Oklahoma Department of Corrections, James Saffle, to the post of president. The firm now had 14 facilities, which housed 2,060 inmates, and also provided management services to two other correctional facilities. The company's alternative programs served another 1,000 individuals with substance abuse treatment, vocational training, work release, and other services.

Continued Growth in 2002

In early 2002 Avalon bought the 180-bed Austin Transitional Center, a halfway house and substance abuse treatment center located in Del Valle, Texas. The company also expanded the size of one of its Colorado halfway houses early in the year, and in the fall won a three-year contract to manage the 48-bed Roy K. Robb Post Adjudication Facility in San Angelo, Texas, which offered substance abuse treatment to juvenile males.

Budget cuts by the state of Oklahoma led to the early 2002 cancellation of the firm's contract to house 80 offenders at the Union City Juvenile Center, at the same time that a state report charged that inmates there had been mistreated. The boom in private prisons that had begun during the 1990s was now cooling off, as the projected cost savings and need for larger capacity were proving less than originally envisioned.

In November Avalon suffered another blow when its Public Inebriate Alternative Program in Tulsa was canceled due to underuse. The leased facility would continue to house 100 inmates for the state Department of Corrections Prison Public Works Program. Following several escapes, the firm recently had spent $35,000 to improve security there. For 2002, Avalon recorded revenues of $27.5 million and net earnings of $1.12 million (as it later restated).

In the spring of 2003 the company lost its contract to house inmates for the Tulsa jail. Although Avalon charged $30 per day, less than the $45 that jail operator Corrections Corporation of America (CCA) did, the inmates' medical costs at Avalon's facility were paid for by the County of Tulsa, while CCA provided its inmates with partial coverage.

In June a $1.5 million, 100-bed expansion to the firm's Phoenix Center operation in Colorado was completed. Several months later four former workers at that facility and two of Avalon's other Colorado halfway houses sued the company and Colorado state corrections officials. They alleged that state officials had refused to investigate problems that included staffers having sex with inmates or selling them drugs, broken or missing security equipment, and billing for services not actually rendered.

During 2004 the company restructured its debt in conjunction with an $8 million bond offering. Revenues for the year increased to $27.2 million from $25.3 million, while earnings fell to $433,000 from $1.2 million.

Citing the high cost of complying with Securities and Exchange Commission (SEC) accounting rules, in February 2005 Avalon moved its stock from the NASDAQ exchange to the Pink Sheets, where less rigorous rules were in effect. The firm put the cost of preparing and filing documents with the SEC at $1 million annually, approximately equal to its net income. Avalon was one of several companies to take this route following implementation of the Sarbanes-Oxley Act in 2004. During 2005 the firm also reached an agreement to sell its closed Oklahoma City assisted living center for $1.3 million, and leased the vacant Union City juvenile facility to the Oklahoma Department of Central Services.

After 20 years Avalon Correctional Services, Inc. had narrowed its focus to the operation of halfway houses and minimum-security prisons and providing alternative sentencing programs. The firm was taking a number of steps to remain profitable, while continuing to serve the needs of its clients and society as a whole.

Principal Subsidiaries

Southern Corrections Systems, Inc.

Principal Competitors

Corrections Corporation of America; The GEO Group, Inc.; Cornell Companies, Inc.; Management & Training Corporation.

Further Reading

Abbott, Karen, ''Halfway House Staffers File Suit,'' *Rocky Mountain News,* November 8, 2003, p. 12A.
''Avalon Completes El Paso Facility,'' *Journal Record,* June 9, 1999.
''Avalon Correction Services Completes Colorado Center Expansion,'' *Journal Record,* June 19, 2003.
''Avalon Earnings, Revenues Improve,'' *Journal Record,* November 16, 1999.
''Avalon Opens New Correctional Facility,'' *Journal Record,* June 15, 2000.
Davis, Kirby Lee, ''Avalon Checks Goals with New Center,'' *Journal Record,* October 21, 1996.
Davis, Melissa, ''Oklahoma City Correctional Services Firm Reports Profit Rise in 2001,'' *Daily Oklahoman,* March 28, 2002.
Hobercock, Barbara, ''Juvenile Center Flaws Cited,'' *Tulsa World,* October 18, 2002, p. A18.
——, ''State Ends Contract with Juvenile Facility,'' *Tulsa World,* October 11, 2002, p. A18.

Hylton, Susan, "Jail Contract Won't Be Renewed," *Tulsa World,* April 26, 2003, p. A22.

——, "Underuse Signals Last Call for Public Drunk Program," *Tulsa World,* November 16, 2002, p. A19.

Latham, Amy, "Escapes Prompt Review," *Tulsa World,* March 16, 1996, p. A1.

Mecoy, Don, "Costs Send Avalon Out of Public Sector," *Daily Oklahoman,* February 4, 2005.

Morrow, Darrell, "Avalon to Give Facelift to Park," *Journal Record,* September 15, 1993.

Page, David, "Okla. City-Based Avalon Correctional Services' Profits, Revenues Up," *Journal Record,* March 22, 2001.

Parrott, Susan, "Avalon to Build Centers," *Journal Record,* June 24, 1995.

Pearson, Janet, "Firm Touts Private Tulsa Jail," *Tulsa World,* September 26, 1994, p. N1.

Peterson, Heidi, "Pre-Release Center to Open," *Tulsa World,* July 10, 1995, p. N1.

Tatum, Lisa, "Corrections Experts Lead Oklahoma City-Based Firm to Profitability," *Daily Oklahoman,* October 30, 2001.

Wiley, Elizabeth Camacho, "Oklahoma City-Based Company Fills Need for Private Prisons," *Daily Oklahoman,* October 1, 2002.

—Frank Uhle

AVIS®

Avis Group Holdings, Inc.

6 Sylvan Way
Parsippany, New Jersey 07054-3826
U.S.A.
Telephone: (973) 496-3500
Fax: (888) 304-2315
Web site: http://www.avis.com

Wholly Owned Subsidiary of Cendant Corporation
Incorporated: 1946 as Avis Airlines Rent-A-Car System
Employees: 18,000
Sales: $2.57 billion (2004)
NAIC: 532111 Passenger Car Rental; 532112 Passenger
    Car Leasing

Avis Group Holdings, Inc. and its subsidiaries own and operate or franchise approximately 1,900 car rental locations in the United States, Canada, Puerto Rico, the U.S. Virgin Islands, Argentina, Australia, and New Zealand. Avis Group is one of two companies that comprise the Avis System, which ranks as the second largest general use car-rental business in the world, trailing Hertz Corporation. (The independent Avis Europe Holdings Ltd. is responsible for the Avis System in Europe, Africa, the Middle East, and parts of Asia, where it owns or franchises more than 3,000 locations.) Known throughout its history for quality service, Avis Group caters primarily to business travelers (who account for about 65 percent of the company's domestic revenue), and has therefore traditionally concentrated on airport rental locations. Although, as a result, 84 percent of revenue is still derived from the airport sites, the company in the early 21st century has made a concerted effort to target the local market and to this end has opened numerous off-airport locations. Avis Group has been owned by Cendant Corporation since March 2001, but late in 2005 Cendant announced that it intended to split itself up into four separate companies. One of the four would focus exclusively on the car rental business and would be comprised of Avis Group and its sister company, Budget Rent A Car System, Inc. This would mark only the latest of more than a dozen ownership changes for Avis over a convoluted six-decade history.

Early History

Avis Airlines Rent-A-Car System was founded in 1946 by Warren E. Avis, a former Army Air Corps flyer. The owner of an automobile dealership in Detroit, Avis had the idea of providing car-rental services at airports, surmising that air travel would quickly become more popular than travel by rail. Using savings, dealership profits, and a $75,000 loan, he opened Avis Airlines Rent-A-Car System in two locations, at Willow Run Airport near Detroit and at Miami Airport in Florida. Avis's idea proved successful and his business grew quickly. Airports in New York, Chicago, Dallas, Washington, Los Angeles, and Houston were soon serviced by car-rental franchises licensed to use the Avis name.

By 1948, Avis was nationally known. In that year, the company dropped the "airlines" designation from its name, expanding operations beyond airports to serve hotels and businesses in urban areas. During the next six years, Avis also expanded internationally. In addition to its 185 locations in the United States, Avis acquired ten in Canada and one in Mexico, and established ties with car-rental agencies throughout Europe and the United Kingdom. Warren E. Avis sold the company in 1954 to Richard S. Robie, a car-rental system owner operating in New England. Robie encouraged continued expansion, introducing a one-way car-rental system and a company charge card. Although Avis had revenues of $4 million in 1956, Robie was plagued by problems of cash flow incurred during his expansion efforts, and was forced to sell the company that year. Avis's new owners, the Amoskeag Company and other investors, continued to foster its growth, creating a new entity, Avis, Inc., as a holding company for the various operations. Business operations were consolidated through the formation of a wholly owned subsidiary, Avis Rent A Car System, Inc.; electronic data processing was introduced to facilitate the company's innovative corporate charge card billing system; car leasing was established; and the licensee system was extended to include markets in Austria, Belgium, Norway, and Spain.

By 1962, Avis owned a fleet of 7,500 vehicles generating annual revenue of $25 million. The company was purchased that year by Lazard Freres & Company, an investment banking firm in New York City, and its corporate headquarters was

Company Perspectives:

Our mission: We will ensure a stress-free car rental experience by providing superior services that cater to our customers' individual needs . . . always conveying the "We Try Harder" spirit with knowledge, caring and a passion for excellence.

moved to Garden City, New York. Under the direction of newly appointed President Robert Townsend, Avis launched a highly successful advertising campaign emphasizing its status as number two contender for car-rental market share. The slogan "We're only No. 2. We try harder" appealed to the public and contributed greatly to Avis's subsequent growth. In 1965, having attained annual revenues exceeding $74 million, Avis was acquired by International Telephone & Telegraph Corporation (ITT); Winston V. Morrow, Jr., was appointed chief executive officer. During this time, international expansion again assumed paramount importance, and Avis increased its operations throughout Europe and Africa, becoming the leading car-rental company in Europe within eight years.

Strong Growth in the 1970s

Keeping pace with technological advances, in 1972 Avis introduced the first and largest computerized information system to be used in a U.S. car-rental business. The Wizard System, subsequently overhauled several times, made reservations and processed rentals, maintained preventive maintenance schedules for Avis's vehicles, and generated for auto manufacturers lists of customers who purchased Avis's used cars. The system also provided electronically transmitted billing reports for use with corporate accounts.

During the same year, Avis became a public company when ITT was ordered to sell several of its businesses. Forty-eight percent of Avis's shares were sold to the public; the balance was held in trust by a court official. During this time, Avis, along with other car-rental companies, began to sell their used cars directly to the consumer rather than to wholesalers. This became a lucrative source of income; by 1987, Avis was marketing approximately 50,000 used cars each year. In 1976 Colin M. Marshall became chief executive officer of Avis, and in the following year the company was purchased by Norton Simon, Incorporated for $174 million. James F. Calvano succeeded Marshall as chief executive officer in 1979; that same year, Avis concluded an advertising and marketing agreement with General Motors Corporation, agreeing to feature GM cars in its worldwide fleet. The 1970s was a decade of enormous growth for Avis both domestically and internationally. Several factors, including greater airline use, airline deregulation, and the increasing strength of Avis's European, African, and Middle Eastern operations, contributed to its jump in revenues from $162 million in 1970 to $673 million in 1979.

1980s: Difficulties, Leading to Several Ownership Changes

The strong growth of the 1970s slowed in the early 1980s as high oil prices, soaring interest rates, and inflation plagued the global economy, reducing the volume of air travel and weakening the closely connected car-rental market. Price competition among the leading car-rental companies contributed to a $50 million loss for Avis in 1982; 2,400 jobs were cut as a result. J. Patrick Barrett, who became chief executive officer of the company in 1981, along with Joseph V. Vittoria, who became president and chief operating officer in 1983, and Alun Cathcart, who became group managing director and chief executive of the Europe/Africa/Middle East Division in the same year, provided new direction for the company. They reorganized management, reemphasized the company's "We try harder" image, and introduced new technology, such as Avis Express service. Designed to facilitate fast passage through airline terminals, Avis Express processed rental agreements before customers deplaned, allowing the consumer a speedy departure from the airport. Earlier, Avis had introduced a computerized checkout system to its operations in Europe; by 1983, after further enhancements, only a few seconds were required for this system to produce a completed rental agreement. In 1984, Avis introduced Rapid Return, an automated self-service check-in device, to its U.S. franchises. A similar innovation called Rapid Rental, a credit-card prompted, computer-assisted transaction, followed shortly thereafter at testing locations in the United Kingdom and France. By 1987, all Avis's domestic and international operations were connected to its main computer in Garden City, New York.

Avis also changed owners a number of times in the 1980s. After being acquired by Esmark, Inc. in 1983, Avis was purchased along with Esmark by Beatrice Companies in 1984. Kohlberg Kravis Roberts & Co., a New York investment firm, acquired Beatrice Companies and Avis the following year in a leveraged buyout. In another leveraged buyout in 1986, Kohlberg sold Avis to Wesray Corporation, a New Jersey-based investment company, and its partner Avis management for $265 million and the assumption of $1.34 billion in debt. Avis's revenues for that year were $1 billion, a 26.2 percent share of the car-rental market. Wesray next sold Avis's domestic car leasing fleet to PHH Group, Incorporated of Hunt Valley, Maryland, the industry leader in corporate car leasing, for approximately $134 million. During 1986, Avis sold 65 percent of its European operations, known as Avis Europe PLC, to the public on the London Stock Exchange for approximately $290 million. Alun Cathcart remained as group managing director and chief executive of what was now a public company, becoming chairman in 1988. Under his direction, Avis Europe grew tremendously, diversifying and updating its services by purchasing such related companies as car leasing businesses and distributorships. In the United States, Avis introduced another technological advance in 1987 with Roving Rapid Return, a portable computer with a printer that allowed Avis employees to move around a rental lot and assist customers at their cars in easy, one-step checkout procedures. Also at this time, Avis's Wizard computer system developed the capacity to allow travel agents direct access to Avis rental vehicles for their customers through computerized communications with airline reservation centers.

Era of Employee Ownership, 1987–96

Avis was sold once again in 1987, this time to an employee stock ownership plan (ESOP) for $750 million and the assump-

---

Key Dates:

1946: Warren E. Avis founds Avis Airlines Rent-A-Car System at Willow Run Airport near Detroit.

1948: Company is renamed Avis Rent-A-Car System.

1954: Avis sells his company to Richard S. Robie.

1956: Robie sells the firm to an investment group led by Amoskeag Company; new owners reorganize the operations under a new holding company, Avis, Inc.

1962: Lazard Freres & Company purchases Avis and moves its corporate headquarters to Garden City, New York.

1963: The company slogan "We try harder" is used for the first time.

1965: Avis is acquired by International Telephone & Telegraph Corporation (ITT).

1972: Company introduces its Wizard System; ITT takes Avis public.

1977: Norton Simon, Incorporated acquires Avis.

1979: Avis enters into a worldwide advertising and marketing agreement with General Motors Corporation (GM).

1983: Avis becomes a subsidiary of Esmark, Inc. after that firm acquires Norton Simon.

1984: Rapid Return automated check-in system is introduced; Avis becomes subsidiary of Beatrice Companies following that company's takeover of Esmark.

1986: Kohlberg Kravis Roberts & Co. takes over Beatrice, then sells Avis to Wesray Corporation; Wesray sells Avis's domestic car leasing fleet to PHH Group, Inc.;

Avis sells majority stake in its European operations, Avis Europe, to the public.

1987: Avis becomes employee owned.

1989: A 29 percent stake in Avis held by Wesray is sold to GM.

1996: HFS Incorporated acquires full control of Avis in an $800 million deal.

1997: HFS creates Avis Rent A Car, Inc. (ARAC) as a system franchisee and spins it off to the public; HFS retains rights to the Avis name, the Wizard system, and reservations operations; ARAC acquires the number two Avis franchisee in North America, First Gray Line Corporation.

1999: Avis acquires the vehicle-leasing unit of Cendant Corporation.

2000: Avis Group Holdings, Inc. is set up as a holding company for the various Avis operations.

2001: Cendant acquires the 88 percent of Avis it did not already own in a $937.4 million deal; Avis moves its headquarters from Garden City, New York, to Parsippany, New Jersey.

2002: Cendant acquires Budget Group, Inc.; certain operations of Avis and Budget are later integrated.

2005: Cendant announces plan to split up into four firms, one focusing on car rentals and comprising Avis and Budget.

---

tion of $1 billion in debt. Under the plan, both buyers and lenders received tax breaks, and employees of the company became its owners, with Wesray retaining a 29 percent stake. Financing for the ESOP was provided by General Motors Acceptance Corporation, Chrysler Credit Corporation, and Pittsburgh National Bank, who loaned a combined $395 million; Irving Trust Company and a group of banks, who loaned $1 billion; Drexel, Burnham, Lambert, Incorporated, and Kleinwort, Benson Limited, who advanced a $255 million bridge loan; and stockholders, who purchased preferred stock for $135 million. A trustee, Citizens & Southern Trust Company of Atlanta, now known as NationsBank, held employees' shares.

The ESOP proved highly successful, boosting employee morale and prompting better service to consumers. When the plan went into effect, Avis's management introduced employee participation groups whose members included workers from all levels of the company. These groups met periodically, generating ideas that were frequently implemented to improve Avis's operations. For example, Avis employees suggested that the company provide managers with Avis charge cards for their expenses, which would save the cost of fees normally paid to charge card creditors. They also suggested such innovations as rental cars to be used specifically for nonsmokers and compilations of traffic law tips for each rental area. Joseph V. Vittoria, who became chairman and chief executive officer of Avis in 1987, commented enthusiastically about the ESOP in *Fortune:* "Believe me, the ESOP works, and it works very well." In another *Fortune* article Charles Finnie, an analyst at the Baltimore brokerage firm of Alex, Brown & Sons and an expert on

the car-rental business, concurred: "Right now Avis is on a roll. The ESOP has really improved their morale and productivity and service." Robert W. Anderson, a director of corporate travel for Unisys Corporation, said in the same publication: "Employee ownership has got to be a winner. Avis is absolutely superior in customer service, though they were pretty good to begin with." Official figures underscored the success of the ESOP. Profits for the first half of 1988 were 35 percent higher than those of the same period a year earlier, market share increased to 27 percent, and customer complaints were down 35 percent from 1,918 in 1987 to 1,238 in 1988.

As the 1980s drew to a close, Avis, which had been exhibiting greater profit-sales ratios than Hertz Corporation since 1984, challenged Hertz's position as the number one car-rental agency in the United States. Internationally, relations between Avis, Inc. and Avis Europe PLC remained strong, as the companies' shared resources contributed to growth and prosperity for both. In addition, such programs as Avis Europe's "Avis in Touch," which provided travelers with travel planning guides, an answering service, and toll-free information numbers, and Avis, Inc.'s Preferred Express, which expedited rental procedures for frequent renters, enhanced customer service throughout the world. In 1987 Avis began to market its computer technology to the hotel industry through a newly formed subsidiary, WizCom International, Limited. The following year, Avis purchased its licensee in New Zealand, broadening the company's influence in the Pacific. Avis Europe became private in 1989, when it was purchased by Cilva Holdings PLC, comprised of Avis, Inc., which owned 8.8 percent of the shares;

General Motors, 26.5 percent; and Lease International SA, 64.7 percent. Also in 1989, General Motors bought out Wesray's 29 percent stake in Avis, Inc.

Avis continued to emphasize innovation as it entered the 1990s. Company training programs in customer service, as well as comprehensive vehicle safety checks, were implemented. Meanwhile, the recession of the early 1990s initially provided benefits to the rental-car industry in North America as automakers, saddled with large inventories of cars they could not unload, sold the vehicles to Avis and other car renters at steep discounts. This in turn, however, brought numerous new competitors into the industry, which drove down rental prices. When the economy recovered in 1993 and 1994, the automakers were able to increase the prices they charged rental-car companies for the cars the companies needed. Rental-car companies in turn raised their rental rates, which dampened demand, leading to heavy losses by Avis and other companies and to an industry shakeout.

It was in this environment that after nine years under employee ownership Avis changed hands yet again. HFS Incorporated, the largest hotel franchiser in the United States and a franchiser of real estate companies as well, paid $800 million for Avis in October 1996, purchasing both the ESOP interest and that of General Motors to gain full control. The buyout provoked controversy among some Avis employees who felt that their shares were being undervalued, but the deal went through nonetheless.

Brief Period As Public Company, 1997–2001

As a franchiser, HFS from the start planned to spin off the company-owned car-rental operations gained from the purchase of Avis, while retaining the rights to the Avis name and control of WizCom and the Wizard System. Along these lines, a new stripped-down company called Avis Rent A Car, Inc. (ARAC) was soon created, which comprised the company-owned car-rental operations. At the same time, HFS set up subsidiary HFS Car Rental, Inc., to which it assigned the rights to the Avis name and which thus became the franchiser of the worldwide Avis rental system. Avis Rent A Car then entered into a 50-year franchise agreement with HFS Car Rental, thereby becoming an Avis system franchisee, the largest in the world. In return for the right to use the Avis name, ARAC agreed to pay HFS a royalty fee of between 4 and 4.5 percent of its revenues. WizCom International and Wizard Co., Inc. became subsidiaries of HFS; Avis Rent A Car thereby entered into a 50-year computer services agreement with WizCom for use of the Wizard System.

As HFS was laying plans for an initial public offering (IPO) of Avis Rent A Car stock, Vittoria retired as head of the company in February 1997. The following month R. Craig Hoenshell, a former American Express executive, was named chairman and chief executive of ARAC. In August 1997 ARAC acquired First Gray Line Corporation for about $195 million in cash. First Gray Line was the second largest Avis franchisee in North America, having 70 locations in southern California, Arizona, and Nevada.

In September 1997 Avis Rent A Car went public through the long-planned IPO, with about 75 percent of the company sold to the public and the remaining 25 percent staying in HFS's hands.

The resulting $330 million proceeds were mainly to be used to pay down ARAC's large long-term debt of nearly $3 billion.

Avis Rent A Car began its new era as a public company with public relations problems and investigations hanging over it. From November 1996 to October 1997, accusations that Avis franchisees racially discriminated against minorities who sought rental cars were raised in North Carolina, Florida, and Pennsylvania. In October 1997 the U.S. Department of Justice launched an investigation into these allegations, as well as into Avis management knowledge of the accusations, the latter being an issue that had the potential to raise uncomfortable questions about the IPO. This issue was quickly resolved, however, after ARAC agreed in December 1997 to pay nearly $3.3 million to settle a class-action lawsuit that had been filed by minority customers and the Justice Department ended its investigation the following May without taking any legal action.

In both 1998 and 1999 Avis Rent A Car made several purchases of Avis franchisees, significantly expanding its operations. The most significant of these was Hayes Leasing Company, Inc., which operated a fleet of about 8,000 cars in Dallas, Fort Worth, San Antonio, and Austin, Texas, and was acquired in 1998. Hoenshell resigned abruptly in December 1998, ushering in an 11-month period of interim leadership at the company. During this period, in June 1999, Avis acquired the vehicle-leasing unit of Cendant Corporation for $1.8 billion in cash and preferred stock and the assumption of $3.2 billion in debt. Cendant had been formed in December 1997 from the merger of Avis's former owner, HFS, and CUC International Inc., and it still owned the Avis brand name and reservations system. Its stake in Avis jumped from 19 percent to 34 percent when Avis's purchase of the vehicle-leasing unit was complete. Among the assets Avis gained were PHH Vehicle Management Services Corp., Cendant's fleet-leasing business, and Wright Express Corp., a fuel-card management services firm. PHH was the world's largest fleet manager, with 700,000 cars and 1998 revenues of $425 million.

In November 1999 Avis filled its vacant CEO position by naming A. Barry Rand to that post and the chairmanship as well. Rand was a 31-year veteran of Xerox Corporation, having left that company in January 1999 as executive vice-president for worldwide operations. In early 2000, soon after Rand took over, Avis restructured itself to reflect its wider range of operations. Avis Group Holdings, Inc. was created as a holding company for the car rental operations, PHH, Wright Express, and other subsidiaries. Also in 2000, Avis sold an 80 percent stake in its U.K. fleet-management business to BNP Paribas SA for $800 million.

Subsidiary of Cendant: 2001–06

In March 2001 a new chapter in Avis's history began, one with reverberations from the recent past. Cendant, successor to HFS, former owner of PHH, and owner of a travel empire that included the Travelodge, Days Inn, and Ramada lodging brands, acquired the 88 percent of Avis it did not already own in a $937.4 million deal. Rand resigned upon completion of the deal; David N. Siegel, a former executive at Continental Airlines, Inc., was named Avis CEO in September 2001. One month later, Avis shifted its headquarters from Garden City,

New York, to Parsippany, New Jersey, the base for most of Cendant's operations. At this time, Avis was managing a system of 1,700 rental locations, including about 900 company-owned outlets.

The new era at Avis got off to a rough start. Siegel left the company in March 2002 to become president and CEO of US Airways Group, Inc. F. Robert Salerno headed Avis as president, a position he had held since 1996. Salerno, who had spent his entire career in the car rental industry, was named CEO in June 2003. In November 2002 he was also given responsibility for Budget Group, Inc., which Cendant bought out of Chapter 11 bankruptcy. At the time, the entire travel industry, including the car rental sector, was in a severe slump because of the drop-off in corporate travel that accompanied the recession and followed the terrorist attacks on the United States on September 11, 2001.

Avis responded to the tough times by initiating cost-cutting measures such as slashing its workforce by 10 percent and its fleet by 20 percent. The company also pushed to pick up more business from vacationers and at-home leisure renters, and toward that end began an aggressive expansion program concentrating on opening new locations in local residential markets. By 2004 Avis had committed itself to opening 100 new locations per year.

During this same period, Cendant was working to wring efficiencies out of its dual-brand car rental operations. Cendant positioned Avis as its premium brand and Budget its value-oriented brand, and the two companies continued to operate separate counters. By 2004, however, Cendant had integrated a large portion of their operations. Avis and Budget now shared a common rental system, fleet, and back-office operation, and field maintenance support had been partially integrated. This integration yielded annual cost savings of $100 million. In another important development, the PHH and Wright Express businesses were separated from Avis Group Holdings, and in early 2005 PHH was spun off to Cendant shareholders and Wright was sold off via an initial public offering.

But Cendant had even more earth-shaking plans for Avis and all of its many other subsidiaries. In October 2005 Cendant announced plans to break itself up into four publicly traded companies. One of the four would focus exclusively on the car rental business and be comprised of Avis Group and Budget. Ronald L. Nelson, the president and chief financial officer of Cendant, was slated to become chairman and CEO of this company, with Salerno serving as president and chief operating officer. Its headquarters were to remain in Parsippany. The breakup was expected to be completed in the summer of 2006, ushering in yet another new era in the ever shifting history of Avis.

Principal Subsidiaries

ARAC Management Services, Inc.; Avis Asia and Pacific, Limited; Avis Car Holdings LLC; Avis Car Holdings, Inc.; Avis Car Rental Group, Inc.; Avis Caribbean, Limited; Avis Enterprises, Inc.; Avis International, Ltd.; Avis Management Pty. Limited (Australia); Avis Rent A Car de Puerto Rico, Inc.; Avis Rent A Car Limited (New Zealand); Avis Rent A Car System, Inc.; Aviscar Inc. (Canada).

Principal Competitors

The Hertz Corporation; National Car Rental System, Inc.; Alamo Rent-A-Car, Inc.; Dollar Rent A Car, Inc.; Thrifty Rent-A-Car System, Inc.; Enterprise Rent-A-Car Company.

Further Reading

Abelson, Reed, "Avis Vs. Hertz: Investors, Start Your Calculators," *New York Times,* September 14, 1997, p. BU4.

"Acquisition of Avis, Inc. Completed by IT&T," *New York Times,* July 23, 1965.

"Avis Is Now Offering Autos That Use Variable Fuels," *Wall Street Journal,* May 6, 1992.

Avis: The Avis Story, Garden City, N.Y.: Avis, Inc., 1991.

"Beatrice Sheds Fat," *Fortune,* October 28, 1985.

Bernstein, Aaron, "Should Avis Try Harder—For Its Employees?," *Business Week,* August 12, 1996, pp. 68–69.

Bigness, Jon, "HFS Plans to Offer Avis to Public, Investigates Purchase of Alamo," *Wall Street Journal,* August 26, 1996, p. B4.

Brecher, John, "Avis: An Orphan in a Merger War," *Newsweek,* July 11, 1983, p. 67.

Chaker, Anne Marie, "Cendant Is Expected to Buy Avis for As Much As $1 Billion," *Wall Street Journal,* November 13, 2000, p. B4.

Chittum, Ryan, "Cendant to Split Up into Four Firms," *Wall Street Journal,* October 24, 2005, pp. A3, A10.

Collingwood, Harris, "With Its ESOP, Avis Tries Even Harder," *Business Week,* May 15, 1989.

Dahl, Jonathan, "Tracking Travel," *Wall Street Journal,* March 13, 1992.

Dahl, Jonathan, and John D. Williams, "Beatrice to Sell Avis to Group Led by Wesray," *Wall Street Journal,* April 30, 1986.

DeMarrais, Kevin G., "Cendant's Breakup: Franchiser to Split into Four Companies," *Hackensack (N.J.) Record,* October 25, 2005, p. L9.

Employees Take the Wheel: A Study of Employee Ownership at Avis, Inc., New York: New York State Industrial Cooperation Council, 1989, 17 p.

Franz, Julie, "Beatrice Sells Avis, Cuts Staff," *Advertising Age,* May 5, 1986.

Goetz, Thomas, "Chairman, CEO of Avis Rent a Car Resigns Abruptly," *Wall Street Journal,* December 17, 1998, p. B22.

Hawkins, Chuck, "Is Avis Moving into the Passing Lane?," *Business Week,* May 9, 1988, p. 100.

Kirkpatrick, David, "How the Workers Run Avis Better," *Fortune,* December 5, 1988, p. 103.

Lublin, Joann S., "Avis to Name Rand, Ex-Xerox Official, to Chairman and Chief-Executive Posts," *Wall Street Journal,* November 9, 1999, p. B12.

Maynard, Micheline, "Avis Is Courting Leisure Travelers," *New York Times,* July 16, 2002, p. C7.

——, "Car Rental Industry Is Forced to Shift Ways," *New York Times,* November 28, 2002, p. C1.

"Meanwhile, Back at the Airport," *Fortune,* October 28, 1996, p. 126.

Miller, Gay Sands, and Laurie P. Cohen, "Avis Inc. Is Sold for Fifth Time in Four Years," *Wall Street Journal,* September 29, 1987.

Miller, Lisa, and Martha Brannigan, "Car-Rental Mergers Leave Consumers in the Back Seat," *Wall Street Journal,* January 7, 1997, p. B4.

Pacelle, Mitchell, and Thomas Goetz, "Cendant to Sell Its Leasing Unit to Avis," *Wall Street Journal,* May 25, 1999, p. A3.

Perone, Joseph R., "Avis Bringing the Fight to Hertz's Turf: No. 2 Rental Car Firm Joining Rival in Jersey," *Newark (N.J.) Star-Ledger,* June 24, 2001, p. 1.

Reeves, Scott, "Kick the Tires and Drive It Out: Avis to Benefit from Cross-Marketing," *Barron's,* September 15, 1997, p. 40.

Rogers, Michael, ''Beatrice Sheds Fat,'' *Fortune,* October 28, 1985, p. 10.

Spragins, Ellyn E., with Chuck Hawkins, and James E. Ellis, ''When You Own the Company, You Try Harder,'' *Business Week,* September 28, 1987.

Stancavish, Don, ''Cendant Adds Another Brand with Avis Buy,'' *Hackensack (N.J.) Record,* November 14, 2000, p. B1.

Starkman, Dean, ''BNP Paribas SA to Acquire 80% of Avis U.K. Unit,'' *Wall Street Journal,* April 19, 2000, p. B15.

Tannenbaum, Jeffrey A., and Stephanie N. Mehta, ''Bias at Single Store Can Taint Franchise Chain's Image: HFS's Avis Rental Unit Faces Allegations, But It Says Results Remain Strong,'' *Wall Street Journal,* March 6, 1997, p. B2.

Ward, John T., ''Cendant Trims the Fat by Selling Car Business,'' *Newark (N.J.) Star-Ledger,* May 25, 1999, p. 21.

—Grace Jeromski
—update: David E. Salamie

Barnes & Noble, Inc.

122 Fifth Avenue
New York, New York 10011-5605
U.S.A.
Telephone: (212) 633-3300
Fax: (212) 675-0413
Web site: http://www.barnesandnobleinc.com

Public Company
Incorporated: 1894 as C.M. Barnes Company
Employees: 42,000
Sales: $4.87 billion (2004)
Stock Exchanges: New York
Ticker Symbol: BKS
NAIC: 451211 Book Stores; 451220 Prerecorded Tape, Compact Disc, and Record Stores; 454111 Electronic Shopping; 511130 Book Publishers

Barnes & Noble, Inc. operates the largest chain of bookstores in the United States. The company revolutionized bookselling by introducing giant, supermarket-style stores with deeply discounted books in the 1970s, and by the early 2000s it operated more than 660 such superstores across the country. Barnes & Noble is also a leading operator of mall bookstores, running the well-known B. Dalton chain, and Doubleday, Bookstop, and Bookstar stores. The company also operates one of the top online bookselling operations, barnesandnoble.com, and is itself a rapidly growing book publisher. In addition to reissuing affordable editions of out-of-print titles under the Barnes & Noble Classics imprint, the company owns Sterling Publishing Co., Inc., one of the top 25 book publishers in the United States and the nation's largest publisher of how-to books.

Early Decades

The Barnes family's history in the book business started in 1873, when Charles Montgomery Barnes went into the second-hand book business in Wheaton, Illinois. Barnes soon moved to Chicago, selling new and used books. By 1894 Barnes's firm, reorganized as C.M. Barnes Company, dealt exclusively in school books. In 1902 C.M. Barnes's son, William R. Barnes, became president of the firm, and he continued the business in partnership with several other men. The younger Barnes sold his interest in his father's company in 1917, when he moved to New York. In New York, he acquired an interest in the educational bookstore Noble & Noble, partnering with G. Clifford Noble. The bookstore was soon renamed Barnes & Noble. Though Mr. Noble withdrew from the business in 1929, the name Barnes & Noble stuck.

The company's early business was wholesaling, selling mainly to schools, colleges, libraries, and dealers. Barnes & Noble entered the retail textbook trade somewhat reluctantly. A report in *College Store* magazine recounted that single book customers were tolerated, but that the store's counters and display shelves functioned as barricades against their encroachment. Eventually the store took a building on Fifth Avenue that included a small retail space. The public then "launched a campaign of book buying that soon banished all doubt as to the need for a general retail textbook house in New York." In 1932 Barnes & Noble opened a large retail store on Fifth Avenue and 18th Street, and this became the company's flagship. The quarters were enlarged and remodeled in 1941, and the store set the standard for college bookstores.

Barnes & Noble served the students of hundreds of New York City schools and colleges, and the store had to operate at top efficiency to accommodate the rush for textbooks at the beginning of each semester. In 1941 the store instituted a "book-a-teria" service that was soon picked up by other college bookstores. A clerk handed the customer a sales slip as he entered the store. Purchases were recorded on the slip by one clerk, money taken by another, and wrapping and bagging done by another. Barnes & Noble installed a telephone service that was quite advanced for the time, with five lines manned by specially trained staff. The New York store was also a pioneer in the use of "Music by Muzak," with the piped-in music interrupted at 12-minute intervals by announcements and advertising. Staff during the textbook rush season sometimes numbered over 300, and the store boasted a stock of two million books.

The successful retail division continued alongside Barnes & Noble's original business of wholesaling to schools and librar-

Company Perspectives:

Our mission is to operate the best specialty retail business in America, regardless of the product we sell. Because the product we sell is books, our aspirations must be consistent with the promise and the ideals of the volumes which line our shelves. To say that our mission exists independent of the product we sell is to demean the importance and the distinction of being booksellers.

As booksellers we are determined to be the very best in our business, regardless of the size, pedigree or inclinations of our competitors. We will continue to bring our industry nuances of style and approaches to bookselling which are consistent with our evolving aspirations.

Above all, we expect to be a credit to the communities we serve, a valuable resource to our customers, and a place where our dedicated booksellers can grow and prosper. Toward this end we will not only listen to our customers and booksellers but embrace the idea that the Company is at their service.

ies. The company also ran an import and an export division, an out-of-print book service, and published several series of non-fiction books, including the *College Outline Series* of study guides. In 1944 Barnes & Noble began putting out children's educational books after it took over the publishing firm Hinds, Hayden & Eldredge. The company also opened branches in Brooklyn and Chicago, and managed an outlet for used books and publishers' remainders called the Economy Book Store.

Barnes & Noble operated on a grand scale from the 1940s onward. Its wholesale textbook division bought used books from around 200 campus bookstores all across the East and Midwest. The flagship retail store earned a place in the *Guinness Book of World Records* in 1972 as "the World's Largest Bookstore," and Barnes & Noble also claimed this store did the largest dollar volume of any retail bookstore in the country.

But Barnes & Noble began to grow in more ways when it came under the sway of a new young owner, Leonard Riggio. Riggio began his stellar career in the book business at age 18, when he was a poorly paid clerk at the New York University (NYU) bookstore. Riggio initially studied engineering at night at the university, and in some sense he was unprepared for working with books. He recalled being embarrassed by a customer who asked for a copy of *Moby Dick*—Riggio had never heard of it. Nevertheless, he caught on to bookselling like no one else. In 1965, when he was only 24, Riggio borrowed $5,000 to open his own college bookstore, the Waverly Book Exchange. Though his store was only one-eighth the size of the official NYU bookstore, he soon rivaled his old employer's sales. He offered exceptional service to his student customers, airlifting textbooks to the store if necessary. The success of the Waverly Book Exchange allowed Riggio to buy or open ten more college bookstores over the next several years.

Arrival of Riggio: 1971

When Leonard Riggio set his sights on Barnes & Noble, the venerable bookstore was in a slump. President John Barnes,

grandson of the founder, had died in 1969, and the retail and wholesale divisions of the company were purchased by a conglomerate called Amtel, Inc., which made toys, tools, and various other products. Business declined under the new management, and Amtel decided to sell. In 1971 Leonard Riggio purchased Barnes & Noble from Amtel for $750,000. He quickly changed the names of his ten other bookstores to Barnes & Noble, and revitalized the old Fifth Avenue store.

The new owner made Barnes & Noble an educational bookstore with a broader focus that included all kinds of how-to and nonfiction books. Riggio believed that more people read books for information than for entertainment, and he changed the setup of the flagship store to give customers easier access to books they might want. He organized the stock into new, more specific categories, for example dividing the traditional category of philosophy into yoga and mysticism. Other sections of special interest books included cooking, Judaica, handyman books, study aids, and dictionaries. Riggio also opened a special children's section in the Fifth Avenue store, which, like the adult sections, emphasized educational books.

Under Leonard Riggio's management, Barnes & Noble expanded to include stores in New York, New Jersey, and Pennsylvania. By 1976, the company leased and operated 21 campus bookstores, and the combined retail and wholesale divisions brought in $32 million in sales. His early success led Riggio to gamble on a new kind of bookstore, the book supermarket. Across the street from the old Fifth Avenue Barnes & Noble, Riggio opened a giant sales annex that sprawled over three buildings. All books at the annex were discounted between 40 and 90 percent, even new books and bestsellers. Shoppers spent hours piling bargains into shopping carts, as Riggio explained to *Publishers Weekly* that he had "set the customer free in an unintimidating atmosphere to roam over a vast space." The prairie-like annex included fiction, textbooks, children's books, reference books, art books, and gift books. Corners were devoted to books on special topics ranging from Latin America to transportation, and huge black and yellow signs directing customers to different categories could be read from 176 feet away. Riggio claimed that most of Barnes & Noble's customers did not intend to read the books they bought, and the casual, warehouse atmosphere of the sales annex was geared to the everyday shopper, not the scholar or bibliophile. It was a marketing technique that worked brilliantly.

Barnes & Noble's thriving sales encouraged the company to grow and innovate. In 1979 Barnes & Noble acquired a chain of retail stores called Bookmasters, and then bought Marboro Books, Inc., a remainder company with discount retail outlets. Barnes & Noble operated a chain of Supermart Books that serviced drugstore and supermarket book departments, and ran the Missouri Book Co., selling used college textbooks. Barnes & Noble also more than tripled its college store leases in the mid-1980s, increasing from 40 in 1983 to 142 in 1986.

B. Dalton Acquisition: 1986

Total sales grew to about $225 million in 1985, and the next year Barnes & Noble made a major acquisition. For a price estimated at around $300 million, Barnes & Noble bought B. Dalton Bookseller, a bookstore chain with 798 outlets, from

---

Key Dates:

1873: Charles Montgomery Barnes enters the second-hand book business in Wheaton, Illinois, soon shifting operations to Chicago.

1894: Barnes's business is reorganized as C.M. Barnes Company.

1917: The founder's son, William R. Barnes, sells his interest in his father's firm and moves to New York, where he acquires an interest in the educational bookstore Noble & Noble (partnering with C. Clifford Noble), soon renamed Barnes & Noble.

1929: Noble withdraws from the business, but the Barnes & Noble name sticks.

1932: Company's flagship retail store is opened on New York's Fifth Avenue and 18th Street.

1969: John Barnes, grandson of the founder, dies, and the company is sold to Amtel, Inc., a conglomerate.

1971: Leonard Riggio purchases Barnes & Noble.

1986: Company acquires the B. Dalton Bookseller chain.

Early 1990s: The modern generation of Barnes & Noble superstores is introduced, followed by rapid expansion.

1993: Company goes public.

1997: Barnesandnoble.com, the firm's bookselling web site, is launched.

1998: Bertelsmann AG acquires a 50 percent stake in barnesandnoble.com.

1999: Barnesandnoble.com is taken public; company enters the video game retailing sector by acquiring Babbage's Etc. LLC.

2002: Stephen Riggio, Leonard's brother, is named CEO, with the elder Riggio remaining chairman.

2003: Company expands its book publishing operations with the purchase of Sterling Publishing Co., Inc.; Barnes & Noble acquires Bertelsmann's interest in barnesandnoble.com.

2004: Barnes & Noble acquires full control of barnesandnoble.com; company's foray into video game retailing ends when its remaining shares in GameStop Corp. are distributed to Barnes & Noble shareholders.

Dayton Hudson Corporation. B. Dalton was the second biggest chain bookstore, behind Waldenbooks, and its sales were estimated at $538 million in 1985. The acquisition put Barnes & Noble in the second place spot, and the company continued to acquire chains. In March 1990 Barnes & Noble purchased an upscale chain of 40 bookstores, Doubleday Book Shops, for an estimated $20 million. A few months later, the company became sole owner of a Texas and Florida chain of discount bookstores called Bookstop.

Barnes & Noble had used the name BDB Corp. for the holding company that owned Barnes & Noble, Inc., B. Dalton, and its other businesses. Leonard Riggio was the majority owner, and had a financial partner in a Dutch conglomerate called Vendex. The name of the holding company changed back to Barnes & Noble, Inc. in 1991, and the company reacquired

rights to publish under the Barnes & Noble name. These rights had been sold after John Barnes died in 1969.

Opening of Numerous Superstores: Early 1990s

Barnes & Noble, Inc. had grown enormously in the 1980s through acquisitions. The company embarked on a new growth strategy in the 1990s, opening new ''superstores'' at a breathtaking pace. The superstores differed somewhat from the earlier Fifth Avenue ''book supermarket'' Barnes & Noble sales annex. The superstores were large, carrying as many as 150,000 titles, or six times the size of a typical mall bookstore, but they had amenities such as coffee bars and children's play areas, and were designed to be pleasant public spaces where people would browse, read, and mingle. Wide aisles and scattered chairs and benches encouraged customers to linger, and local managers had the autonomy to arrange poetry readings and puppet shows. The discounted (usually by 10 to 40 percent) superstore stock was vast, yet the space was as posh and inviting as that of many independent bookstores. Barnes & Noble operated 23 superstores in 1989. Three years later there were 105, and the company intended to open 100 more each year through 1994. On one day in August 1992, Barnes & Noble opened five superstores, and two months later opened three more.

The superstores cost more than $1 million apiece to build, outfit, and stock, and Barnes & Noble lost money by opening so many so quickly. Though sales for 1991 were more than $892 million, Barnes & Noble, Inc. posted a loss of close to $8 million that year. But overall sales continued to rise, and the superstores contributed some impressive revenues. Eighty percent of new superstores contributed to company profits in their first year of operation. A Barnes & Noble superstore on the Upper West Side in Manhattan was expected to bring in $12 million in sales its first year, but it proved so popular with New Yorkers that it actually brought in between $16 million and $18 million. The average superstore commanded a much more modest $3.5 million. The superstores generated on the average twice the sales of mall bookstores, and in 1992 superstore sales rose by 114 percent.

Other booksellers complained about Barnes & Noble's rapid growth, believing that the market could not hold so many bookstores. But Leonard Riggio went on the record repeatedly to dispel claims that his growing chain was predatory. The amount Americans spent on books rose a hefty 12.5 percent in 1992, and Riggio believed the market would continue to grow. But the expansion of Barnes & Noble prompted competitive chains to build more stores, too. Waldenbooks planned to more than double the size of its mall stores, from 3,000 to between 6,000 and 8,000 square feet. Borders Inc., a chain of superstores then owned by Kmart Corporation, planned to open two new stores a month in 1993.

Going Public: 1993

With its growth so enormous and debt so high, Barnes & Noble, Inc. decided to raise cash by selling its stock to the public. An initial stock offering in 1992 was postponed because of adverse market conditions. Wall Street analysts had been skeptical of the company's ability to sustain its profits, but a year after the first offering was withdrawn, superstore sales had continued to climb. These sales accounted for almost half the company's total revenue, up from 26 percent in 1992, and the company seemed more solid. Barnes & Noble stock began trading on the New York Stock Exchange on September 28, 1993, and demand was so high that brokers were unable to purchase as much as they wanted. The stock had been expected to sell for around $17 a share: it closed at $29.25 its first day. Leonard Riggio retained about a third of Barnes & Noble, Inc., and another third was controlled by his Dutch partner Vendex.

For the fiscal year ending in January 1994, Barnes & Noble reported an 87 percent gain in revenue at its superstores. The textbook area of the company continued to be quite profitable too, and the company ran almost 300 college bookstores across the country. Children's books also sold very well, and Riggio made plans to expand the square footage of the Barnes & Noble Jr. stores that were a part of the superstores. The growth of the Barnes & Noble chain under Leonard Riggio had been spectacular.

In spite of critics' fears that the company's rapid expansion would saturate the book market or set off vicious wars for market share, Barnes & Noble seemed able to keep abreast of what the public wanted in a bookstore, and supply just what was needed. The discount sales annex had been a radical step, eliminating the high-brow atmosphere long associated with bookstores. The superstores managed to combine the savings and huge selection of the discount store with an environment tailored equally well to book lovers, socializers, and bargain hunters. In many ways Barnes & Noble set the standard for its competitors from the early textbook store to the 1990s, by innovating in areas such as store design and marketing of software, and by its pioneering efforts such as providing books for children with disabilities, and offering a literary award to first-time novelists.

During the 1995 fiscal year, Barnes & Noble opened 97 additional superstores, bringing the total to 358. This growth increasingly led to declining sales for mall bookstores, including the company's own. Barnes & Noble had been closing between 50 and 60 B. Dalton stores per year since 1989, but in late 1995 decided to step up its mall closings. The company took a charge of $123.8 million for a restructuring program aimed at developing a core of more profitable mall bookstores (the charge led to a $53 million net loss for the year). During 1995, 69 B. Dalton stores closed and another 72 were shuttered the following year. At the same time, Barnes & Noble expanded the size of many B. Dalton outlets and opened a small number of new, larger B. Dalton stores each year, seeking to place them in locations that offered increased visibility and higher traffic flow. The new and enlarged units performed better than their predecessors, but all mall bookstores continued to be hurt by competition from nearby superstores. By 1998 Barnes & Noble operated more superstores than mall bookstores.

Entering Internet Bookselling: Late 1990s

In 1996 Barnes & Noble bought a 20 percent stake in Chapters Inc., the largest book retailer in Canada, but sold it three years later. For the fiscal year ending in January 1997, revenues soared past the $2 billion mark, reaching $2.45 billion, an increase of more than 23 percent over the previous year. In early 1997 the company entered the burgeoning market for Internet bookselling through a venture with America Online Inc. (AOL), whereby Barnes & Noble became the exclusive bookseller for the more than eight million AOL subscribers. Later that year the company launched its bookselling web site, barnesandnoble.com. These moves came following the emergence of a new competitive threat, namely Seattle-based Internet bookselling upstart Amazon.com, Inc., which had been founded in 1995 and had sales of $147.8 million by 1997, although it had yet to make a profit. The e-commerce battle between Amazon.com and barnesandnoble.com intensified in 1998 when German media behemoth Bertelsmann AG purchased 50 percent of Barnes & Noble's Internet operation for $200 million, a sizable capital fund for the nascent undertaking. For the fiscal year ending in January 1999, barnesandnoble.com saw its sales increase 381 percent, from $14.6 million to $70.2 million; it also developed an in-stock inventory of 750,000 titles ready for immediate delivery, which the company claimed was the largest in the industry. It also boasted the world's largest overall selection, with more than eight million new, out-of-print, and rare books available for ordering. In May 1999 Barnes & Noble and Bertelsmann took barnesandnoble.com public, selling 18 percent of the company and raising another $421.6 million for its war chest. The Internet bookseller's joint venture partners retained equal 41 percent shares in barnesandnoble.com. In July 1999 barnesandnoble.com announced the launch of an online "music store," with heavy discounts of as much as 30 percent off retail prices. Here again, Barnes & Noble was following trailblazer Amazon.com, which began selling music online a year earlier.

In March 1998 the American Booksellers Association joined with 26 independent bookstores in suing Barnes & Noble and Borders. The suit claimed that the large chains had violated antitrust laws by using their buying power to demand from publishers "illegal and secret" discounts. Barnes & Noble said it would vigorously defend this and similar actions that were subsequently brought against it. Antitrust concerns of a different nature scuttled Barnes & Noble's attempt to purchase Ingram Book Group Inc., the largest book wholesaler in the United States, a deal that was announced in November 1998. Barnes & Noble was interested in Ingram for its system of 11 distribution centers spread throughout the country. The acquisition of this system would have cut distribution costs and enabled Barnes & Noble to speed delivery of books to its growing legion of online customers. The acquisition, however, drew strong opposition from independent booksellers as well as from Amazon.com. Federal Trade Commission officials ended up siding with the opponents, and recommended in June 1999 that the agency oppose the deal, having concluded that it would stifle competition in both online and offline book retailing. Barnes & Noble soon withdrew its takeover bid rather than enter into protracted litigation.

At the turn of the millennium, the biggest threat to Barnes & Noble's position as the number one U.S. bookseller was clearly Amazon.com, which in mid-1999 had a market value of $18 billion, more than three times the value of Barnes & Noble and barnesandnoble.com combined. In the Internet-crazed world of the late 1990s, the fact that Barnes & Noble held 15 percent of the total U.S. book market versus Amazon's 2 percent mattered less than the companies' respective online bookselling shares:

15 percent for Barnes & Noble, 75 percent for Amazon. Part of Barnes & Noble's response to its upstart challenger was to slow its rapid rate of store expansion.

New Ventures in the Early 2000s

From 1999 to 2004 Barnes & Noble made a brief foray into the video game retailing sector. In October 1999 the company acquired Babbage's Etc. LLC for $215 million. Babbage's, which at the time was operating nearly 500 stores under the Babbage's, Software Etc., and GameStop names, had been owned since 1996 by an investor group led by Riggio. In June 2000 Barnes & Noble acquired Funco, Inc., operator of 400 FuncoLand video game stores. Eventually, all of these operations were organized within a subsidiary called GameStop Corp., and a gradual conversion of the stores to the GameStop name began. In February 2002 Barnes & Noble sold one-third of GameStop's stock to the public via an initial public offering, and in October 2004 its remaining GameStop shares were distributed to Barnes & Noble shareholders. Although the company counted the foray into the video game as a success, having turned a $400 million investment into more than $850 million, management eventually concluded that the values of Barnes & Noble and GameStop would be enhanced by trading separately and not as a conglomerated entity.

During this period the shrinking of the B. Dalton chain continued apace, as the number of outlets fell from 400 in 1999 to just 154 at the end of 2004. Revenues from B. Dalton dropped from $426 million to $176.5 million over this period, while revenues from the Barnes & Noble superstores were jumping from $2.82 billion to $4.12 billion. The number of superstores increased from 542 to 666. During 2000 the company recorded a charge of $106.8 million, primarily to write down the value of its B. Dalton assets. This led to a net loss for the year of $52 million.

In February 2002 Stephen Riggio, Leonard's younger brother, was named CEO of Barnes & Noble. Stephen Riggio had been with the company since 1975, serving as chief operating officer from February 1995 through January 1997 and then as vice-chairman until his appointment as CEO. The company credited him with playing instrumental roles in Barnes & Noble's move into book publishing, its shift to the superstore format, and its entry into electronic commerce. With the shift in leadership, Stephen Riggio assumed responsibility for the day-to-day operations of Barnes & Noble, while Leonard Riggio remained actively involved at the company as chairman of the board overseeing strategic matters such as mergers and financings.

To the consternation of many publishers, Barnes & Noble moved more aggressively into book publishing starting in 2003. In January of that year the firm acquired Sterling Publishing Co., Inc. for $115 million. The closely held Sterling, based in Manhattan and founded in 1949, was the nation's largest publisher of how-to books and ranked among the top 25 publishers overall. Sterling claimed a backlist (inventory) of 4,500 titles, with its biggest sellers including *The Illustrated Dream Dictionary* and *Biggest Riddle Book in the World*. Barnes & Noble followed this purchase with the April 2003 launch of Barnes & Noble Classics, a new line of literary classics positioned to be lower-priced competition to such established lines as the Modern Library, produced by Bertelsmann's Random House, and Penguin Classics, issued by Pearson plc. Publishing was attractive to Barnes & Noble because the firm could book profits on both the publishing and selling of a particular book, and it provided the stores with exclusive products. Book publishing offered a way for the company to boost its profitability at a time when margins in book retailing were being squeezed by a sluggish economy, flat book sales, and growing competition from discounters such as Wal-Mart Stores, Inc. selling books as loss leaders. Barnes & Noble was aiming to increase the portion of revenue derived from sales of its own books to 10 percent by 2008 from the 4 percent level of 2003.

On the online side, Barnes & Noble in September 2003 bought out Bertelsmann's interest in barnesandnoble.com. The company paid Bertelsmann $165.4 million to increase its stake in the venture to 75 percent. Then the following May, Barnes & Noble took full control of barnesandnoble.com, buying the publicly traded shares for an aggregate price of $158.8 million. The shareholders received about $3 per share for a stock that had debuted at $18 a share during the Internet bubble and briefly traded above $25 a share. The online bookseller had yet to turn a profit, but its performance was steadily improving, and in 2004 its net loss narrowed by 18 percent. Its revenues of $419.8 million were nevertheless far below those of Amazon.com, which remained the clear leader with about 70 percent of the online book market compared to Barnes & Noble's 20 percent.

For the fiscal year ending in January 2005 total sales amounted to $4.87 billion, with 85 percent coming from Barnes & Noble superstores. Despite continued softness in the book market, the superstores managed to achieve a 3.1 percent increase in comparable store sales (that is, sales at stores open more than 15 months). An additional 32 superstores opened during the year, and the company planned to continue opening a similar number annually over the succeeding several years, estimating that there was room for 300 to 400 more Barnes & Noble stores. In 2005 the opening of a new store in Morgantown, West Virginia, provided the chain with a presence in all 50 states. The company's publishing program was another key component of future growth, and a line of children's classics was released in late 2004 followed in 2005 by a series of abridged editions of children's classics, for kids with reading disabilities.

Principal Subsidiaries

Barnes & Noble Booksellers, Inc.; B. Dalton Bookseller, Inc.; Doubleday Book Shops, Inc.; B&N.com Holding Corp.; barnesandnoble.com inc.; barnesandnoble.com llc.; Barnes & Noble Publishing, Inc.; CCI Holdings, Inc.; Calendar Club L.L.C. (75%); Sterling Publishing Co., Inc.; Altamont Press, Inc.; Marketing Services (Minnesota) Corp.; Barnes & Noble Services, Inc.; Marboro Books Corp.; Chelsea Insurance Company LTD (Bermuda); Barnes & Noble BookQuest, LLC.

Principal Competitors

Borders Group, Inc.; Books-A-Million, Inc.; Amazon.com, Inc.; Wal-Mart Stores, Inc.; Costco Wholesale Corporation.

Further Reading

"Barnes & Noble, Educational Bookstore, Celebrates 75 Years of Service," *Publishers Weekly,* February 12, 1949, pp. 901–04.

"Barnes & Noble Encouraged by Software Sales," *Publishers Weekly,* October 26, 1984, p. 69.

"Barnes & Noble Remodels Its Quarters for Efficiency," *Publishers Weekly,* December 6, 1941, pp. 2090–093.

"Barnes & Noble's Revitalization Program," *Publishers Weekly,* September 28, 1970, pp. 69–70.

"Barnes & Noble Stock Soars," *Publishers Weekly,* October 4, 1993, p. 14.

"Barnes & Noble to Buy Doubleday Book Shops," *Publishers Weekly,* March 2, 1990, p. 8.

"BDB Corp. Becomes Barnes & Noble Inc. and Plans to Expand," *Wall Street Journal,* January 9, 1991, p. B5.

Berreby, David, "The Growing Battle of the Big Bookstores," *New York Times,* November 8, 1992, sec. 3, p. 5.

Bhargava, Sunita Wadekar, "Espresso, Sandwiches, and a Sea of Books," *Business Week,* July 26, 1993, p. 56.

Breen, Peter, "Fulfilling Dreams: Why Is Barnes & Noble Trying to Buy Ingram Co. for $600 Million?," *Chain Store Age,* May 1999, pp. 244, 246, 248.

Carvajal, Doreen, "Superstore's Online Unit Seeks Stability," *New York Times,* April 17, 2000, p. C1.

Cox, Meg, "Barnes & Noble Boss Has Big Growth Plans That Booksellers Fear," *Wall Street Journal,* September 11, 1992, p. A1.

——, "Barnes & Noble Cancels Proposal to Offer Stock," *Wall Street Journal,* September 30, 1992, p. A4.

Dugan, I. Jeanne, "The Baron of Books," *Business Week,* June 29, 1998, pp. 108–12, 114–15.

Freilicher, Lila, "Barnes & Noble Success Spawns New Mall Stores," *Publishers Weekly,* August 5, 1974, pp. 43–44.

——, "Barnes & Noble: The Book Supermarket—Of Course, Of Course," *Publishers Weekly,* January 19, 1976, pp. 71–73.

Furman, Phyllis, "Profits, but Little Respect: Despite Stellar Rise, Barnes & Noble Exec Remains Outsider," *Crain's New York Business,* February 26, 1996, p. 1.

Kirkpatrick, David D., "Barnes & Noble Makes Bid for Shares of Online Unit," *New York Times,* November 8, 2003, p. C2.

——, "Barnes & Noble's Jekyll and Hyde," *New York,* July 19, 1999.

——, "A Shifting of Leadership at Bookseller: Barnes & Noble Chief Steps Aside for Brother," *New York Times,* February 14, 2002, p. C1.

Knect, G. Bruce, "Independent Bookstores Are Suing Borders Group and Barnes & Noble," *Wall Street Journal,* March 19, 1998, p. B10.

Labaton, Stephen, and Doreen Carvajal, "Book Retailer Ends Bid for Wholesaler," *New York Times,* June 3, 1999, p. 1.

"Literary Supermarket," *Forbes,* May 15, 1976, p. 49.

"Marboro Sells Part of Assets to Barnes & Noble," *Publishers Weekly,* October 29, 1979, p. 28.

McDowell, Edwin, "Book Chain Refinances, Easing Debt," *New York Times,* November 18, 1992, p. D4.

Milliot, Jim, "B&N Priming Publishing Pump," *Publishers Weekly,* September 20, 2004, p. 8.

——, "B&N to Open 30 Stores, Consolidate Warehouses," *Publishers Weekly,* March 29, 2004, pp. 5, 8.

——, "Barnes & Noble Reports Strong Superstore Sales—Up 114% in '93," *Publishers Weekly,* April 26, 1993, p. 17.

——, "Riggio: Books Remain B&N's Focus," *Publishers Weekly,* January 19, 2004, p. 10.

——, "Superstores Success Spurs New Try at B & N Offering," *Publishers Weekly,* September 13, 1993, p. 12.

Munk, Nina, "Title Fight," *Fortune,* June 21, 1999, pp. 84–86, 88–90, 92, 94.

Mutter, John, "Crown Sells Interest in Bookstop to BDB for $8.3 Million," *Publishers Weekly,* June 1, 1990, p. 15.

Prial, Dunstan, "Barnes & Noble Books an IPO for Web Unit," *Wall Street Journal,* August 21, 1998, p. B1.

Quick, Rebecca, "Barnes & Noble Makes Another Play in Video Games," *Wall Street Journal,* May 8, 2000, p. B6.

Reda, Susan, "Barnes & Noble Forays Open Battle for On-Line Bookselling," *Stores,* May 1997, pp. 50+.

Reilly, Patrick M., "Barnes & Noble Closes Book on Attempt to Buy Ingram, Amid FTC Objections," *Wall Street Journal,* June 3, 1999, p. B16.

——, "Barnesandnoble.com to Join a Crowd of Firms Offering 'Online Music Stores,'" *Wall Street Journal,* July 7, 1999, p. B2.

——, "Barnes & Noble Draws Fire over Plan to Buy Ingram Book for $600 Million," *Wall Street Journal,* November 9, 1998, p. B10.

——, "Barnes & Noble Likely to Build Centers for Distribution If Ingram Deal Fails," *Wall Street Journal,* June 2, 1999, p. B8.

——, "Barnes & Noble Sues Amazon.com over Rival's Book-Selling Claims," *Wall Street Journal,* May 13, 1997, p. B3.

——, "Bertelsmann to Buy a 50% Interest in Web Bookseller," *Wall Street Journal,* October 7, 1998, p. B8.

——, "Booksellers Prepare to Do Battle in Cyberspace," *Wall Street Journal,* January 28, 1997, p. B1.

——, "Online Bookseller's Shares Increase by 27% in IPO," *Wall Street Journal,* May 26, 1999, p. C19.

——, "Street Fighters: Where Borders Group and Barnes & Noble Compete, It's a War," *Wall Street Journal,* September 3, 1996, pp. A1+.

Reilly, Patrick M., and John R. Wilke, "FTC Staff Opposes Barnes & Noble's Ingram Bid," *Wall Street Journal,* June 1, 1999, p. B3.

Sandler, Linda, and Patrick M. Reilly, "Barnes & Noble Slows Its Evelyn Wood Pace of Store Openings: A Twist in Bookseller's Plot," *Wall Street Journal,* September 2, 1997, p. C2.

Schoenberger, Chana R., "Chapter Two," *Forbes,* April 15, 2002, p. 44.

Stankevich, Debby Garbato, "A Noble Concept," *Retail Merchandiser,* May 2002, p. 46.

Strauss, Lawrence C., "Book Values," *Barron's,* August 29, 2005, pp. 16–17.

Strom, Stephanie, "Barnes & Noble Goes Public: Vol. 2," *New York Times,* September 3, 1993, p. D1.

Stross, Randall E., "Why Barnes & Noble May Crush Amazon," *Fortune,* September 29, 1997, pp. 248, 250.

Symons, Allene, "Barnes & Noble to Buy B. Dalton: Will Become Largest Chain," *Publishers Weekly,* December 12, 1986, p. 17.

Tangora, Joanne, "Major Chains Set New Software Strategies," *Publishers Weekly,* August 24, 1984, pp. 38–39.

Tarquinio, J. Alex, "With Fancy Footwork, Barnes & Noble Surprises the Naysayers," *New York Times,* January 4, 2004, sec. 3, p. 5.

Trachtenberg, Jeffrey A., "Barnes & Noble Buys Out Interest of Online Partner," *Wall Street Journal,* July 30, 2003, p. B3.

——, "Barnes & Noble Pares GameStop," *Wall Street Journal,* October 5, 2004, p. B6.

——, "Barnes & Noble Pushes Books from Ambitious Publisher: Itself," *Wall Street Journal,* June 18, 2003, p. A1.

——, "Barnes & Noble's Stephen Riggio to Become CEO," *Wall Street Journal,* February 14, 2002, p. A3.

——, "Barnes & Noble to Buy Sterling, Boosting Book-Publishing Effort," *Wall Street Journal,* December 13, 2002, p. B7.

——, "Book Chain to Take a Video-Game Retailer Public," *Wall Street Journal,* February 12, 2002, p. B1.

——, "Investors Brace for Barnes & Noble Plot Twist," *Wall Street Journal,* May 27, 2004, p. C1.

—A. Woodward
—update: David E. Salamie

Baumax AG

Aufeldstrasse 17-23
Klosterneuburg
A-3400
Austria
Telephone: + 43 2243 410 0
Fax: + 43 2243 380 13
Web site: http://www.baumax.at
Private Company
Incorporated: 1976
Employees: 5,634
Sales: EUR 1.0 billion ($1.3 billion) (2004)
NAIC: 423390 Other Construction Material Merchant Wholesalers; 423310 Lumber, Plywood, Millwork, and Wood Panel Merchant Wholesalers; 423320 Brick, Stone and Related Construction Material Merchant Wholesalers; 423330 Roofing, Siding, and Insulation Material Merchant Wholesalers

Baumax AG is Austria's leading operator of Do-It-Yourself (DIY) hardware stores, and one of the leading and fastest-growing DIY chains in the Central European region. Based in Klosterneuburg, in lower Austria, Baumax operates some 70 stores in Austria itself, providing complete national coverage. Many of the company's Austrian stores feature the MegaMax building format. These stores reach nearly 135,000 square feet of selling space, including garden centers of more than 43,000 square feet, and even in-store cafes. The MegaMax format targets not only the consumer DIY market and small trade circuit, but also the professional building segment, with a mix of consumer goods and construction materials. Baumax's Central European expansion has led it into most of Austria's neighboring Eastern and Central European markets, including the Czech Republic, the largest of the group's international network, with 23 stores. The company is also expanding in Hungary (14 stores), Slovakia (ten stores), Slovenia (three stores), and Croatia (three stores). Altogether, the company operated 53 stores outside of Austria in 2005. Further international expansion is a central part of the group's strategy, particularly as

competition heightens in its home market. In 2005, the company began preparing its entry into the increasingly stable Bulgarian market, and launched plans to expand into Rumania as well. These entries are part of the company's ambitious expansion program for the second half of the 2000s, intending to double its revenues. In 2004, the company's total sales topped EUR 1 billion ($1.3 billion). Publicly listed throughout the 1990s, the founding Essl family, which had previously controlled nearly 85 percent of the company's shares, bought out its minority shareholders and took the company private in 2004. Founder Karlheinz Essl remains active in the company as chairman of the board, while son Martin Essl guides the group's operations as managing director.

Forming a Family Business in the 1970s

Baumax stemmed from the Fritz Schömer company, founded in Klosterneuburg, Austria, in 1923. Schömer originally operated as a small coal-selling business. By the late 1950s, however, the company had expanded into the sale of building and construction materials. Nonetheless, the company remained small, with less than 30 employees.

The arrival of Karlheinz Essl as part of the business, and the Schömer family, marked the beginning of a new era for the family-owned business. Born in 1939, Essl came from a family with a background in food retailing. In the 1950s, after finishing his studies at Graz Business School, Essl was sent by his family to Germany, Switzerland, and, especially, the United States, to observe the growing supermarket culture in those countries. While in New York, Essl met his wife, daughter of Fritz Schömer.

Returning to Austria, Essl decided to join his father-in-law in his construction materials business, rather than join his family's food wholesale and distribution operation. Essl and Schömer worked together to build up their operation, extending into building supplies, as well as construction and related materials. By 1973, the company's growth led it to restructure its operations into two businesses, one dedicated to building materials, the other focused on its coal and other mineral distribution operation. In that same year, the company also extended its scope into the cement and aggregates market, founding Schömer L + S Beton Werke.

Company Perspectives:

Our mission is to spread the do-it-yourself philosophy throughout Central Europe. We want to help our customers to realise their home improvement dreams.

Essl took over control of the family business in 1975. By then, he had developed an interest in a relatively young retail market. The Fritz Schömer company continued to grow strongly over the next decades, becoming a major Austrian company in its own right, with sales of more than EUR 1.5 billion by the mid-2000s. Yet Essl's new interest turned toward the Do-It-Yourself (DIY) market. If the traditional hardware stores already existed, the DIY market represented a step further, appealing to the growing trend among consumers toward making their own home repairs and home improvements. The DIY center became part of a trend toward ''category killer'' stores that had emerged in the United States during the 1970s. The category killer, by focusing a narrow product category, promised a far larger selection than the typical department store, as well as the potential for lower pricing. The new DIY retail centers, therefore, developed a similar ''one-stop shopping'' concept, offering products for nearly all of a consumer's home improvement needs under a single roof, from basic construction materials to home furnishings to gardening supplies and plants.

The oil crisis and related economic difficulties of the 1970s, further exacerbated in Austria by the near total lack of significant oil reserves in the country, provided a fertile ground for the development of a DIY culture. Indeed, elsewhere in Europe, the DIY market eventually grew to become one of the most popular consumer pastimes, rivaled only by gardening (which also featured prominently in the typical DIY center). Essl recognized the DIY center as a natural extension of the family's main business, and in 1976, he began developing a DIY retail format, and established a new company, Baumax.

The first Baumax store opened in the town of Kindberg. The Baumax concept caught on quickly, and the company's early entry into the segment allowed it to gain an early and lasting lead in the Austrian DIY market. The company became the country's top DIY retailer in 1983, a position it would not relinquish through the mid-2000s. By the end of the 1980s, the Baumax name was said to have become as well known as McDonald's or Coca-Cola in Austria.

Essl was joined by son Martin Essl in 1983; like his father, the younger Essl had been sent to the United States to study the retail climate there. Baumax began extending its presence throughout Austria, backed by a public offering and a listing on the Vienna Stock Exchange at the end of the decade. The Essl family nonetheless remained in firm control of the company, holding nearly 85 percent of Baumax's stock. The company built its new headquarters in 1987, called the Schömer house in honor of Fritz Schömer.

Central European Expansion in the 1990s

As it approached the 1990s, Baumax drafted a new expansion and marketing strategy, dubbed BauMax 2000. The company's

objective was not only to complete building out its growing national network of retail stores, but also to launch its first efforts at international expansion. The decision to direct its international efforts at the Central and Eastern European market came in 1989, with the collapse of Soviet domination of the region.

In the early 1990s, Baumax went in search of its first foreign expansion prospects. At the same time, the company began implementing a new business and marketing strategy. A prominent part of this strategy was the company's decision to expand its store format. Into the middle of the 1990s the company's stores boasted an average selling space of nearly 3,500 square meters, a 30 percent advantage over the rest of the Austrian DIY market. Yet the company's new format called for the development of far larger stores, featuring 10,000 square meters of DIY selling space, with an additional 4,000 square meters devoted to gardening tools, supplies, and equipment. The larger format stores were dubbed BauMax 2000, and began shifting the company's average store space upward through the end of the decade.

Baumax's first foreign store opened in Prague in 1992. The Czech Republic quickly became the company's most enthusiastic foreign market, and by the mid-2000s was also its largest market outside of Austria, with 23 stores. The company also entered Hungary in 1992, where the success of the company's format enabled it to expand its network to 14 stores over the next decade. Slovakia became Baumax's next target, with the first store opening in Bratislava in 1994.

In that year, Baumax made an important acquisition, buying construction materials, tiles, and retail group Buettinghaus. The acquisition helped boost Baumax's revenues by some 65 percent for the year, allowing the company to top sales of ATS 5.7 billion. Following the acquisition, Baumax split up Buettinghaus's operations into its separate businesses, ultimately divesting the tiles and building materials businesses. Part of these went to the Fritz Schömer company.

The Buettinghaus acquisition not only boosted the company's retail network in Austria, but it also gave Baumax its first retail store in Slovenia. The company began converting its Buettinghaus stores to the BauMax 2000 format, a process in large part completed by 1997. In the meantime, the company began stepping up its international expansion. By 1995, the company's foreign network already numbered 12 stores, and its international sales nearly doubled. Into 1997, the company's expansion remained brisk, as the company pursued an ATS 1.1 billion investment program, including the opening of 14 new stores, and the completion of 32 store refittings.

Facing the Competition in the New Century

Baumax had put into place a new logistics network in 1994, boosting its efficiency. This became all the more important in the late 1990s as the company faced a new level of competition both for the Central and Eastern European market, but in Austria as well. Indeed, into the late 1990s, a number of Europe's largest DIY specialists, especially leading German groups including Obi, Praktiker, and Hornbach, had begun to eye these markets. The increased competition took its toll on Baumax, shrinking its Austrian market share from a high of

Key Dates:

1923: Fritz Schömer establishes a coal trading business.
1959: Karlheinz Essl joins father-in-law Fritz Schömer.
1975: Essl takes over as head of the Fritz Schömer business.
1976: Essl launches a DIY retail store concept, Baumax.
1983: Baumax becomes a market leader in Austria.
1989: Baumax goes public, launches new larger-format BauMax 2000 stores, and announces plans to begin international expansion.
1992: The first foreign store is opened in Prague; a store opens in Hungary.
1994: Baumax opens a new logistics center; its first store in Slovakia is opened; the company acquires Beuttinghaus, which gives it a new store in Slovenia.
1999: The company forms a purchasing alliance named tooMax with Rewe's Toom DIY business.
2000: The company opens its first store in Croatia; the new large-scale Megabaumax store format is launched.
2004: The Essl family acquires full control of the company and Baumax is delisted from the stock exchange.
2005: The company announces plans to open its first store in Bulgaria and to enter Rumania.

35 percent in the mid-1990s to a still respectable 29 percent in the mid-2000s.

Baumax's response came in two parts. On the one hand, the company sought out a number of purchasing alliances, such as that formed with Cologne, Germany-based Rewe in 1999. That alliance, called tooMax, bundled Baumax's purchasing strength with that of Rewe's own DIY retail operation, Toom.

The second part of Baumax's strategy into the 2000s was the development of a new retail format designed to appeal to both the consumer/small trade and professional contractor markets. The new format was called Megabaumax and easily lived up to its name: The new store design featured more than 135,000 square feet of selling space, including a garden department boasting more than 43,000 square feet.

Into the 2000s, Baumax began rolling out the Megabaumax format, building new stores and converting or replacing an in-creasing number of its existing stores. The company also exported the Megabaumax format to its foreign markets, and especially the Czech Republic, which saw the opening of three new large-format stores in 2001 and 2002. The company also launched plans to add eight new stores to its Slovakia network; by 2005, the company had succeeded in expanding its retail operations in that country to ten stores. Hungary, too, proved a strong market for the group. By 2005, the company operated 14 stores in that country, including its latest and largest, a 12,500-square-meter store opened in Obuda, in North Budapest, in 2004. At the same time, Baumax expanded into another new market, neighboring Croatia, opening three stores there by mid-decade.

As it turned toward the second half of the 2000s, Baumax remained confident in its growth strategy. In 2005, the company announced its intention to enter the Bulgarian market, as that country's economy showed signs of reaching stability. The company also indicated its desire to establish a presence in Rumania in the near future, and asserted plans to double its sales, from EUR 1 billion ($1.3 billion) before the end of the decade. In the meantime, the Essl family had moved to take the company private, buying out its minority shareholders in 2004. The family-owned company represented an Austrian, and increasingly international, success story.

Principal Competitors

Franz Haniel and Company GmbH; Castorama Dubois Investissements S.C.A.; BayWa AG; Hagebau Handelsgesellschaft fur Baustoffe mbH und Company KG; AB Lithun; INTERPARES MOBAU Handelsgesellschaft mbH und Company KG.

Further Reading

"BauMax Expects Gross Revenue of HUF 32.5bn in 2004," *Hungarian News Agency (MTI),* September 20, 2004.
"DIY Abroad: Austria," *National Home Center News,* August 7, 2000, p. 135.
"International Retailers Set to Enter Bulgaria," *Europe Agri,* May 4, 2005.
Levering, Robert, and Milton Moskowitz, "10 Great Companies to Work For: Baumax," *Fortune,* January 24, 2005, p. 38.
Pinter, Gejza, "Only a Satisfied Customer Comes Back," *Euro Forum,* January 1999.
Pleininger, Hans, "Baumax ist Niederösterreichs bester Familienbetrieb," *Wirtschaftsblatt,* May 17, 2005.

—M.L. Cohen

Beacon Roofing Supply, Inc.

1 Lakeland Park Drive
Peabody, Massachusetts 01960
U.S.A.
Telephone: (978) 535-7668
Toll Free: (877) 645-7663
Fax: (978) 535-7358
Web site: http://www.beaconroofingsupply.net

Public Company
Incorporated: 1997
Employees: 1,205
Sales: $652.9 million (2004)
Stock Exchanges: NASDAQ
Ticker Symbol: BECN
NAIC: 423330 Roofing, Siding, and Insulation Material
Merchant Wholesalers

Beacon Roofing Supply, Inc. owns regional distributors of roofing and related building materials, maintaining a leadership position in an estimated $10 billion U.S. market. The regional affiliates owned by Beacon Roofing operate under their own identities, giving their parent company a presence in 16 states in the Northeast, Mid-Atlantic, Southeast, and Southwest regions of the United States and in eastern Canada. Beacon Roofing affiliates include: West End Lumber Co.; The Roof Center; Best Distributing Co.; Quality Roofing Supply, Inc.; Beacon Sales Company; Coastal Metal Service; JGA Corp.; Commercial Supply, Inc.; and Shelter Distribution, Inc. The company operates in Canada through Beacon Roofing Supply Canada Co. Beacon Roofing operates 83 branches in North America.

Origins

Because it owned a number of regional roofing companies, each with distinct founding dates and places of origin, Beacon Roofing could lay claim to historical roots stretching back to the late 19th century, but the core of the company, and its namesake, was founded in 1928. In 1928, a company named Beacon Sales Company, Inc. began operating as a commercial roofing supply business in Somerville, Massachusetts. Beacon Sales became the foundation of Beacon Roofing—the principal constituent of a family of regional roofing firms owned by Beacon Roofing—but the process by which a small New England roofing firm developed into a company with national aspirations did not begin until more than a half century after operations first began in Somerville. The individual responsible for transforming Beacon Sales into Beacon Roofing was Andrew R. Logie, whose leadership and vision created the makings of a company advancing toward $1 billion in annual sales.

Logie's influence on the stature of the Beacon name in the roofing industry was profound, highlighted by impressive geographic expansion and a nearly 70-fold increase in annual revenues. Logie, who attended Nichols College in Dudley, Massachusetts, brought with him more than a dozen years of experience in the roofing business when he took the helm at Beacon Sales, spending five years at GAF Corporation and nine years at Bradco Supply. Logie and a group of investors acquired Beacon Sales in 1983, taking control of a company with slightly more than $10 million in annual sales. In the 55 years since its founding, Beacon Sales had achieved modest growth, adding branch offices in Worcester, Massachusetts, and Lewiston, Maine. The pace of expansion increased considerably after the arrival of Logie, who was appointed as Beacon Sales' new chief executive officer after the investment group acquired the company. Logie began shaping Beacon Sales into a regional distributor serving all of New England, establishing each new branch near contractors to facilitate deliveries to job sites. In less than 15 years, he turned Beacon Sales from a three-office into a nine-office company, developing, during this period, a distribution model on the local, branch-office level that would become the basis of Beacon Roofing's operating strategy. Sales growth reflected Beacon Sales' physical expansion, as the company's annual revenue volume swelled from approximately $11 million to $70 million during Logie's first decade-and-a-half of leadership.

The development of the company during the 1980s and 1990s marked a period of tremendous growth, but it paled in comparison to the growth achieved at the turn of the millennium. A new era for the Beacon name began in 1997, one that,

---

Company Perspectives:

The mission of Beacon Roofing Supply Inc. is to be a leading North American supplier to commercial and residential roofing and exterior building contractors through a family of long-established regional suppliers and to add value to our contractor customers' businesses, to our employees' careers, to our investors' assets, and to our suppliers' products.

---

like the company's first era of aggressive growth, continued to be dominated by Logie.

Formation of Beacon Roofing in 1997 Leading to Acquisition Spree

In 1997, after turning Beacon Sales into a genuine regional player in the roofing industry, Logie gained the support of new financial backers. In September, a Chicago investment banking firm named Code Hennessy & Simmons, LLC acquired a controlling interest in Beacon Sales, entrusting the firm's investment to the proven managerial skills of Logie. Logie was named chairman, chief executive officer, and president of a newly formed company, Beacon Roofing Supply, Inc., which became the parent company of Beacon Sales and the maypole around which other regional roofing companies would revolve. The expectations of the first investment group in the early 1980s had been to make Beacon Sales a prominent player in New England's roofing industry. The expectations of Logie's second investment team were far more ambitious, involving not only the expansion of Beacon Sales but also the acquisition and expansion of other roofing companies operating outside New England. Beacon Roofing, with Logie as its chief architect, set its sights on becoming a national force in a highly fragmented industry, scoring noticeable success within the first decade of pursuing its ambitious goal.

Beacon Roofing's expansion strategy depended heavily on acquisitions. Although the company expanded by internal means as well, the primary source of its physical and financial growth was the addition of other regional roofing concerns, which retained their identity after being acquired by Beacon Roofing. Logie began his acquisition campaign in 1998, purchasing Quality Roofing Supply, Inc. Founded in 1949, Quality Roofing opened his first branch in Reading, Pennsylvania, offering shingles, siding, gutters, windows, and doors to contractors involved in the residential roofing market. The company remained focused on residential exterior products until it was acquired by Roofers Mart in 1988, a transaction that broadened its exposure in the roofing market and fueled its physical expansion. Roofers Mart operated as a coalition of independent commercial roofing contractors, giving its members enhanced purchasing power. For Quality Roofing, joining Roofers Mart gave the company the opportunity to offer commercial roofing product lines, making it a comprehensive supplier to contractors involved in both segments of the roofing market. With its product lines expanded, Quality Roofing spent the ensuing decade adding new branch offices throughout Pennsylvania and into Delaware.

Quality Roofing was one of seven regional roofing distributors purchased by Beacon Roofing between 1998 and 2001. The oldest of the companies purchased during this period was Best Distributing Co., a Goldsboro, North Carolina-based company founded in 1880 as Best and Thompson by Marcellus J. Best and B.G. Thompson. The business, which began as a single retail store in Goldsboro, was governed by the Best family during the ensuing decade, with each generation of leadership altering the strategic focus of the company. During the 1930s, the second generation of the family, under the leadership of William H. Best, began focusing on building supplies as the store's main line of merchandise. The next generation, under the leadership of William Best's sons, Mark and Munroe, made the most profound change in the history of the family business, abandoning the retail trade and recasting the company as a wholesaler of building supplies. By 1948, Mark and Munroe Best had made Best Distributing one of the leading building supply wholesalers in North Carolina, serving as a major supplier of wire fencing, cement, sheet metal, roll roofing, and paint to contractors. By the time Beacon Roofing acquired Best Distributing, the company was under the control of the fourth generation of the family, led by Munroe Best, Jr., who narrowed the company's focus to roofing supplies and materials. The acquisition of Best Distributing also included Coastal Metal Service, a company started by Best Distributing in 1991. Coastal Metal began as a metal shop in Goldsboro, where it provided contractors with custom metal roofing systems.

As Logie neared the end of the first stage of his acquisition campaign, he completed several deals that reflected the ambitious nature of his plans for the company. The acquisition of Exeltherm Supply Inc., in particular, offered evidence of a company pursuing expansion plans far grander than the growth strategy developed under the aegis of Beacon Sales. Exeltherm Supply, founded in 1994, became Beacon Roofing Supply Canada Co., the international arm of Beacon Roofing, an entity with commercial and residential roofing distribution offices in Toronto, Ottawa, and Winnipeg. Logie's reach into Canada extended farther with the addition of Groupe Bedard, a commercial and residential roofing material supplier based in Quebec that operated as part of Beacon Roofing Supply Canada Co. In 2001, Logie added two more roofing distributors to Beacon Roofing's stable of companies, strengthening the company's presence on the East Coast and extending its presence into the Southwest. The older of the two companies was West End Lumber Co., founded in Houston, Texas, in 1923 by R.W. Peckham. Peckham founded West End as a lumber company, registering his greatest financial success during World War II, when his business's most profitable products were roofing shingles and shakes. In 1974, a descendant, William H. Peckham, sold the company to Bob Burns and Bebe Burns, who expanded the company during the 1980s when the demand for roofing materials increased. In 2000, the Burnses merged their company with The Roof Center, a building materials distributor based in Gaithersburg, Maryland, that began operating in 1977.

Initial Public Offering in 2004

A lull in acquisitive activity followed the purchase of West End Lumber and The Roof Center. During the respite, the company turned to internal means of achieving growth, expand-

<table>
<tr><td colspan="2">Key Dates:</td></tr>
<tr><td>1928:</td><td>Beacon Sales Company is founded.</td></tr>
<tr><td>1983:</td><td>An investment group headed by Andrew R. Logie acquires Beacon Sales.</td></tr>
<tr><td>1997:</td><td>Beacon Roofing Supply, Inc. is formed after a Chicago investment firm, Code Hennessy & Simmons LLC, acquires Beacon Sales.</td></tr>
<tr><td>1998:</td><td>The acquisition of Quality Roofing Supply, Inc. touches off an ambitious acquisition campaign.</td></tr>
<tr><td>2001:</td><td>After acquiring its seventh regional roofing products distributor, Beacon Roofing's sales eclipse $500 million.</td></tr>
<tr><td>2004:</td><td>Beacon Roofing completes its initial public offering of stock.</td></tr>
<tr><td>2005:</td><td>Beacon Roofing acquires Shelter Distribution, Inc.</td></tr>
</table>

ing by opening two branches in 2002 and 2003. The growth achieved was not much, but the seven acquisitions completed produced stunning growth for the five-year period between 1998 and 2003. Sales increased at a compounded annual growth rate of nearly 49 percent during the period, mushrooming from $76.7 million to $559.5 million. Beacon Roofing, after its initial surge of growth, stood as a formidable competitor in half of North America, projecting sufficient strength for Logie to consider selling the company on Wall Street. In 2004, the company began preparing for its initial public offering (IPO) of stock, seeking to raise capital to continue its acquisition campaign. In September, when Beacon Roofing operated 66 branches in 12 states and three Canadian provinces, the company completed its IPO, selling 8.5 million shares at $13 per share, which raised $102 million in net proceeds.

In the wake of its IPO, Beacon Roofing struck out on the acquisition trail again. In December 2004, the company acquired JGA Corporation, a distributor of roofing and other building products. Based in Atlanta, Georgia, JGA operated eight offices in Georgia and Florida, offering a comprehensive line of residential and commercial roofing products. The company generated $74 million in revenue in 2003, its 26th year of business. Beacon Roofing completed two more acquisitions

before the end of its fiscal year in September 2005, acquisitions that were expected to be followed by other additions in the years ahead. In August, the company completed one of the largest acquisitions in its history, purchasing Shelter Distribution, Inc., a McKinney, Texas-based distributor of roofing and other building products. Shelter Distribution operated 50 branches in 14 states in the Midwest, Central Plains, and Southwest regions, providing Beacon Roofing with entry into a dozen new states. Shelter Distribution, which focused on the residential segment of the roofing market, generated $248 million in sales in 2004. The acquisition of Shelter Distribution was followed by the purchase of Commercial Supply, Inc. in September 2005. Commercial Supply, a fraction of the size of Shelter Distribution, posted $1.4 million in sales in 2004 from its sole branch office in Holyoke, Massachusetts.

Principal Subsidiaries

Beacon Sales Acquisition, Inc.; Quality Roofing Supply, Inc.; Beacon Canada, Inc.; Best Distributing Co.; The Roof Center, Inc.; West End Lumber Company, Inc.; Beacon Roofing Supply Canada Company.

Principal Competitors

The Home Depot, Inc.; Lowe's Companies, Inc.; Stock Building Supply Inc.

Further Reading

"Beacon Adds The Roof Center and West End Lumber to Its Affiliation of Regional Suppliers," *Roofing Contractor,* August 2001, p. 10.

"Beacon Roofing Acquires Shelter Distribution," *Home Channel News NewsFax,* August 15, 2005, p. 1.

"Beacon Roofing Buys JGA Corp.," *UPI NewsTrack,* December 16, 2004.

"Beacon Roofing Supply Inc. Announces Strategic Acquisition," *Roofing Contractor,* January 2005, p. 8.

Romans, Christine, "Beacon Roofing Supply Prices IPO of $13.5 Million at $13 Each," *America's Intelligence Wire,* September 22, 2004.

—Jeffrey L. Covell

The Bernick Companies

P.O. Box 7008
St. Cloud, Minnesota 56302
U.S.A.
Telephone: (320) 252-6441
Fax: (320) 656-2121
Web site: http://www.bernicks.com

Private Company
Incorporated: 1916 as Granite City Bottling Works
Employees: 550
Sales: $81.3 million (2004)
NAIC: 312110 Soft Drink Manufacturing; 424810 Beer
and Ale Wholesalers; 424810 Vending Machine
Operators

The Bernick Companies with its three divisions, Charles A. Bernick Inc., Bernick's Pepsi-Cola Bottling, and Bernick's Full-Line Vending, is one of the largest privately owned beverage bottlers and distributors in the Midwest. With over 40 acquired businesses in its recent history the company services over 10,000 regional accounts that add up to over one million customers throughout its geographic region.

1916–29: The Beginnings of Soda Pop Bottling in St. Cloud

Charles A. and Elizabeth Bernick could be considered pioneers when they bought out a small bottling company in St. Cloud, Minnesota, in 1916. The young married couple launched into a business that was relatively new to central Minnesota. Soda pop was considered a fancy treat, not your standard Minnesota fare. Although owning a soda pop company was exciting, it was not the first adventure for the young married couple.

Charles Bernick left home at 16 with some friends to fulfill his dream of becoming a cowboy out in Colorado. From Colorado he ventured to Teddy Roosevelt's ranchland in Medora, North Dakota, where he continued to pursue his love of horses and his interest in herding cattle.

It was not long before his cowboy lifestyle proved too solitary and decidedly male. Bernick indulged other interests when he met and married Elizabeth Kraemer in 1891. They moved to the Iron Range of northern Minnesota, settling first in Tower and then in Biwabic, where they opened a general store. When a fire destroyed the store in 1892 the Bernicks moved back to Stearns County in central Minnesota, and settled in Cold Spring. There, Charles opened a livery stable.

In 1916 the couple moved to St. Cloud and bought a 720-square-foot concrete block building and its contents of bottling equipment. Ironically, the building stood at the very spot where Elizabeth's father had built a brewery years before and which a fire destroyed in 1864. Unbeknownst to them, the couple's venture would become their lives' work and continue to remain family owned and operated for at least five generations.

For the first few years the company continued operation under the name Granite City Bottling Works. Its inventory included a pop filling machine, a crown cork and seal machine, a bottle soaker, a carbonator made by the Niagra Company, a pot-bellied wood stove for heat, a horse named Queen, a wagon, a sleigh, and less than 200 cases of beverage bottles and five ceramic syrup crocks.

Charles Bernick proved to be a good businessman. He was known to be personable, hard working, and adept at numbers; under his leadership the company steadily grew.

Despite his love for horses, when the horse and wagon would not get somewhere quickly enough he relied on an old motorcycle. With the advent of the automobile it was not long before Charles realized that a truck would make much shorter work of his 30-mile delivery route. He sold Queen and the wagon and bought a Model T delivery truck with side curtains. When the weather was too snowy to make his way with the truck Bernick would rent a horse and sleigh to deliver his goods.

Early fashionable soda pop flavors were ginger ale, grape, blackberry, and orange. Bottled soda pop with such names as Cherry Blossom, NuGrape, Eskimo Pop, and Green River were recognizable brands around Stearns County. In the 1920s Coca-Cola was a popular new choice.

Company Perspectives:

The Bernick Companies is a fourth-generation family-owned, business, providing full service beverage, vending and food service solutions to the Central Minnesota area since 1916. The Bernick Companies is a proud partner in improving the quality of life in the communities they serve, with a rich tradition of community support through financial and in-kind contributions and Team Member volunteerism.

Producing a large volume of carbonated beverages was a labor intensive and messy process in the early years. The procedure involved mixing syrup that came in 55- and 25-gallon color-coded wooden barrels, filling the bottles one at a time largely by hand, using a primitive machine the workers nicknamed ''The One-Armed Bandit.'' Bottles were delivered and picked up again when their contents were emptied. They were then washed and reused, leaving the floor in a constant state of disorder and dampness.

Success was slow but steady and the company added inventory to meet the needs of its growing customer base. Choices in the 1920s and 1930s included Hires Root Beer, Bernick's Chocolate, Wineberry, Howdy Orange, and ''near beers'' named Schmidts City Club, Malta, Kato Beer, Rock Springs, and Pale Dry Ginger Ale.

1930s–50s: The Repeal of Prohibition and a Nation Ready for Beer

The company gained a foothold in the newly reopened beer market with the 21st constitutional amendment. The prohibition of the sale and distribution of alcohol was repealed and the bottling works was poised to capitalize on the new freedom. Charles Bernick approached the Jacob Schmidt Brewing Company with an offer to distribute the newly legal beer. He was the first local salesperson to reap a profit from the long awaited return to legalized alcohol.

On May 25, 1934 tragedy struck the Bernick household when Charles Bernick drowned while fishing up north, leaving his son Francis J. Bernick to take his place as head of the company in 1935. Francis Bernick was named manager and continued to establish Bernick Companies' reputation for community public service. Throughout the decades Francis Bernick received numerous awards and citations for his involvement in charitable activities around St. Cloud and its neighboring communities. The company established itself as a supporter of many family-centered activities at local festivals throughout its market.

The 1940s were a time of corporate expansion both in the types of goods the company provided and in the equipment and production facilities the company built. Bernick Companies added Dr. Pepper and Orange Crush franchises. The company began its automated production by purchasing new machinery. Although the 1940s brought the company new growth opportunities, these were tempered by raw material shortages brought on by World War II. Sugar for flavoring and metal for bottle caps were particularly hard to procure, and kept industrial growth in check. Still the company in 1941 bottled over 100,000 cases of soft drinks, employed 22 men, operated 14 trucks, served 1,300 accounts in a 60-mile radius of St. Cloud, and grossed $300,000 annually.

Growth continued when Bernick Companies bought area franchises to distribute the cherry cola flavored Dr. Pepper and the orange soda pop labeled as Orange Crush, two very popular beverages in the retail market. The company sold beer under common midwestern labels including Schmidt's City Club, Peerless, and Budweiser. In 1940 12,000 barrels of beer were sold through the company.

The 1950s were a time of unparalleled growth and wealth. The baby boom following World War II brought a level of prosperity never before experienced in the United States. Times changed and people who were once satisfied drinking coffee, water, or milk, now could afford soda pop. Soda pop, once a special occasion drink, was now preferred as an everyday affordable luxury.

In 1952 the company took a gamble on a relatively unknown cola product by the name of Pepsi. At the time Coca-Cola had become an international phenomenon. Pepsi was giving away its franchise in St. Cloud. A local company that also distributed beer had decided to discontinue its soft drink products. Bernick Companies accepted the offer, since it was free; however, there was significant risk involved: in the first years of its operation Pepsi twice went bankrupt.

Additionally, when Bernick Companies became a Pepsi-Cola bottler and distributor, the company had to drop Pepsi's competitor, Dr. Pepper, from its product offerings. It was no doubt a dicey move, but one that eventually paid off in a big way for the company. By 1953 Bernick Companies had sold 28,965 cases of Pepsi, a number that would grow substantially throughout the decades. Pepsi continued to gain recognition and became the number two most popular soft drink of all time. Recognizing Pepsi's potential market, Bernick Companies bought three additional Pepsi franchises in Minnesota and Wisconsin.

In the 1960s Pepsi introduced the soft drink Mountain Dew, which became a great seller for the Pepsi-Cola Company and its bottler/distributors. Mountain Dew grew in popularity, becoming one of the leading soft drinks in the U.S. market.

1970s–2005: Acquiring Companies and Adding Vending

In 1976 a 40,000-square-foot distribution center was constructed at the newly acquired Willmar site. By 1980 Bernick Companies had already outgrown its 1976 facility and added an additional 80,000-square-foot building. The company acquired the Pepsi franchise in Duluth, Minnesota, that same year and continued buying up both beverage and vending companies throughout the region.

Consolidation in the industry and streamlined operations to increase profit share led Bernick Companies to help develop Wis-Pak, a cooperative of 50 Pepsi bottlers that centralized production and distribution.

Key Dates:

1916: Charles and Elizabeth Bernick buy Granite City Bottling Works.
1925: Granite City Bottling adds NuGrape, Green River, Cherry Blossom, Eskimo Pop, and Hires Root Beer.
1930: Company buys five new delivery trucks, expands its workforce, and adds several types of ''near beer'' to its product line.
1935: Francis Bernick becomes head of Chas. A. Bernick, Inc.
1940: Company buys Dr. Pepper and Orange Crush franchises.
1952: Company buys distribution rights for a then relatively unknown brand of soda pop, Pepsi-Cola.
1970s: New office and distribution center in Waite Park are completed.
1980s: Bernick Companies adds sparkling water and new beer offerings; new full-line vending division is acquired.
2004: Bernick Companies receives the Donald M. Kendall Bottler of the Year Award.

The company continued to add new products in the 1980s, including Moosehead, Pabst, Special Export, Grain Belt, and several other imported beers. More soft drink choices were also added, including A&W, Canada Dry, La Croix water, and Motts juice.

In 1988 Bernick Companies acquired St. Cloud Full-Line Vending and renamed the operation Bernick's Full-Line Vending. From 1970, when the company acquired the Willmar, Minnesota Pepsi franchise, a series of acquisitions had added to the size and customer base of the company. Significant purchases were made in the vending machine business. The company now sold sandwiches produced by a commissary and added snack food items to its already growing pop, juice, and water vending merchandise. The company expanded its territory into Wisconsin and as far north as the Canadian border.

In 1992 Bernick Companies purchased the 7 Up distributorship in St. Cloud and added several additional 7 Up businesses in Wisconsin and other areas of Minnesota. In 1996 the company acquired Rubald Beverage Company, a distributor of Pigs Eye, Olympia, Strohs, Old Milwaukee, Molson, Grain Belt, Premium, and Cold Spring beers.

By 1997 Bernick Companies employed over 400 people in its Waite Park, Minnesota facility and maintained over 200,000 square feet of corporate and warehouse buildings. The company had over 350 vehicles for its daily operations and was in the process of adding 40,000 square feet of additional space to its Willmar operation.

President and CEO Dick Bernick commented on the beverage industry's consolidation and change in a 1998 *Marketplace Momentum* article, stating,'' Oh, things are changing faster today than they ever have in the past. There are now more changes in a year than there used to be in ten years. . . . The consolidation of beer distributors has been quite dramatic across the country. We've lost a lot of bottlers to consolidation as well—there just aren't that many left. For example, we have some forty-five acquisitions. With new technologies, packaging and so many things happening, in order to stay in business, you've really got to be out front.''

In 1999 Bernick Companies announced it would discontinue production at its downtown St. Cloud site. The company regretted having to close such an integral part of its historical operation but made the decision based on financial data. Bernick's relationship as a co-owner in Wis-Pak made bottling through the massive production facility more cost-effective than keeping the old facility with its associated costs for re-tooling, maintenance, and repair.

Despite industrywide consolidation in the beverage market, the local Dr. Pepper business in St. Cloud and Little Falls had maintained its independence until 2001. Bernick Companies purchased the Dr. Pepper Bottling Company in March 2001 for an undisclosed amount. Bernick's Pepsi-Cola Bottling Company added the right to distribute Dr. Pepper, Sobe beverages, and Big Red Energy Drink, throughout a ten-county region. In addition to distribution rights the company added to its warehouse space, vending machine supply, and delivery vehicles through the acquisition.

By the year 2000 Bernick Companies was servicing over 10,000 accounts and serving over one million customers. The company employed over 500 people and had a fleet of delivery and company vehicles numbering close to 400.

In April 2004, Bernick's Pepsi received one of the highest honors Pepsi-Cola North America bestowed upon its bottlers when the local distributorship was named the Donald M. Kendall Bottler of the Year for 2003. The Donald M. Kendall Award was named for the cofounder and chairman of Pepsi and was considered its most prestigious award for excellence.

It was clear that Bernick Companies had carved out a significant niche in the beverage market in Minnesota and Wisconsin by 2005. Through its acquisitions it had reconstructed itself as one of the largest beverage and vending companies in the region.

The company controlled both a large part of the soft drink market and significant brands for beer distribution. The company was still family owned and operated and appeared to be grooming leadership for the next generation of Bernicks to take their place in the family enterprise.

Principal Divisions

Bernick's Full-Line Vending; Charles A. Bernick Inc.; Bernick's Pepsi-Cola Bottling.

Principal Competitors

Viking Coca-Cola.

Further Reading

''Bernick Buys Local Dr. Pepper Distributorship,'' *St. Cloud Times*, March 8, 2001.

"Bernick's Pepsi Cola a Tradition of Quality and Service," *Daily Times*, March 1, 1998.

Hierlmaier, Christine, "Bottler Builds on Long History, "*St. Cloud Times*, August 6, 1997, p. 5C.

Lindblad, Sr. Owen, "Bottler Pops onto Scene," *St. Cloud Times*, May 29, 2000.

—Susan B. Culligan

Bharti Tele-Ventures Limited

Qutab Ambience (at Qutab Minar)
Mehrauli Road
New Delhi - 110 030
India
Telephone: +91 11 5166 6000
Fax: +91 11 5166 6011/12
Web site: http://www.bhartitele.com

Public Company
Incorporated: 1995
Employees: 5,189
Sales: INR 78.76 billion ($1.8 billion) (2005)
Stock Exchanges: National Stock Exchange of India
Ticker Symbol: 532454
NAIC: 517212 Cellular and Other Wireless
    Telecommunications; 517110 Wired
    Telecommunications Carriers

Bharti Tele-Ventures Limited, part of the Bharti Enterprises group, is India's leading wireless telecommunications provider, with a 25 percent share of the national market, and market share of as much as 50 percent or more in the group's target market "circles." Bharti Tele-Ventures is also one of the world's fastest-growing mobile telephone companies, in part due to the rapid growth of the Indian cellular market as a whole. The Indian mobile telephone market is expected to top 250 million subscribers before 2010, rising from just more than nine million in the early years of the 2000s. Bharti itself has grown from an initial subscriber base of less than 120,000 in the mid-1990s to more than 11.4 million by 2005. The company owes much of its success to its commitment to offering cutting-edge services, while maintaining low pricing policies, an important component in generally impoverished India. The group's GSM-based mobile telecommunications operations span 23 of India's mobile "circles," typically encompassing both major urban and outlying areas. In 2005, the company completed the national rollout of its network. Bharti groups its mobile telecommunications operations under the Mobility Leaders division. Through its Infotel Leaders business division, Bharti also has entered the

fixed-line telephony market, building its own 12,000-kilometer fiber-optic network for selected markets; the company also provides national long distance and broadband services. Most of Bharti's telecommunications services operate under the Airtel brand. Bharti is listed on the Mumbai Stock Exchange and the National Stock Exchange of India, and is led by founder and Chairman Sunil Mitall. In 2005, Bharti's sales topped INR 78.76 billion ($1.8 billion).

From Bicycle Parts to Cellular Phones in the 1990s

Sunil Mittal was an unlikely candidate to become the leader of India's mobile telephone sector. Mittal started his business career in 1976 with the opening of a small factory manufacturing bicycle crankshafts in Ludhiana, in the northwest of Punjab. Mittal, then just 18, started the business with only $400; before long, the factory employed 25 workers. To gain greater scale, and access to bank credit, Mittal added other manufacturing operations, such as hosiery and household utensils.

As his manufacturing capacity grew, Mittal continued exploring other business opportunities. His attention turned to the import-export sector. By the end of the 1970s, Mittal had moved to Delhi and established a new business importing portable generators from Japan, among other items. The generator business flourished, adding operations in Mumbai as well, in large part because of Mittal's ability to navigate the often tortuous windings of Indian regulations governing the sector. Yet in the early 1980s, the government, seeking to develop homegrown industries, placed a ban on the import of a number of items, including portable generators.

The ban, however, encouraged Mittal, joined by his brothers, to explore new business opportunities, setting the stage for his greatest success. Into the early 1980s, India's telephone system still relied on the rotary dial telephone. The development of new types of telephone services, however, demanded the use of push-button telephones. In 1983, Mittal reached an agreement with Germany's Siemens to manufacture the company's push-button telephone models for the Indian market.

Mittal became the first in India to offer push-button telephones, establishing the basis of Bharti Enterprises. This first-

Company Perspectives:

Mission: To be globally admired for telecom services that delight customers.

mover advantage allowed Mittal to expand his manufacturing capacity elsewhere in the telecommunications market. By the early 1990s, Mittal also had launched the country's first fax machines and its first cordless telephones.

In the early 1980s, Mittal had continued to explore other areas of operations; in 1982, for example, he set up Bharti Healthcare in order to produce capsules for medicines. (The word Bharti came from the Hindi word for "Indian.") By the end of the 1980s, however, Bharti's focus had narrowed to the telecommunications market. As Mittal told *Rediff:* "From 1986 to 1992, we manufactured telephone instruments, fax machines and cordless telephones. There has been a method to this growth. We didn't stray even then. No steel mills, no paper mills, no mini-cement plants, cinema halls or hotels—all these opportunities did come to us. Every entrepreneur was getting into these things. But we single-mindedly concentrated on telecom."

At the beginning of the 1990s, the Indian government began preparing for the launch of a new generation of wireless telecommunications standards. Bharti quickly recognized the potential for the development of products such as pagers and cellular telephones. Yet the company's interest now reached beyond manufacturing, and instead focused on becoming a telecommunications services provider. As part of its own preparations, Bharti requested the results of a survey from Feedback Ventures determining the market potential for cellular phone services in the Delhi "circle," as the Indian licensing regions were called.

The results were less than encouraging. As Mittal recalled to *Rediff:* "It said that there would be a market for 5,000 cellular phones in Delhi. That was one more confirmation that these reports were silly and nonsensical, so we tore it up and threw it away. Even before the project was up, I was sure that on the first day of booking, we would have 5,000 connections, leave alone the market being that size!"

The survey nonetheless succeeded in dissuading a number of larger groups from competing for the Delhi license. At the same time, stipulations from the government required that any bids be made by groups with prior telecom experience, which effectively eliminated another class of competitors. Bharti's background in telephone and fax machine manufacturing, however, provided it with the experience sufficient to meet the requirement. Mittal quickly lined up an equipment and support agreement with France's Vivendi and launched its own bid.

The bid from the relatively minor company raised eyebrows, and few gave the company any hope of succeeding. Indeed, even Vivendi developed cold feet, and at the last minute decided to switch its backing to the larger Modi group. Yet Mittal managed to convince Vivendi to stick to their agreement, and Bharti won the Delhi license.

Building a Mobile Telephone Network in the Late 1990s

Bharti began installing its network, a process completed in 1995. With Vivendi's backing, the group was able to convince Ericsson to supply the equipment to build its network on credit. *Time International* reported that Mittal told Ericsson that Bharti would pay "when the customers are happy." In that year, the company founded a subsidiary for its cellular telephone business, called Bharti Cellular, which was placed under the holding company, Bharti Tele-Ventures Limited. Bharti Cellular launched its service, branded Airtel, in Delhi that year. The company immediately began bidding for other markets, adding Himachal Pradesh in 1996.

Bharti's growth was rapid and, in an industry requiring high investment, the company was among the fastest, and very few, in the country to enter profitability. A big part of the group's success in this matter was its willingness to break down traditional subscription-based services. Instead, Bharti emphasized a prepaid card-based model as well. The company then began selling its prepaid cards in a large variety of venues, from grocery stores and other shops, and even to street peddlers. Shopkeepers were given free phone calls and other gifts in exchange for promoting Bharti's service over rivals' networks.

The model worked, and Bharti's growth was rapid. By the end of the 1990s, the company had succeeded in attracting more than 100,000 subscribers, a significant number given the slow pace of the cellular phone industry as a whole in the country.

Bharti began branching out in the 1990s as well. In 1997, the company won a license for providing fixed-line telephone services in Madhya Pradesh. The company also joined with British Telecom, which acquired a 21 percent stake in Bharti Cellular, to launch new services, including Internet services, in 1998. In that year, also, Bharti became the first private company in India to launch fixed-line services.

Bharti was one of the rare profitable cellular phone companies in India in the late 1990s. By then, a number of the country's 30 or so cellular phone operators had begun to struggle. Bharti once again rose to the opportunity, and in 1999, the company launched a series of significant acquisitions. The first of these came with the purchase of more than 63 percent of SC Cellular Holdings, which in turn controlled nearly two-thirds of JT Mobiles. Renamed as Bharti Mobile, the acquisition enabled the company to extend its reach into the Karnataka and Andhra Pradesh circles.

In 2000, Bharti moved again, buying up 40.5 percent of Skycell Communications, which operated under a license for the Chennai circle. That company was renamed as Bharti Mobinet. That year, the company also acquired full control of Bharti Mobile.

Into the 2000s, Bharti increasingly moved toward its goal of national coverage. A major step forward came in 2001 with the purchase of Spice Cell, which provided services to the highly prized Calcutta circle. That service was then rebranded as Bharti Mobitel. At the same time, Bharti increased its control of Bharti Mobinet to more than 95 percent. The company also successfully bid for cellular licenses to enter eight new circles

Key Dates:

1976: Sunil Mittal establishes his first business manufacturing bicycle parts in Ludhiana, Punjab.

1983: Mittal begins manufacturing touch-tone telephones, and later adds fax machines and wireless telephones.

1992: Mittal wins a bid to build a cellular phone network in Delhi.

1995: Mittal incorporates the cellular operations as Bharti Tele-Ventures and launches service in Delhi.

1996: Cellular service is extended to Himachal Pradesh.

1999: The company acquires control of JT Holdings, extending cellular operations to Karnataka and Andhra Pradesh.

2000: Bharti acquires control of Skycell Communications, in Chennai.

2001: The company acquires control of Spice Cell in Calcutta.

2002: The company goes public on the Mumbai Stock Exchange and National Stock Exchange of India.

2003: The cellular phone operations are rebranded under the single AirTel brand.

2004: The company acquires control of Hexacom, entering Rajasthan.

2005: Bharti extends its cellular network to Andaman and Nicobar; rolls out expansion of its network, doubling its number of base stations.

that year. Bharti also was developing its fixed-line business, adding licenses for Haryana, Delhi, Tamil Nadu, and Karnataka in 2001. The company then began rolling out its TouchTel fixed-line service in these markets, starting with Haryana. In addition, Bharti received the right to offer national long distance services, launching IndiaOne.

A large part of Bharti's success had been based on Mittal's ability to raise private investment capital; by the early 2000s, the company had built up a war chest of more than $1.2 billion by bringing in investors such as Singapore Telecommunications and Warburg Pincus. This enabled the company to back its growth through a spending spree; by 2002, the company had spent some $1 billion. That investment had enabled the company to quadruple in size, and to capture the leading share of the Indian mobile telephone market, just as the market was finally beginning to take off in the early 2000s.

Indeed, from just more than nine billion subscribers at the beginning of the decade, the Indian market was expected to grow to as much as 250 million or even more by 2010. Already in the early 2000s, the cellular phone market had begun showing growth rates as high as 80 percent per year.

Bharti prepared for its transformation into a truly national telecommunications provider by merging all of its cellular brands under a single unified brand, AirTel, in 2003. AirTel also continued attracting new subscribers by rolling out a wider and wider range of services, such as free multimedia messaging services, free incoming calls, and voice-mail for prepaid subscribers. As a result, the company's new subscriber rate continued to outpace the industry, topping three million by mid-2003 and more than 12 million by 2005.

Into mid-decade, Bharti continued to expand into new circles. At the end of 2003, the company acquired a stake in Hexacom, which allowed the company to enter the cellular services market in Rajasthan in 2004. By 2005, the company had extended its services to Andaman and Nicobar as well. At the same time, Bharti had been developing its fixed-line services, including a rollout of broadband services over its fixed-line network in 2005.

By mid-2005, Bharti had extended its presence to some 23 circles across India. In August of that year, the company announced a vast expansion effort to be completed by the end of the year, with plans to double its number of base stations to 20,000. The expansion was expected to double the number of towns and cities within the company's network, with a corresponding increase in subscribers. In less than a decade, Bharti had claimed the leading position in the Indian market and was expected by many to become one of the world's largest telecommunications markets before decade's end.

Principal Subsidiaries

Bharti Hexacom Ltd.; Bharti Aquanet Limited; Satcom Broadband Equipment Ltd.; Bharti Broadband Ltd.; Bharti Comtel Ltd.

Principal Competitors

Bharat Sanchar Nigam Ltd.; Mahanagar Telephone Nigam Ltd.; Hughes Software Systems Ltd.; BT India Worldwide Ltd.; BTA Cellcom Ltd.; Videsh Sanchar Nigam Ltd.

Further Reading

"Bharti Does Branding, Puts All Under Airtel," *Times of India,* September 17, 2004.

"Bharti Kicks Off National Long-Distance Telephony," *India Business Insight,* December 18, 2001.

"Bharti Tele-Ventures," *Economic Times,* December 6, 2004.

Chandramouli, Rajeesh, "Bharti Tele Keen on US Bourses Listing," *Times of India,* July 25, 2003.

"A Date with India," *Global Telecoms Business,* February 2003, p. 14.

Hanssen, Benoit, "Evolutionary Thinking: Managed Capacity Network Solution Allows Bharti to Capitalize on Tremendous Market Growth in India," *Global Telecoms Business,* November-December 2004, p. 35.

Hibberd, Mike, "Indian Philosophy," *Mobile Communications International,* May 1, 2005.

"Interview: Sunil Bharti Mittal," *Rediff,* February 9, 2000.

Kripalani, Manjeet, "Asking the Right Questions," *Business Week,* August 22, 2005, p. 64.

Schuman, Michael, "Speed Dialing," *Time International,* December 2, 2002, p. 13.

"Sunil Bharti Mittal, Chairman, Bharti Group," *Medianet,* 2005.

"Take It Easy, Televentures," *India Business Insight,* February 3, 2002.

"Why Phones Are Ringing for Sunil Mittal," *Business Week,* December 27, 1999, p. 21.

—M.L. Cohen

bioMérieux S.A.

Chemin de l'Orme
Marcy l'Etoile
F-69280
France
Telephone: +33 4 78 87 20 00
Fax: +33 4 78 87 20 90
Web site: http://www.biomerieux.com

Public Company
Incorporated: 1963 as BD Mérieux
Employees: 5,400
Sales: EUR 931 million ($1.3 billion) (2004)
Stock Exchanges: Euronext Paris
Ticker Symbol: BIM
NAIC: 339112 Surgical and Medical Instrument
    Manufacturing; 325414 Biological Product (Except
    Diagnostic) Manufacturing

bioMérieux S.A. is one of the world's largest specialists in the development of in vitro diagnostic methods, systems, and applications. The company's products are used to identify, measure, and quantify bacteria, viruses, and body substances, in order to help identify the appropriate course of treatment. bioMérieux develops and manufactures automated testing instruments and their software as well as the reagents and in vitro systems used to identify substances. Clinical diagnosis forms the largest part of the group's activities, at nearly 87.5 percent of total revenues. The company also has expanded into the field of industrial microbiological control, providing diagnostic and measurement systems to determine air, food, water, and other environmental quality levels. bioMérieux has developed a highly international business, with a presence in more than 130 countries and a worldwide network of sales and manufacturing subsidiaries. The company also operates nine research and development centers throughout the world. bioMérieux traces its origins to Marcel Mérieux, who served as an assistant to Louis Pasteur. The Mérieux family remains highly involved in the company, with Alan Mérieux serving as company chairman. The family also retains control of more than 60 percent of

shares following the company's initial public offering on the Euronext Paris Stock Exchange in 2004. In that year, the company posted sales of EUR 934 million ($1.3 billion).

Vaccine Offshoot in the 1960s

The Mérieux name was closely connected with the field of diagnostics and vaccine research almost from the sector's beginnings at the turn of the 20th century. Marcel Mérieux served as an assistant to Louis Pasteur during Pasteur's groundbreaking research in the late 19th century. In 1897, Mérieux set up his own laboratory, Institut Mérieux, which became a world-renowned producer of vaccines, a position the institute would retain into the 21st century.

As part of its work, Institut Mérieux began developing testing methods and, especially, reagents in order to identify the presence of and the quantity and quality of bacterial and viral infections. The use of reagents became an important element in the fight against disease, and Institut Mérieux's reagents operations grew into an important division within the institute. Joining Marcel Mérieux in the institute was his son, Charles, who later became the institute's head.

The discovery of penicillin led to the development of other antibiotics and especially the recognition that many antibiotics were more effective against certain bacteria than other bacterial types. Reagents, used to identify and quantify the source of an infection, became an increasingly important diagnostic tool. The need for investment in developing and producing new reagents and diagnostic systems led Institut Mérieux to spin off its reagents division into a joint venture with the United States' Becton, Dickinson. Created in 1963, the new company, known as BD Mérieux, was led by a new generation of the Mérieux family, Alain Mérieux.

BD Mérieux's separation from Institut Mérieux took place toward the end of the 1960s. In 1968, Rhone Poulenc acquired a stake in Institut Mérieux, which would have given the French pharmaceuticals giant control of 50 percent of BD Mérieux. Yet Becton, Dickinson was not interested in continuing the joint venture with Rhone Poulenc, then controlled by the French government. Instead, the American company asked Alain

---

Company Perspectives:

Mission & Strategy: Become a key player in the in vitro diagnostics field.

bioMérieux's ambition is to become a key player in the in vitro diagnostics field of infectious diseases and other pathologies, such as cardio-vascular diseases or cancers. It has implemented the following strategy: focusing its development on applications with a high potential; launching new products to better satisfy the needs of patients and the imperatives of public health in general; reinforcing its worldwide network to seize growth opportunities; continuing with its sustained effort in research and development; investing in new technologies via strategic alliances and targeted purchases that guarantee growth and technological independence; pursuing a balanced financial strategy to seize on growth opportunities.

Mérieux to buy out Institut Mérieux's 50 percent of the joint venture.

Alain Mérieux's purchase of the stake in BD Mérieux proved to be a first step toward the reagent company's transformation into an independent entity. By 1974, Becton, Dickinson had reduced its own position in the company to that of minority shareholder. With majority control of the company, Alain Mérieux changed the company's name, to bioMérieux.

By the late 1980s, bioMérieux had expanded onto an international scale. The company became one of the leaders of the in vitro diagnostics market. Although still quite small in comparison with the in vitro and reagents operations of many of the pharmaceuticals industry's giants, bioMérieux emerged as one of the largest specialist companies in the field.

Acquiring Scale into the 2000s

Nonetheless, bioMérieux needed to gain sufficient scale to compete in the increasingly global market. Through the 1990s, the company adopted a two-pronged approach toward growth. On the one hand, the company made a small number of acquisitions. On the other hand, the company began developing a worldwide network of research partnerships and alliances.

Among the company's first acquisitions was that of API Systems. Based in France, API had become a world-leading developer and producer of manual testing systems for bacterial identification and, of importance, bacterial susceptibility to antibiotic compounds. The acquisition of this technology was particularly important into the 1990s, as the overuse and nonspecific use of antibiotics had resulted in the development of more and more strains of antibiotic-resistant bacteria. Indeed, by the turn of the 21st century, hospitals found themselves increasingly confronted with bacterial strains that proved resistant not only to traditional antibiotics, but also to many of the more powerful modern antibiotics. Susceptibility testing played an important role in helping to prevent the development of resistant bacteria.

bioMérieux made a second significant acquisition in the late 1980s. In 1988, the company turned to the United States, where it acquired VITEK Systems. That company had pioneered and become a world leader in the development of automated bacterial testing and diagnostic systems.

Into the 2000s, bioMérieux completed two more acquisitions. The first of these came at the end of 1998, with the purchase of Micro Diagnostics Inc. That U.S. company, based in Chicago, was a specialist in diagnostic and testing media for industrial applications. The addition of Micro Diagnostics enabled bioMérieux to expand beyond its focus on the healthcare and pharmaceuticals markets to include reagent and testing systems for areas such as environmental control, waste and water management, the food industry, and the like.

The next major acquisition was completed in 2001, when bioMérieux purchased the diagnostics division of Akzo Nobel subsidiary Organon Teknika. This purchase helped to boost bioMérieux's presence not only in the United States but on a global level. The Organon acquisition also played a significant part in the development of bioMérieux's new polycarbonate-based testing system, BacT/Alert 3D, launched in 2002.

Public Company in the New Century

During this period, bioMérieux had been actively seeking out partnerships and alliances to expand its product range as well as its scope of operations. An early alliance formed by the company came in 1996, between the group's bioMérieux Vitek subsidiary in the United States and Affymetrix, Inc. That alliance provided for the joint development of genotyping testing procedures. In 1998, the companies strengthened their alliance by extending it to include clinical diagnostic tests using Affymetrix gene variation testing systems.

A new alliance came in 1999, when bioMérieux joined with Lyonnaise des Eaux in France to launch a joint research and development program in order to extend Affymetrix's Gene-Chip system to water testing and management. Into the early 2000s, bioMérieux continued signing up partnerships, notably with Celera, CEA, and Eli Lilly.

The need for scale nonetheless remained an important issue for the company. At the end of 2000, the company came up with an answer to that problem, announcing an agreement to merge with fellow French company Pierre Fabre. Like bioMérieux, Fabre was a family-owned company, specialized in the dermatological and cosmetics industries and headed by its founder, Pierre Fabre, who enjoyed a friendship with Alain Mérieux. Fabre's company, with revenues of nearly EUR 1.2 billion, was also nearly twice the size of bioMérieux. The two companies touted the potential of synergies between their merged operations, to be named bioMérieuxPierre Fabre.

The merger quickly unraveled, however, as the purported synergies failed to materialize. Meanwhile, Fabre and Mérieux were unable to agree on the direction of the newly enlarged company, which reportedly caused a deterioration in the friendship between the two men. In the end, Fabre and Mérieux chose friendship, and in 2002 the companies agreed to split up again.

Instead, bioMérieux went public, listing its stock on the Euronext Paris Stock Exchange in 2004. The initial public offering proved to be one of the more successful for the year, and

Key Dates:

1897: Marcel Mérieux established Institut Mérieux in order to develop vaccines.

1963: Institut Mérieux spins off reagents division into BD Mérieux, a joint venture with Becton Dickinson, and Alain Mérieux becomes head of BD Mérieux.

1968: Alain Mérieux buys out Institut Mérieux's stake in BD Mérieux after the institute is acquired by Rhone Poulenc.

1974: Becton Dickinson becomes minority shareholder in BD Mérieux, which changes its name to bioMérieux.

1987: bioMérieux acquires API Systems in the United States.

1988: The company acquires VITEK Systems in the United States.

1996: bioMérieux forms an alliance with Affymetrix, Inc. in the United States.

1999: bioMérieux forms an alliance with Lyonnaise des Eaux in France.

2000: The company merges with Pierre Fabre to form bioMérieuxPierre Fabre.

2002: bioMérieux and Pierre Fabre agree to split up.

2004: bioMérieux goes public on the Euronext Paris Stock Exchange.

2005: The company extends alliances with Affymetrix and ExonHit Therapeutics.

was oversubscribed by some five times. The newly public company continued to seek out partnerships as well as extensions to its existing alliances. In March 2005, for example, the company reached an agreement with the Chinese Academy of Medical Sciences to launch an R&D center in Beijing. By October of that year, the company also had extended its alliance with Affymetrix and strengthened a cancer detection alliance with ExonHit Therapeutics. bioMérieux intended to remain at the forefront of the in vitro diagnostics market into the new century.

Principal Subsidiaries

bioMérieux Argentina; bioMérieux Australia; bioMérieux Austria; bioMérieux Belgium; bioMérieux Brazil; bioMérieux Canada; bioMérieux Chile; bioMérieux China; bioMérieux Columbia; bioMérieux Denmark; bioMérieux Germany; bioMérieux Greece; bioMérieux Finland; bioMérieux Inc. (USA); bioMérieux India; bioMérieux Italy; bioMérieux Japan; bioMérieux Korea; bioMérieux Mexico; bioMérieux New Zealand; bioMérieux Norway; bioMérieux Poland; bioMérieux Portugal; bioMérieux Russia; bioMérieux Spain; bioMérieux Sweden; bioMérieux Switzerland; bioMérieux Thailand; bioMérieux The Netherlands; bioMérieux B.V. (The Netherlands); bioMérieux Turkey; bioMérieux United Kingdom; bioMérieux West Africa.

Principal Competitors

Siemens AG; Abbott Laboratories; Sanofi-Aventis; Eli Lilly and Co.; Asahi Kasei Corporation; GE Medical Systems; Baxter International Inc.; Medtronic Inc.; Otsuka Pharmaceutical Company Ltd.

Further Reading

"bioMérieux Buys Akzo Diagnostics Arm," *Chemical Week*, May 2, 2001, p. 10.

"BioMérieux Develops New Listeria Test for Food Laboratories," *Quick Frozen Foods International*, October 2002, p. 21.

"BioMérieux Five Times Sold As IPO Prices in Upper Range," *Euroweek*, July 9, 2004, p. 26.

"BioMérieux Innovates in Food Quality Testing," *Food Trade Review*, June 2005, p. 384.

Dunham, Dottie, "bioMérieux's Philippe Sans Translates Challenges into Delivery," *Medical Laboratory Observer*, June 2004, p. 28.

Jones, Amanda, "French Firm Bestows New Jobs," *Business Journal*, October 12, 2001, p. 1.

"Pierre Fabre and bioMérieux Split Up," *European Cosmetic Markets*, June 2002, p. 197.

"Southern Belle," *European Cosmetic Markets*, April 2002, p. 149.

Vollmer, Sabine, "BioMérieux Expected to Grow," *News & Observer*, March 18, 2005.

—M.L. Cohen

Brigham Exploration Company

6300 Bridge Point Parkway, Building 2, Suite 500
Austin, Texas 78730
U.S.A.
Telephone: (512) 427-3300
Fax: (512) 427-3400
Web site: http://www.bexp3d.com

Public Company
Incorporated: 1997 as Brigham Oil & Gas, L.P.
Employees: 55
Sales: $72.23 million (2005)
Stock Exchanges: NASDAQ
Ticker Symbol: BEXP
NAIC: 211111 Crude Petroleum and Natural Gas
   Extraction; 211112 Natural Gas Liquid Extraction;
   213111 Drilling Oil and Gas Wells; 213112 Support
   Activities for Oil and Gas Operations; 541360
   Geophysical Surveying and Mapping Services

Brigham Exploration Company is an independent oil and natural gas exploration, development, and production company. It specializes in using 3-D seismic imaging technology to find onshore deposits. The company is no giant in the industry, despite its three million barrels of proven crude oil reserves and 100 billion cubic feet of natural gas reserves. However, it has been quite successful in its niche. Focused on exploration in its early years, the company in the late 1990s began to add substantial development activities. (Brigham hires subcontractors to handle drilling and production.) The company drilled 120 wells in 2004, more than half of them development wells. The family of founder Ben Brigham owns about 7 percent of stock; about 30 percent is held by Credit Suisse First Boston.

Origins

Brigham Oil & Gas, L.P., the operating subsidiary of Brigham Exploration Company, was formed in Dallas in 1990 by Ben M. ''Bud'' Brigham. Brigham was a native of Midland who had earned a degree in geophysics from the University of

Texas at Austin. He started out as a seismic data processing geophysicist for Western Geophysical, Inc., which specialized in 3-D seismic services, and was an exploration geophysicist with Rosewood Resources from 1984 to 1990. Brigham would be the company's chairman, president, and CEO. His brother, David T. Brigham, an oil and gas attorney, would also be an executive in the company beginning in 1992.

Ben Brigham told the *Austin American-Statesman* that his namesake firm was founded with $25,000 and the support of his wife Anne, an oil industry lawyer. In 1992, after some promising early findings, Brigham secured $10 million in venture capital from General Atlantic Partners.

The company's mission was to explore proven oil fields using advanced 3-D seismic technology. This used sound waves to produce detailed maps of underground formations. While the industry did not generally feel this to be a cost effective approach, using it only to probe the borders of proven finds, Brigham believed it would make its money on the much improved chances of drilling success, as a well could cost up to several million dollars to drill. The company's initial efforts were concentrated in west Texas. It then ventured into the Anadarko Basin of Oklahoma and Texas and the onshore Gulf Coast of Texas.

The Anadarko Basin proved a rich source of natural gas. Brigham entered the area around 1994 and soon amassed more experience in 3-D exploration there than anyone (some of its staff had been involved in the area since the mid-1980s, Brigham told *Oil & Gas Investor*).

Brigham typically held up to a 60 percent or more working interest in the projects in which it was acquiring 3-D seismic data. In drilling projects its average working interest was about 21 percent.

Public in 1997

Brigham Exploration Company, a holding company for Brigham Oil & Gas, L.P. (which hired subcontractors to handle drilling and production), was established as a Delaware corporation in 1997 and went public on the NASDAQ that May. Proceeds from the initial public offering (IPO) were earmarked for

Company Perspectives:

Brigham Exploration Company's strategy is to achieve superior growth in shareholder value by applying 3-D seismic and other advanced technologies to reduce the risks and finding costs in drilling for oil and natural gas reserves.

Key Dates:

1990: Brigham Exploration Company is formed in Austin by Ben Brigham.
1997: Company goes public on the NASDAQ, relocates to Austin.
1998: Energy industry experiences major downturn, sending company scrambling for capital.
1999: Brigham makes a major discovery at Home Run Field.
2003: Secondary offering nets $40 million.
2004: Increasing oil prices fuel a profitable year.

continued exploration and development and for paying off the company's $13 million debt. According to *Platt's Oilgram News,* as a smaller company, Brigham braved a bearish market, pricing its offering at $8 a share versus the $9.50 to $11.50 it had anticipated. The company raised about $24 million in the IPO.

Brigham had 40 employees and soon relocated its headquarters from Dallas to the state capital of Austin, a city with a reputation as a liberal-leaning, high-tech island. The move was made largely over quality of life issues; many of the company's staff had gone to school in the area, CEO Ben Brigham told the *Austin American-Statesman.* It also made sense culturally, since Brigham's business was built around advanced technology. "We have invested approximately $2 million in cutting-edge computer hardware and software," he told the *Austin Business Journal.* The company also maintained an office in Houston.

By the time of its IPO, Brigham had acquired more than 3,300 square miles of 3-D seismic data and interpreted more than 2,800 square miles of that, locating 1,200 potential drilling spots. The company had drilled 330 wells and struck oil or gas 63 percent of the time, well above the industry average of 20 percent or less.

1998 Industry Downturn

Brigham had difficulty funding its drilling program when oil prices took a hit in 1998. The company unsuccessfully tried to garner interest in a secondary offering. Instead, it obtained financing from Enron Corp., which bought $50 million of debt and equity securities, ending up with a 14 percent holding.

In April 1999, Brigham sold two of its Anadarko Basin properties to two different buyers for $17.1 million. These fields had been operated by third parties. CEO Ben Brigham told *Petroleum Finance Week* that the company was raising money to fund higher quality prospects. More capital also allowed the company to retain larger shares in wells that went into production.

Brigham ended the year with its largest find to date at the Home Run Field on the Texas Gulf Coast. This was part of the Diablo Project, a joint venture with Exxon Mobil in which Brigham had a 34 percent interest. Another significant discovery for Brigham followed in the Anadarko Basin in 2000.

New Technology for the New Millennium

Brigham added directional drilling technology to complement its 3-D seismic expertise. Directional drilling allowed for unprecedented precision in drill bit guidance. It allowed Brigham to revisit abandoned wells. In 2000, Brigham reentered one, the Mills Ranch Field Discovery on the eastern edge of the

Texas Panhandle. It had been abandoned 19 years earlier at a depth of 15,000 feet. Brigham drilled an additional 10,000 feet for Texas's deepest well that year. The company saved about $1.5 million off its usual $8 million drilling and completion costs by entering an existing well.

Despite the company's impressive track record, CEO Ben Brigham complained it was undervalued in a September 2000 interview with *Oil & Gas Investor.* This was a lingering effect of the capital crunch in the 1998 industry downturn. "Optimally capitalizing our company has proven difficult ever since." However, its debt situation was improving with the recent finds and rising commodity prices. In 2000, Brigham had revenues (as restated) of $19.2 million and net income of $16.7 million.

By 2001 the company was boasting a 65 percent success rate at the 500 wells it had drilled using 3-D seismic imagery. It had discovered more than 500 billion cubic feet of equivalent gross reserves, Brigham told the *Wall Street Transcript.* Brigham's drilling expenses rose to $18 million in 2000 from $11 million the year before. After 1999, the company had begun drilling more development projects versus exploration-oriented ones, Brigham told the *Transcript.* Revenues reached $32.3 million (as restated) in 2001 while net income was $9.2 million.

In 2002 and 2003 Brigham reported several discoveries on the Texas Gulf Coast, Anadarko Basin, and in west Texas. However, it went into the red in 2002, when revenues (as restated) were $35.2 million.

Breaking Out in 2003

Oil & Gas Investor called 2003 a "breakout year" for Brigham Exploration. A secondary offering in September brought in $40 million, substantially alleviating the company's debt load. It continued to increase its reserves and production. "We were pure exploration when we went public, but now with our discoveries, production has mitigated the volatility of our cash flow," CFO Gene Shepherd, Jr., said. Revenues were $51.5 million (as restated) for 2003, and the company posted a net income of $14.6 million after losing $676,000 the previous year.

Brigham's fortune continued to rise with energy prices in 2004. At $50 a barrel, crude oil was fetching well over the $18 to $20 needed to be profitable, Ben Brigham told the *Austin American-Statesman.* He added that the company's operating costs were rising; Brigham was spending $35,000 to $70,000 per square mile for seismic surveys. The company's stock was rising, too; it had a market capitalization of $350 million at the end of the year. Revenues were $72.23 million in 2004, with net income of $19.7 million.

The company's large inventory, successful wells, and high commodity prices allowed it to drill more while holding larger stakes in the projects, Brigham told *Natural Gas Week*. It planned to drill 36 wells in 2005, with an average working interest of 63 percent. While its activities were focused on the Anadarko Basin, onshore Gulf Coast, and west Texas, in the fall of 2005 Brigham acquired property in North Dakota to complement an existing area of exploration in Montana. Revenues for the year were expected to exceed $100 million, with net income around $40 million.

Principal Subsidiaries

Brigham Oil & Gas, L.P.

Principal Competitors

Anadarko Petroleum Corporation; Apache Corporation; Burlington Resources, Inc.; KCS Energy Inc.

Further Reading

"Brigham Announces Two New Financings," *Petroleum Finance Week,* December 2, 2002.

"Brigham Braves the Bear, Falls Short of IPO Target," *Platt's Oilgram News,* May 12, 1997, p. 2.

"Brigham Exploration Co.," *Oil & Gas Investor,* September 2000, p. 2.

Brulliard, Nicholas, "Small Austin Oil and Gas Company Is Cashing in on Energy Prices; Brigham Digs Up a Winner; Founder Took a Chance on 3-D Seismic Method, and Now His Maverick Approach Is Paying Off," *Austin American-Statesman,* November 7, 2004, p. J1.

"CEO/Company Interview: Ben M. Brigham, Brigham Exploration Company," *Wall Street Transcript,* CIBC World Markets Energy Special, March 2001.

"Enron to Take Stake in Brigham Exploration," *Platt's Commodity News,* August 14, 1998.

Fowler, Tom, "Energy Group Drills for Local Identity, Focus," *Austin Business Journal,* November 27, 1998.

Haines, Leslie, "Momentum Is Building at Brigham Exploration," *Oil & Gas Investor,* April 1, 2004, p. 121.

Janes, Daryl, "Dallas Oil Exploration Firm to Relocate Here," *Austin Business Journal,* December 6, 1996.

Snow, Nick, "Mid-Size Producers Quietly Build Up Balance Sheets with Asset Sales," *Petroleum Finance Week,* July 5, 1999.

Sullivan, John A., "Brigham Exploration Boosts 2005 Spending Plan," *Natural Gas Week,* October 17, 2005.

Williams, Peggy, "The Deep Hunton," *Oil & Gas Investor,* November 2004, p. 83.

—Frederick C. Ingram

BRINKER
INTERNATIONAL.

Brinker International, Inc.

6820 LBJ Freeway
Dallas, Texas 75240
U.S.A.
Telephone: (972) 980-9917
Fax: (972) 770-9593
Web site: http://www.brinker.com

Public Company
Incorporated: 1975 as Chili's Grill & Bar, Inc.
Employees: 96,600
Sales: $3.91 billion (2004)
Stock Exchanges: New York
Ticker Symbol: EAT
NAIC: 533110 Owners and Lessors of Other
   Nonfinancial Assets; 722110 Full-Service Restaurants

Brinker International, Inc. operates several popular American restaurant chains: Chili's Grill & Bar, Romano's Macaroni Grill, On the Border Mexican Grill & Cantina, and Maggiano's Little Italy. The mainstay of the company is Chili's, a chain of more than 1,000 eateries featuring Southwest decor and inexpensive meals. Under the direction of Norman E. Brinker, for whom the company was named, the Chili's chain expanded and other theme restaurants were added. To stay near the top of the increasingly competitive casual-dining niche, Brinker has tweaked both concept and strategy.

1975: The Birth of the Chili's Concept

Brinker traces its origins to the first Chili's Grill & Bar, opened on Greenville Street in Dallas in March 1975. Chili's was established by Dallas restaurateur Larry Levine, who sought to provide an informal full-service dining atmosphere with a menu that focused on different varieties of hamburgers offered at reasonable prices. Levine's concept proved successful, and 22 more Chili's restaurants, featuring similar Southwest decor, were opened in the late 1970s and early 1980s. In 1983, Levine's restaurant chain was taken over by Norman E. Brinker.

Brinker had a long and illustrious history in the restaurant business. He had begun his career in 1957 working for the Jack-in-the-Box fast-food chain, which then had just seven outlets. Nine years later, Brinker left the greatly expanded Jack-in-the-Box operation to found Steak & Ale, an informal, full-service restaurant chain with a menu that emphasized inexpensive steak dinners and friendly service. Responsible for introducing the salad bar, an innovation that soon swept the restaurant industry, this new, casual dining concept became a favorite among the baby boomer generation.

By the 1970s, Brinker's nearly 200 restaurants, including the Steak & Ale and Bennigan's chains, were overseen by his S&A Restaurant Corporation. When S&A was sold to the Pillsbury Company in 1976, Brinker became an executive at Pillsbury, in charge of that company's restaurant group, which now had four chains, including Burger King and Pillsbury's Poppin' Fresh Restaurants. Together, the operations of this group represented the second largest restaurant company in the world.

By 1983, however, Brinker had decided to leave Pillsbury to strike out again on his own. "I wanted to see if I could take a very small company and develop it against the big chains," Brinker recalled in a 1992 article in *Food & Service* magazine. Toward this end, Brinker purchased a significant share in the Chili's chain, becoming its chairperson and chief executive officer. At this time, Chili's had less than $1 million in equity, was $8.5 million in debt, and was earning less than $1 million a year. Planning to expand, Brinker took Chili's public in 1984, selling stock under the ticker symbol EAT. On the basis of Brinker's strong reputation in the restaurant industry, Chili's stock offering received strong support from the investment community.

Franchise Expansion in the 1980s

In 1984, Chili's 23 restaurants were generating $40 million in sales from their menu of gourmet burgers, french fries, and margaritas. To improve the chain's profitability and thereby allow for expansion, Brinker began the process of fine-tuning Chili's operations. Seeking input from Chili's customers, as well as from customers of competing restaurants, Brinker made a practice of strolling around the parking lots of eating establishments, informally asking customers how they liked their meals and what changes they would like made. On the basis of

Company Perspectives:

Serving the World a Great Taste of Life—Generosity of Spirit. Brinker International is a global business, but our heart is rooted in the communities we serve. Serving a great taste of life to the world is about great food. It is also about sharing the fruits of our success and improving the quality of life of our employees, shareholders, and business partners around the world.

this feedback, he began to shift the focus of Chili's menu away from burgers to include a broader array of salads and chicken and fish entrees.

Throughout the mid-1980s, Brinker and his associates expanded Chili's steadily, opening new restaurants across the country and further adapting the eatery's offerings. By the end of the decade, burgers accounted for just 10 percent of the company's sales, as new items, such as ribs and fajitas, proved more popular. The company counted on its loyal customers, dubbed "chiliheads," to keep revenues high, while also striving to maintain its rapid rate of customer turnover; the average length of time a customer spent in a Chili's restaurant was just 35 minutes, which allowed for more profitable and efficient use of space and wait staff.

By the late 1980s, the company was ready to branch out into new restaurants and began to consider several different acquisitions. A plan to attempt regaining control of Brinker's former S&A Restaurant Corporation was vetoed, as was an idea to take on several fast-food chains, such as Taco Cabana and Flyer's Island Express. Chili's eventually decided to focus on the casual, low-priced restaurant niche, in which it was already a strong player. In February 1989, the company purchased Grady's Goodtimes, a Knoxville, Tennessee-based restaurant chain owned by a family named Regas, who had been in the restaurant business in Tennessee since 1919. In 1982, the Regas family had opened the first of its Grady's Goodtimes outlets, which served primarily beef, seafood, salads, and sandwiches.

Since the Dallas restaurant market already had a chain called Grady's, Chili's executives decided to call their new chain "Regas." This new name eventually proved unsuccessful, however, as some customers expressed confusion over its pronunciation and others associated it with "regal," leading them to suspect that it was an expensive restaurant. Moreover, Regas faced tough competition from established steakhouse chains in Texas. As a result, Chili's faced unexpected difficulties in expanding the acquisition.

Nine months after purchasing Regas, Chili's acquired another restaurant concept, which it also planned to expand into a chain. With $41 million in capital obtained through a stock sale, Chili's purchased the rights to the Romano's Macaroni Grill concept. Texas restaurateur Phil Romano had opened the prototype restaurant in 1988 in a location north of San Antonio, Texas. He based the eatery's atmosphere and menu on the communal style of dining that he remembered from growing up in an Italian family. Just as his grandfather had always kept a four-liter jug of wine on the dinner table, patrons in Romano's

restaurant were provided with casks of house red wine. Customers were invited to serve themselves throughout the meal and then to inform their waiter of how much they had consumed; the waiter would then charge them accordingly. This "honor system" for wine was modified in areas where liquor laws forbade patrons to serve themselves, but on the whole, it helped to keep sales high at Romano's.

Other innovations at Romano's restaurants included glass walls through which patrons could see kitchen workers creating the evening's meals. The unique interior design of Romano's created a cavernous effect, with strings of bare light bulbs illuminating high, wooden, vaulted ceilings and tables placed between fieldstone arches. Daily specials were displayed in deli cases near the restaurant's front door, and crates of wine and canned tomato products were hung on the walls, serving as decoration and storage space.

Chili's planned for Romano's to compete with the extremely successful Olive Garden chain of Italian restaurants owned by General Mills. Rapid expansion of Romano's and Regas was anticipated, and Brinker set a goal for the Chili's company to earn annual revenues of $1 billion by 1995. Brinker planned to pattern the growth of the new acquisitions after the Chili's chain expansion. In just seven years under Brinker's leadership, Chili's had grown to include 215 restaurants; although a large percentage of these were directly owned by the company, a franchising program also had proved useful in opening new restaurants.

The Early 1990s: New Challenges

To help Romano's and Regas achieve similar growth, Brinker decided to keep the identities and priorities, even the administration, of its three restaurant chains distinct. Each restaurant was designed to appeal to a middle-class customer, between the ages of 25 and 55, and prices were kept reasonable: the average bill for a Chili's customer was $7.50; the average for a Regas customer was $9.50; and at Romano's, a slightly more upscale property, average bills per customer were $13.50. By the end of 1990, Chili's was operating 240 Chili's outlets, 14 Regas Grill restaurants, and three Romano's Macaroni Grill eateries. Together, these operations reported $438 million in revenues.

In May 1991, Chili's announced that it was changing its corporate name, to better reflect the newly diversified nature of its operations. The company's name became Brinker International, Inc., and Brinker told the *Dallas Morning News* that "this new name is a way to bridge our past with our future as a multi-concept corporation in the midst of international expansion." The first foreign countries targeted for Chili's operations were Canada and Mexico, where the company planned for restaurants to open in 1992.

Again, Brinker undertook extensive market research to adapt restaurant offerings to suit customer preferences. As U.S. demographic studies and customer feedback began to suggest that the average age of a Chili's customer had increased, the restaurant took steps to make itself more appealing to this segment of the public. The volume of music played over restaurant loudspeakers was lowered, the size of the print on Chili's

Key Dates:

1975: Larry Levine opens first Chili's Grill & Bar in Dallas, Texas.
1983: Norman Brinker takes over Chili's restaurant chain.
1988: First Romano's Macaroni Grill opens in San Antonio, Texas.
1991: Chili's is renamed Brinker International, Inc.
1992: Brinker reaches an agreement with Pac-Am Food Concepts to expand Chili's franchise to the Far East.
1995: Brinker establishes a strategic partnership with Lettuce Entertain You Enterprises.
2000: Norman Brinker steps down as company chairman.
2005: Company announces international expansion plans.

menus was enlarged, sizes of some portions were reduced, and more low-fat entrees were added. At the same time, the company promoted Chili's as a friendly place for younger couples with children, providing fast and efficient service and low prices. ''You have to stay in the energetic group of customers, but you try to tone it down enough so that you don't turn off the older group,'' Brinker explained to *Food & Service* magazine.

To keep the company's operations as efficient and cost-effective as possible, Brinker also invested in an elaborate computer system. Computers were used to schedule workers' shifts and to help company headquarters determine the amount of supplies each restaurant needed. In addition, Brinker invested in extensive kitchen staff training programs, which were designed to minimize waste in company operations.

By the end of 1991, Brinker's had sales totaling $426.8 million and earnings of $26.1 million, a 44 percent increase over the previous year. Already operating a total of 271 restaurants by the spring of 1992, Brinker was opening one new restaurant a week, as the company chalked up a 23 percent rate of growth in sales, despite a general recession in the restaurant industry. Many of the Chili's restaurants opened in early 1992 showed a higher rate of sales than older properties, reflecting the company's growing expertise in the industry. Moreover, Brinker established Chili's restaurants in less populous areas, reflecting the widespread popularity of the Chili's concept.

Despite these strong signs of continuing financial health, Brinker executives estimated that the market for its Chili's chains would mature by the late 1990s. To take the pressure off the Chili's concept, and lessen the number of new restaurant openings needed to maintain brisk growth in corporate profits, Brinker looked for expansion in its newer properties.

By mid-1992, Brinker had opened 17 Regas restaurants, and, in response to the problems surrounding the chain's name, he had rechristened all of these outlets as Grady's American Grill. The company continued to experiment with different formats for the eatery, redesigning its interiors as more casual and being careful to distinguish Grady's from Chili's. As part of this effort, Grady's menu was centered on beef, seafood, and pasta, rather than the Mexican-based entrees that had become popular at Chili's.

Brinker also looked to Romano's to bolster corporate earnings. By May 1992, eight of these restaurants were in operation, each contributing about $3 million a year in sales, up from $2.4 million the year before. A Romano's restaurant cost no more to build than a Chili's and brought in revenues that were twice as high, since its menu featured higher-priced items, and Brinker planned to nearly triple the number of Romano eateries over the next 12 months. The company's strategy was to enter as many markets as soon as possible, reap the rewards of novelty in areas without moderately priced Italian eateries, and then decide on which markets could support two or more Romano's outlets.

The success of Romano's prompted Brinker to test a second, less expensive Italian eatery concept, also developed by restaurateur Phil Romano. In July 1992, Spageddies, a low-priced, casual pasta restaurant, was opened at a test location in Plano, Texas. The prototype restaurant seated 216 patrons, had a decor featuring bright colors, decorative canned goods, and colorful billboards, and included two bocce ball courts to keep customers amused while they waited for seats. As in Romano's restaurants, exhibition kitchens at Spageddies allowed patrons to watch their food being prepared. With the two chains, Brinker hoped to flank its competitor Olive Garden, with Spageddies engaging a slightly less expensive niche and Romano's occupying a more costly segment of the market.

At the end of June 1992, Brinker posted annual revenues of $519.3 million, with earnings of $26.1 million; 300 Chili's Grill & Bars, 20 Grady's American Grills, and 17 Romano's outlets were in operation. Later that year, Brinker announced plans for further foreign expansion, signing an agreement with Pac-Am Food Concepts, based in Hong Kong, to franchise 25 Chili's restaurants in the Far East over the next 15 years. Pac-Am planned to duplicate the Chili's decor and menu in locations such as Jakarta, Indonesia, and Seoul, South Korea, with some changes to satisfy local tastes.

Brinker also began to test another theme restaurant, Kona Ranch Steakhouse, in Oklahoma City. A small Tex-Mex restaurant in San Antonio, called Nacho Mama's, also was considered a possible avenue for expansion, although Brinker's executives vowed to change that restaurant's name in the event of an acquisition. In the midst of its aggressive plans to expand all four of its principal restaurant chains, the company encountered an unexpected obstacle on January 21, 1993, when Norman Brinker suffered a serious head injury while playing polo. Brinker was comatose for two weeks, during which time he was temporarily replaced at the company by his second in command. Despite an initially unfavorable prognosis, Brinker made a rapid recovery and returned to resume his positions of chairperson and CEO in May 1993.

Shortly thereafter, Brinker International moved to expand its Spageddies property, buying out the interest of its partner Romano in the prototype Spageddies restaurant and announcing that two more Texas locations, in Tyler and Mesquite, would be opened. To provide a corporate structure that would enhance growth in all areas of the company, Brinker reorganized its headquarters staff into concept teams, which were designed to act as small companies within the framework of the larger corporation. As Brinker approached the mid-1990s, it appeared well positioned for strong growth, enhanced by an experienced management team and a track record of success with a variety of different restaurant concepts.

Restaurant Concepts for the Millennium

The year 1995 was pivotal for Brinker. By mid-decade it had become clear that the traditional casual dining concept was losing momentum, while other, more specialized niches, in particular Italian and Mexican cuisine, promised a much larger potential for growth. Observing the success of The Olive Garden, which remained the only major chain of Italian restaurants in the United States, Brinker recognized the need to retool its own Italian concept. In July 1995 the company announced a strategic partnership with Lettuce Entertain You Enterprises, a restaurant developer in the Chicago area. The joint venture enabled Brinker to acquire three of Lettuce's Maggiano's Little Italy restaurants and five of its Corner Bakeries, in addition to establishing a creative development deal between the two companies. Dubbed the "Dream Team" by executives from both sides, this arrangement brought together two men who were widely considered to be the best creative talents in the restaurant industry: Brinker's Phil Romano, "an oracle" in the restaurant business, according to the *Dallas Morning News,* with Lettuce's Rich Melman, whom *Business Week* had called the "Andrew Lloyd Weber of the Industry." The two companies agreed to come up with at least one new concept within the first year, over which Lettuce would retain control. The company also created an Italian Concepts Division in 1996, naming Gerard Centioli as president.

In the meantime, Brinker also made some strategic changes in its holdings. In December 1995 the company sold Grady's and Spageddies to Quality Dining Inc.; then, in January 1996 it opened its first Eatzi's in Dallas. Catering to the public's demand for restaurants that also featured prepared foods and groceries, Eatzi's was an immediate success, earning $12 million in the first year, more than double its predicted sales. By November 1997 a second location had opened in Houston, and a third opened in Atlanta the following February. During this same period, the company set out to modify its Romano's Macaroni Grill concept, with the aim of transforming it into a more casual, less expensive restaurant in order to attract a broader clientele. The new Romano's opened in November 1998 and promptly showed increased sales. In March 1999 Romano's debuted in the United Kingdom, the first of a projected 20 restaurants to be established in England through a joint venture with Queensborough Holdings PLC of London.

Brinker was equally determined in carving out its niche in the Mexican cuisine market. In February 1994 it acquired the On the Border restaurant chain, comprised of 21 units, and in May it opened the first Cozymel's Coastal Mexican Grill. The success of Cozymel's in Texas led to the announcement in May 1995 of the opening of an additional 12 locations nationwide. The following March the company embarked on an aggressive marketing campaign to promote the franchising of On the Border, and by early 1997 it announced the opening of two new On the Border locations in Columbus, Ohio.

By the end of the decade Brinker had nearly doubled its sales over a five-year period, from $1.2 billion in 1996 to nearly $2.2 billion in 2000, and increased its restaurant total to more than 1,000. Although economic indicators suggested a decline in the casual restaurant market in the future, the prognosis for the industry in general remained encouraging, and Brinker's proven talent for adaptation and innovation promised that the company would be able to confront its future challenges head on.

CEO Ron McDougall succeeded Norman Brinker as chairman in December 2000. Concurrently, the company announced plans to purchase the remaining interest in Big Bowl from Let Us Entertain You Enterprises while selling back the Wildfire Steak and Chophouse concept. Six Big Bowl and three Wildfire units were in operation.

Striving to Keep Them Coming in the Door: 2001–05

In 2001, Brinker bought a 40 percent stake in the seafood restaurant endeavor Rockfish Partnership. Brinker pulled out of the Eatzi's gourmet market chain the next year, a move costing more than $10 million. Phil Romano's home-meal replacement concept had inspired imitators, but according to *Restaurant Business* "the brand failed to find widespread acceptance." In September 2002, just four of the stores remained in operation.

In 2003, Brinker upped its stake in Rockfish, to 43 percent with an additional $1.8 million investment. Another $4 million in loans was earmarked for further development of the Rockfish concept. The small chain grew from ten to 16 locations from 2002 to 2003, according to *Restaurant Business.*

The unprofitable upscale-Mexican brand Cozymel's went on the sales block in 2003, and Brinker took a $15.1 million asset impairment charge. The concept created by Phil Romano, *Restaurant Business* recalled, was "fashioned loosely after seaside cantinas on the Yucatan." Brinker ended its fiscal year, in June 2003, with $3.3 billion in revenue and $168.6 million in profit.

Doug H. Brooks, a 26-year veteran of Brinker, was named CEO in January 2004, succeeding Ron A. McDougall, who continued to serve as chairman. Brooks's task, along with the presidents of each brand, was to keep the company relevant in a segment of the market that had become increasingly competitive and more health conscious. Customers who walked in their doors, or by them, might be seeking a low-fat or low-carb meal or one large enough to insure the need for a doggy bag.

Chili's, the chain producing in excess of 70 percent of profits in the early 21st century, had faltered a decade earlier. Brinker's stock fell to $11 per share when customers started going elsewhere. A revamp revived share price and helped put Brinker into the number two spot in the casual dining industry. Darden Restaurants Inc., parent of the Red Lobster and Olive Garden chains, held the top spot. Brinker stock traded around $36 per share in late February 2004.

In addition to tuning into dietary concerns, Brinker tapped into the trend toward increased purchases of takeout meals. Chili's to-go sales climbed to 10 percent of sales, up from practically nil just a decade earlier.

As the company worked to keep its profitable Chili's brand fresh, it continued to search for the best recipe for its smaller brands. Corner Bakery, for example, was changed from a cafeteria format to limited service, to better fit the suburban family's needs.

Another Brinker veteran succeeded Brooks as CEO. Todd Diener joined Chili's in 1981 as a manager trainee. He rose through the ranks and served as Chili's president from 1998 to 2003. When he entered his new role, Diener was confident the success of Chili's could be translated to its other concepts. But not all the brands were destined to continue under the Brinker banner. In November 2004, the company's ''emerging brands'' executive departed. The smaller concepts would no longer have one executive designated to shepherd them along, according to the *Dallas Morning News*. Big Bowl and Cozymel's both had been sold during the year and the value of Brinker's Rockfish investment had been written down.

Fiscal 2005 had begun with elevated operating costs and lagging sales. To get back on the right track, Diener was returned to his position as president of Chili's. Other top management changes occurred at Romano's Macaroni Grill and Maggiano's Little Italy. A new position was created to head up international growth. Initiatives to improve customer satisfaction and employee performance were also implemented.

In August 2005 Brinker disclosed plans to sell Corner Bakery. Lettuce Entertain You Enterprises, its creator, had bought back Big Bowl in 2004, but did not plan on buying the fast-casual bakery-café chain, according to *Nation's Restaurant News*. More than one-third of the 90 Corner Bakery units operated in the Chicago area. Analysts estimated the sale price to range between $140 million and $170 million. Richard Melman, founder and chairman of Lettuce Entertain You Enterprises, was a Brinker consultant and its single largest shareholder.

In September 2005, Brinker announced plans for international expansion and the payment of its first quarterly dividend. ''The company boosted its prediction of the 'universe potential' of its four strongest brands by about 85 percent—to almost 5,000 restaurants. That includes 2,100 outside the United States,'' the *Dallas Morning Star News* reported. During fiscal 2006 about 10 percent of its new units would be opened in international markets. Brinker hoped to grow its international profits from a current 2 percent to 20 percent by 2012. Casual dining in Latin America and the Middle East had been on an upswing, outstripping the rate of U.S. sales growth.

In October 2005, Brinker announced the sale of Corner Bakery; the deal was expected to be completed by the end of the calendar year. Chili's, Romano's Macaroni Grill, On the Border, and the Maggiano's chains remained in the Brinker fold.

Principal Competitors

Applebee's International Inc.; Darden Restaurants, Inc.; Outback Steakhouse, Inc.

Further Reading

Bell, Sally, ''Norm!,'' *Food & Service,* January, 1992.

Bernstein, Charles, ''Brinker's Three-Way Combination: A Bid for Full-Service Dominance,'' *Nation's Restaurant News,* October 29, 1990.

Bertagnoli, Lisa, ''On-the-Job Training: Brinker's Todd Diener Builds on His Chili's Experience to Fine-Tune Emerging Brands,'' *Chain Leader,* May 2004, pp. 76+.

''Brinker Boosts Stake in Rockfish,'' *Restaurant Business,*'' March 1, 2003, p. 10.

''Brinker Dumps Eatzi's Stake . . . and Asks Cozymel's Schmille for Aid,'' *Restaurant Business,*'' September 1, 2002, p. 11.

''Brinker Gives Up on Cozymel's,'' *Restaurant Business,*'' September 1, 2003, p. 14.

Chaudhry, Rajan, ''Ron McDougall's Winning Ways,'' *Restaurants & Institutions,* July 1, 1993.

Fairbank, Katie, ''Eating Profits: Home-Style Restaurants Losing Out in the Battle for Dining Dollars,'' *Dallas Morning News,* November 5, 2000.

Fox, Valerie, and Lisa Y. Taylor, ''Chili's Makes 1,000,'' *Dallas Business Journal,* February 11, 2000.

Gutner, Toddi, ''Norman Brinker Scores Again,'' *Forbes,* January 6, 1992.

Hall, Cheryl, ''Brinker International Runs on Good Game Plan,'' *Dallas Morning News,* February 21, 1993.

——, ''The Brinker Touch,'' *Dallas Morning News,* May 10, 1992.

''Il Fornaio, Bruckmann Rosser Buy Corner Bakery,'' *Nation's Restaurant Business,* October 10, 2005, p. 3.

Oppel, Richard A., Jr., ''A Return Performance,'' *Dallas Morning News,* May 5, 1993.

Rigsby, G.G., ''Analysts Predict Slowdown in Casual-Dining Earnings,'' *Tampa Bay Business Journal,* August 4, 2000.

Robinson-Jacobs, Karen, ''Brinker Plans to Expand Overseas,'' *Dallas Morning News,*'' September 16, 2005.

——, ''Dallas-Based Restaurant Firm Brinker Reports Departure of Small-Brand Executive,'' *Dallas Morning News,* November 30, 2004.

Robinson-Jacobs, Karen, and Victor Godinez, ''Restaurant Company Brinker International Looks to Next Growth Concept,'' *Knight-Ridder Tribune Business News,* February 22, 2004.

Ruggless, Ron, ''Brinker Inks Deal for Chili's Units in Asia,'' *Nation's Restaurant News,* November 16, 1992.

——, ''Brinker to Sell Off Corner Bakery Chain, Renew Focus on Chili's,'' *Nation's Restaurant News,* August 29, 2005, pp. 1+.

——, ''Norman Brinker Hits the Comeback Trail,'' *Nation's Restaurant News,* March 29, 1993.

Sherbert, Felicia M., ''Beyond Chili's,'' *Market Watch,* July/August, 1992.

''Stirring the Bowl,'' *Restaurants & Institutions,* December 15, 2000, p. 14.

—Elizabeth Rourke
—updates: Stephen Meyer; Kathleen Peippo

CAPITAL SENIOR LIVING CORPORATION

Capital Senior Living Corporation

14160 Dallas Parkway
Suite 300
Dallas, Texas 75254
U.S.A.
Telephone: (972) 770-5600
Fax: (972) 770-5666
Web site: http://www.capitalsenior.com

Public Company
Incorporated: 1996 as Capital Senior Living Corporation
Employees: 2,795
Sales: $93.26 million (2004)
Stock Exchanges: New York
Ticker Symbol: CSU
NAIC: 623110 Nursing Care Facilities; 623990 Other
    Residential Care Facilities

Capital Senior Living Corporation is a leading operator of residential communities for seniors, primarily aged 75 and over. It runs more than 40 communities (39 company owned and 15 managed for third parties) in 20 states with a capacity of about 7,000 residents, most of whom live independently. Meals, housekeeping, and transportation are available. The company also offers assisted living services, making it possible for residents to ''age in place'' as their needs change without having to move to different facilities.

Origins

Dallas-based Capital Senior Living Corporation has been involved (through its precursors) in the senior housing industry since 1990. Independent living and assisted living developments bridged a gap between traditional housing and nursing homes. Beyond mere residences, these communities provided meals and transportation. Capital originally focused on the younger, more active seniors of the independent living market. Annual revenues were about $20 million in the mid-1990s.

Jeffrey L. Beck and James A. Stroud were the group's cofounders and cochairmen. Beck also served as CEO while Stroud was chief operating officer. Each would head an industry trade group.

Another investor in one of the companies that would make up Capital Senior Living Corporation, Quality Home Care, Inc., was Lawrence A. Cohen, who would be vice-chairman, CFO, and later CEO of the corporation. Other entities that were part of the formation transactions that created Capital Senior Living Corporation were Capital Senior Living, Inc.; Capital Senior Management 1, Inc.; Capital Senior Management 2, Inc.; and Capital Senior Development, Inc., which were each owned by Beck and Stroud. Capital Senior Living Corporation was incorporated in October 1996 in preparation for its initial public offering.

1997 IPO

The company listed on the New York Stock Exchange on October 31, 1997, raising $130 million. The initial public offering (IPO) was carried out in spite of a 554-point dip in the market just days before. The company's track record, profitability, and niche were key selling points, Beck told the *Dallas Business Journal*.

At the time of the IPO, Capital had 5,000 residents in its communities, which were 95 percent full. Most paid an average of $1,500 a month for independent living quarters and about $600 more for assisted living. Capital did not provide specialized services such as dialysis, and more than 90 percent of residents paid out of private funds, freeing the company of the hassle of dealing with Medicare and Medicaid. Capital was said to be the second largest supplier of senior living services in the United States.

Proceeds from the IPO were earmarked to fund two years of expansion plans, including consolidating partnerships in which the company had an interest. In October 1998 Capital bought out four retirement communities it had been managing from NHP Retirement Housing Partners I. Capital paid $40.6 million for the properties in California, Florida, and Michigan, which together had a capacity of 706 residents.

The company was also buying communities in Nebraska and Missouri. At the time, Capital was expanding nine other facili-

Company Perspectives:

Capital Senior Living Corporation is committed to providing quality housing and services based on the highest standards of excellence in the industry. Our goal is to enrich the daily lives of our senior residents by providing an environment that stimulates them physically, mentally, and emotionally. Therefore, each community offers a relaxed atmosphere of warmth and caring that promotes companionship among residents and staff. Each community's employees are personally committed to serving residents and treating them with dignity and respect.

Key Dates:

1990: Company enters senior housing business.
1997: Initial public offering raises $131 million.
2000: ILM I Senior Living Inc. is acquired.
2001: Blackstone housing joint venture is formed.
2003: A dozen Triad communities are acquired.
2004: CGI Management Inc. is acquired from The Covenant Group of Texas Inc.

ties and building about 30 new ones. The company typically located them in large urban centers, and preferred large developments of more than 100 units. The company's target demographic, according to the *Dallas Business Journal,* was those age 75 and above with $25,000 in disposable income.

Late 1990s Shake-Up

The senior housing industry had a banner year in 1997 followed by a crash the next year. Still, Capital was able to provide shareholders a return of more than 33 percent in 1998, according to one source. With large numbers of the population entering retirement, many expected the industry to grow in the long term. As one of the best capitalized companies in the industry, Capital was able to finance its developments as capital became scarce. Smaller operators in the fragmented industry had difficulty finding bank financing and the state of the capital markets dissuaded them from going public for a few years, an industry insider told *National Real Estate Investor.* Capital took advantage of the industry shakeup to acquire companies and bring in management talent. Another factor in Capital's favor was the general decline of the nursing home industry.

While there would be justifiable concerns about overbuilding in certain segments of the senior housing market, Capital was focusing on affordable, independent living, which it felt to be an underserved niche. Capital had been expanding its offerings to provide more services to those who required more assistance. This allowed the company to promote an ''age in place'' philosophy wherein aging residents could remain in the same setting as their needs changed. Capital's focus remained on private pay residents; nursing services providers who relied on Medicare had been hammered by the 1997 Balanced Budget Act.

Lawrence A. Cohen became Capital's president and CEO in 1999 after serving as vice-chairman and chief financial officer for about three years. Prior to that, he had been CEO of PaineWebber Properties Incorporated.

2000 and Beyond

Capital acquired ILM I Senior Living Inc., a Virginia REIT, in August 2000. The deal included eight communities in Omaha, Nebraska; East Lansing, Michigan; Peoria, Illinois; Raleigh, North Carolina; Wichita Kansas; Hot Springs, Arkansas; Winston-Salem, North Carolina, and one in Santa Barbara, California, that was co-owned by ILM II Senior Living Inc.

The acquisition added capacity for 1,300 residents and increased revenues by $22 million a year. Capital had been managing the properties since 1996. A planned merger with the ILM II fund was terminated over a tax issue.

Capital had total revenues of $59.7 million in 2000. The senior population in Texas was booming, putting it third behind Florida and California as a choice of retirement area.

Capital formed a joint venture with Blackstone Real Estate Advisors in late 2001 to increase its involvement in the housing market for seniors. Blackstone owned 90 percent of the venture and provided significant financial resources from its $1.5 billion Blackstone Real Estate Partners III fund. Capital's role was to manage the properties. The partnership intended to acquire $200 million of senior housing communities, Cohen told the *Wall Street Transcript.*

The purchase of a dozen communities under the Triad name was announced in 2003. They had a capacity of 1,670 residents and were owned by five partnerships, in which Capital had previously held a 1 percent interest. However, according to the *Dallas Morning News,* as the industry dealt with lingering overcapacity, Capital was looking for new growth by gaining more management contracts and keeping existing communities full.

Capital was also making some divestments as its share price slipped to a fraction of its 1998 peak. It sold a community in Sacramento, California, to an investment group, raising $11.7 million. The company sold a 90 percent holding in a Cottonwood, Arizona development to the Blackstone joint venture.

In 2004 Capital acquired CGI Management Inc. (CGIM) from The Covenant Group of Texas Inc. (TCG) for $2 million, plus up to another $1.6 million in performance-linked consideration. CGIM operated 16 senior communities, seven of them owned by TCG. The company expected management contracts to continue at 13 properties in four states (Arkansas, Mississippi, Oklahoma, and Texas), which had a capacity of 1,600 residents.

Stroud told the *Dallas Business Journal* the senior housing industry was seeing more emphasis on affordability in a lethargic economy. Operators were allowing residents to save money by unbundling such services as meals and transportation. By this time Capital had 2,500 employees and about 8,500 residents.

Capital and other operators were also adding new amenities to attract residents in a competitive market. Some communities featured gyms, health centers, beauty salons, and libraries. At least one site even sported an aviary stocked with finches.

There were projections for the number of 65- to 74-year-olds to reach 37 million by 2030, more than twice as many as in 1990, when Capital started out in the senior housing market. The over-75 bracket was growing even faster, outpacing any other segment of the population.

Principal Subsidiaries

Capital Senior Living, Inc.; Capital Senior Development, Inc.; Capital Senior Management 1, Inc.; Capital Senior Management 2, Inc.; Capital Senior Living Properties, Inc.; Capital Senior Living Properties 2, Inc.; Capital Senior Living Properties 2, - Atrium of Carmichael, Inc.; Capital Senior Living Properties 2, - Crossword Oaks, Inc.; Capital Senior Living Properties 2 - Gramercy, Inc.; Capital Senior Living Properties 2, - Heatherwood, Inc.; Capital Senior Living Properties 2 - NHPT, Inc.; Capital Senior Living Properties 2, - Tesson Heights, Inc.; Capital Senior Living Properties 2 - Veranda Club, Inc.; Capital Senior Living Properties 3, Inc.; Capital Senior Living Properties 4, Inc.; Capital Senior Living Properties 5, Inc.; Capital Senior Living Properties 6, Inc.; Capital Senior Living A, Inc.; Capital Senior Living, ILM-A, Inc.; Capital Senior Living P-B, Inc.; Capital Senior Living ILM-B, Inc.; Capital Senior Living P-C, Inc.; Capital Senior Living ILM-C, Inc.; Capital Senior Living Acquisition, LLC; CGI Management, Inc.; HealthCare Properties, L.P. (57%); Quality Home Care, Inc.

Principal Operating Units

Owned: Canton Regency (4), Canton, Ohio; Crosswood Oaks, Sacramento, California; Gramercy Hill, Lincoln, Nebraska; Heatherwood, Detroit, Michigan; Independence Village, East Lansing, Michigan; Independence Village, Peoria, Illinois; Independence Village, Raleigh, North Carolina; Independence Village, Winston-Salem, North Carolina; Sedgwick Plaza, Wichita, Kansas; Tesson Heights, St. Louis, Missouri; Towne Centre (4), Merrillville, Indiana; Veranda Club, Boca Raton, Florida; Waterford at Columbia, South Carolina; Waterford at Deer Park, Texas; Waterford at Edison Lakes, South Bend, Indiana; Waterford at Fairfield, Ohio; Waterford at Fort Worth, Texas; Waterford at Highland Colony, Jackson, Mississippi; Waterford at Huebner, San Antonio, Texas; Waterford at Ironbridge; Springfield, Missouri; Waterford at Mansfield, Ohio; Waterford at Mesquite, Texas; Waterford at Pantego, Texas; Waterford at Plano, Texas; Waterford at Shreveport, Louisiana; Waterford at Thousand Oaks, San Antonio, Texas; Wellington at Arapaho, Richardson, Texas; Wellington at North Richland Hills, Texas; Wellington at Oklahoma City, Oklahoma; Affiliates: BRE/CSL; SHPII/CSL; Managed: Atrium of Carmichael,

Sacramento, California; Covenant Place of Burleson, Texas; Covenant Place of Waxahachie, Texas; Covenant Place of Abilene, Texas; Crescent Point, Cedar Hill, Texas; Good Place, North Richland Hills, Texas; Harding Place, Searcy, Arkansas; Meadow Lakes, North Richland Hills, Texas; Mountain Creek, Grand Prairie, Texas; Meadow View, Arlington, Texas; Saint Ann, Oklahoma City, Oklahoma; Southern Plaza, Bethany, Oklahoma; Sunnybrook Estates, Madison, Mississippi; Tealridge Manor, Edmond, Oklahoma; The Arbrook, Arlington, Texas.

Principal Competitors

American Retirement Corporation; Brookdale Living Communities; Emeritus Corporation; Holiday Retirement Corporation; Sunrise Senior Living, Inc.

Further Reading

''CEO/Company Interview: Lawrence A. Cohen, Capital Senior Living Corp.,'' *Wall Street Transcript*, July 31, 2000.

''Company Interview: Lawrence A. Cohen, Capital Senior Living Corporation,'' *Wall Street Transcript*, May 13, 2002.

''Dallas-Based Developer Buys Four Retirement Communities,'' *Dallas Morning News*, October 6, 1998.

Holman, Kelly, ''Blackstone in JV for Senior Housing,'' *Daily Deal*, January 2, 2002.

Johnson, Ben, ''Assisted Living's Crossroads: Public vs. Private Rages On,'' *National Real Estate Investor*, April 30, 1999.

Lennhoff, David C. and Peter A. Wolman, ''Valuation of Continuing Care Retirement Communities: Worth Another Look,'' *Appraisal Journal*, January 2000, pp. 57, 63.

McCarthy, Edward, ''Avoiding the Pitfalls of Assisted Living Development,'' *Urban Land*, February 1997, pp. 45, 55.

Patrick, Stephanie, ''Capital Merger Ups Resident Capacity,'' *Dallas Business Journal*, August 18, 2000, p. 8.

——, ''Capital to Manage Sites It Sells, CEO Says,'' *Dallas Business Journal*, December 15, 2000, p. 26.

——, ''Capital Senior Buying Two REITs,'' *Dallas Business Journal*, July 14, 2000, p. 1.

——, ''Merger Snag,'' *Dallas Business Journal*, July 28, 2000, p. 3.

——, ''Senior-Housing Market Heats Up in Metroplex,'' *Dallas Business Journal*, March 31, 2000, p. 37.

——, ''Two Minutes with James A. Stroud,'' *Dallas Business Journal*, November 12, 2004.

Strauss, Lawrence, ''Capital Senior Living May Improve with Age,'' *Barron's Online*, December 16, 1998.

Tanner, Lisa, ''Capital Senior Living Raises $131 Million for Expansion,'' *Dallas Business Journal*, November 14, 1997, pp. 1+.

——, ''Capital Senior Living Rides Wave of an Aging Population,'' *Dallas Business Journal*, January 22, 1999.

Yu, Roger, ''Senior Housing Industry Changing with Times,'' *Dallas Morning News*, October 26, 2003.

—Frederick C. Ingram

Capstone Turbine Corporation

21211 Nordhoff Street
Chatsworth, California 91311
U.S.A.
Telephone: (818) 734-5300
Fax: (818) 734-5320
Web site: http://www.microturbine.com

Public Company
Incorporated: 1988 as NoMac Energy Systems
Employees: 202
Sales: $16.96 million (2005)
Stock Exchanges: NASDAQ
Ticker Symbol: CPST
NAIC: 335312 Motor and Generator Manufacturing

Capstone Turbine Corporation is a Chatsworth, California company that develops, manufactures, and markets 30-kilowatt and 60-kilowatt microturbine generators, capable of supplying the electricity needs of commercial and small industrial users. The units, roughly the size of a refrigerator, can be connected to the utility grid or operated as stand-alone units. They are also versatile in terms of the fuels they use, including natural gas, diesel, kerosene, propane, and waste gases from sewage plants, landfills, and oil and gas drilling operations. The turbine generators operate in much the same way as a jet engine. Fuel is mixed with air to create combustion. A magnet generator, compressor, and turbine wheel, all fitted on a single shaft, is then turned, generating electricity. The exhaust from the units can also be used in a cogeneration system, producing both heat and power. Other advantages of the microturbines are low emissions and no need for water. All told, there are more than 3,200 Capstone microturbine generators in the field worldwide. Although yet to produce a profit, the company is cash-rich and has no debts, the recipient of backing from such deep-pocketed investors as Microsoft's Paul Allen and Compaq Computer's Benjamin Rosen. Capstone is a public company listed on the NASDAQ.

Formation in Late 1980s

Capstone was cofounded in 1988 as NoMac Energy Systems by James C. Noe and Robin Mackay, who fused their last names to coin "NoMac." Both men brought considerable experience with turbines to the venture. Noe worked at Douglas Aircraft company from 1957 to 1961, involved with aircraft thermodynamic systems. He then spent 17 years at the Garrett Corporation, which became Allied Signal Aerospace, and where Mackay was a colleague. At Garrett, Noe held a number of engineering positions, working on aircraft environmental systems as well as seeking out commercial and industrial applications for the company's high technology aerospace systems. In 1979 he became president of Alpha National, Inc., a California company that pursued turbines that could use alternate fuels. Two years later he became president of parent company Alpha United, Inc., which developed compact plate-fin heat exchangers and cold plates for electronic cooling in the automotive and aerospace industries. Noe struck out on his own in 1986, establishing Creative Energy Concepts in Los Angeles, California, to work on low-cost turbines that could be used in a range of industrial and aerospace applications. Mackay, who held a degree in mathematics and economics from Canada's McGill University, had worked for The Boeing Company's Industrial Products Division, which made small gas turbines for use in cars and industrial applications. His job was to develop concepts and markets for the turbines, the same role he would play during his 24-year tenure at Garrett (Allied Signal), where he served as Director of Industrial Market Development.

When Noe and Mackay teamed up in 1988 to form NoMac they obtained three master patents related to work the men had done together at Allied Signal. The patents related to a heat pump, a solar power generator, and an interruptible power unit, basic elements of a turbine engine. Noe became president of the start-up and Mackay vice-president of marketing. NoMac's mission was to research and develop innovative energy concepts. In particular, the company wanted to mass produce microturbines. In the early years NoMac received financing from Ford Motor Company, NASA, and a few others, but it faced a difficult task in creating a microturbine. As the *Huber*

Company Perspectives:

With over 3,200 Capstone MicroTurbines worldwide, Capstone Turbine is the leading provider of microturbine cogeneration systems for clean, continuous energy management, energy conservation and biogas-fueled renewable energy.

Mills Digital Power Report indicated in a 2000 article, "A turbine certainly *looks* simpler [than a reciprocating internal combustion engine], and once it's finally built right, it indeed is. A reciprocating engine has far more moving parts . . . but the parts themselves are pretty simple. A turbine's complex, curved blades, by contrast, are very difficult to machine. And they have to be exceptionally strong, because they just don't generate any serious power until they're rotating very fast. A car engine redlines at 5,000 rpm; Capstone's microturbine spins at 96,000 rpm. This required advanced materials, very sophisticated machining, and superb, high-speed bearings." But NoMac struggled to develop such an engine, its early prototypes consuming more energy than they produced. At this stage the focus was on stationary applications, such as providing backup power for a building.

Running out of money in 1992 NoMac was fortunate that its efforts caught the eye of Harold Rosen, former chief engineer for Hughes Electronics who had done pioneering work on geostationary satellites, making possible contemporary global communications. After Hughes was acquired by General Motors in 1986 some of his colleagues began work on electric-powered cars. Rosen's contribution to the project was a controller, entitling him to a ride in an early experimental vehicle. He found the concept intriguing, but believed that it would never be viable until something better than batteries provided the power. According to *Fortune* in a 1996 article, he began looking for an energy system that would be emission-free like batteries but would produce more power. Soon he zeroed in on hybrids. A friend at NASA passed along a paper by an engineer who described a proposed high-speed turbogenerator that could be used in a hybrid. Recalls Harold: "It had on paper everything I was looking for." The author was Robin Mackay. Rosen paid him a visit and was won over by Mackay's presentation, so much so that he pitched the NoMac turbine to Hughes's automotive section. Because GM was committed to batteries, however, Hughes passed. Next, Rosen called his brother, Benjamin Rosen, an electronics engineer who had switched to investing and founded Compaq Computer Company.

Rosen Brothers Buying into Company: 1993

In semi-retirement Benjamin Rosen was closing out his investment fund and looking for a new challenge, having already whittled down his golf handicap to 18. A car enthusiast— he owned a Porsche 928 and Mercedes-Benz SL600—he readily agreed to start a company with his brother and pursue the development of a turbine-powered electric hybrid car. Together, along with funding from venture capital firms Sevin Rosen Funds and Canaan Partners, the Rosen brothers bought NoMac in 1993.

After the Rosens took over NoMac, they installed their own man as CEO, a Hughes' retiree, Paul Craig. The company name did not meet with approval from the new owners, but they struggled to think of an alternative. Ben Rosen had always enjoyed good fortune investing in companies with two-syllable names that started with "C," such as Compaq, Cyrix, Citrix, and Cypress Semiconductor. With some help from a CEO of a company that sold naming software he finally decided on Capstone Turbine Corporation. Noe now became vice-president of engineering, but left in 1994 to become president of another microturbine company, Creative Energy Concepts, Inc. Mackay left in 1995, eventually founding Agile Turbine Technology, LLC to work on advanced gas turbines. The Rosens also wasted little time in forming a car company, Rosen Motors, incorporated in May 1993, to develop a complete power train while Capstone developed the engine.

With Craig in charge, Capstone moved quickly to complete its first prototype, a 24-kilowatt turbine (the equivalent of 32 horsepower) unveiled in 1994. The company now attracted additional investors. In 1995 New Zealand conglomerate Fletcher Challenge Ltd. acquired a 20 percent stake, and a year later the company completed a $50 million private placement of stock with such investors as Microsoft billionaire Paul Allen's Vulcan Northwest, as well as his old partner Bill Gates, who took $5 million of the action. The Capstone microturbine also caught the attention of Ford Motor Company, which bought a unit to evaluate for use in its hybrid vehicles.

But Capstone was also attracting interest from parties looking to use the microturbine to generate power. Fletcher's involvement proved to be a turning point for the company, since Fletcher was looking for ways to bring power to remote oil and gas fields, far removed from the electrical grid. Utilities were also interested in trying out the microturbines as satellite power plants, and some industrial customers wanted to test the units as part of cogeneration systems, providing both electricity and heat, and others sought to make use of garbage dump methane to produce power through the microturbines. In 1996 Capstone placed 37 beta units in the field. The company was still banking on the automotive market in the long run, viewing the power market as a means to an end: lowering costs and contributing to the development of technology that could apply to the automotive units that were expected to emerge around 2005. Although Rosen Motors successfully tested an automotive power train that used a Capstone turbine in 1997, it was unable to convince any of the major automakers to back the company and it ceased operations later in the year. For Capstone, it meant that its focus was now completely directed toward power generation.

In 1998 Capstone named a new CEO, Ake Almgren, a Swede who had been president of Power Systems for ABB, the giant European engineering conglomerate. He had been involved in the development of such cutting-edge technology as fuel cells, flywheels, and mega-powerchip systems. He recognized that utilities were turning to smaller power plants but was unable to convince ABB to become involved in distributed generation, producing power on a small-scale basis at multiple locations rather than in massive installations. In 1997 he bought a Capstone microturbine, was won over by the technology, and a year later, in July 1998, he became Capstone's CEO. He soon made key contributions to the refinement of the

Key Dates:

1988: Company founded as NoMac Energy Systems.
1993: Benjamin and Harold Rosen and investors acquire NoMac, renamed Capstone Turbine Corporation.
1994: Prototype is unveiled.
1998: First commercial units are sold.
2000: Initial public offering is completed.
2003: John Tucker is named CEO.

turbine's design, in particular the addition of solid-state electronics that allowed the turbines to perform seamless hand-offs between the microturbine and the electric grid it might be connected to or between a cluster of microturbines. Capstone sold its first three commercial units in 1998 to Southern Union in Galveston, Texas. The company shipped more than 200 units the following year.

Taken Public in 2000

As Capstone geared up for an initial public offering of stock in 2000, the state of California, where electricity had been deregulated, suffered from a power shortage that resulted in rolling blackouts. As a result Capstone received a great deal of attention from Wall Street. With Goldman, Sachs & Co. and Merrill Lynch & Co. acting as underwriters, the company sold 9.1 million shares at $16 a share on June 29, 2000. The stock immediately shot upwards, closing at $48 by the end of the day, and as the energy crisis grew worse Capstone continued to surge, peaking at $98.50 in August, giving the company an astounding market capitalization of $7.5 billion. Capstone also found no difficulty in lining up alliances with major resellers. In March 2000 it reached an agreement with Meidensha Corp. and Sumitomo Corp. to distribute the microturbines as part of co-generation systems. Later, Mitsubishi agreed to distribute the generators in Japan and Asia. In addition to 16 U.S. distributors, Capstone now had 27 distributors in seven countries and more deals in the works.

Capstone sold 790 30-kilowatt units in 2000 and introduced a larger 60 kilowatt microturbine as well. Enthusiasm for the company's prospects quickly waned, however. The stock price tumbled to less than $18 in late November, rallied back to the $40 level, but as sales tailed off in 2001, due in large measure to an economy slipping into recession, the company's future became uncertain and the price of its stock plummeted below $3.50.

The economy continued to struggle in 2002, as did Capstone, whose stock dipped to the $1 level. The company did receive some good news when United Technologies Corp., a $28 billion company serving the aerospace and building systems industries and a major player in the commercial fuel cell sector, bought a 4.9 percent stake. But Capstone also had to contend with the uncertainty that came with turnover at the top ranks. In October 2002 Almgren announced that he planned to retire.

One factor in Capstone's favor in what was an otherwise bleak year was the reported $126 million it held in cash or cash equivalents in 2003. It was not until August 2003 that the company finally settled on Almgren's replacement, hiring John Tucker, a mechanical engineer by training who had previously served as CEO and chairman of Daimler Benz Aerospace Motoren & Turbine Union in Germany. He had also worked at Allied Signal Aerospace. Less than two weeks later, Capstone received a great deal of renewed interest following the power outage that affected large portions of the Northeast and Midwest. Once again the ideas of distributed generations, or buildings generating their own electricity, began gaining currency, just as they had during the California crisis and other major outages. "Now, in the wake of last week's more-sudden blackout, the biggest in U.S. History," reported the *Wall Street Journal,* "distributed-generation backers are arguing that their time has come." Tucker commented, "One couldn't ask for a more exciting marketing and advertising campaign than what happened in the Northeast."

Tucker set to work on refining Capstone's distribution operation, paring down the network of distributors and hiring more in-house salespeople who were microturbine experts. New York City soon became Capstone's largest growth market, spurred in 2005 by Manhattan's Department of Buildings approval of the company's microturbines without permits. The dramatic rise of fuel price also bolstered the company's prospects, but in 2005 Capstone posted sales of just $17 million and a loss of $39.4 million. At the very least, its future was uncertain.

Principal Competitors

Caterpillar Inc.; Cummins, Inc.; Ingersoll-Rand Company Limited.

Further Reading

Alper, Bill, "Fired Up," *Barron's,* June 18, 2001, p. 19.

Ball, Jeffrey, "Energizing Off-Grid Power," *Wall Street Journal,* August 18, 2003, p. B1.

Cole, Benjamin Mark, "Generating Power Without Much Fuss," *Los Angeles Business Journal,* October 28, 1996, p. 1.

——, "Plugging into Energy Needs Sends Firm's Stock Soaring," *Los Angeles Business Journal,* September 11, 2000, p. 49.

Ho, Rodney, "California's Power Crisis May Give Juice to 'Microturbines,' " *Wall Street Journal,* January 23, 2001, p. B2.

Huber, Peter, and Mark Mills, "Jet Engines for Dot.coms," *Huber Mills Digital Power Report,* July 2000.

Pondel, Evan, "CEO of Chatsworth, Calif.-Based Capstone Turbine Announces Retirement Plans," *Daily News, Los Angeles,* October 29, 2002.

——, "Troubled Capstone Corp. of Chatsworth, Calif., Names New CEO," *Daily News, Los Angeles,* August 5, 2003.

Taylor, Alex III, "Gentlemen, Start Your Engine," *Fortune,* September 30, 1996, p. 156.

Wadman, Bruce, "New Concept Gs Turbine Generator," *Diesel Progress Engines & Drives,* December 1995, p. 40.

Zuckerman, Laurence, "Company Hopes Its Small Unit Will Dominate Power Market," *New York Times,* December 2, 1997, p. D1.

—Ed Dinger

Casas Bahia Comercial Ltda.

Avenida Conde Francisco Matarazzo 100, Centro
Sao Caetano do Sul, Sao Paulo 09520-900
Brazil
Telephone: (55) (11) 4225-6000
Fax: (55) (11) 4225-6431
Web site: http://www.casasbahia.com.br

Private Company
Founded: 1957
Employees: 21,425
Sales: BRL 9 billion ($3.08 billion) (2004 est.)
NAIC: 443111 Household Appliance Stores; 443112
   Radio, Television, and Other Electronics Stores;
   442110 Furniture Stores

Casas Bahia Comercial Ltda. is the largest nonfood retailer in Brazil. A mass marketer, it achieves very high turnover by selling furniture, appliances, and other household goods at low prices, chiefly on credit, to some of the poorest people in the urban parts of the Western Hemisphere. Conceived, created, and presided over by Samuel Klein, a rags-to-riches immigrant sometimes called the Sam Walton of Brazil, the retail chain remains privately held.

Selling to Brazil's Poor: 1957–89

One of nine children of a Polish-Jewish carpenter, Samuel Klein was sent to a German labor camp at the age of 19 during World War II. He escaped two years later as Soviet troops advanced westward, but his mother and five younger siblings did not survive deportation to a death camp. After the war he worked on his own—chiefly selling cigarettes and vodka to Soviet soldiers—in Germany for five years before immigrating to Bolivia with his wife and eldest son. Settling in the Sao Paulo industrial suburb of Sao Caetano do Sul in 1952, he became a backpack peddler armed with a list of 200 customers for bed linens, blankets, and towels obtained from another Jewish immigrant. After a while he was able to make his rounds in a horse-drawn cart. His clients were working-class people, many of them natives of impoverished northeastern Brazil who had migrated to the Sao Paulo metropolitan area looking for comparatively well-paid factory work. By 1957 he had 5,000 customers buying a large variety of merchandise.

Klein, in 1957, purchased a store in Sao Caetano with about 800 customers. It was named Casa Bahia because many of the customers came from the state of Bahia. He sold furniture and clothing, chiefly on installment payments (including 3 to 5 percent monthly interest) that he calculated on the spot to people who otherwise did not qualify for credit. "The poorer the customer, the more punctual his payments," Klein told Miriam Jordan for an article published in the *Wall Street Journal* in 2002. "The poor know they need to guard their reputations. . . . My talent is trusting the poor and giving the poor good service." When he opened a second store, restricted to clothing and tended by his wife, the two units became "Casas Bahia." In 1964 he opened a much larger store, specializing in furniture and appliances.

The growth of the business required more capital than Klein had been able to assemble, even though he was borrowing money from three lenders. The turning point in his career, as he saw it, came in 1970, when he purchased a half-share in a consumer-loan company named Financeira Intervest. Before the year was out, the capital from this company had enabled him to do so much more business that he was able to buy out his partner and, in effect, self-finance Casas Bahia. Klein then bought stores in neighboring cities and had 15 units in 1972. Before the year was out he had acquired a five-store chain in the port of Santos, about 60 miles southeast of Sao Paulo. He also secured a steady source of merchandise by purchasing a major furniture manufacturer, Bartira, in 1981. Casas Bahia continued to sell goods door to door until 1984, but all installment buyers had to make monthly payments at the nearest store, where other goods might catch the customer's eye. About two-thirds then made more purchases.

Klein practically doubled his chain in 1981, when he bought about 20 Lojas Colúmbia stores in the greater Sao Paulo metropolitan area. There were 43 Casas Bahia stores in early 1983. Although the Brazilian economy was sunk in recession and other chains cut back on credit to their customers, Klein forged ahead, stepping up spending freely to advertise his wares in newspapers and on radio and television and hiring the legendary

Key Dates:

1957:   Samuel Klein purchases his first Casas Bahia store.
1970:   Purchase of a stake in a consumer-loan company enables Klein to self-finance his stores.
1981:   Purchase of a furniture manufacturer gives the chain a reliable source of merchandise.
1988:   The Casas Bahia chain has grown to 56 stores with two million registered customers.
1990:   Now a 100-store chain, Casas Bahia brings in $874 million in sales.
1996:   With 250 stores in six states, Casas Bahia has become Brazil's largest nonfood retailer.
1997:   The chain's too-rapid expansion results in its first recorded loss, about $7 million.
1998:   A return to profitability and a sale of debentures restore the chain to financial health.
2004:   The 400-odd Casas Bahia stores have estimated sales of BRL 9 billion (about $3 billion).

soccer star Pelé as a pitchman. By 1990 Casas Bahia was the second largest advertiser in Brazil, spending $50 million a year but producing its ads in-house to save money.

By the end of 1988 the Casas Bahia chain had grown to 56 stores and had penetrated the interior of the state of Sao Paulo. Its number of registered customers had reached two million, and the number of sales transactions 100,000 monthly, of which 75 percent involved installment purchases, financed by Intervest. The chain kept in stock 2,000 different items, with enough merchandise on hand in a 40,000-square-meter warehouse for its fleet of 150 trucks to supply the stores for two months.

Expansion on His Own Terms in the 1990s

By 1990 Brazilian journalists were describing Klein as the Sam Walton of Brazil. His chain now came to 100 stores, which in that year brought in $874 million in sales, 60 percent more than in 1989. His personal empire also included two Volkswagen auto dealerships; Bartira, the furniture manufacturer; Intervest; a brokerage named Interbens; and the house advertising agency, Interjob. Casas Bahia was now Brazil's fifth largest nonfood retailer. Yet Klein looked anything like a tycoon, receiving journalists in the modest headquarters of his enterprise, still located in Sao Caetano, clad in a cheap open-neck sports shirt and slacks, with sandals on his feet.

Because Klein hated to pay rent, almost half of Casas Bahia's stores were the company's own property. In buying merchandise from about 300 suppliers, Klein preferred to pay immediately in cash, if possible. In dealing with them he had powerful leverage, since the chain was buying more than 10 percent of the production of the principal national manufacturers of home appliances. Even so, the suppliers liked dealing with him because he came to a decision immediately and paid on the spot. Much of this work was being conducted by his younger son, Saúl, while the older one, Michael, concentrated on finance. But Klein was not averse to micromanaging his enterprise by such means as personally determining the price of

sale for any of the thousands of items that the chain was selling, using as a guide the newspaper ads of competing chains.

All Klein's efforts could not, however, keep Casas Bahia's sales from sinking during the economic crisis of the early 1990s. Sales dropped to $618 million in 1991 and nosedived to $353 million in 1992, almost, but not quite, putting the company in the red. Klein closed 15 stores, citing high rents, and slashed employment from 9,500 to 6,000. However, the units closed were in places where Casas Bahia already had a presence, and he opened in five more cities in the interior of the state of Sao Paulo while contemplating entering the neighboring state of Minais Gerais.

The year 1993 saw little improvement, but in 1994, when a reform program ended the hyperinflation that had eroded purchasing power, sales of $841 million came close to matching the 1990 peak. The following year Casas Bahia entered Rio de Janeiro by paying almost $60 million for the 33-unit Casas Garson chain. By the end of 1996 there were some 250 Casas Bahia stores in six states, with sales that year reaching an amazing $2.83 billion, making the chain the largest nonfood retailer in Brazil. One of the units was said to be the biggest in Latin America, with almost 150,000 square meters of space. But this headlong expansion did not come without problems. The expenses needed to field so many more units and extend credit to so many more customers had stretched the chain's finances to the point that ten banks refused to loan it more money without auditing the books. Greater transparency was also needed so that the firm could issue $250 million in debentures, since even Klein conceded that his firm's debt of $800 million was almost as large as its assets.

Buffeted by the fluctuating fortunes of the Brazilian economy, Casas Bahia sustained a 17 percent drop in sales in 1997 and its first recorded loss, about $7 million. "They had problems, but they adopted an intelligent strategy," an executive of a rival chain told José Roberto Caetano for an article in *Exame*. "They kept their prices high, at least 15 percent higher than ours. They relied on the loyalty of their clients. A majority of their customers . . . continued buying from Bahia because they were afraid of losing credit and not being able to get it from another store." After opening its books to outsiders for the first time, Casas Bahia successfully floated its debentures and a six-month promissary note. The firm made a comfortable profit in 1998 and, according to Klein, reduced its debt to only 15 percent of its assets. He continued to operate by his own rules, determined not to take on shareholders or deal with banks any more than absolutely necessary. Only he, his wife, and his sons had the authority to sign checks. Rejecting widespread just-in-time practices, he stocked his warehouse (at 230,000 square meters, the biggest in South America) with 60 days of merchandise and transported it to the stores solely in the company's own trucks.

Still Doing It His Own Way: 2000–05

Casas Bahia had over 340 stores in seven states and the federal district of Brasilia in 2002, when its sales came to BRL 4.2 billion ($1.44 billion, based on the average currency rate for the year), and its profit to BRL 53 million ($18.15 million). The company had 20,000 employees, 500 suppliers, and 10,000 merchandise items, of which 4,500 were available online. A fleet of 1,040 trucks delivered the goods to the stores. The company had ten million registered customers, seven million of them active. Seventy percent of its sales were of home appliances, and the chain was buying and selling 30 percent of all home appliances manufactured in Brazil. Furniture accounted for another 25 percent of sales, and miscellaneous goods such as clothing and bicycles for the remaining 5 percent.

The Casas Bahia customer had an income ranging from virtually nothing to ten times the monthly minimum wage of BRL 200 (about $70), a range that comprised 84 percent of Brazil's population. The typical customer was only earning twice the minimum salary, and half were not formally employed at all. Ninety percent of all sales were on credit, with the rest in cash or by credit card, an option that Casas Bahia had only recently (and reluctantly) introduced, the last major Brazilian retailer to do so. Using information technology, the chain had transformed its assessment of customer creditworthiness to a near science. If a new customer applied for credit to buy merchandise costing less than BRL 600 (about $200), no proof of income was required, only a permanent address. Those applying for more credit were quickly evaluated, using a computerized system, and offered a credit limit based on occupation, income, and presumed expenses. Those rejected were directed to a credit analyst for further evaluation.

The company's 900 credit analysts had been trained to formulate questions and interpret responses carefully and with subtlety. If an applicant presented himself as a manual laborer, the analyst checked his hands for calluses and his clothing for stains. A stonemason might, for example, be asked to explain why he wanted to buy a computer. Perhaps he wanted it for his children, but perhaps he really intended to purchase it for another person, a practice that accounted for about half of all the chain's defaulted debts. In the end, an estimated 16 percent of applicants were being denied credit. The company's default ratio of 8 to 8.5 percent was only about half that of its competitors. A team of ''reminders'' made phone calls and wrote letters to customers whose payments were past due but also made it clear that the company would support them in difficulties and might allow them to renegotiate their debts. A 2001 ''amnesty'' canceled the debts of a million customers blacklisted since 1997. Those customers who paid promptly received a yellow preferred-client card, sometimes proudly displayed, as in the case of the hot-dog vendor who Jordan visited in a two-room shack that she described as ''a veritable Casas Bahia showroom, with a bed, bookcase, sofa and kitchen cabinet from the chain.''

Installment payments were made over a period of one to 15 months, with the average term being six months and the average interest rate 4.13 percent a month. Furniture accounted for 31 percent of the goods purchased, with television sets accounting for 14 percent and audio equipment for 10 percent. The interest portion of consumer loans was sold to banks and consumer-loan companies, since Casas Bahia had sold Intervest by this time.

Casas Bahia retained its reputation for frugality and simplicity, operating with only three levels between store manager and top executive. Managers enjoyed significant freedom as long as they met predetermined revenue and profit targets. A store manager had the right to cut prices by as much as 10 percent, and a regional manager by up to 25 percent, without calling Michael

Klein. Salespeople were guaranteed a salary of BRL 500 (about $165) a month, in conformity with the law, but expected, and were expected, to make their living instead by a 2 percent commission on sales. The average salesperson was earning about BRL 1,500 (about $500) a month. Deliverymen, as well as sales clerks, were held to a company standard of deportment and dress and expected to make all deliveries within 48 hours, carrying away old appliances or furniture if requested.

All Casas Bahia stores were linked electronically so that headquarters could monitor sales by product and store. Store and distribution-center inventories were monitored the same way. If a store did not meet sales or profit targets, a team was assembled at headquarters to address the problem. About 30 stores were closed in 2003, but about the same amount were opened, based on a standard of attracting at least 100,000 customers to any given store. A few Casas Bahia stores were in neighborhoods that catered to customers with incomes above the chain's target level, but these were not considered attractive because high rents and the tendency of buyers to pay in cash rather than seek credit resulted in lower profits.

Casas Bahia's sales rose to almost BRL 6 billion (about $2.11 billion) in 2003 and to an estimated BRL 9 billion (about $3.08 billion) in 2004, when its profit nearly doubled to about BRL 150 million (about $50 million). Its sales exceeded those of its next four competitors combined. There were about 400 stores. Furniture from the group's own Bartira unit provided a profit margin twice as high as from the appliances sold by Casas Bahia but made by others. A second, $25-million, furniture production facility opened in 2003. There were three distribution centers: the largest in Sao Paulo, the others in Rio de Janeiro and Ribeirao Preto. The company was planning to build four more in the biggest northern cities: Belém, Fortaleza, Recife, and Salvador.

Casas Bahia's amazing growth put the chain's finances under strain and led to a contract with Banco Bradesco S.A., the nation's largest bank, whereby the bank assumed the direct financing of part of the chain's customer purchases, freeing funds for further expansion. Michael Klein said that Casas Bahia wanted to have 1,000 stores and annual sales of BRL 20 billion by the end of 2010. But to do so the chain would have to expand into unexploited terrain, that of Brazil's tropical north and northeast, a task one competitor compared to Napoleon invading Russia. The chain's growth was also having an effect on the Brazilian economy at large. An article in *Exame* by Tiago Lethbridge quoted Michael Klein in these words; ''Today, in Brazil, whoever wants to have relevant participation in his market has to sell to us. If a large company doesn't approve our conditions, others will form a line to seek a place on our shelves.'' One of these suppliers told Lethbridge: ''Negotiations always take place at the end of the month, when the industry seeks to meet its sales goals and empty its stock. Therefore, hard-pressed, the suppliers offer big discounts.'' Some firms were willing to take a loss simply to maintain their share of the market. Casas Bahia was accounting for 36 percent of all the washing machines, 25 percent of the refrigerators, and 20 percent of the television sets and DVDs made in Brazil.

With Casas Bahia having little to fear from its traditional competitors, the company was looking over the horizon to do battle with a perhaps more dangerous rival than it had ever faced, the hypermarkets. One of the great unknowns was the capability of such hypermarket chains as Carrefour, Extra, and Big to meet the needs of lower income Brazilians. Another potential problem was the rapid spread of credit card use, which by 2005 had grown to account for one-fifth of Casas Bahia's sales and thus threatened both its considerable income from interest and new purchases by customers reentering the stores to make installment payments. Finally, there was the question of succession, since the chain's founder had passed the age of 80. Michael, who cited Jewish tradition favoring the eldest son, was in day-to-day-charge of finance, stores, distribution, fleet, technology, and employees. Saúl was in charge of supplies, customer sales, and marketing.

Principal Competitors

Globex Utilidades S.A.; Lojas Cem S.A.; Lojas Colombo S.A. Comércio de Utilidades Domésticos; Magazine Luíza.

Further Reading

Awad, Elias, *Samuel Klein e Casas Bahia,* Sao Paulo: Novo Século Editora, 2003.

Blecher, Nelson, ''Máquina de vender,'' *Exame,* February 8, 2004, pp. 44–54.

Caetano, José, ''Na Contramao,'' *Exame,* September 22, 1999, pp. 40–42, 44.

Jordan, Miriam, ''A Retailer in Brazil Has Become Rich by Courting Poor,'' *Wall Street Journal,* June 11, 2002, pp. A1, A8.

Lethbridge, Taigo, ''O avanço da Casas Bahia,'' *Exame,* February 2, 2005, pp. 54–56.

Prahalad, C.K., *The Fortune at the Bottom of the Pyramid,* Upper Saddle River, N.J.: Wharton School Publishing, 2005, pp. 117–46.

Vassallo, Cláudia, ''Rindo do qué?'' *Exame,* January 29, 1997, pp. 56–58.

Watanabe, Mário, ''Dedicaçao total a você - e à properidade,'' *Exame,* May 1, 1991, pp. 54–60.

—Robert Halasz

Central European Distribution Corporation

2 Bala Plaza, Suite 300
Bala Cynwyd, Pennsylvania 19004
U.S.A.
Telephone: (610) 660-7817
Fax: (610) 667-3308
Web site: http://www.ced-c.com

Public Company
Incorporated: 1990 as Carey Agri International Poland
    Sp. z.o.o.
Employees: 2,015
Sales: $580.7 million (2004)
Stock Exchanges: NASDAQ
Ticker Symbol: CEDC
NAIC: 424810 Beer and Ale Merchant Wholesalers

Although a public company listed on the NASDAQ that maintains its headquarters in Bala Cynwyd, Pennsylvania, Central European Distribution Corporation (CEDC) operates in Poland, where it imports and distributes nearly 800 brands of beverages and other products. CEDC maintains 52 regional distribution centers in Poland's major urban areas, distributing its products to some 20,000 outlets, including hotels, restaurants, bars, nightclubs, supermarkets, gas stations, and duty free stores. The company's product mix includes imported and domestic beer; Polish vodka, which accounts for three-quarters of all sales; imported spirits, including vodka; wines; soft drinks, including water; and cigars. Over the years, especially early on, CEDC tried its hand at importing a number of products but focused on spirits because of the prodigious drinking habits of Poles. The 2005 acquisition of Polish distilleries has positioned the company to move beyond distribution to production, giving it the potential to become a powerhouse in the company's liquor industry.

Background Leading to Founding in 1990

CEDC was founded by William O. Carey and his partner Jeffrey Peterson. A Wisconsin native, Carey moved to Florida where in the 1950s he became a dairy farmer. In the late 1950s he began exporting cattle to South America, but it was not until he became partners with Jeffrey Peterson that he began expanding his horizons to the global market, a move that would one day lead the pair to Poland. Peterson had seen a good bit of the world, as a child visiting Guatemala with his grandmother, a United Fruit Company teacher. After a tour of duty in Vietnam he attended the University of South Florida in the early 1970s and earned credits by spending several quarters traveling to such countries as Greece, Egypt, and Ecuador. Upon returning to the university he rented a house from Carey and the two became friends. At the time, 1976, Carey was shipping cattle to Costa Rica on propeller-driven DC-3 airplanes, and on occasion Peterson tagged along for weekend getaways. Peterson then went to work on the political campaigns of Ronald Reagan and George H.W. Bush and launched a company that taped speeches. After selling it he approached Carey about going into business together. "I said, 'You've been sending cattle to South America, but you ought to form a company and we'll go after the world,' " Peterson recalled in a 1999 interview with the *Sarasota-Herald Tribune.* "Bill said, 'Okay, as long as it doesn't cost me anything.' "

In the early 1980s Carey and Peterson formed Carey Agri International and began shipping cattle, mostly dairy, around the world. Business in Nigeria was good until a military coup took place and their partner, the country's oil minister, was imprisoned. In the mid-1980s Carey Agri began shipping dairy cattle to Iraq, which was then at war with Iran. Following the end of that contract in 1987, the company did smaller deals in Morocco, Egypt, and the Philippines. Yet when the United States ended a shipping credits program, and tariff restrictions continued, Carey Agri began searching for a market offering new opportunities. In January 1990 the company decided on Poland, and later in the year formed Carey Agri International Poland Sp. z.o.o.

With the fall of the Iron Curtain in the late 1980s the former Soviet Block countries attracted Western businessmen. Poland was much quicker than Russia and other Eastern European countries to adapt to the Western free enterprise system, due in large part to the influence of the Solidarity labor movement. Carey and Peterson were already familiar with Poland because

Company Perspectives:

CEDC is one of the leading importers and distributors of alcoholic beverages in Poland.

they had previously bought cattle there. They were also familiar to the U.S. Department of Agriculture, which helped Carey Agri establish itself in Poland through the embassy, becoming one of Poland's first private exporters. Peterson and a translator named ''Ziggy'' now began to travel across Poland buying cattle from state-owned farms and later individual farmers. During the course of his travels Peterson took note that nowhere in the country could they find a cold beer. In the first year the company bought 10,000 cattle, as well as some horses, which were then shipped to such countries as Croatia, Italy, Serbia, Slovenia, Turkey, and Yugoslavia for use as food.

Chance Encounter in Early 1990s

During this time Peterson took a trip to Paris to attend a food show. Tired of talking to cattle people, Peterson wandered around and met up with some people who worked for Australia's Foster beer. Fond of Australians from his Vietnam days, Peterson enjoyed a few beers with his new friends, who soon convinced him to buy a couple truckloads of beer to sell in Poland. When he returned to Poland, Peterson sold the 4,000 cases in an hour. Sensing an opportunity he scrounged 100,000 cases of Foster from Spain, then ordered 32,000 cases of Grolsch, 20,000 cases of Michelob, and 50,000 cases of Busch. He also convinced the struggling Pittsburgh Brewing Company to make ''American Beer'' on an exclusive basis for Carey Agri.

At the same time that Carey Agri was beginning to make the shift from cattle to spirits, the company received a new man in Poland, Carey's son, William V. Carey. The younger Carey had graduated with a degree in economics from the University of Florida in 1987 and was an aspiring professional golfer who failed to make it on the South African tour and other small tours. After his father, who was sponsoring his golfing career, urged him to get a real job, Carey decided to join Peterson in Poland, expecting to stay just two or three months. He would end up relocating to the country, marrying a Polish woman, and starting a family.

The decision to distribute beer proved to be well timed, given that increased competition in the cattle business had virtually eliminated any chance for a profit, prompting Carey Agri to exit that business. In addition to beer, the company for a time tried importing any number of products, including used cars, but it was beer that Poles wanted. According to the *Tampa Tribune,* ''there were moments in the early years when running a liquor business in Poland was the equivalent of running a saloon in Dodge City. 'You had to watch your back,' Peterson said. 'The KGB was still around, and it was unclear whether Russia would try to come back in. . . . It was like the wild, wild West.' '' The company also faced problems with the government. At one point taxes on imported beers were significantly increased, and the company managed to pull strings to get a major shipment through under the previous rate. Although it

was just a one-time arrangement, the higher taxes did little to blunt the company's momentum. Carey Agri added imported spirits and wines, catering to the Poles' increasing preference for beverages other than the country's traditional vodka. When Poland began to accelerate the privatization of retail outlets in 1993, the company was quick to establish a distribution network that could offer next-day delivery service. Over the next four years it opened seven branches to provide regional coverage. Because of Poland's inadequate road infrastructure, however, the company had to limit the number of distribution branches it operated. It concentrated on the country's major cities, serving in particular the country's fast growing chains of hypermarkets (combination supermarket and department stores). To make sure it was not dependent on the transportation services of local companies, which were hardly established ventures, Carey Agri began assembling its own fleet of delivery trucks.

Carey Agri became the exclusive distributor of a number of brands, then took a major step in 1996 when it began to distribute domestic vodka in Poland. In that same year, the company formed an alliance with United Distillers, which produced Johnnie Walker, in a deal that included financing. Carey Agri looked for additional funding in 1997, when it also suffered a severe setback, as the elder Carey was killed when a train struck his car near his Florida farm. His son succeeded him as chief executive officer and chairman of the company, and continued to operate from Poland. In the United States, Peterson would maintain the company's legal headquarters in Alexandria, Virginia, later moving to Sarasota, Florida, and finally to Bala Cynwyd, Pennsylvania. The need for a U.S. headquarters was part of the company's next step: going public to raise funds needed to acquire rival distributors.

Taken Public in 1997

In September 1997 Central European Distribution Corporation was incorporated in Delaware and the Carey Agri operations were folded into it. Arranging an initial public offering of stock proved difficult, however. According to *Business Week* in a 2005 article, ''CEDC was a tough sell. Carey and Peterson pounded on the doors of more than 20 investment banking houses in New York. All of them took a pass. 'They didn't know Poland, and the business was small,' Carey recalls. 'We were ready to give up.' Then New York Investment banking boutique Brean Murray & Co. took a flier on Carey, helping him raise $10.8 million in an IPO in 1998.''

Also of note in 1998, CEDC opened its first retail store, soon followed by two others. The company also began carrying such products as Camus Cognac, DeKuyper Liquers, Dunhill Cigars, and Evian Water. All told, in 1998 the company recorded sales of $54 million, the start of a period of exceptional growth as CEDC began acquiring other companies to expand market share. In March 1999 it acquired Multi Trade Company for $2.9 million and stock, picking up Poland's largest distributor of domestic vodka as well as expanding the distribution of CEDC's other products to northeastern Poland where Multi Trade was based. Its increased size also provided CEDC with a pricing advantage with suppliers. Two months later CEDC spent $1.8 million and issued another 100,000 shares of stock to acquire The Cellar of Fine Wines Sp. z.o.o., a major importer and distributor of premium wines. With the addition of a number of fine wines, CEDC

Key Dates:

1990: Carey Agri International Poland Sp. z.o.o. is founded by William O. Carey Jeffrey Peterson.
1996: Company begins distributing Polish vodka.
1997: Carey is killed in traffic accident.
1998: Company is taken public as Central European Distribution Corporation.
2005: Company acquires Bols Sp. z.o.o., Poland's third largest distiller.

created an opening to sell its beer and spirits portfolio to better restaurants, bars, nightclubs, and hotels.

In the early 2000s CEDC continued to expand its operations. In early 2000 it acquired Jama Co. in a $5.2 million cash and stock deal that added 2,000 customer accounts and bolstered CEDC's position in western Poland, a key market enjoying strong growth because of its proximity to Germany. Also in 2000 CEDC became the exclusive supplier of beer, wine, and spirits to CPN, Poland's largest operator of gas and convenience stores with 1,400 outlets, of which 800 sold alcoholic beverages. In addition, CEDC looked to spur sales by becoming Poland's first e-commerce company, launching a web site to sell products directly to consumers. The acquisition of competing distributors continued in 2001 and 2002. Astor Sp. z.o.o. was added in April 2001, strengthening CEDC's business in north central Poland. In April 2002 Damianex S.A., a distributor in southeastern Poland, was purchased for approximately $9 million in cash and stock, as AGIS S.A., a distributor in northern Poland, was acquired at the cost of $6.7 million in cash and stock. CEDC completed three acquisitions in 2003, paying $1.8 million for Dako Galant, a distributor in northwest Poland; picking up Panta Hurt Sp. z.o.o., a Warsaw-area distributor for $2 million; and Multi-Ex Sp. z.o.o., a distributor in the city of Kalisz, at a cost of $1.45 million in cash and stock.

CEDC continued in 2004 to identify and acquire key regional distribution companies. It paid $1.6 million for Miro Sp. z.o.o., based in Poland's second largest city, Miro, and nearly $2.4 million for Polnis Distribution, strengthening CEDC's position in Poland's third largest city, Lodz. In 2004 CEDC also acquired Saol Sp. z.o.o., a major distributor in the Krakow region. As a result of its acquisition spree, CEDC generated sales of $580 million in 2004 and net income of $21.8 million.

CEDC took important steps in 2005 to establish itself as a manufacturer and a player in the international spirits market. It forged a strategic alliance with French company Remy Cointreau, then negotiated the $270 million purchase of Bols Sp. z.o.o., Poland's third largest distiller, from Remy. Later in the year CEDC agreed to pay $312 million for a 61 percent interest in Polmos Bialystok, a government owned distiller and Poland's second largest vodka producer. Also in 2005, CEDC acquired Delikates, a central Poland distributor, the addition of which solidified the company's position in the western part of the country. It was an important part of the continuing strategy to dominate the Polish market, but was clearly overshadowed by CEDC's move into production. To help finance the distillery acquisitions, the company took on considerable debt, issuing $396 million worth of euro bonds to help pay for the purchase. CEDC had the potential to become a regional powerhouse, perhaps fulfilling a longstanding goal of doing business in such neighboring countries as Hungary or the Czech Republic, but whether it could succeed with its new strategy remained to be seen.

Principal Subsidiaries

Carey Agri International Poland Sp. z.o.o.; Multi Trade Company Sp. z.o.o.; Mira Sp. z.o.o.; Fine Wines and Spirits, Sp. z.o.o.

Principal Competitors

Carlsberg A/S; Heineken NV; SABMiller plc.

Further Reading

Barrett, Amy, ''Bottoms Up—And Profits, Too,'' *Business Week,* September 12, 2005, p. 80.

Passariello, Christina, ''Poland's Alcohol Market Increases Its Appeal to Large Spirits Firms,'' *Wall Street Journal,* May 4, 2005, p. 1.

''The Polish Connection,'' *Tampa Tribune,* November 22, 1999, p. 8.

Rigsby, G.G., ''Importer Quenches Poland,'' *Tampa Bay Business Journal,* May 10, 2002.

Sauer, Matthew, ''From Bovine to Beer,'' *Sarasota Herald Tribune,* June 14, 1999, p. 10.

——, ''Sarasota-Based Company Having Banner Year in Poland,'' *Sarasota Herald Tribune,* March 30, 1999, p. 1D.

—Ed Dinger

Chi Mei Optoelectronics Corporation

1 Chi-Yeh Road
Tainan Science Based Ind'l Park
Tainan
Taiwan
Telephone: +886 6 505 1888
Fax: +886 6 505 1800
Web site: http://www.cmo.com.tw

Public Subsidiary of Chi Mei Group
Incorporated: 1998
Employees: 12,400
Sales: $3.21 billion (2004)
Stock Exchanges: Taiwan
Ticker Symbol: CMO
NAIC: 334419 Other Electronic Component
  Manufacturing

Established only in 1998, Chi Mei Optoelectronics Corporation (CMO) is one of the world's leading manufacturers of thin-film transistor liquid crystal displays, better known as TFT-LCD flat-panel displays. The company produces more than 4.5 million flat-panel displays per year, and expects to top five million panels annually before 2006. CMO operates four LCM (liquid crystal display module) plants in Taiwan's Southern Taiwan Science Park (STSP). That complex was subsidized by the Taiwanese government as part of its decision to make LCD displays one of the island's key manufacturing areas. The company's production operations include a 5.5G (generation) plant for production of 27-inch displays and a 6.0G plant for production of 32-inch displays. In 2005, CMO announced its intention to open an LCM plant in mainland China, in part because of a labor shortage in Taiwan. The opening of that plant will help CMO reclaim the industry's top spot from chief rival AU Optronics. In addition to TFT-LCDs, CMO has been developing its own organic light-emitting diode (OLED) display capacity; the company also produces color filters. Chairman and founder Hsu Wen-lung, who suffered criticism from Beijing because of his support for Taiwan's independence-minded government, stepped down from his position in 2005 as part of the company's decision to enter the

mainland. CMO is listed on the Taiwan Stock Exchange but remains controlled by Chi Mei Group, a petrochemicals conglomerate established by Hsu's father in 1950.

Made in Taiwan in the 1950s

Few companies so closely mirrored Taiwan's evolution in the second half of the 20th century as Chi Mei Group and its publicly listed subsidiary Chi Mei Optoelectronics (CMO). Taiwan's economy was virtually non-existent at the end of the 1940s, as the newly established government set out to convert itself from a predominantly agrarian base. The country turned toward the industrial sector, investing heavily to begin producing low-cost, and often low-quality, consumer items. With low wages and a vast workforce, Taiwan quickly became a source for discount goods the world over.

Chi Mei played a major role in this transition. The company originally focused on the retail sector, and was founded as a small children's clothing store by Shu-Ho Shi in 1950. Shu chose the name Chi Mei, from the Chinese words for "Unique Beauty," for his store. Yet Chi Mei's focus quickly expanded beyond retail sales.

A number of factors converged in the early 1950s to present a major opportunity for the company. Taiwan's interest in developing its industrial sector, as well as the strong role the government played in directing the country's economic and corporate policy, created a fertile environment for a new breed of entrepreneurs. At the same time, the development of new plastic technologies had opened up an extraordinarily large range of production possibilities. The timing for the new materials was perfect; the Western world was undergoing a period of sustained economic growth. The booming economies of the West not only created unprecedented levels of disposable income, but also steady advances in leisure time. Yet another factor came into play in the 1950s and 1960s: with more and more women joining the workforce, families began to shrink in size. Fewer children meant that parents were willing to spend more on each individual child, stimulating a surge in demand for children's toys. Meanwhile, the use of plastics opened up a whole new range of potential shapes and colors, introducing one of the most creative eras of toy-making ever known.

Company Perspectives:

Mission Statement: Business as a Way to Pursue Fulfillment. Human Management and Harmony are the most important and have been the operating principles of the whole Chi Mei Group.

Chi Mei entered the children's toy market in 1953, setting up Chi Mei with its own manufacturing plant. The initial facility was quite modest, occupying just 26 square meters, manned by four employees. The company began producing toys and other household items, and the words "Made in Taiwan" quickly became ubiquitous throughout the Western world. Shu was joined by son Hsu Wen-lung, who became the driving force behind the company's conversion into an industrial powerhouse.

By the late 1950s, however, Chi Mei had recognized a greater opportunity in producing the basic plastics materials themselves. In 1957, the company launched a research and development effort in order to establish its own methods for the production of acrylic sheets. This led to the creation of a new subsidiary, Chi Mei Industrial Co., led by Hsu Wen-lung. The company built a new industrial complex at Yen Chen Tainan, and launched production in 1960.

Chi Mei brought its acrylic sheets to the export market in 1963. Soon after the company launched production of one of its most successful products, Kibi Board, plywood sheets coated with decorative paper, sealed under a layer of polyester resin. By 1967, the company had developed a second, similar product, Mega Board, which differed from Kibi Board in that it was coated with an aminoalkyd resin. By then, too, the company also had begun to produce buttons, starting in 1964, and quickly became one of the world's leading suppliers of buttons.

The success of its finished products enabled Chi Mei to begin its transformation into one of Taiwan's leading petrochemicals groups toward the end of the 1960s. This effort began in 1965, with the creation of the company's first technology transfer joint venture with Mitsubishi. The following year, Chi Mei launched a new research and development effort to build expertise in the production of expandable polystyrene (EPS). In 1968, Chi Mei turned to Mitsubishi again for technology, forming a new joint venture for the production of a larger range of polystyrene types, including general purpose polystyrene and high-impact polystyrene resins.

By the early 1970s, Chi Mei had established its first overseas plant, in the Philippines. The company's polystyrene operations also became its largest component, topping its acrylic sheets sales by the middle of the decade. Through the next decade, the company continued to develop new plastics and petrochemicals capacity, becoming a leading producer of acrylic granulates and acrylic extrusion sheets. Into the 1990s, Chi Mei expanded its technology to include production of TPE rubber and other plastics. By then, the company had, in large part, exited its former finished goods production, dropping buttons in 1982 and both the Kibi and Mega Boards in 1985.

TFT-LCD Leader in the 2000s

By the mid-1990s, however, Taiwan faced increasing competitive pressure from other emerging, low-cost markets. The country's relatively high wages meant that it increasingly was unable to compete against the growing industrial strength of the developing markets. The gradual emergence of mainland China as a low-cost consumer goods producer especially promised to transform the industrial landscape on a global scale.

In recognition of the shifting situation, the Taiwanese government began encouraging the transformation of its economy toward higher-end technological sectors. Into the mid-1990s, the TFT-LCD market had becoming one of the most promising of the high-tech growth markets. The development of new generations of portable telephones, the promise of digital cameras, and the increasing development of portable computers as a consumer and even household appliance, but especially the development of the first generation of LCD-based televisions, encouraged the Taiwanese government to target that sector for its new technology initiatives.

Another factor played a role in Taiwan's development as a center for world TFT-LCD production. Liquid crystals had been discovered as early as 1888 by Friedrich Reinitzer, a botanist in Austria. Yet the first practical application of liquid crystals did not take place until the late 1960s, when the United States' RCA launched the first display utilizing LCD technology. During the 1970s, however, the center of LCD technology shifted to Japan, and the country emerged as the global center for LCD production. The Japanese jealously guarded their technology, maintaining control of the market into the late 1990s.

Yet the collapse of the Japanese economy during the decade left the country's TFT-LCD manufacturers cash-strapped just at a time when the world saw a surge in demand for TFT-LCD displays. In order to ensure the continued growth in production, the Japanese manufacturers began seeking joint ventures elsewhere, in South Korea and especially Taiwan. There, the Japanese companies found a ready list of cash-rich companies willing to enter TFT-LCD production.

Chi Mei decided to enter the market in 1997, setting up operations for the production of color filters, under Chi Mei Electronics (CME), and TFT-LCD displays, under Chi Mei Optoelectronics (CMO). By 1998, the company had signed on its first technology partner, Fujitsu, which entered into an alliance with CME. This was soon followed by the group's first TFT-LCD partnership, again with Fujitsu. By 1999, CMO and Fujitsu had strengthened their partnership to include an agreement to co-develop new large-screen LCD technologies. Chi Mei also began production of LCD monitors, under a new subsidiary set up that year, Arch Technology Inc. By the end of that year, as well, CMO had succeeded in producing 14-inch TFT-LCD panels. This led the company to sign a new long-term development supply alliance with Dell Computer.

CMO took over the operations of CME in 2000 as the company geared up its vertical integration model, an important part of its strategy for its future display technologies growth. The company also was gaining expertise in large-sized panels, launching its first 18-inch display panel early the next year.

Key Dates:

1950: Shu-Ho Shi sets up the Chi Mei retail store selling children's clothing in Taiwan.
1953: Chi Mei launches industrial production of plastic toys and household goods.
1957: Under son Hsu Wen-lung, Chi Mei begins production of acrylic sheeting.
1968: The company launches production of polystyrene.
1997: The company announces its intention to begin production of TFT-LCD panels.
1998: Chi Mei Optoelectronics (CMO) is created.
1999: A technology transfer agreement is made with Fujitsu.
2001: The company acquires an LCD fab in Japan from IBM.
2004: Hsu Wen-lung steps down as chairman after the mainland Chinese government labels him "a shameless anti-Chinese bigot."
2005: CMO receives approval to set up production facilities in mainland China.

The year 2001 marked a new milestone for CMO's development into one of the world's leading producers of TFT-LCD panels. In August of that year, the company agreed to take over IBM of Japan's Yasu Industrial Complex, acquiring not only its Japanese production capacity, but especially its technology. This acquisition led the company to focus on its panel display development, selling off the consumer-oriented Arch Technology.

By 2002, CMO had unveiled its first 30-inch TFT-LCD television display. In that year, CMO went public, the first member of the Chi Mei Group to do so. By then, CMO had become the motor for Chi Mei's overall growth, serving as the group's largest revenue generator.

The maturation of Taiwan's LCD industry was clearly in place in the early 2000s. Not only had the island become the center of worldwide LCD production, boasting most of the world's top five producers, the country also had emerged as a leading technological center. This development was highlighted by CMO's announcement in 2003 that it had decided to develop its own color-filter technology for new generation display panels, becoming the first of the big six Taiwanese producers to set up its own color filter facilities.

CMO launched a new fifth-generation production facility in 2003, and began preparations to open a sixth generation and seventh generation plant at mid-decade. By 2005, the company had developed its expertise in the production of panels up to 32 inches in size. This led the company to reach an agreement with Sony Corporation to sell its 3G plant in Japan in 2004.

CMO remained the last of the major Taiwanese LCD producers to enter the mainland Chinese market, in part because of founder and Chairman Hsu Wen-lung's open support for Taiwan President Chen Shui-ban. Yet difficulties in recruiting new workers, especially the lower wages of the Chinese mainland, left CMO in a vulnerable position vis-à-vis its competitors.

When CMO launched plans to develop production capacity in the mainland, however, it found itself in the middle of the political battle being waged between Beijing and Taiwan. After the Chinese government's newspaper, the *People's Daily,* branded Hsu as "a shameless anti-Chinese bigot," and further indicated that the country would not welcome "these sort of Taiwanese business people," Hsu conceded defeat and resigned from his post as chairman of CMO. Then in 2005, Hsu gave a speech in which he publicly stated that Taiwan and the mainland were part of "one" China. Soon afterward, CMO received permission to build its first LCD module plant in China. The move was expected to help the company reclaim its title as industry leader, which was captured by rival AU Optronics in August of that year. From toy maker to global technological leader, Chi Mei, with its publicly listed subsidiary CMO, had established itself as a quintessential member of Taiwan's industrial community.

Principal Subsidiaries

International Display Technology Ltd.

Principal Competitors

Samsung Corporation; LG-Philips; Sharp Corporation; AU Optronics; Chungwha Picture Tubes, Ltd.

Further Reading

"AUO Outstripped CMO in 32-Inch TV Panel Shipment in July," *Taiwan Economic News,* August 25, 2005.
"Chi Mei Corp. Stresses Vertical Integration, R&D in TFT-LCD," *China Post,* October 7, 2002.
"Chi Mei to Raise Up to TWD 120 Billion in Latest Fundraising, Expansion Effort," *China Post,* March 29, 2005.
"CMO to Set Up LCM Plant in Mainland China," *Taiwan Economic News,* July 25, 2005.
Hille, Kathrin, "Chi Mei Optoelectronics Chairman Steps Down," *Financial Times,* June 16, 2004, p. 23.
"IBM Becomes Chi Mei's Second Japanese Partner," *New Materials Japan,* August 2001, p. 7.
"Japanese Giants Turn to Taiwan for LCD Displays," *Computergram International,* March 8, 1999.
Norris, Graham, "Chi Mei Expects End to Large Panel Glut," *Financial Times,* July 30, 2005, p. 8.
"Taiwan Seen to Emerge As World's No. 1 Maker of Large-Sized TFT-LCD Panels," *Taiwan Economic News,* March 14, 2005.
"Taiwan's Display Panel Giant Plans to Build More Plants," *AP Online,* October 30, 2003.

—M.L. Cohen

Chicago Mercantile Exchange Holdings Inc.

20 S. Wacker Drive
Chicago, Illinois 60606-7499
U.S.A.
Telephone: (312) 930-1000
Toll Free: (800) 331-3332
Fax: (312) 466-4410
Web site: http://www.cme.com

Public Company
Founded: 1898 as The Chicago Butter and Egg Board
Employees: 1,283
Sales: $732.5 million (2004)
Stock Exchanges: New York
Ticker Symbol: CME
NAIC: 523210 Securities and Commodity Exchanges

Chicago Mercantile Exchange Holdings Inc. is the parent company of Chicago Mercantile Exchange Inc. (CME), which specializes in the trading of futures (contracts to buy or sell something on a specified future date) and options on futures. At its core, the CME, also known as ''the Merc,'' plays an important role in global risk management. It is involved in four major product areas: commodities, the CME's original focus; foreign exchange; interest rates; and stock indexes. The CME is famous for its hectic trading floors where ''price discovery'' is pursued by traders practicing the open outcry system, shouting out prices and quantities and also using hand signals to make themselves understood over the din. The system has been abused in the past, resulting in a major Federal Bureau of Investigation (FBI) sting operation in the late 1980s, but traditionalists cling to open outcry nonetheless. In recent years, however, the method has been undercut by the rise of electronic trading, including CME's Globex round-the-clock electronic trading system. Many traders now trade electronically as well as in the pits. The CME is a public company listed on the New York Stock Exchange.

The Merc: An Outgrowth of Chicago's 19th-Century Rise to Power

The opening of the Erie Canal in 1825 not only transformed New York City into the United States' commercial and financial capital, it gave rise to the country's ''Second City.'' Chicago, advantageously located on the shores of Lake Michigan and, later, a major railroad hub, became the bridge between the farm products of the Midwest and New York and the other major cities of the East Coast. In the mid-1800s Chicago emerged as the country's largest market for corn, wheat, lumber, and meat. It was through the grain market that the futures market became a key factor in the city's financial system. Because transporting grain from the farm to the city was dicey, with rain in the summer and snow in the winter often making country roads impassable, Chicago sometimes found itself bereft of grain or glutted with it. The result could be economic chaos. If there was no grain, livestock could not be fed, resulting in meat shortages and people going hungry. If there was an overabundance of grain on the market, prices would plummet, farmers could not buy equipment, manufacturers faced bankruptcy, and workers were laid off. Forward contracting was a way to instill some certainty into the market to level off the peaks and valleys that could have such a devastating effect on the economy. Chicago's grain traders began using forward contracting in the early 1830s. In 1848 the Chicago Board of Trade was formed, providing a place, an exchange, where buyers and sellers could negotiate prices on the future delivery of grain, as well as a forum where business issues could be resolved.

Far less prominent than grain, livestock, or lumber, the butter and egg business also found its center in Chicago in the 1800s. This sector was served by the Chicago Produce Exchange, founded in 1874, but the butter-and-egg dealers grew dissatisfied with the exchange and the way it allowed its secretary to determine prices by querying merchants in a haphazard way. In 1895 they formed the Produce Exchange Butter and Egg Board as part of the Chicago Produce Exchange, its only purpose being to provide a better way to determine butter and egg prices. But in the next couple of years the exchange suffered from a civil war, as the butter merchants battled with their hated

Company Perspectives:

Since 1919, when it evolved into the Chicago Mercantile Exchange, the Merc has traded futures on over 50 products, from frozen pork bellies and live cattle to Eurodollar and index futures.

rivals, the margarine men or oleo faction. The butter merchants tried to use the exchange to influence state legislators to limit the sale of margarine in Illinois. The oleo producers thwarted them, and so in February 1898 the butter-and-egg men walked out, forming their own organization: The Chicago Butter and Egg Board, destined to one day become the Merc.

Launching the Merc in 1919

The board was part trade association, part marketing. Initially its members were not overly enamored with the concept of egg futures, instead preferring the cash market. In 1915 the trading of futures contracts was banned for a brief period, then limited for the next year before the progressives prevailed and time contracts were restored. Government restrictions due to the United States' entry into World War I soon resulted in the suspension of time contracts in butter and eggs, however, and normal trading was not resumed until 1919. It was also in 1919 that some egg dealers banded together to look deeper into the idea of futures trading. They then convinced the Butter and Egg Board to amend its rules book to include organized futures trading and permit a new organization under the rubric of the board to engage in futures trading. Because the members expected to deal in commodities other than just butter and eggs, the unit took the name of the Chicago Mercantile Exchange. In October 1919 the Chicago Butter and Egg Board went out of existence, and the next day the Chicago Mercantile Exchange (CME) was launched, although it would not be until December that it actually began trading in butter-and-egg futures, when three contracts were traded in less than an hour. At the end of the first week, only eight contracts were negotiated.

In the beginning CME relied on a chalkboard method, with offerings on one board, bids on another, and the final transactions listed on the sales board. Traders worked off of the posted information to negotiate the deals, with the market sometimes closing in a matter of minutes after its 10 a.m. opening. The blackboard method was far from satisfactory but it was the standard for an entire generation, not replaced until 1945 when the trading pit was introduced. In addition to eggs and butter, by now the CME was trading in potatoes and onions and, occasionally, involved in frozen eggs and cheese. It even tried a contract in animal hides as a trial.

The CME struggled to survive the war years 1941 to 1945, barely able to pay its mortgage, as a planned wartime economy handcuffed the country's futures exchanges. In eggs, for instance, there was no trading in futures in 1942 and 1943, and only minor business during 1944 and 1945 due to an imposed price ceiling. The exchange's leadership took the time to plan for the postwar period, installing new leadership that would seek to add new commodities to the trading mix. Shortly after

World War II ended in 1945, the CME added a turkey contract. In 1949 it began trading in apples and dressed poultry. But just as it appeared to be gaining momentum the CME took some backward steps in the 1950s. Price supports ended futures trading in butter, then in 1958, after pressure was brought to bear on Congress by disgruntled onion growers, the practice of futures trading in onions was banned. Onions were the CME's second most heavily traded futures contract. Its loss meant that the Merc was essentially a one-commodity exchange, trading in eggs.

As the CME entered the 1960s, its prospects appeared bleak, especially since the exchange's attempts over the years to trade in other products, including apples, potatoes, turkey, hides, cheese, and even scrap iron, had never met with a great deal of success. The potato business was meager and the egg business was no longer a seasonal business conducive to futures trading, the result of modern technology that offered a consistent supply of eggs year-round. The CME was on the verge of closing its doors, but discontent among the membership led to some changes and the exchange introducing three successful new contracts between 1960 and 1966. In 1961 the exchange added a frozen pork belly (used to make bacon) futures contract, a major innovation since it was the first futures contract related to frozen, stored meats. Few of the members knew what a pork belly was, and fewer investors, so that it was not until 1965 that the business took off, resulting in a significant rise in the price of a CME membership, from $3,000 in 1964 to $8,500 a year later. (In 1968 the price climbed to $38,000.) Another important contract also had been launched in 1964, a live cattle futures contract, notable because it was the first futures contract related to a nonstorable commodity.

Broker's Club Taking Charge in 1968

A group of CME's younger traders, who had forced the Board of Governors to take action in the beginning of the 1960s, were still not satisfied with the direction the Merc was taking. The group, known as the Broker's Club, launched a revolt in 1967 to force the board to be more responsive to the desires of membership. A showdown between the old guard and the dissident traders resulted in the latter winning the day, and in January 1968 a new chairman was installed and the CME entered a new era, governed by new bylaws. The dissidents also would spearhead the move into the financial markets that would transform the old Chicago Butter and Egg Board into a global exchange.

Always on the lookout for an opportunity, the CME found one in foreign currency in the early 1970s. It engaged the services of economist Milton Friedman, who wrote a paper on the possibility of doing business on foreign currency futures. Not only was there money to be made on money, he argued, the ongoing growth of foreign trade actually required a futures market in which currencies could be hedged and risk managed. Thus in 1972 the CME introduced the first financial futures market, involved in futures contracts on seven foreign currencies. The exchange's International Monetary Market would soon add gold, other precious metals, and Treasury Bills to the mix of financial instruments in which it dealt.

Key Dates:

1898: The Chicago Butter and Egg Board is formed.
1919: The Chicago Butter and Egg Board is dissolved; the Chicago Mercantile Exchange (CME) begins operations.
1945: The trading pit is introduced.
1961: The trading of pork belly futures is introduced.
1972: The world's first financial futures are traded.
1989: FBI sting results in the indictment of CME traders.
1992: The Globex electronic trading system is introduced.
2000: The CME is demutualized.
2002: The CME is taken public, listed on the New York Stock Exchange.

As a result, the CME was poised for a period of explosive growth in the 1980s. In 1981 it introduced CME Eurodollar futures, a highly successful market. A year later the CME S&P 500 Index futures contract was first offered, and it too attracted a great deal of interest. The 1980s was a period of innovation for the exchange on other fronts as well. The CME began developing an electronic trading system to operate when the trading floors in Chicago were closed, mostly to benefit the Japanese. According to *Euromoney,* "When originally announced in September 1987 this system was hard to take seriously. Even its name, Post-Market Trading, or PMT, was a joke: the initials PMT are more frequently used in the English speaking world to signify Pre-Menstrual Tension." The idea of electronic trading also met with opposition from old school Merc members who were worried that the venerable outcry system of trading would be imperiled. The new high-tech system would take years to develop, however. In the meantime, the CME had to contend with a scandal that not only called into question the outcry system but sullied the reputation of the institution.

In January 1989 federal agents surprised 40 CME and Chicago Board of Trade traders with subpoenas, the culmination of an undercover sting operation conducted by the FBI to determine if traders had defrauded customers. Four agents, wired with tape recorders, had infiltrated the Merc's trading pit, befriended traders, and recorded them both there and at places where they socialized. As *Time* explained, "Federal law requires that traders and brokers must try to get the best possible price for their customers when executing trades. But because the deals are conducted orally, illegal trades are difficult to catch." A "typical shady deal," according to *Time,* was the " 'bucket trade,' in which a broker slices an extra profit margin by buying a contract from a confederate at a bit more than the going price in the pit, or selling one for a bit less. For example, if a customer asks the broker to sell a soybean contract of 5,000 bushels and the market price is $7.50 per bushel, the crooked broker may sell the contract to a colleague for $7.40. That gives the colleague a discount of 10 cents per bushel, or $500, some of which he kicks back to his partner. The customer probably cannot challenge the price because there is no record of precisely when the deal occurred." Scores of traders and brokers would be indicted, and over the next two years the vast majority would plead guilty and the rest go to jury trial.

The CME spent much of the 1990s trying to rectify the damage caused by the FBI sting. Reforms were introduced, as was Globex, the CME's renamed electronic after-hours trading system, which made its debut in 1992. A virtually round-the-clock electronic trading system, Globex2, was introduced in 1998. Another innovation from this period was the CME E-mini S&P 500 contracts, electronically traded products that were much smaller than the standard S&P 500 Index futures, the first product of its kind to trade during regular trading hours on a U.S. exchange. It also opened the way for other E-Mini products, such as the E-mini S&P 500 futures and the E-mini NASDAQ-100 futures contracts.

As the 1990s came to a close, the CME unveiled a new strategic plan. It introduced more electronic order routing to the trading floor and approved side-by-side electronic and open outcry trading of Eurodollar contracts, a bid in large part to fend off the challenge of foreign exchanges that were dropping actual trading floors for cheap, electronic ones. The Merc also decided to become the first U.S. financial exchange to demutualize in order to become a public company, raise money, and invest in the kind of electronic infrastructure that would be a key to the exchange's future growth.

In 2000 membership shares in the CME were converted into shares of stock, which could be bought and sold apart from trading privileges. A year later a parent company was formed, Chicago Mercantile Exchange Holdings Inc. The stock of this holding company was then offered in an initial public offering in December 2002, raising $191 million for the CME and other selling stockholders. The stock then gained a listing on the New York Stock Exchange, as the CME became the first publicly traded exchange in the United States.

The Merc was on the verge of a new era in the early 2000s. Although many of its members were loath to give up the open outcry system, it was clear that the exchange was moving toward a totally electronic system over the next few years. Such a move, according to *Institutional Investor,* "likely would make for cheaper, more efficient trading for the exchange's 6,000 customers, speed new product development and allow the CME to market more aggressively across borders for new customers, leading to volume gains and bigger profits." When, if ever, open outcry would be eliminated was far from certain, because in the end customer preference ruled the day, and many of the customers still found a great deal of value in the old system, especially when it came to complex deals. The Merc was also in the market to grow in other ways. In the words of *Crain's Chicago Business* in 2004, "Flush with cash, Chicago Mercantile Exchange Holdings Inc. will consider acquisitions, joint ventures and other partnerships in a consolidating futures industry." Given its history of a willingness to adopt to changing times and an eagerness to seize opportunities when they presented themselves, there was every reason to expect the Merc to find a way to prosper for many years to come.

Principal Subsidiaries

Chicago Mercantile Exchange Inc.; GFX Corporation.

Principal Competitors

CBOT Holding, Inc.; Deutsche Börse AG; LIFFE (Holdings) PLC.

Further Reading

Abbott, Susan, and Giner Szala, ''How FBI's Sting Has Changed Pit Life,'' *Futures,* June 1991, p. 46.

Gorman, Christine, ''Crackdown on the Chicago Boys,'' *Time,* January 30, 1989, p. 52.

Lewis, Janet, ''Up from the Pits,'' *Institutional Investor,* December 2004, p. 78.

McWhirter, William, ''A Bid to Salvage a Go-Go Legacy,'' *Time,* February 6, 1989, p. 52.

Osborn, Neil, ''Running Scared in Windy City,'' *Euromoney,* February 1989, p. 38.

Strahler, Steven R., ''Cash to Spare, Merc Intends to Spend,'' *Crain's Chicago Business,* April 26, 2004, p. 26.

Tamarkin, Bob, *The Merc: The Emergence of a Global Financial Powerhouse,* New York: Harper Business, 1993.

—Ed Dinger

Chunghwa Picture Tubes, Ltd.

1127 Hopin Road
Danan Village, Padeh City
Taoyuan
Taiwan
Telephone: +886 3 367 5151
Fax: +886 3 377 31115
Web site: http://www.cptt.com.tw

Public Company
Incorporated: 1971
Employees: 20,000
Sales: TWD 117 billion ($3.67 billion) (2004)
Stock Exchanges: Taiwan
Ticker Symbol: CPT
NAIC: 334411 Electron Tube Manufacturing; 334419
   Other Electronic Component Manufacturing

Chungwha Picture Tubes, Ltd. (CPT) is one of Taiwan's, and the world's, leading manufacturers of thin-film transistor liquid crystal displays, or TFT-LCDs. Ranked number three in the Taiwan TFT panel market, the company is also a leading producer of cathode ray tubes (CRTs), color picture tubes, and electron guns used for CRT-based monitors and televisions. While those markets represent the group's traditional business, CPT responded quickly to the rise of flat-panel technologies at the dawn of the 21st century, embracing both LCD and plasma-based technologies. The company has manufacturing operations in Taiwan (including a 6G plant expected to reach full production by the end of 2005) and in mainland China and Malaysia. Listed on the Taiwan Stock Exchange, CPT was founded by Taiwan's Tatung Corporation, which remains its major shareholder with more than 32 percent of the company's stock. The bruising competition with Japanese and especially Korean flat-panel producers has left CPT, like most of the Taiwanese flat-panel sector, struggling to keep up and maintain profitability. As a result, CPT has long been rumored to be seeking a merger with a fellow Taiwanese LCD producer in order to gain greater scale. In 2004, CPT posted sales of TWD 117 billion ($3.67 billion).

Tatung Offshoot in the 1970s

Chungwha Picture Tubes had its origins as an offshoot of the fast-growing Tatung Corporation, one of the motors of Taiwan's industrial development in the second half of the 20th century. Tatung's roots lay in the post-World War I period, when Shan-Chih Lin went into business, founding the Shan-Chih Business Association in 1918. Lin's business flourished and by 1939 Lin's interests had grown to include the newly founded Tatung Iron Works. That company became known as Tatung Steel and Machinery Corporation following World War II.

Tatung was to play an important role in the development of the new Taiwanese state in the 1950s. The company diversified, adding an appliance manufacturing component. In 1949, Tatung launched production of its first appliance, an electric fan. That product soon brought the company to the export market, with its first international sales shipping to the Philippines.

By the early 1960s, Tatung had added refrigerators and automatic steamers to its list of appliances. The company then began construction of two new factories, one for the production of air conditioners, and another for the manufacture of television sets. This latter category represented Tatung's introduction to the large electronics sector. Production of televisions began in 1964; the following year, the company incorporated a new subsidiary, Tatung Electronics.

By 1968, Tatung had extended its television production expertise to the production of color televisions. The company also began to explore the potential for broadening its technology, namely for the production of the cathode ray tubes at the heart of the television industry. This effort led the company to create a new dedicated subsidiary, Chungwha Picture Tubes (CPT), in 1970. Construction of the company's first production facility in Taoyuan began in 1971.

CPT initially focused on the black and white tube sector, launching a test production run in 1972. By 1973, the company had perfected its production technique, and began full-scale production. CPT's prior export experience enabled it to gain a solid foothold in international markets, shipping CRTs to the

100

Company Perspectives:

Corporate Vision: Be the global leader for visual telecommunication products and the all-rounded innovator for optoelectronic technique.

Americas and to Europe, as well as to Thailand and other Asian markets. In 1974, as well, CPT added production of another important television component, the electron gun. In that year, the group's tubes received certification by the United States, giving the company entry into that market as well.

The rise of new graphics-based computers in the late 1970s gave CPT a fresh outlet for its cathode ray tubes. While computer monitors remained black and white, the television market had by then largely switched over to the color television standard. CPT responded by launching production of its own color CRTs at a new dedicated production facility in Taoyuan in 1978. Sales of the new tubes were swift; by the early 1980s, the company had produced more than one million color CRTs.

The Taiwanese government adopted a new policy in the early 1980s of encouraging Taiwan's shift away from its position as a low-cost, low-technology industrial producer toward a high-technology model. Tatung and CPT responded by expanding their operations to include the fast-growing computer sector, and especially the personal computer market. In 1983, CPT sought to extend its own display expertise into a new and promising display type, a flat-panel display based on liquid crystals. Whereas liquid crystals had been discovered in the 19th century, practical applications of the material only appeared toward the end of the 1960s, when RCA in the United States developed the first liquid crystal displays. By the end of the 1970s, however, Japan had become the focal point for LCD technologies.

Chungwha became the first Taiwanese company to attempt to enter the LCD market in 1983. Yet CPT proved unable to develop the necessary technology on its own, and the Japanese LCD industry jealously guarded its own technology advantage. Instead CPT returned its focus to the CRT market. In 1985, the company succeeded in developing a technology transfer partnership with Japan's Toshiba, not for the production of LCDs, but rather for the production of 14-inch color CRTs for computer and other monitor displays. By the end of that year, CPT had begun producing medium-resolution 14-inch CRTs as well as related components.

CPT launched its first flat-screen CRT in 1986 based on a 5.5-inch tube. By the end of that year, the company also ramped up production of a 14-inch flat rectangular CRT. In order to meet rising demand for its CRT, the company built a new facility in Yang Mei, started in 1987 and completed in less than a year. That facility began producing 14-inch high-resolution displays, as well as 21-inch flat rectangular CRTs.

LCD Beginnings in the 1990s

CPT followed Tatung overseas in the early 1990s. While Tatung built a new construction facility in Thailand, CPT turned to Malaysia, where it began building a plant for the production of color electron guns in 1990. The Malaysian subsidiary reached full production by 1991, then quickly expanded to eight production lines by the middle of the decade. The addition of the Malaysian production capacity helped CPT claim the leading position in the global CRT industry.

The mid-1990s also marked a new effort by CPT to enter the LCD market. In 1994, the company began building a dedicated facility in Fuzhou. In the meantime, the company continued to boost its CRT capacity. A major step in the group's development came with a new technology transfer agreement with Toshiba in 1995, enabling CPT to launch production of 28-inch and larger color picture tubes. The following year, CPT established a manufacturing presence in the European market, opening a production subsidiary in Scotland.

Yet the future of the display industry lay in the fast-developing LCD technology. CPT's efforts paid off by 1996 with the production of the group's first LCD module. By 1996, the company's factory prepared to launch full-scale production.

CPT's efforts to crack the LCD sector were aided by the economic downturn in Japan. Into the late 1990s, that country's LCD giants began to find it difficult to raise the funds needed for further investment. These companies risked falling behind in the newly launched LCD race, as new competitors, especially in Korea, emerged. Meanwhile, the LCD industry was set to take off, as more and more users adopted portable computers, but especially as the world prepared for the sudden explosion in portable telephones. Slightly further down the road lay the promise of new high-definition television standards, which would require consumers to upgrade their sets, and the coming of the flat-screen televisions as well.

In search of funding, the Japanese LCD makers turned to Taiwan for investment capital, launching a series of technology transfer agreements with the island's manufacturers. CPT proved to be among the first to find a partner, signing an agreement with Mitsubishi in 1997. By 1999, the company had completed its new production facility and it became the first in Taiwan to produce 14-inch and 15-inch LCD modules.

Display Leader in the 2000s

CPT's LCD production gained quickly, and by 2001, the company had added a second factory, in Fu Chou. The following year, the company added two more production facilities, in Wujiang, in mainland China, and in Lungtan. The company continued to produce CRTs, but the future clearly lay in flat-panel technologies.

In the early 2000s, CPT began developing production capacity for plasma screens as well. By 2001, the company had successfully launched production of display panels ranging up to 46 inches in size. The company continued to develop its technology, and by 2004, CPT debuted its first high-definition large-screen panels.

As for its Taiwanese counterparts, including AU Optronics and Chi Mei Optoelectronics, the early 2000s proved a difficult period for CPT. The economic downturn had suppressed sales; at the same time, the company faced heavy competitive pressure

Key Dates:

1971: Tatung of Taiwan begins manufacturing cathode ray tubes, establishing Chungwha Picture Tubes.
1974: The company begins production of electron guns.
1978: The company launches production of color CRTs.
1983: The company first attempts to enter LCD production.
1985: The company enters a technology transfer agreement with Toshiba.
1990: A subsidiary in Malaysia is established.
1994: The company re-enters the LCD sector and begins construction on a new factory.
1997: The company reaches an LCD technology transfer agreement with Mitsubishi.
1998: The company becomes the first in Taiwan to produce 14-inch TFT-LCD panels.
2001: New factories are added in Wujiang and Lungtan.
2005: Construction begins on a sixth generation TFT-LCD plant; CPT is rumored to be considering a merger with another display producer in Taiwan.

from its deep-pocketed rivals in South Korea. The result was a swift drop in the prices of LCD and flat-panel displays. Although this stimulated massive consumer demand for these display types, the falling prices sent most of the Taiwanese sector into losses. In order to compete, CPT, like the other Taiwanese display leaders, was forced to invest heavily in expanding its production, building new fifth-generation plants. By 2005, the company had also committed to expanding production with a new sixth-generation plant, to be completed by the end of that year.

Continued losses (CPT's losses topped $226 million for the first half of 2005 alone) made it difficult for CPT to raise needed investment capital. At the same time, Tatung was said to be seeking to offload its money-losing subsidiary, which had been dragging down its own profits. Into the mid-2000s, rumors began to circulate that Tatung was preparing to merge CPT with one of its rivals. By September 2005, the rumor, although denied by Tatung, appeared to become more of a certainty. At that time, two likely candidates emerged. The first was Hon Hai-owned Innolux Display Corp., the current number six in Taiwan. The second was Quanta Display Inc., the market's number five, part of the Quanta Group. The merger with either of these candidates was expected to boost CPT, the market's number three, into the industry's number two position, ahead of Chi Mei Optoelectronics, and trailing only AU Optronics. CPT remained a key player in Taiwan's effort to lead the global flat-panel display market.

Principal Subsidiaries

CPT (Malaysia) Co. Ltd.; Kamper Plant Co. Ltd.; CPTF Optronics Co., Ltd.; Wujiang Plant Co., Ltd.; CPTF Visual Display (Fuzhou) Ltd.; CPT Display Technology (Fujian) Ltd.

Principal Competitors

Samsung Corporation; LG-Philips; Sharp Corporation; AU Optronics; Chi Mei Optoelectronics Corporation.

Further Reading

"Chungwha Picture World's No. 1 Maker of 15-Inch TFT-LCD Panels," *Taiwan Economic News,* May 6, 2004.
"Chunghwa to Build Gen6 LCD Plant," *EBN,* August 11, 2003, p. 16.
"CPT to Decide Merger with Local Counterpart in One Month," *Taiwan Economic News,* September 12, 2005.
"CPT to Expand LCM Capacity at Mainland China Plants," *Taiwan Economic News,* August 19, 2005.
"CPT to Inaugurate 6G TFT-LCD Panel Line," *Taiwan Economic News,* September 19, 2005.
Einhorn, Bruce, and Ihlwan Moon, "A Fierce Fight to Stay in the Flat-Panel Game," *Business Week,* September 16, 2002, p. 23.
Wang, Lisa, "Chunghwa Picture Tubes Shares Rise on Talk of Merger," *Taipei Times,* September 09, 2005, p. 10.

—M.L. Cohen

Comtech Telecommunications Corp.

105 Baylis Road
Melville, New York 11747
U.S.A.
Telephone: 9631) 777-8900
Fax: (631) 777-8877
Web site: http://www.comtechtel.com

Public Company
Incorporated: 1967 as Comtech Laboratories, Inc.
Employees: 842
Sales: $307.9 million (2005)
Stock Exchanges: NASDAQ
Ticker Symbol: CMTL
NAIC: 334110 Radio and Television Broadcasting and
    Wireless Communications Equipment Manufacturing

Based on Long Island, New York, Comtech Telecommunications Corp. develops communications equipment in three business segments through a number of subsidiaries, serving customers such as defense contractors, satellite systems integrators, communications service providers, and oil companies. In the Telecommunications Transmission area, Comtech owns five subsidiaries (Comtech EF Data Corp.; Comtech Systems, Inc.; Comtech AHA Corp.; Comtech Antenna Systems, Inc.; and Comtech Vipersat Networks Inc.) providing products and services for voice, video, and data transmission in satellite, wireless line-of-sight, and over-the-horizon microwave telecommunication systems. Products include modems, amplifiers, satellite transceivers, fiberglass and aluminum antennas, software to optimize satellite bandwidth usage, and forward error correction technology. Comtech's RF Microwave Amplifiers business is conducted through a single subsidiary, Comtech PST Corp., which in turn operates Hill Engineering. Comtech PST supplies broadband high-power, high-performance RF microwave amplifiers used in a variety of military applications as well as medical oncology systems. Hill designs and produces high-power switches, limiters, and duplexers. Comtech's third business segment is Mobile Data Communications Services, conducted through a pair of subsidiaries: Comtech Mobile Datacom Corp. and Comtech Tolt Technolo-

gies, Inc. Comtech Mobile develops mobile data communications systems for the U.S. military, with its primary focus on the Movement Tracking System (MTS). MTS uses satellite, terrestrial, and Internet-based communications to create a way to keep track of military vehicles, ships, and aircraft while also providing two-way, real-time communications between command bases and the field. Comtech Tolt provides this technology to the civilian market, such as trucking fleets that want to track the precise location of their vehicles. Although it has been in operation for decades, the company did not begin to enjoy exceptional growth until the late 1990s. Revenues have increased from $30.1 million in 1998 to more than $300 million in 2005. Comtech is a public company listed on the NASDAQ.

Company's Founding in the 1960s

Comtech was founded in Smithtown, New York, in 1967 as Comtech Laboratories, Inc. by Jack C. Greene, who also served as the company's chief executive. The company started out by designing and manufacturing satellite communications receiving equipment and related subsystems for commercial purposes. In March 1972 Comtech was taken public at $5 a share. Sales topped $10 million in 1974 and reached $16.5 million in 1975.

Greene stepped down as CEO in 1976, replaced by Comtech's current chairman, president, and CEO, Fred V. Kornberg. Born in Poland, Kornberg earned a bachelor's degree in electrical engineering at New York University in 1958 and a year later received a master's degree from the same school. He worked as a staff engineer at Radio Engineering Laboratories until 1962, and then became director of research, a position he held until 1969, when he became general manager at Nardcom Group. Kornberg joined Comtech in 1971 as an executive vice-president and general manager of the telecommunications transmission unit. Under Kornberg, Comtech expanded beyond satellite communications to become involved in the microwave transmission field through the 1977 acquisition of R.F. Systems, Inc.

Early 1980s: Verge of Disaster

Over the next several years Comtech prospered as a manufacturer of telecommunications components and subsystems,

Company Perspectives:

Comtech designs, develops, produces and markets innovative products and services for advanced telecommunications solutions.

but it suffered a significant setback in the early 1980s serving the military market. It won a contract to install 21 satellite communication earth stations for the U.S. Army's Signal Corps, but its $52 million bid proved to be a major miscalculation. On the verge of ruin, Comtech began in March 1981 to pursue a merger with Aeroflex Laboratories Inc. Talks continued for a full year before breaking off after the Army granted Comtech another $17.5 million to complete the contract. The price of Comtech's stock soared on the news, making it a much less attractive deal to Aeroflex.

Comtech was fortunate to break even on the Signal Corps contract and now installed safeguards to make sure there was no repetition of such a blunder. Kornberg also began to tap the financial markets to fuel an expansion drive and to become involved in the end-user segment of the telecommunications market. In 1983 the *New York Times* reported that Comtech offered 750,000 shares at $8.50 each through Drexel Burnham Lambert Inc. The money was used to acquire Premier Microwave Corp. and Storage Technology Corp., a Colorado manufacturer of voice communications products. Comtech raised another $12 million to pay down debt by selling off Comtech Data Corp., which made communications equipment for the satellite, microwave, broadband, and cable markets, to Fairchild Industries.

Despite efforts to diversify its product offering, Comtech became overly dependent on large military contracts, which through much of the 1980s accounted for more than 70 percent of revenues. With the demise of the Soviet Union, however, the United States began to cut back on defense spending, forcing Comtech to make some adjustments. Having already sold Comtech Communication Corp. for $4 million in 1985, Comtech now unloaded Premier Microwave in 1987, adding $7.5 million in cash and notes to the coffers. Also in 1987 Comtech decided that its future lay overseas. The company had been dividing its focus between the United States and foreign markets, but now decided to concentrate on the international telecommunications sector, which was growing much faster than was that of the United States. The strategy worked so well that by 1991, about two-thirds of the company's $13 million in revenues were the result of export sales, primarily from sales to South America and the Pacific Rim. Of that $10 million, some 95 percent was contributed by subsidiary Comtech Systems Inc., which sold tropospheric scatter communications systems, a less expensive alternative to satellites. Tropo systems bounced radio waves off the upper atmosphere rather than a satellite. Although sales to the U.S. military may have fallen off, the foreign military market heated up for Comtech, as some countries began to expand their military forces to compensate for a cutback in U.S. protection.

The early 1990s was a period of transition for Comtech. Reductions in military spending continued to cut into sales,

making the decision to focus on foreign markets a wise one. Domestically, Comtech saw opportunities in the expanding wireless and satellite telecommunications as well as microwave transmissions industries. Revenues crested at $22.3 million in 1993, then plunged in 1994 to $14.9 million. Comtech began to rebound due in large part to the creation of subsidiary Comtech Communications Corp., a satellite communications equipment manufacturer formed in February 1994. Products included frequency converters, solid-state power amplifiers, low noise amplifiers, and satellite subsystems. By the latter part of 1995 the unit was making a major contribution to the company's domestic commercial sales. In fiscal 1995 revenues increased to $16.5 million.

The upward arc continued in 1996, when sales improved to $20.9 million, due mostly to robust international sales, which for the year accounted for 56 percent of all revenues. This was a significant improvement over the 37 percent in 1995. International sales remained strong in 1997, when revenues climbed to $24.7 million, due to a continuing global demand for wireless and satellite telecommunications. It was a fortunate trend for Comtech, because sales to the U.S. government continued to slip, representing 20 percent of all sales in 1996 but only 17 percent in 1997. Increased international sales of over-the-horizon microwave equipment fueled business in 1998, with revenues topping $30 million. It was at this point that Comtech was poised to enjoy exponential growth as it began to transform itself into a product-driven company.

Forming Key Subsidiaries in the Late 1990s

In the autumn of 1998 (fiscal 1999) Comtech formed a pair of subsidiaries. Comtech Wireless, Inc. was established to design and manufacture Wireless Local Loop systems for the rural and remote telephony market. Comtech Mobile Datacom Corp. grew out of the acquisition of Germantown, Maryland-based Mobile Datacom Corp. to provide packet data communication services between remote mobile and fixed assets and home-base using high-tech tracking technology. Applications included remote meter reading, inventory/asset in-route management, messaging, and position reporting. Although the focus of the unit was intended to be the energy and transportation markets, its Movement Tracking System (MTS) product would find a ready customer in the U.S. military. As a result, the amount of government sales, which decreased to just 9 percent of Comtech's total revenues in 2000, now began to surge. In June 1999 the U.S. Army signed an eight-year, $418 million contract with Comtech to install MTS in its vehicles. The system would permit vehicles in the field to communicate with one another and to a command center. As a result, commanders would be able to know where everyone was located at any moment and maintain a constant line of communication. Aside from the income the Army contract brought in, it allowed Comtech a chance to work out any bugs in the technology, which could then be sold to trucking companies without any major changes. The first order of the contract, representing $3.1 million, was received in August 2000 to deploy MTS to 460 U.S. Army logistic vehicles and mobile control stations. By the end of 2000 Comtech announced that it was now ready to offer MTS to commercial truck fleets as well.

The pace of the Army's rollout of MTS would increase sharply with the start of the Iraq War in 2003. In the meantime,

Key Dates:

1967: The company is incorporated as Comtech Laboratories, Inc.
1972: The company is taken public.
1976: Fred Kornberg is named chief executive.
1981: A miscalculated bid puts Comtech on the verge of ruin.
1994: Comtech Communications Corp. is formed.
1998: Comtech Mobile Datacom is formed.
1999: Comtech is awarded a $418 million contract.
2005: Sales top $300 million.

Comtech made strides on other fronts. In May 2000 Comtech acquired EF Data, the satellite communications division of Adaptive Broadband, at a cost of $54.2 million. With annual revenues in the $100 million range, EF Data was larger than Comtech, which posted $37.9 million in 1999. The EF Data business was merged with Comtech Communications to become Comtech EF Data Corp. The capabilities of the two units complemented one another, resulting in the creation of a powerhouse player in the telecommunications transmission field. Also of note in 2000, Comtech acquired Hill Engineering for stock. Furthermore, the company gained some recognition in 2000, named by *Forbes* magazine as one of the top 200 best small companies in the United States, ranked 131st based on five-year and 12-month return on equity, and five-year sales and earnings per share.

Sales increased to $66.4 million in 2000, then soared to $135.9 million in 2001. Net income of $6.7 million in 2001 also set a record for Comtech. Much of these increases were due to the EF Data acquisition, but the company's two other businesses also achieved record revenues, this despite the difficulties experienced by many of its telecommunications' customers. The Mobile Data unit continued to deploy MTS to the Army and also received its first foreign sale, a contract with a value-added reseller in Venezuela to provide MTS technology to commercial truck fleets.

The telecommunications slump finally caught up to Comtech in 2002, when revenues fell to $199.4 million and net income dipped below the $2 million mark. Compared with other telecommunications companies, however, it still turned in a solid year, with all segments of its business turning a profit. Moreover, Comtech bounced back quickly in 2003, achieving a record year with sales increases across the board as the efforts of previous years came to fruition. For the year, the company posted sales of $174 million and net income of more than $9.7 million. Comtech enjoyed another record year in 2004, as sales increased to $223.4 million and net income more than doubled to $21.8 million. The trend continued in 2005 when Comtech's revenues topped the $300 million mark, totaling $307.9 million, and net income soared to $37.8 million. To many Comtech was an overnight success, but in truth the hard work of several decades was finally paying off and the Long Island-based company appeared well positioned to enjoy strong growth for some time to come.

Principal Subsidiaries

Comtech EF Data Corp.; Comtech Systems, Inc.; Comtech AHA Corp.; Comtech Antenna Systems, Inc.; Comtech Vipersat Networks Inc.; Comtech PST Corp.; Comtech Mobile Datacom Corp.; Comtech Tolt Technologies, Inc.

Principal Competitors

EMS Technologies, Inc.; Gilat Satellite Networks Ltd.; ViaSat, Inc.

Further Reading

Angell, Mike, "Military Supplier Finds Its Way to a Windfall," *Investor's Business Daily,* September 8, 2003, p. A08.

Citrano, Virginia, "Telecom Contracts Spur N.Y. Exporters," *Crain's New York Business,* March 8, 1993, p. 17.

"Comtech Receives $8.9 Million in New Orders for U.S. Army's Movement Tracking System," *EDP Weekly's IT Monitor,* February 25, 2002, p. 8.

Conroy, Michael P., "Comtech Nails $3.1M Army Satellite Contract," *Long Island Business News,* August 11, 2000, p. A5.

Frederickson, Tom, "Company Becomes Soldier of Fortune," *Crain's New York Business,* September 19, 2005, p. 30.

Rosenblum, Michael, "Defense Play," *Barron's National Business and Financial Weekly,* August 9, 1982, p. 62.

Shaw, Craig, "Army Spending Boosts Telecom Firm's Profit," *Investor's Business Daily,* August 27, 2003, p. B08.

Solnik, Claude, "Comtech Takes Aim at Trucking Biz," *Long Island Business News,* December 29, 2000, p. A5.

Sonenclar, Robert, "Coming Off the Floor: The Cautionary Tale of Comtech Telecommunications," *Financial World,* November 15, 1983, p. 35.

—Ed Dinger

Concurrent Computer Corporation

4375 River Green Parkway, Suite 100
Duluth, Georgia 30096
U.S.A.
Telephone: (678) 258-4000
Toll Free: (877) 978-7363
Fax: (678) 258-4300
Web site: http://www.ccur.com

Public Company
Incorporated: 1966 as Interdata, Inc.
Employees: 425
Sales: $78.7 million (2005)
Stock Exchanges: NASDAQ
Ticker Symbol: CCUR
NAIC: 334111 Electronic Computer Manufacturing

Concurrent Computer Corporation is a global supplier of high performance computer systems. The company has been a pioneer in the field of real-time computing and parallel processing. Formed in the 1960s to serve the scientific and engineering market, Concurrent has expanded its reach to the financial and medical administration industries. Its hardware and software powers a wide variety of applications including video-on-demand, process control, data acquisition, and simulators. Leading products include the MediaHawk video-on-demand and RedHawk, a Linux-based, real-time processing system. The company is active in more than 30 countries.

Origins

Interdata, Inc. was established in 1966 by former IBM engineer Daniel Sinnott and others. A pioneer in the minicomputer industry, Interdata focused on the technical market and was turning a profit by the end of the decade.

In 1974 Perkin-Elmer Corporation, a Norwalk, Connecticut producer of scientific instruments, optics, and semiconductor manufacturing equipment, acquired Interdata Communications Inc. for $63.6 million. By this time, Interdata had annual sales of $19 million; Perkin-Elmer's were about 12 times greater.

Interdata soon moved into a new headquarters in Oceanport, New Jersey.

Later in the decade, Interdata underwent a management shift and focused on the high end of the market for 32-bit minicomputers, which included applications in flight simulation, seismic analysis for the energy industry, and transaction processing for the financial services industry, noted the *New York Times*.

Interdata claimed the first full 32-bit computer in 1974. The company then became a proponent of the parallel processing approach to number crunching, wherein multiple tasks were performed at once, rather than one by one as in serial processing. This made real-time computing a possibility, with a plethora of applications in business and other markets.

The Interdata name was lost as the company became the basis for Perkin-Elmer's Data Systems Group. The business had a bad year in 1982 and underwent some cost-cutting before the parent company decided to spin it off.

Spun Off in 1985

Concurrent Computer Corporation (formerly Interdata) became an independent company in November 1985. Its initial public offering on the NASDAQ raised $37 million; Perkin-Elmer retained about 80 percent of equity.

Concurrent soon entered a partnership with Nippon Steel Corp. to develop a presence in Japan. However, the newly independent company was experiencing a difficult start. A nine-month product delay of a new $1 million parallel processing system compounded the company's troubles in a slow market. Sales slipped 7 percent to $244.8 million as profits were halved to $6 million in the company's first year of independence.

Perceiving a market shift towards cheaper open systems, in October 1988 Concurrent merged with Massachusetts Computer Corp. (Masscomp), a $76 million producer of UNIX-based microcomputers whose equipment had been used in the Space Shuttle program. Though smaller, Masscomp was the surviving entity, and changed its name to Concurrent. The deal cost Masscomp $240 million, two-thirds of it borrowed.

106

Company Perspectives:

Concurrent is a worldwide leader in providing digital on-demand systems to the broadband industry and real-time computer systems for industry and government. The company's two business areas, On-Demand and Real-Time, leverage the best of Concurrent's technology and mission-critical experience to deliver solutions to a diverse global customer base.

Key Dates:

1966: Interdata, Inc. is formed.
1967: Datacraft is formed.
1971: Harris-Intertype acquires majority interest in Datacraft.
1974: Perkin-Elmer Corporation acquires Interdata.
1985: Concurrent Computer Corporation (formerly Interdata) is spun off.
1988: Concurrent merges with Masscomp.
1994: Harris Computer Systems (formerly Datacraft) is spun off.
1996: Concurrent acquires Harris Real-Time Computer Systems.
1998: Concurrent's MediaHawk Video Server is introduced.
1999: Headquarters moves to Atlanta area as company pursues video-on-demand (VOD) market.
2002: VOD accounts for half of total revenues.

The original Concurrent had about 2,800 employees then, four times as many as Masscomp. James K. Sims, the president and CEO of the original Concurrent, also headed the merged company. He had originally joined Interdata in 1974 as a sales representative.

The newly combined company had the ambition of becoming number one in the real-time computing market. However, in spite of unique tax advantages, some cost savings from layoffs, and a leading position in the $5 billion real-time systems market, there were signs of danger from the beginning.

Early 1990s Debt Crisis

Sales were about $300 million in 1990. Concurrent went through some hard times in the early 1990s as defense spending fell. A new CEO, former Penn Central Industries Group Inc. head Denis Brown, arrived in September 1990 just as the company was going into default on its heavy debt from the Masscomp merger. There were reportedly also considerable corporate culture differences to overcome after moving Masscomp production to Concurrent's New Jersey facility, leading to a significant delay in a new UNIX product.

To put the company back on track, Brown stalled with the company's lenders and bondholders (some of which, including the Bank of New England and a couple of troubled thrifts, were facing insolvency themselves) while letting go of more than a quarter of Concurrent's 3,200-strong workforce and cutting back on research and development and real estate. (Company CFO James P. McCloskey discussed the contentious financial negotiations in some detail with *American Banker* in early 1992.)

Revenues were down to $222 million by fiscal 1992. Brown was looking for growth from more advanced battlefield simulators as well as a new line of administrative products for hospitals. Concurrent had sales of $179 million in 1994. It would soon grow with a major acquisition, the purchase of the rival real-time business of Harris Corporation in 1996.

This business had been formed in 1967 as Datacraft. Harris bought it in the early 1970s and renamed it the Harris Computer Systems Division. It was spun off as Harris Computer Systems Corp. in 1994. In June 1996, Concurrent acquired the spinoff's $40 million-a-year real-time computer business in a stock swap worth $30 million. (Harris Computer Systems was subsequently renamed CyberGuard Corp. after its remaining firewall product.) Concurrent had previously rebuffed an offer to itself be acquired by Harris Computer.

Concurrent introduced its MediaHawk Video Server in 1998. This soon became the basis for video-on-demand services from several leading cable operators. It could also provide streaming content for distance learning, video conferencing, and in-flight entertainment.

New Home in 1999

In 1999 Concurrent relocated its headquarters to the Atlanta area, which was also the site of its new video-on-demand (VOD) division, dubbed XStreme. The Integrated Solutions unit remained in Fort Lauderdale. (Concurrent later did away with the divisional structure a few years later.) Also in 1999, Concurrent acquired a competitor in VOD servers, Vivid Technologies of Chalfont, Pennsylvania.

The company soon claimed the leading position in the emerging broadband video-on-demand market. VOD business with cable operators as far away as Asia accounted for $12 million of the company's fiscal 2000 sales ($68 million). By fiscal 2002, VOD revenues had quadrupled, and accounted for more than half the company's total sales of $89 million.

Concurrent was also maintaining its legacy real-time computing business. It was involved with the Aegis radar system that monitored threats for the Navy. The company was beginning to outfit Navy ships entirely with UNIX-based, COTS (commercial off-the-shelf) technology.

In 2005, Concurrent was acquiring Cleveland's Everstream Holdings in a stock swap worth $15 million. Everstream, formed in 1999, produced business intelligence software. The two companies had been involved in a VOD advertising joint venture.

Principal Subsidiaries

Concurrent Computer Asia Corporation; Concurrent Computer Canada, Inc.; Concurrent Computer Corporation (France) (USA); Concurrent Computer Corporation Pty. Ltd. (Australia); Concurrent Computer France S.A.; Concurrent Computer GmbH (Germany); Concurrent Computer Hispania, S.A. (Spain); Concurrent Computer Holding Corporation; Concurrent Computer Hong

Kong Limited; Concurrent Computer New Zealand Limited; Concurrent Realisations Limited (U.K.); Concurrent UK Ltd.; Concurrent Federal Systems, Inc.; Concurrent Nippon Corporation (Japan); Concurrent Securities Corporation.

Principal Competitors

C-COR Incorporated; Silicon Graphics, Inc.; SeaChange International, Inc.; Sun Microsystems, Inc.

Further Reading

Alper, Alan, ''Perkin-Elmer's Year-Old Data Systems Spin-Off Floundering,'' *Computerworld,* November 17, 1986, p. 118.

Appleton, Elaine L., ''Concurrent Computer Corp.,'' The Datamation 100, *Datamation,* June 15, 1992, p. 154.

Barnes, Peter W., ''Perkin-Elmer Organizes New Computer Firm—Up to 19% of Growing Line Will Be Sold to Public; Better Visibility Sought,'' *Wall Street Journal,* November 14, 1985.

Baumgartner, Jeff, ''Getting in the Game: A New Crop of VOD Players Want to Crack Cable's Starting Lineup, But Will There Be Enough Business to Sustain Them?'' *CED,* June 2003, pp. 28+.

''Company Interview: Walt Ungerer, Concurrent Computer Corporation,'' *Wall Street Transcript,* May 2003.

''Company Interview: Walt Ungerer, Concurrent Computer Corporation,'' *Wall Street Transcript,* June 2004.

''Company Profile,'' *Computer Weekly,* January 30, 1986, p. 20.

''Concurrent Computer, Formerly Perkin-Elmer's Data Systems Group, and Before That Interdata, Is Now Establishing Itself in a Technical Niche,'' *Computer Weekly,* October 15, 1987, p. 46.

Dickson, Glen, ''VOD Gains Ground,'' *Broadcasting & Cable,* May 1, 2000, p. 81.

Fisher, Lawrence M., ''Concurrent Chief to Get Top Jobs After Merger,'' *New York Times,* Sec. D, August 3, 1988.

French, Desiree, ''MASSCOMP Lays Off 225 As Part of Merger Deal,'' *Boston Globe,* August 2, 1988, p. 46.

Goodwin, William, ''Banks on the Brink Test CFO's Mettle,'' *American Banker,* February 3, 1992, pp. 1+.

Haber, Carol, ''Harris Computer Systems, Concurrent Square Off in Deal Talks Gone Awry,'' *Electronic News,* March 6, 1995, p. 14.

Harris, Catherine L., ''Perkin-Elmer Tries to Become Two Household Words,'' *Business Week,* December 9, 1985, p. 86.

Knowles, Ann, ''A Slow Start for Start-Up Concurrent,'' *Electronic Business,* September 1, 1986, pp. 32+.

Kozma, Robert J., ''Perkin-Elmer Unleashes Its Data Systems Group; New Independent Concurrent Computer Corp. Plans to Build on Its Past Minicomputer Success,'' *Electronics,* November 25, 1985, pp. 64+.

Lacob, Miriam, ''Concurrent Solos on Parallel Flight,'' *Computer Decisions,* July 15, 1986, pp. 49+.

Lubove, Seth, ''Cleanup Man,'' *Forbes,* November 9, 1992, pp. 66+.

Margolis, Nell, ''Can Concurrent Make a Comeback?'' *Computerworld,* December 10, 1990, pp. 103+.

——, ''Masscomp Buys Concurrent; Merged Company to Target Top Real-Time Slot,'' *Computerworld,* August 8, 1988, p. 6.

McNair, James, ''Harris Computer Systems Closes Sale to Concurrent Computer Corp.'' *Knight Ridder/Tribune Business News,* June 28, 1996.

''Perkin-Elmer's Big Growth Started with a Small Research Contract,'' *New York Times,* Financial Sec., July 18, 1981.

Saunders, Christopher, ''Everstream, Concurrent Eye Video-On-Demand,'' *ClizkZ News,* November 21, 2001, http://www.clickz.com/news/article.php/927741.

Shandle, Jack, ''Concurrent Is Sitting Pretty After an Unconventional Buyout,'' *Electronics,* April 1989, pp. 119+.

''Sims' Challenge,'' *Management Today,* July 1987, p. 14.

Stedman, Craig, ''Concurrent Chairman/CEO Exits; Firm Loses $38M in 4th Quarter,'' *Electronics News,* September 17, 1990, p. 13.

——, ''Concurrent Layoff Raises '90 Total to Near 800,'' *Chilton's Electronic News,* December 17, 1990, p. 21.

——, ''Concurrent UNIX Effort Snagged,'' *Electronic News,* November 19, 1990, p. 1.

''Two 'Low-Profile' Vendors Make Bids for the IS Spotlight,'' *Infosystems,* May 1986, pp. 20+.

Verity, John W., ''This Computer Tracks Flicks—and Flack,'' *Business Week,* December 19, 1994, p. 116.

—Frederick C. Ingram

Corus Bankshares, Inc.

3959 N. Lincoln Avenue
Chicago, Illinois 60613-2431
U.S.A.
Telephone: (773) 832-3088
Toll Free: (800) 555-5710
Fax: (773) 832-3267
Web site: http://www.corusbank.com

Public Company
Incorporated: 1958 as River Forest Bancorp, Inc.
Employees: 471
Sales: $273.5 million (2004)
Stock Exchanges: NASDAQ
Ticker Symbol: CORS
NAIC: 522110 State Commercial Banks

Based in Chicago, Corus Bankshares, Inc. is a holding company for Corus Bank, N.A., which maintains 11 branches in the Chicago metropolitan area. With more than $6.5 billion in assets, Corus is involved in two main banking activities: deposit gathering (checking, savings, money market, and time deposit accounts) and commercial real estate lending. The bank finances real estate projects across the United States, concentrating on loans that range from $20 million to $135 million. In addition, Corus is the largest provider of services to Chicago's check cashing industry, offering clearing, depository, and credit services to some 525 area check cashing locations, as well as another 20 locations in Milwaukee, Wisconsin. Although Corus is a public company listed on the NASDAQ, it is controlled by Chairman Joseph Glickman and his family, who together own about half of the holding company. Glickman's son, Robert J. Glickman, is the longtime president and chief executive officer. He is known for running a lean operation and taking a hands-on approach to business. *Crain's Chicago Business* once described him as "brilliant and tyrannical, reflective and blunt."

Company Heritage Dating to the 1950s

Corus was incorporated in Minnesota in 1958 as River Forest Bancorp by Minneapolis financier Carl R. Pohlad, who was to become better known as the owner of the Minnesota Twins Major League Baseball team than as a banker. He was born in 1915, the son of a railroad brakeman who struggled to support his family of eight. To help bring some money into the house Pohlad during high school began milking cows on a farm owned by a banker, who took him under his wing and made the young man his driver as he collected loan payments. Pohlad was soon handling the rounds by himself and taking on other chores at the bank. He put that experience to use in the early 1930s during his college career at Gonzaga University in Spokane, Washington. A high school football star, he attended Gonzaga on an athletic scholarship, but, in need of spending money, he began selling used cars repossessed by banks. The profits from this venture then allowed him to buy a small finance company in Dubuque, Iowa. He quit school after football season during his senior year and ran the business until a stint in the Army during World War II. When he returned he found that his partner had purchased Minnesota-based Bank Shares Inc., owners of three banks. Pohlad moved to Minneapolis to help run Bank Shares and when his partner died in 1955 he became CEO and expanded the operation by buying more community banks, including River Forest State Bank, located in a Chicago suburb. In October 1958 he formed another holding company in Minnesota called River Forest Bancorp.

Younger Generation Taking Charge in the Early 1980s

A Minnesota businessman named Joseph C. Glickman led a group of investors who in 1966 bought the $18-million-asset River Forest bank from Pohlad. Three years later, in 1969, Glickman was joined by his son, Robert J. Glickman, who had just graduated with an undergraduate degree from Cornell University. He became a director of the company in 1972 and took on an increasing amount of responsibility at River Forest. In the mid-1970s he recruited longtime friend and high school classmate Robert Heskett to join him. In the early 1980s the two men took the reins of the company, as Joseph Glickman, now in his late 60s, stepped back from the day-to-day running of River Forest, content to serve as its chairman.

According to *Crain's Chicago Business,* the young Glickman and Heskett were referred to by analysts as the "Bob and

┌───┐

Company Perspectives:

Corus has established a strong track record of profitability, made possible by a number of factors, including efficiency and entrepreneurship.

└───┘

Bob Show.'' Glickman was the chief executive and Heskett served as vice-president and the bank's chief lending officer. *Crain's* also reported, ''Observers say Mr. Heskett's more outgoing personality and his ability to cut quickly to the heart of a complex deal complemented Mr. Glickman's more reserved and reflective characters. . . . Bankers described Mr. Heskett as Mr. Glickman's alter ego and the only executive to whom he delegated authority. 'Bob (Glickman) runs a very autocratic organization,' says a banker who knows them both. 'No one could go to the bathroom without asking Glickman. The only other person who could give permission was Heskett.' ''

In 1982 Illinois changed its banking laws to allow for multi-bank holding companies and the two-man team at River Forest soon took advantage of the new conditions to grow through acquisitions, pursuing a strategy of targeting modestly priced banks that were either in trouble or not performing particularly well, then turning them around quickly. First they borrowed $16 million in 1984 to acquire Chicago's Lincoln National Bank. In just two years they were able to repay the money and set their sites on an even larger target, Commercial National Bank of Chicago. This time they borrowed $35 million of the $43.7 million they paid in cash for the bank.

In March 1988 River Forest caught the attention of *Barron's National Business and Financial Weekly,* which profiled the company as the favorite stock of Kurt L. Linder, a well respected mutual fund manager. *Barron's* noted that since 1982 River Forest had grown its total assets from $190 million to around $750 million. During that time earnings also had increased from 57 cents a share to $2.05, adjusted for a pair of stock splits. The article also reported that River Forest was again in the market for further bank acquisitions: ''Of course, they have to meet pretty high standards to mesh with River Forest. 'One thing that's impressive,' Linder finds, 'is its rather high percentage of passbook savings,' which in '86 accounted for almost 15% of deposits.''

Another key factor in the success at River Forest, not mentioned by *Barron's,* was the bank's lean staff, which increased earnings by keeping down overhead. Glickman's hard-charging style was a key factor in this regard. He was known, according to *Crain's* in a 1995 article, ''for churning through employees. He hires young executives and pays them well. But they burn out fast. The cost-conscious Mr. Glickman keeps an eye on the bottom line by keeping head count low and expecting more than 100% from each hire. The strategy works: River Forest is recognized as one of the most efficient banking companies in the country, spending 47 cents for every dollar of revenues it brings in, vs. 63 cents for the average Midwest bank.''

River Forest's next acquisition was completed at the end of 1989 when it paid nearly $9 million for Calumet City Bancorp, picking up First State Bank of Calumet City. This was followed a year later by the purchase of Madison Financial Corp., Illinois's first multi-bank holding company, now boasting assets of $185 million. In the $14.6 million cash deal, River Forest picked up three Chicago-area banks: Madison Bank & Trust Co. of Chicago, Madison National Bank of Niles, and First National Bank of Wheeling. As a result River Forest became a $1 billion banking company. Two more acquisitions followed in the early 1990s. Aetna Bancorp, Inc., holding company for Aetna Bank, was acquired for about $22 million in 1991. Then, in July 1993 River Forest bought Belmont National Bank, located on Chicago's north side, from Water Tower Bancorp for $12.5 million in cash.

A major business for River Forest was student loans, but the company ran afoul of the government program in 1994. According to the rules of U.S. government-guaranteed loans, when a student defaulted on a loan, the lending bank was required to contact the student by phone to seek payment, and only then could a claim for insurance compensation be filed. River Forest learned that since 1988 some of its employees had been cutting corners, falsely documenting calls to students that were not actually made, resulting in 2,200 invalid insurance claims. River Forest reported the misconduct to the Department of Education, which resulted in a lengthy investigation. Finally, in 1999 the U.S. Justice Department filed a civil lawsuit against the company, and another year would pass before a $7.8 million settlement payment was agreed to by both parties.

Heskett's Departure in the Mid-1990s

The student loan flap was little more than a minor distraction in 1994 compared with another development that took place. In early March 1994, the ''Bob and Bob Show,'' according to *Crain's,* ended abruptly ''in a rift that sparked Mr. Heskett's sudden and unexplained resignation, rattling investors and sending River Forest's stock tumbling by 9% to around $33.50 late last week. Neither will comment on the matter, nor on reports that Mr. Heskett was escorted out of River Forest's Northwest Side headquarters by a security guard.'' *Crain's* further reported, ''According to the accounts of several bankers, Mr. Heskett resisted Mr. Glickman's proposal to change a golden parachute agreement that provides Mr. Heskett 299.9 percent of his base $280,000 salary in the event of a takeover. However, a takeover is highly unlikely because of the Glickman family's controlling interest.'' The two boyhood friends now battled each other in court over the terms of Heskett's payout, with the matter not settled for three more years, at which point Heskett was paid $1.5 million over five years.

Heskett's departure came at a difficult time for $1.4 billion River Forest, which found earnings squeezed on a number of fronts and the kind of bank acquisitions that had fueled the company's growth for the past decade more difficult to find and too expensive. Glickman installed himself as chief lending officer and River Forest began assuming more risk in its lending practice in hopes of a higher reward. According to *Crain's,* ''The bank began dealing with mortgage-broker generated prospects for home-equity loans, a process that effectively raised many loan-to-value ratios to 100% instead of the more prudent 80%.'' The company enjoyed success in the first year—''It lulled us into a sense of complacency,'' Glickman admitted— but the company was soon saddled with a large amount of

---

Key Dates:

1958: River Forest Bancorp, Inc. is incorporated.
1966: Joseph C. Glickman investor group acquires the company.
1984: Lincoln National Bank is acquired.
1986: Commercial National Bank is acquired.
1990: Madison Financial Corp. is acquired.
1996: The subsidiaries are consolidated, resulting in Corus Bankshares, Inc.
2000: Corus Asset Management is sold.

---

nonperforming residential loans. River Forest also had to contend with a loss of key personnel in the 18 months after Heskett resigned, including his senior lender and chief financial officer. Glickman continued to hire young talent, paying high wages, and also invested money to upgrade River Forest's account system, introduce telephone banking, and provide customers with home banking software. Moreover, he took steps to rein in costs in 1995 by consolidating four bank subsidiaries into one and closing one of the company's 12 branches. The consolidation was completed in June 1996, resulting in a name change, as River Forest Bancorp became Corus Bankshares, Inc.

By March 1997, three years after Heskett's abrupt exit, Glickman publicly admitted that the less restrictive lending policy he had pursued had not worked. The ''minefield that tripped Corus,'' according to *Crain's,* was ''surging delinquencies by borrowers it had never met.'' After a successful first year, ''non-performing residential loans tripled to $22.7 million and total delinquencies nearly doubled to $35.2 million—while the company's overall net-interest margin remained stuck at 5.4%.'' As a result, Corus took a major writeoff in the fourth quarter of 1996. The company still retained its low cost structure, giving it a competitive edge, but it also meant that the executive ranks were thin and bereft of experience. Corus simply lacked the personnel to consider new acquisitions or the kind of fee income opportunities rival banks were now avidly pursuing.

Corus in 1998 acquired Lawton/Russell Inc. and Moss Lawton Co., two Chicago investment advisory firms owned by Gregory M. Lawton. The assets were combined into a new unit headed by Lawton called Corus Asset Management, providing Corus with a significant revenue driver in trust and asset management. Also in 1998 Corus reentered the residential loan market; Glickman believed that the company had learned its lessons of the mid-1990s. But the most important business for the company remained commercial real estate loans, which totaled $761 million in 1998, or about half of the total loan portfolio. Wall Street firms and other lenders had pulled out of the field because of fast-growing Real Estate Investment Trusts (REITs) that were able to offer lower rates, but when REITs experienced a serious drop in stock prices in the summer of 1998, forcing them to regroup, Corus and other suburban banking groups filled the void and began backing high-profile pro-

jects, such as apartment buildings and downtown Chicago office buildings.

At the start of the new century Corus sold Corus Asset Management and became even more committed to commercial real estate lending, and as the economy slipped into recession, and the terrorist attacks of September 11, 2001 hurt the travel industry and the hotel sector, there was some concern that the company might be vulnerable. ''Given Corus' practice of making large loans on big projects—many of them approaching the bank's $65-million lending limit to a single borrower,'' *Crain's* speculated in 2003, ''just a few bad loans can wipe out a year's worth of earnings.'' Glickman stuck to his strategy, however, and it paid off. Despite being involved in such tricky sectors as hotels and apartments, Corus by the summer of 2005 had not suffered any credit losses for several years. The main reason for the company's success was that by focusing on commercial real estate it had become quite good at evaluating projects in this area. In addition, Glickman proved to be a good stock picker, at least when it came to gauging the potential of other banks. Corus invested in more than two dozen bank stocks across the country and was paid off handsomely when several of the banks were acquired during a consolidation spree.

In was likely that Corus was due for a rough patch in the commercial real estate field. ''People who invest with us should anticipate having some large losses over one or two years,'' Glickman told *Crain's.* ''If they don't have the stomach for that, they shouldn't come along for the ride.''

Principal Subsidiaries

Corus Bank, N.A.

Principal Competitors

Bank of America Corporation; Harris Bankcorp, Inc.; LaSalle Bank Corporation.

Further Reading

Daniels, Steve, ''Corus Bets Big on Other Banks,'' *Crain's Chicago Business,* November 15, 2004, p. 4.

Eaton, Leslie, ''Banking on River Forest,'' *Barron's National Business and Financial Weekly,* March 7, 1988, p. 68.

Healy, Beth, ''Profits—And Top Execs—Run Through River Forest Bancorp,'' *Crain's Chicago Business,* September 25, 1995, p. 4.

Johnsson, Julie, and Tom Corfman, ''Small Banks Rush in Where Other Lenders Fear to Tread,'' *Crain's Chicago Business,* January 11, 1999, p. 3.

Miller, James P., ''Corus Bankshares Settles U.S. Lawsuit Alleging Fraud on Student Lending,'' *Wall Street Journal,* April 10, 2000, p. 1.

Murphy, H. Lee, ''Corus Clicking with Condos,'' *Crain's Chicago Business,* May 2, 2005, p. 16.

Rose, Barbara, ''Inside Breakup of Star Bank Duo: Mysterious Rift at River Forest,'' *Crain's Chicago Business,* March 28, 1994, p. 1.

Strahler, Steven R., ''Of Corus There Are Lessons When a Star Bank Stumbles,'' *Crain's Chicago Business,* March 17, 1997, p. 3.

—Ed Dinger

CPI Aerostructures, Inc.

60 Heartland Boulevard
Edgewood, New York 11717
U.S.A.
Telephone: (631) 586-5200
Fax: (631) 586-5814
Web site: http://www.cpiaero.com

Public Company
Incorporated: 1980 as Composite Products International, Inc.
Employees: 67
Sales: $30.27 million (2004)
Stock Exchanges: American
Ticker Symbol: CVU
NAIC: 336413 Other Aircraft Parts and Auxiliary Equipment Manufacturing

CPI Aerostructures, Inc. (CPI Aero) produces structural aircraft parts, primarily for the U.S. Air Force and other branches of the military. The company outsources most of its manufacturing; its niche is combining components from third parties into complex assemblies. Major programs for the company include the massive C-5A freighter, the T-38 jet trainer, the A-10 Thunderbolt attack aircraft, and the E-3 AWACS. CPI is little known outside the aerospace industry but has been growing both organically and by acquisitions.

Origins

CPI Aero was formed in Farmingdale, New York, in 1980 as Composite Products International, Inc. It had been started by Arthur August, a 25-year veteran of Grumman Corp., as a technical consulting firm. CPI was manufacturing components within three or four years. In 2003, CPI President Edward J. Fred told the *Wall Street Transcript* that the idea was to create a company with the technical expertise of a prime contractor but the flexibility of a much smaller organization.

CPI assembled replacement parts for U.S. military aircraft under contract to the government. Projects included wind-screens for the Fairchild A-10 attack jet. Annual sales were about $2–$3 million in the early years. In the late 1980s CPI became a subcontractor to San Diego-based Rohr Industries, putting together structural components and subassemblies for a number of civil airliner projects.

"We call ourselves a mini-prime," Arthur August told *Long Island Business News.* CPI brought a high level of skills to jobs that were too small ($10 million to $50 million) for prime contractors. August added that the new availability of electronic data via floppy disk closed the "information gap" between large and small companies. "It used to be that huge staffs of people had to be utilized to access the information in government files," he explained.

CPI was able to find a ready supply of aerospace talent after the closing of Fairchild Republic's Long Island factory in 1987. August praised Long Island as "a hotbed of excellent machine shops." Another official explained to *LI Business News* that CPI was an assembler, rather than a parts manufacturer.

Sales for 1988 were reportedly between $5 million and $7 million. The firm had grown to 50 employees by this time and was adding another 10,700 square feet to its 15,000-square-foot plant in Islip, New York. In 1989, the company's name was changed to Consortium of Precision Industries, Inc.

Military Emphasis in the 1990s

The company went public in 1992 in an offering, raising about $4 million. Its name was changed to CPI Aerostructures, Inc. At the time, business was split 60–40 between commercial and military. The latter component would eventually make up virtually all revenues.

There were a couple of aborted deals in the mid-1990s. CPI canceled the acquisition of Valentec International, a producer of stamped metal parts and ammunition components. An agreement to merge CPI with VTX Electronics Corp., parent company of Vertex Technologies, was allowed to lapse.

CPI bought precision electronics parts manufacturer Kolar Machine, Inc. for $14.5 million in 1997. Based in Ithaca, New

Company Perspectives:

Our ability to offer large contractor capabilities with the flexibility and responsiveness of a small company, while staying competitive in cost and delivering superior quality products, is what defines CPI.

Key Dates:

1980: Company is incorporated in New York as Composite Products International, Inc.
1989: Name is changed to Consortium of Precision Industries, Inc.
1992: Company goes public; name is changed to CPI Aerostructures, Inc.
1997: Clinton administration outsourcing spurs growth boom.
2004: CPI wins record contract to supply wingtips and other parts for the C-5A Galaxy.
2005: Company begins doing business as CPI Aero.

York, Kolar employed about 60 people. This operation was terminated in 2001. CPI had announced plans to acquire another precision machining company but this deal was canceled. In 2000 CPI called off an acquisition of another New York aerospace manufacturer due to the equity interest demanded by a financier.

Though the acquisition plans faced such setbacks, CPI was displaying strong organic growth spurred by a military shift towards more outsourcing under the Clinton administration. This produced new demand for CPI's program management services. The company ended the 1990s with record revenues of $21.3 million in spite of the Asian financial crisis and cancellation of a major airliner program, the MD-90.

Record Contracts After 2000

CPI's shares migrated from the NASDAQ SmallCap Market (ticker: CPIA) to the American Stock Exchange in September 2000. "We believe that moving to the American Stock Exchange will increase the Company's support and visibility within the investment community" said Chairman Arthur August. The company's new ticker symbol, CVU, was an acronym for "ceiling and visibility unlimited"—pilot talk for clear skies ahead.

Most of CPI's contracts were relatively small. Arthur August described a $2 million award from Tinker Air Force Base to supply nose cowls for the E-3 Sentry as the largest single military contract the company had landed in two years. Revenues, $8.3 million in 2000, would almost double annually in the first few years of the millennium as CPI landed increasingly larger contracts.

While the U.S. Air Force was spending billions on new stealth aircraft, Vietnam era warhorses made up a large segment of its fleet. The service planned to keep these planes flying for many more years, supplying an increasing source of business for CPI.

In 2001, CPI landed a ten-year, $61 million contract to supply structural inlets for the T-38 Propulsion Modification program. The award size was a record for the company, which typically dealt in contracts worth $200,000 or so.

Chief Financial Officer Edward J. Fred took the role of CEO from company founder Arthur August in 2003. Fred, a ten-year veteran of Grumman, had joined CPI in 1994. Eric S. Rosenfeld succeeded August as chairman in late 2004.

CPI had a record sales year in 2004, as revenue rose 11 percent to $30.3 million. However, net income slipped $3 million, though gross margins remained in the 33 to 34 percent range. CPI employed a little more than five dozen employees at year end and was eligible for preferential treatment as a small business.

This helped CPI win its largest contract to date, which was also the largest government set-aside for small business: a seven-year contract to supply components including wingtips and panels for the Lockheed C-5A Galaxy. The deal had a potential value of $215 million. From 1995 to 2004, CPI had received awards of $71 million related to the program. The C-5, one of the world's largest freighters, was first delivered in 1970 and the Air Force was planning to keep them operational until 2040. Rival Vought Aircraft Industries Inc. was also farming out some of its C-5 production to CPI.

CPI initially profited from the U.S. occupation of Iraq. Its share price boomed and the company was able to raise $9 million in a secondary offering, eliminating its debt. However, heavy use of the C-5 kept the aircraft out of routine maintenance, resulting in a temporary fall off in CPI's spares sales. Aerospace industry giants such as The Boeing Company and Northrop Grumman Corp. were increasingly outsourcing their production of replacement parts to smaller companies.

CPI moved into new quarters in January 2005. At 75,000 square feet, the new facility was almost double the size of its previous plant. CEO Edward Fred told *Newsday* the company was remaining in Edgewood, New York, after several decades due to the availability of skilled workers and Long Island's aviation legacy.

Long Island Business Journal reported that local machine shops handled 30 to 40 percent of CPI's subcontracting requirements. The company patronized retired workers as well as its neighbors. In *Inc.* magazine, Fred credited his over-65 hires with improving the work ethic of his younger employees.

In a 2003 interview with the *Wall Street Transcript,* Fred compared the CPI's corporate culture to that of "The Grumman Family." Staff operated on a first-name basis. "There are no politics," said Fred. "We will not allow it." The company enjoyed low turnover. Underpinning it all was the importance of their work to the U.S. air fleet.

CPI was not well-known in the investment community, and had been working with an IR firm to raise its profile. The company also got a new logo and a new name in 2005, abbreviating its trade name to CPI Aero. Its rise landed it a spot on the *Fortune Small Business* fastest growing companies list. With virtually no similar competitors, a number of long-term contracts, and a supporting role every time C-5s delivered U.S. military resources abroad, more growth seemed likely for CPI. CEO Edward Fred told the *Long Island Business Journal,* "We don't consider ourselves a mini-prime anymore. ... We do everything the primes do."

Principal Competitors

The Boeing Company; Lockheed Martin Corporation; The Nordham Group; Northrop Grumman Corporation; Vought Aircraft Industries, Inc.

Further Reading

Anastasi, Nick, "CPI Deal Dies Over Lender's Equity Demands," *Long Island Business News,* May 5, 2000, p. 5A.

Bernstein, James, "CEO of Aircraft Parts Maker Prefers Edgewood, N.Y., Location," *Newsday,* January 4, 2005.

——, "Edgewood, N.Y., Aerospace Contractor Gets Its Largest-Ever Air Force Contract," *Newsday,* May 6, 2004.

——, "Still Up for the Job; For Veteran Aircraft Workers, The Sky's No Limit at CPI," *Newsday,* February 10, 2003.

"Company Interview: Edward Fred—CPI Aerostructures Inc.," *Wall Street Transcript,* May 5, 2003.

Conroy, Michael, "CPI Aerostructures Moves Holdings to ASE," *Long Island Business News,* September 8, 2000, p. 8A.

——, "CPI Lands Air Force Deal," *Long Island Business News,* August 25, 2000, p. 16A.

Corry, Carl, "CPI Aero Sets Buy, Bulks Up," *Long Island Business News,* November 19, 1999, p. 5A.

——, "CPI Aerostructures to Get Acquisition Funds," *Long Island Business News,* April 7, 2000, p. 10A.

"CPI Aero Expects More Contracts from Peers," *Reuters News,* April 7, 2005.

"CPI Aerostructures, Inc.," *Going Public: The IPO Reporter,* July 27, 1992.

Fahnley, John, "CPI: Inventing the Mini-Prime," *Long Island Business News,* April 3, 1989, p. 22.

Fenn, Donna, "Respect Your Elders," *Inc.,* September 1, 2003.

Gold, Jacqueline S., "NY Companies War Winners: Military Suppliers See First Benefits; Construction Contracts to Come," *Crain's New York Business,* March 24, 2003, p. 1.

Negron, Edna, "Bond to Expand Aerospace Firm; Islip Issue Will Allow More Room, New Jobs," *Newsday,* February 2, 1988, p. 27.

Schachter, Ken, "CPI Aerostructures Eyes Expansion in Wake of $215M Order," *Long Island Business News,* May 7, 2004.

——, "Gaffe Clouds CPI's $7.8M Stock Offering," *Long Island Business News,* February 28, 2003, pp. 1A+.

"6 Long Island Firms Named As *Forbes* 'Hot Shots'," *Long Island Business News,* October 17, 2003.

—Frederick C. Ingram

Cray Inc.

411 First Avenue South, Suite 600
Seattle, Washington 98104-2860
U.S.A.
Telephone: (206) 701-2000
Fax: (206) 701-2500
Web site: http://www.cray.com

Public Company
Incorporated: 1972 as Cray Research
Employees: 889
Sales: $149.2 million (2004)
Stock Exchanges: NASDAQ
Ticker Symbol: CRAY
NAIC: 334111 Electronic Computer Manufacturing

Cray Inc. is one of the world's premier producers of super-computers, a term rather loosely used to denote the fastest computers at any give time. The company's high-performance supercomputers, which are capable of performing billions of operations per second, are used by governmental agencies for classified and nonclassified applications, by governmental and academic research laboratories for scientific research, by weather centers for forecasting, and in the automotive and aerospace industries for vehicle design. Its product line includes both vector and massively parallel supercomputers. Now based in Seattle, Cray has its main manufacturing operations in Chippewa Falls, Wisconsin, and also maintains offices in Mendota Heights, Minnesota, and Burnaby, British Columbia, for software and hardware development, sales, and marketing operations. Although as a legal entity, the Cray of the early 21st century was founded in 1987 as Tera Computer Company, the company traces its earliest roots back to Cray Research, founded in 1972. A pioneer in vector supercomputing, Cray Research was acquired by Silicon Graphics, Inc. in early 1996 and then was acquired in April 2000 by Tera Computer. Following the deal, Tera renamed itself Cray Inc.

Early History

Cray Research was formed through the efforts of Seymour Cray, a recognized genius in the design of supercomputers.

Cray was born in 1925 in Chippewa Falls, Wisconsin, and spent a boyhood devoted to tinkering with electronic gear. After service in World War II working as a radio operator and then functioning as a specialist in breaking Japanese codes, he attended the University of Minnesota, earning a bachelor of science degree in electrical engineering and another in applied mathematics, both in 1950. He decided to enter the computer industry and took a job with Engineering Research Associates, founded by William C. Norris. Through a series of mergers, Engineering Research Associates was brought under the control of Sperry Rand Corporation. Norris left Engineering Research Associates and established Control Data Corporation in 1957. Cray soon followed him to the new company. Among his early projects at Control Data, Cray developed the 1604, one of the first computers to use transistors in place of vacuum tubes.

Control Data shared in the booming computer industry of the 1960s, experiencing a period of rapid growth. Cray became disenchanted with the bureaucracy that this growth created and insisted that the company build him a separate research facility in his home town of Chippewa Falls. In this new facility, he came up with the CDC 6600, the first commercial computer capable of handling three million program instructions per second. Cray's special talent was in putting the circuits of a computer very close together, reducing the time taken for electric signals to pass between them. This closeness, however, increased the heat generated by the circuits. Cray was able to introduce innovative ways of removing this heat.

Cray's success at Control Data eventually hit a stumbling block. In 1972 top management at the corporation halted his plans for a new computer, telling him he could continue working on it only after another computer project was completed.

Instead of waiting, Cray and a group of followers left Control Data to set up Cray Research. Their purpose in starting the new company was to design the first supercomputer, which they ultimately named the CRAY-1. Cray Research situated its research and development and manufacturing operations in Cray's laboratory in Chippewa Falls while establishing a headquarters in Minneapolis, Minnesota. After several years of work on the supercomputer project, the company delivered its first computer to the Los Alamos National Laboratory in 1976 for a six-month trial. Cray Research's first official customer, how-

---
Company Perspectives:

Cray Inc.'s mission is to be the premier provider of super-computing solutions for its customers' most challenging scientific and engineering problems. Cray systems are used to design safer vehicles, create new materials, discover life-saving drugs, predict severe weather and climate change, analyze complex data structures, safeguard national security, and a host of other applications that benefit humanity by advancing the frontiers of science and engineering.
---

ever, was the National Center for Atmospheric Research, which took delivery of a CRAY-1 in July 1977. This sale, totaling $8.86 million, enabled Cray Research to earn back its original investment.

The CRAY-1 was the fastest computer then available. It used the technique of vector processing, which employs a system wherein a series of operations are manipulated at once as opposed to scalar processing where operations take place one at a time. The CRAY-1 could execute 32 operations simultaneously, making it able to complete ten times the work of some larger systems. While it was delivering its first sale, the company also made its first public offering of stock. The company complemented its supercomputers with software programs, releasing its Cray Operating System (COS) and Cray Fortran Compiler in 1977.

During its early years of operation, Cray Research sold its supercomputers to government laboratories and agencies. The main application of supercomputers was in physical simulation, wherein computer models were used to analyze and forecast the response pattern likely to take place in a system composed of physical variables. Early applications of these models were in gauging the effects of nuclear weapons and in meteorology. Because these types of applications were performed under the aegis of the government, it was felt that the market for supercomputers would be very limited. In 1978, however, Cray Research was given its first order from a commercial organization.

Second Generation Systems: Early 1980s

The CRAY-1 system became the CRAY-1/S and the CRAY-1/M systems. As the 1980s began, the company decided to begin development of the next generation of supercomputers. To concentrate his efforts on that development, Seymour Cray resigned as CEO in 1980, and in 1981 he stepped down as chairman. John Rollwagen became CEO in 1980 and chairman in 1981. Cray retained his ties with the company as an independent contractor and as a member of the board of directors. The new project called for the design and development of the CRAY-2, intended to be the first computer on the market that used chips made of gallium arsenide. When the gallium arsenide chips were not available, Cray returned to silicon. The CRAY-2 system was completed in 1985, achieving a performance level ten times that of the CRAY-1.

Because the CRAY-2 project contained an element of risk due to its innovative technology, Rollwagen had the company initiate a second project based on a further upgrade of the

CRAY-1 technology. Under the direction of Steve S. Chen, the CRAY X-MP system was devised. This system marked the first use of multiprocessors, where a number of microprocessors are linked together to take on bigger jobs. Introduced in 1982, the CRAY X-MP was originally a dual processor, with a speed three times that of the CRAY-1.

As had been done with the CRAY-1, both the CRAY-2 and the CRAY X-MP supercomputers evolved into more sophisticated systems. The CRAY X-MP served as the basis for a series that consisted of 11 models. The more innovative CRAY-2 design had three-dimensional circuit interconnections linking circuit boards within a module. Software enhancements were also made available, with the 1986 introduction of a new operating system, UNICOS, which combined the COS system with the AT&T UNIX System V. This advance was especially important because UNIX was well established as the industry standard, especially in areas of scientific application, where supercomputing was so useful; meanwhile an advanced Cray Fortran Compiler, named CF77, was also made available.

Third Generation Systems: Late 1980s

By the mid-1980s Cray Research embarked on producing another generation of supercomputers, again following several paths. In 1986, Chen began working on a new system of highly innovative design, relying on significant technological advances in five different areas. After spending nearly $50 million on the project, the company decided to discontinue it. Chen left the company in 1987, taking 45 engineers from Cray Research, to form Supercomputer Systems, Inc., with plans to build a supercomputer using as many as 256 microprocessors.

Seymour Cray completed design work on the CRAY-3 supercomputer system in 1987. The CRAY-3 marked another effort to use gallium arsenide chips, a prospect made more feasible by the production of the first of the new type of chips suitable for computer production in the 1980s. While awaiting the CRAY-3, the company developed and introduced the CRAY Y-MP system, which combined the power of eight central processing units to give it 30 times the power of the original CRAY-1. The CRAY Y-MP was the first supercomputer to sustain a speed of more than one gigaflops (that is, one billion floating-point operations per second) on many applications.

Cray Research passed two important milestones in 1987. First, it delivered its 200th computer system, especially noteworthy since it had taken from 1976 to 1985 to reach a total of 100 computer shipments. This rapid expansion made possible the second milestone, the inclusion of Cray Research among the nation's largest companies, listed in the *Fortune* 500. During this period, the company was able to market its supercomputer systems to commercial corporations engaged in petroleum exploration, automobile production, and the aerospace industry.

Cray Research underwent a major restructuring in 1989. Delays in the development of the CRAY-3 system were creating very high research costs, and the scheduled date for completing the project was reportedly postponed. In addition, the company had embarked on another project, the C-90, as a new stage in the CRAY Y-MP product line. Rather than discontinue one of the projects, Rollwagen decided to create a new company, Cray Computer Corporation, to be headed by Seymour Cray. Located in Colorado Springs, Colorado, Cray Computer would continue the development of the CRAY-3 supercomputer. On November 15, 1989, Cray Research issued shares of Cray Computer to its stockholders, retaining a 10 percent ownership in the new company (which it later sold). Seymour Cray resigned from the board of directors of Cray Research, severing formal connections with the company he had formed, although he remained a stockholder.

Even after this spinoff Cray Research retained a solid position as the leading company in the production of supercomputers, with about two-thirds of the world market. In 1989, it phased out the CRAY-2 and CRAY X-MP as new models of the CRAY Y-MP were coming on line. There were continuing plans for development of the C-90 project, which was renamed the CRAY Y-MP/16. The company also began development of enhanced systems for supercomputer networking to facilitate scientists' access to Cray supercomputers from a variety of other types and brands of computers. In addition, there were plans to bring to the market an entry-level supercomputer, which would use the technology of the CRAY Y-MP, but would have a much lower price with reduced installation and operating costs.

As the market for supercomputers expanded, Cray Research diversified its sales efforts both in terms of type of customers and geographic region. In 1989 governments remained the largest customers, buying 31 percent of Cray Research's output; other important purchasers of Cray machines included universities; aerospace, petroleum, and automotive companies; energy producers; and weather and environment analysts. Sales in North America that year were 61 percent of the total. Approximately 75 percent of revenue between 1987 and 1989 was derived from sales of computer systems, with remaining income from leased systems and service fees.

Cray Research also took measures to provide for better distribution of its products. It entered into an arrangement with Control Data to make Cray supercomputers available to Control Data's customers, using Cray products to replace Control Data's line of supercomputers. Marcelo Gumucio, who directed Cray Research's marketing operation, was named president and chief operating officer in 1988. By placing more emphasis on the marketing of its products, with less attention paid to product development, Cray Research anticipated that it would be better able to meet the challenges of international competition in the supercomputer industry.

Surviving the Shakedown Period of the Early 1990s

The early 1990s were a shakedown period in the industry, particularly for independent firms in the United States, and for a time Cray itself seemed very vulnerable. Increasing competition from Japanese computer giants Fujitsu Limited, Hitachi, Ltd., and NEC Corporation, and from U.S. giant Intel Corporation, had by 1990 already cut Cray's market share to about 65 percent; this compared to the 80 percent level for the number of installed supercomputers that were Cray models. Looming on the horizon were several upstart companies seeking to build less expensive but still very powerful models—such companies as Alliant, Convex Computer, Kendall Square Research, nCube, Supercomputer Systems, and Thinking Machines—or create high-end models such as Seymour Cray's Cray Computer. At the same time, with the end of the Cold War and cutbacks or slowdowns in government spending worldwide, Cray Research faced the decline of its core market, government agencies and laboratories, the military, and government-supported entities such as universities and research centers.

Facing these threats, Rollwagen reportedly realized in 1990 that he had put the wrong man in charge in the person of Gumucio. Just when Cray needed more than ever to tap into its engineers' expertise, Gumucio's formal management style stifled their creativity and dampened morale. The more inspiring figure of Rollwagen resumed operating responsibilities.

At the end of 1990, Cray's install base stood at 262 systems in 20 countries. With little chance to expand within its core governmental market, Rollwagen knew that future growth would have to come from the commercial sector, notably the aerospace, automotive, financial, healthcare, and telecommunications industries; in order to penetrate these new markets, Cray itself would have to start offering lower-priced models.

Initially, Cray moved into the low-end supercomputer market through acquisitions. In early 1990 it made its first move by acquiring Supertek Computers, Inc., a troubled California-based maker of Cray-compatible minisupercomputers, general-purpose scientific computers that are not as powerful as standard super-computers. Since minisupercomputers sold for as little as $250,000, Cray viewed them in part as an entry level for new customers who might later be tempted to invest in a multimillion-dollar supercomputer. Also on the low end was the 1991 purchase of the superserver (high-end servers within a client-server environment) assets of the bankrupt Floating Point Systems, which became Cray Research Superservers, Inc. The following year this new subsidiary introduced its first product, the Cray S-MP, which was designed for the widely used Sun Microsystems, Inc.'s SPARC processor client-server environment.

Meanwhile, Cray's newly energized product development program produced results on both the low and high end. Within one month in late 1991, Cray introduced an entry-level system priced at about $340,000 called the Y-MP EL and its fastest vector supercomputer to date, the C90, with operational speed four times that of its previous fastest model. Cray had also begun work on a new type of supercomputer (at least for Cray), a massively parallel processing (MPP) system. Long touted by some analysts as the inevitable successor to the vector systems pioneered by Cray, MPP systems linked a number of standard microprocessors to create a virtual supercomputer at a potentially much lower cost than vector systems. MPP systems were the type that the upstart supercomputer companies were developing.

In 1992, even though its entry level system resulted in 70 new customers and exceeded the company's sales projections, Cray posted a net loss of $14.86 million. Its new products and acquisitions not yet paying off in full, the firm had to take a $42.8 million restructuring charge late in the year to cut costs; it closed one plant and eliminated 650 jobs, or one-eighth of the workforce.

Early in 1993, Rollwagen resigned after President Bill Clinton nominated him for the position of deputy secretary of commerce (a position for which he was never confirmed). Rollwagen was replaced by John F. Carlson, a 16-year Cray veteran. Later that year, Cray's first MPP system was rolled out, the T3D. Although scoffed at by rivals because it had to be linked to a standard Cray vector system, the T3D outperformed other MPP systems and helped put a number of the upstart firms out of business (such as Thinking Machines and Kendall Square Research) or into the arms of larger firms (such as Convex Computer which was acquired by Hewlett-Packard Company in 1995).

Although Cray returned to profitability in 1993, additional restructuring was needed to improve the company's operations. In 1994, which saw the resignation of Carlson, an $8.3 million charge was incurred, while in 1995, when J. Phillip Samper, former vice-chairman of Eastman Kodak and former president of Sun Microsystems, became chairman, $187.7 million in charges were booked. The 1995 charges contributed to a full-year loss of $226.4 million, but were incurred within a critical year in which three major new products were introduced: a new low-end J90 series; a new high-end vector system, the T90 series (touted as the first wireless supercomputer and five times faster than its predecessor, the C90 series); and Cray's second-generation MPP system, the T3E. The last of these, unlike its predecessor, did not need to be connected to a traditional vector supercomputer and had a top theoretical speed of one teraflops (one trillion operations per second), a long sought after speed

level. On the basis of these introductions, Cray built up by year-end 1995 a $437 million order backlog. Even without having filled the backlogged orders, Cray could still boast of having increased its installed base to 758 systems in 37 countries (nearly three times the level of 1990).

1996–99: The Silicon Graphics Interregnum

By early 1996, Cray Research was the only independent supercomputing firm left. Among the victims was Cray Computer, which declared bankruptcy early in 1995. (In September 1996 Seymour Cray died at age 71 as the result of an automobile accident in Colorado Springs.) Cray Research had survived and now had a range of products to offer from lower-end superservers and minisupercomputers to entry-level supercomputers to high-end vector and MPP supercomputer systems. But it now competed directly with several firms with much deeper pockets, the Japanese computer giants and Intel on the high end and Hewlett-Packard, IBM, Sun Microsystems, and Silicon Graphics, Inc. (SGI) on the lower workstation end. Thus when SGI, a leader in high-powered workstations with a particular emphasis on graphics-oriented systems, made a friendly take-over offer early in 1996, Samper and other Cray executives decided to accept the offer rather than attempt to continue to compete against such giants. The $745 million deal, completed in June 1996, bolstered SGI's position in the technical-computing arena and simultaneously ended the era of independent supercomputer companies, at least for a time.

Although no longer independent, Cray Research had survived the early 1990s and counted on tapping into SGI's deep pockets to develop future systems. It had to do so, however, without Samper, who resigned shortly after the takeover and who had been credited with turning Cray around in his brief tenure to the point that it was desired by SGI. Robert H. Ewald, who had been Cray's president and chief operating officer, was named general manager of Cray, in charge of day-to-day operations for the now wholly owned subsidiary of SGI.

Nearly concurrent with SGI's acquisition of Cray, SGI engineered the sale of Cray's unit that focused on high-end computers based on Sun Microsystems's UltraSparc microprocessor (the unit having evolved out of Cray's 1991 acquisition of Floating Point Systems). The machines produced by this unit competed directly with one of SGI's existing lines, so it was sold to Sun for an undisclosed sum.

Ironically, at the time of SGI's purchase of Cray, this unit was one of few thriving areas at Cray. The company's core vector supercomputer operations were already beginning to slump, and that sector of the market continued to decline over the next few years. Rather than investing in Cray, SGI instead pulled the plug on successors to both the T90 and T3E and allowed Cray to develop only one new supercomputer, the SV1, which debuted in 1998 and was about twice as fast as previous Cray models. Cray was at the same time expending much energy fighting legal battles against its Japanese rivals, particularly NEC, accusing the firm of ''dumping,'' selling its super-computers below cost in the U.S. market. In September 1997 the U.S. Commerce Department ruled in favor of Cray, imposing dumping duties of 454 percent on NEC supercomputers, effectively barring the firm from the U.S. market. Cray and

NEC continued to battle over this dispute in various venues, but in the meantime SGI, attempting to turn around its now struggling operations, was in near continuous restructuring mode, including overhauls that slashed Cray's workforce from more than 4,500 to around 800 employees. About the only positive development of this dark period in Cray's history, which some Cray staffers later derisively dubbed "the occupation," was a deal that the company struck in 1998 with the National Security Agency and other federal agencies to develop a new vector supercomputer initially dubbed the SV2. In August 1999 Silicon Graphics announced that it would sell Cray as part of yet another restructuring.

Creation of the New Cray Following 2000 Acquisition by Tera Computer

The SGI "occupation" ended in rather surprising fashion in April 2000. That month a much smaller, upstart supercomputer firm, Tera Computer Company, acquired Cray Research for less than $100 million ($50.3 million in cash plus one million shares of Tera's common stock). Tera was founded in 1987 in Washington, D.C., by James Rottsolk and Burton Smith, the former taking the operational lead and the latter serving as chief scientist. One year later, the founders moved the operation to Seattle, Washington, in order to be near the University of Washington and its first-rate computer science department and because they thought a location in the trendy Pacific Northwest would make it easier to attract top computing talent. Tera was established to develop a new kind of supercomputer, an MPP machine, but one with "shared memory." This type of computer was designed to split a problem into many smaller pieces, which are sent to many processors at once for simultaneous computation, an approach that was often compared to the way a secretarial pool works. The Tera design held out the promise of greater speed because the processors would be used more efficiently.

As it worked to develop its first model, Tera stayed afloat through a variety of funding sources, including a contract from the Defense Advanced Research Project Agency (DARPA), an arm of the U.S. Department of Defense; a public offering of stock in 1995, after which Tera was listed on the NASDAQ; and a number of private placements of stock and warrants. In early 1998 Tera finally delivered its first computer, called the MTA, to the San Diego Supercomputing Center in a deal underwritten by the Defense Department and the National Science Foundation. When it bought Cray Research two years later, this was still the firm's sole installation.

Immediately upon completing its takeover of Cray Research, Tera renamed itself Cray Inc. in an acknowledgment of Cray's longer legacy and greater name recognition. The new Cray kept its Seattle headquarters but retained a significant presence in Chippewa Falls, which remained the hub for research and development and manufacturing. While continuing to sell the old Cray's T3E and SV1 models, the new Cray focused its initial efforts on developing the SV2, soon redubbed the X1. As sort of a stopgap measure while developing the X1, Cray resolved its longstanding dispute with NEC in early 2001. NEC invested $25 million in Cray in exchange for Cray becoming a distributor of the NEC SX series of supercomputers, with exclusive North American rights and nonexclusive rights elsewhere. This deal lasted just two years: in 2003 NEC sold its investment in Cray and canceled the company's exclusive distribution rights, although Cray continued as a nonexclusive distributor of NEC supercomputers worldwide.

In the meantime, Cray hired an IBM executive, Michael Haydock, as president and CEO in October 2001, with Rottsolk remaining chairman. Just five months later, however, Haydock resigned after clashing with the board of directors on the company's direction. Rottsolk reassumed Haydock's former positions. Late in 2002 Cray released the long-awaited X1, which enabled the company to eke out a profit of $5.4 million on revenues of $155.1 million following years of losses. The first version of the X1 had a top speed of 51 teraflops, 25,000 times faster than a Pentium 4 personal computer, achieved via an architecture that was vector-based but that enabled the processors to share each other's memory. Early in 2003 Cray received $62 million in orders for the X1 from the U.S. government, one of the largest contracts in company history. Concurrently, Cray in October 2002 had entered into a $90 million contract with Sandia National Laboratories of Albuquerque, New Mexico, to develop a new supercomputer seven times more powerful than the lab's existing model, a project dubbed Red Storm. Emboldened by these successes, Cray completed a secondary offering of its stock in early 2003, raising about $50 million.

In July 2003 Cray was awarded a $49.9 million contract by DARPA to develop a prototype of a supercomputer with a balanced vector/scalar design and capable of sustained performance of more than one petaflops (one quadrillion floating-point operations per second) by 2010. This award was part of a contest sponsored by DARPA, the other two contestants being Sun Microsystems and IBM. Financial results for 2003 were promising: net income of $63.2 million on revenues of $237 million.

The Red Storm project came to fruition in 2004 as Cray began shipping the computer hardware to Sandia in installments, with the final shipment coming in the first quarter of 2005. In October 2004 Cray introduced a commercial version of Red Storm, which it dubbed the XT3, positioning it as the company's third-generation MPP system, following the T3D and T3E. The XT3 combined Cray's traditional high-bandwidth connections on the chips and circuit boards and between the cabinets that comprise the supercomputer with a number of inexpensive, off-the-shelf processing units, particularly the 64-bit Opteron processor from Advanced Micro Devices, Inc., using a Linux-based operating system.

In April 2004 Cray went down market when it acquired OctigaBay Systems Corporation for about $115 million in stock and cash. Based in Burnaby, British Columbia, OctigaBay was in the process of developing a supercomputer comparable in design, but not power, to other Cray products but at a much lower price. Cray subsequently renamed the acquired firm Cray Canada Inc. and in October 2004 released the firm's product as the Cray XD1 system. Another important development came in May 2004 when Cray was selected by the U.S. Department of Energy to provide most of the hardware for a new supercomputer at Oak Ridge National Laboratory that planners hoped would be the fastest civilian research computer in the world. The goal was to create a machine with a sustained speed of 50 teraflops, which would surpass the then world leader, Japan's

40-teraflop Earth Simulator (installed in 2002). IBM and Silicon Graphics were also selected as partners in the project.

In addition to working feverishly on the XT3 and XD1 projects, Cray was also hard at work in 2004 developing a major upgrade to the X1, the X1E, sales of which began in March 2005. The new model boasted a top speed of 147 teraflops. Cray's transition from just the one model, the X1, to its three-supercomputer lineup was unfortunately a rough one. The firm missed several of its delivery dates, cutting 2004 revenues to just $149.2 million. Cray was forced to restructure, announcing in July that about 100 employees (out of a workforce of 925) would be laid off. Various charges totaling more than $62 million, coupled with the revenue shortfall, led to a net loss for the year of $204 million.

Cray's difficulties continued in 2005, when customer delays for several large supercomputer orders adversely affected cash flow. In June the company announced the layoff of an additional 90 employees and temporary pay cuts for the remaining U.S. employees making more than $50,000 per year. By this time a leadership transition was also well underway. In March 2005 Peter J. Ungaro was promoted to president, having joined Cray in August 2003 as senior vice-president of sales, marketing, and service; he came to Cray from IBM, where he had been vice-president of worldwide deep computing sales. Ungaro was named CEO in August 2005, when Rottsolk announced his retirement. Taking over as nonexecutive chairman was Stephen C. Kiely, a company director since 1999 and a tech executive serving simultaneously as chairman of Stratus Technologies Inc. The other cofounder of Tera Computer, Burton Smith, remained Cray's chief scientist. Cray's new leaders seemed confident that a return to profitability was in the offing, once production of the new product lineup had been fully ramped up.

Principal Subsidiaries

Cray Federal Inc.; New Technology Endeavors, Inc.; Cray Australia Pty Ltd.; Cray Brazil, Inc.; Cray Computadores do Brasil Ltda. (Brazil; 99.9%); Cray Canada Inc.; Cray Canada (Washington), Inc.; Cray Canada Corp./Societe Cray Canada; Cray China Limited; Cray Computer Finland Oy; Cray Computer SAS (France); Cray Computer Deutschland GmbH (Germany); Cray Supercomputers (Israel) Ltd.; Cray Italy S.r.l.; Cray Japan, Inc.; Cray Korea, Inc.; Cray Netherlands B.V.; Cray Computer South Africa (Proprietary) Limited; Cray Computer Spain, S.L.; Cray-Tera Sweden AB; Cray Computer GmbH; Cray Taiwan, Inc.; Cray U.K. Limited.

Principal Competitors

International Business Machines Corporation; NEC Corporation; Hewlett-Packard Company; Silicon Graphics, Inc.; Dell Inc.; Sun Microsystems, Inc.; Intel Corporation; Advanced Micro Devices, Inc.

Further Reading

Alexander, Steve, "Cray Says Oregon Business Unit Is No Longer Needed," *Minneapolis Star Tribune,* May 8, 1996, p. 1D.

——, "Seymour Cray Dies of Injuries from Accident," *Minneapolis Star Tribune,* October 6, 1996, p. 1A.

——, "Struggling Firm Buys Struggling Cray Research," *Minneapolis Star Tribune,* March 3, 2000, p. 1D.

Basil, Richard, "The Origin of PCs (and Descent of Cray)," *PC Magazine,* May 15, 1984, p. 128.

Bulkeley, William M., "NEC, Cray Reach Supercomputer Deal for Sales of Japanese Machines in U.S.," *Wall Street Journal,* February 28, 2001, p. A3.

——, "Pact to Buy Cray Marks 'End of an Era' of Independent Supercomputing Firms," *Wall Street Journal,* February 27, 1996, p. B9.

Churbuck, David, "Cray Versus Japan Inc.," *Forbes,* September 4, 1989, pp. 118–19.

Clark, Don, "Cray to Unveil Systems Based on New Chip Line from AMD," *Wall Street Journal,* October 27, 2003, p. B6.

——, "Tera Computer to Acquire Cray in Surprise Bid," *Wall Street Journal,* March 2, 2000, p. B8.

Cook, James, "War Games," *Forbes,* September 12, 1983, p. 108.

Corr, O. Casey, "The Need for Speed: Local Firm's Target Is to Build Prototype of World's Fastest Computer," *Seattle Times,* August 5, 1991, p. B1.

Donlan, Thomas G., "Cray's Lament: Stock Sags As Industry Grows," *Barron's,* July 19, 2004, pp. 17–18.

——, "Dream Machines: Cray, the Pioneer of Supercomputers, May Have a New Winner," *Barron's,* June 23, 2003, pp. 38–39.

——, "Not So Super Outlook: For Cray Research, Competition Looms," *Barron's,* February 5, 1990, p. 39.

Dudley, Brier, "Cray Co-Founder, CEO Steps Down," *Seattle Times,* August 9, 2005, p. D1.

Finley, Michael, "Cray's New Way," *PC Week,* September 18, 1995, p. A5.

Gohring, Nancy, "Cray Fills Need for Computer Speed: Seattle Company's X1 Supercomputer Expected to Regain 'World's Fastest' Title," *Seattle Times,* November 18, 2002, p. C1.

Gomes, Lee, "Silicon Graphics to Lay Off Up to 1,500, Sell or Spin Off Units, Including Cray," *Wall Street Journal,* August 11, 1999, p. A3.

Gordon, Greg, "Trade Ruling Favors Cray in Rift with Japan Firms," *Minneapolis Star Tribune,* September 27, 1997, p. 1D.

Greenberger, Robert S., "Supreme Court Rejects NEC's Appeal of Supercomputing Price-Dump Ruling," *Wall Street Journal,* February 23, 1999, p. B17.

Haines, Thomas W., "It's Make-or-Break Time for Tera Computer," *Seattle Times,* October 23, 1996, p. D1.

Johnson, Jan, "A Look Inside Cray," *Datamation,* May 1982, p. 57.

"Jurassic Pact," *Economist,* March 2, 1996, pp. 58–59.

Lohr, Steve, "Silicon Graphics Reported Ready to Rescue Cray," *New York Times,* February 26, 1996, p. D1.

Markoff, John, "A Maverick Builds a New Supercomputer in a PC World," *New York Times,* February 9, 1998, p. D1.

——, "Seymour Cray, Computer Industry Pioneer and Father of the Supercomputer, Dies at 71," *New York Times,* October 6, 1996, sec. 1, p. 47.

——, "Supercomputing's New Idea Is Old One," *New York Times,* August 4, 2003, p. C1.

"Megaflopolis: Supercomputers," *Economist,* November 28, 1992, p. 79.

Mitchell, Russell, "Can Cray Reprogram Itself for Creativity?," *Business Week,* August 20, 1990, p. 86.

——, "The Genius: Meet Seymour Cray, Father of the Supercomputer," *Business Week,* April 30, 1990.

——, "Now Cray Faces Life Without Cray," *Business Week,* May 29, 1989, p. 31.

——, "What? Cray Computers Eating Dust?," *Business Week,* November 25, 1991, p. 88.

Mitchell, Russell, and Gary McWilliams, "Cray Eats Crow," *Business Week,* October 4, 1993, p. 108.

Murray, Charles J., *The Supermen: The Story of Seymour Cray and the Technical Wizards Behind the Supercomputer,* New York: Wiley, 1997, 232 p.

——, "The Ultimate Team Player: Lester T. Davis, Winner of the *Design News* Special Achiever Award, Supplied the Technical Vision That Helped Cray Research Dominate the Supercomputer Industry," *Design News,* March 6, 1995, pp. 88–95.

Murray, Chuck, "Changing Customers Fuel Supercomputing Shifts," *Chicago Tribune,* December 18, 1994.

"Perilous Descent: Cray and Supercomputers," *Economist,* April 21, 1990, pp. 81–82.

Port, Otis, and Hiroko Tashiro, "Gunning for Speed: Japan Still Has the Fastest Supercomputers, but U.S. Companies Are Closing In," *Business Week,* June 7, 2004, pp. 132–34, 136.

"The Race Is Not Always to the Gigafloppiest," *Economist,* April 15, 1989.

Rigdon, Joan E., and William M. Bulkeley, "Silicon Graphics Inc. Agrees to Acquire Cray Research in $739.2 Million Deal," *Wall Street Journal,* February 27, 1996, pp. A3, A4.

Schatz, Willie, "Who's Winning the Supercomputer Race?," *Datamation,* July 15, 1989.

Stedman, Craig, "Cray Fights for New Users," *Computerworld,* March 6, 1995.

Werner, Larry, "The City and the Supercomputer," *Minneapolis Star Tribune,* January 4, 2004, p. 1D.

—Donald R. Stabile
—update: David E. Salamie

CSG Systems International, Inc.

7887 E. Belleview Avenue, Suite 1000
Englewood, Colorado 80111
U.S.A.
Telephone: (303) 796-2850
Toll Free: (800) 366-2744
Fax: (303) 804-4088
Web site: http://www.csgsystems.com

Public Company
Incorporated: 1994 as CSG Holdings, Inc.
Employees: 2,549
Sales: $529.7 million (2004)
Stock Exchanges: NASDAQ
Ticker Symbol: CSGS
NAIC: 518219 Data Processing, Hosting, and Related Services

CSG Systems International, Inc. provides billing and customer care services to cable television, direct broadcast satellite (DBS), Internet, and telecommunications customers. Business is divided between two divisions: Global Software and Broadband. The NASDAQ-listed company serves more than 230 clients in some 40 countries, working in nearly two dozen languages and 35 different currencies. In addition to its headquarters in Englewood, Colorado, CSG maintains offices in Omaha, Nebraska; Cambridge, Massachusetts; and Miami, Florida. International offices are located in Toronto, London, Paris, Rome, Madrid, Buenos Aires, Rio de Janeiro, Mexico City, Singapore, Sydney, Tokyo, Kuala Lumpur, and Beijing. Major clients include AOL-Time Warner, Comcast, DirecTV, eBay, EchoStar Communications, Time Warner, and Verizon.

Parent Company's Founding in the Early 1970s

Before becoming an independent company, CSG was part of First Data Resources, cofounded in 1971 by CSG's first chairman, Neal Hansen. First Data started out serving the financial sector, and by 1976 had become the data processor for both Visa and MasterCard. In 1980 American Express acquired First Data in an effort to establish a financial services operation. With American Express's deep pockets, First Data, over the next decade, became the largest bank-processing company in the United States. The company branched into other sectors as well. In 1982 Hansen launched a new First Data division, called Cable Services Group, to serve the cable television industry. Hansen left a year later to become chairman and chief executive officer of Applied Communications, Inc. (ACI), an Omaha-based developer of customer-written software to process the electronic transfer of funds. It was here that he began working with George Haddix, who held a doctorate in mathematics and served on the faculties of three universities before devoting himself to a full-time business career. They sold the business to US West Inc. in 1987, stayed on, then in 1989 teamed up to start a consulting business, Hansen, Haddix and Associates, providing advisory management services to suppliers of software products and services.

Cable Services Group, in the meantime, became a dominant player in the cable television billing sector along with category leader CableData, but the unit was not performing nearly as well as First Data's core business. In 1992 American Express spun off First Data, which now faced the decision of whether to invest in its steady but complacent cable billing operation or put that money to better use by supporting its faster-growing financial business. In 1994 it placed Cable Services Group, Inc. on the block. Hansen and Haddix put together an investor group and bought the business for $137 million.

Cable Services Group took the name CSG Systems International, Inc. in November 1994. Hansen became chairman and CEO, and Haddix was named president and chief technical officer. The company started out with a reasonably good client list and two products: statement processing services and basic cable processing. CSG may have been profitable but was still in need of a turnaround. Haddix's eventual replacement as president, Jack Pogge, told *Broadcast & Cable* in a 1997 profile, "Neil Hansen is fond of saying that if there were a law against selling, none of the previous sales staff would have been convicted. Every few years, the local sales staff would take the local cable company representative out to play golf and drink beer and renew the contract—maybe." According to *Broadcast & Cable,*

Company Perspectives:

Yesterday. Today. Tomorrow. You need solutions that aren't just focused on your billing processes, but that directly impact business and how you're able to get it done. At CSG Systems, we understand more than just billing. We understand business. More importantly, we understand your business.

Hansen and Haddix made it clear it would no longer be business as usual: "The new attitude prompted a lot of departures. Of the 550 employees in CSG at the time of the buyout, 350 hit the road in the weeks and months following the deal. . . . More than just the sales department adopted a gung-ho attitude. Software development—essentially R&D—got religion and began work on new products and enhancements of existing products." CSG spent more than $37 million in two years on software development, resulting in a pair of key products: ACSR (Advanced Customer Service Representative), a cross-referencing tool that not only kept track of billing but also provided customer service reps with instant account information presented in an easy-to-navigate graphical user interface for accessing information as well as inputting an order or service call; and CSG VantagePoint, a cross-marketing tool to take advantage of the information available from the billing system.

Going Public: 1996

With its house in order, CSG was soon ready to go public to raise funds and have stock available to grow the company through acquisitions. In February 1996, the company sold 2.9 million shares at $15 a share in an initial public offering of stock led by Alex. Brown & Sons. CSG's first acquisition came in June 1996 when it paid $4.7 million for Bytel Limited, a provider of customer management software systems to the cable industry in the United Kingdom, where it served 850,000 customers. The addition of Bytel gave CSG a base on which to grow its European business. Because it was so dependent on its domestic client base, CSG wanted to expand international sales, which did not even exist in 1995 and at the end of 1996 had increased to 8 percent of the company's $132 million in revenues. In addition, CSG's software and professional services revenues grew from less than 1 percent in 1995 to 14 percent in 1996.

The company's strong domestic growth, according to *Broadcasting & Cable*, was "largely a function of rapid change in telecommunications. There's more competition than ever before as cable companies, DBS providers and Baby Bells try to carve a chunk out of each other's traditional territories. It's no longer enough to provide a single service; all major players are jockeying to offer one-stop shopping for video, voice and data services, since those who are first to market often gain a strategic advantage." Pogge explained, "Convergence and the advent of DBS—that's what generated all the activity in the billing world. . . . People had to be able to bill for new product lines so they could start packaging products to compete with new entrants in the field. To do either you have to have a billing system." As companies came to realize how difficult it was to develop and operate such a billing system, they terminated their in-house efforts and hired companies including CSG, which by

the end of 1997 emerged as the leader in cable television billing, due in large measure to a 15-year, $1.8 billion Master Subscriber contract it signed with Tele-Communications Inc., expanding the number of billed homes by nearly 50 percent. CSG also was helped by CableData's missteps. CableData, according to *Broadcasting & Cable*, "effectively shot itself in the foot on the digital cable front by charging excessively for its billing services. Indeed, that likely was what drove TCI and CSG together." In a separate but related transaction, CSG acquired the SummiTrak back-office billing system TCI had been developing for three years in a deal worth about $172 million. Although CSG did not need a new back-office system, it was able to cherry-pick specific applications from SummiTrak and also add a number of talented software engineers. The end of the year also brought the retirement of Haddix, with Pogge becoming president and COO. Revenues continued to trend upward, totaling $171.8 million in 1997, while net income improved from $25.2 million in 1996 to more than $36.1 million in 1997.

In the final two years of the 1990s, CSG completed another acquisition, paying $6 million and assuming $1.3 million in debt for US Telecom Advanced Technology Systems, Inc. CSG also continued to invest heavily in research and development, leading to the introduction of new products such as CSG Work-Force Express, an automated dispatch system for technicians; CSG Care Express, an Internet-based bill payment and customer do-it-yourself system; and CSG Real-Time Rating Engine, a system that allowed a transaction to be rated on a number of criteria. Some of the new systems were specifically geared toward the developing broadband market, which offered a great deal of promise for new business, although no one was certain when it would become a must-have product for consumers. Despite the delay in the expansion of that market, CSG enjoyed strong growth nevertheless. Sales increased to $236.6 million in 1998 and topped $322 million in 1999.

Y2K: Not an Issue

CSG entered the new century, after addressing the Y2K scare with relative ease, by enhancing the capabilities of existing products and introducing new ones and launching a new international sales effort. ACSR was web-enabled, giving it a Windows look, which helped to cut down on the training time of customer service reps. CSG also introduced CSG.net, a customer care and billing solution for the Internet protocol (IP) marketplace. Another product, CSG NextGen, was designed specifically with the international markets in mind, able to support multiple languages and currencies. CSG targeted "three-play" providers in Europe, Latin American, Asia—companies that used the same pipe to deliver voice, video, and data. Another development of note in 2000, AT&T Broadband acquired TCI, thus inheriting the 15-year Master Subscriber contract. AT&T submitted an arbitration claim questioning provisions of this agreement, and after the claim was dismissed the two sides worked out a new 12-year agreement.

Revenues approached $400 million in 2000, and net income totaled an impressive $90.5 million. With three-quarters of its sales under contract, CSG was well positioned for 2001, which saw sales increase to $477 million and net income to $113.9 million—this in spite of an economy lapsing into recession (proving that consumers were loathe to give up their cable or

Key Dates:

1982: The business is launched as Cable Services Group, a division of First Data Resources.
1994: Neal Hansen and George Haddix lead an investment group to acquire Cable Services Group, creating CSG Systems International Inc.
1996: CSG is taken public.
1997: Haddix retires.
2002: Lucent Technologies Inc. is acquired.
2005: Hansen retires.

satellite television). During the course of the year, CSG also completed three important acquisitions. It picked up Athene Software's churn management software group and its Profit-Now product. (Churn is the number of participants who discontinue their use of a service divided by the average number of total participants.) CSG also paid $16.7 million in cash to acquire Planet Consulting, an e-business consulting firm that was involved in the development of secure, real-time transaction enablement on the Internet. Finally, CSG negotiated an acquisition that would be completed in early 2002, the $261.6 million cash purchase of the billing and customer care assets of Lucent Technologies Inc., known as Kenan Systems when Lucent acquired the business in 1999 for $1.48 billion. Now it was shed as Lucent tried to raise cash to focus on core activities. Kenan had been smothered under Lucent and looked to regain some momentum with new ownership. For CSG, the addition of Kenan was a major boost, bringing with it a great deal of credibility as well as market penetration in Europe, Asia, and South America, where Kenan had more than 200 service provider customers. Also in 2002 CSG completed the acquisition of the customer care and billing assets of IBM, thereby forging a key relationship with IBM and picking up more than 34 telecommunications customers spread across every sector.

As a result of these acquisitions, CSG experienced a significant increase in revenues, which totaled $611 million in 2002. But the company's expectations were higher, leading to the stock being bid down by investors. CSG responded by imposing steep job cuts. CSG also would come under something of a cloud in 2002 when in May AT&T filed a demand for arbitration, claiming that CSG should have been charging AT&T Broadband "most-favored nation" rates, instead of charging more than many other CSG customers were paying. Later in the year Comcast Corporation became involved when it merged with AT&T Broadband. CSG sued Comcast, accusing it of conspiring with AT&T Broadband to break CSG's contract with AT&T Broadband. CSG soon dropped its suit, but the arbitration matter went forward. In October 2003 the arbitrator ruled that CSG must pay $120 million in damages to Comcast, which inherited the dispute. CSG would continue to process former AT&T Broadband customers, but not new customers

acquired by Comcast. It was a significant hit to absorb, prompting CSG to initiate new cost-cutting measures.

The deterioration in the global telecommunications industry finally had a significant impact on CSG, resulting in declining revenues in 2003 and 2004 to $529.7 million. But after recording a net loss of $26.3 million in 2003, CSG earned nearly $47.2 million in 2004. The year 2004 also saw changes in leadership. Pogge left the company, and at the end of the year Hansen announced his retirement. Pogge was replaced by John Bonde. Hansen was replaced as CEO in March 2005 by Ed Nafus, president of the company's Broadband Services Division. Hansen then retired as chairman of the board in July 2005, although he stayed on as a director. He was succeeded in this post by Bernard W. Reznicek, who had more than 40 years of experience in the electric utility industry, as the former chairman, president, and CEO of Boston Edison Company and president and CEO of Omaha Public Power District. Business was improved through the first half of 2005 and the company's new management team was optimistic about CSG's chances of achieving long-term sustainable growth. In October 2005 CSG padded its coffers by selling its billing services unit, which made software-based billing systems, to Comverse Technology Inc. for $251 million in cash.

Principal Subsidiaries

CSG Systems, Inc.; CSG Systems Software, Inc.; CSG Services, Inc.

Principal Competitors

Amdocs Limited; Convergys Corporation; DST Systems, Inc.

Further Reading

Colman, Price, "Making Billing the Bottom Line," *Broadcasting & Cable,* December 8, 1997, p. 101.
Higgins, John M., "New CSG Owners See Company Offering Broader Services," *Multichannel News,* November 21, 1994, p. 77.
Larson, Virgil, "CSG Systems Names New Chief Executive," *Omaha World-Herald,* March 9, 2005.
Lubove, Seth, "Have We Got a Dirty Movie For You!," *Forbes,* February 23, 1998, p. 70.
McElligott, Tim, "CSG's New Framework Integrating Acquisitions," *Telephony,* September 15, 2003, p. 15.
——, "With CSG As Its New Owner, Kenan Hopes to Regain Focus," *Telephony,* January 7, 2002, p. 16.
Parker, Akweil, "Comcast Settles Dispute with Englewood, Colo.-Based Billing Service," *Philadelphia Inquirer,* October 9, 2003.
Starkman, Dean, "TCI Billing System Is Bought by CSG for $106 Million," *Wall Street Journal,* August 12, 1997, p. B4.
Vuong, Andy, "Arapahoe County, Colo.-Based Telecom Services Firm's Stock Hits 52-Week Low," *Denver Post,* July 31, 2002.
Zeiger, Dinah, "CSG Systems Profits from Bundled Billing Statements Covering Cable, Phone, Internet," *Denver Business Journal,* June 20, 1997, p. 10A.

—Ed Dinger

EXPERTS IN
NAVAL SYSTEMS

DCN S.A.

2 rue Sextus Michel
Paris
F-75732 Cedex 15
France
Telephone: 33 1 40 59 50 00
Fax: 33 1 40 59 56 48
Web site: http://www.dcn.fr

State-Owned Company
Incorporated: 2003
Employees: 12,280
Sales: EUR 2.2 billion (2004)
NAIC: 336611 Ship Building and Repairing; 541710
Research and Development in the Physical,
Engineering, and Life Sciences

DCN S.A., or Direction des Constructions Navales (formerly Direction des Chantiers Navals), is a French manufacturer of warships and submarines, and the largest naval shipyard in Europe. In addition to design and engineering of naval systems and warships, and supervising their assembly, it provides maintenance and other services. One unit specializes in Combat Management Systems (CMS).

DCN's naval heritage goes back to the 17th century. Work is completed at a handful of France's ancient shipyards, including Brest, Toulon, Lorient, Ruelle, Nantes-Indret, and Saint Tropez. Cherbourg is the site for submarine construction.

DCN S.A. is at the heart of the DCN Group, Europe's largest naval manufacturer. Although owned by the French government, DCN became an independent company in 2003 and has been moving closer to defense electronics giant Thales in order to remain competitive in a consolidating industry. Although its main client has always been the French navy, DCN serves customers on all continents; international sales account for about one-third of revenues.

Origins

France has had naval shipyards at the ports of Brest and Toulon for centuries. One of the earliest shipyards was estab-

lished at Rochefort in 1631 but was shut down in 1926. The port of Toulon, east of Marseille, was built in large part around its naval dockyards, according to *Toulon in War and Revolution.* It had been Henry IV's *port de guerre* in the Mediterranean. Brest, on the peninsula of Breton, housed another important arsenal in an enduring rivalry with Great Britain. From 1660 to 1790, reports the *Histoire de Brest,* 360 ships were built there, more than half of them large warships. Employment there grew from 1,500 workers under Louis XIV to 9,360 at the peak of the Revolutionary War in America. Brest remained an important source of ships and men to fuel France's colonial ambitions in the 19th century.

A number of other facilities was established as France developed its naval power. A foundry for producing cannons was established in Ruelle in 1751. Twenty years later, a shipyard opened in Nantes-Indret, which would become a steam engine and boiler center. A shipyard at the Lorient headquarters of the Compagnie des Indies was taken over by the French navy in 1778.

18th- and 19th-Century Technology

Construction consumed an enormous amount of natural resources. In the 18th century, the largest battleships each consumed 4,000 mature oak trees in their construction, notes *Toulon in War and Revolution.* Vast forest holdings were required to support the shipyards; France also traded with other nations, the Baltics in particular, for mast timbers. More than 100 tons of metal and untold measures of hemp (for rope and sails) were needed as well. These ships cost more than one million *livres* (a livre was equivalent to a pound of silver at the time; the currency was discontinued late in the 18th century) to build. Prison hulks docked at Toulon, Brest, and Rouchefort provided a source of cheap labor. Toulon had up to 1,000 convicts and about 2,000 free men employed in shipbuilding during the American War in the 1780s. During this time, spending on naval shipbuilding at Toulon reached the unprecedented level of ten million *livres* per year. The town's dependence on the industry resulted in mass unemployment in the Seven Years War a couple of decades earlier.

A large 19th-century warship could take more than ten years to complete. Thousands of arsenal workers were em-

Company Perspectives:

DCN is a major player in the European and world markets for high-added-value naval defence systems. With its long and proud history, the DCN group provides the French Navy and other client forces with direct access to proven capacity for innovation and vast experience in naval and naval air arm systems, through life support and related services.

DCN delivers products meeting its customers' priority requirements, including high-level integration, cost control and interoperability with joint and allied systems.

DCN is one of the few naval defence companies in the world to propose an integrated approach to warships and services. As a prime contractor, shipbuilder and systems integrator, the company offers resources and expertise spanning the entire naval defence value chain and product lifecycles, from design concept to decommissioning.

ployed in trades that were passed down from generation to generation. Warships had evolved to iron by the mid-1800s, though features such as sails and battle tactics such as ramming were still in evidence (the latter was said to be suited to the Gallic disposition).

In the late 1800s France worked to keep its fleet competitive in the age of steel, at one point trying out a couple of American-supplied ironclads. The country had a new threat in innovative ship and gun designs from Italy. While there were private armorers, they had difficulty meeting the expense of developing new steel guns, according to Theodore Ropp's study of the period, *Development of a Modern Navy.*

Yet another shipyard was added, at Cherbourg, in 1813. This would eventually become the center of submarine production. In 1937, the government acquired a torpedo boat factory at Saint Tropez that had been privately founded by the Schneider group in 1907.

Powering Gaullist Policy After World War II

France's defense industry was, in large part, state-controlled in the latter half of the 20th century. Although a fraction of the size of that in the United States, the country maintained an independent defense establishment, including a nuclear component. Under the DGA (Direction Générale pour l'Armement), the country's centralized procurement agency, DCN (Direction des Constructions Navales), produced a range of vessels for the navy, including ballistic missile submarines, attack subs, nuclear-powered aircraft carriers, and some frigates. (Smaller craft were built by Chantiers de l'Atlantique, Constructions Méchaniques de Normandie, and the Société Française de Constructions Navales.)

Exports became an important source of funds to maintain French technical independence. In 1970 Sofrantem formed to facilitate international sales for DCN. DCN International, a private subsidiary, was created in October 1990 to handle DCN's international sales efforts and partnerships. Another subsidiary called DCN Log also was established from the logistics department of the Navfco company.

1990s Restructuring

DCN began the 1990s with about 26,800 employees who had lifetime job security. Annual sales were about FRF 20 billion ($4 billion). France's defense industry was restructured during the decade after post-glasnost budget cuts and dwindling foreign sales. In 1997, the DGA established separate divisions for procurement (SPN) and shipbuilding; DCN was responsible for the latter.

International sales picked up in the mid-1990s as DCN landed large orders with Saudi Arabia and other nations. DCN successfully broke into the South American submarine market in the late 1990s when it led a group building two conventional subs for Chile. DCN was Europe's largest naval group, and had turnover of FRF 13 billion ($2.2 billion) by the late 1990s.

Independence After 2000

DCN was made independent of the DGA in 2000. In June 2003 the company became a state-owned commercial enterprise under private law.

Armaris, a joint venture with defense electronics firm Thales Naval France, was formed in 2002 to produce products for export. DCN and Thales continued drawing nearer; a plan to group Thales Naval France with DCN and Armaris was approaching completion in the fall of 2005. Thales was acquiring a 35 percent holding in government-owned DCN in September 2005. Sources estimated DCN's valuation at up to EUR 3 billion (it had revenues of EUR 2.6 billion in 2004); it was considered the largest naval shipyard in Europe. Defense Minister Michèle Alliot-Marie told *La Tribune* it was necessary for DCN to participate in the consolidation of the European naval shipbuilding industry to remain competitive against southeast Asia and others. A partnership between DCN-Thales and Germany's Thyssenkrupp-HDW grouping was proposed. DCN had considered buying HDW (Howaldtswerke Deutsche Werft) earlier.

In October 2005 the company began the largest (worth EUR 11 billion overall) shipbuilding program Europe had ever seen: 17 multirole frigates for France and ten for Italy (frégates multimissions or FREMM). DCN would get 75 percent of the EUR 3.5 billion award for this first phase, which would keep the company occupied until 2015.

The European Multi-Mission or FREMM program had been started in 1993 as a joint study of air defense frigates with the United Kingdom. Italy joined the partnership in 1994 and the United Kingdom stepped out five years later. DCN International launched its first Horizon-class frigate in March 2005.

Another large order came from India in October 2005: six Scorpene submarines worth EUR 2.4 billion ($3 billion). These were being supplied with a Spanish partner for final assembly at the Mazagaon docks in Mumbai (Bombay).

DCN also was awaiting news for awards to build a half-dozen Barracuda class nuclear subs and a second aircraft carrier codenamed PA2 to supplement France's *Charles de Gaulle*. DCN had formed a joint venture with Thales called MOPA2 to build the latter project. DCN also was working with another French shipbuilder, Chantiers de l'Atlantique, which had been

Key Dates:

1631: One of France's earliest shipyards is established at Rochefort.
1751: A cannon foundry is created at Ruelle.
1771: A shipyard opens at Nantes-Indret.
1778: The navy takes over the Lorient shipyard from Compagnie des Indes.
1813: Cherbourg begins building ships.
1907: Schneider & Cie. forms a torpedo plant in Saint Tropez.
1926: The Rochefort shipyard closes.
1937: The government acquires the Saint Tropez torpedo plant.
1970: Sofrantem is formed to handle international sales.
1990: DCN International is formed to sell products in the world market.
1997: Naval shipbuilding is reorganized into separate divisions for procurement (SPN) and manufacturing (DCN).
2002: The Armaris joint venture is formed with Thales.
2003: DCN becomes a state-owned company under private law.

primarily involved in making commercial vessels. DCN subcontracted construction of fore sections of a pair of Mistral-class projections and command vessels to Chantiers.

The French navy had ordered a half dozen new Barracuda class nuclear powered attack subs for delivery by 2022 to replace its Rubis class. Other subjects of research included a modular submarine called the SMX-22 and a new generation of Gowind corvettes. DCN also was studying ways to integrate the increasingly complex electronic equipment carried by warships in new lightweight masts. Although labor unions had initially viewed the company's transformation into a société anonyme with unease, employment at the Toulon site was growing due to its considerable order book.

Principal Subsidiaries

Armaris (50%); DCN International; DCN Log.

Principal Divisions

DCN Warships & Systems; DCN Services & Equipment.

Principal Operating Units

DCN Engineering; DCN Cherbourg; DCN Lorient; DCN Services Brest; DCN Services Toulon; DCN Underwater Weapons; DCN CMS; DCN Equipment; DCN Propulsion.

Principal Competitors

BAE Systems Ltd.; Blohm + Voss GmbH; General Dynamics Corporation; German Submarine Consortium; Howaldtswerke-Deutsche Werft GmbH; Northrop Grumman Corporation.

Further Reading

"A Brest, le *Mistral* prend forme," *Ouest France,* May 6, 2003.

Browning, E.S., "France's Military Shipbuilders Trying to Cut Bureaucracy—Their Goal Is to Establish Commercial Export Unit for Flexibility and Profit," *Wall Street Journal,* September 24, 1990.

Cathala, Anne-Sophie, "DCN met le cap sur l'emploi," *Le Figaro,* September 12, 2005.

Cloître, Marie-Thérèse, ed., *Histoire de Brest,* Brest: Centre de Recherche Bretonne et Celtique, Université de Bretagne Occidentale, 2000.

Crook, Malcolm, "City and Dockyards," in *Toulon in War and Revolution: From the Ancien Régime to the Restoration, 1750–1820,* Manchester and New York: Manchester University Press, 1991, pp. 7-25.

"DCN-Thales: le government promet un dénouement rapide," *Agence France Presse,* September 30, 2005.

Fiszer, Michal, "Horizon/Orizonte Frigates Near Service: France and Italy Launch a New Class of Capable Air-Defense Ships," *Journal of Electronic Defense,* July 2005, pp. 51+.

"French Break German Lock on S.A. Sub Market," *Navy News & Undersea Technology,* January 26, 1998.

"India, France Sign 2.4-bln-euro Submarine Deal," *Agence France Presse,* October 6, 2005.

"Lessons in Restructuring Defense Industry: The French Experience," Washington, D.C.: Congress of the U.S., Office of Technology Assessment, 1992.

Michaud, Bernard, "Mariage reporté entre DCN et Thales," *Sud Ouest,* August 22, 2005.

"Le rapprochement DCN-Thales doit être bouclé à l'automne," *La Tribune,* September 30, 2005.

Ropp, Theodore, *The Development of a Modern Navy: French Naval Policy 1871–1904,* Annapolis, Md.: Naval Institute Press, 1987.

"Saudi Deal Makes Big Splash," *Middle East Economic Digest,* September 15, 1995, pp. 13+.

"Le Terrible sort des ordinateurs," *Ouest France,* September 30, 2005.

Tieman, Ross, "France Targets Defence Industry for Overhaul," *Sunday Business* (London), October 13, 2002.

—Frederick C. Ingram

DIRECTV, Inc.

2230 East Imperial Highway
El Segundo, California 90245
U.S.A.
Telephone: (310) 535-5000
Toll Free: (800) 531-5000
Fax: (310) 535-5225
Web site: http://www.directv.com

Private Company
Incorporated: 1993
Employees: 1,400
Sales: $7.19 billion (2004)
NAIC: 515210 Cable and Other Subscription
Programming

DIRECTV, Inc. is the world's largest satellite television provider, serving nearly 15 million subscribers in the United States and 1.5 million subscribers in Latin America. DIRECTV is owned by The DIRECTV Group, Inc., a publicly traded company that is 34-percent owned by News Corp. subsidiary, Fox Entertainment Group, Inc.

Origins

Residential satellite television got its start in the early 1980s, but it would be years until the business developed into a legitimate industry. Early efforts failed largely because of poor signal quality and insufficient programming, which generally consisted of sporting events. Sports as a mainstay of programming was not at fault—the market appeal of sporting events represented an all-powerful force in the broadcast industry—but the depth and diversity of the programming offered by satellite broadcasters paled against the content provided by cable operators. One of satellite broadcasting's advantages was that it could reach markets and communities cable lines had not reached, which freed satellite operators from competing head to head with cable in some locations. However, catering to the sliver of potential customers in hard to reach areas would never be enough to cover operating costs. To develop into genuine competitors within the broadcast market, satellite operators had to steal business away from cable companies, something their meager programming offerings and scratchy picture quality could not do in the early 1980s. Consumers, by and large, opted for cable boxes on top of their television sets rather than for high-priced, massive satellite dishes in their backyards. The era of residential satellite service, it became apparent, had arrived prematurely. Hughes Electronics Corporation, a unit of General Motors, realized the fundamental flaws of direct broadcast satellite (DBS) service when it first began to develop DBS plans in 1985. The problem of programming could be overcome by forging distribution deals, but the inherent problems of signal clarity and capacity were inescapable. Hughes's position, and with it the market feasibility of DBS service, was transformed by the development of digital compression technology. Digital compression increased the broadcast capacity of satellites by as much as eightfold. Perhaps more important, the new technology produced a much sharper image than earlier satellite broadcasting efforts, sharper, satellite operators could claim, than the picture received by cable customers. The ramifications were profound, suddenly giving DBS operators a chance to profit in a multibillion-dollar market. Hughes, as the largest satellite company in the world, wanted to dominate the market potential created by digital compression technology. Beginning in 1990, Hughes started forming DIRECTV to fulfill its objective, allocating $750 million to fund the company's start-up.

To steward Hughes's entry into DBS, the company picked Eddy W. Hartenstein, a senior project engineer for scientific, commercial, and classified satellite programs for Hughes Aircraft Co. Hartenstein, as the orchestrator of DIRECTV's formation and development, championed the cause of satellite television, acting as the industry's vocal and influential promoter. His first priority as the 1990s got underway was to forge partnerships with other companies, alliances that would give DIRECTV the hardware, software, and the programming to become operational. During the company's formative years, Hartenstein allied DIRECTV with high-profile concerns such as Sony Corporation and Digital Equipment Corporation. Thomson Consumer Electronics (a subsidiary of Thomson S.A.), for instance, entered into an agreement with DIRECTV to manufacture the satellite dishes that would eventually be marketed to consumers. Aside from such major tasks as perfecting the home receiving equipment, getting the

Company Perspectives:

DIRECTV is continuing to redefine the world of television entertainment. Advances in technology are enabling our viewers to have greater control over their viewing and experience new services on their television, such as digital video recording (DVR), high-definition TV, expanded multi-cultural programming, interactive programming and more.

programming in place, and, of course, launching a satellite, there were equally important projects such as developing the software systems to control programming, scheduling, billing, and other functions. "This is probably the single most complex television start-up in history," Hartenstein remarked in a March 28, 1994 interview with *Broadcasting & Cable*. "There is an incredible amount of detail work that we need to do and make sure is working correctly before we turn this on-line and generate revenues," he explained.

As Hartenstein set out, only the problem of picture quality had been resolved from satellite television's previous flawed existence. The problems of programming and hardware costs incurred by the customer remained to be solved, representing two of the most important factors that would determine DIRECTV's fate. The company needed programming that would justify in the minds of consumers the expense of a $700 to $900 satellite dish, and it needed programming capable of luring customers away from cable television providers. The cost of dishes, according to Hartenstein, would fall as more and more people became DIRECTV subscribers, which left obtaining programming as the company's primary objective. Good programming would attract customers, which would drive down the cost of dishes, and, in turn, attract even more customers.

Toward this end, Hartenstein scrambled to secure the programming that would serve as the foundation for DIRECTV's success. In 1993, the company signed distribution agreements with several leading entertainment programmers. The agreements gave DIRECTV the right to distribute programming services owned by The Sci-Fi Channel, TNN: The Nashville Network, CMT: Country Music Television, The Family Channel, USA Network, and Turner Broadcasting. The pursuit of distribution agreements did not stop there, nor would they ever. The company was actively negotiating with other cable programmers, professional and collegiate sports leagues, and movie studios, part of its constant effort to offer satellite viewers more content than cable operators.

First Satellite Launch: 1993

As the deal-making waged on and the operational aspects of DIRECTV's infrastructure gradually came together, a pivotal moment in the company's existence arrived before the end of the year. In December 1993, the company's first satellite was launched, ascending then resting 23,000 miles above the earth. Approximately five times stronger than traditional satellites and capable of transmitting up to eight times as many video signals, the company's first Hughes-built "bird" was soon ready to beam programming and information directly to a DIRECTV

home receiving unit, its high-power capabilities requiring a dish, or antenna, measuring only 18 inches. All that remained for the company to become a revenue-generating enterprise was the completion of the 13 major software systems on Earth that controlled DIRECTV's programming, scheduling, and billing.

The date for DIRECTV's DBS service to begin was set for May 1, 1994. In preparation for the momentous event, agreements were reached with 2,000 dealers and 1,000 electronics stores, including Sears and Circuit City, to sell the equipment required for DIRECTV service. Agreements were in place for another 2,000 outlets, including Ward's and Best Buy stores, to sell the service beginning in the fall of 1994. By the end of 1995, Hartenstein wanted to have 8,000 retailers selling the company's pizza-sized satellite dishes. Hartenstein had other target numbers he was trying to reach as the DBS-1 satellite sat positioned in geosynchronous orbit, none more important than the projected break-even point for his pioneering company. According to the company's estimates, three million subscribers paying $30 in monthly subscription fees would push DIRECTV past the point of operating at a loss and usher in profitability. Hartenstein hoped to reach this threshold by late 1996 or early 1997. By 2000, Hartenstein projected there would be ten million DIRECTV subscribers.

Initially, DIRECTV's DBS service was sold in five markets. Expansion into seven states was completed by June 1994, setting up the coast-to-coast launch of DBS service in the fall of 1994. By the time the company rolled out national service, its broadcast capabilities had been bolstered considerably. The DBS-2 satellite was launched in early August 1994, increasing the company's broadcasting capacity to 40 channels of cable programming and 50 pay-per-view channels. A third satellite was launched in mid-1995, making DIRECTV's basic lineup roughly four times the size of cable's offering.

The sale of DIRECTV dishes was brisk at first, aided by the launch of DBS-1 just before the holiday season. The company boasted approximately 350,000 subscribers by the end of 1994, exceeding its expectations, and was gaining new subscribers at a rate of 3,000 per day. It was a promising start, but there was still much to accomplish before Hartenstein could claim a lasting hold on the broadcast market.

The obvious need was to gain as many new subscribers as possible to reach the point where the company was profitable. How to gain new subscribers proved to be a murkier question, posing a problem with no easy solution and sparking debate among industry analysts and satellite broadcasters alike. The dilemma centered on the long-term value of offering potential customers subsidies on the hardware required to receive DBS service. By reducing the cost of dishes, so the thinking went, more people would be willing to subscribe to satellite service. The greater the subsidies, however, the greater the operating losses became, as the difference between manufacturing costs and what the customer paid for the hardware widened. Considering that DIRECTV was backed by Hughes and General Motors, the company could absorb financial losses that other, less-endowed companies could not sustain, but the use of subsidies had another drawback, one perceived to be more menacing to a company's fortunes than escalating operating losses. Consensus maintained that if subscribers paid less up-front costs, they were

Key Dates:

1990: Hughes Electronics Corporation begins formulating plans for DIRECTV.
1993: First DIRECTV satellite is launched.
1994: DIRECTV's programming is beamed to subscribers for the first time.
1996: A record one million subscribers sign up during the year.
1999: Primestar and United States Satellite Broadcasting are acquired.
2003: Rupert Murdoch's News Corp. acquires a 34 percent, controlling interest in DIRECTV.
2004: DIRECTV acquires Pegasus Communications and the National Rural Telecommunications Cooperative, gaining 1.4 million new subscribers.

likelier to later cancel their subscriptions, or "churn out," because they had made less of a financial investment in the service. Gaining new subscribers in this respect represented artificial growth, causing greater operating losses and a higher churn-out rate, which could render a DBS service provider financially moribund.

The catch-22 of subsidizing subscriber growth presented Hartenstein with a difficult challenge as he set out to increase DIRECTV's subscriber base. Nevertheless, he could take comfort in DIRECTV's stalwart industry position. Roughly a year after launching its service the company ranked as the largest competitor in the DBS television market, far ahead of its closest competitor, Primestar. By June 1995, DIRECTV had more than 500,000 subscribers scattered across the United States, with projections calling for the company to slip past the one-millionth-subscriber mark by the end of 1995. In early 1996, the company gained its first major partner when AT&T Corp. paid $137.5 million for a 2.5 percent stake in the company, kicking off a banner year in which one million new subscribers signed up for DIRECTV. By the end of 1996, revenues reached $621 million, but profitability still eluded the company.

Chasing Growth in the Late 1990s

DIRECTV performed remarkably well in its fourth year of operation, but the celebratory mood that should have pervaded company headquarters in El Segundo, California, was tempered by an anticlimactic air. During the year, the company signed up its three millionth subscriber, reaching the point of projected profitability, but 1997 ended with a loss. In other respects, the company was demonstrating enviable strength. DIRECTV had nearly one million more subscribers than its closest competitor, it controlled nearly 50 percent of the U.S. DBS market, and the company's revenues had more than doubled in 1997, reaching $1.28 billion. The cost of luring new subscribers, however, meant jeopardizing profitability. In an effort to stimulate demand, the company lowered the price of its dish and set-top box to $199, further distancing itself from the threshold of profitability. Although DIRECTV was recording robust growth, some analysts wondered whether the company would accumulate too much in operating losses while it hotly pursued new subscribers.

As the company entered 1998, the word from Hughes was that the company would sacrifice profits to gain new subscribers. One of the major factors prompting the decision was the expected implementation of digital compression technology by the cable industry. In early 1998, the cable industry was beginning to embrace the technology, which as it had for DBS operators, would increase capacity and picture quality. DIRECTV believed it needed to act fast before an important marketing advantage began to lose its strength. In a March 1998 interview with the *Los Angeles Business Journal*, Mike Smith, Hughes's chairman and chief executive officer, explained: "We have decided to postpone profitability in our DIRECTV business another year because we think it's better to lower our prices and add more subscribers while cable is still vulnerable. They haven't yet gone to digital . . . we are trying to take advantage of this window that we now have."

The actions of DIRECTV during the last years of the 1990s demonstrated its determination to sign up new subscribers. In March 1999, the company began a national retail and marketing promotion to new subscribers that included free installation and three months of free service. The offering helped DIRECTV sign up 120,000 new subscribers in March alone, leading to a record first quarter of 1999 during which more than 300,000 subscribers signed up. A bigger boost to the company's subscriber rolls arrived via acquisition. In January 1999, Hughes announced the acquisition of DIRECTV's major partner, United States Satellite Broadcasting, and DIRECTV's closest competitor, Primestar, as well as the purchase of two high-power satellites. After the deals were completed, DIRECTV's programming selection exceeded 200 channels and its subscriber count swelled to more than seven million.

By August 2000, DIRECTV had more than 8.5 million subscribers, trailing only cable behemoths AT&T Broadband and Time Warner in the number of multichannel video subscribers. According to company projections, DIRECTV expected to reach ten million subscribers by the end of the year. Although the company was close to turning a profit, some analysts were worried by slackening new subscriber growth, while other analysts offered a more optimistic perspective, pointing to potential growth that could witness DIRECTV catapulting past AT&T Broadband and Time Warner by 2005.

A New Owner in the 21st Century

The first half of the new decade saw dramatic changes in the U.S. pay-television market, as competition intensified, new technologies emerged, and new management teams battled against one another for supremacy. The period was most noteworthy for the massive deals completed that put new owners in charge of the country's premier cable and satellite companies. On the cable side, AT&T Broadband bowed out after Comcast Corporation acquired its cable and Internet operations for a staggering $54 billion in late 2002, giving DIRECTV's most formidable foe a new name. On the satellite side, DIRECTV found itself to be the object of someone else's fancy as well after General Motors put Hughes Electronics on the auction block in 2000. The announcement attracted the attention of media mogul Rupert Murdoch, who had been trying to establish a presence in the U.S. DBS market since 1983. Murdoch, through his company, News Corp., owned or controlled media businesses that generated $30 billion in annual revenue, presiding over an empire that published 175 newspapers, delivered television programming in five continents, and, in the United States, owned 35 television stations, the Twentieth Century Fox studio, and the Fox Network. Murdoch desperately wanted DIRECTV, but the pursuit took persistence, resulting in a three-year chase that underscored the value of DIRECTV's hold on the DBS market.

Murdoch and General Motors struggled to come to terms over the fate of DIRECTV. For 18 months, the parties negotiated the particulars of the deal, but they were unable to agree on a price. At this point, EchoStar Communications Corp., led by Charles Ergen, entered a bid for Hughes Electronics, exacerbating Murdoch's frustration. In 1997, Ergen and Murdoch had attempted to join forces in the satellite business, one of a handful of attempts by Murdoch to secure a foothold in the U.S. DBS market, but the partnership flared, according to reports, into a bitter rivalry. Ergen surprised industry onlookers by raising $26 billion, enough to gain General Motors' nod of approval in October 2001, but Murdoch refused to give up his fight. He marshaled his forces to mount a challenge against the proposed transaction, sending lobbyists to the U.S. Congress and to the Federal Communications Commission to undermine Ergen's attempt to acquire DIRECTV. Murdoch prevailed, achieving his objective in December 2002 when the U.S. Justice Department ruled that the combination of the two satellite companies would be anti-competitive. With the interdictive assault by Ergen brushed aside, Murdoch renewed talks with General Motors, reaching an agreement with the car maker to acquire a 34 percent controlling stake in Hughes Electronics in April 2003. After review by regulatory authorities, the deal closed in December 2003, giving Murdoch control of a U.S. satellite company after 20 years of failed attempts.

In the aftermath of the pivotal deal, DIRECTV entered a new era of existence, one supported by the massive resources at Murdoch's disposal. The name of the company's parent company was changed from Hughes Electronics Corp. to The DIRECTV Group, Inc. Ownership of The DIRECTV Group, and by extension, DIRECTV, Inc., was passed from News Corp. to one of its subsidiaries, Fox Entertainment Group, Inc. Mitchell Stern, the chief executive officer of the Fox TV Stations Group, was assigned to head DIRECTV's operations, working under Chase Carey, who was appointed chief executive officer of The DIRECTV Group. Carey ordered sweeping changes for the operations he inherited, shedding nearly every asset that was not related to satellite broadcasting. He sold DIRECTV's 80 percent interest in satellite-launch service PanAmSat for $2.6 billion, divested the company's set-top-box manufacturing division, and cut its holdings in XM Satellite Radio. After the streamlining efforts, which included reducing DIRECTV's headquarters payroll by roughly 50 percent, Carey spent $1.4 billion to acquire two rural satellite companies, Pegasus Communications and the National Rural Telecommunications Cooperative.

Under Murdoch's control, DIRECTV's subscriber rolls swelled at an accelerated rate, but it continued to suffer from a high churn rate and a lack of profits. The company's strategy of adding new subscribers at the expense of short-term profitability, essentially subsidizing its expansion, continued under

Murdoch's rule, aping the strategy he employed with the British Sky Broadcasting Group (BSkyB). Once Murdoch gained a controlling interest in BSkyB, he invested heavily in technology as a lure to attract customers, at one point losing $1 billion to provide viewers with digital boxes. He was expected to do the same with DIRECTV by wresting subscribers away from cable with technological offerings. In many respects, the strategy underpinning DIRECTV before and after News Corp. took control was the same, but with the enormous financial resources and renowned managerial skills of Murdoch supporting and guiding DIRECTV's fortunes, the company's hopes for a successful future were brighter than at any point in its past.

Principal Subsidiaries

DIRECTV Holdings, LLC; DIRECTV Financing Co., Inc.; DIRECTV Enterprises, LLC; DIRECTV Customers Services, Inc.; DIRECTV Programming Holdings I, Inc.; DIRECTV Programming Holdings II, Inc.; DIRECTV Merchandising, Inc.; DIRECTV Operations, LLC; DIRECTV International Inc.; DIRECTV Latin America Holdings, Inc.; DIRECTV Mexico Holdings, LLC; DIRECTV Trinidad Limited (Trinidad/Tobago); DIRECTV Latin America, LLC.

Principal Competitors

Comcast Corporation; EchoStar Communications Corporation; Time Warner Cable Inc.

Further Reading

Albiniak, Paige, "Growth Comes at a Cost: DIRECTV Is Growing but Needs Expensive Customer Incentives to Do IT," *Broadcasting & Cable,* November 29, 2004, p. 26.

——, "Murdoch's 21-Year Quest: That's How Long It Took News Corp. Titan to Gain Control of a DBS Operation," *Broadcasting & Cable,* November 29, 2004, p. 30.

Amdur, Meredith, "Fox Stations Chief Set to Head DIRECTV," *Daily Variety,* November 24, 2003, p. 6.

Brown, Rich, "Dishing Up Full Power," *Broadcasting & Cable,* March 28, 1994, p. 48.

Colman, Price, "A Mixed Bag for DBS: While Subscribers and Revenue Are Growing, Industry Faces Variety of Challenges," *Broadcasting & Cable,* June 9, 1997, p. 41.

——, "No Laurel-Resting for DirecTV's Hartenstein," *Broadcasting & Cable,* November 3, 1997, p. 52.

Crespo, Mariana, " 'You Get More Eyeballs,' " *Financial World,* February 14, 1995, p. 94.

"DIRECTV Launches First of 4 Next-Gen HD Satellites," *Online Reporter,* April 30, 2005, p. 3.

"DIRECTV Turns Quarterly Profit, Keeps Adding Subscribers," *Online Reporter,* August 6, 2005, p. 5.

Dziatkiewicz, Mark, "The One to Watch," *America's Network,* June 15, 1995, p. 55.

"Eddy Hartenstein," *Satellite Communications,* July 1993, p. 26.

Fine, Howard, "Smith on Mission to Beat Cable with DirecTV," *Los Angeles Business Journal,* March 9, 1998, p. 3.

Gorchov, Jolie, "Satellite TV Gets Boost, but Cable Still Has an Edge," *Los Angeles Business Journal,* December 13, 1999, p. 8.

Green, Michelle Y., "The DirecTV System, How It Works," *Broadcasting & Cable,* May 31, 1999, p. 24.

——, "Sitting on Top of the World," *Broadcasting & Cable,* May 31, 1999, p. 4.

Grover, Richard, "Rupert's World," *Business Week,* January 19, 2004, p. 52.

Krause, Reinhardt, ''Murdoch's Channeled His DIRECTV Efforts into Taking Subscribers from Cable Firms,'' *Investor's Business Daily,* August 6, 2004, p A1.

——, ''Satellite TV Plans an Offensive Aimed at Better Local Channels,'' *Investor's Business Daily,* August 30, 2005, p. A4.

La Franco, Robert, ''The Unlikely Mogul,'' *Forbes,* November 30, 1998, p. 52.

Lashinsky, Adam, ''Murdoch's Air War,'' *Fortune,* December 13, 2004, p. 130.

Maney, Kevin, ''Revolution from on High,'' *Canadian Business,* June 1995, p. 81.

Mermigas, Diane, ''Hughes Denies DirecTV Spinoff; Parent Company Seeks Acquisitions to Complement Its Satellite Service,'' *Electronic Media,* June 12, 2000, p. 3.

''News Corp. to Sell Sky Latin America to Partly-Owned DIRECTV,'' *AsiaPulse News,* October 12, 2004.

Potkewitz, Hilary, ''Leaner DIRECTV Facing Challenges of Churn,'' *Los Angeles Business Journal,* March 14, 2005, p. 1.

Sherman, Jay, ''DIRECTV Churn Dismays Wall St.,'' *TelevisionWeek,* November 8, 2004, p. 15.

—Jeffrey L. Covell

Energy Conversion Devices, Inc.

2956 Waterview Drive
Rochester Hills, Michigan 48309
U.S.A.
Telephone: (248) 293-0440
Toll Free: (800) 528-0617
Fax: (248) 844-1214
Web site: http://www.ovonic.com

Public Company
Incorporated: 1964
Employees: 721
Sales: $66.3 million (2004)
Stock Exchanges: NASDAQ
Ticker Symbol: ENER
NAIC: 335911 Storage Battery Manufacturing

Energy Conversion Devices, Inc. (ECD) is a Rochester Hills, Michigan-based company that despite producing few profits in more than 40 years of operation has made great contributions to a number of technologies and materials taken for granted today, including fax machines, rewritable CD-ROMs, photocopy drums, flat-panel crystal displays, solar panels, and batteries used in cell phones, digital cameras, laptop computers, and hybrid cars. Since the beginning, the company's research has centered on phase change technology, the use of amorphous, or structureless, materials that can be charged by electricity or a laser beam to assume an ordered structure. Because such materials can be switched on and off, they have the ability to be used as a digital medium: the amorphous structure becomes zero (off), while the ordered structure becomes one (on). Perhaps of more importance is the switching speed of the material, so fast that timing equipment is unable to provide a precise measurement. Amorphous materials (chalcogenide alloys), which the company calls Ovonics after its founder, are therefore suitable for use in semiconductors, computer processors and memory, and optical devices such as computer flat-screen monitors and high-definition televisions. ECD divides its business among three primary segments. Ovonic Battery Company, Inc. concentrates on battery technol-

ogy. United Solar Ovonic Corp. makes thin-film photovoltaic products. The parent company itself is involved in microelectronics, fuel cell technology, and hydrogen storage technology.

Founder Born to Immigrant Parents in 1920s

Energy Conversion Devices was founded by self-taught, maverick scientist Stanford Robert Ovshinsky and his wife, Iris L. Miroy. Ovshinsky was born in Akron, Ohio, in 1922, the son of a Lithuanian immigrant who supported his family as a scrap-metal dealer. Although uninterested in formal higher education, Ovshinsky grew up with a wide range of interests, including astronomy, biology, and chemistry, and read widely. After graduating from high school, as well as a trade school where he trained as a toolmaker and machinist, he opened his own Akron machine shop, which led to him becoming president of Robert Manufacturing Company in 1946. An inveterate tinkerer, Ovshinsky did a great deal of work on high-speed cutting machines, along the way experimenting with a wide variety of materials, eventually resulting in the first of some 300 patents he received: the invention in the 1940s of the Stanford Roberts automatic lathe. The high-speed lathe was ten times faster than previous tools, became used widely and attracted the attention of Connecticut-based New Britain Machine Company, which bought out Ovshinsky in 1950 and used the lathe to make automobile parts. He stayed on for two years before relocating to Detroit, where he became director of research at Hupp Corporation, an automotive supply company.

While at Hupp in the early 1950s Ovshinsky began thinking about ways to mimic how the brains of mammals worked, in particular how the neurons in brain cells functioned like on-off switches. He guessed that it was possible to design an energy-information system that worked in the same way. In 1955 Ovshinsky shared his ideas with the chairman of the medical college at Detroit's Wayne State University, who encouraged him to continue his work. Ovshinsky then began to experiment with amorphous substances, essentially glassy materials, and soon discovered that once they received a certain voltage of energy they changed phase and became an ordered structure. In 1957 he developed his first switch, which he called an ovonic switch, coining the word "ovonic" by fusing the beginning of his name with "electronics." It was a radical approach at a time

Company Perspectives:

The research and development team at ECD Ovonics, its subsidiaries, and joint ventures are focused on the development of new products and technology that will benefit our commercial partners. At ECD Ovonics, we invent the technology, the products, and production technology that will bring our vision to life.

when scientists often viewed disorder as little more than a nuisance. The early work being done on semiconductor technology was based on crystalline solids, dependent on atoms arranged in symmetrical patterns. Initially Ovshinsky's ideas were considered heretical to the academic world, due in large part to his lack of credentials. But the stark difference between what crystals and ovonic materials had to offer eventually won over the skeptics. According to a 2003 profile of Ovshinsky in *World and I,* "Unlike crystals, which are meticulously 'grown' and 'doped' with impurities, ovonic materials can be mixed to order and poured out by the square foot. The materials then can be used to store and release both energy and information."

Company Taken Public in 1964

During the 1950s Ovshinsky also found his life partner in Iris Miroy, who made up for his lack of credentials with a string of degrees. From the University of Michigan she received a bachelor's in zoology, followed by a master's in biology. She then received a Ph.D. in biochemistry from Boston University. They were married in 1959 and a year later founded Energy Conversion Devices to find practical uses for his breakthrough work with ovonic materials. To gain much needed money for research the Ovshinskys incorporated ECD in 1964 and made a public offering of stock.

Aside from his brilliance as an intuitive scientist, Ovshinsky also proved to be a natural salesman, a man not afraid to promote himself or his ideas. From the start of ECD he was able to attract funding even though he was never quite able to finally deliver on his promises. The company's standard operating procedure over the next 40 years was to forge a joint venture with a deep-pocketed corporation, which put up the money while the Ovshinskys contributed the ideas. Once the partner tired of waiting for a payoff in the form of a commercial product and backed out of the relationship, the Ovshinskys kept the technology, which they continued to develop with the next willing joint venture partner. In addition, ECD was also adept at attracting government research grants.

The Ovshinskys launched their major partnerships after the splash they made in 1968 by announcing ECD had succeeded in making a switch out of amorphous silicon that could be changed by varying the levels of electrical current. According to a 2003 *Forbes* article, "Ovshinsky said the switch would compete with silicon crystalline transistors, and in the space of a day ECD stock shot from $57 to $150. The transistor never made much money and the company's stock never returned to those heights, but Ovshinsky did manage to get the word Ovonics (and his name) into the dictionary." A less exotic application of ECD

technology developed in the 1960s was chemical vapor deposition (CVD), followed later by physical vapor deposition (PVD) coating techniques. They would be used initially to coat watch parts with lubricants and later cutting tools with such materials as titanium carbide and titanium nitride. The process added greatly to the life of watch parts and tools.

ECD attracted the attention of IBM, which in 1972 provided funding for research in erasable Ovonic recording devices, work that would one day lead to optical laser disks but not aid ECD in developing a viable product and turning a profit. In 1976 the company struck a deal with 3M to distribute rewritable microfilm, prompting Ovshinsky to tell *Forbes* at the time, "We're finally moving to become a profit-oriented company." In 1979, however, 3M canceled the deal when the six prototype file machines ECD delivered failed to meet specifications and 3M demanded back its advance payment, which according to *Barron's* ECD kept.

The 1980s followed a similar track as the 1970s, as ECD continued to make scientific breakthroughs and burn through money. The company did manage to turn a profit in 1981, but that was due to a $3 million payment from Standard Oil of Ohio (Sohio) connected to one of two joint ventures, Sovonics Solar Systems and Sovonics Solar Technology, the two companies set up to continue ECD's research in solar cells. The money was received to transfer product licenses and technology to one of the joint ventures and did not actually represent true sales of any products or licenses. Over the next four years Sohio invested $90 million into the two partnerships, then in April 1985, after a change in leadership, Sohio decided to pull out of the joint venture, and converted its interests into common stock. Another partner ECD recruited in the early 1980s was Detroit-based American Natural Resources Company. Together, they formed Ovonic ThermoElectric Company and Ovonic Battery Company to develop battery technology and thermoelectric generators. All told, ANR invested $23 million before it too backed out in 1985 after concluding the joint ventures were not close to offering commercially viable products. As a result, ECD bought ANR, paying $8 million in a combination of stock and notes.

According to *Business Week,* less than $1 million of ECD's reported revenues of $30.1 million in 1985 were related to product sales. Despite its inability to make money, ECD continued to produce tantalizing products and technologies. It developed flexible solar cells in the form of roof shingles, consumer NiMH batteries, and the first commercial use of Ovonic phase-change optical recording technology. Nevertheless, the company was coming under pressure to move products to market and finally turn a profit after 20 years of promises. ECD consolidated its synthetic materials technologies into a subsidiary, Ovonic Synthetic Materials Co., in hopes of better exploiting its CVD and PVD technologies, which were finding increased usage in coating cutting tools. Other ECD coatings had decorative applications, and the company also developed multi-layer X-ray mirrors for use in microscopes, telescopes, and lasers that were not only durable but could be made in a variety of shapes and offered better reflectivity. The unit also offered new hard magnets with automotive, computer, and home appliance applications.

To help prod ECD to profitability, the Ovshinskys cut their own salaries and gave up more than half their voting power. They

Key Dates:

1960: Energy Conversion Devices (ECD) is founded.
1964: Company is incorporated and taken public.
1972: Joint venture with IBM is formed.
1987: Takeover bid is thwarted.
1995: Robert Stempel is named chairman.
2000: Texaco acquires 20 percent stake in ECD.
2004: ECD receives $10 million in patent settlement.

soon faced a takeover bid in 1987 mounted by Manning & Napier Advisors Inc., a Rochester, New York investment company that opposed a management-nominated slate of directors. According to *Crain's Detroit Business* in a 1992 article, ''A New York court decision gave Ovshinsky control but at a price. Under a complex agreement, ECD eventually sold controlling interest in a promising subsidiary, Troy-based OIS Optical Imaging Systems Inc., in order to meet financial obligations to Manning.''

In the early 1990s ECD once again appeared to be on the verge of profitability. This time the product that was going to change the company's fortunes was an environmentally safe rechargeable battery, which used nickel and metal hydride rather than rely on lead and acid or nickel and cadmium. Not only were ECD batteries safer, they stored more energy than competing batteries. Although developed for use in laptop computers, cell phones, and other portable electronic devices, they became a serious candidate for use in electrical vehicles. Back in the early 1980s Ovshinsky began promoting the potential of ECD batteries to power vehicles, only to find Detroit uninterested. Instead, ECD began working with Korea's Hyundai Motor Company and an unnamed Japanese automaker. The green battery's promise was so great that it was chosen by a consortium of Detroit's Big Three automakers in its effort to develop an electric car, the greatest impediment of which was the battery. Traditional batteries had limited range, a short life, and high replacement cost. The Ovonic battery, although expensive, offered a power density three times that of lead-acid batteries, which translated into greater range and better performance, and they could be recharged quickly. The batteries would be used in the 1999 model of General Motors EV-1, the first American electric car to be sold to the general public, able to travel 150 miles before recharging.

Robert Stempel Taking Charge in 1990s

ECD also attracted the attention of Robert Stempel, former chairman and chief executive officer of General Motors Corporation, ousted in a boardroom coup after a 34-year career at GM. A trained engineer, Stempel joined ECD as an adviser in 1993 and became ECD's chairman in 1995, bringing with him stature and contacts that led to more joint venture partners, who were also greatly influenced by the credibility ECD received by the Big Three bestowing their blessing on the company. Not surprising, ECD forged a joint venture with GM. Stempel also had considerable executive experience and began to instill discipline into the company, which continued to find profits elusive but now began making a serious effort to become a manufacturing company rather than a mere licensor of technology.

One of those new partners was giant Intel, which helped in the research conducted on Ovonic Unified Memory technology. In 2000 ECD formed a joint venture with Texaco Energy Systems Inc. called Texaco Ovonic Fuel Cell Co. LLC, to develop regenerative fuel cell technology. In addition Texaco bought GM's 60 percent stake in GM Ovonic, which made nickel metal hydride auto batteries, and a 20 percent stake in ECD itself. GE Plastics also allied itself with ECD, establishing a joint venture, Ovonic Media, to develop optical media technology that would allow for high-volume DVD production. Another partner was Belgium-based N.V. Bekaert S.A., which joined forces with ECD to form Bekaert ECD Solar Systems L.L.C. in 2000.

Despite Stempel's presence, history appeared to be repeating itself for ECD in early 2003 when joint venture partners once again decided to stop funding the projects. ChevronTexaco Corp. cut off investments to Texaco Ovonic, as did GE Plastics and Bekaert. ECD cast about for new partners and announced that it would focus its fuelcell research on non-transportation applications, such as cameras and other consumer products that were more likely to produce near-term sales. With a steep rise in gas prices, however, the company soon resumed its work on hybrid car technology.

ECD received a much welcomed $10 million windfall in the summer of 2004 when it reached a settlement in a patent dispute regarding the use of nickel metal hydride battery technology. At the same time, Stempel announced that ECD would undergo a restructuring that included laying off employees and a redoubled effort to convert core technologies into commercial products. The goal was to achieve sustained profitability by the middle of 2006. Well into his 80s, Stanford Ovshinsky remained highly involved in the company, spending much of his time in the development of the Ovonic Cognitive Computer, which hoped to mimic the working of the biological brain.

Principal Subsidiaries

United Solar Ovonic Corp.; United Solar Ovonic LLC; Ovonic Fuel Cell Company LLC; Ovonic Battery Company, Inc. (91.4%); Cobasys LLC (50%); Ovonys, Inc. (41.6%); Ovonic Media, LLC (49%); Texaco Ovonic Hydrogen Systems LLC (50%); Ovonic Cognitive Computer, Inc.

Principal Competitors

Applied Films Corporation; FuelCell Energy, Inc.; Kyocera Solar, Inc.

Further Reading

Berry, Bryan H., ''Energy Conversion Devices Produces New Supermagnets,'' *Iron Age,* May 2, 1986, p. 65.

Bishop, Jerry E., ''New Generation of Electric-Car Batteries to Be Unveiled—Consortium Chooses Between Two Contenders for Development Contract,'' *Wall Street Journal,* May 15, 1992, p. B3.

Buss, Dale, ''Glasses for the Masses,'' *World and I,* June 2003, p. 130.

——, ''Out of Obscurity,'' *Sales and Marketing Management,* January 2002, p. 42.

Dietderich, Andrew, ''Company Conversion,'' *Crain's Detroit Business,* October 21, 2002, p. 1.

——, ''ECD Short of Cash at Critical Time As Partners Pull Out of Ventures,'' *Crain's Detroit Business,* February 24, 2003, p. 4.

Fahey, Jonathan, ''Repeat Pretender,'' *Forbes,* November 24, 2003, p. 86.

Hornblower, Margot, ''Heroes for the Planet/Design,'' *Time,* February 22, 1999, p. 80.

McGrayne, Sharon, ''Sohio Gone, R&D Firm Needs Cash,'' *Crain's Detroit Business,* June 16, 1986, p. 1.

Porter, Martin, ''Ovshinsky: Optical Storage Pioneer,'' *Computers & Electronics,* July 1984, p. 64.

Richardson, Karen, ''Hybrid Cars Drives C Company and Its Stock,'' *Wall Street Journal,* October 13, 2004, p. C1.

Rublin, Lauren R., ''A Different Kind of Company,'' *Barron's,* June 13, 1983, p. 6.

Sanoff, Alvin P., ''Inventive Genius Is Alive and Well in the U.S.,'' *U.S. News & World Report,* June 13, 1983, p. 61.

Smith, Emily T., and Russell Mitchell, *Business Week,* May 19, 1986, p. 108.

—Ed Dinger

Fanuc Ltd.

3580, Shibokusa Aza-Komanba
Oshino-mura
Minamitsuru-gun
Yamanashi 401-0597
Japan
Telephone: (0555) 84-5555
Fax: (0555) 84-5512
Web site: http://www.fanuc.co.jp

Public Company
Incorporated: 1972 as Fujitsu Fanuc Ltd.
Employees: 2,000
Sales: ¥330.35 billion ($3.09 billion) (2005)
Stock Exchanges: Tokyo OTC
Ticker Symbols: 6954; FANUF
NAIC: 335314 Relay and Industrial Control
    Manufacturing

Headquartered at the base of Japan's Mount Fuji, Fanuc Ltd. is the world's leading manufacturer of computerized numerical control (CNC) equipment for machine tools, devices that put the automation into automated factories. CNC devices also serve as the ''brains'' of industrial robots, and Fanuc, whose name is an acronym for Fuji Automatic Numerical Control, has been a world leader in robotics since the 1970s. Much of the company's sales are channeled through GE Fanuc, a 50–50 automated machinery joint venture with General Electric Company. Countering the prevailing outsourcing trend in global business, Fanuc does all of its manufacturing in Japan at highly roboticized factories; nevertheless, its business is consistently and highly profitable, racking up double-digit profit margins that often approach and sometimes exceed 20 percent.

Founded As a Subsidiary of Fujitsu

Fanuc was founded as a wholly owned subsidiary of Fujitsu Limited in 1955 after that electronics giant decided to enter the factory automation business. Its first employees were a team of 500 engineers, and Fujitsu chose from among them a young executive engineer named Seiuemon Inaba to head the subsidiary. It was a move that would prove beneficial for both the company and the man. Inaba, who received a doctorate in engineering from Tokyo Institute of Technology after joining Fujitsu in 1946, remained at the top of Fanuc's chain of command until June 2000 when he was named honorary chairman. His name became virtually synonymous with that of the company.

At first, Fujitsu Fanuc devoted itself solely to research and development. U.S. companies led the way in automation technology at that time; in fact, no Japanese company produced numerical control (NC) machine tools until the mid-1960s. Once the Japanese NC industry entered the field of play, however, Fujitsu Fanuc dominated the game. By 1971, it controlled 80 percent of the domestic market for NC equipment. In 1972 Fujitsu spun off its highly successful subsidiary as Fujitsu Fanuc Ltd., retaining a substantial minority interest. The remaining shares were put on the open market. In 1975 Seiuemon Inaba became president of the new company.

Fujitsu Fanuc, as it continued to call itself until 1982 (when it changed its name to Fanuc Ltd.), began its life as an independent company with numerous marketplace advantages. As a major Japanese NC manufacturer, it was well suited to spearhead the Japanese NC industry's entry into the export market. In 1975 it licensed U.S. manufacturer Pratt & Whitney to market its NC drilling machines in North America. In the same year it entered into a licensing agreement with German engineering firm Siemens AG, which was also a minority shareholder in the company, giving Siemens the exclusive right to market Fujitsu Fanuc products in Europe. In 1985 the European Economic Community would find that the deal violated its rules regarding monopolies and fined the companies $840,000. In 1978 Fujitsu Fanuc took its manufacturing operations abroad, building a plant in South Korea. By 1982, it had captured half of the world NC market.

Leading Position in Robotics: 1980s

Its position as an NC manufacturer notwithstanding, the company's commitment to the related field of robotics brought it the most attention and acclaim. Fujitsu Fanuc started selling robots in 1975, but they accounted for only a tiny percentage of

137

Company Perspectives:

There is a Japanese proverb which says, "Breeding counts for more than birth," meaning that any underprivileged person can make up for his or her disadvantages at birth through rigorous effort and personal initiative. In the engineering world, however, FANUC believes that birth is more important than breeding. In other words, without a good, solid design from the beginning, it would be more difficult and costly to produce low-cost, high-quality products for today's markets. No matter how hard we strive to make improvements at a later stage of a product's life cycle, a weak initial design is difficult and costly to overcome. This is the reason why FANUC has always placed Research & Development as its top priority and as the foundation of its management practice for the entire enterprise.

sales at first, Kawasaki and Hitachi being the leading Japanese robotics companies at the time. Inaba sought to change that situation in the 1980s. In January 1981 Fujitsu Fanuc opened a showcase plant in Yamanashi Prefecture, in which robots and NC machine tools made parts for other robots. The factory, which would otherwise require 500 workers, was run by a staff of 100 people, whose duties consisted of maintaining the robots and assembling the parts into finished products.

This vision of robots manufacturing other robots caught the fancy of the press and, evidently, other robotics companies. A string of joint ventures followed the opening of the new plant. In 1982 Fujitsu Fanuc granted Taiwan's Tatung Co. sole import rights for its robots. In 1983 it also joined with the 600 Group, a British machine tool manufacturer, to form 600 Fanuc Robotics, which would sell Fanuc robots in the United Kingdom.

Fanuc's most important move in 1982 was to enter into a joint venture with General Motors Corporation (GM), called GMFanuc Robotics Corporation, to produce and market robots in the United States. The new company was 50 percent owned by each partner and was based in Detroit, with GM providing most of the management and Fanuc the products. This was not the first alliance between Japanese and U.S. robotics concerns; Japanese companies on the whole lacked the advanced technology necessary to create sophisticated robots, while the U.S. plants lacked Japanese manufacturing skill. By linking up with its largest single potential customer in the United States, Fanuc all but assured itself of a lucrative share of the U.S. market. In its early years, GMFanuc Robotics chiefly made automobile assembly robots and sold them to GM. Although both companies denied it at the time, few industry observers doubted that GM gave preferential treatment to GMFanuc robots when considering bids from suppliers. GMFanuc sales described a steep upward curve, and within six years it became the world's largest supplier of robots.

Inaba's goal of increasing Fanuc's robot sales was not simply a business matter, but a reflection of his personal interest in robots. Known in Japan as the Emperor of Robots, Inaba said in 1981 that it was his dream to develop within four years a robot that would help assemble Fanuc's robot-made robot parts into finished robots. By the middle of the decade, Fanuc had indeed developed assembly robots, which were used to put together parts for motors at its motor factory.

Fanuc's success in robotics brought Inaba to the attention of the U.S. financial press. There was his passion for the color yellow, for instance, because, as he put it, "In the Orient, yellow is the emperor's color." Fanuc factories, offices, and assembly lines were all painted in such a shade. The workers' jumpsuits were also yellow, head to toe. Inaba was known for his demanding and authoritarian management style; at meetings, his subordinates were not allowed to speak unless spoken to.

In the mid-1980s, sales of automation equipment dropped substantially. Manufacturers who pumped large amounts of capital into automation equipment suddenly found themselves with weak cash flows and were unwilling to invest further. GM cut back on its commitment to robotics, GMFanuc sales fell, and Fanuc was further hurt by the relative strength of the yen against the dollar, making its products more expensive in the United States. Fanuc, nevertheless, managed to maintain a healthy profit margin despite these difficulties, and it kept expanding its activities.

In 1987 it tightened its grip on the U.S. market by entering into a joint venture with another pillar of U.S. industry, General Electric Company (GE). The two companies formed GE Fanuc Automation to manufacture computerized numerical control (CNC) devices. The deal marked something of a defeat for GE, which had failed in its attempt to become a factory automation powerhouse. GE stopped making its own CNC equipment and turned its Charlottesville, Virginia, plant over to the new company, which equipped it to produce Fanuc CNC devices.

In 1988 Fanuc once again joined forces with General Motors, this time to form GMFanuc Robotics Europa, to market robots in Europe. In 1989 it took advantage of relaxed East-West tensions to increase its presence in the Soviet Union. It joined with Mitsui & Co., Ltd., a huge Japanese trading company and with Stanko Service, a Soviet machine-tool service organization, to form Stanko Fanuc Service, which would maintain and repair Fanuc products there.

Fanuc's success had always stemmed from the perception that its products were the most reliable as well as the least expensive on the market. In a cutting-edge field such as automation, a huge commitment to research and development was required, and fully one-third of Fanuc's nearly 1,800 employees were engaged in such activity in the late 1980s, the highest ratio of any Japanese manufacturer. As with every other facet of the company's operations, Fanuc's R&D bore the personal stamp of Seiuemon Inaba. He once gave his Product Development Laboratory a clock that ran ten times faster than normal, as a gentle reminder of the importance of staying ahead of the competition. Inaba made the German engineering slogan *Weniger Teile,* which means "fewer parts," Fanuc's slogan; machines with fewer parts are cheaper to produce and easier for automatons to assemble.

Difficult Years in the 1990s

Inaba also garnered publicity for the extensive benefits he provided his employees. At the Yamanashi Prefecture plant, located in a rural setting at the base of Mount Fuji, Inaba included a

Key Dates:

1955: Fujitsu Limited enters the factory automation field by forming Fujitsu Fanuc, headed by Seiuemon Inaba.

1972: Fujitsu spins off the subsidiary as Fujitsu Fanuc Ltd., retaining a substantial minority stake.

1975: Fujitsu Fanuc begins the sale of robots.

1982: Company changes its name to Fanuc Ltd.; enters into a joint venture with General Motors Corporation called GMFanuc Robotics Corporation.

1987: Fanuc forms GE Fanuc Automation joint venture with General Electric Company.

1992: Company purchases GM's half-interest in GMFanuc, which is renamed Fanuc Robotics Corporation.

2000: Inaba steps down from the company board, becoming honorary chairman.

2003: Yoshiharu Inaba, son of the founder, is named president and CEO.

medical center, gymnasium, 25-meter heated swimming pool, culture center, employee living quarters, and restaurant. In the late 1980s and early 1990s, these attractive benefits helped Fanuc counter a labor shortage affecting many Japanese firms.

In the early 1990s, however, Fanuc faced more than just a difficult labor market. Revenues and earnings declined as the entire machine tool industry in Japan suffered from slackened demand compared to the heyday of the 1970s and 1980s. In 1992, in the midst of this downturn, Fanuc gained an increased presence in foreign markets when it purchased GM's half-interest in GMFanuc and renamed it Fanuc Robotics Corporation, which became a wholly owned subsidiary of Fanuc Ltd. Fanuc Robotics, in turn, held two subsidiaries: Fanuc Robotics North America, Inc., based in Auburn Hills, Michigan, and serving the North American and Latin American markets; and Fanuc Robotics Europe GmbH (formerly GMFanuc Robotics Europa), based in Luxembourg, which served the European market. Also in 1992 Fanuc moved into the emerging market of China through Beijing-Fanuc Mechatronics Co., Ltd., a joint venture with the Beijing Machine Tool Research Institute created to manufacture, sell, and provide service on CNCs.

To maintain Fanuc's dominant position in automation technology in the face of the industry slump, Inaba determined to further bolster Fanuc's R&D. In 1994 the Fanuc Berkeley Laboratory was established in Union City, California. Inaba also sought to reduce costs by purchasing more raw materials outside of Japan, taking advantage of the strength of the yen. Longer term, Inaba committed Fanuc to a strategic emphasis on robots.

Unlike other Japanese robotics firms, Fanuc did not shift production to the United States during this period. Demand for robots was growing dramatically in North America in the early 1990s thanks to a rebounding automobile industry. Fanuc could continue to profitably manufacture in Japan based on two factors. First, Fanuc's production process was cheaper than competitors because of its highly automated "lights out" plant, which was capable of producing one thousand robots a month.

Second, Fanuc could take advantage of its world leadership in production of CNCs, a key component in robots, to keep its production costs down.

These strategies seemed to pay off as Fanuc's revenues and earnings rebounded in 1994 and 1995. Sales and profits remained on an upward trajectory through the fiscal year ending in March 1998. In 1997 Fanuc entered into a second joint venture in China, Shanghai-Fanuc Robotics Co., Ltd. This partnership with Shanghai SMEC Corporation was involved in robotics manufacturing, sales, and service. Fanuc ended the 1990s with its sales and profits on the decline due to the worsening economic climate at home. The firm nevertheless set a goal of boosting its share of the worldwide robot market from 20 percent to 50 percent.

Leadership Changes and a Strong Rebound in the Early 2000s

The new decade began with a historic change in leadership at Fanuc. In June 2000, at age 75, Inaba stepped down from the board of directors, while remaining involved at the company he largely built, as honorary chairman. Ryoichiro Nozawa was named chairman, while Shigeaki Oyama assumed the presidency. Earnings fluctuated early in the decade as the worldwide economic downturn cut into demand for CNCs and robots, and Fanuc faced increasing competition, particularly from those manufacturers setting up shop in low-wage China. Fanuc responded not by shifting its own factories to China but by making its factories in Japan more efficient. In the summer of 2002 production began at a fully automated plant in Oshino that was capable of 720 hours of uninterrupted operation.

Fanuc's ability to remain strongly profitable through a most difficult economic period for Japan enabled the firm to build up a huge hoard of cash: ¥385.51 billion ($2.89 billion) by March 2002. At this same time Fujitsu and other Japanese electronics companies were struggling in a highly competitive, profit-poor environment, and for this reason seeking to raise cash by dismantling at least a portion of Japan's complicated tangle of interlocking shareholdings. In August 2002, then, Fujitsu began gradually selling off its 39 percent stake in Fanuc, eventually reducing it to 7.8 percent by March 2005. Fanuc used part of its pile of cash to buy back some of these shares itself.

In June 2003 Oyama was named chairman of Fanuc, and Yoshiharu Inaba was elevated to president and CEO. Inaba, the only son of the company founder, had been groomed for company leadership from an early age and had earned a Ph.D. in engineering from the University of Tokyo. He took over at an auspicious time as the Japanese economy rebounded strongly from its prolonged doldrums, prompting Japanese companies to finally resume their capital spending and leading to robust sales of CNC systems and industrial robots. Shipments elsewhere in Asia, particularly to China, India, and South Korea, expanded strongly as well. Net sales at Fanuc jumped from ¥214.26 billion ($1.78 billion) in 2003 to ¥330.35 billion ($3.09 billion) in 2005. Net income nearly doubled during this period, hitting ¥75.76 billion ($708.1 million) by 2005.

In order to bolster its production capacity and develop ever more sophisticated robots, the still cash-rich Fanuc significantly increased its capital investment program starting in fiscal 2005. It began populating its factories with so-called intelligent robots, ones equipped with sight and force sensors, enabling them to recognize shapes and positions in three dimensions and to fine-tune their grips on objects, thereby increasing manufacturing efficiency and precision and enabling robots to handle entire assembly operations. Late in 2004 Fanuc began soliciting orders for sets of robots capable of assembling car parts, home appliances, and medical equipment. The company was also working to develop larger robots able to assemble entire car bodies. As demand for its products was increasing, the Japanese market continued its recovery, and such markets as China, India, and Russia were expected to grow strongly, Fanuc significantly raised its medium-term sales forecast, now aiming to achieve sales of ¥500 billion by the fiscal year ending in March 2008.

Principal Subsidiaries

Fanuc FA Service Ltd.; Fanuc Robot Service Ltd.; Fanuc Laser Service Ltd.; Fanuc Pertronics Ltd.; Fanuc Servo Ltd.; Fanuc DD Motor Ltd.; Fanuc Robotics America, Inc. (U.S.A.); GE Fanuc Automation Corporation (U.S.A.; 50%); Fanuc America Corporation (U.S.A.); Fanuc Robotics Europe S.A. (Luxembourg); GE Fanuc Automation CNC Europe S.A. (Luxembourg); Fanuc Robomachine Europe Sales GmbH (Germany); Fanuc Robomachine Deutschland GmbH (Germany); Fanuc Europe Service GmbH (Germany); Fanuc France S.A.S.; Fanuc U.K. Limited; Fanuc Italia S.p.A. (Italy); Fanuc Iberia, S.A. (Spain); Fanuc Turkey Ltd. (80%); Fanuc Bulgaria Corporation; Fanuc Czech s.r.o. (Czech Republic); Fanuc South Africa (Proprietary) Limited; Fanuc Mitsui Automation CIS LLC (Russia; 50%); Fanuc Korea Corporation; Fanuc Taiwan Limited; Beijing-Fanuc Mechatronics Co., Ltd. (China; 50%); Fanuc India Private Limited (95%); Shanghai-Fanuc Robotics Co., Ltd. (China; 50%); Fanuc Robomachine (Shenzhen) Ltd. (China); Fanuc Thai Limited (Thailand); Tatung-Fanuc Robotics Company (Taiwan); Fanuc Mechatronics (Malaysia) Sdn. Bhd.; PT. Fanuc GE Automation Indonesia (50%); Fanuc Singapore Pte. Ltd. (50%); Fanuc Oceania Pty. Limited (Australia); Fanuc Philippines Corporation.

Principal Operating Units

FA Group; Robot Group; Robomachine Group.

Principal Competitors

Siemens AG; IWKA AG; ABB Ltd.; Rockwell Automation, Inc.; Comau S.p.A.

Further Reading

Bylinsky, Gene, "Japan's Robot King Wins Again," *Fortune,* May 25, 1987.

"Fanuc Edges Closer to a Robot-Run Plant," *Business Week,* November 24, 1980.

"Fanuc Throws One-Third of Its Entire Labor Force into the Most Powerful R&D Setup of the Industry," *Business Japan,* April 1989.

Glain, Steve, "Competitive Drill: Fanuc Faces a Challenge from PC-Driven Systems," *Asian Wall Street Journal,* May 20, 1997, p. 1.

——, "Open Systems Narrow Fanuc's Lead in Sector," *Asian Wall Street Journal,* June 13, 1997, p. 13.

"GM to Sell Its 50% Stake in GMFanuc, a Robotics Firm, to Japanese Partner," *Wall Street Journal,* June 4, 1992, p. B4.

Guth, Robert A., "Fujitsu May Lower Its Fanuc Stake," *Asian Wall Street Journal,* June 18, 2002, p. M1.

Imada, Toshihiko, "CEO Puts Fanuc on Growth Path," *Nikkei Weekly,* June 7, 2004.

Inaba, Seiuemon, *Walking the Narrow Path: The FANUC Story,* translated by Inyong Ham, n.p., 1992, 91 p.

Kodaki, Mariko, "Fanuc Goes on Offensive with Robots," *Nikkei Weekly,* February 24, 2003.

Marsh, Peter, "Green Tea with Yellow Robots," *Financial Times,* September 5, 2003, p. 14.

Nakamura, Minoru, "Trouble in the Robot Kingdom," *Tokyo Business Today,* June 1994, pp. 44–45.

Sugawara, Toru, "Fanuc Stuck with Excess Funds," *Nikkei Report,* June 18, 2002.

Wiegner, Kathleen K., "The Dawn of Battle," *Forbes,* October 26, 1981.

Winter, Drew, "Eastward Ho: Japanese Robot Builders Shift Production to U.S.," *Ward's Auto World,* July 1995, p. 81.

—Douglas Sun
—update: David E. Salamie

Federal Agricultural Mortgage Corporation

<table>
<tr><td>

1133 Twenty-First Street N.W., Suite 600
Washington, D.C. 20036
U.S.A.
Telephone: (202) 872-7700
Toll Free: (800) 879-3276
Fax: (202) 872-7713
Web site: http://www.farmermac.com

Public Company
Incorporated: 1987
Employees: 38
Total Assets: $3.84 billion (2004)
Stock Exchanges: New York
Ticker Symbol: AGM
NAIC: 522298 All Other Non-Depository Credit
    Intermediation

</td></tr>
</table>

Federal Agricultural Mortgage Corporation (Farmer Mac) was chartered with the intention of creating a secondary market for agricultural real estate and rural housing mortgage loans. The Government Sponsored Enterprise (GSE) buys both conventional and government guaranteed loans, then packages and sells them to investors as securities to encourage the flow of funds through the mortgage system. Farmer Mac moved at a crawl during nearly all of its first decade of existence, reaping hordes of critics. Following the lifting of restrictions on its terms of operation in 1996, the agency moved into profitability but faced a new round of scrutiny.

Farm Crisis Prompting Creation of New GSE: 1987–95

The Federal Agricultural Mortgage Corporation (Farmer Mac) was created to bring some relief to the struggling U.S. farm economy through a secondary market for agricultural and rural housing loans. American farmers were losing their land to high interest rates and wanted long-term fixed-rate agricultural loans.

The government sponsored enterprise (GSE) was more than a half decade in the making, according to a 1989 *ABA Banking Journal* article, finally being realized in January 1988 following

its authorization through the 1987 Agricultural Credit Act. Farmer Mac's first annual meeting was held on March 2, 1989. As mandated by law, the entity then had 120 days to issue operating regulations and rules. A New Yorker, Henry D. Edelman, was named president in April 1989.

As chartered, banks could not sell loans directly to Farmer Mac. Selling to a pooler, a large commercial bank or insurance company, drove up costs to the banker and in turn interest rates for farmers and ranchers. Moreover, banks had to retain the riskiest 10 percent of their loans.

Subsequently, Farmer Mac's harvest was less than abundant during its first few years of operation. "The agency has yet to assemble a single pool of loans or guarantee a security under its flagship program," wrote Debra Cope for *American Banker* in November 1991. Company stockholders, including banks, insurance companies, and Farm Credit Banks, waited for a return on their $23 million investment. The money-losing agency's six employees, meanwhile, received a total of $1.3 million in salaries, bonuses, and benefits during 1990.

President and CEO Henry D. Edelman, a former PaineWebber investment banker, remained optimistic about the future. He pointed to Fannie Mae and Freddie Mac, drivers of the secondary market for home loans, telling *American Banker* they, too, were slow to develop.

Others had their doubts, including J. Ken Goodmiller, a General Accounting Office (GAO) manager, who told *American Banker* lenders were hanging on to their farm mortgages instead of selling them to poolers ready to assemble loans into guaranteed securities for Farmer Mac.

Many commercial bankers, benefiting from a shift in economic conditions, viewed the program as a backup plan for creating liquidity. Furthermore, the farm real estate market had shrunk from its 1987 level of $87.7 billion of debt outstanding to $78.4 billion at year-end 1990. Less than $27.1 billion of the 1990 farm property debt even qualified for the Farmer Mac program.

For its part, Farmer Mac planned to issue debt and buy the loan-backed securities in hope of creating some momentum for

---

Company Perspectives:

Farmer Mac accomplishes its public policy mission primarily by purchasing, or committing to purchase, qualified loans from agricultural mortgage lenders, thereby replenishing their source of funds to make new loans.

---

the secondary market for farm loans. Farmer Mac's regulator, the Farm Credit Administration, and the GAO questioned the GSE's authority to use debt in this way.

By the end of 1991, Farmer Mac had issued $10 million in securities under the Farmer Mac II program. Created in 1990, following a request by the United States Department of Agriculture, the program securitized government, not commercial, farm loans. Farmer Mac's first mortgage-backed security was issued in late 1991, according to the *US Banker* article.

During 1991, the Farm Credit Administration's Office of Secondary Market Oversight was established as Farmer Mac's financial regulator, overseeing the agency for financial safety and soundness. Additionally, minimum regulatory capital requirements were set and its ability to purchase guaranteed securities was to be clarified.

New Rules and New Opportunities: 1996–99

Farmer Mac received some assistance in its effort to create a secondary farm loan market in 1996 legislation signed by President Clinton. The changes allowed Farmer Mac to buy loans directly from lenders and issue guaranteed securities representing 100 percent of the principal of the purchased loans. A 100 percent backing of securities by Farmer Mac enabled banks to lower their loan rates. The legislation also modified Farmer Mac's capital requirements. Farmer Mac was given two years to reach a minimum capital requirement level of $25 million.

New rules aside, according to *American Banker*, the GES still had to demonstrate that it could be as successful as its cousins Fannie and Freddie. Questions lingered regarding farm program oversight, loan originators, underwriting standards, and loan backing.

Among the GSEs, the multibillion-dollar operations Freddie Mac and Fannie Mae reigned supreme. Fannie Mae, established during the Depression, and Freddie Mac, formed in 1970, produced billions in profits annually while keeping the U.S. non-farm mortgage market pumped up. By comparison, Farmer Mac had securitized less than $1 billion in farm mortgages during its entire existence, according to a late 1997 *US Banker* article.

The Farm Credit System Reform Act of 1996 helped lift Farmer Mac into profitability for the first time. In addition to being granted the authority to work directly with lenders, the entity could now set its own price and terms and develop new loan products, according to *US Banker*. The result was a regular offering of securities.

Farmer Mac recorded profits of $777,000 in 1996 versus a loss of $1.3 million in 1994. A stock offering in December

1996 brought in enough funds to carry it over current capital requirements. An expanding ag credit market also aided Farmer Mac's cause.

Looking for liquidity and a vehicle for making larger loans, ag bankers had begun to turn to Farmer Mac. "The dollar total of loans bought by the Federal Agricultural Mortgage Corp. has risen nearly 64 percent in the last two years, and the formerly money-losing corporation turned a profit in 1997 for the second consecutive year. What's more, Farmer Mac's class C stock has soared to more than $60 a share, from a low of $4.25 in 1995," Annie Sullivan reported for *American Banker* in January 1998.

The potential market for the enterprise was considerable: $40 billion of eligible loans. Farmer Mac had tapped into just a small percentage of that total. Besides allowing bankers to move long-term, fixed-rate ag loans off their books by selling to Farmer Mac, they could earn fees from the GSE by retaining servicing rights on the loans. Farmer Mac drew bankers to its program through workshops, direct mail, and cold calls. In 1998, Farmer Mac began holding agricultural mortgage loan-backed securities on its own books, thus increasing its business volume.

Trading on the NASDAQ, Farmer Mac applied to make the move to the New York Stock Exchange in 1999, seeking greater visibility and liquidity and less volatility for its stock. The move was made possible by an increase in volume of its loan purchases and loan guarantees plus its ongoing fees from previously guaranteed loans, according to a May 1999 *National Mortgage News* article. Farmer Mac and the other GSEs guaranteed timely payment of principal and interest on the mortgage-backed securities.

Low commodity prices at the time were putting pressure on farmers and ranchers, driving up delinquency rates and putting the agency at risk. But Farmer Mac said the combination of its underwriting standards and reserves would counter any possible losses.

In the Pubic Eye: 2000–05

GSEs were in the sights of some in Congress. Louisiana Republican Representative Richard H. Baker, remembering the damage the Savings and Loan crisis had inflicted on his state, attempted but failed to find support for the overhaul of the GSEs in 2000.

Farmer Mac recorded $17.1 million in operating income in 2001, up from the 2000 level of $10.4 million. The company also reported record earnings gains. President and CEO Henry Edelman said the gains were made in spite of volatile interest rates, a stressed ag economy, and a nationwide recession. Outstanding guarantees at year-end of $4.2 billion topped 2000 by $1.1 billion. Farmer Mac held almost $1.9 billion of loans in its portfolio. Past due loans were also up among those made after 1996, when Farmer Mac began holding 100 percent of the credit risk.

Edelman's salary and stock options for 2001 approached an estimated $1.8 million, according to an April 2002 article in the *New York Times*. He controlled $27.6 million in stock: an additional $2.8 million had been sold since the summer of 2001. The board of directors had begun awarding themselves stock options in 1997 and accumulated an average holding of $816,249. Insiders held 13 percent of the company via stock

Key Dates:

1987: Agricultural Credit Act of 1987 creates the Federal Agricultural Mortgage Corporation (Farmer Mac).
1990: Farmer Mac II program is established.
1991: New oversight and capital requirements are set.
1996: Farmer Mac receives more flexibility in operating structure and records first profits.
1988: Company begins holding agricultural mortgage backed securities.
1999: Farmer Mac applies for listing on New York Stock Exchange.
2002: Congress announces call for scrutiny of Farmer Mac.
2004: Farmer Mac declares it will seek a formal rating from a credit agency.

institutions. In effect loan risks were being shifted from one federal agency to another.

In July 2004, Farmer Mac's stock slid again with the news that its federal regulator proposed rules eliminating its competitive advantage over commercial banks or thrifts. Under the changes, the agency would be required to seek a formal rating from a credit agency, thus driving up its cost of borrowing money. The GSE would have to set aside more capital to cover its obligations. Farmer Mac later announced that it would get a credit rating regardless of the outcome of the proposal. For the entire year, Farmer Mac's volume fell, but so did the level of past due loans. Net income and stockholder equity, on the other hand, climbed.

Principal Competitors

Citigroup Inc.; Washington Mutual, Inc.; Wells Fargo & Company.

Further Reading

Cope, Debra, ''A Life Struggle Looms in '92 for Farmer Mac,'' *American Banker*, November 6, 1991, pp. 1+.

Cornwell, Ted, ''Farmer Mac Reports Record 2001,'' *National Mortgage News*, February 18, 2002.

Cowan, Alison Leigh, ''Big-City Paydays at 'Farmer Mac,' '' *New York Times*, April 28, 2002, p. BU1.

——, ''A Bipartisan Call in Congress for Scrutiny of Farmer Mac,'' *New York Times*, June 27, 2002, p. C9.

——, ''One Man Stands Watch on Billions in Farm Loans,'' *New York Times*, June 20, 2002, p. C1.

''Farmer Mac Seeks NYSE Listing,'' *National Mortgage News*, May 10, 1999.

Fogarty, Mark, ''Farmer Mac Gets Boost,'' *US Banker*, November 1997, pp. 81+.

Jackson, Ben, ''GSE Rejects Claims of Straying from Mission,'' *American Banker*, September 10, 2002.

Naylor, Frank W., ''Farmer Mac Gets Ready to Roll,'' *ABA Banking Journal*, May 1989, pp. 73+.

O'Hara, Terence, ''Proposal Hurts Farmer Mac Shares,'' *Washington Post*, July 30, 2004, p. E1.

Richard, Christine, ''Farmer Mac Seeks First Credit Rating,'' *Wall Street Journal*, October 13, 2004, p. 1.

Sullivan, Annie, ''Gaining Acceptance by Ag Bankers, Farmer Mac Plows Deeper into Black,'' *American Banker*, January 5, 1998, pp. 1+.

Talley, Karen, ''Law Gives Farmer Mac a Boost in Securitizing, but Hurdles Remain,'' *American Banker*, February 28, 1996, p. 18.

—Kathleen Peippo

options and restricted stock grants. That figure could be expected to rise to 35 percent based on the number of additional shares available to insiders.

As a GSE Farmer Mac received some advantages over the general marketplace, an exemption from most state and local taxes and an interest rate break on borrowed money. The company used its money borrowing capacity to give the secondary market a jumpstart, but the risks Farmer Mac assumed elevated over time, Cowan reported.

Farmer Mac had yet to develop a thriving secondary market for ag loans, holding more mortgage-backed securities in its portfolio than it had sold. But its earnings growth drew the interest of investors in its stock.

With its securities sales weak, Farmer Mac had turned to other endeavors, including ag loans to part-time and hobby farmers and guarantees on loans retained by banks. Some of the biggest customers for that product were companies with connections to the Farmer Mac board, according to the *New York Times*.

In June 2002, a bipartisan call by members of the Senate Agriculture Committee arose for the GAO to look into Farmer Mac's financial stability, independence of its directors, compensation of insiders, and performance of its mission. Farmer Mac shares fell in response to the questions regarding its business practices. One concern facing the GSE was the level of business it engaged in with other government farm credit

On a Higher Plane

Flight Options, LLC

26180 Curtiss Wright Parkway
Cleveland, Ohio 44143
U.S.A.
Telephone: (216) 261-1454
Toll Free: (877) 703-2348
Fax: (216) 797-6024
Web site: http://www.flightoptions.com

Private Company
Incorporated: 2002
Employees: 1,400
Sales: $700 million (2005 est.)
NAIC: 481211 Nonscheduled Chartered Passenger Air
Transportation; 532411 Commercial Air, Rail, and
Water Transportation Equipment Rental and Leasing;
488190 Other Support Activities for Air Transportation

Flight Options, LLC is a leading U.S. provider of fractional ownership of business aircraft. It has a fleet of approximately 200 planes. The company, formed through the merger of an Ohio charter operation's fractional business and that of Raytheon Company, has done much to lower the cost of business aviation and widen the market.

Formation of Raytheon Travel Air in 1997

For those with the means, owning a plane presents a very appealing alternative to commercial air travel. In addition to offering freedom from a slew of airline industry hassles, including lost luggage, time-consuming check-ins, and inflexible timetables, private aircraft can fly to more than twice as many U.S. airports than the 4,950 served by the scheduled carriers. The main drawback to owning business aircraft is their enormous cost, for the multimillion-dollar plane itself, plus thousands of dollars per hour for maintenance, fuel, and crew. Owning an aircraft in partnership with others allows most of the freedom at a fraction of the cost.

As the fractional aircraft ownership market developed in the 1980s and 1990s, it seemed natural for manufacturers to enter the business. Raytheon Aircraft Company, a subsidiary of con-

glomerate Raytheon Company, launched its fractional ownership unit, Raytheon Travel Air, in August 1997. Raytheon owned Beech and Hawker and the start-up fleet included three types of planes for a variety of budgets: three Beech King Air B200 turboprops, three Beechjet 400A jets, and three Hawker 800XP jets.

Raytheon Travel Air was based in Wichita, Kansas, and led by Gary Hart, hired from rival Bombardier's FlexJet program. Fourteen FBOs (fixed-base operators) from another Raytheon unit were available to support the fleet across the United States. The King Airs, which had a shorter range than the jets, were based in five hubs: Atlanta, Chicago, Dallas, New York, and Van Nuys. As the least expensive business aircraft available for fractional purchase among the major suppliers, the turboprops widened the circle of those who could now afford to fly private planes. Travel Air kept a portion of its fleet in reserve (initially 40 percent, later much less) to resolve scheduling conflicts.

At the time of its August 1997 launch, noted *Flight International,* the company had sold a one-eighth share in a Beechjet 400A, to professional golfer Fred Couples. It took little more than one year for the company to reach 100 fractional shares sold. By this time, Travel Air had 180 employees, more than 110 of them pilots.

In October 1998, the company made a $90 million order for 22 new Premier I entry-level business jets for delivery beginning in 2001. This order was doubled within a year, and the company also ordered 27 Horizon mid-size jets worth $425 million.

Launch of Flight Options, Inc. in 1998

As Travel Air was wrapping up its first year, another company was preparing to be the first to offer fractional ownership of previously owned jets. Flight Options, Inc. of Cleveland, a unit of charter and maintenance company Corporate Wings, Inc., began selling shares in October 1998. Flight Options, Inc. was led by Darnell Martens, former vice-president of finance at Executive Jet.

The company's 11 jets ranged from three to five years in age. The company charged $625,000 for a one-fourth share in a

Company Perspectives:

Focus on Safety, Service, and Consistency. Luxurious, state-of-the-art aircraft aren't the only highlight of flying with Flight Options; in addition, our flight crews are trained to the highest industry standards. Each aircraft is operated by dual-captain certified pilots who each have received annual simulator training and biannual practical training in their aircraft—in addition to their extensive flight time. Add to this exceptional customer service, and you can see why Flight Options has emerged as a leader in the fractional jet industry.

Key Dates:

1997: Raytheon Aircraft launches its fractional ownership unit, Raytheon Travel Air.
1998: Flight Options, Inc. is formed to market fractional shares in previously owned business jets.
2002: Raytheon Travel Air and Flight Options combine their fractional businesses in Flight Options, LLC.
2003: Raytheon Co. acquires majority control of Flight Options, LLC.
2005: Raytheon Co. raises ownership interest to 95 percent.

seven-seat Cessna Citation II jet, plus $12,900 a month for maintenance and $1,200 per hour for actually riding in it. This represented a 60 percent savings over buying a share in a new jet, Martens told *Crain's Cleveland Business.*

Flight Options grew quickly. By the end of 1998, its fleet had 21 planes and the company had secured new capital enabling it to order another two dozen. Flight Options announced its 150th customer at its first anniversary. The operation had hangars in Ohio, Indiana, and New York. In October 1999 it began an expansion of its 100,000-square-foot Operations Control Center.

Kenneth Ricci, a pilot who had bought Flight Options' parent company Corporate Wings in 1981, told the *Plain Dealer* that business was coming not just from business executives but from affluent baby boomers looking to make the most of their leisure and family time.

Flight Options was providing a web site for owners by the time of its second anniversary. The site included scheduling tools for booking flights and calculating trip costs.

A Year of Change in 2001

At the beginning of 2001, Raytheon Travel Air, with 93 planes and more than 700 owners, was the third largest fractional ownership program in the United States. Flight Options, which was preparing to open operations centers in Denver and Sacramento, was a close fourth.

In 2001, Raytheon Travel Air took a page out of Flight Options' book and began buying used Challenger 601 jets. This aircraft, which had been out of production since 1995, had a larger cabin and longer range than Travel Air's other planes.

The September 11, 2001 terrorist attacks on the United States had American executives fleeing commercial airlines in droves. Security made private aircraft more attractive than ever. New, lengthy screenings at airport check-ins made scheduled transportation even more of an ordeal.

A year of major change ended with a new beginning for Raytheon Travel Air and Flight Options, Inc., which announced they were joining forces in a new company called Flight Options, LLC. Flight Options Inc. owned 50.1 percent of the new venture with Raytheon holding the remainder. Part of the deal included a $900 million order for 115 new planes from Raytheon over five years, although it was not an exclusive arrangement. Flight Options, Inc. had just ordered 25 new Envoy 7 aircraft worth $775 million from Fairchild Corp.

The combined business had more than 200 aircraft and 1,600 customers, making it the world's second largest fractional aircraft ownership company and the only competitor of comparable size to Executive Jet's NetJets program. Sales were reportedly between $700 million and $1 billion in 2002 and 2003. Flight Options employed more than 1,500 people, including 900 pilots and 200 mechanics. Flight Options Inc. head Kenn Ricci would also be chairman and CEO of the new venture, which was based in Cleveland.

Ricci told the *Weekly of Business Aviation* that his outfit was superior to NetJets in several key ways. He emphasized the importance of dispatch reliability, or keeping as many planes in the fleet available as possible.

Raytheon-Controlled in 2003

John Nahill, formerly vice-president of corporate strategy at Raytheon Company, replaced Kenn Ricci as CEO in February 2003. (Ricci returned to Corporate Wings while remaining an advisor to Flight Options.) Raytheon Co. was acquiring majority control of Flight Options, LLC, raising its holding from 49.9 percent to 65 percent.

The main challenge for Flight Options was becoming profitable as the once-booming fractional market lost momentum in a slowing economy. Nahill reduced the number of suppliers as one way to trim costs, he told *Crain's Cleveland Business.*

The company also was increasing its product offerings to raise its top line. Following an industry trend, in the summer of 2004, it began offering jet card memberships in 25-hour blocks beginning at about $100,000 (plus tax). This made jets affordable to many more people, some of whom later converted to fractional ownership. Another program allowed both fractional owners and members access to aircraft in Europe and Asia. It also introduced a program allowing customers to split their shares 75–25 between two different aircraft. At least one incentive was aimed at keeping aircraft available during peak periods. Owners of 1/16th shares could save money by agreeing to fly off-peak only.

Another area of cost savings was standardizing the fleet. In 2005 Flight Options, LLC was cutting its aircraft types from 11 to four (the Beechjet 400A, Hawker 800XP, Citation X, and Legacy). This lowered expenses in maintenance and training while producing a reliable, efficient fleet of aircraft.

Raytheon increased its stake in Flight Options again in the summer of 2005. It invested $50 million to raise its holding to 95 percent.

Principal Operating Units

Mid-Atlantic; Midwest; Northeast and NYC; Northwest; South Central; Southeast; Southwest.

Principal Competitors

Bombardier Flexjet; CitationShares; NetJets Inc.

Further Reading

Carey, Susan, "Raytheon-Owned Firm Offers Rental Time on Corporate Jets," *Wall Street Journal,* July 27, 2004, p. D2.

Charlton, Brian, "Time-Share Jets Taking Off; Local Company Second-Largest in New Industry," *Plain Dealer* (Cleveland), June 22, 2005, p. C1.

Clarke, Susan Strother, "Private, Charter Airline Companies See Business Increase Dramatically," *Orlando Sentinel,* September 30, 2001.

Collogan, David, "Flight Options Transitioning Fleet, Service Offerings," *Weekly of Business Aviation,* August 22, 2005, p. 79.

——, "Poised for Continued Growth, Flight Options Launches New Pricing, Support Strategies," *Weekly of Business Aviation,* April 15, 2002, p. 175.

Gerdel, Thomas W., "Flight Options: Offering Time Shares in the Sky," *Plain Dealer* (Cleveland), December 31, 1999, p. 1C.

Grant, Alison, "Pilots at Merged Company Agree on Seniority System," *Plain Dealer* (Cleveland), October 9, 2002, p. C3.

Krouse, Peter, "Flight Options Shareholders Withdraw Opposition to Deal," *Plain Dealer* (Cleveland), August 13, 2005, p. C1.

"Larger Cabins Prompt Travel Air Challenger Buy," *Flight International,* February 6, 2001, p. 24.

Lopez, Ramon, "Raytheon Travel Air Boosts Fleet and Eyes Overseas Markets," *Flight International,* August 18, 1999, p. 23.

McMillin, Molly, "Wichita, Kan., Aircraft Company Buys Used Jets to Add to Fleet," *Knight Ridder Business News,* January 27, 2001.

Mortland, Shannon, "Flight Options Adds New Choices for Jet Customers," *Crain's Cleveland Business,* September 20, 2004, p. 18.

"Nahill Abruptly Departs Flight Options," *Weekly of Business Aviation,* November 8, 2004, p. 207.

Paradis, Tim, "Flight Options, Raytheon Unit Combine in Aircraft Venture," *Dow Jones News Service,* December 20, 2001.

"Raytheon, Flight Options Finalize Joint Business Plans," *Weekly of Business Aviation,* March 25, 2002, p. 141.

"Raytheon Fractional Scheme Exceeds Initial Targets," *Flight International,* October 1, 1997, p. 40.

Rimmer, David, "Ricci: Fractionals a Two-Horse Race; Flight Options Looking to Expand Through Acquisition," *Business & Commercial Aviation,* May 1, 2002, p. 46.

Sarsfield, Kate, "Flight Options Slashes Ageing Fleet As It Seeks Economies of Scale," *Flight International,* March 8, 2005.

Seidenman, Paul, "Raytheon Travel Air: Up-Front About Downtime," *Overhaul & Maintenance,* October 1, 2000, p. 38.

Serres, Christopher, "Companies Can Take Flight with Fractional Shares in Used Jets," *Crain's Cleveland Business,* October 5, 1998, p. 6.

——, "Flight Options Jetting Ahead: Fresh Cash Lets Corporate Wings Unit Pursue Expansion," *Crain's Cleveland Business,* January 4, 1999, p. 2.

Stacklin, Jeff, "Changes in Wings for Flight Options," *Crain's Cleveland Business,* January 6, 2003, p. 1.

——, "Flight Options Lands in West: Company Opens Sacramento, Denver Sites," *Crain's Cleveland Business,* August 13, 2001, p. 23.

——, "Flight Options Looking to Soar: Fractional Jet Biz Plans to Be Top in the Field," *Crain's Cleveland Business,* June 10, 2002, p. 4.

——, "Raytheon to Pilot Flight Options," *Crain's Cleveland Business,* April 7, 2003, p. 3.

Summers, Graham, "Raytheon Travel Air Orders 22 Premier I Entry Level Jets," *Airclaims,* October 16, 1998.

Suttell, Scott, "Prepare for Takeoff: Flight Options Ready to Fly High After Securing $20M," *Crain's Cleveland Business,* August 23, 1999, p. 1.

Thomas, Paulette, "Case Study: Flight Company Owner Knows Trust Is Mutual," *Wall Street Journal,* July 30, 2002, p. B5.

Vanac, Mary, "Brantley Gets Delay in Investment Case," *Plain Dealer* (Cleveland), July 14, 2005, p. C3.

——, "Jet Company to Decide on Restructuring," *Plain Dealer* (Cleveland), July 9, 2005, p. C1.

Warwick, Graham, "Raytheon Launches Fractional Ownership," *Flight International,* June 11, 1997, p. 8.

Zesiger, Sue, "The Fractional Jet Set," *Fortune Magazine,* April 27, 1998, pp. 489 + .

—Frederick C. Ingram

Forward Air Corporation

430 Airport Road
Greeneville, Tennessee 37745
U.S.A.
Telephone: (423) 636-7000
Fax: (423) 636-7279
Web site: http://www.forwardair.com

Public Company
Incorporated: 1981 as Landair Transport, Inc.
Employees: 1,623
Sales: $282.2 million (2004)
Stock Exchanges: NASDAQ
Ticker Symbol: FWRD
NAIC: 484121 General Freight Trucking, Long-Distance,
    Truckload

Forward Air Corporation is a Greeneville, Tennessee-based company that specializes in the surface transportation of deferred air freight, a less expensive alternative to air freight. Unlike time-sensitive air freight, deferred air freight is time definite, a less specific category. Forward Air receives cargo transported by air and sorts it at nearby facilities, where the shipments are consolidated and then sent to the terminal closest to the final destination. All told, Forward Air operates some 80 terminals in the United States and Canada, located on or near airports, a central sorting facility in Columbus, Ohio, and eight regional hubs located in key markets. The company focuses on shipments of 200 pounds and greater. Hence, it does not compete with overnight or small package delivery services, and it primarily markets its services to passenger and cargo airlines, integrated air cargo carriers, and air freight forwarders. Forward Air does not own its own fleet of trucks, preferring to operate as a non-asset based provider. Instead, the company contracts with truck owner-operators and truckload carriers. Because at its core Forward Air is a coordinator, the company offers to others some of the services it provides to itself, including truck brokerage, warehousing, customs brokerage, and shipment consolidation and handling. Forward Air is a public company listed on the NASDAQ.

Parent Company's Founding in the 1980s

Forward Air was originally part of Landair Transport before a split in 1998. Landair was cofounded by Forward Air's chairman and longtime chief executive officer, Scott M. Niswonger. Born in Ohio, Niswonger graduated from Purdue University in 1968 with a degree in aviation technology. An avid flyer, he went to work as a pilot for the president of the Magnavox Company (which maintained a factory in Greeneville, Tennessee, and led to Niswonger's connection to the community) and later graduated from United Airlines Training Academy and the Fairfield Aircraft Factory School. (In the 1980s he returned to college as a chief executive officer, earning a degree in business administration from Tusculum College.) He became a certified airline transport pilot, able to fly small airplanes as well as jumbo jets. Having gained an understanding of the transportation industry, Niswonger decided to strike out on his own in 1974, founding General Aviation, Inc., an all-cargo airline that he headed as president and chief executive officer for the next seven years. In 1980 the trucking industry was deregulated, leading to many air-freight operators seeking to create a reliable ground transport system. Sensing an opportunity, Niswonger in 1981 invested $2,000 along with partner Ed Saylor who invested a similar amount and cofounded Landair Transport as a truckload carrier and contractor to the air cargo industry on a time-definite basis. Saylor would soon die of bone cancer, leaving Niswonger as the sole owner of the business.

Although air freight operators were Landair's first major customers, the company received an increasing amount of business from manufacturers who were employing just-in-time inventory systems. Under Niswonger's leadership, Landair spent heavily to make sure it could deliver goods exactly as they were required, allowing customers to organize their operations as efficiently as possible. In order to meet this goal, Landair assigned two drivers instead of one on longer trips and replaced its tractors every three years, much faster than the norm in the trucking industry. Niswonger also began investing in satellite tracking equipment in the late 1980s, allowing Landair to track the status of its trucks and provide an even greater level of precision to its customers.

Company Perspectives:

Forward Air Corporation is a leading provider of time-definite surface transportation and related logistics services to the North American deferred air freight market. We provide scheduled surface transportation of cargo as a cost effective, reliable alternative to air transportation.

Company Growing Out of 1988 Contract

Forward Air established its roots in 1988 when Landair contracted with North American Van Lines to provide less-than-truckload scheduled air cargo service. It was through this venture that Columbus, Ohio housed a central sorting facility and served as the heart of a hub-and-spoke network. Two years later the business transcended the North American Van Lines contract, and the Forward Air unit came under Landair's direction and control.

Landair generated about $30 million in revenues by the end of the 1980s. That amount would grow to $95.3 million in 1993 to go along with net income of nearly $2 million. It was in 1993 that Landair Transport became Landair Services and was taken public. The business was divided between two units: Forward Air and Truckload, a high-service operation providing short- to medium-haul deliveries on an "on demand" basis. By now Forward Air was the larger of the two subsidiaries.

For the next five years Landair continued to house two separate transportation businesses and sales grew steadily, reaching $148 million in 1995 and $190.4 million in 1997. Net income also kept pace, totaling $8.6 million in 1997. To remain competitive, Forward Air made significant investments in high technology during this period. In 1995 the company began work on a new comprehensive real-time system to log freight orders, track them, and bill customers. The first phase was ready to be rolled out in mid-1997, and the installation was complete in early 1998. As a result, all of Forward Air's terminals were linked together and every shipment could be traced from the moment it was received to the time it was delivered. In addition, the system provided management with a detailed financial picture of the organization on a daily basis, allowing information to be assembled about a specific terminal, customer, or even a particular shipment.

Forward Air's growth was internal, the result of significant growth in the deferred domestic air freight market, until 1997 when it acquired the air cargo assets of Adams Air Cargo, Inc., an Arbuckle, California-based surface transportation contractor to the air cargo industry. It was an important acquisition, given that the West Coast was becoming the most important part of Forward Air's business. The company was well positioned to enjoy further growth through acquisitions, as consolidation in the deferred domestic air freight market was on the horizon, with hundreds of regional less-than-truckload carriers ready to sell their air cargo operations. But first Niswonger restructured Landair Services.

In July 1998 Landair announced that it would split into two separate, publicly traded companies. As had been rumored in the industry for some time, the Truckload and Forward Air operations would go their separate ways. Although older, the Truckload unit was now smaller, generating revenues of about $96 million a year while Forward Air was doing $112 million in business. The Truckload unit was spun off and named Landair Corporation. Landair Services would then take the name of its remaining subsidiary, becoming Forward Air Corporation. According to a *Traffic World* article, "The decision to split the two companies [was] meant to bring a higher profile to the fast-growing Forward Air division. Industry analyst Alex Brand was quoted as saying that the two divisions were 'more or less run as separate companies now. It's a hard sell as a combined company. The Forward Air business is a cleaner story. It's neat and easy, like an airline that moves over land.' " Niswonger explained his strategy in a press release, stating, "We believe investors, analysts and lenders will be better able to assess the different operating characteristics, capital requirement and growth expectations of each business." He added, "The strategic separation will enable both businesses to motivate their key employees and attract new employees by offering economic incentives such as stock options whose value will be directly related to the performance of the truckload business of the Forward Air business." Niswonger became chairman of both companies, but it was clearly Forward Air that emerged from the split as the stronger of the two entities. Within a year, Landair was struggling; its president resigned and Niswonger had to step in to run the company until a replacement was hired.

Forward Air, in the meantime, continued to grow at a steady clip, pursuing a consolidation strategy. In October 1999 it acquired the air cargo operations of Quick Delivery Services, a Mobile, Alabama-based carrier that focused on the Southeast. Forward Air expanded its reach and could not provide greater coverage to its existing customers while adding new customers. Later in the month, Forward Air added the air cargo operating assets of Tennessee-based LTD Express, again adding reach and revenues. After 1999 came to a close, Forward Air reported revenues of $170.8 million for the year, a 30 percent increase over 1998, and a 62 percent improvement over 1997.

Market Downturn at the Close of the 1990s

In December 1999 freight levels dropped sharply, a foreshadowing of a downturn in the economy that would soon visit the country, but it did little to blunt Forward Air's momentum. Once again the company produced record results, with sales increasing more than 25 percent to $214.9 million and net income increasing 46.2 percent to $23.4 million. Forward Air also completed another acquisition during 2000, purchasing the assets of Dedicated Transportation Services, Inc., a subsidiary of Professional Transportation Group, at a cost of $10.7 million. A Chattanooga-based freight hauler and Dedicated's line hauler, U.S. Xpress Enterprises Inc. also had tried to acquire the assets, and after failing began using the "Dedicated" name on another business. Forward Air sued U.S. Xpress for antitrust violations in federal court in 2001, and a year later the two parties reached a settlement, with U.S. Xpress agreeing, without admitting guilt, to pay Forward Air $1.3 million and dropping the Dedicated name on its air transport business.

Another acquisition followed early in 2001 when Forward Air acquired assets of Expedited Delivery Services, Inc., a

Key Dates:

1981: Scott M. Niswonger and Ed Saylor found Landair Transport, Inc.
1988: The roots of Forward Air are planted with a North American Van Lines contract.
1990: Forward Air becomes a Landair business unit.
1993: Landair goes public as Landair Services, Inc.
1998: Landair Services spins off its Truckload business unit and changes its name to Forward Air Corporation.
2003: Niswonger steps down as CEO.

Dallas-based deferred air freight contractor. Overall the year proved to be problematic, despite the company again producing record sales, improving to $227.5 million. The company's technology subsidiary, LogTech, experienced problems, which led its operations to be folded into Forward Air's existing sales operations. On the positive side, Forward Air made strides in expanding its national sales presence and landed significant national accounts with Northwest Airlines and British Airways. In addition, the carrier expanded its service from St. Louis to the Southwest in 2001 and launched a three-day service from San Francisco to ten cities. Investors grew somewhat concerned and the price of Forward Air dropped 9.1 percent. Given that the NASDAQ composite was down 20.7 percent, it was not an entirely dismal performance, however.

Challenges continued in 2002, as Forward Air had to contend with the effects of a sputtering economy that resulted in a soft air freight market. The company was able to make the best of a poor situation, as it experienced a 1 percent decline in revenues to $226 million but still managed to post net income of $21.6 million, the company's second most profitable year in its history. Wall Street, on the other hand, was not impressed, as shares of Forward Air lost 43 percent of their value in 2002.

Forward Air experienced a changing of the guard in October 2003. Niswonger announced that he would step down as CEO at the end of the year, opting to devote more of his time to his many philanthropic endeavors. Replacing him was Bruce Campbell, who had served as chief operating officer since 1990. Niswonger stayed on as the non-executive chairman of the board. He left the company in excellent shape, due in no small measure to a significant rebound in the expedited domestic freight shipping market. Sales increased to $241.5 million and net income improved to $25.8 million. Moreover, the company had $87 million of cash on hand and less than $1 million in debt

at the end of the year. Investors took note and bid up the price of Forward Air stock by 37 percent in 2003.

Demand for shipping continued in 2004, prompting Forward Air to recruit more truck owner-operators. In addition, for the first time in 13 years, the company increased the pay of its owner-operators, adding three cents a mile to their compensation. For the year 2004, sales increased to $282.2 million and net income jumped to $34.4 million. The company was the clear leader in its category and reaping the benefits. In 2005 it bought the customer list used by Xpress Global Systems, which had tried to copy the Forward Air business model and failed. Another rival, Maryland-based Air Cargo, also had exited the field, providing Forward Air with even greater opportunities. The company opened its 81st service facility, located in Harrisburg, Pennsylvania, in June 2005 and also began expanding its Columbus hub facility. There was every indication that Forward Air would continue to enjoy strong growth for some time to come.

Principal Subsidiaries

FAF, Inc.; Forward Air, Inc.; Forward Air International Airlines, Inc.; Forward Air Royalty Company; Forward Air Systems Technology, Inc.; Forward Air Licensing Company; Transportation Properties, Inc.

Principal Competitors

BAS Global Inc.; International Cargo Marketing Consultants; New Penn Motor Express, Inc.; Old Dominion Freight Line, Inc.

Further Reading

Armbruster, William, "Forward to Buy Air Cargo Assets," *Journal of Commerce,* September 30, 1999, p. 16.

Flessner, Dave, "Two Tennessee Trucking Companies Reach Settlement in Anti-Trust Suit," *Chattanooga Times/Free Press,* November 26, 2002.

Krause, Kristin S., "Forward Shares Tumble," *Traffic World,* February 26, 2001, p. 36.

——, "Landair Splits Off Unit," *Traffic World,* July 27, 1998, p. 25.

McKenna, Ed, "Forward Air's Kick Start," *Traffic World,* August 8, 2005, p. 1.

——, "Forward Air's Stable Records," *Traffic World,* February 28, 2005, p. 1.

——, "Profits and Capacity Up," *Traffic World,* November 8, 2004, p. 1.

Posner, Bruce G., "Prime Time: Landair Transport Inc.," *Inc.,* December 1989, p. 125.

Saccomano, Ann, "Seizing the High Ground," *World Trade,* January 2002, p. 20.

—Ed Dinger

FuelCell Energy, Inc.

3 Great Pasture Road
Danbury, Connecticut 06813
U.S.A.
Telephone: (203) 825-6000
Fax: (203) 825-6100
Web site: http://www.fuelcellenergy.com

Public Company
Incorporated: 1969 as Energy Research Corporation
Employees: 346
Sales: $31.4 million (2004)
Stock Exchanges: NASDAQ
Ticker Symbol: FCEL
NAIC: 335999 All Other Miscellaneous Electrical
   Equipment and Component Manufacturing

FuelCell Energy, Inc. develops and manufactures high-temperature hydrogen fuel cells for electric power generation. In essence, fuel cells are like a continuous fuel battery, converting the chemical energy of a fuel directly into electricity without the need for generators, turbines, or any other mechanical equipment. As long as they are supplied with fuel and air they generate a steady stream of electricity. Also like batteries, the cells can be combined, "stacked," to create more powerful units. These fuel cells should not, however, be confused with automobile fuel cells, which start and stop generating power instantaneously without throwing off excess heat. The company's fuel cells take much longer to get up to speed but are designed to run for as long as five years. Its Direct FuelCell product line features three primary units: a 300 kilowatt plant designed for small building and light industrial customers and 1.5 megawatt and 3 megawatt versions suitable for larger buildings, such as hospitals, schools, and factories. The fuel cells do not require an external hydrogen supply or reactor. Rather, they can use a variety of ready fuels, including coal gas, coal-mine methane, methanol, natural gas, biogas, propane, and diesel. Moreover, the products are environmentally friendly, producing few emissions. They are also simple to maintain and inexpen-

sive to operate. FuelCell is a public company listed on the NASDAQ and based in Danbury, Connecticut.

Origins of Fuel Cell Technology: 1800s

Regarded as cutting edge, fuel cell technology is in fact about as old as steam power. Although Sir Humphrey Davy discovered the principles of fuel cells as early as 1802, they were not properly applied until the work of British scientist William Grove, who was better known as the inventor of the "Grove Battery," a voltaic battery that was widely used by the telegraph industry. Less celebrated at the time, however, was his 1839 discovery that water decomposed through electrolysis could be reunited with hydrogen and oxygen atoms to produce electricity and water. This research led to Grove developing a "gas voltaic battery," the predecessor of contemporary fuel cells. It was actually a later scientist, William White Jaques, who coined the term "fuel cell." It was difficult technology to harness and it was not until the 1950s that fuel cells began to become a viable power alternative. In the 1960s they came of age when NASA chose fuel cells over nuclear power to provide electricity and water for the Gemini and Apollo spacecrafts.

FuelCell's founder, Dr. Bernard S. Baker, became exposed to fuel cells in the late 1950s. The son of a chemicals salesman, Baker was born in Philadelphia, Pennsylvania, in 1936. He received both bachelor's and master's degrees in chemical engineering from the University of Pennsylvania. He then became a Fulbright Fellow and went to work for Dutch scientist G.H.J. Broers at the Laboratory for Electrochemistry at the University of Amsterdam. Broers was a pioneer in the advancement of fuel cell technology. While typical fuel cells of the period relied on a "reformer," an external device to extract hydrogen from a hydrocarbon fuel such as natural gas, Broers eliminated the reformer entirely. He developed a high-temperature fuel cell that relied on molten salts to extract the hydrogen from the fuel inside the cell itself. When Baker returned to the United States he devoted his career to making fuel cells a practical and commercial technology. He went to work on fuel cells for Lockheed Aircraft Corporation as a senior scientist in the missile and space divisions, then moved to Chicago, where he became director of basic sciences at the

Company Perspectives:

FuelCell Energy, Inc. based in Danbury Connecticut, is a world leader in the development and manufacture of high temperature hydrogen fuel cells for clean electric power generation.

Institute of Gas Technology while also completing his doctorate at the Illinois Institute of Technology in 1969.

Baker moved his family to Bethel, Connecticut, in 1969 and with partner and fellow chemical engineer Martin Klein founded a company to conduct research on electrochemical technologies for both fuel cells and rechargeable batteries. Klein's field of expertise was in advanced battery technology. Prior to joining forces with Baker, he had worked on batteries for the U.S. Army Signal Corps, Yardney Electric Corp., Electrochimica Corp., and Electro Optical Systems. The start-up company was incorporated as Energy Research Corporation (ERC) in 1969, and a year later the four-person operation set up shop in rented lab space in Danbury, Connecticut.

ERC's financial backing in the 1970s came from the U.S. military and utility companies. In the fuel cell area the company focused initially on low temperature systems (less than 400 degrees Fahrenheit). Following the oil embargo in 1973 that drove up fuel prices, fuel cells and other forms of alternative energy sources received a great deal of attention. "In those early days of the fuel cell," Baker wrote to shareholders in the company's annual report in 1997, "a euphoria existed based on the belief that low temperature fuel cells would become a universal panacea for power generation. It soon became apparent to us, however, that low temperature systems were highly unlikely to become commercially viable." Such systems were complex, requiring a great deal of extra, and expensive, equipment.

ERC enjoyed better success with battery development in the 1970s. With funding from the U.S. Navy, the company developed a new type of battery. Instead of lead acid and nickel cadmium, ERC batteries used silver and zinc. The silver-zinc batteries were used by the Navy in a variety of ships, including the Trieste, a bathyscaph that held the record for the world's deepest ocean dive. But as was the case with ERC's fuel cells, the silver-zinc battery offered limited commercial appeal.

Change of Focus in 1980s

ERC changed its focus in both fuel cells and batteries in the early 1980s. The company now pursued high temperature carbonate fuel cell technology, which would lead to the development of the flagship product, the Direct Fuel Cell. It offered greater commercial possibilities because it was able to use such readily available fuels as natural gas. It was also more efficient at producing electricity than low temperature systems and did not require the costly support equipment of the earlier system. In batteries, ERC built on its experience with silver and zinc to develop a battery that relied on nickel oxide and zinc. This new system offered a high energy density, allowing for a much lighter battery, making it easier to transport and ideal for marine applications. In addition, the materials had less an impact on the environment, important for a battery used on the water. As Baker wrote to shareholders in 1997, "By the early 1980s, ERC had developed full size electric vehicle batteries and tested them in various types of electric vehicles. While vehicle performance was good, cycle life was limited to about 150 cycles or about 20,000 miles of normal driving."

After 20 years in operation, ERC in the 1990s continued to build on its research and neared the goal of developing commercially viable products that could complement one another. In a nutshell, the fuel cell generated electricity and rechargeable batteries became the electrical energy storage component of an integrated power system. Fortunately, the company did not lack for funding. In 1990, for example, ERC won a $32 million Department of Energy contract to design, build, and test fuel cells in the 100-kilowatt range that could operate on natural gas or coal-derived gas. It also appeared in the early 1990s that fuel cells were on the verge of coming into their own. As the *Wall Street Journal* noted in a 1992 article, "Tighter environmental regulations are forcing power producers to install expensive anti-pollution equipment. That had shrunk fuel cells' capital-cost difference to 25% more than a coal-fired plant, for example. With high-volume production, fuel-cell makers say, the technology will become competitive with conventional energy sources." A pioneer in the field, ERC now faced competition from Westinghouse Electric Corporation and Japanese giants Mitsubishi Heavy Industries Ltd. and Toshiba Corporation, as well as a dozen other companies interested in fuel cells.

Taken Public in 1992

ERC took advantage of the growing interest in fuel cell technology to go public in 1992, making an initial offering of stock that raised $6.5 million. While forecasts about the imminent arrival of fuel cells proved wrong, ERC continued to plug away, refining its Direct FuelCell unit, targeting the 2 megawatt range, which the company felt was a practical size to fit into a grid-connected utility environment. ERC reached a significant milestone in 1992 when it successfully tested a 120 kilowatt Direct FuelCell unit. A year later an improved version was tested in Denmark by the Elkraft Power Company. Then, in 1996, a 2 megawatt Direct FuelCell power plant went online in Santa Clara, California, connected to the grid of the Santa Clara municipal electric system. Partners in the effort included the City of Santa Clara, the Electric Power Research Institute, the Los Angeles Department of Water and Power, the Sacramento Municipal Utility District, Southern California Edison Company, and the U.S. Department of Energy's Morgantown Energy Technology Center.

In batteries during the early 1990s, ERC worked on extending cycle life. In 1990 Martin Klein resigned as executive vice-president, and remained as director for two more years before selling his stake in the company. During his 20 years at ERC, Klein headed all research concerning silver-zinc, nickel-zinc, nickel-cadmium, nickel-hydrogen, silver-hydrogen, zinc-oxygen, and zinc-bromine rechargeable batteries. In 1992 Klein founded another company, Electro Energy Inc., to develop batteries for the military.

By 1997 ERC, in the opinion of Baker, was in need of a more commercially oriented executive to take the company to the next level. He was also thinking of the day he would have to retire and wanted to make sure a succession plan was in place. "My first love was research and development," he told the *Wall Street Journal* in a 2001 article. "I wasn't a business man and I knew I wasn't a business man." In the fall of 1997 he hired Jerry D. Leitman to become ERC's chief executive officer. Leitman's previous experience included a stint with Swedish multinational FLAKT AV and serving as president of Asea Brown Boveri's global air pollution control business. Leitman told the *Wall Street Journal* that he was wary about taking the job because he was worried about Baker looking over his shoulder. The transition proved to be a smooth one, however. Reported the *Wall Street Journal,* "According to Messrs. Baker and Leitman, the two have been successful because they recognize their unique skill sets and try to use them to their advantage. For example, Mr. Baker will talk to the public whenever technology is the focus, but Mr. Leitman handles presentations to investors who are more concerned about how the company is operated on a day-to-day basis."

Under Leitman's leadership ERC began a concerted effort to commercialize its fuel cell and battery technologies. In 1998 the company successfully demonstrated its nickel-zinc batteries for use in electric cars, bicycles and scooters, wheelchairs, trolling motors, and lawn motors. The batteries offered 2.5 times the range of a lead acid battery. Although batteries and fuel cells shared much of the same technology, they were generally marketed to different customers. As a result, the company found its focus increasingly divided, leading to the battery business being spun off as a separate company, Evercel, Inc. in 1999. As the *Fairfield County Business Journal* explained in an article at the time, "selling an expensive, tennis court-sized, megawatt power plant with four fuel cell stacks is a vastly different matter than selling a rechargeable battery designed to power an electric scooter."

Because fuel cells were now ERC's sole focus, the company changed its name to FuelCell Energy, Inc. in 1999. In that same year, the company's first 250 kilowatt power plant began operations. Again, there was no shortage of willing partners. In Germany DaimlerChrysler's MTU division fired up a cogeneration power plant using a FuelCell unit. Then, in 2000, Mercedes-Benz U.S. International Inc., Southern Company, and Alabama Municipal Electric Authority agreed to team up with FuelCell to install a 250-kilowatt fuel cell power plant at the Mercedes-Benz plant in Tuscaloosa, Alabama, in a pilot demonstration project. Also in 2000 FuelCell was awarded a Department of Energy contract for product design and improvement, as well as commercial contracts to install power plants in Washington state, Los Angeles, Asia, and elsewhere.

There was a great deal of enthusiasm for fuel cell technology in general, due almost entirely to the energy crisis in California, which brought the idea of alternative sources of power generation to the forefront. As a result, FuelCell's stock surged as it became the darling of Wall Street within the large fuel cell category. But once energy supplies rebounded, enthusiasm waned and the price of the company's stock plummeted. Fuel-Cell had been in the business for a long time, however, was well stocked with cash, and continued to follow its own game plan. Yet it would have to do so without Baker. He retired in June 2002, handing over the chairmanship to Leitman. Two years later he died just short of his 68th birthday from a series of strokes related to cancer.

By now FuelCell had a commercially viable product in hand but had to wait for market acceptance. Because of an energy glut the fuel cell industry was in disarray in 2003, and FuelCell was forced to cut costs by reducing payroll. Nevertheless, the company was healthy enough to acquire a Canadian company, Calgary-based Global Thermoelectric Inc., in a stock deal valued at $80 million. At the same time, FuelCell also paid $2 million for a 16 percent stake in an Illinois fuel cell company, Versa Power Systems. Global's focus was on thermoelectric generators intended to supply electricity to rural and other remote locations. Several months later, FuelCell sold off the Global generator product line that did not fit with its focus, pocketing $17 million.

FuelCell was hardly in need of extra money. In the fall of 2004 it was reported to have $170 million in cash and a few weeks later announced that it planned to make a private placement of $75 million in stock, the money earmarked for further development and commercialization of its fuel cell products. In 2005 the company branched into a different area of fuel cell technology, teaming up with Pennsylvania-based Air Products and Chemicals as part of a Department of Energy project to develop a new type of pumping station for hydrogen-powered cars. Fuel was to be fed through a fuel cell to produce hydrogen that could be purified for use in hydrogen-powered cars.

As oil prices soared in 2005, fuel cells and other forms of alternative power generation, received a boost, just as they had every time energy costs soared. Whether fuel cells would finally find their place in the power field remained to be seen, however. What was not questioned, after 35 years of commitment, was that FuelCell was in for the long haul.

Principal Subsidiaries

Xiamen-ERC High Technology Joint Venture, Inc. (24.5%)

Principal Competitors

Ballard Power Systems Inc.; Energy Conversion Devices; Honeywell International Inc.

Further Reading

Blumenau, Kurt, "Companies Join Forces to Build New Type of Hydrogen Fueling" *Morning Call* (Allentown, Pa.), August 4, 2005.

Cheddar, Christina, "Boardroom Vets Move to Power Technology," *Wall Street Journal,* September 11, 2001, p. B8A.

Feder, Barnaby J., "Bernard S. Baker, 67, a Pioneer in the Development of Fuel Cells, Dies," *New York Times,* June 4, 2004.

Hegarty, Liam, "ERC Poised for a Radical Power Trip," *Fairfield County Business Journal,* May 10, 1999, p. 1.

Ludlum, David, "Fuel Cell Companies Offer Choice and Risk," *New York Times,* December 23, 2001, pp. 3, 9.

Naj, Amal Kumar, "Clean Fuel Cells Sparking New Interest," *Wall Street Journal,* March 19, 1992, p. B1.

Roberts, Jim, "ERC Powers Up for a Field Test of Unique Fuel Cells," *Fairfield County Business Journal,* November 30, 1992, p. 1.

Silvestrini, Marc, "FuelCell Energy Founder to Retire As Chairman," *Waterbury Republican-American,* June 22, 2002.

Smith, David A., "Danbury, Conn.-Based FuelCell Energy Increases Stake in Growing Industry," *Waterbury Republican-American,* August 6, 2003.

——, "FuelCell Energy of Torrington, Conn., Cuts 25 Percent of Jobs to Save Money," *Waterbury Republican-American,* May 2, 2003.

—Ed Dinger

Genentech, Inc.

One DNA Way
South San Francisco, California 94080-4990
U.S.A.
Telephone: (650) 225-1000
Fax: (650) 225-6000
Web site: http://www.gene.com

Public Subsidiary of Roche Holding Ltd.
Incorporated: 1976
Employees: 7,646
Sales: $3.98 billion (2004)
Stock Exchanges: New York
Ticker Symbol: DNA
NAIC: 325412 Pharmaceutical Preparation Manufacturing; 325414 Biological Product (Except Diagnostic) Manufacturing; 541710 Research and Development in the Physical, Engineering, and Life Sciences

Genentech, Inc. is the oldest and second largest biotechnology company in the world. Genentech discovers, develops, manufactures, and markets human pharmaceuticals for significant medical needs. The company fabricates organisms from gene cells, organisms that are not ordinarily produced by the cells. Conceivably, this process, referred to as gene splicing or recombinant DNA, may lead to cures for cancer or AIDS. Genentech markets a host of pharmaceuticals, but several of its drugs stand above the rest, serving as the revenue-generating engines that propel the company forward. Rituxan, used to treat non-Hodgkin's lymphoma; Herceptin, designed to treat breast cancer; and Avastin, developed to treat colon cancer, rank as the company's most important products developed in its oncology franchise.

Early Years

Founded in 1976, Genentech was financed by Kleinman, Perkins, Caufield and Byers, a San Francisco high-tech venture capital firm, and by its cofounders, Robert Swanson and Herbert Boyer. Swanson, a graduate of the Sloan School of Management at the Massachusetts Institute of Technology, was employed by Kleinman, Perkins, where he learned of the achievements of Cetus, a biotechnology firm founded in 1971; he decided to investigate the prospect of marketing DNA products. Initially, the concept was met with little enthusiasm, but in Herbert Boyer, a distinguished academic scientist, Swanson found someone who enthusiastically supported his plan. One of the first scientists to synthesize life (he had created gene cells with Stanley Cohen), Boyer wanted to take his research further and to create new cells.

Boyer and Swanson decided to leave their respective jobs and to found Genentech (genetic engineering technology). Thomas J. Perkins, a partner with Kleinman, Perkins, who became Genentech's chairman, suggested that the new company subcontract its early research. Swanson followed Perkins's advice and contracted the City of Hope National Medical Center to conduct the company's initial research project.

Boyer and Swanson, desiring to achieve credibility for Genentech, wanted to exhibit their grasp of the relevant technology before they attempted to market products. To accomplish this goal, Boyer intentionally selected an easily replicated cell with a simple composition, Somatostatin. The first experiment with Somatostatin required seven months of research. Scientists on the project placed the hormone inside E. coli bacteria, found in the human intestine. The anticipated result was that the bacteria would produce useful proteins that duplicated Somatostatin, but that did not happen. Then a scientist working on the project hypothesized that proteins in the bacteria were attacking the hormone. Somatostatin was protected, and the cell was successfully produced. Although it established credibility for the company, the experiment brought no real financial returns. Boyer and Swanson intended to produce human insulin as Genentech's first product.

Early in the summer of 1978 Genentech experienced its first breakthrough in recreating the insulin gene. This development required an expenditure of approximately $100 million and 1,000 human years of labor. By 1982 the company had won approval from the Food and Drug Administration (FDA). Eli Lilly and Company, the world's largest and oldest manufacturer of synthetic insulin, commanded 75 percent of the U.S. insulin market, and Swanson knew that Genentech stood little chance

Company Perspectives:

Our mission is to be the leading biotechnology company, using human genetic information to discover, develop, manufacture and commercialize biotherapeutics that address significant unmet medical needs. We commit ourselves to high standards of integrity in contributing to the best interests of patients, the medical profession, our employees and our communities, and to seeking significant returns to our stockholders, based on the continual pursuit of scientific and operational excellence.

of competing with them. He informed Lilly's directors of Genentech's accomplishments, hoping to attract their attention: he believed that the mere threat of a potentially better product would entice Lilly to purchase licensing rights to the product, and he was correct. Lilly bought the rights and marketed the product as Humulin. This maneuver provided ample capital for Genentech to continue its work. By 1987 the company was earning $5 million in licensing fees from Lilly.

Swanson pursued a similar strategy with the company's next product, Alpha Interferon. Hoffmann-La Roche purchased the rights to Interferon—which it marketed as Roferon-A—and paid approximately $5 million in royalties to Genentech in 1987. Revenues from these agreements helped to underwrite the costs of new product development, which ran from $25 million to $50 million per product prior to FDA approval. Meanwhile, Genentech went public in 1980, raising $35 million through an initial public offering.

Entering the Marketing Arena in the Middle to Late 1980s

The first product independently marketed by Genentech, human growth hormone (HGH) or Protropin, generated $43.6 million in sales in 1986. Demand for HGH increased as the medical profession learned more about the drug's capabilities and diagnosed hormone inadequacy more frequently. Protropin enjoyed record-setting sales over the next six years, topping $155 million by 1991. Approved by the FDA in 1985, Protropin helped prevent dwarfism in children. Genentech's entry into the market was facilitated by an FDA decision to ban the drug's predecessor because it was contaminated with a virus. By the end of the 1980s a "new and improved" version of HGH patented by Eli Lilly also had received approval from the FDA. Lilly's drug, unlike Genentech's version, actually replicated the growth hormone found in the human body. To counter this potential threat to their market, Genentech sued the FDA to force the agency to determine which company held exclusive rights to the product. At the end of 1991, Genentech's Protropin maintained an impressive 75 percent share of the HGH market.

Such legal disputes were not unusual for biotechnology firms still in their infancy. Because the products of the industry duplicated substances found in nature, they challenged long-established patent laws. Traditionally, products and discoveries determined as not evident in nature receive patent awards. Biotechnology firms contested these standards in the court-

room, attempting to force alterations in the law, to make it conform to the needs of the industry. Companies applied for broad patents to secure against technological innovations that could undermine their niche in the marketplace. For start-up firms such as Genentech, patent battles consumed large sums of money in both domestic and foreign disputes.

Genentech introduced tissue plasmogen activator (t-PA) in 1987 as Activase, a fast-acting drug that helped to break down fibris, a clotting agent in the blood. At $2,200 per dose, t-PA was marketed as a revolutionary drug for the prevention and treatment of heart attacks. When Genentech failed to provide the FDA with evidence that Activase prolonged the lives of heart attack victims, the federal agency delayed approval until 1988. The drug brought in almost half of the company's $400 million in 1989 revenues.

But Activase was soon battered with legal and clinical setbacks. Genentech's claim to exclusive ownership of natural t-PA and all synthetic variations on it was struck down in Britain when the British firm Wellcome Foundation Ltd. challenged Genentech's patent in the British courts, claiming it was overly broad. In 1993, however, Genentech won a court victory against Wellcome, preventing the U.K. firm from marketing t-PA in the United States until 2005, when Genentech's patent was due to expire. Clinical data showed that the drug caused serious side effects, including severe internal bleeding. A European study indicated that the drug was faster, but no more effective, than some competitors costing just $200 per dose. The troubles continued when a controversial study comparing Activase, SmithKline Beecham plc's Eminase, and another firm's streptokinase was released in March 1991. The International Study of Infarct Survival (ISIS-3) found all three drugs to be equally effective at keeping people alive, which again reflected badly on Activase's high cost. Genentech discounted several of the research methods used, then commissioned its own 41,000-patient comparative trial (at a cost of $55 million), which was completed in 1993 and vouched for the superiority of Activase over streptokinase. By the mid-1990s, however, Genentech was selling just $300 million worth of Activase per year, a far cry from the $1 billion annual sales it had projected for the product in the late 1980s.

Early to Mid-1990s: From Roche Merger to CEO Controversy

The regulatory, legal, and clinical roadblocks that stymied Genentech's introduction of Activase, combined with competition from large pharmaceutical and chemical companies that bought into biotechnology in the late 1980s, culminated in Genentech's 60 percent acquisition by Switzerland's Roche Holding Ltd. The merger was one of many in 1989 and 1990, which resulted in such pharmaceutical giants as SmithKline Beecham plc and Bristol-Myers Squibb Company. Genentech used the $2.1 billion influx of capital to fund research, finance patent disputes, and invest in cooperative ventures to develop synthetic drugs using biotechnological discoveries. Also in 1990, G. Kirk Raab, whom the *Wall Street Journal* described as a "master marketer," was named CEO of Genentech. That year, the company launched the first commercial life sciences experiment in space when it sponsored research aboard the space shuttle *Discovery*, and it received FDA approval to ex-

Key Dates:

1976: Robert Swanson and Herbert Boyer found Genentech, Inc.

1978: Company scientists recreate the insulin gene, Genentech's first marketable product.

1980: Company raises $35 million through an initial public offering (IPO).

1982: Human insulin clone wins FDA approval and is marketed as Humulin under license by Eli Lilly.

1985: Protropin, the first product independently marketed by Genentech, receives FDA approval for the treatment of dwarfism.

1987: Company begins marketing Activase as a way to dissolve blood clots in heart attack victims.

1990: Switzerland's Roche Holding Ltd. purchases a 60 percent stake in the company for $2.1 billion.

1993: Pulmozyme receives FDA approval for the treatment of cystic fibrosis.

1994: Company begins marketing a second human growth hormone (HGH), Nutropin.

1995: Roche agrees to extend its option to buy remainder of Genentech for four more years; Genentech board forces CEO G. Kirk Raab to resign after allegations of ethical improprieties arise; Dr. Arthur Levinson is named as successor.

1996: Nutropin AQ, the first liquid HGH and Genentech's third HGH product, receives FDA approval.

1997: Company begins marketing Rituxan for the treatment of non-Hodgkin's lymphoma; revenues surpass $1 billion for the first time.

1998: FDA approves Herceptin in the treatment of breast cancer.

1999: Company pays $50 million to settle charges that it had illegally marketed Protropin for unapproved uses; Roche exercises option to buy remainder of the company, then sells about 34 percent of its stock back to the public through two public offerings; Genentech agrees to pay the University of California at San Francisco $200 million to settle a patent dispute involving Protropin.

2004: Levinson's emphasis on oncology produces two new drugs, Tarceva and Avastin.

pand the marketing of Activase to include the treatment of acute massive pulmonary embolism (blood clots in the lungs).

Activase had faced stiff competition when it first entered the market in the late 1980s. Delays in approval gave competitors such as Biogen and Integrated Genetics the opportunity to catch up with the industry leader. A dozen or so companies filed patents for similar drugs. Genentech could not expect to easily secure foreign markets for its new drug, either. Competition was stiff; this relatively new industry had little time to carve out established markets, and there were important competitors, particularly in Western Europe. In 1991, however, Genentech won an exclusive patent for recombinant t-PA in Japan. Genentech also had several new products in FDA trials in 1991. An insulin-like growth factor for the treatment of full-blown AIDS patients and relaxin, an

obstetric drug, were in development that year. Genentech's DNase (pronounced dee-en-ayse), for use in the management of cystic fibrosis and chronic bronchitis, entered Phase III FDA trials. The firm's HER2 antibody entered clinical trials in 1991 as well. This treatment for breast and ovarian cancer was first developed from mouse cells. Genentech also was able to begin marketing of interferon gamma, or Actimmune, in 1991. The product's relatively meager sales of $1.7 million were connected to the small number of patients suffering from chronic granulomatous disease, an inherited immunodeficiency.

In 1993 Genentech received regulatory approval to market Pulmozyme, its brand name for DNase, in the United States, Canada, Sweden, Austria, and New Zealand, for the treatment of cystic fibrosis. The company's relationship with Roche led to the establishment of a European subsidiary of Genentech to develop, register, and market DNase in 17 primary European countries. Genentech also allotted Roche an exclusive license to sell DNase anywhere but Europe, the United States, Canada, and Japan. DNase was considered the first major advance in the treatment of cystic fibrosis in 30 years. Sales of Pulmozyme—which had gone from conception to market in just five years, half the industry average—reached $76 million by 1996.

Genentech continued to expand its product line during the 1990s. In March 1994 the FDA approved a new Genentech human growth hormone, Nutropin, for the treatment of growth failure in children. Other uses for Nutropin soon followed, including the treatment of adults suffering from growth hormone deficiency and of short stature associated with Turner syndrome. A third Genentech HGH, Nutropin AQ, the first liquid HGH, received its first FDA approval in 1996. That year the company's line of growth hormone products generated $218.2 million in revenues.

By mid-1995 Roche's holding in Genentech had increased to about 65 percent. As part of its original stake purchased in 1990, Roche had received the option of purchasing the remainder of the company at $60 per share, an option that expired June 30, 1995. In May 1995, however, Genentech and Roche reached an agreement whereby the option would be extended to June 30, 1999. The option was set to begin at $61.25 per share, then increase each quarter by $1.25 until expiring at $82.50. As part of the agreement, Roche took over Genentech's Canadian and European operations, with Genentech agreeing to receive royalties on sales of Pulmozyme in Europe and on sales of all of the company's products in Canada.

In the midst of the negotiations on this deal, Raab approached Roche to seek a $2 million guarantee of a personal loan. When Genentech's board found out about this improper move, it conducted a broad review of his leadership. Finding other problems, including ongoing federal regulatory investigations into charges that Genentech was promoting the use of its products in unapproved ways, the board forced Raab to resign in July 1995. Named to replace him as president and CEO was Dr. Arthur Levinson, a molecular biologist who had headed the company's research operations. One outcome of the federal probes came in April 1999, when Genentech finalized an agreement to pay $50 million to settle charges that it had illegally marketed Protropin for unapproved uses, such as a kidney disorder and severe burns, from 1985 to 1994. The company also pleaded guilty to a criminal violation, "introducing mis-branded drugs in interstate commerce."

Revitalizing the Product Pipeline in the Late 1990s

Although many questioned the wisdom of appointing as CEO a scientist who had never before run a company, Levinson helped restore the company's reputation by shifting its focus away from the marketing arena and back to the laboratory. Genentech reached new heights in the late 1990s, with revenues surpassing the $1 billion mark for the first time in 1997 before reaching $1.15 billion the year after. The reemphasis on research revitalized the company's product pipeline, leading to a substantial increase in the sales of products Genentech marketed itself. In 1998 such sales reached $717.8 million, an increase of nearly 23 percent from the previous year. The growth was attributable to the sales of two new products. In November 1997 Genentech began selling a monoclonal antibody called Rituxan, the first such entity approved to treat a cancer, specifically a form of non-Hodgkin's lymphoma (a cancer of the immune system). Sales of Rituxan, which was codeveloped with La Jolla, California-based IDEC Pharmaceuticals Corporation, were $162.6 million in 1998, the first full year of sales. Monoclonal antibodies are designed to zero in on cancer cells and kill a tumor without harming healthy tissue. A second Genentech-developed monoclonal antibody, Herceptin, was approved by the FDA in September 1998 to treat breast cancer. In clinical trials at this time was a third cancer treatment, called Anti-VEGF, which was being studied as a treatment for several types of solid-tumor cancers.

In June 1999 Roche exercised its option to acquire the 33 percent of Genentech it did not already own for $82.50 per share, or about $3.7 billion. Just one month later, however, Roche sold about 16 percent of Genentech stock back to the public in an initial public offering (IPO) that raised about $2.13 billion at the offering price of $97 per share. Genentech thereby resumed trading on the New York Stock Exchange but under a new symbol, DNA. In October 1999 Roche made a secondary offering of 20 million Genentech shares at $143.50, raising $2.87 billion in the largest secondary offering in U.S. history. Following the offerings, Roche held a 66 percent stake in Genentech, which retained the operational autonomy through which it had thrived.

In November 1999 Genentech agreed to pay $200 million to the University of California at San Francisco (UCSF) to settle a nine-year dispute over a patent underlying Protropin. The university had charged that Genentech scientists had stolen a DNA sample from a lab in 1978 and used the specimen to develop Protropin, which by the end of the 1990s had generated $2 billion in sales over its lifetime. The university had sought $400 million in lost royalties and other damages.

The UCSF lawsuit was not the only legal blemish on Genentech's record at the turn of the century, but overall the period was more noteworthy because it validated the decision to put Levinson at the helm. In 2002, a Los Angeles County Superior Court jury awarded the Duarte, California-based City of Hope National Medical Center $500 million in royalty payments and punitive damages for Genentech's failure to pay royalties connected to a licensing agreement in 1976. Specifically, the law-suit charged that Genentech had hidden licensed sales and not paid royalties on a process for inserting genes into bacteria and inducing them to produce proteins, a process developed by two City of Hope scientists. The jury's decision was a blow, to be sure, but with a market capitalization of nearly $30 billion and $2.5 billion in cash and long-term marketable securities, the company could incur the loss without fear of financial collapse. Of a bigger concern were the delays in bringing several drugs to market, which cast a pall over Genentech's immediate future at the time the jury's decision was announced, at least as indicated by Wall Street's estimation of the company.

A Focus on Cancer for the Future

Levinson's most vital contribution to Genentech was steering the company toward oncology, a decision that promised to define his legacy. He wanted to make Genentech the world's leader in developing drugs to treat cancer, setting 2005 as the target date for the company to achieve such status. The introduction of Rituxan and Herceptin provided an intoxicating start to the emphasis on cancer treatments, with each registering stunning success. Herceptin generated $152 million sales during its first year on the market, making it the most successful cancer drug ever, and exhibited fantastic growth with each passing year, building a business volume that grew to $347 million in sales by 2001. Rituxan demonstrated even greater sales growth, quickly becoming a financial boon for Genentech. Between 1999 and 2001, Rituxan's sales mushroomed from $263 million to $818 million.

Herceptin and Rituxan became the two major sources of growth for Genentech during the first years of the decade, replacing the company's traditional core business of growth hormones and Pulmozyme as the financial foundation of the company. Levinson's decision to focus on oncology sparked impressive financial growth, but early in the decade the company was beset with delays for its next wave of drugs to enter the market. Xolair, an asthma drug, was supposed to be released in 2001, but the FDA demanded more tests midway through the year, which pushed back the release of the drug to the end of 2003. A psoriasis drug, Xanelim, was slated for debut in 2002, but the company did not submit an application until mid-2002, delaying its introduction. Further, a promising cancer drug known as Tarceva was still years away from being released, offering no immediate source of revenue. One drug was progressing through the development pipeline faster than expected—Avastin, scheduled to be released in 2003—but the absence of any new drugs entering the market prompted the investment community to voice its displeasure. Genentech's stock peaked in March 2000 before beginning to drop in value substantially. By the end of 2001, the company's stock had dropped 40 percent. By mid-2002, the stock was trading for 75 percent of its value in March 2000. Despite the negative reaction from Wall Street, there remained an air of optimism. Genentech, the company that had invented its industry, had legions of admiring fans, including supporters who worked on Wall Street. "These guys are very, very good," an analyst remarked in a December 18, 2001 interview with *Investor's Business Daily*. "Wall Street has very high expectations for them. So when they miss on expectations, one way or another, the response seems to be magnified."

Levinson and his team fulfilled the expectations of Wall Street by ending the lull in new drug introductions with a flurry of new pharmaceuticals. Xolair, the first humanized therapeutic antibody for the treatment of asthma, received FDA approval in 2003, the same year the company's psoriasis drug, which was launched as RAPTIVA, received approval. In 2004, the company's lung cancer drug, Tarceva, which was developed with OSI Pharmaceuticals, won approval, but the year's biggest introduction was a drug the company developed on its own. In February 2004, Avastin, which was designed to choke the blood supply that feeds tumors, was approved for sale by the FDA, the first drug of its kind to enter the market. The expectations for Avastin put the drug on the same level of Herceptin and Rituxan, both of which continued to serve as the lifeblood of the company nearly a decade after their release. Sales of Avastin in the third fiscal quarter of 2005 reached $325 million, nearly 80 percent more than the drug had generated during 2004's third quarter. With Avastin's sales expected to surpass $1 billion within a few years and roughly 30 projects in the company's development pipeline, optimism for the future ran high at the company's central offices on One DNA Way in South San Francisco. In the years ahead, with an emphasis on oncology delivering enviable results, Genentech promised to remain one of the most successful biotechnology companies in the world.

Principal Subsidiaries

Genentech Espana, S.L. (Spain).

Principal Competitors

Abbott Laboratories; American Home Products Corporation; Amgen Inc.; Bayer AG; Biogen, Inc.; Bristol-Myers Squibb Company; Chiron Corporation; E.I. du Pont de Nemours and Company; Eli Lilly and Company; Genzyme Corporation; Glaxo Wellcome plc; Hoechst AG; Immunex Corporation; Johnson & Johnson; Merck & Co., Inc.; Novartis AG; Novo Nordisk A/S; Pfizer Inc.; Pharmacia & Upjohn, Inc.; Rhone-Poulenc Rorer Inc.; Schering-Plough Corporation; SmithKline Beecham plc.

Further Reading

Abrahams, Paul, "Biotech Veteran Seeks a Formula for Growth," *Financial Times,* July 10, 2002, p. 13.

Arancibia, Juan Carlos, "Genentech Keeping Pipeline Full," *Investor's Business Daily,* August 29, 2005, p. B2.

Arnst, Catherine, "After 27 Years, a Big Payoff," *Business Week,* June 1, 1998, p. 147.

Baum, Rudy, "Knotty Biotech Issues Receive Attention," *Chemical & Engineering News,* April 27, 1992, pp. 30–31.

Blumenstyk, Goldie, "U. of California Patent Suit Puts Biotech Powerhouse Under Microscope," *Chronicle of Higher Education,* August 6, 1999, pp. A45–A46.

Bylinsky, Gene, "Got a Winner? Back It Big," *Fortune,* March 21, 1994, pp. 69–70.

Chase, Marilyn, "Hedged Bet: As Genentech Awaits New Test of Old Drug, Its Pipeline Fills Up," *Wall Street Journal,* April 30, 1993, p. A1.

Crabtree, Penni, "Oceanside Plant Purchase Shows Genentech Is Sailing," *San Diego Union-Tribune,* June 19, 2005.

Darmiento, Laurence, "Settlement Possible After Huge City of Hope Verdict," *Los Angeles Business Journal,* June 17, 2002, p. 9.

Fisher, Lawrence M., "Rehabilitation of a Biotech Pioneer," *New York Times,* May 8, 1994, Sec. 3, p. 6.

"Genentech's Winning Formula," *Business Week Online,* May 17, 2005.

Grabarek, Brooke H., "Genentech: Still Nowhere But Up?," *Financial World,* June 21, 1994, pp. 16, 18.

Hamilton, Joan, "How Long Can Biotech Stay in the Stratosphere?," *Business Week,* November 25, 1991, p. 224.

——, "It Ain't Over Till It's Over at Genentech," *Business Week,* July 24, 1995, p. 41.

——, "A Miracle Drug's Second Coming," *Business Week,* June 3, 1996, p. 118.

——, "A Star Drug Is Born," *Business Week,* August 23, 1993, p. B6.

"Heart Attack Drugs: Trials and Tribulations," *Economist,* March 19, 1991, pp. 86–87.

King, Ralph T., Jr., " 'Assembly Line' Revs Up Genentech," *Wall Street Journal,* March 12, 1998, p. B1.

——, "Genentech Inc. Names Its CEO As Chairman," *Wall Street Journal,* September 23, 1999, p. B18.

——, "Genentech to Pay $200 Million to End Suit Over Patent," *Wall Street Journal,* November 17, 1999, p. B7.

——, "Profit Prescription: In Marketing of Drugs, Genentech Tests Limits of What Is Acceptable," *Wall Street Journal,* January 10, 1995, p. A1.

——, "Roche to Unload As Much As 17% of Genentech," *Wall Street Journal,* October 11, 1999, p. B2.

Levine, Daniel S., "Genentech Finds a Swiss Cure for Its Wall Street Ills," *San Francisco Business Times,* June 16, 1995, p. 6.

McCoy, Charles, "Genentech's New CEO Seeks Clean Slate," *Wall Street Journal,* July 12, 1995, p. B6.

"Mergers and Acquisitions: Strategic Is the Word," *Institutional Investor,* January 1991, pp. 74–81.

Moukheiber, Zina, "The Great White Hunter," *Forbes,* July 26, 1999, pp. 133–36.

"A Natural Selection," *Chief Executive,* May 1992, pp. 34–39.

Reeves, Amy, "Genentech Inc. South San Francisco, California Hey, Investors: We're Still Turning a Profit," *Investor's Business Daily,* December 18, 2001, p. A12.

Rigdon, Joan E., "Fatal Blunder: Genentech CEO, a Man Used to Pushing Limit, Exceeds It and Is Out," *Wall Street Journal,* July 11, 1995, p. A1.

Shinkle, Kirk, "Genentech Beats Q3 Profit," *Investor's Business Daily,* October 11, 2005, p. A1.

Silber, Judy, "Shares of Biotech Company Genentech Fall on Cancer Medication Side-Effect News," *Contra Costa Times,* August 14, 2004.

Slutsker, Gary, "Patenting Mother Nature," *Forbes,* January 7, 1991, p. 290.

Thayer, Ann, "Biotech Firms' Revenues Up But Earnings Win First Half," *Chemical & Engineering News,* August 31, 1992, pp. 15–16.

Weintraub, Arlene, "Another Pain for Genentech," *Business Week Online,* June 17, 2002.

——, "Giving Birth to Biotech," *Business Week,* October 18, 2004, p. 16.

Westphal, Christoph, and Sherry Glied, "AZT and t-PA: The Disparate Fates of Two Biotechnological Innovations and Their Producers," *Columbia Journal of World Business,* Spring/Summer 1990, pp. 83–100.

—April S. Dougal
—updates: David E. Salamie; Jeffrey L. Covell

Global Hyatt Corporation

71 South Wacker Drive
Chicago, Illinois 60606-4637
U.S.A.
Telephone: (312) 750-1234
Fax: (312) 750-8550
Web site: http://www.hyatt.com

Private Company
Incorporated: 1957 as Hyatt Hotels Corporation
Employees: 41,000
Sales: $3.7 billion (2004 est.)
NAIC: 721110 Hotels (Except Casino) and Motels;
    721120 Casino Hotels

Global Hyatt Corporation is one of the leading luxury hotel companies in the world. Owned by the Pritzker family of Chicago, Hyatt manages or licenses the management of more than 210 hotels and resorts (with a total of more than 90,000 rooms) in 43 countries around the world. In addition to the core Hyatt Regency brand, Hyatt has also developed other special hotel concepts, including the Grand Hyatt, the Park Hyatt, and Classic Residence by Hyatt. Grand Hyatts are large-scale, higher priced hotels located in culturally rich cities; Park Hyatts are modeled after small European hotels; and Classic Residence by Hyatt properties offer luxury retirement apartments for rental. Hyatt also operates six casino hotels located in Aruba; Thessaloníki, Greece; Mendoza, Argentina; Rising Sun, Indiana; and Henderson and Incline Village, Nevada. The company's U.S., Canadian, and Caribbean hotels are organized under the Hyatt Corporation subsidiary, while Hyatt International Corporation handles the international locations. Other Global Hyatt subsidiaries include Hyatt Vacation Club, Inc., specializing in time-shares; Hyatt Equities, L.L.C., involved in hotel ownership; and U.S. Franchise Systems, Inc., franchisor of the Hawthorn Suites, Microtel Inns & Suites, and Best Inns & Suites chains.

The Founding Family

While Hyatt's history as a corporate entity dates from 1957, the Pritzker family, who built and control Hyatt, has been active

significantly longer. In the late 19th century, the Pritzkers immigrated to the United States from Ukraine. Patriarch Nicholas Pritzker led them to Chicago, and in 1902 he founded Pritzker & Pritzker (P&P), the law firm that was to evolve into a management company and the center of the Pritzkers' many and varied investments.

P&P grew, and by the late 1920s it had become a respected local firm. At that time, the Pritzkers' best client was Goldblatt Brothers, the low-priced Chicago department store chain. Through the Goldblatts, Abram (A. N.) Pritzker, Nicholas Pritzker's son, met Walter M. Heymann, then a leading Chicago commercial banker and an officer at the First National Bank of Chicago. In succeeding years A.N. Pritzker and Walter Heymann became business associates, and the powerful First National Bank of Chicago became the financial cornerstone of the Pritzker family empire.

Using a line of credit from the First National Bank, A.N. Pritzker began acquiring real estate, something he already knew about from P&P's concentration on real estate reorganization. As his and the family's investments grew, the law practice shrank, and in 1940 P&P stopped accepting outside clients, concentrating solely on Pritzker family investments. At the same time A.N. Pritzker began the family practice of sheltering his holdings within a dizzying array of interrelated family trusts.

Emergence of Hyatt in the 1950s

The story of Global Hyatt Corporation begins with the succeeding generation of Pritzkers. By the early 1950s, A.N. Pritzker's oldest son, Jay, had become active in the family business. Something of a prodigy, Jay Pritzker had graduated high school at 14. He finished college soon thereafter and then took a law degree from Northwestern University. During World War II he worked first as a flight instructor and later for the U.S. government agency that managed German-owned companies. In that position, he sat on corporate boards with men many years his senior. An accomplished deal-maker even in his earliest years, Jay would later become well known for his quickness at sizing up balance sheets and offering deals. Jay, beginning in 1957, made the initial deals that formed the basis for what was initially called Hyatt Hotels Corporation.

Company Perspectives:

Today, Hyatt Hotels & Resorts specialize in deluxe hotels with meeting facilities and special services for the business traveler, operates hotels in major and secondary cities, airport locations, and leading resort areas throughout the world. In many cities Hyatt Hotels & Resorts has made a significant contribution to revitalizing the area and spurring business and population growth. With the new hotels under development, Hyatt International Corporation will be creating more than 20,000 job opportunities throughout the world. Hyatt Hotels & Resorts have a reputation not only for their physical distinctiveness, incorporating local art and design, but also for the amenities and services provided. These special services include Hyatt Gold Passport, Hyatt's renowned recognition and award program for the frequent traveler; Regency Club and Grand Club, VIP concierge floors; complimentary morning newspaper; specialty restaurants; and custom catering.

Jay's youngest brother, Donald Pritzker, finished law school in 1959, whereupon he joined P&P. Meanwhile, the middle brother, Robert Pritzker, earned an industrial engineering degree at the Illinois Institute of Technology in Chicago, and later he and Jay would found and manage the Marmon Group.

In 1957 Jay Pritzker bought a small Los Angeles International Airport motel named Hyatt House after its original owner, Hyatt R. von Dehn. Within four years, Jay expanded the single property into a chain of six hotels and brought Donald Pritzker to California as manager of operations, reporting to Jay. The two made a good team, with Jay's deal-making skills and Donald's managerial ability and gregarious personality.

Hyatt grew rapidly during its first decade, opening small motor inns on the West Coast and one outside Chicago. The fledgling company went public in 1967, but the more important event of that watershed year was the opening in Atlanta of its first hotel with an atrium tower lobby, designed by architect John Portman. The Portman atrium was a 21-story interior courtyard, designed so that each hotel room entered off the high-rise open space, set off with a central glass elevator leading to all floors, and hanging green vines growing from each floor's balcony. The overall effect was revolutionary, because the Portman interior eliminated the impersonal hallway with rows of doors and brought to the hotel interior an open-air congeniality, with the spinoff of greater safety, feeling of security, and warmth. The Portman lobby became the hotel's signature and brought Hyatt to widespread notice for the first time, as well as advancing the concept of public space in buildings.

What became the Hyatt Regency Atlanta was part of the 15-building Peachtree Center. The developers of the large hotel property were in financial trouble and both Hilton and Marriott passed up opportunities to purchase the property before Hyatt did and finished construction. Soon after the hotel opened, its occupancy rate reached 94.6 percent.

Hyatt grew to a chain of 13 hotels by 1969. That year, the Pritzkers set up a separate company called Hyatt International

Corporation to expand the chain overseas, with its first hotel the Hyatt Regency Hong Kong. In 1972 Donald died of a heart attack at the age of 39. Jay installed his brother-in-law, Hugh M. "Skip" Friend, Jr., as the new president.

Growth in the 1970s

The company grew rapidly during the 1970s, aided by the signature Hyatt design and the innovations that a young staff was able to devise. Management went awry, however, when it was discovered in 1977 that Friend had spent $300,000 of company money on personal expenses. After Jay Pritzker demoted him, Friend left the company. Jay took over the duties of president, in addition to his responsibilities as chairman and chief executive officer. He also moved corporate headquarters to Chicago, where he could more closely oversee matters. Then, Jay gradually bought back the public shares of stock, taking the company private in 1979. Jay reportedly was distressed by the meager valuation Hyatt was receiving on Wall Street, and, according to a September 30, 2002, *Fortune* magazine article, purchased the 25 percent publicly traded stake for a mere $12.5 million.

The 1980s

In 1980 Thomas Jay Pritzker, Jay's son, became president, with Jay remaining chairman and CEO. The decade started promisingly with three significant firsts in 1980: the openings of the first Park Hyatt, the first Grand Hyatt, and the first Hyatt resort. Park Hyatts were designed as smaller luxury hotels with a European style, featuring personalized service, privacy, and elegance; the first one opened in Chicago near the Water Tower. Grand Hyatts were designed for the high-end market in culturally rich destinations, and featured sophisticated leisure, banquet, and conference facilities utilizing the latest technology. Hyatt Resorts were specially designed to reflect their area of location and offered numerous activities and facilities for their guests; the first Hyatt resort was the Hyatt Regency Maui in Hawaii.

Then in 1981, two skywalks at the Kansas City Hyatt Regency Hotel collapsed, killing 114 people and injuring 229 in what the National Bureau of Standards called the most devastating structural collapse ever to take place in the United States. Between 1981 and 1986, more than 2,000 resulting lawsuits were settled for a total of $120 million. In June 1986, 900 individuals remaining in a federal class-action suit against the hotel settled all claims for $1,000 each. Ultimately, "gross negligence and misconduct" were attributed to engineers Daniel Duncan, Jack Gillum, and their former company, G.C.E. International Inc., whose "hurry-up" design system caused them to be pouring concrete on one part of the building while finishing the design on the rest of the building. As was the case with most Hyatt hotels at this time, Hyatt was managing the hotel for its owner and builder, Hallmark Properties, so Hyatt was not held liable. Still it did not help to have the Hyatt name associated with such a disaster.

Hyatt's growth slowed somewhat as the 1980s progressed, in part because hotel property owners began to object to the high fees Hyatt (and other hotel managers) received for managing the hotels without taking on any ownership risks. In order to keep the company growing, the Pritzkers launched a separate

Key Dates:

1957: Hyatt Hotels Corporation has its start when Jay Pritzker buys the Hyatt House motel at Los Angeles International Airport.

1961: Pritzker has expanded Hyatt into a chain of six hotels.

1967: Company goes public and opens its first hotel with an atrium tower lobby, the Hyatt Regency Atlanta.

1969: To expand the chain overseas, the Pritzker family sets up a separate company called Hyatt International Corporation, which opens its first hotel, the Hyatt Regency Hong Kong.

1979: The Pritzker family takes the company private.

1980: The first Park Hyatt, the first Grand Hyatt, and the first Hyatt resort open.

1981: Two skywalks collapse at the Kansas City Hyatt Regency Hotel, killing 114 people.

1987: Classic Residence by Hyatt is launched.

2000: A group led by the Pritzker family acquires U.S. Franchise Systems, Inc. (USFS).

2004: All of the Pritzkers' lodging operations, including Hyatt Hotels, Hyatt International, and USFS, are amalgamated under a new holding company, Global Hyatt Corporation.

2005: Global Hyatt acquires the AmeriSuites hotel chain, which is later rebranded Hyatt Place.

company to develop and build hotels and resorts, with Jay's cousin Nick in charge.

During the decade, Hyatt Corporation also became involved in an indirect way in some of the Pritzkers' nonlodging activities. Most notable was the 1983 purchase of the troubled Braniff airline through Dalfort, a Hyatt subsidiary. Under Dalfort, and with Jay Pritzker taking the lead, Braniff's losses were cut. But after a proposed merger with the also troubled Pan Am Corp. failed in 1987, Braniff was sold the following year.

During this time, Darryl Hartley-Leonard was named president of Hyatt Hotels Corporation, which had been reorganized as a subsidiary of the parent Hyatt Corporation. Another subsidiary was launched in 1987 under the name Classic Residence by Hyatt, with Donald Pritzker's daughter Penny Pritzker as president. The Classic Residence properties were designed as luxury retirement centers with large rental apartments, housekeeping and gourmet meal service, and such activities as lectures by university professors. Aimed at the growing population of senior citizens, many of whom were looking for alternatives to institutional settings, Classic Residence centers opened initially in Reno, Dallas, and Teaneck, New Jersey. They were somewhat slow to fill, however, and the properties were typically half empty six months after opening.

In 1989 Hyatt introduced the Camp Hyatt program to attempt to attract more families to its somewhat business-oriented facilities. Under the program, Hyatt hotels began to offer numerous activities geared toward the toddler to preteen set, gave parents the option of taking a half-priced second room for their kids, and added menus and room service tailored for children.

Innovations and Growth Opportunities in the 1990s

As the 1990s began, Hyatt's growth was somewhat challenged by what analysts regarded as the reluctance of some owners of new hotels to hire Hyatt as managers, given the relatively high cost of running a glitzy Hyatt hotel. In fact, Hyatt was beginning to run the risk of losing existing contracts. Seeking to streamline operations, the company laid off more than 1,000 employees from its workforce and then embarked on a detailed appraisal of the services it was offering at its hotels. Major cost savings were realized in several ways, such as moving to a centralized purchasing system, changing the turning down of beds from an automatic service to one that a guest had to request, cutting down on the number of choices offered on restaurant and room service menus, and outsourcing housekeeping and valet parking. The company also sought ways to attract frequent business travelers by augmenting its Gold Passport frequent stayer program and by offering additional business-oriented amenities such as in-room fax machines. By 1994, Hyatt's gross operating profits had increased 45 percent from 1990 and the company was hearing fewer complaints from hotel owners about costs.

In 1994 Douglas G. Geoga, a lawyer who had served as head of development, was named president and CEO of Hyatt Hotels, with Hartley-Leonard remaining chairman. At about the same time, Hyatt began to pursue several new opportunities for growth, as competition from other chains grew fierce. Starting in 1994, the company moved cautiously into franchising for the first time. The first two franchised Hyatts were older hotels— the Hyatt Sainte Claire in downtown San Jose and the Hyatt Regency Pier Sixty Six in Fort Lauderdale. A third franchised Hyatt, the Hyatt Regency Wichita, a new downtown convention hotel, opened in 1997. Hyatt also entered, again cautiously, the crowded time-share property market with the opening in June 1995 of a resort known as Hyatt's Sunset Harbor Key West.

Freestanding golf courses and casinos were additional ventures Hyatt entered in the mid-1990s. In January 1995 it opened on the island of Aruba its first freestanding golf course, which was also the island's first golf course. In addition to developing freestanding courses, Hyatt also intended to manage existing golf courses near its hotels. Already involved in gaming through casinos it operated at some of its resorts, Hyatt moved into the riverboat gambling industry in 1994 with the opening of the Grand Victoria Casino in Elgin, Illinois, which generated revenues of $37 million during the last three months of that year.

In addition to its pursuit of these growth opportunities, Hyatt also strived through innovation to retain its role at the forefront of the industry. In 1994 the company tested automated check-in kiosks in a number of its hotels. The kiosks, which allowed guests to check themselves in—in less than one minute—and even dispensed room keys, proved a success and were subsequently expanded to other Hyatts. The company also successfully introduced a telephone check-in system.

In 1995 and 1996, Hyatt spent $200 million in renovating more than 30 of its hotels in North America. Among the enhancements were the replacement of worn-out furnishings, the improvement of access for peoples with disabilities, the addition of coffee kiosks and convenience stores to hotel lobbies, and the installation of modem ports, larger desks, and better lighting in guest rooms. Also in 1996 Hartley-Leonard left the company in order to continue running a Hyatt affiliate that he had founded, Regency Productions, which specialized in sports events production. Hyatt elected to sell Regency to narrow its focus to its hotel and franchising operations. Thomas Pritzker reassumed the chairmanship.

In 1997 Hyatt Hotels launched an aggressive expansion program, earmarking $1 billion to acquire 20 to 30 hotels by the end of the decade. Serving as a vehicle for this expansion was the newly established Hyatt Equities, L.L.C., a real estate acquisition company headed by Nicholas Pritzker, a cousin of Thomas Pritzker. Hyatt Equities also assumed the ownership interests of those properties already owned by Hyatt. In addition to buying non-Hyatt hotels, such as Nikko Hotel in Atlanta's Buckhead section, which was converted to the Grand Hyatt Atlanta, Hyatt Equities was also charged with buying existing Hyatt properties. By mid-1998 Hyatt had already purchased the Grand Hyatts in New York and San Francisco as well as the Hyatts in Deerfield, Illinois, and Miami. By this time, Hyatt owned about one-third of the rooms in the various Hyatt properties. At the end of 1999 Geoga left Hyatt Hotels to take charge of a new financing venture for the Pritzker family. Scott D. Miller took the presidency of Hyatt Hotels.

Early 2000s: Diversifying and Consolidating Under Global Hyatt Corp.

Jay Pritzker died in early 1999 at age 76, having suffered a stroke two years earlier, after which his son Thomas gained increasing influence over the family's various businesses. For Hyatt, the post–Jay Pritzker era ushered in many changes, starting with what many industry observers felt was a long-overdue diversification into the faster-growing lower end of the lodging business. In 2000 a group led by the Pritzker family acquired U.S. Franchise Systems, Inc. (USFS), the franchisor of three chains: Microtel Inns & Suites, budget-priced, limited-service hotels; Hawthorn Suites, upscale, extended-stay hotels; and America's Best Inns & Suites, mid-market economy hotels. Initially at least, USFS was independent from Hyatt Hotels, just as Hyatt International continued to be. The timing for this diversification, however overdue, turned out to be quite auspicious as Hyatt and the entire luxury lodging market, already feeling the effects of the economic slowdown, was further depressed by the travel downturn that followed the terrorist attacks of September 11, 2001. In this environment Hyatt Hotels curtailed expansion in the United States, opening just two new properties in 2002.

Behind the scenes, meantime, the Pritzker family was reshuffling its assets following the death of Jay Pritzker. Amid a great deal of acrimony—and a couple of lawsuits—the Pritzkers eventually worked out a deal to split up the family fortune (by some estimates as large as $15 billion) into 11 equal pieces by 2011. In order to facilitate this division of the Pritzker empire, the family in March 2003 announced plans to consolidate all of its lodging operations within one company called Global Hyatt Corporation. Under this umbrella company were placed not only Hyatt Hotels (renamed simply Hyatt Corporation) and Hyatt International but also Classic Residence by Hyatt, Hyatt Vacation Club, Inc. (specializing in time-shares),

Hyatt Equities, and USFS. Once this major restructuring was completed and Global Hyatt formed in 2004, all 200 Hyatts around the world—120 in North America and the Caribbean and 80 elsewhere—were brought together for the first time. By consolidating all the lodging assets under one balance sheet, Global Hyatt was now better positioned to raise financing for potential mergers and acquisitions and for organic growth as well, and better positioned to take the long-rumored step of returning to public ownership. Thomas Pritzker remained in charge as chairman and CEO of Global Hyatt, Nicholas Pritzker was named vice-chairman, and Geoga was brought back into the fold as president. Global Hyatt soon moved its headquarters into a new 49-story tower, the Hyatt Center, located in Chicago's financial district and developed by Penny Pritzker.

Many observers viewed a public offering of Global Hyatt stock as a necessity for the Pritzkers to complete their planned breakup of the family assets. But the Pritzkers felt that before any such offering Global Hyatt had to get much larger. The company thus embarked on a huge hotel-building spree. In the fall of 2005 Global Hyatt had no fewer than 35 Hyatt hotels and resorts under development and scheduled to open by mid-2008. The vast majority of these were international locations, but two of the five planned for the United States were particularly large properties: the 1,100-room Hyatt Denver Convention Center Hotel, slated to open in late 2005, and the 2,700-room Grand Hyatt Las Vegas casino resort, with a planned early 2008 opening. Internationally, in addition to new Hyatts in such far-flung locales as Ankara, Turkey; Quito, Ecuador; Kabul, Afghanistan (that nation's first luxury hotel); Cairo, Egypt; and Colombo, Sri Lanka, Global Hyatt was making a major push into the burgeoning Chinese market, with 12 new hotels under development. Similarly ambitious plans for expanding the USFS chains were also in place, and Global Hyatt set aside $237 million to renovate 13 company-owned Hyatts in the United States in 2005 and 2006, aiming to make each property reflect its city.

At the same time, Global Hyatt filled in a major gap in its lodging portfolio in early 2005 when it acquired the AmeriSuites hotel chain from the Blackstone Group for a price estimated at more than $600 million. This propelled the company into a fast-growing sector of the industry—limited-service, all-suites hotels where the entrenched competition included the Courtyard by Marriott and Hilton Garden Inn chains. At the time of the deal, there were more than 140 AmeriSuites properties. Late in 2005 Hyatt launched a plan to take AmeriSuites upscale under the name Hyatt Place, earmarking $175 million for the makeover, and to open 50 to 60 new Hyatt Places per year.

Principal Subsidiaries

Hyatt Corporation; Hyatt International Corporation; Classic Residence by Hyatt; Hyatt Vacation Club, Inc.; Hyatt Equities, L.L.C.; U.S. Franchise Systems, Inc.

Further Reading

Adams, Bruce, ''Global Hyatt's Plan Includes AmeriSuites,'' *Hotel and Motel Management,* January 10, 2005, pp. 1, 58.

——, "Hyatt Refocuses: Company to Curtail New Hotel Development," *Hotel and Motel Management,* February 17, 2003, pp. 1, 30.

——, "Narrowing the Gap: Global Initiative More Closely Aligns Hyatt Hotels, Hyatt International," *Hotel and Motel Management,* April 7, 2003, pp. 3, 38.

Bergen, Kathy, "Hyatt Readies to Go Public, Grow by Acquisition, Document Says," *Chicago Tribune,* July 31, 2004.

Binkley, Christina, "Hyatt Joins Industry Spending Spree, Setting Plans to Buy Up to 30 Hotels," *Wall Street Journal,* February 24, 1997, p. A12.

Borden, Jeff, "Hyatt Has No Reservations About Four-Star Strategy," *Crain's Chicago Business,* April 13, 1998, pp. 3+.

Chandler, Susan, and Kathy Bergen, "Inside the Pritzker Family Feud," *Chicago Tribune,* June 12, 2005.

Cohen, Warren, "Hotels Check in Profits: After Years of Struggle, the Lodging Business Makes a Comeback," *U.S. News and World Report,* October 16, 1995, pp. 78–79.

Drell, Adrienne, "Jay A. Pritzker Dies: Built Business Empire," *Chicago Sun-Times,* January 24, 1999.

Fitch, Stephane, "Shaking the Family Tree: The Pritzkers Are Reorganizing Their Fortune and Weighing a Public Offering for Hyatt," *Forbes,* September 30, 2002, pp. 48, 50.

Gimbel, Barney, "Conquer and Divide: Suddenly Hyatt Is on a Building Spree. Why? Heirs to the $15 Billion Empire That Owns It Want Out," *Fortune,* October 17, 2005, pp. 175–76+.

Heller, Robert, "The Pritzker-Hyatt Phenomenon," *Management Today,* February 1987, pp. 72–75.

Higley, Jeff, "Hyatt Plans for Succession," *Hotel and Motel Management,* July 5, 1999, pp. 1, 43.

Kilman, Scott, Christina Binkley, and William Bulkeley, "An Empire on the Brink," *Wall Street Journal,* December 12, 2002, p. B1.

Maremont, Mark, "Hyatt to Buy AmeriSuites Hotel Chain," *Wall Street Journal,* December 9, 2004, p. A3.

——, "Pritzkers Settle Family Lawsuit," *Wall Street Journal,* January 7, 2005, p. B1.

Maremont, Mark, and Christina Binkley, "Pritzkers to Reorganize Hyatt Chain," *Wall Street Journal,* March 4, 2003, p. A3.

Melcher, Richard A., "Jay Pritzker's Mantle Fits Pretty Well," *Business Week,* February 15, 1999, p. 40.

——, "Why Hyatt Is Toning Down the Glitz," *Business Week,* February 27, 1995, pp. 92, 94.

"Quiet Makeover," *Hotels,* June 2005, pp. 12–13, 16, 18.

Rowe, Megan, "Hyatt Does a Reality Check," *Lodging Hospitality,* September 1994, pp. 30–34.

——, "Hyatt: Plotting a Solo Course," *Lodging Hospitality,* June 1998, pp. 18–19.

Sanders, Peter, "Global Hyatt Joins Industry Rivals with High Style, No-Frills Service," *Wall Street Journal,* September 21, 2005, p. D4.

Sidron, Jorge, "Hyatt Plans to Consolidate Its Operations," *Travel Weekly,* March 10, 2003, p. 83.

Strauss, Karyn, "Hyatt Acquires AmeriSuites," *Hotels,* January 2005, p. 14.

"The Times Have Changed," *Advertising Age,* January 11, 1993, p. 5.

Weber, Joseph, "The House of Pritzker," *Business Week,* March 17, 2003, pp. 58+.

——, "Hyatt: Quite a Housecleaning," *Business Week,* December 20, 2004, p. 40.

Weber, Joseph, and Lorraine Woellert, "An Empire Trembles: Can a New Generation of Pritzkers Halt the Slide in the Family's Fortunes?," *Business Week,* September 10, 2001, pp. 92–94, 96.

Wolff, Carlo, "Hyatt Hotels Goes Global," *Lodging Hospitality,* May 1, 2003, pp. 18–20, 22.

Worthy, Ford S., "The Pritzkers: Unveiling a Private Family," *Fortune,* April 25, 1988, pp. 164–83.

—Claire Badaracco
—update: David E. Salamie

Gluek Brewing Company

219 Red River Avenue North
P.O. Box 476
Cold Spring, Minnesota 56320
U.S.A.
Telephone: (320) 685-8686
Fax: (320) 685-8318
Web site: http://www.gluek.com

Private Company
Incorporated: 1997
Employees: 45
NAIC: 312120 Breweries; 312111 Soft Drink Manufacturers

Gluek Brewing Company, the largest brewery in Minnesota, has a two-part history, the second beginning in 1997 when the brand was revived following a change in ownership of debt-ridden Cold Spring Brewing. Gluek makes and markets beer, water, and non-alcoholic beverages, producing hundreds of products for national and international companies as well as its own brands. The company is the top U.S. producer of energy drinks for major beverage companies, and its head brewmaster has won national competitions against the country's brewing giants.

First Time Around: 1850s–1960s

German immigrant Gottlieb Gluek used the brewing methods of his home country in the brewery he established along the northern reaches of the Mississippi River in 1857. The business preceded the establishment of the state of Minnesota and the city of Minneapolis. The next year, Gluek produced 3,996 barrels of beer.

A March 1880 fire destroyed the brewery. No lives were lost directly but the founder died the following October at the age of 52, taxed by the loss and the effort to rebuild. Only partially covered by insurance, the Gluek family lost $20,000 and used their funds to rebuild a larger, more modern facility and continue the operation.

By 1901, the company ranked third among area brewers in annual capacity, following Minneapolis Brewing Company (later

Grain Belt) and Theo. Hamm Brewery of St. Paul. Between 1878 and 1920, 114 breweries were established in the area.

During these early days, distribution was limited by the mode of transportation. At its peak the company stabled 110 draft horses to pull its beer wagons. Prior to Prohibition, which went into effect in 1920, 95 percent of sales were in the city of Minneapolis.

Gluek was among 51 breweries in operation when Prohibition began. Just over half that number survived until the law was repealed in 1933. Gluek like many others turned to "near beer," soft drinks, and other products to make ends meet.

Following the resumption of production, Gluek began selling beer in one-way containers: disposable cans. The company also introduced Stite; the malt beverage was a forerunner of light beer. Fans of the product nicknamed it "Green Lightning," claiming it had a better than average kick.

In 1941, Gluek held 7 percent of the Minnesota beer market. During World War II the horse-drawn wagons hit the streets again for a time. The war effort was first in line for gas and rubber allotments.

Minneapolis's oldest continuously operating business shut its doors in 1964, holding just 3.6 percent of the market. The family sold the brewery to the G. Heileman Brewing Company of LaCrosse, Wisconsin, and the building was demolished in 1966. Heileman in turn sold the label to Cold Spring Brewing Co. for the rights to Cold Spring mineral water, according to the *Star Tribune* (Minneapolis). When Cold Spring Brewing fell on hard times of its own in the mid-1990s, the Gluek brand was revived.

Something New Brewing: Mid-1990s

The Cold Spring brewery, built in 1894, had produced Cold Spring, North Star, and for a time, Billy beer, named for President Jimmy Carter's brother. The brewery had a 180,000-barrel annual capacity. Colorado-based Beverage International acquired Cold Spring Brewing from the family owners in early 1995. A planned initial pubic offering was scuttled by a glut of competition seeking to cash in on the hot market for small breweries.

Company Perspectives:

The Gluek Brewing Company of today is much like its namesake, dedicated to brewing the finest beer from the finest ingredients, regardless of cost. The Gluek water source is world famous, bubbling from deep within the crystalline granite of Stearns County, Minnesota. The water, which requires no additional filtration, produces a beer of extraordinary taste and purity.

By December 1996 it was clear Beverage International had abandoned its obligations to workers, lenders, and suppliers, as well as for city services, payroll, and property taxes. The company left a debt estimated at $11 million.

First National Bank of Cold Spring gained possession of the brewery when a $300,000 loan went into default. Maurice Bryan, former vice-president of packing operations for Coors and head of Cold Spring operations, was retained as consultant to the bank.

Bryan set out to reopen the brewery, forming an investment group. According to the *Star Tribune* the group bought the bank's position for about $300,000, paid about $400,000 in back taxes, and negotiated a settlement over city water charges.

In mid-1997, the business reopened as Gluek Brewing Company. Then in December 1997, the brewery bought the Naked Aspen brand, which it had been producing under contract for Littleton, Colorado's Alpine Brewing Company. The brewery had produced about 5,000 barrels of Naked Aspen during the year. Overall, during 1997 the operation was at one-third of capacity.

The new owners wanted their 34 employees to re-establish Gluek "as a quality regional beer brand in the Upper Midwest," according to a February 1998 *St. Paul Pioneer Press* article. Regional brews had been finding success by producing a specific product for a narrowly defined market rather than going up against such national brands as Busch, Miller, Coors, Stroh, and Pabst. Other regional breweries in the area included 1.2 billion barrel capacity Minnesota Brewing; 140-year-old August Schell Brewing Company; and proprietary brewer Summit Brewing. Gluek was the second largest brewery in the state of Minnesota in terms of annual capacity.

"Dennis Nielsen, securities analyst at R.J. Steichen in Minneapolis, said regional breweries are starting to emerge as the survivors in the specialty beer market. At the same time, would-be beer tycoons keep bringing new brands and products to the market and are running into resistance from both distributors and retailers," Lee Egerstrom reported for the *St. Paul Pioneer Press*.

Late July 1998 marked the end of legal troubles for the brewery and the assumption of full control by the new owners for the first time. "We were like squatters for a year," Bryan told the *Star Tribune*. "Now our legal problems are behind us."

Majority shareholder Judy Charles, a turnaround specialist from Colorado with experience in other beverage ventures, headed the five-person ownership group. Local investors were

also on board. Mabel and Dan Coborn, owners of the successful regional grocery and liquor store corporation Coborns, Inc., had helped bring the brewery back to life, and were negotiating with Gluek to bottle a beverage line sold in their stores. The contract would be the largest ever for the company, in excess of a half million cases. But business was not the only thing on Mabel Coborn's mind when it came to saving the brewery. "Growing up we had the Cold Spring Granite Co. and the Cold Spring brewery, that was it," Coborn told Tony Kennedy of the *Star Tribune*. "It means something personally to keep it open." It also meant 30 jobs in a town of 3,000.

Other brewers or their hometowns had not fared that well. Competition drove Stroh Brewery to shut the doors on its St. Paul plant in 1997, eliminating 365 jobs. Minnesota Brewing, also in St. Paul, remained open but was piling on losses.

The 130-year-old Cold Spring Brewing plant had survived, but not the brand name. Gluek's Stite took center stage, backed by the core business of contracting beer and non-alcoholic beverage production for other companies. The first modern barrel of Stite, popular in the 1940s and 1950s, was tapped in October 1998. Gluek planned to introduce bottles in December that year and then bring out the original-style eight-ounce cans if bar and liquor store demand warranted.

The production of private label beers was a low margin venture but helped to pay fixed costs. Von's, a large California supermarket chain, was one of the brewers top accounts. Gluek was the sole producer of the bargain priced beer Eureka. Another budget brand, 9-0-5, was produced for Shop'n Go stores in Missouri.

Energized: 2000–05

The private owners wanted to increase market share of the wholly owned brands, Stite, in particular. By 2001, Gluek was producing Gluek Pilsner, Dark, Golden, Golden Light, Stite, and Naked Aspen beers.

The state's breweries made strong gains in 2003 despite a drop in consumption. Total beer sales in Minnesota, based on taxed production, had fallen by more than 41,000 barrels. Softened national brand and import sales and the closing of Minnesota Brewing Co. came into play.

Anheuser-Busch, which held 45 percent of the state's beer market, had increased its sales. But August Schell made the largest gain of market share, thanks to the popular Grain Belt regional brand purchased from bankrupt Minnesota Brewing. Its state share rose to 1.45 percent in 2003, up from 0.64 percent. Gluek produced and sold 10,372 barrels in Minnesota, up by 4,106 barrels. The company held 0.28 percent of the market.

Gluek stepped up promotion of its proprietary line of beer in Minnesota in March 2004. The company had also begun making a beer for distribution in Puerto Rico. Gluek made plant improvements the following winter and planned a warehouse addition.

Gluek annual capacity had been increased to 300,000 barrels of beer, six million cases of beer, and six million cases of non-alcoholic beverages. The products it produced were dis-

Key Dates:

1857: Gottlieb Gluek establishes Mississippi Brewing Company, later renamed Gluek Brewing Company.
1858: Company brews 3,996 barrels of beer.
1880: Brewery burns down.
1901: Company ranks third in annual capacity among Minneapolis/St. Paul brewers.
1920: Prohibition forces product changes.
1933: Company returns to beer production.
1941: Company holds 7 percent of Minnesota market.
1964: Oldest continuously run business in Minneapolis shuts doors.
1966: Brewery is torn down.
1997: Gluek name and business are revived.
1998: First barrel of Stite is tapped.
2005: Gluek earns contract to produce energy drink containing alcohol.

tributed primarily though not exclusively in the Midwest. Specialty brands were exported to Mexico, Russia, China, Korea, and Japan.

Hard E Beverage Co. of Corona, California, contracted with Gluek in 2005 to produce an alcoholic version of an energy drink targeting the 20- and early 30-year-old market. The first year of production was expected to be about 20 percent of the brewery's total. Gluek already produced about 47 other styles of beer for companies in the United States and abroad. "This would be a huge product for anybody," Bryan told *Modern Brewery.* "This product has never been produced in the world and for them to bring it to Cold Spring is remarkable."

Reportedly the first energy drink to come pre-mixed with alcohol, Hard E contained beer, vodka, citrus flavor, ginseng extract vitamins A, B and C, along with other nutrients. Hard E's parent company made Hansen's Energy drink. The fortified energy drink trend began in Asia, then moved to Europe, reaching the United States around 2002.

Hansen's Energy and Red Bull were U.S. market leaders. Gluek and Hard E had a two-year extendable contract. Gluek expected to produce a minimum of 500,000 cases during the first year, equaling the total number of cases produced in 2004. Employees climbed to 45 during mid-summer 2005 and were expected to climb to more than 100 by the end of 2006.

Principal Competitors

Red Bull GmbH; South Beach Beverage Company; The Boston Beer Company, Inc.; Miller Brewing Company.

Further Reading

Core, Richard, "Battle Brewing Over Distribution by Beer Importer," *San Diego Business Journal,* April 19, 1993, pp. 1+.
Egerstrom, Lee, "Minnesota Breweries Report Strong Sales During 2003," *Duluth News-Tribune* (Minnesota), June 4, 2004, p. 8A.
——, "Regional Brewers Buck the Trend," *St. Paul Pioneer Press,* February 22, 1998, p. 1D.
"Gluek Makes Energy Drink, with Alcohol," *Modern Brewery,* July 21, 2005.
Hanson, Eric, "The Six Pack," *Star Tribune* (Minneapolis), June 8, 2001, p. 24.
Kennedy, Tony, "Cold Spring Revival Thrills Brew Believers," *Star Tribune* (Minneapolis), November 19, 1998, p. 1D.
——, "Gluek Brewing Acquires Naked Aspen Brand," *Star Tribune: Newspaper of the Twin Cities,* December 23, 1997, p. 3D.

—Kathleen Peippo

Goodby Silverstein & Partners, Inc.

720 California Street
San Francisco, California 94108
U.S.A.
Telephone: (415) 392-0669
Fax: (415) 788-4303
Web site: http://www.goodbysilverstein.com

Wholly Owned Subsidiary of Omnicom Group Inc.
Incorporated: 1983 as Goodby, Berlin & Silverstein
Employees: 300
Gross Billings: $850 million (2004 est.)
NAIC: 541810 Advertising Agencies

Best known for its "Got Milk" campaign for the California Fluid Milk Producers Advisory Board, Goodby Silverstein & Partners, Inc. operates as a subsidiary of advertising services conglomerate Omnicom Group, which consists of BBDO Worldwide, DDB Needham Worldwide, TBWA International, and Diversified Agency Services. It has won every major advertising award, most of them many times over.

1980s: Creating a Distinctive Style of Advertising

Jeff Goodby, Andy Berlin, and Rich Silverstein cofounded Goodby, Berlin & Silverstein in 1983. Rich Silverstein was raised in New York where he attended the Parsons School of Design. When he graduated in 1973, he moved to San Francisco and began working at *Rolling Stone* magazine as a graphic designer and, later, as an art director. After his stint at *Rolling Stone*, he worked at various advertising agencies throughout San Francisco, including Bozell & Jacobs, McCann/Erickson, Foote, Cone & Belding, and Ogilvy & Mather. Silverstein met Jeff Goodby in 1980 while the two were working under Hal Riney at Ogilvy & Mather.

A graduate of Harvard University and a staffer at the *Harvard Lampoon*, Goodby had originally intended to become a journalist. After college, he worked as a city hall reporter at a small daily newspaper in Massachusetts. However, when he relocated to San Francisco with his wife, he decided to try his hand at advertising. "[I] opened the Yellow Pages and started with "A". . . . Along the way someone advised me to create a resume of myself that would show a sense of humor. So I did a parody of an encyclopedia entry of myself, as if I were dead. And that got me a job at J. Walter Thompson," Goodby recalled in *Inc.* in 2004.

As collaborators on various projects, Silverstein and Goodby won numerous prizes for their groundbreaking advertising campaigns at Ogilvy & Mather. They came up with the idea of starting their own agency while working on a freelance project with Andy Berlin. With barely enough money to cover operating expenses and only one client, the Electronic Arts Software Co., the three opened Goodby, Berlin, & Silverstein in 1983.

Soon after, Goodby met Will Hearst, the grandson of William Randolph Hearst, who at the time was the publisher of the *San Francisco Examiner*. Hearst invited Goodby and his partners to compete for the newspaper's account. Goodby recalled in a 2004 *San Francisco Chronicle* article: "The idea we presented was a parody of the film *Citizen Kane*, which was of course a damning indictment of Will's grandfather. . . . [H]e liked it and even agreed to act in the commercials, playing the tortured figure who ran the newspaper. The campaign really got a lot of notoriety and we were on our way."

With the *Examiner* ad, the company began building a reputation for creating unusual, humorous, and provocative ads. Looking back over the company's history, Goodby described the creative philosophy in a 2004 *San Francisco Chronicle* article: "[We tried] to approach people with respect, to treat them as if they have a sense of humor, as if they are paying attention, as if they are smart, and look for the highest common denominator rather than the lowest common denominator, like most advertising does." During the company's early years, Goodby, Berlin & Silverstein gained recognition for a variety of innovative ads. Examples of the company style include commercials for Isuzu, in which a driver plunges his off-road vehicle into the middle of a room-sized birthday cake, and its Norwegian Cruise Line account, where a passenger vows: "I will be naked more often." One billboard they created for the *San Francisco Examiner*, in which TV newscasters are portrayed as Barbie and Ken dolls, was so provocative that a TV station manager broadcast

Company Perspectives:

We believe that this is a time of great upheaval in the way brands are created, and our company is evolving to antici- pate and take best advantage of the new environment around us. The old model, in which advertisers address captive audiences with unavoidable messages, is a thing of the past. To be successful in a faster, more voluntary world, we have to engage our audiences, creating messages, often in unex- pected places, that people welcome and even seek out. This kind of communication will have elements of entertainment and avant-garde media thinking not presently associated with advertising.

an angry rebuttal. The partners also distinguished Goodby, Ber- lin & Silverstein from their bigger rivals by promising their clients that one of the agency's founders would personally head up every account.

In the late 1980s, the London agency Boase Massimi Pollit (BMP) purchased a minority stake in Goodby, Berlin & Sil- verstein. Through BMP, the partners met Colin Probert and Jon Steel, who later became Goodby, Berlin & Silverstein's presi- dent and director of planning, respectively. The relationship between BMP and Goodby, Berlin & Silverstein proved profit- able to both companies and lasted until BMP was sold, includ- ing its minority stake in Goodby, Berlin & Silverstein, to Omni- com Group, a holding company of ad agencies and design firms, in 1991. That same year, *Advertising Age* named Goodby, Berlin & Silverstein Agency of the Year for the second time. In 1990 (and again in 1992 and 1994), *Adweek* named Jeff Goodby and Rich Silverstein National Creative Directors of the Year. In addition to this prestigious award, Goodby, Berlin & Silverstein also won *Adweek's* West Coast Agency of the Year award in 1992 and again in 1993 and 1994.

Early 1990s: Experiencing Steady Growth As Part of Omnicom

Soon after the sale, Omnicom's chairman and CEO, Bruce Crawford, offered to sell Goodby, Berlin & Silverstein's shares back to the agency, but the partners declined the offer. Instead, in 1992, Goodby, Berlin & Silverstein sold Omnicom its re- maining shares. The deal included a stipulation that Goodby, Berlin & Silverstein would retain full managerial and creative control of the agency, while Omnicom would operate solely as a silent partner. "We made sure the company continued to have [our] name on the door. . . . And we tried to show everyone that we were still going to make business decisions on the basis of whether we were doing good work and having fun. We still pitched the accounts we wanted to pitch and resigned the ones we didn't want to work on. And Omnicom didn't interfere . . . ," Goodby recalled in a July 2004 *Inc.* article. At the time, Goodby, Berlin & Silverstein's accounts included American Isuzu Motors, Norwegian Cruise Line, the National Baseball Association, and Sega of America.

Goodby, Berlin & Silverstein's sale to Omnicom did not improve relations between the agency's founders, and by

mid-1993, trade publications were frequently reporting tensions between Berlin and his two partners. By August of that year, Berlin left Goodby, Berlin & Silverstein to become chairman and CEO of Berlin Wright Cameron in New York. The agency immediately reorganized around Berlin's absence. In 1994, three new partners joined the agency: Colin Probert and Jon Steel, formerly of Boase Massimi Pollit, and Harold Sogard. The agency changed its name to Goodby, Silverstein & Partners to reflect their arrival.

Also in 1993, the company reached the full expression of its trademark humor with the introduction of the "Got Milk?" campaign for the Fluid Milk Processors Advisory Board. One ad won the agency "Best in Show" at the annual Clio Awards in 1994. In it, an Aaron Burr expert loses a phone contest when he can not answer the question "Who shot Alexander Hamilton?" because his mouth is clogged with a peanut butter sandwich, and he has no milk to wash it down. This and other ads in the series departed obliquely from former advertising attempts to sell milk by promoting its ability to "build strong bones." Instead, the ads focused on foods that would be inedible without milk, reaching consumers on a gut rather than intellectual level. "The time you most notice milk is when it's gone," Goodby reflected in a 1994 *Los Angeles Times* article. "We could make ads until we're blue in the face, but not many people are going to come in from jogging on a hot day and drink a tall glass of milk."

After the "Got Milk?" ads began appearing on grocery carts, bus shelters, billboards, and television, milk consumption among teenagers and young adults in the state of California increased for the first time in ten years, according to the Milk Processors Board. The following year, in 1994, Wisconsin and Hawaii paid to use portions of the campaign, at which point the Milk Processors Board devised a secondary strategy: building alliances with consumer product companies including cereal and cookie makers. Soon, the Board began to underwrite 50 percent of the cost of in-store sampling in return for manufac- turers, such as General Mills and Mother's Cookies, distributing cents-off coupons for milk. Wheaties, Total, and Cheerios car- ried the tag line: "Got Milk?"

Late 1990s: The Move to a More Horizontal Structure

By the mid-1990s, business was booming for Goodby, Sil- verstein & Partners, which had billings upwards of $260 mil- lion. Yet despite this success, the agency's staff of 160 writers, artists, and directors still wore t-shirts and tennis shoes to work, and the agency maintained its headquarters in a modest brick building in San Francisco's Embarcadero. Goodby himself, known for his long, graying hair, continued to write poetry and screenplays. "Some people take this business so seriously," he averred in a 1994 *Chronicle* article. "I think I have enough of a sense of humor about it that it helps me keep my perspective. I haven't taken it too seriously and I still have fun doing it." He and Silverstein signed contracts with Omnicom in 1995 to stay at the helm through 2000.

Two years after earning its prestigious "Best in Show" award at the Clios, the agency dominated the awards competi- tion again in 1995, receiving two gold and 12 silver statuettes, the largest number of Clios for a single shop. Goodby, Sil-

Key Dates:

1983: Jeff Goodby, Andy Berlin, and Rich Silverstein co-found Goodby, Berlin & Silverstein.
1992: Omnicom, Inc. purchases the company.
1993: Berlin leaves the company.
1994: The company changes its name to Goodby, Silverstein & Partners.
2004: Goodby and Silverstein are inducted into The One Club Hall of Fame for advertisers.

verstein & Partners also won the most awards at the annual National Addy Awards sponsored by the American Advertising Federation for the second year in a row in 1995. In 1995 and again in 1998, six of its campaigns were finalists in the Kelly Awards, the most for any one agency in history. Also in 1995, the Norwegian Cruise Line campaign was awarded that competition's Grand Prize, and in 1996, Goodby, Silverstein & Partners' campaign for Porsche was awarded the Grand Prize.

By 1996, Goodby, Silverstein & Partners was finally attracting large, high-profile accounts: the Bud Ice beer brand of Anheuser-Busch, Polaroid Corporation's Polaroid instant cameras, and Porsche A.G.'s sports cars. Billings soon surged to $360 million, making the agency the second largest shop (along with Hal Riney & Partners) in San Francisco behind Foote, Cone & Belding. Although, according to Goodby in a 1996 *New York Times* article, his agency had not made expansion a goal, the agency's increased visibility caught the attention of Omnicom managers, who started contemplating national and international expansion.

In 1997 and 1998, the agency was named Clio Agency of the Year. Also in 1998, its Nike skateboarding campaign received the Cannes Festival's Grand Prix award for "Best Advertising Campaign in the World." However, there were also negative aspects of the agency's success. Around this time, a new group of small, energetic ad agencies began to emerge in San Francisco. As a result, Goodby, Silverstein & Partners soon lost a number of its top creative staffers who were eager to step out on their own by taking jobs at other agencies. Additionally, some of its executives left to form their own competing agency, Grant, Scott & Hurley. These defections were difficult for Goodby, who said in a 2004 *San Francisco Chronicle*, "It took me a while to stop being angry at people who left. I don't anymore. . . . [T]he guys who have a good batting average are going to be taken away at large sums. We can't keep 15 people at large salaries. . . ."

By 1999, the agency was earning a gross income of $58 million on billings of $670 million. To confront its challenges, it surveyed its employees to find out what they liked and disliked about the company. In 2000, it implemented a streamlined approach to new business. Some of the new changes included creating, for the first time, the position of group account director and the development of an in-house school, GS&P University, which offered employees classes that covered topics such as design and public speaking. In addition, a policy of flex time and formal mentoring for new employees was started.

The early years of the new century were years of significant change at Goodby, Silverstein & Partners. To grapple with the challenge of maintaining the agency's corporate culture and retaining talented people, Goodby and Silverstein instituted a more horizontal structure. Wanting to empower staffers and motivate them to do their best work, they handed over many day-to-day creative responsibilities to their creative staffs.

In 2001, this move was followed by the layoff of 35 to 40 workers and salary cuts for employees in order to trim expenses in the face of major client SBC Communications' departure and the loss of $100 million or 10 percent of the agency's business. Notwithstanding this setback, the agency continued to grow over the next several years. *Campaign* magazine, Britain's industry publication, named it one of the ten "hottest shops," and in 2004 awarded it International Advertiser of the Year for work on Hewlett-Packard. Also in 2004, both Goodby and Silverstein were inducted into The One Club Hall of Fame for advertisers.

Looking to the future, Goodby, Silverstein & Partners continued to try to find a way to repay people for their attention, to create advertising that "[rewarded] with delight, with humor, insight or an emotional giveback that is not fundamentally dishonest." According to a *Los Angeles Times* article in 1996, "The creative pair still avowed the desire to 'have an impact on popular culture and maybe change the way people think about advertising.' "

Principal Competitors

Arnold Worldwide; Carmichael Lynch Inc.; Colby & Partners; Crispin Porter; Dailey & Associates; Fallon Worldwide; Leo Burnett; McCann Worldgroup; Ogilvy & Mather; Publicis & Hal Riney; Red Cell; Wieden + Kennedy.

Further Reading

Adelson, Andrea, "A New Campaign Focused on the Utility of Milk Does the Product a Lot of Good," *New York Times*, June 14, 1994, p. D19.

Berger, Warren, "How I Did It with Jeff Goodby," *Inc.*, July 2004, p. 84.

Chiang, Harriet, "A Playful Sense of Advertising: Bay Area Company Produces Creative Campaigns Like 'Got Milk?,' " *San Francisco Chronicle*, October 25, 1994, p. A13.

Cuneo, Alice Z., "Goodby Grows Up; Next Generation: Agency Co-founders to Change Philosophy Yet Preserve Culture As They Turn Over Creative Duties," *Advertising Age*, June 12, 2000, cover p.

Elliott, Stuart, "As Goodby, Silverstein Raises Its Profile, It's Still Different Out There," *New York Times*, February 23, 1996, p. D2.

Emert, Carol, "Ad Agency Nursery: But Does SF Have Enough Work to Feed the Brood?," *San Francisco Chronicle*, February 5, 1998, p. C1.

Fahey, Alison, "Jeff Goodby on the Spot," *Adweek.com*, May 2, 2005.

"Meet the Milk Man," *Los Angeles Times*, May 27, 1994.

"New Age Hucksters," *Los Angeles Times*, June 9, 1996.

Raine, George, "S.F. Advertising Agency to Cut Jobs, Salaries," *San Francisco Chronicle*, September 21, 2001, p. C3.

—Carrie Rothburd

GOODYEAR

The Goodyear Tire & Rubber Company

1144 East Market Street
Akron, Ohio 44316-0001
U.S.A.
Telephone: (330) 796-2121
Fax: (330) 796-2222
Web site: http://www.goodyear.com

Public Company
Incorporated: 1898
Employees: 84,786
Sales: $18.37 billion (2004)
Stock Exchanges: New York Midwest Pacific
Ticker Symbol: GT
NAIC: 326211 Tire Manufacturing (Except Retreading); 325212 Synthetic Rubber Manufacturing; 326212 Tire Retreading; 326220 Rubber and Plastics Hoses and Belting Manufacturing; 326299 All Other Rubber Product Manufacturing; 811111General Automotive Repair

---

The Goodyear Tire & Rubber Company ranks third among the world's tire manufacturers, trailing only Bridgestone Corporation and Compagnie Générale des Établissements Michelin. Nearly 90 percent of Goodyear's revenues are generated via the development, manufacturing, marketing, and distribution of tires for most applications. The firm's tire brands include Goodyear, Dunlop, Kelly, Fulda, Lee, Sava, and Debica; the Dunlop brand is offered by Goodyear through an alliance with the Japanese firm Sumitomo Rubber Industries, Ltd. Goodyear also manufactures and sells other rubber products, including belts and hoses, and synthetic rubber chemicals for the transportation industry and various other applications, and these activities account for the remaining revenue. The company is also one of the world's largest operators of commercial truck service and tire retreading centers, and runs a network of more than 1,700 tire and auto service centers that sell and install tires and provide automotive repair services. On the manufacturing side, Goodyear operates more than 90 plants, of which 30 are in the United States, the balance being in 27 other countries. The company's marketing reach extends to 185 countries, with about 54 percent of revenues generated outside the United States.

After Founding in Late 19th Century, Goodyear Quickly Became Household Name

Without the discovery by U.S. inventor Charles Goodyear of vulcanization (the process by which extreme heat renders rubber flexible and strong) the modern rubber industry would not exist. Goodyear had nothing to do with the company that bears his name. He died insolvent in 1860, 38 years before Frank A. Seiberling founded Goodyear in Akron, Ohio, destined to be the world's first rubber concern to post $1 billion in sales. It reigned as the world's largest tire maker for seven decades.

Bicycle and carriage tires were the company's major products until the start of automobile tire production in 1901. Seiberling's 1899 application to make carriage tires under Consolidated Tire Company's patent was refused, so he started manufacturing a similar tire without a license, claiming it was monopolistic for Consolidated to grant patent licenses selectively. The ensuing legal battle meant that Goodyear's first- and second-year profits from the sale of carriage tires were held in escrow until the court decided, in Goodyear's favor, in 1902.

Goodyear introduced its straight-side tire under the Wing-foot trademark adopted in 1900, with a full-scale national magazine advertising campaign in 1905. The tire was quickly detachable from its rim, and this popular tire made Goodyear a household name.

Seiberling followed David Hill to the presidency in 1906, with Paul W. Litchfield, George M. Stadelman, and Frank Seiberling's brother Charles Seiberling composing the formative management team. In 1907 Goodyear opened its Detroit shop, providing 1,200 tires to equip Henry Ford's new Model T. By 1909 auto tire production jumped to 36,000, and Goodyear's sales reached $4.25 million, double that of the previous year. By 1910 Goodyear provided one-third of all original tires on U.S. cars. In 1909 Goodyear started production of airplane tires.

In 1910 Litchfield acquired a method for bonding rubber over fabric from North British Rubber Company in Edinburgh,

Company Perspectives:

Goodyear is a truly global organization and the bearer of a universally recognized brand name. With worldwide production and technological resources, it offers customers unparalleled international experience and the capacity to respond to the particular needs of local markets. The Goodyear name stands for unquestioned quality and diversity in the tire and rubber products business.

Scotland. Goodyear's rubberized fabric, soon used for planes, including the Wright brothers', also formed the shell of early dirigibles, the production of which commenced in 1910.

By 1916 Goodyear had grown to become the world's largest tire company. It adopted a longstanding company slogan that year: "More people ride on Goodyear tires than on any other kind."

Goodyear's tire production rose from 250 per day in 1916 to nearly 4,000 per day by the end of World War I. The company made 1,000 balloons and 60 airships during the war, as well as 715,000 gas masks and some 4.75 million other military supply parts, such as tire valves. It also provided many of the tires used on aircraft. Wages rose, and both the company and its employees ended the war years in prosperity. Sales had jumped from $110 million in 1916–17 to $172 million in 1918–19, and to $223 million in 1920.

Nearing Bankruptcy in Early 1920s

Only two days after the November 1918 armistice, the government canceled its contracts and decontrolled prices. The economy swelled as industry rushed to meet postwar demand, but sales fell in late 1920 as unemployment and bankruptcy soared. Goodyear felt the squeeze as early as 1918, when it made its first attempt to recapitalize by a direct sale of stock to customers and employees.

As the recession deepened, Goodyear was forced to turn to bankers, a position Frank Seiberling in particular was loathe to assume. In 1920, nonetheless, the company accepted temporary refinancing of $18 million from a banking syndicate headed by Goldman, Sachs & Co. of New York and A.G. Becker of Chicago. The effort was not sufficient, and bankruptcy loomed imminent as the book value of its common stock, at $75 million in early 1920, was reduced to zero. By 1921 sales had fallen to $105 million with a $5 million loss.

In early 1921 the New York law firm of Cravath, Henderson, Liffingwell & De Gersdorff connected Goodyear with an investment bank, Dillon, Read, & Co., that agreed to manage Goodyear's refinancing and reorganization. Of the original officers, only Litchfield and Stadelman remained with the company. Frank Seiberling left and soon thereafter incorporated Seiberling Rubber Company, later acquired by Firestone. President E.G. Wilmer and a new management team were brought in. Wilmer focused on creating financial vigor at Goodyear, making few changes, if any, in the production and sales realms. One month after his appointment, in June 1921, he had reduced debt

from $66 million to $26.5 million. Of 469 creditor claims in 1921, all but seven were settled. Sales picked up to $123 million in 1923, from $103.5 million in 1921. In 1923 Stadelman moved into the presidency, Wilmer assumed the board chairmanship, and Litchfield moved into the first vice presidency. Wilmer would resign from Goodyear to head Dodge Brothers, the forerunner of the Dodge Motor Company, in 1926.

The world's largest tire producer since 1916, Goodyear became the world's largest rubber producer by 1926. By 1928 the company operated in 145 countries and sales reached $250 million. Stadelman did not live to see the company reach that point, as he died in January 1926. Litchfield assumed the presidency, commencing a 30-year tenure as chief executive officer. He spent his first year resolving litigation begun in 1922 by Goodyear common stockholders to increase their power and improve the position of common and preferred stock. The battle was concluded in 1927, on terms satisfactory to the stockholders.

Goodyear had produced all of the significant U.S. dirigibles since 1911, and it was commissioned in 1928 to build two huge dirigibles for the U.S. Navy. The enormous Goodyear airdock, then the world's largest building without internal supports, was erected to accommodate the project. Despite Litchfield's personal interest in the field of lighter-than-air craft, the industry came to an end in 1937 with the crash of the *Hindenburg*. Goodyear's famous fleet of smaller, nonrigid blimps continued to enjoy recognition at outdoor events since they were first floated as a friendly company trademark in the 1930s.

Goodyear was the defendant in one of the most famous antitrust cases of all time beginning in 1933 when the Federal Trade Commission (FTC) charged that its cost-plus-6-percent purchasing contract with Sears, Roebuck and Co. discriminated against independent dealers in violation of the Clayton Act, a U.S. antitrust law. The FTC issued a cease-and-desist order in March 1936, and Goodyear appealed to the courts. Later that year, however, the Clayton Act was stringently amended, in large part because of the Goodyear case. In light of the stricter law, Goodyear voluntarily terminated its Sears contract. The federal Circuit Court of Appeals planned to drop the case, but Goodyear wanted its name cleared and the commission wanted a precedent set for other cases, so the court was pushed to make a firm decision. In 1939 it came out for Goodyear, relieving any threat of future damage claims by dealers. Goodyear's one-time loyal buyer, Sears, became a serious competitor as it took its business to manufacturers selling only to mass distributors.

Prior to the 1930s Goodyear's labor conflicts had been limited. In 1913 some Goodyear workers joined 15,000 other rubber workers in a strike against Akron's other rubber companies organized by the Industrial Workers of the World (IWW). The strike was terminated after 48 days by worker vote, but it did mark the beginning of employee-initiated gains in Akron. The following year Goodyear instituted the eight-hour work day and a paid vacation plan for workers of five to nine years' tenure. A number of employee benefit programs were established, including an in-factory hospital, a worker-oriented company newspaper called *Wingfoot Clan,* and athletic leagues that attracted many a sports-minded employee. In 1915 Litchfield donated an amount equal to his first 15 years' salary, about $100,000, to the factory workers to be used at their discretion.

Key Dates:

1898: Frank A. Seiberling founds The Goodyear Tire & Rubber Company in Akron, Ohio, naming it after Charles Goodyear, discoverer of the vulcanization process; the firm initially focuses on bicycle and carriage tires.

1901: Production of automobile tires begins.

1910: Company ventures outside United States for the first time, establishing a plant in Canada.

1916: Goodyear becomes the largest tire company in the world.

1921: After approaching bankruptcy, Goodyear is refinanced and reorganized.

1926: Goodyear becomes the world's largest rubber company.

1935: Kelly-Springfield Tire Company is acquired.

1951: Revenues exceed the $1 billion mark.

1977: Goodyear introduces its Tiempo radial, its most successful tire yet.

1986: Company thwarts a takeover bid by Sir James Goldsmith, then restructures by selling off most of its nontire assets.

1990: Goodyear suffers its first net loss since the Great Depression.

1991: First outsider is selected to lead Goodyear: Stanley C. Gault; Aquatred radial debuts.

1999: Goodyear cements a broad alliance with Sumitomo Rubber Industries, Ltd.

2002: Company reports a record net loss of $1.25 billion, bringing the firm close to bankruptcy.

2004: Assurance tire is introduced; Goodyear returns to profitability after three straights years in the red.

In later decades this fund provided scholarships to children of Goodyear employees or retirees.

Labor Strife Marking 1930s

In 1919 under Litchfield's direction, Goodyear formed the industrial assembly, a representative body of 60 employees that voiced worker interests to management. The assembly existed for 16 years, until its place was challenged by newly organized chapters of the American Federation of Labor (AFL). Coleman Claherty, a major force in the AFL, began organizing in Akron in 1933 and, within the year, won 20,000 members throughout the city, 1,000 of whom formed Goodyear's Local 2. The first international convention of the United Rubber Workers (URW) was held in September 1935.

In 1935 the local union chapters demanded that the companies recognize them as bargaining representatives for all employees. The companies refused, and the unions threatened to strike. At Goodyear a companywide vote carried out by the industrial assembly voted down a strike 11,516 to 891. The unions threatened to strike based solely on member vote, and the federal government resolved tensions by establishing the Perkins agreement, which essentially required management to consult the unions on all wage and scheduling issues.

Goodyear had established a six-hour work day in 1932 to lessen the effects of the Great Depression among workers, by reducing layoffs and distributing work as evenly as possible among remaining employees. When national price controls were removed in 1935, however, Goodyear reestablished the eight-hour work day to increase productivity, decrease its prices, and make its products more competitive. The industrial assembly requested a return to the six-hour shift, and when this was denied it appealed to the board of directors. Local 2, encouraged by the industrial assembly's tenacity, appealed to the secretary of labor, who ruled in January 1936 that Goodyear was unjustified in its reversion to the eight-hour shift because it had voluntarily established a shorter day. The government also charged Goodyear with discriminating between industrial assembly and union workers. At the time, union membership was at 10 percent.

Goodyear returned to the six-hour day as suggested, but layoffs became necessary as tire sales decreased, and the union struck in February 1936. Goodyear's strikers were supported by union sympathizers from other rubber companies and by Ohio and West Virginia coal miners from John L. Lewis's Committee for Industrial Organization (CIO). Within two days, thousands were picketing Goodyear's three major Akron plants. More than 1,000 employees, including Litchfield, moved into the factories to maintain as much production as possible. The union strategy was to break Goodyear, the largest rubber factory, so that the other companies would be more compliant. After 34 days the strike was settled by direct negotiations.

With a three-month stock of goods, Goodyear did not suffer financially from the strike, but the show of union muscle upped URW membership throughout Akron and increased Goodyear union members to 5,000. The Wagner Act, or National Labor Relations Act, was affirmed by the U.S. Supreme Court in April 1937. The industrial assembly was categorized as a company union and had to be disbanded. Workers supported the move to URW representation by a ratio of more than two to one.

Sitdowns and interworker violence frequently disrupted production after the 1935 strike, culminating in a May 1938 sitdown that attracted picketers even though none were formally requested. Police were summoned to disperse the demonstrators, and in an ensuing riot 100 people were injured. The company and union negotiated three days later and sitdowns decreased. Goodyear had decreased employees in Akron from 58,316 in 1929 to 33,285 in 1939. In 1941, after three years of cooperation, Goodyear signed its first formal contract with Local 2.

Despite labor and litigation difficulties during the 1930s, Goodyear continued its expansion. An Alabama plant and two textile mills were built in 1929, followed by another textile mill in 1933. In 1935 the company acquired a bankrupted company, Kelly-Springfield Tire Company. Another plant was acquired in Akron in 1936, and a Vermont factory was purchased to centralize shoe sole-and-heel production.

Goodyear's foreign expansion, begun in 1910 with its first of two Canadian plants, continued during the 1930s. In addition to its London and Australian plants, operative since 1912, Goodyear had distributors located throughout northern Europe, Russia, Central and South America, and the Caribbean. In 1931 a tire plant was opened just outside Buenos Aires, Argentina. The sixth foreign factory went up in Bogor, on Java in Indonesia in 1935, and the seventh was built in 1938 in Sao Paolo, Brazil. A Swedish plant was opened in 1939. Rubber plantations were established during the 1930s in Indonesia, Costa Rica, and the Philippines. Goodyear Foreign Operations was created to manage the company's 18 foreign subsidiaries, seven factories, seven plantations, 37 branches, 28 depots, and hundreds of distributors located outside of the United States.

Goodyear patented its first synthetic rubber, Chemigum, in 1927. It was first mass produced in 1935, and tires were made of it in 1937. In 1934 the company introduced Pliolite, a compound that cemented rubber to metal, and Pliofilm, a packaging material. Other popular Goodyear products were rubber floor tiles; many new models of tires; Airfoam, a cushioning material for seats and mattresses; and Neolite, a synthetic heel-and-sole material.

Return to Military Contracting During World War II

Goodyear began producing 200,000 gas masks a month for the U.S. Army after Adolf Hitler's April 1939 invasion of Poland. The same year, Goodyear Aircraft Corporation (GAC) was established, and the Goodyear airdock, unused since the demise of the giant airships, housed wartime airplane and parts production, as well as the construction of 132 blimps for coastal submarine defense. In 1941 Goodyear joined other manufacturers to produce parts for 100 B-26 bombers a month. In 1943 some of GAC's 32,000 employees worked on the plane that dropped A-bombs on Hiroshima and Nagasaki in 1945, a B-29 Superfortress. GAC also produced 4,008 Vought Corsair FG1 fighter planes, beginning in 1943.

In 1940 Edwin J. Thomas, who began as Litchfield's secretary and assistant in the 1920s, ascended to the presidency as Litchfield continued as chairman of the board. The company took on management of a government-owned factory producing propellant charges for 600 types of artillery shells in 1940. In 1941 the U.S. government required each of the "big four" rubber producers—Goodyear, General Tire, Firestone, and Goodrich—to construct plants that would produce 400,000 tons a year of GRS, or government rubber, a synthetic compound including styrene and butadiene. Goodyear supervised the construction of three synthetic rubber plants for the government. Two of the plants became owned and operated by the company. Goodyear sales increased 52 percent over 1940.

Goodyear also produced the top-secret phantom fleet, used to confuse Nazi reconnaissance before the D-Day invasion of Normandy. The "fleet" was made of rubberized material, from which Goodyear constructed life-sized inflatable replicas of amphibious invasion craft, PT boats, tanks, combat vehicles, and heavy artillery. These impostors were inflated and deployed in one coastal English base, then rapidly deflated and moved by night to another. To Axis surveillance, the apparent serial establishment and abandonment of fighting bases was inexplicable and may have contributed to their unstable coastal defense.

Extraordinary Growth Following World War II

When the war concluded, the government canceled $432 million in Goodyear contracts. GAC released almost 27,000 employees, reducing its payroll to 2,000 by 1946. Demobiliza-

tion increased demand for consumer tires, and sales increased to 25 million in 1946–47. Goodyear established factories in Colombia and Venezuela in 1945, in Cuba in 1946, and in South Africa in 1947. A Japanese-occupied factory in Indonesia was regained in 1945, as well as a rubber plantation in 1949. In its 50th year, 1948, Goodyear reached a peacetime sales record of $705 million. It employed 72,000 workers worldwide and was poised to expand its international presence.

In its first 50 years, Goodyear total sales had been $9 billion; in the decade from 1949 to 1958, sales would top $11.5 billion. In 1951 Goodyear became the first rubber company to exceed $1 billion in sales in one year. Goodyear's World War II production record garnered it several government contracts associated with the Korean War in 1950. A subsidiary, Goodyear Atomic Corp., was founded in 1952 when the government selected the company to operate a $1.2 billion atomic plant under construction in Pike County, Ohio. The facility opened in 1954.

In 1954 Goodyear acquired its first new plantation in 20 years in Belem, Brazil. The following year it acquired two government-owned rubber factories it had operated during the war. That same year, at Goodyear's Gadsden, Alabama, plant, an $11.5 million investment elevated it to the largest tire-making facility in the United States. In 1957 it also built a 7,200-acre tire testing site with 18.5 miles of multisurface roads.

Rubber consumption after World War II was double that of prewar production. Much of the increase was due to new rubber products such as foam rubber, film, and plastics, and growth was fueled by newly developing synthetic rubbers such as polyisoprene, introduced by Goodyear in 1955 and called Natsyn, for commercial purposes. In 1960 Goodyear built a $20 million synthetic rubber plant in Beaumont, Texas; its annual production of 40,000 tons of Natsyn equaled the annual generation of 15,000 acres of rubber trees.

In 1958 Thomas became chairman of the board, and Litchfield moved to honorary chairman. Russell DeYoung became Goodyear's ninth president; his first full-time Goodyear position had been that of a tire inspector. DeYoung appointed Robert H. Lane as public relations director in 1958. Lane was largely responsible for the makeover of Goodyear's public profile from a somewhat stodgy, though quality, tire maker, to a contemporary innovator. The key to this image update was Goodyear's reentry into racing. Once it overcame Firestone's domination of the field, Goodyear was able to equip winning cars in the Daytona 500 and other popular U.S. and European races. Lane also clearly defined the role of the Goodyear blimp as a corporate goodwill ambassador, capitalizing on the company's historic association with airships.

Foreign operations were consolidated in February 1957 under Goodyear International Corporation (GIC). In 1959 GIC initiated its European expansion program with construction of a plant in Amiens, France. Tire plants were built in 1965 at Cisterna di Latina, Italy, and in 1967 in Phillipsburg, Germany, giving Goodyear production sites in Europe's three major markets within ten years.

In the United States, Goodyear's expansion was partly by acquisition. In 1959 the company added a $3 million aeronautics research and development laboratory in Litchfield Park,

Arizona, to supplement GAC's activities. The subsidiary received a $65 million contract in 1958 to produce Subroc, an antisubmarine missile. Goodyear would continue to derive much of its business from U.S. military and space program contracts, including production of equipment for several of the Apollo moon missions. In 1961 the company bought Geneva Metal Wheel Company, a maker of specialty wheels, and in 1964 acquired Motor Wheel Corporation, the world's largest maker of styled auto wheels. That same year, it was the first rubber corporation to exceed $2 billion in annual sales. Its profits were in excess of $100 million, with foreign subsidiaries contributing more than one-third.

In 1966, two years after Victor Holt assumed the presidency, Goodyear opened its tenth U.S. tire plant, in Danville, Virginia. This was followed in 1967 by a $73 million facility at its 593-acre site in Union City, Tennessee. Goodyear's sales doubled during the 1960s, topping $3 billion in 1969—Goodyear was the first rubber company to hit that mark. Net income rose from $71 million to $155 million.

1970s: Achieving Position As the World's Leading Radial Tire Producer

Goodyear's biggest challenge in the 1970s was overhauling its factories to produce radial tires. The radial, with its excellent reinforcement system and extra belt of steel, was introduced by France's Michelin in 1948, and by 1972 it equipped 8 percent of U.S. cars. Recognizing the superiority of the radial, Goodyear introduced a transitional fiberglass reinforced tire in 1967, and by 1972, 50 percent of U.S. cars rode on them. When Charles J. Pilliod assumed the presidency in 1972, he insisted that Goodyear bear the expense of adapting to full radial technology. The radial tire equipped 45 percent of U.S. cars by 1976, and Goodyear was the world's largest radial producer. In 1977, with a media blitz extolling its all-season tread, Goodyear introduced its Tiempo radial, the company's most successful tire to that time.

Goodyear's 75th anniversary year, 1973, was marred by the debilitating Middle East oil crisis. In 1974, Pilliod became chairman and chief executive officer, John H. Gerstenmaier assumed the presidency, and Goodyear, prompted by the government, formed a joint project to stimulate domestic propagation of guayale, a native North American bush that provided 50 percent of U.S. rubber until 1910. As oil prices declined, however, the project slowed. In 1975 Mark Donohue, a well-known car racer, was killed when a tire blew out during prerace preparations. In 1984 his estate was awarded a $9.6 million settlement from Goodyear, one of the largest wrongful death payments in history.

In 1976 Goodyear suffered its longest strike ever when URW workers walked out on Goodyear, Goodrich, Uniroyal, and Firestone after talks at Firestone, the target company, failed. Goodyear's 22,000 strikers and their cohorts at the other companies returned to work some 130 days later, having obtained an agreement that wages and benefits would be increased 36 percent over the following three years.

In 1979 Goodyear fought hard and succeeded in avoiding the ''neutrality'' clause accepted by the other three rubber companies, which guaranteed that companies would not interfere with URW organizing. This was motivated by its desire to create a nonunion shop at its newly built Lawton, Oklahoma, facility. Pilliod's new labor relations policies required individual workers, rather than supervisors, to be responsible for quality control. The new policies also provided regular and ongoing communications between management and laborers as well as worker involvement in problem solving. The factory was considered 50 percent more efficient than older facilities, and, by 1983, factory worker turnover was down to less than one-third of 1 percent.

In 1977 the Securities and Exchange Commission (SEC) accused Goodyear of maintaining a clandestine fund of $1.5 million to make foreign and domestic political contributions and government and labor bribes. The SEC charged that the company had made $500,000 in dubious payments since 1970 in 20 foreign countries. Goodyear agreed, without admitting guilt, to a permanent court injunction against violations of federal securities laws, providing a report of its activities in the countries in question. Two years prior, in 1975, Goodyear said it made political contributions of at least $242,000 between 1964 and 1972.

Robert E. Mercer assumed the presidency in 1978, when Gerstenmaier retired. That year Goodyear tire production was terminated in Akron, but the company began building Goodyear Technical Center, a $750 million research and design complex located on 3,000 acres in Akron. By 1980 despite national and global recession, Goodyear had record earnings of $264.8 million and had reduced debt to its lowest level in 17 years. By 1984 it supplied one-third of the U.S. tire market and one-fifth of the world tire market. In 1983 Pilliod retired, Mercer became chief executive officer, and Tom H. Barrett was voted president.

Briefly Focusing on Diversification in the 1980s

Having won the ten-year battle to remain leader of the tire market, Goodyear entered the 1980s planning to scale some other peaks. Its diversification goal was to reduce tire revenues to one-half of corporate earnings and generate the other half through its GAC subsidiary and Celeron Corp., a Louisiana oil and gas concern purchased in 1983. GAC had expanded at a compound annual rate of 17 percent from 1973 to 1983, providing a 20 percent return on investment. In 1983 its annual sales were $617 million, despite a questionable $50 million investment in the production of centrifuges to enrich uranium for nuclear power plants. Celeron, although its sales slipped the year after it was purchased, began construction of the then promising $750 million All American Pipeline, a 1,200-mile tube used to transport 300,000 barrels per day of offshore California crude oil to Texas refineries.

The diversification came to an abrupt end in 1986, when takeover specialist Sir James Goldsmith made a bid for Goodyear. The company was able to beat off this takeover, but only by selling most of its nontire concerns, including GAC, which went to Loral Company for $588 million, and parts of Celeron, which went to Exxon Corporation for $650 million. Barrett became chief executive officer in 1988 and remained president. In 1989 the company divested its South African operations, which it had maintained despite the social protest against apartheid during the 1980s.

1990s Rebound, Backed by Aquatread and Global Expansion

In 1990 Goodyear took its first loss since 1932 and surrendered its position as the world's largest tire maker to Michelin, when the French company bought out Goodrich's tire business, which had been merged with Uniroyal's. Firestone and General, weakened by Goodyear's dominance in the radial market, were absorbed, respectively, by Japan's Bridgestone and Germany's Continental AG, forcing upon Goodyear competition of its own size. Its All American Pipeline, prevented from operating at full capacity by environmental restrictions, continued to produce losses; the company's $3.3 billion long-term debt, largely incurred by the Goldsmith battle, was also a weakness. Analysts pointed to Goodyear's sluggish internal efficiency as a major problem. For the first time since 1921, Goodyear went outside company ranks to choose a chairman and chief executive officer, as Stanley C. Gault succeeded Barrett in June 1991. Gault had been chairman and chief executive of Rubbermaid, Incorporated, while serving on Goodyear's board.

Between 1989 and 1991, Goodyear eliminated 12,000 jobs, or 10 percent of its workforce, with more than one-half of that coming from the salaried sector. In combination with the $1.4 billion investment in modernization and consolidation of factories, these cuts added up to an estimated savings of $250 million annually. Yet Goodyear remained committed to its annual research and development budget of more than $300 million a year, confident in this as a source of quality tires, such as 1990's Eagle GA and Eagle GT+4, successful luxury car models. By restructuring its U.S. marketing tactics, the company regained its lost market share and was holding its own in the tougher international market. Goodyear was also able by 1992 to reduce its long-term debt to a much healthier $1.47 billion.

More important, however, were the new tires rolling out of the company's research and development department. In 1991 alone four new Goodyear tires for the replacement market were introduced, the flagship of which was the Aquatread, an all-season passenger tire specially designed to provide better traction on rain-slickened roads. The tire proved to be a huge and immediate success. More troubling was Gault's 1992 decision to sell, once again, Goodyear-brand tires at Sears, more than half a century after it had stopped doing so. The following year the company began to sell its name-brand tires through Wal-Mart Stores and the Discount Tire chain. These moves angered Goodyear dealers, especially because some of their new competitors undercut their prices on Goodyear tires.

From 1993 to 1995, Goodyear enjoyed healthy profits, which increased from $387.8 million in 1993 to $567 million in 1994 to $611 million in 1995, and sales that increased from $11.64 billion in 1993 to $12.29 billion in 1994 to $13.17 billion in 1995. Some of this growth was fueled by global expansion through acquisitions and joint ventures. In 1993 the company entered into a joint venture in India with Ceat Ltd. to form South Asia Tyres Private Limited and build a $150 million tire plant in India. The following year Goodyear purchased a 60 percent stake in Gold Lion (subsequently renamed Goodyear Qingdao Engineered Elastomers Company Ltd.), an automotive hose factory based in Qingdao, China, as well as a 75 percent

stake in Dalian International Nordic Tire Co. (later known as Goodyear Dalian Tire Company Ltd.) based in Dalian, China.

In 1996 the Egyptian-born Samir F. Gibara, who had been president and chief operating officer, replaced Gault as chairman and CEO. That year, Goodyear acquired majority control of TC Debica, the leading passenger tire maker in Poland; the company planned to take advantage of Debica's central location and lower-wage environment as it expanded in Europe. This acquisition also meant that Goodyear now had manufacturing facilities in four of the world's most important developing areas: Eastern Europe, India, China, and Latin America. Late in 1996, Goodyear reentered South Africa with the $121 million purchase of 60 percent of Contred Ltd., a unit of Anglovaal Industries Ltd. and a maker of tires, power transmissions, and conveyor belts.

The company's global spending spree continued in 1997. Early that year Goodyear entered into a manufacturing agreement with Sumitomo Rubber Industries Ltd. of Japan, through which the companies would manufacture tires for each other in Asia and North America. Goodyear's presence in eastern Europe was bolstered in May 1997 when Goodyear signed agreements with the Sava Group, based in Kranj, Slovenia, to form two joint ventures through which Goodyear would acquire a 60 percent interest in Sava's tire business and a 75 percent interest in its engineered products business.

Goodyear was not idle at home either. In 1995 the company's retail tire presence was beefed up through the purchase of 860 Penske Auto Centers and more than 300 Montgomery Ward-operated auto centers. The following year Goodyear unveiled the Infinitred, the first passenger tire with a manufacturer's lifetime treadwear limited warranty. In the spring of 1997 Goodyear had to endure its first strike in more than 20 years, when 12,500 United Steelworkers of America members went out on strike. This proved to be a brief setback as a contract agreement (an unusually long six-year pact) was reached after only 18 days of picketing. In June of that year Goodyear's Kelly-Springfield Tire unit entered into a long-term supply agreement with Lincolnton, North Carolina-based J.H. Heafner Co., whereby Kelly-Springfield would make at least one million Winston tires annually to be sold through Heafner's network of tire distributors, one of the country's largest. Goodyear in July 1997 unveiled a line of "run-flat" tires called EMT ("extended mobility tire" or "empty"), which enabled a car to be driven between 50 and 200 miles at speeds up to 55 miles per hour on a deflated, even punctured, tire. Such tires also eliminated the need for a spare tire.

In early 1998 Goodyear finally offloaded its troubled and noncore Celeron unit and its All American Pipeline, selling the operations to Plains Resources for $420 million. In anticipation of this divestiture, Goodyear in the fourth quarter of 1996 had taken a $572.2 million charge, most of which was a write-down of Celeron assets. Continuing to invest overseas, Goodyear acquired full control of both Contred in South Africa and India's South Asia Tyres in 1998. The company that year also launched a new manufacturing system called Impact that by making greater use of automation was expected to improve uniformity, cut production times by 70 percent, use 15 percent less material, and slash labor costs by 35 percent. In another efficiency initiative, Goodyear was working to integrate its

Kelly-Springfield operations, which had been run as an independent company based in Cumberland, Maryland, into the parent company's North American operations based in Akron. By mid-1999 this process was complete, and the Kelly-Springfield offices were shut down.

The key development of the late 1990s, however, was the broad alliance cemented in 1999 between Goodyear and Sumitomo Rubber. The complex deal centered around six joint ventures, the largest one consisting of 14 Goodyear and Sumitomo factories in Western Europe and selling Goodyear brand tires and tires under Sumitomo's Dunlop and Sumitomo brands. Initial revenues for this venture were $4 billion. Goodyear controlled 75 percent of this venture, which had initial revenues of $4 billion, and the company assumed the same percentage stake in a U.S. venture that took control of Sumitomo's two U.S. factories, in Huntsville, Alabama, and Buffalo, New York, and that had $800 million in sales. The two partners also combined their global purchasing and research and development operations into two joint ventures majority owned by Goodyear, and Sumitomo took majority ownership of two joint ventures in Japan. The deal also involved the two firms taking small stakes in each other and Goodyear paying Sumitomo nearly $1 billion for the latter's contributions to the ventures. The alliance was projected to yield annual cost savings of more than $300 million after three years. Simultaneous with the announcement of the Sumitomo deal, Goodyear revealed plans to cut more than 2,500 jobs worldwide and shut down its 70-year-old tire plant in Gadsden, Alabama, and a Kelly-Springfield plant in Freeport, Illinois, yielding another $100 million to $150 million in savings annually. Manufacturing was also to be consolidated at several plants in Asia and Latin America, where demand had fallen off in tandem with regional economic travails.

For Goodyear, the key to the Sumitomo deal was gaining much broader rights to market Dunlop brand tires, which Goodyear positioned as its midprice brand, between the premium Goodyear brand and the inexpensive Kelly. The deal also temporarily vaulted the company back into first place among global tire makers, surpassing Bridgestone and Michelin. In a clear blow, however, Goodyear suffered the ignominy of being booted out of the prestigious Dow Jones Industrial Average late in 1999 after 59 years on the index, as part of a periodic rejiggering of the Dow to better reflect the overall U.S. economy.

Early 2000s: Bouncing Back from Near Bankruptcy

The first years of the 21st century were dire ones at Goodyear. The company barely eked out a profit in 2000 as it struggled under the weight of high raw materials costs, a strong dollar, a heavy debt load (largely attributable to the Sumitomo deal), and slowing orders from automakers. These negatives more than offset the additional business that Goodyear had garnered in the wake of a huge tire recall Bridgestone/Firestone had been forced to initiate in August 2000. Goodyear responded in early 2001 with another restructuring plan, this one involving 7,200 job cuts and additional plant closings.

Further job cuts followed later in 2001 as Goodyear moved somewhat belatedly to restructure its enlarged overseas operations. In North America, the company sharply increased its prices to its large distributors, but this sparked a backlash as disgruntled

distributors cut back on their tire orders. Business in the U.S. market was hurt further by the economic recession, and in this down climate American consumers increasingly elected to purchase cheaper tires made by companies using low-wage overseas labor. Continuing its program to exit from noncore businesses, the company sold its France-based specialty chemical business late in the year. Early in 2002 Goodyear reported a net loss of $203.6 million (later restated to $254.7 million) for 2001, its first red ink since 1992. Investors abandoned the company's stock: shares ended the year at $23.81, down from the high of $76.75 recorded in 1998. A further blow came in January when the company's credit rating was downgraded to ''junk'' status, reflecting the heavy debt load and the lack of earnings.

The crisis at Goodyear accelerated in 2002 as the company suffered a net loss of $1.11 billion (later restated to $1.25 billion), its largest annual loss ever. Substantially contributing to the loss was a fourth-quarter charge of $1.08 billion taken to write down deferred tax credits the company could not use while losing money in North America. At the beginning of 2003 Robert J. Keegan took over as president and CEO, succeeding Gibara, who remained chairman. Keegan had joined Goodyear in October 2000 as president and chief operating officer, having previously spent 28 years at Eastman Kodak Company, where he rose to president of the company's global consumer imaging business. Keegan added the chairmanship as well in July 2003. Early in the year, meanwhile, Goodyear shares fell below $4, the lowest level in at least four decades as the company grappled with a liquidity crisis that threatened bankruptcy. In April, however, Keegan succeeded in restructuring $2.9 billion in bank debt and stretching out the payments. Further breathing room came in September when the United Steelworkers ratified a new contract with Goodyear that entailed the slashing of labor costs by $1.15 billion over three years and 3,000 job cuts. In return, the company promised to keep open and invest in all but two of its U.S. factories and to limit imports from its factories in Brazil and Asia. Late in 2003 Goodyear closed its Dunlop tire plant in Huntsville, Alabama.

As the company struggled to recover, it suffered the further embarrassment of having to restate its earnings several times because of accounting irregularities. The restatements, eventually covering the years from 1997 to 2004, cut reported earnings by more than $280 million. In May 2004 Goodyear belatedly released its results for the previous year, and despite record revenues of $15.12 billion, the firm posted its third straight loss, $807.4 million. But by this time the company was in the midst of turning its fortunes around. Goodyear patched relations with its dealers, and in February 2004 introduced a new line of tires, dubbed Assurance, which proved to be hot sellers. The company also cut back on the number of tires it sold to automakers as original equipment and sought better deals from automakers on what had historically been a low-profitability business for tiremakers. Goodyear also improved its balance sheet through a further restructuring of its debt, substantially increasing cash flow. Through these and other measures, and with the return of its North American Tire unit to profitability, Goodyear returned to the black in 2004, recording net income of $114.8 million on record sales of $18.37 billion.

As part of its ongoing efforts to divest noncore businesses, Goodyear in July 2004 had announced its intention to sell its chemical products division. The company later changed course, concluding it made more sense to keep the business, and at the beginning of 2005 the division was integrated into the North American Tire unit. During 2005 Goodyear sold its Indonesia rubber plantations and its Wingtack adhesives resin business and reached an agreement to sell its farm tire operations to Titan International, Inc. for about $100 million. In September 2005 the company put its engineered products business up for sale. The unit, producer of rubber hoses, conveyor belts, air springs, and tracks for military vehicles, generated $1.47 billion in revenue in 2004.

In a hangover from its dark days of the near past, Goodyear in August 2005 received a so-called Wells Notice from the U.S. Securities and Exchange Commission indicating that the commission was ready to take either civil or administrative action against the firm because of the various accounting problems that had led to the restatements. In September the company announced that it was seeking to reduce expenses by up to $1 billion and planned to close additional plants and increase sourcing from low-wage Asian markets. In what was becoming a familiar lament at U.S. industrial concerns, Goodyear was grappling with paying the mounting pension and healthcare costs of current and former employees in the United States. It thus appeared that negotiations for a new labor agreement with the United Steelworkers were likely to center around plant closures, jobs cuts, and cuts to worker benefits. The union's contract was slated to expire in July 2006. In the meantime, Goodyear's turnaround continued apace as the firm reported net income of $142 million for the third quarter of 2005, the best quarterly result since 1998, and sales of $5.03 billion, the firm's highest quarterly sales ever.

Principal Subsidiaries

Allied Tire Sales, Inc.; Belt Concepts of America, Inc.; Celeron Corporation; Cosmoflex, Inc.; Dapper Tire Co., Inc.; Goodyear Dunlop Tires North America, Ltd. (75%); Goodyear Farms, Inc.; Goodyear International Corporation; The Goodyear Rubber Plantations Company; Goodyear-SRI Global Purchasing Company (80%); Goodyear-SRI Global Technology LLC (51%); Goodyear Western Hemisphere Corporation; The Kelly-Springfield Tire Corporation; Laurelwood Properties Inc.; Retreading L Inc.; Retreading L, Inc. of Oregon; Utica Converters Inc. (75%); Wheel Assemblies Inc.; Wingfoot Commercial Tire Systems LLC; Wingfoot Corporation; Abacom (Pty.) Ltd. (Botswana); Compania Anonima Goodyear de Venezuela; Compania Goodyear del Peru, S.A. (78%); Compania Goodyear, S.A. de C.V. (Mexico); Corporacion Industrial Mercurio S.A. de C.V. (Mexico); Dackia Partners AB (Sweden; 75%); Dunlop Airsprings (France; 75%); Dunlop GmbH & Co. KG (Germany; 75%); Dunlop Grund und Service Verwaltungs GmbH (Germany; 75%); Dunlop Tyres Limited (U.K.; 75%); Dunlop Versicherungsservice GmbH (Germany; 75%); Fit Remoulds (Ireland) Limited (75%); Fulda Reifen GmbH & Co. KG (Germany; 75%); GD Furstenwalde Vermogensverwaltungs GmbH (Germany; 75%); GHS Goodyear Handelssysteme GmbH (Germany; 75%); Goodyear Australia Pty Limited; Goodyear Aviation Japan, Ltd. (85%); Goodyear Belting Pty Limited (Australia); Goodyear Brokers Limited (Bermuda); Goodyear Canada Inc.; Goodyear Chemical Products SAS

(France); Goodyear Dalian Tire Company Ltd. (China; 75%); Goodyear de Chile S.A.I.C.; Goodyear de Colombia S.A.; Goodyear do Brasil Productos de Borracha Ltda (Brazil); Goodyear Dunlop Financial Service GmbH (Germany; 75%); Goodyear Dunlop Tires Austria GmbH (75%); Goodyear Dunlop Tires Baltic A.S. (Estonia; 75%); Goodyear Dunlop Tires Belgium N.V. (75%); Goodyear Dunlop Tires Czech s.r.o. (Czech Republic; 75%); Goodyear Dunlop Tires Danmark A/S (Denmark; 75%); Goodyear Dunlop Tires Espana S.A. (Spain; 75%); Goodyear Dunlop Tires Europe B.V. (Netherlands; 75%); Goodyear Dunlop Tires Finance Europe B.V. (Netherlands; 75%); Goodyear Dunlop Tires Finland OY (75%); Goodyear Dunlop Tires France (75%); Goodyear Dunlop Tires Germany GmbH (75%); Goodyear Dunlop Tires Hellas S.A.I.C. (Greece; 75%); Goodyear Dunlop Tires Ireland Limited (75%); Goodyear Dunlop Tires Italia SRL (Italy; 75%); Goodyear Dunlop Tires Hungary Trading Ltd. (75%); Goodyear Dunlop Tires Nederland B.V. (Netherlands; 75%); Goodyear Dunlop Tires Norge A/S (Norway; 75%); Goodyear Dunlop Tires Polska Sp z.o.o. (Poland; 75%); Goodyear Dunlop Tires Portugal, Unipessoal, Lda. (75%); Goodyear Dunlop Tires Romania Srl (75%); Goodyear Dunlop Tires Slovakia s.r.o. (75%); Goodyear Dunlop Tires Slovenia d.o.o. (75%); Goodyear Dunlop Tires Suisse S.A. (Switzerland; 75%); Goodyear Dunlop Tires Sverige A.B. (Sweden; 75%); Goodyear Dunlop Tyres UK Ltd. (75%); Goodyear Earthmover Pty Ltd (Australia); Goodyear Engineered Products Europe d.o.o. (Slovenia); Goodyear Finance Holding S.A. (Luxembourg); Goodyear France Aviation Products S.A.; Goodyear GmbH & Co. KG (Germany; 75%); Goodyear India Limited (74%); Goodyear Industrial Rubber Products Ltd. (U.K.); Goodyear Italiana S.p.A. (Italy; 75%); Goodyear Jamaica Limited (60%); Goodyear Korea Company; Goodyear Lastikleri Turk Anonim Sirketi (Turkey; 74.61%); Goodyear Luxembourg Tires S.A. (75%); Goodyear Malaysia Berhad (51%); Goodyear Marketing & Sales Snd. Bhd. (Malaysia; 51%); Goodyear Maroc S.A. (Morocco; 55%); Goodyear Middle East FZE (Dubai); Goodyear Nederland B.V. (Netherlands); Goodyear New Zealand, Ltd.; Goodyear Orient Company (Private) Limited (Singapore); Goodyear Philippines, Inc. (88.54%); Goodyear Productos Industriales S. De R.L. De C.V. (Mexico); Goodyear Productos Industriales, C.A. (Venezuela); Goodyear Qingdao Engineered Elastomers Company Ltd. (China; 60%); Goodyear Russia LLC; Goodyear Sales Company Limited (Taiwan; 75.5%); Goodyear S.A. (France); Goodyear S.A. (Luxembourg); Goodyear Servicios Comerciales S. De R.L. De C.V. (Mexico); Goodyear Servicios Y Asistencia Tecnica S. De R.L. De C.V. (Mexico); Goodyear Singapore Pte Limited; Goodyear Solid Woven Belting (Pty) Limited (South Africa); Goodyear South Africa (Proprietary) Limited; Goodyear South Asia Tyres Private Limited (India; 99.4%); Goodyear SRI Global Purchasing Yugen Kaisha & Co. Ltd (Japan; 80%); Goodyear Taiwan Limited (75.5%); Goodyear (Thailand) Public Company Limited (66.8%); Goodyear Tyres Pty Ltd (Australia); Goodyear Tyre and Rubber Holdings (Pty.) Ltd (South Africa); Goodyear Wingfoot KK (Japan); Gran Industria de Neumaticos Centroamericana, S.A. (Guatemala; 79%); Hi-Q Automotive (Pty.) Ltd. (South Africa); KDIS Distribution (France; 75%); Kelly-Springfield Puerto Rico, Inc.; Kelly-Springfield Tyre Co. (Australia) Pty. Ltd.; Magister Limited (Mauritius); Multimarkenmanagement GmbH & Co KG (Germany; 75%); Neumaticos Goodyear S.R.L. (Argentina); Nippon Giant Tire Co., Ltd. (Japan; 65%); Pneu Holding (France; 75%); Property Leasing S.A. (Luxembourg); P.T. Goodyear Indonesia Tbk (85%); Rubber & Associated Manufacturing (Pty) Ltd. (South Africa); RVM Reifen Vertriebsmanagement GmbH (Germany); Sava Tires, d.o.o. (Slovenia; 75%); S.A. Vulco Belgium N.V. (75%); Servicios Y Montjes Eagle, S. de R.L. (Mexico); South Pacific Tyres (Australia; 50.01%); South Pacific Tyres New Zealand Limited (50.01%); SP Brand Holding GEIE (Belgium; 75%); Three Way Tyres (Botswana); Tire Company Debica S.A. (Poland; 59.87%); Tredcor Export Services (Pty) Ltd. (South Africa); Tredcor Southern Zimbabwe (Pvt.) Limited (60%); Tredcor (Zambia) Limited; Trentyre Limited (Mozambique); Trentyre Holdings (Pty) Ltd (South Africa); Trentyre (Pty.) Ltd. (South Africa; 92%); Trentyre North Zimbabwe (Pvt.) Limited (51%); Tyre Services (Botswana); Vulco Development (France; 62.2%); Vulco France; Wingfoot de Chihuahua, S. de R.L. de C.V. (Mexico); 4 Fleet Group GmbH (Germany; 75%).

Principal Operating Units

North American Tire; European Union Tire; Eastern Europe, Middle East & Africa Tire; Latin America Tire; Asia/Pacific Tire; Engineered Products.

Principal Competitors

Bridgestone Corporation; Compagnie Compagnie Générale des Établissements Michelin; Continental AG; Cooper Tire & Rubber Company; Pirelli & C. S.p.A.; Toyo Tire & Rubber Co., Ltd.; The Yokohama Rubber Company, Limited; Kumho Tire Co., Inc.; Hankook Tire Co., Ltd.

Further Reading

Aeppel, Timothy, ''Deflated: How Goodyear Blew Its Chance to Capitalize on a Rival's Woes,'' *Wall Street Journal,* February 19, 2003, p. A1.

——, ''Goodyear, Expecting Loss for Year, May Snub Car Makers,'' *Wall Street Journal,* February 8, 2002, p. B2.

——, ''Goodyear Is Told It Could Be Hit with SEC Case,'' *Wall Street Journal,* August 17, 2005, p. A6.

——, ''Goodyear Says Keegan to Succeed Gibara As Chief Executive Officer,'' *Wall Street Journal,* October 2, 2002, p. A10.

——, ''Goodyear Tire to Restate Results for Past Five Years,'' *Wall Street Journal,* October 23, 2003, p. A6.

——, ''Goodyear to Restate 1997–2003 Profits,'' *Wall Street Journal,* April 13, 2004, p. A3.

Allen, Hugh, *The House of Goodyear: A Story of Rubber and of Modern Business,* Cleveland: Corday & Gross, 1943, reprinted, Arno Press, 1976, 417 p.

Byrne, Harlan S., ''Gaining Traction,'' *Barron's,* June 7, 1999, pp. 17, 19.

Cimperman, Jennifer Scott, ''After 59 Years on the Dow, Goodyear Gets Bounced,'' *Cleveland Plain Dealer,* October 27, 1999, p. 1A.

——, ''Goodyear Plans 7,200 Job Cuts,'' *Cleveland Plain Dealer,* February 15, 2001, p. 1C.

Donlon, J.P., ''A New Spin for Goodyear,'' *Chief Executive,* December 1995, pp. 34–35, 38–40.

Fahey, Jonathan, ''Blowout!,'' *Forbes,* March 3, 2003, p. 40.

Gerdel, Thomas W., ''Goodyear Riding on Assurances: New Line of Tires Is Fueling Firm's Turnaround Bid,'' *Cleveland Plain Dealer,* September 22, 2004, p. C1.

——, ''Goodyear's Bumpy Ride: CEO Gibara Deals with Competition, Global Uncertainty,'' *Cleveland Plain Dealer,* March 24, 2002, p. G1.

Labich, Kenneth, ''The King of Tires Is Discontented,'' *Fortune,* May 28, 1984.

Love, Steve, and David Giffels, *Wheels of Fortune: The Story of Rubber in Akron,* edited by Debbie Van Tassel, Akron, Ohio: University of Akron Press, 1999, 359 p.

Lubove, Seth, ''The Last Bastion,'' *Forbes,* February 14, 1994, pp. 56, 58.

Magnet, Myron, ''The Marvels of High Margins,'' *Fortune,* May 2, 1994, pp. 73–74.

McNulty, Mike, ''Goodyear Plans to Make Major Cost Cuts,'' *Automotive News,* October 17, 2005, p. 8.

Narisetti, Raju, ''For Two Tire Makers, a Flat-Out Pitch for Safer Wheels,'' *Wall Street Journal,* July 3, 1997, p. B4.

Neely, William, *Tire Wars: Racing with Goodyear,* Tucson, Ariz.: Aztex Corp., 1993, 192 p.

O'Reilly, Maurice, *The Goodyear Story,* Elmsford, N.Y.: Benjamin Company, 1983, 223 p.

Rodengen, Jeffrey L., *The Legend of Goodyear: The First 100 Years,* Ft. Lauderdale, Fla.: Write Stuff Syndicate, 1997, 251 p.

Schiller, Zachary, ''After a Year of Spinning Its Wheels, Goodyear Gets a Retread,'' *Business Week,* March 26, 1990.

——, ''And Fix That Flat Before You Go, Stanley,'' *Business Week,* January 16, 1995, p. 35.

——, ''Goodyear May Be Getting Some Traction at Last,'' *Business Week,* October 7, 1991, p. 38.

——, ''Stan Gault's Designated Driver,'' *Business Week,* April 8, 1996, pp. 128, 130.

Taylor, Alex, III, ''Goodyear Wants to Be No. 1 Again,'' *Fortune,* April 27, 1998, pp. 130–32, 134.

White, Joseph B., ''Goodyear Moves to Cut Capacity, Jobs: U.S. Tire-Making Factory Will Close as Alliance with Sumitomo Is Set,'' *Wall Street Journal,* February 4, 1999, p. A3.

—Elaine Belsito
—update: David E. Salamie

H.B. Fuller Company

1200 Willow Lake Boulevard
St. Paul, Minnesota 55110-5101
U.S.A.
Telephone: (651) 236-5900
Toll Free: (800) 214-2523
Fax: (651) 236-5165
Web site: http://www.hbfuller.com

Public Company
Incorporated: 1887 as Fuller Manufacturing Company
Employees: 4,500
Sales: $1.41 billion (2004)
Stock Exchanges: New York
Ticker Symbol: FUL
NAIC: 325510 Paint and Coating Manufacturing; 325520
   Adhesive Manufacturing; 325998 All Other
   Miscellaneous Chemical Product and Preparation
   Manufacturing

A top performer among specialty chemicals firms, H.B. Fuller Company markets adhesives, sealants, coatings, paints, and several other specialty chemical products in 34 countries. Fuller's international markets, which have been aggressively pursued since the 1970s, account for more than 45 percent of the company's overall revenue. The company originated during the late 19th century as the first paste and glue manufacturer in Minnesota. Despite a long list of successes, Fuller ranked as the second smallest adhesive firm in the country up until World War II, at which time majority ownership and management of the company was passed from one of the founder's sons, H.B. Fuller, Jr., to Elmer Andersen, a highly successful sales manager. Andersen inaugurated a ''double it in five'' strategy, a systematic campaign for decentralized growth that would ensure 14 percent annual sales increases, or the doubling of sales every five years. By 1950, the company had become the fourth largest adhesives manufacturer in the country. When Andersen's son, Tony, assumed leadership of the company in 1971, further rapidly paced growth came through overseas expansion. Since the early 1980s, Fuller's growth has generally slowed,

and net earnings have tended to fluctuate. Albert Stroucken, who took over the helm in the late 1990s, becoming the first outsider to lead H.B. Fuller, thoroughly restructured the company, leading by 2004 to a healthy, nearly 10 percent, jump in revenues.

Early Years

The company was launched in 1887 when Harvey Benjamin Fuller, Sr., traveled from Chicago to St. Paul, Minnesota, with the sole intention of inventing and selling glue. In Chicago Fuller had experimented with glue mixing, while successfully buying, repackaging, and marketing an existing adhesive that was guaranteed to ''cement everything.'' His marketing took the form of various promotional rhymes, including clever Mother Goose spoofs: ''Maid was in the garden, hanging out her clothes/Along came a blackbird, and nipped off her nose/When she found her nose was off, what was she to do/But go and stick it on again with FULLER'S 'PREMIUM GLUE.' '' Fuller regarded St. Paul, together with its ''twin city'' Minneapolis, as the ideal urban center to establish his business, because general industry was thriving there and competition was scarce. In addition, flour, then a key ingredient in gluemaking, was in abundant supply because of a strong agricultural base and such rising concerns as Pillsbury and General Mills's precursor, Washburn-Crosby Company.

Fuller's business plan was simple. ''What the world needed,'' according to *A Fuller Life* and H.B. Fuller, Sr., ''was a convenient, economical, strong adhesive—an adhesive so versatile that homemakers and manufacturers could both use it.'' His equipment was also simple: an iron kettle and the family's wood-burning stove. Soon Fuller concocted a wet, flour-based paste with which he was satisfied. He then began selling the mixture in small batches to local paperhangers, who were generally glad not to have to make their own glue. As the Fuller brand name gained recognition, Fuller realized his business required outside capital to sustain growth. The company was incorporated when three Minneapolis lawyers agreed to invest a total of $600. Thereafter, Fuller Manufacturing Company marketed its glue to a wide variety of customers, including flour mills, shoe companies, box manufacturers, bookbinders, printers, and households. The company also made and sold laundry blueing and did a brisk business

---

Company Perspectives:

Our mission is to be a leading worldwide formulator, manufacturer and marketer of technology-driven specialty chemical products and related services and solutions. We are committed to the balanced interests of our customers, employees, shareholders and communities. We will conduct business ethically and profitably, and exercise leadership as a responsible corporate citizen.

---

in ink for the city schools. By 1888, the company, which was really just Fuller serving as jack-of-all-trades, added its first employee, Fuller's oldest son, Albert. Two years later the company moved into its own manufacturing facility, where Albert assumed primary responsibility for filling orders and discovering new formulas while Harvey generated more revenues by expanding his sales areas.

In 1892 the company acquired a Minneapolis competitor, The Minnesota Paste Company, for $200. Although several decades later such acquisitions would become regular occurrences, Fuller meanwhile was destined to grow by internal development, particularly through a succession of inventions by the founder that greatly expanded both its product line and its manufacturing capabilities. In late 1893 Harvey successfully produced Fuller's Cold Water Dry Wall Cleaner, intended for use on wallpaper (at that time it was customary to clean walls twice yearly, but existing cleaners tended to decompose under warm conditions), and applied for a patent. The item was in wide production by the following spring and became enormously popular. The elder Fuller's next invention was Fuller's Cold Water Dry Paste, which became even more successful than Fuller's Cleaner. Because it was packaged dry, without the added weight of water, the product could be shipped at lower cost, saving both the manufacturer and the customer money. In addition, Fuller's Paste was remarkably easy to work with, and advertisements boasted that ''a child can mix and use it.'' By 1898, Fuller Manufacturing was posting annual sales of $10,000. By 1905, the company was not only shipping its paste and cleaner to both coasts, it also had entered markets in England, Germany, and Australia.

One setback for the firm, however, was the lack of an obvious successor to the post of president, for Albert and Roger, Fuller's middle son, both left the business. Furthermore, Fuller's youngest son, Harvey, Jr., was more inclined to a career in art than manufacturing. Nevertheless, upon his graduation from the University of Chicago in 1909, Harvey, Jr., joined the company full time and made an immediate impact by bolstering advertising and creating the first comprehensive catalog of Fuller products.

Increasing its workforce to include an experienced bookkeeper, a stenographer, and a sales manager, Fuller Manufacturing entered the 1910s prepared for heightened growth. In 1915 the firm reincorporated as H.B. Fuller Company and issued stock valued at $75,000. World War I, already underway, was to be the primary impetus for Fuller's short-term growth. With the engagement of American troops came the need for shipping

mass quantities of food overseas. U.S. canneries were ready to comply but had a need for a quality adhesive that would speed the labeling process. Fuller filled that need and prospered. After the war, however, Fuller's sales dropped off and Harvey, Sr., fell ill, dying late in 1921.

Struggles in the 1920s and 1930s

During this difficult period, when the company faced the possibility of bankruptcy, Harvey, Jr., made what was undoubtedly his greatest decision: that of hiring a full-time chemist named Ray Burgess. By the time Harvey inherited the presidency from his father, the company had regained its momentum, due in large part to Burgess's self-taught genius and his ability to develop customized adhesives and formulas for the industrial market. The list of Fuller products expanded to several dozen by the mid-1920s and record-setting sales of $157,000 capped the end of the decade.

In 1930, following the stock market crash, Fuller acquired The Selvasize Company of St. Paul, the maker of a combination plaster and wallpaper adhesive, for $2,000. Fuller, with steady customers in 38 states and a near monopoly on glue production in the Twin Cities, remained relatively healthy throughout the Great Depression. A number of events highlighted the 1930s. The company hired its first degreed chemist, who became responsible for several new patents, such as Ice Proof, a glue resistant to cold water. In addition, a research team was formed, Fuller began a full-scale entry into international markets, and Elmer Andersen, a business administration graduate and budding salesman, joined the company, which celebrated its 50th anniversary in 1937.

Also during this time, Burgess developed an important new product known as Nu-Type Hot Pick-Up. Until Burgess's invention, the company, like its competitors, had marketed several hot pick-up glues for use in automated labeling; all such glues, however, were notoriously difficult to work with, either too hard or too sticky in bulk form, and always cumbersome to apply in measured amounts. Nu-Type Hot Pick-Up was the first glue that solved each of these problems. Consequently, Fuller cornered the hot glue market nationwide.

Not all the corporate news was as favorable, however. The company, with just half of one percent of industry sales, was still conspicuously overshadowed by such giants as National Adhesives Corporation, which controlled approximately 65 percent of the market. Every new sale, therefore, mattered greatly, which made all the more devastating the revelation in late 1937 that three of Fuller's regional salesmen had been undercutting the company's orders through the creation of a bogus firm, which they now claimed to represent. Sales, depressed already by the still struggling economy, dropped from $212,000 that year to $165,000 the following year. Even more devastating to the company's long-term prospects was the debilitating stroke Harvey Fuller suffered in 1939.

In March 1941 a large Chicago competitor named Paisley Products approached the ailing St. Paul firm with an acquisition offer. Both Fuller, then in his mid-50s, and Andersen, 32, attended a meeting with Paisley's representatives, who formally proposed to purchase H.B. Fuller Company for $50,000. Fuller

Key Dates:

1887: Fuller Manufacturing Company is founded by Harvey Benjamin Fuller, Sr.

1915: Firm is reincorporated as H.B. Fuller Company.

1921: Harvey B. Fuller, Jr., takes over presidency upon the death of his father.

1941: Elmer Andersen takes majority position in and leadership of the company.

1958: H.B. Fuller Company (Canada) Ltd., based in Winnipeg, is launched.

1968: Company goes public.

1971: Tony Andersen, son of Elmer, becomes company president.

1974: Sales reach $100 million.

1984: Company is named to the *Fortune* 500 list.

1992: Walter Kissling is named president of Fuller.

1994: Sales surpass $1 billion.

1998: Albert Stroucken is named president and CEO, becoming the first outsider so named; major restructuring is launched.

2002: Fuller initiates a further restructuring effort.

was prepared to retire but was also discouraged by the low offer he had received. Andersen provided an alternative solution. His plan involved assuming leadership of and a majority position in the company himself, while still allowing Fuller to retain at least a 25 percent stake. The deal was completed in July after Andersen borrowed heavily to finance a $10,000 down payment on the stock he was required to purchase. Mere months later, Pearl Harbor was attacked.

World War II and Postwar Growth

Far more so than the previous war, World War II afforded the company a chance to develop a broad line of adhesives that the government demanded for an equally broad array of uses. Fuller became one of the nation's first companies to specialize, among other areas, in waterproof adhesives. It thus earned a place on the government's recommended suppliers list which, in turn, brought it enhanced recognition nationally. The company scored another victory when it was able, during the midst of rationing, to supply Nabisco with raw glucose from its inventory, which had been dramatically enlarged by Andersen as a cost-saving measure. Nabisco subsequently became a major user of Fuller's adhesives for its boxed foods and other products. Both during and following the war, the company focused on decentralizing operations—bringing the product closer to the customer—by establishing a number of branch plants, beginning with Kansas City in 1943. At the close of the decade, Fuller ranked fourth among U.S. adhesives companies, behind National Starch (later owned by Unilever, then Imperial Chemical Industries PLC), Paisley Products (acquired by Fuller in 1975), and Swift.

In 1949, Andersen was elected to the state senate and became a part-time company president. Al Vigard assumed control of day-to-day operations in Andersen's absence; he later became president when Andersen extended his political career

by winning the governorship of Minnesota in 1960. A steady introduction of new products, a systematic development of a strong nationwide sales force, and a greater attention to international expansion typified this transitional era. In 1958, the company launched H.B. Fuller Company (Canada) Ltd. in Winnipeg. Shortly thereafter, Fuller Adhesives International of Panama was established. Numerous other international subsidiaries followed, each of which conformed to the Fuller blueprint for growth. A three-stage process, this blueprint called for: (1) building export volume to a high level; (2) forming or acquiring a subsidiary, or sometimes establishing a co-venture with a noncompetitor, in a clearly defined market; and (3) sustaining the business by hiring and training a local workforce to produce customized products.

One of Fuller's most significant ventures outside the United States was Kativo Chemical Industries Ltd. A promising but nearly bankrupt paint, inks, plastics, and chemicals business based in Costa Rica, Kativo was begun by a Kansas inventor named Dr. Frank Jirik. During the early 1960s, Fuller acquired a minority interest in the company, but by early 1967 Jirik approached Elmer Andersen with a proposal that Fuller assume a majority interest to fuel the company's plans for expansion. In *A Fuller Life,* Andersen recounted the visit that clinched his decision: "It was Kativo's people who made all the difference to us. . . . We trusted them. We had confidence in them and we cut them loose. We decided to send no U.S. Fuller employees to work in the Kativo operation." In addition, Andersen awarded the 13 Kativo executives the right to own stock in the company they had helped build. Soon Kativo became the heart of Fuller's Latin American operations, from Mexico to Argentina. Surviving plant and monetary losses from both the June 1979 revolution in Nicaragua and General Manuel Noriega's rampages during the U.S. invasion of Panama ten years later, Kativo and its related businesses ranked among the fastest growing in the Fuller fold into the 1990s. One of Kativo's original executives, Costa Rican native Walter Kissling, eventually served as president and chief operating officer of Fuller.

Late 20th Century: International Growth and Restructuring

In 1971, three years after Fuller went public, Tony Andersen became company president. International sales accounted for around 15 percent of total revenues, and Andersen was given the primary responsibility for boosting this figure, while increasing overall volume. Consequently, he became a president routinely in transit, flying from one country to the next. Not until 1980 did he return to head U.S. operations full-time. During the interim, he oversaw some two dozen acquisitions—half in foreign countries—and, significantly, the first of these provided important new market entries into Japan and Europe. From 1971 to 1980, sales grew from $60 million to $296 million (reaching $100 million in 1974). Andersen's greatest contribution to the company, however, came shortly after his return to the St. Paul headquarters. In what was then an unpopular maneuver, he decided to revamp the company's entire infrastructure, which because of rapid geographic-oriented expansion had become both inefficient and inconsistent. A market-driven organization stressing product and price uniformity was Andersen's answer. Because of an economic downturn, the payoff was slow to come. By 1985, however, earnings had improved dramatically, and three years later, Andersen was named executive of the year by *Corporate Report Minnesota*. H.B. Fuller, meanwhile, became a *Fortune* 500 company in 1984 when revenues hit $425 million.

Fuller inaugurated the 1990s by broadening its Asia/Pacific operations with a hot-melt production plant in Guangzhou, China. Plant expansions around the globe, as well as continuing investment in research and development, typified the company through 1992. In April of that year, Elmer Andersen officially stepped down as company chairperson. In a speech to shareholders, he optimistically stated, "The past is prologue: you ain't seen nothing yet." During this time, however, Andersen's statement was somewhat eclipsed by publicity surrounding Fuller's Resistol glue and its use as an inhalant by children in Latin America. Widely respected for its sponsorship of charitable and educational causes, Fuller pulled the product from markets in Honduras and Guatemala in the fall of 1992 and continued to fund social programs that helped minimize such abuse. Despite these moves, the Resistol issue simply would not go away. More negative publicity came in 1996 when the company was sued for negligence by the family of a 16-year-old Guatemalan boy. The suit, brought in U.S. District Court in St. Paul, claimed that the boy died as a result of years of inhaling Resistol. The judge in the case dismissed the suit, having concluded that it lacked jurisdiction.

When Elmer Andersen retired in 1992, Tony Andersen took over as chairman and Kissling became president. Kissling added the CEO position as well in 1995. Under Kissling's leadership, Fuller in the mid-1990s worked to reduce its operating expenses through the closure and consolidation of plants, particularly in Europe and Latin America. The company was aided in these efforts by the liberalization of tariffs in these regions. Whereas previously the company was forced to locate a plant in nearly every country in which it hoped to sell its products, it could now consolidate its factories on a regional basis. In concert with these moves came a reorganizing of the European and Latin American operations into strategic business units that were based on product lines rather than on geography. Company sales, meantime, surpassed the $1 billion mark for the first time in 1994 and then grew to $1.28 billion by 1996.

In 1997 Fuller joined its automotive adhesives, sealants, and coatings operations (with annual sales of $100 million to $115 million) with the automotive adhesives business of Zurich-based EMS-Chemie Holding AG to form EFTEC. The Detroit-based joint venture had revenues of about $250 million, making it the second largest automotive supplier, after Dow's Essex, and enabling it to operate on a global basis.

The following year Kissling retired from the company. His successor as president and CEO was Albert Stroucken, the first outsider in the company's 111-year history to take over the top positions. A native of the Netherlands, Stroucken was a 29-year veteran with Bayer A.G. Stroucken's first major task as head of Fuller was to improve the company's net earnings, which had for years stood at around 3 percent. The investment community had long complained that Fuller's corporate culture, which helped earn the company a consistent place on lists of the best places to work, did not place enough emphasis on the bottom line. The company had a longstanding pledge that "its responsibilities, in order of priority [are] to its customers, employees, stockholders and communities."

It became immediately clear that this outsider would bring startling changes to Fuller and propel it into a new era. Most strikingly, in 1998 the Stroucken-led Fuller changed its mission statement, which now read in part, "H.B. Fuller is committed to the balanced interests of its customers, employees, shareholders and communities." In August 1998, a mere four months after his arrival, Stroucken announced a major restructuring aimed at reducing costs by $30 million per year and improving net margins to 5 percent through the closure of about a dozen plants, the divestment of underperforming units, and the elimination of about 600 jobs worldwide—all over an 18-month period. Stroucken also took a more aggressive stance toward acquisitions, aiming to displace Imperial Chemical Industries' National Starch subsidiary from the number one position in the global adhesives market. During 1998 Fuller spent $92.4 million on acquisitions, purchasing the Australian and New Zealand adhesives business of Croda International PLC and Peterson Chemicals Adhesives from Ecolab Inc. Stroucken told analysts in mid-1999 that he was identifying acquisition targets with sales of at least $100 million, a huge jump from the $5 million to $10 million companies that Fuller typically purchased. The new leader's moves were quick to pay off as 1999 revenues increased 2 percent to $1.36 billion and profits jumped from $16 million to $43.4 million. Late in 1999 Stroucken succeeded Andersen as chairman of H.B. Fuller.

Developments in the Early 2000s

In 2000 and 2001 the company's results suffered first from the rapidly rising cost of petroleum-based raw materials and then from the economic downturn, which weakened demand for H.B. Fuller's products. Early in 2002 Stroucken launched another major restructuring to slash the firm's existing manufacturing capacity by 20 percent and yield annual savings of more than $10 million. By 2003 the company had shut down 14 manufacturing plants, mainly in North America, eliminated 556 positions from the payroll, and recorded pretax restructuring charges of more than $40 million. Since taking over, Stroucken had cut the number of Fuller plants from 70 to 39 and trimmed the workforce from 6,400 to 4,600; he also improved the company's efficiency by slashing the number of its product offerings from 8,000 to approximately 2,700.

On the strategic front, EFTEC, the 70 percent owned automotive joint venture, acquired a 48 percent stake in Autotek Sealants, Inc., a provider of bonding, sealing, and coating technology within the automotive industry. After switching its stock from the NASDAQ to the New York Stock Exchange in December 2002, Fuller completed the first significant acquisition of the Stroucken era in February 2004. Acquired that month were the adhesives and resins businesses of Probos, S.A., a firm based in Oporto, Portugal. The purchased product lines, with annual revenues of about $30 million, mainly derived from the Portuguese and Spanish markets, included water-based, hot melt, reactive, and solvent-based adhesives for the assembly, woodworking, and converting industries, and emulsions for the paints, textiles, and food product industries. The businesses were incorporated into H.B. Fuller's European operations.

During 2004 another dramatic run-up in raw material prices was at least partially offset by the beneficial weakness of the U.S. dollar. When coupled with improved sales volume and gains from the Iberian acquisition, these factors led to the company's best revenue gain in many years. The $1.41 billion in revenues were nearly 10 percent more than the previous year. Profits, however, fell $3 million, totaling just $35.6 million. Fuller was also embarrassed to discover irregularities in the financial statements of its operations in Chile and was forced to reduce its net income for the year by $3.8 million.

In the spring of 2005 Fuller shifted its operations in Japan and China into joint ventures with Sekisui Chemical Co., Ltd., a Japanese construction supplier and house manufacturer. The two firms merged their Japanese adhesives businesses to form Sekisui-Fuller Company, Ltd., initially 60 percent owned by Sekisui and 40 percent by Fuller (with the latter holding an option to buy a further 10 percent in 2007 for $12 million). The new entity, with annual sales of about $150 million, ranked as one of the leading adhesive firms in Japan. Fuller also sold a 20 percent stake in its China operations to Sekisui. As these transactions were being completed, H.B. Fuller continued to struggle with the effects of rising raw material costs. The company increased the prices of its products but could not do so enough to offset the rising raw material burden. Fuller thus faced additional pressure to cut costs and improve efficiency.

Principal Subsidiaries

H.B. Fuller International Inc.; Specialty Constructions Brands, Inc.; H.B. Fuller Licensing & Financing, Inc.; Adalis Corporation; Stratyc, Inc.; H.B. Fuller Automotive Company; EFTEC North America, LLC (70%); EFTEC Latin America (Panama; 88.5%); EFTEC Europe Holding AG (Switzerland; 30%); EFTEC Asia Pte. Ltd. (Singapore; 60%); H.B. Fuller Canada Holding Co.; H.B. Fuller Mexico, S.A.; H.B. Fuller Benelux B.V. (Netherlands); H.B. Fuller Austria Produktions GesmbH (90%); H.B. Fuller Austria GesmbH (90%); H.B. Fuller Belgium N.V./S.A. (99.8%); H.B. Fuller Deutschland Holding GmbH (Germany); H.B. Fuller Deutschland Produktions GmbH (Germany); H.B. Fuller Deutschland GmbH (Germany); H.B. Fuller France SAS; H.B. Fuller Finance (Ireland); H.B. Fuller Italia Holding s.r.l. (Italy); H.B. Fuller Italia Produzione s.r.l. (Italy); H.B. Fuller Italia s.r.l. (Italy); H.B. Fuller Portugal - SGPS, Lda.; Proadec Productos Quimicos, S.A. (Portugal); Isar-Rakoll Chemie Portuguesa, S.A. (Portugal); Isar-Rakoll, S.A. (Portugal); H.B. Fuller Sverige AB (Sweden); H.B. Fuller Espana, S.A. (Spain); Proadec Quimicos Espana, S.A. (Spain); H.B. Fuller Europe GmbH (Switzerland); H.B. Fuller Holdings Limited (U.K.); H.B. Fuller Group Limited (U.K.); H.B. Fuller U.K. Operations Ltd.; H.B. F. Ltd. (U.K.); H.B. Fuller U.K. Ltd.; H.B. Fuller Powder Coatings Limited (U.K.); Powderstore Limited (U.K.); Datac Ltd. (U.K.); H.B. Fuller U.K. Manufacturing Limited; H.B. Fuller Company Australia Pty. Ltd.; H.B. Fuller (China) Adhesives Ltd. (99%); H.B. Fuller (Shanghai) Trading Ltd. (China); H.B. Fuller (Shanghai) Consulting Ltd. (China); H.B. Fuller Japan Company, Ltd.; H.B. Fuller Korea, Ltd.; H.B. Fuller Company (N.Z.) Ltd. (New Zealand; 99.9%); H.B. Fuller (Philippines), Inc. (93.68%); H.B. Fuller Taiwan Co., Ltd.; H.B. Fuller (Thailand) Co., Ltd. (99.9%); Centro de Pinturas Glidden-Protecto, S.A. (Panama); Fabrica de Pinturas Glidden, S.A. (Panama); H.B. Fuller Holding Panama Co.; Glidden Panama S.A.; Kativo Chemical Industries, S.A. (Panama).

Principal Competitors

Henkel KGaA; Eastman Chemical Company; Ashland Specialty Chemical Company; Sovereign Specialty Chemicals, Inc.; National Starch and Chemical Company; Dow Corning Corporation; Rohm and Haas Company.

Further Reading

Carlson, Scott, "U.S. Judge Dismisses Suit Against St. Paul-Based H.B. Fuller," *St. Paul Pioneer Press,* September 25, 1996.
Croghan, Lore, "Family Values: Why Paternalistic H.B. Fuller Gives Wall Street Fits," *Financial World,* November 7, 1995, pp. 46–47, 50.
Davis, Riccardo A., "New President Targets Net Profit Margin at Minnesota's H.B. Fuller," *St. Paul Pioneer Press,* July 2, 1998.
Feyder, Susan, "Fuller Plans Cost-Cutting Effort," *Minneapolis Star Tribune,* December 22, 1995, p. 1D.
A Fuller Life: The Story of H.B. Fuller Company, 1887–1987, St. Paul: H.B. Fuller Company, 1986.
"Fuller's Brush with Fame," *Corporate Report Minnesota,* June 1984, p. 23.
Fuller World, January/February 1992 (full issue).
Gelbach, Deborah L., "H.B. Fuller Company," in *From This Land: A History of Minnesota's Empires, Enterprises, and Entrepreneurs,* Northridge, Calif.: Windsor Publications, 1988, pp. 358–61.
Hayes, Brian, "Branching Out: H.B. Fuller Widens Its Scope with Venture Fund," *Adhesives and Sealants Industry,* May 2005, pp. 36–37.
"Glue Issue Dominates Fuller Meeting," *Minneapolis Star Tribune,* April 16, 1993, p. 3D.
"H.B. Fuller Co.," *City Business,* March 26, 1993, p. 18.
"H.B. Fuller Forms Two Asian JVs," *Chemical Market Reporter,* February 21, 2005, p. 2.
"H.B. Fuller Jockeys for Position to Become No. 1 Adhesives Player," *Chemical Marketing Reporter,* June 14, 1999, p. 7.
"H.B. Fuller Net Falls 51% in Quarter; Nonrecurring Sales Adjustment Cited," *Minneapolis Star Tribune,* March 23, 1993, p. 5D.
"H.B. Fuller Reports Lower Second-Quarter Earnings," *Minneapolis Star Tribune,* June 23, 1993, p. 5D.
Henriques, Diana B., "Suit Against Fuller Over Death of Guatemalan Youth Dismissed," *New York Times,* September 25, 1996, p. D5.
Kelly, Marjorie, "Though H.B. Fuller May Wish It, Resistol Issue Won't Go Away," *Minneapolis Star Tribune,* December 4, 1995, p. 3D.
Kunz, Virginia Brainard, *St. Paul: A Modern Renaissance,* Northridge, Calif.: Windsor Publications, 1986, pp. 142–45.
Levering, Robert, Michael Katz, and Milton Moskowitz, *The 100 Best Companies to Work for in America,* Reading, Mass.: Addison-Wesley, 1984, pp. 112–14; new edition, New York: Doubleday, 1993, pp. 136–40.
Malamud, Steven, "H.B. Fuller: A Different Record Home and Abroad," *Business and Society Review,* January 1, 1996.
McEnroe, Paul, and Susan E. Peterson, "H.B. Fuller Sued in Teen's Death," *Minneapolis Star Tribune,* January 4, 1996, p. 1D.
Mundale, Charles I., "H.B. Fuller's Caribbean Initiative," *Corporate Report Minnesota,* July 1983, pp. 55–60.
Papa, Mary Bader, "Executive of the Year (Anthony L. Andersen): Building for the Future by Sticking to the Basic Values of the Past," *Corporate Report Minnesota,* January 1988, pp. 31–39.
Peterson, Susan E., "The Andersen Legacy: Over a Period of Almost Six Decades, Elmer Andersen and Son Tony Andersen Built H.B.

Fuller from a Small St. Paul Glue Maker into a $1 Billion *Fortune 500 Company*," *Minneapolis Star Tribune,* February 7, 2000, p. 1D.

——, "Fuller Names Bayer Exec to Replace Kissling As CEO," *Minneapolis Star Tribune,* March 28, 1998, p. 1D.

——, "H.B. Fuller Honors Outgoing Chairman Andersen, Celebrates Company's Continuing Good Health," *Minneapolis Star Tribune,* April 17, 1992, p. 1D.

——, "H.B. Fuller President Kissling to Retire from Post in 1998," *Minneapolis Star Tribune,* July 19, 1997, p. 1D.

——, "H.B. Fuller Will Cut 600 Jobs," *Minneapolis Star Tribune,* August 12, 1998, p. 1D.

——, "Judge to Decide Venue of Fuller Case," *Minneapolis Star Tribune,* May 30, 1996, p. 1D.

——, "This Al's No 'Chainsaw,' " *Minneapolis Star Tribune,* July 6, 1998, p. 1D.

Pitzer, Mary J., "Fuller's Worldwide Strategy: Think Local," *Business Week,* November 16, 1987, p. 169.

"Remaking H.B. Fuller," *Adhesives Age,* March 2000, p. 11.

Schafer, Lee, "H.B. Fuller and the Indignities of War," *Corporate Report Minnesota,* March 1990, p. 14.

Scheraga, Dan, "Fuller Acquires Coating Technologies from NiTech," *Chemical Marketing Reporter,* October 19, 1998, p. 16.

——, "Fuller Poised to Reap Rewards from Restructuring," *Chemical Marketing Reporter,* February 22, 1999, p. 20.

——, "Fuller's Success Based on European and Latin Support," *Chemical Marketing Reporter,* April 12, 1999, pp. 4, 26.

——, "H.B. Fuller Streamlines to Counteract Effects of Economic Slowdown," *Chemical Marketing Reporter,* August 17, 1998, pp. 3, 18.

Schmitt, Bill, "H.B. Fuller Prepares for Deals," *Chemical Week,* December 11, 2002, p. 39.

Teresko, John, "Too Fast a Pace? Andersen Has a Strategy for the Next Leg of the Race," *Industry Week,* September 15, 1986, pp. 59–60.

Valero, Greg, "The Risk Taker," *Adhesives Age,* January/February 2003, pp. 28, 30, 32.

Walsh, Kerri A., "A Fresh Start for H.B. Fuller," *Chemical Week,* February 3, 1999, pp. 39, 41.

—— "Fuller, EMS—Chemie Stick Auto Adhesives Together," *Chemical Week,* May 28, 1997, p. 14.

——, "Fuller to Scale Back Capacity," *Chemical Week,* January 23, 2002, p. 10.

Zemke, Ron, and Dick Schaaf, "H.B. Fuller," *The Service Edge: 101 Companies That Profit from Customer Care,* New York: Penguin, 1989, pp. 458–61.

—Jay P. Pederson
—update: David E. Salamie

HealthExtras, Inc.

800 King Farm Boulevard
Rockville, Maryland 20850
U.S.A.
Telephone: (301) 548-2900
Toll Free: (800) 323-6640
Fax: (301) 548-2980
Web site: http://www.healthextras.com

Public Company
Incorporated: 1999
Employees: 227
Sales: $521.3 million (2004)
Stock Exchanges: NASDAQ
Ticker Symbol: HLEX
NAIC: 524298 All Other Insurance Related Activities

HealthExtras, Inc. is a Rockville, Maryland-based healthcare company that is primarily involved in the management of pharmacy benefits. Services include claims processing, mail-order drug delivery, benefit design consultation, drug utilization evaluation, formulary management, and drug data analysis services. The company also operates a national retail pharmacy network of more than 54,000 pharmacies. All told, it serves more than two million members. A major factor in HealthExtras' strong growth in this field is its full disclosure policy, revealing both the price it pays for drugs and the amount of profit it takes. In addition, HealthExtras sells supplemental health benefits insurance, the company's original focus, through American Express and retailers such as J.C. Penney and Sears Roebuck. HealthExtras is a public company listed on the NASDAQ.

Launching the Business in 1997

HealthExtras grew out of the business of United Payors and United Providers, a preferred provider organization (PPO) and healthcare credit card company founded by Thomas L. Blair in 1995. From 1977 until 1988 Blair was a partner at Jurgovan & Blair, Inc., developing and managing health maintenance organizations. In 1989 he founded America's Health Plan, Inc., and then in 1992 became president of Initial Managers & Investors, Inc., which was eventually folded into United Payors. Serving as his financial manager was his son, David T. Blair, who started his business career working for the management consulting firm of Kelly, Anderson, Petchick and Associates. He left in 1994 to cofound Continued Health Care Benefit Program to market health insurance to people leaving the U.S. military. A year later this business merged with United Payors and Blair became financial manager. He was still in his 20s when he played a significant role in United Payors going public in 1996. Then, in October of that year he took the lead in a marketing research campaign for the development of a supplemental benefits program. In July 1997 the Blairs launched HealthExtras, LLC, along with Edward S. Civera, a 25-year veteran of Coopers & Lybrand who joined United Payors in 1997 as chief operating officer and co-CEO. David Blair became the chief executive officer of HealthExtras.

Market research and product development work continued in 1998 and the company began offering insurance in January 1999, marketing directly through its web site, www.healthextras.com, and becoming the first company to offer a tax-free payment of up to $1 million in the event of a permanent accidental disability. HealthExtras actually assumed no underwriting risks; Reliance National Insurance provided the products and another insurer provided the out-of-area coverage. These products included catastrophic disability; excess medical, supplementing the limit on a member's primary health insurance coverage; organ transplant, to supplement limited coverage offered by many health insurance policies; out-of-area expense reimbursement, to cover costs incurred when members were more than 100 miles from home; emergency evacuation and repatriation, providing as much as $50,000 for air ambulance transportation; 24-hour nurse consultation; and provider network access, allowing members to take advantage of discounts United Payors had arranged through its network of more than 2,500 hospitals and 150,000 physicians. HealthExtras was also very much dependent on United Payors for office space, equipment, and personnel. The start-up paid for these services on a cost basis until arranging a sublease in 1999 and eventually hiring United Payors personnel who worked on HealthExtras' business fulltime.

Company Perspectives:

The Company operates and reports in two segments; pharmacy benefit management and supplemental health, and while both segments are profitable, the Company's primary focus is the expansion of its pharmacy benefit management business.

Early on, HealthExtras established a relationship with actor Christopher Reeve, best known for his film work as Superman, who had been paralyzed in an equestrian accident in 1995. He assumed that he had top-shelf health insurance, only to discover that his disability insurance coverage had a cap of $1.2 million. "He suffered the precise problem that one of our products is designed to alleviate," David Blair told *Advertising Age.* As a result of his experience, Reeve became the spokesman for HealthExtras in July 1997 (for a three-year term later extended to five), making the case that basic health insurance had its limitations and urging people to consider HealthExtras' supplemental coverage to provide their families with financial security should they suffer a debilitating accident like his. Initial advertising efforts included an insert in Citibank statements featuring a picture of Reeve and the caption: "In an instant your life can change. Mine did."

Going Public in 1999

To take full advantage of Reeve's celebrity and to drive traffic to its web site, however, HealthExtras needed more money, and in 1999 took steps to make an offering of stock. In July 1999 HealthExtras, Inc. was incorporated in Delaware. An initial public offering of stock was then conducted, underwritten by Warburg Dillon Read LLC, PaineWebber Incorporated, Prudential Vector Healthcare, and SG Cowen Securities Corp. It was completed in December 1999, raising $55 million. HealthExtras, LLC and HealthExtras, Inc. were then merged. The stock began trading on the NASDAQ at $11 but quickly lost value, dropping to the $5 range. In the letter to shareholders that accompanied the 1999 annual report, David Blair expressed his disappointment in the stock's performance: "Unfortunately HealthExtras has been categorized with a number of e-health companies that are focused on owning 'space' rather than making a profit. HealthExtras has a sound business model, we do not sell information or banner ads; we sell a product that is inherently profitable." But he would soon come to change his mind about the viability of the company's business model.

Some of the proceeds of the stock offering were used to pay off debt and $20 million to $25 million was earmarked for an integrated advertising campaign featuring Reeve that was launched in the spring of 2000. It included three black-and-white, documentary-style television ads in which Reeve talked about his immediate thoughts of suicide after his riding accident and then the realization that "the people around you still love you and need you . . . that, that's the first big breakthrough. . . . But, having made that breakthrough . . . and decided it's worth staying around . . . you still have the problems of . . . how are we going to make ends meet?" The tag at the end of these spots was as follows: "Even if you have health insurance, you need

HealthExtras.'' To some observers the ads were sensational and perhaps exploitive. *Advertising Age*'s longtime critic of commercials, Bob Garfield, opined, "Nobody wants to see the man's affliction turned into a cottage industry, and nobody wants to watch Christopher Reeve in a one-man freak show. But in this particular campaign from Focused Image, Alexandria, Va., nothing freakish is afoot. It's just a man—a famous, handsome movie star—reminding you that what can happen to him can happen to anyone." The campaign also included radio, print, and Internet elements, targeting women, upper-income families, and small businesses.

Due in large measure to Reeve's effort, HealthExtras signed up members at a much faster than expected clip, and they not only signed up for the $10-a-month basic product but bought additional products as well. Despite selling a product with a high profit margin and facing little competition, David Blair had misgivings about the direction the company was headed. According to a *Washington Post* profile in 2004, "The Internet, it turned out, was a poor place to sell insurance to provide benefits after debilitating injuries or illnesses. The company spent about $100 in marketing costs, such as direct mail and Web advertising, for each customer it signed up. It charged roughly that amount for an annual policy."

First Step in Prescription Management: 2000

It was at this point that the company changed gears, diversifying its revenue base and moving into the business of managing prescription drug benefits. In November 2000 HealthExtras acquired International Pharmacy Management, Inc. (IPM) in a $9.2 million stock and cash deal. Based in Birmingham, Alabama, IPM offered pharmacy benefit management services and operated a mail-order pharmacy. Launched in 1995, it now had $30 million in annual sales. Blair commented in a press release, "The IPM acquisition gives our company the opportunity to further expand our reach from direct-to-consumer to direct-to-employer groups by highlighting a benefit which is increasingly valuable in employee recruitment and retention."

HealthExtras was now competing in a field that was dominated by three larger players: Caremark Inc., Express Scripts Inc., and Medco Health Solutions Inc. In order to compete, HealthExtras had to narrow its marketing focus. According to the *Washington Post,* "It chose to court mid-size employers, promising strong customer service, flexible prescription plans and big savings. Compared with its larger competitors, Blair said, HealthExtras relies less on payments from major pharmaceutical companies promoting their drugs. 'It allows us to be objective,' said Michael Donovan, the company's chief financial officer."

HealthExtras also tried to diversify its supplemental insurance products in 2001 by partnering with Oklahoma insurer Globe Life and Accident Insurance, taking advantage of its direct-mail program that reached 2.5 million people, and with AtYourBusiness.com, a Rockville-based company that marketed insurance services to small businesses. But increasingly HealthExtras' focus was on growing its pharmacy business. The company completed another acquisition in this sector in 2001. In November it bought 80 percent of Catalyst Rx and Catalyst Consultants, Inc. in a transaction worth about $14.3 million.

The remaining 20 percent would be purchased in early 2002. HealthExtras also began to cut back on its investments in the development of new supplemental insurance products, as well as reducing its marketing budget. The company was now content to use the original thrust of the company as a base of revenues and, by reducing overhead, turned it into a cash cow to support the expansion of its pharmacy benefits business.

To fund expansion opportunities, HealthExtras in early 2001 decided to make a private placement of about $30 million in stock and hired SG Cowen to place the shares with investors, a so-called PIPE (private investments in public equity) offering. As the *Wall Street Journal* explained in a 2002 article, ''These investors are offered shares at a discount because the new shares are unregistered. But the risk with PIPE offerings is that if other investors hear of the offering, they may sell the firm's shares short, betting that the deal will trigger a drop in the issuer's stock price. Because unregistered shares are worth less than the publicly traded stock, opportunistic investors can take advantage of the price discovery.'' While Cowen was placing the shares, HealthExtras' shares lost about half their value on the NASDAQ, unlike the experience of its competitors. In October 2001 HealthExtras asked Cowen to investigate the matter. Four months later Cowen reported that Managing Director Guillame Pollet had been short-selling HealthExtras shares and had been terminated. Not satisfied with Cowen's response, HealthExtras sued Cowen in federal court in December 2002, alleging that Cowen had profited by misusing client information. The two parties reached a settlement in 2004, and then in April 2005 Pollet pleaded guilty to insider trading for short-selling HealthExtras stock. The Securities and Exchange Commission next filed a civil lawsuit against Pollet, accusing him of fraud and insider trading involving ten companies in other PIPE offerings.

Revenues totaled $118.2 million in 2001 and more than doubled in 2002 to $248.4 million. HealthExtras also recorded its first profitable year, with nearly $13.5 million in earnings. Much of the increase in sales was the result of the Catalyst Rx acquisition, and HealthExtras set itself up for even more growth by completing another acquisition late in 2002, paying $20.2 million for Raleigh, North Carolina-based Pharmacy Network National Corporation, which focused on the Carolinas and Tennessee.

Sales improved to $384.1 million in 2003 and net income totaled $10.3 million. HealthExtras received a major boost in the spring of 2004 when it won a contract from the state of Louisiana to manage pharmacy benefits for state employees and retirees, worth between $40 million to $50 million in annual sales. HealthExtras also was reported to be on the short list for a similar and even larger contract from the state of North Carolina, news that caught the attention of Wall Street, which bid up the price of HealthExtras' stock. The company continued to build momentum in June 2004 when it acquired another PBM, Florida-based Managed Healthcare Systems Inc. in a cash and stock deal worth $44 million. On a sad note, Christopher Reeve died in October 2004, leaving the company without its chief spokesperson. If HealthExtras had continued to focus on supplemental insurance, his death would have likely caused serious problems. But, in reality, supplemental insurance accounted for just 10 percent of revenues, making the impact of Reeve's loss decidedly more personal than financial for HealthExtras.

Revenues reached $521.3 million in 2004 while net income increased to $16.4 million. In 2005 HealthExtras experienced a change in the boardroom, as Thomas L. Blair was replaced as chairman by Civera. Blair stayed on as a director, and the change was not likely to interfere with HealthExtras' pattern of steady growth.

Principal Subsidiaries

Catalyst Rx; Catalyst Consultants, Inc.; HealthExtras Benefits Administrator, Inc.; International Pharmacy Management, Inc.; Pharmacy Network National Corporation; Pharmacy Providers of Georgia, Inc.; U.S. Scripts, Inc.

Principal Competitors

Caremark Rx, Inc.; Express Scripts, Inc.; Medco Health Solutions, Inc.

Further Reading

Barbara, Michael, ''New Business Plan Led to Profitability,'' *Washington Post,* July 19, 2004, p. E10.

Benesh, Peter, ''Pharmacy Benefits Manager Enjoys the Benefits of Being Small,'' *Investor's Business Daily,* November 3, 2003, p. A08.

——, ''Recent Deal Is the Right Financial Rx for Pharmacy Benefit Manager,'' *Investor's Business Daily,* June 1, 2004, p. A07.

Craig, Susanne, ''HealthExtras Sues SG Cowen, Alleging Misuse of Private Data,'' *Wall Street Journal,* December 4, 2002, p. C9.

Garfield, Bob, ''Christopher Reeve's Credibility Connects for Disability Insurer,'' *Advertising Age,* April 24, 2000, p. 101.

Goetzl, David, ''Spokesman Reeve Stars in Effort for Disability Insurer,'' *Advertising Age,* February 21, 2000, p. 4.

Higgins, Marguerite, ''Rockville, Md.-Based Pharmacy-Benefits Management Firm Sees Stock Price Rise,'' *Washington Times,* May 4, 2004.

Keaveney, Bob, ''HealthExtras Poised for Growth,'' *Daily Record,* March 6, 2000, p. A1.

Lemke, Tim, ''Christopher Reeve Symbolized Rockville's HealthExtras,'' *Daily Record,* October 12, 2004, p. 1.

''S.E.C. Accused Former Official at SG Cowen in Fraud Suit,'' *New York Times,* April 22, 2005, p. C6.

Thompson, Stephanie, ''Insurers Direct Tactic: Buy or Beware,'' *Brandweek,* April 12, 1999, p. 50.

—Ed Dinger

Hillenbrand Industries, Inc.

700 State Route 46 East
Batesville, Indiana 47006
U.S.A.
Telephone: (812) 934-7000
Fax: (812) 934-7371
Web site: http://www.hillenbrand.com

Public Company
Incorporated: 1969
Employees: 10,400
Sales: $1.82 billion (2004)
Stock Exchanges: New York
Ticker Symbol: HB
NAIC: 337127 Institutional Furniture Manufacturing; 337214 Nonwood Office Furniture Manufacturing; 337910 Mattress Manufacturing; 339995 Burial Casket Manufacturing; 551112 Offices of Other Holding Companies

Hillenbrand Industries, Inc. is a holding company for two major operating businesses, Batesville Casket Company and Hill-Rom Company. Batesville Casket manufactures caskets and cremation-related products, selling its products to funeral homes in North America, the United Kingdom, Australia, Mexico, and Puerto Rico. The company ranks as the largest coffin manufacturer in the United States, controlling nearly half of the domestic market. Hill-Rom operates in the healthcare industry, selling and renting hospital beds, furnishings and accessories, and systems for wound, pulmonary, and circulatory care.

Origins

"The first generation starts a company, the second builds it, and the third generation destroys it," recalled August (Gus) Hillenbrand, president and CEO of Hillenbrand Industries, in the *Cincinnati Business Courier* in 1993. A family friend had offered those words in jest to Hillenbrand when he was boy. "That has just stuck with me all my life . . . and that's why we work so dang hard." Indeed, in the mid-1990s Hillenbrand was

sustaining a legacy of success which his grandfather, John A. Hillenbrand, initiated in the late 1800s.

John A. Hillenbrand's father, a German immigrant and woodworker, settled in the German-speaking community of Cincinnati, Ohio, before the Civil War. He was soon drawn, however, to the enormous timber stocks of southeastern Indiana. Shortly after moving to Batesville, Indiana, in 1861, the 16-year-old Hillenbrand found himself orphaned with two infant sisters. Realizing that timberland was abundant and inexpensive in comparison to farmland, he abandoned his family's unprofitable farm and began purchasing small sections of woodland. He cut and sold the rich hardwood to the railroads for track ties, and then sold the cleared land to farmers.

Like his father, John A. Hillenbrand combined hard work and ingenuity to create several Hillenbrand family enterprises, including a general store. In 1906, Hillenbrand seized an opportunity to rescue the Batesville Coffin Company, a local casket manufacturer founded in 1884, from bankruptcy. He employed German woodworkers, carvers, and cabinet makers to craft his high quality coffins, and used his business acumen to turn the company around. Steady coffin demand, a swelling population, and Hillenbrand's success at increasing his share of the regional casket market allowed the company to realize healthy profit growth throughout the early 20th century.

Part of John A. Hillenbrand's unique recipe for success was close cooperation with his four talented sons. For example, John W., the eldest son, eventually assumed his father's role as president, and guided company expansion during the mid-20th century. George C. became the company's manufacturing genius. His numerous patents and his insistence on continuous product improvement made innovation a Hillenbrand hallmark. Daniel A., the youngest son, is credited with extending the company's reach nationally and, during the late 20th century, globally.

William A., the second oldest son, vastly broadened the scope of the Hillenbrand operations into the healthcare field. In an attempt to start a furniture business, he founded the Hill-Rom Company in 1929, during the Great Depression. Determined to set himself apart from other furniture makers, William decided to enter the hospital market. He spent almost a full year visiting

---
Company Perspectives:

People turn to our products, services and companies for positive outcomes. We help deliver a mother's newborn infant; speed a boy's recovery from a biking injury; make a military veteran's funeral more meaningful to his family with personalized products; and we deliver value to our shareholders. We are proud that our products and services are making a meaningful difference in people's lives everyday.

---

hospitals throughout the United States to determine how he could improve furniture in patient's rooms. The end result was his development of the first wood and metal hospital bed, which soon replaced the prevailing white tubular steel beds.

Hill-Rom, a division of Hillenbrand Industries, prospered along with the Batesville Casket Company during the 1930s, and especially during the post-World War II economic expansion in the United States. The company combined high-quality hardwoods, including cherry, mahogany, oak, and walnut, with expert craftsmanship and design to broaden its share of regional casket and hospital bed markets. Importantly, though, it was the companies' completely new product innovations that vaulted them past their competitors.

In 1940, for example, Hillenbrand pioneered the mass production of metal caskets, which became considerably less expensive to manufacture than traditional wooden coffins. The company eventually integrated stainless steel, bronze, and copper into its products. Metal caskets, many of which are warranted against corrosion for 75 years, grew to dominate U.S. coffin sales. By the 1990s, wood caskets represented only 15 percent of global industry sales.

Hillenbrand also led changes in the hospital furniture business. In 1950, for instance, Hill-Rom introduced the first electronically controlled bed. A slew of advancements followed, such as beds that monitored patients, maternity beds, and special beds for burn victims. The company later boasted that it had developed virtually every meaningful innovation in the hospital room furniture and equipment industry since World War II.

Besides high-quality materials and craftsmanship, inventiveness, and family cooperation, other important factors influenced Hillenbrand Industries' success. For example, the company prided itself on a heritage of fiscal responsibility. Prudent management allowed the Hillenbrand brothers to expand the company almost entirely from cash flow instead of debt. Even during the 1980s, when many other corporations were assuming large debt loads, Hillenbrand minimized its debt ratio. The Hillenbrand family retained a 60 percent ownership share of the corporation in 1993.

The company attributed its past achievements to a strong work ethic and a cooperative relationship between management, labor, and the local community. Hillenbrand poured millions of dollars into the local community, and in 1993 employed about 60 percent of Batesville's 4,500 residents. "If it weren't for the Hillenbrands, this wouldn't be the town that it is," remarked Mary Gauck, a 20-year Hillenbrand veteran, in the

Cincinnati Business Courier. "We wouldn't have the YMCA, the swimming pool, or the library." In explaining his company's success, Gus Hillenbrand returned the praise: "The work ethic [in Batesville] is phenomenal."

After serving as president of the Batesville Casket Company for seven years, Daniel took the reins from his eldest brother in 1971 when he became chairman of the board of Hillenbrand Industries. In an effort to continue his brother's successful leadership and to parlay the company's numerous competitive advantages into new achievements, Daniel sought to expand Hillenbrand's market presence.

Diversification Beginning in the Late 1970s

Besides taking the company public in 1971, Daniel led the company into completely new arenas. The company purchased American Tourister, Inc., of Warren, Rhode Island, in 1978. American Tourister was a major U.S. luggage manufacturer with a reputation for producing high-quality, affordable goods. In 1984, Hillenbrand made Medeco Security Locks, Inc. of Salem, Virginia, the fourth company operating under its corporate umbrella. Medeco was a leading producer of high-performance locking devices and security systems.

In 1985, Hillenbrand entered the insurance business when it organized the Forethought Group, Inc. This group of companies was established to provide advance funeral planning services, in the form of insurance policies, through funeral homes. In a bid to increase its healthcare presence, Hillenbrand also purchased SSI Medical Services, Inc. of Charleston, South Carolina, in 1985. SSI was a leading provider of specialized therapeutic products and services. By 1994, SSI and Hill-Rom were being integrated under the Hill-Rom name.

Hillenbrand's diversification strategy began to pay off in the late 1970s and early 1980s. As revenues multiplied from about $60 million in 1970 to over $325 million in 1980, the company's net income surged from less than $10 million per year to $25 million. Moreover, by 1985 the company netted almost $35 million in income from about $440 million in sales.

Besides new lines of business, Hillenbrand's profit growth during the 1980s reflected the continued success of its core casket and hospital furniture segments. New products and manufacturing techniques allowed both Hill-Rom and Batesville Casket Company to achieve greater market dominance. Hill-Rom broadened its product line to include items such as infant warmers, special stretchers, and nurse communication systems. Its hospital bed offerings grew to encompass a variety of specialty devices, including critical care beds, sleep surfaces for ulcer patients, and birthing beds.

Like Hill-Rom, the Batesville Casket Company increased its offerings during the 1980s to include over 400 products sold to more than 16,000 funeral homes. By the end of that decade, the company was manufacturing caskets in several states, including Kentucky, Mississippi, New Hampshire, and Tennessee. Its Kentucky plant, which employed advanced robotics, was one of the world's most automated metal casket production facilities.

Hillenbrand also developed new marketing techniques during the 1970s and 1980s, emphasizing customer service and

---

Key Dates:

1906: John A. Hillenbrand acquires a troubled casket manufacturer, Batesville Coffin Company, and changes its name to Batesville Casket Company.

1929: One of Hillenbrand's sons, William A. Hillenbrand, founds Hill-Rom Co., which begins making hospital beds.

1940: Hillenbrand Industries pioneers the mass production of metal caskets.

1950: Hill-Rom unveils the first electronically controlled hospital bed.

1971: Hillenbrand Industries completes its initial public offering of stock.

1978: American Tourister, Inc. is acquired.

1984: A fourth operating company, Medeco Security Locks, Inc., is acquired.

1985: Forethought Group, Inc. is formed, marking the company's entrance into the insurance business.

1991: A French manufacturer of hospital beds, Le Courviour S.A., is acquired, the first of three foreign businesses acquired by the company during the first half of the decade.

1993: Hillenbrand Industries' American Tourister division is divested.

1999: Fredrick Rockwood is appointed president, ushering in a series of senior management changes.

2004: Forethought Financial Services is sold to FFS Holdings, Inc.

2005: Ray Hillenbrand announces his retirement.

---

satisfaction. The company's sales pitch to prospective hospital furniture clients often entailed a trip to Batesville, a stay at a company farm and conference center, and product demonstrations between rounds of food and drink. Similarly, the company hosted thousands of funeral directors annually at its Batesville headquarters.

As Hillenbrand widened its scope, improved its products, and boosted marketing efforts during the 1970s and 1980s, it also benefitted from favorable demographic and economic trends. The number of annual deaths in the United States rose about 12 percent between 1970 and 1990, resulting in gradual growth in the combined demand for caskets and cremation products and services. Furthermore, U.S. expenditures on hospital beds and other medical equipment rose at a rate of roughly 15 percent per year throughout much of the 1970s and 1980s.

When Gus Hillenbrand replaced his uncle as president and CEO of Hillenbrand Industries in 1989, he presided over the culmination of 83 years of immense growth and prosperity. His grandfather's fledgling casket business had grown into a national corporation with six separate operating companies and nearly 10,000 employees. Hillenbrand's 1989 net income topped $71 million, as revenues vaulted past $870 million, up an extraordinary 98 percent since 1985. Furthermore, the Hillenbrand umbrella could boast dominance of over 90 percent of the entire U.S. hospital bed market and over 30 percent of the total casket business.

In addition to its business accomplishments, the Hillenbrand organization had also achieved success in its local community. Aside from donating money for various recreational and educational facilities and contributing the lion's share of Batesville's operating budget, Hillenbrand prided itself on emphasizing employee satisfaction and personal development. Indeed, the Hillenbrand family was credited locally with having a direct and positive impact on the lives of the Batesville citizenry.

Hillenbrand in the 1990s

Motivated in part by the prophetic jest of his childhood—that the third generation destroys a company—Gus Hillenbrand entered the 1990s determined to quash that Germanic myth. To boost sales in its casket division, for example, Hillenbrand initiated an aggressive campaign in the early 1990s to expand into its first line of cremation products and services. It also strove to elevate its presence in the African-American and Hispanic burial market.

To jump-start shipments in the slowing hospital furniture market, Hill-Rom focused on the development of niche products. One of the company's most notable achievements in 1993 was its introduction of the first voice-activated control system for hospital beds. Using a new high-tech attachment, a quadriplegic patient, for example, could operate the bed, call a nurse, adjust a television or radio, make a telephone call, or activate a light switch. The system was designed to pick up sounds from only one direction, and could be trained to respond only to the patient's voice.

In 1991 Hillenbrand acquired Block Medical, Inc., of Carlsbad, California, a leading manufacturer of infusion pumps. Block introduced a portable home infusion pump and was experiencing significant productivity gains under Hillenbrand management.

Perhaps Gus Hillenbrand's greatest aspiration was the globalization of Hillenbrand Industries. To continue the 16 percent revenue growth rate that the company had averaged since 1972, he believed that Hillenbrand would have to expand its international presence. In 1991, Hill-Rom acquired French manufacturer Le Courviour S.A., a leading European supplier of hospital beds and furniture. In 1993 Batesville Casket Company acquired leading casket producers in both Canada and Mexico, strengthening its dominance of the North American market, and in 1994 Hill-Rom bought L. & C. Arnold S.G., a major German hospital manufacturer.

Although burgeoning domestic markets and proliferating global opportunities boded well for the company, a few impediments threatened to slow Hillenbrand's momentous growth. Federal proposals for government intervention in the U.S. healthcare system, for example, meant that technological advancements in the Hill-Rom and SSI subsidiaries might require more extensive government approval before healthcare providers could purchase their equipment. In addition, the entrance of Michigan-based Stryker Corp. into the hospital bed market posed a potential threat to Hill-Rom's command of that segment.

Hillenbrand jettisoned its lagging American Tourister division in 1993, while its Medeco lock company benefitted from renewed consumer spending and concerns about crime during that year. Late in 1993, Hill-Rom became the target of a federal antitrust probe. Noting its almost unequaled reputation for integrity, analysts suspected the charges were of little relevance.

Despite minor hindrances, Gus Hillenbrand's multifaceted growth strategy successfully guided the corporation through the perilous early 1990s. Indeed, Hillenbrand's unprecedented growth and profitability between 1989 and 1993 seemed almost staggering, particularly in light of a relentless world economic recession that lingered into 1993. Sales jumped an impressive 13 percent in 1990 and 10 percent in 1991, to $1.08 billion, and 1991 net income jumped 18 percent, to more than $89 million. In 1992, moreover, net income rocketed 30 percent as sales ballooned to more than $1.3 billion. Explosive growth continued in 1993, as sales jumped 11 percent to $1.45 billion and net income soared 25 percent to $146 million. About 40 percent of the company's revenues came from its funeral-related subsidiaries, while the other 60 percent were derived from healthcare divisions.

Sweeping Changes with the New Millennium

As Hillenbrand neared the end of the 20th century, maintaining its firm grip on its two primary markets proved to be a challenge. The company enjoyed a commanding market lead with both Batesville Casket and Hill-Rom, but it was buffeted by changes in the industries the two companies served. During the 1990s, the funeral service industry consolidated, giving increasing power and influence to two firms in particular, Service Corp. International and Loewen Group Inc. As the two companies grew into dominant players, large volume sales for Batesville Casket increased, but the considerable purchasing power wielded by Service Corp. and Loewen Group drove the price of coffins downward, forcing Hillenbrand to discount its prices. Further, with significantly fewer funeral operators buying its coffins, the Batesville Casket subsidiary was beset with an oversupply of certain models of coffins; those models not preferred by Service Corp. or Loewen Group became excess inventory stacked in the company's manufacturing facility. On the healthcare side of Hillenbrand's business, unwelcome change came in the form of the Federal Balanced Budget Act of 1997, which led to changes in Medicare payments. "It wreaked havoc and uncertainty on the budgets of hospitals and nursing homes," an analyst explained in an August 23, 2001 interview with *Investor's Business Daily*. Hillenbrand felt the blow delivered to both sides of its two main businesses, as sales began to stagnate by the end of the decade and, worse, earnings began to decline.

Hillenbrand responded to the changing dynamics of the funeral and healthcare industries by implementing its own sweeping changes. The first, and perhaps most profound, set of changes involved putting a new leader in charge of the company, including the first non-Hillenbrand to hold the titles of president and chief executive officer. Fredrick Rockwood, who joined the company in 1977 as director of corporate strategy and spearheaded the formation of the company's insurance subsidiary in the mid-1980s, was named president in 1999. When Gus Hillenbrand retired in late 2000, Rockwood added the title of chief executive officer, representing just one of a slew of leadership changes made at the time. In January 2001, Dan Hillenbrand retired, vacating his post as chairman and handing it to his nephew, Ray Hillenbrand. A new chief financial officer was appointed soon afterwards, as well as new department heads for each of the company's three operating companies, Batesville Casket, Rom-Hill, and Forethought, which had been renamed Forethought Financial Services, Inc. in 1997.

Under a new management team led by Rockwood, Hillenbrand reassessed its operations, making alterations to combat problems with profitability and stagnant sales. "The euphemism we use is 'weed and seed,' " the company's vice-president and treasurer explained in an August 23, 2001 interview with *Investor's Business Daily*. "We're weeding out those not producing the results we expect. The businesses that are producing results, we're seeding with additional investment to grow them faster." Rockwood pared back the company's selection of coffins, reducing the company's product line by 20 percent, and, with fewer products to manage, was able to improve manufacturing and distribution efficiency. Hill-Rom's operations underwent a product-by-product review as well, leading to the closure of its home-care and long-term-care rental bed business in January 2001, the closure of certain facilities, and a reduction in payroll of 400 workers.

In the wake of the reductions, Hillenbrand began to build its business strategically, "seeding" after the "weeding" had been completed. By 2003, annual sales had remained flat for five years, hovering below $2 billion. To invigorate revenue growth, the company looked to the medical care side of its business, deciding that the best opportunities for future growth were to be offered to Hill-Rom. Toward this end, the company struck out on the acquisition trail, completing a series of deals that extended the reach of Hill-Rom in the medical equipment market. In February 2003, Hillenbrand acquired St. Paul, Minnesota-based NaviCare Systems Inc., a healthcare management firm. Another St. Paul company joined the fold in September 2003, when a home-therapy equipment provider, Advance Respiratory Inc., was purchased. In November 2003, the company announced an agreement to acquire Pennsauken, New Jersey-based Mediq Inc., which provided outsourcing services to nearly 80 percent of acute-care hospitals in the nation. Mediq, which generated $166 million in annual sales, offered a line of portable medical equipment, selling and renting infusion pumps, ventilators, incubators, and oxygen regulators.

After building up its healthcare business, Hillenbrand was leaner and more profitable. In 2004, the company decided to sell its Forethought Financial Services business, divesting a substantial portion of its business to sharpen its focus on the funeral services and healthcare markets. The company completed the sale in July, when FFS Holdings, Inc. acquired Forethought Financial Services. As the company plotted its future course, it intended to pursue growth opportunities primarily on the healthcare side of its business. The company's dominance in the casket business offered little opportunity for growth. Hillenbrand's centennial celebrations promised to coincide with the appointment of a non-Hillenbrand as chairman. In late 2005, Ray Hillenbrand announced his plans to retire in 2006, paving the way for Rolf A. Classon, who succeeded Rockwood as president and chief executive officer, to become the company's chairman. To Classon and the senior managers beneath him fell the responsibility of ensuring Hillenbrand's legacy of success continued into the company's second century of business.

Principal Subsidiaries

Batesville Services, Inc.; Hill-Rom, Inc.; Hillenbrand Properties, Inc.; Travel Services, Inc.; Memory Showcase, Inc.; Sleep Options, Inc.; The Acorn Development Group, Inc.; Hill-Rom International Inc.; Batesville Casket de Mexico, S.A. de C.V.

Principal Operating Units

Batesville Casket Company, Inc.; Hill-Rom Company, Inc.

Principal Competitors

Matthews International Corporation; Medline Industries, Inc.; Stryker Corporation.

Further Reading

Boyer, Mike, "Hillenbrand Plans to Sell American Tourister," *Cincinnati Enquirer,* August 4, 1993.

Elliot, Alan R., "Hillenbrand Industries Inc.," *Investor's Business Daily,* August 23, 2001, p. A10.

Evanoff, Ted, "Batesville, Ind.-Based Manufacturer's Stock Rises on Possible Subsidiary Sale," *Indianapolis Star,* February 14, 2004.

Faris, Charlene, "Batesville Casket Co.: The Nation's Largest Casket Manufacturer," *Indiana Business,* April 1993.

Head, Lauren Lawley, "Rockwood to Take Top Spot at Hillenbrand," *Business Courier Serving Cincinnati—Northern Kentucky,* October 13, 2000, p. 4.

"Hillenbrand Agrees to Acquire Mediq for $330 Million," *Indianapolis Business Journal,* November 3, 2003, p. 36.

"Hillenbrand Hospital-Bed Unit, German Company Link," *Indianapolis Business Journal,* June 28, 1993.

Larking, Patrick, "Analysts Downplay Inquiry of Hill-Rom Co.," *Cincinnati Post,* October 19, 1993.

Lubove, Seth, "Dancing on Graves," *Forbes,* February 28, 1994, p. 64.

Lundegaard, Karen M., "At Home with Hillenbrand," *Cincinnati Business Courier,* June 28, 1993.

Pletz, John, "Hillenbrand Puts Unusual Twist on S&L," *Indianapolis Business Journal,* June 15, 1998, p. 3.

Song, Kyung M., "Indiana Hospital-Bed Maker Is Target of Probe," *Louisville Courier-Journal,* October 20, 1993.

Tortora, Andrea, "Hillenbrand Hunting Buys," *Business Courier Serving Cincinnati—Northern Kentucky,* November 9, 2001, p. 3.

—Dave Mote
—update: Jeffrey L. Covell

Hungarian Telephone and Cable Corp.

<table>
<tr><td>

1201 Third Avenue, Suite 3400
Seattle, Washington 98101
U.S.A.
Telephone: (206) 654-0204
Fax: (206) 652-2911
Web site: http://www.htcc.hu

Public Company
Incorporated: 1992
Employees: 900
Sales: $60.3 million (2004)
Stock Exchanges: American
Ticker Symbol: HTC
NAIC: 517110 Wired Telecommunications Carriers;
    518110 Internet Service Providers and Web Search
    Portals

</td></tr>
</table>

Hungarian Telephone and Cable Corp. (HTCC) is a holding company for subsidiaries involved in providing local and long-distance telephone service and Internet access to businesses and residences principally in Hungary. Through Hungarotel Tavkozlesi Rt., HTCC provides local and long-distance telephone service to a population base of 668,000 in the regions of Bekes, Nograd, and Papa/Sarvar. Hungarotel also offers broadband and dial-up Internet access under the name "Globonet." The company's other primary operating subsidiary is PanTel Tavkozlesi Rt., which provides voice, data, and Internet services to businesses throughout Hungary. PanTel's network, through a combination of owned and leased capacity, extends beyond Hungary's borders into Austria, Bulgaria, Croatia, the Czech Republic, Romania, Slovakia, Slovenia, and Ukraine. A third, smaller subsidiary, PanTel TechnoCom, provides telecommunications services to the Budapest-based oil firm Mol Magyar Olaj-es Gazipari Rt., the country's largest company. HTTC is majority owned by the Danish telecommunications company TDC A/S.

Origins

HTCC was created to seize a business opportunity created by the collapse of a centrally planned economy in Hungary.

Shortly after World War II, the Hungarian communist party, with Soviet support, established a communist dictatorship patterned after the Soviet model, setting in place one-party rule, land collectivization, and the nationalization of banks, industrial concerns, utilities, and scores of private firms. The country joined the Council for Mutual Economic Assistance, a Soviet-bloc economic organization, in 1949 and for the next four decades adhered to the precepts of Soviet-style communist rule, including the nationalization of any private industrial firm with more than ten employees. When the Eastern European bloc severed its ties to the Soviet Union between the late 1980s and early 1990s, Hungary led the way, becoming the first satellite nation to transition to Western-style parliamentary democracy and a free market economy. Hungary also enjoyed what was considered to be the smoothest transition of all the Soviet-bloc countries, easing relatively trouble free into a private-enterprise-based economy that attracted the likes of HTCC and other firms seeking to take part in the country's large-scale privatization effort.

Beginning in 1988, Hungary began establishing the foundation for a market economy, a process that, in part, involved dismantling government-owned and -operated monopolies and allowing the private sector to step in and take control. In the telecommunications sector, Magyar Tavkozlesi Rt. (Matav) ruled supreme during the communist era, operating as a government-controlled monopoly in charge of the country's entire telecommunications system. In 1992, the Hungarian government began the process of privatizing the country's telecommunications industry by selling a 30 percent stake in Matav to MagyarCom, a company owned at the time by Deutsche Telekom AG, a German public telephone company, and Ameritech, a U.S. based telecommunications company. Over the course of the ensuing decade, Matav's ownership changed. In 1995, MagyarCom increased its stake in Matav to 67 percent. In 1997, Matav completed its initial public offering of stock, which reduced the interests held by MagyarCom and the Hungarian government to 60 percent and 6 percent, respectively. In 1999, the Hungarian government sold its 6 percent stake. In 2000, Deutsche Telekom purchased the stake in MagyarCom owned by Ameritech's successor, SBC Communications Inc., which left MagyarCom, a German-controlled company, in majority control of Matav.

Company Perspectives:

With competition fully in place in Hungary, the Company faces new opportunities and challenges. The Company's goal is to provide the broadest array of telecommunications services with exceptional quality and service at reasonable prices by becoming the most efficient full service telecommunications provider in Central and Eastern Europe.

The initial 30 percent stake sold in 1992 to MagyarCom coincided with two other events, one that reshaped Hungary's telecommunications landscape and the other, the formation of HTTC. The Hungarian government divided the country into 54 telecommunications service areas, thereby creating a way to sell the rights, the concessions, to private interests and remove the service areas from Matav's network of local, wireline telephone service. Matav was allowed to continue its monopoly in providing domestic and international long-distance services for another decade and it would continue to own the concessions to local wireline service in some areas, but the privatization of the company and the division of the country into telecommunication fiefdoms made room for other interested parties to enter Hungary's telecommunications industry. HTCC was one of the interested parties that joined the fray, a company formed in March 1992 to acquire concession rights to operate as a local, wireline operator. Although it intended to operate only in Hungary, the company established its headquarters in the United States, occupying offices in New Jersey and Connecticut before moving to its main offices in Seattle, Washington. The company's business was conducted through a Budapest-based company, Hungarotel Tavkozlesi Rt., HTCC's primary operating subsidiary.

The process of determining whom Hungary's new local telephone operators (LTOs) were going to be began in 1993. The Hungarian government started soliciting bids for concessions to build, own, and operate telecommunication networks in 25 of the 54 service areas not controlled by Matav. The government awarded 23 of the 25 concessions, allowing Matav to retain the rights to the two service areas for which there were no successful bidders. The winning bidders represented the new face of Hungary's telecommunications industry, the companies against whom HTCC would compete in the coming years. HTCC acquired the concession rights to five service areas. Matav acquired the rights to eight service areas. Monor Communications Group, part of Denver, Colorado-based UnitedGlobalCom, Inc., acquired rights to one service area. A joint venture company, Invitel Telecommunications Services Rt., controlled by AIG Emerging Europe Infrastructure Fund and GMT Communications Partners Limited, acquired the rights to nine service areas.

Mid-1990s: HTCC Building Its Backbone

For HTCC, one year old when it received the nod of approval from the Hungarian government, winning the bid did not mean the company could immediately enjoy a revenue stream to offset its operating costs. HTCC began as a development-stage enterprise, a status that would continue for three years after its formation. The years were spent raising debt and equity

financing, assembling its management team, and obtaining the all-important concession rights. The company paid $11.5 million for the rights to its five service areas, a territory of operation comprising three regions: Bekes, Nograd, and Papa/Sarvar. Of the three regions, Bekes was the largest in terms of population, home to 391,700 of the company's total population base of 668,000. Nograd was slightly larger than Papa/Sarvar, with the two regions claiming 147,900 and 128,400 residents, respectively. For the money paid for its concession rights, HTCC received a 25-year license to provide local, wireline telephone service to its service areas and an agreement to have exclusive rights to its service areas for a decade, the same terms accorded to Monor, Invitel, and Matav. To become a fully operational company, HTCC needed the infrastructure to put its concessions to use. In the first fiscal quarter of 1995, the company acquired 15,500 telephone access lines from the Hungarian government, the first phase of an acquisition program that saw HTCC pay $23.2 million between 1995 and 1996 for existing telecommunications infrastructure, which included 61,400 access lines. The initial acquisition enabled the company to generate revenue for the first time in 1995, a year in which revenues reached $4 million. The acquisition of additional access lines in 1996 increased revenues to $20.6 million, but the end of HTCC's development-stage period of existence did not confer profitability to the company. HTCC lost $20 million in 1995 and $54.7 million in 1996, which, when added to the losses incurred during the company's developmental stage, brought total losses to more than $80 million.

Although the acquisition of access lines and infrastructure assets from the Hungarian government put HTCC in business, much remained to be accomplished before the company could take full advantage of its service areas and turn its losses into profits. The infrastructure acquired in 1995 and 1996 needed to be upgraded, requiring millions of dollars to replace antiquated manual exchanges and analog lines, and the telecommunications network needed to be expanded to serve all the residences and businesses in the company's operating areas. Between 1996 and 2000, HTCC's capital expenditures totaled $190 million, contributing to a net loss of $36 million in 1997 and $50 million in 1998, but by the end of the period the bulk of the improvement and expansion effort was completed. By the end of 2000, the company had the capacity to provide basic telephone service to all of the 283,300 homes and 38,400 businesses in its three operating areas, fueling hopes for a more profitable future.

HTCC began to perform encouragingly well during the first years of the 21st century, enjoying financial success for the first time, which gave it the ability to expand the scope of its business. After recording its first annual profit in 1999, a $3.1 million gain, the company lost $5.3 million in 2000, but went on to post a profit for four consecutive years. HTCC reported net income of $11.1 million in 2001, $27.3 million in 2002, $12.4 million in 2003, and $16.2 million in 2004. Revenues during the period increased from $42.9 million in 2000 to $60.3 million in 2004, supporting the feeling that the company, after years of investment, had established a stable business foundation. Against the backdrop of improved financial results, the first half of the decade included several significant events. In 2002, the company's exclusive operating rights to its service areas expired, but the year also marked the end of Matav's absolute control over providing long-distance service, which opened a

Key Dates:

1992: Hungarian Telephone and Cable Corp. (HTCC) is formed to take part in the privatization of Hungary's telecommunications industry.
1993: HTCC acquires the rights to operate in five service areas.
1995: HTCC begins providing local telephone service.
2000: All major expansion and improvement work on the company's infrastructure is completed.
2005: PanTel is acquired.

new avenue of growth for HTCC. The period's most noteworthy event occurred on the acquisition front, when a new addition to HTCC's holdings substantially strengthened the company's role in Hungary's telecommunications industry.

Acquisition of PanTel in 2005

In 2004, HTCC took the first step toward adding a new operating subsidiary. In November, the company acquired a 25 percent stake in PanTel Tavkozlesi Kft., a company founded in 1998 by the Hungarian state railroad company to compete with Matav. Using the railroad company's rights-of-way, PanTel built a fiber-optic telecommunications network spanning 3,700 kilometers that was capable of carrying voice and data traffic, as well as voice and data over Internet Protocol. PanTel, unlike Hungarotel, served the entire country, including Budapest, where nearly one-fifth of the country's population resided. Further, once Matav's monopoly rights for long distance voice services expired in 2002, PanTel began serving customers in neighboring countries, including Austria, Bulgaria, Croatia, the Czech Republic, Romania, Slovakia, Slovenia, and Ukraine. PanTel offered its telecommunications services to business customers, and through PanTel TechnoCom, provided service to the Hungarian oil company Mol Magyar Olaj-es Gazipari Rt. In February 2005, HTCC completed the acquisition of PanTel, acquiring the 75 percent of the company it did not already own from the Dutch telecommunications company Royal KPN NV. The acquisition represented a major addition to HTCC's operations, combining PanTel's $128 million in revenues to HTCC's $60 million in revenues and giving the company national and international exposure to the telecommunications market.

In the wake of the acquisition, HTCC stood poised to play a more prominent role in Hungary's telecommunications industry. Belief in the company's potential increased, particularly in the minds of executives at the Danish telecommunications giant TDC A/S, formerly known as Tele Danmark. TDC had been an early investor in HTCC, increasing its stake in the company to 21.3 percent by 2000 before taking a 63 percent interest in March 2005. Executives at TDC were convinced HTCC had the potential to become a legitimate competitor to Deutsche Telekom's Matav, a belief that pitted a Danish company against a German company for control of Hungarian telecommunications services. In mid-2005, once under Danish control, HTCC began integrating Hungarotel, PanTel, and PanTel TechnoCom into a single company to be housed in the same offices and managed by the same executive team. The process was expected to be completed by the end of 2006. As the company prepared to increase its stature and wage a more competitive battle against Matav, there was much ground to be gained. Matav, with annual revenues eclipsing $3 billion, boasted local wireline service areas covering 72 percent of Hungary's population and 70 percent of its geographic area. HTCC could not expect to overtake its much larger rival in the near future, but the TDC-controlled company was intent on narrowing the gap separating the two telecommunications providers.

Principal Subsidiaries

Hungarotel Tavkozlesi Rt.; PanTel Tavkozlesi Rt.; PanTel TechnoCom Rt.

Principal Competitors

Magyar Telekom Telecommunications Company Ltd.; BT Group PLC; Deutsche Telekom AG.

Further Reading

"HTCC Continues Integration of Pantel and Hungarotel," *Europe Intelligence Wire,* September 2, 2005.
"HTCC Puts One Management Team in Charge of All Units," *Europe Intelligence Wire,* June 9, 2005.
"Hungarian Telephone and Cable Revamps with New Management Team," *Wireless News,* June 9, 2005.
Smyth, Robert, "Bolstered by PanTel Buy, HTCC Readies to Rival Matav," *Europe Intelligence Wire,* May 24, 2004.
——, "HTCC Integrates Operations to Challenge for Telecom Top Spot," *Europe Intelligence Wire,* June 13, 2005.
"TDC Acquires Majority Stake in HTCC," *Europe Intelligence Wire,* March 30, 2005.
"TDC Plans to Turn HTCC into No. 2 Fixed-Line Company in Hungary," *Europe Intelligence Wire,* September 21, 2004.

—Jeffrey L. Covell

intel ®

Intel Corporation

2200 Mission College Boulevard
Santa Clara, California 95052-8119
U.S.A.
Telephone: (408) 765-8080
Toll Free: (800) 628-8686
Fax: (408) 765-9904
Web site: http://www.intel.com

Public Company
Incorporated: 1968 as N M Electronics
Employees: 70,200
Sales: $34.21 billion (2004)
Stock Exchanges: NASDAQ
Ticker Symbol: INTC
NAIC: 334413 Semiconductor and Related Device
   Manufacturing; 334210 Telephone Apparatus
   Manufacturing

Intel Corporation is the largest semiconductor manufacturer in the world, with 11 fabrication facilities and six assembly and test facilities around the world. Intel has changed the global marketplace dramatically since it was founded in 1968; the company invented the microprocessor, the ''computer on a chip'' that made possible the first handheld calculators and personal computers (PCs). By the early 21st century, Intel's microprocessors were found in approximately 80 percent of PCs worldwide. The company's product line also includes chipsets and motherboards; flash memory used in wireless communications and other applications; networking devices and equipment for accessing the Internet, local area networks, and home networks; and embedded control microchips used in networking products, laser printers, factory automation instruments, cellular phone base stations, and other applications. Intel has remained competitive through a combination of clever marketing, well-supported research and development, superior manufacturing proficiency, a vital corporate culture, prowess in legal matters, and an ongoing alliance with software giant Microsoft Corporation often referred to as ''Wintel.''

1968–79: From DRAM to the 8086

Intel's founders, Robert Noyce and Gordon Moore, were among the eight founders of Fairchild Semiconductor Corporation, established in 1957. While at Fairchild, Noyce and Moore invented the integrated circuit; in 1968, they decided to form their own company. They were soon joined by Andrew Grove, a Hungarian refugee who had arrived in the United States in 1956 and joined Fairchild in 1963. Grove would remain president and CEO of Intel into the 1990s.

To obtain start-up capital, Noyce and Moore approached Arthur Rock, a venture capitalist, with a one-page business plan simply stating their intention of developing large-scale integrated circuits. Rock, who had helped start Fairchild Semiconductor, as well as Teledyne and Scientific Data Systems, had confidence in Noyce and Moore and provided $3 million in capital. The company was incorporated on July 18, 1968, as N M Electronics (the letters standing for Noyce Moore), but quickly changed its name to Intel, formed from the first syllables of ''integrated electronics.'' Intel gathered another $2 million in capital before going public in 1971.

Noyce and Moore's scanty business proposal belied a clear plan to produce large-scale integrated (LSI) semiconductor memories. At that time, semiconductor memories were ten times more expensive than standard magnetic core memories. Costs were falling, however, and Intel's founders surmised that with the greater speed and efficiency of LSI technology, semiconductors would soon replace magnetic cores. Within a few months of its startup, Intel produced the 3101 Schottky bipolar memory, a high-speed random access memory (RAM) chip. The 3101 proved popular enough to sustain the company until the 1101, a metal oxide semiconductor (MOS) chip, was perfected and introduced in 1969. The following year, Intel introduced the 1103, a 1-kilobyte (K) dynamic RAM, or DRAM, which was the first chip large enough to store a significant amount of information. With the 1103, Intel finally had a chip that really did begin to replace magnetic cores; DRAMs eventually proved indispensable to the personal computer.

The company's most dramatic impact on the computer industry involved its 1971 introduction of the 4004, the world's

196

Company Perspectives:

For over 35 years, Intel Corporation has developed technology enabling the computer and Internet revolution that has changed the world. Founded in 1968 to build semiconductor memory products, Intel introduced the world's first microprocessor in 1971. Today, Intel supplies the computing and communications industries with chips, boards, systems, and software building blocks that are the "ingredients" of computers, servers and networking and communications products. These products are used by industry members to create advanced computing and communications systems. Intel's mission is to do a great job for our customers, employees, and stockholders by being the preeminent building block supplier to the worldwide digital economy.

first microprocessor. Like many of Intel's innovations, the microprocessor was a byproduct of efforts to develop another technology. When a Japanese calculator manufacturer, Busicom, asked Intel to design cost-effective chips for a series of calculators, Intel engineer Ted Hoff was assigned to the project; during his search for such a design, Hoff conceived a plan for a central processing unit (CPU) on one chip. The 4004, which crammed 2,300 transistors onto a one-eighth- by one-sixth-inch chip, had the power of the old 3,000-cubic-foot ENIAC computer, which depended on 38,000 vacuum tubes.

Although Intel initially focused on the microprocessor as a computer enhancement that would allow users to add more memory to their units, the microprocessor's great potential—for everything from calculators to cash registers and traffic lights—soon became clear. The applications were facilitated by Intel's introduction of the 8008, an 8-bit microprocessor developed along with the 4004 but oriented toward data and character (rather than arithmetic) manipulation. The 8080, introduced in 1974, was the first truly general purpose microprocessor. For $360, Intel sold a whole computer on one chip, while conventional computers sold for thousands of dollars. The response was overwhelming. The 8080 soon became the industry standard and Intel the industry leader in the 8-bit market.

In response to ensuing competition in the manufacture of 8-bit microprocessors, Intel introduced the 8085, a faster chip with more functions. The company was also developing two more advanced projects, the 32-bit 432 and the 16-bit 8086. The 8086 was introduced in 1978 but took two years to achieve wide use and, during this time, Motorola, Inc. produced a competing chip (the 68000) that seemed to be selling faster. Intel responded with a massive sales effort to establish its architecture as the standard. When International Business Machines Corporation (IBM) chose the 8008, the 8086's 8-bit cousin, for its personal computer in 1980, Intel seemed to have beat out the competition.

During the 1970s, Intel had also developed the erasable programmable read-only memory (EPROM), another revolutionary but unintended research byproduct. Intel physicist Dov Frohman was working on the reliability problems of the silicon gate used in the MOS process when he realized that the discon-

nected, or "floating," gates that were causing malfunctions could be used to create a chip that was erasable and reprogrammable. Since conventional ROM chips had to be permanently programmed during manufacture, any change required the manufacture of a whole new chip. With EPROM, however, Intel could offer customers chips that could be erased and reprogrammed with ultraviolet light and electricity. At its introduction in 1971, EPROM was a novelty without much of a market. But the microprocessor, invented at the same time, created a demand for memory; the EPROM offered memory that could be conveniently used to test microprocessors.

Another major development at Intel during this time was that of peripheral controller chips. Streamlined for specific tasks and stripped of unneeded functions, peripheral chips could greatly increase a computer's abilities without raising software development costs. One of Intel's most important developments in peripherals was the coprocessor, first introduced in 1980. Coprocessor chips were an extension of the CPU that could handle specific computer-intensive tasks more efficiently than the CPU itself. Once again, innovation kept Intel ahead of its competition.

Intel's rapid growth, from the 12 employees at its founding in 1968 to 15,000 in 1980, demanded a careful approach to corporate culture. Noyce, Moore, and Grove, who remembered their frustration with Fairchild's bureaucratic bottlenecks, found that defining a workable management style was important. Informal weekly lunches with employees kept communication lines open while the company was small, but that system had become unwieldy. Thus, the founders installed a carefully outlined program emphasizing openness, decision-making on the lowest levels, discipline, and problem solving rather than paper shuffling. Moreover, the company's top executives eschewed such luxuries as limousines, expense account lunches, and private parking spaces to establish a sense of teamwork with their subordinates.

In an interview with the *Harvard Business Review* in 1980, Noyce remarked on the company's hiring policy, stating, "we expect people to work hard. We expect them to be here when they are committed to be here; we measure absolutely everything that we can in terms of performance." Employee incentives included options on Intel stock, and technological breakthroughs were celebrated with custom-bottled champagne—"Vintage Intel" marked the first $250 million quarter, in 1983—the year sales reached $1 billion for the first time.

1980s: From 286 to 486

During the 1974 recession, Intel was forced to lay off 30 percent of its employees, and morale declined substantially as a result. Thus, in 1981, when economic struggles again surfaced, instead of laying off more employees, Intel accelerated new product development with the "125 Percent Solution," which asked exempt employees to work two extra hours per day, without pay, for six months. A brief surge in sales the following year did not last, and, again, instead of more layoffs, Intel imposed pay cuts of up to 10 percent. Such measures were not popular among all its workforce, but, by June 1983, all cuts had been restored and retroactive raises had been made. Moreover, in December 1982, IBM paid $250 million for a 12 percent

Key Dates:

1968: Robert Noyce and Gordon Moore incorporate N M Electronics, which is soon renamed Intel Corporation.
1970: Company develops DRAM, dynamic RAM.
1971: Intel introduces the world's first microprocessor (the 4004) and goes public.
1974: Company introduces the first general purpose microprocessor (the 8080).
1980: IBM chooses the Intel microprocessor for the first personal computer.
1983: Revenues exceed $1 billion for the first time.
1992: Net income tops $1 billion for the first time.
1993: The fifth generation chip, the Pentium, debuts.
1996: Revenues surpass $20 billion, net income exceeds $5 billion.
1997: Company introduces the Pentium II microprocessor.
1999: Intel debuts the Pentium III and is added to the Dow Jones Industrial Average.
2000: The Pentium 4 hits the market.
2003: The Centrino technology for mobile computers is launched.

share of Intel, giving the company not only a strong capital boost, but also strong ties to the undisputed industry leader. IBM would eventually increase its stake to 20 percent before selling its Intel stock in 1987.

During the early 1980s, Intel began to slip in some of its markets. Fierce competition in DRAMs, static RAMs, and EPROMs left Intel concentrating on microprocessors. While competitors claimed that Intel simply gave away its DRAM market, Moore told *Business Week* in 1988 that the company deliberately focused on microprocessors as the least cyclical field in which to operate. Customer service, an area Intel had been able to overlook for years as it dominated its markets, became more important as highly efficient Japanese and other increasingly innovative competitors challenged Intel's position. In addition, Intel's manufacturing record, strained in years past by undercapacity, needed fixing. Fab 7, Intel's seventh wafer-fabrication plant, opened in 1983 only to face two years of troubled operations before reaching full capacity. Between 1984 and 1988, Intel closed eight old plants, and in 1988 it spent some $450 million on new technology to bring its manufacturing capacity into line with its developmental prowess.

Despite these retrenchments, the company continued to excel in the microprocessor market. In 1982 Intel introduced its 80286 microprocessor, the chip that quickly came to dominate the upper-end PC market, when IBM came out with the 286-powered PC/AT. The 286 was followed in 1985 by Intel's 80386 chip, popularized in 1987 by the Compaq DESKPRO 386, and which, despite bugs when it first came out, became one of the most popular chips on the market. While the 286 brought to the personal computer a speed and power that gave larger computers their first real challenge, the 386 offered even greater speed and power together with the ability to run more than one program at a time. The 386 featured 32-bit architecture and 275,000 transistors, more than twice the number of the 286.

In 1989 Intel introduced the 80486, a chip *Business Week* heralded as "a veritable mainframe-on-a-chip." The 486 included 1.2 million transistors and the first built-in math coprocessor, and was 50 times faster than the 4004, the first microprocessor. In designing the i486, Intel resisted an industry trend toward RISC (reduced instruction-set computing), a chip design that eliminated rarely used instructions in order to gain speed. Intel argued that what RISC chips gained in speed they lost in flexibility and that, moreover, RISC chips were not compatible with software already on the market, which Intel felt would secure the 486's position. A new chip, the 64-bit i860 announced in early 1989, however, did make use of RISC technology to offer what Intel claimed would be a "supercomputer on a chip."

Also in 1989, a major lawsuit that Intel had filed against NEC Corporation five years before was decided. Intel had claimed that NEC violated its copyright on the microcode, or embedded software instructions, of Intel's 8086 and 8088 chips. Although Intel had licensed NEC to produce the microcode, NEC had subsequently designed a similar chip of its own. At issue was whether microcode could be copyrighted. The court ruled that it could but that NEC had not violated any copyright in the case at hand. The suit made public some issues surrounding Intel's reputation. Some rivals and consumers, for example, claimed that Intel used its size and power to repress competition through such tactics as filing "meritless" lawsuits and tying microprocessor sales to other chips. Other observers, however, praised Intel's protection of its intellectual property and, subsequently, its profits. The Federal Trade Commission conducted a two-year investigation of Intel's practices and did not recommend criminal charges against the company, but two rival companies, Advanced Micro Devices, Inc. (AMD) and Cyrix Corporation, filed antitrust lawsuits against Intel in 1993.

1990s: The Pentium Decade

Intel's annual net income topped $1 billion for the first time in 1992, following a very successful, brand-building marketing campaign. Intel ads aggressively sought to bolster consumer interest in and demand for computers that featured "Intel Inside." By late 1993, the company's brand equity totaled $17.8 billion, more than three times its 1992 sales. Also during this time, Intel began to branch out from chipmaking. In 1992 the company's Intel Products Group introduced network, communications, and personal conferencing products for retail sale directly to PC users.

In 1993 Intel released its fifth-generation Pentium processor, a trademarked chip capable of executing over 100 million instructions per second (MIPS) and supporting, for example, real-time video communication. The Pentium processor, with its 3.1 million transistors, was up to five times more powerful than the 33-megahertz Intel 486 DX microprocessor (and 1,500 times the speed of the 4004), but, in an unusual marketing maneuver, the company suggested that "all but the most demanding users" would seek out PCs powered by the previous chip. The Pentium's reputation was initially sullied by the revelation of an embedded mathematical flaw, but Intel moved quickly to fix the problem.

The company enjoyed a dramatic 50 percent revenue increase in 1993, reaching $8.78 billion from $5.84 billion in

1992. Moreover, Intel's net income leapt 115 percent to $2.3 billion, repudiating Wall Street's worries that competition had squeezed profit margins. While Intel faced strong competition both from chip makers such as Motorola's PowerPC and former partner IBM, its place at the leading edge of technology was undisputed.

A key initiative that kept Intel ahead of its competitors was the company's move beyond chip design into computer design. With the advent of the Pentium, Intel began designing chipsets and motherboards, the latter being the PC circuit board that combined a microprocessor and a chipset into the basic subsystem of a PC. With the company now selling the guts of a PC, dozens of computer manufacturers began making and selling Pentium-based machines.

In the mid-1990s, as sales of PCs accelerated and multimedia and the Internet were beginning to emerge, Intel continued developing ever more powerful microprocessors. In 1995 the Pentium Pro hit the market sporting 5.5 million transistors and capable of performing up to 300 MIPS. Intel next added MMX technology to its existing line of Pentium processors. MMX consisted of a new set of instructions that was designed specifically to improve the multimedia performance of personal computers. Fueled by exploding demand, revenues hit $20.85 billion by 1996, while net income soared to $5.16 billion.

At this point Intel was continuing its longtime strategy of designing new, more powerful chips for the top end of the market while allowing previous-generation microprocessors to migrate down to the lower segments of the market. With the introduction of the Pentium II in May 1997, however, the company adopted a new strategy of developing a range of microprocessors for every segment of the computing market. The Pentium II, with 7.5 transistors, debuted with a top-end model that clocked at 300 megahertz. Originally designed for high-end desktop PCs, the Pentium II was soon adapted for use in notebook and laptop computers. With the following year came the launch of the Celeron processor, which was designed specifically for the value PC desktop sector, a rapidly growing segment of the market ever since the early 1997 debut of a sub-$1,000 PC from Compaq. Also in 1998 Intel for the first time designed a microprocessor, the Pentium II Xeon, especially for midrange and higher-end servers and workstations. At the same time Intel was moving into another burgeoning sector, that of embedded control chips for networking and other applications, such as digital set-top boxes.

Meanwhile Intel settled a dispute with Digital Equipment Corporation (DEC) over the development of the Pentium chip by acquiring DEC's semiconductor operations. In May 1997 Craig R. Barrett was named president of Intel, having joined the company in 1974, serving as head of manufacturing starting in 1985, and being named chief operating officer in 1993. Grove remained chairman and CEO for one year, whereupon Barrett was named president and CEO, with Grove retaining the chairmanship. In early 1999 Intel reached a settlement with the Federal Trade Commission on an antitrust suit, thereby avoiding the protracted litigation and negative publicity that beset its Wintel partner, Microsoft, in the late 1990s. Reflecting the increasing importance of technology to the U.S. economy, Intel was added to the Dow Jones Industrial Average in November 1999.

During the late 1990s Intel made several strategic acquisitions that rapidly gave the company a significant presence in areas outside its microprocessor core: wireless communications products, such as flash memory for mobile phones and two-way pagers; networking building blocks, such as hubs, switches, and routers; and embedded control chips for laser printers, storage media, and automotive systems. Intel also entered the market for e-commerce services, rapidly building up the largest business-to-business e-commerce site in the world, with $1 billion per month in online sales by mid-1999. The company was not neglecting its core, however; in 1999 Intel had its largest microprocessor launch ever with the simultaneous introduction of 15 Pentium III and Pentium III Xeon processors.

New Strategies in the Less Buoyant Early 2000s

The new product launches continued in 2000, but they were accompanied by an uncharacteristic series of blunders. In February arch-rival AMD had bested Intel by releasing the first 1-gigahertz chip, the Athlon, which had the added benefit of being cheaper than the Pentium III. Intel responded by speeding a 1.13-gigahertz version of the Pentium III to market, but the processor simply did not work right and thousands had to be recalled. Further embarrassment came when the firm had to recall a million motherboards because of a faulty chip. Intel had also underestimated growth in PC sales, leaving its production capacity insufficient to meet the demands of computer makers, and it also cancelled plans to develop a low-end microprocessor called Timna that had been slated for budget PCs. Intel continued to encounter problems developing the complex Itanium 64-bit processor, the company's first, which was specifically designed, in partnership with Hewlett-Packard Company, to meet the needs of powerful Internet servers. The long-delayed Itanium, seven years in the making at a cost of $2 billion, finally reached the market in 2001, receiving a rather muted initial reception. (The Itanium line was later shifted from servers to high-end computers.) On the bright side, Intel successfully released the Pentium 4 in November 2000. This processor included 42 million transistors and ran at an initial speed of 1.5 gigahertz, enabling Intel to regain the lead in the ongoing chip-speed battle with AMD. Despite all of the year's travails, Intel reached new heights in financial performance, earning $10.54 billion in profits on revenues of $33.73 billion.

The bursting of the Internet bubble posed new challenges for Intel in 2001 as consumer spending on computers dropped off and corporate information technology managers pulled back as well. The fierce competition from AMD prompted Intel to initiate a brutal price war, which cut both revenues and profits, and it also slashed Intel's worldwide share of the microprocessor market to below 80 percent, compared to the 86.7 percent figure from 1998. In 2001 Barrett began jettisoning many of the new ventures and acquisitions that were part of the late 1990s diversification drive, in a renewed refocusing on microprocessors. Revenues for 2001 fell 21 percent to $26.54 billion—the first such drop since the mid-1980s tech recession—while profits plummeted 87 percent to $1.29 billion. Early the following year, Paul Otellini was named president and chief operating officer, with Barrett remaining CEO. Otellini had served in a variety of marketing and management positions since joining the company in 1974, most recently serving as head of Intel's core operating unit, the architecture group, which was responsible for developing microprocessors, chipsets, and motherboards for desktop and notebook computers and for servers.

As the technology downturn continued in 2002, Intel cut thousands of workers from its payroll to reduce costs. Behind the scenes, an important change occurred in the company's approach to designing chips. Since the 1980s Intel had maintained its leading position by creating ever-faster processors. But by the early 2000s speed was becoming less important to the majority of PC users, who were mainly employing their desktop PCs and laptops to surf the Internet and run basic programs, such as word processors. Intel decided to deemphasize speed in favor of designing chips to better fit the way people were actually using their computers and to do so using technology ''platforms,'' which were composed of several chips rather than a single microprocessor. The first fruit of this endeavor was Centrino, launched in early 2003. Centrino was a combination of chips specifically designed for portable computers. It included the Pentium M microprocessor, which while not sporting top speeds consumed much less power than the typical chip, providing for longer battery life (and reduced energy consumption when installed in desktop computers). The Pentium M was also smaller in size, making it less expensive to manufacture. Centrino also included a supporting chipset to further improve battery life and graphics performance as well as a wireless radio chip for connecting to the burgeoning number of wireless (Wi-Fi) networks being installed at corporate offices, in retail outlets, and within homes.

Buoyed by the success of Centrino, Intel's revenues hit a new high in 2004, $34.21 billion, despite a number of manufacturing glitches, product delays, and schedule changes during the year. Intel abandoned its efforts to develop television display chips and also scrapped plans to introduce the first 4-gigahertz processor because of problems with overheating. The profits of $7.52 billion were an impressive 33 percent higher than the previous year but below the peak reached in 2000.

In May 2005 Otellini became only the fifth CEO in Intel history and the first non-engineer. At the same time, Barrett succeeded Grove as chairman. One of the key legacies of Barrett's tenure was surely the huge outlay of capital, as much as $32 billion over six years, expended to rebuild Intel's manufacturing base and enabling the firm to increase capacity to meet chip demand and add capabilities to the products. At the same time, Otellini was credited with leading the push toward platforms, and this approach was institutionalized in a 2005 reorganization that divided the company into five market-focused groups: corporate computing, the digital home, mobile computing, healthcare, and channels (PCs for small manufacturers). Otellini was also shifting the product development effort toward so-called dual-core technology featuring two computing engines on a single piece of silicon. In this realm, Intel was competing fiercely with, and playing catchup to, AMD, which released its first dual-core chips for PCs in 2005, whereas Intel was aiming to produce three lines of dual-core processors, for notebooks, desktops, and servers, during the second half of 2006. Like the Centrino technology, dual-core chips were being developed to extend battery life in laptops and cut power costs for desktop PCs and servers. They were also intended to improve performance while avoiding the problems with overheat-

ing that had plagued some of the fastest single-processor models. Intel was simultaneously beginning work on multicore platforms with three or more ''brains.'' Two other developments from mid-2005 held potential long-term significance. AMD filed a wide-ranging antitrust suit in U.S. federal court accusing Intel of using illegal inducements and coercion to discourage computer makers from buying AMD's computer chips. This action followed an antitrust ruling against Intel in Japan, earlier in the year. In the meantime, in what seemed a significant coup, Intel reached an agreement with Apple Computer, Inc. whereby Apple would begin shifting its Macintosh computers from IBM's PowerPC chips to Intel chips.

Principal Subsidiaries

Components Intel de Costa Rica, S.A.; Intel Americas, Inc.; Intel Asia Finance Ltd. (Cayman Islands); Intel Capital Corporation (Cayman Islands); Intel Copenhagen ApS (Denmark); Intel Corporation (UK) Ltd.; Intel Electronics Finance Limited (Cayman Islands); Intel Electronics Ltd. (Israel); Intel Europe, Inc.; Intel International; Intel International B.V. (Netherlands); Intel Ireland Limited (Cayman Islands); Intel Israel (74) Limited; Intel Kabushiki Kaisha (Japan); Intel Malaysia Sdn. Berhad; Intel Massachusetts, Inc.; Intel Overseas G.C. Ltd. (Cayman Islands); Intel Overseas Funding Corporation (Cayman Islands); Intel Phils. Holding Corporation; Intel Products (M) Sdn. Bhd. (Malaysia); Intel Puerto Rico, Ltd. (Cayman Islands); Intel Semiconductor Limited; Intel Technology Finance Limited; Intel Technology Phils., Inc. (Philippines); Intel Technology Sdn. Berhad (Malaysia); Mission College Investments Ltd. (Cayman Islands).

Principal Operating Units

Mobility Group; Digital Enterprise Group; Digital Home Group; Digital Health Group; Channel Platforms Group.

Principal Competitors

Advanced Micro Devices, Inc.; Samsung Electronics Co., Ltd.; Texas Instruments Incorporated; International Business Machines Corporation; STMicroelectronics N.V.

Further Reading

Brandt, Richard, Otis Port, and Robert D. Hof, ''Intel: The Next Revolution,'' *Business Week,* September 26, 1988, p. 74.

Bylinsky, Gene, ''Intel's Biggest Shrinking Job Yet,'' *Fortune,* May 3, 1982, pp. 250+.

Clark, Don, ''AMD Files Broad Suit Against Intel,'' *Wall Street Journal,* June 28, 2005, p. A3.

——, ''Change of Pace: Big Bet Behind Intel Comeback; In Chips, Speed Isn't Everything,'' *Wall Street Journal,* November 18, 2003, p. A1.

——, ''Intel's New CEO Signals Shift for Chip Maker,'' *Wall Street Journal,* November 12, 2004, p. A6.

Clark, Don, and Gary McWilliams, ''Intel Bets Big on Wireless Chips,'' *Wall Street Journal,* January 9, 2003, p. A3.

Clark, Don, Nick Wingfield, and William M. Bulkeley, ''Apple Is Poised to Shift to Intel As Chip Supplier,'' *Wall Street Journal,* June 6, 2005, p. A1.

Clark, Tim, ''Inside Intel's Marketing Machine,'' *Business Marketing,* October 1992, pp. 14–19.

Corcoran, Elizabeth, "Reinventing Intel," *Forbes,* May 3, 1999, pp. 154–59.

Intel: 35 Years of Innovation, Santa Clara: Intel Corporation, 2003.

Edwards, Cliff, "Getting Intel Back on the Inside Track," *Business Week,* November 29, 2004, p. 39.

——, "Intel: What Is CEO Craig Barrett Up To?," *Business Week,* March 8, 2004, pp. 56–62, 64.

——, "Shaking Up Intel's Insides," *Business Week,* January 31, 2005, p. 35.

Edwards, Cliff, and Ira Sager, "Intel: Can CEO Craig Barrett Reverse the Slide?," *Business Week,* October 15, 2001, pp. 80–86, 88, 90.

Edwards, Cliff, and Olga Karif, "This Is Not the Intel We All Know," *Business Week,* August 16, 2004, p. 32.

Garland, Susan B., and Andy Reinhardt, "Making Antitrust Fit High Tech," *Business Week,* March 22, 1999, p. 34.

Gottlieb, Carrie, "Intel's Plan for Staying on Top," *Fortune,* March 27, 1989, pp. 98 + .

Grove, Andrew S., *Swimming Across: A Memoir,* New York: Warner, 2001, 290 p.

Heller, Robert, *Andrew Grove,* New York: Dorling Kindersley, 2001, 112 p.

Hof, Robert D., Larry Armstrong, and Gary McWilliams, "Intel Unbound," *Business Week,* October 9, 1995, pp. 148 + .

"Is the Semiconductor Boom Too Much of a Good Thing for Intel?," *Business Week,* April 23, 1984, pp. 114 + .

Jackson, Tim, *Inside Intel: Andy Grove and the Rise of the World's Most Powerful Chip Company,* New York: Dutton, 1997, 424 p.

Kirkpatrick, David, "Intel Goes for Broke," *Fortune,* May 16, 1994, pp. 62–66, 68.

——, "Intel's Amazing Profit Machine," *Fortune,* February 17, 1997, pp. 60 + .

——, "Mr. Grove Goes to China," *Fortune,* August 17, 1998, pp. 154–61.

Lashinsky, Adam, "Is This the Right Man for Intel?," *Fortune,* April 18, 2005, pp. 110–12 + .

Palmer, Jay, "Zero Hour," *Barron's,* October 4, 1999, pp. 33–34, 36.

Reinhardt, Andy, "Intel Inside Out: After a Year of Bloopers, Can the Chipmaker Get Its House in Order?," *Business Week,* December 4, 2000, pp. 116–17, 120.

——, "The New Intel: Craig Barrett Is Leading the Chip Giant into Riskier Terrain," *Business Week,* March 13, 2000, pp. 110 + .

——, "Who Says Intel's Chips Are Down?," *Business Week,* December 7, 1998, p. 103.

Reinhardt, Andy, Ira Sager, and Peter Burrows, "Intel: Can Andy Grove Keep Profits Up in an Era of Cheap PCs?," *Business Week,* December 22, 1997, pp. 71–74, 76–77.

A Revolution in Progress: A History of Intel to Date, Santa Clara, Calif.: Intel Corporation, 1984.

Ristelhueber, Robert, "Intel: The Company People Love to Hate," *Electronic Business Buyer,* September 1993, pp. 58–67.

Roth, Daniel, "Craig Barrett Inside," *Fortune,* December 18, 2000, pp. 246 + .

Schlender, Brent, "Intel's $10 Billion Gamble," *Fortune,* November 11, 2002, pp. 90–94, 98, 100, 102.

——, "Intel Unleashes Its Inner Attila," *Fortune,* October 15, 2001, pp. 168–70 + .

Wilson, John W., "Intel Wakes Up to a Whole New Marketplace in Chips," *Business Week,* September 2, 1985, pp. 73 + .

Yu, Albert, *Creating the Digital Future: The Secrets of Consistent Innovation at Intel,* New York: Free Press, 1998, 214 p.

—April Dougal Gasbarre
—update: David E. Salamie

[INTER PUBLIC GROUP]

The Interpublic Group of Companies, Inc.

1114 Avenue of the Americas
New York, New York 10036
U.S.A.
Telephone: (212) 704-1200
Fax: (212) 704-1201
Web site: http://www.interpublic.com

Public Company
Incorporated: 1961
Employees: 43,000
Gross Billings: $6.39 billion (2004)
Stock Exchanges: New York
Ticker Symbol: IPG
NAIC: 541810 Advertising Agencies

Once the world's largest advertising company, The Interpublic Group of Companies, Inc. fell on hard times in the early 2000s, dropping to third in worldwide standing behind rivals Omnicom Group and WPP Group. Set to rebound in 2006 and 2007, Interpublic through its numerous subsidiaries still ranks among the world's top advertising and marketing firms, with offices in 120 countries and employees numbering more than 43,000. Through its independently operating agencies, Interpublic provides advertising programs, direct marketing, market research, and other media services. Although Interpublic's advertising agencies compete against one another for clients, all benefit from the resources and connections of their parent company. With worldwide billings of $6.39 billion, Interpublic remains a force to be reckoned with in the advertising world.

In the Beginning: 1910s–60s

The history of Interpublic began 50 years before its incorporation in 1961. In 1911 the U.S. Supreme Court dismantled the Rockefeller Standard Oil Trust and divided it into 37 different companies. The largest of these was Standard Oil of New Jersey (now Exxon). Harrison McCann, who had been advertising manager at the Rockefeller Trust for a number of years, opened up his own ad agency and took on Jersey Standard as his first client. The age of the automobile was soon to come and with it

an increase in the demand for refined petroleum products. As the advertising man for the world's largest oil company, McCann was poised for success.

In 1930 McCann merged his agency with that of Alfred Erickson to form the McCann-Erickson Company. Despite the Depression and World War II, the newly conjoined firm managed to grow in billings and importance; by 1945 McCann-Erickson was doing close to $40 million in business, making it the fifth largest advertising firm in the United States.

Marion Harper began working at the McCann-Erickson agency in the 1930s as a clerk in the mailroom. After delivering the day's mail he would visit the research department and learn what he could. He proved a remarkable student; he was made manager of copy research at the age of 26 and then promoted to director of research at 30. Two years later, Harrison McCann promoted Harper again, this time to president of McCann-Erickson Advertising.

During Harper's rise from mail clerk to president, McCann-Erickson experienced the most lucrative decade of its history. In 1954 the agency surpassed $100 million in billings for the first time. Between 1955 and 1956 the agency added over $45 million worth of new business, including the Westinghouse appliance division, Chesterfield tobacco, and Mennen personal hygiene products. These accounts, however, were overshadowed by the fourth new customer gained by McCann at this time, Coca-Cola. Though Coke was a $15 million account in 1956, it was the soft drink company's potential for future growth that made it such an attractive customer. For McCann-Erickson, Coca-Cola was an investment in the coming era of "recreation and refreshment."

During this heady era, Harper, as chief executive officer and chairman of McCann-Erickson, began to implement his vision of fashioning an advertising company modeled after General Motors, a vigorous conglomerate consisting of equally vigorous but largely autonomous divisions. He arranged for McCann-Erickson to buy the Marshalk advertising firm of New York. The move was unprecedented because Harper declared that the two agencies (McCann-Erickson and Marshalk) would be operated as competing companies. Harper's intention was to avoid

202

Company Perspectives:

From McCann to Draft, from Jack Morton to R/GA, the companies of Interpublic add color to local and global brands and breathe life into their relationship with consumers. The work our agencies produce can move markets or change behavior; our agencies inform, entertain and ultimately make powerful connections on behalf of our clients.

the conflict of interest problem that plagued all agencies attempting to procure accounts from competing clients. He felt if Marshalk and McCann were run separately, a camera manufacturer looking to hire McCann would not care that Marshalk did the advertising for another camera manufacturer. Most people within the industry viewed the idea with skepticism, but Harper proved them wrong. Both agencies continued to grow while often servicing rival clients.

McCann-Erickson had also moved to establish itself in a variety of less conventional foreign advertising markets. Long the leading agency in Latin America and Europe, the company purchased the third largest ad firm in Australia and began to actively pursue business in Asia. By 1960 McCann-Erickson had billings of $100 million outside the United States, with a substantial portion coming from the Asia-Pacific area.

The Formation of Interpublic: 1960s–70s

In January 1961 Interpublic was established as a holding company with McCann-Erickson becoming its largest subsidiary. What followed was a rapid, occasionally reckless, six-year period of expansion and acquisition. Harper purchased majority interests in a variety of advertising firms all over the world. The network of affiliates was global, but it was also chaotic, mismanaged, and unprofitable. In 1966 Harper's sprawling conglomerate included 24 divisions, 8,300 employees, a fleet of five airplanes, and billings of $711 million. The following year Interpublic incurred a $3 million deficit and defaulted on agreements with two New York banks. At one point in 1967 a group of investment bankers offered to buy Interpublic in its entirety for the small sum of $5 million, but the deal was never finalized.

Unable to repay its loans, the company nearly went into receivership. Only through a radical restructuring of management practices and sales of subsidiaries was the agency saved. One of the casualties was Marion Harper himself; he was ousted from the chairmanship of the company by the governing board. The man responsible for instituting Interpublic's changes was Robert Healy, an executive at the firm for a number of years, who had gone into voluntary exile in Switzerland over managerial differences with Harper. In the autumn of 1967 the board brought Healy back from Geneva to reverse the company's mismanaged expansion. Healy was put in charge and given a short time by Interpublic's creditors to stabilize the company. He persuaded his employees to loan the company $3.5 million in return for convertible debentures. In addition, a number of clients agreed to pay in advance for future advertising services. These two factors permitted Interpublic to remain in business. With the help of an additional $10 million in loans, the company went public in 1971.

By selling public stock and reducing its high payroll costs, Interpublic stabilized its finances. It began operating again at a profit. In 1973 Paul Foley succeeded Healy as chief executive and chairman, ushering in a new era of growth at the company. Billings topped $1 billion for the first time in 1974 and plans were drawn up for renewed expansion. The Campbell-Ewald company, longtime ad agency for Chevrolet, was acquired in 1973. This move was followed five years later by the $32 million purchase of the SSC&B firm, the largest merger in advertising history at the time. These two acquisitions, along with Interpublic's strong overseas presence at a time when the American dollar was weak, led the company to record profits. At the end of 1978 Interpublic was billing in excess of $2 billion.

New Management: 1980s–90s

In the early 1980s Philip Geier was appointed chief executive and chairman of Interpublic, which angered two of the firm's most distinguished ad men, Bill Backer and Carl Spielvogel. Backer and Spielvogel had worked wonders with such prominent clients as Coke and Miller Beer. When Geier took the reins of Interpublic, Backer and Spielvogel left to start their own agency and took the Miller Beer account with them. News of their departure made Interpublic's stock price fall five points.

Coca-Cola, feeling pressure from Pepsi and upset with the departure of Backer and Spielvogel, issued an ultimatum to McCann-Erickson to come up with a new campaign in three months or the company would take its $750 million account elsewhere. Fortunately, the account was saved by the phrase ''Have a Coke and a smile,'' and a commercial featuring Pittsburgh Steeler football player ''Mean'' Joe Green giving a young fan the uniform off his back.

After this initial scare Geier became more comfortable in his post as chief executive, though Interpublic's billings had begun to decline in Europe. The offices in Great Britain and France lost a variety of important clients, including Bass Ale and Gillette, and Campbell-Ewald's European division was operating at a loss. These difficulties were particularly troublesome to Interpublic since 65 percent of its billings were outside of the United States. Geier fought back, increasing Interpublic's expansion in Asia where the firm ranked as the number one American-based agency.

By the end of the decade Interpublic had 166 offices in 50 countries. The four company divisions created advertising for such products as: Coca-Cola, Buick, Viceroy cigarettes, Inglenook wine, Exxon, Early Time bourbon, and Kentucky Fried Chicken (McCann-Erickson); Pall Mall and Lucky Strike cigarettes, Johnson & Johnson baby shampoo, Lipton tea, Noxzema, and Bayer aspirin (SSC&B); Chevrolet and Smirnoff vodka (Campbell-Ewald); as well as Minute Maid, Sprite, A-1 Steak Sauce, and Grey Poupon mustard (Marshalk).

Growth in the 1990s

As Interpublic entered the 1990s Geier and his chief financial officer, Eugene Beard, had made impressive financial gains after their first decade in control of the company. Revenues had more than tripled between the early 1980s and early 1990s, rising to $1.9 billion in 1992. Interpublic's stock demonstrated a

---

Key Dates:

1930: McCann-Erickson advertising agency is formed.
1961: Interpublic Group is incorporated as a holding company.
1971: Interpublic goes public on the New York Stock Exchange.
1974: Earnings top $1 billion for the first time.
1989: Interpublic has 166 offices in 50 countries worldwide.
1995: The company fuels growth through international expansion.
2000: Interpublic announces it will buy Deutsch.
2001: True North Communications agrees to merge with Interpublic, creating the world's largest advertising conglomerate.
2002: Accounting irregularities at McCann spark an SEC investigation.
2005: Interpublic has to restate its financials or be delisted from the New York Stock Exchange.
2006: Interpublic begins to regain its footing in the advertising industry.

---

more animated leap, increasing 15-fold between 1982 and 1992. Much of this growth had been achieved during the 1980s, when the advertising industry grew robustly. It was only when the advertising industry's years of vigorous growth came screeching to a halt in 1990, that the full measure of Geier's influence could be gauged.

During the recessive early 1990s, other international advertising conglomerates suffered miserably. Companies such as WPP Group and Saatchi & Saatchi watched their business evaporate and their earnings erode, as an era of corporate cutbacks and wholesale downsizing began. In contrast to the decade before, the early 1990s were years in which advertising agencies were forced to sell not only advertising ideas to corporate America, but the value of advertising itself. For many of Interpublic's ilk, the transition was not a smooth one: business was down on all fronts and advertising agencies floundered. Interpublic, however, distinguished itself from the industry pack and continued to radiate remarkable financial health.

The company's success during the transition in the 1990s was attributed to Geier, whose penchant for cost control maintained the momentum built up during the 1980s. Further, Geier was lauded for his practice of ceding creative authority to Interpublic's four agencies, which by this point served 4,000 clients in 91 countries. As the recession intensified, Interpublic continued to shine. In late 1993 the company registered one of the most prolific growth spurts in the history of the media industry, landing $1 billion worth of business during a three-day period. On a Monday in early December 1993, McCann-Erickson was awarded a $200 million Johnson & Johnson account for national television advertising. Two days later, General Motors handed McCann-Erickson its $300 million national print advertising account and Lintas delivered its $500 million national television advertising account, giving all those at Interpublic, and particularly those at McCann-Erickson, ample cause for celebration.

In early 1994 Geier exercised his role as chief strategist for all Interpublic agencies by advising the company's subsidiaries to develop interactive media capabilities. Geier was intent on securing a leading position in a burgeoning area of advertising, and McCann-Erickson was the first to respond by forming a business unit called McCann Interactive. Other Interpublic agencies followed suit, until all of Interpublic's interactive operations were organized into one entity in early 1995, an Interpublic subsidiary christened Allied Communications Group.

On the heels of this development, Interpublic suffered its first meaningful setback during the first half of the decade. In mid-1995 McCann-Erickson lost Coca-Cola's advertising contract, an account it had held for 40 years. Although McCann-Erickson retained Coke's media account, the news was devastating. Following the worrisome news, Interpublic proved to be more resilient than some expected. Financially, the company did not miss a beat, registering strong gains in revenues in 1995 and 1996. Interpublic eclipsed the $2 billion in commissions and fees in 1995 and collected more than $2.5 billion in revenues the following year.

Interpublic's continued good fortune was primarily attributable to Geier's worldwide expansion, in particular several key acquisitions over the next three years, including the purchase of DraftDirect Worldwide, the largest independent direct marketing firm in the world; the United Kingdom's International Public Relations, plc; the Atlanta, Georgia-based Austin Kelly Advertising; NFO Worldwide, Inc. of Greenwich, Connecticut; and one of the country's leading Hispanic agencies, Casanova Pendrill Publicidad. By the end of the decade, Geier had masterminded the acquisition of some 400 companies of varying size. Interpublic finished 1999 with 28,000 employees in 120 countries and gross income of $4.5 billion. There was, however, trouble on the horizon.

Trouble Looming in the New Millennium: 2000s

Interpublic started the new century as it had ended the previous one: with more acquisitions. In January the firm acquired a stake in Suissa Miller, a Los Angeles-based advertising agency, as Geier unveiled plans for his retirement. John Dooner, chief executive of McCann-Erickson Worldgroup, had been handpicked by Geier as Interpublic's new president and chief operating officer and took up the posts in March 2000. As the end of the year neared, Geier went out with a bang, managing to convince Donny Deutsch to join the Interpublic fold and announcing year-end worldwide revenues of $5.6 billion with earnings topping $349 million.

In January 2001 Dooner took over as CEO as Geier left the firm after 20 years at the helm. Interpublic made big news soon after by announcing it would acquire Chicago-based True North Communications and become the world's largest advertising holding company. The acquisition of True North ushered in a new era at Interpublic; it was not, however, one of continued prosperity or worldwide domination of the advertising industry. In the third quarter Interpublic posted its largest loss ever ($477 million) amidst falling revenues and steep restructuring costs; the company's stock, however, surged 20 percent to over $29 a share. The losses were a harbinger of what was to come, as Interpublic ended the year with worldwide revenues of $6.7 billion, down over 6 percent from the previous year's $7.2 billion.

In early 2002 Dooner was replaced as chief executive by David Bell, who had come to Interpublic from True North. Dooner remained chairman but relinquished his Interpublic CEO duties to return to his former stomping grounds, McCann. At McCann, however, a series of billing irregularities had been discovered. As trouble brewed at McCann over years of financial mismanagement, it led to scrutiny of Interpublic as a whole as well as its many independent units. Once the Securities and Exchange Commission (SEC) got wind of the financial irregularities, Interpublic went from worldwide advertising leader to fighting for its very survival.

In 2003 Interpublic was given an ultimatum: provide restated financials by November 2005 or face delisting from the New York Stock Exchange. Bell and Dooner vowed to have the numbers ready and worked hard at not only keeping Interpublic's clients but redeeming its reputation throughout the next year. As 2004 ended with rumors flying about criminal misdeeds and widespread accounting imbalances, Michael Roth, formerly of MONY and a member of Interpublic's board since 2002, was brought in as the company's chairman. In January 2005 Roth added the duties of chief executive as the firm faced the final months before the SEC's deadline.

When Roth presented Interpublic's restated financials, the documents revealed years of unreconciled accounts, liberal "media credits" (i.e., kickbacks), and a string of losses, including a staggering loss of $558 million for the first three quarters of 2004. Roth issued a public mea culpa and Interpublic's annual meeting was held in November (delayed from May). At the meeting, former CEOs and Chairmen David Bell and John Dooner were kicked off the board amid accusations of mismanagement. In addition, shareholders discussed but did not force the issue of breaking up the company and selling it to rivals.

Interpublic's stock hit a low of $10 per share in late 2005, but Roth took this in stride, reminding anyone who would listen that Interpublic's troubles were behind it and a number of its agencies were actually gaining ground and making a profit. Though Interpublic's overall financial performance remained weak, Roth firmly believed the venerable behemoth was poised for a turnaround.

Principal Subsidiaries

Campbell-Ewald; Campbell Mithun; Carmichael Lynch; Casanova Pendrill; Dailey & Associates; Deutsch; DeVries Public Relations; Draft Healthcare; Draft Worldwide; DraftDigital; Foote Cone & Belding; FutureBrand; GolinHarris International; Gotham Inc.; Hill Holliday; Hill Holliday Hispanic; Initiative Media; IW Group; Jack Morton Worldwide; Jay Advertising; Kaleidoscope; Lowe Worldwide; MAGNA Global; MRM Worldwide; McCann Erickson Worldwide; McCann WorldGroup; Media Partnership Corporation; MWW Group; Newspaper Services of America; Octagon; R/GA; Siboney USA; The Sloan Group; Springer & Jacoby; Universal Worldwide McCann; Walhstrom

Group; Weber Shandwick; Women2Women Communications; Zipatoni.

Principal Competitors

Omnicom Group Inc.; Publicis Groupe S.A., WPP Group, Plc.

Further Reading

Bulik, Beth Snyder, "Dooner, Geier to Reinvent Interpublic," *Advertising Age,* March 27, 2000, p. 69.

Creamer, Matthew, "IPG's New CEO Must Make the Tough Calls," *Advertising Age,* January 24, 2004, p. 3.

Davis, Wendy, "Deutsch Now Part of Interpublic Empire," *Advertising Age,* December 4, 2000, p. 1.

Dougherty, Philip, "Backer and Spielvogel Set the Standard for Growth," *New York Times,* June 1, 1980.

Feuer, Jack, "Omnicom & IPG: A Continental Divide," *ADWEEK,* May 26, 2003, p. 18.

Fox, Stephen, *The Mirror Makers,* New York: Morrow, 1984.

Harrington, John, "Interpublic Looks North for True Growth," *Crain's New York Business,* March 26, 2001, p. 46.

Hughes, Laura K., "Interpublic Still Faces Hurdles in True North Deal," *Advertising Age,* March 26, 2001, p. 3.

Khermouch, Gerry, "IPG: Synergy—or Sinkhole?," *Business Week,* April 21, 2003, p. 76.

"Late News: Bell, Dooner to Exit IPG Board," *ADWEEK Eastern Edition,* October 24, 2005, p. 1.

MacArthur, Kate, "The Dooner Party: Interpublic's CEO Inherited a Global Giant," *Advertising Age,* July 30, 2001, p. 1.

Machan, Dyan, "I Will Not Be Denied: Interpublic Group Companies CEO John Dooner, Jr.," *Forbes,* October 16, 2000, p. 166.

Marshall, Caroline, "Quiet American Stays Mum As Coke Loosens Ties," *Campaign,* July 14, 1995, p. 10.

McMains, Andrew, "Critics Get Louder on IPG Board," *ADWEEK Midwest Edition,* January 27, 2003, p. 3.

——, "Interpublic Posts Quarterly Loss of $327 Million," *ADWEEK Online,* November 11, 2003.

——, "IPG Stock Sinks to 52-Week Low," *ADWEEK Online,* October 18, 2005.

——, "IPG to Report on Restructuring Plan," *ADWEEK,* August 11, 2003, p. 7.

Morgenson, Gretchen, "Sibling Rivalry," *Forbes,* February 15, 1993, p. 119.

O'Leary, Noreen, "Above It All? Can a Confident Michael Roth Save the Faltering IPG?," *ADWEEK,* October 3, 2005, p. 34.

——, "Damage Control at IPG," *ADWEEK,* June 28, 2004, p. 8.

——, and Andrew McMains, "Criminal Confessions Rock IPG Shops," *ADWEEK Online,* September 19, 2005.

Snyder, Beth, "Mating Mania. . . . With the Landscape Picked Clean of Independents, the Giants Circle Each Other," *Advertising Age,* April 5, 1999, p. 3.

Steinberg, Brian, "Interpublic's Troubles Mount As Revenues Fall at Key Units," *Wall Street Journal Eastern Edition,* November 10, 2005, p. B5.

Wall, Kathleen, "At Interpublic, Family Feud Over Motorola," *ADWEEK Eastern Edition,* November 13, 1995, p. 5.

Willott, Bob, "IPG Braces for Next Round of Troubles," *Campaign,* October 7, 2005, p. 6.

——, "The Grapes of Roth: How It All Went Sour at IPG," *Campaign,* April 1, 2005, p. 19.

—updates: Jeffrey L. Covell; Nelson Rhodes

ITC Holdings Corp.

39500 Orchard Hill Place, Suite 200
Novi, Michigan 48375
U.S.A.
Telephone: (248) 374-7100
Fax: (248) 374-7140
Web site: http://www.itc-holdings.com

Public Company
Incorporated: 2002
Employees: 118
Sales: $126.4 million (2004)
Stock Exchanges: New York
Ticker Symbol: ITC
NAIC: 221121 Electric Bulk Power Transmission and
    Control

ITC Holdings Corp. (ITC) is a Michigan-based public company whose wholly owned subsidiary, International Transmission Company, is recognized as the first independent electricity transmission company in the United States. International Transmission's fully regulated, high-voltage system links generating stations in Michigan and neighboring areas to local distribution points, serving a population of nearly five million people in 13 southeastern Michigan counties, including the Detroit metropolitan area. Following a 2005 initial public offering of stock, ITC shares are traded on the New York Stock Exchange. ITC hopes to expand beyond Michigan by acquiring other Midwest electricity transmission systems.

Tracing Roots Back to the
1800s Invention of Electric Light

The transmission system that formed the backbone of International Transmission was once part of Detroit Edison. After Thomas Edison successfully introduced electric lighting in 1879, electric companies cropped up all over the country to provide street lighting as well as commercial and residential service. Even in the sleepy town of Detroit, years before the automobile industry transformed it into a thriving metropolis, a number of competing electric companies were launched and jockeyed for position.

During the final 15 years of the 1800s, two companies emerged in the market: Edison Illuminating Company of Detroit, founded in 1886 to serve businesses and homes, and Peninsular Electric Light Company, established in 1891 to focus on street lighting. In January 1903 the two companies were combined to create The Detroit Edison Company. Like all utility companies at the time, it was a vertically integrated operation, controlling all aspects of the business, from power generation to transmission to distribution. Over the ensuing decades, Detroit Edison acquired smaller Michigan utilities, steadily increasing the area it covered, all the while adding generating capacity and a network of transmission lines. During the 1990s, however, the longtime utility model became obsolete.

In 1992 the U.S. Congress passed the Energy Policy Act, which created competition in the wholesale sector of electricity by requiring utilities to make their power lines available for the transmission of electricity generated by outside producers. Next, in 1996, the Federal Energy Regulatory Commission (FERC) established new rules regarding transmission, and a year later the industry was deregulated, eliminating the monopoly status only as it pertained to transmission access of such longtime utility companies as Detroit Edison, which by now had been reorganized into a holding company called DTE Energy Company. This new structure created separation between nonregulated subsidiaries and those business units that remained regulated, such as the power transmission system.

There was a clear advantage to the public for a company such as DTE to spin off its transmission system into a separate company. According to a case study published in the *Journal of Structure and Project Finance,* "Transmission investments traditionally have been seen as a necessary, but largely uninteresting, segment of the vertically-integrated utility business. . . . [focusing] only on reducing costs for consumers in a specific service territory. In determining whether it could recover the costs of transmission through its rate base, a vertically-integrated utility looked only at the benefits which would accrue to its native load customers." As a result, there was little incentive to make improvements that would benefit the larger regional transmission system. An independent transmission company, on the other hand, operated under a different set of circumstances. While it was still concerned about the impact of an investment on its customers, who of course would be footing the bill, it also had to consider the contribution of the investment to the regulated regional transmission network on which it depended. Consequently, according to the study, investment incentives were "more focused on improving the overall value of transmission than [were] those of a vertically-integrated utility. The return on equity for a transmission-only company [was] measured strictly from its transmission business, as opposed to the vertically-integrated company whose return on equity [was] measured from a portfolio of regulated and unregulated activities in generation and energy delivery." In short, an independent transmission company had more incentives than an old-guard utility company to make the kind of infrastructure investments that benefited the public. FERC supported the idea of independent operators, which the agency believed were likely to make the kind of upgrades needed to ensure the reliability of the country's overall transmission system. In addition, FERC hoped that independents would have more incentive to eliminate the "bottlenecks" that existed between systems and lead to an overall smoother delivery of electricity.

Formation of the International Transmission Company in 2000

For DTE, transmission was not a growth business, a major reason why in 2000 DTE began the process of exiting from transmission, forming a new subsidiary called International Transmission Company. It then sought approval from FERC and notified the U.S. Securities and Exchange Commission regarding plans to spin off its transmission system into the subsidiary with assets worth $440 million. These assets included approximately 6,500 miles of both 120,000-volt cable and 345,000-volt electric cable, rights-of-way, and interconnections with other utilities. Although a subsidiary of DTE, International Transmission would become a common carrier, open to all suppliers of electricity. Some protests arose, however, after International Transmission made its initial rate request from federal regulators. Customers who chose to buy power from a supplier other than Detroit Edison would pay a higher rate, which opponents charged would discourage customers from choosing a different electricity supplier, in effect helping Detroit Edison to retain business. International Transmission disagreed, maintaining that it was not in the company's interest to hinder open access: In fact, the new company needed it simply to survive. In October 2000, FERC approved the rate request, imposing only minor modifications. The stage was now set for DTE's board of directors to approve the actual transfer of transmission assets to International Transmission.

Selected to serve as International Transmission's president and chief executive officer was Joseph L. Welch, the manager of transmission for Detroit Edison. Welch earned a Bachelor of Science degree in Electrical Engineering from the University of Kansas and was a Licensed Professional Engineer in Michigan. He began his career at Detroit Edison in 1971 and worked his way up through the organization. Although International Transmission was a DTE subsidiary, it was understood from the outset that it was soon likely to be sold off and become an unaffiliated, separate company. It would be Welch who would be called upon to supply the vision for the new company finding its way in a new environment for the energy industry.

The momentum for separating transmission assets from power companies was blunted somewhat, due in some degree to the financial difficulties caused in the industry by the Enron scandal and the time needed to adjust to the new relaxed regulatory environment. In 2001 DTE merged with MCN Energy Group Inc. and a year later was eager to sell off assets that no longer fit in with the company's new strategy, one of which was International Transmission. In preparation for a deal, ITC Holdings Corp. was formed in November 2002. On January 1, 2003, DTE announced that it had a buyer in New York City investment firm Kohlberg Kravis Roberts & Co. and asset management firm Trimaran Capital Partners LLC, which teamed up to acquire International Transmission for $610 million. The deal closed on February 28, 2003, and International Transmission became a stand-alone transmission company. It would go on later to be recognized as the first fully independent transmission company in the country when it completed the last piece of transition of maintenance, construction, and operations responsibilities from DTE in early 2004.

International Transmission had been a stand-alone transmission company for less than six months when it became caught up in the major power outage of August 14, 2003 that affected a large portion of the northeastern United States and eastern Canada and some 50 million people in all, the third largest blackout in North American history. The outage began in Ohio around 2:00 p.m. when a generating plant owned by FirstEnergy shut down in Eastlake, Ohio, resulting in transmission line failures that caused a cascading series of events. As voltage dipped in Ohio, and Pennsylvania utilities disconnected to save their own systems, a massive amount of power, about 2,500 megawatts, was drawn out of Michigan through the International Transmission system, which was given no warning. " 'We got hit by the equivalent of a tsunami and we didn't have a clue that it was coming,' said Joseph Welch," according to *Northeast Power Report*. The publication also reported that International Transmission told the Michigan Public Service Commission in a Powerpoint presentation that after the FirstEnergy transmission lines failures, "Northern Ohio becomes electrically isolated from the rest of Ohio. FirstEnergy is suddenly 2,000 MW short and the shortest route for the power to flow is through Michigan. In less than 10 seconds the flows on the International Transmission-FirstEnergy intertie jump by 2,000 MW. FirstEnergy starts to pull the equivalent of 20% of Detroit Edison's load from Michigan. The blackout is inevitable at this point. Flow around Lake Erie reverses, pulling power from New York and Ontario through Michigan."

In light of the August outage, International Transmission began reassessing its 2004 spending plans to upgrade its system. "What is it going to take, if an event like this happens again, so that the state of Michigan isn't impacted?," Welch commented to *Crain's Detroit Business.* According to *Crain's,* "Improvements to make the transmission system more reliable, relieve congestion, meet customer needs and reduce energy costs are the backbone of the business plan for ITC." Now the company began to think that it would have to increase its budget for improvements on its system as well as sharing in the cost of a regional, multistate transmission upgrade. All told, International Transmission was likely to spend three to four times as much on the transmission system than had DTE, but FERC also allowed it to charge higher rates to make those types of investments.

An example of upgrades that benefited the public was the building of a $9.5 million substation in Washington Township. Begun in 2004 and completed in 2005, the substation removed a traffic jam in the system. As a result, all utilities in Michigan could switch more quickly to cheaper sources of electricity as they became available, something that could not be done previously because of congestion. Cheaper power, of course, translated into lower rates for customers. Other improvements to the system during this period included an $8 million control center and a $16.1 million project to install new cable in downtown Detroit. In the summer of 2004, International Transmission also hosted a meeting with a number of midwestern transmission and electrical utility companies to help prevent the kind of blackout that visited the country the previous year. According to *Energy User News,* "The group examined ways to restore the electrical system from a wide area perspective, reviewed emergency and system restoration plans, and conducted a tabletop drill."

Public in 2005

Coming off a year in which it generated revenues of $126.4 million and net income of $2.6 million, ITC took another major step in its development in 2005 when the company made an initial public offering of stock, raising more than $330 million. Kohlberg Kravis Roberts remained the majority shareholder, owning a 55 percent stake. With its share of the proceeds, ITC paid down some of its debt, which was reduced to $508.5 million. It also earmarked money for capital improvements, expected to total $105 million in 2005 and grow to $120 million in 2006. ITC also looked to make use of its stock as currency to fund the purchase of other Midwest electricity transmission systems. No immediate deals were in the offering, but there was every reason to expect that in the near future ITC would be expanding beyond southeast Michigan.

Principal Subsidiaries

International Transmission Company; New York Transmission Holdings Corporation.

Further Reading

Bell, Dawson, and Chris Christoff, "Ohio Left Michigan in Dark, Utility Executives Say," *Detroit Free Press,* September 3, 2003.

Bodipo-Memba, Alejandro, "ITC Offering Surpasses Expectations," *Detroit Free Press,* July 27, 2005.

Lane, Amy, "DTE Asks for Approval to Spin Off Detroit Edison Transmission System," *Crain's Detroit Business,* June 26, 2000, p. 1.

——, "Edison Spinoff's Rate Proposals Raise Customer's Ire," *Crain's Detroit Business,* September 11, 2000, p. 21.

——, "ITC Holdings Aims to Juice Up Its Profits by Acquisition," *Crain's Detroit Business,* August 22, 2005, p. 4.

——, "Transmission Company Plant to Spend More on Grid," *Crain's Detroit Business,* August 25, 2003, p. 24.

"Search for Sources of Blackout Continues As FirstEnergy Seeks to Deflect Blame," *Northeast Power Report,* August 25, 2003, p. 1.

Sikora, Martin, "Transmission Carve-Outs Generate M&A Transactions," *Dealmaker's Journal,* January 1, 2003.

Tabors, Richard D., "Evaluating the Benefits of Independently-Owned Transmission Companies," *Journal of Structured and Project Finance,* Winter 2004, p. 48.

—Ed Dinger

Jean-Georges Enterprises L.L.C.

111 Prince Street
New York, New York 10012
U.S.A.
Telephone: (212) 358-0688
Fax: (212) 358-0685
Web site: http://www.jean-georges.com

Private Company
Founded: 1990
Employees: 2,000
Sales: $50 million (2004 est.)
NAIC: 722110 Full-Service Restaurants

Based in New York City, Jean-Georges Enterprises L.L.C. is the privately owned holding company for the global restaurant portfolio of master chef Jean-Georges Vongerichten. New York properties are anchored by his signature restaurant, Jean Georges, one of the most respected establishments in the city. Area restaurants also include JoJo, Vong, Mercer Kitchen, Perry Street, Vsteak, The Lipstick Café, and 66. Jean-Georges Enterprises also operates Vong restaurants, featuring Thai-inspired French cuisine, in Hong Kong and Chicago. In addition, the company's portfolio includes Prime Steakhouse in Las Vegas, Dune in the Bahamas, Market in Paris, and JG in Shanghai. Although less well known than Wolfgang Puck and Emeril Lagasse, Vongerichten "hasn't played to the Mall of America culture," according to Paula Disbrow, writing for *Restaurant Business* in 1999. "Vongerichten largely has maintained the halo of master culinary artist. His signatures include cooking with vegetable juices and herb oils, or incorporating Asian influences into unlikely fusion match-ups. Yet it has worked so well that one food authority has called him the most influential chef of the decade."

Early 1970s Experience Key
to Vongerichten's Career

Born in 1957, Vongerichten grew up in Strasbourg, France. He was the eldest son and expected to take over the family fuel business, but early on his passion became cooking, as he helped his mother and grandmother prepare the daily lunch served to 40 hungry coal handlers. "It was like a minirestaurant at home," he told *Nation's Restaurant News* in a 2003 profile. "I'd wake up, and there would be all these smells, and it really started there." Perhaps the seminal moment in his life came on his 16th birthday in 1973, which he would call the best day in his life, when his parents treated him to dinner at one of the region's finest restaurants, the Michelin three-star Auberge de L'Ill in Illhaeusern. It was during the meal that he decided he would not follow in the footsteps of his father and grandfather but would cook professionally. Several months later he entered hotel school and began a three-year apprenticeship at Auberge de L'Ill, learning from the restaurant's well-known owners, Paul and Jean-Pierre Haberlin. Here he gained an appreciation for the way restaurants were once commonly run: He visited local farms to pick up fresh milk each morning and witnessed hunters bringing in fresh game.

Known to be a very serious and focused student, Vongerichten completed his apprenticeship in 1976, and then posted the highest score in the province that year in the required technical examination given to apprentices. The Haberlins arranged for their star pupil to work in the south of France as a commis at another Michelin three-star restaurant, L'Oasis, in La Napoule, headed by Louis Outhier. An exacting chef, Outhier insisted that everything had to be made from scratch; service was not to be begun with anything on the stove. In essence, Vongerichten started his education from scratch as well, and over the next two years learned the importance of making everything as fresh as possible, while also opening his palate to herbs, olive oils, and salads. Vongerichten then moved to the north to work as saucier for another major chef, and taskmaster, Paul Bocuse, and once more felt as if he were beginning his education all over again. "Each night I had to make 12 sauces according to [Bocuse's] palate," Vongerichten told Paul Frumkin of *Nation's Restaurant News.* "He made me throw them out if they weren't right. I went through hell. But I learned real discipline and consistency."

Vongerichten took a job at a three-star restaurant in Munich, Germany, after ten months with Bocuse, but was soon summoned by Outhier, who had become a consultant to the Oriental Hotel in Bangkok, Thailand, and wanted to install the 23-year-old Vongerichten as the chef of Normandie, the French dining room in the hotel. Over the next two years Vongerichten gained

Company Perspectives:

Internationally reputed for his innovative, ground-breaking cuisine, Jean-Georges Vongerichten has emerged as one of the country's leading chefs.

valuable experience in the running of a fine restaurant and managing staff. Moreover, he was exposed to the multitude of exotic ingredients used in Thai food that would play such a major role later in his career. But his time in Thailand was also an ordeal by fire. Having never managed a kitchen, he felt lost when Outhier left after two weeks. "I had no idea how to do anything. All I had was my palate—everything else was weak. It was the toughest six months of my life. Some days I came home crying," he told Amana Mosle Friedman, writing for *Nation's Restaurant News.*

Vongerichten Coming to the United States in the Mid-1980s

All told, Vongerichten worked for Outhier for ten years, opening restaurants for him in Singapore, Hong Kong, Tokyo, Geneva, Lisbon, and London. Then, in 1985, Vongerichten came to the United States to open a restaurant in Boston. A year later he was in New York, where he opened Restaurant Lafayette inside the Drake Swissotel. He quickly realized that classic French cuisine and its reliance on butter and cream was falling out of favor in New York, which was being taken over by Italian cuisine. Vongerichten changed pace, and introduced more salads and vinaigrettes, relying on infused oils and juices. The switch proved magical, as the restaurant became a hit within a matter of months, and a year later it was named a four-star restaurant by the *New York Times,* only one of a handful in the city to receive the honor.

In 1989 Outhier's contract with the Drake Swissotel came to a close, and as a result Vongerichten was at loose ends. His wife hated New York and wanted to return to France. When he refused to leave, she took the two children, returned home, and the couple divorced. He was not able to buy Lafayette but his reputation was by now well established in New York, and so he decided to strike out on his own, but in a direction different from the four-star cuisine of Lafayette. He approached television producers and restaurant investors Phil Suarez (for whom he had previously consulted) and Bob Giraldi about opening a new restaurant that was more in keeping with the times. With the New York economy mired in recession, Vongerichten wanted to open a bistro-style restaurant, offering reinvented bistro-style classics priced under $20. The result was JoJo (Vongerichten's childhood nickname), which opened in 1991. Located in an Upper Eastside townhouse, JoJo was launched on a modest scale: six burners, one oven, and 15 employees. Suarez was responsible for arranging the financing, dealing with the landlord, and essentially freeing up Vongerichten to concentrate on creating the menu. It was a partnership that worked well and proved to be a key element of the success of Jean-Georges Enterprises. An intimate restaurant featuring tables covered in brown paper, JoJo cost just $150,000 to launch. "We thought we would do about 40 lunches and 60 dinners a day," Vonge-

richten told the *New York Times*' Florence Fabricant. "But when we opened the door, it was a madhouse." JoJo earned three stars from the *Times* and was named by *Esquire* as the Best New Restaurant of the Year.

Already with one major success in his solo career, Vongerichten was soon eager to pursue new ideas. In 1993 he and his partners opened a pair of restaurants: Vong and The Lipstick Café in Midtown Manhattan's Lipstick Building. For Vong, the chef drew on his experience in Thailand, combining Thai flavors with French cooking techniques to create his own version of Thai cuisine. Next door he opened an upscale salad-and-sandwich eatery that catered to the business crowd. As was the case with JoJo, both were immediate hits. Vong, because its recipes were exact and could be easily produced, became a vehicle for licensed operations. Over the next few years Vong restaurants opened in Chicago, London, Hong Kong, and Mexico City. Due primarily to a faltering economy, the Mexico City operation folded after six months.

By the mid-1990s the New York economy was beginning to boom once again and Vongerichten began looking for a chance to return to haute cuisine and regain four-star status. He and his partners found a valuable ally in real estate developer Donald Trump, who was converting the Old Gulf Western skyscraper at Columbus Circle into the Trump International Hotel & Tower and looking to house a major new restaurant. The demand for the restaurant space was intense, and Trump was supposedly in serious talks with a West Coast group when Suarez convinced him that as someone who personified New York Trump needed to open a New York restaurant. Trump was won over by the argument and leased the 15,000-square-foot space to Jean-Georges Enterprises, which spent the next two years developing a pair of restaurants in the building. One was Nougantine, a modestly priced café-type eatery serving breakfast, lunch, and dinner, and the second space, known as the main dining room, became Jean Georges, offering lunch five days a week and dinner six nights. The opening was repeatedly delayed but Jean Georges was worth the wait. Vongerichten refused to categorize its cuisine, but diners and critics alike raved about it, and the chef won back his fourth star from the *New York Times.* The Trump International Hotel & Tower actually provided four profit centers to Jean-Georges Enterprises. In addition to Nougantine and Jean Georges, the company also ran room service and an employees' cafeteria.

John Mariani of *Esquire* named Vongerichten Chef of the Year in 1997, but the businessman-chef was not content to rest on his plaudits. In 1998 he opened a pair of new restaurants. In downtown Manhattan he introduced the Mercer Kitchen, a chic eatery that offered Mediterranean-inspired cuisine. Vongerichten also opened a Las Vegas steakhouse called Prime in the new Bellagio Hotel. In addition, as if that did not keep him busy enough, he found time to pen a book for Broadway Books called *Cooking at Home with a Four Star Chef.* The honors also kept coming his way in 1998, when the James Beard Foundation named Jean Georges the "Best New Restaurant" and named Vongerichten the "Outstanding Chef."

New Century, More Openings

Vongerichten resumed his impressive record of restaurant openings with the start of the 2000s. In 2000 he opened Dune in

Key Dates:

1986: Jean-Georges Vongerichten opens Restaurant Lafayette in New York.
1991: Vongerichten strikes out on his own with JoJo in New York.
1993: Vong and The Lipstick Café open in Manhattan.
1997: Jean Georges opens and becomes a four-star restaurant.
2001: Market opens in Paris.
2003: 66 opens in TriBeCa.
2004: JG opens in Shanghai.

the Bahamas, focusing on fresh local ingredients, including seafood and fruit. A year later he opened JoJo a second time. After the owner of the East 64th Street townhouse decided to make the property his home, Vongerichten began to relocate to the TriBeCa section of Manhattan. Instead, the townhouse was bought by another party who insisted on JoJo remaining. Vongerichten took the opportunity to remodel the space and revamp the menu, although he retained some signature dishes to provide continuity. In reviewing JoJo after its reopening, William Grimes of the *New York Times* commented, "It's older now, but still new in all the ways that count."

In 2001 Vongerichten reached a significant milestone, opening his first restaurant in his native France. Called Market, it was located off the Champs-Elysees in Paris. "As you grow older, you go back toward your roots," he explained to Suzanne Daley of the *Times.* "Paris always was a dream. I have always loved this city—its architecture, its energy." Vongerichten brought his style of fusion cuisine to the French capital, a mix of dishes pulled from some of his other restaurants as well as new items such as a pizza with black truffles. The initial review from *Le Figaro* was harsh, but subsequent reviews were better. Vongerichten refined the menu, and Market was soon among the most popular restaurants in all of Paris.

Vongerichten's next venture was a Chinese restaurant called 66, located at 66 Leonard Street in TriBeCa, unveiled in 2003. It was inspired by a trip he took to Shanghai, where he also planned to launch a restaurant. Whereas Vong was Thai in flavor but French in technique, Vongerichten decided to make 66 more authentic. He told the *Times* shortly before the restaurant's opening, "We're using Chinese techniques here even though we're breaking some rules."

The Shanghai eatery opened in 2004. Called JG and modeled after Jean Georges, it offered light French cuisine, relying mostly on locally grown organic produce and local seafood. Three other restaurants also were launched by Jean-Georges Enterprises in 2004. Bank, a steak and seafood restaurant,

opened in the Hotel Icon, a boutique hotel, in Houston. In Manhattan's Chelsea area, the old meatpacking district, Vongerichten offered Spice Market, the food of which was influenced by the street food Vongerichten discovered during his travels in Southeast Asia. The last of the restaurants was called Vsteak, a pricey steakhouse located in Manhattan's new Time Warner Center. Vsteak struggled to survive, however, and there were some concerns in the summer of 2005 that it might be unable to meet its rent payments and was in danger of being forced to close, making it the first Vongerichten restaurant to fail.

Forever active, Vongerichten and his partners always had a number of projects in the works. In the spring of 2006 he planned to open a restaurant in the Chambers Hotel, a small luxury boutique hotel in downtown Minneapolis. After enjoying success with Houston's Hotel Icon, Vongerichten and his partners were increasingly interested in the boutique hotel sector. There was even talk in the press of extending the Vongerichten brand to a line of luxury hotels. As Vongerichten told *Nation's Restaurant News,* "I have to stay excited about projects. I have to keep it fresh."

Principal Operating Units

Jean Georges; JoJo; Mercer Kitchen; The Lipstick Café; Vong New York; Market; JG.

Principal Competitors

Restaurant Associates Corporation; Levy Restaurants, Inc.; Wolfgang Puck Fine Dining Group.

Further Reading

Brewer, Bonnie, "Jean Georges: Cool Color Palette for NYC's Hottest Restaurant," *Nation's Restaurant News,* August 18, 1997, p. 20.

Claridge, Laurann, "Seeing Stars," *Houston Chronicle,* October 9, 1998, p. 1.

Daley, Suzanne, "Adopted New Yorker's Latest Isn't Chopped Liver," *New York Times,* November 21, 2001, p. A4.

Disbrowe, Paula, "The Vong Show," *Restaurant Business,* June 1, 1999, p. 38.

Duecy, Erica, "Vongerichten, Suarez Expand Upscale Group in U.S., China," *Nation's Restaurant News,* March 1, 2004, p. 1.

Fabricant, Florence, "Trum and Le Cirque Are Players in Two Major Restaurant Deals," *New York Times,* February 10, 1996, p. A27.

Friedman, Amanda Mosie, "The NRN 50L R&D Culinarians—Jean-Georges Vongerichten," *Nation's Restaurant News,* January 27, 2003, p. 198.

Frumkin, Paul, "Jean Georges," *Nation's Restaurant News,* May 24, 2004, p. 152.

——, "Jean-Georges Vongerichten: No Longer in the Shadows, This Visionary Sheds Light on the Latest Food Trends," *Nation's Restaurant News,* January 2000, p. 190.

—Ed Dinger

Johnson & Johnson

One Johnson & Johnson Plaza
New Brunswick, New Jersey 08933-0001
U.S.A.
Telephone: (732) 524-0400
Fax: (732) 524-3300
Web site: http://www.jnj.com

Public Company
Incorporated: 1887
Employees: 109,900
Sales: $47.35 billion (2004)
Stock Exchanges: New York
Ticker Symbol: JNJ
NAIC: 322291 Sanitary Paper Product Manufacturing;
325412 Pharmaceutical Preparation Manufacturing;
325413 In-Vitro Diagnostic Substance Manufacturing;
325414 Biological Product (Except Diagnostic)
Manufacturing; 325611 Soap and Other Detergent
Manufacturing; 325620 Toilet Preparation Manufacturing; 334516 Analytical Laboratory Instrument Manufacturing; 339112 Surgical and Medical Instrument
Manufacturing; 339113 Surgical Appliance and
Supplies Manufacturing; 339115 Ophthalmic Goods
Manufacturing; 339994 Broom, Brush, and Mop
Manufacturing; 541710 Research and Development in
the Physical, Engineering, and Life Sciences

Johnson & Johnson (J&J) is one of the largest healthcare firms in the world and one of the most diversified. Its operations are organized into three business segments: pharmaceutical, which generates 47 percent of revenues and 58 percent of operating profits; medical devices and diagnostics, which accounts for 36 percent of revenues and 31 percent of operating profits; and consumer, which contributes 17 percent of revenues and 11 percent of operating profits. J&J's pharmaceutical products include drugs for family planning, mental illness, nervous system diseases, gastroenterology, oncology, immunotherapy, cardiovascular disease, pain management, allergies, and other areas. The medical devices and diagnostics segment includes surgical and patient care equipment and devices, diagnostic products, joint replacements, coronary stents, and contact lenses. The company's well-known line of consumer products includes the Johnson's baby care line, the Neutrogena skin and hair care line, o.b. and Stayfree feminine hygiene products, the Reach oral care line, Band-Aid brand adhesive bandages, Imodium A-D diarrhea treatment, Mylanta gastrointestinal products, Pepcid AC acid controller, Tylenol, Motrin, and St. Joseph pain relievers, and Benecol and Splenda sweeteners. J&J generates about 40 percent of its revenues outside the United States, through its network of 200 operating companies in 57 countries, selling products around the world.

Early History: From Surgical Dressings to Baby Cream

J&J traces its beginnings to the late 1800s, when Joseph Lister's discovery that airborne germs were a source of infection in operating rooms sparked the imagination of Robert Wood Johnson, a New England druggist. Johnson joined forces with his brothers, James Wood Johnson and Edward Mead Johnson, and the three began producing dressings in 1886 in New Brunswick, New Jersey, with 14 employees in a former wallpaper factory.

Because Lister's recommended method for sterilization, spraying the operating room with carbolic acid, was found to be impractical and cumbersome, Johnson & Johnson (which was incorporated in 1887) found a ready market for its product. The percentage of deaths due to infections following surgery was quite high, and hospitals were eager to find a solution.

J&J's first product was an improved medicinal plaster that used medical compounds mixed in an adhesive. Soon afterward, the company designed a soft, absorbent cotton-and-gauze dressing, and Robert Wood Johnson's dream was realized. Mass production began and the dressings were shipped in large quantities throughout the United States. By 1890 J&J was using dry heat to sterilize the bandages.

The establishment of a bacteriological laboratory in 1891 gave research a boost, and by the following year the company

Company Perspectives:

Our Credo: We believe our first responsibility is to the doctors, nurses and patients, to mothers and fathers and all others who use our products and services. In meeting their needs everything we do must be of high quality.

had met accepted requirements for a sterile product. By introducing dry heat, steam, and pressure throughout the manufacturing process, J&J was able to guarantee the sterility of its bandages. The adhesive bandage was further improved in 1899 when, with the cooperation of surgeons, J&J introduced a zinc oxide-based adhesive plaster that was stronger and overcame much of the problem of the skin irritation that plagued many patients. J&J's fourth original design was an improved method for sterilizing catgut sutures.

From the beginning, J&J was an advocate of antiseptic surgical procedures. In 1888 the company published *Modern Methods of Antiseptic Wound Treatment,* a text used by physicians for many years. That same year, Fred B. Kilmer began his 45-year stint as scientific director at J&J. A well-known science and medicine writer, and father of poet Joyce Kilmer, Fred Kilmer wrote influential articles for J&J's publications, including *Red Cross Notes* and the *Red Cross Messenger*. Physicians, pharmacists, and the general public were encouraged to use antiseptic methods, and J&J products were promoted.

R.W. Johnson died in 1910 and was succeeded as chairman by his brother James. It was then that the company began to grow quickly. To guarantee a source for the company's increasing need for textile materials, J&J purchased Chicopee Manufacturing Corporation in 1916. The first international affiliate was founded in Canada in 1919. A few years later, in 1923, Robert W. Johnson's sons, Robert Johnson and J. Seward Johnson, took an around-the-world tour that convinced them that J&J should expand overseas, and Johnson & Johnson Limited was established in Great Britain a year later. Diversification continued with the introduction in 1921 of Band-Aid brand adhesive bandages and Johnson's Baby Cream (Johnson's Baby Powder had debuted in 1893) and the debut of the company's first feminine hygiene product, Modess sanitary napkins, in 1927.

1932–63: The General at the Helm

The younger Robert Johnson, who came to be known as "the General," had joined the company as a mill hand while still in his teens. By the age of 25 he had become a vice-president, and he was elected president in 1932. Described as dynamic and restless with a keen sense of duty, Johnson had attained the rank of brigadier general in World War II and served as vice chairman of the War Production Board.

The General firmly believed in decentralization in business; he was the driving force behind J&J's organizational structure, in which divisions and affiliates were given autonomy to direct their own operations. This policy coincided with a move into pharmaceuticals, hygiene products, and textiles. During Robert Johnson's tenure, the division for the manufacture of surgical packs and gowns became Surgikos, Inc.; the department for

sanitary napkin production was initially called the Modess division and then became the Personal Products Company; birth control products were under the supervision of the Ortho Pharmaceutical Corporation; and the separate division for suture business became Ethicon, Inc. Under the General's leadership, annual sales grew from $11 million to $700 million at the time of his death in 1968.

Following his father's lead as a champion of social issues, Johnson spoke in favor of raising the minimum wage, improving conditions in factories, and emphasizing his business's responsibility to society. Johnson called for management to treat workers with respect and to create programs that would improve workers' skills and better prepare them for success in a modern industrial society. In 1943 Johnson wrote a credo outlining the company's four areas of social responsibility: first to its customers; second to its employees; third to the community and environment; and fourth to the stockholders. On the heels of the credo came the company's change from family-owned firm to public company, as J&J was listed on the New York Stock Exchange in 1944.

In 1959 J&J acquired McNeil Laboratories, Inc., maker of a non-aspirin (acetaminophen) pain reliever called Tylenol, which was at that time available only by prescription. Just one year after the acquisition, McNeil launched Tylenol as an over-the-counter (OTC) medication. Also in 1959, Cilag-Chemie, a Swiss pharmaceutical firm, was purchased, followed in two years by the purchase of Janssen Pharmaceutica, maker of the major antipsychotic drug Haldol, which had been introduced in 1958.

In 1963 Johnson retired. Although he remained active in the business, chairmanship of the company went outside the family for the first time. Johnson's immediate successor was Philip Hofmann, who, much like the General, had started as a shipping clerk and worked his way up the ladder. During Hofmann's ten-year term as chairman, J&J's domestic and overseas affiliates flourished. Hofmann was another firm believer in decentralization and encouraged the training of local experts to supervise operations in their respective countries. Foreign management was organized along product lines rather than geographically, with plant managers reporting to a person with expertise in the field.

1960s and 1970s: Increased Promotion of Consumer Products

In the early 1960s federal regulation of the healthcare industry was increasing. When James Burke, who had come to J&J from the marketing department of the Procter & Gamble Company, became president of J&J's Domestic Operating Company in 1966, the company was looking for ways to increase profits from its consumer products to offset possible slowdowns in the professional products divisions. By luring top marketing people from Procter & Gamble, Burke was able to put together several highly successful advertising campaigns. The first introduced Carefree and Stayfree sanitary napkins into a market that was dominated by the acknowledged feminine products leader, Kimberly-Clark Corporation. Usually limited to women's magazines, advertisements for feminine hygiene products were low-key and discreet. Under Burke's direction, J&J took a more open approach and advertised Carefree and Stayfree on television. By 1978 J&J had captured half of the market. Meantime, the company expanded its feminine hygiene line through the 1973 acquisition of the German firm Dr. Carl Hahn G.m.b.H., maker of the o.b. brand of tampons.

One of Burke's biggest challenges was Tylenol. Ever since J&J had acquired McNeil Laboratories, maker of Tylenol, the drug had been marketed as a high-priced product. Burke saw other possibilities, and in 1975 he got the chance he was waiting for. Bristol-Myers Company introduced Datril and advertised that it had the same ingredients as Tylenol but was available at a significantly lower price. Burke convinced J&J Chairman Richard Sellars that they should meet this competition head on by dropping Tylenol's price to meet Datril's. With Sellars's approval, Burke took Tylenol into the mass-marketing arena, slashed its price, and ended up beating not only Datril, but number one Anacin as well. This signaled the beginning of an ongoing battle between American Home Products Corporation, maker of Anacin, and McNeil Laboratories.

Sellars, Hofmann's protégé, had become chairman in 1973, and served in that position for three years. Burke succeeded Sellars in 1976 as CEO and chairman of the board, and David R. Clare was appointed president. J&J had always maintained a balance between the many divisions in its operations, particularly between mass consumer products and specialized professional products. No single J&J product accounted for as much as 5 percent of the company's total sales. With Burke at the helm, consumer products began to be promoted aggressively, and Tylenol pain reliever became J&J's number one seller.

At the same time, Burke did not turn his back on the company's position as a leader in professional healthcare products. In May 1977 Extracorporeal Medical Specialties, a manufacturer of kidney dialysis and intravenous treatment products, became part of the corporation. Three years later, J&J acquired Iolab Corporation, maker of ocular lenses for cataract surgery, and effectively entered the field of eye care and ophthalmic pharmaceuticals. In 1981 the company extended its involvement in eye care through the acquisition of Frontier Contact Lenses. The increased in-house development of critical care products resulted in the creation of Critikon, Inc., in 1979, and in 1983 Johnson & Johnson Hospital Services was created to develop and implement corporate marketing programs.

1980s Tylenol Tampering Tragedy

In September 1982 tragedy struck J&J when seven people died from ingesting Tylenol capsules that had been laced with cyanide. Advertising was canceled immediately, and J&J recalled all Tylenol products from store shelves. After the Food and Drug Administration (FDA) found that the tampering had been done at the retail level rather than during manufacturing, J&J was left with the problem of how to save its number one product and its reputation. In the week after the deaths, J&J's stock dropped 18 percent and its prime competitors' products, Datril and Anacin-3, were in such demand that supplies were back-ordered.

J&J was able to recoup its losses through several marketing strategies. The company ran a one-time ad that explained how to exchange Tylenol capsules for tablets or refunds and worked closely with the press, responding directly to reporters' questions as a means of keeping the public up to date. The company also placed a coupon for $2.50 off any Tylenol product in newspapers across the country to reimburse consumers for Tylenol capsules they may have discarded during the tampering incident and offer an incentive to purchase Tylenol in other forms.

Within weeks of the poisoning incidents, the FDA issued guidelines for tamper-resistant packaging for the entire food and drug industry. To bolster public confidence in its product, J&J used three layers of protection, two more than recommended, when Tylenol was put back on store shelves. Within months of the cyanide poisoning, J&J was gaining back its share of the pain-reliever market, and soon regained more than 90 percent of its former customers. By 1989 Tylenol sales were $500 million annually, and in 1990 the line was expanded into the burgeoning cold remedy market with several Tylenol Cold products; the following year saw the launch of Tylenol P.M., a sleep aid. James Burke's savvy, yet honest, handling of the Tylenol tampering incident earned him a spot in the National

Business Hall of Fame, an honor awarded in 1990. Litigation over the incident was finally resolved in 1991, almost a decade after the initial tampering. McNeil Labs settled with over 30 survivors of the poisonings for more than $35 million.

In 1989 Bristol-Myers launched an aggressive advertising campaign that positioned its Nuprin brand ibuprofen pain reliever in direct competition with Tylenol. The move compounded market share erosion from American Home Products' Advil ibuprofen. Both products claimed to work better than Tylenol's acetaminophen formulation.

There were a number of other important developments in the second half of the 1980s. In 1986 J&J acquired LifeScan, Inc., maker of at-home blood-monitoring products for diabetics. That same year, the company expanded its world leading position in baby care products through the acquisition of Penaten G.m.b.H., the market leader in Germany. Following the acquisition of Frontier Contact Lenses, which was renamed Vistakon, J&J introduced the Acuvue brand of disposable contact lenses in the United States in 1988. The popularity of the Acuvue lenses helped propel Vistakon into the number one position in contact lenses worldwide. In 1989 J&J and drug giant Merck & Co., Inc. entered into a joint venture, Johnson & Johnson-Merck Consumer Pharmaceuticals Co., to develop OTC versions of Merck's prescription medications, initially for the U.S. market, later expanded to Europe and Canada. One of the first product lines developed by this venture was the Mylanta brand of gastrointestinal products.

Burke and Clare retired in 1989 and were succeeded by three executives: CEO and Chairman Ralph S. Larsen, who came from the consumer sector; Vice-Chairman Robert E. Campbell, who had headed the professional sector; and President Robert N. Wilson, who had headed the pharmaceutical sector. The three men were responsible for overseeing the network of 168 companies in 53 countries.

Larsen moved quickly to reduce some of the inefficiencies that a history of decentralization had caused. In 1989 the infant products division was joined with the health and dental units to form a broader consumer products segment, eliminating approximately 300 jobs in the process. Over the next two years, the reorganization was extended to overseas units. The number of professional operating departments in Europe was reduced from 28 to 18 through consolidation under three primary companies: Ethicon, Johnson & Johnson Medical, and Johnson & Johnson Professional Products. In 1990, meantime, J&J formed Ortho Biotech Inc. to consolidate the company's research in the burgeoning biotechnology field, an area J&J had been active in since the 1970s.

Dealmaking in the 1990s

J&J was able to counter increasing criticisms of rising healthcare costs in the United States and around the world in the 1990s due in part to the company's longstanding history of social responsibility. The company pioneered several progressive programs including child care, family leave, and "corporate wellness" that were beginning to be recognized as healthcare cost reducers and productivity enhancers. In addition, weighted average compound prices of J&J's healthcare products, including prescription and OTC drugs and hospital and professional products, grew more slowly than the U.S. consumer price index from 1980 through 1992. These practices supported the company's claim that it was part of the solution to the healthcare crisis. In 1992 J&J instituted its "Signature of Quality" program, which urged the corporation's operating companies to focus on three general goals: "Continuously improving customer satisfaction, cost efficiency and the speed of bringing new products to market."

J&J grew at a relatively slow pace in the early 1990s, in part because of the difficult economic climate. Revenues increased from $11.23 billion in 1990 to $14.14 billion in 1993, an increase of just 26 percent. A series of acquisitions in the mid-1990s, however, ushered in a period of more rapid growth, with revenues hitting $21.62 billion by 1996, a leap of 53 percent from the 1993 level. The skin care line had received a boost in 1993 through the purchase of RoC S.A. of France, a maker of hypoallergenic facial, hand, body, and other products under the RoC name. More significant was the acquisition the following year of Neutrogena Corporation for nearly $1 billion. Neutrogena was well-known for its line of dermatologist-recommended skin and hair care products. J&J spent another billion dollars in 1995 for the clinical diagnostics unit of Eastman Kodak Company, which was particularly strong in the areas of clinical chemistry, which involves the analysis of simple compounds in the body, and immuno-diagnostics. In 1997 J&J combined its existing Ortho Diagnostics Systems unit with the operations acquired from Kodak to form Ortho-Clinical Diagnostics, Inc. (LifeScan remained a separately run diagnostics company.)

Another subsidiary that grew through acquisitions in this period was Ethicon Endo-Surgery, Inc., which had been spun off from Ethicon in 1992 to concentrate on endoscopic, or minimally invasive, surgical instruments. J&J acquired Indigo Medical, which specialized in minimally invasive technology in urology and related areas, in 1996, while Biopsys Medical, Inc., specializing in minimally invasive breast biopsies, was purchased in 1997. Another large acquisition occurred in 1996 when J&J spent about $1.8 billion for Cordis Corporation, a world leader in the treatment of cardiovascular diseases through its stents, balloons, and catheters. In 1997, in exchange for several consumer products, J&J acquired the OTC rights to the Motrin brand of ibuprofen pain relievers from Pharmacia & Upjohn. Other important developments during this period included the 1995 introduction of an Acuvue disposable contact lens designed to be worn for just one day but priced at a reasonable level, and the 1995 U.S. approval of the antacid Pepcid AC, an OTC version of Merck's Pepcid that was developed by the Johnson & Johnson-Merck joint venture.

The company's aggressive program of acquisition continued in the late 1990s, beginning with the 1998 purchase of DePuy, Inc. for $3.7 billion in cash, J&J's largest acquisition yet. DePuy was a leader in orthopedic products, such as hip replacement devices. J&J already marketed one of the leading knee replacement devices in the United States, making for a nice fit between the two companies. On the negative side, J&J was forced to initiate a restructuring in 1998 following a number of difficulties. J&J had been a pioneer in the market for coronary stents, devices used to keep arteries open following angioplasty, but its stent sales fell from $700 million in 1996 to just over $200 million in 1998 after competitors introduced second-generation stents and J&J did not. Also troubled was the firm's pharmaceutical operation, which in 1997 and 1998 had seen nine drugs in the development pipeline fail in testing, fail to get government approval, or be delayed. In late 1998 J&J announced that it would reduce its workforce by 4,100 and close 36 plants around the world over the succeeding 18 months. Taking $697 million in restructuring and in-process research and development charges, J&J aimed to save between $250 million and $300 million per year through this effort.

To bolster its drug R&D efforts, J&J completed its first major pharmaceutical deal since the 1961 purchase of Janssen Pharmaceutica. In October 1999 J&J merged with major biotechnology firm Centocor, Inc. in a $4.9 billion stock-for-stock transaction, the largest such deal in company history. With Centocor and Ortho Biotech under its wing, J&J was now one of the world's leading biotech firms. Soon after the merger with Centocor was completed, the FDA approved a key Centocor-developed drug, Remicade, for the treatment of rheumatoid arthritis. Centocor was also developing other pharmaceuticals in the areas of cancer, autoimmune diseases, and cardiology. Also in 1999 J&J acquired the dermatological skin care business of S.C. Johnson & Son, Inc., which was primarily made up of the Aveeno brand, for an undisclosed amount. Finally, the company introduced Splenda, a no-calorie sweetener that by 2003 would garner the top position in U.S. retail sales of tabletop sweeteners. Despite its late 1990s troubles, J&J reported record results for 1999, earning $4.17 billion on revenues of $27.47 billion. Net earnings had nearly quadrupled since 1989, while net sales nearly tripled over the same period.

Early 2000s Developments: ALZA, Cypher, Guidant

The year 2000 got off to a rough start for the company, as it was forced to withdraw from the market a prescription heartburn medication, Propulsid, after the drug had been linked to 100 deaths and hundreds of cases of cardiac irregularity. Propulsid had garnered nearly $1 billion in sales in 1999. By 2004 the number of persons who had allegedly died from the use of the drug had risen to more than 415, and more than 400 lawsuits representing the interests of about 5,900 plaintiffs had been filed against J&J's Janssen unit, the maker of Propulsid. In early 2004 Janssen reached an agreement to settle lawsuits involving approximately 4,000 plaintiffs, whereby it would pay compensation totaling between $69.5 million and $90 million as well as administrative and legal fees amounting to $37.5 million. On a more positive note, J&J's pharmaceutical business was led in the early 2000s by a true blockbuster, Procrit (marketed as Eprex in Europe), an anemia medication licensed from Amgen, Inc. and introduced by J&J in 1991. Sales of Procrit exceeded $3 billion per year in the first years of the new century. It accounted for as much as 10 percent of the company's overall revenues, which surpassed the $30 billion mark for the first time in 2001 and $40 billion just two years later.

In the meantime, Johnson & Johnson expanded its OTC pain reliever lineup in 2000 by acquiring the St. Joseph brand, best known for its orange-flavored, low-dose aspirin, which was in wide use as a doctor-recommended daily therapy. Several more key acquisitions followed. In June 2001 J&J acquired ALZA

Corporation in a $12.3 billion stock-swap transaction, the company's largest purchase yet. ALZA, based in Mountain View, California, was a leading developer of drug-delivery technologies, such as time-release capsules and transdermal patches. Sales of the firm's two biggest-selling drugs, Concerta, a treatment for attention deficit/hyperactivity disorder, and Ditropan XL, a urinary incontinence remedy, were expected to surge based on J&J's worldwide marketing prowess. Also in 2001, J&J's LifeScan unit was bolstered through the $1.3 billion purchase of the diabetes-care-products business of Inverness Medical Technology Inc., producer of devices used by diabetes patients to monitor their blood-sugar levels.

Larsen retired from the company in early 2002. Taking over as CEO and only the sixth chairman in the history of Johnson & Johnson was William C. Weldon, who had joined the firm in 1971 and had most recently served as head of the pharmaceuticals side since 1998. Weldon took over at a time when some of J&J's top-selling drugs, including Procrit, were faced with plateauing sales because of increased competition. One of the company's key achievements of 2003 was the receipt of FDA approval for Cordis's Cypher, a stent coated with a drug designed to reduce reblockage of blood vessels. Though J&J succeeded in being first to market with a drug-coated stent, and the product achieved strong first-year sales of $1.4 billion, Cypher quickly faced stiff competition from Boston Scientific Corporation's Taxus drug-coated stent. In pharmaceuticals, J&J once again turned acquisitive to bolster a somewhat somnolent drug-development pipeline, buying Scios Inc. in April 2003. Scios, a biotech firm specializing in treatments for cardiovascular and inflammatory disease, brought with it Natrecor, touted as the first new treatment for congestive heart failure in 15 years. Sales of Natrecor rose to $384 million by 2004, but the potential blockbuster status of the drug came into question following reports that it was damaging patients' kidneys. In mid-2005 a panel composed of independent experts recommended that use of Natrecor be restricted to acutely sick hospitalized patients and endorsed J&J's plans for additional studies of the drug.

During 2004 revenues reached $47.35 billion and increased for the 71st consecutive year. That year, J&J also continued its record of issuing dividends to shareholders every quarter since 1944, increased its dividend for the 43rd straight year, and achieved a double-digit increase in earnings for the 19th consecutive year. The firm now ranked as the fourth largest pharmaceutical company in the world, trailing only Pfizer Inc., Glaxo-SmithKline plc, and Sanofi-Aventis, and the number two biotech company, after Amgen. Johnson & Johnson also held sway as the largest manufacturer of medical devices and diagnostics tools in the world, a position it aimed to bolster by acquiring Indianapolis-based Guidant Corporation (and merging Cordis into it), in a deal announced in December 2004 that was initially valued at $25.4 billion. Guidant, with annual sales of about $3.8 billion, focused on implantable devices to treat abnormal heart rhythms, including implantable cardiac defibrillators and pacemakers, as well as catheters and stents. The deal, expected to be completed in late 2005, became questionable after Guidant was forced to recall tens of thousands of its defibrillators and pacemakers because of malfunctions. Further clouding Johnson & Johnson's future were reports that the drug-coated stents being produced by both J&J and Boston

Scientific might pose a higher long-term risk of life-threatening blood clots than the old-fashioned bare-metal type.

Principal Subsidiaries

ALZA Corporation; BabyCenter, L.L.C.; Biosense Webster, Inc.; Centocor, Inc.; Codman & Shurtleff, Inc.; Cordis Corporation; DePuy, Inc.; Ethicon Endo-Surgery, Inc.; Ethicon, Inc.; Independence Technology, L.L.C.; Janssen Pharmaceutica Products, L.P.; Johnson & Johnson Consumer Products Company; Johnson & Johnson Development Corporation; Johnson & Johnson Gateway, LLC; Johnson & Johnson Health Care Systems Inc.; Johnson & Johnson - Merck Consumer Pharmaceuticals Co. (50%); Johnson & Johnson Pediatric Institute, L.L.C.; Johnson & Johnson Pharmaceutical Research & Development, L.L.C.; Johnson & Johnson Sales and Logistics Company; Johnson & Johnson Vision Care, Inc.; LifeScan, Inc.; McNeil Nutritionals, LLC; Neutrogena Corporation; Noramco, Inc.; Ortho Biotech Products, L.P.; Ortho-Clinical Diagnostics, Inc.; Ortho-McNeil Pharmaceutical, Inc.; Scios, Inc.; Therakos, Inc.; TransForm Pharmaceuticals, Inc.; VISTAKON Pharmaceuticals, L.L.C.; Cilag AG (Switzerland); Greiter (International) AG (Switzerland); Janssen Animal Health BVBA (Belgium); Janssen-Cilag B.V. (Netherlands); Janssen-Ortho Inc. (Canada); Janssen Pharmaceutica N.V.; Johnson & Johnson AB (Sweden); Johnson & Johnson Comércio e Distribuiçao Ltda. (Brazil); Johnson & Johnson Consumer France SAS; Johnson & Johnson de Argentina, S.A.C.e I.; Johnson & Johnson de Colombia S.A.; Johnson & Johnson Gesellschaft m.b.H. (Austria); Johnson & Johnson GmbH (Germany); Johnson & Johnson Inc. (Canada); Johnson & Johnson K.K. (Japan); Johnson & Johnson Korea, Ltd.; Johnson & Johnson Limited (India); Johnson & Johnson, s.r.o. (Czech Republic); McNeil Consumer Healthcare (Canada); McNeil Europe (Germany); McNeil Limited (U.K.); PENATEN (Germany); Tibotec Pharmaceuticals Ltd. (Ireland); Virco BVBA (Belgium); Xian-Janssen Pharmaceutical Ltd. (China).

Principal Operating Units

Consumer; Medical Devices and Diagnostics; Pharmaceutical.

Principal Competitors

The Procter & Gamble Company; Bayer AG; Merck & Co., Inc.; Pfizer Inc.; Unilever; Novartis AG; AstraZeneca PLC; Abbott Laboratories; Medtronic, Inc.; Boston Scientific Corporation; Amgen, Inc.; Eli Lilly and Company; Kimberly-Clark Corporation.

Further Reading

Abelson, Reed, ''Johnson Takes Ally to Try to Keep Lead in Stents,'' *New York Times,* February 25, 2004, sec. C, p.1.

Alpert, Bill, ''Bitter Pills: Once Invincible, J&J Faces Fresh Competition Across Its Product Spectrum,'' *Barron's,* June 9, 2003, pp. 17–18.

——, ''Breach of Discipline?: Possible J&J Buy of Guidant Draws Skeptics,'' *Barron's,* December 13, 2004, p. 14.

Alsop, Ronald, ''Johnson & Johnson (Think Babies!) Turns Up Tops,'' *Wall Street Journal,* September 23, 1999, p. B1.

Barker, Robert, ''Picture of Health: Johnson & Johnson Seems to Have Cured What Ailed It,'' *Barron's,* March 30, 1987, pp. 15+.

Barrett, Amy, ''J&J Stops Babying Itself,'' *Business Week,* September 13, 1999, pp. 95–97.

——, ''Johnson & Johnson: A Shopping Spree Waiting to Happen,'' *Business Week,* June 17, 2002, pp. 58, 60.

——, ''Staying on Top,'' *Business Week,* May 5, 2003, pp. 60–63, 68.

''Changing a Corporate Culture,'' *Business Week,* May 14, 1984, pp. 130+.

Dumaine, Brian, ''Is Big Still Good?'' *Fortune,* April 20, 1992, pp. 50–60.

Easton, Thomas, and Stephan Herrera, ''J&J's Dirty Little Secret,'' *Forbes,* January 12, 1998, pp. 42–44.

Fannin, Rebecca, ''The Pain Game,'' *Marketing and Media Decisions,* February 1989, pp. 34–39.

Foster, Lawrence G., *A Company That Cares: One Hundred Year Illustrated History of Johnson & Johnson,* New Brunswick, N.J.: Johnson & Johnson, 1986, 175 p.

Guzzardi, Walter, ''The National Business Hall of Fame,'' *Fortune,* March 12, 1990, pp. 118–26.

Harris, Roy J., Jr., and Elyse Tanouye, ''Johnson & Johnson to Buy Neutrogena in Bid to Boost Consumer-Products Unit,'' *Wall Street Journal,* August 23, 1994, p. A3.

Hensley, Scott, ''J&J Say New-Drug Pipeline Is Filling After Four-Year Push,'' *Wall Street Journal,* May 27, 2005, p. B3.

——, ''Johnson & Johnson Agrees to Buy Alza in $12 Billion Stock Deal,'' *Wall Street Journal,* March 28, 2001, p. B15.

Hensley, Scott, Thomas M. Burton, and Dennis K. Berman, ''Johnson & Johnson to Buy Guidant,'' *Wall Street Journal,* December 16, 2004, p. A3.

Hwang, Suein L., ''J&J to Acquire Unit of Kodak for $1.01 Billion,'' *Wall Street Journal,* September 7, 1994, p. A3.

Jacobs, Richard M., ''Products Liability: A Technical and Ethical Challenge,'' *Quality Progress,* December 1988, pp. 27–29.

Johnson & Johnson: Global Expansion in the Face of Intense Competition, Mountain View, Calif.: Frost & Sullivan, 1993.

Kador, John, *Great Engagements: The Once and Future Johnson & Johnson,* New Brunswick, N.J.: Johnson & Johnson, 2004, 268 p.

Kardon, Brian E., ''Consumer Schizophrenia: Extremism in the Marketplace,'' *Planning Review,* July/August 1992, pp. 18–22.

Keaton, Paul N., and Michael J. Semb, ''Shaping up That Bottom Line,'' *HRMagazine,* September 1990, pp. 81–86.

Langreth, Robert, and Ron Winslow, ''At J&J, a Venerable Strategy Faces Questions,'' *Wall Street Journal,* March 5, 1999, p. B1.

Leon, Mitchell, ''Tylenol Fights Back,'' *Public Relations Journal,* March 1983, pp. 10+.

Matthes, Karen, ''Companies Can Make It Their Business to Care,'' *HR Focus,* February 1992, pp. 4–5.

McLeod, Douglas, and Stacy Adler, ''Tylenol Death Payout May Top $35 Million,'' *Business Insurance,* May 20, 1991, pp. 1, 29.

Moore, Thomas, ''The Fight to Save Tylenol,'' *Fortune,* November 29, 1982, pp. 44+.

Moukheiber, Zina, and Robert Langreth, ''J&J: An Unfinished Symphony,'' *Forbes,* December 10, 2001, p. 62.

Murray, Eileen, and Saundra Shohen, ''Lessons from the Tylenol Tragedy on Surviving a Corporate Crisis,'' *Medical Marketing and Media,* February 1992, pp. 14–19.

O'Reilly, Brian, ''J&J Is on a Roll,'' *Fortune,* December 26, 1994, pp. 178–80+.

Rublin, Lauren R., ''More Than a Band-Aid: Johnson & Johnson's Has a Strong Prescription for Growth,'' *Barron's,* April 17, 2000, pp. 37–38, 40, 42.

Silverman, Edward R., ''J&J Will Slash 4,100 Positions,'' *Newark Star-Ledger,* December 4, 1998.

——, ''More Than Medicine: Johnson & Johnson's CEO Defends the Company's Slow-Growing Divisions,'' *Newark Star-Ledger,* June 18, 2000.

Smith, Lee, ''J&J Comes a Long Way from Baby,'' *Fortune,* June 1, 1981, pp. 58+.

Taylor, Alex, III, "Can J&J Keep the Magic Going?," *Fortune,* May 27, 2002, pp. 117–18+.

Tully, Shawn, "Blood Feud," *Fortune,* May 31, 2004, p. 100.

Waldholz, Michael, "Johnson & Johnson Defends Emphasis on Long-Term Growth As Profit Surges," *Wall Street Journal,* August 8, 1985.

Warner, Susan, "From Band-Aids to Biotech," *New York Times,* April 10, 2005, sec. 14NJ, p. 1.

Weber, Joseph, "A Big Company That Works," *Business Week,* May 4, 1992, pp. 124–32.

——, "No Band-Aids for Ralph Larsen," *Business Week,* May 28, 1990, pp. 86–87.

Winslow, Ron, "Head Start: Johnson & Johnson Finds an Elusive Gene and Races to Exploit It," *Wall Street Journal,* May 26, 2000, pp. A1+.

——, "J&J Agrees to Buy DePuy for $3.5 Billion," *Wall Street Journal,* July 22, 1998, p. A3.

Winters, Patricia, "J&J Sets Nighttime Tylenol," *Advertising Age,* February 18, 1991, pp. 1, 46.

——, "Tylenol Expands with Cold Remedies," *Advertising Age,* August 27, 1990, pp. 3, 36.

—Mary F. Sworsky
—update: April S. Dougal; David E. Salamie

j2) Global Communications

j2 Global Communications, Inc.

6922 Hollywood Boulevard, Suite 500
Hollywood, California 90028
U.S.A.
Telephone: (323) 860-9200
Toll Free: (888) 438-5329
Fax: (323) 464-1446
Web site: http://www.j2global.com

Public Company
Incorporated: 1995 as JFax.com Inc.
Employees: 202
Sales: $106.3 million (2004)
Stock Exchanges: NASDAQ
Ticker Symbol: JCOM
NAIC: 517110 Wired Telecommunications Carriers

j2 Global Communications, Inc. is a Hollywood, California-based provider of messaging and communications services to both individuals and companies around the world. Originally designed as a computerized system to allow travelers to access their faxes and voice messages by phone, j2 Global now offers a range of value-added web-based unified messaging services, including message retrieval by either phone or email, web-initiated conference calls, complete fax sending and retrieving capabilities, fax broadcasting, email marketing campaign services, and document transfer and archiving services. All told, j2 Global has 400,000 paying subscribers and about 8.5 million users of its advertising-supported services. j2 Global is a public company listed on the NASDAQ.

Company's Genesis Dating to the Early 1990s

The man who spawned the idea for j2 Global was a musician born in East Germany named Jaye Muller. Growing up in East Berlin before the Communist system crumbled, Muller wanted to pursue a career in rock and roll but was required by the state to take night career training courses. He studied electronics, another area of interest and one that would pay dividends later in life. By the time he was 18 and the Berlin Wall had been toppled in dramatic fashion, Muller moved to Paris, where he furthered his musical career. He found a producer and manager in Jack Rieley,

a former producer of the Beach Boys, and signed a record deal with A&M records. In January 1993, under the name J., he released his first album, *We Are the Majority*. *Fortune* described it as "a hip-hop rant about the supposedly Gestapo-like takeover of J.'s native East Germany by the West German government, with lyrics that got the album banned in Bonn." Despite the ban, the album did well in Europe, selling 350,000 copies. He toured widely to support the album, and it was during a swing through colleges in England that Muller received the inspiration that led to the birth of j2 Global. Because he was changing hotels every day, his faxes and voice messages were always a day or two behind. Not only were messages getting lost, Muller was disturbed that the hotel staff was reading his confidential faxes. A technophile, Muller had a laptop with Internet capabilities and was always able to keep up with his email messages. He thought that voice mail and faxes should be equally portable. When he realized that there was no such commercial service available, he and Rieley decided to start a business to fill that need.

In downtime during the rest of the tour Muller began sketching out an idea for an email-based retrieval system for voice mail and faxes, drawing heavily on his technical training. He then put his music career on hold, postponing work on his second album to turn his concept into a business, working closely with an Australian telecommunications software development company to develop a prototype. Muller relocated to New York City and in December 1995 he and Rieley incorporated JFax.com Inc. The need for $2 million in seed money, according to the Scottish newspaper, the *Scotsman*, pitched "Muller headlong into a maelstrom of accountants and meetings at a point when the 23-year-old musician knew virtually nothing about the ways of business. He coped with the situation, he says, by relying on a blend of instinct and 'how to' books. 'I literally picked things up as I went along. A lot of big numbers were being talked about, but for much of the time they were only on paper and didn't matter that much. I just mentally removed the zeroes from every figure they threw at me and didn't take anything too seriously.'"

Launching Operations in 1996

Muller and Rieley raised the necessary $2 million from a pair of "industrialists" (according to *Global Finance*), and com-

Company Perspectives:

j2 is the result of a marriage of a revolutionary patented suite of services and a financially strong and disciplined organization. This success benefits our customers, who are looking for a stable service provider for their advanced messaging needs; our shareholders, who look for increasing financial growth and value; and our employees, who work in a creative, positive and success-driven environment.

menced operations in April 1996. Within a matter of months JFax caught the attention of *The New York Times*, which in September 1996 published a lengthy profile on the start-up. The service at the time cost $12.50 a month plus a $15 setup fee. Already the company was offering local telephone numbers for New York, Los Angeles, San Francisco, Atlanta, Silicon Valley, and London. The rest of the United States could also use the service through toll-free numbers. A number of other messaging companies also were cropping up, but JFax's product and business model gave it a decided edge, even though the company was still months away from being able to answer voice messages through email or "reading" email over the phone. The technology was robust enough to support business customers, and unlike the competition, JFax did not give away its service and began to build a base of paying customers. Moreover, by carving out a significant share of the market in the early days, the company was gaining an edge that would make it difficult to be dislodged later.

JFax continued to successfully raise necessary funds. In April 1997 the company received venture funding from Orchard Capital Corporation, a firm run by Richard Ressler, who now took the reins of the start-up. According to *Barron's*, Ressler was "a former Drexel Burnham banker who had spent a number of years running companies controlled by corporate raider Bennett Lebow." Muller was able to back away and return to music, although he would remain as the company's co-chairman along with Rieley. In 2000 he would resign from that post as well, although he remained a major stockholder and continued to play a role, using his charismatic personality in making presentations for the company.

Ressler raised more money for JFax in 1998, arranging with Donaldson, Lufkin & Jenrette for a private placement of stock, which according to *Fortune* amounted to $100 million. By now JFax had introduced its Telephone Access option, which allowed subscribers to access messages by way of a regular or cellular phone. Using text-to-speech software, email messages could be read aloud, and by using the telephone keypad subscribers could redirect faxes to a fax machine close at hand. The company also offered local phone numbers in some 60 cities around the world, especially attractive to companies looking to establish a foreign presence and a local identity. Customers in that market could use the local phone number and their messages would be instantly sent to the company wherever it was located.

Public in 1999

In 1999 Ressler was ready to take JFax public. With Donaldson, Lufkin & Jenrette, BancBoston Robertson Stephens, CIBC World Markets, and DLJdirect Inc. serving as underwriters, JFax sold 8.5 million shares of common stock at $9.50 per share in July 1999. The offering netted the company $73.9 million, earmarked to pay down debt, expand its international network, and fund advertising and marketing efforts. Unlike other initial offerings of the late 1990s, JFax did not enjoy an immediate surge, ending the first day of trading unchanged at $9.50. As a result a number of investors ignored the stock and it began to languish. Moreover, dot-coms were losing favor and the entire e-commerce market was on the verge of a major collapse. Unlike other companies with dot-com in their names, however, JFax had paying customers and was not pursuing a business model dependent on advertising revenues that might or might not develop over time. Nevertheless, JFax was lumped in with the rest of the dot-com companies, leading management to begin thinking about a name change.

In 2000 JFax began to use some of its stock to fuel growth through acquisitions. It also changed CEOs. The company traded $12 million in common stock in January 2000 to acquire Carlsbad, California-based SureTalk.Com, Inc., another Internet-based messaging and communications company. SureTalk's CEO, Steven J. Hamerslag, then took over as JFax's CEO, while Ressler stayed on as chairman. Hamerslag was a seasoned chief executive, the founder and head of MIT Technologies, a global provider of data storage management products and services, before joining SureTalk in July 1999. JFax completed another acquisition in March 2000, paying $1.1 million in common stock for TimeShift, Inc., a San Francisco company that brought with it web-based technology that allowed JFax subscribers to create impromptu conference calls, as point-to-point calls could be expanded on the flow. Finally, in November 2000, JFax used another $8.2 million in stock to acquire one of its chief rivals, eFax, a free Internet faxing service. The original deal, announced in April, called for JFax to pay $74 million, a far cry from the $787 million a comparable competitor, Onebox.com, had fetched in February 2000. But the carnage that took place on the NASDAQ in April changed everything, and eFax, running low on cash, had no options but to take what JFax had to offer. In fact, while the deal was being worked out, eFax had to borrow $5 million from its suitor in order to keep the doors open. eFax had built up a sizable base of users, nearly three million, for its free receive-only service. Since advertising revenues were eroding in the wake of the dot-com meltdown, and had never been high enough to make eFax commercially viable, the challenge for JFax was to convert as many of those people as possible to paying customers. JFax closed the year by dropping the dot-com from its name, becoming j2 Global Communications, Inc. For the year 2000, the company recorded sales of $13.9 million, resulting in a net loss of $22.2 million.

Sales continued to grow in 2001 while the company's net loss decreased significantly, and j2 Global also received a patent on its core technology (accepting incoming messages over a circuit-switched network and transmitting them over a packet-switched network), but the investment climate was such that none of this mattered much. The price of the company's stock dipped into penny stock status, prompting j2 Global to buy back shares to support the price and to eventually engineer a 1-for-4 reverse split to decrease the number of outstanding shares and boost the price over the $1 hurdle for listing requirements.

Key Dates:

1995: The company is incorporated as JFax.com Inc.
1996: The company begins operations.
1999: An initial public offering of stock is made.
2000: The name is changed to j2 Global Communications, Inc.
2002: The company turns its first profit.
2005: CEO Scott Jarus resigns.

However, many of its rivals were in far worse shape, going out of business to the benefit of j2 Global.

In July 2001 Hamerslag left the company, replaced as CEO by Scott M. Jarus. A former executive at Metromedia Communications, Jarus also had held senior positions at RCN Telecom and OnSite Access, Inc. before joining j2 Global. Jarus took over a company that was on the verge of a significant rebound. j2 Global posted sales of $33.2 million in 2001, an increase of almost 300 percent. The company's net loss also was cut by nearly two-thirds at $7.8 million. Sales continued to grow at a strong clip so that in the early months of 2002 j2 Global turned in the first profitable quarter in its history. Wall Street took notice and by the middle of the year the price of j2 Global stock, which stood at $5 at the start of the year, approached $17 a share, and in November topped the $27 mark. When the numbers for 2002 were tallied, revenues had increased to $48.2 million (due in no small measure to the company's ability to convert eFax's free subscribers into paying customers) and instead of a loss j2 Global posted net income of $14.3 million.

To take advantage of its position in the marketplace, j2 Global resumed its acquisition strategy, completing a pair of deals. Early in the year it bought Cyberbox, a Hong Kong-based message management company, gaining 40,000 local telephone numbers in Hong Kong, which j2 Global considered the gateway to the coveted market of mainland China. Later in the year j2 Global acquired San Mateo-based M4Internet, provider of corporate high-volume, personalized, permission-based email marketing campaigns. The addition of new territory and new services helped j2 Global to continue its upward financial trend. Sales increased to $71.6 million and net income climbed to $35.8 million.

More acquisitions followed in 2004. The Electric Mail, a Canadian-based provider of outsourced email and value-added messaging services, was purchased in March 2004. Its acquisition gave j2 Global an advanced email platform on which to build additional service offerings. The company added other technologies by acquiring the Onebox unified communications assets of Call Sciences, Ltd. These included full-featured unified communications software, and a ''find me/follow me''

feature that j2 Global hoped to incorporate into future product offerings. In addition, j2 Global also picked up a new group of customers. Sales improved to $106.3 million in 2004 and the company continued to realize a healthy net profit, which totaled $31.6 million for the year.

j2 Global completed yet another acquisition in July 2005, picking up the UniFax brand of Data on Call, LLC, and its subscriber base, as well as the technology for features such as dynamic delivery options via FTP, web-post with XML, and barcode data capture. The company would carry on without Jarus, who decided in 2005 to move on to ''pursue other challenges,'' but stayed to help in a transition. In August 2005 the company named co-presidents: Hemi Zucker, who also served as chief operating officer, and Scott Turicchi, who also held the title of chief financial officer. They took over a company with $100 million in cash and stock approaching $40 per share. More than likely j2 Global would remain in the mood to entertain further acquisitions.

Principal Subsidiaries

SureTalk.com, Inc.; The Electric Mail Company; Call Science, Inc.

Principal Competitors

CommTouch Software Ltd.; Critical Path, Inc.; Multi-Link Telecommunications, Inc.

Further Reading

Biddle, RiShawn, ''Short Sellers Take Their Licks As J2 Global Shares Hit a High,'' *Los Angeles Business Journal,* September 1, 2003, p. 25.

Bruce, Iain S., ''The Fax of Life—According to a German Rock Star,'' *Scotsman,* March 9, 1999, p. 7.

Ewing, Terzah, ''How the Other Half Lives; Tales of IPO Losers,'' *Wall Street Journal,* December 20, 1999, p. C1.

Palazzo, Anthony, ''J2 Global's Changing Fortunes Getting Noticed on Wall Street,'' *Los Angeles Business Journal,* October 28, 2002, p. 36.

Powell, Nigel, ''Rock Star's Way of Tuning In,'' *Times* (London), June 17, 1998, p. 18.

Rombel, Adam, ''Musician's Online Messaging Firm Isn't Singing the Blues,'' *Global Finance,* July/August 2002, p. 8.

Savitz, Eric J., ''Partying Like It's 1999,'' *Barron's,* November 11, 2002, p. 22.

Spruell, Sakina, ''Just the Fax, Please,'' *Black Enterprise,* July 1999, p. 48.

Sreenivasan, Sreenath, ''Expanding the Boundaries of E-Mail,'' *The New York Times,* September 23, 1996, p. D5.

Warner, Melanie, ''JFAX Personal Telecom,'' *Fortune,* July 7, 1997, p. 90.

—Ed Dinger

Jupitermedia Corporation

23 Old Kings Highway South
Darien, Connecticut 06820
U.S.A.
Telephone: (203) 662-2800
Fax: (203) 655-4686
Web site: http://www.jupitermedia.com

Public Company
Incorporated: 1999 as Internet.com Corporation
Employees: 339
Sales: $71.9 million (2004)
Stock Exchanges: NASDAQ
Ticker Symbol: JUPM
NAIC: 541513 Computer Facilities Management Services

One of the first companies devoted to the Internet, Darien, Connecticut-based Jupitermedia Corporation is one of the few to survive the dot-com meltdown, due in large measure to the willingness of Alan M. Meckler, the company's founder, chief executive, and chairman, to adapt to changing conditions. Jupitermedia's business is organized within three divisions. Jupiterimages offers a wealth of stock graphics, photos, and footage to both industry professionals and general consumers, either by subscription basis or as a single image download. The unit also produces two print magazines for design professionals: *Dynamic Graphics Magazine* and *STEP Inside Design Magazine*. JupiterWeb operates four online networks for Information Technology professionals: Internet.com, which offers 12 content channels; EarthWeb.com, offering content for six different professional audiences (including IT managers, software developers, and Web developers); DevX.com, providing software development information for international professionals; and Graphics.com, a network devoted to creative professionals, offering news, tutorials, a forum where professionals can communicate, and a gallery where work can be displayed. The third division is Jupiterresearch, providing research, analysis, and consulting services to help businesses get the most out of the Internet and other emerging consumer technologies. Jupitermedia is a public company listed on the NASDAQ. Meckler owns a 37 percent stake.

Meckler Becoming Involved in Publishing in the Early 1970s

Alan Marshall Meckler was born in Queens, New York, in 1945. Despite suffering from dyslexia, a condition not diagnosed until he was well into his 50s, he earned three degrees in American history from Columbia University. He was able to turn his disability into an advantage: Learning how to listen closely rather than taking notes in class provided him with the skill of focusing on what was important and avoiding getting sidetracked. It was a skill that would become key to his business career, as Meckler was quick to identify business trends well ahead of the competition. One of those trends was the rise of the Internet. After completing his education, Meckler became involved in the publishing field. In 1971 he founded his own company, Microform Review, Inc. in Weston, Connecticut, which subsequently became part of a larger concern, Meckler-Media Corporation. He also found time to author several books on American history as well as other subjects, such as *The Complete Guide to Winning Lotteries by Mail.*

In 1990 Meckler was quick to realize the potential of the Internet, well before the graphic interface made it easy to navigate and only the heartiest of souls were willing to learn the arcane programming language necessary to "telnet" and "ftp" their way through cyberspace. Meckler believed the Internet was an ideal way to deliver computer-related content to librarians, information end-users, and specialists. His first notion was to create an electronic storefront of technology publishing resources, including books, magazines, and newsletters, the first step in establishing a complete electronic publishing division.

Meckler started out in October 1990 with the launch of *Internet World* newsletter, and he soon enjoyed solid success organizing Internet World trade shows, but in the first couple of years he struggled to make money. In 1992 and 1993 he was on the verge of corporate as well as personal bankruptcy, but he managed to hang on through a loan from Union Trust and by selling a third of his company for $1.25 million.

In February 1994 Meckler was able to take MecklerMedia public, raising nearly $5 million. His first Internet acquisition, the first of dozens over the next few years, was the $50,000

Company Perspectives:

Jupitermedia Corporation, headquartered in Darien, CT, is a leading global provider of images, original information, and research for information technology, business and creative professionals.

purchase of The List, a directory of Internet service providers (ISPs). He then attempted to launch MecklerWeb, which he envisioned as a "knowledge exchange," targeting a wide swath of companies and organizations, including think tanks, finance firms, and entertainment companies, which were to pay $25,000 to $50,000 each for a slot on the site. The goal was to attract an upscale online audience to which participants could market. However, only one customer, Anderson Consulting, was willing to pay a $25,000 fee to participate, prompting Meckler to kill the idea. He then sought to impose a more traditional publishing model on MecklerWeb supported by advertising. The content of three MecklerMedia magazines, *CD-ROM World, Internet World,* and *Virtual Reality World,* were put online, with the hope that other specialized publications would be recruited to participate in the future. In November 1994 Meckler sold *CD-ROM World,* and a month later reorganized MecklerMedia, packaging mecklerweb.com and another site, iworld.com, into a separate division, Internet.com.

Internet World also was revamped and began to shift away from a technical audience to a more mainstream one, as user-friendly web browsers including Netscape became available. The publication alerted readers to interesting new web sites, maintained its own home page, and sponsored the hottest trade show in the industry. Other Meckler print publications also focused on the tech sector, such as the quarterlies *Web Developer* and *Web Week,* an Internet trade paper of record.

As forward-thinking and ambitious as Meckler was, however, he lacked the financial resources of much larger media companies. In November 1998 Meckler sold MecklerMedia Corporation to Penton Media, Inc. for $274 million, pocketing a 1,000 percent return on his investment. As part of the deal, Penton immediately sold Meckler an 80.1 percent interest in Internet.com L.L.C., a subsidiary created by Penton to house MecklerMedia's Internet assets. As a result, Meckler was fully committed to the Internet and had the money he needed to become more competitive.

Internet.com Going Public in 1991

In April 1999 Meckler incorporated Internet.com Corp. in Delaware and two months later took the company public at $14 a share in an initial public offering of stock underwritten by U.S. Bancorp, Piper Jaffray Inc., William Blair & Co., and DLCdirect Inc. Internet.com netted $42.8 million. Almost $5 million of the money was used to pay down debt and the rest was earmarked for strategic acquisitions. In addition to using Internet.com to acquire web sites and other online assets, Meckler used it to launch venture capital funds to invest in early-stage content-based web site businesses that focused on business-to-business markets and did not compete directly with Inter-

net.com. The company also launched a pair of complementary web sites, InternetVCLinx.com and InternetVCWatch.com, to provide information on venture capitalists and track investments in Internet companies.

The close of the 1990s and start of the new century were heady days for Meckler and Internet.com. It operated a network of advertisement-supported web sites, e-mail newsletters, online discussion forums, and began hosting a number of face-to-face forums. (In keeping with the sale to Penton, Meckler was prohibited from entering the trade show business for two years.) In December 1999 Internet.com opened news bureaus in Boston and Washington, D.C., to provide local coverage on industry news and Internet investments. Although the company was posting net losses, sales were growing as Meckler proved adept at converting his content and web sites into a number of diversified revenue streams, such as syndication, licensing, and e-commerce partnerships. The price of Internet.com also grew at a strong clip, eventually topping $70. About $6 million of that stock would be put to use in September 2000 when Meckler completed his largest acquisition since 1994: the $16 million purchase of ClickZ Corp., which through its ClickZ.com web site provided online marketing industry analysis.

The dot-com bubble soon burst, and although Internet.com was better established than the vast majority of Internet ventures and boasted actual revenues, more than $52 million in 2000, and was at its heart a publishing company, it was punished along with the rest of the players in the sector. In February 2001, as ad revenues tailed off, the company was forced to lay off about 15 percent of its 400 employees. (About two years later that number would be reduced to 260.) "We have been the whipping boy because of the name," Meckler told the *Wall Street Journal,* which also interviewed Edward Saenz, founder of naming consultant Gravity Branding, who commented, "Anything today that says Internet only or dot-com only has warning and hazard signs all over it." He added that a name including both, like Internet.com, suffered "a double whammy." It was not surprising, therefore, that Meckler changed the name of the company to INT Media Group Inc. in May 2001.

Adopting the Jupitermedia Name in 2002

Despite the name change the price of the company's stock continued to slide until bottoming out at $1.50 in September 2002. By this time the company had changed its name once again, the result of an acquisition. A month earlier Internet.com paid $250,000 for the Jupiter Research and Events business of New York City-based Jupiter Media Metrix Inc., which had been selling off its assets in recent months after failing to negotiate a merger with competitor Nielsen/NetRatings. Jupiter Research had been in business since 1986 as an international research organization that was now a widely respected research firm specializing in Internet-related market research in a number of business areas. Not only did the acquisition mark Meckler's return to the trade show business, it also provided him with a brand name to exploit. In September 2002, INT Media Group, a name Meckler dismissed as "not memorable," became Jupitermedia Corporation.

Meckler was quick to build on Jupiter Research's trade show business, which was launched at the end of 2001 and quickly

---

Key Dates:

1990: MecklerMedia launches the first Internet-related publication.
1994: MecklerMedia establishes the Internet.com division.
1998: MecklerMedia is sold, and its Internet assets are spun off into Internet.com Corp.
1999: The company is taken public.
2001: The name is changed to INT Media Group Inc.
2002: The name is changed to Jupitermedia Corporation.

---

spread from the United States to Germany and Australia. Recast as Jupitermedia's 802.11 Planet trade shows, they were geared toward the promotion of the Wi-Fi revolution for Internet access service providers. Meckler told the *Hartford Courant,* "This thing is a real horse; Kentucky Derby material, Triple Crown material." He also decided to launch a computer industry trade show to challenge the one conducted by Comdex. At the same time, Meckler was not neglecting his other Internet interests. In June 2003, Jupitermedia acquired ArtToday.com, a subscription service for photographs and commercial art, paying $13 million in cash plus stock and other considerations. Two weeks later, Jupitermedia acquired the assets of DevX.com for $2.25 million and 200,000 shares of stock. DevX operated a network of web sites serving the international software community by focusing on software development issues concerning specific products and areas, such as Windows programs, Web development, Java, XML, .NET, c/c + +, Visual Basic, wireless applications, and database applications. Clients included corporate giants such as Microsoft, IBM, Intel, and Nokia.

Sales grew to $71.9 million in 2004 and Jupitermedia also turned a profit of $15.7 million. Meckler was not about to become complacent, however, forever adjusting Jupitermedia's business mix to take advantage of opportunities in the marketplace. He became particularly aggressive in the stock photo and image field. In February 2005 Jupitermedia paid $64.4 million in cash and stock to acquire Creatas L.L.C., which owned Dynamic Graphics Inc. and PictureQuest Acquisition Group. Then, in July, Jupitermedia bought PictureArts Corp. for approximately $63.2 million in cash. Meckler was clearly enamored with the potential of this line of business. All told, Jupitermedia spent $200 million in acquiring seven online photography companies since 2003, and they were a large reason for Jupitermedia becoming profitable. Trade shows, on the other hand, provided lackluster growth, with revenues in 2004 just short of $10 million and a net profit of $1.4 million. In August 2005 Jupitermedia sold its Search Engine Strategies

(SES) trade shows, SearchEngineWatch.com web site, and ClickZ.com network of web sites to London-based Incisive Medias for $43 million in cash, with the money earmarked to pay down the debt incurred from the recent acquisitions. SES was the only Jupitermedia trade show brand to show much promise, and Meckler was eager to sell the business while it was hot. "This sale is evidence of our intent to be even more aggressive in the licensing and distribution of commercial images," Meckler explained in a press statement. "The Funds received from the sale will strengthen our balance sheet and allow us to have greater buying power for more image acquisitions." Meckler, as reported by *Tradeshow Week,* told analysts during an earnings call, "Essentially, with the sale of SES, for all intents and purposes, we are out of the tradeshow business." He was quick to add, "We'll keep our options open, since we have shown great skill in coming up with tradeshow ideas over the years." Given Meckler's track record for ferreting out new opportunities, there was no way to predict in what direction he would take Jupitermedia in the future.

Principal Subsidiaries

Jupiterimages Corporation; Creatas, L.L.C.; Dynamic Graphics, Inc.; PictureQuest Acquisition Company, L.L.C.

Principal Competitors

CNET Networks, Inc.; International Data Group, Inc.; Ziff Davis Media Inc.

Further Reading

Bryan-Low, Cassell, "By Any Other Name, a Dot-Com Would Be Sweeter to Investors," *Wall Street Journal,* April 18, 2001, p. B1.
Callahan, Sean, "Jupitermedia Banks Future on Stock Images," *B to B,* August 8, 2005, p. 3.
Crabb, Cheryl, "Jupitermedia Seeks to Make New Mark in Internet World with Wi-Fi Trade Shows," *Hartford Courant,* June 26, 2003.
McCall, Margo, "Primedia, Jupitermedia Exit Events Biz," *Tradeshow Week,* August 15, 2005, p. 1.
Meeks, Brock N., "MecklerWeb: It's On; It's Off; It's On," *InterActive Week,* November 7, 1994, p. 39.
Pack, Thomas, "Meckler's Media Methods," *EContent,* February/March 2001, p. 66.
Quint, Barbara, "MecklerMedia Sold to Penton Media," *Information Today,* November 1998, p. 18.
Stempel, Dan, "INT Media to Acquire Events Segment of Jupiter Media," *Fairfield County Business Journal,* July 15, 2002, p. 7.
——, "Internet.com Goes Public with Eye on the Long-Term," *Fairfield County Business,* July 26, 1999, p. 2.
——, "Meckler Stands by the Web," *Fairfield County Business Journal,* July 23, 2001, p. 8.

—Ed Dinger

Kintera, Inc.

9605 Scranton Road, Suite 240
San Diego, California 92121
U.S.A.
Telephone: (858) 795-3000
Fax: (858) 795-3010
Web site: http://www.kintera.com

Public Company
Incorporated: 2000 as VirtualDonors.com, Inc.
Employees: 473
Sales: $23.7 million (2004)
Stock Exchanges: NASDAQ
Ticker Symbol: KNTA
NAIC: 511210 Software Publishers

Kintera, Inc. provides software and services to help nonprofit organizations raise money online and manage their fundraising activities. Kintera generates revenue by taking a percentage of each donation and by charging monthly maintenance fees for operating web sites. The principal products offered by the company are the "Friends Asking Friends" fundraising program and "Kintera Sphere," a web-based service providing nonprofit organizations with the tools to put together a complete marketing infrastructure. Kintera serves more than 15,000 accounts in the nonprofit, government, and corporate sectors.

Origins

Much of the financial support, faith in, and future hopes of Kintera rested on the reputation of its cofounder and principal executive, Harry E. Gruber. For many of those who studied Kintera, analyzing its moves and progress, the individual behind the company was more important than what the company did—Gruber's accomplishments, his track record, overshadowed Kintera's business model. Gruber completed his medical training in internal medicine, rheumatology, and biochemical genetics at the University of California, San Diego (UCSD). After earning his medical degree, he joined the faculty at UCSD's School of Medicine, serving as a geneticist, rheumatologist, and a researcher until 1986, when he left to start a

second career as an entrepreneur. The change in direction eventually netted Gruber an immense personal fortune measured in the hundreds of million of dollars and earned him a reputation on Wall Street as a shrewd and skillful businessman.

When Gruber left UCSD, he started Gensia Pharmaceuticals, Inc., a biotechnology firm that became the first of five companies he founded before starting Kintera. Gensia, later renamed SICOR, Inc. and sold to Teva Pharmaceutical Industries LTD. for $3.4 billion in 2003, established Gruber as an entrepreneur of note, fueling his confidence to try other ventures. Over the course of the ensuing decade, he developed the technology for three publicly traded companies focused on human genetics. Gruber founded Aramed, Inc., a central nervous system drug discovery company; Metabasis, Inc., a company developing drugs to treat diabetes and liver disease; and Viagene, Inc., a gene therapy company. After selling Viagene to Chiron Corp. for $150 million, Gruber readied himself for another start-up venture of the same ilk. "I thought I'd take some time off and then do another genetics project," he reflected in a May 15, 2003 interview with *Investor's Business Daily*. Gruber's plans soon changed, however. After a conversation with a friend, he decided to leave the healthcare field and start a company based on the then nascent technology of the Internet.

In 1995, Gruber started INTERVU Inc. after a friend suggested forming a business that offered online videos to help real estate agents. "The idea," Gruber said in his interview with *Investor's Business Daily*, "was to put together little video vignettes so brokers could look at the clips without having to visit the properties." At the time, the Internet had yet to become the bustling hub of information and commerce its proponents promised it would become, but advances in technology would soon turn their vision into reality. Advances in technology, aside from moving the Internet into the mainstream, propelled INTERVU in a new direction shortly after its formation. The advent of streaming technology, which enabled users to watch video as it was being downloaded, prompted Gruber to address a new, larger customer base. INTERVU began offering its service to enable companies to provide audio and video broadcasts of their quarterly financial conference call meetings with analysts and investors. Gruber struck gold with the idea, quickly

Company Perspectives:

Kintera is dedicated to helping nonprofit organizations fulfill their mission by providing Knowledge Interaction technology to build vibrant communities of supporters, beneficiaries and staff. By sharing a set of dynamic data and content, organizations can motivate and engage community members to achieve marketing, programming and fundraising success. With leading edge technology and innovative leadership, Kintera is committed to making a difference in the nonprofit sector.

gaining numerous corporate clients. Television companies NBC and CNN used INTERVU's services to provide video of breaking news stories online. In the midst of the company's widely heralded success and the phenomenal growth of the Internet as a virtual destination, Microsoft Corp. invested $30 million in INTERVU to promote the use of its media player software. "We got a lot of adoption from that relationship," a Microsoft executive said in a May 15, 2003 interview with *Investor's Business Daily.* "It's one of the reasons we're the No. 1 media player." Gruber took INTERVU public in 1997 and, at the height of the Internet fervor, sold the company in February 2000 to Akamai Technologies, Inc. in a $3.5 billion deal, a transaction that netted Gruber $245 million worth of stock.

In his late 40s at the time he sold INTERVU, Gruber possessed more than enough wealth to last a lifetime, but he was ready to strike out again on his own. "The bubble Internet was about creating communities, getting people to show up," he said in a May 15, 2003 interview with *Investor's Business Daily.* "The post-bubble Internet is about transactional communities, getting people to spend money on the Internet." Although his interpretation of the two periods segued to an age decidedly more capitalistic in nature, Gruber adopted a somewhat philanthropic stance with his next company. He decided to start a company that would help charities raise money online, an idea that sprang from his work with Senator John McCain. Gruber, who served as chairman of the development committee responsible for fundraising at UCSD between 1994 and 1999, was organizing online town hall meetings through INTERVU for McCain's 2000 presidential campaign when he realized the potential for online fundraising. "At the time," he explained in a September 28, 2004 interview with the *Daily Deal,* "we were also delivering live music from the House of Blues, but I couldn't get people to spend $10 to hear concerts. But we got people to pay $100 to spend an hour in a town hall meeting with John McCain." Gruber, intent on running a company that sold software and related services to help nonprofits build web sites and collect donations, enlisted the help of his brother Allen Gruber, a physician and early investor in INTERVU, and Dennis Berman, with whom he had attended the University of Pennsylvania during the early 1970s, and started his sixth company. The company was incorporated in February 2000 as VirtualDonors.com, Inc. and changed its name to Kintera, which stood for "Knowledge Interaction," in July 2000.

As Gruber and his two partners set out, the goal was to develop comprehensive capabilities for Kintera. U.S. nonprofit organizations collected more than $200 billion annually, obtaining a fraction of that total—slightly more than $1 billion—online. Gruber was convinced online donations would increase exponentially in the years ahead, and he intended to make Kintera the premier provider of interactive software and services across all sectors of the industry. The company eventually targeted 14 markets that covered the spectrum of nonprofit, government, and corporate sectors: arts and culture; associations; foundations; corporate workplace giving; education, environmental and animal causes; faith-based groups; federations; financial services; governments; health and hospitals; human and social services; international affairs; and advocacy and politics. To meet the needs of clients in each of these sectors, Gruber needed to broaden Kintera's portfolio of services, an objective he pursued by employing an aggressive acquisition strategy. "We're trying to build a substantial company in a short period of time," Gruber explained during a December 6, 2004 interview with the *San Diego Business Journal.* "We're building a brain trust and acquiring the best and brightest management teams in the industry."

Acquisitions Fueling Growth During Kintera's First Years

Kintera's growth during its formative years was fueled by acquisitions. The company followed a particular strategy, surveying the industry landscape, which was populated with scores of firms, and identifying its acquisition targets. "The number one reason is the quality of the management team," Gruber said in his interview with the *San Diego Business Journal,* "and number two is [management's] knowledge of a particular sector. The technology itself is less important because we rebuild it anyway to fit our platform." Gruber agreed to acquire one of his first companies in November 2000, when he purchased Give Power, Inc., a two-person firm based in San Diego that offered online services for athletic fundraising activities. After a lull in acquisitive activity, Kintera began purchasing competing firms with regularity, tailoring each acquisition to fit its platform. Two flagship products, which constituted the company's platform, emerged, "Kintera Sphere" and "Friends Asking Friends." Kintera Sphere, a web-based service, gave clients the ability to manage their web sites, organize individuals, advocate causes, and implement marketing campaigns. Friends Asking Friends, which the October 13, 2003 issue of *Forbes* described as "a kind of do-gooder pyramid scheme," served as a way for volunteers to solicit donations from their friends.

Kintera's acquisition campaign began in earnest in 2002. During the ensuing two years, the company acquired more than a dozen companies, significantly broadening its capabilities. Most of the acquired properties were rival software designers with expertise in particular sectors, but one acquisition stood out from the rest. In February 2002, Kintera acquired Masterplanner Media, Inc., a company founded and owned by Elisabeth Familian. In 1986, Familian published the Los Angeles Masterplanner, a publication that offered a comprehensive calendar of social and civic events in Los Angeles, thereby enabling fundraisers and party planners to avoid conflicts with events targeting the same crowd. Familian added a version for New York City in 1997. In November 2002, eight months after acquiring Masterplanner Media, Gruber published a 28-page, glossy magazine for San Diego, charging a $225 per year

---

Key Dates:

2000: Kintera is founded as VirtualDonors.com, Inc.
2002: Kintera begins acquiring companies at a rapid pace.
2003: Kintera completes its initial public offering of stock.
2005: Kintera's payroll is reduced by 10 percent.

---

subscription rate. A version for Washington, D.C., was slated for release in 2003, part of Gruber's plan to add two to four markets a year until Masterplanner Media's coverage encompassed ten major markets.

Public Offering of Stock in 2003

Thanks largely to acquisitions, Kintera's revenue increased substantially during the first years of the decade, but profits eluded the company. After losing $12.4 million in 2001, the company lost $9.4 million in 2002, a year in which revenues totaled $1.9 million. As the company's acquisition rate picked up pace, its revenue swelled. By August 2003, Kintera was managing monthly donations totaling more than $5.6 million, significantly more than the $65,000 it was managing two years earlier. At this point, Gruber chose to take the company public, filing for an initial public offering (IPO) of stock in October 2003 to reduce nearly $30 million of debt. The IPO was completed in December 2003, raising roughly $35 million, but the year ended with another substantial loss. Kintera generated $7.5 million in revenue and posted a $9.8 million loss. In 2004, a flurry of acquisitions coupled with online donations spurred by the U.S. presidential election, helped revenues nearly triple to $23.7 million, but the year ended with another substantial loss, putting Kintera $19.2 million further in debt.

As Kintera plotted its future course, its inability to post a profit worried some analysts. Gruber remained confident, however, offering advice to those who claimed Kintera was destined to be a perennial money-loser. "I don't think it's a wise bet considering the last two companies I owned were each sold for $3 billion," he said in a September 28, 2004 interview with the *Daily Deal*. "Those who bet on the jockey own my stock," he added. The company was expected to record another major increase in revenue in 2005. Further acquisitions combined with the outpouring of donations for the damage caused by the December 26, 2004 tsunami in Southeast Asia and Hurricane Katrina in August 2005 promised to fuel dramatic revenue growth for the year. Increased revenue offered no guarantee of profitability, however. To help make Kintera a profitable company, Gruber turned his attention to streamlining operations and trimming the company's workforce by 10 percent in August

2005. As it had since the company's formation, success for Kintera rested on the skill and reputation of Gruber. He offered no guarantee that he would end his career at Kintera, only mildly dismissing speculation that he was planning to leave. "I've never started a company to be acquired," he stated in his interview with the *Daily Deal*. "They're more like children—you don't want them to leave, but they grow up."

Principal Competitors

Blackbaud, Inc.; Convio, Inc.; gomembers inc.

Further Reading

Allen, Mike, "Kintera Buys Consultancy," *San Diego Business Journal,* March 29, 2004, p. 8.
——, "Kintera Inc. Agrees to Buy Give Power, Inc." *San Diego Business Journal,* November 13, 2000, p. 5.
——, "Kintera Inc., Provide Ready to Test IPO Market," *San Diego Business Journal,* October 6, 2003, p. 11.
——, "Kintera Revenue and Loss Grow," *San Diego Business Journal,* May 16, 2005, p. 59.
——, "Local Firm Builds Brain Trust Through Acquisitions," *San Diego Business Journal,* December 6, 2004, p. 14.
Barlas, Pete, "Doctor Turned Dot-Com Founder Returns, with Focus on Charities," *Investor's Business Daily,* May 15, 2003, p. A6.
Bigelow, Bruce V., "Kintera, Which Aided in Tsunami Relief, Hit Hard by Quarterly Loss," *San Diego Union-Tribune,* May 11, 2005, p. B1.
——, "Online Fund-Raiser Kintera Posts Record Revenue," *San Diego Union-Tribune,* February 18, 2005, p. B2.
——, "Trading Debut Is Success for San Diego Nonprofit-Services Firm Kintera," *San Diego Union-Tribune,* December 20, 2003, p. B2.
Cecil, Mark, "For Kintera, Why Compete When Buying Is Better?," *Mergers & Acquisitions Report,* November 10, 2003.
Freeman, Mike, "Cost-Cutting Kintera Plans 10 Percent Work-Force Layoffs," *San Diego Union-Tribune,* August 12, 2005, p. B3.
"Fundraising Made Easy," *Health Management Technology,* September 2001, p. 64.
Graves, Brad, "S.D. Tech Firm Jumps into Social Scene with Magazine," *San Diego Business Journal,* November 25, 2002, p. 10.
"Kintera Cutting Workforce; to Report Results Next Week," *America's Intelligence Wire,* August 11, 2005, p. 43.
"Kintera Quarterly Loss Widens; Post Wider Restated 1Q Loss," *America's Intelligence Wire,* August 15, 2005, p. 54.
Lubove, Seth, "I Gave on the Internet," *Forbes,* October 13, 2003, p. 54.
Sanchez, Rick, "Donations Flood Tsunami Web Sites," *America's Intelligence Wire,* January 3, 2005, p. 14.
Shabelman, David, "CEO's Rep Bodes Well for Kintera," *Daily Deal,* September 28, 2004, p. 32.

—Jeffrey L. Covell

Kyokuyo Company Ltd.

3-3-5 Akasaka, Minato-ku
Tokyo
107-0052
Japan
Telephone: +81 3 5545 0701
Fax: +81 3 5545 0751
Web site: http://www.kyokuyo.co.jp

Public Company
Incorporated: 1937
Employees: 1,145
Sales: ¥152.64 billion ($1.45 billion) (2004)
Stock Exchanges: Tokyo
NAIC: 311712 Fresh and Frozen Seafood Processing;
   311412 Frozen Specialty Food Manufacturing

Kyokuyo Company Ltd. is one of Japan's leading seafood products companies. Originally focused on the whaling industry in the 1930s, Kyokuyo has since abandoned that activity in order to transform itself into a full-fledged marine foods company. Kyokuyo's operations include worldwide marine products purchasing and marketing, as well as seafood processing through a global network of more than 220 factories, including seagoing processing facilities. The company also produces food products such as frozen foods and canned seafoods. In addition to its purchasing and processing activities, Kyokuyo remains active in commercial fishing, with a fleet of four tuna seiners. Kyokuyo also has boosted its position in the Japanese sushi market through its partnership with Thailand's Union Frozen Products Co. (UFP). In 2005, that partnership was strengthened with the creation of a joint venture, K&U Enterprise, which began producing sushi for the Japanese and other markets. Kyokuyo is listed on the Tokyo Stock Exchange and is led by Chairman Kiyokazu Fukui.

Whaler in the 1930s

Kyokuyo's history dated back to the beginnings of the Japanese whaling industry in the early 20th century. Ayukawa rap-idly became the center of the country's whaling industry, following the establishment of the first slaughterhouse there in 1906. At the beginning of the next decade, nearly all of the country's major whalers were based in Ayukawa.

By the 1920s, the Japanese whaling fleet had expanded operations to include many of the world's primary whale hunting regions. A number of new companies sprang up, such as Ayukawa Hogei, founded in 1925, as Japan began asserting itself among the world's most active whalers. The new company, like many others in the industry, began focusing on hunting smaller whale species in the early 1930s. This led to further expansion in the Japanese whaling industry, with increasing interests in the northern polar region. Ayukawa Hogei's own expansion into polar whaling led it to change its name, to Kyokuyo Hogei KK (literally, Polar Seas Whaling Ltd.), in 1937.

Although Kyokuyo remained an active whaler through the next decades, by the 1950s the company had begun its transformation into a seafood processor. This process was begun in 1954 when the company launched its own fleet of factory ships, providing onboard fish processing facilities. The company then began fishing and processing salmon and ocean trout in the northern Pacific region.

Kyokuyo's success in fish processing encouraged the company to expand its food production operations in the early 1960s. The first food production facilities were built in the Hokkaido and Miyagi regions in 1960. Kyokuyo then launched production of canned goods, and at the same time extended beyond seafood to include production of cured meats and sausages, among others.

Yet seafood remained at the heart of the company's business. In 1963, Kyokuyo set up what was to become one of its core business areas, establishing a marine products imports business. The company then launched its worldwide seafood purchasing activity, with a special focus on the Alaskan market and its highly prized salmon roe and other fish products. By 1970, Kyokuyo also had entered the frozen foods market, building a cold-storage facility in Hiratsuka, Kanagawa. The company also expanded its overall production with the opening of a new factory in Hachinohe, Aomori.

<table>
<tr><td colspan="2">

Company Perspectives:

In keeping with our mission ''growing along with society as we contribute to a healthy and abundant lifestyle and diet'' our entire group of companies will continue to strive to the utmost to keep the satisfaction and trust of our business partners and consumers by supplying safe and secured food. We look forward to a continuance of your support and cooperation.

</td><td>

Key Dates:

1925: The whaling company Ayukawa Hogei is established.
1937: The company changes its name to Kyokuyo Hogei KK.
1954: The company enters the fish processing business with the launch of a fleet of factory processors for salmon and ocean trout.
1960: The company launches food production with factories in Hokkaido and Miyagi.
1963: The company begins marine food products purchasing and imports operations.
1970: Production of frozen foods begins.
1971: The company changes its name to Kyokuyo KK; cold-storage operations are launched in Osaka.
1973: Kyokuyo launches a fleet of purse seine vessels for tuna and skipjack.
1976: The company abandons the whaling industry.
1980: A frozen shrimp and prawn subsidiary is established in Miyagi.
1984: A new frozen crab-flavored food products facility is opened in Ehime.
1988: Kyokuyo expands its frozen food activities with the creation of another production subsidiary, Sapport Foods Co., in Hokkaido.
1991: The company abandons deep-sea trawling and liquidates its trawling fleet; a research and development laboratory is established in Shiogama, in Miyagi.
1994: A new factory is opened in Shiogama.
1996: Kyokuyo America Corporation is established.
1997: The company launches Kyokuyo Suisan Co., operating purse seine fishing vessels.
1999: A new factory is opened in Hitachinaka, Ibaraki.
2004: The company launches a ship-owning subsidiary in Panama.
2005: Kyokuyo forms the K&U Enterprise joint venture with UFP in Thailand.

</td></tr>
</table>

Kyokuyo's expansion into food production helped shield it from the intensifying competition and dwindling whale population in the global whaling industry. By then, the whaling industry had shifted away from its interest in small-type whaling, in favor of larger species and larger vessels. Nonetheless, Kyokuyo remained in the whaling trade into the 1970s. As part of its effort to remain competitive, the company formed a new subsidiary, Hokuyo Hogei, which began operating large-type whalers within the company's fleet.

Shift to Food Production in the 1970s

By then, however, Kyokuyo's shifting emphasis to food production led it to change its name, to Kyokuyo KK, in 1971. In that year, as well, the company added another cold-storage subsidiary, Kyoikuyo Akitsu Reizo, in Osaka, helping to expand its coverage of the Japanese market. Kyokuyo also boosted its purchasing and imports operations with the creation of Kyokuyo Shoki Co. That company began purchasing and selling not only marine products, but livestock and agricultural products as well.

Kyokuyo further solidified both its production and sales operations with the launch of its own fleet of tuna and skipjack seiners in 1973. The company's fleet sailed under the Wakaba Maru name. At the same time, Kyokuyo also entered a new shipping category, launching a fleet of refrigerated transporters, Satsuki Maru. The successful development of these lines of business, coupled with intensifying international pressure on the Japanese government to restrict, and even ban, international whaling, led Kyokuyo to exit the whaling industry in 1976.

Kyokuyo sought new expansion areas into the 1980s. In 1980, for example, the company founded a new subsidiary, Kyokuyo Shokuhin Co. in Miyagi, which began processing frozen seafood, especially shrimp and prawn. This was followed by the launch of another subsidiary, in Ehime, in 1984, which began processing crab-flavored frozen food products, such as kamaboko. In 1986, the company added to its international shipping operations with the establishment of Kyokuyo Shipping Co., which included the transport of fruits and vegetables, as well as dairy foods, in addition to marine products. Two years later, Kyokuyo expanded its frozen food activities with the creation of another production subsidiary, Sapport Foods Co., in Hokkaido.

In the late 1980s, Kyokuyo boosted its international presence with an entry into a number of foreign markets. In the United States, for example, the company set up a number of operations involved in marine products purchasing, fish paste marketing (on the East Coast), and the oversight of a seafood processing company. The company also entered the South American market, notably through the operation of a fish-paste processing vessel. In 1991, the company expanded that business through the creation of a joint venture with fellow Japanese company Mitsui & Co. The joint venture took over Kyokuyo's fish-paste processor, with production levels slated at 6,000 tons per year. By January 1992, the company had expanded its partnership with Mitsui to include another joint venture, together with local partner Harengus, the leading fish-exporter in Argentina, to process surimi for the Japanese market.

The continued development of its food production wing encouraged Kyokuyo to abandon its deep-sea trawling business at the beginning of the 1990s as well. By 1993, the company had discontinued its operations in this area, selling off most of its fleet. Nonetheless, the company remained involved in fishing, and continued to operate a small fleet of tuna seiners into the mid-2000s.

Major Japanese Seafood Company in the 2000s

Kyokuyo took the lead in the establishment of new food quality and hygiene control standards, especially the internationally recognized HACCP system. As part of this effort, the company launched its own research and development laboratory in Shiogama, in Miyagi, in 1991. Miyagi remained the focus of continued expansion by the company, with the establishment of a second plant in Shiogama in 1994. That facility received HACCP certification the following year.

The year 1995 also saw the addition of a new subsidiary to the ever expanding Kyokuyo group, with the creation of Hachinohe Seafood Co., in 1995. That company launched processing operations for various marine products, including cuttlefish and salmon. Further development of the group's Japanese production facilities continued into the 2000s, including the opening of a new factory in Hitachinaka, in Ibaraki, in 1999. That plant received HACCP certification in 2003.

Yet Kyokuyo also had begun efforts to develop its international operations as well. This led the company to found a new subsidiary in the United States, Kyokuyo America Corporation, in 1996. That company served as the group's marine products purchasing agent for exports to Japan. Kyokuyo also returned to international fishing waters with the establishment of a new purse seiner subsidiary, Kyokuyo Suisan Co., in 1997. That subsidiary not only operated its own tuna and skipjack fishing vessels, but also provided processing and sales operations and cold-storage warehousing facilities. In 2004, the company opened a new shipping subsidiary in Panama, Kyokuyo Shipping Panama.

Kyokuyo moved to boost its presence in the Japanese sushi market into the mid-2000s. This led the company to form a strategic alliance with Thailand's Union Frozen Products Co. (UFP), one of that country's leading suppliers of sushi products, which was then making an effort to penetrate the Japanese market. The two companies had long conducted business together, starting in the mid-1980s. The companies moved toward a more formalized alliance in the early 2000s, as Kyokuyo, which relied on UFP for the bulk of its sushi products, sought to head off competitors. This effort resulted in the creation of a joint venture between the two companies in 2005.

The new company, called K&U Enterprise, was based on UFP's supply of raw product and Kyokuyo's expertise in sushi production techniques and technology. K&U began marketing its products under a number of brand names, including Kyokuyo in Japan, Prantalay in Thailand, and K&U and UFP elsewhere. In this way Kyokuyo emerged as a leader in the Japanese sushi market. As it moved into the 21st century, Kyokuyo had completed its transition from whaler to dedicated seafood processor.

Principal Subsidiaries

Kyokuyo America Corporation; Kyokuyo Suisan Co., Ltd.; Kyokuyo Shoji Co., Ltd.; Kyokuyo Shokuhin Co., Ltd.; Hachinohe Seafood Co., Ltd.; Kyokuyo Foods Co., Ltd.; Sapport Foods Co., Ltd.; Kyokuyo Akitsu Reizo Co., Ltd.; Kyokuyo Shipping Co., Ltd.; Kyokuyo Shipping Panama S.A.; K&U Enterprise Co., Ltd.; Kyokuyo Sougou Service Co., Ltd.

Principal Competitors

Antarktika Fishing Co.; Mar Fishing Company Inc.; ENACA; Maruha Group Inc.; Unilever Deutschland GmbH; Mavesa S.A.; Mukorob Fishing Proprietary Ltd.; Hanwa Company Ltd.; Nichiro Corporation.

Further Reading

Arunmas, Phusadee, "Joint Venture Will Market Sushi," *Bangkok Post,* April 8, 2005.
"New Surimi Venture Set Up," *Seafood International,* January 1992, p. 4.
Somporn Thapanachai Smarn Sudto, "Firm Wins Deal to Supply Sushi to Japanese Importer," *Bangkok Post,* June 3, 2002.
"Tuna Flakes from Kyokuyo," *Japan Food Service Journal,* June 25, 2003.

—M.L. Cohen

Laboratoires Arkopharma S.A.

BP 28
Carros
F-06511 Cedex
France
Telephone: + 33 4 93 29 11 28
Fax: + 33 4 93 29 11 62
Web site: http://www.arkopharma.com

Public Company
Incorporated: 1980
Employees: 1,600
Sales: EUR 253.9 million (2004)
Stock Exchanges: Euronext Paris
Ticker Symbol: ARK
NAIC: 325412 Pharmaceutical Preparation Manufacturing

Laboratoires Arkopharma S.A. is France's leading producer and distributor of phytotherapeutic medicines—that is, medicine based on plants. The Nice-based company also has built up a leading position on the worldwide market, with subsidiaries in 12 countries, and sales to more than 65 countries. The largest part of Arkopharma's product range targets the over-the-counter (OTC) market, with treatment for commonly self-medicated conditions such as headache, pain relief, cold relief, insomnia, and the like. Arkopharma also is a leading producer of appetite control and diet-related products, vitamins and minerals, and skin care treatments, and also produces a line of veterinary products. In addition to its OTC range, the company also develops a range of prescription-strength medicines, including supplemental treatments for AIDS, cancer, and other diseases. Phytotherapy remains the group's largest market, at 65 percent of sales of EUR 247 million ($280 million) in 2004. Europe represents the group's core market, at nearly 90 percent of total sales. North America accounted for just 6 percent of sales, while the Asian Pacific (in large part through Australian subsidiary Nutrasense) added 3 percent. Colette Robert is the group's president, and founder Max Rombi is chairman of the board of directors. Sons Olivier and Philippe Rombi serve as co-CEOs. Arkopharma is listed on the Euronext Paris Stock Exchange.

The Rombi family controls approximately 54 percent of the group's shares.

French Phytotherapy Pioneer in the 1980s

The use of plants for healing purposes had its roots in mankind's earliest history. The earliest known records of attempts to classify plants according to their medicinal properties dated back to ancient Sumer, and the earliest Chinese dynasties also developed a system of medicine based on plants and herbs. In this way, hundreds of species had been classified as medicinal plants.

In the West, the first classification attempts appeared in Greece, and included the efforts of such noted figures as Hippocrates, Dioscorides, and Galen. Yet the use of plants and herbs for their medicinal and pharmaceutical effects appeared universal among cultures and civilizations around the world.

Modern medicine itself grew out of the use of plants. A major step came following the work of Swiss alchemist Philippus Aureolus Paracelsus (1493–1541), who developed the idea of the "active principal," that is, the part of the plant that contributed its medicinal effect. The notion of the active principal was to give rise to a global pharmaceutical industry, which developed new drugs and medicines through the identification, and ultimately, the artificial synthesis of the active molecules in plants and other substances found in nature.

For many, however, the development of the pharmaceutical industry and of such highly targeted molecules had unpleasant consequences, not the least of which were the often unpleasant side effects of many, if not most, modern medicines. By the late 1960s and especially during the 1970s, a growing number of people had begun to question the basis of the pharmaceutical industry, particularly as it grew into one of the most powerful sectors of the global economy. The highly symptom-oriented nature of Western medicine also came under criticism, particularly as many common drug therapies were known to cause symptoms, and even illnesses, as painful as the treated disease itself.

This led to a growing interest in a return to more traditional healing techniques, and particularly, an interest in the use of the

Company Perspectives:

ARKOPHARMA—The science of health, naturally.

whole plant, rather than a single identified "active" substance contained in the plant, for the treatment of many common ailments. The branch of phytotherapy, that is, plant-based medical therapies, became part of a trend toward the development of gentler and less toxic treatment methods. Unlike many competing "alternative" therapies, however, such as homeopathy, among others, phytotherapeutic preparations presented clear active ingredients that were capable of being identified and quantified.

In France, Dr. Max Rombi had become part of the movement toward more holistic medical treatment by the late 1970s. In 1980, Rombi went into business for himself in order to produce his own phytotherapeutical preparations. Rombi founded Laboratoires Arkopharma that year, and was joined by chemist Colette Robert, among others.

Rombi's idea was to break from traditional delivery methods of plant-based medicines, which generally were presented in liquid form, and were heated and/or dissolved in water or alcohol. Rombi recognized that a market existed for a more convenient form of delivery. Inspired by the tablets and capsules of mainstream medicine, Arkopharma sought a method for encapsulating its plant preparations. By 1982, the company's efforts resulted in the launch of its line of Arkogélules, which featured powdered, whole plant in gelatin capsules. The capsules were an immediate success, not least because they seemed to capture the spirit of the times, and the "on-the-go" nature of French society in the early 1980s.

The launch of the Arkogélule enabled Arkopharma to claim an early lead in the French phytotherapy sector. By the end of 1982, sales had topped the equivalent of EUR 8 million. Arkopharma extended its product range into the mid-1980s, adding a line of vitamins and minerals, as well as a line of veterinary products. Among the company's biggest sellers, however, was its line of dietary and appetite control preparations.

Arkopharma's research and development effort also worked toward a new breakthrough, inventing the Cryobroyage method of plant preparation. Launched in 1985, the new method employed liquid nitrogen to deep freeze plants and enabled them to be ground at temperatures below −196 degrees Celsius. In this way, the totality of the plant and its active ingredients was conserved, in contrast to traditional plant preparation techniques. The method also permitted the plants to be ground more finely, enabling them to be more efficiently digested.

Arkopharma's breakthrough came in 1986, when the Health Ministry of the French government recognized phytotherapy as a legitimate branch of medicine. The ministry put into place a certification system, called the "Autorisation de Mise sur Marché" (or AMM), as a means of legislating the marketing of phytotherapeutical medicines. Arkopharma quickly took advantage of the new legislation, achieving AMMs for 18 of its products by the following year. In 1987, as well, the company launched a new line, Arkofluides, featuring encapsulated oils.

Acquiring Scale in the 1990s

The French government's recognition of phytotherapy not only boosted the branch's profile in France, but also enhanced its legitimacy elsewhere in Europe. Arkopharma moved to capture a share of the growing European market for plant-based therapies, creating subsidiaries in Spain, Italy, and the United Kingdom by 1987. The rising interest in plant-based treatments in North America also encouraged the company to set up a subsidiary in the United States. By the end of 1988, the company's sales had topped the equivalent of EUR 31 million.

Arkopharma made a number of strategic expansion moves in the early 1990s. In 1990, for example, the company acquired one of its chief French rivals, Laboratoires Phytodif. Another acquisition, of Homéopathie Ferrier, enabled the company to boost its range with Ferrier's production of homeopathic medicines. By 1991, Arkopharma also had expanded its sales network to include Germany. To meet its production needs, the company added a new 15,000-square-meter facility that year as well.

By 1994, Arkopharma had expanded its international sales reach by forming a series of distribution agreements. In this way, the company entered the Danish, Finnish, and Portuguese markets in Europe, and also added sales in Hong Kong, Malaysia, Taiwan, Singapore, and China. Part of the success of the company's international expansion was due to the launch, in 1993, of a new line of diet products, called Arkoline, which became a strong seller for the company both at home and abroad. In that year, as well, the company added the Nutriline family of nutritional therapy products.

Arkopharma continued rolling out new products into the mid-1990s. A significant milestone for the company came with the launch of its Mincifit line of "slimming" creams and oils in 1995. In this way the company became an early entrant into what was to become one of the fastest-growing cosmetics categories at the dawn of the 21st century.

At the same time, the company entered the dental care field, launching its own brand, Arkofresh, in 1995. That year, as well, the company acquired Laboratoires Veterinaire ICC, a manufacturer of veterinary products, and especially anti-parasite collars. The purchase of ICC made Arkopharma the number two maker of tick and flea collars in France.

Arkopharma's sales had topped the equivalent of EUR 80 million by the middle of the 1990s. The company then prepared for the next phase of its development by listing its stock on the Paris Bourse's Secondary Market in 1996. The public offering enabled Arkopharma to make a new acquisition, of Laboratoires Homéopathie Complexe, that year. The company also acquired a new logistics center, a 15,000-square-meter facility in Carros.

Arkopharma returned to innovation the following year with the launch of the market's first 100 percent vegetable-based capsule coating. Until then, the company's capsules had been based on gelatin, derived from cows. Yet rising concerns over mad cow disease in the late 1990s, and the inherent conflict between the company's plant-based therapies and the animal-based delivery method, as well as the natural tendency of the company's core consumer market to reject the latter, had encouraged the company to commit to the development of the new capsule type, based on cellulose fibers.

The launch of the new capsule coincided with a boom in the company's international development. Arkopharma added to its foreign network, buying up its Belgian distributor in 1998, and setting up a subsidiary in The Netherlands that year as well. The following year, the company established a true presence in the U.S. market with the purchase of New Hampshire-based Oakmont Investments, Inc., and its Health from the Sun and Oakmont Laboratories brands. The acquisition gave Arkopharma control of Oakmont's line of vegetarian essential fatty acid capsules and, still more important, access to Oakmont's distribution network among the 6,000 some stores in the U.S. health food market.

Phytotherapy Leader in the 2000s

Arkopharma relied on outside sources for most of the raw products used in its preparations. In 1999, however, the company launched a new subsidiary, called Burgundy, dedicated to the production of certain plants and plant extracts for use in the group's phytotherapy products. The company expanded its product line again in 2000, buying up a 75 percent stake in

Nutrasense, based in Australia. The acquisition enhanced the company's access to the Australian, New Zealand, and related Pacific markets, and also extended its product range to include the strong Nutrasense brand of plant-based arthritic and rheumatic medications.

The Nutrasense and Oakmont acquisitions played a major role in the shifting geographic focus of Arkopharma's sales. From a purely French company at the beginning of the 1980s, Arkopharma had grown into a truly international phytotherapy leader. By the early 2000s, international sales represented nearly 80 percent of the company's sales of almost EUR 184 million in 2001.

Arkopharma moved to boost its position in the cosmetics market, taking advantage of growing concerns over the massive use of often dangerous chemicals by the mainstream cosmetics and skin care leaders. In 2002, the company launched a new brand, Laboratoires Plante System, featuring 16 plant-based skin care and cosmetics products. The following year, the company had a new major success, this time in the diet-related segment, with the launch of its drinkable appetite control beverage, 4.3.2.1 Minceur. By 2004, that product had become the company's top seller.

Arkopharma maintained its growth momentum into the middle of the 2000s. In 2003, the company moved into Switzerland, acquiring that country's PAD and Phyto Pharma Medika. That same year, Arkopharma added a Canadian subsidiary to boost its North American presence. By the end of 2004, Arkopharma's sales had grown again, nearing EUR 250 million.

In the mid-2000s, Arkopharma and the growing phytotherapy industry faced new pressures. In 2003, Arkopharma was forced to withdraw one product, Exolise, launched in 1999, from the market because of reports that the product had caused liver damage in a number of people. Then in October 2005, Max Rombi, who had since retired as chairman of the company, was charged with involuntary manslaughter because a reported mix-up between two Chinese herbs, one innocuous, the other toxic, used in one of the company's weight-loss preparations allegedly had caused the deaths of two women.

These cases highlighted for many the potential danger of plant-based medicines, and especially the risks involved in the tendency for consumers to self-medicate using phytotherapeutic formulations. For others, however, the pressure to enforce stricter legislation on the phytotherapy sector, and the alternative healthcare sector in general, represented an attempt by the global pharmaceuticals industry to gain control of, if not eliminate, a growing competitive threat. Arkopharma's strong growth since its founding highlighted the appeal of alternative treatment methods to mainstream medicine.

Principal Subsidiaries

Arkopharma UK Ltd.; Arkopharma GmbH (Germany); Arkopharma LLC (U.S.A.); Nutrasense Australia Pty. Ltd.; Arkochim España; Arkopharma Nederland B.V; Arkofarm S.R.L. (Italy); Arkopharma Benelux; Arkopharma Ireland Ltd.; Arkopharma Canada.

Principal Competitors

Nature's Sunshine Products, Inc.; Pure World, Inc.

Further Reading

"Arkopharma Announces EUR 23m Expansion Plan for 2003 to 2006," *Chemical Business NewsBase,* April 14, 2003.

"Arkopharma Invests in Australian Firm," *Nutraceuticals International,* December 2000.

"Arkopharma Posts 16.4% Sales Increase," *Nutraceuticals International,* October 2004.

"Arkopharma's Exolise Suspended from Sale," *Nutraceuticals International,* May 2003.

Crochet, V., "Gros plan sur: Le groupe pharmaceutique Arkopharma, leader français de la phytotherapie," *Gazette Labo,* April 1999.

"French Supplement Maker Acquires Health from the Sun," *Natural Foods Merchandiser,* April 1999.

"Les 15 patrons les plus influents: Colette Robert, la reine des plantes médicinales, *L'Expansion,* May 2005.

"Ouverture du 'procès des plantes chinoises' d'Arkopharma à Nice," *AFP,* October 5, 2005.

"Patrons moins," *Challenges,* October 6, 2005.

—M.L. Cohen

A RICOH COMPANY

Lanier Worldwide, Inc.

2300 Parklake Drive, NE
Atlanta, Georgia 30345-2902
U.S.A.
Telephone: (770) 496-9500
Toll Free: (800) 708-7088
Fax: (800) 252-9703
Web site: http://www.lanier.com

Wholly Owned Subsidiary of Ricoh Corporation
Founded: 1934 as The Lanier Company
Employees: 4,000
Sales: $1.1 billion (2004)
NAIC: 423420 Office Equipment Merchant Wholesalers; 423410 Photographic Equipment and Supplies Merchant Wholesalers; 423439 Computer and Computer Peripheral Equipment and Software Merchant Wholesalers

A subsidiary of Ricoh Corporation, Atlanta-based Lanier Worldwide, Inc. supplies customers with copiers, fax machines, scanners, digital duplicators, and printers, as well as parts and supplies and document management software. The Lanier Professional Services unit offers consulting services, facilities management, systems integration, reprographics services, and outsourcing. In response to a downturn in the copier field Lanier has begun to develop market-specific applications for industries such as healthcare and real estate.

Company Roots Dating to the 1930s

Lanier was founded by brothers Hicks, Sartain, and Thomas Lanier in Nashville, Tennessee, where the family settled after the three boys and a sister were born. Fascinated with the new dictation machines, the Dictiphone brought out by Columbia Graphophone and Thomas Edison's Ediphone, the brothers started The Lanier Company in Nashville in 1934 to serve as the southeastern distributor of Ediphone. They soon began producing their own dictation machines, as well as business forms. The business prospered and spread throughout the region, but growth was interrupted by World War II, when the components they needed were commandeered by the military. As a result,

the Lanier brothers were forced to find a more suitable business for the times, intended merely as an interim measure.

Through a friend they learned about Oxford of Atlanta, which sold clothing for men and boys. Despite knowing nothing about the apparel industry, they bought a stake in the company in 1942, established themselves in Atlanta, and took the lead in expanding the company. A year later Oxford acquired the Rome, Georgia-based Champion Garment Company, which they renamed Oxford Manufacturing Company, and before the war was over they added three more plants to the operation. In 1944 the Lanier brothers bought out their partners and became the sole owners of Oxford, which they no longer viewed as a temporary occupation. Hicks Lanier, however, was never overly comfortable with the apparel trade and its constant changes in fashion. After the war he decided to return to his prior business, telling Sartain that apparel was too complex: "I'm going back to the dictating machine, where customers only want one model, one size, and one color."

The major break for the Lanier Company, now based in Atlanta, came in 1947 when it revolutionized the dictation industry with the introduction of plastic discs that replaced the bulky wax cylinders that had been used for decades as the recording medium. The company entered the new copier field in 1955, again embracing new technology when it became an independent distributor for Minnesota Mining and Manufacturing Company (3M) and its "thermofax" copiers, which relied on semitransparent and heat-sensitive paper. An original was covered with the Thermofax paper, placed under a glass contact frame and exposed to light, which was absorbed by the black images on the original and heated up the Thermofax paper to create a copy. Offering just a single copy at a time, Thermofax copiers were crude by contemporary standards, yet they were a godsend to offices at a time when carbon paper was an office staple. They also established a lasting relationship between Lanier and 3M that would benefit both companies over the decades.

Acquired by Oxford Industries in the 1960s

In 1960 Oxford Industries became a public company. Two years later Thomas Lanier was killed in a plane crash, leaving Sartain to run the apparel business and Hicks to head what had

Company Perspectives:

Lanier is among the world's largest global providers of document management solutions. We specialize in products and services that help customers improve productivity and reduce the cost of document creation, distribution, replication and retention.

become Lanier Business Products. In 1965 Gene Milner, who married into the Lanier family, took over as Lanier's president and would become known for his tough management style. Three years later, in 1968, Oxford acquired Lanier Business Products in a stock swap. It proved to be a good addition for Oxford, which saw its apparel sales decline due to inflation and a recession. With Oxford's backing Lanier grew into a national player in the 1970s, able to buy many of its key suppliers. However, less than ten years after acquiring Lanier, Oxford decided it was better off focusing on apparel, and in July 1977 Lanier business products was spun off as a public company listed on the New York Stock Exchange.

As Lanier regained its independence it also changed leadership, with Milner replaced by Wesley E. Cantrell, a man of opposite personality, described as warm and gregarious, who would head Lanier for the next 25 years. Milner's son, Hicks L. Milner, told *Atlanta Business Journal* in 1998 that Cantrell "had more of a calmer approach" than his father, adding, "Dad would kick you in the pants, and Wes would come around and pat you on the back and tell you he loved you."

Cantrell was born in Georgia in 1935, the son of an itinerant Baptist minister who moonlighted as a school teacher or principal to help make ends meet. A child of the Depression, Cantrell grew up with a well-ingrained work ethic and an abiding Christian faith. By the time he was 14 he had his own checking account and paid his expenses, working seasonally as a chicken catcher for a local poultry processor and an order picker at a drugstore. He dreamed of becoming an inventor and was determined, despite his modest circumstances, to attend college. After graduating as valedictorian of his high school class, Cantrell joined the Naval Reserves to help finance his studies at Southern Technical Institute in Georgia, from which he graduated in electronics with honors in June 1955 after just two years. Cantrell was hired by IBM as a field engineer, but the job did not start until the fall and he looked for a summer job. He came across a Lanier ad at his school's placement office and took a position as a repairman for the office equipment distributor. He was sent to work in Louisiana, where in addition to repairs he began to work in sales. His personality was well suited to the task of building customer relations and he soon discovered the potential of commissions, realizing that the more products he sold the more money he could make. Not only was his job at IBM to be salary only, he noticed that a lot of young people were quickly moving up the ranks at Lanier, a fast-growing company after forging its alliance with 3M. At the end of the summer, he decided to stay at Lanier and gave up the job offer at IBM and the life of a field engineer. Although his focus would shift to sales, for many years he carried a tool kit in his car in case a Lanier copier needed fixing.

Cantrell steadily moved up the corporate ladder at Lanier over the next 20 years. He was named a district sales manager in 1962 and by 1966 was made vice-president and sales manager for dictating products. From there he became an executive vice-president and national sales manager in 1972, and two years later secured a seat on Oxford's board of directors. Although he took charge of Lanier after it was spun off in 1977, the company, which was generating sales of less than $100 million, remained very much influenced by the Lanier family, which continued to own a stake in the company through Oxford. Sartain Lanier served as Oxford's CEO and chairman until his retirement in 1981, when he was succeeded by his son, John Hicks Lanier. Then, in 1983 Lanier Business Products was acquired by Harris Corporation, an international communications and electronics company, ending the Lanier family connection and also bringing with it a stricter environment. "I didn't like it at first," Cantrell told *Atlanta Business Chronicle* in a 1990 profile. "It was different. I wasn't sure I could get along with these people. . . . They didn't see the world from the same vantage point we did." According to the *Chronicle,* "Eventually, Cantrell saw the advantages of working for a new boss. Today he calls the buyout by Harris 'one of the best things that ever happened to me.' "

Two years after acquiring Lanier, Harris opted to merge Lanier's unit that sold copiers, laser printers, and fax machines with 3M operations to create a joint venture called Harris/3M Document Products Inc. Harris continued to control the Lanier business systems and Lanier voice products divisions, which sold dictating equipment, telephone systems, and document processing systems. The 3M venture lasted until May 1989, when Harris bought out its partner. Two months later, Harris restructured its business products operations, housing them under a new wholly owned subsidiary called Lanier Worldwide, Inc. The $1 billion company was divided into three product divisions: copying systems, fax, and voice products. Lanier would now be able to take advantage of the global sales network of 1,600 offices set up by Harris/3M to sell copiers, printers, and fax machines in order to sell dictating equipment around the world. Previously, just 5 percent of Lanier's dictating equipment sales were outside the United States.

Lanier was a major component of Harris Corporation, accounting for about one-third of its revenues at the start of the 1990s. Having the deep pockets of a corporate parent also proved beneficial to Lanier's growth, as it was able to take advantage of Harris's research and development capabilities as well as its cash. According to *Atlanta Business Chronicle,* Lanier grew its revenues 32.5 percent to $1.3 billion and nearly doubled its earnings from $36.6 million in 1994 to $62.8 million in 1998. At this stage, the company generated about a third of its revenues overseas, from operations in more than 100 countries. All told, Lanier employed 9,400 people around the world.

Cantrell announced in 1998 that he planned to retire in 2000. (Aside from approaching the mandatory retirement age of 65, Cantrell also had been diagnosed with prostate cancer, which he managed through lifestyle changes such as adopting a vegetarian diet.) "There comes a time for the old guy to step aside and let the young guys run things," he told *Atlanta Business Chronicle.* Before leaving, however, he planned to reorganize the company to ensure it was able to make the adjustment to a shift in technologies, as the industry moved from analog to digital.

He named C. Lance Herrin as Lanier's first chief operating officer, positioning him as his successor. Structurally Cantrell wanted to organize the company by function and do away with the split between domestic and international operations. He wanted to negotiate global distribution rights from suppliers and be able to offer the same products around the world. As part of the effort to bolster its global business, Lanier in 1998 acquired an Australian company and later paid $162 million for the Agfa-Gevaert Group's copying systems business unit from Germany's Bayer Group, a deal that gave Lanier access to Canon, Minolta, and Xerox products in Europe. Lanier also began to target industries, including healthcare and the legal field, with products and services geared specifically for them. The company was also increasingly promoting multifunctional equipment rather than dedicated copiers, fax machines, and printers.

Late 1990s Spinoff

Cantrell's retirement plans were put on hold, however. In April 1999 Harris decided to spin off Lanier as a public company in the form of a tax-free dividend of Lanier stock. As part of the plan, Harris, which would retain a 10 percent stake in Lanier, asked Cantrell to commit to serving another two years as CEO and chairman. Since being the chairman of a publicly traded Lanier had been his ''last unfulfilled dream,'' Cantrell agreed. Splitting Harris and Lanier was believed to be in the best interests of both companies. Their value as two pure-play companies was expected to be greater because narrowly focused companies generally outperformed conglomerates. In exchange for gaining its independence Lanier took on $700 million in debt, but because the economy was booming and the global market for document imaging and management products was projected to enjoy strong growth, the company was not expected to have any difficulty in generating the cash it needed to repay its debt.

The joy of being a separate company was short-lived for Cantrell and Lanier, however. His cancer flared up once again, which he suspected was related to the pressures of splitting the company from Harris. In March 2000 he had the cancer removed and stayed away from the company for a month. ''But back at Lanier,'' according to *Atlanta Business Chronicle* in a

2000 article, ''the situation was deteriorating. The copier industry is making a transition from the older analog technology to the newer digital technology, putting great pressure on prices. Lanier buys the office machines it distributes from Japanese manufacturers, and a stronger yen has meant falling profit margins. Price increases are unheard of, and the entire industry is looking at declining revenues.'' In order to cut costs and remain competitive, Cantrell eliminated some 500 jobs.

Although not close to going bankrupt, Lanier, saddled with heavy debt, found itself in a difficult situation. As a result, it was open to overtures from five companies who were interested in buying Lanier. Cantrell decided he should at least listen to the offers and concluded that Japan's Ricoh Corporation's bid of $3 per share of stock, which at this point had plunged to the 50 cent range, was too good to pass up. In late November 2000, Ricoh paid about $260 million for Lanier and took on its remaining $650 million in debt. Lanier not only gained financial security but was now tied to one of its chief manufacturer/suppliers.

Cantrell stayed on until January 2001, when Ricoh officially acquired the company and installed Nori Goto as the new chief executive officer. A seasoned international businessman, Goto had been with Ricoh for nearly 20 years and had previously served as president of Ricoh Germany GmbH. Under Goto, Lanier continued to pursue a strategy of developing market-specific applications. In 2002 the company introduced a slate of document management systems intended for healthcare organizations, such as encryption features to ensure that copying and faxing of patient records (protected health information or PHI) were secure. Also in 2002 Lanier unveiled a pair of products geared toward the real estate market: Email-Enable Fax, to allow a home office to send letters and contracts to agents in the field, and Color Print Tracking for Real Estate, an application that allowed brokers to produce full-color publications in-house. Lanier added to its healthcare applications in 2003 with the introduction of PHI Release, an integrated, comprehensive system for copying, filing, and retrieving sensitive documents. To help it develop more state-of-the-art document management solutions, Lanier in 2003 opened the Atlanta Technology Center, a 10,000-square-foot facility where customers and Lanier engineers could work together to conceive of and shape new product development from Lanier and Ricoh. Although Lanier had once again given up its independence, it had always benefited from its relationship with corporate parents. Its tie to Ricoh appeared to be yet another case in point.

Principal Subsidiaries

Lanier Professional Services.

Principal Competitors

Canon Inc.; Hewlett-Packard Company; Konica Minolta Holdings, Inc.

Further Reading

Allison, David, ''Lanier Worldwide's Wesley Cantrell Perseveres Amidst Great Challenges,'' *Atlanta Business Chronicle,* May 26, 2000.

Coleman, Zach, ''Copying for the Future,'' *Atlanta Business Chronicle,* September 11, 1998, p. 1A.

Gove, Matt, "Ricoh Rescues Ailing Lanier," *Atlanta Business Chronicle,* December 8, 2000, p. A1.

Jones, Robert Snowdon, "Harris Merging Lanier, Copier Sales Units Costs Cuts Seen As One Benefit," *Atlanta Journal; Atlanta Constitution,* July 12, 1989, p. B7.

"The Lanier Name Returns As a Billion-Dollar Leader," *Managing Office Technology,* September 1, 1989. p. 38.

Molis, Jim, "Lanier Worldwide Set to Fly Solo," *Atlanta Business Chronicle,* July 9–July 15, 1999, p. A1.

Morris, Chris, "Wes Cantrell: From Copier Repairman to CEO," *Atlanta Business Chronicle,* August 30, 1990, p. 1B.

"Oxford Fiftieth Anniversary," Atlanta: Oxford Industries, Inc., 1992.

—Ed Dinger

Linens 'n Things, Inc.

6 Brighton Road
Clifton, New Jersey 07015
U.S.A.
Telephone: (973) 778-1300
Fax: (973) 815-2990
Web site: http://www.lnt.com

Public Company
Incorporated: 1958 as Great Eastern Linens, Inc.
Employees: 18,300
Sales: $2.66 billion (2004)
Stock Exchanges: New York
Ticker Symbol: LIN
NAIC: 442299 All Other Home Furnishing Stores

Linens 'n Things, Inc. is one of the nation's leading large-format specialty retailers of home textiles, housewares, and decorative home accessories. In 2005, the company operated more than 500 stores in 45 states and five Canadian provinces. The retailer maintained impressive growth during the 1990s but stalled out during the early years of the 21st century. When a series of initiatives failed to turn things around, the merchandiser opened the door to potential suitors in 2005, agreeing to be acquired in November by a newly formed entity controlled by Apollo Management, L.P.

Creating a Retail Prototype: 1958–83

Eugene Wallace Kalkin laid the initial groundwork for Linens 'n Things, Inc. when he was only 22 years old and began what would be a seven-year stint with Allied Purchasing Corp., the buying office for the second largest department store chain in the United States. In 1958 he entered into a partnership with the retail discount chain known as Great Eastern Mills, Inc.; in that company's stores, called Great Eastern Linens, Inc., Kalkin set up leased-linen departments. Meanwhile, Great Eastern Mills sold its business and its 50 percent share of Great Eastern Linens to Diana Stores Corporation, a ladies' apparel store chain with a strong market position in the southern United States. Thereupon, Diana Stores opened a chain of stores,

named Miller's Discount Department Stores, in which Great Eastern Linens operated the linen and curtain department.

Diana Stores later sold its company and its 50 percent interest in Great Eastern Linens to Beverly Hills-based Daylin Inc., a national chain of department stores that leased departments for health and beauty aids. In 1970 Daylin bought Kalkin's share of Great Eastern Linens in exchange for Daylin stock. In 1975, however, Daylin filed for bankruptcy, and Kalkin's stock became almost worthless. During an interview reported in the May 1998 issue of the *UVM Record,* a University of Vermont publication, Kalkin recalled how this bankruptcy affected both his finances and his self-esteem: "It was absolutely a devastating blow to my life. To me, there was no alternative but to go back into business," said Kalkin.

Kalkin did just that. In 1975, from the Daylin bankruptcy court, he bought seven of the leased departments and specialty stores he had started for that company. This seven-unit retail chain with annual sales of $2 million was the beginning of Linens 'n Things, Inc., one of the country's first specialty retail stores dedicated to home furnishings and decorative accessories. Having experienced the unpredictable consequences related to dependency on landlords, Kalkin turned away from the operation of leased departments and applied a novel set of merchandising techniques to the development of Linens 'n Things as a chain of specialty retail stores.

Eugene Kalkin had learned about the European *hypermarchés,* stores in which storage cubes filled with food or general merchandise were piled up to the ceiling, thereby saving space and reducing expenses. This merchandising concept later became popular in the United States in discount chain stores, such as those of Sam's Club, BJ's Wholesale Club, and Home Depot. Influenced by the concept of the *hypermarché* no-frills warehouse environment, Kalkin used his retailing experience to create the retail industry's off-price prototype. He opted for stores with high ceilings in order to save space by installing ten-foot high, warehouse-type shelving for piling up storage cubes. He could then display in 7,000 square feet the quantity of merchandise that previously would have taken 12,000 to 13,000 square feet. In this way, Linens 'n Things cut expenses—especially for rent, lighting, and taxes—and turned a profit

---

Company Perspectives:

Our business strategy is to offer a broad selection of high quality, brand name home furnishings merchandise at exceptional everyday values, provide superior guest service, and maintain low operating costs. Our mission is to exceed the expectations of our guests in every store, every day.

---

while selling quality products at discount prices. "When I went into off-price, the timing was right and we had the right physical format," Kalkin later commented in an interview for a June 1990 story in *Home Fashions Magazine.*

The soft economy of the 1970s did elicit enthusiastic consumer response to Linens 'n Things' off-price stores. Other retailers in the home textiles industry kept an eye on the chain's rapid growth. For instance, Bloomingdales' Norman Axelrod—who would later serve as Linens 'n Things' CEO, president, and chairman—remembered that "Gene Kalkin was very dynamic." "Selling brand names in a low-cost environment was a groundbreaking concept," Axelrod commented in a 1995 interview for *Business News New Jersey.*

Transition and Refocus: 1983–95

By 1983 Melville Corporation (later known as CVS Corporation) was also attracted to Linens 'n Things—by then a 55-store chain with sales of over $85 million—and soon acquired the chain. After the sale, Kalkin stayed on to direct the company for two years and was succeeded by his longtime assistant, Robert L. Karan. Sales from 116 stores reached $145.3 million for 1985; $163.4 million from 131 stores for 1986; $175.8 million from 144 stores in 1987; and $180 million from 140 stores by 1988.

Karan's marketing philosophy, however, was very different from that of Kalkin, who was attuned to the volatile, evolutionary nature of the retail industry and had noted an emerging trend to larger stores. In fact, before Kalkin's departure, the company already had experimented with the profitable operation of an 18,000-square-foot store and had begun to increase the "things" side of the business in order to meet customer requests for a larger selection of decorative home accessories. Karan, however, held back on making changes and, according to Lasseter's article, he "scrimped on spending to keep prices low, and sales stagnated." In January 1988, Melville Corporation asked Norman Axelrod—then senior vice-president at Bloomingdales in New York City—if he would run Linens 'n Things. Axelrod reportedly hesitated because the company had "a lot of problems," but Stan Goldstein, Melville's chairman, agreed to invest more money in Linens 'n Things, and in 1988 Axelrod joined the company as chief executive officer.

Axelrod had kept abreast of the radical and dramatic changes taking place in industry and individual lifestyles during the 1980s. Corporate structures were crumbling. Banks, brokerage houses, department stores, and specialty stores were undergoing bankruptcy, acquisitions, and/or consolidation. As for lifestyles, as Barbara Solomon pointed out in an August 1991 article in *Realities of Retailing,* during the 1980s many married people had

settled in the suburbs and their discretionary buying power was reduced by mortgages, children, medical bills, and the need to save for the future. Moreover, many women had entered the workforce and had less time to visit downtown banks and stores; instead, they went to branch locations in the malls near their homes and increasingly frequented specialty stores. In addition, department stores had become less efficient; more often than not it took several months for new merchandise to reach the shelves. In short, many retailers had lost touch with consumers.

Consequently, Axelrod's initial undertaking was to iron out some of Linens 'n Things' wrinkles and to learn about the needs and spending habits of its "guests," as the company called its customers. With a new management team, Axelrod guided the major part of Melville's first $15 million investment into upgrading the technology in the company's stores; a highly sophisticated point-of-sale system encompassing application of the Universal Product Code (UPC) and electronic data interchange (EDI) was installed. These UPC and EDI systems allowed the stores to track exactly what was selling on a day-to-day basis, thereby making it possible to keep lower levels of inventory and to have a more precise policy of maintaining what people wanted. This line of thinking was underscored by Daniel Raff, an industry analyst quoted in Solomon's 1991 article: "Some of the success of specialty stores has to do with the fact that they have a more sophisticated way of knowing what they're selling. A big part of retailing is having the product in stock and having it out on the floor."

However, maintaining an inventory large enough to meet consumer demand and having products out on the floor required much space. Axelrod recognized that the superstore concept that had inspired Kalkin might solve the space problem. In September 1988 Linens 'n Things opened its first superstore in Rockville, Maryland. In 1989 the company started to convert its store base to superstores ranging in size from to 35,000 to 40,000 square feet and began to close all but the most profitable and traditional stores.

The superstore format was meant to save a customer's time by having inventory visible and accessible on the selling floor for immediate purchase. To further enhance customer satisfaction and loyalty, Linens 'n Things strove to provide prompt, knowledgeable sales assistance and enthusiastic customer service. The company offered competitive wages, training, and personnel development in order to attract and retain well-qualified, highly motivated employees dedicated to providing efficient customer service. Recognizing the increasing propensity of consumers to spend more on home decor, Linens 'n Things targeted its product selection to reflect the broadening trends of the 1990s.

The breadth and depth of Linens 'n Things' extensive merchandise offerings enabled guests to select from a wide assortment of styles, name brands, colors, and designs within each of the company's six major product lines. An effort was made to present merchandise in a more visually appealing, customer-friendly manner. The company emphasized its "won't be undersold" policy and explored opportunities to increase sales in its "things" merchandise without sacrificing market share or customer image in the "linens" side of the business. "Linens did not engage in high/low discounting but held two clearance events

Key Dates:

1975: Personally affected by the bankruptcy of Daylin Inc., Eugene Wallace Kalkin forms a seven-unit retail chain with annual sales of $2 million.
1988: Linens 'n Things opens its first superstore, in Rockville, Maryland.
1998: Sales top $1 billion for the first time.
2002: Company begins closing underperforming stores.
2005: Company announces agreement to be acquired.

annually, in January and June,'' noted James Mammarella in *Discount Store News,* an industry publication. He also commented that the company did distribute seasonal fliers containing promotional offers but that ''the main message, expressed in the store's slogan, was consistent: 'We give you more for less. Everyday'.''

From 1988 through 1995 Linens 'n Things introduced 101 superstores, resulting in the closing of 85 traditional stores. However, although the total number of stores increased only by 15, the company's gross square footage more than tripled, going from 1.4 million square feet on January 1, 1992, to 4.8 million square feet by the end of 1995. Net sales, after slow growth from 1988 to 1992, increased annually with added momentum.

With a view toward maintaining a low-cost operating structure, the company also instituted centralized management and operating programs and also invested significant capital in its infrastructure for distribution and management-information systems. In 1995 the company began full operation of its 275,000-square-foot, state-of-the-art distribution center in Greensboro, North Carolina. The center's EDI capabilities optimized allocation of products to the sites having the highest potential for sales and inventory productivity. Use of this center resulted in lower freight expense averages, more timely control of inventory shipment to stores, improved inventory turnover, better in-stock positions, and improved data flow. Freed from the responsibility of receiving inventory, sales associates had more time to be present on the selling floor to serve the company's guests.

Expanding and Refining: 1996–99

In October 1995 CVS Corporation, Linens 'n Things' parent company, decided to spin off some of its subsidiaries. On November 26, 1996, Linens 'n Things effected an initial public offering (IPO) of its common stock; CVS retained approximately 32.5 percent of the shares, but sold them during 1997.

In response to consumer demands for one-stop shopping destinations, Linens continued to balance its merchandise by bringing in a fuller assortment of ''things.'' This shift significantly impacted net sales; the ''things'' side of its business increased from less than 10 percent of net sales in 1991 to 35 percent in 1996. The company's long-term goal was to increase the sale of ''things'' merchandise to approximately 50 percent of net sales. The chain also moved toward more upstairs brands and more elegant presentations of its merchandise.

In a continual effort to offer the best possible customer service, Linens 'n Things also installed satellite transmission for credit card authorizations and upgraded its point-of-sale (POS) system. The company also further refined its planning process through a comprehensive EDI system used for substantially all purchase orders, invoices, and bills of lading. Combined with automatic shipping notice technology used in the distribution systems, the EDI system created additional efficiencies by capturing data through bar codes, thereby reducing clerical errors and inventory shrinkage.

By the end of 1996, net sales increased 25.4 percent to $696.1 million, as compared to $555.1 million in 1995. The company opened a total of 36 superstores in 1996, increasing gross square footage by 28 percent to approximately 4.6 million square feet.

Linens 'n Things superstores continued to grow in size, number, and product line. The operative strategy was to expand market share in new and existing markets, to increase store-productivity levels at existing units, and to penetrate new markets in which the company could become a leading operator of superstores for home furnishings. New markets were located primarily in the western region of the United States, in trading areas of 200,000 persons within a ten-mile radius and having the demographic characteristics that matched the company's target profile. According to Alan M. Rifkin and Kevin M. Hunt's *Home Furnishings Handbook,* Linens 'n Things targeted its product selection ''to reflect the broad trends of the 1990s, with an emphasis on consumers' increasing propensity to spend more on home decor.'' The company succeeded in making ''its stores an exciting experience for today's consumer, who continued to prefer home-related goods at the expense of apparel,'' wrote Rifkin and Hunt.

Linens 'n Things' net sales for 1997 increased 25.6 percent to $874.22 million, compared with $696.1 million for the same period in 1996. During 1997, the company opened 25 new stores and closed 18 stores. Total square footage of stores increased 16.2 percent to 5.5 million square feet; sales from traditional stores represented less than 5 percent of total sales. In April 1998 the Linens 'n Things board of directors approved a two-for-one split of the company's common stock to be effected in the form of a stock dividend distributed on May 7, 1998. Commenting on the results of the first quarter of 1998, Chairman and CEO Axelrod declared that the company began 1998 ''with an improved sales and earnings performance, which carried over from a strong 1997 performance. . . . The operating margin for the quarter showed meaningful improvement over the prior year as a result of the increase in comparable store net sales, improved selling mix, and lower markdowns.''

The surprise to the bedding industry was that although sales of bedding-specialty chains dropped to 11 percent in 1997 from 13 percent in 1996, ''superspecialists Bed Bath & Beyond, Inc. and Linens & Things, Inc. have been growing, both financially and in importance to the whole textiles industry,'' wrote David Gill in a 1998 issue of *Home Textiles Today.* By way of explanation, Gill quoted Chip Fontenot, president and CEO of New York-based Decorative Home Accents: ''You have to understand that there are only two specialty chains that are of any size, Linens 'n Things and Bed Bath & Beyond and both of these are emphasizing 'things.' Fewer and fewer customers are running to these stores to buy sheets, while more and more of them are running there to buy kitchen magnets,'' quipped Fontenot. Linens 'n Things' broad mix of ''things'' was obviously in sync with the increasing trend of consumer spending for the home.

In 1998 the company was operating 176 stores (153 superstores and 23 smaller, traditional-size stores) in 37 states. The traditional stores averaged approximately 10,000 square feet in size while the superstores ranged from 38,000 to 50,000 square feet. The stores carried brand name ''linens,'' that is, home textiles, such as bed linens, towels, and pillows, and ''things,'' such as housewares and home accessories. The superstores were located predominantly in power-strip centers and, to a lesser extent, in shopping malls. More than 25,000 stock-keeping units (SKUs) supported the company's six product categories: bath, home accessories, housewares, storage, top-of-the-bed, and window treatments. The company bought its inventory from approximately 1,000 suppliers, 95 percent of whom were in the United States. The superstores represented Linens 'n Things' desire to create a compelling one-stop shopping experience for the time-pressed consumer. The company carried many name brands, including Wamsutta, Martex, Fieldcrest, and Waverly in domestics; Libbey, Ravel, Lancaster Colony, Zwiesel Glas, and Luminarc in glassware; Sango, Mikasa, Sakura, Tienshen, and Gibson in stoneware; Calphalon, Circulon, and Farberware in cookware; and Braun and Krups in appliances. Linens 'n Things also sold an increasing amount of merchandise (about 10 percent) under its own private label, *LNT,* in order to supplement the offering of brand name products with other high-quality merchandise sold at value pricing below regular department store prices and comparable with, or below, sale prices at department stores.

The company planned to open 30 superstores in 1998 while closing 13 traditional stores, thereby expanding its square footage by 17 percent, and to maintain this expansion rate through the next several years by opening 35 to 40 superstores annually. Moreover, the company's ability to keep in step with changing trends and lifestyles, its flexible merchandising strategy, and its continually updated POS and MIS systems all allowed the company to increase market share through expansion and increased productivity. In the late 1990s, the company was within reach of increasing ''things'' by up to 50 percent and was gradually closing its remaining traditional stores as the annual increase of its superstores kept consumers coming to Linens 'n Things for quality home textiles, housewares and home accessories ''at everyday low prices.''

During 1998, Linens 'n Things sales topped $1 billion for the first time in its history. Sales climbed to $1.07 billion, up 22 percent from 1997. As for net income, it jumped 47.6 percent to $38.1 million. The company posted strong figures the next year as well. Net income increased by 36.8 percent and sales by 22 percent.

Changing Linens: 2000–05

Confident in the light of three years of uninterrupted growth, Linens 'n Things moved to extend its chain of stores even further. The company planned to open at least 50 new stores.

The first Canadian units were also on the docket for 2000. Chairman and CEO Norman Axelrod predicted the market north of the border could sustain a total of 40 to 50 of the home-goods stores.

As far as the company's Internet strategy, Axelrod told *HFN The Weekly Newspaper for the Home Furnishing Network:* ''We want to make sure a Web site won't negatively impact our sales, and we see no significant advantage to rush to market.'' He explained, ''We want to keep the e-commerce site integrated with store operations.''

However, the chain's outlook experienced a reversal in the early years of the 21st century. As part of its self improvement drive, Linens 'n Things planned to close 17 of its 343 locations during 2002, eliminating the underperforming stores. Problems in the crucial linens end of the business needed to be ironed out. The company introduced a series of initiatives they hoped would work out the wrinkles. *Home Textiles Today* reported in February 2002, ''This effort, headed by Steve Silverstein, president, will build on introducing new products, sharpening price points, strengthening the accessories business and increasing marketing support.''

During early 2003, Axelrod set forth a corporate goal of growing revenues from $2 billion to $4 billion within three years. The pronouncement came in the wake of the departure of the company's president who had headed Linens 'n Things for less than two years. The highly hands-on Chairman and CEO Norman Axelrod was in no hurry to bring in a new president, according to *Home Textiles Today*.

To meet the goal, sales per square foot, which had been on the slide, would have to improve. Linens 'n Things sales per square foot lagged behind Bed Bath & Beyond to a tune of $60, according to the February 2003 *Home Textiles Today* article.

A new chief merchandising officer was appointed in 2003 to aid Axelrod in his quest to improve performance, Mike Duff reported in a September 2003 *DSN Retailing Today* article. In addition, another set of initiatives were set in place: more ''things'' to join the product offering mixture; the number of store-level personnel increased, linens continued to receive added attention; and managers gained greater control over the items they carried in their stores, tuning in to regional preferences. Moreover, new labels, including Yankee Candle, Waverly, and Nautica Home, added in 2002, continued to help results.

The merchandising moves served to intensify head-to-head competition with the company's more powerful rival, a challenging position. ''Bed Bath & Beyond has been among the most successful retailers in the United States over the past several years and shows no signs of slowing down. Yet in this case, differentiation may not be an option. Stroud's, Lechters, HomePlace and Waccamaw all have, in one way or another, tried to drive a business strategy based on differentiating from Bed Bath & Beyond. Each suffered so severely that only one, Stroud's, still exists—and that as a scaled-back privately held remnant,'' Duff wrote.

The search for the key to improving the company's position continued. In March 2005, Jack Moore, president and chief operating officer, announced that Linen 'n Things would move its product lines toward the ''better'' segment of the retail world, citing the dominance of mass marketers in the ''good'' category. By September, a possible sale had been added to its list of strategic alternatives. Two months later, the company formally announced that it had agreed to be acquired by Apollo Management, L.P. for a price of $28 per share.

Principal Competitors

Bed Bath & Beyond, Inc.; Pier 1 Imports, Inc.; Target Corporation.

Further Reading

Corral, Cecile B., ''Linens 'N Things Plans to Get 'Better,' '' *Home Textiles Today*, March 28, 2005, p.16.

Denitto, Emily, ''Meeting the Street,'' *Crain's New York Business,* April 14, 1997, pp. 3–5.

Duff, Mike, ''Is Linens Buyer Waiting in the Wings?,'' *DSN Retailing Today,* October 10, 2005, pp. 5+.

——,''Linens 'N Things Earns Notice for Consistent Performance,'' *DSN Retailing Today,* July 24, 2000, p. 6.

——, ''Linens 'N Things Grows Up,'' *Discount Store News*, April 5, 1999, p. 17.

——, ''Plan to Empower Local Managers Makes Top Brass Shine, Top Line Glimmer,'' *DSN Retailing Today*, September 8, 2003, pp. 18+.

Gill, David, ''Specialty Losing Its Steam,'' *Home Textiles Today,* February 16, 1998, pp. 10, 14.

Hartnett, Michael, ''Linens 'n Things Sale Shakes up Home Furnishings Superstores,'' *Stores,* February 2, 1997, pp. 51–52.

Hogsett, Don, ''Fourth Quarter Profits up 38 Percent at Linens 'n Things,'' *Home Textiles Today,* February 9, 1998, pp. 2, 23.

Lasseter, Diana G., ''A Retailer Tries to Blanket Its Market,'' *Business News New Jersey,* November 15, 1995, pp. 1–2.

Lickteig, Mary Ann, ''Kalkins' Service to UVM Knows No Boundaries,'' *UVM Record,* May 8–21, 1998, p. 7.

Lillo, Andrea, ''Axelrod: 'We'll Nearly Double Biz,' '' *Home Textiles Today,*'' February 10, 2003, p. 1.

——, ''To Shutter 17 Stores: Boxed in: LNT Slowed by Competition,'' *Home Textiles Today,* February 4, 2002, p. 1.

Mammarella, James, ''Freedom Fuels Linens 'n Things,'' *Discount Store News,* May 5, 1998, pp. H6–H7.

Page, Melinda, ''Linens 'N Things Records Strong Year,'' *HFN The Weekly Newspaper for the Home Furnishing Network,* February 7, 2000, p. 4.

Rifkin, Alan M., and Kevin M. Hunt, *The Home Furnishings Handbook: A Portfolio Manager's Guide to Understanding and Investing,* Minneapolis: Piper Jaffray Inc., 1998, p. 15.

Solomon, Barbara, ''Kalkin's Back,'' *Home Fashions Magazine,* June 1990, pp. 17–20.

——, ''Madness in Store: The New Realities of Retailing,'' *Management Review,* August 1991, pp. 4–9.

——, ''What's Up at Retail,'' *Home Furnishings Daily,* June 11, 1990, p. 40.

Verdon, Joan, ''Sale Potential Boosts Stock of Linens 'N Things,'' *Record* (Hackensack, N.J.), October 20, 2005.

Wright, J. Nils, ''Linens 'n Things Likes the Looks of Roseville Power Center,'' *Business Journal Serving Greater Sacramento,* June 24, 1996, p. 10.

—Gloria A. Lemieux
—update: Kathleen Peippo

Marco Business Products, Inc.

3000 Division Street
St. Cloud, Minnesota 56301
U.S.A.
Telephone: (320) 259-3000
Toll Free: (800) 892-8548
Fax: (320) 259-3087
Web site: http://www.marconet.com

Private Company
Incorporated: 1973
Employees: 188
Sales: 40.5 million (2004 est.)
NAIC: 541512 Computer Systems Design Services;
   541519 Other Computer Related Services; 443120
   Computer and Software Stores

Marco Business Products, Inc. stands out among the largest business services and business product companies in Minnesota and North Dakota. The company operates out of six satellite offices throughout Minnesota and a branch office in Fargo, North Dakota. Marco Business Products partners with such companies as Cisco Systems and Microsoft to offer data networking solutions. The company assists other companies with Information Technology services including systems integration, data migration, and software programming. Marco also serves companies with telecom services including IP telephony, Internet access, and web site hosting. In addition to its services, Marco sells products for the office, including digital copiers and printers, video systems, and office furniture.

1972–90: Looking for Opportunity

In the early 1970s Gary Marsden was a young salesman eager to step out on his own. Marsden teamed up with a partner named Dave Marquardt to buy a typewriter shop in St. Cloud, Minnesota, that had been advertised in the newspaper. The Typewriter Shop was an established business with 14 employees and sales of approximately $500,000 a year. The business appealed to Marsden because he had worked for IBM when he was first out of college and knew a bit about business machinery.

There was one significant drawback to the company that Marsden learned after inquiring further. The advertisement for The Typewriter Shop had been listed in the wrong section of the paper. Marsden had been looking for business opportunities in the Twin Cities metro area and The Typewriter Shop was in St. Cloud, over 100 miles from where Marsden had wanted to establish his business.

Though reluctant to leave the Twin Cities of Minneapolis and St. Paul, Gary Marsden believed that the opportunity to begin his own operation was good enough to draw him to the smaller city of St. Cloud. The Typewriter Shop held promise, and it was priced right. Marsden and Marquardt spoke of the impetus behind the purchase in *Twin Cities Business Monthly* saying, ''We thought we could do something good with a sleepy business like this, and so we bought it in January 1973.''

Knowing they had plans for expansion on the horizon, Marsden and Marquardt changed the name of the company from The Typewriter Shop to Marco Business Products and began to expand the inventory from typewriters to an assortment of business products, machines, and services.

In 1974 Marco had begun selling CPT word processing systems and the following year the company began marketing Savin copiers. Business machinery was rapidly changing during the 1970s as innovations industrywide were replacing products that had long been the staple of offices for many decades. Mimeograph machines, manual typewriters, and the like had become obsolete in a few short years.

By 1977 sales had increased to $3 million. Marsden and Marquardt's gamble was paying off. While expanding its machinery offerings, Marco also focused on office furniture systems and opened a facility in 1977 at 609 E. St. Germain in St. Cloud. The company became a distributor of Steelcase office furniture systems. By 1979 Marco signed an agreement to carry

Company Perspectives:

Marco's vision is total customer satisfaction for integrated information solutions—guaranteed. Marco's mission is to help our customers understand and apply information technology that contributes to their success. Our philosophy is that any organization in order to survive and achieve success, must adhere to a sound set of beliefs. These basic precepts provide the foundation for Marco's principles, policies, practices, procedures and rules. We believe the success of our customers and our company is interdependent. Our mutual well being is best achieved through the establishment of long-lasting business relationships.

Sharp copiers. The sales and service of copiers became one of its most profitable areas of business.

The 1980s were an ideal time to own a business machine company. Technological advancements related to business instruments had occurred at a rate unparalleled in history. The advent of personal computers revolutionized the workplace and Marco Business Products was in place to capitalize on the PC's success.

In 1983 the company became a marketplace for IBM typewriters. The typewriters were still in demand despite the trend towards computer systems in the workplace. Nonetheless, from the mid-1980s home and business computer use had become a worldwide trend. Marco Business Products was connected and established in central Minnesota and was the logical choice for many businesses converting their business systems over to the latest technological wave. Throughout the decade the company focused a large part of its inventory on business software for both commercial and personal use.

In 1985, Marco sold Epson personal computers and Sharp facsimile machines. By 1988 the company continued its emphasis on the emerging personal computer market by becoming a computer franchise for IBM, Compaq, and Hewlett Packard.

In 1987 Marco consolidated its offices into one corporate headquarters based in St. Cloud. The company opened its facility on Division Street, one of the main thoroughfares in town. The company maintained satellite offices in Brainerd and Fargo.

The company experienced rapid growth toward the end of the 1980s. One of the defining moments in its history came in 1989 when the company began its employee ownership plan. Partner Dave Marquardt decided to sell his share of the company. An ESOP (Employee Stock Ownership Plan) was established allowing employees to own a part of the company. Management at Marco credited the ESOP with making the company more stable over time. The fact that employees worked for themselves led to less employee turnover and greater employee satisfaction. Those two elements contributed to greater customer satisfaction, according to CEO Marsden. He stated in *Business Central:* "The ESOP helps attract and retain good people. We've had eight percent turnover at Marco compared to 20-plus percent in the industry."

Marco Business Products was also one of the earliest Minnesota Keystone Companies. The Keystone program recognized businesses that contributed 2 to 5 percent of pretax profits to charity. Marco had maintained its status as a 5 percent donor since the program's founding.

From 1989 to 1990 Marco had more than doubled its number of employees, jumping from 57 to 117. By 1991, however, the company faced its first financial setback since its founding. In that year, the company failed to turn a profit for the first time ever.

President Gary Marsden's analysis of the loss of revenue led to a restructuring and retraining of his employees. Marsden provided the training himself, focusing on customer service. The push for customer satisfaction paid off when in subsequent years the growing company recorded a profit once again. According to an article in the St. Cloud Area Chamber of Commerce magazine, *Business Central,* Marsden described the loss as a "wake-up call." The article continued by pointing out the success Marco experienced because of the retraining program: "What emerged at the end of the year was a newly awakened giant poised for high speed growth in a high tech environment."

The company sold off its office supply division in March 1997 to U.S. Office Products. U.S. Office Products set out to acquire 11 different company's holdings. The consolidation of the office products industry had been a trend consistent with many industries in the 1980s and 1990s and Marco decided to concentrate its work on the growing information systems industry and rising e-business sector.

Later that year, Marco began a partnership with Microsoft. The company became a Certified Solutions Partner, teaming up with the software giant to provide business software to its regional customer base. The company continued to expand its products and services when Cisco Systems certified engineers and network professionals, through rigorous training in the current technologies available, at Marco in 2000.

With years of experience and a regionally and nationally recognized company to his credit, Marsden received statewide recognition in 2001 when the corporate leader was selected for the Minnesota Entrepreneurial Success Award. The previous year Marsden had been lauded as the recipient of the St. Cloud Area Entrepreneurial Success Award. The same year, Marco Business Products distinguished itself by becoming 100 percent employee owned. In anticipation of his January 2005 retirement, Marsden had sold his own share in the company.

In June 2004, Marco Business Products received one of its highest honors when it was named one of the top 25 Best Small Companies to work for in the United States. The ranking was done by the Great Places to Work Institute, a research and management agency that provided human resource consultancy.

Marsden spoke of his company's success in a December 2004 article in *Twin Cities Business Monthly,* "Our strength has been that we've been able to adapt and change over time, from a seller of office products to a technology solutions provider."

The corporate culture at Marco Business Products had always been one of giving back to the community and the

---

Key Dates:

1973: Gary Marsden and partner Dave Marquardt buy The Typewriter Shop and rename it Marco Business Products.

1977: Marco expands its products and services and adds second location.

1981: Marco adds third location and shifts product emphasis to personal computers and copiers.

1987: Marco opens corporate headquarters on Division Street in St Cloud.

1991: Sales decline after rapid growth; Marco leaders restructure.

1994: Company rebounds and wins industry awards.

1997: Company forges partnership with Microsoft.

2000: Cisco Systems certifies Marco network professionals.

2001: Gary Marsden is selected for Minnesota Entrepreneurial Success Award; Marco becomes 100 percent employee owned.

2004: Marco is honored as one of the top 25 Best Small Companies to work for in the United States.

---

recognition that Marsden and Marco received was the community's way of acknowledging the service and leadership the company promoted.

In January 2005 Gary Marsden retired and Jeff Gau, a Marco employee since the mid-1980s, took over the helm as president and CEO.

Twin Cities Business Monthly honored Marco as a small business success story in January 2005. The company was among nine companies chosen from approximately 60 nominations. The criteria for selection included entrepreneurial insight, management ability, marketing acumen, and a marked sense of purpose and drive.

Marco Business Products has been a successful venture for many reasons. The company excelled because of excellent leadership, adaptability, consumer trends, and a generosity of spirit that helped endear it both to its employees and to its customer base. Its ties with the latest technology provided by cutting edge partners including Microsoft and Cisco Systems ensured it a strong position in its market area in the future.

Principal Competitors

International Business Machines Corporation; Ingram Micro Inc.; Tech Data Corporation

Further Reading

Clements, Bill, "Marco, from Typewriters to VoIP, the St. Cloud-Based Firm Has Nimbly Followed Changes in Communications Technology." *Twin Cities Business Monthly,* December 2004, p. 75.

Ivers, Gail, "From Typewriters to E-Commerce, Long-Time Entrepreneur Says "the Fun Has Just Begun!," *Business Central, St. Cloud Area Chamber of Commerce,* May/June 2000, p. 20.

—Susan B. Culligan

Marine Products Corporation

2170 Piedmont Road, Northeast
Atlanta, Georgia 30324
U.S.A.
Telephone: (404) 321-7910
Fax: (404) 321-5483
Web site: http://www.chaparralboats.com

Public Company
Incorporated: 2000
Employees: 1,200
Sales: $252.4 million (2004)
Stock Exchanges: New York
Ticker Symbol: MPX
NAIC: 336612 Boat Building

Marine Products Corporation is a manufacturer of fiberglass, motorized boats, selling Chaparral stern-drive and inboard pleasure boats and Robalo outboard fishing boats. Marine Products' boats are marketed through its independent dealer network domestically and internationally. Chaparral boats are manufactured at the company's production plant in Nashville, Georgia. Robalo fishing boats are manufactured in Valdosta, Georgia. The Rollins family in Atlanta, Georgia, who spun off Marine Products from one of its holdings, RPC, Inc., controls 67 percent of Marine Products' stock.

Origins

For the first four decades of its existence, the company known as Marine Products operated as Chaparral Boats, Inc., the name given to the company by William ''Buck'' Pegg. Pegg's attraction to building boats was developed during his youth in his hometown of Union Lake, Michigan, where each spring thaw presented Pegg with abandoned rowboats released from the lake ice. Pegg used tar to patch the holes in the boats, an annual salvaging ritual he performed until he was 15 years old, when his father retired and moved the family to Fort Lauderdale, Florida.

Although he had retired, Pegg's father kept busy by opening a shop called Fiberglass Fabricators in 1961. Pegg, meanwhile,

made a half-hearted attempt at becoming a dentist, spending a couple of years at Troy State and Florida State University before joining his father's business in 1964. Sitting in a classroom, Pegg explained years later, did not suit him. By the time Pegg joined his father, Fiberglass Fabricators had blossomed into a manufacturer of custom fiberglass parts, producing marine mufflers, swimming pool panels, planters and fountains, and parts to repair cars and boat hulls. The same year father and son began working together, a new boat company in south Florida named Fish & Ski called Fiberglass Fabricators and asked Pegg to build molds and boats. Pegg agreed and began making one or two boats a day, which were sent to Fish & Ski to be finished and rigged. Within a year, Pegg decided to begin manufacturing complete boats, introducing his first model in 1965, the 15-foot, tri-hull Chaparral 15. The name Chaparral, taken from the Chevy Chaparral, was suggested by a Fiberglass Fabricators employee who was an auto-racing enthusiast. The Chaparral 15, like other Pegg designs to follow, was purposely simplistic, made without upholstery, rugs, or other creature comforts. Pegg liked boats that could be washed with a hose: bare-boned boats that exuded substance over style. The Chaparral 15 lacked dash, but it was manufactured according to exacting standards, which attracted a loyal following. Pegg sold thousands of Chaparral 15s before the model was discontinued in the early 1980s, earning recognition as a trusted boat-builder that underpinned the success of his company.

Not long after establishing his credentials with the Chaparral 15, Pegg stopped making custom fiberglass parts and focused Fiberglass Fabricators' efforts exclusively on boat manufacture. In 1968, after Fiberglass Fabricators introduced an 18-foot Chaparral, one of the most important events in the company's history occurred: the day Buck Pegg met Jim Lane, a Wauchula, Florida, native who earned an accounting degree at the University of Florida. The pair met on the city paddleball courts in Hollywood, Florida. Lane, who was the chief financial officer of a mobile home financing company in Miami at the time, recalled his introduction to Pegg in an interview with *Powerboat Magazine* in July 1990. ''We were the same age,'' he said, ''and we both had a wife and kids. We talked about my business and his business.'' Both were competitive paddleball players, pairing up at one point to win the Hollywood city championship, and their friendship grew. Lane, who had owned several boats before meeting Pegg,

---

Company Perspectives:

Every day you see companies displaying awards and touting their accomplishments. How do you sort out the claims and counterclaims? At Chaparral, building award winning boats isn't a bolt out of the blue. We've been building the marine industry's finest sportboats, deckboats, and cruisers for more than four decades. We're proud to let our record speak for itself. For almost a quarter-century, Powerboat Magazine*'s team of experts have tested our boats against the leading names on the water. The fact that we've won 27 awards including nine Boat of the Year trophies shows an unmatched level of consistency. And if that's not enough, turn to the International Standards Organization. Two years ago Chaparral earned ISO 9001:2000 certification for consistent quality management systems. Completing the ISO certification sends a signal to customers worldwide that Chaparral is dedicated to achieving the ultimate advantage in customer satisfaction through design innovation, manufacturing process excellence, and dealer network support.*

---

purchased a boat from Fiberglass Fabricators, the first twin-engine Chaparral made by Pegg, but for nearly a decade each pursued his occupation separately. They eventually joined forces in 1976, a significant year in Pegg's boat-building career.

Chaparral Moving to Georgia in 1976

After nearly a decade focused solely on building boats, Fiberglass Fabricators was flourishing. Pegg needed to expand his manufacturing plant, and he was preparing to do so when he learned Larsen Boat Company was on the verge of declaring bankruptcy and preparing to vacate its production plant in Nashville, Georgia. Pegg wanted to move Fiberglass Fabricators to Nashville, but his financial partner had no desire to move to Georgia. Pegg asked Lane to join the business and Lane agreed, buying out Pegg's partner's interest in the business. In 1976, Pegg acquired the 37,000-square-foot Nashville plant, shuttered the Florida operations, and moved to Florida with Lane in tow, re-incorporating the company as Chaparral Boats, Inc.

The decade-long friendship between Pegg and Lane developed into an effective business partnership. Their contrasting skills and desires formed the basis of a complementary working relationship. ''It works out real well,'' Pegg explained in a July 1990 interview with *Powerboat Magazine*. ''I didn't want to be in the office, so Jim said, 'Good. I'll do that.' He didn't really want to be in the plant, so I said, 'Good. I'll do that.' '' Pegg relished the opportunity to spend all his time designing new boats and improving manufacturing methods. Lane threw himself into managing Chaparral Boats' public relations efforts and controlling the company's costs, focusing his attention on profits and efficiency. With Lane's contributions, Chaparral Boats became a perennial profit maker, among the first boat companies to use computer-controlled inventory tracking. With Pegg cloistered in the Nashville plant, production quality took center stage, yielding a slew of Chaparral boat models that withstood the rigors of use and won the business of boating enthusiasts throughout the country.

Soon after Pegg and Lane assumed their respective managerial roles, Pegg relented to the pressure of consumer demand. Despite his belief that accoutrements such as rugs and upholstery were destined to rot, Pegg strayed from his no-frills approach to boat manufacture in 1978, introducing the Chaparral 198, the first model bearing stylish lines and a plush interior. Subsequently, Pegg began to broaden the company's selection of boats, designing models to appeal to the entire powerboat community. The Cruiser line was introduced in 1984, the high-performance Villain in 1986, and the wide-beam Cruiser and the SX line in 1988.

The 1980s proved to be a significant decade for Chaparral Boats. Pegg's willingness to broaden the selection of the company's boats helped fuel tremendous financial growth, making Chaparral Boats one of the largest powerboat builders in the country. At the end of the 1970s, after the company had settled into its new facilities in Nashville, annual sales reached $4 million. During the 1980s, annual sales leaped upward, reaching nearly $100 million by the end of the decade. The exponential growth in business required the company to significantly expand its manufacturing plant, resulting in a facility that was ten times its original size by the end of the decade. In the midst of this energetic growth, Pegg and Lane took an important step to ensure their company's financial security, despite all outward signs of a company free from any financial concerns. In 1986, they sold their company to RPC Inc., an oil and gas services firm controlled by the Rollins family in Atlanta. In his July 1990 interview with *Powerboat Magazine*, Lane explained the reasoning behind the deal. ''By 1986,'' he said, ''we'd had the longest upcycle the industry had ever been through. Who knew how long it would last? We wanted to have a big brother to protect us.'' The big brother came in the form of a deep-pocketed parent company, but Chaparral Boats' acquisition by RPC did nothing to lessen the control or influence of Pegg and Lane over the company. The Rollins family expressed no interest in interfering in the management of the company, ceding virtually all authority to the proven partnership of Pegg and Lane.

Spinoff in 2001

Chaparral Boats operated as a component of RPC's business for 15 years, years that saw the company earn dozens of industry awards for the quality of its powerboats while recording steady financial growth. The next major corporate event that had a significant effect on Chaparral Boats involved the creation of Marine Products Corporation. At the close of the century, members of the Rollins family and senior executives at RPC decided it was in the best interests of both RPC and Chaparral Boats to separate the two companies. News of the separation first emerged in early 2000, by which point Chaparral Boats' annual sales totaled nearly $150 million, ranking it as the third largest manufacturer of stern-drive, fiberglass boats in the United States. In an interview with the *Oil Daily* on January 18, 2000, R. Randall Rollins, RPC's chairman and chief executive officer, commented on the proposed spinoff of Chaparral Boats. ''This is a major step in strategically positioning our oil-field service companies and our leisure boat manufacturing company to successfully grow and compete in the 21st century,'' he said. Roughly a year later, the spinoff was completed, a maneuver that necessitated the formation of Marine Products in 2000 as

Key Dates:

1965: A year after joining his father's fiberglass parts business, William "Buck" Pegg introduces the Chaparral 15.
1976: Pegg is joined by Jim Lane; the company moves to Nashville, Georgia.
1986: Chaparral Boats is acquired by RPC, Inc.
2000: Marine Products Corporation is formed to facilitate the spinoff of Chaparral Boats one year later.
2001: Marine Products Corporation acquires fishing-boat manufacturer Robalo.
2005: The Chaparral brand name celebrates its 40th anniversary.

the parent company of Chaparral Boats. At the end of February 2001, shares in Marine Products were sold to RPC shareholders, with the Rollins family coming away from the spinoff owning 67 percent of Marine Products' stock.

Chaparral Boats' new era of existence as a subsidiary of Marine Products began with one of the most significant events in the company's history. In June 2001, Marine Products acquired Robalo, a manufacturer of fishing boats, which became a subsidiary alongside Chaparral Boats. Founded in 1969, Robalo was a company on the decline at the time it was acquired. The company's first boat was a 19-foot, saltwater fishing boat that was among the first to feature a so-called unsinkable hull. As its business grew, the company attracted the attention of a corporate suitor and major competitor of Chaparral Boats, Brunswick Corporation, which acquired Robalo in 1991, organized it within its U.S. Marine division, and relocated the company to Tallahassee, Florida. Robalo fared well for the ensuing decade, but its production of 600 boats in 2000 represented its peak production. A downturn in boating production delivered a crippling blow to Robalo, forcing it to cease production of its boats in early 2001. "Production was virtually zero when we bought the company," Marine Products' president and chief executive officer, Richard Hubbell, remarked in a May 23, 2004 interview with the *Atlanta Journal-Constitution.* "We had to build it from scratch." When Marine Products acquired Robalo, it moved its headquarters to Valdosta, Georgia, where the task of rebuilding the company began. Under Marine Products' guidance, the company began producing two 23-foot models, recording its first sales at the end of 2001. Expansion of the company's product lines followed, resulting in a total of eight models ranging from 19 feet to 26 feet in length by 2003.

When Robalo regained its footing as a going enterprise, it began to contribute to the financial health of Marine Products,

although the line of fishing boats represented only a small percentage of the parent company's business. By the time Robalo was producing eight models of boats, its sales accounted for 6 percent of Marine Products' total sales. Robalo was estimated to control less than 1 percent of the outboard fishing market. The strength of Marine Products was found in Chaparral Boats, which spent the first years of the new century displaying its signature traits: production excellence and financial health. Thanks largely to Chaparral Boats' contribution, Marine Products' sales increased from $134 million in 2001 to $252 million in 2004. The company's profits recorded a more impressive increase, jumping from $8.5 million to $23.7 million during the period. As the company planned for the future, Robalo offered another avenue of growth, but much of Marine Products' success in the years ahead depended on its line of Chaparral boats. In 2005, the subsidiary celebrated the 40th year since the introduction of the Chaparral 15 in quarters far more elaborate than the fiberglass parts shop where Buck Pegg made his first boat. Chaparral Boats occupied nearly one million square feet of manufacturing space on 57 acres in Nashville, producing 150 sport boats, deck boats, and cruisers each week. As the Chaparral name headed toward its first half-century of existence, there was every indication that its legacy of success would continue into the future.

Principal Subsidiaries

Chaparral Boats, Inc.; Chaparral Marine Inc.; Robalo Acquisition Company, LLC; Marine Products Investment Company, LLC.

Principal Competitors

Brunswick Corporation; Genmar Holdings, Inc.; Yamaha Motor Co., Ltd.

Further Reading

Harmon, Jim, "Chaparral Is Jim Lane and Buck Pegg," *Powerboat Magazine,* July 1990, p. 32.
Hirschman, Dave, "Georgia Boat Builder Marine Products Sets Sales, Profit Records," *Atlanta Journal-Constitution,* May 23, 2004, p. B2.
——, "Georgia 100," *Atlanta Journal-Constitution,* May 23, 2004, p. B1.
Kempner, Matt, "Georgia 100," *Atlanta Journal-Constitution,* June 12, 2005, p. B1.
"RPC Board of Directors Approves Spin-Off," *Advanced Materials & Composites News,* February 19, 2001, p. 13.
"RPC to Unload Boat Subsidiary," *Oil Daily,* January 18, 2000, p. 21.

—Jeffrey L. Covell

Maruha Group Inc.

1-1-2 Otemachi, Chiyoda-ku
Tokyo
100-8608
Japan
Telephone: +81 3 3216 0821
Fax: +81 3 3216 0342
Web site: http://www.maruha.co.jp

Public Company
Founded: 1880 as Tosa Hogei
Employees: 12,000
Sales: ¥757.96 billion ($40 billion) (2004)
Stock Exchanges: Tokyo
NAIC: 551112 Offices of Other Holding Companies;
    311412 Frozen Specialty Food Manufacturing; 311712
    Fresh and Frozen Seafood Processing; 424420
    Packaged Frozen Food Merchant Wholesalers; 424460
    Fish and Seafood Merchant Wholesalers; 493120
    Refrigerated Storage Facilities

Maruha Group Inc. is Japan's leading importer and processor of seafoods, and a leading producer and processor of frozen, canned, fresh, and convenience foods. Maruha's operations span the full range of seafood production, from managing its own fishing fleet, to extensive global fish purchasing and processing operations, cold-storage facilities, food production and packaging, and distribution, including restaurant operations. Formed in the late 19th century, Maruha developed into one of Japan's major whaling companies, under its former name of Taiyo Gyogyo KK (Taiyo Fishery Co.), and also built up one of the country's largest fleets of trawlers. The worldwide moratorium on whaling forced the company to exit that industry, and the company has responded to increasing conservation pressures on the global fishing industry by reducing its own fishing fleet and relying instead on an international network of supply partnerships. Maruha also has established some 60 international subsidiaries, including in the United States, Thailand, China, Spain, Chile, New Zealand, Indonesia, Mozambique, and Mad-

agascar. The company also operates nearly 110 subsidiaries in Japan. In addition to seafoods, Maruha produces meat and poultry products, pet foods, and feed. The company ended a longstanding presence in the sugar industry through the sale of its stake in Ensuiko Sugar Refining Co. in 2005. This followed the company's move to restructure itself as a holding company in 2004, part of a wider reorganization and consolidation of its operations. The company is listed on the Tokyo Stock Exchange. Yuji Igarashi is company president and CEO.

Fishmonger in the 19th Century

Maruha's origins reach back to the late 19th century, when Ikujiro Nakabe began a business buying fish from local fishermen and delivering the product to wholesalers in Osaka. The company, originally known as Tosa Hogei, remained a small family-owned business into the 20th century. Yet the importance of fish to the Japanese diet—the country was to distinguish itself as the world's single largest market for fish—encouraged the company's growth. By 1904, Nakabe had moved his company to Shimonoseki, in the Yamaguchi Prefecture.

The move precipitated the Nakabe family's entry into the whaling industry. Shimonoseki had by then been a center of Japanese whaling for more than a century, and Nakabe's company rapidly established itself among the pioneers of modern whaling methods. The launch of Japanese whaling in Antarctica provided a new opportunity for the company, which went public in 1924 as KK Hayashikane Shoten. By 1926, the company had launched its own fleet of whaling vessels in Antarctica.

The group's whaling operations led it to develop an expanded range of businesses, including its own fishing fleet and fish processing businesses. The company also added diversified activities such as restaurant operation, shipbuilding, transport, and even the operation of its own hospitals. In 1943, the company changed its name to recognize its expanded focus, becoming Nishi Taiyo Gyogyo Tosei KK. Two years later, however, at the end of World War II, the company shortened its name to Taiyo Gyogyo KK (Taiyo Fishery Co.). Following the war, the

---

Company Perspectives:

Group Vision: For almost a century, Maruha has delivered the seafood bounties of the world's oceans to customers' dining tables through all stages of the business from fisheries and aquaculture to processing, storage, logistics, and sales.

In addition to fulfilling customer needs through high-quality foodstuffs, materials, and services, our vision is to provide the innovation of the Maruha Group as well as "value" to a variety of dining settings.

---

company moved its headquarters to Tokyo in 1949. In that year, the company also became involved in Japanese baseball, forming its own professional baseball team, the Taiyo Whalers (later changed to the Yokohama Bay Stars).

World War II, however, had had drastic consequences for the company. With much of its domestic operations damaged during the war, the company lost nearly all of its assets and businesses overseas as well. Forced to rebuild, Taiyo developed a two-pronged business focus. The company reentered whaling and fishing, boosting its operations with the 1955 acquisition of Nippon Kinkai Hogei, formed in a merger between three prominent Japanese whalers just a year earlier. The company also contributed to the rebuilding of Japan's whaling fleet, once again targeting the Antarctic region. By the beginning of the 1960s, Taiyo was one of the country's leading whalers, with its own fleet hunting whales in the Antarctic, supported by its own factory ship.

During this period, as well, Taiyo began rebuilding its overseas fishing fleet. By 1951, the company had returned to salmon fishing and processing operations, including in the Alaskan region. The company became one of the first to enter the West African fishing market, when the region was opened for trawling in 1958.

Yet Taiyo also had begun to develop its food production arm, emerging as one of Japan's longtime leading seafood importers, producers, and processors. In 1963, the company launched its own aquaculture business. By 1960, Taiyo also had begun to expand its production beyond seafood and marine products into other food areas, as well as into the production of pet foods and feeds (which served as a means of making use of the waste byproducts of its seafood processing operations) and livestock production. In 1964, the company made another significant extension of its operations when it acquired a stake in Ensuiko Sugar Refining Co. That company grew into one of Japan's top-five sugar producers.

Leading Seafoods Group in the New Century

Conservationist pressures began building on a global scale in the late 1960s and early 1970s. The voracious Japanese appetite for whale meat had brought on a drastic reduction in the world's whale populations. Japanese aggressive, industrialized fishing methods also were called into question as fish stocks began to dwindle around the world. A massive lobbying effort to ban whaling grew during the 1970s. At the same time, the international community began placing restrictions on international fishing operations, leading to the adoption of 200-mile protection zones by many countries in an effort to protect their local fishing industries from large-scale international fishing companies.

The prospect of a whaling ban led Taiyo to merge its whaling operations with those two other prominent Japanese whalers, Nihon Suisan and Kyukyuo Hogei, in 1976, forming Nihon Kyodo Hogei. At the height of the Japanese whaling industry in the 1960s, the three companies had operated a combined fleet of more than 140 vessels, including nearly 90 whaling ships. The new company, however, started operations with a far reduced fleet of just 20 whaling ships and three factory ships. During the company's first post-merger whaling campaign, the company sent out 18 whaling ships. By the 1977 whaling season, however, the company fielded just four whalers. In support of the whaling fleet, though, Taiyo founded a new subsidiary, Nihon Hogei, which began processing and distributing whale meat to the Japanese market. By 1987, however, Taiyo had exited the whaling industry altogether, transferring the remains of Nihon Hogei to a new company, Kyodo Senpaku.

Continued restrictions also had forced the company to slim down its fishing fleet. Instead, during the 1980s and 1990s, the company began building up a network of international partnerships and local affiliates. By the mid-2000s, the company had developed joint ventures in some 15 countries. An early example was the creation of Solomon Taiyo Ltd. (STL) in a joint venture with the government of the Solomon Islands in 1973. Under that agreement, Taiyo supplied the fishing vessels and equipment, as well as the construction of a processing and cannery facility, in exchange for the right to fish off of the Solomon Islands waters, as well as a 75 percent stake in STL. The venture was a success, and STL rapidly became the Solomon Islands' largest employer.

Taiyo looked for other international expansion opportunities into the 1990s. In 1990, for example, the company acquired control of Kingfisher Holdings Limited in Thailand. That company had been formed in 1972 as SAFCOL Thailand, the first tuna processor in the country. SAFCOL later developed a wider line of frozen, canned, and other value-added seafood products, with an emphasis on the export market, before changing its name to Kingfisher in 1989.

Other investments brought Taiyo to the United States, where it acquired control of Trans-Ocean Products, based in Bellingham, Washington. That company was one of the first in the United States to begin producing and marketing surimi to the U.S. market.

Taiyo changed its name to Maruha Corporation, and developed a new logo, in an effort to shake off its past as a whaling company and to emphasize its new focus as a major seafood importer and processor. By the early 1990s, fishing accounted for just 10 percent of the company's sales, while the sale of fish and shellfish had become its core business, representing more than 70 percent of its revenues. The company also had developed a strong aquaculture business, with 20 fish farms in operation in Japan.

Key Dates:

1880: Ikujiro Nakabe founds a fish purchasing business to supply Osaka-area wholesalers.

1904: Nakabe moves the business to Shimonoseki and enters the whaling and fishing industry.

1924: The company goes public and changes its name to KK Hayashikane Shoten.

1926: The company launches an Antarctic whaling fleet and later diversifies into shipbuilding, restaurant operation, and other businesses.

1943: The company changes its name to Nishi Taiyo Gyogyo Tosei.

1945: The name is shortened to Taiyo Gyogyo (Taiyo Fishery Company, Limited); the company loses its overseas whaling and fishing fleet and other assets.

1949: Company headquarters are moved to Tokyo; the company forms a professional baseball team, the Taiyo Whalers.

1951: The company relaunches international fishing and whaling operations, and helps rebuild the Japanese whaling fleet; the company relaunches the salmon fishing fleet.

1953: Fish farming operations begin.

1958: The company launches West African trawl fishing operations.

1960: Operations are extended into pet foods, feed, and livestock production.

1964: The company acquires control of Ensuiko Sugar Refining Co.

1973: Joint venture Solomon Taiyo Limited is formed in the Solomon Islands.

1976: The whaling fleet merges into Nihon Kyodo Hogei.

1978: The company opens new headquarters in Tokyo.

1990: Kingfisher Holdings in Thailand is acquired.

1993: The company changes its name to Maruha Corporation.

1994: The Zhousan Industrial Co. joint venture is formed in China.

1999: The company begins a sell-off of its stake in Ensuiko Sugar.

2002: The company launches a restructuring, divesting its cold-storage operations, trawler fleet, and baseball team.

2004: The company restructures as Maruha Group Inc.; a frozen food partnership is formed with Japan Tobacco.

2005: The company sells its remaining stake in Ensuiko Sugar.

Maruha sought an entry into the Chinese market in the early 1990s as well. This led the company to form a joint venture, Zhousan Industrial Company Ltd., in 1994. The Zhousan company, held at 49 percent by Maruha, then took over its partner's original fishery business, Zhousan No. 2 Fishery Corporation, which had been founded in 1978.

Maruha launched a restructuring effort at the end of the 1990s and into the 2000s. As part of that process, the company began selling its stake in Ensuiko Sugar Refining, which had been hit by declining sugar consumption in Japan. That process was completed in 2005, when Maruha sold its remaining 24 percent stake to Mitsubishi, which also controlled the number two sugar producer in Japan, Dai-Nippon Meiji Sugar Co. In 2001, the company spun off its pet food business into a new company, Maruha Pet Food Co. Ltd., as part of a management buyout.

Maruha's restructuring continued into 2002. The company sold off its share of the Yokohama Bay Stars baseball team that year. Also in 2002, the company disposed of its trawling fleet, and spun off its cold-storage business into a new company. On a positive note, the company's restaurant business had been growing strongly, and in 2002 the company announced its intention to triple its number of restaurants. A step in that direction came in 2003 when the company opened its new Oregon Bar & Grill in Tokyo in a partnership with the Oregon state government.

Maruha's restructuring effort was completed, in large part, in 2004, capped by its own reorganization as a holding company, Maruha Group Inc., that year. The newly formed company then began taking steps to exert tighter control over its somewhat loosely linked federation of more than 170 subsidiaries worldwide. Maruha also formed new partnerships, such as a link with Osaka Uoichiba Co. in 2003, and a frozen foods development partnership with Japan Tobacco at the end of 2004. Maruha Group looked forward to another century as a leading name in the Japanese seafood industry.

Principal Subsidiaries

Alyeska Seafoods Inc (U.S.A.); Bengal Fisheries Ltd. (Bangladesh); Cixi Yongching Frozen Foods Co., Ltd. (China); Cixi Young-shin Foods Co., Ltd. (China); Dalian Riken Maruha Foodstuff Co., Ltd. (China); Entreposto Frigorifico de Pesca de Mocambique, Ltda.; Gill & Duffus S.A. (Switzerland); Kingfisher Holdings Limited (Thailand); Maruha (N.Z.) Corporation Ltd. (New Zealand); Maruha (Shanghai) Trading Corporation (China); Maruha Capital Investment, Inc. (U.S.A.); P.T. Nusantara Fishery (Indonesia); Raoping Younglian Foodstuffs Factory Co., Ltd. (China); Sociedad Pesquera Taiyo Chile Ltda.; Société Malgache de Pêcherie (Madagascar); Société Malgache de Pecherie du Boina (Madagascar); Southeast Asian Packaging & Canning Ltd. (Thailand); Supreme Alaska Seafoods Inc. (U.S.A.); Taiyo (U.K.) Ltd.; Taiyo (U.S.A.) Inc.; Trans Ocean Products Inc. (U.S.A.); TransEurope Seafood Sales B.V. (Netherlands); Viver-Atun Cartagena, S.A. (Spain); Westward Seafoods Inc. (U.S.A.); Zhoushan Industrial Co., Ltd. (China).

Principal Competitors

Antarktika Fishing Co.; Mar Fishing Company Inc.; ENACA; Kyokuyo Company Ltd.; Unilever Deutschland GmbH; Mavesa

S.A.; Mukorob Fishing Proprietary Ltd.; Hanwa Company Ltd.; Nichiro Corporation.

Further Reading

''Japan Seafood Giant Maruha Boosts Production of Dried Bonito, Mackerel,'' *Knight Ridder/Tribune Business News,* March 17, 2004.

''Japan's Maruha Expanding Ship Repair Operations in China,'' *Asia Pulse,* March 8, 2005.

''Japan's Maruha Gets Out of Sugar Production,'' *Asia Pulse,* March 16, 2005.

''Japan's Maruha Sees US$144 mln Net Loss on Property Liquidation,'' *Asia Pulse,* December 21, 2004.

''Japan's Maruha to Raise Seafood Output in China,'' *Asia Pulse,* October 27, 2004.

''Japan's Maruha to Withdraw from Trawl Fishing,'' *Asia Pulse,* September 27, 2004.

''Maruha, Japan Tobacco Team Up on Frozen Food Biz,'' *Jiji,* December 20, 2004.

''Maruha Restaurant Systems Opens Restaurant with Support of State of Oregon,'' *New Food Products in Japan,* June 25, 2003.

''Maruha Tripling Number of Restaurants,'' *Japan Food Service Journal,* August 25, 2002.

—M.L. Cohen

McDATA Corporation

310 Interlocken Crescent
Broomfield, Colorado 80021
U.S.A.
Telephone: (72) 558-8000
Toll Free: (800) 545-5773
Fax: (720) 566-3860
Web site: http://www.mcdata.com

Public Company
Incorporated: 1982
Employees: 1,008
Sales: $399.7 million (2004)
Stock Exchanges: NASDAQ
Ticker Symbol: MCDT
NAIC: 334290 Other Communications Equipment
    Manufacturing

McDATA Corporation (McData) provides storage area networking (SAN) products and services that help large organizations build Global Enterprise Data Infrastructures (GEDIs), consolidating computer networks and tying together data centers that may be spread around the world. The company's main product is the director-class Fibre Channel switch, essentially a traffic director that connects mainframe computers to storage devices, or multi-mainframes to multiple storage devices. The switch creates a "dynamic" connection, a temporary point-to-point connection for data transfer. In addition, McData sells switch cabinets, SAN management and security software, and offers training and support services. Most of its sales are indirect, accomplished through a wide range of original equipment manufacturers, including Dell, EMC, IBM, Hitachi Data Systems, Hewlett-Packard, Sun Microsystems, as well as system integrators and distributors. Based in Broomfield, Colorado, McData is a public company listed on the NASDAQ.

Offspring of 1960s Storage Pioneer

McData is one of dozens of data storage companies that grew out of Storage Technology Corporation (STC), founded in Boulder, Colorado, in 1969 by Israeli immigrant Jesse Aweidi, an IBM engineer who convinced three colleagues to launch a company at a time when leaving IBM, which maintained a plant in Boulder where they worked, to form a startup was tantamount to treason. The founders were familiar with IBM's approach to the tape storage business and sensed there was an opportunity in the market. Their gamble paid off and inspired any number of workers at STC to start their own storage-related companies, which in turn spawned other companies. As a result, Boulder County became the center of the computer storage industry even after IBM relocated its storage development operation to Arizona.

One STC employee who caught the entrepreneurial bug was John F. (Jack) McDonnell, who attended California State University at Long Beach before working at Computer Communications Inc. and moving from California to take a position at STC in its networking division in 1980. Two years later, however, he found himself laid off when a project he was working on was cancelled. Rather than move out of state in search of employment, McDonnell and five of his out-of-work colleagues (Wil Behl, Jim Fugere, Bruce Walsh, Paul Lilly, and Gary Flauaus) decided to start a company to build their own data communications devices. That was the extent of the business plan they mapped out in McDonnell's garage in August 1982.

McDonnell became chief executive officer of the new company. It was only when he went to the Colorado Secretary of State's office to file the incorporation papers that he realized that he and his partners had neglected to name the company. He remembered that while he was at STC a secretary had labeled one of his projects "McDATA," a play on his last name. McDonnell submitted the name, never intending it to be anything more than a stop-gap choice. "We all agreed that we would find a really nifty name, some kind of clever acronym, later," McDonnell told the *Denver Post* in 2002. "But we never did. So here we are 20 years later still with that name that just popped up. We've kind of gotten used to it."

Operating on a shoestring, McData set up shop in McDonnell's garage, where the engineers developed the company's first product, cluster controls that linked computer terminals to mainframe computers even if the individual operating systems

Company Perspectives:

McDATA products are designed to help you create a unified infrastructure—They bring together multi-vendor, multi-protocol, multi-location resources so that your data is available anytime, anywhere, across the global enterprise.

were not compatible. It was not long before McDonnell's wife, Pat, kicked them out of the garage and the company found accommodations in Gunbarrel, Colorado, six miles outside of Boulder, and soon became a tenant at Interlocken Business Park in Broomfield where the company would have room to grow. The founders raised the seed money among themselves, cashing in retirement funds and savings accounts, and taking out second mortgages on their homes. After a year money was so tight that McDonnell was on the verge of putting his house up for sale in order to meet payroll. Before that came to pass, however, he was able to attract $3.2 million in venture capital money in September 1983. In a second round held two years later, McData raised another $4.6 million. In 1984 the company introduced its first product, generating sales of $295,000, and in 1985 it showed its first profit.

McData enjoyed tremendous growth during its first five years. By the autumn of 1987 the company employed about 250 people and the space it leased at Interlocken grew from less than 10,000 square feet to nearly 120,000 square feet. Sales approached $30 million. In addition to cluster controllers, McData built multiplexers to allow a large number of terminals to share a printer and local area network (LAN) gateways. The products were sold primarily through distributors, available in 29 countries, but they were marketed under the name of others. In 1989 the company decided to sell products under the McData name directly to corporate computer users, hiring scores of sales and support people. Employment swelled to 500 by the end of the year. While the industry began to accept the products with McData's label, the transition to direct selling did not proceed as rapidly as hoped. As a result, in 1990 McData underwent a "resizing," as many workers were terminated.

Technology Changes Leading to 1990s' Restructuring

What was more important than sales channels to the future direction of McData were changes in technology and the marketplace. The demand for cluster controllers was fading as companies phased out systems that tied dumb terminals to mainframes in favor of networking personal computers. By November 1993 McData's workforce was reduced to just 140. With a change in strategy clearly in order, the company sold off its channel gateway product lines in March 1993. It also dropped the idea of direct sales to end-users, a poor idea given that the company was trying to sell into an already mature market, opting instead to sell to original equipment manufacturers. With the money received from the sale of its business, McData was able to invest in the development of what it called the Model 3 project, which was pursued confidentially in a collaborative effort with IBM. That product was the Escon Director. *Denver Business Journal* described it in October 1994 as "a piece of equipment that is half the size of a refrigerator and priced at about $250,000. It provides

switching capabilities between the channels of mainframe computers and peripherals such as tape drives, hard drives and printers." The product also offered fail-safe backup systems to protect companies from the crippling loss of data. Under the terms of its agreement with IBM, McData would only sell the Escon Director to IBM, which would use the product in its own mainframes and sell it to other OEMs. IBM would soon account for 90 percent of McData's business.

In 1995 McData was purchased by IBM rival EMC Corporation for $235 million in stock. The leading provider of storage devices for mainframe computers, EMC viewed the addition of McData as a way to ease its entry into storage devices used in networked computer systems. According to *Network World,* "The bundling of the switch and storage products could give EMC a leg up against storage rivals and provide a boost for McData's technology." While the relationship with EMC did not prove as fruitful as anticipated, McData's founders and backers enjoyed a significant payoff for their investments in the garage startup.

Uncomfortable with being overly dependent on a single product sold to a single customer, McData entered the Fibre Channel switch market in 1997. As part of this change in direction, EMC restructured its ownership, resulting in a new McData Corporation with its own separate board of directors and the freedom to act independently of the parent company, although EMC remained the majority shareholder. The new McData's focus was on the development and marketing of products using Fibre Channel networking technology. The Escon Director business with IBM was packaged into a shell entity called McData Holdings Corp., which remained a wholly owned EMC subsidiary and through which EMC held a 90 percent stake in McData Corp. The major reason for the change in structure was that EMC had been holding back McData's growth and if the company was to realize its potential, and maximize its investment for EMC, it needed to be independent. "EMC is a very powerful, influential storage company," McData's Director of Communications Linda Reed told *Computer Canada.* "Other storage companies said that as long as we were a subsidiary of EMC, they weren't really interested in working with us." According to *Rocky Mountain News,* "the relationship with EMC was both a blessing and a curse. McData saw substantial revenue growth in those years as well as missed opportunities. The deal kept the company from selling to competitors and hampered its long-held desire to go public."

Break from EMC in 2001

Independent once more, McData could move beyond mainframes and bring fibre channel solutions to new markets while not jeopardizing its relationship with IBM. In short order it was able to develop end-to-end SAN solutions, teaming up with large corporations, such as Microsoft and Hewlett-Packard, which began incorporating McData's SAN solutions. The Chinese wall erected between McData Holdings and McData Corp. was eventually rendered moot. In 2000 the company reached an agreement with EMC that allowed it to make a public offering of stock and gave EMC shareholders one share of McData stock for every share they owned of EMC. In August 2000 McData completed a public offering of stock, raising $350 million, and in February 2001 EMC made the distribution of McData stock

Key Dates:

1982: Company is founded by John F. McDonnell and partners.
1983: Venture capital is raised.
1984: First product is unveiled.
1993: Focus changes to Escon Director product.
1995: EMC Corporation acquires McData.
1997: McData restructures, emphasizes Channel Fibre switches.
2000: McData makes public offering of stock as part of spinoff.
2004: McDonnell retires.
2005: Computer Network Technology Corporation is acquired.

to its shareholders. As a result, McData was truly independent and EMC rivals could feel more comfortable doing business with it. As part of the arrangement, EMC also signed a two-year noncompete agreement.

Even before the break with EMC, McData began to diversify, imperative because of its agreement with EMC, as it looked ahead to the day when the noncompete agreement came to an end, knowing full well that there was no guarantee that EMC would continue to buy products and that it would be wise to line up new customers as soon as possible. In late 2000 McData launched a line of lower cost fibre switches, followed by the addition of software products offering clients what it called "Enterprise to Edge" data storage solutions. Several months later, in 2001, McData acquired SANavigator Inc., a San Jose developer of storage network management software.

McDonnell launched a succession plan in 2001, handpicking John A. Kelley, a former Qwest Communications vice-president, to serve as president and chief operating officer. A year later Kelley became chief executive officer, while McDonnell retained the chairmanship. Two years later, in January 2004, McDonnell gave up the chairmanship to Kelley, but six months later McDonnell was once again launching a storage-related startup, Crosswalk Inc. One of its first customers was McData, in which McDonnell continued to hold a significant stake.

As Kelley was assuming control, McData had to contend with difficult business conditions that resulted in disappointing earnings and led to a severe erosion in the price of its stock. McData performed better than most storage companies, enjoying solid growth in the mid-range market for its products. Wall Street, though, was not suitably impressed and failed to reward the company's stock, due in some measure to powerhouse Cisco Systems Inc. entering the market. In an effort to stay ahead of Cisco, as well as longtime rival Brocade Communications Systems, Inc., McData added new products by acquiring a pair of companies in 2003, paying $83 million for Sunnyvale, California-based Nishan Systems and $102 million for San Jose, California-based Sanera Systems. Through Nishan, McData gained software and hardware used to back up stored information in emergency or disaster situations. Sanera brought with it an advanced networking switch, linking computer servers and

storage devices. At the same time, McData invested $6 million to buy a 15 percent stake in San Jose, California-based Aarohi Communications, developer of silicon solutions for intelligent storage networks. According to *Computerworld*, "Together, the three deals are designed to help McData broaden its existing line of directors for Fibre Channel storage-area networks (SAN) to include storage-over-IP capabilities. The technology additions will also expand the port count on the devices it sells from a maximum of 140 now to 256."

Conditions were still difficult in 2003 and 2004 for McData, which made significant job cuts to control costs. Not only did the company have to contend with lower sales, its competition cut prices. In addition Cisco became even more formidable by forging a partnership with EMC in early 2005. McData responded by acquiring Minneapolis-based Computer Network Technology Corporation (CNT) in a stock and debt deal valued around $235 million. The hope was that McData would become more competitive by adding CNT services and products related to wide-area network technology. Moreover, the deal strengthened its relationship with IBM, its second largest customer. IBM was CNT's largest customer. The acquisition was not well received by all parties, however, as reflected by an article in Boulder's *Daily Camera* that maintained, "Whether the purchase is enough for McData to hold its ground and grow remains to be seen. One analyst says the business—itself the subject of speculation as an acquisition target in recent months—was likely better off focusing on its own turnaround, rather than attempting to swallow another company working to reverse its fortune."

Principal Subsidiaries

SANavigator, Inc.; Nishan Systems, Inc.; Sanera Systems, Inc.

Principal Competitors

Brocade Communications Systems, Inc.; Cisco Systems, Inc.; QLogic Corporation.

Further Reading

Branaugh, Matt, "Broomfield, Colo.-Based Data Storage Firm Buys Competitor for $235 Million," *Daily Camera,* January 19, 2005.
——, "CEO Steps Aside from Broomfield, Colo.-Based Storage Networking Firm," *Daily Camera,* June 12, 2002.
Cooney, Michael, "Consuming McDATA Satisfied EMC's Hunger for Networking," *Network World,* October 30, 1995, p. 16.
Forgrieve, Janet, "McDATA Changes with Tech World," *Rocky Mountain News,* October 5, 2001, p. 4B.
Locke, Tom "McData's Back on Line," *Denver Business Journal,* October 14, 1994, p. 3A.
McGhee, Tom, "McData Leaving the Nest," *Denver Post,* January 22, 2001, p. C1.
Nachman-Hunt, Nancy, "Its Name May Sound Generic, But McDATA's Sales Growth Is Anything But," *Boulder County Business Report,* October 1987, p. 3.
Nowak, Pete, "McDATA Targets Fibre Channel After EMC Spinoff," *Computing Canada,* November 24, 1997, p. 41.
Olgeirson, Ian, "McDATA Attempts to Reach Past IBM's Coffers," *Denver Business Journal,* August 1, 1997, p. 8A.

—Ed Dinger

Merix Corporation

1521 Poplar Lane
Forest Grove, Oregon 97116
U.S.A.
Telephone: (503) 359-9300
Fax: (503) 357-9755
Web site: http://www.merix.com

Public Company
Incorporated: 1994
Employees: 1,533
Sales: $186.99 million (2005)
Stock Exchanges: NASDAQ
Ticker Symbol: MERX
NAIC: 334412 Printed Circuit Board Manufacturing

Merix Corporation is a leading manufacturer of advanced printed circuit boards that are used in sophisticated electronics equipment. Merix serves the data and wireless communications, computer, and test and industrial instrumentation markets, supplying "interconnect" devices that link microprocessors, integrated circuits, and other components. The company operates two manufacturing facilities in Oregon, one at its headquarters complex in Forest Grove and another in Wood Village. Merix's Data Circuit Holdings subsidiary operates in San Jose, California. Overseas, manufacturing operations are maintained at four plants in southern China and at one facility in Hong Kong. Merix serves original equipment manufacturers (OEMs), deriving the majority of its revenue from customers such as Cisco Systems, Juniper Networks, Motorola, Nokia, and Silicon Graphics. The company generates nearly 80 percent of its sales from the data and wireless communications markets.

Origins

Merix was born from the corporate structure of Tektronix, Inc., a troubled *Fortune* 500 company that freed itself from several of its divisions as part of a reorganization plan implemented during the early 1990s. Before being beset by the problems that triggered Merix's formation, Tektronix had developed into one of Oregon's most important and largest enterprises.

Founded in 1946 and based in Beaverton, Oregon, the company established a lasting presence in the business world by developing a way to accurately measure and display high-speed electrical signals. Tektronix's pioneering developments in the testing, measurement, and calibration of electric signals served it well during the postwar period, creating one of the largest concerns of its kind in the country. The company leveraged its mainstay business to branch out into other businesses, notably the formation of a circuit board operation in 1959.

Tektronix's circuit board business blossomed in the years to follow, eventually earning distinction by occupying a separate facility in 1983 in Forest Grove. From Forest Grove, the circuit board division served a distinguished clientele, supplying products to IBM, NCR, and Rockwell International, among others. Tektronix, meanwhile, was beginning to show its age. Throughout the 1980s, the company was hobbled by declining sales from its core products and, significantly, its strategic focus became blurred by numerous side ventures. Tektronix management took action in the early 1990s, and part of the solution for the company's ills was the creation of Merix.

As Tektronix entered the 1990s, its chief executive officer and chairman, Jerry Meyer, began formulating a plan to rid his company of the unflattering tag of a moribund former powerhouse. An important part of his plan hinged upon narrowing the company's focus on its core product lines. Those businesses deemed outside the company's strategic pale were to be either divested or spun off as separate entities. To assist him in his restructuring efforts, Meyer hired John Karalis, a former vice-president and general counsel at Apple Computer, Inc. who joined Tektronix in 1992 as vice-president for corporate development. Karalis was one of the first of a group of former Apple executives who migrated to Tektronix in the early 1990s, a group that included Deborah Coleman, an 11-year Apple veteran who joined Meyer and Karalis in 1992 as vice-president of materials operation.

By the time Coleman joined Tektronix to head the company's circuit board division, she was already a renowned figure in the corporate world. A native of Providence, Rhode Island, Coleman earned a Bachelor of Arts degree in English literature from Brown University in 1974 and an M.B.A. from Stanford Business

---

Company Perspectives:

Selecting the right supplier who has the technical expertise and knowhow can be difficult. Our customers have found that superior quality and reliability do not happen by chance. It is a result of the cumulative efforts of a focused group of talented people, guided by a skilled management team.

School four years later. During college, she worked at Texas Instruments before beginning her post-academic career at Hewlett-Packard as a financial manager. In 1981, in what she later hailed as her best business decision, Coleman joined Apple as part of founder Steve Jobs's Macintosh management team. At Apple, Coleman established her reputation as an ambitious, indefatigable, and sometimes over-ardent executive. She logged 100-hour work weeks while at Apple, drove a car bearing the personalized license plate "GECEO2B"—proclaiming her goal to be chief executive officer of General Electric Company one day—and struck one of her greatest admirers as being "too bossy, too loud, too rough around the edges, too everything," as quoted in the May 1996 issue of *Oregon Business*. Coleman's supporters acknowledged she had a somewhat abrasive managerial style, but they also applauded her rise within the executive ranks at Apple. She started at Apple developing Macintosh and LaserWriter products, before being selected to manage the Macintosh manufacturing plant. Coleman was named vice-president of operations and later, at the age of 34, she became the youngest chief financial officer of a *Fortune* 500 company in the country.

Merix's 1994 Spinoff

Not long after Coleman joined Tektronix, Meyer and Karalis began implementing their plan to spin off non-strategic internal components operations. The restructuring that ensued included the sale of Tektronix's ceramic packaging operation to VisPro Corp., a combination joint venture and divestiture of its integrated circuits operation, and the spinoff of its Forest Grove circuit board manufacturing plant. Coleman was selected to serve as the chief executive officer and chairperson of the new company created by the March 1994 spinoff, a company named Merix Corporation that began as a $78.5 million-in-sales company. Although Merix was created as a distinct business, its ties to Tektronix remained strong after the spinoff. Tektronix ranked as Merix's largest customer, accounting for nearly half of the circuit board maker's sales immediately following the separation. Further, Tektronix owned a considerable portion of Merix. Merix converted to public ownership in June 1994, with Tektronix retaining a 43 percent interest in its former division.

Despite Merix's financial connections to its former parent company, the Forest Grove-based concern was an independent enterprise capable of standing on its own in its industry. The company was a leading supplier of printed circuit boards, backplanes, and flexible circuits—devices referred to as "interconnect" products because they are used to link microprocessors, integrated circuits, and other components. Armed with approximately $30 million raised from Merix's initial public offering, Coleman was intent on greatly increasing the company's stature, hoping to create a $500-million-in-sales business by the

end of the 1990s. She wasted little time adding to the production capacity and technological expertise of the firm, acquiring a printed circuit board manufacturing facility in Loveland, Colorado, from Hewlett-Packard in 1995. The following year, Coleman acquired the Soladyne division belonging to Rogers Corporation. The acquisition gave Merix a printed circuit board manufacturing facility in San Diego, California. Following the Soladyne acquisition, Merix's sales reached $155.6 million, nearly twice the amount collected two years earlier when Coleman was just beginning to navigate on her own.

Faltering in the Late 1990s

As Coleman prepared for further expansion during the late 1990s, her hopes were dashed for a spurt of explosive growth to catapult the company toward the $500 million mark. Merix, like other companies in its industry, was buffeted by the collapse of markets in the Far East. The impact of the Asian economic crisis was exacerbated by an industrywide oversupply of electronics components, causing scores of electronics firms to adopt defensive postures. Coleman was forced to retreat as well, as Merix's profits plummeted in 1997 and again in 1998. As the industry downturn dragged on, Merix's losses increased, prompting Coleman to scale down the company's operations, lay off workers, and cut costs wherever possible. A $28 million restructuring program was begun in mid-1998 that saw the company shutter its manufacturing facility in Loveland in October 1998. Coleman conceded that the acquisition of the printed circuit board facility was the worst business decision of her career, declaring that she had paid too much for the plant. Coleman also rid Merix of its manufacturing facility in San Diego, selling the former Soladyne business in early 1999 to Tyco Printed Circuit Group Inc., a subsidiary of Tyco International Ltd.

Shortly after Merix's structural changes were complete, the company underwent managerial changes. In the midst of the restructuring process, Mark Hollinger, the company's senior vice-president of operations, was named chief operating officer. In May 1999, Hollinger was promoted to president and promised the chief executive position by September 1999. His ascension was triggered by a decision Coleman made in January 1999 to step down as Merix's chief executive officer, ending her reign five years after it had begun. Coleman professed a desire to devote more time to investing in emerging technology companies. She remained CEO until September 2001. Hollinger, meanwhile, inherited a company poised to emerge from a worldwide surfeit of circuit board manufacturing capacity.

As the company waited for conditions to improve, having done what it could to position itself for the market's return to equilibrium, Hollinger declared his intentions to diversify Merix's customer base and to pursue strategic alliances with other concerns in the electronics industry. At the time he took the helm as president in May, there were already signs that recovery was on its way. Merix completed the expansion of its Forest Grove facility, a project that had commenced at the beginning of 1998, and began to hire employees after months of trimming its payroll. By late 1999, when Hollinger added the title of chief executive officer, there were tangible signs of recovery on the company's balance sheet. During Merix's second quarter in 2000, which represented the last months of

Key Dates:

1959: Tektronix, Inc. forms circuit board division.

1983: Tektronix moves circuit board operations to a separate facility in Forest Grove, Oregon.

1992: Deborah Coleman joins Tektronix to manage the circuit board operations.

1994: Tektronix spins off its circuit board division as Merix Corporation.

1995: Merix acquires Hewlett-Packard's circuit board manufacturing plant in Loveland, Colorado.

1996: A third manufacturing facility is added through the acquisition of Rogers Corp.'s Soladyne division in San Diego, California.

1998: Declining sales and mounting losses force Merix to close its Loveland plant.

1999: Soladyne plant is sold to Tyco International Ltd.

2000: A three-year expansion project begins that will double production capacity.

2004: Merix acquires Data Circuit Systems Inc.

2005: Eastern Pacific Circuits Limited is acquired, establishing a manufacturing presence in China and Hong Kong.

calendar 1999, the company recorded $1.2 million in net income, a figure that compared favorably to the $1.9 million loss registered during the same period a year earlier. A significant contributor to the financial results was increased orders from manufacturers of communications equipment, a market segment that grew from 30 percent to approximately 50 percent of Merix's revenue during the previous year. The company's stock recorded an encouraging gain as well, increasing from $5 per share in May 1999 to $14 per share by the end of 1999.

Merix at the Beginning of the 21st Century

As Merix entered the new century, the company appeared to have put the difficult years of the late 1990s behind it. One positive outcome of the industrywide downturn was the consolidation it triggered, as a form of corporate Darwinism played itself out. Those printed circuit board manufacturers that proved less resilient to the harsh market conditions either exited the business or were acquired by other firms, thereby reducing the number of competitors Merix faced as it plotted its course in the 21st century. Hollinger, who continued to steer the company toward an increased presence in the data communications and wireless communications markets, stood to gain from the return to more favorable market conditions. "The order rate for high-technology printed circuit boards continues to be very strong," he noted in a June 19, 2000 interview with *Electronic News,* "and capacity in the industry is definitely tightening. Demand from both new and existing customers in the communications market segment is driving much of our sales growth."

Hollinger's optimism soon faded as Merix entered the new century. Like Coleman, Hollinger was preparing for growth and expansion when market conditions soured, forcing him to retreat instead of advance. Not long after announcing plans to build a new production plant in Wood Village, Oregon, Merix felt the blows delivered by the dot-com industry's collapse and a nationwide recession. During the first two years of the decade, the company lost money, forcing another series of layoffs, which eventually reduced the company's payroll to 850, and forcing it to suspend plans for constructing the Wood Village plant. The cumulative effect of the Asian economic crisis and domestic economic problems, occurring in quick succession, left the company battered, but after Merix had endured its latest challenge, Hollinger prepared to lead the company toward a brighter future.

Market conditions began to improve by the end of 2003. After recording eight consecutive money-losing quarters, the company posted a profit of $707,000 at the end of November, which drove the price of its stock up to heights not reached in more than two years. Encouraged by the result, Hollinger pressed forward with plans to build a new manufacturing plant in Wood Village, a facility that eventually increased manufacturing capacity by 50 percent. Sales increased by 100 percent or more in each of the ensuing quarters, as the company enjoyed renewed demand from electronics manufacturers, but it continued to struggle with consistent profitability. "The big issue for them has always been execution," an analyst remarked in an April 15, 2005 interview with the *Oregonian.* Merix registered two profitable quarters in 2004 and lost money in the other two quarters, a record repeated in 2005.

To give his company a firmer footing, Hollinger completed two significant deals as the company began its second decade of independence. At the end of 2004, he acquired Data Circuit Systems Inc., paying $43 million for the San Jose, California-based printed circuit board manufacturer. Data Circuit, a $27.7 million-in-sales company, specialized in quickly completing small orders of circuit boards used for prototypes and new products, serving customers such as Boeing, Hewlett-Packard, and Intel. The company's ability to produce circuit boards quickly, known as "quick-turn" in the industry, gave Merix a new skill. Data Circuit could print a new board design within 24 hours, while it took Merix at least three days to accomplish the same feat. After enhancing his company's ability to produce small numbers of circuit boards quickly, Hollinger next turned to strengthening Merix's high-volume capabilities. For years, he had wanted to establish a presence in Asia, where lower labor costs were conducive to the high-volume segment of Merix's industry. In April 2005, Hollinger achieved his goal, signing an agreement to acquire Eastern Pacific Circuits Limited for roughly $120 million. The acquisition of Hong Kong-based Eastern Pacific, which was completed in September 2005, gave Hollinger four manufacturing plants in southern China and one facility in Hong Kong, operations that generated $143 million in sales in 2004. For Merix, which was generating $186 million in sales at the time of the purchase, the addition of Eastern Pacific promised to increase its revenue volume substantially, but the more pressing need for the company was to improve its bottom-line performance. As the company prepared for the future, consistent profitability represented its single greatest challenge, putting Hollinger in the position of accomplishing something none of his predecessors had achieved.

Principal Subsidiaries

Merix San Jose, Inc.; Data Circuit Holdings, Inc.; Merix Nevada, Inc.; Merix Europe B.V.

Principal Competitors

Dynamic Details Inc; Multek; Sanmina-SCI; TTM Technologies, Inc.; Tyco International Ltd., Viasystems, Inc.

Further Reading

"Debi Coleman," *Business Journal-Portland,* February 25, 2000, p. 6.

Dolan, Kerry A., "Fairfield Bound?," *Forbes,* February 27, 1995, p. 142.

"Forest Grove's Merix Corp. Acquires Data Circuit Systems," *Daily Journal of Commerce,* December 30, 2004.

Holt, Shirleen, "Business Unusual," *Oregon Business,* May 1996, p. 27.

Keuchle, Jeff, "Good Apples," *Oregon Business,* December 1994, p. S12.

Kosseff, Jeffrey, "Investment Fuels Forest Grove, Ore., Circuit Board Makers Growth," *Knight-Ridder/Tribune Business News,* July 12, 2000,

——, "Oregon Tech Companies Tektronix, Merix Show Signs of Recovery," *Oregonian,* December 19, 2003.

LaBarre, Polly, "The Seamless Enterprise," *Industry Week,* June 19, 1995, p. 22.

Levine, Bernard, "Merix Completes Soladyne Sale to Tyco," *Electronic News,* February 15, 1999, p. 34.

Manning, Jeff, "Stock Drops Sharply As Forest Grove, Ore., Tech Supplier Merix Projects Loss," *Oregonian,* May 15, 2004.

"Merix Corporation Acquires Data Circuit Systems, Inc.," *EDP Weekly's IT Monitor,* December 13, 2004, p. 5.

"Merix Moves to Cut Costs," *Electronic News,* August 24, 1998, p. 48.

"Merix to Acquire Eastern Pacific Circuits," *Wireless News,* April 14, 2005.

Rogoway, Mike, "Forest Grove, Ore., Circuit Board Maker Merix to Gain Speed with Buyout," *Oregonian,* December 11, 2004.

Sickinger, Ted, "Latest Acquisition Gives Merix Gateway to Asia," *Oregonian,* April 15, 2005.

Williams, Elisa, "CEO of Forest Grove, Ore.-Based Circuit Board Maker Departs," *Knight-Ridder/Tribune Business News,* May 25, 1999.

Woodward, Steve, "Oregon-Based Circuit Board Maker Credits Restructuring for Sales Rise," *Knight-Ridder/Tribune Business News,* December 24, 1998.

Zimmerman, Rachel, "Merix CEO Prevails in Male-Dominated Industry," *Business Journal-Portland,* September 30, 1994, p. 16.

—Jeffrey L. Covell

Moog Music, Inc.

2004 E. Riverside Drive
Asheville, North Carolina 28804
U.S.A.
Telephone: (828) 251-0090
Toll Free: (800) 948-1990
Fax: (828) 254-6233
Web site: http://www.moogmusic.com

Private Company
Incorporated: 1978 as Big Briar, Inc.
Employees: 18
Sales: $3 million (2004 est.)
NAIC: 339992 Musical Instrument Manufacturing

Moog Music, Inc. produces electronic musical instruments and accessories. The firm's flagship product is the Minimoog Voyager synthesizer, a keyboard instrument that can produce a wide range of different sounds. Other products include electronic instruments called theremins; Moogerfooger audio effects boxes; and the Moog PianoBar, a device that enables an acoustic piano to play and record a wide range of synthesized sounds. Company founder Dr. Robert Moog died in 2005, and the company is now headed by his business partner, Mike Adams.

Beginnings

Moog Music traces its origins to 1954, when 20-year-old Robert Moog (rhymes with "vogue") formed the R.A. Moog Company in Flushing, Queens, New York to produce theremins, instruments that were played by manipulating an electric field in the air above them. From a young age Moog, whose father was an electronics hobbyist, had built radios and simple musical instruments from kits, and in 1949, at the age of 14, he had built a theremin after reading an article on the subject in *Radio News* magazine. The instrument had been invented three decades earlier by Russian Leon Theremin, and was used as much for music (a few classical pieces had been written for it) as for creating eerie audio effects in movies including *The Day the Earth Stood Still* and Alfred Hitchcock's *Spellbound*.

To help earn money while he studied physics at Queens College, in 1954 Moog and his father decided to sell theremins through the mail. The instrument had not been manufactured for a number of years, and the new company found a small market for them by placing ads in electronics magazines. A ready-to-assemble kit cost $59.95, and a pre-assembled unit was $87.95.

The late 1950s saw Moog study electrical engineering at Columbia University in New York. He continued to sell theremins from his parents' basement, and by 1960 his offerings ranged from a $75 basic kit to a $650 fully assembled professional model. In January 1961 he published an article in *Electronics World* magazine on building a new transistorized theremin, which helped him sell more than 1,000 kits. During that year production moved to Trumansburg, New York, near the city of Ithaca, where he had begun attending Cornell University to earn a Ph.D. in engineering physics. While continuing to build and sell theremins, Moog also experimented with making a battery-powered amplifier, though this effort proved unsuccessful.

In the fall of 1963 Moog was invited to demonstrate his theremin at a music educators' convention in Rochester, New York, by Walter Sear, a composer and tuba player who was selling Moog's kits. One of the attendees, teacher and experimental musician Herbert Deutsch, approached him with the idea of creating a new kind of electronic instrument.

Creating the Moog Synthesizer in 1964

In the summer of 1964, six months after Moog's interest had been heightened by a performance of electronic music in New York, the pair began working together at his home in Trumansburg. With Deutsch suggesting ideas for sounds, Moog built electronic circuits to create them. His intent was to build the most useful tool possible for a musician, and he valued the input of an end-user such as Deutsch. Moog himself, though he had taken years of piano lessons as a child, considered himself a passable musician at best.

Within two weeks the basic idea for the synthesizer was established, and Moog began working to complete a prototype. His was not the first device to synthesize sound electronically; its predecessors ranged from Thaddeus Cahill's 1906 Telharmonium (which weighed 200 tons) to a room-sized instrument constructed in the 1950s by RCA in collaboration with

Company Perspectives:

Here at the beginning of the 21st century Moog Music is still producing the quality tools to create music that could not otherwise exist without them, making instruments so unique that they represent a genre of their own: Moog Music. Perhaps back in 1954, Bob Moog and his father were only trying to make something cool, to create a sound that as of yet was only in the realm of imagination, never dreaming how far their invention would take the Moog name. Whatever the original purpose, there is no doubt that Bob Moog has made his mark, and that modern music has been forever changed for the better.

Columbia and Princeton Universities, which used holes punched in rolls of computer-readable paper to define sounds. Although it filled a table with black boxes sporting many knobs, patch cords, and switches, Moog's invention (which at Deutsch's suggestion also incorporated a 3½-octave, 44-note keyboard) was much smaller than its predecessors.

Moog's device passed the notes through voltage-controlled oscillators, amplifiers, and filters that could be adjusted to produce tones that ranged from an organ-like sound to others that were otherworldly. It had several unique features including attack-delay-sustain-release envelopes that gave notes the ability to swell and fade, and its relatively small size allowed it to be transported to public performances, something not feasible with previous synthesizers.

In October 1964 a primitive version was demonstrated at the Audio Engineering Society Convention in New York, which immediately resulted in orders for instruments from Alwin Nikolais, a prominent New York dance choreographer/composer, and Eric Sidey, who operated a studio for recording commercial "jingles." Over the next several years avant-garde musicians and recording studios would be the primary buyers of Moog's synthesizers, which were considered esoteric devices far outside the realm of mainstream music.

These early models, each custom made, sold for between $2,000 and $10,000, depending on the degree of complexity desired. By the summer of 1965, when he completed his doctorate, Moog had a staff of six building synthesizers and theremins, which he also continued to make. Orders came in only sporadically, however, and by 1967 he was close to giving up the business to take a job in the corporate world. Before throwing in the towel he decided to make one last push, and with his wife Shirleigh took a new version of the synthesizer to the Audio Engineering Society Convention in Los Angeles, which helped generate enough sales to keep the business afloat.

Moog's biggest boost would come the following year, when classical musician and composer Walter (later known as Wendy) Carlos released an album called *Switched on Bach.* The recording of some of Johann Sebastian Bach's most famous compositions with the unusual tonality of the Moog (done through multiple overdubs, because only one note could be played at a time) was a smash hit, selling more than one million copies and spawning dozens of copycats. Although some of the

recordings were serious attempts to use the capabilities of the new instrument, many others (with such names as "The Electric Cow Goes Mooog" and "Switched On Santa") utilized it as a gimmick. Regardless, Moog was soon swamped with orders, and production of synthesizers jumped from 23 in 1967 to 49 in 1968 and 99 in 1969.

At this time the psychedelic music era was in full bloom, and rock musicians were beginning to discover the synthesizer as well. The Beach Boys had approached Robert Moog in 1966 to build a theremin soundalike for concert performances of their hit "Good Vibrations" (which had been recorded using a similar-sounding instrument called an electro-theremin), and in the fall of 1967 Monkees drummer Mickey Dolenz became the first rock musician to buy a Moog synthesizer, which he used on the group's fourth album. In 1968 the Rolling Stones and Byrds both purchased Moogs, and they were followed in 1969 by Jimi Hendrix, Simon & Garfunkel, and The Beatles, who used one on their last recorded album, *Abbey Road,* as well as for a George Harrison solo project called "Electronic Sound." By decade's end the R.A. Moog Co. had grown to employ 42 and had annual sales of $750,000.

Debut of the Minimoog in 1970

In 1970 the company introduced a much smaller synthesizer, the Minimoog. Weighing less than 50 pounds, it was mounted in an attractive hardwood cabinet and featured a flip-up effects panel above the keyboard. Although initial sales were promising, the inventor's lack of business skills, aggressive new competitors including ARP, and an economic recession all combined to bring the firm close to bankruptcy.

To stay in business, in 1971 Robert Moog sold controlling interest in the company to investor Bill Waytena for the assumption of $250,000 in debt, and the firm was merged into his muSonics, Inc. to form Moog muSonics, with its manufacturing operations relocated to the Buffalo suburb of Williamsville. In 1972, the company became known as Moog Music, Inc.

The year 1973 saw Waytena sell control of Moog Music for several million dollars to Norlin Industries, a conglomerate that was the largest producer of musical instruments in the United States via brands including Gibson guitars and Lowery organs. Minority stakeholder Robert Moog would continue to serve as president of its Moog Music division.

During the early 1970s further refinements were made to the Minimoog and new variations were introduced, including the Micromoog and Polymoog. The latter, which debuted in 1977, was the first of the firm's synthesizers that could play more than one note at a time, and accounted for a third of the approximately $10 million Moog Music took in during the year.

The disco era brought new uses for synthesizers, with such hits as Donna Summer's 1977 "I Feel Love," featuring a throbbing Moog bass line. Other Moog users of the period included fusion jazz musicians Herbie Hancock and Chick Corea; rhythm and blues artists James Brown, Stevie Wonder, and Parliament/Funkadelic; and rock performers Emerson Lake & Palmer, Yes, and Kraftwerk. Moogs also were starting to see use on "new wave" hits by Gary Numan, Devo, and others, but the company was struggling to keep up with several dozen competitors, including makers of inexpensive digital synthesizers that stayed in tune better than their analog kin.

Robert Moog's Departure from the Firm in 1977

Other engineers were being assigned to design Moog's synthesizers by Norlin, and in 1977 the company's disillusioned founder sold his ownership stake and left the firm. In 1983 Moog Music executives bought the company from Norlin for $2.2 million, and under the name Moog Electronics made diminishing numbers of synthesizers while servicing older Moog instruments and performing contract manufacturing of products including subway door openers and climate control systems. In 1987 the company was purchased by electronics maker EJE Research, which quietly shut it down in 1993.

Meanwhile, in 1978 Robert Moog had moved from Buffalo to a remote area outside Asheville, North Carolina, where he formed a new company, called Big Briar, to provide consulting services and make theremins and other custom audio equipment. In 1984 he moved to Boston to work full time for instrument maker Kurzweil Music Systems, but in 1989 he quit and returned to Asheville to teach music at the University of North Carolina.

In 1989 Moog met nonagenarian inventor Leon Theremin for the first time, and two years later he introduced a new theremin instrument, the Series 91 model. He quit teaching in 1992 to devote his full attention to Big Briar, and in 1996 added the Etherwave theremin, followed in 1998 by the Moogerfooger effects module. The latter unit incorporated original Moog synthesizer technology and allowed musicians to plug in guitars or other instruments to alter their sounds. Moog also worked with longtime associate David Van Koevering to create the Van

Koevering Interactive Piano, a keyboard instrument that incorporated a computer that could synthesize the sounds of more than 120 different instruments while creating a digital record of the performance.

By 1994 the Moog Music trademark had been inactive for enough time that, according to U.S. law, it was up for grabs. Several individuals began seeking to use it, and a legal wrangle took shape. Robert Moog, immersed in a divorce, was at first unaware of the news, but when he found out he went to court to win it back. In 2000 he succeeded, and began laying plans to introduce a new Moog synthesizer, which would offer the sound of the Minimoog with select modern improvements. Original examples of his synthesizers, in particular the Minimoog, had begun increasing in value as a new generation of musicians sought their unique qualities.

Big Briar Becoming Moog Music and the Debut of the Voyager in 2002

In 2002 Big Briar changed its name to Moog Music, Inc., with new partner and CEO Mike Adams running the business end. In the fall the company introduced the new Moog Voyager synthesizer. It was the first keyboard-based synthesizer Robert Moog had marketed under his own name since the 1970s (though in the United Kingdom, it was sold as "Voyager—by Bob Moog," as a Welsh entrepreneur had obtained rights to the Moog trademark there).

The instrument combined the best features of the Minimoog with more recent technological advancements, but its sound remained totally analog. Moog believed, as did many musicians, that digital synthesizers had a cold, "soulless" sound, and he preferred the warmth of analog technology. The new synthesizer resembled the Minimoog, with a hardwood cabinet and flip-up control panel, but it could make more sounds than the original model, and had 128 programmable presets to store specific ones for future use. Like its predecessor, it was able to play only one note at a time. Priced at nearly $3,200, it received rave reviews from industry publications.

All but two of the components of the new Voyager were sourced from the United States, with Moog's small staff assembling a completed instrument in approximately one-half hour's time. Seeking to improve manufacturing efficiency, CEO Adams trained his employees in the use of Demand Flow Technology production, a manufacturing philosophy in which inventory of completed products was kept to a minimum and new orders were built and shipped out quickly. He also worked to improve the financial aspects of the business, which under Robert Moog had been notoriously underdeveloped.

In the summer of 2003 the firm introduced the Moog PianoBar, a $1,500 device designed by fellow synthesizer pioneer Don Buchla. When attached to an acoustic piano, it could synthesize the sounds of more than 200 instruments or sound effects while making a digital record of keystrokes for later playback or use with software that created musical notation. It was targeted to composers who wished to experiment with different sounds but preferred to use an acoustic piano, or solo performers who wanted to add layers of sound to the piano.

In 2004 the company introduced the Etherwave Pro, a $1,500 professional-grade theremin, and the MuRF, a new addition to the Moogerfooger line. The year also saw numerous tributes to Robert Moog, including several concerts and a documentary film. In 2005 new variations on the Minimoog were introduced including a rack-mountable version and the Minimoog Electric Blue, which featured a strikingly backlit front panel. The company's synthesizers were once again a hot item, with orders coming from high-profile pop musicians hip-hopper Snoop Dogg and alternative rock band Wilco.

On August 21, 2005, Dr. Robert Moog died from brain cancer at the age of 71. Prior to his death he had begun working with Cyril Lance, a Cornell-educated physicist, who would take his place as senior design engineer. Business partner Mike Adams would continue to serve as Moog Music CEO.

More than 50 years after Robert Moog began selling theremins by mail, the revitalized Moog Music, Inc. was successfully manufacturing Minimoog Voyager synthesizers, Etherwave theremins, Moog PianoBars, and Moogerfooger effects boxes. Despite the recent death of its founder and guiding light, the firm remained dedicated to serving musicians around the world with high-quality, innovative products.

Principal Competitors

Yamaha Corporation; Korg, Inc.; Roland Corporation; Casio Computer Co., Ltd.; E-MU Systems, Inc.; Analogia, Inc.; Clavia DMI; Alesis.

Further Reading

Bernstein, David, "A Comeback for Another Classic Rocker: The Moog Synthesizer," *The New York Times,* September 29, 2004, p. E3.

Bledsoe, Wayne, "Robert Moog Flipped the Switch on Bach," *Knoxville News-Sentinel,* May 29, 1994, p. 3.

Cane, Alan, "Survey—Creative Business—Robert Moog," *Financial Times,* June 12, 2001.

Henahan, Donal, "Is Everybody Going to the Moog?," *The New York Times,* August 24, 1969, p. D15.

Horowitz, Joseph, "In the Moog for Electronic Music," *The New York Times,* January 28, 1979, p. L19.

Keenan, David, "Electric Dreams," *Sunday Herald,* February 24, 2002, p. 6.

Kozinn, Allan, "Robert Moog Dies at 71; Created a Synthesizer That Revolutionized Music," *The New York Times,* August 23, 2005, p. C16.

Luxenberg, Stan, "Norlin Seeks to Scale Up Profits," *The New York Times,* April 23, 1978, p. F1.

——, "The Vicissitudes of the Moog," *The New York Times,* April 23, 1978, p. F4.

Miller, Nancy, "This Man Rocks," *Entertainment Weekly,* September 17, 2004, p. 32.

Myers, Paul, "Smells Like Moog Spirit," *Globe and Mail,* August 3, 1996, p. C1.

Pinch, Trevor, and Frank Trocco, *Analog Days,* Cambridge, Mass.: Harvard University Press, 2002.

Rideout, Ernie, "Fantastic Voyager—The Making of a Minimoog for the Millennium," *Keyboard,* May 1, 2003, p. 32.

Vail, Mark, *Vintage Synthesizers,* San Francisco: Miller Freeman, 2000.

—Frank Uhle

MTR Gaming Group, Inc.

State Route 2 South
Chester, West Virginia 26034
U.S.A.
Telephone: (304) 387-5712
Toll Free: (800) 804-0468
Fax: (304) 387-2167
Web site: http://www.mtrgaming.com

Public Company
Incorporated: 1988 as Secamur Corporation
Employees: 2,750
Sales: $315.2 million (2004)
Stock Exchanges: NASDAQ
Ticker Symbol: MNTG
NAIC: 711212 Race Tracks; 551112 Offices of Other
     Holding Companies; 721110 Hotels (Except Casino
     Hotels) and Motels

MTR Gaming Group, Inc. owns and operates thoroughbred and harness racetracks, casinos, and properties called ''racinos,'' which are racetracks offering forms of gambling other than pari-mutuel wagering. The company's flagship property is the Mountaineer Racetrack & Gaming Resort in Chester, West Virginia, 35 miles west of Pittsburgh. The Mountaineer property is a year-round thoroughbred racetrack with a 359-room hotel, golf course, theater and events center, convention center, and more than 3,000 slot machines. MTR also owns Scioto Downs, a harness racing facility in Columbus, Ohio; the Ramada Inn in Reno, Nevada; the Speedway Casino and Binion's Gambling Hall & Hotel in Las Vegas; and a license to build Presque Isle Downs, a thoroughbred racetrack in Erie, Pennsylvania. MTR holds a 50 percent interest in North Metro Harness Initiative, LLC, which has a license to construct a harness racetrack 30 miles north of Minneapolis. The company also has signed a definitive agreement to acquire a 90 percent stake in Jackson Trotting Association, which owns and operates Jackson Harness Raceway in Jackson, Michigan.

Origins

MTR struggled mightily during its first decade in business, trying in vain for years to find a business model that worked. The company operated under several different names and it delved into several different markets, floundering financially and strategically until its path crossed with a former tax accountant named Edson ''Ted'' Arneault.

The years before Arneault's arrival were pocked by the failings of a rudderless company. MTR was incorporated in March 1988 as Secamur Corporation, starting out as a wholly owned subsidiary of Buffalo Equities, Inc. until Buffalo Equities spun the company off to its shareholders in January 1989. Secamur was not on its own for long, gaining a new parent company six months later when Pacific International Industries, Inc. acquired it. Pacific International, only 11 months older than Secamur, was attempting to carve a niche for itself in Southern California's contract security guard market. Its name was changed to Excalibur Security Services, Inc., but the experiment soon failed. Excalibur Security filed a voluntary petition with the U.S. Bankruptcy Court for the Central District of California in December 1990, giving its management time to develop a new strategy. In May 1991, the company sold its moribund security guard business and decided to focus on the odd business mix of acquiring gambling and oil and gas properties. The bankruptcy court approved the plan in December 1991, an event marked by a name change to Excalibur Holding Corporation. It was while the newly named company was beginning its new corporate life as an acquirer of gambling and oil and gas properties that Arneault entered the scene. Within a few short years, the company's strategic scope was narrowed and Arneault emerged as the chief architect of its execution.

Arneault wore many hats during his professional career. Aside from his experience as a tax accountant, he ran an oil and gas company at one point and served as a partner in a jewelry chain, a knife company, and a steel processing plant. In 1992, a friend asked him to assist in the sale of a thoroughbred racetrack in Chester, West Virginia, named Mountaineer Park. Arneault agreed and served in the capacity of a consultant, helping to sell the property to an interested suitor, Excalibur Holding. After the

---

Company Perspectives:

We are optimistic about the prospects for our expansion opportunities, which leverage the Company's expertise in the gaming and racing markets and should provide additional long-term value for shareholders.

---

sale, Arneault remained a consultant, offering advice on the installation of slot machines at the racetrack. Not long afterwards, Excalibur Holding's management decided to shelve plans to acquire any additional oil and gas properties and to focus exclusively on the gaming industry, a sharpening in strategic focus that prompted another name change. In August 1993, Excalibur Holding changed its name to Winners Entertainment, Inc., a change in identity that occurred at roughly the same time the company was engulfed in controversy that threatened its existence.

The deal that allowed the installation of slot machines at Mountaineer Park had been struck with the state lottery commission. It formed the basis of Winners Entertainment's new business strategy: add casino-style gambling to the racing venue to increase profits and revenue. Unfortunately for Winners Entertainment's management, the lottery director was convicted of insider trading and fraud several weeks after the acquisition of Mountaineer Park was completed. In the investigation into the director's malfeasance, it was discovered that the testing of slot machines at Mountaineer Park had no legal standing, which prompted the state supreme court to order for their removal, significantly lessening the value of the property to Winners Entertainment.

Arneault, still serving as a consultant, decided to fight for Winners Entertainment's cause. He dug in, renting a room in the state capital at the Charleston Marriott, and began lobbying for state approval of slot machines. He spent three months working out of his hotel room, first asking the court for a stay on the initial agreement before petitioning state representatives to legalize slot machines. He asked that slot machines be allowed at all four racetracks in West Virginia, arguing that establishment of slot machines would create new jobs and improve the local economy. As the October 29, 2001 issue of *Forbes* noted, "The odds could hardly have been worse: Get a Bible Belt state to support gaming legislation in the wake of a lottery scandal." Despite the negative publicity surrounding his lobbying efforts, Arneault prevailed in March 1994, when the state legislature passed the bill by a narrow margin.

Arneault Taking the Helm in 1995

Arneault's troubles did not end after he fought for the passage of gaming legislation. Winners Entertainment had hired a management firm, American Gaming, to oversee the operation of Mountaineer Park, but after American Gaming chewed through a $10 million loan with not much to show for the expenditure, Winners Entertainment cut its ties to the management firm. For a replacement, Winners Entertainment's management turned to Arneault, who accepted the titles of chairman and chief executive officer in April 1995. The company lost $5.3 million during Arneault's first year as a senior executive, but he had a plan for

reversing the company's financial fortunes. Arneault wanted to build a casino near the racetrack to lure more serious gamblers, the first part of an overall plan to turn Mountaineer Park into a full-scale entertainment resort. Arneault's vision led to another name change in October 1996, when Winners Entertainment, Inc. became MTR Gaming Group, Inc.

Arneault succeeded in turning MTR into a profitable company soon after focusing its efforts on racing, gaming, and entertainment. In 1996, revenues increased 61 percent to $40 million, but the most impressive financial result was the $1.1 million the company recorded in net income, a figure that offered evidence Arneault was steering MTR in the right direction. Arneault was beginning the process of turning Mountaineer Park into the "Mountaineer Race Track & Gaming Resort," a project that entailed adding scores of new slot machines, the primary reason for the encouraging financial results in 1996, and a host of other attractions. The expansion project took years to complete, as Arneault built the company's signature property on 2,600 acres of land on the banks of the Ohio River, intending to lure customers from neighboring Ohio and Pennsylvania to MTR's gaming and entertainment complex in Chester. While the mammoth construction project was underway, Arneault began acquiring other properties for MTR, shaping the company into a geographically diversified company. First, he sold the last of the company's remaining oil and gas properties in 1998, the same year he established a presence in Nevada. Through two subsidiaries, Speakeasy Gaming of Las Vegas, Inc. and Speakeasy Gaming of Reno, Inc., MTR acquired the Cheyenne Hotel & Casino in Las Vegas for $5.5 million and the Reno Ramada in Reno for $8 million. The Cheyenne Hotel & Casino property included a 131-room hotel and casino that Arneault intended to expand and to design with a motor-racing theme to attract patrons from the Las Vegas Motor Speedway, located five miles away from the Cheyenne property. The Reno Ramada was a 262-room hotel with an adjoining casino earmarked for a $500,000 expansion project. After the expansion of the hotel and casino, the property was renamed the "Speakeasy Hotel & Casino."

Arneault's decision to establish a presence in Nevada yielded mixed results, but his efforts to turn the Mountaineer property into a full-fledged resort mitigated the difficulties experienced in Reno and Las Vegas. By 2001, the Mountaineer property had been developed into a sprawling complex with a 140,000-square-foot slots casino, seven bars, a 70,000-square-foot arena for live entertainment, and a 100-room hotel. In August 2001, a 28,000-square-foot convention center and a spa and fitness center opened, while the expansion of the hotel, expected to be completed in April 2002, was underway, adding 260 rooms. The property was driving the company's revenue growth, helping push revenues to $218 million by the end of 2001, nearly ten times the total recorded during Arneault's first year as the company's leader. "The scene is more NASCAR than diamond pinkie rings," an analyst remarked in a June 22, 2001 interview with *Investor's Business Daily,* offering his impression of the Mountaineer property. Arneault, in the same article, offered his description of MTR's signature property. "I like to consider us a middle-class outfit," he said. "We're not looking for the Las Vegas whales. Our whales would probably be keeper bass."

The resort in Chester stood as a remarkable success story for MTR, enabling the company to accomplish what it had been unable to accomplish in the pre-Arneault years: record significant revenue growth and post steady profits. The foray into Nevada had been made because of uncertainty about how the expansion effort in Chester would evolve, but during the first years of the new decade the operations in Nevada presented their own uncertainty. The company closed the casino in Reno in May 2001 after it and the hotel lost $1.4 million during the first half of the year, a blemish on its otherwise impressive earnings record. Aside from correcting the lackluster operations in Nevada, Arneault's greatest challenge was protecting Mountaineer Race Track & Gaming Resort from a new threat on the horizon. Both Pennsylvania and Ohio were discussing legislation to legalize gaming, the promulgation of which promised to take business away from the company's complex in Chester. "The biggest threat for this company," an analyst said in a February 8, 2002 interview with *Investor's Business Daily,* "is the potential for legalized gaming in Pennsylvania and Ohio." Arneault responded to the threat by preparing for entry into Pennsylvania and Ohio, one phase of an expansion strategy that saw MTR greatly broaden its geographic scope of operations during the first half of the decade.

Expansion in the 21st Century

By early 2002, Arneault was preparing to take MTR to far greater heights. He had filed an application with Pennsylvania's racing commission for approval to build a new thoroughbred racetrack. MTR received approval to build a racetrack in Erie, Pennsylvania, a facility it anticipated naming Presque Isle Downs, but the scope of the project increased after Pennsylvania passed a law legalizing slot machines in July 2004. Arneault filed to gain a gaming license from the Pennsylvania Gaming Control Board, holding off construction of Presque Isle Downs until he received a gaming license. Meanwhile, Arneault made a move into Ohio, purchasing Scioto Downs in Columbus in July 2003. A harness horse racing facility, Scioto Downs featured pari-mutuel wagering. Next, Arneault increased MTR's presence in Nevada, undaunted by the troubles experienced after the acquisition of the Cheyenne Hotel & Casino and Reno Ramada in 1998. In March 2004, MTR acquired Binion's Horseshoe, a hotel and casino located in downtown Las Vegas, for $20 million. One year later,

the company began independently operating the property, renamed "Binion's Gambling Hall & Hotel," after concluding its joint operating agreement with an affiliate of Harrah's. Several months after making his initial investment in the Binion's property, Arneault added Minnesota to MTR's ever expanding geographic profile by acquiring a 50 percent interest in North Metro Harness Initiative in June 2004. In January 2005, the Minnesota Racing Commission awarded North Metro a license to build, pending judicial review, a harness racetrack in Anoka County, 30 miles north of Minneapolis. While plans were being developed to build a racetrack and card-room operations in Minnesota, Arneault expanded further, signing a definitive agreement to acquire a 90 percent stake in Jackson Trotting Association, LLC. Jackson Trotting operated the Jackson Harness Raceway in Jackson, Michigan, 70 miles away from Detroit.

After a decade of leading MTR, Arneault achieved much, inheriting a floundering company and giving it a precise strategic direction to pursue. The company's financial gains during his first decade of leadership were enormous, with annual revenues increasing from $25 million to $315 million. Profitability, once a perennial struggle for the company, was achieved with regularity, averaging roughly $15 million per year between 2000 and 2004. The second half of the decade promised to be a busy period for the company, with properties in Pennsylvania, Minnesota, and Michigan slated to debut. As Arneault worked toward adding these properties to MTR's fold, his success in Chester offered a blueprint for expansion in the years ahead.

Principal Subsidiaries

Mountaineer Park, Inc.; Speakeasy Gaming of Las Vegas, Inc.; Speakeasy Gaming of Freemont, Inc.; Speakeasy Freemont Street Experience Operating Company; Scioto Downs, Inc.; Presque Isle Downs, Inc.; MTRCHarness, Inc.; Jackson Racing, Inc.

Principal Competitors

Colonial Holdings, Inc.; Magna Entertainment Corp.; Penn National Gaming, Inc.

Further Reading

Elliott, Alan R., "MTR Gaming Group Inc.; Chester, West Virginia; There's Gold in Them Thar Hills," *Investor's Business Daily,* February 8, 2002, p. A10.
Gallagher, Leigh, "On Track," *Forbes,* October 29, 2001, p. 146.
Guerriero, John, "Erie, Pa., Businessman Fails in Bid to Budge Convention Center from Bayfront," *Erie Times-News,* July 12, 2005, p. A1.
——, "Penn National Gaming Sells Erie, Pa., Off-Track Betting Parlor," *Erie Times-News,* October 16, 2004, p. B1.
Jones, Chris, "MTR Gaming Group to Take Reins of Binion's Horseshoe Casino in Las Vegas," *Las Vegas Review-Journal,* November 9, 2004, p. B1.
Marcial, Gene G., "A Lagging MTR May Catch a Buyer's Eye," *Business Week,* September 30, 2002, p. 120.
Shinkle, Kirk, "MTR Gaming Group Inc.," *Investor's Business Daily,* June 22, 2001, p. A7.

—Jeffrey L. Covell

Natura Cosméticos S.A.

Rodovia Régis Bittencourt, Km 293 - Edificio 1
Itapecerica da Serra, Sao Paulo 06882-700
Brazil
Telephone: (55) (11) 4147-8300
Toll Free: 0800-704-5566
Fax: (55) (11) 4147-8370
Web site: http://www.natura.net

Public Company
Founded: 1969
Employees: 3,495
Sales: BRL 2.46 billion ($839.59 million) (2004)
Stock Exchanges: Bolsa de Valores de Sao Paulo
Ticker Symbol: NA
NAIC: 325611 Soap and Other Detergent Manufacturing;
      325620 Toilet Preparation Manufacturing

Natura Cosméticos S.A. is a leading player in sales of cosmetics, fragrances, and toilet products in Brazil, which is the world's fifth largest market for these products. With an army of more than 450,000 salespeople (whom the company calls ''consultants''), it relies on direct sales to the home and ranks a close second to Avon Products Inc.'s Brazilian subsidiary, Avon Cosméticos Ltda. Natura has direct-sales operations in other Latin American countries and has opened retail stores in Paris and Mexico City. Active in disseminating new products, the company keeps up to date with the latest pharmaceutical, chemical, and biochemical research in its field and is said to be Brazil's largest investor in scientific techniques. It has an enviable reputation for ethical corporate behavior. While exploiting Brazil's bountiful plant resources for its Ekos line of products, it uses only sustainable ingredients from special reserves in remote areas and strives to aid community development in these areas.

Beauty a la Brazil: 1969–89

Antonio Luiz da Cunha Seabra was working as an economist in the Brazil office of the Remington Electric Shavers Division of Sperry Rand Corp. when he founded Natura in 1969 with $9,000 in cash and a handful of cosmetic formulations by Jean-Pierre Berjeaut. The small shop that Seabra opened in Sao Paulo was a kind of luxury boutique, with a staff of four promoting Berjeaut's creams and lotions, which were based on natural products. Seabra gave consultations there, coaching clients on how to use the products correctly and promising therapeutic benefits. ''They were difficult years,'' he recalled, speaking in 1998 with Nelson Blecher of Brazilian business magazine *Exame*. ''Sometimes there wasn't even money to pay the light bill.''

This changed in 1974, when Natura abandoned retailing in favor of direct sales by door-to-door salespeople working on commission. During this period the company developed a network of 2,000 salespeople and raised its annual sales to $5 million. Among the benefits of direct sales, according to one of Seabra's partners, was that it enabled Natura to anticipate consumer trends in this fickle field before retailers could do so. In addition, this marketing method was said to make it easier for the company to promote and sell all of its products, whereas retailers tended to concentrate their efforts on only a few hot-selling items.

As the business grew, Seabra and Berjeaut financed expansion by founding, between 1979 and 1981, related companies with outside entrepreneurs. Four distributorships and a makeup firm called L'Arc en Ciel operated independently. Guilherme Peirao Leal, a distributor who had invested $40,000 in the business, became a partner in 1979. In 1983 Leal brought in Pedro Luiz Passos, an engineer who became superintendent of production and later was made a junior partner. By 1986 Natura was fielding 16,000 ''consultants,'' averaging growth of 40 percent a year, and dominating high-end door-to-door sales of cosmetics in Brazil. That year, the company introduced Chronos, a facial skin-care treatment for fine lines and wrinkles that was the first in Brazil to promote cell renewal. This line exceeded the company's own expectations by accounting for sales of 90,000 units in scarcely its first month and a half. Chronos remained a Natura staple, but not all of the company's endeavors were successful. Another line, called Númina, was a failure. Taking the enterprise into neighboring countries proved premature. Natura also tried retailing again, but abandoned the effort after losing $2 million in 1987. A crisis involving company shares in the late 1980s resulted in

Company Perspectives:

Natura, for its business behavior, the quality of its relationships and its products and services, shall become a worldwide brand, identified with the community of people engaged in building a better world through a better relationship with themselves and others, with nature, of which they form part, and with the whole.

Berjeaut's departure, and the five autonomous enterprises were merged into Natura in 1989.

Natura's Way in the 1990s

Natura's sales reached $180 million in 1990, then fell sharply the next two years because of an economic recession in Brazil. As a result, the company dismissed 15 percent of its 1,800 employees. However, taking advantage of an opportunity created by their company's difficulties, Seabra and Leal purchased the 26 percent share of the company held by Yara Pricolli for $25 million. Seabra thereby raised his stake to 38 percent, and Leal to 36 percent. During this period the two established Natura's basis for further growth by recruiting experienced executives from larger competitors such as Johnson & Johnson Indústria e Comércio Ltda., Gillette do Brasil Ltda., Procter & Gamble do Brasil & Cia., Shell Brasil Ltda., and Unilever Brasil Ltda.'s Indústria Gessy Lever Ltda., and also by investing heavily in technology and quality control.

Natura surpassed its 1990 revenues in 1993. In that year Chronos announced a new line of anti-aging creams, based on two years of trial and $1.5 million in development expenses. The complete line, consisting of liquid toilet soap, tonic lotion, peeling gel, creme gel, emulsion for the eye area, and a cellular renovator, cost 32,000 cruzeiros (almost $100). It proved a smashing success, selling 70,000 units a month. Natura also introduced a new perfume, Shiraz, developed by Brazilian, French, Mexican, and Swiss researchers. It sold for $28 per container. The company was again venturing outside Brazil, having entered Portugal in 1991 and having just established subsidiaries in Argentina and Chile.

Natura's revenues reached $350 million in 1994. The following year the company had a 14 percent share of the Brazilian market for cosmetics and personal hygiene products and was offering 250 kinds of perfumes, shampoos, creams, and lipsticks. It was fielding 105,000 salespeople, mostly in Brazil but also in Argentina, Bolivia, Chile, and Peru. The next year, 1996, was even better. Natura's revenues reached $580 million, of which some 20 percent came from third-party goods such as lingerie and jewelry. Its sales force, now up to 160,000, had three million customers in Brazil alone. They sold 61 million units of 270 products, with each salesperson averaging $5,760 worth of goods, on which they received a commission of 30 percent. For Natura the payoff was even sweeter: a 28.3 percent return on the company's net worth.

Natura's rapid growth created both new opportunities and daunting challenges. In the company's early days, such multinational giants as Procter & Gamble and Unilever confined them-selves to marketing the cheap mass products found in Brazilian drugstores and supermarkets, leaving fragrances and artisanal creams to smaller, specialized enterprises. Then the giants moved into their territory, attracted by its high profit margins. They were willing and able to spend large sums on research and development for a torrent of the new products demanded by a fickle public. Between 1992 and 1996, cosmetic sales in Brazil grew from $2.6 billion to $5.7 billion. Natura hired a French-based Vietnamese scientist, Anh Tuan Tran, to furnish technology and introduced 108 new products in 1996. Forty percent of its sales came from products not in existence two years earlier. In addition, the company began work on a new factory in Cajamar, five times larger than the existing one in Itapecerica da Serra, and nearer to Sao Paulo (about 19 miles away). It was completed in 1999 at a cost of $110 million.

Although Natura followed the lead of big multinational competitors in some respects, it remained a most unusual company that reflected its idiosyncratic founder. Greatly influenced by the thinking of psychiatric pioneer Carl Gustav Jung, Seabra spent more than a decade in Jungian psychoanalysis and shared the master's interest in mythology as a manifestation of what Jung called the collective unconscious. In his garden Seabra erected a Buddhist and a Taoist temple; nearby he placed a chapel in homage to St. Francis. Each day of the week, he believed, was influenced by a different force of nature. For example, Monday, the day of Aphrodite, favored intuition and was suitable for considering new products. Although his company relied on opinion surveys and experiments to launch its highly successful Essencial line of perfumes, it initiated its popular Mamae e Bebê (Mother and Baby) line for babies, pregnant women, and new mothers despite a survey indicating that the market for infant products was too small.

According to Seabra, cosmetics were so associated with superficiality that most people did not realize the power of these products to transform personality by reestablishing self-esteem. Unfortunately, Leal told Blecher, "In the world of cosmetics, in particular, there prevails deception, illusion, falsehood, in the quest for success at any price." Natura sought to avoid false promises for its products, preferring the word *antisinais* (antisigns—i.e., of aging), rather than "rejuvenation," since nothing can reverse the march of time. The company did not hire supermodels but instead employed advertising featuring ordinary women older than 30.

An admirer of Levi Strauss & Co. as a corporate model, especially for ethical conduct, Seabra earmarked a percentage of Natura's dividends to finance social projects and refused to do business with companies that employed child labor. Also a follower of business guru Peter Drucker, he championed accessible, responsive management that would break down hierarchy, work in teams, and make decisions by consensus. Officially, the firm had three presidents by 1998: Seabra, "president-founder"; Leal, "executive president"; and Passos, "operational president." Seabra took a six-month sabbatical in Paris in 1996, and Leal took one the following year in Boston, where he attended business courses at Harvard University. Responsiveness also extended to the public, and Natura directed hundreds of service personnel to field calls from its clients and salespeople. Employees were paid a median monthly salary 16 times the national minimum, with the lowest about five times the minimum level. They shared in the

Key Dates:

1969: Natura is founded by Antonio Luiz da Cunha Seabra.
1974: Natura abandons retailing in favor of selling its products door to door.
1986: Sales of the company's new Chronos line exceed all expectations.
1990: Natura's sales reach $180 million a year.
1996: Natura is selling 270 products to three million Brazilians.
1999: The company moves into a new factory built at a cost of $110 million.
2000: The new Ekos line consists of products mainly derived from Brazil's tropical forests.
2004: Natura goes public, selling 22 percent of its equity on the Borsa de Valores de Sao Paulo.
2005: Natura opens retail outlets in Paris and Mexico City.

profits and held a portion of the company shares (17 percent in 1998). Natura also made a major investment in its salespeople, who were sent to classes in cutaneous biochemistry and physiology and were not permitted to work for competitors.

By 2000 Natura had about 300 items in its portfolio, divided into men's and women's fragrances; hair care; color cosmetics; facial skin care; body care; sun care; bath products; children's products; mother and baby products; and vitamin and mineral supplements. Chronos, now extended to include body-care products, remained one of its most popular lines, along with Mamae e Bebê, Natura color cosmetics and fragrances, and Natura Homem for men's grooming. The company claimed to have one of the largest cosmetics research-and-development centers in Brazil, with access to universities and international study centers that kept its researchers up to date with the latest techniques in the fields of dermatology, chemistry, biochemistry, and related subjects. Natura also was reported to be Brazil's largest investor in scientific testing, in order to introduce an average of 120 new products a year.

Another recession, in 1998 and 1999, took a heavy toll on Natura's revenues and profits and led to a 10 percent drop in employees. Nevertheless, in 1999 the company bought Flora Medicinal J. Monteiro da Silva Ltda., a company almost a century old, which had 300 products and was researching 280 species of Brazilian plants. This was an essential part of what the company called its "Manhattan Project," which resulted in the Ekos line, introduced in 2000 with 21 products and developed at a cost of BRL 185 million (about $100 million). In 2002 this line accounted for 10 percent of company revenues.

The Ekos line consisted of a range of body-care products such as shampoos, bath soaps, massage and moisturizing oils, and perfumes, made from exotic fruits, roots, and nuts obtained from the Amazon rainforest and other Brazilian forests or small, traditional plantations. In addition to its commercial advantages for Natura, the indigenous products initiative was seen by the company as offering an alternative to the destruction of fragile environments by the clearing of forests for the logging of

tropical timber or for mining, cattle raising, or intensive farming of soybeans and other cash crops. In Brazil's Xingu national park, Leal and other Natura executives participated in a festival, sleeping in native huts. Two months later, 13 indigenous leaders visited company headquarters, seeking assurances that Natura was committed to buying their products for the long term and not only for the life cycle of a single cosmetic, at the most, only five years.

Natura, which had established an Internet site for sales in 2000, added a printed catalog in 2003, with a circulation of 800,000. It was updated every three weeks. The company also was producing a television program broadcast twice weekly on an over-the-air channel. In May 2004 Natura issued the first initial public offering of stock by a Brazilian company in more than two years, selling $240.9 million worth of shares, or 22 percent of total equity, on the Borsa de Valores de Sao Paulo. The company announced an impressive net profit of BRL 300.41 million ($102.5 million) in 2004 (compared with BRL 65.16 million, or $21.16 million in 2003) on net income of BRL 1.84 billion ($627.99 million). Gross sales, before deducting for commissions, came to BRL 2.46 billion, or $839.59 million. It held a 19 percent share of the cosmetics, fragrance, and toiletries market in Brazil, second only to Avon.

A weakness for Natura was its failure to make an impact abroad; foreign sales came to only 3 percent of the total in 2004. The following year the company opened a retail outlet in Paris. This boutique, on the Left Bank, a two-level store created to resemble a Brazilian home, initially marketed only the Ekos line, now a collection of at least 72 units, and showcased fragrant bowls of grains, flowers, herbs, and other raw ingredients used in its products, which it arranged by scent and color rather than by function. Natura opened another retail outlet, in Mexico City, later in the year. It also was planning to expand its direct-sales operations into Colombia, Costa Rica, Ecuador, Mexico, Uruguay, and Venezuela by 2007. The company's sales staff had swelled to 481,000.

Although Seabra, Leal, and Passos all had grown children, none of them were working for Natura when they announced in 2005 that they would yield the presidency to Alessandro Carlucci, a 38-year-old executive who had been with the company since completing business school 15 years earlier. As chief executive officer, Carlucci would be in charge of day-to-day management, while Seabra, Leal, and Passos would be co-presidents of the administrative council (that is, cochairmen of the board).

In addition to the Chronos, Ekos, and Mamae e Bebê lines, Natura was fielding, in 2005, the Tododin line, a broad range of products for daily use, employing natural ingredients such as milk, sugar, and honey, in cosmetics, fragrances, and toiletries; the Natura Unica line of makeup products for the face, lips, and eyes; and Faces de Natura, consisting of skin treatment products, cosmetics, and fragrances for young women.

Principal Subsidiaries

Commodities Trading S.A. (Uruguay); Indústria e Comércio de Cosméticos Natura Ltda.; Natura Brasil Cosmética Ltda. (Portugal); Natura Cosméticos S.A.(Argentina); Natura Cosméticos S.A. (Chile); Natura Cosméticos S.A. (Peru).

Principal Competitors

Avon Cosméticos Ltda.; Botica Comercial Farmaceutica Ltda.; Indústrias Gessy Lever Ltda.

Further Reading

Blecher, Nelson, "Excelência perfumada," *Exame,* July 1, 1998, pp. 21–28.

Costello, Brid, and Jennifer Joan Lee, "Paris Welcomes La Maison Natura," *WWD/Women's Wear Daily,* May 2, 2005, p. 17.

Galloway, Jennifer, "When the Going's Good," *Latin Finance,* July 2004, p. 35.

"Going Back to Natura," *Brand Strategy,* September 8, 2005, p. 28.

Kapp, Michael, "Best Face Forward," *Latin Trade,* June 2005, pp. 25.

——, "Taking Stock of *Natura* Success," *WWD/Women's Wear Daily,* Jun 21, 2004, p. 15.

"Natura Born Thriller," *Soap, Perfumery & Cosmetics,* May 2000, p. 45.

Netz, Clayton, "Até onde a Natura consegue ir?," *Exame,* September 10, 1997, pp. 116–22, 124.

Smith, Tony, "Grass Is Green for Amazon Farmers," *New York Times,* October 8, 2003, p. W1.

Vassallo, Cláudia, "Um jeito diferente de fazer negócios," *Exame,* March 12, 2003, pp. 32–40.

—Robert Halasz

New Seasons Market

5320 NE 32nd Avenue
Portland, Oregon 97211
U.S.A.
Telephone: (503) 288-3838
Fax: (503) 292-6280
Web site: http://newseasonsmarket.com

Private Company
Incorporated: 1999
Employees: 900
Sales: $24.8 million (2004)
NAIC: 445110 Grocery Stores

New Seasons Market has carved a niche for itself in the Portland grocery store market, carrying a wide range of natural and organic products, grown or produced in the Northwest, alongside basic brand-name products. Approximately two-thirds of each of its six stores' product mix is natural or organic, while the remaining products are conventional brands. About 11 percent of its product mix is produced locally. New Seasons also has a socially responsible ethic that permeates every level of its business.

1999: A New Kind of Food Store

In 1999 Brian Rohter, Stan Amy, and Chuck Eggert, with the backing of their families and about 50 friends, opened the first New Seasons Market in Portland, Oregon. Their mission was to make people aware of healthy food and the benefits of sustainable agriculture. Their plan was ambitious: To become a key player in the Portland grocery field with five stores serving Portland neighborhoods by 2001. The three wanted to create a company that had a "true commitment to its community, to promoting sustainable agriculture, and to maintaining a progressive workplace," according to the company's web site.

All three men were veterans of the grocery business: Amy had owned another Portland-area chain called Nature's Northwest until he sold it to General Nutrition Corporation in the mid-1990s.

Eggert was the president of Pacific Foods, a manufacturer of soup and soy drinks, located in nearby Tualatin, Oregon. Rohter had worked as a consultant for Nature's and, once the store became an independent subsidiary of General Nutrition Corporation, as its executive vice-president for three years. Rohter left that job when Wild Oats of Boulder, Colorado, purchased Nature's then seven-store chain in the spring of 1999. "My heart wasn't in it anymore," he explained in the *Oregonian* in 2000, referring to the fact that General Nutrition Corporation had allowed him the authority to make decisions he deemed appropriate, while Wild Oats set policies at headquarters.

Following retailing trends, the first New Seasons store had a bakery, a delicatessen, and a salad bar and take-out meal area, including a "Hot Wok," where customers picked from fresh ingredients for a meal cooked especially for them. The deli did not get its food from offsite industrial commissaries; instead, New Seasons hired a well-known local sous chef to make everything from scratch. The atmosphere of the new store was friendly and interactive with well-labeled aisles and shelves, eye-catching displays, and countless signs instructing customers to "Smell me!" or informing, "We tried this one on vacation—it's great!"

Joining the trend led by Nature's Northwest and later embraced by Whole Foods out of Austin, Texas, and Trader Joe's of California, New Seasons was part of a new generation of grocery stores. Unlike the mega-supermarket, according to The Hartman Group, a Washington-based market research and consulting firm for the wellness industry, the new groceries sold an experience as much as they did food or other products. "[W]hen we talk to consumers who get a babysitter so that they can spend a couple hours roaming around Whole Foods, it's a whole different scenario than when grocery shopping was a pain, and you wanted to spend as little time there as possible . . . ," offered the president of The Hartman Group in a 2002 *Oregonian* article.

But what set New Seasons apart from the other markets in its category was that it refused the label of either traditional supermarket or health food store. "We're not a natural foods store. We have everything from free-range chicken to Frosted

Company Perspectives:

We'll do whatever it takes to make New Seasons the best shopping experience in town.

Flakes,'' Rohter explained in a 2000 *Oregonian* article, referring to the store's philosophy to have locally owned stores serving local people and to cater to all food preferences. New Seasons also made a point of promoting local economic and ecological sustainability by showcasing community vendors and farmers as well as national producers.

In keeping with their emphasis on community, New Season's founders chose sites for their planned stores that had the potential of becoming commercial and social centers for neighborhoods. They settled on a smaller store footprint than other supermarkets, with doors that opened onto sidewalks and streets, and added a second story for storage and offices. They planned benefit events, such as bento barbeques and slice-of-cake days, to raise money for local nonprofits.

New Seasons was also different from most other markets in its emphasis on customer service. Every employee at New Seasons had the authority to make whatever decision necessary to keep the customer happy. These employees, also viewed as part of the New Seasons community, were well taken care of; anyone working 20 hours or more received full-time benefits, which included medical and dental insurance for the employee and his or her family.

Of course, not everyone was as happy with New Seasons as those who shopped or worked there. After many Nature's Northwest employees joined the exodus led by Rohter and other higher-ups, Wild Oats Markets Inc. sued Rohter in November 1999 for ''misappropriating Wild Oats' confidential and proprietary information,'' using inside knowledge to unfairly compete with Wild Oats, stealing away Nature's managers, and acquiring leases for store locations that Wild Oats had targeted. Rohter filed his own legal action, and eventually both companies dropped their claims.

2000–01: Three New Stores in Portland

New Seasons opened its second store in Portland in 2000, and then its third and fourth stores in 2001. At 29,000 square feet, stores three and four were bigger than the first two, but were still small compared to other supermarkets, which averaged 50,000 square feet. The new, larger size was required to include more conventional products, such as cereals, diapers, and over-the-counter cold remedies. ''To truly be a neighborhood store, we really needed to expand the center of the store,'' Rohter explained in *Gourmet News* in 2002. Onsite bakeries baked 17 different kinds of organic breads daily (a portion of which were donated to local Meals on Wheels programs) and offered in-store dining. The third store also housed the company's new corporate headquarters.

Neighborhood leadership participated in lobbying for the fourth store, which included gaining approval from the Portland

Planning Commission for permanently closing one block of a city street. A local committee also weighed in on the store's exterior design, its lighting and maintenance, hours of delivery and operation, landscaping and parking, prices, and security. Situated on a lot that had been vacant since 1994, this new store featured the then standard deli bar with soups, salads and sandwiches, ''Hot Wok,'' as well as an in-store bakery. There was also a store nutritionist available daily for free consultations and tours of the store, which employed 110 workers, many from the surrounding neighborhood.

Some neighbors voiced reservations about the fit between New Seasons and the area's working class community. One community member, quoted in a 2001 *Oregonian* article, said, ''I wonder sometimes how well that store, being the kind of store it is, is going to serve some of the poorer people.'' Some of the banks from which New Seasons sought to borrow money for the project also wondered. However, according to Rohter in the *Seattle Skanner*, ''Completion of this project is a real tribute to the strength of the Concordia Neighborhood Association in this community. Those folks had a vision of what they wanted to see happen here—they wanted a full-service grocery store, and they just dug in and wouldn't let go until it was accomplished.''

With the addition of its fourth metro store, New Seasons became able to spread the costs of doing business across more operations, making it easier to achieve profits. ''We have a lot of overhead for a business our size,'' Rohter explained in the *Oregonian* in 2001, referring to the number of employees on the store floor and the large number of buyers New Seasons employed to negotiate with local vendors as well as national suppliers.

2004–05: Leading the ''Slow Foods'' Movement in Portland

A fifth store in 2004 added to the company's economies of scale and created an additional 120 jobs. This store, like the last, opened in a neighborhood that had no local supermarkets and drew criticism from those worried that the building was too big and would lead to gentrification of another working class community. In addition, supporters of an established neighborhood grocery coop protested that it would steal business away from that store. But the $3 million, 25,000-square-foot market, with a 12,000-square-foot office and storage space, was under construction in December 2003 and reached completion as planned. Store five was the first New Seasons Market to include an onsite pharmacy.

By 2004, New Seasons had become one of the cornerstones in the ''slow food'' movement in Portland. This movement celebrated groceries that were fresh, local, and peddled in a progressive workplace. An article in the *Oregonian* in 2004 quoted legendary environmentalist Paul Hawken, who in *Grist Magazine* had hailed New Seasons as ''successfully forging new, sustainable corporate practices . . . a model of what a grocery store can do to help farmers and citizens and communities.'' A year before in the *Oregonian*, Rohter himself had acknowledged, ''We're pleased because our social mission and our business mission are aligned. There is growing interest in the origin of foods. People want their dollars to support local farmers.''

Key Dates:

1999: Rohter, Amy, and Eggert open the first New Seasons grocery store.
2000: New Seasons opens its second store.
2001: The company opens its third and fourth stores.
2004: The fifth company store is opened.
2005: Lisa Sedlar becomes the company's president and Brian Rohter becomes the chief executive officer.

In 2005, New Seasons hired Lisa Sedlar as its new president when Brian Rohter became the company's chief executive officer. Sedlar had been the former vice-president of sales and merchandising for Colorado-based Pharmaca Integrative Pharmacy. At the close of the year, New Seasons had 900 employees and was planning to add another two stores in 2006. The company's continued growth, attributable in part to smart marketing, in part to maturation, in part to the fact that people had begun spending more money on premium food and less on dining in recent years, now seemed well assured.

Principal Competitors

QFC; Wild Oats Markets, Inc.; Whole Foods Market, Inc.; Zupan's Markets; Trader Joe's Company; Fred Meyer Stores, Inc.

Further Reading

Barnett, Erin Hoover, "Super Markets," *Oregonian*, July 7, 2002, p. B1.

Brinckman, Jonathan, "A Seasoned Independent," *Oregonian*, May 29, 2003, p. B1.

Colby, Richard, "Kienow's Morphs into Another Kind of Food Store," *Oregonian*, February 25, 2000, p. D2.

Goldfield, Robert, "A Bit Bigger Is Better for New Seasons Markets," *Portland Business Journal*, December 7, 2001, p. 3.

——, "New Seasons Meets Southeast Neighborhood Resistance," *Portland Business Journal*, September 12, 2003, p. 3.

"Grow, Think, Sell Locally," *Portland Business Journal*, June 27, 2005.

Loving, Lisa, "Concordia Store Nearly Ready: The New Season's Market on Northeast 33rd Avenue Opens December 5," *Skanner*, November 28, 2001, p. 1.

Nkrumah, Wade, "North/Northeast Portland Concordia Greets Long-Wanted Grocery," *Oregonian*, December 5, 2001, p. C3.

Starke, Amy Martinez, "The Monday Profile: Grocer's Lust Is a Passion for Real Food," *Oregonian*, December 9, 2002, p. A1.

Strom, Shelly, "Grow, Think, Sell Locally," *Portland Business Journal*, June 24, 2005.

Wolfe, Anna, "New Seasons Markets Opens Store No. 4," *Gourmet News*, February 2002, p. 1.

—Carrie Rothburd

NFL Films

One NFL Plaza
Mount Laurel, New Jersey 08054
U.S.A.
Telephone: (856) 222-3500
Fax: (856) 722-6779
Web site: http://www.nflfilms.com

Wholly Owned Subsidiary of National Football League Inc.
Founded: 1962 as Blair Motion Pictures
Employees: 200
Sales: $50 million (2004 est.)
NAIC: 512110 Motion Picture and Video Production

"NFL Films is perhaps the most effective propaganda organ in the history of corporate America," opined *Sports Illustrated* in 1999. The family-run Mount Laurel, New Jersey-based subsidiary of the National Football League (NFL) films every NFL game each year. The material is then packaged in a multitude of ways: providing highlight packages for distribution on television and the Web, programming for outlets such as ESPN, HBO, and NFL Network, and DVD and videocassette titles. Profits flow back to the clubs in the form of royalties. The winner of more than 90 Emmy awards, NFL Films has been a pioneer on a number of fronts since its founding in the early 1960s. It was the first to put a microphone on coaches, referees, and players; the first to diagram plays on the screen; the first to use a reverse-angle replay; the first to put popular music to sports footage; the first to use 600-mm telephoto lenses in sports; the first to produce a bloopers video. Moreover, NFL Films' groundbreaking presentation of action in slow-motion photography, combined with montages and driving music, has had a profound impact on contemporary filmmaking. The company's projects have attracted such notable stars as Orson Welles, Vincent Price, Burt Lancaster, and Roy Scheider, who have all lent their vocal talents to the narration of NFL Films' productions. Although filming NFL football games remains the company's focus, over the years it has branched into the filming of other sporting events, filming sports sequences for feature films, and providing commercial and corporate video production services. NFL Films is the largest purchaser of Kodak film in the world.

Origins with Gift of Movie Camera in 1940

The man behind the founding of NFL Films was Ed Sabol, born in Atlantic City, New Jersey, and raised in Philadelphia, Pennsylvania. He was an athlete with a theatrical bent. He lettered in football, track, and swimming in high school, and became an accomplished swimmer at The Ohio State University. After graduation he appeared on Broadway in one of Oscar Hammerstein's less successful musicals, *Where Do We Go From Here,* set in a college fraternity house. It closed after just 15 performances. Sabol then appeared as an extra with the vaudeville comedy team the Ritz Brothers, a stint that ended his brush with show business. Sabol found an outlet for his creativity when he received a 16-mm Bell & Howell movie camera in 1940 as a wedding present from his mother-in-law. The camera quickly became his hobby and passion, and his favorite subject became his son, Steve, whom he filmed growing up. When Steve began playing high school football, Sabol filmed all of his games. People who saw his work were impressed and asked him to film their football games as well. Other than his family life, his camera was about the only source of joy in Sabol's life. According to *Fortune,* "In 1962, Ed Sabol was 45 years old and miserable. Selling overcoats in Philadelphia for his father-in-law, a tough, frugal immigrant businessman, Ed hated his job. 'It was like going to the dentist every morning,' he grumbles." Sabol learned from the newspapers that an area company called Telra had paid $1,500 for the rights to film the 1961 NFL championship game. He became determined to win the rights for the 1962 championship game and doubled the bid to $3,000. Although he only had high school footage to show the NFL, his high offer at least accorded him a chance to sell himself to NFL Commissioner Pete Rozelle. They met for lunch at "21," and according to company lore, Ed Sabol the accomplished salesman won over Rozelle by the end of the fourth martini.

From the start Sabol wanted to be innovative. Rather than just film the championship game between the New York Giants and the Green Bay Packers from a single camera located high in the

Company Perspectives:

Stunning cinematography. Exclusive all-access sound. Stirring orchestral music. Poignant storytelling. These hallmarks define the NFL Films style ... often imitated, but never equaled.

stands at the 50-yard line, he wanted to film up close to catch the intensity of the game. He hired free-lance cameramen and stationed them in a way that has hardly changed since. To the stationary camera at the 50-yard line, he added a "Mole" to film the sidelines and a "Weasel" to wander around the stadium to collect moments of opportunity. Sabol also had one of the men speed up his camera to produce slow-motion footage. His son, a college student by then, also worked the game as a "Gopher," helping out the cameramen but not filming himself. It was a frigid day, with the wind chill at 20 degrees below zero, and the cameras kept freezing up. The film broke, and until it was developed Ed Sabol was not sure he would have anything with which to work. The film did develop and the result was "Pro Football's Longest Day," which premiered at Toot Shor's restaurant in New York. Rozelle was pleased, calling it the greatest football film ever made. However, there was a limited market for the film, and Sabol had to travel to Kiwanis Club and Boy Scout meetings, packing his own projector and screen, to find an audience.

The NFL's Acquisition of Blair Motion Pictures in 1964

Ed Sabol called his fledgling company Blair Motion Pictures (named after his daughter), setting up shop above a Philadelphia delicatessen and doing some educational films during football's off-season. He filmed the 1963 championship game, again received praise and again lost money. Having proven himself, he now pestered Rozelle with the idea of the NFL owning its own film company. Rozelle, who possessed a background in public relations, recognized that the epic way Sabol captured the NFL could be used to sell tickets, and he presented the idea to the club owners. The NFL considered other companies, including Telra and New York-based producers, but Ed Sabol closed the deal. Rather than using a slide presentation, like his rivals, he simply talked to the owners and convinced them to buy out his company for a one-time payment of $280,000, amounting to $20,000 each from the league's 14 teams. His film company would become a house organ, renamed NFL Films, and he promised to produce a championship game film each year and a film for each team highlighting their past season. The teams were already spending that much money to produce their own highlight films and, by having a single production company involved, they could control quality. Turning a profit was not an important consideration, but not losing money was. As Sabol rode down the elevator following his successful pitch, the owner of the Baltimore Colts, Carroll Rosenbloom, told him, "Good luck on your new endeavor, but if you even come back and ask for money, we'll close you down in a second."

Blair Motion Pictures became NFL Films in 1964 and Sabol turned to Steve to help him avoid the wrath of Rosenbloom and the other owners. Steve Sabol, aside from growing up a football

fan, loved movies. As a youngster he was enamored with the award-winning television documentary series *Victory at Sea,* which chronicled World War II with an innovative score by composer Richard Rodgers and became a key influence on NFL Films' style. The younger Sabol also developed an eye from his mother, an art collector. He had been a disinterested college student, however, as a varsity football player and art major at Colorado College who spent much of his free time watching movies. He returned to Philadelphia and father and son quickly proved to be a good combination. The elder Sabol knew how to run a business and was an accomplished schmoozer, and his son was filled with ideas about how to bring the reality of the game to the screen.

Over the next few years the key elements of the NFL style, and in turn the reputation of NFL Films, was forged. A Japanese editor who did not know football but did understand film language moved the company away from the tradition of showing a football play from beginning to end. Instead, NFL Films began to break a play into parts, and as a result developed a montage approach that was given full expression in the 1965 film *They Call It Pro-Football,* which also featured the narration of John Facenda, a longtime Philadelphia news anchor whose rich voice and commanding delivery elevated the material. *The New York Times* called it the *Citizen Kane* of sports movies. According to *Business Journal of New Jersey,* the film was unique because it "wasn't written in complete sentences; it was written in sentence fragments. The music wasn't march music; it was contemporary. The whole concept was completely new, adding a sense of drama and glory." With Facenda becoming the voice of NFL Films, a year later the company hired composer Sam Spence to provide background music in the manner of a Hollywood film. He provided a muscular soundtrack that became another hallmark of an NFL Films production. Spence continued to work for the company for many years despite living in Munich. According to Steve Sabol, he would hum a few bars of what he was looking for over the phone and Spence would take it from there.

With a few championship game films, dozens of team season summaries, and *They Call It Pro-Football* to its credit, NFL Films began finding more ways to package all the film it shot. By this time the company was spending a considerable amount of money on film because every play was shot in slow motion. People loved the slow-motion shots, and Ed Sabol, who came from the school of "the customer is always right," decided to give the people what they wanted. In 1967 NFL Films produced its first feature for a network pre-game show, *CBS Countdown to Kickoff,* and began producing a weekly highlight show, *This Is the NFL,* which premiered on television on a syndicated basis. In the beginning it was shown late at night and other odd hours, but eventually moved into better time slots. Also in 1967, NFL Films found a way to make use of some of the film that never made it into the highlights, especially the more unusual plays, including the fumbles and mistakes. The humorous result was called the *Football Follies,* which a league official initially rejected because he thought it humiliated the players. But Rozelle decided to show the film to some players to see what they thought. The Philadelphia Eagles players who viewed the film at training camp roared their delight. The *Follies* was released, and would one day become a video bestseller that not only spawned *Follies* sequels but launched the bloopers genre that became a TV mainstay. Other firsts in the 1960s included

Key Dates:

1962: Ed Sabol launches Blair Motion Pictures to film the 1962 NFL Championship game.

1964: The company is bought by the National Football League and becomes NFL Films.

1970: *Monday Night Football* begins airing NFL Films' halftime highlights.

1974: Association with HBO begins.

1978: Association with ESPN begins.

1980: The first home video is sold.

1987: Steve Sabol succeeds his father as president.

1995: Ed Sabol retires.

2002: The company moves into a new state-of-the-art facility.

the use of graphics to explain strategy, the miking of the first coach (the Philadelphia Eagles' Joe Kuharich), filming inside a locker room before a game, and the first use of 600-mm telephoto lenses in sports.

NFL Films had gained a solid enough reputation in the 1960s to attract the attention of Major League Baseball and the National Basketball Leagues, which both approached the company about doing work for them. Ed Sabol, however, did not want to be stretched too thin, electing instead to continue to focus on football. By the end of the decade professional football had made great strides in popularity. At the start of the 1960s it trailed baseball, college football, and boxing, but the sport flourished as perfect television programming. A major factor in the changing perception of professional football was the way in which NFL Films portrayed it, a treatment that television would begin to emulate and that would make the game even more popular. A major step for both the NFL and its filmmaking subsidiary was the 1970 launch of *Monday Night Football.* Not only did it bring the game to a larger, prime-time audience, it spiced up the coverage with some of the NFL Films trademarks, including an abundance of slow motion. It also dispensed with the traditional halftime fare of marching bands and showed highlights of the previous day's games, courtesy of NFL Films, narrated off the cuff by the flamboyant Howard Cosell who was generous in his praise for the work of the company.

NFL Films enjoyed steady growth in the 1970s, finding new outlets for its work while retaining an innovative spirit. It also did a little work for Hollywood, shooting footage for the football film *Brian's Song.* In 1974 it forged a partnership with HBO, providing material for a weekly highlight show. The rise of cable television also brought another key long-term partner: all-sports channel ESPN, which began using NFL Films-produced content in 1978. In that same year, the company produced its first *Road to the Superbowl* television special. Along the way, NFL Films began using the reverse-angle play in 1971, and employed ''The Way We Were'' in 1973 as the first popular song to accompany football footage. In 1977 the first Sports Emmy Awards were held and, not surprisingly, NFL Films took home a statue, the first of dozens. The company closed the decade by moving into larger accommodations, relocating to Mount Laurel, New Jersey.

Innovations Continuing in the 1980s

NFL Films introduced the first sports home video in 1980, and also began to expand beyond football. In 1980, working in conjunction with NASA, it produced a PBS documentary called *Greatest Adventure: Man's Journey to the Moon.* Astronaut Buzz Aldrin was so impressed he commented that if NFL Films worked for NASA full-time the agency would never have suffered a budget cut. NFL camera crews also began filming rock concerts for Bruce Springsteen and Michael Jackson and produced MTV videos, but Ed Sabol made sure the company never placed too much emphasis on projects outside its bread-and-butter football business. In 1987 he turned over the presidency to Steve and stayed on as chairman of NFL Films, a post he held until 1995 when he retired.

Under Steve Sabol's leadership, little changed at NFL Films, which continued to produce a staggering amount of programming each year. It also remained committed to taking advantage of the best equipment and technology available. In 1987, for example, the company began to log the contents of its extensive film vault in a computer database. NFL Films under Steve Sabol formed a new division in 1993, NFL Films Commercial Production, to take advantage of the company's state-of-the art production facilities. The focus of the unit was on commercials, infomercials, corporate films, and video annual reports. Over the next two years more than 30 commercials for local and national companies were produced at the NFL Films facility.

By 1995 NFL Films had long since turned every available closet and conference room into usable space and the company began making plans to relocate to a larger facility. It was a long-term project that required approval from the NFL, and it was not until 2002 that the company moved into a new 200,000-square-foot, 26-acre site in Mount Laurel that included production studios and a massive film library. NFL Films hoped to use the new facility as a launching pad for even more non-NFL work, which still only accounted for 10 percent of its revenues. The extra space would also be necessary as NFL Films began providing programming for the NFL Network, a new cable TV venture launched by the league. In essence the company now had a Hollywood-caliber studio at its disposal, which was soon put to use in making a pair of feature-length war dramas for the History Channel: *My Father's Gun* and *Blood from a Stone.*

The new facilities also positioned NFL Films to take its football franchise into the future. The company began the long-term project of digitizing its massive film library, so that theoretically all of NFL Films' highlights could be available on the Web. Digital technology also allowed NFL Films content to become available on a new generation of cell phones. In 2005 Sprint Nextel Corp. agreed to a five-year deal to provide a variety of NFL programming to customers, including the ''best of NFL Films.''

Although NFL Films was sure to continue its evolution, for the time being at least it would continue to be led by Steve Sabol. ''I have no line of succession,'' he told the *New York Times* in 2000. ''I will be taking care of this place every day when I'm 85, I assure you. I haven't gotten tired of it yet, so I can't see it ever happening. I fell into this, and I can't believe how lucky a life I've lived.''

Principal Subsidiaries

NFL Films Commercial Production.

Further Reading

Clarke, Norm, ''As CC Student, Sabol Began to Roll for NFL Films,'' *Rocky Mountain News,* January 20, 1998, p. 23N.

George, John, ''NFL Films Kicks Off New Digs,'' *Philadelphia Business Journal,* October 4, 2002, p. 1.

Goldstein, Scott, ''Running to Daylight,'' *NJBIZ,* October 28, 2002, p. 20.

Lidsky, David, ''This Is NFL Films,'' *Fortune Small Business,* September 16, 2002, p. 176.

Macnow, Glen, ''NFL Films Is Scoring High,'' *Nation's Business,* September 1988, p. 44.

Sorcher, Jamie Ann, ''In a League of Its Own,'' *Business Journal of New Jersey,* February 1992, p. 37.

Strauss, Robert, ''Catching Football on Film,'' *New York Times,* October 29, 2000, p. 14NJ4.

——, ''One On One: Steve Sabol,'' *Electronic Media,* December 4, 2000, p. 16.

Taafe, William, ''Footage That Can Go to Your Head,'' *Sports Illustrated,* September 5, 1984, p. 84.

Van Allen, Peter, ''Game Plan of NFL Films Goes Beyond Football,'' *Philadelphia Business Journal,* December 20, 2002, p. 3.

—Ed Dinger

nike

NIKE, Inc.

One Bowerman Drive
Beaverton, Oregon 97005-6453
U.S.A.
Telephone: (503) 671-6453
Toll Free: (800) 344-6453
Fax: (503) 671-6300
Web site: http://www.nike.com

Public Company
Incorporated: 1968 as BRS, Inc.
Employees: 26,000
Sales: $13.74 billion (2005)
Stock Exchanges: New York Pacific
Ticker Symbol: NKE
NAIC: 316219 Other Footwear Manufacturing; 339920
   Sporting and Athletic Goods Manufacturing; 422340
   Footwear Wholesalers; 448190 Other Clothing Stores;
   448210 Shoe Stores

Founded as an importer of Japanese shoes, NIKE, Inc. (Nike) has grown to be the world's largest marketer of athletic footwear, holding a global market share of approximately 37 percent. In the United States, Nike products are sold through about 22,000 retail accounts; worldwide, the company's products are sold in more than 160 countries. Both domestically and overseas Nike operates retail stores, including NikeTowns and factory outlets. Nearly all of the items are manufactured by independent contractors, primarily located overseas, with Nike involved in the design, development, and marketing. In addition to its wide range of core athletic shoes and apparel marketed under the flagship Nike brand, the company also sells footwear under the Converse, Chuck Taylor, All Star, and Jack Purcell brands through wholly owned subsidiary Converse Inc. and sells under the brands Starter, Shaq, and Asphalt in the discount retailer channel through another subsidiary, Exeter Brands Group LLC. The firm also sells Nike and Bauer brand athletic equipment; Hurley surfing, skateboarding, and snowboarding apparel and footwear; and Cole Haan brand dress and casual footwear. Nike has relied on consistent innovation in the design of its products and heavy promotion to fuel its growth in both U.S. and foreign markets. The ubiquitous presence of the Nike brand and its Swoosh trademark led to a backlash against the company by the late 20th century, particularly in relation to allegations of low wages and poor working conditions at the company's Asian contract manufacturers.

BRS Beginnings: 1960s

Nike's precursor originated in 1962, a product of the imagination of Philip H. Knight, a Stanford University business graduate who had been a member of the track team as an undergraduate at the University of Oregon. Traveling in Japan after finishing business school, Knight got in touch with a Japanese firm that made athletic shoes, the Onitsuka Tiger Co., and arranged to import some of its products to the United States on a small scale. Knight was convinced that Japanese running shoes could become significant competitors for the German products that then dominated the American market. In the course of setting up his agreement with Onitsuka Tiger, Knight invented Blue Ribbon Sports to satisfy his Japanese partner's expectations that he represented an actual company, and this hypothetical firm eventually grew to become Nike, Inc.

At the end of 1963, Knight's arrangements in Japan came to fruition when he took delivery of 200 pairs of Tiger athletic shoes, which he stored in his father's basement and peddled at various track meets in the area. Knight's one-man venture became a partnership in the following year, when his former track coach, William Bowerman, chipped in $500 to equal Knight's investment. Bowerman had long been experimenting with modified running shoes for his team, and he worked with runners to improve the designs of prototype Blue Ribbon Sports (BRS) shoes. Innovation in running shoe design eventually would become a cornerstone of the company's continued expansion and success. Bowerman's efforts first paid off in 1968, when a shoe known as the Cortez, which he had designed, became a big seller.

BRS sold 1,300 pairs of Japanese running shoes in 1964, its first year, to gross $8,000. By 1965 the fledgling company had acquired a full-time employee and sales had reached $20,000.

Company Perspectives:

The Nike Mission: "To bring inspiration and innovation to every athlete* in the world."
    *If you have a body, you are an athlete.

The following year, the company rented its first retail space, next to a beauty salon in Santa Monica, California, so that its few employees could stop selling shoes out of their cars. In 1967 with fast-growing sales, BRS expanded operations to the East Coast, opening a distribution office in Wellesley, Massachusetts.

Bowerman's innovations in running shoe technology continued throughout this time. A shoe with the upper portion made of nylon went into development in 1967, and the following year Bowerman and another employee came up with the Boston shoe, which incorporated the first cushioned midsole throughout the entire length of an athletic shoe. Also in 1968 the company was incorporated as BRS, Inc.

Emergence of Nike: 1970s

By the end of the decade, Knight's venture had expanded to include several stores and 20 employees and sales were nearing $300,000. The company was poised for greater growth, but Knight was frustrated by a lack of capital to pay for expansion. In 1971, using financing from the Japanese trading company Nissho Iwai Corporation, BRS was able to manufacture its own line of products overseas, through independent contractors, for import to the United States. At this time, the company introduced its Swoosh trademark and the brand name Nike, the Greek goddess of victory. These new symbols were initially affixed to a soccer shoe, the first Nike product to be sold.

A year later, BRS broke with its old Japanese partner, Onitsuka Tiger, after a disagreement over distribution, and kicked off promotion of its own products at the 1972 U.S. Olympic Trials, the first of many marketing campaigns that would seek to attach Nike's name and fortunes to the careers of well-known athletes. Nike shoes were geared to the serious athlete, and their high performance carried with it a high price.

In their first year of distribution, the company's new products grossed $1.96 million and the corporate staff swelled to 45. In addition, operations were expanded to Canada, the company's first foreign market, which would be followed by Australia, in 1974.

Bowerman continued his innovations in running-shoe design with the introduction of the Moon shoe in 1972, which had a waffle-like sole that had first been formed by molding rubber on a household waffle iron. This sole increased the traction of the shoe without adding weight.

In 1974 BRS opened its first U.S. plant, in Exeter, New Hampshire. The company's payroll swelled to 250, and worldwide sales neared $5 million by the end of 1974. This growth was fueled in part by aggressive promotion of the Nike brand name. The company sought to expand its visibility by having its shoes worn by prominent athletes, including tennis players Ilie Nastase and Jimmy Connors. At the 1976 Olympic Trials these efforts began to pay off as Nike shoes were worn by rising athletic stars.

The company's growth had truly begun to take off by this time, riding the boom in popularity of jogging that took place in the United States in the late 1970s. BRS revenues tripled in two years to $14 million in 1976, and then doubled in just one year to $28 million in 1977. To keep up with demand, the company opened new factories, adding a stitching plant in Maine and additional overseas production facilities in Taiwan and Korea. International sales were expanded when markets in Asia were opened in 1977 and in South America the following year. European distributorships were lined up in 1978.

Nike continued its promotional activities with the opening of Athletics West, a training club for Olympic hopefuls in track and field, and by signing tennis player John McEnroe to an endorsement contract. In 1978 the company changed its name to Nike, Inc. The company expanded its line of products that year, adding athletic shoes for children.

By 1979 Nike sold almost half the running shoes bought in the United States, and the company moved into a new world headquarters building in Beaverton, Oregon. In addition to its shoe business, the company began to make and market a line of sports clothing, and the Nike Air shoe cushioning device was introduced.

1980s Growth Through International Expansion and Aggressive Marketing

By the start of the 1980s, Nike's combination of groundbreaking design and savvy and aggressive marketing had allowed it to surpass the German athletic shoe company adidas AG, formerly the leader in U.S. sales. In December 1980, Nike went public, offering two million shares of stock. With the revenues generated by the stock sale, the company planned continued expansion, particularly in the European market. In the United States, plans for a new headquarters on a large, rural campus were inaugurated, and an East Coast distribution center in Greenland, New Hampshire, was brought on line. In addition, the company bought a large plant in Exeter, New Hampshire, to house the Nike Sport Research and Development Lab and also to provide for more domestic manufacturing capacity. The company had shifted its overseas production away from Japan at this point, manufacturing nearly four-fifths of its shoes in South Korea and Taiwan. It established factories in mainland China in 1981.

By the following year, when the jogging craze in the United States had started to wane, half of the running shoes bought in the United States bore the Nike trademark. The company was well insulated from the effects of a stagnating demand for running shoes, however, because it gained a substantial share of its sales from other types of athletic shoes, notably basketball shoes and tennis shoes. In addition, Nike benefited from strong sales of its other product lines, which included apparel, work and leisure shoes, and children's shoes.

Given slowing growth in the U.S. market, however, the company turned its attention to foreign markets, inaugurating

Key Dates:

1962: Philip H. Knight founds Blue Ribbon Sports (BRS) to import Japanese running shoes.

1963: BRS takes its first delivery of 200 shoes from Onitsuka Tiger Co.

1964: BRS becomes partnership between Knight and William Bowerman.

1966: The company's first retail outlet opens.

1968: Company is incorporated as BRS, Inc.; the Bowerman-designed Cortez shoe becomes a big seller.

1971: BRS begins manufacturing its own products overseas, through subcontractors; the Swoosh trademark and the Nike brand are introduced.

1972: At the U.S. Olympic Trials, the Nike brand is promoted for the first time; company enters its first foreign market, Canada.

1978: Company changes its name to Nike, Inc.

1979: First line of clothing is launched and the Nike Air shoe cushioning device debuts.

1980: Nike goes public.

1981: Nike International, Ltd. is created to spearhead overseas push.

1985: Company signs Michael Jordan to endorse a version of its Air shoe, the ''Air Jordan.''

1988: Cole Haan, maker of casual and dress shoes, is acquired; ''Just Do It'' slogan debuts.

1990: First NikeTown retail outlet opens in Portland, Oregon.

1994: Company acquires Canstar Sports Inc., the leading maker of skates and hockey equipment in the world, later renamed Bauer Nike Hockey Inc.

1995: Company signs golfer Tiger Woods to a $40 million endorsement deal.

1996: The Nike equipment division is created.

1999: Company begins selling its products directly to consumers via its web site.

2003: Converse Inc. is acquired for $305 million.

Nike International, Ltd. in 1981 to spearhead the company's push into Europe and Japan, as well as into Asia, Latin America, and Africa. In Europe, Nike faced stiff competition from adidas and Puma, which had a stronghold on the soccer market, Europe's largest athletic shoe category. The company opened a factory in Ireland to enable it to distribute its shoes without paying high import tariffs, and in 1981 bought out its distributors in England and Austria, to strengthen its control over marketing and distribution of its products. In 1982 the company outfitted Aston Villa, the winning team in the English and European Cup soccer championships, giving a boost to promotion of its new soccer shoe.

In Japan, Nike allied itself with Nissho Iwai, the sixth largest Japanese trading company, to form Nike-Japan Corporation. Because Nike already held a part of the low-priced athletic shoe market, the company set its sights on the high-priced end of the scale in Japan.

By 1982 the company's line of products included more than 200 different kinds of shoes, including the Air Force I, a basket-ball shoe, and its companion shoe for racquet sports, the Air Ace, the latest models in the long line of innovative shoe designs that had pushed Nike's earnings to an average annual increase of almost 100 percent. In addition, the company marketed more than 200 different items of clothing. By 1983, when the company posted its first ever quarterly drop in earnings as the running boom peaked and went into a decline, Nike's leaders were looking to the apparel division, as well as overseas markets, for further expansion. In foreign sales, the company had mixed results. Its operations in Japan were almost immediately profitable, and the company quickly jumped to second place in the Japanese market, but in Europe, Nike fared less well, losing money on its five European subsidiaries.

Faced with an 11.5 percent drop in domestic sales of its shoes in the 1984 fiscal year, Nike moved away from its traditional marketing strategy of support for sporting events and athlete endorsements to a wider-reaching approach, investing more than $10 million in its first national television and magazine advertising campaign. This followed the ''Cities Campaign,'' which used billboards and murals in nine American cities to publicize Nike products in the period before the 1984 Olympics. Despite the strong showing of athletes wearing Nike shoes in the 1984 Los Angeles Olympic games, Nike profits were down almost 30 percent for the fiscal year ending in May 1984, although international sales were robust and overall sales rose slightly. This decline was a result of aggressive price discounting on Nike products and the increased costs associated with the company's push into foreign markets and attempts to build up its sales of apparel.

Earnings continued to fall in the next three quarters as the company lost market share, posting profits of only $7.8 million at the end of August 1984, a loss of $2.2 million three months later, and another loss of $2.1 million at the end of February 1985. In response, Nike adopted a series of measures to change its sliding course. The company cut back on the number of shoes it had sitting in warehouses and also attempted to fine-tune its corporate mission by cutting back on the number of products it marketed. It made plans to reduce the line of Nike shoes by 30 percent within a year and a half. In addition, leadership at the top of the company was streamlined, as founder Knight resumed the post of president, which he had relinquished in 1983, in addition to his duties as chairman and chief executive officer. Overall administrative costs were also reduced. As part of this effort, Nike also consolidated its research and marketing branches, closing its facility in Exeter, New Hampshire, and cutting 75 of the plant's 125 employees. Overall, the company laid off about 400 workers during 1984.

Faced with shifting consumer interests (i.e., the U.S. market move from jogging to aerobics), the company created a new products division in 1985 to help keep pace. In addition, Nike purchased Pro-form, a small maker of weightlifting equipment, as part of its plan to profit from all aspects of the fitness movement. The company was restructured further at the end of 1985 when its last two U.S. factories were closed and its previous divisions of apparel and athletic shoes were rearranged by sport. In a move that would prove to be the key to the company's recovery, in 1985 the company signed basketball player Michael Jordan to endorse a new version of its Air shoe, introduced four years earlier. The new basketball shoes bore the name "Air Jordan."

In early 1986 Nike announced expansion into a number of new lines, including casual apparel for women, a less expensive line of athletic shoes called Street Socks, golf shoes, and tennis gear marketed under the name "Wimbledon." By mid-1986 Nike was reporting that its earnings had begun to increase again, with sales topping $1 billion for the first time. At that point, the company sold its 51 percent stake in Nike-Japan to its Japanese partner; six months later, Nike laid off 10 percent of its U.S. employees at all levels in a major cost-cutting strategy.

Following these moves, Nike announced a drop in revenues and earnings in 1987, and another round of restructuring and budget cuts ensued, as the company attempted to come to grips with the continuing evolution of the U.S. fitness market. Only Nike's innovative Air athletic shoes provided a bright spot in the company's otherwise erratic progress, allowing the company to regain market share from rival Reebok International Ltd. in several areas, including basketball and cross-training.

The following year, Nike branched out from athletic shoes, purchasing Cole Haan, a maker of casual and dress shoes, for $80 million. Advertising heavily, the company took a commanding lead in sales to young people to claim 23 percent of the overall athletic shoe market. Profits rebounded to reach $100 million in 1988, as sales rose 37 percent to $1.2 billion. Later that year, Nike launched a $10 million television campaign around the theme "Just Do It" and announced that its 1989 advertising budget would reach $45 million.

In 1989 Nike unveiled several new lines of shoes and led its market with $1.7 billion in sales, yielding profits of $167 million. The company's product innovation continued, including the introduction of a basketball shoe with an inflatable collar around the ankle, sold under the brand name Air Pressure. In addition, Nike continued its aggressive marketing, using ads featuring Michael Jordan and actor-director Spike Lee, the ongoing "Just Do It" campaign, and the "Bo Knows" television spots featuring athlete Bo Jackson. At the end of 1989, the company began relocation to its newly constructed headquarters campus in Beaverton, Oregon.

Market Dominance in the Early to Mid-1990s

In 1990 the company sued two competitors for copying the patented designs of its shoes and found itself engaged in a dispute with the U.S. Customs Service over import duties on its Air Jordan basketball shoes. In 1990 the company's revenues hit $2 billion. The company acquired Tetra Plastics Inc., producers of plastic film for shoe soles. That year, the company opened NikeTown, a prototype store selling the full range of Nike products, in Portland, Oregon.

By 1991 Nike's Visible Air shoes had enabled it to surpass its rival Reebok in the U.S. market. In the fiscal year ending May 31, 1991, Nike sales surpassed the $3 billion mark, fueled by record sales of 41 million pairs of Nike Air shoes and a booming international market. Its efforts to conquer Europe had begun to bear fruit; business there grew by 100 percent that year, producing more than $1 billion in sales and gaining the second place market share behind Adidas. Nike's U.S. shoe market had, in large part, matured, slowing to 5 percent annual growth, down from 15 percent annual growth from 1980 and 1988. The company began eyeing overseas markets and predicted ample room to grow in Europe. Nike's U.S. rival Reebok, however, also saw potential for growth in Europe, and by 1992 European MTV was glutted with athletic shoe advertisements as the battle for the youth market heated up between Nike, Reebok, and their European competitors, Adidas and Puma.

Nike also saw growth potential in its women's shoe and sports apparel division. In February 1992 Nike began a $13 million print and television advertising pitch for its women's segment, built upon its "Dialogue" print campaign, which had been slowly wooing 18- to 34-year-old women since 1990. Sales of Nike women's apparel lines Fitness Essentials, Elite Aerobics, Physical Elements, and All Condition Gear increased by 25 percent in both 1990 and 1991 and jumped by 68 percent in 1992.

In July 1992 Nike opened its second NikeTown retail store in Chicago. Like its predecessor in Portland, the Chicago NikeTown was designed to "combine the fun and excitement of FAO Schwartz, the Smithsonian Institute and Disneyland in a space that will entertain sports and fitness fans from around the world" as well as provide a high-profile retail outlet for Nike's rapidly expanding lines of footwear and clothing.

Nike celebrated its 20th anniversary in 1992, virtually debt free and with company revenues of $3.4 billion. Gross profits jumped $100 million in that year, fueled by soaring sales in its retail division, which expanded to include 30 Nike-owned discount outlets and the two NikeTowns. To celebrate its anniversary, Nike brought out its old slogan "There is no finish line." As if to underscore that sentiment, Nike Chairman Philip Knight announced massive plans to remake the company with the goal of being "the best sports and fitness company in the world." To fulfill that goal, the company set the ground plans for a complicated yet innovative marketing structure seeking to make the Nike brand into a worldwide megabrand along the lines of Coca-Cola, Pepsi, Sony, and Disney.

Nike continued expansion of its high-profile NikeTown chain, opening outlets in Atlanta, Georgia, in the spring of 1993 and Costa Mesa, California, later that year. Also in 1993, as part of its long-term marketing strategy, Nike began an ambitious venture with Mike Ovitz's Creative Artists Agency to organize and package sports events under the Nike name, a move that potentially led the company into competition with sports management giants such as ProServ, IMG, and Advantage International.

Nike also began a more controversial venture into the arena of sports agents, negotiating contracts for basketball's Scottie Pippin, Alonzo Mourning, and others in addition to retaining athletes such as Michael Jordan and Charles Barkley as company spokespersons. Nike's influence in the world of sports grew to such a degree that in 1993 *Sporting News* dubbed Knight the most powerful man in sports.

Critics contended that Nike's influence ran too deep, having its hand in negotiating everything in an athlete's life from investments to the choice of an apartment. But Nike's marketing executives saw it as part of a campaign to create an image of Nike not just as a product line but as a *lifestyle,* a "Nike attitude."

Nearly everyone agreed, however, that Nike was the dominant force in athletic footwear in the early to mid-1990s. The company held about 30 percent of the U.S. market by 1995, far outdistancing the 20 percent of its nearest rival, Reebok. Overseas revenues continued their steady rise, reaching nearly $2 billion by 1995, about 40 percent of the overall total. Not content with its leading position in athletic shoes and its growing sales of athletic apparel, which accounted for more than 30 percent of revenues in 1996, Nike branched out into sports equipment in the mid-1990s. In 1994 the company acquired Canstar Sports Inc., the leading maker of skates and hockey equipment in the world, for $400 million. Canstar was renamed Bauer Nike Hockey Inc., Bauer being Canstar's brand name for its equipment. Two years later Bauer Nike became part of the newly formed Nike equipment division, which aimed to extend the company into the marketing of sport balls, protective gear, eyewear, and watches. Also during this period, Nike signed its next superstar spokesperson, Tiger Woods. In 1995, at the age of 20, Woods agreed to a 20-year, $40 million endorsement contract. The golf phenom went on to win an inordinate number of tournaments, often shattering course records, and was on pace to eclipse golf legend Jack Nicklaus's illustrious lifetime record of winning 18 majors, more than validating the blockbuster contract.

Late 1990s Slippage

For the fiscal year ending in May 1997, Nike earned a record $795.8 million on record revenues of $9.19 billion. Overseas sales played a large role in the 42 percent increase in revenues from 1996 to 1997. Sales in Asia increased by more than $500 million (to $1.24 billion), while European sales surged ahead by $450 million. Back home, Nike's share of the U.S. athletic shoe market neared 50 percent. The picture at Nike soon turned sour, however, as the Asian financial crisis that erupted in the summer of 1997 sent sneaker sales in that region plunging. By 1999, sales in Asia had dropped to $844.5 million. Compounding the company's troubles was a concurrent stagnation of sales in its domestic market, where the fickle tastes of teenagers began turning away from athletic shoes to hiking boots and other casual "brown shoes." As a result, overall sales for 1999 fell to $8.78 billion. Profits were falling as well, including a net loss of $67.7 million for the fourth quarter of 1998, the company's first reported loss in more than 13 years. The decline in net income led to a cost-cutting drive that included the layoff of 5 percent of the workforce, or 1,200 people, in 1998, and the slashing of its budget for sports star endorsements by $100 million that same year.

Nike was also dogged throughout the late 1990s by protests and boycotts over allegations regarding the treatment of workers at the contract factories in Asia that employed nearly 400,000 people and that made the bulk of Nike shoes and much of its apparel. Charges included abuse of workers, poor working conditions, low wages, and use of child labor. Nike's initial reaction, which was highlighted by Knight's insistence that the company had little control over its suppliers, resulted in waves of negative publicity. Protesters included church groups, students at universities that had apparel and footwear contracts with Nike, and socially conscious investment funds. Nike finally announced in mid-1998 a series of changes affecting its contract workforce in Asia, including an increase in the minimum age, a tightening of air quality standards, and a pledge to allow independent inspec-

tions of factories. Nike nonetheless remained under pressure from activists into the 21st century. Nike, along with McDonald's Corporation, the Coca-Cola Company, and Starbucks Corporation, among others, also became an object of protest from those who were attacking multinational companies that pushed global brands. This undercurrent of hostility burst into the spotlight in late 1999 when some of the more aggressive protesters against a World Trade Organization meeting in Seattle attempted to storm a NikeTown outlet.

Seeking to recapture the growth of the early to mid-1990s, Nike pursued a number of new initiatives in the late 1990s. Having initially missed out on the trend toward extreme sports (such as skateboarding, mountain biking, and snowboarding), Nike attempted to rectify this miscue by establishing a unit called ACG, short for "all-conditions gear," in 1998. Two years later, the company created a new division called Techlab to market a line of sports-technology accessories, such as a digital audio player, a high-altitude wrist compass, and a portable heart-rate monitor. Both of these initiatives were aimed at capturing sales from the emerging Generation Y demographic group. In early 1999 Nike began selling its shoes and other products directly to consumers via the company web site. The company finally earned some good publicity in 1999 when it sponsored the U.S. national women's soccer team that won the Women's World Cup. In December 1999 Nike cofounder Bowerman died, and the company later introduced a line of running shoes in his honor.

Early 21st-Century Comeback

Nike's struggles continued into the early 2000s, but by 2002 the company appeared to have turned a corner. Surprisingly, the turnaround stemmed in large part not from clever marketing or new high-tech sneakers but from concentrating more attention on the more mundane aspects of running a business, such as investing in start-of-the-art information systems, logistics, and supply-chain management. Equally important was Knight's willingness to cede more control of the company to a number of underlings, some recruited from the outside. Donald W. Blair was brought onboard from PepsiCo, Inc. to become chief financial officer in 1999 after Nike inexplicably had been without a CFO for two years. In 2001 Knight named two longtime company insiders, Mark G. Parker and Charles D. Denson, as copresidents with responsibility for day-to-day operations. On the product side, Nike successfully overhauled its apparel operations, garnered surging sales of its golf equipment after Woods began using Nike golf balls in 2000, and made a big push in the soccer shoe market, where it gained the top spot among European soccer shoe buyers, leapfrogging over Adidas, by 2003. Nike also continued to score endorsement coups, inking high school basketball phenom LeBron James to a $90 million contract in 2003.

The Nike comeback also centered around a commitment to lessen its dependence on the volatile market for high-performance shoes by owning a portfolio of brands covering different market sectors and price points. In 2002 the company bought Hurley International, a teen lifestyle brand, for an estimated $95 million. Based in Costa Mesa, California, Hurley was a designer and distributor of action sports apparel and footwear for surfing, skateboarding, and snowboarding. Nike next bought Converse Inc. for $305 million in September 2003. The 95-year-old Converse of North Andover, Massachusetts, was best known for its retro, low-tech Chuck Taylor All-Star sneakers, a product that for many teenagers and young adults had come to be viewed as the very antithesis of everything Nike. Converse's management team remained in place following the takeover, with the company operating as an autonomous subsidiary. In August 2004 Nike bought Official Starter Properties LLC and Official Starter LLC for approximately $47 million. These companies marketed athletic apparel, footwear, and accessories under the Starter, Team Starter, Asphalt, Shaq, and Dunkman brands (the latter two featuring NBA star Shaquille O'Neal), primarily through discount chains such as Wal-Mart Stores, Inc. These brands were placed within a new wholly owned subsidiary, Exeter Brands Group LLC, focusing on developing products for value-conscious consumers.

While these acquisitions were unfolding in the United States, Nike was pushing hard into overseas markets, and by 2003 international sales exceeded domestic sales for the first time. Starting in 2002 the company also concentrated on building an extensive program to address the perennial charges of labor exploitation. Nike began allowing a monitoring organization it had cofounded, the Fair Labor Association, to conduct random factory inspections. It also built an in-house staff of approximately 100 employees to inspect hundreds of factories and grade them on labor standards. In early 2005 Nike took an unprecedented step toward greater transparency by issuing a list of its more than 700 contract factories. Such moves provided the basis for an improving relationship between Nike and its critics. There were even a few cases in which activists worked with the company to resolve specific issues at certain factories.

Nike enjoyed record results in the fiscal year ending in May 2004, posting profits of $945.6 million on revenues of $12.25 billion. Profits surged past the $1 billion mark the next year, hitting $1.21 billion, while revenues jumped to a new high of $13.74 billion. Late in 2004 Knight stepped aside from his executive position, while remaining chairman, to bring William D. Perez onboard as president and CEO. Perez, a marathon runner and avid golfer, was hired away from S.C. Johnson & Son, Inc., the family-controlled consumer products company, where he spent 34 years and rose to the top as president and CEO. His vast international experience was expected to help Nike as it continued its expansion abroad, and Perez was known as an excellent marketer with a stellar reputation of acquiring and managing well-known brands. Within months of Perez's appointment, Nike's need for such an experienced hand appeared to grow when adidas-Salomon AG agreed to buy Reebok International Ltd. for approximately $3.8 billion. The deal, announced in August 2005, promised to combine two of Nike's biggest rivals, giving the newly enlarged company about 30 percent of the worldwide athletic footwear market, compared to Nike's 37 percent. A revitalized Nike nevertheless seemed to have the strategies in place to fend off this new threat and stay on top of the global sneaker heap.

Principal Subsidiaries

Bauer Nike Hockey Inc.; Cole Haan Holdings Incorporated; Converse Inc.; Hurley International LLC; Exeter Brands Group LLC.

Principal Competitors

Reebok International Ltd.; adidas-Salomon AG; Fila USA, Inc.; PUMA AG Rudolf Dassler Sport; Skechers U.S.A., Inc.

Further Reading

Buell, Barbara, "Nike Catches Up with the Trendy Frontrunner," *Business Week,* October 24, 1988, p. 88.

Collingwood, Harris, "Nike Rushes in Where Reebok Used to Tread," *Business Week,* October 3, 1988, p. 42.

Dash, Eric, "Founder of Nike to Hand Off Job to a New Chief," *The New York Times,* November 19, 2004, p. C1.

Dowdell, Stephen, "No Finish Line," *Footwear News,* November 25, 2002, p. 12.

Eales, Roy, "Is Nike a Long Distance Runner?," *Multinational Business,* 1986, pp. 9+.

"Fitting the World in Sport Shoes," *Business Week,* January 25, 1982.

Gallagher, Leigh, "Rebound," *Forbes,* May 3, 1999, p. 60.

Gilley, Bruce, "Sweating It Out," *Far Eastern Economic Review,* December 10, 1998, pp. 66–67.

Gold, Jacqueline S., "The Marathon Man?," *Financial World,* February 16, 1993, p. 32.

Grimm, Matthew, "Nike Vision," *Brandweek,* March 29, 1993, p. 19.

Heins, John, "Looking for That Strong Finish," *Forbes,* May 4, 1987, pp. 74+.

Holmes, Stanley, "The New Nike," *Business Week,* September 20, 2004, pp. 78–82, 84, 86.

Holmes, Stanley, and Christine Tierney, "How Nike Got Its Game Back," *Business Week,* November 4, 2002, pp. 129–31.

Jenkins, Holman W., Jr., "The Rise and Stumble of Nike," *Wall Street Journal,* June 3, 1998, p. A19.

Kang, Stephanie, and Joann S. Lublin, "Nike Taps Perez of S.C. Johnson to Follow Knight," *Wall Street Journal,* November 19, 2004, p. A3.

Katz, Donald R., *Just Do It: The Nike Spirit in the Corporate World,* New York: Random House, 1994, 336 p.

"Kennel Mates: Nike Bites into Fogdog Ownership," *Sporting Goods Business,* October 11, 1999, p. 10.

Klein, Naomi, *No Logo: Taking Aim at the Brand Bullies,* Toronto: Knopf Canada, 2000, 490 p.

Labich, Kenneth, "Nike vs. Reebok: A Battle for Hearts, Minds, and Feet," *Fortune,* September 18, 1995, pp. 90+.

LaFeber, Walter, *Michael Jordan and the New Global Capitalism,* rev. ed., New York: Norton, 2002, 220 p.

Lane, Randall, "You Are What You Wear," *Forbes 400,* October 14, 1996, pp. 42–46.

Lee, Louise, "Can Nike Still Do It?," *Business Week,* February 21, 2000, pp. 120–22+.

Loftus, Margaret, "A Swoosh Under Siege," *U.S. News and World Report,* April 12, 1999, p. 40.

McGill, Douglas C., "Nike Is Bounding Past Reebok," *The New York Times,* July 11, 1989, p. D1.

Murphy, Terence, "Nike on the Rebound," *Madison Avenue,* June 1985, pp. 28+.

"Nike Pins Hopes for Growth on Foreign Sales and Apparel," *New York Times,* March 24, 1983.

"Nike Sports Shoes: Winged Victory," *Economist,* December 2, 1989, pp. 83+.

"Nike Versus Reebok: A Foot Race," *Newsweek,* October 3, 1988, p. 52.

Richards, Bill, "Just Doing It: Nike Plans to Swoosh into Sports Equipment but It's a Tough Game," *Wall Street Journal,* January 6, 1998, pp. A1+.

——, "Tripped Up by Too Many Shoes, Nike Regroups," *Wall Street Journal,* March 3, 1998, p. B1.

Robson, Douglas, ''Just Do . . . Something,'' *Business Week,* July 2, 2001, pp. 70–71.

Roth, Daniel, ''Can Nike Still Do It Without Phil Knight?,'' *Fortune,* April 4, 2005, pp. 59–62, 64, 66, 68.

Saporito, Bill, ''Can Nike Get Unstuck?,'' *Time,* March 30, 1998, pp. 48–53.

Sellers, Patricia, ''Four Reasons Nike's Not Cool,'' *Fortune,* March 30, 1998, pp. 26–27.

Steinhauer, Jennifer, ''Nike Is in a League of Its Own: With No Big Rival, It Calls the Shots in Athletic Shoes,'' *The New York Times,* June 7, 1997, Sec. 1, p. 31.

Strasser, J.B., and Laurie Becklund, *Swoosh: The Unauthorized Story of Nike, and the Men Who Played There,* San Diego: Harcourt Brace Jovanovich, 1991, 682 p.

Stroud, Ruth, ''Nike Ready to Run a More Traditional Race,'' *Advertising Age,* June 18, 1984, pp. 4 + .

Tharp, Mike, ''Easy-Going Nike Adopts Stricter Controls to Pump Up Its Athletic-Apparel Business,'' *Wall Street Journal,* November 6, 1984.

Thurow, Roger, ''Shtick Ball: In Global Drive, Nike Finds Its Brash Ways Don't Always Pay Off,'' *Wall Street Journal,* May 5, 1997, pp. A1 + .

Tkacik, Maureen, ''Nike to Swoosh Up Old-Line Converse for $305 Million,'' *Wall Street Journal,* July 10, 2003, p. A3.

——, ''Rubber Match: In a Clash of Sneaker Titans, Nike Gets Leg Up on Foot Locker,'' *Wall Street Journal,* May 13, 2003, p. A1.

''Where Nike and Reebok Have Plenty of Running Room,'' *Business Week,* March 11, 1991.

Williams, Christopher C., ''The Now and Future King,'' *Barron's,* June 13, 2005, pp. 18, 20.

Wrighton, Jo, and Fred R. Bleakley, ''Philip Knight of Nike—Just Do It!,'' *Institutional Investor,* January 2000, pp. 22–24.

Wyatt, John, ''Is It Time to Jump on Nike?,'' *Fortune,* May 26, 1997, pp. 185–86.

Yang, Dori Jones, et al., ''Can Nike Just Do It?,'' *Business Week,* April 18, 1994, pp. 86–90.

—Elizabeth Rourke; Maura Troester
—update: David E. Salamie

Nissin Food Products Company Ltd.

1-1, 4-chome, Nishinakajima, Yodogawa-ku
Osaka
532-8524
Japan
Telephone: +66 3057711
Fax: +66 3041288
Web site: http://www.nissinfoods.co.jp

Public Company
Incorporated: 1948 as Chukososha Co., Ltd.
Employees: 6,176
Sales: ¥320.02 billion ($2.87 billion) (2004)
Stock Exchanges: Tokyo
Ticker Symbol: 2897
NAIC: 311823 Pasta Manufacturing; 551112 Offices of
  Other Holding Companies

Nissin Food Products Company Ltd. is the world's leading producer of instant ramen noodles. The Osaka-based company controls more than 40 percent of the Japanese market, despite competition from some 500 other noodle-makers, and some 9 percent of the worldwide market. Nissin founder Momofuku Ando is credited with inventing the instant noodle, considered by many to feature among the most important Japanese inventions of all time. The company produces a large range of instant noodle flavors, introducing some 100 new flavors each year. Since the 1990s, Nissin also has expanded its business to include fresh and frozen noodles, and other products, such as cereals. The company has responded to increasing consumer demand for ready-to-eat meals by launching its own line of fresh and frozen prepared foods. The company was also the first in Japan to launch retort-packaged foods. Nissin's products reach more than 100 countries worldwide. In support of its international business, the company operates some branches and subsidiaries, including manufacturing facilities, in ten countries, including the United States, Germany, The Netherlands, Hong Kong, the Philippines, Thailand, Singapore, and China. Nissin is listed on the Tokyo Stock Exchange but remains controlled by the Ando family. In 2005, Momofuku

Ando announced his decision to retire as company chairman at the age of 91.

Japanese Food Revolutionary in the 1950s

Momofuku Ando started his career as a wholesaler for foodstuffs in the Osaka area. Ando also became managing director of a credit union. Yet in the aftermath of World War II, the credit union went bankrupt and Ando lost all of his assets. The loss of his livelihood, coupled with the extreme scarcity of food in postwar Japan, led Ando to recognize the importance of food—and to decide to begin a new career in food production. In 1948, Ando founded a new company, Chukososha Co., Ltd.

Ando was inspired by the sight of the long lines of people waiting to purchase ramen noodles on the black market. Noodles, however, remained difficult to produce, time-consuming to cook, and especially difficult to preserve. Ando set up a small laboratory in his home and began experimenting with the production of a new type of noodle that could be preserved indefinitely and cooked easily. As a basic ingredient, Ando chose to use wheat, instead of the traditional rice flour. The introduction of wheat, in the form of U.S. aid shipments, had already begun to transform the Japanese diet, and schools had begun to serve bread to children. Ando, however, saw a greater nutritional benefit from transforming wheat into noodles, which then can be used in soups along with other ingredients.

By 1958, Ando had succeeded in developing a method for creating the world's first instant noodle soup. Consumers had only to add water, wait two minutes, and stir. Ando's method involved salting and seasoning the noodles themselves, then deep-frying them in order to dry them. Frying the noodles also introduced pores in them, further facilitating the rehydration process.

Ando named his first, chicken-flavored instant soup "Chikin Ramen" and set up a sales booth in a department store in Tokyo, providing samples to customers. The noodles, despite being several times more expensive than ordinary noodles, quickly caught on with Japanese consumers, earning the nickname "Magic Ramen." Always eager to embrace new novelties, the Japanese market was especially ripe for Ando's instant soup. As the Japanese economy entered its extended boom

Company Perspectives:

The Philosophy of Nissin Foods

Nissin Foods was established in 1948 by the visionary Mr. Momofuku Ando, who foresaw the rise of the fast-paced modern lifestyle in our post war society. Our daily habits were being streamlined for speed and efficiency, and that included our eating habits. Based on this, he founded Nissin Foods and put his heart and soul into developing the instant food industry.

Through innovation and the continuous search for excellence, the delicious taste of Nissin Foods was quickly accepted by consumers all over the world.

Nissin Foods is still the No. 1 manufacturer of instant food in Japan and is gaining huge popularity overseas. Mr. Momofuku Ando can truly be called a great man in the food industry, as he brings great tastes to the world!

period in the 1950s and through the 1960s, ''Magic Ramen'' became a symbol of sorts of the country's industriousness.

Ando relaunched his company as Nissin Food Products and began developing additional recipes. By 1961, the company was selling some 500 million packets of soup per year. Just five years later, that figure had leapt to 2.5 billion—and by the mid-2000s had soared to more than 47 billion annually. Supporting the company's growth was its early decision to go public, placing its stock on the Tokyo and Osaka Stock Exchanges in 1963.

Success in a Cup in the 1970s

Nissin faced a great deal of competition, however, as an increasing number of companies sprang up with their own instant noodle recipes. Nissin responded to the competition by staying one step ahead, introducing new recipes and noodle types. Among the company's new products was the launch of ''Nissin Yakisoba'' in 1963, which was the first ramen soup to include a separate flavoring packet. The company introduced the so-called ''pillow'' type of noodle, which floated at the top of soup, in 1968. That brand, Damae Ramen, became Nissin's strongest seller in the Japanese market. Nissin's market share remained strong into the next century, and by the mid-2000s the company continued to claim some 40 percent of the Japanese instant noodle market.

Nonetheless, the Japanese market for instant noodles began to soften toward the end of the 1960s. This led Nissin toward two very important developments that not only solidified Nissin's position as Japan's dominant instant noodle producer but also established the ramen noodle as a global fast-food phenomenon. The first of these was the decision to introduce its instant ramen noodles to an international market, starting with the launch of a subsidiary in the United States in 1970.

The move into the United States proved fortuitous in another way. During his visits to the United States, Ando had been introduced to the country's fast-food industry, and particularly the widespread use of paper cups and containers. Ando recognized the potential for developing a new type of packaging for his company's instant soup. By 1971, the company had pre-

pared to launch what was to become the other important component of Nissin's growth: the Cup o' Noodles brand (later renamed as Cup Noodles) of soup. Nissin's packaging was something of a revolution in the global food industry, presenting a food product that could be distributed, cooked, and eaten all in the same container.

Cup Noodles paved the way for the company's expansion throughout the world. The company entered South America with the establishment of a Brazilian sales subsidiary in 1975. At the same time, Nissin added new factories in Kanto in 1971, Shiga in 1973, and Shimonoseki in 1975. In 1978, Nissin launched production in the United States, with the completion of its first U.S. plant in Lancaster, Pennsylvania. The company added to its overseas production capacity with the opening of a Brazilian plant in 1981. In that year, as well, Nissin entered Singapore.

Through the 1980s, Nissin's international expansion continued. The company entered Hong Kong in 1984, launching production there the following year. Nissin also expanded through acquisitions, acquiring a frozen and fresh noodle operation in Hong Kong in 1987 and adding U.S. frozen burrito maker Camino Foods in 1988. The company returned to Hong Kong the following year, buying up Beatrice Hong Kong and 74 percent of Winner Food Products there. In 1991, the company entered India, forming a joint venture with Brooke Bond to produce noodles for that market.

Diversification in the 1990s

Nissin entered the European market in the 1990s as well, starting with the creation of a sales subsidiary in The Netherlands in 1991. The company launched production in that country in 1993, and later expanded its European operations to include a subsidiary in Germany as well. Other markets followed through the 1990s, including Thailand, Indonesia, and the Philippines, which the company entered through local joint ventures. Nissin also entered the mainland Chinese market for the first time. For this expansion, the company chose to form its own network of wholly owned subsidiaries, establishing its first production plant in Guangdong in 1994. That was followed by plants in Shanghai in 1996, then Beijing in 1998. By the early 2000s, the company operated some 12 subsidiaries in the Chinese mainland. Yet the company's decision not to enter China through local joint ventures was credited with the group's relatively slow penetration of the vast Chinese market. In contrast with its strong share of the global market, some 9 percent worldwide, the company barely managed a 3 percent market share in China into the 2000s.

Global Noodle Leader in the 2000s

At the same time as it built its international network, Nissin backed up its increasingly global business with a continued commitment to product innovation, as well as a drive toward diversification. As early as 1986, the company entered the frozen foods business. That unit was boosted with the acquisition of frozen foods specialist Pegui Foods Co. (later renamed as Nissin Frozen Foods) in 1991. The company also entered the breakfast cereals market with the purchase of Cisco Co. That company had been the first to introduce breakfast cereals in Japan in 1963; under Nissin, the Cisco unit developed a ''cup''

Key Dates:

1948: Momofuku Ando founds the Chukososha Co. in Osaka and begins developing a method of producing instant noodles.

1958: The company changes its name to Nissin Food Products and launches Chikin Ramen, the first instant ramen soup.

1963: Nissin goes public on the Osaka and Tokyo Stock Exchanges.

1968: Nissin launches ''pillow'' type of noodles.

1970: The company establishes its first international subsidiary in the United States.

1971: Nissin launches Cup o' Noodles (later Cup Noodles), which becomes an international hit.

1975: A sales subsidiary is established in Brazil.

1978: Nissin launches production in its first U.S. plant.

1981: The company launches production in Brazil; a subsidiary is established in Singapore.

1984: Nissin enters the Hong Kong market.

1986: Production of frozen foods begins.

1988: Nissin acquires frozen burrito maker Camino Foods in the United States; the first retort pouch products are launched.

1991: Nissin establishes its first European subsidiary in The Netherlands; the company acquires frozen foods specialist Pegui in Japan.

1992: The first long-life fresh noodles are launched.

1994: Nissin enters the Chinese market with a subsidiary in Guangdong.

1999: The company launches production in India.

2001: The Chinese subsidiaries are consolidated under a single holding company.

2004: Nissin becomes the world's instant noodle market leader through a stake in Hebei Hualong F&N Industry Group.

2005: Founder Ando retires from the company.

version of its breakfast cereals, which proved popular with Japanese consumers.

Nissin also maintained its tradition of innovation. In 1988, the company became the first to develop new food preparation technology based on retort pouches. This led to the launch of LL cup noodles in 1992, which quickly became one of the company's hottest sellers. By 1995, the company had launched its SpaO brand of retort pouch spaghetti. In the meantime, Nissin also had solved an important obstacle in the development of the fresh noodle market, that of preservation. In 1992, the company launched the first of its long-life noodle products.

Nissin took steps to correct its slow growth in China at the beginning of the 2000s, merging its 12 Chinese subsidiaries under a single holding company in 2001. The company also continued to seek out new food areas. In the early 2000s, the company entered the ''functional food'' category, receiving approval to market a new line of health-promoting soups containing psyllium dietary fibers. The company also launched a dedicated Food Safety Research Institute in 2002.

Nissin's acquisition of a stake in Hebei Hualong F&N Industry Group in 2004 allowed the company to claim the global leadership position in the instant noodle soup category that year. Nissin also continued to seek ways of building its brand name. Starting in 1996, for example, the company's billboard, of a bowl of soup putting out real steam, had become a fixture in New York's Times Square. By 2005, the company had set its advertising sights still higher, launching a newly developed zero-gravity ''Space Ram'' for Japanese astronaut Soichi Noguchi's trip into space aboard the Discovery. In that year, as well, Nissin, now led by Koki Ando, announced that Momofuku Ando was retiring from his position as chairman of the board. Ando was by then acknowledged as one of the most influential figures in the 20th-century global food industry.

Principal Subsidiaries

Accelerated Freeze Drying Co., Ltd. (India); Camino Real Foods, Inc. (U.S.A.); Guangdong Shunde Nissin Foods Co., Ltd. (China); Indo Nissin Foods Ltd. (India); Miracle Foods Co., Ltd. (Hong Kong); Nissin Cisco Co., Ltd.; Nissin Food Products Co., Ltd. (Mexico); Nissin Foods (China) Holding Co., Ltd.; Nissin Foods (HK) Management Co., Ltd. (Hong Kong); Nissin Foods (Huabei) Co., Ltd. (China); Nissin Foods (Thailand) Co., Ltd.; Nissin Foods (U.S.A.) Co., Inc.; Nissin Foods B.V. (Netherlands); Nissin Foods Co., Ltd. (Hong Kong); Nissin Foods GmbH (Germany); Nissin Frozen Foods Co., Ltd.; Nissin Plastics Co., Ltd.; Nissin-Ajinomoto Alimentos Ltda. (Brazil); Nissin-Universal Robina Corporation (Philippines); NITEC (Europe) B.V. (Netherlands); NITEC (H.K.) Ltd. (Hong Kong); NITEC (U.S.A.), Inc.; P.T. NISSINMAS (Indonesia); Sapporo Nissin Co., Ltd.; Shandong Nissin Foods Co., Ltd. (China); Shandong Winner Food Products Co., Ltd. (China); Shanghai Nissin Foods Co., Ltd. (China); Winner Food Products Ltd. (Hong Kong); Zhuhai Golden Coast Winner Food Products Ltd. (China).

Principal Competitors

Toyo Suisan Kaisha Ltd.; House Foods Corporation; Nong Shim Company Ltd.; Tingyi Cayman Islands Holding Corporation; Asia Food and Properties Ltd.; Ottogi Corporation; Myojo Foods Company Ltd.; Tokatsu Foods Company Ltd.; Bing-Grae Company Ltd.

Further Reading

Al-Badri, Dominic, ''Oodles of Noodles,'' *Japan, Inc.,* June 2003.

Beech, Hannah, ''Instant Success,'' *Time Asia,* August 23, 1990.

Fong, Ricky, ''Nissin: Oodles of Chinese Noodles,'' *Daily Deal,* April 14, 2004.

Kageyama, Yuri, ''Food Innovator Still Taking on the World,'' *Enquirer,* February 13, 2001.

Katayama, Hiroko, ''The Last Noodle Emperor,'' *Forbes,* May 30, 1988, p. 306.

''Nissin Launches Space Ram,'' *Taipei Times,* July 28, 2005, p. 12.

''Nissin Seeks Recipe for Cup Noodle Sales in Asia,'' *TDC Trade,* March 25, 2004.

Yakushiji, Sayaka, ''Recipe for Success,'' *IHT/Asahi,* January 5, 2005.

—M.L. Cohen

Norfolk Southern Corporation

Three Commercial Place
Norfolk, Virginia 23510-9227
U.S.A.
Telephone: (757) 629-2600
Toll Free: (800) 531-6757
Fax: (757) 664-5069
Web site: http://www.nscorp.com

Public Company
Incorporated: 1980
Employees: 28,475
Sales: $7.31 billion (2004)
Stock Exchanges: New York
Ticker Symbol: NSC
NAIC: 482111 Line-Haul Railroads; 488210 Support
    Activities for Rail Transportation; 488510 Freight
    Transportation Arrangement; 551112 Offices of Other
    Holding Companies

Norfolk Southern Corporation (NS) is a holding company that owns and operates one of the nation's biggest railroad systems, the Norfolk Southern Railway Company. Its lines run through 22 states, mostly in the South and East, and extend into Ontario, Canada, covering approximately 21,300 miles of rail. About one-third of its rail was acquired in a 1998 takeover of lines formerly owned by Conrail Inc. Norfolk Southern also operates a coal, natural gas, and timber company through its subsidiary Pocahontas Land Corporation. Approximately one-quarter of Norfolk Southern's revenues come from the transportation of coal, coke, and iron ore. Intermodal services (the movement of trailers and containers on railroad freight cars) generates about 20 percent, with the remainder well balanced among the following sectors: automotive; chemicals; metals and construction; agriculture, consumer products, and government; and paper, clay, and forest products. The railway's predecessors, principally Norfolk and Western Railway Company and Southern Railway Company, in addition to Conrail, date back to the 1820s and 1830s.

19th-Century Roots of Norfolk and Western

Norfolk and Western Railway Company was the result of numerous mergers. It started as a ten-mile line, City Point Railroad, which served two small Virginia towns beginning in 1838. William Mahone orchestrated the company's first mergers. He was elected president of a successor, the Norfolk and Petersburg Railroad (N&P), in 1860. He joined the company on its founding in 1853 as chief engineer and was the innovator of a roadbed through swampland that continues to hold up under the huge tonnages of coal traffic. After the Civil War, N&P linked up with South Side Railroad and Virginia & Tennessee Railroad, forming Atlantic, Mississippi & Ohio Railroad (AM&O). In 1870 this line extended from Norfolk to Bristol, Virginia. The combined railroads were damaged during the war and reconstruction was slow and expensive. Half of the railroads in the South failed between 1873 and 1880. Mahone borrowed heavily and three years after the crash and financial panic of 1873, the company was put into receivership by its creditors. A private Philadelphia banking firm, E.W. Clark and Company, purchased the AM&O in 1881, changing its name to Norfolk and Western Railroad Company.

A partner in the firm, Frederick Kimball, took charge of Norfolk and Western, merging it with the Shenandoah Valley Railroad in 1882. Kimball's interest in minerals led to lines being built with access to coal deposits, although at this time the railroad was mainly an agricultural line, cotton being its primary freight. Four years later, the coal handled by Norfolk passed the one-million-ton mark. Within a decade, coal would account for the line's greatest traffic.

Henry Fink became president when the company emerged from bankruptcy in 1896 as Norfolk and Western Railway Company (NW). For the next three decades, NW expanded aggressively. Building through West Virginia, north to Ohio and south to North Carolina, NW established its trademark route. Between 1895 and 1905 railroads across the nation consolidated and improved operations. In 1901 NW acquired about 400,000 acres of coal reserves owned by the Philadelphia-based Flat-Top Coal Land Association; these properties were vested in a subsidiary called Pocahontas Coal & Coke Company

---

Company Perspectives:

Norfolk Southern's mission is to enhance the value of our stockholders' investment over time by providing quality freight transportation services and undertaking any other related businesses in which our resources, particularly our people, give the company an advantage.

(renamed Pocahontas Land Corporation in 1939). In 1904 Lucius Johnson became president of NW.

War Years

During World War I, traffic was heavy and equipment condition and upkeep suffered from material shortages. Government control of the railroads took place in 1917 and was relinquished in 1920. For the next ten years, NW consolidated its strength as a coal carrier. The early 1920s saw increased Interstate Commerce Commission (ICC) involvement in the industry and increased union activity. The drive for greater efficiency and reduced costs, as well as the company's coal revenues, helped NW through the Great Depression, but unprofitable branch lines were abandoned and equipment purchases were delayed.

With the start of World War II, NW rebounded. Traffic volume reached a peak in 1944. Robert H. Smith assumed the presidency in 1946. Between 1945 and 1950, $14 million was spent on improvements. During this same time, diesel locomotives were becoming an indelible presence in the industry. Although NW had great investments in coal-burning power and steam engines, the greater economy and efficiency of diesel were decisive; the company ordered its first diesel engines in 1955.

Mergers Through the Early 1980s

The 1950s were marked by union battles, the abandonment of steam power, and a decline in coal traffic, but growth nonetheless. Stuart Saunders became president in 1958. A lawyer, he stepped up the company's mergers through complicated transactions, beginning with Virginian Railway in 1959. In 1964 NW acquired two railways: Wabash, Nickel Plate, Pittsburgh & West Virginia and Akron, Canton & Youngstown. With this, NW gained a Midwestern presence, providing service between the Atlantic, the Great Lakes, and the Mississippi River. Saunders expected expansion to reduce the company's reliance on coal as a revenue source.

Following the flurry of merger activity in the 1960s, the ICC authorized rights to NW in 1971 for portions of the tracks of the Atchison, Topeka & Santa Fe Railway. NW began merger talks with Southern Railway in 1979. The year before the consummation of the NW-Southern merger in 1982, NW acquired the Illinois Terminal Railroad.

History of Southern Railway

Like NW, Southern Railway was the result of many railroad lines combined and reorganized, nearly 150 lines. The earliest of these lines was the South Carolina Canal & Rail Road Company, a nine-mile line chartered in 1827. It was the first regularly scheduled passenger train in the United States in 1830. It was also the first to carry U.S. troops and mail. Within three years, it was 136 miles long, the longest in the world.

Prior to the Civil War, rail expansion crossed the South. By 1857 Charleston, South Carolina, and Memphis, Tennessee, were linked by rail, but growth was stopped by the Civil War. With the devastation of the Southern economy and railroads by the war, rebuilding of the industry was slow. Repairs and reorganization took place during the postwar period, and new railroads were built along the Ohio and Mississippi Rivers.

Southern Railway (SR) was formed in 1894, when the Richmond & Danville merged with the East Tennessee, Virginia & Georgia Railroad. The company's first president was Samuel Spencer. Its line spread over 4,400 miles, two-thirds of which SR owned. The Alabama Great Southern Railway, and the Georgia Southern and Florida were also under SR's control. Over the span of Spencer's 12-year presidency, SR acquired many more lines and equipment, and revenues went from $17 million to more than $153 million. The company shifted from dependency on tobacco and cotton to more involvement with the South's industrial development. By 1916 SR had an 8,000-mile line over 13 states, establishing its territory for the next half century.

Fairfax Harrison became president in 1913. World War I traffic was substantial but was offset by inflation, and the postwar boom period helped pay for repairs and equipment replacement delayed by the war. In 1922 SR invested $77 million in improvements. The stock market crash of 1929 came two months after SR moved into lavish new headquarters. Many U.S. railroads were forced into bankruptcy in the early 1930s. SR operated at a loss for the first time in 1931 and began amassing debts. The company did not show a profit again until 1936.

Under Ernest Norris, SR recovered, paying its debts to the Reconstruction Finance Corporation in 1941. That same year SR purchased its first diesel equipment, and World War II began. Wartime traffic led to increased efficiency and safety. By 1951 SR owned a fleet of almost 850 diesel-electric units that drove nearly 92 percent of its freight service and 86 percent of its passenger service. SR became the first U.S. railroad to convert entirely to diesel-powered locomotives in 1953, closing the era of the steam locomotive.

SR prospered as a result of dieselization. The southern economy led the nation in growth in the late 1950s. SR took advantage of this growth by acquiring railroads and gaining access to developing industrial areas beginning with the 1952 purchase of the Louisiana-Southern Railway. In 1957 it acquired the Atlantic & North Carolina Railroad and in 1961 the Interstate Railroad, which brought SR to new coal fields in southwest Virginia. In 1963 the Central of Georgia merged with SR.

W. Graham Claytor became president in 1967, instituting the streamlined management and tough budgets that saw the company through the 1974 recession. An unrelated company called Norfolk Southern Railway was acquired in 1974, adding 622 miles of line in an area marked for economic growth. At this time, SR was thriving. There was a 70 percent increase in revenue between 1974 and 1978. In 1979 Harold Hall became president and later ushered the company through its merger with Norfolk and Western. SR was considered one of the best

Key Dates:

1827: South Carolina Canal & Rail Road Company, earliest forerunner of Southern Railway Company, is chartered.

1838: City Point Railroad, the earliest predecessor of Norfolk and Western Railway Company, is chartered.

1853: Norfolk and Petersburg Railroad (N&P), a successor to City Point, is organized.

1870: N&P is merged with Southside Railroad and Virginia & Tennessee Railroad to form Atlantic, Mississippi & Ohio Railroad (AM&O).

1881: The AM&O is bought out of receivership and renamed Norfolk and Western Railroad Company.

1894: Southern Railway Company (SR) is formed from the amalgamation of the Richmond & Danville and the East Tennessee, Virginia & Georgia Railroad.

1896: Norfolk and Western emerges from bankruptcy as Norfolk and Western Railway Company (NW).

1959: NW acquires Virginian Railway.

1963: SR acquires the Central of Georgia.

1964: Two railways—the Wabash, Nickel Plate, Pittsburgh & West Virginia and the Akron, Canton & Youngstown—are consolidated into NW.

1974: SR acquires Norfolk Southern Railway.

1980: Norfolk Southern Corporation (NS) is incorporated.

1982: NW and SR are consolidated within the NS holding company.

1985: NS acquires North American Van Lines, Inc.

1986: After several years of negotiation, NS's bid to acquire Consolidated Rail Corporation (Conrail) falls through.

1990: NS restructures its rail operations, changing SR's name to Norfolk Southern Railway Company and transferring ownership of NW to the newly named subsidiary.

1998: North American Van Lines is divested.

1999: Norfolk Southern and archrival CSX Corporation complete their carve-up of Conrail.

managed railroads in the industry. In 1980 the company enjoyed its fifth consecutive year of record profits.

At the time of the merger, both NW and SR were among the most profitable firms in the industry. Between 1971 and 1981, net income at NW had increased fivefold. At SR it had tripled. Prior to merging, both railroads had added many miles and much time to their transportation routes to avoid using each other's tracks; the amount of overlap was small but affected operations significantly. In some cases three days of transportation time was added just to circumvent ten miles of track operated by the other system. SR operated a 10,000-mile line between Washington, D.C.; New Orleans, Louisiana; Cincinnati, Ohio; and St. Louis, Missouri. NW had a 7,000-mile line between Norfolk and Kansas City.

1980s: Creation of Norfolk Southern Corp. and Subsequent Acquisitions

In 1980 Chessie System Inc. and Seaboard Coast Line Industries, Inc. merged, forming CSX Corporation. This provided

some impetus for the Norfolk Southern merger. Equally compelling was the complementary territories and corporate objectives of NW and SR. Norfolk Southern Corporation, incorporated in 1980 and completing its acquisition of the railroads in 1982, became the lowest cost, highest profit corporation in the industry. Merging also made NS the nation's fourth largest system in terms of track line. Robert Claytor, who had been president of NW, became the first chairman of Norfolk Southern Corporation. Huge assets and conservative investments kept NS sound in 1982, when the steel and coal businesses slowed, but NW's revenues dipped as a result. It was expected that SR's merchandise traffic would help offset NW's coal business if it slowed, and vice versa. Both slumped, however, in the early 1980s.

With an eye toward becoming the country's first integrated transportation company, NS moved to purchase North American Van Lines, Inc. (NAVL) in 1984. The acquisition was completed in 1985. NAVL was known mostly for its household moving, which, however, constituted only one-third of its revenues. Other services offered included commercial transport, moving general commodities from manufacturer to distributor, and transporting high-value products such as computers. NAVL was founded in Ohio in 1933, moved to Indiana in 1947, and was purchased by PepsiCo, Inc. in 1968. The purchase of NAVL by NS for $369 million put the recent industry deregulation policy of the ICC to the test. NS became the dominant railroad in trucking, developing a transportation system that provided both motor carrier and rail service.

In the mid-1980s, NS aggressively pursued the purchase of Consolidated Rail Corporation (Conrail) from the U.S. government. Conrail was founded in 1976 from six bankrupt northwestern railroads and subsequently became profitable. The purchase would have made NS the nation's largest railroad, but after several years of negotiations, it fell through. The unsuccessful bid to take over Conrail, however, resulted in 1986 in a profitable cooperation between the two companies, including an interchange agreement that allowed NS and Conrail to offer competitive services over the same areas.

In the mid-1980s NS's principal revenue-producing commodities, aside from fuel, were paper, chemicals, and automobiles. In 1985 NS had revenues of $3.8 billion and was the most profitable railroad in the nation. The following year NS formed Triple Crown Services Company as a subsidiary specializing in intermodal services. In 1987 Arnold McKinnon succeeded Robert Claytor as CEO and chairman and Harold Hall became vice-chairman.

The company further profited from its investments in Santa Fe Southern Pacific and Piedmont Aviation, both of which it sold later at huge profits. By 1988 coal and merchandise traffic began to increase after a long slump. McKinnon worked on cutting costs and smoothing the way for increased intermodal traffic, traffic that shifts easily between railroad and highway. Only 6 percent of NS's business in 1988, intermodal traffic posed great growth potential.

With the recession in 1989, automobile and steel industries suffered, as did housing and, therefore, lumber shipments and coal. The decline in industrial freight shipments hit railroads hard. NS's revenues were down by about 3 percent because of traffic declines early in 1989. At the same time fuel prices and insurance costs rose.

Growth in the 1990s, Particularly Through Conrail Carve-Up

Although heavy freight and merchandise revenues remained lower in 1990, increased shipments of coal, coke, and iron ore helped the company offset losses. Profits dipped in 1990, the result of higher fuel costs and the expense of employee layoffs and early retirements. At the end of 1990, NS restructured its rail operations, changing Southern Railway's name to Norfolk Southern Railway Company and transferring ownership of Norfolk and Western to it. The company spent $20 million in the early 1990s to improve its routes for double-stacked containers and vied with the trucking industry for freight. NS entered a joint venture with Conrail in 1993 to run a hybrid truck and rail service. It used vehicles called Road-Railers, which could convert quickly from truck to rail car, and ran these on a network that joined Chicago, Atlanta, and Harrisburg, Pennsylvania. NS also acquired more varied business in its home southern territory as auto companies built new plants. Toyota expanded a plant in Georgetown, Kentucky, and BMW built a new factory in Greer, South Carolina, in the early 1990s, giving NS a lucrative new product, automobiles, to ship. In August 1992, meanwhile, McKinnon retired, and David R. Goode took over as chairman, president, and CEO.

NS was a remarkably stable and profitable company despite the downturn in coal exports, and it was known for its low costs and efficient management. Much of its profits came from running the easy downhill route from the coal mines in the Appalachians to the port of Hampton Roads, Virginia, where waiting tankers took its freight abroad. One snag on its profitability, however, was its trucking unit, North American Van Lines, which continued to do poorly. The company sought to sell off two of its trucking unit's divisions in 1993, after trucking operations came in with a loss of close to $40 million in 1992. The rest of its trucking operations was sold off in 1998.

Meanwhile, NS began merger talks with its old friend Conrail. Conrail controlled 12,200 miles of rail, particularly in the industrial Northeast and Midwest. Heavy traffic between Chicago and Philadelphia and from East St. Louis to Boston gave the firm much of its profits. When Conrail and NS began to talk in 1994, Conrail was valued at around $4 billion. Negotiations between the two companies broke down in the summer of 1994, however, apparently because Conrail wanted a price substantially higher than that of market value. After talks between the companies broke off, Conrail's CEO James Hagen told *Forbes* magazine in a November 21, 1994, interview, "We don't need a merger." Yet two years later, in November 1996, Conrail was on the verge of accepting a merger offer from rival railroad CSX. NS topped CSX's bid, offering $9 billion for the company that had been too expensive at more than $4 billion in 1994. In March 1997 a new deal was cemented, involving all three companies: CSX bought Conrail for $10.3 billion and then sold half of Conrail's routes (58 percent of the company) to NS for $5.9 billion. This led to what one analyst, transportation curator of the Smithsonian Institution William Withuhn called "the most complicated merger in history," according to a *Wall Street Journal* article from June 10, 1998. Norfolk Southern and

CSX had to divide up the thousands of miles of Conrail track, despite daunting physical and administrative problems. The two companies spent more than a billion dollars each expanding tracks, terminals, and equipment, and had other headaches such as working their computer systems into Conrail's. The breakup of Conrail was carefully plotted, yet myriad problems led to delays. By January 1999 NS was paying out approximately $1 million every day in interest costs on the roughly $6 billion it had borrowed for its share of Conrail. Finally, the merger was physically complete on June 1, 1999, when Conrail's rail lines went into use by its respective owners. The many expenses incurred by the merger dampened income for that year, but to NS it seemed a wise long-term investment. The company was now about evenly matched with CSX, splitting the eastern United States between them, just as two other railroads dominated the West. NS was convinced it would be a stronger company with Conrail's addition, as the expanded mileage opened many more markets to it.

Early 2000s: Post-Conrail Indigestion Followed by a Turnaround

Norfolk Southern's difficulties digesting the Conrail lines were more than evident in the dropoff in profits that followed the deal. The company had netted $734 million in 1998, but this figure dropped to $239 million in 1999 and then $172 million in 2000. After the 1999 carve-up, the NS system suffered from widespread service breakdowns, including blocked tracks, lost freight cars, and delivery delays. Many customers switched their shipments to trucks, cutting into revenues. At the same time, a sharp decline in coal exports, stemming largely from stiff competition from Australia, hurt NS's core business of hauling coal. Further reductions in profits were incurred from charges taken to slash the workforce in order to cut expenses. The payroll was trimmed by 3,500 in 2000 and then a further cut of 1,000 was announced in January 2001. The latter cutback included the closure of several rail years and repair facilities identified as "redundant." That same month, Norfolk Southern suffered another black eye when it agreed to settle a class-action lawsuit filed in 1993 by African American employees who alleged they were denied promotion to management on the basis of race. NS agreed to pay $28 million to the plaintiffs and to establish new promotion policies.

To turn matters around, Norfolk Southern, among other initiatives, launched the Thoroughbred Operating Plan in the summer of 2001. Named after the firm's longtime logo of a speedy black stallion, this effort aimed to fix NS's customer service problems by implementing new train schedules, operating trains over shortened, more direct routes, and bypassing as many freight yards as feasible to reduce delays. By February 2002 Norfolk Southern's on-time delivery rate had improved from 57 percent to 86 percent. By another key rail industry yardstick, the operating ratio, a measure of efficiency, and profitability, comparing expenses with revenues (the lower the figure the better), NS seemed to have completely turned the corner by 2004. That year, the firm's operating ratio stood at 76.7 percent, the best showing since 1998 (and therefore since the Conrail split-up). Indeed, 2004 was a record year for Norfolk Southern: $7.31 billion in revenues and net income of $923 million. In part, NS was riding a significant increase in demand for rail transport, at the expense of the trucking industry, propelled by a combination of several factors: increasing highway congestion, rising fuel prices, demand for more environmentally friendly transportation options, and changes in trucking regulation. In this shifting climate, the surging demand for NS's intermodal services, the firm's fastest-growing sector, came as no surprise. Intermodal revenues jumped 24 percent in 2004, reaching $1.54 billion, second only to the $1.73 billion generated by coal shipments.

The year 2004 also saw Norfolk Southern and CSX reorganize the structure of their Conrail holdings. Since 1999 the two firms had jointly owned Conrail, and NS had operated the routes and assets of a Conrail subsidiary called Pennsylvania Line LLC (the former Pennsylvania Railroad, incorporated in 1846), while CSX did the same for New York Central Lines LLC. In August 2004, with the approval of the Surface Transportation Board (the regulatory successor to the now abolished ICC), NS and CSX took direct ownership and control of these subsidiaries, and Pennsylvania Line was merged into Norfolk Southern Railway Company. The Conrail joint venture nevertheless continued to exist, owning, managing, and operating certain shared assets, such as switching facilities and terminals, used by both railways.

Late in 2004 a succession plan appeared to be in place for the eventual retirement of Goode. In October, Charles W. Moorman IV was named president of Norfolk Southern, marking him as the likely heir apparent. A civil engineer by training who had spent his entire career at NS, Moorman had most recently headed up Thoroughbred Technology and Telecommunications, Inc., a unit that had developed fiber optic lines along the railroad's routes and that had been forced to take an $84 million writedown of assets in 2003 following the implosion of the telecom sector stemming from its overbuilding of capacity. In January 2005, just months after Moorman's promotion, a Norfolk Southern freight train carrying deadly chlorine gas crashed and derailed in the small textile town of Graniteville, South Carolina, killing nine people, sending more than 200 to the hospital, and forcing the evacuation of all 5,400 people within a mile of the crash. A little more than a week later, Norfolk Southern offered an official apology to the town, and the company later set aside $35 million to cover expenses related to the accident. In August 2005 a federal judge approved an agreement whereby NS would compensate persons evacuated from the accident vicinity and those suffering minor injuries. The company still had to contend with lawsuits filed by people who incurred more serious injuries and the families of those who died.

Principal Subsidiaries

Conrail Inc. (58%); Lambert's Point Docks, Incorporated; Norfolk Southern Properties, Inc.; Norfolk Southern Railway Company; Pocahontas Land Corporation; Thoroughbred Technology and Telecommunications, Inc.; Transworks Inc.; Triple Crown Services Company.

Principal Competitors

CSX Corporation.

Further Reading

"All Steamed Up over Conrail," *Business Week,* November 4, 1996, p. 54.

Byrne, Harlan S., "Right on Track," *Barron's,* July 11, 2005, p. 23.

Cooper, Mason Y., *Norfolk and Western's Shenandoah Valley Line,* Forest, Va.: Norfolk and Western Historical Society, 1998, 214 p.

Davis, Burke, *The Southern Railway: Road of the Innovators,* Chapel Hill: University of North Carolina Press, 1985, 309 p.

Dinsmore, Christopher, "Norfolk Southern, CSX Announce Date for Conrail Breakup," *Knight-Ridder/Tribune Business News,* January 20, 1999.

——, "Norfolk Southern Reports Record Year," *Norfolk (Va.) Virginian-Pilot,* January 27, 2005, p. D1.

——, "Norfolk, Va.-Based Railroad Company Looks Forward to Conrail Takeover," *Knight-Ridder/Tribune Business News,* May 13, 1999.

——, "One-Time Charges Suppress Norfolk Southern Earnings," *Norfolk (Va.) Virginian-Pilot,* January 29, 2004, p. D1.

——, "A Railroad on the Rebound: One Year After the Conrail Deal, Norfolk Southern Is Bouncing Back," *Norfolk (Va.) Virginian-Pilot,* May 28, 2000, p. D1.

——, "Railroad's Earnings Off Track," *Norfolk (Va.) Virginian-Pilot,* January 27, 2000, p. D1.

——, "Riding a Renaissance," *Norfolk (Va.) Virginian-Pilot,* January 30, 2005, p. D1.

Gilbert, Nick, "The Road Not Taken," *Financial World,* March 14, 1995, p. 28.

Machalaba, Daniel, "Conrail Carve-Up Turns Toward Its Real Uphill Climb," *Wall Street Journal,* June 10, 1998, p. B4.

——, "Conrail Faces Labor Unrest After Walkout," *Wall Street Journal,* August 17, 1998, p. B4.

——, "Norfolk Southern Aims to Get Back on the Golden Track," *Wall Street Journal,* January 30, 2001, p. B4.

——, "Norfolk Southern Charts New Course As Coal Profits Slip," *Wall Street Journal,* April 27, 1993, p. B4.

——, "Norfolk Southern Corp. Seeks Buyers for Two of Its Trucking Unit's Divisions," *Wall Street Journal,* June 28, 1993, p. A9C.

——, "Norfolk Southern Is Revamping Its Rail Freight Network," *Wall Street Journal,* March 28, 2002, p. B3.

Norman, James R., "Choose Your Partners!," *Forbes,* November 21, 1994, pp. 88–89.

O'Brien, Dennis, "Norfolk Southern Fourth-Quarter Earnings Up," *Norfolk (Va.) Virginian-Pilot,* January 25, 2001, p. D1.

——, "Norfolk Southern Settles Lawsuit for $28 Million," *Norfolk (Va.) Virginian-Pilot,* January 10, 2001, p. D1.

——, "Norfolk Southern to Restructure," *Norfolk (Va.) Virginian-Pilot,* January 24, 2001, p. D1.

Shapiro, Carolyn, "Profits Up for Quarter, Year at Norfolk Southern," *Norfolk (Va.) Virginian-Pilot,* January 30, 2003, p. D1.

Striplin, E.F. Pat, *The Norfolk and Western: A History,* rev. ed., Norfolk, Va.: Norfolk and Western Historical Society, 1997, 234 p.

Thomas, David St. John, and Patrick Whitehouse, *SR 150: A Century and a Half of the Southern Railway,* Newton Abbot, Devon, U.K.: David & Charles, 2002, 207 p.

Vantuono, William C., "David Goode Keeps Norfolk Southern Ahead of the Curve," *Railway Age,* January 2005, pp. 23 + .

Weber, Joseph, "Highballing Toward Two Big Railroads?," *Business Week,* March 17, 1997, pp. 32–33.

Zellner, Wendy, "Steep Grade for a Rail Deal: Taking Over Conrail Has Snarled CSX and Norfolk Southern," *Business Week,* July 5, 1999, p. 29.

—Carol I. Keeley
—updates: A. Woodward; David E. Salamie

OfficeTiger, LLC

475 5th Avenue, 16th Floor
New York, New York 10016
U.S.A.
Telephone: (212) 629-9275
Fax: (212) 629-9276
Web site: http://www.officetiger.com

Private Company
Incorporated: 1999
Employees: 3,000
Sales: $100 million (2005 est.)
NAIC: 561210 Facilities Support Services

OfficeTiger, LLC is a New York City-based global provider of business support services, with the work done in India and Sri Lanka. Although a practitioner of offshore outsourcing, OfficeTiger does not simply transfer high-paying jobs from the United States and the United Kingdom to India and Sri Lanka as a way to save money for its clients. Rather, the firm tries to provide what it calls judgment-based Business Process Outsourcing (BPO) solutions. Indian workers, well educated and highly skilled, provide support to Western employees who can concentrate on higher value tasks and enhance their productivity. OfficeTiger offers a variety of support services, including document preparation and desktop publishing, market research, financial analysis, and a full range of accounting functions. Clients include investment banks, law offices, and consulting and accounting firms. OfficeTiger's India facility operates 24 hours a day, structured to provide quick turnaround on client requests. In addition to its corporate headquarters in New York, OfficeTiger maintains offices in London and Frankfurt, Germany. The company is run by co-CEOs Randolph Altschuler and Joseph Sigelman. Altschuler operates out of New York, while Sigelman spends most of his time in Chennai, India, where the firm maintains a pair of large offshore services facilities.

Cofounders College Friends in the 1990s

OfficeTiger was founded by Altschuler and Sigelman, both raised in New York City and accepted at Princeton University. As freshmen they met in the cafeteria and became best friends, and later went on to Harvard Business School together. Afterward they both landed high-paying jobs on Wall Street with investment banks, Altschuler at Blackstone Group Inc. and Sigelman with Goldman, Sachs & Co., working in London. Late one night in 1999 Sigelman was working on a PowerPoint presentation and growing increasingly frustrated with the work coming back from the typing pool, fraught with fresh errors every time it was returned. Sigelman called Altschuler in New York and discovered that his friend was enduring the same kind of clerical horrors. It was clear that typing pool employees and temps lacked the drive and focus necessary to turn out the kind of work business people required. The two men in their mid-20s felt that there must be a better way to provide business support services and a more dedicated source of labor than artists and out-of-work actors. Sigelman thought of India, which he had visited with his family as a child. He had always been impressed with the country. "You met people in factories or running the elevator who had the intelligence and spirit to do so much more," he told Kate Boo of *The New Yorker.* "We thought, why not release that talent?"

Founders Quitting High-Paying Jobs in the Late 1990s

Sigelman and Altschuler decided to launch a business to provide word processing to financial services firms on an outsourced basis, drawing on the labor that India had to offer at inexpensive rates. It was all made possible by contemporary technology that allowed people in New York and India to work together on a real-time basis. "No one thought it was a viable idea," Sigelman told *Business Week,* "but we decided to do it anyway." They quit their jobs in 1999 and spent several months working up a business plan. They named their start-up company OfficeTiger after the Princeton mascot, the Tiger, and lined up $18 million in funding from U.K. venture capital funds Mountgrange Capital and Elwin Capital.

Since Altschuler was married, it was decided that he would remain in New York to build up the sales operations, while Sigelman would spend most of his time in India. In the beginning, however, both men came to India to establish the outsourcing operation. They had to negotiate a difficult course in obtaining regulatory approval in India, steering clear of corrupt

---

Company Perspectives:

OfficeTiger's vision is to change the way the world does business by leading the new generation of industry-focused, judgment-based Business Process Outsourcing (BPO) solutions.

---

officials, before finally setting up in the city of Madras with its high concentration of talent. OfficeTiger also received a ten-year "tax holiday" from the Indian government.

The company's first facility was just a sheet-metal shed. Its first service line was Enterprise Document Services, offering to do PowerPoint presentations for investment banks and other firms and word processing for law firms. "We had virtually no business," Altschuler told *The New Yorker*. "At the time people thought it was crazy to be sending work to India. So we had a hundred people sitting in a room and we'd get one fax a day to type. When the fax came through, it was like a five-alarm fire. . . ." Altschuler returned home to New York, opened an office above a Dunkin' Donuts, and began pestering former Wall Street colleagues to give their service a try.

As work began to come in and the Indian operation found its feet and performed well, OfficeTiger attracted repeat business. In a case study written for WorldTrade Executive Inc., Altschuler recalled, "We began to see a lot more opportunities. Bankers started saying, 'You know, I'd like to really understand some background on the companies that I'm going to be talking about in this presentation. Can you help me do some research on that?' " After OfficeTiger established itself in research, clients asked if the firm could also provide some financial analysis. In this incremental way, OfficeTiger added more demanding services. "We were really the first company that was focused on what we call 'judgment dependent services,' " Altschuler explained. "So it wasn't just inputting a spreadsheet or doing a rote transactional task, but the professional had to step back and think, 'What is the appropriate thing for me to do here?' Even in a PowerPoint presentation, the customers come to me and they've got an idea what they're looking for, but they're looking for me to really make the call."

OfficeTiger began to add staff at a rapid clip, hiring employees a team at a time to serve clients as they contracted services. The company established offices in a shopping mall in Chennai, and had no difficulty in attracting highly skilled people to occupy bank after bank of cubicles. According to *The New Yorker*, the company sometimes received "fifteen hundred applicants a day, many of them accompanied by parents who pray as their sons and daughters take one test after another in the hope of earning an interview." Only a small percentage of applicants, the cream of the crop, would find employment. Sigelman and Altschuler had one simple rule of thumb: Hire people smarter than themselves. OfficeTiger paid well above the market rate by Indian standards, about $1,000 a month, but a far cry from the $8,000 a month some of their employees might earn doing the same kind of judgment dependent work on Wall Street. It was that price difference as well as the work ethic of Indians, who were committed to performing even the most mundane task with "full sincerity," as the locals called it, that combined to make OfficeTiger such an

immediate success in New York and London. In Chennai OfficeTiger quickly achieved a status afforded few employers. According to *The New Yorker*, "Workers were so pleased by their affiliation that they put it on their wedding invitations, just below their fathers' names."

There were some cultural miscommunications to smooth out along the way. To motivate the staff, Sigelman made the mistake of offering on-the-spot payments, not realizing that the employees considered it to be demeaning to accept wads of cash in front of others. Sigelman also had to contend with life at the hotel where he resided. He enjoyed a great deal of success recruiting employees from the reception desk, but had less luck, according to *The New Yorker*, in reprogramming "the hotel coffee-shop pianist, who, having realized that Joe is perhaps the only Jew in Chennai, routinely serenades him with 'Have Nagila' when he sits down to lunch, even when his companion is a Kuwaiti investor." There was no compromise in terms of dress at the office, however. Only Western business attire was accepted. Women were not allowed to wear saris, and men wore ties, sometimes passed from one shift to the next, since not everyone owned one.

Because OfficeTiger landed the business of competing firms it had to go to great lengths to make sure teams assigned to handle their business were kept separate. Regardless, security issues were a major concern of all clients. The first step in providing security was the implementation of a thorough screening procedure, which was just as unforgiving as the testing process in weeding out unacceptable employees. In the end less than 2 percent of applicants found employment at OfficeTiger. When they reported to work, it was to a single point of entry, manned by guards who checked each employee. No personal belongings were allowed inside, and women were allowed to bring in a handbag only. Swipe cards were used to control access within the facility. In addition, if a client required, OfficeTiger maintained a secured environment within its secured environment, with more guards on duty to man another single point of access and a second set of swipe cards required. In addition, computer drives were locked, Internet access limited to people working directly with clients, and two levels of confidentiality agreements put in place, between OfficeTiger and its employees and between clients and OfficeTiger personnel.

Acquiring Devonshire in 2004

By 2004 OfficeTiger was generating annual revenues of $20 million and adding employees at a rapid pace. The company received an influx of cash in June 2004, raising $50 million from private equity firm Francisco Partners and earmarking the money for acquisitions to expand the company's range of service. Some of that money was soon put to use in the October 2004 acquisition of Devonshire, a British outsourcing company with some 200 clients in the financial, legal, consulting, design, and pharmaceutical fields. The funds also were used to establish an operation in Colombo, Sri Lanka, an effort to achieve geopolitical risk diversification. In addition, OfficeTiger expanded its Indian operation, opening a new 65,000-square-foot, six-floor dedicated building to supplement the original location in Chennai.

OfficeTiger continued to pursue an expansion strategy in 2005, completing a pair of significant acquisitions. In a deal

<table>
<tr><td colspan="2">**Key Dates:**</td></tr>
<tr><td>**1999:**</td><td>The company is founded.</td></tr>
<tr><td>**2000:**</td><td>The company's first revenues are booked.</td></tr>
<tr><td>**2004:**</td><td>Devonshire is acquired.</td></tr>
<tr><td>**2005:**</td><td>MortgageRamp Inc. is acquired.</td></tr>
</table>

valued between $25 million and $30 million, OfficeTiger bought General Motors Acceptance Corporation Commercial Services' Atlanta-based MortgageRamp Inc., the addition of which was expected to increase sales by about 35 percent and add greatly to the firm's real estate back-office business. Some of OfficeTiger's clients were already involved in the equity side of real estate, but MortgageRamp brought with it clients from the debt side of the industry as well. Services to this sector were expected to begin shifting overseas, and OfficeTiger was well positioned to reap a large portion of that business. The increase in size also set up OfficeTiger to make a public offering of stock, something Altschuler and Sigelman had dismissed in the past. Moreover, the MortgageRamp acquisition was important to the future of OfficeTiger because it was becoming increasingly apparent that the outsourcing industry was ripe for a shakeout and size would not matter a great deal. OfficeTiger hoped to be one of the companies that emerged from the pack. It also was looking to new countries to establish operations and improve its geographic diversity, eyeing the Philippines and possibly Eastern Europe. "It's not about India," Altschuler told *Securities Industry News.* "It's about global sourcing."

Principal Subsidiaries

Devonshire; MortgageRamp Inc.

Principal Competitors

WNS Global Services; ICICI OneSource Ltd.

Further Reading

Agnihotri, Ameeta, "Tiger on the Prowl," *Hindu,* February 24, 2003.

Ante, Spencer E., "OfficeTiger Roams Toward an IPO," *Business Week,* September 12, 2005, p. 92.

Barrie, Giles, "When Manish and Martin Went East: OfficeTiger Is a 'Hedge' by Two of Property's Best-Known Entrepreneurs Against the Threat to the UK Office Market from Asia," *Property Week,* October 3, 2003, p. 40.

Boo, Kate, "The Best Job in Town," *The New Yorker,* June 28, 2004.

Kripalani, Manjeet, "OfficeTiger: Hear It Roar," *Business Week,* July 11, 2005, p. 68.

Merchant, Khozem, " 'Business Is Roaring' at Office Tiger," *Business Standard,* August 21, 2003.

"Showing Its Stripes—A Conversation with OfficeTiger's Randy Altschuler," *Offshore Business Sources: Special Report on Law and Strategy,* World Trade Executive Inc., 2004.

Slater, Joanna, "Calling India. . . . Why Wall Street Is Dialing Overseas for Research," *Wall Street Journal,* October 2, 2003, p. C5.

Zunitch, Victoria, "Ivy Leaguers Book Passage to India," *Securities Industry News,* April 18, 2005.

—Ed Dinger

Changing Lives One Smile at a Time

Operation Smile, Inc.

6435 Tidewater Drive
Norfolk, Virginia 23509
U.S.A.
Telephone: (757) 321-7645
Toll Free: (888) 677-6453
Fax: (757) 321-7660
Web site: http://www.operationsmile.org

Private Company
Incorporated: 1987
Employees: 50
Revenues: $43.8 million (2004)
NAIC: 813410 Civic and Social Organizations

Operation Smile, Inc. is a private, nonprofit volunteer medical services organization that provides free reconstructive surgery and related healthcare to children of developing countries and the United States, with special attention to cleft lips and cleft palates. In addition, Operation Smile provides medical training to physicians and other healthcare professionals around the world in order to encourage self-sufficiency. Through these efforts, the organization brings together healthcare professionals within the public and private medical sectors to provide volunteer care in order to improve the quality of life of the children treated by Operation Smile.

Humble Beginnings: 1967–82

Bill Magee intended to be a dentist. The son of a general practitioner and one of 12 children, he had modest plans for his life. His high school sweetheart, Kathy, planned to be a nurse. "We had pretty conventional goals," Bill said, "We thought we'd get married, have a bunch of kids and live in New Jersey."

After getting married in 1967, Bill and Kathy moved to Maryland so that Bill could finish his last year of dental school. Kathy became a public health nurse, working with those in the poorest neighborhoods of Baltimore. Then Bill was introduced to facial surgery and was intrigued by it. "I liked the artistry," he said, "Moving people's jaws around; making an attractive

face." Over nine years of study followed, including advanced studies in Switzerland, Germany, and Scotland. In addition, he was awarded the Hays-Fulbright Scholar Grant and received training under Dr. Paul Tessier, the father of craniofacial surgery. After his studies, Magee and his wife settled down in Norfolk, Virginia, presumably to begin the life they had initially planned. Bill began a private practice, while also performing surgery for economically challenged children in Virginia. In so many ways, they had come far from their working-class neighborhood in Fort Lee, New Jersey. Nonetheless they had no idea what lay ahead and how much further they would be stretched.

In 1982, a trip to the Philippines changed Bill and Kathy's life forever. The trip consisted of a group of American healthcare professionals volunteering their time in order to operate on children who were suffering from cleft lips and cleft palates. Bill's intent for the trip was to learn. "I wanted to become better as a surgeon," recalled Bill, "but what I saw changed my life." During the five-day trip, with the surgical team working 16-hour days, nearly 150 children in three cities were operated on. They had changed the lives of these children and their families, but Bill Magee felt wracked with guilt. Each operation took less than an hour, a fact that he was struck with every day when taking his lunch break. In the time it took him to eat his lunch, another child's life could be completely changed. For the good they had done, the experience was heartbreaking and emotionally exhausting. "Everywhere we turned, there was a sea of deformities," Kathy said. "People pushed their babies at us, tugged at our sleeves with tears in their eyes and begged us to help their children."

Arriving back in Norfolk, the question was not whether to continue helping those children in need, but how to do so. They gave their undertaking a name, Operation Smile, and decided that the best way to start was with a grassroots effort. Their flame of excitement quickly lit a fire and soon Operation Smile became a citywide mission. There were bake sales and potluck dinners, and, armed with donated surgical supplies and equipment, the Magees arrived back in Manila with 18 volunteer doctors, nurses, and technicians. This time they were able to help 200 children, but hundreds more remained on the waiting list and thousands more were just beginning to hear of their

Company Perspectives:

Throughout the world, Operation Smile volunteers to repair childhood facial deformities while building public and private partnerships that advocate for sustainable healthcare systems for children and families. Together, we create smiles, change lives, heal humanity.

efforts. Although it seemed nearly impossible, the Magees were determined to return again. It was clear that Operation Smile was to become a permanent endeavor.

Dead tired, the Magees were spurred ahead by the visions of those who waited for them to return. They went about asking for help. They searched for volunteers for the missions, surgeons, nurses, dentists, speech therapists, psychologists, and physical therapists. They searched for private donors and corporate sponsors and help from every organization they could think of. The goals of the mission spread by word-of-mouth. The astonishing fact that each cleft lip and palate surgery cost about $250 and took only about 45 minutes to perform moved many people. The volunteers that they had taken on their second trip went home with their own stories of those whom they had helped and the hundreds more waiting to be helped. The response was overwhelming.

Dream Growing into Reality: 1982–2002

Many prominent companies, including Johnson & Johnson and Abbott Laboratories, committed to providing long-term gifts-in-kind. These donations, consisting of pharmaceuticals, surgical instruments, and medical supplies, were not only appreciated, but were inherent to the success of each mission. In 2005, Operation Smile was in need of anesthesia for trips to Lima, Peru. Abbott Labs quickly donated the needed medicine and sent a representative to witness how the product contributions benefited the children treated by Operation Smile. In addition, the company donated an annual supply worth about $500,000.

Service organizations also quickly became an integral part of Operation Smile's success. Groups such as the General Federation of Women's Clubs raised money for missions and, according to Operation Smile, donated many personal hygiene products, quilts, toys, and hospital gowns. Members of Rotary International also raised hundreds of thousands of dollars of support over the years, as well as giving countless hours of time.

On one of the first missions, Bridgette Magee, Bill and Kathy's daughter, accompanied them. Touched by Bridgette's compassion and unique strength on the mission, Kathy asked her daughter and her daughter's friend, Danny Rosen, to host a fundraiser. They would be raising money for the school in the Filipino community that they had served in. Together, Bridgette and Danny were able to assemble a group of students willing to give their time and efforts to children in need. This group collected money and books for the school. Far surpassing their original goals, they raised enough funds to build an entire wing on the school. In the grassroots tradition of Operation Smile, word spread of this student group and quickly other groups were formed around the world. Thousands of high school and college

students created Student Associations in the United States, Asia, Africa, and Latin America and, according to Operation Smile, "annually contributed approximately $400,000 to the surgical costs of children, as well as donating hundreds of toys and school supplies for the patients and their families."

In 1996, Operation Smile received the first Conrad N. Hilton Humanitarian Prize, a $1 million donation. According to *Management Review*, the Hilton Prize was about one-quarter of Operation Smile's annual cash budget at the time. "We were really humbled by [the Hilton Prize]. There were a large number of major organizations in the world that had applied for it," said Bill Magee. "I've often said that Operation Smile is like a funnel, and at the top of the funnel are literally thousands of people—many of whom never have a name—and as the funnel narrows, it comes down to an operating table with a surgeon, anesthesiologist and a nurse." Magee explained that the prize would allow the organization to offer medical care to more than 17,500 youths.

In 1999, Operation Smile completed the largest ever surgical mission dedicated to correcting and treating cleft lips and cleft palates. The mission, called *World Journey of Hope '99*, brought "3,000 volunteers to 18 countries to treat more than 5,000 children," according to Operation Smile. Medical technology companies such as Becton, Dickinson & Company donated items including catheters, ACE bandages, and surgical instruments. "Supporting this journey is one way we continue our strong tradition of commitment to meeting the health and medical needs of communities around the world," said Clateo Castellini, president, chairman, and CEO of Becton, Dickinson. Operation Smile was then able to donate medical and educational equipment to each of the host countries in an effort to encourage better healthcare.

Unfortunately, also in 1999, Operation Smile faced some anonymous allegations regarding the charity's management and the quality of its medical care. Prompted by the death of a patient in China and charges of shoddy surgical practices, the organization underwent an independent review. According to *The New York Times*, "the charity came under increasing criticism from volunteers, members of its board and foreign doctors, who said the charity was practicing assembly-line medicine by putting volume ahead of patient safety." In early 2000, Operation Smile acknowledged that there had been some improper oversight, and promised its worldwide chapters "sweeping changes." Amid some controversy, the organization continued its missions.

The year 2000 brought some exposure for Operation Smile and Bill Magee in the Information Technology (IT) industry. Speaking at the World Congress 2000 on Information Technology (WCIT), Magee lobbied for the use of IT within the medical services world. The *Central News Agency* (Taiwan) quoted Magee as saying that Operation Smile "has already conducted 'long-distance, cross-continent' craniofacial surgical procedures through the medium of television conferencing and the Internet." Magee noted that several surgical procedures had been performed in Cambodia by local surgeons with direction from plastic surgeons in the United States. The direction was received via a broadband Internet system. Magee also stated that he planned to create an online college for medical personnel in underdeveloped countries in the hopes that through Internet

---

Key Dates:

1982: Operation Smile is founded by Dr. William and Kathleen Magee.
1996: Operation Smile receives the first Conrad N. Hilton Humanitarian Prize.
1999: *World Journey of Hope '99* mission commences.
2002: Operation Smile celebrates 20th anniversary.
2005: Movie *Smile* is released.

---

teaching, they would be able to "upgrade their practices." Magee's speech was well-received, and, according to the *New Straits Times*, "captured the hearts of his audience."

20th Anniversary and Beyond

In 2002, Operation Smile celebrated its 20th anniversary, marking it with a trip to the Philippines. The anniversary mission involved four sites, including the site of the original mission in 1982. Since its inception, the operation had expanded to cover many other cities in that country as well as outreach to 19 other nations.

Over the next years, the Magees' vision continued to grow much in the way it was begun. The grassroots efforts that were so much a part of the operation's beginning continued to be an essential aspect of its continuation. In 2003, hikers from Atlanta, Georgia, climbed Mount Kilimanjaro in an effort to raise $100,000 for Operation Smile. Student groups had bake sales and car washes with the belief that every little bit helped. Women's groups sewed hospital gowns and held Bingo nights. On a larger scale, Sephora introduced a lip balm whose net proceeds benefited Operation Smile.

In 2005, a man named Jeffrey Kramer wrote and directed a film called *Smile*. The movie was loosely based on the work done by Operation Smile. Kramer stated that the film was fiction, but, in his words, "based on 80,000 true stories." Some of the film's proceeds were slated to be donated to Operation Smile, but, "more importantly," Kathy Magee said, "is the inspiration the film could evoke in young people." According to her, "they become volunteers for the future." That year, Operation Smile could proudly state that "more than 90,000 children have been treated by thousands of volunteers in 25 countries and more than 10,000 healthcare professionals have been trained."

According to the Cleft Palate Foundation, one of every 700 newborns born in the United States is affected by cleft lip and/or cleft palate. However, there were very few studies indicating the amount of children born with such defects in countries such as the Philippines and Iraq. Regardless of the numbers, Operation Smile vowed that "the promise Bill and Kathy Magee made years ago will not be fulfilled until every child with a correctable facial deformity is given a chance to smile."

Principal Competitors

The American Red Cross; Boys & Girls Clubs of America; Make-A-Wish Foundation of America; March of Dimes Birth Defects Foundation; United Way of America; Volunteers of America, Inc.; YMCA of the USA.

Further Reading

Abelson, Reed, "Charity Promises Sweeping Changes After Review," *The New York Times*, April 12, 2000, p. C1.
Blaney, Retta, "Dr. William P. Magee, Jr.—Smile Maker," *Spirituality & Health*, Fall, 1999.
Brazino, Joyce, "Smiles on Kids' Faces Match Those in Volunteer Hearts," *Nursing Spectrum*, April 7, 2005.
Briggins, Angela, "Where There's a Will . . . ," *Management Review*, October, 1996, p. 6.
Lacayo, Richard, "No One Will Ever Laugh at Me Again," *People Weekly*, Fall, 1991, pp. 18 + .
Moore, Anne, "Giving Children Smiles: Dr. William Magee," *ToDoInstitute.org*, September 13, 2004.
Simpson, Elizabeth, "Norfolk-Based Charity Gets a Boost from Movie 'Smile'," *Virginian-Pilot*, August 12, 2005.
Wackerman, Daniel T., "OpSmile," *America*, August 31, 1996, p. 4.

—Sara Poginy

OraSure Technologies, Inc.

220 East First Street
Bethlehem, Pennsylvania 18015
U.S.A.
Telephone: (610) 882-1820
Fax: (610) 882-1830
Web site: http://www.orasure.com

Public Company
Incorporated: 2000
Employees: 193
Sales: $54.0 million (2004)
Stock Exchanges: NASDAQ
Ticker Symbol: OSUR
NAIC: 325413 In-Vitro Diagnostic Substance
    Manufacturing

OraSure Technologies, Inc. is the leading supplier to the life insurance industry and public health markets of oral fluid collection devices for the detection of antibodies to HIV. OraSure is a company that develops and manufactures medical devices and diagnostics. Using their four-platform technologies, OraSure provides an ever growing number of diagnostic capabilities, including tests for HIV and drugs-of-abuse. These medical diagnostics are built for and marketed to physician's offices, clinical laboratories, workplace sites, insurance companies, public health agencies, and criminal justice and drug rehabilitation agencies. OraSure's primary focus is the oral fluid, point-of-care market. The company is striving to improve the current methods of testing and provide ways for conducting tests by using oral fluid samples that return results in a matter of minutes.

Early Beginnings: 1979–93

Epitope, Inc. was an Oregon-based company that focused on oral fluid diagnostics specifically for the detection of HIV infection and for drugs of abuse. Epitope was formed as a private company in 1979, as Immunologic Associates, and became a public company in 1986, mainly in order to raise money for AIDS research. Prior to becoming a public company,

Epitope's main funding came through private stock placement and research contracts. Through its initial offering, Epitope raised over $2.7 million in cash, which was used to finance development of a more reliable way to test for the AIDS virus.

In 1989, Epitope reported that it had developed technology for an oral fluid-based, rather than blood-based, diagnosis of infectious disease, allowing for rapid "on-the-street" testing. The Food and Drug Administration (FDA) approved a request by Epitope to begin human testing of an oral fluid-based HIV test in 1990. The system from Epitope included an oral fluid collection kit called "OraSure" that would collect an oral fluid called oral mucosal transudate (OMT) from the mouth. OMT contains large quantities of antibodies and is free of many of the contaminants that saliva contains. Specimens would be taken from between the gums and cheek; the sample was then placed in a tube and sent to Epitope's laboratory for results. The company cited the convenience of using oral fluid as opposed to blood-based tests. Although the actual product lacked full FDA approval and the company had yet to make a penny, its stock was valued at $160 million on the American Stock Exchange.

Approval Granted: 1994–97

In 1994, after a three-and-a-half year journey, Epitope finally received FDA approval for its oral fluid collection device, OraSure, specifically to be used for the detection of the AIDS virus. OraSure became the first medical diagnostic test of its type to be approved by the FDA for use in disease detection. The company projected that it would sell a million products monthly, with the cost being $2 to $4 per unit, a fraction of the cost of blood tests. However, because the oral fluid test was far less accurate than a blood test, the FDA outlined that the test would only be available through physician's offices and administered by trained personnel. Under the guidelines for approval, the FDA stated that the test could not be administered at home and could not be used to screen donors. Epitope acknowledged that the test was not as accurate as a blood test but stated that its hope was that the test would broaden HIV testing and help people to become aware of their AIDS status earlier. Now that FDA approval had been received, the question was whether Epitope could begin to make a profit.

Company Perspectives:

Create, combine and collaborate to be the world's best oral fluid diagnostics company. Deliver superior diagnostic solutions through the use of the most user-friendly and technologically advanced sample collection, detection and information technologies. Be entrepreneurial, build a culture based on our Core Values, and exceed Stakeholder Expectations.

Epitope concluded an exclusive licensing agreement with SmithKline Beecham Consumer Healthcare, one of the world's largest healthcare companies, in 1995, for distribution of OraSure. Unfortunately Epitope experienced a major loss and stocks hit a new low in the fall of 1995. This was due largely to SmithKline Beecham's reluctance to heavily market the oral fluid device. SmithKline cited the need for a confirmatory test prior to seriously distributing the test. An oral confirmatory test would allow for the use of the same sample when doing a second test for patients who tested positive for the HIV virus. Without an oral confirmatory test, patients would need to undergo a blood test in order to confirm a positive result.

In 1996, the first oral HIV antibody confirmatory test was approved by the FDA, making a single oral fluid sample adequate for the preliminary test and confirmatory tests in samples that tested positive for the HIV antibody. SmithKline Beecham announced plans to begin heavily marketing the OraSure test to health professionals and the insurance industry. By 1997, sales of the oral fluid diagnostic test had doubled, following an article in the *Journal of the American Medical Association (JAMA)* that declared OraSure's convenience and comparability (with regards to accuracy) to blood testing. In the fall of 1997, attempting to recover from damage incurred during problems with its Agritope subsidiary, Epitope reacquired the OraSure diagnostic from SmithKline Beecham. Epitope announced that it would market the diagnostic through the use of its own distribution channels.

Promising Agreements and New Developments: 1998–2000

The year 1998 brought several new agreements with marketing companies. First there was an agreement with LabOne, Inc., a company that marketed clinical, substance abuse, and insurance laboratory testing services. The agreement was for LabOne to provide oral testing for the HIV antibody to customers in the public health, corrections, military, and college health markets using the OraSure device. Second, Epitope made an agreement with Altrix Healthcare, plc, a U.K.-based medical diagnostic provider. The agreement was that Altrix would be responsible for the marketing and sales of OraSure in the United Kingdom and Ireland. Under the terms of the agreement, Altrix was required to meet minimum sales goals in order to maintain the relationship with Epitope. Having succeeded in increasing product sales, Epitope reported record product revenues and a small profit in late 1998.

Late 1998 also brought another agreement and a variation on the use of the OraSure fluid collection device. Epitope announced a five-year supply and distribution relationship with

STC Technologies, a privately held company that developed and supplied medical devices and clinical lab products for use in workplace testing, clinical labs, and physician's offices. Under the terms of the agreement, Epitope's OraSure device would be packaged with STC's substance abuse tests. The kit would be called "Intercept" by STC. Epitope would be the exclusive supplier of its collection device for use with STC's drugs-of-abuse tests in the United States and Europe, excluding the United Kingdom and Ireland. In turn, STC would be the exclusive distributor of the substance abuse tests in the same area. The agreement stated that Epitope would sell the OraSure device at a per-unit price to STC. Epitope would then receive a percentage of STC's gross revenue from the resale of the Intercept substance abuse tests. It would also be entitled to a percentage of any of STC's revenues that occurred from any future related activities where the OraSure device was incorporated. This collaboration of Epitope's OraSure oral fluid collection device and STC's drugs-of-abuse tests was considered by both companies to be an ideal one, convenient and less invasive for employers and employees without sacrificing accuracy.

Early 1999 brought the formation of an alliance between Epitope and two of its partners: STC Technologies and LabOne. LabOne agreed to provide oral fluid analysis of STC's Intercept substance abuse tests (which were performed using Epitope's OraSure oral fluid collection device). STC voiced excitement over the alliance, saying that it was an important step necessary to truly market the Intercept device. LabOne also appreciated the relationship, stating that the market was continuously attempting to find ways to improve the collection of samples. In turn, sales of Epitope's OraSure collection device were sure to increase, thereby increasing revenue.

The year also brought an agreement with Organon Teknika, Ltd., of Dublin, Ireland, to work together on the final development of OraQuick, Epitope's one-step, rapid-result oral specimen testing kit. OraQuick would allow health providers to supply results to patients within ten minutes, forgoing the use of a laboratory. Organon Teknika touted expertise with tests similar to OraQuick and planned to manufacture OraQuick at its factories in Ireland. Both companies hoped to reach a future agreement for the manufacturing and distribution of the kit upon completion of development.

In the fall of 1999, Epitope reported that it was supplying the OraSure oral fluid collection device to seven of the top ten insurance companies in the United States. Those seven companies accounted for 21 percent of ordinary life insurance purchased in the United States in 1998. Epitope attributed that growth to the industry's increased comfort with oral fluid testing devices, cost efficiency as compared to blood testing, and the non-invasive aspect of the OraSure device.

Also in 1999, Epitope announced that it had received a two-phase $1.1 million grant from the National Institutes of Health (NIH) to develop a test for syphilis using either oral fluid samples or blood samples. Epitope hoped to modify the OraSure device so that it could collect samples for the syphilis test. The addition of a blood-based alternative would come as a response to Epitope's expression of a need to broaden its product base. Under terms of the grant, the first phase would include the company reaching certain, outlined goals. The second phase included clinical trials

Key Dates:

1986: Epitope, Inc. becomes a public company.
1989: Epitope announces new oral-fluid, point-of-care technology called "OraSure."
1994: Food and Drug Administration (FDA) approves OraSure fluid collection device.
1998: Epitope enters into supply and distribution relationship with STC Technologies, Inc.
2000: Epitope merges with STC Technologies to form OraSure Technologies, Inc.
2004: Company receives FDA approval to market OraQuick test for both HIV-1 and HIV-2.

and submission to the FDA for approval. The test for syphilis would allow patients to find out a positive or negative result quickly, and, if necessary, get treatment sooner.

In early 2000, Epitope, along with LabOne and STC Technologies, announced the introduction of Intercept, the first laboratory-based substance abuse test that would look for and find illicit drugs in oral fluid samples. The Intercept test was expected to make a large impact in workplace drug testing, with negative results being available within 24 hours of receipt at the laboratory and positive results being confirmed within 72 hours of receipt. In addition, it would also be marketed to the criminal justice and public health markets. The Intercept drugs-of-abuse test was marketed as one of the most efficient, cost-effective drug testing alternatives available.

An Integration of Technologies; OraSure Is Born: 2000–02

In May 2000, STC Technologies and Epitope announced that they had signed a merger agreement. The newly formed company would be called OraSure Technologies, Inc. and would combine the developers of the foremost oral fluid collection device and the leaders in oral fluid analysis. STC Technologies was the owner of the Histofreezer Cryosurgical product line, a safe, effective means for removing skin lesions, and of the Uplink products, one of which was a point-of-care product used to detect the use of illicit drugs through oral fluid samples. Joining Epitope's OraQuick rapid fluid assay platform and the OraSure collection device along with STC's Histofreezer Cryosurgical and Uplink products created a four-platform technology that would allow for the companies to come together to become the world's utmost oral fluid diagnostic company. In September 2000, the merger was completed.

The new company was off to a running start when, in October 2000, it received the first international order for the OraQuick HIV Rapid test. The order was placed by a sub-Saharan African company and represented OraSure's push to provide the test to all of sub-Saharan Africa. The company cited the opportunities for OraQuick in that area as being enormous and stated that it felt the test was ideal for an area in which an estimated four million AIDS-affected individuals live.

Also in 2000, OraSure announced that it had finished phase one of the NIH grant received in 1999. The NIH approved

almost $1 million in added funding for the oral fluid-based syphilis detection test. The syphilis project focused on developing a device that would both screen and confirm the result using the OraSure oral fluid collection device. In the future, the company hoped to extend to point-of-care syphilis testing using its OraQuick test. OraSure intended to use the OraQuick rapid fluid assay platform, the OraSure collection device, and its Uplink technology to maximize the market coverage achieved from projects including the research on syphilis. In this manner, the company hoped to broaden the range of users, extending from lab-based testing to street corner testing.

Early 2001 brought a new agreement with one of the largest drug testing laboratories, Bendiner & Schlesinger, Inc. of New York, New York. OraSure would be providing its Intercept drug testing system to the company, which would, in turn, offer the system to the drug rehabilitation market of the New York metropolitan area. The annual revenue from this agreement was expected to reach $500,000 annually. OraSure also announced that the FDA had given approval of the Intercept fluid assay for barbiturates and methadone. These new assays would join the test panel that already tested for opiates, cocaine, PCP, marijuana, amphetamines, and benzodiazepines. The new clearance would allow for OraSure to meet the demands of the rapidly growing market of drug rehabilitation customers.

In 2002, OraSure submitted for and received clearance from the FDA for the Uplink test system for detecting opiates in oral fluid. This became the first oral fluid point-of-care test cleared by the FDA. Uplink provided instrument-read results in ten minutes and was expected to increase accuracy and efficiency of drug testing. The company announced its intention to submit for the full five-drug panel of assays in an oral fluid specimen. The drugs in the panel would include cocaine, PCP, marijuana, methamphetamines/amphetamines, as well as opiates.

Advancements in HIV Testing: Late 2002–05

In the fall of 2002, OraSure received approval from the FDA for its OraQuick Rapid HIV-1 test. The test was to be done with whole blood samples acquired from a finger-stick, and was cited as being highly accurate. Clinical studies showed the test to have 99.6 percent accuracy in detecting positive samples and 100 percent accuracy in identifying negative samples. The results would be available in about 20 minutes, making it the fastest test of its kind.

Once FDA approval was received, an agreement made in 2002 allowed for Abbott Laboratories, a leader in HIV/AIDS research, and OraSure to begin co-exclusively distributing the OraQuick Rapid HIV-1 test. Both companies announced the availability of the test to physician's offices, hospitals, and other healthcare facilities in 2003. The Centers for Disease Control and Prevention (CDC) created further acceptance and interest in the product by announcing that it would incorporate the use of the OraQuick test into its new HIV testing initiative. OraQuick was cited as being a convenient test that could conform to nontraditional test settings as well as provide rapid results. Further validating the test, OraSure announced that the OraQuick Rapid HIV-1 test had received the Gold Medical Design Excellence Award in the "In Vitro Diagnostics" category in the sixth annual Medical Design Excellence Awards (MDEA) competition.

Furthering its testing capabilities, in 2004 the OraQuick test was approved by the FDA to test for HIV-2. The approval allowed for simultaneous detection of HIV-1 and HIV-2 antibodies by using one sample. Although the instances of infection with HIV-2 were believed to be relatively low in the United States, HIV-2 testing was part of the required drug testing regimen in many foreign countries. Allowing for simultaneous HIV-1 and HIV-2 testing created an added convenience and quicker detection and treatment of the viruses. Additionally, the OraQuick device was approved by the FDA for use in detecting HIV-2 in oral fluid samples. This made OraSure's OraQuick Rapid HIV-1/2 test the only test approved by the FDA to detect antibodies to the HIV-1 and HIV-2 in oral fluid, whole blood, and in plasma samples.

At the beginning of 2005, OraSure continued to be the market leader in oral fluid technology, signing an agreement with Abbott Laboratories to distribute the OraQuick Rapid HIV-1/2 test. The company announced its long-term goals, namely, moving into global markets, developing more products for point-of-care testing, and seeking government approval to sell products, specifically OraQuick, directly to customers without professional assistance. These goals reflected OraSure's commitment to broadening its product base and constantly looking to the future.

Principal Competitors

Bio-Rad Laboratories, Inc.; Johnson & Johnson; LabOne, Inc.; Laboratory Corporation of America Holdings; Nabi Biopharmaceuticals; Roche Diagnostics Corporation; Schering-Plough Holdings; Trinity Biotech plc; UBS AG.

Further Reading

"Abbott Laboratories and OraSure Technologies Agree to Co-Market a Rapid HIV Test That Detects the Presence of Its Antibodies in As Little As 20 Minutes," *Diagnostics & Imaging Update,* July 2002, p. 14.
"Abbott, OraSure in Pact for Distribution of HIV Tests," *Diagnostics & Imaging Week,* February 17, 2005, p. 7.
Anderson, Michael A., "Epitope Goes Public to Raise Cash for AIDS Work," *Business Journal-Portland,* September 22, 1986, p. 6.
Brock, Kathy, "Epitope Now Faces Biggest Test: Turning a Profit," *Business Journal-Portland,* December 30, 1994, p. 3.
——, "Market Proving Epitope's Toughest Test," *Business Journal-Portland,* October 20, 1995, p. 1.
"CDC Commits $2M for Purchase of OraQuick," *Virus Weekly,* July 22, 2003, p. 12.
"Epitope Inc.," *Drug Detection Report,* September 23, 1999, p. 144.
"FDA Approves OraQuick Rapid HIV Antibody Test for Use with Oral Fluid," *Biotech Week,* April 28, 2004, p. 341.
"FDA Approves Saliva-Based AIDS Test," *CDC AIDS Weekly,* August 27, 1990, p. 7.
"HIV Saliva Test Approved," *AIDS Weekly,* January 9, 1995, p. 22.
"NIH Funds Blood and Oral Fluid Test Development," *Hepatitis Weekly,* November 20, 2000.
"Oral Fluids Specialists Team to Offer Turnkey Product," *Drug Detection Report,* May 20, 1999, p. 78.
"Clearance of Oral Fluid Assays for Barbiturates and Methadone," *BW Healthwire,* January 26, 2001.
"OraSure Technologies Announces Plans to Realign Its Global Manufacturing Operations; Company to Relocate and Expand Manufacturing of OraQuick Product," *BW Healthwire,* February 1, 2001.

—Sara Poginy

Orbotech Ltd.

P.O. Box 215
Yavne
81102
Israel
Telephone: +972 8 942 35 33
Fax: +972 8 943 87 69
Web site: http://www.orbotech.com

Public Company
Incorporated: 1981 as Optrotech
Employees: 1,382
Sales: $305.3 million (2004)
Stock Exchanges: NASDAQ
Ticker Symbol: ORBK
NAIC: 333314 Optical Instrument and Lens
  Manufacturing; 334513 Instruments and Related
  Product Manufacturing for Measuring, Displaying,
  and Controlling Industrial Process Variables; 334516
  Analytical Laboratory Instrument Manufacturing

Orbotech Ltd. is the world's leading developer and producer of automated optical inspection (AOI) and related imaging and computer-aided manufacturing systems. The company's imaging tools are used in the manufacturing of bare printed circuit board (PCB), flat-panel displays, PCB assemblies, and IC packaging, among other applications. These systems aid manufacturers by providing highly accurate, high-speed, and automated optical inspection, allowing faster production speeds with less waste and at lower cost. Orbotech, through its predecessors Optrotech and Orbot, which merged in 1991, pioneered the AOI market and remains its dominant player, with a global market share of some 50 percent. The company's headquarters and main research and manufacturing facilities are located in Yavne, Israel. The company also operates manufacturing and research facilities in the United States, as well as a network of some 30 sales subsidiaries in Germany, Japan, Belgium, Taiwan, and elsewhere. Founded in 1981, Orbotech has been listed on the NASDAQ since 1984. Optrotech founder Shlomo Barak

remains company chairman, and Arie Weisberg serves as CEO. In 2004, the company posted revenues of $305 million.

Inventing an Industry in the 1980s

The development of computer and electronics technologies faced a number of obstacles into the early 1980s. Among these was the need to inspect printed circuit boards (PCBs) as an integral part of the manufacturing process. Yet inspection, which required human operators using microscopes, remained a roadblock in the production process. At the same time, the rapid miniaturization of electronic components presented a still larger future obstacle; before long, PCBs were to become so small that manual inspection would become impossible.

Shlomo Barak had been working for Israel's Electro-Optical Industry Ltd., helping to develop laser and fire-control systems and other electro-optical systems. These were targeted, in large part, at military applications, but saw commercial use as well. Barak recognized that the company's technology could be adapted to provide automated visual inspection applications. The PCB market promised to be particularly receptive to this technology.

In 1981, Barak led a team of fellow engineers at Electro-Optical in the formation of a new company, called Optrotech. Financial backing for the start-up came from Elron Industries, a leading Israeli holding company with interests in a number of industries, especially the electronics industry. Among Elron's other holdings were Elbit Computers, a manufacturer of computers and electronics for military and other markets; Fibronics, based in the United States, which manufactured and sold fiber optics systems; and Elscint, a company that developed and produced medical imaging systems.

Optrotech began developing its automated inspection technology. After 18 months of research and development, the company was finally ready with its first-generation product, dubbed the Vision 104. Although a number of other companies also had been working on their own automated inspection systems, Optrotech became first to market.

Success was immediate. As the first to market, the company was able to maintain its frontrunner status into the middle of the

Company Perspectives:

Orbotech develops and produces the world's most advanced hi-tech equipment for inspecting and imaging circuit boards and display panels—the backbones of today's cutting-edge electronic products.

Orbotech's innovative automated optical inspection (AOI), imaging and computer-aided manufacturing (CAM) technologies enable customers to achieve the increased yields and throughput essential to remaining at the forefront of electronics production.

decade. Overnight, Optrotech had helped transform the PCB industry, enabling companies to begin the first of a series of dramatic productivity improvements. The faster production times and greater volumes helped drive costs down, and the steadily dropping prices of PCBs provided still further stimulation for the development of the global electronics and computer industries. The simple existence of an automated optical inspection system made the Vision 104 indispensable to PCB producers.

Yet the appearance of new rivals, such as fellow Israeli company Orbot, created in 1983, and rival technologies, forced Optrotech to continue to invest heavily in its research and development effort. Despite the success of the Vision 194, Optrotech found itself strapped for cash by 1984. Although still a young company, Optrotech turned to the stock market that year, placing its listing on the NASDAQ. As former Optrotech and Elron Chairman Uzia Galil told *Electronic Business:* "There was no better alternative to bring $10 million into the company. They would have lost the time window." Elron nonetheless retained a major stake in the company.

The initial public offering (IPO) allowed Optrotech to begin development of its next-generation AOI technology, while continuing to refine its initial technology. In 1984, the company launched a new system, the Vision 104X, which was followed by the Vision 105 in 1985. The company also launched an effort to diversify its market, beginning development of its first CAD/CAM system, the Image 2000. This technology targeted the front-end phases of the PCB production process, providing automated capacity to the artwork generation stage.

Heightened competition, however, forced Optrotech to defend its market in 1986, and in that year the company rushed its new-generation AOI system, the 206, to market. The 206 departed from the company's earlier systems, which employed reflective technology, by using a nonreflective imaging technology. The initial release of the 206 proved faulty, however. As Barak told *Electronic Business:* "There was misjudgment of the difficulty in introducing this technology. It was a long way to solve the problems and clean up the machine." During this time, Optrotech found itself outpaced by rival Orbot, which took over as AOI market leader in 1986.

Merging Market Leaders in the 1990s

The loss of its top position allowed Optrotech to shift its focus away from a reliance on core AOI technologies to include more diversified front-end technologies. As such the company added

competence in related areas, including artificial intelligence, machine vision, and systems engineering. By the late 1980s, the company featured two strong product lines: Vision, for its AOI technologies; and Image, for its front-end businesses.

Optrotech also continued to invest heavily in research and development. This led the company to seek additional capital toward the end of the decade. In 1989, the company turned to Canadian-owned Claridge Israel Inc., which agreed to acquire 22 percent of Optrotech for $16 million.

The capital injection provided Optrotech with a new opportunity. At the start of the 1990s, rival Orbot began experiencing its own financial difficulties. Orbot had grown strongly in the late 1980s, in part through the 1988 launch of subsidiary Orbot Instruments Ltd., which developed AOI systems for the booming semiconductor market. Orbot's growth was further supported by its close relationship with IBM, which remained a major customer throughout the decade. At the same time, Orbot developed an early international strategy, looking beyond the U.S. market to target Japan and other Asian markets as early as 1985. In 1990, Orbot hoped to go public in an effort to inject new capital. Yet the collapse of the stock market, and especially the IPO market, forced the company to reconsider.

Instead, Optrotech and Orbot entered talks to merge their complementary operations. Initial discussion failed to find an agreement between the two companies. By 1991, however, the slowdown in the global AOI led the two market leaders to try again. At last, in August 1992, Optrotech and Orbot reached a merger agreement, in which Optrotech absorbed Orbot. The resulting business was then renamed Orbotech.

Orbotech started out as the clear dominant player in the global AOI market; into the late 1990s, the company continued to command some 70 percent of certain market segments. Orbotech also continued to seek new areas for growth. In 1995, for example, the company adapted its technology to provide automatic check reading capabilities for banks and other check processing customers, marking the launch of the company's expansion beyond its focus on the electronics industry. Closer to the electronics field, in 1997, Orbotech launched a new imaging and process control system for use as part of the manufacturing process. In this way, Orbotech's AOI products spanned the range from PCB design to production to testing and inspection.

Global Leader in the 2000s

Into the 2000s, Orbotech launched a new acquisition-based growth strategy. This led the company to form a joint venture with Jenoptik AG, which had developed its own laser-based direct imaging system used for the production of PCB prototypes. Launched in 1997, the partnership came under full ownership of Orbotech in 2000. The company boosted its presence in Japan in 1998, acquiring Toyo Ink Manufacturing's PCB sales and marketing operations.

By then, Orbotech had emerged as the leading producer of AOI systems for the fast-growing LCD industry. The purchase of KLA Acrotec in 1999 allowed Orbotech to firm up its leading position in that market. The acquisition of the Japan-based company cost Orbotech $13.6 million and gave Orbotech as

Key Dates:

1981: Shlomo Barak leads a team of engineers to found Optrotech to produce AOI systems for the PCB industry.
1983: Orbot is founded as an AOI specialist.
1984: Optrotech lists stock on the NASDAQ.
1985: Orbot launches international operations in Japan and the Far East.
1986: Orbot becomes the AOI market leader; Optrotech diversifies into the CAD/CAM market.
1991: Optrotech and Orbot agree to merge, forming Orbotech.
1995: The company launches automated check reading systems for the financial industry.
1997: A joint venture is formed with Jenoptik; the company acquires W. Schuh in Germany.
1998: The PCB sales and marketing business is acquired from Toyo Ink Manufacturing of Japan.
1999: The company acquires KLA Acrotec in Japan.
2000: The company acquires full ownership of the Jenoptik joint venture.
2001: Orbotech launches a venture capital subsidiary, investing in Negevtech, among others.
2004: The company agrees to acquire Negevtech from Clal Industries.

much as 80 percent of the LCD AOI market. By then, Orbotech also had added operations in Europe, with the 1997 acquisition of the AOI business of Germany's W. Schuh GmbH. That company specialized in the production of post-solder inspection equipment.

Orbotech also sought to provide a seedbed for future technology developments. To this end, the company set up a new subsidiary, Orbotech Technology Ventures Ltd., in order to invest in technology start-ups. At the end of 2003, the company had invested nearly $9 million. Among the companies that received investment capital from Orbotech was Negevtech, majority held by Clal Industries and Investments Ltd. In 2004, Orbotech and Clal agreed to transfer ownership of Negevtech to Orbotech for $14.1 million.

Orbotech also continued to attract new customers. After reaching a cooperation agreement with Korean giant Samsung in 2004, the company scored a new sales success with a large-scale order for several AOI systems from Quanta Display Inc. That deal solidified Orbotech's position as a global leader in AOI systems for the LCD market. With sales of more than $300 million in 2005, Orbotech expected to continue to dominate the market it had created just 25 years earlier.

Principal Subsidiaries

Frontline P.C.B. Solutions Limited Partnership; Frontline P.C.B. Solutions Ltd. (50%); Laser Imaging Systems GmbH & Co. KG; Orbograph Ltd. (91%); Orbotech Asia Ltd.; Orbotech B.V.; Orbotech Holding GmbH; Orbotech Japan Ltd.; Orbotech Medical Solutions Ltd.; Orbotech Pacific Ltd.; Orbotech S.A.; Orbotech Schuh GmbH & Co. KG; Orbotech Singapore Corporation Pte. Ltd.; Orbotech Technology Ventures Limited; Orbotech, Inc.

Principal Competitors

Canon Inc.; 3M Co.; Krasniy Gigant; Olympus Corporation; Nikon Corporation; Citizen Watch Company Ltd.; Magna Donnelly Corporation; Hoya Corporation; Showa Electric Wire and Cable Company Ltd.; NeoPhotonics Corporation.

Further Reading

Dorsch, Jeff, "Orbotech to Acquire KLA Acrotec," *Electronic News,* February 15, 1999, p. 26.
Greenberg, Shlomo, "Orbotech and the Doubters," *Israel Business Arena,* August 3, 2004.
Greene, Tony, "Eye to Eye But Head to Head: A Tale of Two AOI Start-ups," *Electronic Business,* November 1, 1988, p. 68.
"Orbotech Gets Major Order from Quanta Display," *CircuiTree,* February 2005, p. 87.
"Orbotech Starts Its Sixth Year," *Israel Business Today,* May 1999, p. 27.
"Orbotech to Acquire W. Schuh Operation," *Electronic News,* July 28, 1997, p. 50.
Shalev, Shai, and Avishay Ovadia, "Orbotech Wants All of Negevtech," *Israel Business Arena,* February 9, 2004.

—M.L. Cohen

Overstock.com

Your Online Outlet™

Overstock.com, Inc.

6350 South 3000 East
Salt Lake City, Utah 84121
U.S.A.
Telephone: (801) 947-3100
Toll Free: (800) 989-0135
Fax: (801) 944-4629
Web site: http://www.overstock.com

Public Company
Founded: 1997 as D2-Discounts Direct
Employees: 426
Sales: $494.6 million (2004)
Stock Exchanges: NASDAQ
Ticker Symbol: OSTK
NAIC: 423220 Home Furnishing Merchant Wholesalers;
423910 Sporting and Recreational Goods and Supplies
Merchant Wholesalers; 423940 Jewelry, Watch,
Precious Stone, and Precious Metal Merchant
Wholesalers; 423990 Other Miscellaneous Durable
Goods Merchant Wholesalers

Overstock.com, Inc. is an online retailer that sells excess inventory at discounted prices. The company, akin to an outlet store that sells the closeout merchandise of manufacturers, distributors, and other retailers, offers brand name bed-and-bath goods, home décor, furniture, kitchenware, watches, jewelry, computers and electronics, sporting goods, and apparel. Overstock.com also sells books, magazines, CDs, DVDs, videocassettes, and video games, items that are classified as "BMV" products. The company sells approximately 500,000 BMV products and 50,000 non-BMV products. Merchandise is obtained either by buying excess inventory, referred to as the company's "direct" business, or by selling the merchandise of other retailers, catalogue companies, and manufacturers on a commission basis, referred to as its "fulfillment partner" business. Overstock.com has fulfillment partner relationships with roughly 380 clients, who supply nearly all of the BMV products and 80 percent of the non-BMV products sold on the company's web site. Overstock.com also maintains an online auction site that allows consumers to buy and sell merchandise, and it operates an online travel store, which sells cruise vacations.

Origins

Overstock.com did not assume a recognizable national profile until the company's path crossed with that of a dynamic and gifted businessman named Patrick Byrne. The company was founded in May 1997 as D2-Discounts Direct, a limited liability company that became a C Corporation at the end of 1998. Byrne first learned of the company's existence in the spring of 1999 when its founder approached him, asking for capital. The company, which had generated slightly more than $500,000 in revenue the previous year by liquidating excess inventory online, was struggling, forcing its founder to ask for Byrne's help. The meeting introduced Byrne to a business idea he would make his own, inspiring him to bring a massive outlet-store concept to the burgeoning world of e-tailing.

Byrne was 36 years old when he became aware of D2-Discounts Direct, having spent the first three decades of his life developing into a singularly accomplished person. His father, Jack Byrne, was an executive of note, serving as chief executive officer of GEICO, Fireman's Fund Insurance, and Fund America, distinguishing himself sufficiently to earn the trust and friendship of the legendary investor from Omaha, Nebraska, Warren Buffett. Buffett met Jack Byrne not long after he became chief executive officer of GEICO, which at the time was a troubled company. Buffett was impressed by Byrne, impressed to the point that he soon bought 500,000 shares in GEICO, and the two became friends. Buffett met Patrick Byrne when he was 13 years old and offered business advice to the teenager in the form of a baseball analogy. "There was no one calling balls and strikes," Byrne recounted in a February 7, 2000 interview with *Fortune,* "and I could take as many pitches as I wanted." Buffett's advice followed: "Every year or two, the perfect pitch comes along and you swing from the heels."

In the years after meeting Buffett, Byrne established a record of excellence, compiling a lengthy list of accomplishments. He received his undergraduate degree from Dartmouth College, translating Lao Tse's *Way of Virtue* during his senior year. He earned a master's degree at Cambridge University as a Marshall Scholar, where he studied moral philosophy, and he received a doctorate in philosophy from Stanford University. Byrne spoke four foreign languages, including Mandarin, earned black belts in hapkido and tae kwon do, and bicycled across the United

307

Company Perspectives:

Closeout merchandise is typically available in inconsistent quantities and prices and often is only available to consumers after it has been purchased and resold by disparate liquidation wholesalers. We believe that the traditional liquidation market is therefore characterized by fragmented supply and fragmented demand. Overstock utilizes the Internet to aggregate both supply and demand and create a more efficient market for liquidation merchandise. We provide consumers and businesses with quick and convenient access to high-quality, brand-name merchandise at discount prices.

States three times. He successfully battled cancer, surviving three appearances of seminoma and 20 surgeries between 1985 and 1988, an ordeal that left the six-foot-five-inch, 240-pound Byrne weighing only 164 pounds. He also possessed an impressive memory, a skill he demonstrated with a deck of cards. After several minutes of studying the cards, he could remember their sequence, one by one, in either direction. Remarkably, Byrne could recall the precise order of the deck six months after performing the trick.

In the months before Byrne first became involved in D2-Discounts Direct, he divided his time between running an investment firm and lending his talents to Buffett. Buffett's Berkshire Hathaway controlled scores of companies, including a uniform manufacturer in Cincinnati named Fechheimer Brothers. The company was struggling, and Buffett asked Byrne to step in as temporary chief executive officer in 1998. Byrne led Fechheimer Brothers for 18 months, gaining admirers who described him as "the greatest motivator ever" and critics who accused him of being "too quick on the trigger," according to reports in the February 7, 2000 issue of *Fortune*. Byrne primarily occupied himself professionally by operating a personal investment company called High Plains Investments, the entity D2-Discounts Direct's founder approached for money. Through High Plains, Byrne had amassed a $100 million portfolio, which gave him more than ample resources to invest in D2-Discounts Direct. "The financials were a joke," High Plains' chief financial officer said in a February 7, 2000 interview with *Fortune,* referring to his initial assessment of D2-Discounts Direct. "But buried in all that was this billion-dollar idea." Byrne was entranced by the potential for an online "closeout" retailer and invested $7 million for a 60 percent stake in the company in the spring of 1999. By September, his faith in the management team had faded, and he stepped in to take over as chief executive officer, renaming the company Overstock.com the following month. Byrne's active presence delivered immediate results, triggering sales growth that saw the company's monthly revenue volume swell from $70,000 in August to $1 million by December.

Liquidated Inventories Giving Overstock.com Its Initial Merchandise Base

Once at the helm, Byrne's principal objective was to expand Overstock.com. At the end of 1999, a year in which the company generated $1.8 million in gross merchandise sales, Overstock.com offered fewer than 100 items, a selection that needed to become exponentially larger if Byrne was to succeed in his goal of making the company larger than Amazon.com, Inc. within five years. The company added to its merchandise selection in two ways, either by acquiring excess inventory for resale, its "direct" business, or by selling other parties' excess inventory for a commission, its "commission" business (later renamed "fulfillment partner"). Overstock.com dealt with manufacturers, distributors, importers, retailers, catalog companies, and e-tailers, giving each type of company a way to get rid of its excess inventory. Initially, Byrne acquired the inventories of failing dot-com companies, which were in great supply during Overstock.com's first years in business. The struggling companies were in desperate need of cash, enabling Byrne to acquire merchandise at heavily discounted prices. During his first two-and-a-half years in charge, Byrne liquidated 18 moribund dot-com companies, giving Overstock.com a product selection that supported its claim of being an outlet store for the nation. In a two-month period in 2000, for instance, Byrne acquired inventories valued at $44 million retail for prices far below retail. (Typically, Overstock.com customers paid wholesale prices.) He paid $860,000 for Adornis.com's jewelry inventory, gaining merchandise that had a retail value of $5 million and a wholesale value of $2.2 million. He paid $50,000 for the inventory of BabyStripes.com, gaining a selection of 500 baby-related products that retailed for $450,000 and had a wholesale value of $180,000. He purchased more than 2,000 hats from eHats.com, paying $70,000 for $550,000 worth of hats.

The liquidation of failing or failed dot-coms provided Byrne with a merchandise selection large enough to justify Overstock.com's debut on Wall Street. The company completed its initial public offering (IPO) of stock at the end of May 2002, when Overstock.com shares debuted at $13 per share, raising $39 million. With the proceeds obtained from the IPO, Byrne continued to broaden the company's offerings, sending representatives to search for bargain buys to build Overstock.com's direct business. He recruited former catalog buyers, traditional retail buyers, and, on some occasions, he hired ticket scalpers he met at rock concerts. "It's people who can think on their feet," Byrne said, referring to the company's buyers in a July 17, 2003 interview with *Investor's Business Daily.* Each purchase completed by a buyer gave the company greater revenue-generating potential, fueling the company's sales growth. Between 2000 and 2003, Overstock.com's revenues increased from $25.5 million to $91.7 million. Profits, however, proved harder to come by. The company lost nearly $40 million between 2000 and 2002, despite generating net income in its first two fiscal quarters as a publicly traded company. Some analysts blamed Overstock.com's profitability problems on Byrne's reliance on a word-of-mouth marketing strategy, but he was not to be swayed. "We're betting the ranch on that," he stated in a July 17, 2003 interview with *Investor's Business Daily.* "We can price cheaper and count on customers to spread the word," he added. "I don't want to spend $200 million on advertising and price it into the products." He later changed his mind about the company's marketing tactics, at least as demonstrated by the enormous attention the company was attracting midway through the decade by turning to expensive television commercials, but before the company hit the airwaves it began to record surging revenue growth.

The merchandise foundation supporting Overstock.com had been established almost exclusively through direct acquisition deals. In the years immediately following its IPO, the company recorded its greatest financial growth by forging commissioned-

Key Dates:

1997: Overstock.com's predecessor, D2-Discounts Direct, is formed.

1999: Patrick Byrne acquires a 60 percent stake in D2-Discounts Direct and changes its name to Overstock.com.

2000: Byrne begins acquiring the inventories of ailing dot-com companies.

2002: Overstock.com completes its initial public offering of stock.

2003: Overstock Mexico, a subsidiary, is formed to distribute merchandise in Mexico.

2004: The company launches an online auction site.

based deals with manufacturers, other retailers, catalogue companies, distributors, and importers. Overstock.com, once it established itself as a legitimate, trustworthy player in the e-commerce sector, was able to form partnerships with companies such as Hewlett-Packard, Kenneth Cole, Simon & Schuster, Samsonite, and Cuisinart. These fulfillment partners, constituting the former commission side of Overstock.com's business, drove the company's revenue growth following its IPO. In 2000, fulfillment partner agreements accounted for $867,000 of the company's $25.5 million in revenue. In 2002, fulfillment partner agreements accounted for $12.3 million of the company's $91.7 million in revenue. In 2003, fulfillment partner revenue skyrocketed to $100.8 million, pushing overall revenue to $238.9 million, before eclipsing the direct side of the company's business in 2004, when partnership agreements generated $281.4 million of the company's $494.6 million in revenue collected during the year.

Post-IPO Diversification

Against the backdrop of energetic revenue growth, the company added new dimensions to its business during the period immediately following its IPO. In July 2003, Overstock Mexico, S. de R.L. de C.V. was formed, a wholly owned subsidiary created to distribute products in Mexico. Several months later, a discount travel store was added to the Overstock.com web site, part of Byrne's plan to provide a one-stop destination for discount shopping for products and services. The travel store was shut down in May 2004, but after improvements were made in the types of services offered, it returned in January 2005, enabling users to book reservations for flights, hotels, cars, and cruises. In September 2004, the company launched a bold bid to take away some of eBay Inc.'s business by adding an online auction function to its web site. Like eBay, Overstock.com operated the site strictly as a consumer-to-consumer marketplace.

As Overstock.com prepared for the second half of the decade, several positive developments mitigated the company's problems with profitability. The company lost $11.8 million in 2003 and $5 million in 2004, but investors hardly seemed to care. During the fourth fiscal quarter of 2004, the company's stock reached a record high of $76.05 per share, an enormous increase from the debut price of $13 per share. Part of the confidence expressed by Wall Street stemmed from the success of the company's marketing campaign midway through the decade, one that strayed far

from Byrne's commitment to word-of-mouth advertising. The campaign featured a 41-year-old model, Sabine Ehrenfeld, dressed in white and surrounded by white consumer items and the tagline, "Have you discovered the secret of the Big O?" The television and radio commercials proved to be surprisingly successful, exceeding the hopes of Overstock.com executives. In a market survey conducted in November 2004, brand awareness of the Overstock.com name reached 46 percent, up substantially from the 12 percent recorded in 2003. "We never expected this kind of interest," the company's vice-president of branding said in a March 5, 2005 interview with the *Salt Lake Tribune*. "This is just bizarre—in a good way," he added.

With public interest stirred and its revenue increasing robustly, Overstock.com stood poised to clear the one hurdle it had been unable to clear during its first six years in business: consistent profitability. Byrne maintained that the company's failure to record steady profits was based in large part on his emphasis on expansion, suggesting that if he ratcheted back growth plans Overstock.com would soon become profitable. Byrne, however, was committed to expansion for the near-term, as he pressed forward with acquiring inventories and forming fulfillment partner agreements, seeking to make Overstock.com the dominant player in re-selling closeout merchandise online.

Principal Subsidiaries

Overstock Mexico, S. de R.L. de C.V.

Principal Competitors

Amazon.com, Inc.; Buy.com Inc.; SmartBargains, Inc.

Further Reading

Alva, Marilyn, "Overstock.com, Inc.," *Investor's Business Daily,* July 17, 2003, p. A8.

"Beating the Bottlenecks: Overstock.com's Strategy," *Chain Store Age,* September 2005, p. 47.

Braunstein, Peter, "Overstock.com Buys Inventories," *WWD,* November 17, 2000, p. 12.

"Gear.com Acquired by Overstock.com," *Puget Sound Business Journal,* October 20, 2000, p. 21.

Horowitz, Alan S., "Overstock.com Vs. eBay: Online Giants Face Off," *Utah Business,* June 2005, p. 42.

McGarvey, Robert, "Sales from the Crypt," *Entrepreneur,* May 2001, p. 22.

Mclean, Bethany, "Is Overstock the New Amazon?," *Fortune,* October 18, 2004, p. 336.

Mims, Bob, "Internet Closeout Retailer Overstock.com Racks Up Sales," *Salt Lake Tribune,* December 29, 2004.

——, "Overstock.com Chief Vows Fight Against 'Sith Lord' on Wall Street," *Salt Lake Tribune,* August 15, 2005.

"New Discount Site Targets Independent Retailers," *Direct Marketing,* November 2001, p. 64.

"Patrick Byrne CEO of Overstock.com," *IPO Reporter,* July 8, 2002.

Stein, Nicholas, "The Renaissance Man of E-Commerce," *Fortune,* February 7, 2000, p. 181.

Stepleman, Robert, "Is Overstock.com a Bargain for Investors?," *Sarasota Herald Tribune,* December 26, 2004, p. D1.

Tucker, Ross, "Tiffany Hits Overstock.com with Five More Lawsuits," *WWD,* January 26, p. 19.

Warchol, Glen, "Overstock.com Is Purring Over Publicity from New Ads," *Salt Lake Tribune,* March 5, 2005.

—Jeffrey L. Covell

Palm, Inc.

950 West Maude Avenue
Sunnyvale, California 94085
U.S.A.
Telephone: (408) 617-7000
Toll Free: (800) 881-7256
Fax: (408) 617-0100
Web site: http://www.palm.com

Public Company
Incorporated: 1992 as Palm Computing, Inc.
Employees: 907
Sales: $1.27 billion (2005)
Stock Exchanges: NASDAQ
Ticker Symbol: PALM
NAIC: 334111 Electronic Computer Manufacturing

Palm, Inc. is a leading producer of handheld computing products. The company that led the market for personal digital assistants (PDAs) has adapted its offerings to be ever more handy. After acquiring rival Handspring, Inc., Palm inherited a top product, the Treo. The company spun off its software unit in 2003, and in 2005 entered separate deals to license software from rivals Microsoft Corporation and Research in Motion Ltd. (RIM) to counter competition from RIM's Blackberry and a slew of competitors from the mobile phone and computer industries.

Silicon Valley Origins

Palm Computing, Inc. was established in January 1992. Its founder, Jeff Hawkins, was formerly vice-president of Grid Systems Corp. and was credited with designing that company's line of pen computers. President and COO Donna Dubinsky was a cofounder of Claris Corp.

Tandy Corporation sponsored Palm Computing's first product: the Zoomer (marketed as the Casio Z-7000 and the Tandy Z-PDA) handheld device that was developed in cooperation with Casio Computing Inc. Three California venture capital firms also backed the company.

Palm soon introduced add-on software for connecting Zoomers to PCs. Other early products were the PalmPrint and PalmOrganizer devices based on the Geos operating system developed by Geoworks of Alameda, California. Sharp used these technologies in its PT-9000 handheld pen tablet machine.

In 1994, Palm began marketing itself as a third-party developer for other makers of handheld computing devices, extending beyond the Geos operating system. Three other platforms were under consideration: Apple's Newton Intelligence, Microsoft's WinPad, and General Magic Inc.'s MagicCap.

In September 1994, Palm debuted its Graffiti handwriting recognition software. Until that time, users of personal digital assistants usually entered information by choosing selections on a tiny screen with a little plastic stylus. Adding any kind of practical keyboard would make the devices too large to carry in one's pocket. Apple's Newton already had a limited handwriting recognition capability, but Palm's Graffiti could be used for taking notes or sending e-mail. It boasted 100 percent accuracy and a speed to rival typing. Graffiti required users to modify their handwriting somewhat, omitting, for example, the cross bar in the letters "A" and "F" and writing the letter "L" in mirror image. Palm claimed the system could be learned in 20 minutes and mastered in a couple of hours. Palm offered the software for the Newton, Magic Cap, and other PDAs. Giant modem manufacturer U.S. Robotics, based in Skokie, Illinois, acquired Palm in September 1995 for $44 million. Palm was based in Los Altos, California.

A New Pilot in 1996

Palm introduced its new, simplified PDA, called the Pilot, in the spring of 1996. Rather than attempting to stand alone as a computer, the Pilot was designed to easily and quickly exchange information with a PC. It sat in a cradle that was plugged into the desktop computer.

According to *Time,* venture capitalists in Silicon Valley doubted users would buy a device with as few features as the Pilot offered. However, the very key to the Pilot's success was its Zen-like simplicity. While designing it, Hawkins carried an uncarved block of wood in his shirt pocket for months, tapping

Company Perspectives:

Palm, Inc. is a leader in mobile computing and strives to put the power of computing in people's hands so they can access and share their most important information. The company's products for consumers, mobile professionals and businesses include Palm Treo smartphones, Palm LifeDrive mobile managers and Palm handheld computers, as well as software, services and accessories. Palm's products are equipped with a comprehensive suite of Personal Information Management (PIM) software, infrared beaming capabilities, calculators, note-taking applications, and games. A range of additional features, including hi-res color screens, wireless capabilities (Bluetooth, Wi-Fi, cellular), MP3 software and digital cameras, ensures that there's a Palm product to meet almost any user's needs.

on it while deciding the key features the Pilot needed. Eventually, four functions emerged: a calendar, address book, to-do list, and memo section.

The tiny new device measured just 4.7 inches long, 3.2 inches wide, and 0.7 inches thick. It used ubiquitous miniature flashlight batteries that lasted for months. The basic Pilot 1000 retailed for $299, half the price of a Newton. It could hold 500 addresses and 600 appointments. The Pilot 5000 had four to five times the memory and sold for $369.

It took a few months for the Pilots to catch on, but soon they were appearing all over. Palm shipped more than a million of them in their first year and a half, a faster launch than Sony Walkmans, pagers, and mobile phones. They certainly outsold all other PDAs. The GridPad that Hawkins had designed nearly ten years earlier was simply too big. The expensive Apple Newton failed in the mass marketplace. The Sharp Wizard and the Hewlett Packard 200LX were limited to tiny niches of gadget enthusiasts.

In the face of Palm's success, Microsoft rushed out its Windows CE 1.0 operating system in its haste to dominate yet another market. The units that used it, equipped with tiny keyboards, offered more features than the Pilot but were difficult to use. They failed to threaten Palm's position; the company controlled two-thirds of the handheld market at the end of 1997.

New Competition and New Ownership in Late 1990s

Microsoft released its updated CE 2.0 software in November 1997 and called its new handhelds "Palm PCs," quickly landing it in court for alleged trademark infringement. Seven companies, including Casio and Philips, allied with Microsoft in developing their own feature-packed handhelds running the CE 2.0 operating system. They generally proved more complex to use than the Pilot. (Palm soon began referring to its devices by company name and model number.)

Palm continuously updated the Pilot's design. It introduced a modem for it in 1997. However, its software was not well received and third party developers moved to quickly fill the void. The Palm III was introduced in March 1998. It could

exchange information with other Palm IIIs via a wireless infrared transmission. *Time* magazine documented the phenomenon of strangers swapping video games, contact information, and subway maps by this "beaming." Other new features included refined styling, a protective lid, and more memory.

Palm kept its own offerings relatively simple, leaving 5,000 outside parties to develop software and hardware add-ons. Users could now link with the Internet, corporate networks, and pagers. The Palm III sold for $399. Wireless modems (supplied by Novatel, JP Systems, and Metricom) sold for $350–$400 and doubled the size of the unit.

3Com, based in Santa Clara, California, had acquired U.S. Robotics in June 1997. 3Com manufactured networking adapters and switches. With sales of $570 million Palm accounted for nearly 10 percent of 3Com's revenues in the 1998/99 fiscal year. 3Com CEO Eric Benhamou saw the unit as the centerpiece of a revitalized 3Com, according to the *Wall Street Journal*. In fact, although Dubinsky claimed it attracted little interest at the time of the acquisition, Palm Computing emerged as the best part of the merger with U.S. Robotics, which had left 3Com with massive excess modem inventories and other difficulties in combining the two product lines.

Dubinsky and Hawkins left 3Com in 1998 because it would not spin off Palm as a separate company. They formed Handspring Inc. and used licensed Palm software in their own, lower-priced device, called the Visor, which was introduced in September 1999. It featured a slot for effortlessly adding a variety of hardware modules, such as digital music players and cameras. (PalmPilots did have a serial port for adding peripherals.)

By this time, Palm held an 85 percent market share, and was aggressively licensing its proprietary Palm OS operating system. *Computer Reseller News* reported that Microsoft had turned its attention towards secondary functions beyond organizing data, such as playing music clips and video games.

The new Palm VII arrived in 1999. The handy organizer had morphed into a full-time wireless telecommunications device. It was priced at $599, plus an additional monthly fee ($10–$40) for Palm.net service based on usage. Although its tiny screen could not display all the contents of a typical web page, Palm had lined up more than 1,000 Internet content developers willing to accommodate the Palm VII.

Compaq Computer Corporation unveiled another lower-priced competitor, the Aero 1500, in September 1999. Hewlett-Packard Co.'s Jornada 430, priced the same as the Palm VII, debuted the same month. The Jornada featured a color screen.

3Com picked a new CEO for Palm in December 1999: Carl J. Yankowski, head of the Reebok Brand athletic shoe division of Reebok International Ltd. He also had experience with Sony Corporation, PepsiCo, Inc., Polaroid Corporation, and General Electric Co.

Palm controlled 70 percent of the organizer market; a few progressive corporate network administrators were buying PalmPilots by the hundreds. Sales were growing 65 percent a year. Organizers still accounted for 99 percent of revenues in spite of the emphasis the company was making on licensing its

---

Key Dates:

1992: Palm Computing, Inc. is founded.
1995: U.S. Robotics acquires Palm for $44 million.
1996: New PalmPilots revolutionize handheld computing.
1997: 3Com acquires U.S. Robotics.
1998: Palm founders leave to start rival Handspring, Inc.
2000: Palm goes public in March with a staggering opening day valuation of $53 billion; 3Com distributes all remaining shares in Palm to its stockholders in July.
2001: Palm begins first layoffs in economic slowdown.
2003: Palm, Inc. spins off PalmSource software unit, acquires Handspring, Inc.; PalmOne, Inc. is formed.
2005: PalmOne renamed Palm, Inc.

---

software to other companies, such as America Online Inc. and Motorola Inc.

Qualcomm Inc. and Nokia used Palm OS in their most advanced mobile phones. However, Palm saw smarter mobile phones as the company's second biggest competitive threat after Microsoft. Nokia was also a member of the Symbian consortium, which was developing its own operating system for wireless Internet devices. Handspring and Telefon AB L.M. Ericsson were also members of this effort.

In this rapidly changing industry, competitors often had to cooperate. For example, Palm's organizers were designed to work with the Windows-based programs running on PCs. Palm's struggles and victories were cited by opposing sides at the Microsoft antitrust trial.

2000 IPO

Palm Inc.'s IPO in March 2000 displayed high-tech speculation at its most febrile. Priced at $38, shares reached $165 each before closing at $95, giving Palm a market valuation of $53 billion—more than that of General Motors and McDonald's, and more than that of its parent company, 3Com, valued at $28 billion. At the time 3Com still owned 94 percent of Palm's stock; however, in July it completed the distribution of its remaining shares to stockholders.

A revamped Microsoft operating system appeared in a series of Pocket PC devices launched by Hewlett-Packard, Compaq, and Casio in April 2000. The Pocket PC enjoyed a sleeker design than the somewhat boxy Pilots. According to the *Wall Street Journal,* independent programmers who developed Palm-based software remained intensely loyal, often refusing to adapt applications for the rival Windows CE systems. Palm claimed to have 70,000 third-party developers registered in the middle of 2000, up from only 3,000 at the beginning of 1999. Many of these had modest operations, some distributing their programs over the Internet as shareware. In contrast, Microsoft had licensed 200 companies to work on Pocket PC programs; many were larger companies.

Revenues in the last quarter of 1999/2000 were more than double those of the previous year. Suppliers of display screens and memory had difficulty keeping up with ever accelerating demand. A few faulty memory chips were allowed into production; Palm offered a software fix. Full-year sales exceeded $1 billion.

2001 Slowdown

Boosting its wireless Internet services, Palm bought Any-Day.com, which produced Internet-based calendars, in June 2000 for $80 million in cash and stock options. It had also bought e-mail provider Actual Software Corp. Palm planned to offer expansion slots in its organizers by early 2001, an area where it lagged behind Visor and Pocket PC devices. Personal electronics powerhouse Sony was preparing to introduce its own PDA.

In a race to develop more advanced features in a shrinking market, Palm and its rivals were buying companies for their technology. Palm bought several over the year. It acquired Portland wireless-synchronization expert WeSync for about $40 million in late 2000. Handspring, Inc. made its first acquisition, picking up Bluelark Systems Inc. of Mountain View, California, in a $16 million stock swap. Bluelark made Internet tools for handhelds.

These purchases were not able to forestall a collapse in the handheld computer market in a slowing economy. A two-months premature announcement of the company's new m500 and m505 models did not help sales of units already in stores.

As Palm's share price began to evaporate, it had to cancel a plan to acquire Boise's Extended Systems, Inc., a wireless technology producer for the corporate market, for $264 million in stock.

In May 2001, the once high-flying Palm laid off employees for the first time and put the brakes on a planned 11-building headquarters complex. As the year progressed, PDA manufacturers introduced deep discounts to keep the machines moving.

Hoping to increase PDA use before the days of widespread wireless Internet, Palm provided infrared beaming stations to a wide range of partners. PDA users at certain sites could beam relevant information at a number of kiosks, including newspaper stories and transit schedules at train stations; special offers at retailers such as Banana Republic; and movie listings at theaters.

Palm acquired the Be operating system of former Apple exec Jean-Louis Gassee in August 2001 for $11 million in stock. Be boasted impressive Internet and multimedia capabilities. The acquisition included engineering talent to bolster Palm's Platform Solutions Group. Palm had divided into two business units dedicated to hardware and software, respectively, in July 2001. The company was hoping the separation would improve operating system sales to other manufacturers. The new software unit was dubbed PalmSource and led by former Apple exec David Nagel. A former Gateway exec led the hardware unit.

Not only did Palm have to deal with the familiar threat posed by Microsoft, but there was a new threat to confront: the Blackberry, a wildly popular handheld pager and wireless e-mail system developed by Ontario's Research in Motion, Ltd. Mobile phone manufacturers were also edging into traditional PDA territory by adding new features to their phones.

Palm and its rivals countered the Blackberry threat by developing their own wireless Internet products. Handspring produced a new hybrid device called the Treo that could make voice calls and check e-mail. However, the expensive new product hit resistance from the mobile phone networks it depended on, and Handspring, too, began losing money.

Palm was also trying to increase its presence in the corporate market by offering features such as wireless database access and high security, noted the *San Francisco Chronicle.* Medical doctors, who appreciated ready access to tons of technical data, formed an important niche market. Palm's hardware business soon developed two main product lines: the high end Tungsten brand for professionals, and the Zire brand for new users and students.

Palm had a relatively broad range of products and leaned toward less expensive price points: a Zire sold for as little as $99. By the 2002 Christmas shopping season, its distribution had expanded to such high volume markets as QVC and Target.

2003 Spinoff

PalmSource, the company's software unit, won control of the Palm brand as the company split into two parts, which relocated into separate headquarters in August 2002. The hardware business was dubbed the Palm Solutions Group.

Palm CEO Carl Yankowski had resigned in November 2001; he was one of numerous executives to leave the company during the restructuring. His duties were taken by company Chairman Eric Benhamou. Benhamou, a native of Algeria, had designed Palm's spinoff from 3Com, noted the *Wall Street Journal.*

In June 2003, Palm, Inc. announced it was purchasing rival Handspring in a stock swap (worth $240 million when the deal closed in October). The *Wall Street Journal* noted Handspring had been valued at $9 billion in its heyday. Both companies' workforces had been greatly scaled back by this time—Handspring had 250 employees to Palm's 800—and there were plans for another round of layoffs at the combined company. In October 2003, Palm, Inc. spun off PalmSource, its software unit, while the original company, which retained the hardware operations, was renamed PalmOne, Inc.

According to *Business Week,* palmOne still led the traditional PDA market with a 40 percent share, while Handspring had become a niche player in the emerging "smartphone" market, which was exploding. Handspring's gamble on these combination devices came too early to pay off for Handspring, but would help save palmOne. The $399 Treo Smartphone became a hit among gadget-rich professionals who could use it to replace their PDAs, mobile phones, cameras, and MP3 players.

PalmOne was renamed Palm, Inc. in July 2005 after it bought the remaining rights to use of the Palm name for $30 million. The software business, PalmSource, had not succeeded in conquering the operating system market, observed the *San Francisco Chronicle;* Palm was still its main customer.

Still more new products were being launched. Palm introduced its LifeDrive line, which featured four gigabyte hard drives, in the spring of 2005. Later in the year, Palm signed

separate deals with two of its archrivals. In September, it announced it was developing a Treo with Microsoft's operating system to help stave off competition from Research in Motion's Blackberry. The next month, it announced a pact to put Research in Motion's wireless e-mail software on its Treo 650.

Principal Subsidiaries

Palm Comércio de Aparelhos Eletrônicos Ltda. (Brazil); Palm Europe Limited (UK); Palm Italy S.r.l.; PalmOne France; PalmOne Germany GmbH; Palm Global Operations Ltd. (Ireland); Palm Asia Pacific Limited (Hong Kong); PalmOne Ireland Investment; Palm Latin America, Inc. (USA); PalmOne Mexico S.A. de C.V.; Palm Benelux B.V. (The Netherlands); Palm Australasia Pty Limited (Australia); Palm Canada Inc.; Palm Singapore Pte. Ltd.; Palm Nordic AB (Sweden); PalmOne, K.K. (Japan); Handspring International SARL (Switzerland); Handspring International Ltd. (BVI); Handspring Facility Company LLC.

Principal Competitors

Dell Inc.; Hewlett-Packard Company; Nokia Oy; Research in Motion Ltd.; Sony Corp.

Further Reading

Alsop, Stewart, "Innovative Graffiti Might Actually Make PDAs Useable," *InfoWorld,* September 26, 1994, p. 130.

Bransten, Lisa, and Scott Thurm, "For Palm Computers, an IPO and a Flashy Rival," *Wall Street Journal,* September 14, 1999, p. B1.

Brewin, Bob, "Palm's Mace Is Officially 'Paranoid' About PocketPC," *Computerworld,* April 17, 2000, p. 12.

Buckman, Rebecca, "Microsoft to Unveil Pocket PCs in Big Rematch with Palm Inc.," *Wall Street Journal,* April 18, 2000, p. B6.

Clark, Don, and Ted Bridis, "Palm Is Cited by Both Sides of Microsoft Case," *Wall Street Journal,* May 4, 2000, p. B6.

Croal, N'Gai, "The World in Your Hand," *Newsweek,* May 31, 1999, p. 22.

Edwards, Cliff, "Palm Reaches Out for a Hand; But Will a Merger with Handspring Be Enough to Fend Off Ferocious Rivals?," *Business-Week,* November 3, 2003, p. 74.

Fost, Dan, "PalmOne to Go Back to Its Old Name," *San Francisco Chronicle,* May 25, 2005, p. C1.

Gore, Andrew, "Never Say Never Again," *Macworld,* July 2000, p. 23.

Guth, Robert A., "Microsoft, Palm Unite to Fight Blackberry," *Wall Street Journal,* September 25, 2001, p. B1.

Hua, Vanessa, "Betting on Beaming; Palm Hopes Infrared Stations Expand Audience for PDAs," *San Francisco Chronicle,* July 5, 2001, p. E1.

——, "Palm Gears Up for New Go-Around in PDA Market," *San Francisco Chronicle,* October 14, 2002, p. E1.

——, "Palm Grabs at Corporate Customers," *San Francisco Chronicle,* June 17, 2002, p. E1.

Hwang, Diana, "Palm Grasps Handheld Market," *Computer Reseller News,* May 2, 1994, p. 62.

Jackson, David S., "Palm-to-Palm," *Time,* March 16, 1998, pp. 42–44.

Mossberg, Walter S., "The PalmPilot Has Some New Rivals But No Competition," *Wall Street Journal,* July 2, 1998, p. B1.

——, "A Palm-Size Computer That's Easy to Use and Cheap, Finally," *Wall Street Journal,* March 28, 1996, p. B1.

Nakache, Patricia, "Secrets of the New Brand Builders," *Fortune,* June 22, 1998, pp. 167–70.

Nasri, Jennifer, "Investor Frenzy Causes Palm Inc.'s Market Valuation to Soar," *Weekly Corporate Growth Report,* March 13, 2000.

Norr, Henry, "Palm Snags Be Assets, Engineering Team," *San Francisco Chronicle,* August 17, 2001, p. B1.

Pui-Wing Tam, "Army of Programmers Helps Palm Keep Its Edge; Loyal Independent Designers Decline to Adapt Software for Rival Microsoft System," *Wall Street Journal,* June 1, 2000, p. B1.

——, "For Palm, Splitting in Two Isn't Seamless," *Wall Street Journal,* June 27, 2002, p. B4.

——, "Handspring Plans Line of Hybrid Devices," *Wall Street Journal,* October 15, 2001, p. B7.

——, "No Room to Hedge—New Tech Dilemma: Big Bets Now Mean Other Projects Die," *Wall Street Journal,* May 14, 2003, p. A1.

——, "Palm Plans Slot for Hand-Held Devices to Offer Memory Boost, More Functions," *Wall Street Journal,* June 27, 2000, p. B8.

——, "Palm Profit Jumps 82 Percent, Beats Forecasts," *Wall Street Journal,* June 29, 2000, p. B10.

——, "Palm's Fortunes Take a Tumble, Pressuring CEO," *Wall Street Journal,* June 4, 2001, p. B1.

——, "Palm's Founders to Get IPO at Handspring," *Wall Street Journal,* June 15, 2000, p. B1.

——, "Palm to Buy Handspring as Hand-Helds Morph into Phones," *Wall Street Journal,* June 5, 2003, p. B1.

——, "Palm to Create Separate Subsidiary for Key Software-Platform Group," *Wall Street Journal,* July 30, 2001, p. B4.

——, "Palm Treo to Use RIM's Software As Rivals Team," *Wall Street Journal,* October 17, 2005, p. B7.

——, "Pilot Error: How Palm Tumbled from Star of Tech to Target of Microsoft," *Wall Street Journal,* September 7, 2001, p. A1.

——, "That Nosy Shopper May Be a Handspring Executive—As Hand-Held Battle Heats Up, Companies' Agents Monitor Store Displays, Sales Spiels," *Wall Street Journal,* November 29, 2000, p. B1.

Pui-Wing Tam, and Mahvish Khan, "Hand-Held Makers Slash Prices and Rev Up Promotions As Sales Slow—Economy and Gadget Fatigue Hurt the Pocket Computers," *Wall Street Journal,* August 2, 2001, p. B1.

Quittner, Joshua, "PCs? Forget 'Em!," *Time,* May 8, 2000, p. 105.

Sears, Steven M., "Palm IPO Soars, Then Retreats a Bit, Pushing Traders to Unwind Options in Parent 3Com," *Wall Street Journal,* March 3, 2000, p. C26.

Stirpe, Amanda, "Can Palm Hold On?," *Computer Reseller News,* October 18, 1999, pp. 117–18.

Thurm, Scott, "Palm Inc. Gets Ready for New Hands," *Wall Street Journal,* February 28, 2000, p. B1.

——, "3Com Faces Bleaker Future Without Palm," *Wall Street Journal,* March 9, 2000, p. B6.

——, "3Com Names Yankowski to CEO Post at Soon-Independent Palm Computing," *Wall Street Journal,* December 3, 1999, p. B5.

Wildstrom, Stephen H., "The PalmPilot Flies Higher," *Business Week,* Industrial/Technology Edition, March 23, 1998, p. 20.

—Frederick C. Ingram

Pegasus Solutions, Inc.

Campbell Centre I
8350 North Central Expressway
Suite 1900
Dallas, Texas 75206
U.S.A.
Telephone: (214) 234-4000
Fax: (214) 234-4040
Web site: http://www.pegs.com

Public Company
Founded: 1989 as THISCO, The Hotel Industry Switch
 Company
Employees: 1,320
Sales: $190.1 million (2004)
Stock Exchanges: NASDAQ
Ticker Symbol: PEGS
NAIC: 514210 Data Processing Services; 511210
 Software Publishers; 541990 All Other Professional,
 Scientific and Technical Services

Pegasus Solutions, Inc. serves the worldwide hotel and travel industry with a medley of technological services. Founded in 1989, the company has evolved to become the hotel industry's largest provider of third-party marketing and reservations services. Pegasus is headquartered in Dallas, Texas, and has regional corporate sites in Scottsdale, Arizona; London; and Singapore, as well as offices in ten other countries. The company provides a number of technological solutions to some 60,000 hotel properties worldwide, and to the vast majority of travel agencies. Pegasus' resources for the hotel and travel industry include central reservation systems, electronic distribution services, commission processing and payment services, and marketing representation services. Pegasus' Utell and Unirez representation services are known and utilized in 140 countries around the world. Pegasus' services are primarily business-to-business, with the exception of Hotelbook.com, serving online consumers with access to independent hotels all over the world.

1989: Founded to Create Technology

The company was founded in 1989 to develop the technology to connect hotel reservation systems to the airlines' global distribution systems. A group of about 15 leading hotel and travel company executives recruited John F. Davis III to launch The Hotel Industry Switch Company (THISCO). Davis's business abilities and entrepreneurial experience and success had come to their attention when Davis established ATC Communications and called on them to offer the services of his call center to manage their overflow reservation calls. Under Davis's leadership, the company was given the goal of developing the "switch" technology to link systems of the THISCO member hotels' systems to global distribution systems used by travel agents.

It did not take long for the company to succeed and be recognized. In 1991, President and CEO Davis was selected by *Travel Agent* magazine as one of their "People of the Year" for solving frequent problems and inefficiencies hotel operators and travel agents deal regularly with by developing the technology to connect the hotels' central reservations systems (CRSs) to the global distribution systems (GDSs).

Finding initial success in the travel and technology niche, Davis developed another service targeted to that same market. He followed up by establishing the Hotel Clearing Corporation (HCC) in 1992. HCC enabled travel agents to consolidate their hotel commissions in one check for a small fee. In addition, in 1994 the company launched the first Internet site for booking hotels in real-time. It was called TravelWeb. Consumers responded well to the new service. A year later Davis created Pegasus Systems as the umbrella under which all three technological travel services operated. Pegasus Systems was the parent company of THISCO, HCC, and TravelWeb.

Going Public: 1997

In 1997 Pegasus Systems had a successful initial public offering of $53.4 million, distancing its ownership from the original small group of investors. Pegasus Systems' public campaign raised $40.5 million for the company and fueled further business growth. The company was listed in the Fast-Tech 50 in both 1998 and 1999.

315

Company Perspectives:

The company's mission is to maximize revenue and profitability for hotels and travel distributors worldwide by providing the most comprehensive and innovative services and technologies in the industry.

By 2000 Pegasus became the power behind the popular travel deal web site Hotwire.com, helping provide Hotwire with one-stop direct access to hotels around the globe, up-to-date price deals, and little hassle. The addition of Hotwire opened another distribution channel to reach Pegasus's hotel clients, including Summit Hotels and Resorts, Utell, Sterling Hotels and Resorts, and Golden Tulip Worldwide. Pegasus also continued to unveil new services for the hotel and travel industry, such as a new Customer Relationship Management tool.

2000: Name Change and Growth Spurt

In April 2000 the company changed its name from Pegasus Systems to Pegasus Solutions to better reflect the breadth of services offered by the company. The company's offerings had grown to include marketing services for independent hotels as well as the technological solutions the industry had come to expect and respect.

Soon after the name change, Pegasus purchased a much larger company called REZsolutions. In the hotel industry, REZsolutions was the biggest third-party marketing and reservations provider. Pegasus acquired REZsolutions for $198 million in cash and stock. The merger enhanced Pegasus' technological capabilities and expanded the company's presence internationally.

As part of the purchase, Pegasus gained access to Utell, a company with a more global reach that was providing reservation services to more than 6,000 hotels. According to *Hotel and Motel Management* magazine, as a result of the acquisition, "Pegasus emerges as the total-solution provider for reservations distribution, whether electronic or voice, for independent hotels as well as for worldwide chains." The company grew from "two offices and 170 employees" to "39 offices in 25 countries." Pegasus not only gained worldwide exposure, it would soon benefit from an experienced sales force and access to more independent hotel brands. *Travel Agent* magazine called the company "the invisible hand behind every type of hotel booking."

Acquisition Fueling Global Expansion

Soon after the company's growth spurt, Pegasus made headlines for global expansion into the travel industry businesses in the U.K. and Japanese markets. In addition, Pegasus realigned its business operations into technology and hospitality divisions. The technology group included information technology development, business intelligence, electronic distribution, application-server computing services, and central-reservation-system software licensing and integration. The hospitality group included Pegasus Commission Processing (which had been HCC) and Hotel Representation Services.

The merger with the larger company was not a smooth one. *Forbes* magazine referred to REZsolutions as a "poorly managed hodgepodge." "The group marketing independent hotels had no idea what the Web-based central reservations systems for the likes of Hilton or Fairmont were up to. The marketing subsidiary, Utell, was positively obese: 2,000 people in 39 offices across 25 countries, managing only 6,400 accounts and miserably at that."

Pegasus saw its stock fall to $7 a share, in contrast to the $40 high enjoyed early the previous year. The company let go of several of REZsolutions' top executives and 100 employees of Utell while working to streamline operations. Pegasus continued its pioneering efforts in developing and implementing new services for the industry.

Growing Recognition: Late 1990s and 2000s

Davis succeeded in getting the larger company back on track, so much so that *Travel Agent* magazine chose him again as one of its People of the Year in 2000, for "doing the same thing [that he had been recognized for in 1991] but on a larger scale." Davis's growing and frequent recognition in the industry was widespread. In 1999 *Business Travel News* named him to its "Travel Industry Hall of Fame," and for five years in the 1990s it cited Davis as one of the travel business's "25 Most Influential Executives." In addition, in 1998 *Interactive Travel Report* named him its "Person of the Year in Interactive Travel." *Computerworld* cited him as an "Agent of Change" in 1995. In 2001 Davis was inducted into the Hospitality and Financial and Technology Professionals International Technology Hall of Fame

By 2001, what started out as the commission payment service, HCC, was proving to be a successful arm of the business. Pegasus was consolidating $42 million each month in commission payments for customers in more than 200 countries, all done through an electronic network. The company was providing those services to nine out of the top ten travel agencies in the United States. In addition, Pegasus was involved in 70 percent of all electronic hotel reservations generated through travel agents and the Internet.

According to a 2001 *Dallas Business Journal* article, Pegasus' customers included nine of the world's largest hotel companies, with some 40,000 hotel properties. Pegasus also powered more than 1,000 web sites for securing hotel reservations. The business world recognized Pegasus' strength in the business-to-business category. *Forbes ASAP* magazine included Pegasus in its list of "Best of the Web: Top B2B Websites" in September 2001.

Pegasus garnered additional attention from the mainstream business world when *Forbes* magazine put the company on its 200 Best Small Companies list. Pegasus was the only company on the list whose business was related to the hotel industry. According to the magazine, Pegasus was "a compilation of profitable, financially strong small-cap businesses." Within the industry, Pegasus' service was gaining recognition and faithful customers. The company's Utell Service was selected as the preferred provider of hotel rooms by nine out of the top 50 travel agencies in the United States. Utell represented independent hotels around the globe.

Key Dates:

1989: Company is founded as THISCO, The Hotel Industry Switch Company.
1992: THISCO CEO creates Hotel Clearing Corporation (HCC).
1994: TravelWeb is launched as the first online site for real-time hotel reservations.
1995: Pegasus Systems is created as parent company of THISCO, HCC, and TravelWeb.
1997: Pegasus Systems goes public.
2000: Pegasus Systems acquires REZsolutions and becomes Pegasus Solutions.
2001: Pegasus Solutions purchases GETS, LLC.
2003: Pegasus Solutions acquires Unirez.
2004: Pegasus Solutions sells TravelWeb stake to Priceline.com.
2005: Pegasus Solutions opens an office in Beijing; launches Hotelbook.com.

2003: Acquiring Competitor Unirez

The company was not done growing. In late 2003 Pegasus Solutions acquired competitor Unirez for $38 million. Unirez was a leading hotel reservation distribution company that delivered lower cost connectivity-only representation services to independent hotels and small groups. At the time, Unirez was a young company, just four years old, with annual sales of $18 million. Its success was partially due to its flexibility and easy-to-use format. With Unirez under its wing, Pegasus could expand the reach of its hotel reservation service, Utell, with its primarily European customers. Formats of the two programs (Utell and Unirez) would eventually be integrated. According to *Travel Agent* magazine, the acquisition was expected to facilitate the company's "growth in the United States customer base and enhance its technology offerings to small hotel chains and independents worldwide."

In 2004 Pegasus was in the selling rather than buying mode. The company sold its TravelWeb stake to Priceline.com, and extended its services agreement with TravelWeb through 2007. Pegasus also released a web-based property management system, PegasusCentral. Another reorganization was in the works as Pegasus worked to integrate its technology and hospitality divisions into one.

By 2005 Pegasus Solutions was successfully expanding its presence in the Asia-Pacific region. The previous year it had brokered a deal with Ctrip, a leading Chinese online travel service provider. The deal was for electronic distribution, and would help increase the company's business presence in China. Pegasus soon opened an office in central Beijing. At the time Pegasus also had offices in Singapore, Tokyo, and Sydney.

The company received additional industry recognition for its growth and success. Accounting firm Deloitte and Touche listed Pegasus Solutions in its prestigious Technology Fast 500 honor roll, indicating it was among North America's fastest growing technology companies. It was the fourth year in a row Pegasus had made that list. The company's RezView central reservation system received a World Travel Award in 2005 for the third consecutive year as the "World's Leading Hotel Reservation Service."

2005: Exploring Strategic Options

Despite the kudos, the company continued to face increased pressure from similar services including Expedia.com. In mid-2005 Pegasus leaders began to explore corporate strategic options as many of the company's competitors were increasing their reach and scope with acquisitions of other related businesses such as Orbitz and Hotwire. Breaking up the company was a possibility; there were some companies interested in acquiring all or part of Pegasus Solutions.

But Pegasus was still in a growth mode. The company reentered the consumer market by establishing Hotelbook.com, a consumer site linking online customers to a cache of some 5,000, mostly independent hotels, with descriptions of their attributes and amenities as well as detailed information about general travel destinations. The company also had plans to launch a similar site targeted toward consumers of high-end, five star hotels. Pegasus also announced it was getting out of the property management system (PMS) business and sold its NovaPlus and Guestview businesses to competitor MSI.

Being a pioneer and innovator in the travel and hotel industry had kept Pegasus Solutions on the cutting edge of the industry since its inception. What started out as the original switch technology, now connected more than 40,000 hotels worldwide to global distribution systems. Under Davis's leadership, Pegasus Solutions had exerted a major impact on the travel and hotel industry. The future of the company and the industry appeared promising since online hotel booking was still a booming business, with no signs of waning.

Principal Subsidiaries

Utell; Unirez.

Principal Competitors

IAC/Interactive Corp. (Expedia); Sabre Holdings Corp. (Travelocity); Cendant Corporation (Orbitz).

Further Reading

Adams, Bruce, "*Forbes* Magazine Selected Pegasus Solutions in the *Forbes* 200 Best Small Companies List," *Hotel and Motel Management,* March 3, 2003, p. 24.
——, "Pegasus Realigns After Acquiring REZsolutions," *Hotel and Motel Management,* June 5, 2000, p. 74.
Bush, Melinda, "Pegasus Leader Is One of the Industry's Technology Gurus," *Hotel and Motel Management,* January 15, 2001, p. 31.
Cecil, Mark, "Pegasus Auction: Expected to Wrap up Soon," *America's Intelligence Wire,* August 1, 2005.
Cook, Lynn, "Some Reservations—John Davis Bets Early and Big," *Forbes,* February 5, 2001, p. 102.
"Ctrip Signs Distribution Agreement with Pegasus Solutions," *China Business News,* December 2, 2004.
Marta, Suzanne, "Dallas-Based Hotel-Reservation Firm Pegasus Solutions to Acquire Rival Unirez," *Dallas Morning News,* November 6, 2003.

——, ''Dallas-Based Pegasus Solutions Inc. Plans Online Hotel Site,'' *Dallas Morning News*, July 25, 2005.

Moyse, Misty, ''Pegasus Solutions, Inc.: Acquisition Led to a Stellar Year,'' *Dallas Business Journal*, May 18, 2001, p. 18C.

''Pegasus Completes Unirez Acquisition,'' *Travel Agent*, December 4, 2003, http://www.travelagentcentral.com.

''Pegasus Peruses Strategic Solutions,'' *Mergers and Acquisitions Report*, April 25, 2005.

''Pegasus Solutions CEO John F. Davis III Appointed Chairman of the Board,'' *123Jump*, April 27, 2001, p. 2141.

''Pegasus Solutions Expands Presence in Asia-Pacific Region,'' *Asia Africa Intelligence Wire*,'' June 15, 2005.

''Pegasus Solutions' Leader Selected for Technology Hall of Fame,'' *Hotel and Motel Management*, June 18, 2001, p. 48.

Webber, Sara Perez, ''Spreading Its Wings,'' *Travel Agent*, January 8, 2001, p. 28.

—Mary Heer-Forsberg

Phelps Dodge Corporation

One North Central Avenue
Phoenix, Arizona 85004
U.S.A.
Telephone: (602) 366-8100
Fax: (602) 366-7329
Web site: http://www.phelpsdodge.com

Public Company
Incorporated: 1885 as Copper Queen Consolidated
    Mining Company
Employees: 15,500
Sales: $7.09 billion (2004)
Stock Exchanges: New York
Ticker Symbol: PD
NAIC: 212234 Copper Ore and Nickel Ore Mining;
    331411 Primary Smelting and Refining of Copper

One of the largest copper mining concerns in the world, Phelps Dodge Corporation operates several manufacturing businesses to insulate the company from the cyclicality of copper prices. Phelps Dodge's copper business is conducted through the company's Phelps Dodge Mining Company subsidiary, which also produces silver, gold, and other minerals as a byproduct of its copper operations. Its Climax Molybdenum Co. unit is the world's largest molybdenum producer. The manufacturing side of the company's business operates through a division called Phelps Dodge Industries, which has expanded aggressively during the 1990s. The manufacturing businesses include Columbian Chemicals Company, one of the world's largest producers of carbon black (used in inks and tires); Phelps Dodge Wire & Cable; and Phelps Dodge High Performance Conductors, which manufactures specialty conductors used by the automotive, computer, and aerospace industries.

19th-Century Origins

In 1834 founder Anson Phelps, a New York entrepreneur thoroughly experienced in the import-export trade and well-connected in his targeted British market, formed Phelps, Dodge & Co. Along with his junior partners, sons-in-law William

Dodge and Daniel James, Phelps supplied his English customers with cotton, replacing it on the homeward journey with tin, tin plate, iron, and copper, for sale to government, trade, and individual consumers in the United States. Before long, Phelps started a manufacturing company in Connecticut called the Ansonia Brass and Battery Company, and in 1845 he helped organize the Ansonia Manufacturing Company, which produced kettles, lamps, rivets, buttons, and other metal items.

Phelps steered his fledgling empire grimly through a seven-year panic that began during 1837. His reward came during the following 14 years of national prosperity, when large numbers of his products went west with new settlers, accompanied travelers on the rapidly expanding railroads, and provided a modicum of comfort for miners at the recently discovered Sierra Nevada gold deposits in California. Even broader markets came from such inventions as the McCormick reaper and the electric telegraph, whose need for cable wire would swell Phelps Dodge coffers well into the next century. By 1849 the company was capitalized at almost $1 million, and its profits were almost 30 percent.

Phelps's death in 1853 gave his son and each of his two sons-in-law a 25 percent interest in the business, with 15 percent going to a younger son-in-law. This second partnership was scarcely five years old when Anson Phelps, Jr., died. On January 1, 1859, the partnership was revised again, to increase the firm's capitalization to $1.5 million and to give William Dodge and Daniel James each a 28 percent share. With reorganization complete, the company turned its attention to developing industries such as mining.

An interest in timber had begun in the mid-1830s, when Phelps, Dodge accepted timberlands in Pennsylvania in lieu of payment for a debt. Later it built the world's largest lumber mill there, establishing a timber agency in Baltimore, Maryland, to send its products to domestic and foreign customers.

Despite these diversifications, the principal interests of the company were still mercantile. However, through the advice of James Douglas, a mining engineer and chemical geologist, Phelps, Dodge was persuaded to take a large block of stock in the Morenci copper mine in what was then the Arizona Territory. Morenci was owned by the Detroit Copper Company,

Company Perspectives:

We are committed to providing superior quality products, produced at internationally competitive costs, to customers around the globe. We seek to prosper by forging partnerships with our customers and suppliers.

Our mission in conducting business is to create and enhance long-term value for our shareholders and our employees, and to do so in an environmentally responsible manner as good citizens of the communities in which we live and work.

which exchanged the stock for a $30,000 loan. Douglas was also enthusiastic about prospects for another claim called Atlanta, situated in Arizona's Bisbee district, about 200 miles southwest of Morenci. In 1881 the company bought the Atlanta claim for $40,000.

Two years later Phelps, Dodge had a chance to purchase the adjoining Copper Queen mine, which was then producing about 300 tons of ore monthly. The partnership decided to buy Copper Queen when Douglas hit the main Atlanta lode in 1884, at almost the same time that a Copper Queen tunnel penetrated the lode from a different spot. Arizona mining operations at the time stuck strictly to the ''rule of the apex,'' according to which a claim owner could follow a vein of ore onto another claim, if the deposit had come closest to the surface on his land. This had occurred with Copper Queen, and Phelps, Dodge, rather than risk losing this strike to the Copper Queen owners, purchased the Copper Queen mine, merging it with the Atlanta claim.

In August 1885 Phelps, Dodge & Co. decided to streamline its operations by incorporating the subsidiary Copper Queen Consolidated Mining Company in New York, with James Douglas as president. Cautiously, Douglas made no major acquisitions for ten years. Then, he bought the Moctezuma Copper Company in Sonora, Mexico, from the Guggenheim family. Two years later he purchased the Detroit Copper Company.

20th Century: A Focus on Copper

A large increase in domestic iron production during the 1890s plus a two cents tariff on each pound of imported tin plate instituted in 1890 combined to make profitable metal markets hard to find. These factors and the fast growth of the company's mining interests forced it to withdraw from most ventures other than copper mining and selling by 1906.

Phelps, Dodge still retained its Ansonia Brass and Copper Company, however, which had become one of the largest U.S. manufacturers of copper wire for the new telephone industry. Other products included brass wire, sheet copper, and rolled brass.

The shift to mining interests led to a need for another reorganization. In 1908 the old Phelps, Dodge & Co. partnership was dissolved, to be replaced by a corporation called Phelps, Dodge & Co., Inc. Capitalized at $50 million, the new concern consolidated all the various Phelps, Dodge mining interests: Copper Queen Consolidated Mining Company; Moctezuma Copper Company; Detroit Copper Mining Company;

and Stag Cañon Fuel Company, a subsidiary consisting of coal and timber properties near Dawson, New Mexico, purchased in 1905 to supply the mines and smelters with fuel.

By this time there were 10,000 employees working in the mines, the smelters, the company railroads, and other ventures. There was also competition from other mining companies, which were able to mine copper, but lacked smelting facilities for processing. To provide these competitors with more efficient service while handling the smelting for its own copper mines, Phelps, Dodge abandoned its old Bisbee smelter and erected a new one some 23 miles away.

Following the 1917 entry of the United States into World War I, demand for copper for munitions and communications exploded. The company smelters turned out 600 to 700 tons daily. Also in 1917, Phelps, Dodge & Co., Inc. transferred its assets and subsidiaries to Copper Queen Consolidated Mining Company. Copper Queen became the operating company and changed its name to Phelps Dodge Corporation.

With all enterprises operating at capacity, the Bisbee miners went on strike in July 1917. One factor was the powerlessness of mine managers to make policy decisions on behalf of top management in New York. Another was the shrinking supply of experienced workers, who were going into the military or being lured away by higher salaries and better working conditions.

The International Workers of the World (Wobblies) easily caught the attention of the miners working for Phelps Dodge. At issue were better working conditions, a wage increase to $6 per day, and abolition of the unpopular physical examination to which all applicants were subjected before obtaining a job. Many suspected the exam was a filter to exclude prospective miners with undesired political affiliations.

When the strike was two weeks old, Phelps Dodge Director Walter Douglas instructed an employee of the El Paso & Southwestern Railroad to transport about 1,200 strikers to Columbus, New Mexico, where they were to be turned loose. After the commander of a nearby army camp refused permission to unload the cars, the workers were released in a small Mexican town called Hermanas, where they lived at starvation level until two carloads of food arrived from the U.S. Army base at nearby El Paso, Texas. Though 25 participants in the Bisbee deportation were indicted, no particular blame was attached to any individual and the matter petered out.

The end of World War I brought a need for downscaling of all operations. Government warehouses were packed with more than 800 million pounds of copper, and more was coming in from Chilean mines at low cost. To counter these new challenges, Phelps Dodge and other large U.S. copper mining companies cut production and formed the Copper and Brass Research Association to seek out and promote new uses for copper. At the same time, the companies founded the Copper Export Association, pooling 400 pounds of copper for exclusive sale in foreign markets.

Suffering acutely from the postwar slump in demand was the Arizona Copper Company, with holdings adjoining the Phelps Dodge Morenci properties. Part of this company's assets was a huge deposit of low-grade ore that it could not afford to de-

Key Dates:

1834: Phelps, Dodge & Co. trading company is formed as a partnership.

1885: Phelps, Dodge incorporates Copper Queen Consolidated Mining Company.

1908: Copper Queen and other companies consolidate into Phelps, Dodge & Co., Inc.

1917: Phelps, Dodge transfers assets to Copper Queen, which is renamed Phelps Dodge Corporation.

1930: Nichols Copper Company and National Electric Products Corporation are acquired.

1931: Calumet & Arizona Mining Company is acquired.

1932: United Verde Copper Company is acquired.

1944: Company begins building the Horseshoe Dam on Arizona's Verde River.

1950: Phelps Dodge is second largest copper producer in the United States.

1963: Phelps Dodge Aluminum Products Corporation is formed.

1969: Phelps Dodge begins acquiring interest in Denver's Colorado-based Western Nuclear, Inc. uranium mining company.

1971: Aluminum business is merged with Consolidated Aluminum.

1982: Headquarters relocates from New York City to Phoenix.

1986: Uranium mining business is sold; carbon black producer Columbian Chemicals Company is acquired.

1988: Wheel producer Accuride Corporation is acquired.

1995: New manufacturing subsidiaries help give company record earnings.

1998: Phelps Dodge closes some mines while building manufacturing capacity abroad; most of Accuride is sold.

1999: Cyprus Amax Minerals Company is acquired for $1.8 billion.

2001: Hundreds are laid off as low copper prices, high energy bills hammer high-cost U.S. operations.

2005: Company increases production, pays dividends and bonuses as copper prices approach $2.

velop. Phelps Dodge bought Arizona Copper and merged it with its Morenci holdings in 1921 in exchange for 50,000 shares of capital stock.

By 1925 business expansion was demanding record amounts of copper. In that year almost 1.75 billion pounds of refined copper were produced all over the country. Arizona's contribution to this total was more than 800 million pounds, a quarter of which came from Phelps Dodge mines. The stock market crash in 1929 brought the bonanza to an end, however. Demand for copper dwindled everywhere, the price falling to 18 cents per pound from a high of 23 cents. Effects of the crash were felt immediately. Sales, which had been $46.1 million in 1928, were down to $38.7 million in 1929, though net earnings were $4 million, up from $2.6 million the year before.

In April 1930 Walter Douglas resigned as chief executive of Phelps Dodge. In his stead came Louis S. Cates. Cates's first priority was to integrate the Phelps Dodge operations and to cut costs and allow for the Arizona tax of two cents on every pound of copper processed. Cates then, also in 1930, acquired the Nichols Copper Company, which had an electrolytic refinery on Long Island, New York.

In another important 1930 acquisition, Phelps Dodge bought National Electric Products Corporation, a large manufacturer of copper products for electrical and building purposes, with an annual capacity of more than 200,000 pounds of fabricated copper products and 150,000 pounds of steel. National Electric brought the company eight plants and a major interest in the Habirshaw Cable and Wire Corporation.

Cates reorganized all subsidiaries into two efficient organizations. The first, the National Electric Products Corporation, consisted only of the National Metal Molding division. This division's main interest was steel products, and it eventually reverted to its original owners by an exchange of stock. The second division was headed by a new subsidiary called the Phelps Dodge Copper Corporation. This division was charged with operating all the fabricating divisions including Habirshaw Cable and Wire.

Cates's next challenge was the long-operative Copper Queen mine, whose high-grade ore was becoming inaccessible and too expensive to mine. Phelps Dodge acquired the Calumet & Arizona Mining Company, a longstanding rival with Bisbee acreage adjoining Copper Queen. Overriding the objections of Calumet President Gordon Campbell, who resigned in April 1931, the purchase became final in September, giving Phelps Dodge title to a low-cost New Cornelia mine 150 miles away at Ajo, Arizona. Phelps Dodge consolidated the Calumet & Arizona and Copper Queen operations to reap economies of scale.

The Depression continued, however; the end of 1932 showed sales of just under $22 million, as opposed to $50.3 million in 1931. In an effort to pare costs and keep pace with lower demand, Cates cut production at the Copper Queen. He also suspended all operations at New Cornelia, and closed both the Stag Canyon coal operations and Morenci.

Nevertheless, Phelps Dodge bought the United Verde Copper Company despite a steep price of $20.8 million. With about 6,100 acres of claims in Arizona, United Verde proved its worth in 1937, when reserves of 6.9 millions tons of ore were produced. In 1937 the company went ahead with long-held plans to expand operations at Morenci, where a clay ore-body was prepared for open-pit copper mining, refining, and smelting, at a cost of $32.6 million.

By 1939 the Depression years were part of the company's history. Sales reached $75.5 million, yielding total income of $15.5 million, and the number of employees, recorded in mid-1938, reached about 9,000.

World War II once again found plants operating at maximum capacity. Stepping in for employees on military service, women and Navajo Indians ran the Morenci mine, smelting facilities, and refining plant. Typical of pay rates was the wage for rock-shoveling: 64 cents per hour.

Once again operating at full capacity, Phelps Dodge supplied condenser tubes for the navy and cables for communications and electric power. Other orders were harder to fill, notably a specialized lead pipe in 50-mile lengths, which was laid under the English Channel to supply Britain's troops with gasoline for the Normandy invasion.

Already looking towards the war's end in 1944, the company began to build the Horseshoe Dam on the Verde River, about 55 miles northeast of Phoenix, Arizona, to allow for water conservation while filling the needs of its Morenci operations. Year-end 1944 sales figures of $168.1 million more than doubled the $80 million figure for 1940.

Post-World War II Expansion

By 1950 Phelps Dodge was the second largest domestic copper producer, contributing 30 percent of the country's output. It was also one of the world's top three, its position as a purely domestic supplier made even more secure by a two cents per pound import duty. Characteristic of the 1950s was government activism in the industry, partly as a result of the Korean War. At the end of 1950, the government instituted price controls for copper, placing a cap of 24.5 cents per pound. Other moves came as a result of a 1947 Federal Trade Commission study, emphasizing the surprisingly low level of competition in the industry, and intimating the power was concentrated in the hands of too few groups.

Though not specified by the report, there was also a belief that copper resources could be exhausted, because copper companies were doing little to find additional reserves, and that this situation should be remedied. Negotiations between the government and the mining companies followed. Over the next two years, the country's copper-mining capabilities increased by 25 percent, thanks to seven new mines.

Phelps Dodge's contribution to this effort was the Lavender Pit mine, opened in 1954 to develop an extension of the Bisbee operations known as the Bisbee East orebody. As was the case with most of the companies, terms of the agreement were that the open-pit mine should be developed and equipped with a smelter at a cost of $25 million, entirely corporate-sponsored. In return, the company asked for a guarantee that the government would buy its copper at protected prices. By 1956 Lavender Pit produced 80.3 million pounds of copper.

Another important development was the Peruvian Project, a joint venture between Phelps Dodge and three other mining companies intended to provide ownership of three southern Peru mines, together containing an estimated one billion tons of low-grade ore. Phelps Dodge's 16 percent share of the costs was $24.3 million. The peak sales year of the 1950s was 1956, when sales reached $540.3 million, yielding a total income of $153.9 million.

At the end of the 1950s, the company spread its wings beyond its Canadian subsidiaries, venturing into several developing countries. A 51 percent interest in a 1957 enterprise called the Phelps Dodge Copper Products Corporation of the Philippines gave it a new source of insulated wire and cable for electrical use. Another venture blossomed in 1960, when the United States Underseas Cable Corporation was established jointly with several U.S. companies and a West German company. There was also a San Salvador affiliation called the Phelps Dodge Products de

Centro America S.A., which manufactured electrical wire and cables for the Central American market.

Despite these overseas connections, however, Phelps Dodge kept its main activities in the United States. This policy protected its copper from politically inspired import tariffs, as well as from taxation, strike activity, and fluctuating prices found in foreign bases including Chile. By the end of 1963, this policy yielded $327 million in sales, from annual production reaching 261,400 tons.

Another advantage of domestic concentration was vertical integration. Now one of the country's three largest copper producers, Phelps Dodge through its fabricating subsidiaries provided outlets for its copper. This hedge against price swings also gave it immunity against purchasing at high prices to make sure that fabricating subsidiaries had an adequate copper supply.

By 1965 the price of copper rose from 34 cents to 36 cents per pound. Plastics, lead, aluminum, and zinc had advanced far enough to threaten long-term copper markets. Phelps Dodge President Robert Page felt it desirable to keep copper prices moderate enough to maintain demand for the metal.

Still, the new opportunities aluminum offered could not be ignored. In 1963 the company formed the Phelps Dodge Aluminum Products Corporation, producing aluminum wire and cable to complement the copper line. Though the aluminum enterprise produced 17 fabrication plants by 1970, the company foresaw little long-term profit in it, and therefore merged its company with the Consolidated Aluminum Corporation in 1971.

In July 1967 an industrywide strike began that lasted until the end of March 1968. The Phelps Dodge operations most affected were the Morenci, Ajo, and Bisbee mines, as well as the El Paso refinery. Run by a coalition of 14 unions led by the United Steelworkers of America, the strike called for company-wide bargaining for all operations, regardless of competitive and geographic differences. Eventually, an average increase of $1.13 per hour in wages and benefits sent workers back to their jobs after the administration of President Lyndon B. Johnson intervened. Post-strike operations recommenced without raw-copper shortages, since most refiners were able to reuse scrap copper to augment their reserves.

Company Chairman Robert Page handed the helm to George Munroe in 1969. Still holding the presidency (the office of chairman was abolished), Munroe oversaw the establishment of a new mine at Tyrone, New Mexico. Formerly known as Burro Mountain, this was a low-grade ore deposit that previously had been too expensive to work. New technology made the mine economically feasible, boosting total capacity by 20 percent annually. The expansion brought its reward; the decade ended with sales of $672.1 million.

In 1969 Phelps Dodge swapped 800,000 of its own shares for a 26 percent interest in Denver, Colorado-based Western Nuclear, Inc., a company concerned with uranium mining, milling, and exploration. Initially, an open-pit uranium mine and mill were erected near Spokane, Washington. Three years later, Western Nuclear became a wholly owned subsidiary, undergoing a $71 million expansion and modernization program to improve its production capacity at other facilities in Wyoming.

With the Clean Air Act of 1970, environmental concerns came to the fore. The most critical problem Phelps Dodge faced was at Douglas, Arizona, where its smelter regularly processed 7 percent of the nation's annual copper production. By 1973 Arizona anti-pollution laws required $17 million worth of emission-control adaptations to this smelter, although the Environmental Protection Agency (EPA) was still undecided about its requirements. This left a strong possibility of conflict between state and federal regulations. Fears of a clash were dispelled when federal standards proved to be lower than those of Arizona; state regulators were still dissatisfied, despite the money spent on emission control equipment. Phelps Dodge officials protested, claiming that these expensive standards would force the company to shut the smelter down, putting almost 2,000 people out of work.

Because of sluggish demand and foreign competition, production cutbacks followed at a new mine called Metcalf, and at Morenci, Ajo, and Tyrone. The shift showed up in net income figures: $121.7 million for 1974, $46.3 million by the following year, and $17.9 million by 1977. The smelters kept operating 24 hours a day, however, to cope with the large amount of ore that had accumulated during the shutdown for the installation of pollution controls.

By 1978 there were voluble industry complaints that piecemeal EPA regulations made long-term antipollution planning impossible. The $2 billion initially spent plus frequent updating added about ten cents per pound to production costs, bringing the consumer's price for copper up to about 75 cents per pound.

Coupled with cheaper foreign competition and sluggish demand, this brought a business-cycle trough to the industry. Company executives blamed the crisis on the waning uranium market (Western Nuclear had lost its biggest customer, the Washington Public Power Supply System), the demand slump caused by the slowdowns in the automobile and housing industries, and environmental protection woes. Many outsiders thought it was time to expand Phelps Dodge interests beyond copper.

In the first quarter of 1982 the company revenues showed a $19.1 million deficit. In April Munroe laid off 3,800 workers and closed all four mines and three out of four smelters. He also instituted salary cuts at all levels, and reluctantly took on short-term debt to cover operating costs.

The following year the United Steelworkers instituted an industrywide strike. Kennecott Corporation, the country's top copper producer, settled quickly, exchanging a three-year wage freeze for a cost-of-living allowance reaching $1.87 per hour at 6 percent inflation. Using this settlement as a model, the strikers then approached Phelps Dodge management. The company counteroffered abolition of the cost-of-living allowance, a three-year wage freeze, and lower wages for new workers.

By the end of August 1983 the stalemate had led many workers to cross picket lines, despite sharp harassment from hard-line strikers. At Morenci, the company called in the National Guard, fomenting more resentment. The strike ended uneasily the following fall, with the company refusing to budge on its position, and the miners voting to decertify the 13 unions that had long been present at the mines and the smelters.

Now, management turned its attention to reorganization. First on the agenda was a strategy to reduce production costs to less than 65 cents per pound, and lessen dependence on copper. The economy drive began with the 1982 move of company headquarters to Phoenix. At the same time, the Morenci, Ajo, and Douglas smelters were closed and replaced by a $92 million solvent extracting-electrowinning plant at Morenci that produced 100 million pounds of copper annually by mid-1987. Electrowinning is a process of recovering metals from a solution through electrolysis.

Electrowinning capacity grew further in 1986, when the company built a $55 million plant after buying a two-thirds interest in New Mexico-based Chino Mines Company from Kennecott (the remaining third was acquired in 2003). In the same year, the company sold a 15 percent interest in the Morenci mine for $75 million. Also sold was the uranium-mining business.

1980s–90s: Diversification into Manufacturing

The 1986 purchase of Columbian Chemicals Company for $240 million diversified Phelps Dodge interests to include the manufacture of carbon blacks, used to strengthen tires and to make toner for copiers. Also providing profitable diversification was Accuride Corporation, a manufacturer of steel wheels and rims for trucks and trailers, which merged with the company in 1988 at a cost of $273 million. That same year, all operations were divided into two new operating divisions, headed by the Phelps Dodge Mining Company and Phelps Dodge Industries.

By the end of 1989, the company had an income of $267 million, on sales of $2.7 billion. A year later, net income leaped to $454.9 million, on sales of $2.6 billion, partly with the help of a joint venture between Phelps Dodge and Sumitomo Electric Industries, to sell magnet wire in the United States.

Although Phelps Dodge continued to expand its copper activities during the 1990s, particularly overseas, an emphasis was placed on developing the manufacturing side of the company's business during the decade. The acquisitions of Accuride, Columbian Chemicals, and Hudson International during the latter half of the 1980s were important forays into new fields, creating a foundation the company would build on during the 1990s as the manufacturing division, operated under the control of Phelps Dodge Industries, took shape. The largest segment of the company's manufacturing business was wire and cable production, governed by Phelps Dodge Magnet Wire Co., the largest magnet wire producer in the world. Expansion of this business was achieved through acquisition and expansion, beginning in 1992 with the purchase of three Venezuelan wire and cable manufacturers and the establishment of a wire and cable plant in Thailand. Two years later, two magnet wire production facilities were acquired, one in El Paso, Texas, and the other in Laurinburg, North Carolina, to serve regional demand not met by the company's Hopkinsville, Kentucky plant, the largest magnet wire plant in the world. Capacity at the El Paso plant was doubled in 1996, followed by a commensurate increase in production at the Laurinburg facility in 1997.

The investment in the Phelps Dodge Industries division paid off handsomely in 1995, as the company's carbon black, truck wheel and rim, and wire and cable businesses each registered a record high in sales. For the year, record financial and production totals led to what Phelps Dodge Chairman, CEO, and President Douglas C. Yearley described as "the best year in the 162-year history of our company." The progress achieved within the Phelps Dodge Industries division played an important part in engendering the banner year, but the company could not claim such a victory without realizing significant gains in its copper business, upon which it was heavily dependent. The average price of copper in 1995 surged to $1.35 per pound, 28 cents higher than the previous year, and Phelps Dodge reaped the benefits, registering record production totals at its Morenci, Candelaria, Chino, and Hidalgo mining facilities. On the heels of this resounding success, the company planned to focus its exploration efforts in South America, Africa, and the Far East, intending to increase its annual copper production total to two billion pounds during the ensuing five years.

In 1996, Phelps Dodge's manufacturing businesses continued to perform admirably, with the exception of Accuride Corporation, which suffered from weak demand for heavy wheels. Phelps Dodge's wire and cable business rallied forward, its progress highlighted by the company's first entry into the People's Republic of China through a joint venture called Phelps Dodge Yantai Cable Company that allowed Phelps Dodge to acquire, expand, and operate the power cable manufacturing facility in Yantai in the Shandong province. As this historic project began, the company initiated a three-year expansion program aimed at increasing Columbian Chemical's carbon black production capacity by 25 percent. Another notable development during the year was the acquisition of Nesor Alloy Corporation, which was combined with Hudson International Conductors to form Phelps Dodge High Performance Conductors, organized as the newest addition to the Phelps Dodge Industries division.

The late 1990s saw copper prices sag from 1995's level, but the company recorded meaningful progress in its manufacturing operations, helping to offset troubling developments in its mining activities. An uncertain regulatory environment concerning mining and exploration prompted Phelps Dodge to close its U.S. exploration offices. Falling copper prices forced the company to close a mine in Chile and another mine acquired in a $105 million hostile takeover of Cobre Mining Co. in 1998. Along with these closures, Phelps Dodge also sold 90 percent of Accuride to Kohlberg Kravis Roberts in 1998, gaining $480 million from the sale. On the positive side, Phelps Dodge opened a new wire magnet plant in Monterrey, Mexico, in 1998 and purchased the carbon black assets belonging to Brazil-based Copebras for $220 million, as well as an 85 percent holding in the carbon black operations of Kumho Group of South Korea.

Ups and Downs in the New Millennium

The company's use of technology was evolving as it entered the new millennium. GPS, first introduced at the Morenci mine in the mid-1990s as a surveying tool, was adapted to new applications such as guiding machinery for bulldozers, electric shovels, and drills.

Copper prices hit unfamiliar lows in 1999, due to the lingering effects of the Asian financial crisis. According to *Barron's*,

while copper was selling for just 61 cents per pound (after a decade of averaging more than $1), the company needed another few cents per pound to break even. However, there was a bright side to the crisis in that the company was able to stake its claim on future leadership of the industry. In the ensuing round of consolidation, Phelps Dodge acquired Cyprus Amax Minerals Company, which had been preparing to merge with ASARCO. However, Grupo México SA de CV bested Phelps Dodge's $700 million bid for ASARCO (which soon stumbled into bankruptcy). The $1.8 billion Cyprus Amax purchase made Phelps Dodge the world's second largest copper producer after Codelco of Chile, and the largest producer of molybdenum. It ended the year with revenues of $3.1 billion.

Douglas C. Yearley retired as chairman in May 2000 and was succeeded by J. Steven Whisler. According to *American Metal Market,* Yearley had been a big advocate of industry consolidation and earning a return on capital. Yearley's hand-picked successor, Whisler, had begun working at a subsidiary in 1978 and had been Phelps Dodge president and CEO since 1995.

In late 2000, as copper prices showed signs of improvement, the company proposed selling off Columbian Chemicals and PD Wire. These businesses presented their own management challenges. "Wire and cable always had problems because they're in developing countries," Yearley told *American Metal Market.* Of the turbulence-free mid-1990s, he said, "It all looked too good—and it was."

In spite of a number of economic difficulties in Asia and South America, the sale of the manufacturing businesses would be called off by mid-2001. The improvement in copper prices stalled. In addition, skyrocketing energy prices and the threat of shortages prompted Phelps Dodge to scale back copper production and cut the workforce at three mines in the western United States.

Company headquarters was relocated from Tempe to ten floors in the new 20-story, $78 million Phelps Dodge Tower in downtown Phoenix in November 2001. The company consolidated other local offices there and eventually employed 400 at the site. It had 13,000 employees worldwide. The company's operations at the Candelaria mine in Chile, in which it owned an 80 percent share, employed 950 people. About half of these workers went on strike in 2003.

Phelps Dodge Corporation had revenues exceeding $7 billion in 2004. Phelps Dodge Mining Company accounted for more than three-quarters of the total. While copper was trading above $1 again, thanks in large part to demand from China's booming economy, energy costs remained a concern. Phelps Dodge announced an $850 million expansion to a Peruvian mine in October 2004.

In 2005, the company was planning to add a new copper processing plant at its Morenci, Arizona, mine. There was a moderate shortage of refined copper, fueled by demand from China's construction and consumer goods industries, Whisler told Reuters. Copper prices were reaching levels not seen since the 1980s, prompting Dodge Phelps to increase production and hand out dividends to shareholders and bonuses to employees. Short of help, Dodge Phelps was mining the Arizona workforce for talent to fill a slew of positions. The company had about 5,000 employees in Arizona.

Principal Subsidiaries

Ajo Improvement Company; Alambres y Cables de Panama, S.A. (78.1%); Alambres y Cables Venezolanos, C.A. (Venezuela); Arizona Community Investment Corporation; Cables Electricos Ecuatorianos, C.A. (Ecuador; 67.1%); Cahosa, S.A. (Panama; 78.1%); Chino Acquisition Inc.; Cobre Cerrillos S.A. (Chile); Columbian Chemicals Company; CONDUCEN, S.A. (Costa Rica; 73.4%); Cyprus Amax Minerals Company; Dodge & James Insurance Company, Ltd. (Bermuda); Electroconductores de Honduras, S.A. de C.V. (59.4%); Habirshaw Cable and Wire Corporation; James Douglas Insurance Company, Ltd. (Bermuda); PD Candelaria, Inc.; PD Cobre, Inc.; PD Ojos del Salado, Inc.; Phelps Dodge Africa Cable Corporation; Phelps Dodge China Corporation (USA); Phelps Dodge Chino, Inc.; Phelps Dodge Corporation of Canada, Limited (USA); Phelps Dodge Development Corporation; Phelps Dodge Dublin (Ireland); Phelps Dodge Energy Services, LLC; Phelps Dodge Exploration Corporation; Phelps Dodge Hidalgo, Inc.; Phelps Dodge High Performance Conductors of SC & GA, Inc.; Phelps Dodge Industries, Inc.; Phelps Dodge Mercantile Company; Phelps Dodge Mining Services, Inc.; Phelps Dodge Molybdenum Corporation; Phelps Dodge Morenci, Inc.; Phelps Dodge Overseas Capital Corporation; Phelps Dodge Refining Corporation; Phelps Dodge Safford, Inc.; Phelps Dodge Sales Company, Incorporated; Phelps Dodge Suzhou Holdings, Inc. (Cayman Islands); Phelps Dodge Thailand Limited (75.5%); Phelps Dodge Wire and Cable Holding de Mexico, SA de CV (99%); Savanna Development Co., Ltd.; Soner, Inc.; The Morenci Water & Electric Company; Tyrone Mining, LLC.

Principal Divisions

Phelps Dodge Mining Co.; Phelps Dodge Industries.

Principal Operating Units

Phelps Dodge Mining Co.; Phelps Dodge Wire and Cable; Climax Molybdenum Co.; Climax Engineered Materials; Columbia Chemicals Co.

Principal Competitors

BHP Billiton; Corporación del Cobre de Chile (Codelco); Rio Tinto PLC.

Further Reading

Cleland, Robert Glass, *A History of Phelps Dodge: 1834–1950,* New York: Alfred A. Knopf, 1952.
Cummins, Chip, "Phelps Dodge Cuts Copper Production; Energy Is Concern," *Wall Street Journal,* March 27, 2001, p. B15.
——, "Phelps Dodge May Shutter Mines As California Saps Power Supplies," *Wall Street Journal,* January 2001, p. B6.
Ducote, Richard, "Copper, PD Make Comeback," *Arizona Daily Star* (Tucson), May 23, 2004, p. D1.
——, "PD Hands Out Bonuses; Asarco Courts Oblivion," *Arizona Daily Star* (Tucson), October 28, 2005, p. A1.
Durham, G. Robert, *Phelps Dodge Corporation: "Proud of Its Past, Prepared for the Future,"* New York: Newcomen Society of the United States, 1989.
Lazo, Shirley A., "Born-Again Payouts: Phelps Dodge, C&W Rebound Dividends After Retreat," *Barron's,* June 7, 2004, p. 31.
Navin, Thomas R., *Copper Mining & Management,* Tucson: University of Arizona Press, 1978.
"Presbyterian Copper," *Fortune,* July 1932.
Reagor, Catherine, "Copper Giant Phelps Dodge's Move to Downtown Phoenix Sealed," *Knight Ridder/Tribune Business News,* November 8, 1999.
Richardson, Karen, "Activist Investor Finds Winning Is Bittersweet— Phelps Dodge's Big Payout May Cut Value of Options Owned by Atticus Capital," *Wall Street Journal,* November 2, 2005, p. C3.
Scholl, Jaye, "Copper King: If the Metal's Price Ever Revives, Phelps Dodge Could Be a Big Winner," *Barron's,* June 21, 1999, p. 19.
——, "Pure Play: Copper Giant Phelps Dodge Gets Back to Basics," *Barron's,* December 18, 2000, p. 13.
Shields, Scott, Janet Flinn, and Andres Obregon, "GPS in the Pits: Differential GPS Applications at the Morenci Copper Mine," *GPS World,* October 2000, pp. 34+.
Stundza, Tom, "Phelps Dodge CEO Sees Red Metal Shortage," *Purchasing,* July 14, 2005.
Watkins, Steve, "Copper Producer Is Making a Pretty Penny," *Investor's Business Daily,* October 21, 2004, p. A8.
Yafie, Roberta C., "Adios, Mr. Yearley," *American Metal Market,* May 2000, p. 16.
——, "Phelps Dodge Basks in Wall Street Glow," *American Metal Market,* May 8, 2000, p. 16.
——, "Phelps Dodge's Whisler: The View from the Top Is Changing," *American Metal Market,* May 3, 2000, p. 9.
——, "Phelps Dodge Tale Rich in US History," *American Metal Market,* December 16, 1999, p. 2.

—Gillian Wolf
—updates: Jeffrey L. Covell; Frederick C. Ingram

Pirelli & C. S.p.A.

Via Gaetano Negri 10
20123 Milan
Italy
Telephone: (02) 85351
Fax: (02) 8535-4426
Web site: http://www.pirelli.com

Public Company
Incorporated: 1872 as Pirelli & C.
Employees: 37,154
Sales: EUR 7.11 billion ($8.96 billion) (2004)
Stock Exchanges: Milan
Ticker Symbol: PC
NAIC: 326211 Tire Manufacturing (Except Retreading)

One of the largest companies in Italy, Pirelli & C. S.p.A. is among the world's leading tire manufacturers, producing and distributing tires for cars, motorcycles, and farm and industrial vehicles. The world leader in tires for high-performance cars, Pirelli produces tires in 22 factories located in Argentina, Brazil, Egypt, Germany, Italy, Spain, Turkey, the United States, the United Kingdom, and Venezuela. Its marketing network covers 120 countries around the world, with about 14 percent of tire sales stemming from the home market, 45 percent from the rest of Europe, 7 percent from North America, 20 percent from South America, and the remaining 14 percent from Africa and the Asia-Pacific region. Among other operations, Pirelli is involved in real estate management, optical research relating to photonics-based telecommunications, and the development of alternative fuels from waste products, and it also holds a 57.7 percent stake in Olimpia S.p.A., which in turn is the leading shareholder of Telecom Italia S.p.A., one of Europe's largest telecommunications companies.

Late 19th-Century Origins

The company's founder, Giovanni Battista Pirelli, a 24-year-old engineering graduate from the Milano Politecnico, formed the company Pirelli & C. with an initial share capital of ITL 215,000. Pirelli had astutely realized that rubber was to become one of the most important commodities in the rapidly industrializing Italy. Less than a year after its inception in 1872, Pirelli's company built its first factory in Milan. There were 45 people employed in the small, 1,000-square-meter building as demand for the company's rubber sheets, belts, slabs, and vulcanized products increased. The rapid growth in the popularity of the motor car, which was now seen as more than a fashionable plaything for the rich, led to contracts to supply pneumatic tubes and transmission belts.

From its earliest years Pirelli demonstrated a willingness to diversify its product range and to produce overseas in order to satisfy its desire for ambitious, yet controlled, expansion. The company began the manufacture of insulated telegraph cables in 1879 and within seven years had developed the technology to produce underwater telegraph cables. In 1890 pneumatic bicycle tires rolled off the production line and were followed in 1901 by the company's first car tires.

Pirelli established a trend that many Italian companies were to follow when it began to expand abroad as early as 1902. The new cable and electrical lead factory set up near Barcelona in Spain was followed by a similar venture in Britain in 1914, and by 1920 factories had also been set up in Brazil, Greece, Argentina, Turkey, and Germany. Product diversification at home was encouraged by the firm's long-term commitment to investing in research and development. Giovanni brought his two sons into the business and they helped to run the new motorcycle tire production plant built at Bicocca in 1908. Forever at the forefront of new technology, the company began to produce rubberized fabrics as early as 1909.

Two major factors were to account for Pirelli's growth in the years immediately preceding World War I. First, between 1900 and 1914, Italy saw increased social reforms and political stability, which created more favorable conditions for trade and industry. Pirelli, which derived much of its demand from newly established ventures, was well placed to benefit from these changes by producing fluid control devices, transmission belts, and fuel distribution machinery. Second, the invention of the internal combustion engine in 1910 made the mass production of cars economically viable. The so-called rubber boom of 1911

Company Perspectives:

The Pirelli Group has a long industrial tradition and is ranked among the world's leaders in every sector in which it operates. For more than a century, we have been developing into a fully-fledged multinational, firmly rooted in various national markets. Our competitive strength lies in technological capabilities and research, and in the quality and the professional expertise of our human resources.

marked the acceptance of the material as a worldwide commodity and ensured the continued success of the company.

Interwar and World War II Era

New factories were opened in Spain in 1917 and Argentina in 1919, but the first major event to affect the company after the end of the war was a change in its organizational structure, implemented in 1920. Pirelli & C., the original company founded by Giovanni Pirelli, changed its status and became an investment rather than a production company. Società Italiana Pirelli, later to become Pirelli S.p.A., was incorporated to act as a holding company to control the group's varied industrial operations based in Italy. Compagnie Internationale Pirelli S.A., incorporated in Brussels, was set up to manage the group's rapidly increasing overseas operations. Pirelli & C. S.a.p.A. was taken public in 1922; Pirelli S.p.A. was listed four years later.

In 1924 Luigi Emanueli, an employee of the company, developed the first commercially viable oil-filled cable. The world's first crossply tire, the Superflex Stella Bianca, was successfully launched in 1927 and within two years a new cable production unit was opened in Brazil and a new tire factory was opened at Burton-on-Trent in England. Initiatives were also made in India and Malaysia to guarantee the supply of natural rubber to Milan and Pirelli's overseas subsidiaries.

This was a period when Pirelli's products, fitted to the Ferraris and Alfa Romeos of Nuvolari and Ascari, became synonymous with success in international Grand Prix racing. Nevertheless, the rise of Mussolini's fascists and Italy's increasingly disastrous foreign policy in the mid-1930s led to a further period of economic and political turbulence. To counteract the impending threat of international boycotts, Compagnie Internationale Pirelli S.A. was transferred into Pirelli Holdings S.A., a holding company incorporated in neutral Switzerland, in 1937.

Postwar Rebuilding and Expansion

World War II left Italy politically and economically crippled. A weak leadership was unable to cope with the severe poverty, rampant inflation, and high unemployment that affected the whole country. Nonetheless, Alcide de Gasperi, the Christian Democrat leader, was able to bring both inflation and the budget deficit under some degree of control, and by 1948 a large-scale public investment program was instigated.

Italian industry had been situated in the north of the country for a number of reasons. Milan, Turin, and Genoa became business centers because of the availability of both capital and raw materials—steel for machinery and railways, coal for power—and again Pirelli, which derived much of its success from the success of others, was well placed to take advantage of the new boom in the north. Pirelli responded to this opportunity by producing the first fabric-belted tire, the Cinturato CF67, introduced in 1948, which revolutionized the tire industry.

In the 1950s and 1960s Italy enjoyed the same kind of economic miracle experienced by many European countries as postwar depression gave way to years of growth and prosperity. An influx of new talent, often from comparatively humble backgrounds, suffused the established upper crust of Italian society and led to an improvement in the quality of management. Pirelli set new records for expansion overseas, opening a cable factory in Canada in 1953, a latex foam plant in France in 1957, and new tire plants in Greece and Turkey in 1960. The company purchased the German tire company Veith in 1963 and reinforced its position in both South America and Australasia when it opened cable manufacturing operations in Peru in 1968 and Australia in 1975. Pirelli was also involved in establishing several turnkey plants during the 1960s to provide tires for Eastern European companies.

Throughout this period of expansion Pirelli followed the strategy, common to most of the Italian multinationals, of eschewing joint ventures and the purchase of minority and majority shares in established companies. Instead, product ranges that had already proved successful in the Italian domestic market were transferred for production and sale overseas. In this way the company was able to retain complete control over its operations abroad while being able to overcome barriers preventing Italian exports.

Surviving Heightened Competition from Michelin and the 1970s Oil Shocks

In the late 1960s Pirelli's reputation for being at the forefront of innovation was usurped by Michelin when the latter introduced steel-belted radial tires. Michelin also entered the U.S. cable market seven years before Pirelli. Some commentators suggested that Pirelli's management was more concerned with producing glossy calendars than tires (the first Pirelli calendar having been produced in 1964). The company responded by embarking on a long-term research and development agreement with the British Dunlop group. This surprising move did not lead to a full merger, and neither party seemed to be too disappointed when the agreement was terminated in 1981.

A personal tragedy hit the firm in the early 1970s when Giovanni Pirelli, a direct descendant of the original founder, was killed in a car crash. This natural leader of the firm was replaced by his younger brother, Leopoldo, who was also severely injured in the accident. Leopoldo led the company through a period of protracted change.

The oil crises of the 1970s brought about a change in attitude towards the role of the motor car. Sales of new cars slumped as the price of gasoline soared, and as a consequence the worldwide demand for tires fell dramatically. Italy, far more dependent on imported sources of energy than most of its European partners, was particularly badly hit by the 1974 crisis, which saw the return of rampant inflation and a massive drop in the value of the lire. The second oil crisis of 1979 followed the withdrawal of the Communists from the "historic compromise" coalition government that had done so much to stabilize Italian political life. The Naples earthquake of November 1980 and the public exposure of P2, the secret Masonic lodge, six months later further damaged the morale of the country.

Reorganizing and a Program of Acquisitions in the 1980s

After the ending of the agreement with Dunlop, Pirelli benefited from the upturn in the European economy of the early 1980s. The Italian and Swiss parent companies were responsible for an extensive reorganization of the group in 1982, which saw an equalization of the shares each company held in the

group's many and varied subsidiary companies. A new management company, Pirelli Société Générale S.A., was created in Basel to ensure that unified policies and centralized objectives were put in place in Pirelli companies throughout the world.

In 1986 Pirelli acquired the share capital of Metzeler Kautschuk GmbH, a German company with many interests in the rubber industry. The acquisition of Metzeler led to a 13 percent increase in consolidated turnover and reinforced Pirelli's position in the market for motorcycle tires and automobile components. Just as important, the move provided Pirelli with a well established distribution chain that dealt with manufacturing activities. This apparent change in strategy, favoring growth through acquisition at the expense of traditional organic growth, was also demonstrated in 1988 when the group acquired Armstrong Tire and Rubber Company, the sixth largest U.S. tire manufacturer. In the same year Pirelli bought Filergie S.A., a cable manufacturer with 13 plants in France and Portugal. Although the pace of technical development appeared to be slowing down and no further radically different tires were introduced, the company did benefit from the increased margins offered by a shift in demand in favor of low-profile and premium radial tires.

A further share restructuring was undertaken in 1988 when Pirelli S.p.A. acquired Société Internationale Pirelli S.A.'s holding in Pirelli Société Générale S.A., thereby accepting direct responsibility for the day-to-day management of the operating companies. In turn, these operating companies were restructured into self-contained divisions in order to facilitate faster responses to financial, production, and employment problems. The three divisions, Pirelli Tire, Pirelli Cavi, and Pirelli Prodotti Diversificati, were each given separate holding companies.

The worldwide tire industry was as badly hit by the recession of the late 1980s and early 1990s as any other manufacturing sector. Worldwide sales of tires stagnated, and producers were unable to pass on increases in the cost of raw materials, especially oil, to the final consumer. Car makers, suffering from reduced demand, cut their costs by forcing tire manufacturers to accept lower prices. A spate of ill-conceived takeovers in the early 1980s and an increasing market dominance by a decreasing number of companies led to pressure on margins in the struggle to gain market share. Excess capacity and oversupply exacerbated the situation.

Pirelli's reaction to these market forces was to engage in two major merger and acquisition exercises. First, the company became involved in an acrimonious battle with Bridgestone Corporation to take control of the U.S. company Firestone Tire & Rubber Company in 1988 and 1989. With the benefit of hindsight, Pirelli should be content to have lost the battle and thereby have avoided what proved to be a costly and largely unsuccessful acquisition for Bridgestone.

Early 1990s: Near Disastrous Attempt to Merge with Continental and a Massive Restructuring

Pirelli's second attempt to increase its market share by entering the world of mergers and acquisitions led to a long series of merger discussions with the German company Continental AG and ultimately, near disaster. The plan to merge the fourth- and fifth-largest tire producers in the world was designed to produce a force powerful enough to achieve critical mass in a fairly stagnant market. Damaging price competition would be avoided and overcapacity would be reduced. This deal seemed a far more attractive proposition than the opportunity to acquire Firestone two years earlier. The proposed merger, however, proved to be problematic from the very first time the two parties met. The board of Continental, led by CEO Horst Urban, angered the Pirelli leadership by publicly revealing details of secret meetings. Pirelli believed that its attempts to follow traditional German merger practice, in which friendly approaches are made to willing partners in order to achieve mutual benefit, was the best way to act in the early stages of the deal. Continental's belligerent defensive strategy, inspired by the aggressive tactics employed by the City of London and Wall Street in the mid-1980s, led Pirelli to hire an investor group to buy up Continental stock. While talks between the two firms dragged on into 1991, Pirelli's financial condition weakened under the strain of the stagnant economy to the point where Continental pulled out of the merger discussions.

It was subsequently revealed that Pirelli lost almost $300 million on the Continental stock its investor group had purchased, further damaging the company's fortunes and instigating a shareholder revolt (after an earnings gain of 11 cents per share in 1990, the company posted a loss of 48 cents per share in 1991). In 1992 Leopoldo Pirelli was pushed aside from day-to-day management (he remained chairman of the board) in favor of his son-in-law Marco Tronchetti Provera, who had opposed the Continental takeover attempt. Tronchetti instigated a massive restructuring effort to forestall threatened bankruptcy. Many of the businesses his predecessors had acquired in preceding decades were sold off, eventually reducing Pirelli to two core divisions, tires and cables, out of the nine it had operated at its peak of diversification. In addition to the sale of such operations as conveyor belt and apparel manufacturing, much of Pirelli's downtown Milan real estate was sold, bringing in $563 million which contributed to cutting the firm's $2.5 billion debt load in half. The company's workforce was cut from 53,500 in 1990 to 38,500 in 1994, or about 25 percent, and the number of factories Pirelli operated was reduced from 103 in 1990 to 74 in 1994.

After its loss of ITL 657 billion in 1991, Pirelli's newfound concentration on its core tire and cable businesses slowly turned the company around. After smaller losses of ITL 69 billion in 1992 and ITL 41 billion in 1993, Pirelli returned to profitability in 1994 with a gain of ITL 72 billion. Its tire operation was boosted by a resurgence in European sales based primarily on Pirelli's emphasis on increasingly popular high-performance tires. By 1995, Pirelli had captured 12 percent of the European tire market, second only to Michelin. The North American market lagged behind, however, because of the poor performance of Armstrong. Pirelli replaced Armstrong's management team in early 1995, giving the new team until 1997 to break even. At the same time, Pirelli began to expand its tire business into East Asia.

On the cable side of its business, Pirelli had built itself into one of the world's top two manufacturers of fiber-optic cables. It aimed to increasingly emphasize telecommunications cables over those used for power. The company was also doing pioneering work in the area of photonics: the use of optical fiber and other components for high-speed transmission of information as pulses of laser light. Pirelli had expressed interest in broadening its telecommunications business by purchasing a stake in the state-owned Telecom Italia, which the Italian government had considered privatizing. However, threats to block any such Pirelli move to further enhance its position in the Italian telecommunications sector were immediately raised by Italian legislators.

Late 1990s: Solidifying the Turnaround

By 1996 net income had jumped to ITL 436 billion on revenues of ITL 10.24 trillion ($6.2 billion), while Pirelli's debt load had been cut to just ITL 1.02 trillion ($617 million). In a further signal of the company's turnaround, Pirelli made its first dividend payment in five years. In June 1996 Tronchetti succeeded the retiring Leopoldo Pirelli as chairman of Pirelli, becoming the first non-Pirelli to chair the group. Early the following year, Tronchetti unwound his predecessor's disappointing acquisition of Armstrong. Pirelli closed the last of the factories inherited from Armstrong, consolidated its North American production at its plant in Hanford, California, and ended its use of the Armstrong brand. The new strategy in North America was to sell high-performance tires under the Pirelli brand and use its Formula brand in the broad-line replacement passenger tire market. Pirelli's main U.S. tire subsidiary, Pirelli Armstrong Tire Corporation, was renamed Pirelli North America Inc.

At the beginning of 1999 Pirelli completed a further simplification and modernization of its ownership structure. Pirelli & C., the principal holding company of the Pirelli family, maintained control of Pirelli S.p.A. through three intermediary holding companies. In a complex series of transactions, these intermediary companies were eliminated, after which Pirelli & C. directly held a controlling 30 percent stake in Pirelli S.p.A. Meanwhile, Pirelli was in the midst of bolstering its position in power cables through several acquisitions. In 1998 the company purchased the power cables operations of Siemens AG for $277 million, gaining businesses in Germany, Hungary, Romania, Turkey, Italy, Spain, Austria, Slovakia, and China and making Pirelli the world's largest producer of energy cables. This deal was followed in 1999 by the purchase of the power and construction cables division of Metal Manufacturers Limited of Australia and in 2000 by the acquisitions of part of the power cable operations of the electricity companies of NKF, a Dutch cable company, and of the energy cable operations of BICCGeneral, a unit of General Cable Corporation. The latter deal included 11 factories, five of which were in the United Kingdom and one in Italy along with additional facilities in Africa and Asia and joint ventures in Malaysia and China. A restructuring announced by Pirelli in late 1999 involving the elimination of 2,800 jobs and the closure of five plants was mainly aimed at streamlining its acquisition-bolstered cable operations.

On the tire side, meanwhile, Pirelli formed alliances with Cooper Tire & Rubber Company in North and South America in 1999. Cooper agreed to distribute and sell Pirelli passenger-car and light-truck tires for the North American replacement-tire markets, while Pirelli agreed to distribute and market Cooper tires in South America. For Pirelli, this alliance was mainly intended to shore up its position in its weakest market, North America. In June 1999 Pirelli acquired majority control of

Alexandria Tire Co. S.A.E., the largest tire manufacturer in Egypt. As part of a drive to cut costs, Pirelli also developed a new production process it dubbed the Modular Integrated Robotized System (MIRS). A highly flexible, robot-run minifactory integrated with the entire supply chain, MIRS made its debut in 2000 at the firm's Milan factory.

Early 2000s: Enter Telecom Italia, Exit Cables

In 2000 Pirelli completed two large divestments that left it with a horde of cash. In February Pirelli sold its terrestrial fiber-optic equipment business to Cisco Systems, Inc. for about $2.2 billion. As part of the deal Cisco invested $100 million for 10 percent stakes in Pirelli's fiber-optic components and submarine-cable businesses. Part of the fiber-optics components business, however, was sold in December 2000 to Corning Inc. for approximately $3.6 billion. In the wake of these deals, which left Pirelli with about $5 billion in cash—Pirelli having sold the assets at the peak of the market—the company split its cables and systems division in two, effective at the end of 2001, creating two new units, one focused on telecommunications cables and systems and the other on energy cables and systems.

In September 2001 Tronchetti stunned the European financial community when he used Pirelli's pile of cash to gain control of Telecom Italia, at the time the fourth largest telecommunications firm in Europe, with interests in the telephone, Internet, and television sectors, and a debt-laden company struggling to shake off its past as a bloated state-owned monopoly. Telecom Italia had been privatized in 1997 and then taken over by Olivetti S.p.A. in 1999 in a highly leveraged hostile takeover engineered by Roberto Colaninno. Tronchetti joined with the Benetton family, Italy's three largest banks, and the investment fund Hopa in a EUR 7 billion ($6.1 billion) deal to take a controlling 27 percent stake in Olivetti, which in turn controlled 55 percent of Telecom Italia. Pirelli set up a new holding company called Olimpia S.p.A. as the vehicle to hold the stake in Olivetti. Pirelli initially held a 60 percent stake in the new company.

This deal was treated quite coolly by investors, and Pirelli's stock was pummeled. Tronchetti's plan was to refocus Pirelli on telecommunications, including the Telecom Italia assets and Pirelli's own fiber-optic cables, components, and networking gear. Toward this end a plan was announced to divest the firm's tire and energy cable operations by the end of 2002. Luckily for Pirelli, this plan was never put into full effect, sparing it the prospect of being fully exposed to a worldwide telecommunications industry gone bust. Instead, Pirelli restructured into four businesses in 2003: tires, energy cables and systems, telecommunications cables and systems, and real estate. Seeking to further simplify its convoluted ownership structure, Pirelli S.p.A. was acquired by and merged into Pirelli & C. S.p.A. in 2003, the latter becoming the main holding company for the Pirelli group. At the same time, Olivetti was merged into Telecom Italia, further reducing the number of companies linking Pirelli to the latter.

While Pirelli's telecommunications and cables businesses suffered from deep slumps, its tire business was doing quite well thanks to an emphasis on high-performance products and the spread of its automated factories. In 2003 a new MIRS plant

in Rome, Georgia, began churning out tires, including a new model called the Scorpion that was intended to reintroduce the Pirelli brand to the U.S. market. During 2004 Pirelli's tire operations enjoyed their best performance in ten years as Pirelli's emphasis on high-end tires continued to pay dividends. The tires unit posted profits of EUR 169 million on revenues of EUR 3.26 billion. Overall net income amounted to EUR 274 million on revenues of EUR 7.11 billion.

By this time, Pirelli had placed both of its cables units up for sale, and in June 2005 it announced their sale to the private equity arm of Goldman Sachs for EUR 1.3 billion ($1.6 billion). This left the group focused primarily on tires, telecommunications, and real estate. With Telecom Italia beginning to perform better and the tires unit riding high, Pirelli's future seemed bright. Not resting on its laurels, the company was actively pursuing new markets for its tires business and by late in 2005 had set up new joint ventures for tire manufacturing in Romania and China.

Principal Subsidiaries

Olimpia S.p.A. (57.7%); Pirelli Labs S.p.A.; Pirelli & C. Real Estate S.p.A. (53.9%); Pirelli Broadband Solutions S.p.A.; Pirelli Ambiente Holding S.p.A. (51%); Pirelli Pneumatici S.p.A.; Pirelli Gesellschaft mbH (Austria); Pirelli Tyres Belux S.A. (Belgium); Pneus Pirelli S.A.S. (France); Pirelli Deutschland GmbH (Germany); Elastika Pirelli S.A. (Greece); Pirelli Hungary Tyre Trading and Services Ltd.; Pirelli Tyre Holding N.V. (Netherlands); Pirelli Tyres Nederland B.V. (Netherlands); Pirelli Polska Sp. Zo.o. (Poland); S.C. Cord Romania SRL (80%); S.C. Pirelli Tyres Romania S.R.L.; Pirelli Slovakia S.R.O.; Pirelli Neumaticos S.A. (Spain); Pirelli Tyre Nordic AB (Sweden); Agom S.A. (Switzerland; 80%); Pirelli Tyre (Europe) S.A. (Switzerland); Çelikord A.S. (Turkey; 50.76%); Türk-Pirelli Lastikleri A.S. (Turkey; 63.05%); Pirelli UK plc; Pirelli UK Tyres Ltd.; Pirelli Tire Inc. (Canada); Pirelli North America Inc. (U.S.A.); Pirelli Neumaticos S.A.I.C. (Argentina); Pirelli Pneus S.A. (Brazil; 99.73%); Pirelli Neumaticos Chile Limitada; Pirelli de Colombia S.A.Pirelli Neumaticos de Mexico S.A. de C.V.; Pirelli Venezuela C.A. (96.22%); Alexandria Tire Company S.A.E. (Egypt; 86.82%); Pirelli Tyre (Pty) Ltd. (South Africa); Pirelli Tyres Australia Pty Ltd.; Pirelli Tyres (NZ) Ltd. (New Zealand); Pirelli Japan K.K.; Pirelli Asia Pte. Ltd. (Singapore).

Principal Competitors

Bridgestone Corporation; Compagnie Générale des Établissements Michelin; The Goodyear Tire & Rubber Company; Continental AG.

Further Reading

Ball, Deborah, "For Telecom Italia, a Sudden Change of Hands," *Wall Street Journal*, July 30, 2001, p. A15.

——, "A Tale of Blue Blood, Sweaters, and Tires: Stylish Telecom Deal Cut by Benetton and Pirelli Marks a Coming of Age," *Wall Street Journal*, July 31, 2001, p. A12.

Banks, Howard, "The (Almost) Perfect Son-in-Law," *Forbes*, May 19, 1997, pp. 106+.

Betts, Paul, "Mogul in a Slicker Mould," *Financial Times*, May 22, 2000, p. 23.

——, "Pirelli Set to Streamline Control Chain," *Financial Times,* March 25, 1998, p. 43.

Edmondson, Gail, "That's Some Corner Pirelli Is Turning," *Business Week,* April 10, 2000, p. 164.

——, "Tronchetti's Coup," *Business Week,* August 13, 2001, p. 42.

Friedman, Alan, "Pirelli Deal Mastermind Promises to Streamline," *International Herald Tribune,* August 3, 2001, p. 1.

——, "Redrawing the Map of Italian Capitalism: Telecom Italia Falls to Pirelli and Benetton," *International Herald Tribune,* July 30, 2001, p. 1.

Galloni, Alessandra, and David Reilly, "Telecom Italia Chairman Faces Revolt on Merger with Olivetti," *Wall Street Journal,* March 13, 2003, p. B5.

"Getting a Grip," *Economist,* April 21, 2001, p. 59.

Hill, Andrew, "Milanese Scion to Pilot Pirelli," *Financial Times,* April 22, 1996, p. 17.

Kapner, Fred, "Italy's Corporate Raider," *Financial Times,* August 4, 2001, p. 11.

——, "Telecom Italia Chief Treads Precarious Path," *Financial Times,* March 12, 2003, p. 26.

King, Russel, *Italy,* London: Harper & Row, 1987.

Kline, Maureen, "Pirelli Says It's Poised for a Recovery Following Painful Restructuring Moves," *Wall Street Journal,* April 8, 1994, p. B6B.

La Pirelli: Vita di una azienda industriale, Milan: Industrie Grafiche A. Nicola, 1946.

Michaels, Adrian, "Italy Fails to Tire of Provera's Manoeuvres," *Financial Times,* November 12, 2004, p. 29.

Michaels, Adrian, and Peter Smith, "Pirelli Sells Cable Unit for EUR 1.3bn," *Financial Times,* June 2, 2005, p. 27.

Onida, Fabrizio, and Gianfranco Viesti, *The Italian Multinationals,* Beckenham: Croom Helm, 1988.

Perulli, Paolo, *Pirelli, 1980–1985: Le relazioni industriali; Negoziando l'incertezza,* Milan: F. Angeli, 1986, 107 p.

Pirelli, Alberto, *Economia e guerra,* Milan: Istituto per gli Studi di Politica Internazionale, 1940.

Pirelli, 1872–1997: Centoventicinque anni di imprese, Milan: Pirelli, 1997, 174 p.

Pirelli, 1914–1980: Strategia aziendale e relazioni industriali nella storia di una multinazionale, Milan: F. Angeli, 1985, 2 vols.

"Plenty of Bravado, but Not Bravo," *Economist,* August 4, 2001, pp. 52-53.

Rossant, John, "How Pirelli Pulled Off a 180-Degree Turn," *Business Week,* November 6, 1995, pp. 160+.

Shaw, David, "Pirelli: Not a Niche Player," *European Rubber Journal,* September 1999, p. 34.

"Still Spinning Its Wheels," *Financial World,* April 13, 1993, p. 64.

Sylvers, Eric, "Pirelli Returns to Basics with Tires Made in U.S.," *The New York Times,* March 20, 2003, p. W1.

——, "Pirelli's Bet on High-Performance Tires," *International Herald Tribune,* April 2, 2005, p. 15.

Tagliabue, John, "Pirelli Tires Rolling Again in Italy," *International Herald Tribune,* July 23, 1994, p. 11.

Ulrich, Bob, "Goodbye, Armstrong: Pirelli Shifts North American Focus," *Modern Tire Dealer,* February 1997, pp. 56+.

White, Liz, "Pirelli Sells Energy and Telecom Cables Operations," *European Rubber Journal,* July 2005, p. 6.

——, "Pirelli to Divest Cables Unit, Emphasise Tyres," *European Rubber Journal,* December 2004, p. 9.

——, "Restructured Pirelli Aims for New Opportunities," *European Rubber Journal,* May 2004, p. 7.

—Andreas Loizou
—update: David E. Salamie

Radeberger Gruppe AG

Darmstadter Landstr 185
Frankfurt am Main
D-60598
Germany
Telephone: +49 69 6 06 5 0
Fax: +49 69 6 06 52 09
Web site: http://www.radeberger-gruppe.de

Wholly Owned Subsidiary of Oetker Gruppe
Incorporated: 1870 as Binding Brauerei
Employees: 2,600
Sales: EUR 990 million ($1.03 billion) (2003)
NAIC: 312120 Breweries; 312111 Soft Drink
    Manufacturing; 722110 Full-Service Restaurants;
    722410 Drinking Places (Alcoholic Beverages)

Radeberger Gruppe AG, formerly known as Binding Brauerei, is one of the largest brewery groups in the highly fragmented German beer market. The company controls a number of top national, regional, and local and "trend" breweries and brands as well as other beverage brands, and produces a total of more than 9.2 million hectoliters per year. Radeberger's portfolio is segmented into three categories. National brands include company flagship Radeberger Pilsner, one of Germany's oldest and best-selling pilsner beers; Clausthaler, a nonalcoholic beer developed by the company in the 1970s; Schoefferhof Weise, the fourth best-selling wheat beer in Germany; and the mineral water brand Selters Mineralwasser. The company's regional brands include Dortmunder Actien7-Brauerei in Dortmund, Radeberger Exportbierbrauerei in Radeberg/Dresden, Krostitzer Brauerei in Krostitz/Leipzig, Binding-Brauerei in Frankfurt am Main, Henninger-Bräu in Frankfurt am Main, Erbacher Brauhaus in Erbach/Odenwald, and Allgäuer Brauhaus in Bavaria. Radeberger also controls Krušovice, a leading beer in the Czech Republic, and Allgäuer Brauhaus (Allgäu District of Bavaria Brewery) as well as the table water producer Selters Mineralquelle (Selters Mineral Spring). In addition to traditional beers, Radeberger produces and distributes a range of Specialty and Trend beers, under brands such as Berliner Kindl, Carolus der Starke, the low-alcohol Henninger Radler, Hovels Original Bitterbier, Binding Flavored Lagers, and, under license, Corona. Once a public company, Radeberger was acquired by German food giant Oetker Gruppe as a number of foreign brewers began entering the German market and acquiring the country's beer brands. Following its acquisition by Oetker, Radeberger was delisted from the Frankfurt Stock Exchange. In 2004, the company posted revenues of approximately EUR 990 million ($1.03 billion).

German Pilsner Beer Origins in the 19th Century

The Radeberger Gruppe entering the 21st century represented the combination of several prominent German breweries, most of which were established in the late 19th century to produce a new beer type, Pilsner, named after the Czech town of Pilsen. Among the most prominent of the new pilsner beers were Radeberger, brewed in the Dresden suburb in what was later to become East Germany, and Binding, based in Frankfurt.

Pilsner beers arrived in Germany from the then-named Bohemia in the mid-1800s and quickly became popular among German beer drinkers in the nearby Saxony region. The rising success of pilsner beers encouraged a group of brewers to form a new brewery in Radeberg, a suburb of the city of Dresden, in 1866. The partnership began brewing that year. While production remained small at first, the Radeberg beer attracted a following. By 1872, the group had transformed the brewery into a shareholding partnership, called Zum Bergkeller.

The so-called German "purity" regulations governing beer production placed strict geographic limits on the country's brewers. Only beers judged to be of very high quality were allowed to produce for markets beyond a local level, with deliveries limited to the distance smoke traveled from a brewery's chimneys. These restrictions were lifted, however, in the case of beers exhibiting high quality and, of importance, longer shelf life.

The Radeberg brewery met the high quality specifications by the 1880s. As the company's pilsner beers reached a wider market, the group changed its name, becoming Radeberger Exportbrauerei. The Radeberger pilsner became a favorite among German beer drinkers on a national level. By the late

Company Perspectives:

Radeberger relies on strong brands, high product quality, and management continuity. The enterprise does business in accordance with the motto "margin over volume." Radeberger is market and customer oriented, views itself as a company that produces pure products and is committed to conservation and preservation of the environment.

1880s, the company's production neared 300,000 cases per year. Yet Radeberger also enjoyed strong international success, especially in the United States and Canada. There, the German immigrant communities helped spread an appreciation for pilsner-styled beers. By the early years of the 20th century, fully one third of Radeberger's production was destined for the North American market.

By the outbreak of World War I, Radeberger's production had topped 2.7 million cases annually. The interwar period also marked a time of strong growth for the company, and by the end of the 1920s, the company's production had reached a peak. Yet the economic crisis at the end of the decade and the turbulence of the 1930s combined to depress the company's sales. World War II and the firebombing of Dresden further shattered the company's fortunes. Then, at the end of World War II, the Radeberger brewery found itself on the Soviet side of the Iron Curtain.

The Soviet-backed East German government took control of Radeberger in 1946. The company became known as the People's Radeberger Export Brewery. Backed by its government owners, Radeberger rapidly became the largest selling beer in East Germany. The maintenance of high quality standards, and continued investments by the government in modernizing the brewery, also led to the beer's return to the export market in 1956. Served by the Communist government at social functions around the world, the brand became especially popular among other Communist bloc countries.

The development of a special export variety of Radeberger, which boasted a shelf life of at least a year, even in tropical climates, led to the brand's wider acceptance beyond Eastern Europe. By the end of the 1960s, half of the brewery's production was destined to the export market, which by then numbered more than 30 countries. Radeberger continued upgrading and expanding its brewery and other facilities through the 1970s and 1980s. By the end of the 1980s, the Radeberger brewery had topped a production capacity of 4.7 million cases per year.

Binding with Binding Brauerei: 1990s

The collapse of Soviet control and the reunification of Germany in 1990 brought a new era for Radeberger. The company now returned to the West German market for the first time in more than 50 years. Demand for the Radeberger brand surged, in part as West Germans embraced certain products of their East German counterparts in the first wave of enthusiasm following reunification. Yet Radeberger, which had lost its government ownership, and its financial backing, was unable to carry out the necessary expansion and upgrade of its production facilities.

For this reason, the company turned to a new partner, Binding Brauerei, which acquired Radeberger in 1990.

Binding's roots also lay in the second half of the 19th century. In 1870, Conrad Binding purchased a small brewery, Ehrenfried Glock, in the old section of Frankfurt. Binding had already gained experience as a master brewer, and under his leadership the brewery grew strongly through its first decade. By 1881, Binding was ready to modernize the operation, and the company moved to a new, larger site in Frankfurt. Binding formally incorporated the brewery as Binding Brauerei in 1884. By then, Binding was the largest in Frankfurt, producing some 45,000 hectoliters each year.

Binding was joined by his younger brother Carl, and together they built the business into a major Frankfurt region corporation. Into the new century, the company began adding to its portfolio of beers. In 1902, for example, the Bindings launched a new extra-strong lager, called Carolus Doppelbock, named after Charlemagne (called Carolus in German), founder of Frankfurt.

The company expanded in the 1920s through a merger with local rival Schoefferhof in 1921. The resulting company adopted a new name, Schoefferhof Binding Buergerbraeu AG. Soon after, the Binding brothers left the business; Carl Binding died in 1925 and Conrad Binding died in 1933. During the 1930s, Binding also prepared the launch of another beer brand, Romerpils, which debuted in 1939. In that year, however, the company's brewery was destroyed during air raids over Frankfurt.

Schoefferhof Binding rebuilt after the war, and expanded during Germany's economic recovery. Leading the company in its postwar growth was a new generation of the Binding family, led by Conrad Binding II, the son of Carl Binding. By the 1960s, the company had drawn up a new expansion strategy, and by 1968 had added a new corporate headquarters as well as a bottle filling plant. This resulted in two highly successful launches for the company. By then, Conrad Binding II had retired, and the control of the company passed to the Oetker family, one of Germany's food production leaders. By the early 1990s, the Oetkers' control of Binding had topped 71 percent.

During the 1970s, the company was particularly active in developing new types of beer. The first of these was the introduction of Schoefferhof Weise, a wheat beer, which quickly became one of Germany's leaders in this category. Launched in 1978, Schoefferhof Weise developed into a national brand and remained one of the pillars of the group's portfolio into the next century.

The second beer represented a true innovation: The 1979 launch of Clausthaler gave the world the first nonalcoholic beer. The company's research had succeeded in producing an alcohol-free beer that nonetheless retained the full flavor of true beer. Clausthaler was an instant success for the company in Germany, and also represented a major new export product. This was especially true in the North American market, where Clausthaler remained more or less the sole nonalcoholic beer for more than a decade.

By the late 1980s, the German government was under pressure to repeal the country's beer purity laws, which shielded the domestic market from the arrival of foreign beer brands and

Key Dates:

1866: A brewery is founded in Radeberg, near Dresden, in order to brew pilsner beer.

1870: Conrad Binding acquires a brewery in Frankfurt.

1872: The Radeberger brewery incorporates as a shareholding partnership.

1881: Binding builds a new, modern brewery in Frankfurt.

1885: As exports increase, the name is changed to Radeberg Exportbrauerei.

1921: Binding merges with Schoefferhof.

1946: The Radeberg brewery is taken over by the Soviet-backed East German government.

1978: Binding launches Schoefferhof Weise wheat beer.

1979: Binding launches alcohol-free Clausthaler beer.

1988: Binding acquires 87 percent of Berliner Kindle Brauerei.

1989: Binding acquires Getranke Hoffmann; construction of a new brewery is launched in Erbach.

1990: After the collapse of communism, Binding acquires two breweries in East Germany, Radeberger and Krostitzer, near Leipzig.

1994: Krusovice in the Czech Republic is acquired.

2002: The group restructures, becoming Radeberger Gruppe AG.

2004: Oetker acquires full control of Radeberger.

2005: Radeberger acquires a 50 percent stake in Stuttgarter Hofbraeu.

companies for the first time. In 1989, the European Commission struck a blow at the purity legislation, demanding that ''impure'' beers be allowed into the country. This effectively led to the repeal of the purity legislation, and ushered in a new era of competition and consolidation for the highly fragmented German market. Indeed, at the beginning of the 1990s, the country still counted more than 1,500 breweries.

Binding played a prominent role in leading a partial consolidation of the market, making a number of significant acquisitions at the end of the 1980s. These included the 1988 acquisition of 87 percent of Berliner Kindl Brauerei, with whom Binding had already developed a close working relationship. The company further added to its interests in the Berlin market with the purchase of Getranke Hoffmann GmbH in 1989, giving it a network of more than 100 wholesale outlets. In that year, as well, the company launched construction of an entirely new brewery in Erbach.

Grouping Around Radeberger in the 2000s

A more significant moment for the company came with the toppling of the Berlin wall and the reunification of Germany. The company's recent Berlin purchases gave it a strong foothold from which to enter the newly liberated East German market, which proved highly receptive to the company's brands. Berliner Kindl, for example, saw a 40 percent rise in sales in that year alone.

Berliner Kindl also led Binding's first acquisition incursion into the former East Germany, buying up Brauerei Potsdam

GmbH in 1990. Soon after, Binding deepened its interests in the region, acquiring Krostitz Brauerei, a brewer of Ur-Krostitzer pilsner near Leipzig. Then, in November 1990, the company acquired Radeberger, the largest brewer in East Germany.

Following the Radeberger acquisition, Oetker, which also controlled DAB (Dortmunder Actien-Brauerei) and Andreas Brauerei, restructured its brewery holdings, transferring the minority shares of both DAB and Andreas to Binding. Binding invested heavily in Radeberger, nearly tripling its production by the end of the 1990s. Radeberger quickly became Binding's national and international flagship brand. The company also added a number of other brands to its portfolio, including a license to brew and distribute Pilsner Urquel, the Czech beer, for parts of the German market, and later an exclusive German franchise for Mexico's Corona. In 1994, Binding went looking for expansion outside of Germany, and purchased its first foreign holding, Krušovice, in the Czech Republic.

For much of the 1990s, German brewers remained more or less safe from foreign competition, in part because of the strong German preference for German-style beers. The market shifted dramatically at the end of the 1990s, however, as a number of foreign players, such as Belgium's Interbrew, The Netherlands' Heineken, and the United States' Budweiser, began buying up a number of Germany's national and regional brands.

Binding responded to the new challenge to its home market in two ways. The first came in 2002, and led the company through a restructuring, creating a new holding company, called Radeberger Gruppe, in order to regroup the company's portfolio under this strong, nationally and internationally recognized identity. The company also moved to consolidate its operations, including merging its various marketing and distribution subsidiaries (which, attached each to its own brewery, had worked independently of one another) into a single corporate-wide unit.

Then in 2004, in an effort to preserve Radeberger Gruppe from the potential threat of a takeover by a foreign company, Oetker bought out the group's minority shareholders. Radeberger then delisted from the stock exchange, becoming a private company. Soon after, Oetker became Germany's leading brewery group through the purchase of a controlling stake in another brewer, Brau und Brunner, based in Dortmund.

In 2005, Radeberger itself entered the consolidation drive, buying up a 50 percent share of Stuttgarter Hofbraeu. As part of that purchase, Radeberger also acquired the option to take full control of Stuttgarter in the future. Radeberger Gruppe's strong brand portfolio and geographic reach gave it confidence that it would remain a German beer leader into the new century.

Principal Subsidiaries

Allgäuer Brauhaus AG; Andreas Brauerei KG; Bärenbier Vertrieb GmbH; Bayerische Brauerei-Schuck-Jaenisch GmbH; Berliner Kindl Brauerei AG; Binding-Brauerei AG; Binding-Brauerei USA Inc.; Brauerei Potsdam GmbH; Brauerei Thier GmbH; Brauerei Wittenberge GmbH; DAB Gaststätten GmbH; DAB Italia S.p.A.; Dortmunder Actien-Brauerei AG; Erbacher Brauhaus J. Wörner & Söhne KG; Erbacher Premium Pils Brau GmbH; Getränke Hoffmann GmbH; Henninger-Bräu AG; Královsk y Pivovar Krušovice A.S. (Czech Republic); Kronen

Privatbrauerei Dortmund GmbH; Krostitzer Brauerei GmbH; Radeberger Exportbierbrauerei GmbH; Schöfferhofer Weizenbier GmbH; Selters Mineralquelle Augusta Victoria GmbH; Victoria Brauerei GmbH.

Principal Competitors

Carlton and United Beverages; Ochakovo Beer and Soft Drinks Joint Stock Co.; Dreher Sorgyarak Rt; Pivovary Staropramen A.S.; Groupe Danone; Fulger S.A.; SABMiller PLC; Heineken Holding N.V.; Budejovicky Mestansky Pivovar A.S.; Carlsberg A/S; Allied Domecq PLC; Interbrew S.A.

Further Reading

"Binding Starts Holiday Promo for Radeberger," *Modern Brewery Age,* October 29, 2001, p. 2.

Bohme, Henrik, "Oetker Gulps Down Brau und Brunnen," *Deutsche Welle,* February 13, 2004.

"German Brewing Managers Expect Further Alliances and Mergers (Radeberger-Chef sagt weitere Fusionen voraus)," *Financial Times Deutschland,* June 18, 2004.

"Oetker Reaches Agreement with Radeberger Shareholders Over Improved Offer (Mehr Abfindung fur Radeberger-Aktionare)," *Suddeutsche Zeitung,* July 8, 2004.

"Possible Radeberger Brewery Closures (Radeberger denkt an Brauereischliesungen)," *Handelsblatt,* January 17, 2005.

"Radeberger Acquires 50% Stake in Hofbrau (Radeberger-Gruppe steigt in Stuttgart ein)," *Die Welt,* December 11, 2003.

"Radeberger Gruppe Squeezes Out Small Owners at Krušovice Brewery," *Czech News Agency,* August 29, 2005.

"Radeberger Takes Stake in Rival Brewer Stuttgarter Hofbrau," *Europe Agri,* December 19, 2003, p. 511.

"Radeberger to Be Removed from Stock Exchange (Radeberger kehrt Borse den Rucken)," *Suddeutsche Zeitung,* August 9, 2004.

—M.L. Cohen

RENTWAY
The Right Way. Right Away.™

Rent-Way, Inc.

One Rentway Place
Erie, Pennsylvania 16505
U.S.A.
Telephone: (814) 455-5378
Toll Free: (800) 736-8929
Fax: (814) 461-5400
Web site: http://www.rentway.com

Public Company
Incorporated: 1981
Employees: 3,929
Sales: $503.8 million (2004)
Stock Exchanges: New York
Ticker Symbol: RWY
NAIC: 532310 General Rental Centers

Rent-Way, Inc. operates a chain of approximately 800 rental-purchase stores in 34 states, renting merchandise such as home entertainment equipment, computers, furniture, major appliances, and jewelry on a weekly or monthly basis. Rent-Way stores are typically located in low- to middle-income neighborhoods in high-traffic strip malls; the typical Rent-Way customer, often with limited credit or cash-on-hand, finds it easier to make weekly or monthly payments than to purchase merchandise outright. The company offers its customers rental agreements ranging from one week to several years, with an average rental agreement lasting 16 weeks. Customers also have the option to purchase merchandise at the conclusion of a rental agreement, or they can return the merchandise at any time during the agreement without penalty. The company offers free pickup and delivery of merchandise and does not charge customers for normal wear and tear. Rent-Way also offers prepaid local phone service to customers on a monthly basis through its subsidiary dPi Teleconnect LLC.

The First Store in 1981

Company cofounders William E. Morgenstern and Gerald A. Ryan opened their first rental-purchase store in Erie, Penn-sylvania, in 1981. Morgenstern was first introduced to the industry in 1979 while he worked as a store manager and then district manager for Rent-A-Center in Fort Worth, Texas. Ryan, on the other hand, came to the new venture from a different background, having been instrumental in forming Spectrum Control, Inc., a company that produced electronic components.

Like other rental-purchase stores, Rent-Way would offer its customers merchandise via weekly or monthly agreements. Agreements could be canceled at any time without penalty, and customers were offered the option to purchase merchandise at the end of a rental agreement. The store made its profit through mark-ups on merchandise. Although the majority of Rent-Way's customers had little or no credit and very little cash on hand and found Rent-Way a financially convenient option, some were furnishing temporary or vacation homes only a few months a year, and some wished to test electronic equipment before purchasing it. Whereas the store offered furniture, appliances, and jewelry, the bulk of its rental agreements were for home entertainment equipment. The average customer returned merchandise after 16 weeks, and most merchandise could be rented several times during its lifetime. Rent-Way did not charge its customers for normal wear and tear and sometimes offered free repairs. The store offered free pickup and delivery of merchandise.

Morgenstern and Ryan had ambitious plans for the company. They believed bigger was better and strove to capture a significant portion of the industry's market share. Since acquired stores generated a profit more quickly than newly opened stores, the company concentrated on acquisitions. By 1993, Rent-Way had 19 stores in three states and had completed its initial public offering (IPO) on the New York Stock Exchange. After the IPO, the company set a goal to capture between 6 and 10 percent of the estimated $4.4 billion rental-purchase industry by the year 2000.

Rapid Expansion in the Mid-1990s

In 1994, the company acquired DAMSL Corporation, which doubled the number of stores it owned from 20 to 40. The following year, Rent-Way purchased a 45-store chain from McKenzie Leasing Corporation. The McKenzie acquisition

Company Perspectives:

Rent-Way's marketing strategy revolves around a unique approach to customer service. Our "Welcome, Wanted and Important" philosophy emphasizes customer satisfaction and positions Rent-Way as a friendly, easy solution to our customers' rental needs.

made Rent-Way the tenth largest rental-purchase company in the United States.

Rent-Way realized that in order to succeed in the competitive rental-purchase market, it needed to offer its customers outstanding service. The company's "Welcome, Wanted, and Important" program was one way it strove to set itself apart from the roughly 1,500 to 2,000 independently owned mom-and-pop rental-purchase shops throughout the country. "We think it's critical that our customers feel satisfied by the products we offer and the treatment they receive," explained Morgenstern in *Management Review*. He added: "In most service industries, customers who have limited purchasing power are viewed pejoratively. Rent-Way puts all its entry-level employees through an intensive 13-week program that puts a strong emphasis on customer service." Customers who experienced problems in Rent-Way stores could call headquarters using a special customer hotline that rang through to the president's office. "Out of 26,000 customers, we average about 15 calls a week," Morgenstern said in *Management Review*. The company also impressed its customers with its clean, well-stocked stores.

During this time, while acquisitions were fast and furious, Rent-Way focused on making its new employees as comfortable as its customers. Whenever Rent-Way acquired a new chain, it initiated a "pal system," where management from Rent-Way stores visited new stores to make employees feel welcome. Their aim was to develop a sense of loyalty rather than risk the usual mistrust that occurred when one company took over another. Explained Morgenstern in *Management Review*, "We want to end up with the best of both cultures and we realize each company can learn from the other."

Rent-Way employees also were allowed to take part in problem-solving task forces made up of three to five people. Regional managers conducted regular meetings with store managers to make upper-level management aware of problems within the company. Upper-level management then organized employee task forces to solve each problem.

Rent-Way continued its breakneck pace in 1996 and 1997. In 1996, the company purchased the 11-store Diamond Leasing Corporation, which had stores in Delaware, Maryland, and Pennsylvania. The purchase expanded Rent-Way's portfolio to 104 stores. In January 1997, the company acquired the 70-store Rental King chain. The move was a good one for Rent-Way; Rental King stores were nearly as profitable as Rent-Way stores. A Rental King store typically earned $400,000 a year as compared with the $500,000 a typical Rent-Way store earned. Also in January, Rent-Way spent $6.7 million for Bill Coleman TV's 15 Michigan-based stores. In July, the company acquired R.A. Wolford, Inc., a four-store chain in Pennsylvania. Rent-

Way paid about ten times the target company's monthly revenue for each acquisition.

Rent-Way believed the smooth integration of its new stores was paramount to its success. Using its point-of-sale software, Rent-Way was able to get an acquisition's operating systems working with its own in a short period of time. "The key to our success has been the way we assimilate companies into our organization," remarked CFO Jeffrey Conway in *Investor's Business Daily*. "We don't put the Rent-Way name on it until it's operating the way we like it," Conway said.

Further Growth in 1998 and 1999

Rent-Way continued its tremendous growth in 1998. In January, the company added 50 more stores to its portfolio when it purchased the South Carolina-based Ace T.V. Rentals; 46 of these stores were in South Carolina and four were in California.

In February, the company acquired the Daytona-based Champion Rentals. The 145 Champion Rental stores gave Rent-Way access to new markets in Alabama, Arkansas, and Georgia. In July, the company acquired Fast Rentals, Inc., a rental purchase chain with six stores in Alabama and two in Georgia. In September, Rent-Way purchased Cari Rentals, a 23-store chain with stores in Iowa, Missouri, Nebraska, and South Dakota.

Also that month, Rent-Way entered into its largest purchase agreement ever, signing a merger agreement with Home Choice Holdings, Inc., an enormous chain with 459 stores in 26 states. The $330 million acquisition opened new markets for Rent-Way in 11 states, including 100 Home Choice stores in Texas. Rent-Way kept the Home Choice name in newly renovated stores but planned to switch eventually to a single banner. Also in September 1998, *Fortune* magazine named Rent-Way the tenth fastest growing stock in the United States and the nation's 56th fastest growing company.

The acquisition program continued in 1999. In June of that year, Rent-Way purchased America's Rent-to-Own Center, a 21-store chain in Arkansas, Kansas, Missouri, and Oklahoma with revenues of $18. Later in the year, Rent-Way purchased rival RentaVision for $250 million. RentaVision had 250 stores.

Since Rent-Way's IPO in August 1993, the company had more than tripled its size and had exceeded its goal of capturing 6 to 10 percent of the industry's market share. As of 1999, it had 11 percent of the estimated $4.4 billion rental-purchase market.

In 2000, the company planned to roll out new products and services, including prepaid telephone service and computers. Toward that end, in January 2000, Rent-Way acquired a 49 percent interest in dPi Teleconnect, a privately held provider of prepaid local phone service. Rent-Way agreed to acquire an additional 21 percent interest upon receipt of regulatory approvals. dPi was licensed to offer prepaid local phone service in 21 states and had planned to expand to more than 40 states by the end of 2000. dPi provided service to customers who could not afford the fees required by their local telephone service. Even though dPi was only one year old, it already had 14,000 customers who were paying about $50 a month for the prepaid phone service. Both dPi and Rent-Way felt the partnership was a good one: About six million households in the United Sates

Key Dates:

1981: The first Rent-Way store opens in Erie, Pennsylvania.

1993: Rent-Way, with 19 stores in three states, completes its initial public offering (IPO) of stock.

1994: The size of the company doubles with the acquisition of DAMSL Corp.

1995: Rent-Way doubles in size again after acquiring a 45-store chain from McKenzie Leasing Corp.

1998: Rent-Way completes its largest acquisition, purchasing Home Choice Holdings, Inc. and its 458 stores.

1999: The company acquires America's Rent-To-Own Center Inc. and RentaVision.

2000: Allegations of accounting fraud are made public in October, touching off a three-year period of federal criminal and civil investigations and shareholder lawsuits.

2003: Three Rent-Way executives plead guilty to manipulating the company's accounting books in an effort to inflate profits; to help reduce mounting debt, 295 stores are sold to rival Rent-A-Center, Inc.

2004: Rent-Way opens ten new stores, its first expansion since 2000.

2005: Founder William Morgenstern steps down as president and chief executive officer.

were wired for phone service but did not have it; a significant portion of these homes were near Rent-Way stores.

Commenting on dPi's mission, David Dorwart, company president, said in a press release, "Historically individuals who for whatever reason could not meet the credit or deposit requirements of the local phone company have done without a phone. The service dPi offers provides them with access to local phone service, 911, and the Internet. Partnering with Rent-Way will allow dPi to grow more quickly and become a leader in the prepaid local phone service industry." Rent-Way would receive the benefit of extra traffic in its locations as well as 10 percent commission from the sale of dPi's service. Rent-Way's investment in dPi was expected to total $7.5 million.

Around the same time, Rent-Way negotiated a deal with Compaq to rent computers to customers on a 15-month contract. Rent-Way paid $950 per Compaq computer and was hoping to negotiate a similar deal with Dell Computer. The company's computer rentals were successful from the start. "We are very optimistic about the potential of bringing computers to our customer base in a much bigger way in the months and years ahead," Conway said in a February 14, 2000 news release. Conway, who was formerly vice-president and chief financial officer of Rent-Way, was promoted to president of the company in January 2000. As it approached a new century Rent-Way looked toward increasing its annual sales to the $1 billion mark.

A Disastrous Start to the 21st Century

Conway did not enjoy his promotion for long, nor did any Rent-Way executive particularly relish the beginning of the new century. The hope of reaching the $1 billion-in-sales plateau was replaced with the hope of staving off bankruptcy, and the agent of the dramatic alteration in intent was Conway. In October 2000, the specter of accounting malfeasance, a trend in corporate America at the turn of the 21st century, hovered over the company, triggering federal criminal and civil investigations, inquiries by the Securities and Exchange Commission (SEC), and a shareholder lawsuit. At the center of the scrutiny was Conway, who, during the course of the investigations and court proceedings that dragged on for three years, was found to be the architect of the accounting scandal. Conway, the allegations charged, began implementing his scheme in 1998 in an effort to meet or to exceed analysts' expectations of Rent-Way's financial performance. He directed Matthew Marini, the company's controller, to understate expenses to inflate profits, court records revealed. Further, Conway enlisted the help of Rent-Way's senior vice-president of operations, Jeffrey Underwood, instructing him to defer the recording of the company's expenses at the end of 1999 and 2000, again in an attempt to make the company appear more profitable than it was. As investigators poured over the company's accounting books, Morgenstern, who was cleared of any involvement in the fraud, watched his company nearly collapse. Rent-Way posted a loss of $63.6 million in 2001. In 2002, its fifth consecutive year of losing money after earnings were restated, the company registered a $76.5 million loss, the largest loss in the five-year period. Amid mounting losses and increasing debt, shareholders filed a lawsuit against the company, venting their fury at the plummeting value of their stock. Rent-Way, battered from all fronts, teetered on the brink of bankruptcy, dethroned from its position among the industry's elite.

Rent-Way's nightmarish ordeal reached its resolution in 2003, leaving Morgenstern with the daunting task of rebuilding his company. In March 2003, the company settled the lawsuit filed by shareholders in a $25 million deal. In July 2003, Conway, Marini, and Underwood pleaded guilty to the charges against them, with Conway receiving the stiffest sentence of 13 months in federal prison. The trio was found to have inflated reported earnings by roughly $60 million and to have made an additional $35 million in fraudulent entries during the fourth quarter of 2000.

Morgenstern began implementing turnaround measures while Rent-Way was embroiled in legal difficulties. The company's merchandising mix underwent an overhaul, its pricing strategy was altered, and a new, more aggressive marketing and advertising campaign was created. Meanwhile, the company began reducing its store count from a peak of 1,147 stores in November 2000 to roughly 750 stores, closing underperforming units and selling others, including the sale of 295 stores to its main competitor, Rent-A-Center, Inc., in February 2003. Morgenstern's actions soon realized their intent, as Rent-Way began to demonstrate renewed vitality. After posting a net loss of $29.4 million in 2003, the company reported a profit of $9.2 million in 2004. Buoyed by its improved financial health, the company opened ten new stores in the fall of 2004, the first expansion since 2000, and announced plans to open 100 more stores in 2005 and 2006. After restoring hope in a profitable future for Rent-Way, Morgenstern left the day-to-day task of fulfilling that objective to the company's chief operating officer. In mid-2005, Morgenstern relinquished the titles of president and chief executive officer, appointing William Short as the company's new leader. Short spent a dozen years at Rent-A-Center before joining Rent-Way in 1996 to manage the company's stores in western New York, earning a promotion to chief operating officer in July 2002. As the company began to expand in earnest midway through the decade, the challenge of returning Rent-Way to the top of its industry fell to Short and his senior managers, all of whom were determined not to repeat the failures of the past.

Principal Subsidiaries

Rent-Way of Michigan, Inc.; Rent-Way of TTIG, L.P.; dPi Teleconnect LLC (83.5%).

Principal Competitors

Rent-A-Center, Inc.; Aaron Rents, Inc.; Wal-Mart Stores, Inc.

Further Reading

Breskin, Ira, ''Rent-Way Tackles Its Market Through Streak of Acquisitions,'' *Investor's Daily,* September 5, 1997.

''How a Winning Strategy Helps Pay the Rent,'' *Management Review,* October 1995, p. S4.

Milite, George, ''Short-Term Teams Yield Long-Term Results,'' *Supervisory Management,* September 1995, p. 7.

Pachuta, Michael J., ''Rent-Way Gobbles Up Rivals to Double Its Market Share,'' *Investor's Business Daily,* May 6, 1998.

Panepento, Peter, ''CEO Vows to Rebuild Erie, Pa.-Based Rent-Way,'' *Erie Times-News,* July 24, 2003.

——, ''Erie, Pa.-Based Rent-to-Own Chain Is Focused on the Future,'' *Erie Times-News,* December 3, 2004.

——, ''Erie, Pa.-Based Rent-to-Own Company Rent-Way to Add New Stores,'' *Erie Times-News,* July 30, 2004.

——, ''Erie, Pa.-Based Rent-Way Looks to Brighter Future,'' *Erie Times-News,* March 11, 2004.

——, ''Erie, Pa.-Based Rent-Way Posts Losses for Fourth-Quarter, Year,'' *Erie Times-News,* December 19, 2002.

——, ''Erie, Pa.-Based Rent-Way Shows Signs of Mending,'' *Erie Times-News,* August 15, 2003.

——, ''Former Rent-Way Executive Gets Prison, Fine in Fraud Case,'' *Erie Times-News,* November 26, 2003.

——, ''Rent-Way's Founder to Step Aside As CEO,'' *Erie Times-News,* March 23, 2005.

——, ''Three Former Rent-Way Executives Plead Guilty,'' *Erie Times-News,* July 23, 2003.

Marcial, Gene G., ''Rent-Way's Black Ink May Lure a Buyer,'' *Business Week,* May 30, 2005, p. 124.

''Rent-Way and Home Choice Merging,'' *Consumer Electronics,* September 14, 1998.

''Rent-Way, Continuing Breakneck,'' *Television Digest,* January 12, 1998, p. 17.

''Rent-Way Stock Offering,'' *Television Digest,* April 29, 1996, p. 20.

—Tracey Vasil Biscontini
—update: Jeffrey L. Covell

Riviera Holdings Corporation

2901 Las Vegas Boulevard South
Las Vegas, Nevada 89109
U.S.A.
Telephone: (702) 734-5110
Fax: (702) 794-9442
Web site: http://www.rivierahotel.com

Public Company
Incorporated: 1955 as Riviera Hotel Company
Employees: 1,639
Sales: $201.35 million (2004)
Stock Exchanges: American
Ticker Symbol: RIV
NAIC: 721120 Casino Hotels; 722110 Full-Service
     Restaurants; 722410 Drinking Places (Alcoholic
     Beverages)

Riviera Holdings Corporation owns and operates the Riviera Hotel & Casino in Las Vegas, Nevada, and the Riviera Black Hawk Casino in Black Hawk, Colorado. The firm's focus is on price-conscious gamblers aged 45 to 65, and its casinos feature reasonably priced lodging, entertainment, and food; hundreds of slot machines (many playable with pennies or nickels); and a variety of card, dice, and roulette tables. The Riviera Hotel offers 2,100 rooms and a 125,000-square-foot casino, as well as restaurants, bars, and clubs where variety, comedy, and "adults-only" performances are offered. One-third of the hotel's revenue comes from business conventions. The Riviera Black Hawk casino, which is restricted to $5 wagers by Colorado law, offers a large gaming area along with several restaurants and entertainment venues. CEO, President, and Chairman William L. Westerman owns 17 percent of the firm's stock.

Beginnings

The roots of Riviera Holdings date to April 20, 1955, when the Riviera Hotel and Casino opened in Las Vegas with a star-studded premiere featuring Hollywood icon Joan Crawford as hostess and showman Liberace performing on the stage of the Clover Room. The nine-story hotel (then Las Vegas's tallest) had been built on the famous Highway 91 "Strip" at a cost of $8.5 million by a group of Miami investors headed by Sam Cohen. Situated on 25 acres of land leased from Gensbro Hotel Co., it featured 300 rooms, several restaurants and bars, an Olympic-size swimming pool, and a casino with 116 slot machines and 18 gaming tables.

Las Vegas was then in a building frenzy, with nearly 100 new hotels opened since 1953, including several luxury ones such as the Dunes and Royal Nevada. With competition so fierce, it was not surprising that the Riviera's owners quickly found profits elusive. As costs soared out of control, including the then unprecedented fees paid to such entertainers as Liberace (earning $50,000 per week), by July the hotel was close to bankruptcy with debts of $2.5 million. In September the Riviera was taken over by a group of Vegas veterans led by Gus Greenbaum, who had formerly run the Flamingo Hotel, built a decade earlier by notorious racketeer Bugsy Siegel. Under Greenbaum's experienced management team, the hotel's financial picture improved markedly, and in early 1956 plans were announced for a $2 million expansion that would add 200 new rooms and enlarge the casino and dining room areas.

In December 1958 Gus Greenbaum and his wife were murdered, allegedly by underworld operatives, and a few months later the Riviera was sold to a group of investors associated with the Fremont and Sands hotels. October 1959 saw a new $2.4 million remodeling announced that would add 114 guest rooms and an atomic-themed three-level rooftop nightclub.

The 1960s was a golden era for Las Vegas, as members of the "Rat Pack" performed in clubs and prowled the lounges in the wee hours. Acts playing the Riviera during the decade ranged from the Duke Ellington Orchestra and Louis Armstrong to Liberace, Engelbert Humperdinck, and Rat Pack member Dean Martin, who later took a 10 percent ownership stake.

The year 1965 saw the hotel's owner, now known as Hotel Riviera, Inc., purchase the land beneath it from Gensbro, and two years later the hotel was expanded with a new 200-room wing, a 9,000-square-foot lobby, and 10,000 square feet of new office and meeting rooms. Organized crime associations contin-

Company Perspectives:

At the Riviera, we take pride in serving our customers in the tradition and style that made Las Vegas famous. Offering top value for your room, food and entertainment dollar with a personal touch is in what we take pride. Our repeat business is indicative of the many fond memories created by a trip to the Riviera Hotel and Casino, the Entertainment Center of Las Vegas.

ued to surface, with several shareholders indicted on charges of ''skimming'' gambling revenues in 1967.

Sale to Riklis in 1973

In 1973 Turkish-born Meshulam Riklis, owner of Boston-based AITS (American International Travel Services), bought the Riviera for $56 million. Two years later the new 17-story Monte Carlo tower was opened, which added 300 guest rooms, 60 suites, and a penthouse. It was followed in 1977 by the San Remo tower, which added 200 rooms and an Italian restaurant.

In August 1983 the hotel's owners filed for bankruptcy protection after they were unable to make payments on a $52 million loan. The following year Riviera management decided to move away from high-rolling gamblers to focus on families, and added a Burger King and a video arcade, along with five-cent slot machines and other low-wager betting options. By now Riklis had married entertainer Pia Zadora, and hotel restaurants Kady's and Kristofer's were named after their two young children.

In 1985, under longtime Riklis associate and new President Arthur Waltzman, the Riviera emerged from bankruptcy. That same year a new entertainment offering, ''Splash,'' debuted. A music and dance variety show starring impersonator and actor Frank Gorshin, its set featured a 20,000-gallon aquarium in which swimming routines were performed. Another show added that year, ''An Evening at La Cage,'' showcased female impersonators and dancers. The year 1987 saw the addition of ''Crazy Girls,'' a topless comedy revue. All three would remain in continuous operation in the ensuing years, with occasional updates to keep them from becoming stale.

In 1988 the Riviera opened the 1,000-room, 24-story Monaco Tower. Built at a cost of $28 million, it gave the hotel a total of 2,100 rooms. Expansion continued in 1989, when a new 70,000-square-foot casino addition was begun. A fire touched off by welders in September forced a complete evacuation of the hotel and caused an estimated $3.5 million in damage. The casino's Burger King and adjoining video arcade were later closed for good. The company had likely been spared worse damage because Nevada had instituted strict safety codes in the wake of hotel fires in 1980 and 1981 that killed nearly 100 people.

In March 1990 the Riviera's newly expanded casino, touted as the world's largest, was opened. With 1,600 slot and video poker machines, 90 table games including blackjack, dice, poker, and roulette, and a 200-seat lounge, the hotel's 125,000-square-foot gambling area now extended from the front of the original 1955 building almost to the sidewalk of the Strip. Soon

afterward a 250-seat race and sports betting parlor, a 24-hour food court, three new restaurants, and a second swimming pool were added as well. The firm, which had spent some $150 million on renovations since 1984, had revenues of approximately $200 million per year at the close of 1996.

1991 Bankruptcy Leading to New Ownership

Increasing competition, an economic recession, and a downturn in travel during the 1991 Persian Gulf War led to a drop in revenues at many Las Vegas casinos, and in December 1991 the Riviera again filed for Chapter 11 bankruptcy protection. The firm had been unable to make payments on its secured debt of $126 million. In early 1992 company head Arthur Waltzman was replaced with William Westerman, another longtime business associate of Riklis, and layoffs were announced that brought the hotel's total workforce down from the mid-1991 figure of 2,300 to less than 2,000.

On July 1, 1993, the hotel officially emerged from Chapter 11 protection, with ownership transferred from the financially troubled Riklis to the Riviera's bondholders. The firm's unsecured debtors also would receive 50 cents on the dollar. The company would now be known as Riviera Holdings Corp., with William Westerman serving as CEO, chairman, and president, after President Al Rapuano had resigned over publicity about his ties to organized crime figure Joey Cusumano.

The new owners soon announced that the Riviera would concentrate on middle-income adult gamblers instead of families, with in-house entertainment emphasized over such well-known headliners as Frank Sinatra and George Burns, both of whom had recently appeared there. The firm also began to step up its marketing efforts, and reached out to travel agents with commissions and other incentives for steering tourists to the hotel.

In December 1995 the firm began working with Donaldson, Lufkin and Jenrette to look for acquisition or merger opportunities, and soon afterward formed a subsidiary in Mississippi to seek approval to operate a casino there. The year 1995 also saw the Splash showroom closed for six months for remodeling. Revenues for the year topped $150 million, down from $154 million a year earlier, though net income rose from $4.8 million to $6.3 million. Occupancy was 98 percent, one of the highest rates in Las Vegas.

In 1996 a new subsidiary, Riviera Gaming Management, took over operations of the bankrupt 700-room Four Queens hotel and casino in Las Vegas for a $1 million annual guarantee versus 25 percent of the increase in cash flow generated through its efforts. The year also saw the company's stock begin trading on the American Stock Exchange.

In March 1997 the firm announced plans to build a $50 million casino in Black Hawk, Colorado, in conjunction with Eagle Gaming L.P., which would own 20 percent of the operation. The limited wager casino (in which no bets over $5 were allowed) would be the largest in the state. Construction would be funded by the sale of 1.5 million new shares in Riviera Holdings.

The year 1997 also saw the Riviera Hotel begin expanding its convention facilities to 150,000 square feet, as well as adding ''Nickel Town,'' a new casino that included several hundred

---

five-cent slot machines. Notes worth $155 million were sold during the year to help fund the new growth. The firm also had recently attempted to win a casino license in Detroit when that city voted to allow gaming, but lost to three other firms.

In the fall of 1997 San Diego-based racehorse owner Allen Paulson struck a deal to buy Riviera Holdings for $75 million in cash and assumption of $175 million in debt, along with the Four Queens, owned by Elsinore Corp., for $54 million. For the year the firm had revenues of $153.8 million and net income of $2.1 million, down from $164.4 million and $8.4 million in 1996. Not long after these figures were released, Paulsen backed out of the deal, alleging he had been given inaccurate information, and sued his financial advisors and the hotels.

In September 1998 ground was broken on the new $75 million Black Hawk Casino, and the following year another $45 million in bonds was sold to finance it. In July 1999 the firm agreed to pay Allen Paulson $5 million, keeping part of the $6 million he had put into escrow before agreeing to buy the hotel. In December the firm's contract to manage the Four Queens ended.

Black Hawk Casino Opening in 2000

In February 2000 the Riviera Black Hawk Casino opened. The 300,000-square-foot facility featured 990 slot machines, 12 gaming tables, a 280-seat restaurant, and a 490-seat entertainment venue. Marketing plans included a "slot club," which gave members various incentives to make repeat visits. Revenues for the Black Hawk's first months of operation were underwhelming, and the firm subsequently boosted its promotional efforts.

The September 11, 2001 terrorist attacks on New York and Washington, D.C., had a devastating impact on tourism, and

Las Vegas, already hurt by the recent economic slowdown, was hit hard. In October the Riviera closed its poker room, which would be remodeled to add more slot machines, and the fourth quarter of the year saw room occupancy fall below 80 percent. The firm had total revenues of $202 million and a loss of $6.4 million for 2001. One bright spot was the Black Hawk casino (whose business came, in large part, from regional gamblers), where revenues were up significantly over the previous year.

Early 2002 saw the firm propose a $152 million riverboat hotel/casino in Missouri on the Mississippi River, with plans also afoot to build a 600-slot racetrack/casino in New Mexico. In the summer the company offered $215 million in new bonds to refinance its existing debt. Results for 2002 were poor, with revenues falling to $188.3 million and losses hitting $24.7 million.

After Donald Trump bought a 10 percent stake in the firm in 2002, in early 2003 Italian investor Fabrizio Boccardi offered $30 million plus assumption of $216 million in debt to purchase it. Sales continued to decline during the year as the start of the Iraq War and the SARS outbreak caused tourism to plummet, but the firm's convention bookings were up, with 298 hosted during the year. In November the company's bid for the New Mexico "racino" was rejected, resulting in a $1.3 million writeoff.

April 2004 saw Donald Trump sell his 10 percent stake in the firm, and in August another takeover bid was received from D.E. Shaw Laminar Portfolios, but it was rejected by the Riviera's board. In September, the firm's bid for a Missouri gaming license was rejected, resulting in another $600,000 writeoff.

At this time the northern end of the Las Vegas Strip was seeing the stirrings of a revival. With Vegas kingpin Steve Wynn pledging $2.4 billion to build a new "megaresort" near the Riviera and other resort and condominium plans on the drawing board, the Riviera began to receive new attention from investors, in part because of the value of its land. Members of management soon broached the possibility of demolishing the hotel and building a new $800 million resort on the site, or refurbishing the existing facilities for $500 million. The company's losses were also narrowing, as both the Las Vegas and Colorado operations saw improved earnings. The firm's stock, which had been threatened with delisting by the American Stock Exchange in 2003, was trading at more than $44 per share by year's end, up from slightly more than $5 in January. In February the company announced a three-for-one stock split, and began looking at options to increase shareholder value with advisor Jefferies & Co.

Early 2005 saw profits continuing to rise, but they fell off again during the second quarter of the year, in part because of complicated new accounting rules, as well as $500,000 spent celebrating the hotel's 50th anniversary. The firm was planning to raise room rates from their average of $59 as activity on the north end of the Strip increased, however, and profits were expected to rise as Wynn's resort neared completion.

After 50 years, the Las Vegas hotel and casino owned by Riviera Holdings Corp. had gone from cutting-edge to retro, and its customer base had evolved downward from high rollers to middle Americans. With new developments nearby making it more attractive to investors and the public, and the firm's

Colorado casino doing well, the company looked to a return to profitability in the near future.

Principal Subsidiaries

Riviera Operating Corporation; Riviera Black Hawk, Inc.; Riviera Gaming Management, Inc.

Principal Competitors

Harrah's Entertainment Inc.; MGM MIRAGE; Boyd Gaming Corporation; Wynn Resorts, Ltd.; Las Vegas Sands Corporation; Isle of Capri Casinos, Inc.

Further Reading

"Addition Scheduled for Las Vegas Hotel," *Los Angeles Times,* November 15, 1959, p. G2.

Ames, Walter, "New Riviera Hotel Opens in Las Vegas," *Los Angeles Times,* April 21, 1955, p. 5.

Benston, Liz, "Offer Spotlights Issues Facing Riviera Holdings," *Las Vegas Sun,* April 4, 2003, p. 1.

Blevins, Jason, "Black Hawk Makes Bet Pay Off," *Denver Post,* September 30, 2001, p. B1.

Burbank, Jeff, and Alan Tobin, "Riviera Hotel Seeks Chapter 11 Again," *Las Vegas Review-Journal,* December 19, 1991, p. 1A.

Havas, Adrian, "Riviera Outlook Sunny, But Faces at the Top Change," *Las Vegas Business Press,* June 28, 1993, p. 3.

Hill, Gladwin, "The 'Sure Thing' Boom at Las Vegas," *The New York Times,* January 30, 1955, p. X29.

Jones, Chris, "Riviera Execs Believe That Better Times About to Land," *Las Vegas Review-Journal,* June 10, 2004, p. 1D.

——, "Riviera Results Go Up, Up, Up As Glitzy New Neighbor Arrives," *Las Vegas Review-Journal,* April 27, 2005.

McKee, David, "Strip's Oldsters Await Mixed Future," *Las Vegas Business Press,* August 22, 2005, p. 1.

"Nevada Board Acts to Save Riviera Hotel," *Los Angeles Times,* September 29, 1955, p. 2.

Palermo, Dave, "Board OKs Riviera's Reorganization," *Las Vegas Review-Journal,* June 19, 1993, p. 1B.

——, "Hundreds Laid Off at Riviera Hotel," *Las Vegas Review-Journal,* February 5, 1992, p. 7C.

——, "Riviera to Manage Four Queens," *Las Vegas Review-Journal,* July 25, 1996, p. 10D.

"Riviera Chapter 11," *The New York Times,* August 26, 1983.

"Riviera Hotel, Las Vegas, Nev, Bought by Travel Company of Aits Inc. Mar. 3," *The New York Times,* March 4, 1973, p. 27.

Simpson, Jeff, "Riviera Holdings Pleased with New Colorado Casino," *Las Vegas Review-Journal,* February 9, 2000, p. 2D.

"Six Nevada Gamblers Answer Indictments," *Los Angeles Times,* May 13, 1967, p. 2.

"Slowdown, Terror Take Toll on LV Riviera," *Las Vegas Sun,* February 12, 2002, p. 3.

Smith, John L., "Despite Age, Debt and Megaresort Trend, Riviera Hangs Tough," *Las Vegas Review-Journal,* February 24, 2004, p. 1B.

Stutz, Howard, "Riviera Shares Rising Fast," *Las Vegas Review-Journal,* December 28, 2004, p. 1D.

"Vegas Hotel Man, Wife Found Slain," *Los Angeles Times,* December 4, 1958, p. 2.

Velotta, Richard N., "Riviera Holdings Board Rejects Offer to Buy Company," *In Business Las Vegas,* August 27, 2004, p. 32.

—Frank Uhle

Roy Anderson Corporation

11400 Reichold Road
Gulfport, Mississippi 39503
U.S.A.
Telephone: (228) 896-4000
Toll Free: (800) 688-4003
Fax: (228) 896-4078
Web site: http://www.rac.com

Private Company
Founded: 1955
Employees: 300
Sales: $225 million (2004 est.)
NAIC: 236220 Commercial and Institutional Building
Construction

Family owned and operated, Roy Anderson Corporation (RAC) is one of the United States' largest construction companies. Based in Gulfport, Mississippi, RAC is involved in a wide variety of hospitality, commercial, government, education, healthcare, industrial, entertainment, and sports construction projects. A major factor in the growth of the company since 1990 has been the building of casinos in the Gulf of Mexico region, which elevated RAC from regional status to a firm with national prominence. In addition to its home office, the company maintains regional offices in Jackson, Mississippi, and Destin, Florida. RAC's founder, Roy Anderson, Jr., serves as chairman, while his son, Roy Anderson III, is president and chief executive officer, responsible for the day-to-day running of the business.

Roots of Company Dating to the 1920s

Roy Anderson Corporation grew out of the real estate business founded by Roy Anderson, Sr., who moved from Purvis, Mississippi, to Gulfport in 1925, launching Roy Anderson Real Estate. He became involved in construction on a small scale, building one or two small houses each year. As a child, his son, Roy Anderson, Jr., often helped out on the construction sites, fetching water and materials for the workmen and eventually learning to do a little carpentry himself. That early experience led him to become interested in engineering, which he studied at the Georgia Institute of

Technology, better known as Georgia Tech, graduating in 1951. Because he was involved in the Reserve Officer Training Corps (ROTC), Anderson then served a four-year stint in the Air Force, in Korea, before returning home to Gulfport with his wife in September 1955 to go into the contracting business.

He set up shop in his father's real estate office and with just a single employee and a pickup truck began drumming up small repair jobs. Later in 1955 his father died, and the real estate business was taken over by his sister, Jane Sawyer, and brother-in-law, Len Sawyer, becoming Sawyer Real Estate and Insurance. Anderson soon graduated from repair and remodeling projects and followed in his father's footsteps by building a few homes. His goal, however, was to become involved in constructing commercial buildings. Two of his earliest large projects were the construction of the Mount Bethel Baptist Church in Gulfport and the Gulfport Chamber of Commerce.

A major step in the history of the company came in 1958 when Anderson bid on the construction of a branch for Hancock Bank. His bid of $106,000 was matched by another area contractor. According to Anderson's recollections in a 2002 interview with the *Mississippi Business Journal,* ''It was quite a dilemma for [Hancock] to decide what to do. I was only a young contractor and the other contractor was an established firm, W.M. Craig & Co. Leo Seal (then president of Hancock Bank) decided the only thing he knew to do was to flip a coin. Since I was the youngest of the group, I suggested that Mr. Craig call the coin. He called heads and it came up tails. You could say we won our first gambling project back then.'' The credibility Anderson gained with the Hancock Bank project led to ever larger jobs. Later in 1958 RAC built the Long Beach High School, a $386,000 contract. Another significant project was the building of a five-story officers' residence at Biloxi's Keesler Air Force Base in 1961. Yet another milestone job in the early years was the $3.8 million contract to build the substructure foundation at Gulfport's Mississippi Power Company power plant in 1969.

Government Contracts Dominating the 1980s

Over the years, RAC proved adept at changing with the times, shifting its focus to different types of projects as they became

Company Perspectives:

Since 1955, performance has been the guiding principle at Roy Anderson Corp. We know it means more than making deadlines. It means dedication. It means professionalism. It means leaving the job site on the last day knowing that the finished project tells all the world the kind of work you do. At Roy Anderson, we're proud to let our work speak for us.

available. In the 1980s, for example, when there was little private construction money in Mississippi and the Reagan and Bush administrations were dramatically increasing defense spending, RAC chased state and federal business, landing a large number of contracts at both Keesler Air Force Base and Stennis Space Center in Hancock County. As the Cold War came to an end at the close of the 1980s, defense spending slowed down and RAC was on the lookout for new opportunities in the area. It found them after Mississippi legalized gambling in 1990.

By this time Anderson was receiving help in the business from his son, Roy Anderson III. The younger Anderson, born in 1957, took a route to the construction industry different from that of his father, although like his father he spent time at construction sites delivering water to the workmen. After earning an undergraduate degree at the University of Alabama, he earned a law degree from the University of Mississippi Law School in 1982. He never practiced law, instead joining his father shortly after graduation. His study of law, however, would prove an asset when dealing with contracts. Although the son of the owner, Anderson III worked his way up in the company, starting out by assisting project managers on a number of jobs. By the time RAC entered the 1990s the company was very much a father and son operation, and in 1993 the younger Anderson took over day-to-day responsibilities as president.

Despite never having built a casino, the Andersons were able to land the contract to build Casino Magic in Biloxi in July 1992, unusual in that it was the first casino built on a barge rather than a riverboat. RAC was able to complete the project in just 83 days, a feat that caught the attention of Park Place Entertainment, owner of Grand Casinos, which was set to build a casino in Gulfport and was intrigued by the barge concept and brought in the Andersons for a meeting at their Minnesota headquarters. Park Place's mid-south region President Tom Brosig, whose own family was involved in the construction business, told Mississippi's *Sun Herald,* "I saw a father and son working together. That was all I needed." The newspaper also reported, "Brosig recalled that the Andersons convinced reluctant Grand Casino executives to build a parking garage next to their casino in Gulfport, something they didn't think was necessary. 'None of us anticipated Gulfport would open as well as it did,' Brosig said. 'Without the garage, we would have been dead.'" By working 24 hours a day, seven days a week, RAC was able to complete the $42 million Grand Casino project in only 156 days. Speed was of great importance to the owners, as casino operators were all vying to open before the competition to establish themselves in the new market.

With two highly successful casino projects under its belt, RAC positioned itself to take full advantage of the region's casino boom in the early 1990s. Casino construction dominated RAC's business until 1996 as employment peaked around 1,000. Other projects included the Grand Casino-Biloxi, Lady Luck-Biloxi, the Palace Casino in Biloxi, and Casino Magic in Bay St. Louis. During this period the company also tackled its largest project, the $260 million contract to build the Grand Casino and Hotel in Tunica, the largest dockside casino in the world. But even as casino building was just beginning to explode, the Andersons knew that the contracts would not last forever. They began taking steps, as early as 1993, to diversify and not place too much emphasis on the hospitality industry. In 1993 RAC opened regional offices in Jackson, Mississippi, and in Memphis, primarily to accommodate the new casino business but also with the idea of scouting for noncasino work after the boom ended. The company was also wise to recognize that the casinos would bring other construction work. Roy Anderson III told the *Mississippi Journal* in a 1997 article, "Gaming is the magnet that brings the people—which results in the ancillary construction. Even in areas that do not have gaming, you're seeing tax revenues go back into the communities through more state building projects."

After casino work petered out in the mid-1990s, RAC shifted its focus to other industries. In 1995 it built the Marshall County Correctional Facility, Mississippi's first privately run prison, for Wackenhut Corrections Corp. Wackenhut was so pleased with the work that it awarded RAC a second contract to build a Virginia facility. Prison projects dominated the company's slate over the next couple of years as it completed eight more prison-related projects in Mississippi and Arkansas. During this period RAC also became involved in the hospital/health facility sector. It built the University Medical Center's perinatal center in Jackson as well as a major project at Rush Medical Center in Meridian, Mississippi.

When prison work dried up in the late 1990s, RAC focused on hotel work through its offices in Jackson and Memphis, as well as an office the company also opened in Dallas. At the end of the decade RAC became involved in the building of sports and entertainment facilities. In 1999 it won the $49 million contract for a 14,000-seat multipurpose arena in Bossier City, Louisiana, suitable for sporting events, concerts, conventions, and other programs. The project was another example of ancillary construction, resulting from the increase of convention business in the Bossier City and Shreveport markets due to casino gambling in the area. But much of RAC's sports business during this period was related to the popularity of college football in the South, as members of the Southeastern Conference (SEC) found themselves funding stadium expansions in order to remain competitive. Major schools including the University of Alabama, Auburn University, and the University of Tennessee led the way, and smaller SEC members such as the University of Mississippi and Mississippi State University felt compelled to follow suit. In 2000 RAC won the $19.7 million expansion of DavisWade Stadium on the Campus of Mississippi State and the $24 million expansion of Caught-Hemingway Stadium on the Mississippi campus in Oxford. The company was not actually looking for stadium work, but because it possessed a great deal of expertise with concrete work, RAC proved to be an ideal candidate for the projects.

As the economy stalled in the early 2000s, RAC's diverse capabilities allowed the company to be opportunistic. While

Key Dates:

1955: The company is founded by Roy Anderson, Jr.
1958: A bank branch is the first major contract.
1969: A Mississippi Power Company power plant contract is won.
1982: Roy Anderson III joins the company.
1992: The firm wins its first casino contract.
1993: Roy Anderson III is named president and CEO.
2003: Harrell Construction Group, LLC is acquired.

large hospitality projects were on the wane, RAC was able to offset that loss of business by taking on healthcare projects such as the $9 million Biloxi Regional Hospital and parking garage, the $24 million ambulatory care facility in Sherman, Texas, and the $12 million medical office building parking garage for Gulfport's Memorial Hospital. RAC also won a pair of judicial projects: the $44 million U.S. Courthouse in Gulfport and the $18 million Justice Court facility in Jackson. A stalwart of the 1980s, military projects became another important source of new work. RAC received contracts to construct a Special Operations Forces facility for the U.S. Navy and a Lockheed Martin Metrology Center, both located in the Stennis Space Center. In September 2002, RAC was awarded the $22.4 million contract for several projects on the Keesler Air Force Base.

Acquiring Harrell Construction in 2003

RAC looked to diversify further in 2003 by way of acquisition, purchasing Jackson-based Harrell Construction Group, LLC (HCG). With sales of $75 million in 2002, HCG employed about 200 people, compared with RAC's $210 million in sales and 500 employees. In addition to its Jackson headquarters HCG maintained a division office in Birmingham, Alabama. Although HCG was formed in 1997, it was the result of a management buyout of a 120-year-old construction firm, giving HCG deep roots in the region: About 60 percent of its work came from repeat customers. Although HCG mostly operated in Mississippi and Alabama, it was capable of handling projects throughout the Southeast. HCG was especially strong in hospitality and retail and brought to RAC a number of experienced construction professionals.

With the incorporation of HCG's operation, RAC continued to win a wide variety of building contracts. In 2003, for example, it was awarded the $5.9 million repair contract at the Pensacola Naval Air Station. In 2005 it returned to the casino market in a major way, teaming up with a partner of Donald Trump to make the winning bid to build the $500 million, 240-acre President Casino Broadwater Resort on the Biloxi Peninsula, with the project to include the first all-suite 638-room hotel on the Mississippi Gulf Coast, and The Villas at Bacaran Bay, featuring 387 one- and two-bedroom luxury condominiums. A wide variety of construction projects also would open up in the reconstruction efforts after Hurricanes Katrina and Rita struck the Gulf Coast in August and September, respectively, of 2005.

Principal Subsidiaries

Harrell Construction Group, LLC.

Principal Competitors

Hunt Construction Group, Inc.; Perini Corporation; Skanska USA Building Inc.

Further Reading

"Casino Work Puts Roy Anderson in Top 400 Contractor's List," *Coast Business,* June 20, 1994, p. 9.
Gillette, Becky, "RAC Grows from One Pickup Truck, One Employee," *Mississippi Business Journal,* August 19, 2002, p. 35.
——, "Roy Anderson, Harrell in Talks to Unite Construction Companies," *Mississippi Business Journal,* February 17, 2003, p. 3.
Hancock, Tammy C., "Million Dollar Anderson Firm Started with a Few, Small Houses," *Coast Business,* October 25, 1993, p. 4.
Jeter, Lynne Wilbanks, "Roy Anderson Corp. Star Player in Sports Facilities Construction," *Mississippi Business Journal,* August 21, 2000, p. 12.
Monti, Lisa, "Gulfport, Miss., Construction-Firm President Latches on to Casino Boom," *Sun Herald,* September 16, 1999.
Simmons, Andi, "Construction with a Conscience," *Mississippi Business Journal,* March 31, 1997, p. 21.
——, "Roy Anderson Corp. Building a Strong, Confident Future," *Mississippi Business Journal,* May 26, 1997, p. 14.

—Ed Dinger

SP ALPARGATAS

Sao Paulo Alpargatas S.A.

Rua Urussui 300
Sao Paulo, Sao Paulo 04542-903
Brazil
Telephone: (55) (11) 4147-8300
Fax: (55) (11) 4147-8370
Web site: http://www.alpargatas.com.br

Public Company
Incorporated: 1907 as Sao Paulo Alpargatas Company S.A.
Employees: 9,966
Sales: BRL 1.23 billion ($419.74 million) (2004)
Stock Exchanges: Sao Paulo; OTC
Ticker Symbols: ALPA3, ALPA4; SAALY, SAANY
NAIC: 314912 Canvas and Related Products Mills;
    314999 All Other Textile Products Mills; 316211
    Rubber and Plastics Footwear Manufacturing; 339920
    Sporting and Athletic Goods Manufacturing

Sao Paulo Alpargatas S.A., one of the largest apparel and textile firms in Brazil, is best known for its Havaiana thong sandal. This humble flip-flop, after long serving as simple light footwear in tropical Brazil, has improbably morphed into international high fashion. But the company also turns out other kinds of footwear; sports clothing and other sporting goods; and a range of industrial textiles. It also operates a chain of retail clothing stores and is active in property development.

Footwear, Jeans, and Much More: 1907–79

The origin of Sao Paulo Alpargatas goes back to 1884, when S.A. Fábrica Argentina de Alpargatas was established in Buenos Aires by Juan Etchegaray, a Basque who had made a shoe with a canvas top and a sole of jute rope or twine, and Robert Fraser, a Scot whose family firm, Douglas Fraser & Sons, made textile machinery. They teamed to produce a version of the footwear known as an alpargata. This traditional Spanish light sandal, worn by peasants and laborers, had a sole of tough fiber (usually hemp) woven to an upper of canvas cloth and was fastened about the ankle with cloth strings. Additional capital for the Argentine alpargata came from a Manchester firm, Ashworth & Co., which was manufacturing cotton textiles.

Fraser and other British and Argentine investors brought this footwear to Brazil in 1907, when they founded Sao Paulo Alpargatas. The Argentine company took a stake of nearly 9 percent in return for its privileges and patents. Production began the next year, and the factory also turned out oilcloth and canvas tarpaulins. These goods were prized on coffee plantations, because laborers clad in the light footwear did not damage the beans on the ground, and the tarpaulins were used in the drying yards (and later for awnings). The company began selling shares on the Sao Paulo stock exchange in 1913.

The Wall Street stock market crash of 1929 and the resulting collapse of coffee prices in the worldwide economic crisis that followed forced the company to stop making alpargatas. It diversified its output with other types of footwear, such as other sandals, leather shoes, and tennis shoes. During the 1940s the company began making alpargatas again and expanded its production of textiles to enter the clothing industry. This output included denim for its first line of jeans, marketed under the Rodeio label. In 1946 Robert M. Fraser, grandson of the founder, sent Keith Bush to Sao Paulo for 15 days as an emissary from the Argentine firm. He stayed for 42 years, becoming president of the company in 1954. The enterprise was a pioneer in publicizing its products on the radio during this era.

SP Alpargatas introduced the Havaiana (Hawaiian) flip-flop in 1962. This rubber-soled sandal, with a V-shaped strap separating the big toe from the others, quickly became ubiquitous in Brazil, thanks to its simplicity, suitability for a tropical climate, and low price. The company, in 1965, introduced its Topeka brand of trousers. Two years later it introduced Madrigal bedspreads. In 1972 it launched a brand of trendy faded jeans called US Top. SP Alpargatas was the dominant Brazilian jeans producer in the 1970s. It added Topper-brand sporting articles in 1976 and purchased a competing company, Raihna Calçados e Materiais Esportivos Ltda., in 1979. SP Alpargatas was Brazil's biggest textile and shoe manufacturer, with $385 million in net sales, in 1980, and factories turning out footwear, jeans, jackets, shirts, bedspreads, denims, canvas, tarpaulins, and sporting goods.

Company Perspectives:

What we want to be: Be a world class company with desired brands of sport products, shoes, and industrial textiles.

Good Times, Then Tough Times: 1980–97

Parent Alpargatas S.A. parted company with SP Alpargatas in 1982, selling its shares. Thousands of individual shareholders now controlled more than 90 percent of the Brazilian enterprise's capital. It was the tenth largest Brazilian-owned private group, with 21 factories in six states and 28,000 employees. That year the company bought Jeaneration, a six-year-old brand of jeans and shirts, and opened a retail chain by that name. In 1983 SP Alpargatas introduced Top Plus, a more expensive jeans line, and Samba, another footwear brand. The company, in 1987, began manufacturing Arrow shirts under license. Because of its superior variation of sleeve lengths and collar sizes, Arrow enjoyed a 10 percent share of the dress-shirt market. Alpargatas also held the Brazil license for Nike footwear from 1987 to 1994.

With revenue of 31.2 billion cruzados ($433 million) and 30,000 employees, SP Alpargatas was still Brazil's biggest textile conglomerate in 1987. The following year Diego Jorge Bush succeeded his father as the company's president. Forty-six percent of the common shares were still owned by 8,000 individual stockholders, but two big blocks of shares were held by the Brasmotor (22.1 percent), and Camargo Corrêa (19.5 percent) industrial groups. The two, each well represented on the board of directors, eyed each other uneasily but agreed not to raise their respective stakes in the company and seek control.

SP Alpargatas was still the leading manufacturer of textiles and ready-made clothing in 1991, but this sector had experienced a 10 percent drop in revenue because of the recession that had gripped Brazil for two years. Indeed, in 1991 the company suffered its first loss in 55 years. Under the impact of the looming economic crisis, Alpargatas, in 1989, had changed its business philosophy, which had always been to turn out more goods, at lower prices, of the products in which it specialized. Some eight factories were closed in 1990 and 1991, and 14,000 employees dismissed. Much of the work needed was outsourced to plants in Argentina, Bolivia, Peru, and Uruguay. Clothing, the second largest division next to footwear, was the area most affected. Two of the company's six clothing factories were sold, and the number of items manufactured was reduced by more than half. However, some new lines were added. In 1991, for example, Alpargatas began manufacturing Polo/Ralph Lauren shirts under license, and the following year it began doing the same for Van Heusen. This was in keeping with the firm's new philosophy: to seek products with major brand recognition. It intended to become more a service than a manufacturing company, concentrating on marketing and on supervising the logistics of distribution.

In spite of these measures, SP Alpargatas suffered catastrophic results in 1992, losing $84 million on flat revenues that were, in dollar terms, less than half the total in 1986. Its share of the Brazilian jeans market was now only 6 percent, while its share of the footwear market had dropped from 70 percent in 1988 to 30 percent. The company's change in policy had not been bearing fruit. By abandoning corner stores for shopping centers and other higher-end venues, Alpargatas had been yielding space to its competitors. Moreover, the hard-pressed public had shown reluctance to pay higher prices for clothing such as the US Top line, which was now twice as expensive as similar jeans. In response, Alpargatas cut costs further by outsourcing even internal areas such as corporate engineering, insurance, and a supermarket chain mounted for its employees. It thereby lowered its fixed costs and its debt by almost half and was able to make money from 1993 to 1995. Another important decision was the joint venture initiated in 1994 to produce indigo denim fabric and twill with a rival textile firm, Santista Têxtil S.A. This seven-factory unit became the largest manufacturer of these products in Brazil and the third largest in the world. In 1995 SP Alpargatas acquired the license to manufacture and sell Timberland Co. sportswear, and the following year, a similar license for the products of Mizuno Corp., a leader in sandals, tarpaulin, and sports shoes.

Camargo Corrêa had raised its stake in SP Alpargatas to about one-third by 1993. In January 1997, after Alpargatas had again lost money, Camargo Corrêa joined with Banco Bradesco S.A., Brazil's biggest privately owned bank, which now held Brasmotor's former share, to oust Bush as chief executive. He was succeeded by Fernando Tigre de Barros Rodrigues.

By this time SP Alpargatas had made a giant step toward recovery in upgrading its familiar Havaiana sandal in 1994. A publicity campaign featuring young, attractive models introduced Havaianas Top, which cost twice as much as the basic-sandal price (BRL 3, or about $1) and sold in 13 colors. Sales of the flip-flop rose from 70 million in 1993 to 105 million in 1999. A Brazilian advertising agency, Almap, launched a highly successful television campaign that always featured a Brazilian celebrity in a comic situation involving a new pair of Havaianas. By the end of the century Alpargatas had also introduced two lines that were twice as expensive as Havaianas Top: Fashion, a thick-soled model for women and girls, and Surf, a line for boys that had a wider sole and different colors.

When Tigre arrived at SP Alpargatas, he later told Eduardo Ferraz for the Brazilian business magazine *Exame,* ''I saw the organization was hierarchical and stagnant, and I doubted that it was possible to change things. After two weeks I told my wife that my career was over.'' Unlike Bush, who had preferred to delegate authority to the company's three virtually autonomous divisions, Tigre involved himself in almost very phase of the organization: the product lines, the positioning of the brands, export strategy, the politics of human resources. The Polo/Ralph Lauren, Arrow, and Fido Dido licensed operations were dropped, and the Jeaneration stores were sold, as were the firm's operations in Argentina. Many executives were fired or demoted, and thousands more workers were dismissed. Six of the 12 floors at headquarters were rented out. Company business was reorganized into five divisions: sports shoes, Havaianas, canvas and other textile coverings, retail strategy, and Timberland shoes.

The Flip-Flop Fueling Profits: 1998–2005

SP Alpargatas returned to profitability in 1998 and stayed in the black. It continued to turn out Rainha, Topper, and Mizuno sports footwear, articles, and clothing, Timberland footwear, and industrial textiles, including almost all Brazil's seat coverings for trucks. Meggashop was now the name of its retail store business. But it was the Havaiana that was attracting the

Key Dates:

1907: Sao Paulo Alpargatas is founded by British and Argentine investors.

1962: SP Alpargatas introduces the Havaiana flip-flop, which quickly becomes ubiquitous.

1972: Introduction of US Top helps make the company Brazil's dominant jeans producer.

1980: SP Alpargatas is Brazil's leading shoe and textile manufacturer.

1991: With the Brazilian economy in recession, SP Alpargatas suffers its first loss in 55 years.

1992: The company's share of the jeans market falls to only 6 percent.

1994: By upgrading the Havaiana sandal, SP Alpargatas takes a giant step toward recovery.

1995–96: The company wins licenses to manufacture and sell Timberland and Mizuno products.

1998: After several years of mixed results, SP Alpargatas returns to the black and stays there.

2003: The company take a sizable stake in Santista Têxtil S.A., a large denim manufacturer.

2004: Havaianas account for 43 percent of the company's sales volume.

world's attention. Some eight million pairs were exported between 2000 and 2002.

Abroad, however, the Havaiana was being marketed as a high-end item. In the United States it was restricted to such chains as Marshall Field's, Saks Fifth Avenue, Bergdorf Goodman, and Nordstrom, and the better-class West Coast surf stores, where fashionistas paid as much as $160 for a customized pair festooned with Swarovski crystals. Sandra Bullock was seen wearing Havaianas with an evening dress. Nicole Kidman, Julia Roberts, and Sting also sported the suddenly trendy flip-flop, and supermodel Naomi Campbell bought dozens for her friends whenever she visited Brazil. In Paris, designer Jean-Paul Gaultier paraded his models down the runway in Havaianas for his summer show, and by mid 2003 jewel-encrusted versions, bearing labels such as Chanel and Gucci, were being marketed in 45 countries, including Japan, where Swarovski-crystal pairs sold for the equivalent of $236. H. Stern, a longtime Brazilian jeweler, offered the sandals with 18-karat gold-feather straps; the price ranged from $2,100 for this "simple" sandal to $17,000 for a pair with both gold feathers and diamonds.

In January 2003 Camargo Corrêa raised its share of SP Alpargatas from 38.5 percent to 61.2 by purchasing Bradesco's stake in the enterprise. In June of that year Alpargatas and Camargo Corrêa bought the 55 percent of Santista Têxtil held by Bradesco and the Bunge group, becoming its sole owners. With five plants in Brazil, two in Argentina, and one in Chile, Santista Têxtil was one of the largest manufacturers of denim in the world. It ranked fourth in sales among Brazilian clothing and textile companies, while Alpargatas ranked third. Alpargatas held 30.67 percent of Santista's shares in 2004 and half of the voting capital.

SP Alpargatas sold 129.7 million pairs of Havaianas in 2004, 16 percent more than in 2003. This unit accounted for 43 percent of the company's sales volume. The sports footwear, articles, and clothing brands Rainha, Topper, and Mizuno were placed under common management in 2004. This business unit accounted for 35 percent of sales volume. The operation of the Meggashop stores and management of Timberland and its associated Sete Léguas, Conga, and Samba brands was now under the business development unit, which accounted for 12 percent of company sales. Alpargatas sold 20.2 million square meters of industrial textiles in 2004, accounting for 10 percent of sales volume. In addition, its principal wholly owned subsidiary, Amapoly Indústria e Comércio Ltda., was producing polyvinyl chloride and polyester laminates for use in the manufacture of a variety of fabrics.

Amapoly's products and Alpargatas's industrial textiles were being made in Manaus. Topper and Rainha sports shoes were being produced in Natal and Santa Rita. Havaiana and Samba sandals were being made in Campina Grande. Soccer balls and Topper, Rainha, Mizuno, and Timberland shoes were being manufactured in Veranópolis. Vulcanized and injection-molded shoes were being produced in Mogi Mirim. Pouso Alegre was the site of tennis and shoe development.

Counting its share of Santista, SP Alpargatas had gross sales of BRL 1.23 billion ($419.74 million, based on the average currency-exchange rate) in 2004 and net income of BRL 93.82 million, or $32.02 million (although Santista lost a small amount). The company's own sales came to BRL 1.08 billion ($368.6 million) and its net income to BRL 95.55 ($32.61 million). Export revenue accounted for 6 percent of the total. The gross debt was BRL 64 million ($21.84 million) at the end of the year.

Principal Subsidiaries

Amapoly Indústria y Comércio Ltda.

Principal Operating Units

Business Development; Industrial Textiles; Sandals; Sports Articles.

Principal Competitors

Cia. de Tecidos Norte de Minas—Coteminas; Grendene S.A.; Vicunha Têxtil S.A.

Further Reading

"Amarrota, desbota e perde ó vinco," *Exame,* January 8, 1992, pp. 40–41.

Balbi, Sandra, "Uma aliança para nao perder o vinco," *Exame,* February 16, 1994, pp. 48–50.

Correa, Cristiane, "Pé lá fora," *Exame,* July 9, 2003, pp. 78–81.

Ferraz, Eduardo, "Operaçao resgate," *Exame,* November 28, 2001, pp. 66–68.

Galanternick, Mary, "Flip-Flop Fly," *Latin Trade,* July 2003, p. 32.

Gutiérrez, Leandro, and Juan Carlos Korel, "La Fábrica Argentina de Alpargatas," in *Siglo XIX,* January/June 1990, pp. 75–104.

"Sai Bush, Entra Bush," *Exame,* May 18, 1988, pp. 75–76.

Smith, Tony, "Sandal From Brazil Is New Fashion Flavor," *The New York Times,* March 25, 2003, pp. W1, W7.

—Robert Halasz

SOURCE
INTERLINK
COMPANIES

Source Interlink Companies, Inc.

27500 Riverview Center Boulevard, Suite 400
Bonita Springs, Florida 34134
U.S.A.
Telephone: (239) 949-4450
Fax: (239) 949-7623
Web site: http://www.sourceinterlink.com

Public Company
Incorporated: 1995 as Source Information Management
    Company
Employees: 2,473
Sales: $1.7 billion (2005 est.)
Stock Exchanges: NASDAQ
Ticker Symbol: SORC
NAIC: 423990 Other Miscellaneous Durable Goods
    Merchant Wholesalers; 424920 Book, Periodical, and
    Newspaper Merchant Wholesalers; 519190 All Other
    Information Services; 541614 Process, Physical
    Distribution, and Logistics Consulting Services;
    541910 Marketing Research and Public Opinion
    Polling; 561499 All Other Business Support Services

Source Interlink Companies, Inc. distributes magazines, CDs, DVDs, and assorted other merchandise to retailers including Kmart, Borders, Kroger, and Walgreens; processes magazine rebate claims and manages sales data for retailers and publishers; designs and makes display units for stores; and provides related services. Two of the firm's largest clients are Barnes & Noble and Borders, each of which accounts for more than a quarter of revenues. Founder S. Leslie Flegel serves as chairman and CEO of the publicly traded firm, which has grown rapidly through acquisitions.

Early Years

The beginnings of Source Interlink date to 1995, when two Missouri-based companies that provided magazine rebate services to retailers merged to form a single entity. Display Information Systems Co. was owned and run by S. Leslie Flegel, and

Periodical Marketing and Management, Inc. was operated by William H. Lee. Flegel would take the titles of CEO and board chairman of the new firm, with Lee serving as its chief administrative officer. The St. Louis-based company soon became publicly traded after a reverse merger with a dormant Montana outfit called Garner Investments, taking the name Source Information Management Co.

Source's income came from relieving store owners of the often-complicated process of obtaining magazine sales rebates from publishers. Beginning in the 1950s, publishers had tried to gain better visibility for their offerings by giving retailers financial incentives, which were paid as a percentage of actual sales. The vast number of different publishers and rebate offers involved made for a large amount of paperwork, and many retailers did not collect what was due them. By the 1970s companies such as those owned by Flegel and Lee had sprung up around the country to take over the work of tallying sales and collecting checks, receiving a percentage of the proceeds for their efforts. As this brought retailers more rebate money, they began paying closer attention to magazines, which served to boost sales and bring more revenues for all concerned. More attention also was given to other products sold in checkout lanes (dubbed the "front end" of a store in the industry), which were typically items purchased on impulse such as candy, film, and batteries.

Source gave retailers two options for payment, one being to wait for checks to be issued directly by publishers, and the Advance Payment Program, in which the firm advanced retailers the money for a slightly larger commission. The company soon began acquiring competitors, including Dixon's Modern Marketing Concepts and Tri-State Stores of Chicago Heights, Illinois, in 1995, and in 1996 Magazine Marketing and Readers Choice of Ohio. In October of that year the firm also launched the Periodical Information Network (PIN), which sold sales information to magazine publishers.

The company initially had sold items including greeting cards and caps to retailers, but now de-emphasized this to concentrate exclusively on rebate processing. By early 1997 the firm was handling the processing and collection of incentive payments for approximately 6,000 magazine titles at more than

<table>
<tr><td>

Company Perspectives:

No other company that we know of has seen or tried to capitalize on the opportunity to build a new model for selling the family entertainment category at mass market retail, until now. No other company can build and install attractive fixtures and procure promotional advertising to draw attention to them, get product to almost any zip code in a timely way and replenish it quickly, provide field level service at the point of purchase to optimize product placement and sales, manage rebate and fulfillment operations on a fully outsourced basis, and then support all of that with information services that tell retailers—and content producers— what is selling and why. In the past year-plus, we have built the structure, developed the critical mass, and obtained the financial wherewithal to in effect reinvent the magazine distribution industry, and then expand it to a new category of family entertainment merchandising and marketing. As we sit here today, we believe the actions we have taken to address this opportunity signal "game over" to the old fashioned way of doing business.

</td></tr>
</table>

700 retail chains with close to 70,000 stores. In its second year of operation, Source recorded annual revenues of $7.3 million and a loss of $603,000.

Acquisitions continued in May 1997 with the purchase of Mike Kessler and Associates of New Jersey, and in July the company broadened its reach by taking over management of the front-end display area for retail giant Kmart. The firm subsequently formed a consulting unit called the Display Group, which assisted retailers in placing magazine display racks and selecting titles for local markets. By the end of 1997 this division was contributing 13 percent of revenues. The firm's customers now included a host of major names including Wal-Mart, Target, Food Lion, W.H. Smith, and Southland 7-Eleven.

In June 1998 the company's stock moved from the NASDAQ SmallCap Market to the National Market exchange. Shortly afterward an additional two million shares of stock were sold, a quarter of which came from existing shareholders. Funds would be used for various purposes, including acquisitions and expanding the Advance Pay Program, which required a sizable pool of money to pay retailers up front before checks from publishers arrived. Also during the summer, the company acquired Periodical Concepts, a Texas-based magazine rebate firm.

In November Source entered yet another new business area with the purchase of Chestnut Display Systems of Florida and MYCO, Inc. of Rockford, Illinois, for a total of $21 million in cash and stock. Both firms made display fixtures for stores. A short time later fixture makers Yeager Industries of Philadelphia and Brand Manufacturing Corp. of New York were purchased, along with Brand affiliates Vail Salvage Co. and T.C.E. Corp., a fixture scrap company and trucking firm, respectively. The deals brought Source a number of new clients, including Ahold USA, Kroger, and Winn Dixie. Revenues for the fiscal year, which ended January 31, 1999, were $21.1 million, and net income reached $3.9 million.

Launching ICN in 1999

In early 1999 Source introduced a new web-based subscription service called Interactive Communication Network (ICN), which offered magazine publishers data about chains' magazine rack sales and their purchasing policies. Retailers were allowed free information about publishers' latest incentive programs and could respond to them online. Early subscribers included Time Distribution Services, Ziff Davis, and Wenner Publications, with retail users including Kmart, Rite-Aid, and Walgreens. Source later expanded the service to cover other checkout lane staples and signed on candy maker Nestlé, battery manufacturer Rayovac, and others. The system helped simplify the process of updating magazine pricing information for retailers, who might receive more than 100 price changes per week via fax, phone, or sales representative visit.

Source was now expanding its presence north of the border by purchasing Canadian magazine rebate firm Promark and fixture maker Aaron Wire and Metal Products, Ltd. for a combined total of $3 million. The company now employed nearly 500, and had approximately 80 percent of the magazine rebate business in the United States. It was serving 1,000 retail chains with 100,000 stores, and handling 7,000 titles.

Acquisitions continued in the fall of 1999 with the purchase of Huck Store Fixture Co. and Arrowood, Inc., both makers of wooden store display fixtures. Huck, the larger of the two, had revenues of $18.8 million and clients that included Kmart and Borders. By year's end display manufacturing accounted for more than three-fourths of the firm's revenues.

The year 2000 saw the company busy signing on new users for its ICN service, such as Hachette Filipacchi, while it expanded ICN's data sourcing to include figures from Efficient Market Services and, later, Barnes & Noble. The company's fixtures unit also was working on major orders from Kmart, Home Depot, and Wal-Mart, for which it would build front-end displays for the North American stores. During the year *Fortune* magazine named Source the fifth fastest-growing company in the United States.

Purchase of Interlink in 2001

In the spring of 2001 the company entered the business of magazine distribution with the acquisition of The Interlink Companies, Inc., which operated through subsidiaries International Periodical Distributors, Inc. (IPD), and Deyco. IPD was a leading distributor to bookstore chains and independent retailers, offering 6,000 titles to more than 5,000 stores, including Borders, B. Dalton, Waldenbooks, and Barnes & Noble. Deyco contracted with printers to drop-ship magazines directly to wholesalers. Total annual revenues for the pair were $217 million, and the acquisition nearly quadrupled Source in size. The merger would increase the efficiency of IPD and Deyco (which had both been losing money) by using point-of-sale information from ICN to reduce the number of unsold magazines returned to publishers, which was sometimes half of the total printed.

The year 2001 also saw Source execute a $25.3 million sale/leaseback transaction with Bentley Forbes Group for five manufacturing and office properties, the proceeds of which would be used to reduce debt. The company's ICN unit signed a five-year agreement with A.C. Nielsen to use that firm's retail sales scan data during the year, as well. On a tragic note, company co-founder William Lee died in February at the age of 50.

For the fiscal year ending in January 2002 the firm had sales of $238 million, up dramatically from $91.7 million the year before, but also recorded a loss of $73.4 million. The flood of red ink was attributed to a reduction in the goodwill valuation of the Huck and Interlink companies to zero ($78.1 million below previous years' figures), which had been done in accordance with new accounting rules. Magazine distribution accounted for 66 percent of revenues, with in-store services making up 27 percent and manufacturing falling to 7.5 percent.

The year 2002 saw the firm boost its presence in the magazine import/export business by signing agreements to handle titles from Seymour International, Future Publishing, and Hudson Group, which helped make Source the largest importer of magazines to the United States, as well as a major exporter via Hudson. The year also saw the acquisition of Innovative Metal Fixtures, Inc. for $2.6 million, and the addition of Hearst Corp. and Condé Nast to the ICN subscriber list. A new service called Cover Analyzer was introduced as well. It allowed for comparisons of magazine sales issue by issue, and the forecasting of future sales based on cover subjects. In August, the company's name was officially changed to Source Interlink Companies, Inc.

Numbers for 2003 (ended in January of that year) showed great improvement, with revenues topping $290 million and profits back up to $7.1 million. The firm now employed 1,300. During the spring Source moved its headquarters from St. Louis, Missouri, to Bonita Springs, Florida, also relocating its claim submission and fixture billing center there from North Carolina. In March the company formed a new magazine export unit, which quickly signed a number of agreements giving it exclusive rights to distribute American magazines overseas. By year's end export of U.S. publications had grown to account for nearly 10 percent of the firm's revenues, while close to 18 percent of the publications it distributed in the United States came from foreign publishers.

Early 2004 saw Source raise $41.1 million via a new stock issue, which was used to help pay down all of its long-term debt.

The company also secured a new line of credit worth $45 million during the year; signed agreements to distribute Marvel comics, *Reader's Digest,* and *Scientific American* magazines; and added candy and other front-end merchandise.

In 2004 the company broadened its magazine distribution to include convenience stores, mass merchandisers, and airport terminal stores, with the initiative soon expanded to more than 1,000 locations. Unlike many of its competitors, Source typically used overnight shipping from Federal Express to distribute goods, giving it a faster and more flexible response time than truck deliveries.

In August 2004 the firm purchased the business operations of PROMAG Retail Services LLC for $13.2 million. PROMAG was a magazine rebate-processing firm that served 14 states in the western United States. A New York-based magazine wholesaler called Empire State News Corp. was acquired in September for $5 million, and in November Source sold Deyco, its secondary wholesale magazine business. The firm also became the exclusive distributor of magazines for PRIMEDIA, Inc. to bookstores during 2004.

Merger with Alliance Entertainment Corp. in 2005

In February 2005 the company merged with Coral Springs, Florida-based Alliance Entertainment Corp. (AEC) in a deal worth $317 million. AEC, with annual revenues of $931 million, distributed CDs, DVDs, and video games to such national chains as Barnes & Noble, Borders, Kmart, Toys 'R' Us, Sears, Circuit City, Best Buy, Blockbuster, and Tower Records, as well as providing mail-order fulfillment to barnesandnoble.com, bestbuy.com, amazon.com, and others. After the merger Source was reorganized into two units, Supply Chain Management and In-Store Services. The company soon began to distribute DVDs, CDs, and other entertainment products to existing magazine markets such as grocery stores.

Shortly after completing the AEC deal, the firm arranged to buy Chas. Levy Circulating Co. for approximately $30 million. Illinois-based Levy was a leading U.S. magazine wholesaler, and the purchase would double the number of stores the firm serviced to approximately 20,000. A ten-year agreement was also signed with parent Levy Home Entertainment to distribute books. Chas. Levy had annual revenues of close to $370 million, and when added to those of Alliance, Source projected sales of more than $1.7 billion for 2005.

In the wake of these major acquisitions, the firm set about consolidating distribution sites and other operations, while reincorporating in Delaware to take advantage of that state's business-friendly laws. In April Source was tapped to distribute CDs to 400 Kmart stores, and in the summer the firm signed an agreement with Walgreens to place DVDs and music CDs in half of that company's 5,000 stores.

In scarcely more than a decade, Source Interlink Companies, Inc. had grown from a small regional magazine rebate firm into a multifaceted powerhouse with more than $1.7 billion in revenues. The firm was working on integrating the recently added Alliance Entertainment DVD/CD and Chas. Levy magazine distribution businesses, while continuing to serve clients in its established information services, display construction, and magazine import/export areas.

Principal Subsidiaries

Alligator Acquisition, LLC; Source Home Entertainment, Inc.; The Interlink Companies, Inc.; Source-U.S. Marketing Services, Inc.; Source-Chestnut Display Systems, Inc.; Source-Yeager Industries, Inc.; Source-Huck Store Fixtures Company; Source-MYCO, Inc.; Source Interlink International, Inc.; Primary Source, Inc.; T.C.E. Corporation; Vail Companies, Inc.; The Source-Canada Corporation; International Periodical Distributors, Inc.; David E. Young, Inc.; Brand Manufacturing Corporation; Source Interlink Canada, Inc. (Canada); Huck Store Fixture Company of North Carolina, Inc.; AEC One Stop Group, Inc.; Distribution & Fulfillment Services Group, Inc.; A.E. Land Corporation; AEC Direct, Inc.; AEC Supermarket Services Group, LLC; Chas. Levy Circulating Co.

Principal Competitors

Anderson News Co.; Anderson Merchandisers, L.P.; Hudson News Co.; News Group; Ingram Book Group, Inc.; Ingram Entertainment, Inc.; Handleman Co.; Baker & Taylor, Inc.; A.C. Nielsen Co.; Information Resources; Audit Bureau of Circulations.

Further Reading

Christman, Ed, ''AEC, Source Interlink See Growth After Merger,'' *Billboard,* December 11, 2004, p. 45.

——, ''Alliance Pries 400 Kmart Stores from Handleman,'' *Billboard,* April 16, 2005.

——, ''Source Interlink Gains National Clout,'' *Billboard,* June 25, 2005.

Clifton, Alexandra Navarro, ''South Florida Merger Will Take Movie DVDs into Supermarkets,'' *South Florida Sun-Sentinel,* November 19, 2004.

Danner, Patrick, ''Coral Springs, Fla., Music, Video Distributor Gets New Partner,'' *Miami Herald,* November 20, 2004.

Elson, Joel, ''Magazines' Price-Update Technology Set for Test,'' *Supermarket News,* March 15, 1999, p. 41.

Guy, Sandra, ''Major Magazine Distributor Buys Chas. Levy,'' *Chicago Sun-Times,* April 6, 2005, p. 87.

Hanford, Desiree J., ''Source Info Expands Weekly Store Sales Collection,'' *Dow Jones Business News,* October 7, 1999.

Milliot, Jim, ''Source to Grow Book Biz,'' *Publishers Weekly,* April 11, 2005, p. 16.

Perrotta, Peter, ''Kroger Taps Source Interlink for Self-Check Displays,'' *Supermarket News,* July 2, 2001, p. 15.

''Source Interlink to Distribute DVDs at More Than 900 Grocery Stores,'' *DVD Insider,* April 11, 2005.

Stroud, Jerri, ''St. Louis Company Offers Online Systems to Manage Magazine Sales,'' *St. Louis Post-Dispatch,* February 20, 1999, p. 30.

—Frank Uhle

Sunterra Corporation

3865 West Cheyenne Avenue
North Las Vegas, Nevada 89032
U.S.A.
Telephone: (702) 804-8600
Fax: (702) 304-7066
Web site: http://www.sunterra.com

Public Company
Incorporated: 1996 as KGK Resorts, Inc.
Employees: 5,000
Sales: $288.7 million (2004)
Stock Exchanges: NASDAQ
Ticker Symbol: SNRR
NAIC: 531210 Offices of Real Estate Agents and Brokers

Sunterra Corporation is one of the largest vacation owner-ship companies in the world, supported by nearly 100 resorts in 13 countries. Sunterra's properties are located in North Amer-ica, Europe, and the Caribbean, where its more than 300,000 customers can use their vacation ownership interests to stay at selected resorts, typically for a one-week stay. The company offers financing services to its customers, referred to as "owner families," and also develops and manages resort properties.

Origins

Sunterra experienced the highs and lows of competing as a timeshare operator during its first decade of business, recording phenomenal growth before falling spectacularly from the heights it had attained. The company's roller-coaster ride began in 1992, when Osamu Kaneko, Andrew J. Gessow, and Steven C. Kenninger decided to delve into the acquisition and develop-ment of timeshare resorts. Kaneko, a native of Japan who was educated in the United States, had spent the previous 25 years developing and acquiring resorts, spending the years immedi-ately preceding the formation of Sunterra working with Kenninger, a business attorney. In 1985, the pair founded KOAR Group, Inc., a Los Angeles-based real estate acquisition and development company. The third member of the founding group, Gessow, brought his own entrepreneurial experience to

the team, having founded Argosy Group, Inc., a Woodside, California-based real estate and acquisition company, in 1990.

When Kaneko, Kenninger, and Gessow started out, a single corporate entity did not exist. Instead, a group of individual limited partnerships and limited liability companies (LLCs), each in charge of a particular resort and each affiliated with the founders, constituted Sunterra's predecessor organization. With each acquisition, a new limited partnership or LLC became part of the organization controlled by the founders, beginning with their first acquisition in November 1992, the purchase of the Cypress Pointe Resort in Lake Buena Vista, Florida. A single corporate entity did not exist until 1996, when KGK Resorts, Inc. was incorporated, a company that at the time of its creation controlled nine resort properties acquired by Kaneko, Kenninger, and Gessow. After the acquisition of the Cypress Pointe Resort, the founders purchased Plantation at Fall Creek, an 82-unit resort in Branson, Missouri. In 1994, two resorts were acquired, a 40-unit property in Hilton Head, South Carolina, called Royal Dunes Resort, and an Embassy Vacation Resort in Koloa, Kauai, Hawaii, with 219 units. In 1995, after acquiring another Florida property, the 72-unit Grand Beach in Orlando, the company acquired its first property in the Caribbean, the Royal Palm Beach Club on St. Maarten in The Netherlands Antilles, a 140-unit resort. A second resort on St. Maarten was acquired the same year, the 172-unit Flaming Beach Club. In 1996, the company added destinations in California, acquiring a property in South Lake Tahoe and the San Luis Bay Resort in Avila Beach.

The nine resorts in operation by the time KGK Resorts was incorporated marked a turning point in the history of Sunterra, the end of the first chapter in the company's story and the beginning of the most eventful period in its development. The same month the company acquired the Avila Beach property it changed its name to Signature Resorts, Inc., the corporate ban-ner under which it completed its initial public offering (IPO) of stock two months later. When Signature Resorts completed its IPO in August 1996, the acquisition program executed during the previous years had produced impressive financial growth, increasing revenue from $11 million in 1992 to $72 million in 1995. Following its IPO, however, the company began acquir-ing resorts more aggressively.

Company Perspectives:

Sunterra's goal is to become the global currency of relaxation. Our key strategies include: expand our channels of distribution in key markets around the world; to complement our current product offerings with an active development program, including strategic partnerships; to increase our brand name recognition; and to provide consistently high levels of quality and reliability so that our current and prospective owner families can look forward to their vacations with trust and pleasure.

Rapid Expansion in the Late 1990s

By the end of 1997, roughly one year after its IPO, Signature Resorts could claim to be the largest vacation ownership company in the world, having spent the previous year acquiring resort properties at a furious pace. In a little more than 12 months, the company increased its stable of resorts from nine to 81, giving its customers the opportunity to vacation in eight North American and European countries. The company's annual sales shot past $300 million, propelled by its torrid acquisition campaign. Its stock value reacted favorably to the expansion drive, reaching a high of $32.17 per share in October 1997. Wall Street, as evinced in the increasing value of Signature Resorts' shares, approved of the company's decision to expand at a rapid clip, but the applause from investors and analysts soon ended. After reaching $32.17 per share, the company's stock value plummeted, falling at one point to five cents per share. "In its quest for growth," an analyst reflected in a March 2, 2005 interview with *Investor's Business Daily,* "financial caution was sacrificed and the company gave loans to people who weren't qualified."

The collapse of Signature Resorts' stock value represented a telling barometer of profound problems, reflecting the financial community's reaction to a company spinning out of control. The severity of the company's problems was not revealed until early 2000, two years after Signature Resorts had changed its name to Sunterra Corporation. In the three years since the major portion of the company's acquisition campaign had ended, annual sales had grown to $500 million, a total derived from the 89 resorts under Sunterra's control at the dawn of the 21st century. Such size had come at a hefty price, however, a price that proved nearly fatal to the company that heralded itself as the largest company of its kind in the world. The scope of its problems—the effect of its acquisition campaign on its financial stability—first became apparent after an in-depth audit in early 2000 discovered that Sunterra would have to write off $43 million in delinquent accounts. From there, the company's situation worsened as the months passed. At the end of its fiscal quarter in March 2000, the company posted an alarming $15.6 million loss, a result that stood in stark contrast to the $10 million profit recorded during the first quarter of 1999. Steven Miller, who was appointed chief executive officer in 1998, was replaced, as the company's board of directors tried to contend with the problems presented to it. In May 2000, the company laid off 12 percent of its workforce, stopped work on several development products, including a partly completed, $22 mil-

lion headquarters complex in Orlando, and hoped to stave off financial ruin. Sunterra's difficulties proved greater than the measures implemented to correct them, however. The company's infrastructure—its customer service operations, central reservations functions, and its accounting department—had not been able to keep pace with the rapid expansion fueled by acquisitions, exacerbating its debt problems. At the end of May, after defaulting on scheduled loan payments, Sunterra admitted defeat and declared bankruptcy, awash in debt totaling $850 million. The company was delisted by the New York Stock Exchange in the summer, and ended the year with a staggering $376 million loss.

Reorganization After Collapse: Emerging from Bankruptcy in 2002

Once under court protection from its creditors, Sunterra focused on reconstituting itself for a return as a participant in the timeshare industry. After several leadership changes, the company found the chief executive officer to spearhead its revival, a former British Army officer, Nicholas J. Benson. Benson was promoted from within the Sunterra organization, having joined the company in 1997 as chief operating officer of its European operations. He was promoted to chief executive officer of the company's international business in January 2000, the post he occupied before the board of directors appointed him as chief executive officer of the entire company in November 2001. Under Benson's guidance, Sunterra reduced the number of properties it owned or managed from 89 to 75 as it worked on developing a reorganization plan to submit to the bankruptcy court. As the plan was being developed, the company announced that it was relocating its headquarters from Orlando to Las Vegas, part of a reorganization that divided the company's operations into two divisions: Sunterra Europe, based in England, and Sunterra USA, based in Las Vegas. After ending 2001 with another loss, $72 million, the company submitted its reorganization plan in January 2002, ready to make a fresh start and to exercise greater financial discipline in the future.

Under Benson's leadership, Sunterra staged an impressive comeback. The company returned to profitability in 2003, achieving financial stability that allowed it to begin rebuilding its portfolio of resorts. By the fall of 2004, Sunterra had regained its pre-Chapter 11 stature, owning or managing more than 90 resorts in 12 countries from which its more than 300,000 owner families could select as their vacation destination. The company's fiscal year ended in September 2004, a year in which sales declined 7 percent to $288 million, but most important, produced another encouraging profit result. For the year, Sunterra collected $21 million in net income, spurring Benson and his management team to continue with their acquisition program.

As Sunterra concluded its first decade as a publicly traded company, it appeared to have put its troubles behind it. On the acquisition front, the company continued to press forward, beginning the start of fiscal 2005 in October 2004 with the announcement of two purchases. The company acquired Jardines de Sol resort at Playa Blanca in Lanzarote, Spain, a property with 54 villas, and signed an affiliation agreement with Alvechurch Waterway Holidays, which operated eight traditional English canal boats moored at a marina in Cheshire on the Trent and Mersey canal. In July 2005, Sunterra announced that

Key Dates:

1992: The first Sunterra resort is acquired, the Cypress Pointe Resort in Lake Buena Vista, Florida.

1996: The company completes its initial public offering of stock, debuting on the New York Stock Exchange as Signature Resorts, Inc.

1998: After acquiring more than 70 properties during the previous year, Signature Resorts changes its name to Sunterra Corporation.

2000: Sunterra declares bankruptcy.

2001: Nicholas J. Benson is appointed chief executive officer.

2002: The company emerges from bankruptcy.

2005: The number of resorts owned or managed by Sunterra reaches 97.

it had entered an agreement to acquire the 69 percent it did not already own in the Embassy Vacation Resort Poipu Point on the Hawaiian island of Kauai, one of the first nine properties in which the company had invested before its IPO. Sunterra completed the deal in September 2005.

In the years ahead, Sunterra's success depended on the attractiveness of the resort properties it owned and managed and its ability to expand its operations in a financially responsible manner. The lessons learned from managerial mistakes made during the late 1990s served as valuable guidelines governing the company's acquisition efforts in the 21st century, making it stronger, more disciplined, and sensitive to the threat of expanding in a careless fashion. Toward this end, much of the responsibility for not falling victim to the same type of problems that beset the company in the late 1990s fell to Benson and Sunterra's chief financial officer, Steven E. West. West joined Sunterra as CFO in September 2002 after serving as the vice-president of finance for Coast Asset Management. In May 2005, he was promoted to the additional post of executive vice-president. As Sunterra plotted its future course, Benson and West were the two principal executives responsible for ensuring

that the company's second decade of existence did not end as the first one had, a challenge both executives appeared well equipped to meet.

Principal Subsidiaries

KGK Investors, Inc.; Lake Tahoe Resort Partners, LLC; Premier Vacations, Inc.; Resort Marketing International, Inc.; Sunterra Centralized Services Global, LLC; Sunterra Centralized Services USA, LLC; Sunterra Financial Services, Inc.; Vacation Time Share Travel, Inc. (Bahamas); Vacation Research Ltd. (U.K.); Sunterra Spanish Sales SL (Spain); Sunterra Sales Italy S.R.L.; Octopus GmbH (Austria); Mercadotechnia de Hospedaje S.A. de C.V.; Kenmore Club Ltd. (U.K.); GVC Deutschland Holding GmbH (Germany).

Principal Competitors

Hilton Grand Vacations Company, LLC; Marriott Vacation Club International; Trendwest Resorts, Inc.

Further Reading

Barker, Tim, "Orlando, Fla.-Based Sunterra Hopes to Shine Again in Time-Share Industry," *Orlando Sentinel,* March 12, 2001.

——, "Orlando, Fla.-Based Time-Share Company Files Bankruptcy," *Orlando Sentinel,* June 1, 2000.

Brennan, Terry, "Sunterra to Emerge from Ch. 11," *Daily Deal,* June 21, 2002.

Foster, Christine, "Short Memories," *Forbes,* September 22, 1997, p. 269.

Isaac, David, "Sunterra Corp. North Las Vegas, Nevada; Back from the Brink, but No Time to Relax," *Investor's Business Daily,* p. A7.

Pack, Todd, "Bankrupt Orlando, Fla., Time-Share Company Names New CEO," *Orlando Sentinel,* October 12, 2000.

——, "Time-Share Operator to Leave Orlando, Fla., for Las Vegas," *Orlando Sentinel,* March 9, 2002, p. B2.

"Signature Resorts Will Change Name," *Hotel & Motel Management,* July 20, 1998, p. 1.

"Sunterra Buys Resort Group," *Travel Weekly,* September 19, 2005, p. 51.

—Jeffrey L. Covell

SYSCO Corporation

1390 Enclave Parkway
Houston, Texas 77077-2099
U.S.A.
Telephone: (281) 584-1390
Fax: (281) 584-2721
Web site: http://www.sysco.com

Public Company
Incorporated: 1969
Employees: 47,800
Sales: $30.28 billion (2005)
Stock Exchanges: New York
Ticker Symbol: SYY
NAIC: 422410 General Line Grocery Wholesalers;
422420 Packaged Frozen Food Wholesalers; 422480
Fresh Fruit and Vegetable Wholesalers; 422490 Other
Grocery and Related Products Wholesalers

SYSCO Corporation (an acronym for Systems and Services Company) is the largest marketer and distributor of foodservice products in North America, holding a market share of approximately 14 percent. With more than 160 distribution facilities located throughout the contiguous United States and parts of Alaska, Hawaii, and Canada, SYSCO provides food and related products and services to approximately 390,000 restaurants, schools, hospitals, nursing homes, hotels, businesses, and other foodservice customers. Restaurant customers account for fully two-thirds of revenues. The company's line of products includes about 275,000 items, including fresh and frozen meats, seafood, poultry, fully prepared entrees, produce, canned and dry foods, desserts, imported specialties, paper and disposable items, china and silverware, restaurant and kitchen equipment and supplies, and cleaning supplies. Founded in 1969, SYSCO has grown steadily ever since, mainly through dozens of acquisitions of smaller distributors, with double-digit increases in sales and earnings nearly every year.

Founded Through Combination of Ten Distributors

John Baugh was the guiding force behind the founding of SYSCO. Baugh had grown up on a ranch near Waco, Texas, and got his start in the food business through a part-time job at a local A&P grocery store when he was in high school. He eventually founded Zero Foods Company of Houston, a Houston-based food distributor. In 1969 Baugh convinced the owners of eight other small food distributors to combine the nine companies, forming what he hoped to mold into a national foodservice distribution organization, one that would be able to distribute any food despite its regional availability. The other eight original companies were: Frost-Pack Distributing Company (Grand Rapids, Michigan); Global Frozen Foods, Inc. (New York); Houston's Food Service Company (Houston); Louisville Grocery Company (Louisville, Kentucky); Plantation Foods (Miami, Florida); Texas Wholesale Grocery Corporation (Dallas); Thomas Foods, Inc. and its Justrite Food Service, Inc. subsidiary (Cincinnati); and Wicker, Inc. (Dallas). The combined 1969 sales for the nine founding companies were $115 million.

SYSCO went public in 1970 and that year made its first acquisition, of Arrow Food Distributor. In its early years the company grew by acquiring a number of small foodservice distribution companies, carefully chosen for their geographic regions. These acquisitions helped to realize Baugh's early goal of providing uniform service to customers across the country. Throughout the 1970s SYSCO Corporation built many new warehouses to deal with this rapid expansion, later incorporating freezers into its warehouses and adding multi-temperature refrigerated trucks to transport produce and frozen foods.

During the 1970s SYSCO grew steadily except for a brief earnings drop in 1976 caused by a canned food glut and excessive start-up costs due to increasing capacity. One reason for such rapid recovery and regular growth was SYSCO's continuing diversification into new products, such as fish, meat, and fresh produce. In 1976 SYSCO acquired Mid-Central Fish and Frozen Foods Inc., expanding the company's distribution capabilities around the nation. In 1979 SYSCO's sales passed the $1 billion mark for the first time; by 1981 the company was rated as the largest U.S. foodservice distribution company. That year SYSCO set up Compton Foods in Kansas City to purchase meat, and began to supply supermarkets and other institutions with meat and frozen entrees.

Company Perspectives:

SYSCO's Mission—Helping Our Customers Succeed. It's the foundation of the decisions and actions taken by our employees on a daily basis.

Attention to detail, going the extra mile and simply being available for any need enhances the level of service each customer receives, and ultimately benefits customers in their daily endeavors to satisfy their patrons.

We are committed to our customers' success and to helping them achieve their goals. Maintaining outstanding service has become even more important as consumers embrace quality dining experiences as they enjoy meals away from home. Our responsibility is not taken lightly—our customers' success is vital to our success.

1980s: Rapid Growth Through Acquisitions

In 1983 John E. Woodhouse, whom Baugh had hired as chief financial officer in September 1969, became CEO of SYSCO, with Baugh remaining chairman. The following year SYSCO continued its strategy of acquiring its competitors when it purchased three operations of PYA Monarch, then a division of Sara Lee Corporation. One of SYSCO's largest acquisitions occurred in 1988, when the company paid $750 million for CFS Continental, at that time the third largest food distributor in the country, which added 4,500 employees and increased the number of markets SYSCO served to 148 out of the top 150 markets. Although much of the United States and especially Texas experienced hard financial times during the 1980s, as a national company in a relatively recession-proof industry, SYSCO Corporation was not adversely affected.

SYSCO also made several smaller acquisitions of foodservice distributors in the late 1980s, including Olewine's Inc. (Harrisburg, Pennsylvania), which was renamed Sysco Food Services of Central Pennsylvania, Inc.; Lipsey Fish Company, Inc. (Memphis, Tennessee); Hall One Chinese Imports, Inc. (Cleveland); and Fulton Prime Foods, Inc. (Albany, New York). By the end of the decade, sales had reached $6.85 billion, making SYSCO twice as large as its closest competitor in foodservice distribution and second only to McDonald's in the overall foodservice industry. Despite its size and growth (through some 43 acquisitions since its founding), SYSCO accounted for less than 8 percent of overall foodservice distributor volume, a testament to the continuingly fragmented nature of the foodservice distribution industry, and evidence that SYSCO had plenty of room for future growth.

1990s: More Acquisitions, SYGMA, and the "Fold-out" Strategy

During the early 1990s, SYSCO made several additional acquisitions, increasing the company's geographic spread still further. Among the more important purchases were the 1990 acquisition of the Oklahoma City-based foodservice distribution business of Scrivner, Inc., which became Sysco Food Service of Oklahoma, Inc.; the 1991 acquisition of four of Scrivner's northeastern U.S. distribution businesses, including

that of Jamestown, New York, which became Sysco Food Services-Jamestown; the 1992 acquisition of Philadelphia-based Perloff Brothers, Inc., which operated as Tartan Foods; and the 1993 acquisitions of the St. Louis Division of Clark Foodservice, Inc. (which became Sysco Food Service of St. Louis, Inc.) and of Ritter Food Corporation of Elizabeth, New Jersey (which was renamed Ritter Sysco Food Services, Inc.).

In 1991 SYSCO created a subsidiary called the SYGMA Network, Inc. to consolidate its chain restaurant distribution systems and improve its service to chain restaurants. By 1997 SYGMA consisted of 11 distribution centers serving customers in 37 states, and posted sales of $1.3 billion.

By 1995 Baugh had assumed the title of senior chairman (he retired in late 1997), Woodhouse was chairman, and Bill M. Lindig, who had joined the company in 1970, had become CEO. SYSCO revenues had grown to $12.12 billion, but the company still held less than 10 percent of the foodservice distribution market. That year, Lindig told the *Houston Business Journal:* ''We could grow at 20 percent a year for the next five years and we'd still have only 20 percent of the market.'' (From 1978 to 1997, the company's compound growth rate was 16.4 percent.)

Also by this time, the company's management structure had grown somewhat unwieldy. SYSCO's operating companies, which by 1995 numbered 58, had always been allowed to function in a largely autonomous manner. This decentralized structure, however, meant that 58 operating company presidents were reporting directly to the corporate staff. With SYSCO expecting to soon have about 75 operating companies, corporate management decided to add four senior vice-presidents of operations, each of whom would have full responsibility for about ten SYSCO operating companies. Nineteen companies would still report directly to corporate headquarters.

In the late 1990s SYSCO slowed its pace of acquisition, although acquisitions were still seen as important for growth in selected new markets, particularly such far-flung areas as Alaska and Canada. In mid-1996 the company purchased Strano Foodservice of Peterborough, Ontario, which gave SYSCO a presence in the Toronto market, while Alaska Fish and Farm, Inc. was bought in early 1997. Beginning in 1995, however, SYSCO added a ''fold-out'' expansion strategy as an additional method of growth. This strategy involved developing a sales base in markets distant from an existing operation, then building a new distribution center, staffing it with transferred staff, and thereby creating a stand-alone operating company serving a new market. In 1995 SYSCO opened its first distribution center in Connecticut through this program. Over the next four years, ''fold-out'' operating companies were added in Tampa and Riviera Beach, Florida; Wisconsin; North Carolina; Birmingham, Alabama; and San Diego.

SYSCO posted record sales of $14.45 billion in fiscal 1997, along with record net earnings of $302.5 million. Although the company's growth had slowed somewhat in the 1990s as fewer acquisitions were made, the ''fold-out'' expansion strategy was still keeping SYSCO growing much faster than the foodservice industry as a whole. These trends continued through decade's end as profits reached $362.3 million on revenues of $17.42 billion. New fold-outs were being created about every six

Key Dates:

1969: John Baugh, owner of Zero Foods Company of Houston, is the guiding force behind the creation of SYSCO Corporation from the combination of nine small food distributors.

1970: SYSCO goes public and makes its first acquisition, Arrow Food Distributor.

1979: Revenues surpass $1 billion.

1981: SYSCO becomes the largest U.S. foodservice distribution company.

1988: CFS Continental is acquired.

1991: SYSCO creates a subsidiary called the SYGMA Network, Inc. to consolidate its chain restaurant distribution systems.

1995: Company launches its ''fold-out'' expansion strategy as an additional method of growth.

2000: SYSCO acquires FreshPoint Holdings.

2002: Canadian operations are vastly enlarged through the purchase of Serca Foodservice.

2005: The first SYSCO regional redistribution centers open.

months, and several significant acquisitions were completed in 1999. As beef enjoyed a resurgence in popularity, SYSCO bought two leading purveyors of beef, Buckhead Beef Company, based in Atlanta, and Newport Meat Company, headquartered in Irvine, California. Also acquired that year was Doughtie's Foods, based in Portsmouth, Virginia, which was renamed SYSCO Food Services of Hampton Roads, Inc.

Early 2000s and Beyond

Lindig took on the additional role of chairman in 1999 but then retired the following year, when Charles Cotros became SYSCO's fourth CEO and chairman as well. Cotros, who had been the firm's president, had joined SYSCO in 1974. One of Cotros's first tasks was shepherding through one of the company's largest deals, the 2000 purchase of FreshPoint Holdings, one of the biggest distributors of wholesale produce in the United States. Based in Dallas, FreshPoint reaped annual sales of approximately $750 million selling to more than 20,000 customers, including restaurants, hotels, cruise ships, and wholesale grocers.

Early in 2001 SYSCO acquired a group of specialty meat supply operations in Texas, doing business under the names Freedman Food Service and Texas Meat Purveyors, that specialized in supplying fresh meat to upscale restaurants. The acquired businesses generated annual revenues in excess of $200 million. Next, SYSCO spent about $200 million to buy Guest Supply Inc., a New Jersey firm supplying guest-care and housekeeping items to hotels. Guest Supply's sales for fiscal 2000 totaled approximately $366 million. Significantly bolstering its presence north of the border, SYSCO bought Serca Foodservice from Sobey's, Inc. for about $280 million in early 2002. Based in Toronto, with annual sales of $1.4 billion, Serca provided 100,000 food products, as well as foodservice supplies and equipment, to 80,000 customers. SYSCO's Canadian distribution operation now covered the entire nation. In May 2002 the company opened its first niche fold-out: a Buckhead Beef branch that began providing fresh-cut meat to the New York metropolitan area. Broad-line fold-out operations were opened in Sacramento, California; Las Vegas; and Columbia, South Carolina, in 2002. In addition, SYSCO was working to expand the FreshPoint produce brand across North America. Late in the year SYSCO moved into the ethnic food market with the acquisition of St. Paul, Minnesota-based Asian Foods, Inc., the largest Asian food distributor in the United States, with annual revenues of more than $100 million.

At the beginning of 2003 Cotros retired and was succeeded as chairman and CEO by Richard J. Schnieders, who had moved up to president and COO since joining SYSCO in 1982. The company stayed the course under CEO number five, continuing its string of acquisitions, mainly seeking to fill in gaps in its geographic reach in the broad-line distribution sector in North America. In July 2004 SYSCO went further afield when it bought International Food Group Inc., of Plant City, Florida, distributor of supplies to quick-service chain restaurants in Central and South America, the Caribbean, Europe, Asia, and the Middle East. International Food reported 2003 revenues of $77.8 million. By late 2004 SYSCO had consummated 121 acquisitions over the course of its 35-year history.

To improve efficiency, SYSCO launched a national overhaul of its supply chain that included the construction of as many as nine regional redistribution centers over a ten-year period. These regional centers were designed to supply a number of SYSCO operating companies within a certain geographic area. The first, opened in February 2005 in Front Royal, Virginia, was slated to serve 14 broad-line SYSCO companies in the firm's northeast region (which encompassed Virginia, Maryland, Delaware, Pennsylvania, New Jersey, and western New York State). Schnieders called this ''the largest strategic project in SYSCO's history.'' In August 2005 SYSCO announced that it had selected Alachua, Florida, as the site for its second redistribution center, which would serve the Southeast with an anticipated opening in the fall of 2006.

By fiscal 2004 SYSCO's steadily rising revenues had reached $29.34 billion, a 12.2 percent increase over the previous year, while earnings rose 16.6 percent, to $907.2 million. Fourth-quarter profits, however, failed to meet Wall Street expectations in part because of a high rate of inflation on the food it bought from suppliers. To control expenses during the next fiscal year, SYSCO cut 1,500 jobs from its payroll late in 2004. SYSCO managed to achieve gains in both sales and earnings for the 29th straight year in fiscal 2005, but the gains were very small, 6 percent for earnings, which totaled $961.5 million, and just 3.2 percent for revenues, which nevertheless passed the $30 billion mark for the first time. SYSCO was likely to keep a close eye on expenses while continuing to emphasize customer service and relying on its strong management team, a team that had been strengthened over the years by a company policy of retaining the managers of acquired firms, to keep the firm moving forward. SYSCO was well-positioned to maintain its record of steady increases in its share of the foodservice distribution sector, which had reached 14 percent by 2005.

Principal Subsidiaries

Abbott SYSCO Food Services; A.M. Briggs Inc.; Baugh Northeast Co-op, Inc.; Buckhead Beef Company; Buckhead Beef Florida; Buckhead Beef Northeast; Freedman Meats, Inc.; Freshpoint, Inc.; Fulton Provision Company; Guest Supply, Inc.; Hallsmith Sysco Food Services; Hardin's Sysco Food Services, LLC; Lankford Sysco Food Services, LLC; Malcolm Meats; Nobel Sysco Food Services; Pegler Sysco Food Services Company; Robert Orr Sysco Food Services Company, LLC; Robert's Sysco Food Services, Inc.; SYGMA Network, Inc. - Columbus Central; SYSCO Asian Foods, Inc.; SYSCO Food Services of Alaska, Inc.; SYSCO Food Services of Albany; SYSCO Food Services of Arizona, Inc.; SYSCO Food Services of Arkansas, LLC; SYSCO Food Services of Atlanta, LLC; SYSCO Food Services of Austin, LP; SYSCO Food Services of Baltimore; SYSCO Food Services of Baraboo; SYSCO Food Services of Central Alabama, Inc.; SYSCO Food Services of Central California, Inc.; SYSCO Food Services of Central Florida, Inc.; SYSCO Food Services of Central Pennsylvania, LLC; SYSCO Food Services of Charlotte, LLC; SYSCO Food Services of Chicago, Inc.; SYSCO Food Services of Cincinnati; SYSCO Food Services of Cleveland, Inc.; SYSCO Food Services of Columbia; SYSCO Food Services of Connecticut; SYSCO Food Services of Dallas, LP; SYSCO Food Services of Detroit, LLC; SYSCO Food Services of Eastern Wisconsin; SYSCO Food Services of Grand Rapids, LLC; SYSCO Food Services of Gulf Coast, Inc.; SYSCO Food Services of Hampton Roads, Inc.; SYSCO Food Services of Houston, LP; SYSCO Food Services of Idaho, Inc.; SYSCO Food Services of Indianapolis, LLC; SYSCO Food Services of Iowa, Inc.; SYSCO Food Services of Jackson; SYSCO Food Services of Jacksonville, Inc.; SYSCO Food Services of Jamestown; SYSCO Food Services of Kansas City, Inc.; SYSCO Food Services of Las Vegas; SYSCO Food Services of Los Angeles, Inc.; SYSCO Food Services of Louisville; SYSCO Food Services of Metro New York; SYSCO Food Services of Minnesota, Inc.; SYSCO Food Services of Montana, Inc.; SYSCO Food Services of New Mexico; SYSCO Food Services of New Orleans, LLC; SYSCO Food Services of Northern New England, Inc.; SYSCO Food Services of Oklahoma, Inc.; SYSCO Food Services of Philadelphia, LLC; SYSCO Food Services of Pittsburgh, Inc.; SYSCO Food Services of Portland, Inc.; SYSCO Food Services of Sacramento, Inc.; SYSCO Food Services of St. Louis, LLC; SYSCO Food Services of San Antonio, LP; SYSCO Food Services of San Diego, Inc.; SYSCO Food Services of San Francisco; SYSCO Food Services of Seattle, Inc.; SYSCO Food Services of South Florida, Inc.; SYSCO Food Services of Southeast Florida, LLC; SYSCO Food Services of Spokane; SYSCO Food Services of Syracuse; SYSCO Food Services of Ventura, Inc.; SYSCO Food Services of Virginia, LLC; SYSCO Food Services of West Coast Florida, Inc.; SYSCO Intermountain Food Services, Inc.; SYSCO Newport Meat Company; Watson Sysco Food Services, Inc.; North Douglas SYSCO Food Services, Inc. (Canada); SYSCO Canada; SYSCO Food Services of Atlantic Canada; SYSCO Food Services of Calgary (Canada); SYSCO Food Services of Central Ontario, Inc. (Canada); SYSCO Food Services of Edmonton (Canada); SYSCO Food Services of Ontario, Inc. (Canada); SYSCO Food Services of Quebec (Canada); SYSCO Food Services of Regina (Canada); SYSCO Food Services of Sturgeon Falls (Canada); SYSCO Food Services of Thunder Bay (Canada); SYSCO Food Services of Toronto (Canada); SYSCO Food Services of Vancouver, Inc. (Canada); SYSCO Food Services of Winnipeg (Canada); SYSCO HRI Supply, LTD. (Canada); SYSCO I & S Foodservices, Inc. (Canada); SYSCO Ontario Produce, Inc. (Canada).

Principal Competitors

U.S. Foodservice, Inc.; Performance Group Company; Gordon Food Service.

Further Reading

Anders, K.T., "SYSCO's Strategy," *Supermarket Business,* September 1998, p. 182.

Bagamery, Anne, " 'Don't Sell Food, Sell Peace of Mind,' " *Forbes,* October 11, 1982, p. 58.

Civin, Robert, "Sysco: Distribution's $7-Billion Entrepreneur," *Institutional Distribution,* April 1990.

"Distribution's Multi-Branch Giants," *Institutional Distribution,* October 1985, p. 169.

Fisher, Daniel, "Little Things Mean a Lot for Giant Sysco," *Houston Business Journal,* August 18, 1995, p. 24.

Geelhoed, E. Bruce, *The Thrill of Success: The Story of SYSCO/Frost-Pack Food Services, Incorporated,* Muncie, Ind.: Bureau of Business Research, College of Business and Department of History, Ball State University, 1983, 96 p.

"Great Distributor Organization Study: SYSCO Corporation," *Institutional Distribution,* June 1980.

Greer, Jim, "First in the Food Chain," *Houston Business Journal,* April 28, 2000, p. 16A.

——, "Sysco Stock Hits Record High, Emerges from Cisco's Shadow," *Houston Business Journal,* March 5, 2004.

Harrison, Dan, "Sysco Eyes $10 Billion," *Institutional Distribution,* April 1989, p. 52.

Hassell, Greg, "The Sage of Sysco: Retired Founder Still at Work," *Houston Chronicle,* July 10, 1998.

——, "Sysco's President Will Be Its Next Chief Executive," *Houston Chronicle,* November 6, 1999.

——, "Sysco Will Purchase FreshPoint," *Houston Chronicle,* January 8, 2000.

Jones, Jeanne Lang, "Keeping Sysco on Course," *Houston Post,* January 8, 1995.

Kreimer, Susan, "Sysco to Expand Presence in Canada," *Houston Chronicle,* December 6, 2001.

Lawn, John, "Sysco's Strategy: 'Divide and Multiply,' " *Foodservice Distributor,* January 1995, p. 32.

Loeffelholz, Suzanne, "Voracious Appetite: Sysco's Ability to Digest Its Acquisitions Can Only Mean More Deals Ahead," *Financial World,* April 18, 1989, p. 72.

Mack, Toni, "V.P.s of Planning Need Not Apply," *Forbes,* October 25, 1993, p. 84.

Reiter, Jeff, "Sysco and Dairy," *Dairy Foods,* October 1995, p. 113.

Ruggless, Ron, "John F. Woodhouse," *Nation's Restaurant News,* January 1995.

Salkin, Stephanie, "Sysco's Schnieders Previews Growth Agenda," *ID,* May 2002, pp. 17–18.

"SYSCO Corporation: Serving Up Steady Growth," *Better Investing,* December 2004, pp. 36–38.

"Sysco Corporation: Since 1980," *Institutional Distribution,* September 15, 1986, p. 60.

"Sysco: Swallowing Up Its Competitors to Grow in Food Distribution," *Business Week,* August 17, 1981, pp. 116+.

—update: David E. Salamie

Taiwan Tobacco & Liquor Corporation

No. 4, Nanchang Road, Section 1
Taipei
Taiwan
Telephone: +886 2 2321-4567
Fax: +886 2 2397-2086
Web site: http://www.ttw.gov.tw

State-Owned Company
Incorporated: 1901 as Monopoly Bureau of Taiwan
    Governor's Office
Employees: 7,000
Sales: TWD 64.23 billion (2004)
NAIC: 312221 Cigarette Manufacturing; 312210 Tobacco
    Stemming and Redrying; 312229 Other Tobacco
    Product Manufacturing; 312120 Breweries; 424810
    Beer and Ale Merchant Wholesalers; 424820 Wine and
    Distilled Alcoholic Beverage Merchant Wholesalers

Taiwan Tobacco & Liquor Corporation (TTL) is Taiwan's leading manufacturer and distributor of beer, wine, and tobacco products. The company, the operational arm of the former Taiwan Tobacco and Liquor Board monopoly, has retained control of more than 80 percent of the island's beer market, 53 percent of the liquor and wine market, and 45 percent of the tobacco market since the total abolition of the government's monopoly on these markets in 2002. TTL's leadership is based on popular and dominant brands such as Taiwan Beer, Long Life cigarettes, YuSan Kaoliang, and other traditional alcoholic beverages. The company operates nine wineries and distilleries and three breweries, as well as cigarette production facilities. TTL also operates its own 135-branch retail chain, and distributes its product through more than 50,000 sales outlets, including other retailers, vending machines, street sellers, and the like. Formed in 2002, TTL is slated to be privatized as part of the Taiwan government's commitment to meeting conditions imposed by its acceptance into the World Trade Organization (WTO). The company public offering is expected to be completed by 2006, but has been slowed by labor union disputes. Although most of TTL's sales remain focused on the Taiwan

market, the company also ships a number of its brands, including flagship Taiwan Beer, worldwide, with major markets including Japan and the United States. TTL has begun an attempt to enter the mainland Chinese market, but has met resistance from the Chinese government.

From Colonial Monopoly to State-Owned Treasure Chest in the 1940s

The Taiwan Tobacco & Liquor Corporation stemmed from the Japanese occupation of the island at the end of the 19th century. The colonial governor quickly set up a monopoly controlling the island's lucrative opium production through the establishment of the Taiwan Pharmaceutical Factory. By the beginning of the 20th century, the colonial government had extended its monopoly to include salt and camphor as well. Initially, these products were placed under separate bodies, including the Taiwan Salt Bureau and the Taiwan Camphor Bureau. In 1901, however, these, together with the opium factory, were placed under a single body, the Monopoly Bureau of the Taiwan Governor's Office.

Taiwan developed its own tobacco industry in the early years of the 20th century, as a large number of Taiwanese farmers converted their lands to growing tobacco. The rise of tobacco use on the island created a lucrative and, in large part, captive revenue stream, and the Monopoly Bureau quickly extended its range, taking control of Taiwan's tobacco monopoly in 1905.

Taiwan's alcoholic beverage market, at least among the native Chinese population, remained dominated by traditional Chinese wine and liquor varieties, such as the rice-based Shaohsing, and Kaoliang, distilled from sorghum. The Japanese taste for beer, imported from Japan, soon began to spread among the Taiwanese, however. By the end of World War I, demand for beer had grown sufficiently to necessitate the construction of a brewery in Taiwan itself. By 1919, the island's first brewery, in Chienguo, had launched production.

Initially, the Chienguo brewery's production was rather limited, at just 1.5 million bottles per year. Yet Chienguo Beer, as it was originally known, became an instant hit among the

Company Perspectives:

Business Mission: To create a dignified working environment for employees; To protect the health of the consumption of tobacco and liquor; To insist on innovation, assertiveness, responsibility, honesty and faith.

island's beer drinkers, and especially among the Japanese, who brought the beer brand home with them. Before long, the Chienguo factory had begun to export its beer to Japan, where the brand rivaled even that market's dominant beer brand, Sapporo. Soon, beer exports had exceeded beer imports.

The popularity of the Chienguo brewery's beer provided the colonial government with a new and fast-growing revenue stream. In 1922, therefore, the Monopoly Bureau extended its reach again, to include production and sale of alcoholic beverages. Throughout the remaining two decades of Japanese occupation, the Monopoly Bureau continued to add new monopolies, including matches and even the standardization of weights and measures used on the island. In 1943, the Monopoly Bureau added petroleum products to complete the scope of its monopoly holdings.

The end of Japanese occupation following World War II spelled the end of the Monopoly Bureau. Yet control of the various sectors under that bureau offered a strong source of revenue for the newly installed Taiwan Government Executive Administration Office. In 1945, the Chiang Kai-shek-led government created a new body, the Taiwan Provincial Monopoly Bureau, which took over the monopolies on tobacco, liquor, camphor, matches, and weights and measures. That body was reformulated as the Taiwan Tobacco and Wine Board in 1947. At this time the board's oversight was reduced to just three monopolies: camphor, wine, and tobacco. In 1951, the board, previously a self-standing entity, was placed under the control of the Finance Department. In 1968, the board's role was further streamlined to its two major revenue streams, alcoholic beverages and tobacco.

Throughout the decades of military dictatorship in Taiwan, the Tobacco and Wine Board played an important role as a financial motor for the country's rapidly evolving economy. The strong revenue stream and consistent profits enabled the government to invest in developing new industries, particularly Taiwan's thrust into the electronics sector in the late 1970s and 1980s. The Tobacco and Wine Board also developed an extensive sales network around Taiwan, setting up its own retail stores (more than 135 by the mid-2000s) and developing a network of more than 50,000 sales outlets throughout Taiwan.

As the sole producer and distributor of alcoholic beverages and tobacco products for Taiwan, the board was responsible for ensuring that production levels met consumer demand. As such, and as Taiwan's population grew, the board added new factories, breweries, and other production sites around the island. The board also built up a portfolio of brand names, not least of which was its Taiwan Beer brand, based at the original Chienguo brewery. Over time the Taiwan Beer brand became the board's international spearhead, following the Taiwanese expatriate community to the United States in particular, but also

rebuilding a following among Japanese consumers as well. Another brand created by the board at this time was the incongruously named, but highly popular, Long Life brand of cigarettes. Other brands included Prosperity Island, Triumph, and President. At the same time, the board oversaw production of the group's other alcoholic beverages. This segment, however, remained limited, in large part, to the traditional Chinese spirits, Shaohsing and Kaoliang.

Free Market Competitor in the 2000s

The end of military dictatorship in Taiwan in the mid-1980s brought about the first steps toward a liberalization of the state's alcoholic beverages and tobacco minority. The creation of a democratic structure led to the creation of a liberalized, market-driven economic policy, and to Taiwan's aspirations for joining the World Trade Organization (WTO). As part of that effort, the government began lowering trade barriers, including abolishing its monopoly over tobacco and alcoholic beverages. In 1987, the government took the first step toward full liberalization of both of these markets by allowing the first imports of wine into Taiwan. Under pressure from the U.S. government, Taiwan also accepted the first imports of U.S. cigarette brands that year. These were followed by imports of European tobacco products soon after.

Consumer acceptance of grape-based and other fruit-based wines was slow; as such the board's control over the Taiwanese alcoholic beverage market remained solid. Nonetheless, as wine drinking grew in popularity in Taiwan, entering a boom phase in the mid-1990s, the board diversified its production as well, adding its own wine varieties.

The Taiwanese consumer responded more quickly to the arrival of the first foreign whiskey imports, authorized in 1991. By 1992, the country had widened its spirits imports to include brandy, gin, and other spirits. Into the 1990s, the board saw its market share shrink rapidly, and by 1998, imports represented nearly 25 percent of the alcoholic beverage market. Helping to offset the board's dwindling market share was a steady increase in Taiwanese alcoholic beverage consumption. At the same time, the board remained relatively protected by a system of tariffs on imports. Although some imports, particularly those from Japan, were less heavily taxed than others, the system nonetheless helped buffer the board from full-scale competition into the late 1990s.

Taiwan's commitment to meeting the requirements of WTO membership by 2002 brought a new effort by the government to liberalize its markets. In 1999, the government implemented a new Tobacco & Alcohol Administrative Law (or TAAL). The new legislation provided the blueprint for the conversion of the board into a private enterprise and the introduction of full-fledged competition in both the tobacco and alcoholic beverage markets. As part of that process, the board was split into two parts. The board's administrative function was regrouped into a new bureau, placed under the Ministry of Finance. Meanwhile, the board's production and distribution units were regrouped into a new state-owned corporation. At the same time, the government leveled import taxes and duties.

The restructuring of the board lasted into the early 2000s. Finally, in 2002, the breakup was completed, and a new corpo-

group's control of the Taiwan beer market had slipped back to 80 percent by 2005.

To shore up its sagging sales at home, TTL began instituting its own international expansion strategy. While continuing to target the U.S., Japanese, and European markets, TTL's main target became the Chinese market. The company chose its Long Life brand as the spearhead for its entry into the Chinese market, sending over a first shipment in late 2004. At the same time, TTL prepared to launch its Taiwan Beer brand onto the mainland. This effort was held up, however, by the Chinese government, apparently in retaliation for the re-election of independence-minded President Chen Shui-bian. Nonetheless, China, which also sought entry into the WTO, was expected to play by the rules. With the world's largest consumer population just a short boat ride away, TTL appeared certain to remain a major name in the tobacco and alcohol markets in the region.

Principal Divisions

Marketing & Sales; Liquor; Beer; Tobacco.

Principal Competitors

Shanghai Cigarette Factory; Sumatra Tobacco Trading Company, N.V.; Chuxiong Cigarette Factory; Ben Thanh Tobacco Co.; Japan Tobacco Inc.; Central Group of Cos.; Itochu-Shokuhin Company Ltd.; Yamae Hisano Company Ltd.; Nanlien International Corporation.

Further Reading

"Beer's Bid for China Market Goes Flat," *Taiwan Headlines.com,* June 29, 2004.

John, Glenn A., "Taiwan's Cigarette Monopoly Charges Ahead," *Tobacco International,* August 1, 1990, p. 26.

Lin, Frances, "Free for All in Taiwan's Deregulated Alcohol Industry," *TDC Trade,* March 14, 2002.

Lin, Josephine, "The Birthplace of Taiwan Beer," *Taiwan Fun Magazine,* April 2002.

"One and Only," *Asiaweek,* November 24, 1995.

"Taiwan Beer Popular at Home Despite Robust Foreign Competition," *Asia Pulse,* August 11, 2005.

"Taiwan Beer's Mainland China Début Appears to Have Gone Flat," *Asia Pulse,* June 29, 2004.

"Taiwan Tobacco and Liquor Corp. Opens Kinmen Outlet," *Asia Pulse,* May 26, 2005.

"Taiwan Tobacco and Wine Board to Put Forward Privatization Plan," *Asia Pulse,* April 6, 2004.

"Taiwan Tobacco and Wine to Be Privatized by End of 2003," *Taiwan Economic News,* September 23, 2002.

"TTL Eyes Chinese Market," *World Tobacco,* November 2003, p. 12.

"Wine Monopolist Turning to Imports," *China News,* December 8, 1999.

Yu-huay Sun, "Top Brewer in Taiwan Is Seeking Partners," *International Herald Tribune,* October 12, 2005.

—M.L. Cohen

Key Dates:

1901: The Monopoly Bureau of Taiwan Governor's Office is established to control opium trade, as well as the salt and camphor monopolies.
1905: Monopoly is extended to include tobacco.
1919: Chienguo Brewery, the first to brew beer in Taiwan, is founded (it later adopts the Taiwan Beer brand).
1922: Alcoholic beverages are placed under government monopoly.
1947: The Taiwan Tobacco and Wine Board, which oversees the tobacco, alcohol, and camphor monopolies, is created.
1968: The board's control over the camphor monopoly ends.
1987: Taiwan accepts imports of wine and cigarettes for the first time.
1991: Imports of whiskey are allowed.
1992: Imports of brandy, gin, and other spirits are allowed.
1999: The government passes a new Tobacco & Alcohol Administrative Law; private domestic production of fermented beverages is allowed.
2001: Private domestic production of spirits is allowed.
2002: TTL is created as a state-owned corporation, including the production and distribution operations of the former board; private domestic production of beer is allowed.
2004: TTL launches the Long Life cigarette brand in mainland China.
2005: TTL prepares for a public offering and privatization.

ration, Taiwan Tobacco & Liquor Corporation, was formed. The creation of TTL also marked the launch of full-scale competition, including the admittance of the production of alcoholic beverages by private companies. That process had been started in 1999, with the production of wine and other fermented beverages. Production of distilled spirits was permitted in 2001. The brewing of beer followed in 2002, and signaled the start of TTL's own move toward private control.

TTL began preparing for a future public offering, targeting 2005 as the date of its transformation into a private enterprise. That process was hampered, however, by the need to reach agreement with the company's labor union, particularly involving projected cuts of more than 1,000 workers from the company's payroll. TTL also was burdened by its obligation to purchase tobacco from Taiwan's tobacco farmers, despite the fact that the company's warehouses were already overstocked.

In the meantime, the appearance of new domestic producers had begun to take a toll on TTL's sales. By 2005, the group's grip on the local liquor and wine market had slipped to 53 percent. The company's share of the tobacco market also had suffered, dropping to 45 percent. Only the group's Taiwan Beer subsidiary appeared to withstand the tide of competition, but the

⏀ Taubman

Taubman Centers, Inc.

200 East Long Lake Road, Suite 300
P.O. Box 200
Bloomfield Hills, Michigan 48303-0200
U.S.A.
Telephone: (248) 258-6800
Fax: (248) 258-7596
Web site: http://www.taubman.com

Public Company
Incorporated: 1973
Employees: 509
Sales: $471.5 million (2004)
Stock Exchanges: New York
Ticker Symbol: TCO
NAIC: 525930 Real Estate Investment Trusts

Taubman Centers, Inc. (TCO) is a publicly traded real estate investment trust (REIT) that holds a controlling interest in one of the United States' leading developers of regional malls, The Taubman Realty Group Limited Partnership, which owns the management company known as The Taubman Company LLC. The group's portfolio includes 21 shopping centers in nine states. Part of the empire founded in 1950 by A. Alfred Taubman, the business has maintained a reputation for innovation and quality. Its malls consistently exceed the industry standard in sales per square foot.

Origins

The Taubman Company was formed in 1950 by A. Alfred Taubman, who would be credited with pioneering the regional mall concept. According to official lore, he started the business with a $5,000 bank loan at the age of 25. Early projects focused on retail establishments in the Detroit area. North Flint Plaza, built in 1953, was a significant increase in scale, with 26 stores anchored by Federated's Department Store.

In 1955, company headquarters was relocated to a boxy, one-story building in Oak Park, Michigan. In 1968, it was relocated to Southfield, Michigan, where it remained for ten years.

Taubman had an office in northern California by the early 1960s. There, it completed its first enclosed regional mall, Southland, in 1964. At 300,000 square feet, it was twice the average size of its contemporaries.

There were other notable new malls in the 1960s and 1970s. Concord, California's Sunvalley was billed as ''the world's largest air conditioned shopping center'' when it opened in 1967. At 2.3 million square feet, Woodfield of Schaumburg, Illinois, was the largest enclosed mall built up to 1971 and remained one of the five largest in the United States through the end of the century. Some early design innovations included parking around the full perimeter of a mall to allow for customer convenience and even distribution of traffic.

Taubman Centers, Inc. was incorporated in 1973. It served as the managing partner of the Taubman Realty Group Limited Partnership.

Taubman was among the first to capitalize upon the improving highway system to bring shopping to the suburbs. He later told *Crain's Detroit Business* that he and other developers were unfairly charged with contributing to the decline of downtown areas. He cited an attempt to build a new mall in downtown Detroit in the mid-1970s that was scuttled under pressure from an existing department store. In fact, notes the company's 1999 annual report, of the nine malls Taubman built in the 1980s, four very successful ones were located in urban areas (Los Angeles; Charleston; Stamford, Connecticut; and Columbus, Ohio).

Taubman engineered many history-making deals. He led a group that acquired the 77,000-acre Irvine Ranch for $337.4 million in 1977. The enterprise also was credited with innovations, such as the first two-story regional mall. Taubman developed a signature style: clean, simple designs that highlighted the tenant stores. Robert Taubman later told the *Wall Street Journal* that the company disdained food courts because their hectic atmosphere discouraged long visits.

Taubman company headquarters moved to a glassy corporate edifice in Troy, Michigan, in 1978. In April 1985, corporate headquarters were relocated to Bloomfield Hills, another suburb of Detroit.

Company Perspectives:

Our mission is to own, manage, develop and acquire retail properties that deliver superior financial performance to our shareholders.

We distinguish ourselves by creating extraordinary retail properties where customers choose to shop, dine and be entertained; and where retailers can thrive.

We foster a rewarding and empowering work environment, where we strive for excellence, encourage innovation and demonstrate teamwork.

Key Dates:

1950: Alfred Taubman launches a shopping center empire.
1973: Taubman Centers is incorporated.
1985: Taubman Realty Group Limited Partnership is formed as Taubman gets financing from GM pensions.
1992: Taubman Centers, Inc. goes public on the New York Stock Exchange.
1998: Restructuring returns control of TCO to the Taubman family.
2003: TCO defeats a hostile takeover from Simon Property Group Inc.

Taubman's growth was financed with $625 million borrowed from General Motors pension trusts in 1985. The Taubman Realty Group Limited Partnership was created in this transaction. The funds would be repaid when Taubman Centers, Inc. went public following the collapse of the freewheeling commercial real estate market of the 1980s.

Public in 1992

Taubman Centers, Inc. (TCO) had its initial public offering (IPO) on the New York Stock Exchange in November 1992, raising $295 million. TCO became a real estate investment trust (REIT) through the offering, owning about 36 percent of the Taubman Realty Group Limited Partnership (TRG). It was TRG that owned interests in the malls.

TCO was led by Robert S. Taubman, who had joined the Taubman group in 1976 and had become its CEO in 1990. Another of Alfred Taubman's sons, William S. Taubman, was also active in management. Both visited their father's construction sites often while growing up.

Taubman had about 400 employees in the mid-1990s. It ran 19 malls across the United States. With high-end anchors such as Saks Fifth Avenue and Nordstrom, it generated per-foot sales far above the industry average. According to *Forbes,* the company's relatively short leases (six years) helped its malls stay on top of retail trends.

According to the *Wall Street Journal,* Taubman did not open any new malls for four years after its IPO. Growth failed to meet expectations, said one analyst. In 1997, however, the company began a plan to open one mall per year for the next six years. During the 1990s, Taubman bought five centers and expanded ten more.

1998 Restructuring

Taubman Centers underwent a restructuring in 1998, a year of many changes. The Taubman family was able to increase its voting control from 7 percent to 33 percent by buying series B preferred shares. This increased—some characterized it as disproportionate—power allowed the family to rebuff several takeover advances.

Taubman ventured into a new type of development in 1998 through a joint venture with The Mills Corporation. The team agreed to develop seven value malls, which had more entertainment and food choices than traditional malls and were intended to attract more tourists. One of these, Great Lakes Crossing near Detroit, would attract ten million visitors a year, making it a leading destination in its own right.

Finally, in 1998 the company instituted a new philosophy of architectural design. Officials told *Chain Store Age* the aim was to differentiate Taubman's centers from traditional boxy malls. "Society is changing, and we are evolving with the changes," said John Simon, senior vice-president and managing director of development. "People are very lifestyle-conscious, unemployment is low and often the cost of an item or money issues are transcended by lifestyle choices." The company was already a pioneer in bringing high-end accoutrements such as marble and artwork to the suburbs. The firm devoted considerable attention to matching the style of its malls to their respective surroundings.

Unprecedented Growth After 2000

TCO benefited from renewed interest in REITs following the collapse of the Internet bubble. Taubman continued to open malls even as the economy staggered after 2000. Four malls were opened in 2001, a record, totaling about 5.5 million square feet of retail space. The opening of so many malls at once was accidental, stressed company officials.

Such developments unfolded even as Alfred Taubman was caught up in a price-fixing scandal at the British auction house Sotheby's Holdings Inc., which he had acquired with an investment group in 1983. He resigned as Taubman Centers chairman in December 2001, but retained about 30 percent of shares, and later served ten months in jail. By this time, Taubman's sons had been running the company's daily operations for years.

Resisting Simon Takeover in 2003

Simon Property Group, Inc. attempted a $1.7 billion hostile takeover of Taubman Centers from November 2002 to October 2003; Westfield America Inc. joined the bid in January. Simon was the country's largest mall owner with about 250 malls to TCO's 30. After a number of legal challenges, the takeover attempt was ultimately derailed after TCO persuaded the Michigan legislature to create a law allowing for the Taubman family to form an alliance with other shareholders.

While Taubman had two traditional malls under development in 2005—Syosset, in New York's Oyster Bay (though it faced legal complications) and Northlake Mall in Charlotte, North Carolina—the company was looking for new types of developments as well as overseas opportunities. In January 2005, the company announced that it was setting up a retail center connected to an Atlantic City casino, Caesars. TCO also was studying the $20 billion New Songdo City project in South Korea, a planned commercial district with ten million square feet of retail space that was expected to open by 2009. Taubman also was looking at opportunities in China and Japan, and had budgeted $100 million a year for development in North America and Asia, its Asia president told the *Vietnam Investment Review.*

Principal Subsidiaries

Dolphin Mall Associates Limited Partnership; Fairlane Town Center, LLC; La Cienega Partners Limited Partnership d/b/a Beverly Center; Lakeside/Novi Land Partnership, LLC; MacArthur Shopping Center, LLC; Northlake Land LLC; Oyster Bay Associates Limited Partnership; Short Hills Associates, LLC d/b/a The Mall at Short Hills; Stony Point Associates, LLC d/b/a Stony Point Fashion Park; Stony Point Land LLC; Tampa Westshore Associates Limited Partnership d/b/a International Plaza; Taub-Co Finance LLC; Taub-Co Finance II, Inc.; Taub-Co Kemp, Inc.; Taub-Co Land Holdings, Inc.; Taub-Co Management, Inc.; Taub-Co Management IV, Inc.; Taubman Auburn Hills Associates Limited Partnership d/b/a Great Lakes Crossing; Taubman Regency Square Associates, LLC d/b/a Regency Square; The Taubman Company, LLC d/b/a The Taubman Company; The Taubman Realty Group Limited Partnership; TJ Palm Beach Associates Limited Partnership d/b/a The Mall at Wellington Green; TRG Charlotte, LLC d/b/a Northlake Mall; Twelve Oaks Mall, LLC; Willow Bend Kemp Limited Partnership; Willow Bend Realty Limited Partnership; Willow Bend Shopping Center Limited Partnership.

Principal Competitors

CBL & Associates Properties, Inc.; General Growth Properties, Inc.; The Macerich Company; The Mills Corporation; Simon Property Group, Inc.

Further Reading

"Against All Odds," *Chain Store Age,* May 2002, pp. 62+.

Barsky, Neil, "Taubman Files New Prospectus to Lure Public," *Wall Street Journal,* October 19, 1992, p. C17.

Brauer, Molly, "Two REITs Team Up to Build Seven Value Malls," *Knight Ridder/Tribune Business News,* May 19, 1998.

Bridgeforth, Art, Jr., "Taubman Builds Success; Great Lakes Crossing Shows Vision," *Crain's Detroit Business,* January 18, 1999, pp. 1+.

Cohen, Nancy E., *America's Marketplace: The History of Shopping Centers,* International Council of Shopping Centers, 2002.

Crump, Constance, "New Era for REITs: Taubman Offering Success Is a Signal," *Crain's Detroit Business,* December 7, 1992, p. 2.

——, "Taubman Co. Still Has Acquiring Mind," *Crain's Detroit Business,* March 29, 1993, p. 1.

Day, Sherri, and Andrew Ross Sorkin, "Simon Group Gives Up Hostile Bid for Taubman Centers," *The New York Times,* October 9, 2003, p. C1.

Eichenwald, Kurt, "Taubman Is Trying Again on Initial Public Offering," *The New York Times,* October 20, 1992, p. 21.

Gearty, Robert, "Convicted Sotheby's Former Chief Steps Down from Helm of Shopping-Mall Empire," *Daily News* (New York), December 12, 2001.

Gentry, Connie Robbins, "Designing Lifestyle Experiences," *Chain Store Age,* August 2000, pp. 131+.

"Goldman's Dangerous REIT Game: Firm Now Defending Unpopular Strategy It Helped Devise," *Investment Dealers' Digest,* February 24, 2003.

Kirkpatrick, David D., "Taubman Centers Revival," *Wall Street Journal,* August 13, 1997, p. B8.

Light, Sara Jo, "HR Strategies and Tactics Help Taubman Weather a Crisis," *Journal of Organizational Excellence,* Spring 2005, pp. 29+.

"Mall Culture to Hit Asia As Operators Start to Set Up Shop," *Vietnam Investment Review,* June 27, 2005, p. 22.

Matnard, Micheline, "If a Name Is Tarnished, But Carved in Stone," *New York Times,* December 9, 2001, p. BU4.

Moukheiber, Zina, "Tempting the Jaded Shopper," *Forbes,* May 20, 1996, pp. 48+.

"My Three Sons," *Retail Traffic,* September 2003.

Norris, Floyd, "Taubman Centers, a Mall Empire, to Go Public; Big Developer to Shed Debt in Stock Sale," *The New York Times,* August 4, 1992, p. 1.

"Shopping Center Magnate Proposes Public Stock Offering," *Associated Press,* August 3, 1992.

Snavely, Brent, "Crash … Or Charge?," *Crain's Detroit Business,* July 23, 2001, pp. 1+.

——, "Failed Takeover Bid Didn't Derail Taubman Centers' Expansion," *Crain's Detroit Business,* October 13, 2003, p. 4.

——, "Taubman Centers' Decision to Go Public Put It at Risk for a Takeover," *Crain's Detroit Business,* November 25, 2002, p. 4.

——, "Taubman Centers' Stock Price Stays Up As Takeover Battle Ends," *Crain's Detroit Business,* November 3, 2003, p. 43.

——, "Taubman Shores Up Its Malls, Prepares to Move Beyond Them," *Crain's Detroit Business,* April 25, 2005, p. 4.

Snavely, Brent, and Jennette Smith, "Making Things Happen; Taubman Speaks on His Legacy in Business, His Time in Prison and the Future of Retail," *Crain's Detroit Business,* April 4, 2005, p. 11.

Starkman, Dean, "After Conviction, Taubman Resigns from Mall REIT," *Wall Street Journal,* December 12, 2001, p. B2.

——, "Taubman's Mall-Building Efforts Raise Eyebrows," *Wall Street Journal,* March 7, 2001, p. B10.

——, "Taubmans Take Law into Their Own Hands," *Wall Street Journal,* June 17, 2003, pp. C1+.

Vincour, Barry, "Refashioned Taubman Offering Still Draws Fire," *Barron's,* October 26, 1992, p. 47.

Vogel, Carol, "Taubman Centers, a Mall Empire, to Go Public; Still Dealing and Living in 80's Style," *The New York Times,* August 4, 1992, p. 1.

—Frederick C. Ingram

Technical Olympic USA, Inc.

4000 Hollywood Boulevard, Suite 500 North
Hollywood, Florida 33021
U.S.A.
Telephone: (954) 364-4000
Fax: (954) 364-4010
Web site: http://www.tousa.com

Public Company
Incorporated: 1983 as Newmark Homes Corporation
Employees: 2,079
Sales: $2.13 billion (2004)
Stock Exchanges: New York
Ticker Symbol: TOA
NAIC: 236116 New Multi-Family Housing Construction (Except Operative Builders); 237210 Land Subdivision; 522292 Real Estate Credit; 524127 Direct Title Insurance Carriers; 551112 Offices of Other Holding Companies

Technical Olympic USA, Inc. (TOUSA) is a designer, builder, and seller of detached, single-family homes, town-homes, and condominiums. The company operates in four regions: Florida, the Mid-Atlantic, Texas, and the West, concentrating its activities in 15 metropolitan markets. TOUSA, which eventually intends to create a single national brand for its homes, operates under several brand names, including Engle Homes, Newmark Homes, D.S. Ware Homes, Masonry Homes, Trophy Homes, and Gilligan Homes. The company sells more than 7,000 homes per year at an average sales price of $275,000. TOUSA also operates a financial services business through three subsidiaries, Preferred Home Mortgage Company, Alliance Insurance and Information Services, LLC, and Universal Land Title Inc. TOUSA's mortgage financing services are used primarily by buyers of its homes, while its closing services and insurance agency operations are used by its customers as well as other clients purchasing or refinancing residential or commercial real estate. TOUSA subcontracts nearly all of its construction work, assigning its own construction superintendents to monitor and to coordinate the construction of each home. Tech-

nical Olympic S.A., a Greek construction firm, owns approximately 70 percent of TOUSA's stock.

Origins

TOUSA represented the efforts of a Greek construction company to enter the U.S. home-building market at the end of the 1990s. The Greek company, Technical Olympic S.A., was founded in Patra in 1965 as Pelops Constructions. Its founder, Konstantinos Stengos, a civil engineer who was a graduate of the National Technical University in Athens, specialized in the construction of apartment buildings and public works projects. Stengos served as chairman of Technical Olympic S.A. and more than two dozen other subsidiaries at the time TOUSA was formed, having spent the previous 30 years creating a massive construction conglomerate. After decades of development, his company held sway as a giant construction firm, operating as a contractor for residential dwellings, tourist resorts, marinas, and large-scale industrial projects throughout Greece. By the 1990s, the extent of Technical Olympic S.A.'s growth had begun to work against the company, leaving it with fewer opportunities for commercial, residential, and industrial construction projects. The company had grown too large to subsist solely on the business available in Greece, a natural consequence of its own success that prompted Stengos to look beyond Greece's borders for work. He began expanding geographically, founding Technical Olympic UK, PLC, based in London, and Eurorom Constructii SRL, a Romania-based subsidiary, in 1997. Next, he plotted the company's foray into the United States, a move to be spearheaded by the newest Technical Olympic S.A. subsidiary and TOUSA's direct predecessor, Technical Olympic Inc.

Technical Olympic Inc. was a company with Greek lineage, but its business was American with its own historical roots. A dual citizen of sorts, Technical Olympic could explain its corporate lineage by following two paths: One led back to Patra in 1965 and followed the development of Stengos's construction business and the other led back to Houston in 1983, to the formation of Newmark Homes Corp. Technical Olympic was formed for the express purpose of buying its way into the U.S. construction industry, an objective completed when the company acquired Newmark in 1999 and became a going enterprise.

Company Perspectives:

We believe that our diversification across a range of fast-growing markets, across a range of product types and prices, and across a range of homebuilding and financial services will enable us to thrive in a variety of economic conditions. We invite you to watch our results as we execute this strategy!

Technical Olympic's development would be shaped almost entirely by the acquisitions it made, with each new addition expanding the company's operations in a significant way, but with no acquisition as important as the Newmark acquisition. Newmark lent Technical Olympic a corporate identity, defining it at its birth, and it gave the company tangible assets for the first time, and because of this, its influence over the company superseded its Greek parentage. Technical Olympic, as it described itself in later years, was a company with historical roots stretching back to Houston in 1983, not to Patra in 1965.

Newmark was a nearly $500 million-in-sales company when Technical Olympic acquired 80 percent of its stock for $86 million. During its first 15 years of business, Newmark had developed into a geographically diverse designer, builder, and seller of single-family detached homes. The company operated as holding company for its Newmark Home, Westbrooke Communities, The Adler Companies, and Pacific United Development subsidiaries, a group of businesses that served seven major markets in the Southwest and Southeast. Newmark built its business in Texas before expanding into Tennessee. In 1995, after a dozen years in business and with a substantial presence in Houston, Austin, Dallas/Fort Worth, and Nashville, the company acquired The Adler Companies, Inc. The Adler Companies, formed in 1990 in Miami, constructed homes in south Florida, tailoring its construction efforts to attract ''move-up,'' or second-time homebuyers. In 1998, Newmark increased its construction activity in Florida by acquiring Westbrooke Communities, Inc., a company founded in Miami in 1976. Once Newmark had completed the purchase of Westbrooke, it merged its two Florida acquisitions into a single operation and expanded into North Carolina, entering Charlotte and the Greensboro/Winston-Salem area. The year of the merger also coincided with Newmark's initial public offering of stock, which made Technical Olympic a publicly traded company once it purchased Newmark in December of the following year.

The purchase of Newmark was a defining event for Technical Olympic, one that was followed by an acquisition of significant size. In November 2000, less than a year after acquiring Newmark, Technical Olympic purchased Boca Raton, Florida-based Engle Holdings Corp. in a deal valued at $465 million. A publicly traded company, Engle Holdings was founded in 1978 by Alex Engelstein, who continued to serve as the company's chairman and chief executive officer when it was acquired by Technical Olympic. Engelstein took Engle Holdings public in 1992, which gave him $27 million to make land acquisitions to accelerate the growth of his company. In the years preceding its acquisition by Technical Olympic, Engle Holdings recorded impressive growth, increasing its revenues from $245 million in 1995 to $742 million by 1999. During the period, the number of homes sold by the company more than tripled, jumping from 1,137 to 3,514, as it expanded its business into Georgia, North Carolina, Virginia, Colorado, Texas, and Arizona. Despite the company's accomplishments, the reaction from Wall Street was less than Engelstein would have hoped for, fueling his disenchantment with running the company. In his mind, Engle Holdings' share price never accurately reflected the value of the company, a perception that led him to sell the company to Technical Olympic. ''It was one of the things,'' he said in an October 13, 2000 interview with the *Miami Herald,* referring to the decision to sell his company to Technical Olympic. ''The frustration that the market, per se, didn't give us full credit for our accomplishments.''

With Newmark and Engle Holdings constituting its operations, Technical Olympic stood as a recognizable force in the nation's home-building industry, having quickly penetrated the U.S. market. Based on the number of homes the company sold in 2001, a year in which revenues reached $1.4 billion, Technical Olympic ranked as the 12th largest homebuilder in the country. The company pressed forward with its strategy of expanding by acquiring local and regional homebuilders, doing so under new leadership appointed in 2001. Antonio B. Mon was named president and chief executive officer, bringing with him 35 years of experience in finance, investment management, consulting, venture capital, and constructing residential properties. In his position before joining Technical Olympic, Mon served as vice-chairman of Pacific Greystone Corp., a company he had cofounded in 1991. During his stay at Pacific Greystone, Mon presided over the company's development into a major homebuilder in the western United States.

Merger in 2002 Creating TOUSA

Technical Olympic resumed its acquisition campaign in 2002, a significant year for the company. In April, the company sold Westbrooke, the south Florida builder it had acquired through the purchase of Newmark, to Standard Pacific Corp., a homebuilder with extensive holdings in California and Florida. In June, the company merged Newmark with its Engle Holdings subsidiary, a transaction that gave birth to a new name for the entire organization, Technical Olympic USA, Inc., or TOUSA, as the company preferred to call itself. Under its new corporate banner, the company added to its portfolio of home-building brands, shoring up its presence in Florida and adding a new market to the geographic scope of its operations. In October, TOUSA purchased D.S. Ware Homes, LLC for $35.6 million. Founded in 1987 by Donald Ware, D.S. Ware operated in Jacksonville, Florida, where it ranked as the city's fourth largest builder, selling between 300 and 400 homes each year. The following month, TOUSA completed a smaller acquisition, paying $17.1 million for Masonry Homes, Inc. Founded in 1971, Masonry constructed homes in the northwestern suburbs of Baltimore and in southern Pennsylvania, selling 250 homes at an average price of $214,000 in the year before its acquisition by TOUSA.

With a substantial foundation in place, Mon added to TOUSA's holdings as if adding pieces to a puzzle. The company was focused on ten states: Florida, Texas, Arizona, Virginia, Colorado, Nevada, Tennessee, Maryland, Pennsylvania, and Delaware. Housing markets deemed to be overpriced,

Key Dates:

1983: Newmark Homes Corp. is founded.
1999: Technical Olympic Inc. is formed to acquire Newmark Homes.
2000: Technical Olympic acquires Engle Holdings Corp.
2001: Antonio B. Mon is named president and chief executive officer.
2002: Newmark and Engle are merged, creating Technical Olympic USA, Inc.
2003: Trophy Homes Inc. and The James Construction Company are acquired.
2004: Gilligan Homes is acquired.
2005: Transeastern Properties, Inc. is acquired.

markets such as San Diego, Boston, and Los Angeles, were avoided, as were markets that lacked employment growth. The company was reluctant, for instance, to establish a presence in the Midwest, where little employment growth existed. Instead, Mon and his management team concentrated on areas where employment growth had been steady for at least five years and where second-time homebuyers could be found. TOUSA's typical customer wanted a three- to four-bedroom home, 3,000 square feet of living space, and a two-car garage. "They're a little older, in their 30s and 40s," Mon said, describing the typical TOUSA customer in an April 18, 2005 interview with *Investor's Business Daily.* "They're more financially successful and have equity in the homes they're selling."

A Single Brand for the Future

Mon selected acquisition candidates that matched the criteria of the company's expansion strategy and fleshed out TOUSA's market presence, making several additions during his first five years of leadership. In 2003, he acquired two builders, completing both purchases in February. First, he acquired The James Construction Company, a homebuilder operating in the greater Denver area, paying $22 million for the company. Next, he acquired Trophy Homes, Inc., paying $36 million for the Las Vegas-based homebuilder. In 2004, he acquired Gilligan Homes, a homebuilder with operations in Maryland, Pennsylvania, and Delaware, gaining control of roughly 1,100 home sites. The company ended the year, its fifth anniversary, eclipsing $2 billion in sales, a total derived from the 7,221 homes it sold during the year.

As TOUSA looked ahead, the company anticipated creating a single national brand out of its local and regional construction firms. As its acquisition campaign continued, it planned to retain the name of the local or regional company it acquired for two years, after which point the acquisition would adopt the single identity of the entire organization, a single corporate banner under which all of the company's firms would operate. As a cohesive whole, TOUSA's construction activities in its four geographic regions—Florida, Mid-Atlantic, Texas, and the West—stood to benefit from the project-management and inventory-flow technology employed by the company. "You can't have the drywall guys come in before the plumbers," Mon said in his April 18, 2005 interview with *Investor's Business Daily.* "Our system allows us to track each stage of construction and alert subcontractors to get ready." To this system, Mon was expected to add additional local and regional homebuilders. The company's acquisition of Transeastern Properties, Inc., a Coral Springs, Florida-based construction firm purchased in August 2005, set the tone for the years ahead: TOUSA would continue to expand through acquisitions, fleshing out its presence in its four major operating regions.

Principal Subsidiaries

Engle Homes Residential Construction, LLC; Alliance Insurance and Information Services, LLC; Preferred Home Mortgage Company; Universal Land Title Inc.; Newmark Homes, L.P.; Trophy Homes; Fedrick, Harris Estate Homes; TOUSA Homes, Inc.; Universal Land Title, Inc.; Woodland Pines, L.P.

Principal Divisions

TOUSA Homes, Inc.; TOUSA Financial Services.

Principal Competitors

Centex Corporation; D.R. Horton, Inc.; KB Home.

Further Reading

Benesh, Peter, "Technical Olympic USA Hollywood, Florida Home Builder Zeros in on Middle America," *Investor's Business Daily,* April 18, 2005, p. A8.

Clifton, Alexandra Navarro, "Technical Olympic USA Acquires Home Builder Transeastern," *South Florida Sun-Sentinel,* June 8, 2005.

Daniels, Earl, "Large Jacksonville, Fla., Homebuilding Firm Is Sold; Few Changes Planned," *Florida Times-Union,* October 8, 2002.

Danner, Patrick, "Subsidiary of Greek Company to Buy Boca Raton, Fla.-Based Home Builder," *Miami Herald,* October 13, 2000.

Field, Kimberly, "Engle Homes, Northstar Break Ground on Retirement Community Joint Venture," *Miami Daily Business Review,* April 30, 2002, p. A3.

Guido, Daniel Walker, "Merger Mania Continues," *Builder,* January 2001, p. 41.

Meullner, Alexis, "Technical to Buy Engle Homes," *South Florida Business Journal,* October 27, 2000, p. 25A.

"Newmark Homes Corp.," *Houston Business Journal,* February 25, 2000, p. 32B.

Wray, Barbara, "Where Have All the—Local—Builders Gone?," *Austin Business Journal,* September 22, 2000, p. 34.

—Jeffrey L. Covell

Thai Union Frozen Products PCL

72/1 Moo 7 Sethakit 1 Road, Tambon Tarsrai,
   Amphur Muangsamutsakorn
Samutsakorn
74000
Thailand
Telephone: + 66 34 816 500
Fax: + 66 34 816 886
Web site: http://www.thaiuniongroup.com

Public Company
Incorporated: 1988
Employees: 5,140
Sales: THB 40.33 billion ($1.19 billion) (2004)
Stock Exchanges: Thailand
Ticker Symbol: TUF
NAIC: 311712 Fresh and Frozen Seafood Processing;
   311711 Seafood Canning; 424420 Packaged Frozen
   Food Merchant Wholesalers; 424460 Fish and
   Seafood Merchant Wholesalers

Thai Union Frozen Products PCL (TUF) is one of the world's leading processors and producers of canned tuna, notably through its control of the Chicken of the Sea brand, and other canned and frozen fish products. Canned tuna makes up 46 percent of the Bangkok-based company's sales, and the United States is the group's biggest customer, representing 60 percent of the company's revenues. Exports dominate TUF's sales; more than 92 percent of revenues are produced overseas, including 13 percent from Japan. Frozen shrimp is TUF's other major product group, accounting for 21 percent of sales. The company also produces frozen cephalopod and other canned seafood, including canned pet food, for the export market. TUF produces a range of domestic brands as well, including the Fisho brand family of products. The company has targeted China for expansion in the mid-2000s. After establishing its own marketing subsidiaries, TUF acquired a 50 percent stake in local producer Century Union Foods in Shanghai in 2005. TUF is led by founder and Chairman Kraisorn Chansiri and his son,

company President Thiraphong Chansiri. The company has been listed on the Thailand Stock Exchange since 1994.

Thai Fishmonger in the 1970s

Kraisorn Chansiri had already established himself as a leading fishmonger in Bangkok by the late 1970s. In 1977, however, Chansiri took a chance and acquired a failing tuna cannery in nearby Samutsakorn. Chansiri was soon joined by members of his family, including son Thiraphong.

The younger Thiraphong traveled to the United States, where he earned an M.B.A. from the University of San Francisco, before returning to Thailand and rejoining the family business. Together the Chansiris invested in developing technology enabling the processing of smaller fish of two kilos and less. In this way the company avoided direct competition with larger canneries in the United States and elsewhere, which tended to avoid this category of fish.

The Chansiris built a dedicated processing facility to house the new production process in 1988, at Mahachi, in the province of Slut Sakhon. The family then launched a new company for the cannery business, called Thai Union Frozen Foods (TUF).

The Chansiris proved fortunate in their timing. In the late 1980s, the larger American fish companies began seeking to shift their canning operations overseas, and especially to the lower-wage, developing markets. TUF's ability to process smaller tuna, coupled with the low wages in the Thai canning industry, placed the company in a strong competitive position. While the company continued to produce for the domestic market, notably through its own Fishy branded products, the United States quickly became the company's most important market.

TUF's expansion began in earnest in the early 1990s. In 1992, the company made a strategic investment by constructing a new and larger cold-storage facility. The company also sought out strategic partnerships, forming joint ventures with Mitsubishi Corporation and Hagoromo Foods corporations. These partnerships enabled the company to step up its product develop-

Company Perspectives:

Mission: Generate steady growth in revenues and net profit. Focus on improving and adding value to products. Build strong business foundation with global product presence. Maintain leadership position in seafood industry. Constantly monitor business risks in response to potentially adverse trading situations. Generate regular returns to shareholders. Support socially and environmentally beneficial activities. Equip workforce and personnel with necessary professional caliber and expertise in core business.

ment, and especially to redevelop its production facilities to meet international standards.

At the same time, TUF began acquiring a number of businesses in Thailand in order to vertically integrate its operations. This effort gave the company operations spanning production of cans and other packaging, label printing, and public relations and marketing businesses. The company also boosted its range of food offerings, acquiring IFC Inter-Food Co., which distributed pies, and a stake in T-Holding Co., which owned the fast-food chain Calico, specialized in seafood. Another purchase, that of a 51 percent stake in a frozen shrimp packaging business in the south of Thailand, became known as Thai Union Seafood. That operation eventually became TUF's second largest product segment, after tuna canning.

TUF went public in 1994, listing its stock on the Thailand Stock Exchange. Soon after, Thiraphong Chansiri was appointed as the company's president, then just 30 years old. The younger Chansiri now became determined to expand the company into one of the world's largest seafood specialists. As Chansiri told *Asiaweek:* "We stick to what we're good at. We didn't go out and buy hotels, didn't branch out into telecommunications. We are in the seafood business."

The single-mindedness meant that the company's share price lingered below the radar as the international investment community sought out other, more visible stocks in the high-flying Thai and Asian markets in the early and mid-1990s. Investors shunned TUF's more conservative approach. "Today it is the right approach, but a few years back we were the stupidest company in the market, you know," Chansiri told *Asiaweek.* "People asked why we did not borrow and expand."

TUF nearly gave into temptation, arranging a loan for $42 million. Yet in early 1997, Chansiri became concerned over the possibility of the devaluation of the Thai baht ahead of the looming Asia economic crisis, and did not go through with the loan. The decision to remain debt-free set the company apart when the Thai government went through with the devaluation of the baht, and the Thai economy crumbled. As many of the country's debt-laden, overly diversified companies collapsed, TUF emerged as one of Thailand's healthiest businesses. The company's long focus on the international market, which accounted for as much as 96 percent of sales, meant that its revenues came in as U.S. dollars, while its costs remained in

baht. As Chansiri told *Forbes:* "The crisis proved we had the right approach to our business."

Canned Seafood Leader in the 2000s

In the meantime, TUF had continued its program of international expansion and its strategy of entering into partnerships. In 1996, the company moved into the U.S. canning market, forming Thai Union International Inc., which then formed a joint, $12 million purchase of Pan Pacific Fisheries. The following year, at the height of the Thai currency crisis, TUF's solid financial position enabled it to form a new joint venture, Tri-Union Seafoods, together with the Gann Family Trust, led by Edmund Gann, a noted tuna boat operator, and Tri-Marine International, a top raw tuna trader. Through that partnership, TUF acquired a 50 percent stake in another important U.S. seafood company, Van Camp Seafoods, owner of the Chicken of the Sea brand. For just $23 million, TUF now found itself among the leaders in the U.S. and international canned seafood markets.

Van Camp was founded in 1914 when the father-and-son team of Frank and Gilbert Van Camp purchased the California Tuna Canning Company, and then became the first in the United States to pack yellowfin tuna. By the 1930s, Van Camp had launched its own tuna fishing operations. The early 1950s, however, marked the company's breakthrough—the launch of the Chicken of the Sea brand. By 1956, Van Camp had opened canneries in San Diego and Terminal Island in California, and in Puerto Rico and American Samoa. In the 1960s, Van Camp became part of the Ralston Purina foods group. Acquired by an Indonesian company in 1988, Van Camp soon became majority owned by Prudential Life Insurance Company.

The Chicken of the Sea brand played a primary role in TUF's new goal of becoming a $1 billion company by 2005. A major step toward meeting this target came at the end of 2000 when the company paid its partners $38.5 million to buy the remaining 50 percent of the Chicken of the Sea brand. The addition of Chicken of the Sea gave TUF a solid U.S. base, and ownership of the country's second largest canned tuna brand. Under TUF's sole control, Chicken of the Sea immediately began its own expansion effort, buying CI Seafoods Inc., which controlled the Jonah, Pacific Pearl, and Perla Pacifica brands of canned seafood.

TUF moved to rationalize its growing U.S. operations in 2001. By then, the tuna fishing market had shifted its center to the Western Pacific. TUF followed that movement by shutting down its California cannery operations in order to step up production at its American Samoa plant. At the same time, TUF made its first effort to expand beyond seafood, launching production of canned chicken that year.

Nonetheless, seafood remained TUF's core market, while expansion of its international sales continued to play the central role in the company's growth strategy. In the United States, TUF profited from the economic slowdown and the depressed climate following the terrorist attacks on September 11, 2001. As Thiraphong Chansiri explained in *Thai Press Reports:* "Our tuna business generally becomes flat when the economy is in high-growth mode, as people opt for other foods. But whenever

Key Dates:

1977: Kraisorn Chansiri buys a failing tuna cannery near Bangkok.

1988: Chansiri is joined by his son Thirophong Chansiri, and develops technology to process small-sized tuna and opens a new cannery company, Thai Union Frozen Products.

1992: The company expands its cold-storage capacity and launches partnerships with Mitsubishi, Hagoromo Foods, etc.

1994: TUF goes public on the Thailand Stock Exchange.

1997: TUF acquires 50 percent of Van Camp Seafoods and its Chicken of the Sea brand in the United States.

2000: Full control of the Chicken of the Sea brand is acquired.

2001: TUF closes its California cannery and shifts production to American Samoa.

2003: The company launches a marketing subsidiary in China; Empress International in the United States is acquired.

2005: Century Union (Shanghai) Foods in China is acquired.

the global economy is in bad shape or grows slowly, our business thrives.''

Yet Chansiri himself played the primary role in TUF's growth, leading the company on its continued acquisition program. In 2003, the company moved into second place in the packaged seafood market through its purchase of Empress International, a New York-based importer and distributor of frozen shrimp, shellfish, and other seafood.

At the same time, TUF began moves to enter a new market, that of mainland China. In 2003, the company set up its first marketing subsidiaries, in an effort to import its own brands into the Chinese market. When that effort failed to take off, however, TUF quickly changed course. Instead, in 2005, the company paid $4 million to acquire a 50 percent stake in Century Union (Shanghai) Foods Co. In this way, the company gained greater access to the Chinese market through Century's FMCG brand family of products.

By then, TUF had achieved its goal of topping the $1 billion mark, with sales of more than THB 40 billion ($1.19 billion) in 2004, and a forecast of more than THB 50 billion ($1.3 billion) by the end of 2005. Under Thirophong Chansiri, TUF had expanded to become one of the world's leading canned and frozen seafood companies.

Principal Subsidiaries

Century Union (Shanghai) Foods Co. (China); Chicken of the Sea International (U.S.A.); Empress International (U.S.A.); Thai Union Manufacturing Co,; Tri-Union Seafoods LLC (U.S.A.).

Principal Competitors

Antarktika Fishing Co.; Juraslicis A.S.; Mar Fishing Company Inc.; ENACA; Primlaks Nigeria Ltd.; Maruha Group Inc.; Unilever Deutschland GmbH; Mavesa S.A.; Mukorob Fishing Proprietary Ltd.; Nichirei Corporation; StarKist Foods, Inc.

Further Reading

''Empress International: Chicken of the Sea Joined Its Sister Company to Roll Out a Retail Shrimp Line Consumers Asked For,'' *Seafood Business,* April 2005, p. S14.

Kittikanya, Charoen, ''Empress Acquisition Strengthens TUF's Hold in US,'' *Bangkok Post,* July 26, 2003.

——, ''TUF Makes Fresh Foray into China,'' *Bangkok Post,* April 13, 2005.

Lao, Jervina, and Julian Gearing, ''Bangkok's Biggest Catch: Why Thai Union Frozen Food Is Very Hot Stuff,'' *Asiaweek,* December 24, 1999.

Phoosuphanusorn, Srisamorn, ''TUF Buys Out World's Third Biggest Tuna Firm,'' *Bangkok Post,* December 28, 2000.

Steinhauer, Peter, ''The Takeover Expert: CEO Thiraphong Chansiri,'' *Asiaweek,* October 26, 2001.

''Thai Seafood Processor, Exporter to Reach Sales Target of $1.2 Billion,'' *Bangkok Post,* November 11, 2004.

''Thai Union Buys 50% Stake in Chinese Company,'' *just-food.com,* April 15, 2005.

''TUF Announces Acquisition of Thai Quality Shrimp,'' *Thai Press Reports,* August 26, 2004.

''TUF Says US Operations Not Affected by Hurricane Katrina,'' *Thai Press Reports,* September 12, 2005.

''Tuna Costs Hit TUF Q2,'' *just-food.com,* August 10, 2005.

—M.L. Cohen

TiVo Inc.

2160 Gold Street
Alviso, California 95002
U.S.A.
Telephone: (408) 519-9100
Fax: (408) 519-5330
Web site: http://www.tivo.com

Public Company
Incorporated: 1997
Employees: 343
Sales: $172.1 million (2005)
Stock Exchanges: NASDAQ
Ticker Symbol: TiVo
NAIC: 515210 Cable and Other Subscription Programming;
334310 Audio and Video Equipment Manufacturing

TiVo Inc. is a leading provider of digital video recorders (DVRs), selling its devices through retailers and licensing agreements with DIRECTV and Comcast Corporation. The company charges a monthly subscription fee for its DVR service, which is paid either directly by the subscriber or through the subscriber's satellite or cable provider. TiVo contracts with third-party manufacturers to produce its devices.

Origins

Few products in the consumer electronics industry generated as much attention as a device built by James Barton and Michael Ramsay. In the years before they built their first prototype machine, Barton and Ramsay worked for two Silicon Valley-based companies, Convergent Technologies and Silicon Graphics. At Silicon Graphics, Ramsay led the company's workstation division and Barton worked as one of the engineers designing an interactive television system for Time Warner. The system relied on using massive, centralized servers to store digitized programs that subscribers could access through their television sets at home, enabling them to watch stored programming whenever they chose. The project, which was rumored to have cost $150 million, was abandoned by Barton before Time

Warner decided to shut down further development. "People come up with all sorts of reasons why interactive television didn't work," Barton said in a September 21, 1998 interview with *Forbes.* "The basic reason is centralized planning does not work. Why did the economy collapse in Russia?," he asked. "Because the Kremlin wasn't able to deliver what people wanted." Barton, along with Ramsay, left Silicon Graphics in 1996, intending to build a device that gave consumers greater control than the Time Warner system offered, endeavoring "to deliver what people wanted."

When Barton and Ramsay founded TiVo in August 1997, they set in motion what promised to be a revolution in consumer electronics, one that would greatly affect the entertainment industry. Few products posed such a threat to the status quo in the broadcasting industry and provoked as much speculation about the future of television as the product they envisioned. The basic idea behind the proposed device was to combine a computer-style hard drive and software with a television tuner, thereby enabling a user to record programs, pause live television, and skip past advertisements. Instead of relying on content stored on a centralized server, the basis of the Time Warner project, the machine proposed by Barton and Ramsay put the power of choosing content in the hands of the user. The cost of hard drives had dropped to the point where Barton believed he could build a machine capable of storing 20 hours of television programming for approximately $300. Convinced their idea would work, Barton and Ramsay began soliciting for the capital required to get their business underway, presenting their idea to venture capitalists in Silicon Valley. "We walked in," Ramsay remembered in a February 17, 2004 interview with the *Financial Times,* describing one meeting with a group of potential investors, "and said: 'We are after a consumer market, not enterprise. It is about entertainment, not technology, and we are going to need several hundred million dollars before we ever turn a profit.' " Ramsay's last statement proved particularly prescient. TiVo, from its start, created a high level of excitement, fueling great expectations, but turning such promise into financial success proved to be a challenge for the company for years to come.

Barton and Ramsay obtained $3 million from venture capitalists to get their company up and running. With the initial seed

Company Perspectives:

Founded in 1997, TiVo, a pioneer in home entertainment, created a brand new category of products with the development of the first digital video recorder (DVR). Today, the company continues to revolutionize the way consumers watch and access home entertainment by making TiVo the focal point of the digital living room, a center for sharing and experiencing television, music, photos and other content. TiVo connects consumers to the digital entertainment they want, where and when they want it. The company is based in Alviso, California.

money, the pair and a team of colleagues developed a prototype device and showed it to a group of network executives, demonstrating a product that allowed viewers to watch whatever programming they liked, whenever they liked, without watching the commercials that funded the programming. The response from the group of network executives, who sat and watched a product that undermined their control, was not surprising. "They asked me if I was the devil," Ramsay said in his February 17, 2004 interview with the *Financial Times*.

Ramsay and Barton pressed forward with bringing their idea to market. They began negotiating with consumer electronics companies, searching for manufacturers to manufacture the TiVo boxes, and they began discussions with content providers, hoping to reach agreements with cable channels and network producers. TiVo raised an additional $4.5 million in July 1998, giving the company the capital to fund an expected product launch in early 1999. When the first TiVo was introduced in March 1999, its debut was heralded as the most important innovation in the home entertainment industry since the introduction of the VHS video recorder. TiVo offered users the ability to locate and record multiple shows and search for programs by actors, genre, and plot lines, and it featured what was called "suggestive viewing." Software offered on-screen suggestions to viewers about possible recording options, basing the recommendations on the viewing habits of the user. If a TiVo customer watched a horror film, for instance, the technology compared certain aspects of the program with other programs, deducing that the viewer might like to record other films of the same genre.

Once their company had a product on the market, Barton and Ramsay faced the challenge of turning expectations into reality. The period for talking about the potential of TiVo had ended, leaving the founders with the task of realizing the potential of their vision through execution, a task that would prove to be extraordinarily difficult in the years ahead. At the time of the launch of TiVo, analysts projected there would be ten million TiVo-like DVRs in use by 2005, but Barton and Ramsay were not alone in attempting to dominate the market. Palo Alto, California-based Replay Networks also was marketing a product with hard drive recording capabilities, marketing itself, like TiVo, as a purveyor of what both companies called "personal television." In September 1999, TiVo completed its initial public offering of stock, turning to Wall Street to fill its coffers for the battle ahead, but as it turned out the company's greatest

challenge was not the threat posed by direct competitors such as Replay Networks' ReplayTV service. Instead, the greatest difficulty was in convincing the public that TiVo was the revolutionary innovation nearly every industry observer claimed it was. "We are about integrating with the traditional television infrastructure and making it better by personalizing the television experience for the consumer," a TiVo executive explained in an April 5, 1999 interview with *Electronic Media*. "We make it possible for them to view shows more akin to their taste and are working with the networks to provide a new frontier, a new portal into the viewing experience." The executive's statement rang true to most ears, particularly early TiVo customers who expressed a deep appreciation of the device in market research studies, but the problem for Ramsay and Barton was getting customers to bring a TiVo into their homes.

TiVo and DIRECTV Joining Forces in 1999

TiVo's efforts to create and to penetrate the market for DVRs were helped substantially by an agreement made during the first year its device was put on the market. Initially, the company's machine retailed for between $499 and $1,499, a price range encompassing models with between 10 and 30 hours of capacity. In addition, TiVo customers were required to pay a $10 per month subscription fee to cover the costs of receiving programming information through TiVo software. Undoubtedly, some consumers were wary of the costs involved in trying out a new type of electronics device, despite its characterization as a revolutionary product, something that would change the way everyone watched television in the future. Barton and Ramsay's hopes of gaining widespread acceptance early on failed, but their company drew much of its financial sustenance from an agreement with DIRECTV, the largest provider of satellite television in the United States. In 1999, DIRECTV agreed to assist TiVo in marketing and delivering TiVo service to the satellite provider's customer base, the beginning of a longstanding agreement between the two companies that provided the primary source of new customers for Barton and Ramsay.

Ramsay's prediction that it would take years and several hundred million dollars of investment before TiVo turned a profit was accurate. The company signed its one-millionth subscriber in November 2003, but had yet to record a profit, racking up more than $550 million of debt in its attempt to bring TiVo to the masses. Although competition from other DVR manufacturers played a part in TiVo's inability to post a profit, the company's lackluster financial performance stemmed in large part from the public's tepid response to DVR technology. By 2004, three million DVRs had been sold, far fewer than the ten million forecast by analysts five years earlier. Of the three million DVRs in use, only one-third bore the TiVo logo. The widely predicted revolution that TiVo was expected to lead had failed to materialize, leaving the company almost entirely dependent on its licensing agreement with DIRECTV for a volume of business that did not generate a profit.

New Leadership for the Future

TiVo's fortunes began to improve in 2005, an eventful year for the company that hinted at the beginning of widespread acceptance of DVR technology. The year began with Ramsay's

Key Dates:

1997:	TiVo is founded by James Barton and Michael Ramsay.
1999:	The first TiVo is introduced.
2003:	TiVo's subscriber base reaches one million customers.
2005:	TiVo signs a licensing agreement with Comcast Corp.

announcement that he would vacate his post as chief executive officer. Several months later, TiVo announced that it had reached an agreement with Comcast Corporation, the largest provider of cable television in the United States. Comcast had begun to offer DVR set-top boxes to its subscribers, but the company signed its joint venture agreement with TiVo because of the strength of the TiVo name. "They are like Kleenex," an analyst said in a March 16, 2005 interview with the *Chicago Tribune.* "Their brand name defines the entire product category. They have a lot of patents and intellectual property, but their real value is their brand." The importance of the agreement with Comcast increased exponentially when TiVo executives learned that their agreement with DIRECTV, the lifeblood of the company, would no longer provide a significant stream of revenue. Roughly a year earlier, Rupert Murdoch's News Corporation had acquired a 34 percent stake in DIRECTV, a deal that threatened to end DIRECTV's relationship with TiVo because News Corp. owned a U.K.-based company named NDS with its own DVR technology. As expected, DIRECTV began to distance itself from TiVo's devices in August 2005, when it started emphasizing the distribution of DVRs made by NDS to new subscribers.

Against the backdrop of the pivotal deal signed with Comcast and the fading importance of the agreement with DIRECTV, TiVo gained new leadership. In July 2005, Tom Rogers was appointed president and chief executive officer. Rogers began his career as an attorney working for a Wall Street firm, a position that eventually led to his appointment as senior counsel to the U.S. House of Representatives subcommittee on Telecommunications, Consumer Protection and Finance. Next, Rogers served as president of NBC Cable and executive vice-president of NBC, spearheading the creation of CNBC and the formation of the MSNBC partnership with Microsoft. He joined TiVo's board of directors in 1999, brokering NBC's original investment in the company, and reportedly presided over the negotiations with Comcast.

Rogers's tenure began on an exceptionally positive note, offering the new leader a moment to savor that Ramsay had never enjoyed during his eight years of leadership. In August 2005, TiVo reported the first profit in its history, posting $240,000 in net income during the second quarter of 2005, an enormous increase from the $10.8 million the company lost during the same period in 2004. "I got to hand it to the team," Rogers said in an August 24, 2005 interview with the *Financial Times.* "They've heard a lot of skeptical comments that TiVo

was never going to see a profit. We've shown the world that we can manage to achieve profitability. Our customer base is generating enough revenue to secure profitability."

Despite Rogers's enthusiasm, there was little expectation that TiVo would begin to operate profitably on a consistent basis after its achievement during the second quarter of 2005. Rogers conceded that the company was expected to lose between $20 million and $25 million in 2005, as it continued to emphasize increasing its business volume over sustaining profitability, something Rogers believed was in the best long-term interest for TiVo. "I am firmly convinced that TiVo can extend its strong brand identity and technology platform to the mass market through broader distribution by various carriers, and through growing its value as an advertising medium," he said in a July 9, 2005 interview with the *Online Reporter.* "After pioneering the digital video category, TiVo is now uniquely positioned to help multi-channel carriers, networks, and advertisers grow their businesses in an environment that presents new realities for how television is watched."

Principal Competitors

Microsoft Corporation; ReplayTV; THOMSON; Comcast Corporation; EchoStar Communications Corporation.

Further Reading

Bulikm, Beth Snyder, "Mr. Rogers Has New Neighborhood," *Advertising Age,* July 18, 2005, p. 31.

Carlson, Scott, "Best Buy Agrees to Be Sole Distributor of TiVo Digital Video Recorders," *Saint Paul Pioneer Press,* March 6, 2002.

"DIRECTV to Switch to Non-TiVo DVR," *Online Reporter,* August 13, 2005, p. 3.

Douglas, Torin, "TiVo—or the Case of the Dog That Never Barked," *Marketing Week,* March 8, 2001, p. 19.

London, Simon, "The Revolution Will Be Televised," *Financial Times,* February 17, 2004, p. 16.

Pitta, Julie, "Interactivity: The Great White Whale," *Forbes,* September 21, 1998, p. 60.

Robins, J. Max, "To TiVo or Not to TiVo," *Broadcasting & Cable,* October 3, 2005, p. 6.

Rothenberg, Randall, "Seeking the Next TV Revolution? Here's the Clue: It's Spelled TiVo," *Advertising Age,* June 5, 2000, p. 28.

Shaw, Russell, "Tapeless VCR Does the Thinking for Viewers," *Electronic Media,* April 5, 1999, p. 14.

Sherman, Jay, "TiVo Shifts Its Strategy Again," *TelevisionWeek,* August 29, 2005, p. 6.

"Sign of Coming DVR War: TiVo Cuts Price to $50," *Online Reporter,* September 10, 2005, p. 12.

Stroud, Jerri, "Move Over TiVo, Moxi's Box Muscles onto the DVR Scene," *St. Louis Post-Dispatch,* September 23, 2005.

"TiVo Cuts Back on Work Force As Subscriber Base Grows," *Silicon Valley/San Jose Business Journal,* April 13, 2001, p. 22.

"TiVo Reorganizes, Gets New Division, New CEO," *Online Reporter,* July 9, 2005, p. 3.

Van, Jon, "TiVo Partners with Comcast," *Chicago Tribune,* March 16, 2005.

—Jeffrey L. Covell

TRW Automotive Holdings Corp.

12001 Tech Center Drive
Livonia, Michigan 48150-2122
U.S.A.
Telephone: (734) 855-2600
Fax: (734) 266-5702
Web site: http://www.trwauto.com

Public Subsidiary of The Blackstone Group, L.P.
Incorporated: 1901 as Cleveland Cap Screw Co.
Employees: 59,900
Sales: $12.01 billion (2004)
Stock Exchanges: New York
Ticker Symbol: TRW
NAIC: 336399 All Other Motor Vehicle Parts
  Manufacturing; 336322 Other Motor Vehicle
  Electrical and Electronic Equipment Manufacturing;
  336360 Motor Vehicle Seating and Interior Trim
  Manufacturing

TRW Automotive Holdings Corp., successor to the conglomerate TRW Inc., is one of the world's largest automotive parts and systems suppliers, with a primary focus on safety systems. The TRW product lines include air bags, seat belts, and safety- and security-related electronics, as well as chassis systems and various automotive components. Nearly 60 percent of revenues are attributable to four large customers: Ford Motor Company, DaimlerChrysler AG, Volkswagen AG, and General Motors Corporation. The company has more than 200 facilities located in 24 countries; Europe accounts for 55 percent of revenues, and North America, another 37 percent.

The old TRW was acquired by Northrop Grumman Corporation in December 2002. Northrop Grumman wanted only TRW's space and defense operations and so sold the TRW automotive business to The Blackstone Group, L.P., a privately held investment firm, in February 2003. Blackstone then took the newly named TRW Automotive Holdings Corp. public through a February 2004 initial public offering, after which Blackstone held a 56.7 percent interest in TRW, Northrop

Grumman, 17.2 percent (later reduced to less than 10 percent), and TRW management, 1.7 percent.

Shaky Beginnings As Conglomerate

The conglomerate structure of the original TRW was deeply rooted in the company's history. In the early 1950s the Cleveland-based Thompson Products Co. was looking for an acquisition. J. David Wright, the company's general manager, and Horace Shepard, a vice-president, thought the auto valve and steering component maker needed more technical sophistication. Thompson, founded in 1901 as Cleveland Cap Screw Co. before adopting the Thompson Products moniker in 1926, had made a name for itself in automotive and aircraft engine parts and had become well known by sponsoring the famed Thompson Trophy Race, the aeronautical equivalent of auto racing's Indianapolis 500. In recent years, however, the company was facing a decline in manned aircraft and saw opportunities in aerospace and electronics.

To break into the young high-tech industry, Wright and Shepard tried to buy Hughes Aircraft Co. Hughes was willing to listen to bids but scoffed at the Thompson offer, which was thought to be ten times too low. Just a few months later, two of Hughes Aircraft's top scientist-executives, Simon Ramo and Dean Wooldridge, decided to leave Hughes to form a new electronic systems company, and Thompson put up $500,000 to bankroll the venture. Not long afterward, in 1953, Ramo-Wooldridge Corporation was established in Los Angeles and quickly gained solid standing in the advanced technology business, being awarded the systems engineering and technical direction contracts for such important missile programs as Atlas, Minuteman, Titan, and Thor.

By 1958 Thompson Products had invested $20 million—20 percent of its net worth at the time—for a 49 percent interest in Ramo-Wooldridge, and the two operations were merged as Thompson-Ramo-Wooldridge Corporation. Though united on paper, the company maintained separate corporate headquarters, with Wooldridge president in Los Angeles and Wright chairman in Cleveland. Ramo and Shepard, a former chief of production procurement for the Air Force, also had an active role in management.

Company Perspectives:

In early 2003, TRW Automotive began a new adventure when it became independent from its former parent company. A new company with a distinguished past, TRW Automotive is now focused solely on the needs of the automotive market.

TRW Automotive is the global leader in automotive safety systems. One of the top 10 automotive suppliers in the world, the company designs, develops and produces one of the broadest arrays of active and passive safety products in the industry. Its active safety systems enhance vehicle control and assist in avoiding collisions—while its passive safety systems are designed to minimize injury in the event of an accident.

While TRW Automotive still has places to go, its Technology Roadmap offers a timeline for getting there—and getting drivers and passengers there more safely. The TRW Automotive team of more than 63,000 employees around the globe is driven by a single vision: Producing the high-quality, safety-enhancing products of today and pioneering the safety systems of tomorrow.

The merger could hardly have started less auspiciously. In the midst of a recession, the Cleveland-based group was hit with a 14 percent drop in automotive business and a 34 percent drop in manned aircraft business. When business improved for the Cleveland division, the Los Angeles division got into trouble. Its venture into semiconductors collapsed in 1961, and the Robert McNamara era was beginning at the Pentagon. The West Coast scientists, who had known only cost-plus-fixed-fee contracts, needed help. They had to learn how to go from spending money to making it. This education was hampered by hard feelings between the two groups. The electronics end was not living up to its promise of being the business of the future. In the first four years following the merger, profit margins, which had been at the 4 percent-plus level in the mid-1950s, dropped to an average of barely 2 percent.

With the company facing such mundane tasks as cost-cutting, Wooldridge, who reportedly never really wanted to be a businessman anyway, resigned in 1962. As Wooldridge was getting settled in at his new job as a professor at the California Institute of Technology, Shepard was promoted to president and Ramo named vice-chairman. With Cleveland now in control of the company, the Los Angeles scientists were quickly reassured when the new management team instituted a number of reforms to get the company back on its feet, including writing off $3 million in inventory.

In 1963 Shepard and Wright began pruning unprofitable divisions. They sold most of the unprofitable Bumkor-Ramo computer division to Martin Marietta. The company retained partial ownership in Bumkor-Ramo but no longer played a large role in the company's plans. Shepard and Wright continued hammering out the company's plans for long-term growth, seeking specifically to raise profit margins. To this end, in 1964 they sold the microwave division and the division that made hi-fidelity components, intercoms, and language laboratories.

To shore up the company's auto parts division, they bought Ross Gear and Tool Company, a maker of mechanical and power steering units, and Marlin-Rockwell, a ball bearings manufacturer. The 7 percent profit margin of the new acquisitions, which had a combined profit of $5.7 million on sales of $76.5 million, helped boost TRW's overall margin to 4 percent in 1964, up a percentage point from a year earlier.

Improving Prospects As TRW Inc.

In 1965, in another look toward the future, Thompson-Ramo-Wooldridge adopted a shorter, less cumbersome name, the now household initials TRW Inc. Also in that year, the company's investment in aerospace and electronics became increasingly clear. In the previous decade, sales in space and electronics shot up from $14 million to $200 million. Despite that dramatic growth, the company's earnings still came mostly from its oldest business, auto parts. New and replacement parts accounted for 34 percent of TRW's $553 million in sales and 40 percent of its earnings. Chief among those products were its steering linkages, valves, and braking devices that it sold to General Motors, Ford, and Chrysler Corporation.

TRW's prospects improved in 1966. An auto parts boom helped the company's profitability. The Cleveland-based automotive group had a return of 6 percent on sales of $350 million. The equipment group, also in Cleveland, had an increase of sales to $200 million in aerospace and ordinance technology but lower profit margins because of start-up costs for unexpected demand in commercial aircraft. The Los Angeles-based TRW Systems had $250 million in sales and a 3 percent profit margin building and designing spacecraft and doing research. Totals were up to $870 million in sales for TRW, producing $36 million in profit for a 4.2 percent return. Even with the upturn in sales, the company was relying less on government contracts, down to about 44 percent from 70 percent ten years earlier.

With the company's finances on the upturn, the wrangling between Los Angeles and Cleveland declined. As *Business Week* reported, the discord was "under control, if not cured." The company continued tightening its operations in 1966. It bought United Carr, producer of automotive electronics, with $122 million in sales and sold its one consumer business, a hi-fi manufacturer. The late 1960s saw TRW pioneer in such auto technologies as rack and pinion steering and antilock braking systems.

TRW had grown into a conglomerate, a term disliked by company management. In 1969 TRW operated six groups that, in turn, administered 55 divisions. The company derived 32 percent of its revenues from aerospace products and systems and computer software, 28 percent from vehicle components for autos and trucks, 23 percent from electronic components and communication, and 17 percent from industrial products ranging from mechanical fasteners to automated controls.

To manage the increasingly far-flung company, TRW maintained strict management control over all operations. By encouraging communication between all levels of management and holding monthly manager meetings, TRW avoided the problems that had plagued other conglomerates. Another of TRW's successful management styles caught *Fortune*'s eye in 1966. The magazine covered in depth the happenings of a TRW

Key Dates:

1901: Cleveland Cap Screw Co. is founded in Cleveland, Ohio.
1926: Company is renamed Thompson Products Co.
1953: Specializing in missile systems, Ramo-Wooldridge Corporation is formed in Los Angeles with backing from Thompson Products.
1958: The two companies merge as Thompson-Ramo-Wooldridge Corporation.
1965: Company is renamed TRW Inc.
1972: Through purchase of the German firm Repa, TRW's auto business enters the field of occupant restraints.
1989: TRW acquires Talley Industries Inc.'s driver-side air bag unit.
1996: TRW divests its Information Systems and Services unit, which is later renamed Experian Corp.
1997: The air bag and steering wheel businesses of Magna International Inc. are acquired.
1999: British auto-parts maker LucasVarity plc is acquired for $7 billion.
2002: Northrop Grumman Corporation acquires TRW in an $11.8 billion deal.
2003: The Blackstone Group, L.P. acquires TRW's automotive unit, which begins operating as TRW Automotive Holdings Corp. and is based in Livonia, Michigan.
2004: Blackstone takes TRW Automotive public.

---

management meeting in Vermont, where 49 of the company's top executives had gathered annually since 1952 at an old farmhouse to think about the company's future.

TRW continued beefing up its auto parts business, acquiring Globe Industries, a Dayton-based maker of miniature AC and DC electric motors. At the same time, TRW's electronics group had grown to more than 20 plants in the United States, Canada, and Mexico. The company continued to evade problems that had plagued other conglomerates, posting a slight pretax gain of 16.4 percent, above the industry average of 13.3 percent.

In 1969 TRW named a new president, Ruben F. Mettler. One of his first big projects was a contract for a laboratory that NASA would send on the Viking probe to Mars. TRW won the challenge to provide one black box weighing 33 pounds with complex instruments capable of making biological and chemical tests to detect the most primitive forms of life. The NASA contract was worth only $50 million, not a big financial risk for a multibillion-dollar company like TRW, but the job was important for the company's prestige.

The auto parts business, in the meantime, was once again proving to be immune to cyclical trends in car output. The market for new parts was in a slump, but it was made up for by the accompanying increase in demand for replacement cars as consumers kept their cars on the roads longer. TRW also announced a move into business credit reporting, challenging Dun & Bradstreet.

The company's sound financial condition was unmistakable. For the five years preceding 1970, the company had average annual earnings and sales increases of 27 percent and 23 percent, respectively. But officials conceded that the company could not keep growing at that rate forever. It had acquired 38 companies through 1968, a pace it would not be able to maintain indefinitely. The company looked for future growth to run about 10 percent.

Risky Ventures in the 1970s and Early 1980s

The company's skillful management again became apparent in 1971, when TRW was forced to make cuts because of an aerospace recession. Its TRW Systems division had to cut the number of employees by 15 percent. Managers were not spared cuts either; 18 percent of the professional staff was laid off. The company's open management style enabled TRW to build a strong enough relationship with its employees that two-thirds of them were nonunion, perhaps preventing the labor squabbles that had appeared in other companies. Meanwhile, in a move more clearly important in hindsight, TRW's auto business entered the field of occupant restraints through the purchase of the German firm Repa.

TRW made a risky venture in 1976, entering the tricky market of electronic point-of-sale (POS) machines. Those machines had boosted profits for retailers, but not for manufacturers. Its proposed 2001 system targeted the general market and cost $4,000 per unit, similar to competitors. TRW's move into POS was largely a defensive tactic. The electronic credit authorization business it had pioneered in the 1960s was coming under increasing competition. Then NCR, the overall leader in POS machines, launched a POS system incorporating credit checking in 1975. TRW attempted to enter the market with an established customer base by acquiring the service contracts for the 65,000 customers Singer had built up during its short, ill-fated move into the POS market. TRW remained cautious, however, delivering only 200 to 300 machines in 1976, mostly to the May Co. Altogether that year nonfood retailers ordered 24,500 POS terminals worth $94 million, and the market was picking up.

In 1976 TRW achieved the moment of glory it had long awaited with Viking's historic landing on Mars. The company took out full-page newspaper ads proclaiming "That lab is our baby." Appropriately, Mettler, 52, who had pushed for TRW to compete for the Viking contract, was named to succeed Horace A. Shepard as chairman and chief executive officer when Shepard retired the next year.

Aerospace ventures continued to play an important role in the company's finances. In 1977 TRW was still the chief engineer for U.S. intercontinental ballistic missiles. Aerospace and government electronic revenues were providing a cool $60 million in profits on revenue of $440 million. The electronics division had $300 million in sales. The data communications unit was also doing well with over $150 million in sales. It had established a retail credit bureau, a business credit system, and was an international maker of data communications equipment. Nevertheless, auto and commercial parts were still accounting for twice as much in sales and five times as much in earnings.

In 1980 TRW and Fujitsu Limited, Japan's largest computer maker, formed a joint venture. TRW had a 3,000-person service organization, reportedly the largest independent network in the

United States for data process maintenance, with a special team to develop software. Each company invested $100 million, with Fujitsu keeping a 51 percent share and TRW, 45 percent. TRW initiated the venture, seeking a foreign partner to perform maintenance work for its POSs. Fujitsu, which earned 68 percent of its revenue from data processing, was eager to expand overseas to increase its economies of scale to compete with International Business Machines Corporation (IBM) back home. Fujitsu named a majority of the directors of the new company so it could qualify for Japanese export and financing tax breaks, but TRW took charge of running it. One of the new company's first moves was to buy TRW's ailing POS and ATM maker division. The company, hoping in the beginning to capture a large segment of the small and medium-sized computer market, predicted sales of $500 million to $1 billion by the decade's end.

Despite TRW's careful planning, the POS and Fujitsu deals both proved unsuccessful. The competition from established POS makers, particularly IBM and NCR, was too great. Nonetheless, TRW remained a strong, highly visible company. *Forbes* in 1983 called it "a paragon" for other conglomerates. It had by then grown to $5 billion in sales spread across 47 different businesses and had 300 locations in 25 countries. It had also grown to be the number one producer of valves for automobiles and aircraft plus a wide range of other products. With a 16 percent return on stockholders' equity as proof, *Forbes* called TRW one of the best managed, most successful American companies. This outward success, however, belied the company's growing inefficiency.

Late 1980s and Early 1990s: Restructuring, Auto Products, Air Bags

By the time Joseph T. Gorman was named president and chief operating officer of TRW in 1985 (he became chairman, president, and chief executive officer in 1988 when Chairman Ruben Mettler retired), the company had grown bloated, inefficient, and overdiversified. It hit a low in 1985 when it lost $7 million on sales of $5.92 billion. Mettler and Gorman instituted a three-year restructuring plan that aimed to focus resources on core businesses, to slash staff, and to increase efficiency. The new TRW would concentrate on three main areas: automotive products, space and defense projects, and information systems and services. Among the noncore businesses divested were the firm's energy division. Staff was reduced from 93,200 in 1985 to 73,200 in 1988.

From 1986 to 1990, TRW's financial outlook improved somewhat with the new corporate structure. Although sales rose each year to a high of $8.17 billion in 1990, profits were stagnant and actually fell from 3.7 percent in 1988 to 3.6 percent in 1989 to 2.6 percent in 1990.

In 1989 TRW made a huge and risky commitment to what at the time was an unprofitable business: air bags. That year it purchased Talley Industries Inc.'s driver-side air bag unit for $85 million, plus royalties on any air bag sold in North America through the year 2001. TRW also began to invest in the development of passenger-side air bags. In total, the company invested more than half a billion dollars in its air-bag business by 1992. Until the fourth quarter of 1991, TRW lost money on air bags. Although Ford had chosen TRW as its sole supplier of the

safety devices in 1989, TRW's fortunes suffered in 1990 because of a Ford recall of 55,000 vehicles with defective air bags and a massive fire at TRW's passenger-side air-bag plant (TRW air bags used sodium azide as its propellant, a chemical prone to explode in the manufacturing process). TRW's automotive business also suffered from a recession in the automotive industry in 1989 and 1990.

The space and defense sectors of TRW were also suffering from the end of the Cold War and the resultant leveling off in defense spending. With its two main sectors down, overall TRW sales for 1991 fell 3.1 percent to $7.91 billion. Gorman embarked on another restructuring late that year, incurring a $365 million charge that resulted in a $140 million loss for the year. This restructuring aimed to remake TRW into primarily an automotive products company, with reduced operations and investments in the space and defense and information sectors. With air bags now profitable and generating $600 million in annual revenue, the company aimed to take advantage of their increasing popularity with consumers and the mandatory inclusion of dual air bags in vehicles by the year 1998. Gorman also set his sights on overseas markets not only for air bags but also for TRW's power-steering systems and engine valves.

By 1994, TRW's automotive operations accounted for 63 percent of total sales, compared to 56 percent in 1992 (and 40 percent in the early 1980s), whereas space and defense accounted for only 31 percent, compared to 35 percent in 1992 (and 50 percent in the early 1980s). The defense operations were also reduced, with sales to the U.S. government falling to 28 percent of total sales, compared to the 45 percent figure of the late 1980s. Meanwhile, international sales accounted for 35 percent of total sales in 1994 (compared to 25 percent in 1985), led by sales to Japanese automakers of $800 million. The 1994 sales total of $9.09 billion represented a 14.3 percent increase over the previous year. On the negative side, Talley Industries brought a lawsuit against TRW in 1994, which resulted in a $138 million judgment against TRW the following year.

Late 1990s: Divesting Info Systems Unit, Bolstering Auto Business Through Acquisitions

Further paring down to the core, TRW in 1996 sold off the bulk of its TRW Information Systems and Services Inc. unit for a little more than $1 billion to a buyout group led by Thomas H. Lee Co. and Bain Capital, Inc. (The new owners quickly resold the unit, now named Experian Corp., to the Great Universal Stores plc, a U.K. firm later renamed GUS plc.) Later in 1996 TRW closed several of its automotive plants and laid off 2,300 workers amid increased competition in the automotive safety system sector. The following year proceeds from the information systems divestiture were used to help fund two significant acquisitions. On the automotive side, TRW bought majority control of the air bag and steering wheel businesses of Magna International Inc. for about $418 million. The units, based in Germany, had 1996 sales of $688 million. Also acquired in 1997 was BDM International Inc., a provider of information technology to the government and defense sectors. BDM, based in McLean, Virginia, was bought for about $975 million, making the deal the largest yet in TRW's history. Late in 1997 TRW pulled the plug on its $3.5 billion Odyssey satellite system, a joint venture with Montreal-based Teleglobe Inc. After years of development, TRW had been unable to secure sufficient backing from other major telecommunications firms for this proposed satellite phone service.

Under intense pressure to cut costs to stay competitive, TRW announced plans in July 1998 to shut down more than a dozen of its automotive plants and cut that sector of its workforce by 7,500, aiming to eliminate about $100 million in annual operating costs. During this period, there was persistent speculation about (and pressure from Wall Street for) a breakup of the company—specifically, a spinoff of the automotive operations that would enable TRW to concentrate solely on the better-performing space, defense, and information operations. There was much surprise and some skepticism as well, then, when TRW in January 1999 agreed to acquire the British autoparts firm LucasVarity plc for $7 billion in cash. LucasVarity, the product of a 1996 merger of Lucas Industries Plc and Varity Corporation, was a leading producer of automotive brakes, and the merger was expected to enable TRW to make integrated systems involving TRW's steering and suspension components and the acquired firm's brakes. The combination was expected to yield annual cost savings of between $200 million and $300 million. The deal closed in May 1999.

The acquisition of LucasVarity pushed TRW's debt load to a staggering $9.3 billion. Gorman had to find ways to relieve the company of some of this burden, and toward a goal of cutting debt by $2.5 billion TRW divested several noncore automotive units by early 2000. The largest unit jettisoned was Lucas Diesel Systems, maker of diesel fuel-injection parts, sold to Delphi Automotive Systems Corporation for $871 million. Late in 1999, in the meantime, David M. Cote was brought onboard as president and chief operating officer as well as heir apparent to Gorman. Cote was a 25-year veteran of General Electric Company (GE), where he most recently served as head of the $5.6 billion appliances unit.

Ending of the TRW Conglomerate Era with 2002 Northrop Grumman Takeover

TRW's automotive operations now generated nearly two-thirds of TRW's sales, which totaled $17.2 billion in 2000. That year, a slowdown in the U.S. auto industry led to a 17 percent drop in profits to $471.2 million. After Cote took over as CEO in February 2001 (and then chairman that summer), he cut several thousands jobs from the payroll, replaced eight key executives, and reduced the massive debt by about $1 billion. In contrast to the more autocratic Gorman, Cote moved to decentralize the TRW operations, consolidating the firm's automotive businesses into one unit, TRW Automotive, based in Livonia, Michigan. Analysts continued to call for the divestment of the automotive unit, but Cote's hands were tied: The still massive debt and a slumping auto industry made such a move next to impossible.

Cote also did not stick around long enough for conditions to become favorable for such a move. In February 2002 he abruptly resigned when offered the chance to succeed Lawrence Bossidy, his mentor at GE, as head of Honeywell International Inc. Cote's stunning departure precipitated a slide in TRW's stock, which opened the door for a near immediate hostile takeover bid by Northrop Grumman Corporation, which offered $47 per share, or about $5.8 billion in stock, plus the assumption

of $5 billion in debt. TRW, now led on an interim basis by Philip Odeen, who had run the firm's Washington office for many years before semi-retiring, quickly rejected the offer and announced plans to sell off its aeronautical systems unit and to spin the automotive unit off to shareholders. Northrop raised its bid to $53 per share in April, bumping the total price up to $11.9 billion, but TRW continued to resist. In June the company reached an agreement to sell the aeronautical unit to Goodrich Corporation for $1.5 billion (a deal completed in October), and it also began soliciting bids for all or parts of the company from other defense firms. BAE Systems plc, General Dynamics Corporation, and Raytheon Company all submitted bids, but in the end Northrop prevailed by boosting its bid again, to $60 a share, or $7.8 billion plus the assumption of $4 billion in debt.

New Beginnings As TRW Automotive Holdings Corp.

Northrop Grumman completed its takeover of TRW in December 2002. In the interim, Northrop found a buyer for TRW Automotive. The Blackstone Group, L.P., a privately held investment firm, agreed to buy the unit in a $4.72 billion deal announced in November and completed in February 2003. The newly named TRW Automotive Holdings Corp. was headed by John C. Plant, who had been president and CEO of the former TRW's automotive business since 2001. He had come to TRW via the LucasVarity acquisition. TRW Automotive, which reported first-year revenues in 2003 of $11.35 billion, stood as one of the ten largest automotive suppliers in North America with significant operations in Europe as well. Primarily focused on active and passive safety- and security-related automotive parts and systems, the new TRW also produced steering systems, engine valves, fasteners, and suspension components.

Blackstone took TRW public in February 2004, selling 24.1 million shares of common stock at $28 per share. This reduced Blackstone's 78.4 percent stake in TRW to 56.7 percent, and Northrop Grumman's interest from 19.6 percent to 17.2 percent. (Northrop sold 7.26 million of its TRW shares in early 2005, further reducing its stake to just under 10 percent.) TRW Automotive got off to a rough start because of the continuing struggles of U.S. automakers, who were placing intense pricing pressure on their suppliers, and because of high raw-material costs. As it sought future growth through emerging areas of auto safety such as side and curtain air bags, front crash sensors, vehicle stability systems, and tire pressure monitoring systems, TRW also was targeting growth in China by setting up several ventures there. TRW worked as well to pay down its still heavy debt load, a hangover from a combination of debt inherited from the former TRW and debt incurred through Blackstone's leveraged buyout. Cost-cutting efforts helped cut long-term debt from $3.71 billion to $3.12 billion during 2004. The following year the company announced the closure of several more plants as well as a modest acquisition. In September 2005 TRW reached an agreement to acquire majority control of Dalphi Metal Espana, S.A. for $240 million. Based in Madrid, Spain, Dalphi produced steering wheels and air bags for a variety of Europan carmakers, making for a nice fit with TRW's existing operations.

Principal Subsidiaries

Kelsey-Hayes Company; Lake Center Industries Transportation Inc.; REMSA of America, Inc.; TRW Automotive Inc.; TRW

Automotive U.S. LLC; TRW Safety Systems Inc.; TRW Vehicle Safety Systems Inc.; TRW Occupant Restraint Systems GmbH (Austria); SM Sistemas Modulares Ltda. (Brazil); TRW Automotive Ltda. (Brazil); Kelsey-Hayes Canada Limited; TRW Canada Limited; CSG TRW Chassis Systems (China); Shanghai TRW Automotive Safety Systems Co., Ltd. (China); TRW Automotive Component Technical Service (Shanghai) Co., Ltd. (China); TRW Automotive Components (Shanghai) Co., Ltd. (China); TRW Automotive Research & Development Co., Ltd. (China); TRW Engine Components (Langfang) Corp. Ltd. (China); TRW Fawer Commercial Vehicle Steering Company Ltd. (China); TRW System Consulting Services Shanghai Co., Ltd. (China); Lucas Autobrzdy s.r.o. (Czech Republic); LucasVarity s.r.o. (Czech Republic); TRW Autoelektronika s.r.o. (Czech Republic); TRW Carr s.r.o. (Czech Republic); TRW-DAS a.s. (Czech Republic); TRW Volant a.s. (Czech Republic); Autocruise SA (France); La Source Composants Moteurs S.A. (France); TRW Automotive Distribution France S.A.S.; TRW Carr France SNC; TRW Composants Moteurs S.A. (France); TRW France S.A.S.; TRW Systemes de Freinage S.A.S. (France); Lucas Automotive GmbH (Germany); TRW Advanced Plastics Technologies GmbH & Co. KG (Germany); TRW Airbag Systems GmbH (Germany); TRW Automotive Electronics & Components GmbH & Co. KG (Germany); TRW Automotive GmbH (Germany); TRW Automotive Safety Systems GmbH (Germany); TRW KFZ Ausrustung GmbH (Germany); TRW Automotive Italia S.p.A. (Italy); TRW Automotive Ricambi Italia SpA (Italy); TRW Aftermarket Japan Co. Ltd.; TRW Automotive Japan Co., Ltd.; TRW Controls & Fasteners Inc. (Korea); TRW Overseas Inc. (Korea); Lucas Automotive Sdn Bdh (Malaysia); LucasVarity (M) Sdn. Bhd. (Malaysia); TRW Steering & Suspension (M) Sdn. Bhd. (Malaysia); Forjas y Maquinas, S.A. de C.V. (Mexico); Frenos y Mecanismos SA de CV (Mexico); Reinvestmientos Especiales de Mexico S. de R.L. de C.V.; TRW Electronica Ensambles S.A. de C.V. (Mexico); TRW Occupant Restraints de Chihuahua SA de CV (Mexico); TRW Sistemas de Direcciones, S.A. de C.V. (Mexico); TRW Steering Wheel Systems de Chihuahua SA de CV (Mexico); TRW Vehicle Safety Systems de Mexico S.A. de C.V. (Mexico); TRW Braking Systems Polska Sp. z o.o. (Poland); TRW Polska Sp. z o.o. (Poland); TRW Steering Systems Poland Sp.z o.o.; Lucas Automotive Pecas e Automoveis, Ltda. (Portugal); TRW Automotive Safety Systems S.R.L. (Romania); TRW Occupant Restraints South Africa Inc.; Eurofren Brakes, S.L.U. (Spain); TRW Automotive Espana, S.L. (Spain); TRW Switzerland GmbH; LucasVarity (Thailand) Co. Ltd.; TRW Steering & Suspension Co. Ltd. (Thailand); TRW Otomotiv Dagitim ve Ticaret A.S.(Turkey); Components Venezolanos de Direccion, S.A. (Venezuela); TRW Automotive Systems Ltd. (U.K.); TRW Fastening Systems Ltd. (U.K.); TRW Limited (U.K.); TRW LucasVarity Electric Steering Ltd. (U.K.); TRW Steering Systems Ltd. (U.K.); TRW Systems Ltd. (U.K.).

Principal Competitors

Delphi Corporation; Robert Bosch GmbH; Continental Teves, Inc.; Visteon Corporation; Koyo Seiko Co., Ltd.; ZF Friedrichshafen AG; Advics Co., Ltd.; Autoliv, Inc.; Takata Corporation; Key Safety Systems, Inc.; Illinois Tool Works Inc.; Raymond Limited; Nifco Inc.; Textron Inc.; Leopold Kostal GmbH & Co. KG; Valeo; Tokai Rika Co., Ltd.; Eaton Corporation.

Further Reading

Ball, Jeffrey, and Robert Frank, ''TRW to Buy LucasVarity for $7 Billion,'' *Wall Street Journal,* January 29, 1999, p. A3.

Berss, Marcia, ''Nothing Is in the Bag,'' *Forbes,* March 4, 1991, p. 97.

Dyer, Davis, *TRW: Pioneering Technology and Innovation Since 1900,* Boston: Harvard Business School Press, 1998, 503 p.

England, Robert Stowe, ''Less Sizzle, More Steak,'' *Financial World,* August 4, 1992, pp. 20–21.

Fehr-Snyder, Kerry, ''TRW Threatens to Fight $138 Million Trial Ruling: Talley Wins Lawsuit over Sale of Air-Bag Business,'' *Phoenix Gazette,* June 8, 1995, p. C1.

Flint, Jerry, ''The TRW Way,'' *Forbes,* July 31, 1995, pp. 45–46.

Galuszka, Peter, ''Air Bags Are Deflating TRW,'' *Business Week,* May 18, 1998, pp. 111, 114.

Gerdel, Thomas W., ''Northrop Bids to Take Over TRW,'' *Cleveland Plain Dealer,* February 23, 2002, p. A1.

——, ''TRW Enters New Era: Purchase Puts Company Back on Growth Path,'' *Cleveland Plain Dealer,* January 31, 1999, p. 1H.

——, ''TRW Plans to Sell Four Major Units,'' *Cleveland Plain Dealer,* May 18, 1999, p. 1C.

——, ''TRW's Heir Apparent,'' *Cleveland Plain Dealer,* April 16, 2000, p. 1H.

——, ''Walking a Tightrope at TRW: Huge Debt Limits Options As New Chief Seeks Profit Boost,'' *Cleveland Plain Dealer,* August 16, 2001, p. C1.

Gerdel, Thomas W., and Peter Krouse, ''The Stewards of TRW: Three CEOs Have Had the Same Title, but Distinctly Different Tasks,'' *Cleveland Plain Dealer,* June 30, 2002, p. G1.

Gerdel, Thomas W., and Sandra Livingston, ''TRW Plans to Close Valve Plant,'' *Cleveland Plain Dealer,* October 19, 2001, p. A1.

Kosdrosky, Terry, ''TRW Purchase Part of Move to Smaller, Targeted Deals,'' *Crain's Detroit Business,* September 12, 2005, p. 3.

Krouse, Peter, ''Buyer Found for TRW Auto Unit,'' *Cleveland Plain Dealer,* November 20, 2002, p. C1.

——, ''TRW to Northrop: Sold! $7.8 Billion Stock Deal to Shut Down Lyndhurst Operation,'' *Cleveland Plain Dealer,* July 2, 2002, p. A1.

Lipin, Steven, ''TRW Reaches Accord to Buy BDM International,'' *Wall Street Journal,* November 21, 1997, p. A3.

Mettler, Ruben F., *The Little Brown Hen That Could: The Growth Story of TRW Inc.,* New York: Newcomen Society, 1982, 24 p.

Nodell, Bobbi, ''Hughes, TRW Offset Defense Cuts with Telecommunications Projects,'' *Los Angeles Business Journal,* April 19, 1993, p. 52.

Norton, Erle, and Gary Putka, ''TRW's Sale of Unit Is Likely to Be Only a First Step,'' *Wall Street Journal,* February 12, 1996, p. B4.

Palmer, Jay, ''Playing It Safe,'' *Barron's,* July 12, 2004, pp. 19–20.

Parker, Jocelyn, ''Newly Independent Auto-Parts Spinoff TRW Automotive Gets Second Chance,'' *Detroit Free Press,* March 20, 2004.

Pasztor, Andy, Joann Lublin, and Anne Marie Squeo, ''Honeywell Names TRW's Cote As Successor to Retiring Chairman,'' *Wall Street Journal,* February 20, 2002, p. A6.

Phillips, Stephen, ''Just Don't Get in Joe Gorman's Way,'' *Business Week,* November 12, 1990, pp. 88–89.

——, ''TRW Forming Air-Bag Alliance,'' *Cleveland Plain Dealer,* December 17, 1996, p. 1C.

Prizinsky, David, ''TRW Expects Global Strategy to Yield Major Sales Growth,'' *Crain's Cleveland Business,* November 18, 1996, p. 7.

Schiller, Zach, ''TRW Puts an End to 'Odyssey','' *Cleveland Plain Dealer,* December 18, 1997, p. 1C.

Sendler, Emily R., ''TRW to Close Plants, Cut Jobs in Auto Segment,'' *Wall Street Journal,* July 30, 1998, p. A3.

Sherefkin, Robert, ''Blackstone Strikes Tentative Deal for TRW Automotive,'' *Automotive News,* November 25, 2002, p. 33.

——, ''TRW Stock Nosedives After IPO,'' *Crain's Detroit Business,* September 13, 2004, p. 4.

Shirouzu, Norihiko, and Robin Sidel, ''TRW Tries to Show Its Automotive Business Is a Good Bet,'' *Wall Street Journal,* March 18, 2002, p. B6.

Sidel, Robin, and J. Lynn Lunsford, ''TRW to Sell Aeronautics Unit to Goodrich,'' *Wall Street Journal,* June 20, 2002, p. B4.

Skeel, Shirley, ''Tracking Satellite Joe,'' *Management Today,* January 1990, pp. 60–66.

Squeo, Anne Marie, ''TRW May Be Considering a Farewell to Cars, Not Arms,'' *Wall Street Journal,* February 15, 2002, p. B4.

Sweetman, Bill, ''Breaking Up Is Hard to Do,'' *Interavia,* April 2002, pp. 11–12, 14.

Thornton, Emily, ''To Sell in Japan, Just Keep Trying,'' *Fortune,* January 25, 1993, pp. 103–04.

Tompor, Susan, ''TRW Leader Says the Future Is All About Safety,'' *Detroit Free Press,* April 11, 2005.

Webb, Alysha, ''TRW Automotive to Bolster Its China Operations,'' *Automotive News,* November 29, 2004, p. 32E.

White, Joseph B., and Gregory L. White, ''Delphi Automotive Agrees to Acquire TRW's Lucas Diesel for $871 Million,'' *Wall Street Journal,* November 24, 1999, p. B14.

—update: David E. Salamie

Ultimate Leisure Group PLC

<table>
<tr><td>

26 Mosley Street
Newcastle upon Tyne NE1 1DF
United Kingdom
Telephone: 0191 261-8800
Fax: 0191 221-2282
Web site: http://www.ultimateleisure.com

Public Company
Incorporated: 1997
Employees: 1,000
Sales: £36.4 million (2005)
Stock Exchanges: London
Ticker Symbol: ULG
NAIC: 722410 Drinking Places (Alcoholic Beverages);
   722211 Limited-Service Restaurants; 721110 Hotels
   (Except Casino Hotels) and Motels

</td></tr>
</table>

Ultimate Leisure Group PLC operates more than 30 bars and nightclubs in northern England and Ireland, most of which it owns. The firm's sites are typically large, stylish venues located in established ''drinking circuit'' areas and geared toward a younger clientele. The company utilizes several different bar concepts, including lounge-styled Chase/Barbacca/Quilted Llama, Western-themed Coyote Wild, and tropical Beach/Blubambu. In 2005 founder and Chairman Allan Rankin, CEO Bob Senior, and several other top managers and directors left the firm under pressure from stockholders who wanted expansion to speed up.

Beginnings

Ultimate Leisure Group was founded in 1997 in Newcastle-upon-Tyne, England, with backing from local businessman Allan Rankin and his family, who operated metal galvanizing concern the Metnor Group and other companies. The firm was chartered to focus on developing large, stylish venues in drinking circuit areas that were already home to numerous bars, with particular emphasis placed on attracting women, which was a time-honored way to lure male customers. The new company would be headed by Bob Senior, who had more than two decades' experience in the pub business.

Newcastle, located on England's northeast coast, was renowned for its nightlife, with some 135 bars in the city's mile-square Bigg Market area. At this time more than half were owned by brewing company Scottish & Newcastle, and because of restrictive local laws new liquor licenses were essentially unavailable, with the only way to enter the market through acquisition.

Shortly after commencing operations, the firm purchased five bars and a hotel in the center of Newcastle along with an undeveloped property on that city's Quayside, where the 560-capacity Chase bar opened the following year. The firm had spent £3 million acquiring and renovating the lounge-style venue, which featured a beer garden nestled under the Tyne bridge. Revenues for 1998 were £5 million, with a profit of £680,000.

After acquiring three more bars and a hotel in nearby Whitley Bay, by early 1999 Ultimate Leisure was operating a total of nine pubs and two hotels. These included the Waterside Hotel and the Vault, Ram Jam, Love Shack, and Chase bars in Newcastle; and the Rex Hotel and Deep Club Cafe in Whitley Bay. The company had 300 employees.

Public Stock Offering in 1999

In late July 1999 the firm's stock began trading on the London Stock Exchange's Alternative Investment Market, after which its name became Ultimate Leisure Group PLC. The initial offering of a one-fourth ownership stake raised £6 million, which would soon be used for upgrading existing facilities and to make new acquisitions. Afterward, the family of co-founder and Commercial Director Allan Rankin continued to hold a controlling interest in the firm.

In November four more Newcastle bars were purchased from Allied Leisure PLC for £3.7 million, and a few weeks later two bars and a restaurant in Sunderland were acquired for £1.3 million from an independent operator. The company also had recently refurbished the Rex Hotel in Whitley Bay and the Yel Bar in Newcastle and begun work on several other new sites. The first of these to open, in early March 2000, was the Sports Bar Cafe in Newcastle, which had been developed at a cost of £1 million.

For the fiscal year ended June 30, 2000, Ultimate Leisure reported revenues of £12 million, up from £8.3 million in 1999,

Company Perspectives:

Quite simply we are owners, designers and operators of atmospheric drinking venues in which enjoyment flourishes.

Ultimate Leisure, predominantly based in the North East of England, is one of the most exciting and innovative bar operators in the country.

The Company's philosophy is to identify under developed, prime sites; to design and develop these into unique, stylish and imaginative drinking venues; and to attract and empower and develop staff who commit to the Ultimate Leisure ethos.

With over 30 trading sites Ultimate Leisure is the predominant bar operator in the North East of England and is expanding its concepts further afield into other towns and cities.

and a profit of £3.2 million. Later that summer the new 995-capacity Sea nightclub opened in Newcastle's popular Quayside area, which featured a dance floor and VIP lounge. Another club in Newcastle, Masters Bar, also had recently been refurbished with modern, stylish fixtures and renamed Bar M.

Expansion Beyond Newcastle Continuing in 2001

As competition in the area increased and national firms began to aggressively seek entrée into Newcastle's prime drinking circuit, Ultimate Leisure began looking at more opportunities for growth further afield. In early 2001 sites were acquired in Sunderland, Durham, and South Shields, and in June the firm reached an agreement to buy a hotel/restaurant called The Gresham in the Jesmond suburb of Newcastle for £570,000. Jesmond recently had become a hot destination for drinkers, and the company began converting the hotel into a large bar. Ultimate Leisure also unveiled the refurbished Chase Bar in Newcastle in June 2001, with capacity increased to 780.

In July the company paid £1.6 million to buy an established bar/nightclub in the college town of Durham called Klute, which could serve 400. At this time Allan Rankin was named to the newly created title of chief executive of the company, with Bob Senior serving as managing director and Jon Pither as board chair. For 2001 sales of £16.6 million were recorded. The firm now had 500 employees.

In October 2001 Ultimate Leisure opened a new 1,300-capacity bar in Sunderland called Beach, which featured a tropical theme that would later reappear elsewhere. Fall also saw more venues purchased outside the Newcastle area, including the Glasshouse bar in Nottingham and a 1,600-capacity venue in Rotherham that was closed for refurbishing.

In early 2002 £13 million of credit was secured through the Royal Bank of Scotland, at the same time that a new license in Newcastle's Bigg Market was acquired. It was the first in the area with a 2 a.m. closing time, later than the British pub's standard last call of 11 p.m. The license would be used for a new 1,300-capacity bar under development on a leased site. In May the company also bought the Venice Bar in South Shields, which was licensed to serve drinks until 2 a.m. as well.

The late summer of 2002 saw Beach Rotherham opened, along with a Sunderland pub that had been converted into a

Chase bar. In September the firm's late-closing Bigg Market property was completed and opened as Blubambu, a variation on the Beach theme.

Debut of Coyote Wild in Autumn of 2002

The fall of 2002 also saw an 800-capacity venue opened in South Shields called Coyote Wild, inspired by the recent Hollywood film *Coyote Ugly* in which lightly clad female bartenders danced on top of a bar and sprayed water on patrons. It was decorated in a western theme and featured a mechanized "bucking bronco" that customers could ride to win drinks. Later in the year a lease also was signed on a property in Belfast, Northern Ireland, and a bar was purchased in Mansfield.

In early 2003 the firm linked up with a pair of British television stars known as Ant & Dec, who invested £175,000 to help convert the firm's Johnny Ringo's bar in Newcastle into The Lodge, which had a license to serve drinks until 1 a.m. April saw the opening of the Bambu Beach club at the recently leased site in Belfast's Odyssey Complex, and in May the firm's second Coyote Wild opened in Mansfield, while a Chase-style bar called The Quilted Llama opened in Nottingham.

Revenues for 2003 topped £26.5 million, with a net profit of £6.8 million before taxes. One-third of earnings had been generated outside of the company's Newcastle stronghold. Employment now stood at more than 1,000.

In August 2003 Ultimate Leisure paid £4.2 million for two neighboring bars and a nightclub with a combined capacity of 1,000 in Belfast. In October the firm raised an additional £20 million through a new issue of 6.9 million shares of stock.

The company was renovating a 140-year-old former post office in Derby that it had recently purchased, which was opened as a Coyote Wild bar in December. A total investment of £3 million had been made in the 900-capacity venue, which would serve alcohol until 1:30 a.m. Other properties also had been acquired recently in Leeds, Ireland, and Derby, and work on converting a former boathouse site in Durham into a new Chase was ongoing.

Gresham Dispute Reaching the High Court in 2003

Although most of the company's acquisitions had been relatively straightforward, the conversion of the Gresham Hotel in Newcastle into a 450-capacity bar had faced particularly strong opposition from neighbors in the upscale Jesmond area. There were already other bars nearby, but protesters voiced fears that the new venue would bring an increase in noise and rowdy, drunken behavior like that associated with Bigg Market. It was in fact legal to transfer the license of a bar that had been demolished by order of the city, as the firm was seeking to do, but in January the transfer request was turned down by local magistrates because of inadequate soundproofing. The case was appealed to the High Court in London, and in the summer, after word surfaced that the anti-Gresham campaign was being funded by a rival firm, the High Court decided in favor of Ultimate Leisure. In December the license transfer was approved, and the venue was finally opened as Barbacca. Several months later, however, the ruling was again overturned, though the company was given permission to continue operating while an appeal was made.

In March 2004 a new Chase bar opened in Durham, which had taken five years to complete due to another lengthy public inquiry. In August the firm opened its refurbished City Vaults bar in Newcastle's Bigg Market area, with capacity for 1,200 and a late license, at a cost of £1.5 million. That same month a nightclub called Halo and a second Quilted Llama bar, with total capacity of 1,600, opened in Leeds in the former Trinity St. David's church building next to the University. September saw the firm buy a site in Cork, Southern Ireland, which it began refurbishing. Also in 2004, board Chairman Jon Pither retired, and Allan Rankin took his place and turned the chief executive duties over to Bob Senior.

Public drinking had been deregulated recently in England after many decades of an 11 p.m. pub closing time, and much media coverage was given to the feared increase in binge and round-the-clock drinking it might cause. Ultimate Leisure responded to such concerns by announcing that it would not offer all-inclusive drink pricing at its bars, and would not change any to 24-hour service.

In the latter half of 2004 and into early 2005 growth began to slow as the firm found suitable new properties harder to acquire, and business declined at some bars due to fierce competition and stepped-up policing in the wake of deregulation. The firm also was experiencing delays in finishing its Cork Blubambu bar, a Chase in South Shields, and Jimmy'z in Newcastle Quayside.

Management Shake-Up in 2005

Rumors about a possible sale of the company began surfacing in the summer of 2005, and after a dispute with shareholders who wanted expansion sped up, in August the firm's top management, including CEO Bob Senior, Chairman Allan Rankin, and several board members, resigned. Rankin sold his holdings in the firm, and Senior and another company executive founded Utopian

Leisure Group to re-enter the bar/restaurant business with £50 million in new funding. Mark Jones was appointed executive chairman of Ultimate Leisure, and pledged to continue making acquisitions in accordance with shareholder wishes.

Less than a decade after its founding, Ultimate Leisure Group PLC had assembled a collection of more than two dozen bars and nightclubs in northern England and Ireland, many of which used the firm's beach, western, or lounge themes. Under new management, the company sought to maintain its pace of expansion in an increasingly challenging market.

Principal Competitors

Luminar PLC; Punch Taverns PLC; JD Wetherspoon PLC; Enterprise Inns PLC; Mitchells & Butler PLC; Spirit Group Ltd.; Rindberg Holding Company; Inventive Leisure PLC; Greene King PLC.

Further Reading

Anderson, Guy, "Record Profits Again at Ultimate," *Journal* (Newcastle, U.K.), February 25, 2005, p. 2.

——, "Ultimate Keeps Moving On," *Journal* (Newcastle, U.K.), September 17, 2004, p. 3.

Armitstead, Louise, and Matthew Goodman, "Investors Push for Ultimate Shake-Out," *Sunday Times,* May 15, 2005, p. 2.

Barr, Gordon, "TV Stars Are Real Lads of Leisure," *Evening Chronicle* (Newcastle, U.K.), February 26, 2003, p. 13.

"Battle of Osborne Road Flares Up," *Journal* (Newcastle, U.K.), July 21, 2004, p. 5.

Clark, Dave, "Large-Scale Pub Is Set for Fish Market," *Evening Chronicle* (Newcastle, U.K.), October 19, 1999, p. 3.

Finn, Moira, "Ultimate Aims for Market Flotation," *Journal* (Newcastle, U.K.), June 28, 1999, p. 41.

——, "Ultimate Works on Its Appeal to Women," *Journal* (Newcastle, U.K.), June 30, 1999, p. 23.

"Flotation Is Key to Ultimate Leisure Expansion," *Journal* (Newcastle, U.K.), July 28, 1999, p. 26.

Hetherington, Peter, "Resident Anger As Bars Exploit Licence to Booze," *Guardian* (London), May 24, 2003, p. 9.

Kendall, Rik, "Ultimate Moves Outside Home Base As Big Player," *Journal* (Newcastle, U.K.), January 12, 2000, p. 34.

Malkani, Gautam, "Newcastle's Pubs Stay Within the Limit," *Financial Times,* April 21, 1998, p. 10.

Morris, Gordon, "Revamp That Breathed New Life into Old Bank Praised," *Journal* (Newcastle, U.K.), April 26, 2000, p. 34.

"Pub Specialists Keep Up Demand," *Journal* (Newcastle, U.K.), March 7, 2001, p. 36.

Quinn, James, "Now Could Be the Time for an Ultimate Party," *Daily Mail* (London), December 4, 2004, p. 91.

"Theme for a Drinker's Dream?," *Journal* (Newcastle, U.K.), January 16, 2002, p. 41.

"Ultimate Revels in Its Success," *Journal* (Newcastle, U.K.), October 24, 2001, p. 30.

Walker, Howard, "Bar Owners Back in Business After Revolt," *Journal* (Newcastle, U.K.), September 28, 2005, p. 21.

——, "Profits Prove Ultimate Tonic for Leisure Group," *Journal* (Newcastle, U.K.), January 7, 2004, p. 2.

—Frank Uhle

Universal Stainless & Alloy Products, Inc.

600 Mayer Street
Bridgeville, Pennsylvania 15017
U.S.A.
Telephone: (412) 257-7600
Fax: (412) 257-7640
Web site: http://www.univstainless.com

Public Company
Incorporated: 1994
Employees: 463
Sales: $120.64 million (2004)
Stock Exchanges: NASDAQ
Ticker Symbol: USAP
NAIC: 331111 Iron and Steel Mills

Universal Stainless & Alloy Products, Inc. is a producer of semifinished and finished specialty steel products. Stainless steel products account for about 80 percent of sales. The company's facilities in Bridgeville and Titusville, Pennsylvania, make up its Universal Stainless & Alloy Products segment. Dunkirk Specialty Steel in New York forms another segment.

Origins

Clarence "Mac" McAninch and Daniel DeCola formed Universal Stainless & Alloy Products, Inc. to acquire the assets of an Armco steel mill in Bridgeville, Pennsylvania, in 1994. (Originally incorporated in Pennsylvania in January of that year, it was converted to a Delaware corporation a few months later.) The pair had been managers at the Armco plant; McAninch, formerly national sales manager, served as the new company's president and DeCola was vice-president of operations.

The history of the Bridgeville plant reflected the ups and downs of the steel industry. In the early 1980s, the Bridgeville facility, known as Universal-Cyclops, had employed more than 500 people; it was subject to intermittent shutdowns, however, as cheap imports flooded the specialty steel market.

Cyclops unsuccessfully tried to sell the unit at least three times from 1985 to 1989. By this time, Cytemp had 1,200 employees at three plants in Bridgeville, Titusville, and Pittsburgh, Pennsylvania, and posted revenues of $168 million.

Cyclops split the Cytemp operation into two parts in 1990; the Bridgeville operation was renamed Bridgeville Stainless & Alloy Products, while Titusville kept the Cytemp name. Titusville had about 700 employees producing high-temperature bars and billets. The Bridgeville plant, with 270 employees, focused on commodity stainless steel bars. Cyclops refocused the Bridgeville plant on semifinished ingots, billets, and blooms while shifting the stainless bars to Titusville.

A plan for Armco Inc. of Parsippany, New Jersey, to buy Cyclops for $156 million collapsed in the spring of 1991. There was difficulty obtaining financing in a sluggish specialty steel market. The deal was not entirely dead, however, and the companies would be combined in April 1992. (Armco also acquired the Cytemp Specialty Steel operation in Titusville.)

In the meantime, in January 1992, Cyclops announced that it was closing Bridgeville Stainless & Alloy Products after having failed to lift income or forge a new agreement with the United Steelworkers union (USW). According to *American Metal Market,* its capacity was 100,000 tons a year.

After the merger, Armco Inc.'s Baltimore Specialty Steels was combined with Bridgeville Stainless & Alloy Products in a new division, Armco Stainless & Alloy Products. The Baltimore unit, which had 735 employees, made stainless steel bars, wire, and rods for sale to steel distributors and machinery manufacturers.

Formation of Universal in 1994

The Bridgeville plant was virtually shut down in late 1993 during a restructuring of Armco. In August 1994 it was bought for $3.7 million by former managers, who had formed a company called Universal Stainless & Alloy Products, Inc. The new owners had a four-year agreement with the labor union, which allowed for lower wages and more flexible work rules while including employees in a profit-sharing plan.

According to the *Pittsburgh Post-Gazette,* the reopening of the Bridgeville operation was part of a renewed interest in

Company Perspectives:

The Company's mission is to be a leading, low-cost domestic provider of premium quality specialty steel products for our chosen markets.

Our mission is accompanied by two essential elements: 1. Work closely with our customers to understand and meet their needs through strategic investments. 2. Maintain a unique alliance with employees and suppliers to enhance productivity.

Key Dates:

1994: Universal Stainless & Alloy Products begins operations at a Bridgeville, Pennsylvania plant.
1995: The Titusville plant is acquired.
1996: Capital improvement is begun by rebuilding the Bridgeville melt shop's 50-ton electric arc furnace.
1998: Bridgeville enters the finished product market with the addition of a round bar finishing facility.
2000: The company enters the plate product markets after acquiring a plate saw.
2002: Dunkirk Specialty Steel is acquired, greatly expanding offerings in finished specialty steel.
2004: Universal posts record revenues and backlog.

steelmaking as the industry experienced its biggest demand since the 1970s. Universal capitalized on that interest in a successful initial public offering on the NASDAQ in December 1994. About 1.6 million shares were sold at $8 each; within a month they hit $10. Universal sold another two million shares at $9 each in a secondary offering in November 1995. Much of the $14 million raised was earmarked for new equipment.

Universal reported a loss of $2.5 million on sales of $7.4 million for 1994. Aside from the usual start-up costs, earnings were hit by a five-week shutdown of its rolling mill because of an electrical fault. Fortunately, the company was able to hold on to customers during the crisis and sign on new ones afterward. The company ended the year with a backlog worth $10 million.

By this time, Universal was employing about 90 workers. The plant continued to produce semifinished ingots, billets, and blooms and tool steel plate. Steam and gas turbine manufacturers were a major market. ''We're going to carve out niche markets,'' McAninch told *American Metal Market.* ''We're not going to be all things to all people.''

Acquiring Titusville in 1995

In 1995, Universal acquired the precision rolled products and remelting operations of Armco's Cytemp Specialty Steel facility in Titusville for $950,000. This business primarily machined parts for the aerospace industry, but also supplied the power generation market. The company also was spending $3 million to upgrade Bridgeville. Equipment included a 50-ton electric-arc furnace, a decarburization vessel, remelt furnaces, and a rolling mill.

Power generation, heavy equipment, and aerospace were Universal's three main markets after the Titusville buy. Stainless steel accounted for the majority of production, though Universal also made tool steel. Revenues were up to $47 million in 1995, with stainless steel accounting for $38 million of sales.

Sales were up to $81 million by 1997, producing net earnings of $7 million. The Bridgeville plant was ISO 9002 certified in 1998 and installed a new $11 million round bar finishing facility. By this time, the company had 290 employees at its two plants. Sales slipped to $72.6 million in 1998 and $66.7 million in 1999 under pressure from imports. The power generation and aerospace industries were experiencing hard times in the wake of the Asian financial crisis.

With natural gas costs escalating, in October 2000 Universal began implementing a surcharge in October 2000. This was

initially rejected by the marketplace, according to *American Metal Market,* but quadrupling energy costs had other specialty steel producers studying similar initiatives. A few years later, producers would add surcharges to cover price increases for iron, chrome, titanium, and other materials.

Acquiring Dunkirk in 2002

Universal acquired a third location in February 2002, buying the Empire Specialty Steel plant in Dunkirk, New York, from the state's Job Development Authority for $4 million. Empire had been formed from AL Tech Specialty Steel, which Universal had considered buying for $38 million before it went bankrupt in 1999. At its mid-1990s peak, the site had produced revenues of $100 million a year. Empire shut the site down in mid-2001. The Dunkirk site dated back to the Atlas Crucible Steel Co., formed in 1907, which was later part of the Allegheny Ludlum Steel Corp. Universal CEO Mac McAninch had reportedly helped launch AL Tech in 1976. It was acquired by Korea's Sammi Steel Co. Ltd. in 1989.

The Dunkirk plant added finished specialty steel rod and wire products to Universal's offerings. Dunkirk mainly served the service center market. Universal was initially investing $6 million in improvements there. Unfortunately, a sluggish economy did not help restore its profitability. Losses there helped lower Universal's overall profits 72 percent to $2 million in 2002.

Universal lost $1.4 million in 2003. Sales were flat at $69 million. The company attributed the results to a poor economy, weak aerospace and power generation business, and price cutting by struggling competitors. The new Dunkirk unit was especially hard hit.

2004 Recovery

Universal benefited from a recovery in the United States in 2004. A weaker dollar helped fight imports, while consolidation among domestic specialty steel producers raised prices. China's expanding economy produced demand for both steel and raw materials. Sales rose enormously in 2004, reaching $120.6 million, with net income of $7.1 million. The company boasted a record backlog of $72 million at the end of the year.

The recovery in the power generation and aerospace markets continued into 2005, and Universal obtained additional financing to go on an expansion path. The company had to contend with a strike at its Titusville plant, however, after its USW contract expired there in September 2005.

Principal Subsidiaries

Dunkirk Specialty Steel, LLC; USAP Holdings, Inc.

Principal Divisions

Dunkirk Specialty Steel; Universal Stainless & Alloy Products.

Principal Operating Units

Bridgeville; Dunkirk; Titusville.

Principal Competitors

Allegheny Technologies; Carpenter Technology Corporation; The Timken Company.

Further Reading

Boselovic, Len, ''New Owners to Revive Armco Plant in Bridgeville,'' *Pittsburgh Post-Gazette,* August 18, 1994, p. B8.

——, ''Reopened Pennsylvania Steelmaker Shares Profits with Employees,'' *Knight Ridder/Tribune Business News,* June 24, 1996.

——, ''Universal Backs Off Buying Al Tech,'' *Pittsburgh Post-Gazette,* November 18, 1998, p. E8.

——, ''Universal Stainless Expanding Business,'' *Pittsburgh Post-Gazette,* January 12, 1995, p. D10.

Gaynor, Pamela, ''Cyclops Merger Dead,'' *Pittsburgh Post-Gazette,* April 29, 1991.

Glynn, Matt, ''Buyer of Empire Steel Plant Confident of Returning It to Profitability,'' *Buffalo News,* February 16, 2002, p. E4.

——, ''Pennsylvania Firm to Reopen Empire Steel Plant,'' *Buffalo News,* February 15, 2002, p. B8.

——, ''Universal Plans $6 Million Outlay at Dunkirk Plant,'' *Buffalo News,* April 2, 2002, p. B6.

——, ''Universal's Dunkirk Plant Losing Money,'' *Buffalo News,* January 25, 2003, p. E4.

Guzzo, Maria, ''Universal's Pa. Workers Strike As Deal Rejected,'' *American Metal Market,* October 4, 2005, pp. 1+.

Lott, Ethan, ''Ellwood's Interest in Universal Proves to Be No Passing Fancy,'' *Pittsburgh Business Times,* August 13, 1999, p. 7.

''McAninch Takes Hard Line on Titusville Strikers,'' *Metal Bulletin News Alert Service,* October 21, 2005.

Moore, Deborah, ''Al Tech Says Parent Forged Illegal Merger,'' *Business Review* (Albany), January 26, 1998.

Pensak, Richard, ''Universal Stainless Moves into Next Century,'' *American Metal Market,* December 8, 1998.

Pollock, Beth, ''Bridgeville Closing Assessed,'' *American Metal Market,* January 27, 1992, p. 3.

——, ''Bridgeville Gets Temporary Stay; Interim Labor Pact Will Keep Plant in Operation Until April 30,'' *American Metal Market,* March 4, 1992, p. 2.

——, ''Cyclops' Shareholders OK Merger with Armco,'' *American Metal Market,* April 24, 1992, p. 1.

——, ''Will to Oversee Steel Operations of Armco, Former Cyclops Units,'' *American Metal Market,* April 30, 1992, p. 2.

Robertson, Scott, ''Universal Completes Stock Offering,'' *American Metal Market,* November 28, 1995, p. 4.

Sacco, John E., ''McAninch Formula in Evidence As Universal Eyes Bid for Slater Plant,'' *American Metal Market,* January 27, 2004, p. 3.

——, ''Metals Firms Struggle with Costlier US Energy; Gas Surcharge on Steel Revived,'' *American Metal Market,* January 8, 2001, p. 1.

——, ''Universal Agrees to Buy AI Tech,'' *American Metal Market,* October 20, 1998.

——, ''Universal Stainless Sets Surcharge for Natural Gas,'' *American Metal Market,* October 6, 2000, p. 1.

Scolieri, Peter, ''Bridgeville Will Modify Approach to Market,'' *American Metal Market,* August 31, 1990, p. 4.

——, ''Cyclops Eyes Cytemp Upgrade,'' *American Metal Market,* May 1, 1980, p. 2.

——, ''Cytemp Sale Seen Stymied by Bid Cut,'' *American Metal Market,* February 6, 1989, p. 2.

——, ''Cytemp Split into Two Separate Units,'' *American Metal Market,* July 9, 1990, p. 1.

——, ''Questions, Issues Raised in Proposed Armco-Cyclops Tie,'' *American Metal Market,* January 24, 1991, p. 1.

——, ''Takeover of Cytemp Dissolves; Asking Price Trips Up USW-Led ESOP Buyout,'' *American Metal Market,* November 30, 1989, p. 1.

Selland, Kerri J., ''Bridgeville Reborn As Universal,'' *American Metal Market,* August 19, 1994, p. 1.

——, ''Execs to Buy Armco Plant; Former Cyclops Unit at Bridgeville May Be Reborn,'' *American Metal Market,* March 1, 1994, p. 2.

——, ''Newborn Universal Set to Start Melting Metal,'' *American Metal Market,* August 22, 1994, p. 2.

Teaff, Rick, ''Universal Stainless Mill Out for 5 Weeks; Electrical Problem Ruins Drive Motor,'' *American Metal Market,* July 20, 1995, pp. 1+.

Tobin, Audrey, ''When Communications Matters Most,'' *Small Business News* (Pittsburgh), May 1, 1996, p. 6.

''Universal Stainless Plans to Raise Production at Dunkirk,'' *Steel Business Briefing,* January 25, 2005.

Welch, David T., ''First-Year Loss for Universal,'' *American Metal Market,* March 29, 1995, p. 3.

—Frederick C. Ingram

Urbium PLC

Vernon House, 40 Shaftesbury Avenue
London
W1D 7ER
United Kingdom
Telephone: + 44 20 7434 0030
Fax: + 44 20 7434 1413
Web site: http://www.urbium.co.uk

Public Company
Incorporated: 1995 as Trocadero PLC
Employees: 1,222
Sales: £75.3 million (2004)
Stock Exchanges: London
Ticker Symbol: URM
NAIC: 722410 Drinking Places (Alcoholic Beverages);
    551112 Offices of Other Holding Companies

Urbium PLC has built up one of the United Kingdom's fastest-growing portfolios of bars and nightclubs, and is the dominant bar owner in London's West End. Essentially launched in 1998, the company has opened a string of some ten Tiger Tiger-branded large-scale nightclubs across the United Kingdom, combining restaurant, bar service, and dancing in a single multifloor complex. The Tiger Tiger clubs feature capacity ranging from 1,300 to 2,000, and target a more affluent 25- to 45-year-old market seeking a less raucous environment than the typical youth-oriented nightclub. Tiger Tiger clubs hold late-night licenses, allowing them to commence restaurant service at noon and continue to operate until as late as 3 a.m. Since 1998, Urbium has opened Tiger Tiger clubs in London (Haymarket), Aberdeen, Croyden, Dublin, Glasgow, Leeds, Manchester, Newcastle, Portsmouth, and elsewhere, and planned to open a new generation of the Tiger Tiger concept in Cardiff before the end of 2005. Urbium, which founded its nightclub operations with the purchase of three West End bars from Luminar in 1998, has continued to build its portfolio of London establishments. The company operates a number of smaller bars and nightclubs throughout the city, including Abacus, Agenda, Alibi, On Anon, Oxygen, Ruby Blue, Strawberry Moons, Sway, Zoo Bar, and others. The dominant bar group in the popular West End section of London, Urbium has been expanding its presence throughout the city into the mid-2000s. Urbium was created through the split of Chorion PLC into its intellectual property and nightclub operations, and subsequently listed on the London Stock Exchange. In October 2005, however, the company agreed to be acquired in a management-led buyout by Electra Partners.

Property Group in the 1990s

Urbium essentially began as a property investment vehicle acquiring the famed Trocadero, on London Piccadilly Circus, in the mid-1990s. The Trocadero itself had been a London landmark for more than 100 years. Located on the corner of Shaftesbury Avenue and Windmill Street, the site had first achieved notoriety as the Argyll Rooms. Opened in 1851, the Argyll Rooms operated as a nightclub, theater, and restaurant. The Argyll Rooms became well known among the city's nobility and other society figures for its masquerade balls, but also for its operation as a brothel in its rooms upstairs. The notoriety of this latter activity, however, led to the loss of the establishment's license in 1878.

Operated by various theater owners until the mid-1890s, the site's true glory came in 1896, when its 99-year lease was acquired by J. Lyons & Co. Lyons refurbished the property as the Trocadero, widely considered as among the world's finest and most lavish restaurants. Indeed, the restaurant and banquet hall inspired the appearance of numerous ''Trocaderos'' throughout the world. A famous feature of the site, the Long Bar, was added in 1901. In 1916, the site hosted its first concert tea. Later, in the 1920s, the Trocadero launched its own cabaret, which remained a popular destination into the early 1940s.

In the years following the end of World War II, however, the Trocadero lost much of its former luster. By the 1960s, the Trocadero had become outmoded. The restaurant shut its doors in 1965. The site, however, remained a highly prized location, particularly with the importance of Piccadilly Circus as a London destination during the period.

In the 1980s, the Trocadero was acquired by the Burford Group, a high-flying properties group created as an offshoot for

Company Perspectives:

Urbium PLC operates premium bars in high footfall venues in major urban markets, with a substantial food offer and corporate business.

a London commodities firm. Led by Nick Leslau and Nigel Wray, Burford set out to transform the Trocadero site into a multifaceted leisure complex, combining retail shopping and various entertainment outlets.

Burford spun off the Trocadero site as a separate company called Trocadero PLC. The new company set out to expand the entertainment portion of the site, adding an Imax theater, an amusement park-styled attraction, the Drop Ride, and, in 1996, the £50 million Segaword, billed as a virtual reality theme park. Yet these failed to attract the desired public.

New management, led by John Conlan and Nick Tamblyn, both formerly of the First Leisure group, took over Trocadero PLC's operation in 1997. The new team decided to take the company into an entirely different direction or, rather, two new directions. The first was intellectual property. The business was to be based on the company's holding of the rights to the characters and works of popular British children's writer Enid Blyton. Acquired in 1996, the former management had intended to incorporate the characters into the Trocadero site.

Instead, the new Trocadero PLC began acquiring other intellectual property holdings and, most notably, the worldwide rights to the Agatha Christie catalog, as well as the rights to the Simenon series of books. In the meantime, the Trocadero itself had run into difficulties, failing to attract a sufficient public. In 1997, Burford Holdings agreed to reacquire the Trocadero site.

Trocadero PLC continued operating under that name into the beginning of 1998, before changing its name to Chorion PLC in April of that year. Part of the impetus for the name change came with the launch of the company's second line of business: bar and nightclub ownership. In 1998, the company reached an agreement with Luminar PLC to acquire three of its West End London bar properties—Oxygen, Zoo Bar/Venom, and Bar Madrid—for £10.9 million. Although observers were somewhat skeptical over the acquisition, Chorion had spotted an opportunity in the bar scene. For Chorion, although the younger market was well served with nightclubs, there were few venues serving the older and more affluent 25- to 45-year-old set. Yet Chorion recognized that this market, with its high level of disposable income, would welcome bars and nightclubs more specifically catering to it.

Chorion then began preparations to launch a new large-scale late-night (that is, open until 2 or 3 a.m.) nightclub concept. Dubbed "Tiger Tiger," the new nightclub, to be opened in London's Haymarket, featured a multifloor concept offering multiple environments, including a restaurant, a bar, and dancing, and a capacity of nearly 2000. The Tiger Tiger club was designed to be contemporary, but not trendy, matching the tastes of its target public, but also in a bid to extend the club's longevity. By not catering to a prevailing trend, the company

hoped to avoid a shift in consumer interest as the next trend came along.

Nightclub Leader in the 2000s

The first Tiger Tiger opened to critical, and popular, acclaim in November 1998. Chorion quickly began plans to expand the brand on a national level. Meanwhile, the company continued acquiring London properties in a bid to become one of the dominant nightclub players in that city.

Chorion soon achieved its aim, and by 2000 the company's strong position in the West End section in particular allowed it to claim leadership in the London market. The company was also highly profitable. By the end of 1999, the company posted a 19 percent profit despite the costs of its acquisition and the £6.5 million price tag involved in the creation of the first Tiger Tiger.

The company's strong balance sheet enabled it to launch a full-scale expansion of its nightclub business. Through 2000 and into 2001, the company opened or acquired a number of new sites, focusing on the London market, with the West End remaining at its core. As such Chorion added names such as Loop, Sway, and On Anon, which offered nightclub concepts similar to those of the Tiger Tiger format; the lounge-led bars Babble, Digress, The Boardwalk, and the Warwick, which provided a smaller and lower key setting, targeting predominantly the after-work professional set; and restaurants, including the Sugar Reef, near Picadilly Circus, and Red Cube, near Leicester Square. The company also maintained its original club acquisitions, including Oxygen, Zoo, and Bar Madrid. These, however, targeted a younger crowd.

Meanwhile, the Tiger Tiger brand led Chorion's expansion to the national, and even international, level. The company opened its first Tiger Tiger outside of London in 2000, in England's second largest city, Birmingham. This initiated a quick rollout of the Tiger Tiger brand, and by 2002, the company operated Tiger Tigers in Manchester, Leeds, Portsmouth, and Newcastle, among others. The company also targeted an introduction into the European market, opening its first Tiger Tiger in Dublin, while planning an extension of the brand to Spain, a popular destination for British holiday-goers.

During this time, Chorion's intellectual property business had also grown strongly, to the point at which the company had become one of the most prominent in this segment as well. In 2002, therefore, the company decided to conduct a "de-merger" of its two different businesses, spinning off its nightclub business into a new, publicly listed entity, Urbium PLC. The intellectual property business retained the Chorion name.

Urbium spent the next year consolidating its holdings. As such, the company put new bar openings on a temporary hold, while it refurbished and upgraded its existing properties. The Tiger Tiger concept received particular attention as the company shifted its model toward still larger capacity venues. Nonetheless, the Tiger Tiger concept proved highly flexible. For example, when the company opened its next new nightclub, in Aberdeen in 2003, it scaled down the Tiger Tiger there to a maximum accommodation of just 1,300 people.

On the whole, the Tiger Tiger concept remained highly successful. Indeed, its flagship club in the London Haymarket

---

<table>
<tr><td colspan="2" align="center">**Key Dates:**</td></tr>
<tr><td>**1851:**</td><td>The Argyll Rooms opens near Picadilly Circus in London.</td></tr>
<tr><td>**1896:**</td><td>The site is reopened as the Trocadero Restaurant under J. Lyons & Co.</td></tr>
<tr><td>**1982:**</td><td>Burford PLC is founded as a properties group, which acquires Trocadero and repositions it as a retail and entertainment complex.</td></tr>
<tr><td>**1995:**</td><td>The Trocadero operation is spun off as Trocadero PLC.</td></tr>
<tr><td>**1997:**</td><td>New management steers Trocadero into intellectual property rights management.</td></tr>
<tr><td>**1998:**</td><td>The company changes its name to Chorion and acquires its first three West End nightclubs; the Tiger Tiger nightclub concept is launched in London's Haymarket.</td></tr>
<tr><td>**2000:**</td><td>The first Tiger Tiger nightclub outside of London is opened, in Birmingham.</td></tr>
<tr><td>**2002:**</td><td>The successful expansion of the nightclub business leads to a ''de-merger'' and creation of Urbium PLC.</td></tr>
<tr><td>**2005:**</td><td>Urbium agrees to a management buyout led by Electra Partners.</td></tr>
</table>

even managed to increase its customer base over its first five years in business, a rarity in the nightclub market. The only negative was the group's experience in Birmingham, where the property's location, at the new Five Point complex, did not attract enough of the relatively upscale clientele targeted by the Tiger Tiger concept.

Urbium returned to expansion in 2004. The company acquired two new London properties at the beginning of the year. The company also opened a new bar, Abacus, in London's Cornhill, that year. By the end of 2004, Urbium had acquired yet another London property, the Strawberry Moons nightclub, located near the city's Regent Street. For that purchase, Urbium paid £1.45 million. The company's expansion continued into 2005, with the purchase of another London bar, the Walkabout. That site, renamed the Alibi under Urbium, also marked the group's entry into the City financial district.

Urbium prepared to launch a still more ambitious expansion to take it into the second half of the 2000s. In February 2005, company Chairman Conlan announced the group's plan to acquire or open another 15 new properties in London, and as many as 50 more nationwide.

In June 2005, however, the company received a takeover offer from rival Regent Inns. The company rejected that offer, yet decided to accept bids for the group from private equity groups. As Conlan told the *Financial Times:* ''The sector is going through a period of consolidation and restructuring and that is easier to do in the private arena.''

As a result, the company was approached by investment group Electra Partners. The two sides ultimately worked out a buyout agreement, involving members of Urbium's management. In October 2005, Electra set up a buyout vehicle, Lightflower, and acquired Urbium for £113 million. Urbium was said to be considering a change of name at the end of 2005 as it prepared to extend its leading position among the British nightclub circuit.

Principal Subsidiaries

Latenightlondon.co.uk.

Principal Competitors

Compass Group PLC; Whitbread PLC; Mitchells and Butlers PLC; J D Wetherspoon PLC; Enterprise Inns PLC; Greene King PLC; Wolverhampton and Dudley Breweries PLC; Spirit Group Ltd.; Luminar PLC; Laurel Pub Company Ltd.

Further Reading

Blackwell, David Harold, ''Urbium Dances to a Steady Upward Beat,'' *Financial Times,* January 8, 2003, p. 24.

''Burning Bright,'' *Birmingham Post,* September 11, 2002, p. 21.

Dorsey, Kristy, ''More Tiger Tiger Venues Planned,'' *Herald,* February 28, 2003, p. 11.

Duckers, John, ''Roaring City Success Spurs National Bars Roll-out Plan,'' *Birmingham Post,* February 28, 2003, p. 27.

Goodman, Matthew, and Mark Kleinman, ''Electra Roars into Talks for Tiger Bars,'' *Sunday Times,* August 14, 2005, p. 3.

Grande, Carlos, ''Urbium Sale Signals Bar Chains' Move to Private Equity,'' *Financial Times,* September 9, 2005, p. 25.

''Urbium Acquires 30th UK Venue,'' *Caterer & Hotelkeeper,* February 17, 2005, p. 12.

''Urbium Agrees £113m Deal with Lightflower,'' *Leisure Report,* October 2005, p. 8.

''Urbium Boss Expects New Venue to Be Roaring Success,'' *Aberdeen Press & Journal,* June 2, 2004.

''Urbium Profits Up on London Expansion As Feel Good Factor Returns,'' *Leisure Report,* April 2005, p. 8.

—M.L. Cohen

Ventana Medical Systems, Inc.

1910 East Innovation Park Drive
Tucson, Arizona 85737
U.S.A.
Telephone: (520) 887-2155
Toll Free: (800) 227-2155
Fax: (520) 229-4207
Web site: http://www.ventanamed.com

Public Company
Incorporated: 1993
Employees: 732
Sales: $166.1 million (2004)
Stock Exchanges: NASDAQ
Ticker Symbol: VMSI
NAIC: 334510 Electomedical and Electrotherapeutic
Apparatus Manufacturing; 334517 Irradiation Apparatus
Manufacturing; 339111 Laboratory Apparatus and
Furniture Manufacturing; 339112 Surgical and Medical
Instrument Manufacturing; 339113 Surgical and
Supplies Manufacturing; 541710 Physical, Engineering
and Biological Research

Ventana Medical Systems, Inc. is an international leader in the development and manufacture of instrument-reagent systems used to automate the process of diagnostic testing of tissue samples on glass microscope slides. The company provides healthcare professionals with superior tools that standardize and speed slide staining in clinical histology, cytology, and drug discovery laboratories across the globe. Ventana's pharma-services and research instruments are used to accelerate the discovery of new drug target systems and evaluate the safety of cancer therapies. The company's instruments are used by most of the top 50 cancer research centers in the United States, including the Mayo Clinic, Johns Hopkins Hospital, and the Memorial Sloan-Kettering Cancer Center.

1985–91: Developing, Manufacturing, Marketing Automated Tissue-Testing Systems

Thomas M. Grogan, M.D., founded Immunodiagnostics Inc. in 1985. A pathologist at the University of Arizona, Dr. Grogan became interested in improving the practice of medicine by creating automated laboratory equipment to speed cancer diagnosis. Grogan first learned about immunohistochemistry (IHC) in the 1970s while doing postgraduate work at Stanford University with a professor who pioneered the field. IHC is based on the discovery that a cancer cell can be characterized by biochemical markers found within and on the cell's surface. Using special reagents and stains, the anatomic pathologist can identify these markers to determine what feeds a particular form of cancer and what types of chemotherapy can be used to treat it.

Grogan arrived at the University of Arizona in 1979. In the following years, as a practicing pathologist and professor of pathology, Grogan began to realize the necessity for automation in the anatomical pathology laboratory. Automation of the tissue preparation and staining process would allow doctors to make diagnoses and present therapy options to patients in a more timely manner than manual processing allowed. However, he lacked business savvy. In 1984, after spending two years looking for investors, he teamed up with Ross Humphreys, and the two launched Immunodiagnostics, Inc. in 1985.

From 1985 to 1995, Immunodiagnostics did not make a profit and operated solely on investments. Humphreys, who had experience heading up an investment firm, shepherded the fledgling business through its early years while Grogan developed the necessary technology. Later, Jim Danehy took over as president and CEO of Immunodiagnostics, and the company secured $20 million in venture capital from investors. By 1989, it had nine employees with plans to reach 300 in five years.

Ventana's first product was an instrument reagent system designed to automate and thereby standardize IHC staining. At the time, all IHC staining was performed manually or via rudimentary automation, with each test taking 40 to 50 manual steps and five to six hours to complete. It was hard to compare results between institutions because there was no standard industry protocol. Moreover, manual testing resulted in a five to 10 percent failure rate.

Grogan became convinced that a machine could do the testing much faster and more effectively. Looking back in a 2005 *Tucson Citizen* article, he explained, ''I realized it needed to be done on every patient. We got obsessive. It should be done by

392

Company Perspectives:

Ventana's mission is to provide Innovations in Science and Medicine that Improve the quality of Life. Our vision is to become the leading provider of solutions to the anatomical pathology laboratory so patient care can move beyond what is to what can be.

an instrument like developing film. I looked at film developing technology.'' Ventana's first commercially marketed system, the Ventana 320, was launched in November 1991. The Ventana 320 could process 40 slides per run, eight runs per day, for a total of 320 slides. The instrument provided automation of a labor-intensive process thereby improving productivity and response time of the anatomical laboratory. The whole process took three steps and was complete in an hour and 20 minutes. Instead of the 10 to 15 percent repeat rate for manual tests, the 320's repeat rate was 1 to 2 percent.

1992–2000: Growth and Product Diversification

In 1992, Immunodiagnostics was renamed Ventana Medical Systems, Inc. Using the Spanish word for ''window,'' the new name reflected the company's focus on developing integrated systems that provide a window on the biochemical characteristics of tumor cells. That year, Ventana began marketing its flagship device to community hospital-based anatomical pathology labs and commercial labs. Revenues for 1992 exceeded $1 million.

By the mid-1990s, Ventana had become a significant competitor in the anatomical pathology industry. From 1995 onward, the company launched at least one instrument per year and developed numerous diagnostic reagents. After Ventana went public in 1996, hospitals, clinics, and research labs quickly discovered the company and began to make use of its revolutionary and constantly improving technology. Ventana also purchased its main competitor, California-based BioTek Solutions, for almost $19 million in 1997. BioTek's more research-oriented products complemented Ventana's, which were more clinically focused.

Henry T. Pietraszek replaced Danehy as head of the company in 1997. Pietraszek had spent most of his professional career at Abbott Laboratories: first at Abbott Diagnostics; then as president of Dainbot, Abbott's diagnostics joint venture in Japan; and finally as president of its pharmaceutical joint venture, TAP Pharmaceuticals. Pietraszek left Abbott in 1994 to head Biostar, Inc., an early stage medical diagnostics company. During the first two years of Pietraszek's leadership, Ventana more than doubled in size, reaching revenues of $47.7 million in 1998 and $69 million in 1999. Under Pietraszek, Ventana signed an agreement to acquire Biotechnology Tools, Inc. of Tucson, which gave the company a second point of entry in the histology market. It also purchased several of Oncor, Inc.'s products for cancer research and treatment, including an FDA-approved test to help doctors decide how aggressively to treat patients with breast cancer.

The year 2000 proved to be the springboard of a new era for Ventana with Christopher M. Gleeson taking charge of the com-

pany upon Pietraszek's departure. Gleeson came to Ventana from Bayer Diagnostics in 1999. From 1993 to 1997, he had worked at Chiron Diagnostics and prior to that, as the founder, owner, and director of Australian Diagnostics Corporation. Under Gleeson's direction, Ventana continued to expand along its traditional lines, acquiring the assets of Quantitative Diagnostics Laboratories, Inc., a specialty lab that provided quantitative IHC services to pathologists and cancer research support in 2000. The company also received FDA approval for its Pathway HER-2/*neu* test in 2000, which aided in identifying patients eligible to receive Herceptin for metastatic breast cancer. Herceptin is a targeted therapeutic developed by Genentech.

In 2001, the company refined its systems, culminating in the development of its ''baking through staining'' technology available on the BenchMark platform, which won the Medical Design Excellence award that year. Ventana also created its Molecular Discovery Systems business to expand the company's revolutionary staining technology to research and drug discovery laboratories. The MDS group provided a direct sales and marketing mechanism to place the Discovery instrument, launched in 1999, and corresponding reagents in research and drug discovery laboratories, in North America, Europe, and Japan. Also in 2001, the company moved to new headquarters in Oro Valley, Arizona.

By 2002, Ventana had successfully reached the international market it first began to seek out with proceeds from its initial public offering in 1995. At this point, it employed 540 people worldwide and its systems were in place in 55 countries. By 2003, 29 percent of its revenue came from international customers. At home, it began working with Pima Community College in Tucson to develop a degree program in histology, the microscopic study of tissue. Histotechnicians run anatomical pathology laboratories. Ventana's involvement included providing guest lecturers at the college, as well as onsite specialty classes and internships for 18 students each year.

After a court ruled that Ventana had unintentionally infringed on competitor CytoLogix's patent in late 2003, Ventana halted the sale of the extremely successful BenchMark instrument, launched in 2000, and began revamping its product line. In its place, the company unveiled the BenchMark XT instrument, a higher-capacity system. It also gained momentum on the development of the Symphony, the first fully-automated instrument to perform primary or hematoxylin and Eosin (H&E) staining and coverslipping on patient samples mounted on glass microscope slides. With the Symphony, Ventana, already a leading provider in the IHC or advanced staining market, which processes the 30 percent of patient samples that require further examination for cancer or infectious disease, entered the front-end of the diagnostic process.

Looking ahead in 2004, Ventana angled to get in on the ground floor of a new generation of drugs targeted at people with certain genetic traits by automating the screening process for such medicines. ''There's a whole host of drugs coming down the pipeline from drug companies, and the indications are . . . that there will be a tissue-based diagnostic required to admit these patients to therapies,'' Gleeson announced in a 2004 *Arizona Daily Star* article. Moving toward this growth, the company increased its Tucson workforce by 10 percent. It also began developing an integrated information management sys-

```
┌─────────────────────────────────────────────────┐
│                 Key Dates:                       │
│                                                  │
│ 1985:  Dr. Thomas Grogan and Ross Humphreys found│
│        Immunodiagnostics Inc.                    │
│ 1992:  The company is renamed Ventana Medical    │
│        Systems.                                  │
│ 1996:  The company holds its initial public      │
│        offering; purchases BioTek Solutions.     │
│ 1997:  Henry T. Pietraszek replaces Danehy as    │
│        president and CEO.                         │
│ 1998:  Ventana acquires Biotechnology Tools,     │
│        Inc.; acquires the key assets of Oncor,   │
│        Inc.                                       │
│ 1999:  Christopher M. Gleeson replaces Pietraszek│
│        as CEO.                                    │
│ 2000:  Ventana acquires the assets of Quantitative│
│        Diagnostics Laboratories, Inc.            │
│ 2001:  Company headquarters move to Oro Valley,  │
│        Arizona.                                   │
└─────────────────────────────────────────────────┘
```

tem that would link its instrument results to hospital information systems.

By 2005, the company expected to reap revenues of just under $200 million. More than 5,000 of its devices were used for cancer diagnosis in at least 1,500 hospitals and clinics in 55 countries. It controlled a 60 percent market share in automated diagnostic and reagent systems. Promising further growth, that same year it also entered into a five-year global supply agreement with TriPath Imaging, Inc., which allowed Ventana to sell and distribute a branded version of TriPath's interactive histology imaging system worldwide. "[W]e are a fraction of what we are going to be," Gleeson announced in a 2005 *Tucson Citizen* article. "We want to be in every hospital in every city in every country in the world."

Principal Subsidiaries

Ventana Medical Systems GmbH; Ventana Medical Systems Japan K.K., Ventana Medical Systems, Pty. Ltd.; Ventana Medical Systems, S.A.

Principal Competitors

Apogent Technologies Inc.; Beckman Coulter, Inc.; Becton Dickinson & Company; BioGenex; DakoCutomation; Diagnostic Products Corporation; Digene; Ortho-Clinical Diagnostics.

Further Reading

"Local Success Story: Ventana Leads World in Tissue Analysis Technology," *Arizona Daily Star*, September 15, 1996.
"Tucson Paid Off for Ventana Founder Grogan," *Arizona Daily Star*, October 10, 2002.
"Ventana Medical Sees Growth," *Arizona Daily Star*, February 21, 2004.
"Ventana Medical Systems Inc.," *Investor's Business Daily*, October 7, 2003.
Vitu, Teya, "Diagnosing Cancer Propels Local Firm," *Tucson Citizen*, May 26, 2005.
Weintraub, Arlene, "These Tests Go Way Beyond the Pap Smear," *BusinessWeek*, October 15, 2001, p. 68.
Wichner, David, "Tucson, Arizona-Based Medical Device Firm to Adjust Production After Patent Suit," *Arizona Daily Star*, January 29, 2004.

—Carrie Rothburd

Vodafone Group Plc

The Courtyard
2 - 4 London Rd
Newbury
Berkshire RG 14 1JX
United Kingdom
Telephone: +44-1635-33-251
Fax: +44-1635-45-713
Web site: http://www.vodafone-airtouch-plc.com

Public Company
Incorporated: 1985 as Racal Telecommunications Group
    Ltd.
Employees: 60,109
Sales £31.55 billion ($64 billion) (2005)
Stock Exchanges: London New York
Ticker Symbols: VOD.L; VOD
NAIC: 513322 Cellular and Other Wireless
    Telecommunications

Vodafone Group Plc is the world's leading cellular telephone operator, boasting more than 165 million subscribers and annual sales of more than £31.5 billion ($64 billion). The Berkshire-based company is not only the largest corporation in the United Kingdom, it is also the world's third largest generator of free cash flow, trailing only GE and Microsoft. Vodafone is also leading the battle to standardize global mobile telephone standards ahead of the expected next-generation boom in the industry, in which voice, video, data, music, games, Internet, payment and other services are expected to merge into users' handsets. Vodafone's success in the 2000s came through its aggressive acquisition strategy, which included the nearly $63 billion purchase of AirTouch Communications in 1999 and the $183 billion takeover of Mannesmann—the world's largest ever acquisition—in 2000. The company is present in more than 30 countries, with a focus on the European markets, as well as Japan, where it is that market's number three mobile telephone player. In the United States, the company holds a 45 percent stake in the Verizon Wireless joint venture with Bell Atlantic. With fewer large-scale acquisitions available to gener-

ate double-digit growth into the second half of the 2000s, Vodafone has begun to concentrate on rolling out so-called 3G services to its markets. The company is listed on the New York and London stock exchanges. Arun Sarin has been company CEO since 2003.

Origins

Vodafone was the brainchild of Racal Electronics Ltd., a modestly prosperous U.K. electronics firm, and Millicom, a U.S. communications company. Developed as a joint venture during the early 1980s, Vodafone was granted a license to develop a cellular network in the United Kingdom and was introduced under the auspices of Racal in January 1985. The new subsidiary's success was stunning. The corporate sector was quick to appreciate the advantages of mobile telecommunications, and individuals were equally quick to spot the status symbol potential of the new technology; fueled by business need and Yuppie culture, the demand for mobile phones skyrocketed.

Vodafone found itself one of only two entrants in the United Kingdom in a virtually unregulated new industry; the other member of the duopoly was Cellnet, which remained Vodafone's principal competitor into the 1990s. Throughout the 1980s the company created much of the technology, and enjoyed most of the profits, of this rapidly expanding field. Racal Telecommunications' profit and loss history from 1985 to 1989 succinctly describes the matter: in the year of its creation, Vodafone was operating at a loss of £10 million; by the end of the decade pretax profits were over £84 million. Racal soon developed allied divisions, including Vodac, Vodata, and Vodapage, to expand the number and type of services the company offered.

By 1988 Racal Telecommunications Group Ltd., as Vodafone and the related subsidiaries were officially known, was by far the most successful player on the Racal Electronics team. The parent company, fearing that the Telecommunications Group was hampered on the stock market by its subsidiary status, and wishing, in addition, to enhance other aspects of its business with profit from Vodafone stocks, proposed a partial flotation of the subsidiary. Millicom, the second largest shareholder, who lobbied for a complete sell-off, opposed the move; in the end, only 20 percent of the share capital of Racal Telecom

Company Perspectives:

We aim to be the world's leading wireless telecommunications and information provider bringing more customers more services and more value than any other of its competitors.

was offered on the market. Three years later, however, Racal Electronics reconsidered, and Racal Telecom was separated from its parent company in 1991, at which time the name was changed to Vodafone Group Ltd.

Dominant in the 1990s

Vodafone was a market leader in the United Kingdom since its inception. Its main competitor, Cellnet, jointly owned by British Telecom and Securicor, was also granted its license in 1985 and grew as steadily as Vodafone. However, it always remained a step or two behind, with Vodafone generally enjoying some 56 percent of the market. The two remained the only companies on the scene for approximately eight years. Although an industry regulator, Oftel, existed, frequent rumors that the duopoly would be subjected to some sort of price regulation never materialized, on the grounds, it is thought, that further competition in such an obviously lucrative industry was bound to eventually appear. As the *Daily Mail* commented in early 1993, ''Profits from mobile phones have been mouthwatering.'' Such competition did appear when Mercury, in a joint venture between Cable & Wireless and the telephone company U S West, issued its challenge in 1993.

Amid much publicity and a flurry of marketing, Mercury's Personal Communications Network, called One-2-One, was launched. Mercury's advertising campaign hammered home a message of lower costs. By offering low prices and even free off-peak local calls, Mercury forced the two telecommunications giants into a price war, but only in the London area, where Mercury's operations began.

One-2-One was seen primarily as a bid for the private market of mobile telephone users, whereas the majority of Vodafone's customer base was in the corporate sector, where demand and the tariffs charged were historically higher. Despite this, the company was clearly not unmindful of the competitors' interest in the vast untapped private market. It first responded to the threat of Mercury's introduction with its own countermarketing. After One-2-One was operating, Vodafone introduced new options such as Low Call, which, with its lower rental costs but higher call charges, was targeted at individuals who used their phones less frequently than business customers. Another new initiative, MetroDigital, a service begun in 1993 that allowed subscribers low rates when calling from an urban ''home cell,'' was aimed at least in part at the personal user market.

Mercury's One-2-One employed the new digital technology rather than the analog systems used until then by Vodafone and Cellnet. Digital technology represented a significant advance in the industry, as its use allowed for higher quality, better security, and lower costs. Not to be outdone, Vodafone too was expanding its digital network, and the company expected operations to be fully digital by the end of the 1990s.

As of the mid-1990s it was too soon to assess the ramifications of Mercury's entry into the market, or indeed that of newcomer Hutchison Microtel, which began operating its Orange network in 1994. Most financial analysts predicted, however, that there was room for all in a market so ripe for expansion; increased competition would thus have little effect on profit margins.

Although Vodafone Ltd. was clearly its flagship company, the Vodafone Group as a whole comprised several wholly owned subsidiaries that supported or complemented the activities of Vodafone Ltd. Vodac was the group's service provider, buying cellular airtime wholesale from Vodafone and selling it, equipment, and services to customers via service centers, retail outlets, dealers, mail order, and special corporate accounts. Another subsidiary, Vodapage, operated a nationwide radiopaging network; among the services it offered were Healthcall Medical Answerline Service; Neighbourhood Watch Information Line, a crime prevention service; and even the Rare Bird Alert News Service. Paknet, a radio-based national public data communications network, had a client base of banks, retailers, utilities, alarm companies, and others, and had a variety of applications. Country councils used it to handle traffic measurements, and British Rail used it for credit card authorization.

Vodafone had been involved as well in a number of other specialized applications of its capabilities. ''SafeLink,'' introduced in 1992 in conjunction with the West Yorkshire Police, gave individuals fast access to the police via the Vodafone network. The ''Callsafe'' service, developed the same year, allowed stranded motorists to contact the Automobile Association. Perhaps the company's highest profile special application, however, came in 1993 when it provided the emergency mobile phone service to environmental rescue workers following the wreck of the tanker *Braer* in the Shetland Islands.

Vodata, another crucial subsidiary, developed and marketed new products and services for Vodafone and Vodapage customers. The company pioneered information services for users such as the Automobile Association's ''Roadwatch'' and the *Financial Times*' ''CityLine.'' ''Recall,'' the world's largest voice messaging service, was introduced in 1992. ''Vodastream'' fax allowed customers access to up-to-date macroeconomic statistics compiled by the Central Statistical Office; ''Met fax'' gave the latest weather bulletins; and ''Vodafax Broadcast'' allowed the facsimile transmission of information to several different destinations simultaneously.

Vodafone Group International was a rapidly growing component of the group. Active in seeking opportunities and implementing projects abroad, Vodafone International looked likely to one day be as important to the group as Vodafone Ltd. itself. In 1993 the company was awarded a license in Australia to operate that country's third digital mobile telephone network. In the same year, consortia of which Vodafone was a member received similar licenses to operate in Greece and Germany. Vodafone also had substantial interests in France, Scandinavia, Hong Kong, Fiji, Malta, and Mexico. Although start-up costs for foreign ventures were obviously high, the field was very lucrative, and Vodafone was continually on the lookout for new possibilities. Analysts predicted that Vodafone would increase its investments with the aim of acquiring more foreign associates and, eventually, subsidiaries.

A digital system that allowed international calls between participating countries was introduced in the early 1990s. Called the Global System for Mobile Communications (GSM), it was first used by Vodafone, whose introduction of EuroDigital in 1991 allowed customers to "roam" throughout Europe and Scandinavia. In 1994 the company acquired a 10 percent stake in Globalstar, an international consortium formed to develop a satellite-based network that would allow mobile telecommunications to operate everywhere in the world (except the polar ice caps) by 1998.

As of 1994, Vodafone operated one of the world's largest cellular networks, with over one million subscribers. This, combined with the company's increasingly high international profile, made it a safe bet that Vodafone would continue its prominent role in the expanding mobile telecommunications industry. The *Mail on Sunday* confidently predicted in 1993: "We're on the verge of a communications explosion. By 2000, nearly all of us will have a phone in our pocket." It was highly likely that for many, that phone would be a Vodafone.

Digital phones took some time to catch on due to a limited service range and reliability problems; they accounted for only 13 percent of mobile phones in Britain in 1995. However, the new wave of digital entrants did force Vodafone and other analog providers like Cellnet to trim their pricing somewhat. Earnings for the fiscal year ending March 1996 fell 4 percent in the face of stiff competition from Orange and One-2-One. However, Vodafone's foreign operations soon began to post positive results.

Thanks to its profitable operations at home, the concept of credit remained foreign to Vodafone until July 1996, when it sought European capital to increase its stake in France's number two mobile phone provider, SFR. It paid FFr 1.8 billion ($346 million) to raise its shareholding from 10 percent to 16.5

percent. Vodafone also had equity positions in a number of other European and Asian cellular companies.

Chris Gent, who had sat on Vodafone's board for a dozen years, was appointed CEO in January 1997. He had never attended college but won a reputation as a shrewd businessman in the banking and computing industries. The company introduced a new corporate identity in the summer of 1997, uniting the six cellular providers it had acquired (Vodac, Talkland, Vodacom, Vodacall, Astec, and People's Phone) under the Vodafone brand. Vodafone began to restructure its network, laying off 250 employees. Its 300 retail outlets dropped competitors' products after the change. The success of One-2-One and Orange prompted regulators to allow Vodafone and top rival Cellnet relative freedom. All four providers promoted heavily during the Christmas 1997 season, each hoping to ensure its fair share of the widening market. The fastest growing segment, low-income clients, was being accommodated through prepayment plans.

The Merger of the Millennium

Beginning January 1, 1999, subscribers became able to retain their phone numbers after switching providers. On the same date, 11 European countries introduced the Euro currency unit, making cross-border acquisitions theoretically more attractive. However, Telecom Italia's shareholders still chose the hostile offer Italian typewriter manufacturer Olivetti tendered in February 1999 over the friendly one of Deutsche Telekom largely due to nationalistic sentiment.

It would be a few months before Vodafone exploited the possibilities of the redefined European financial environment. Meanwhile, it merged with U.S. West Coast cellular company AirTouch in the summer of 1999, paying $68 million. Although this merger thwarted Bell Atlantic from its plans for coast-to-coast wireless coverage, Gent was soon planning a huge new venture with this East Coast company as well.

German telecommunications giant Mannesmann AG bought Orange for $33 billion in October 1999. Some saw the expensive purchase as a move to dissuade potential corporate raiders. However, the teaming of Orange and Mannesmann scuttled plans Vodafone had with Mannesmann's German and Italian mobile phone units and Vodafone launched its own takeover bid on November 16.

Before the takeover was closed, Vodafone had formed a joint venture (Multi Access Portal or MAP) with Vivendi, the French media and telecom group, shutting off a potential white knight from Mannesmann. The German company was also constrained by a lack of poison pill and other takeover defenses in its home country.

After a spirited campaign played out in the media, in February 2000 Vodafone AirTouch acquired Mannesmann AG in the largest corporate takeover ever, surpassing even the merger of AOL and Time Warner in the preceding month. At $180 billion, the final price was nearly twice the original offer. Vodafone shareholders owned 50.5 percent of the new company, Mannesmann shareholders 49.5 percent. Its market value of $314 billion made it the largest British company and the world's sixth largest, according to *Barron's*.

It also entered the millennium as the only truly global wireless phone company. The post-merger Vodafone claimed more than 42 million mobile telephone subscribers in 25 countries. (*Business Week* reckoned Vodafone was paying $9,000 per customer.) However, the real prize was Mannesmann's position in the European Internet market. Gent hoped to use the German company's established ground-based Internet service to grow Vodafone's own new wireless-based Internet service. Although relatively untried at the time, the fusion of mobile telephone and e-commerce technologies offered unprecedented marketing opportunities.

In April 2000, the Verizon Wireless joint venture with Bell Atlantic was launched. The European Commission approved the Vodafone-Mannesmann merger in the same month, stipulating that the combined company sell off its Orange unit and allow competitors access to its international network for three years. Vodafone also planned to sell Mannesmann's old automotive and engineering businesses.

Vodafone was showing strong customer growth in all areas. Its stock had doubled in the previous six months as investors caught on to the group's potential. In May 2000, France Telecom SA announced it was buying Orange for £25.1 billion ($37.4 billion), creating Europe's second largest mobile phone group with 21 million subscribers. Aggressive competition lay ahead. The Globalstar communications satellite, in which Vodafone had an interest, was launched in the same month, and the Vizzavi Internet portal developed with Vivendi debuted.

Ever looking forward, Vodafone was developing new devices offering faster mobile connections than most Americans had on their home PCs. Its control of the tiny screen on millions of such units across Europe and beyond placed it at the center of a telecommunications revolution. More than one analyst expected Vodafone to become the world's largest company.

The first half of the 2000s proved a disappointment for the global mobile telephone market, as the telecommunications sector, and the high-technology market in general, went into an extended slump. The potential of the new high-speed mobile telephone protocol sparked a fierce bidding war that saw most of the industry become heavily indebted. Yet Vodafone, which had maintained a relatively clean balance sheet compared to its heavily indebted competitors, successfully navigated the difficult market. Indeed, between 2000 and 2005, the company more than quintupled its global revenues and more than quadrupled its international subscriber base.

In 2001, Vodafone boosted its position in Japan, acquiring control of Japan Telecom Co. and its mobile carrier J-Phone Co., the number three player in that market. Vodafone also took control of Spain's number two, Airtel, which was subsequently renamed Vodafone Spain. In Ireland, the company bought Eircell in a deal worth EUR 4.5 billion. By 2002, the group's subscriber base already neared 90 million, and revenues had topped $34 billion. The company had also achieved the number one or number two position in a number of core markets, including Britain, Switzerland, France, Italy, Belgium, the Netherlands, and including Verizon's number one position in the United States. However, the company's growth had not yet translated into growing profits; indeed, in 2002, the company posted a loss of £13.5 billion ($21 billion), the largest ever annual loss in U.K. history.

In the meantime, the main growth phase of the mobile communications market appeared to be completed. In Europe for example, mobile telephone penetration had reached 70 percent overall (and higher in individual markets). In the United States, too, analysts estimated that market had already reached 75 percent of its potential. Another difficulty for Vodafone came in 2003, when Chris Gent, described as a "swashbuckler" who had led the company on its $300 billion expansion drive, announced his decision to retire.

Named in Gent's place was Arun Sarin, who had previously led AirTouch before its acquisition by Vodafone. *Business Week* describe Sarin as "a skilled integrator of different businesses." Sarin's skills appeared to be the perfect complement to the post-Gent Vodafone, a sprawling business with 122 million customers and sales of more than $55 billion. Indeed, among Sarin's first moves was to lead Vodafone into an agreement with Microsoft in an attempt to develop a single international mobile handset standard, seen as a crucial development for the future growth of the mobile communications industry.

Yet Sarin quickly surprised observers, launching a takeover bid for AT&T Wireless in the United States in early 2004. Vodafone's bid was topped by Cingular Wireless, however, dashing Vodafone's hopes of becoming a dominant U.S. player independent of the Verizon joint venture.

Elsewhere, Vodafone's difficulties increased. In Japan, the company appeared to have flubbed its bid to position itself in the 3G market there. Vodafone's commitment to handset standardization, which led the company to roll out a limited line of new handsets for its global operations, failed to take into account the highly specific nature of the Japanese market. As competitors launched their own, highly stylish handsets offering cutting-edge services, Vodafone's own handsets appeared quaint. At the same time, competitors' networks boasted download speeds as high as eight times faster than Vodafone's network. The result was a drop in the group's market share, down to 17.8 percent in 2005, and losses in its subscriber base.

In the meantime, with few large-scale acquisition prospects available, at least in the short term, Vodafone's growth prospects appeared to depend on the development of its 3G business. The company launched an aggressive rollout of its new 3G-capable handsets, as well as a range of non-voice services, such as photo messaging, video and music downloads, and the first transmissions of new mobile television programming. Yet the company faced increased competition for the market, as a new range of 3G competitors, including Hong Kong's Hutchison Whampoa, entered the European market. At the same time, a number of other players, notably France Telecom's Orange, had begun a drive to build up scale in order to create a true rival to Vodafone.

With 165 million subscribers and sales of more than £31.5 billion ($64 billion), Vodafone was the outright global leader in the mobile communications market at mid-decade. The company remained interested in further acquisition opportunities. Some analysts suggested that, having failed in its bid to acquire AT&T Wireless, Vodafone might instead launch an effort to take over the combined AT&T and Cingular business. As one of the world's largest companies, Vodafone expected to continue setting the pace for the global telecommunications industry.

Principal Subsidiaries

Airtel Movil SA (21.7%); Belgacom Mobile (Belgium; 25%); Europolitan AB (71.1%); Globalstar L.P. (U.S.A.; 6.5%); Japan Telecom (27%); Libertel (Netherlands; 70%); Mannesmann Mobilfunk GmbH (Germany; 99.1%); MisrFone Telecommunications Co. (Egypt; 60%); Mobilfon SA (Romania; 20.1%); Omnitel Pronto Italia S.p.A. (Italy; 76%); Panafon SA (Greece; 55%); Polkomtel SA (19.6%); RPG Cellcom Ltd. (India; 20.6–49.0%); Safaricom (Kenya; 40%); SFR (France; 20%); Shinsegi Telecom Inc. (South Korea; 11.7%); tele.ring Telekom (Austria; 53.8%); Telecel Comunicacoes Pessoias SA (Portugal; 50.9%); Verizon Wireless (U.S.A.; 45%); Vodacom Pty. Ltd. (South Africa; 31.5%); Vodafone Australia (91%); Vodafone Fiji Ltd. (49%); Vodafone Hungary (50.1%); Vodafone Malta Ltd. (80%); Vodafone New Zealand.

Principal Competitors

British Telecommunications PLC; Deutsche Telekom AG; France Telecom Group; AT&T Corp.

Further Reading

Baker, Stephen, and Kerry Capell, "Chris Gent, King of the Web?," *Business Week,* February 14, 2000, pp. 60–61.

Brewis, Janine, "Vodafone More Than a Match for Mannesmann," *Corporate Finance,* March 2000, pp. 22–26.

Brown, Malcolm, "Slow March of the Mobiles," *Management Today,* December 1993, pp. 54–57.

"Calling the Masses," *Sunday Times,* June 20, 1993.

Capell, Kerry, "Vodafone: Is the Shine Wearing Off?," *Business Week,* June 7, 2004, p. 30.

Carney, Beth, "Will 3G Answer Vodafone's Call?," *Business Week Online,* November 29, 2004.

"Crossed Lines over Survey," *Sunday Times,* March 28, 1993.

Evans, Richard, "The New Microsoft," *Communications International,* April 2000, pp. 29–32.

——, "Tomorrow, the World," *Barron's,* March 6, 2000, p. 28.

Ferguson, Anne, "Securing Racal's Future," *Management Today,* August 1988, pp. 30–31.

Guyon, Janet, "Vodafone's Man on the Line," *Fortune,* July 12, 2004, p. 40.

——, "What Does This Gent Really Want?," *Fortune,* March 6, 2000, pp. 163–66.

"Harrison's Happy Ending," *Daily Telegraph,* June 9, 1993.

Kharif, Olga, "Where Does Vodafone Turn Now?," *Business Week Online,* February 18, 2004.

"The Lex Column: Mobile Market," *Financial Times,* June 8, 1994.

"A Line to the Future," *Mail on Sunday,* February 7, 1993.

"Mobile Telephones: London Calling," *Economist,* August 5, 1995, p. 60.

Naik, Gautam, and Anita Raghavan, "France Telecom Confirms Plan to Buy Vodafone Unit; Purchase of Orange for $37.4 Billion Intensifies a Battle," *Wall Street Journal,* May 31, 2000, p. A21.

O'Sullivan, Tom, "Mobile Phone Rivals Plan Marketing Blitz," *Marketing Week,* December 11, 1997, p. 22.

——, "Vodafone Cuts Lines to Challenge Rivals," *Marketing Week,* July 10, 1997, p. 23.

Palmer, Jay, "Loud and Clear," *Barron's,* December 16, 1996, p. 15.

Reed, Stanley, Kerry Capell, Heidi Dawley, and Stephen Baker, "Ready to Take on the World," *Business Week,* June 12, 2000, pp. 70–71.

Rowley, Ian, "Vodafone's Bad Connection in Japan," *Business Week,* February 21, 2005, p. 20.

Ryan, Vincent, "Vodafone AirTouch's Shock to the System," *Telephony,* February 14, 2000, pp. 35–36.

Schneiderman, Ron, *Future Talk: The Changing Wireless Game,* New York: IEEE Press, 1997.

Shishkin, Philip, and William Boston, "Vodafone Wins EU Clearance to Acquire Mannesmann in Record $180 Billion Deal— Competitors to Get Access to Network for Three Years; Orange Must Be Shed," *Wall Street Journal,* April 13, 2000, p. A14.

"Stay Well Connected for the Phoney War," *Daily Mail,* February 3, 1993.

"Upwardly Mobile," *Economist,* August 13, 1988, pp. 62–64.

"Vodafone: Casting a Worldwide Network," *Investors' Chronicle,* January 7, 1994.

"Vodafone Finds the Right Response," *Corporate Finance,* July 1996, p. 9.

"Vodafone Move Fuels Price War," *Financial Times,* June 17, 1993.

"Vodafone: On Line for a Breakthrough," *Investors' Chronicle,* October 22, 1993.

"Vodafone Signs up for $1.8 Billion Satellite Telecoms Venture," *Independent,* March 25, 1994.

Wallace, Charles P., "A Vodacious Deal," *Time,* February 14, 2000, p. 63.

Wonacott, Peter, and Silvia Ascarelli, "Hutchison Whampoa Sells Stake in Vodafone, Raising $5.03 Billion," *Wall Street Journal,* March 23, 2000, p. A19.

—Robin DuBlanc
—updates: Frederick C. Ingram; M.L. Cohen

Wanadoo S.A.

48 rue Camille Desmoulins
Issy les Moulineaux
F-92791 Cedex 9
France
Telephone: +33 1 58 88 50 00
Fax: +33 1 58 88 50 50
Web site: http://www.wanadoo.com

Wholly Owned Subsidiary of France Telecom Group
Incorporated: 1996
Employees: 6,333
Sales: EUR 3.25 billion ($3.89 billion) (2004)
NAIC: 514191 Internet Service Providers; 513390 Other
    Telecommunications; 511140 Database and Directory
    Publishers; 541512 Computer Systems Design
    Services

Wanadoo S.A. is one of Europe's top three Internet service providers (ISPs), along with rivals T-Online and Tiscali. The company, a subsidiary of France Telecom, boasts nearly ten million customers chiefly in France, the United Kingdom, Spain, and The Netherlands, but also in Morocco, Jordan, Mauritius, and Algeria. France remains Wanadoo's single largest market, accounting for more than four million subscribers. The company is also one of the leading ISPs in the United Kingdom, through its subsidiary Wanadoo UK, formerly Freeserve. The company's Internet services have focused especially on building up its broadband network, based on both the ADSL and ADSL+ protocols. In 2004, the company launched its WIFI-equipped Livebox, combining Internet capability with Internet telephony capacity. Since late 2005, the company also has begun rolling out Internet television services as well. Wanadoo's true strength, however, lies in its strong content and services component. The company's PagesJaunes Internet-based yellow pages directories are a major source of revenues for the group, and include a base of nearly 700,000 business customers. The company also has moved to extend its directories operations into other markets, particularly Spain. Wanadoo also controls online shopping site Marcopoly, spe-

cialized in appliances and electronics, and Alapage, specialized in books, CDs, and video. Another Wanadoo operation, Voila, is France's leading French-language Internet portal and search engine. Parent company France Telecom took full control of Wanadoo, which had previously listed 10 percent of its stock on the Euronext Paris Stock Exchange, in 2004. At the end of 2005, France Telecom signaled its intention to merge Wanadoo with its mobile telephone subsidiary, Orange, in order to create a single overriding brand. Wanadoo is expected to be rebranded as an Orange subbrand following the merger process, which could take as much as 18 months to complete. In 2004, Wanadoo posted revenues of EUR 3.25 billion ($3.9 billion).

Late Internet Entry in the 1990s

France Telecom was a true pioneer in offering online services to the general public. Long before the rise of the Internet and the World Wide Web, France Telecom had developed its own proprietary service, with its own terminals, using ordinary telephone lines. Launched in 1982, Minitel, as the service was called, provided users with directory services, as well as a range of other services, such as paid chat and information services. Unlike the Internet, where users paid for the connection but where content was, in large part, free, Minitel users paid both for their connection time and for the various services they used. A third revenue stream came from the rental of the Minitel terminal to customers. Yet this proved an advantage as well, at a time when personal computers remained an expensive purchase.

As such, Minitel became an important source of revenues, and huge profits, for France Telecom. By the early 1990s, revenues from Minitel neared FRF 9.5 billion (equivalent to $1.5 billion). Understandably, France Telecom saw little interest in developing its own Internet service in the early 1990s. Minitel appeared solidly entrenched in France, despite the inroads made by the arrival of early paid online services, including America Online (AOL), Compuserve, and later, MSN. Part of Minitel's strength lay in the extremely low penetration of personal computers among the consumer population.

A number of factors converged to give a boost to the Internet market in France in the mid-1990s. Prices on personal comput-

Company Perspectives:

We build and develop Internet access products, services and tools and produce great portal content—all to help our customers get the most from the Internet.

ers had started to shift downward. The development of new multimedia features, and especially the addition of soundcards, high-resolution color graphics, and then CD-ROMs as standard equipment, provided a platform for a wider range of uses, and made the personal computer a more appealing consumer appliance. A new generation of higher-speed modems arrived toward the mid-1990s as well; in just a few years, the maximum connection speed had risen from just 1,200 bits per second (bps) to a maximum of 56,000 bps. The faster speeds were particularly attractive given the arrival of a major Internet innovation, namely, the World Wide Web, which provided a graphical interface to the Internet for the first time.

By 1995, a growing number of companies had begun to vie for France's nascent Internet market. As the French telephone monopoly, France Telecom naturally benefited from the steady rise in the use of its telephone lines, all the more so because, like most of its European counterparts (and unlike in the United States), customers were accustomed to paid local calls and to per-minute charges. In addition, a large number of new Internet users living in the country's provinces were forced to connect using higher-priced interregional and long-distance phone numbers.

Yet the rise of the use of the Internet and online services clearly threatened Minitel with extinction. As revenues from Minitel began to drop, especially since many of the services available through Minitel could be had for free through the Internet, France Telecom was forced to rethink its indifference to the Internet. In January 1996, therefore, the company announced that it was setting up its own Internet service provider, called Wanadoo.

Wanadoo went live in May 1996. A major feature of the new service was its use of a single telephone number that was accessible nationwide at local dialing rates. While this service was put into place for the country's other national ISPs, Wanadoo greatly benefited from France Telecom's backing in a number of ways. Wanadoo was given control over the implementation and access to the newly launched online version of the French yellow pages, PagesJaunes. Through the end of the 1990s and into the 2000s, PagesJaunes remained Wanadoo's single largest source of revenues and profits. Another benefit from its relationship with France Telecom was its access to its parent's countrywide network of retail stores, giving the company closer proximity to potential customers.

Pan-European Provider in the 2000s

A major step forward for Wanadoo came in 1997 when it teamed up with MSN, in the midst of a brief bid to rival AOL in France. Rather than set up its own network, however, MSN turned to Wanadoo. This placed Wanadoo in position to scoop up MSN's customer base when the Microsoft-owned company decided to exit France in 1998. Also that year, the company

lowered its subscription rates, undercutting certain of its rivals by as much as 30 percent in a bid to gain market share. By the end of that year, Wanadoo had established itself as the clear Internet leader in France.

In addition to boosting its subscriber base, Wanadoo launched an effort to expand its range of content and services. By the end of 1999, the company had added several services, including the French-language portal and search engine Voila, which rapidly became one of the leading portals in France. The company also launched a direct-marketing wing, Mediatel, while making a series of acquisitions, including Alapage.com, an e-commerce book, music, and video seller; and the Kompass franchises for France, the Benelux market, and Spain. In 2000, the company boosted its content portfolio again with the purchase of Marcopoly, an e-commerce site specialized in home appliances and electronics.

By 2000, Wanadoo counted more than 1.3 million subscribers in France, representing a market share of more than 50 percent. The company's revenues by then had topped EUR 800 million. Some 87 percent of the group's sales, however, were still generated by its Yellow Pages division. Indeed, much of the success of Wanadoo's initial public offering (IPO) in 2000 came from France Telecom's decision to bundle in the PagesJaunes unit as part of the launch.

The IPO, of just 10 percent of Wanadoo's stock, was enough to fuel Wanadoo's drive to become one of Europe's leading Internet groups. The company had initiated this effort in 1999, launching its ISP service in Belgium and The Netherlands, and planning an entry into Denmark as well. Wanadoo also targeted the Spanish market, which was then one of the least developed Internet markets in Europe. For its entry into Spain, Wanadoo acquired a 69 percent stake in Spain's Uni2, an Internet service provider, which served as the backbone for the launch of the Wanadoo Spain service. The company quickly built up a position as number three ISP in Spain.

France Telecom's acquisition of U.K. mobile telephone company Orange in 2001 pointed the way for Wanadoo's next, and largest, expansion effort. Shortly after, Wanadoo acquired Freeserve, the leading ISP in the United Kingdom, in a deal worth more than $2 billion. The addition of Freeserve added more than 1.5 million subscribers to Wanadoo's subscriber base, propelling the company into the top ranks of European ISPs. Eighteen months after the Freeserve purchase, Wanadoo changed its U.K. subsidiary's name to Wanadoo UK.

Freeserve had been set up as part of a trend in Europe that saw the rise of a whole new class of Internet providers offering their services for free. The trend helped encourage the breakthrough in the European Internet penetration rates, which had lagged far behind the United States and Japan. Wanadoo was forced to follow suit, and launched its own free subscription service. The loss of these subscriber revenues encouraged Wanadoo and France Telecom to step up the rollout of the next generation of Internet services, based on the high-speed ADSL protocol. In this way, Wanadoo was able to retain many of its free-subscription customers, shifting them toward paid broadband access.

Wanadoo next turned to Spain, where it paid EUR 360 million ($336 million) to acquire the directory publisher Indice

---

Key Dates:

1982: France Telecom launches Minitel, an online directory service.
1996: France Telecom enters the Internet market with the launch of Wanadoo and online Yellow Pages unit PagesJaunes.
1998: Wanadoo takes over MSN's French subscriber base; the Voila Internet portal is launched.
1999: Wanadoo acquires Alapage.com, an online book, video, and music store; the company enters Spain through the acquisition of 69 percent of Uni2; the company enters The Netherlands and Belgian markets.
2000: Wanadoo is listed on the Euronext Paris Stock Exchange; Marcopoly, specialized in home appliances and electronics, is acquired.
2001: The company acquires Freeserve, the leading Internet service provider (ISP) in the United Kingdom (later re-branded as Wanadoo UK).
2002: The company acquires EresMas in Spain, becoming that market's number two ISP.
2003: Wanadoo exits the Belgian market.
2004: France Telecom acquires full control of Wanadoo.
2005: France Telecom announces its intention to merge the Orange and Wanadoo brands.

Multimedia. By 2002, the company had acquired EresMas, from Grupo Auna, adding more than one million subscribers. The EresMas purchase boosted Wanadoo to the number two spot in the Spanish ISP market. In The Netherlands, the company grew through its purchase of MyWeb B.V., adding 110,000 customers to become that country's number three player.

Not all of Wanadoo's international efforts were successful, however. The company had failed to gain a significant position in Belgium, rising only to fifth place. In 2003, Wanadoo sold off its Belgian arm to Tiscali. Nonetheless, for the most part Wanadoo'ss strategy had paid off. By the end of 2002, the company's sales had topped EUR 2.0 billion. In that year, as well, Wanadoo became the first of the major European ISPs to turn a profit.

France remained the company's stronghold, with more than four million subscribers, including some one million broadband subscribers by 2003. Indeed, the broadband segment was now driving Wanadoo's growth, accounting for some two-thirds of all new subscribers. By 2004, as ADSL modem speeds topped 2 megabits per second (Mbps), with a promise to reach as high as 20 Mbps by the end of that year, Wanadoo launched its Livebox, a WIFI-enabled modem and router featuring Internet telephony services, and the promise of ADSL-based television

transmission. By 2005, Wanadoo's subscriber base neared ten million, and revenues had passed EUR 3.25 billion.

The mid-2000s promised a major shift in the telecommunications market, as the mobile telephone sector prepared its own high-speed networks. "Convergence" became the buzzword, combining traditional voice telephone services with Internet access and a whole new range of services.

France Telecom began to position itself for the new market, and in 2004 acquired the minority shares in Wanadoo. By 2005, France Telecom had revealed its intention to merge its Orange and Wanadoo brands into a single brand identity. As part of that process, which was expected to last as long as 18 months, Wanadoo was expected to be rebranded under the Orange name. In the meantime, Wanadoo continued to play a prominent role as one of the true motors of the European Internet market.

Principal Subsidiaries

Wanadoo UK PLC; Wanadoo Spain S.A.; Wanadoo Netherlands B.V.

Principal Competitors

BT Group PLC; UnitedGlobalCom, Inc.; T-Online International AG; Tiscali S.p.A.; Free S.A.; Yahoo! Inc.; Google Inc.; Cegetel S.A.S.; Telecom Italia Media S.p.A.

Further Reading

Carter, Ben, "Is BT's First Real Rival on the Way?," *Marketing,* October 6, 2004, p. 14.
"France Telecom Hopes for Successful Wanadoo IPO," *Telecoms Deal Report,* July 21, 2000.
Hargrave, Sean, "Wanadoo: Going for the Treble," *New Media Age,* May 5, 2005, p. 18.
Holmes, Mark, "Wanadoo Targets Spain, But Chafes Under Tight Regulation," *Communications Today,* January 4, 2001.
"Orange Weighs Up Sub-brands in Wake of Wanadoo Merger," *New Media Age,* October 6, 2005, p. 3.
"Rebranding Wanadoo," *Campaign,* July 8, 2005, p. 10.
Reinhardt, Andy, "Can Wanadoo Keep Doing It?," *Business Week,* June 23, 2003, p. 80.
"Wanadoo Creates Voice and Video Services Brand," *Marketing,* March 2, 2005, p. 4.
"Wanadoo Netherlands to Build Own Broadband Network," *Online Reporter,* September 11, 2004.
"Wanadoo Reports Over 1 Million 'Livebox' Subscribers," *Tarifica Alert,* October 18, 2005.
"Wanadoo Serves Notice of Its UK Intentions with Freeserve Acquisition," *Telecoms Deal Report,* December 21, 2000.
"Wanadoo Takes on Yahoo! and MSN with Pan-European Boost," *New Media Age,* April 28, 2005, p. 3.
"Wanadoo Tops 4m Customers in France," *EuropeMedia,* February 12, 2003.

—M.L. Cohen

Wieden + Kennedy

224 NW 13th Avenue
Portland, Oregon 97209
U.S.A.
Telephone: (503) 937-7000
Fax: (503) 937-8000
Web site: http://www.wk.com

Private Company
Incorporated: 1982
Employees: 523
Gross Billings: $875 million (2004 est.)
NAIC: 541810 Advertising Agencies; 541830 Media
Buying Agencies; 541850 Display Advertising;
541870 Advertising Material Distribution Services;
541890 Other Services Related to Advertising

Wieden + Kennedy (W + K) is one of the largest independent advertising companies in the world. Best known for the NIKE slogan, "Just Do It," the company's other high-profile clients have included Coca-Cola, ESPN, Subaru, Avon, and America Online. Wieden + Kennedy's offices are located in Portland, New York, Amsterdam, London, Shanghai, and Tokyo. Wieden + Kennedy also has launched "12," a school that offers 13 months of hands-on experience for aspiring advertising professionals.

1982–94: From Relative Obscurity to Wide Acclamation

Dan Wieden and David Kennedy opened their independent advertising agency, Wieden + Kennedy, on April 1, 1982. Wieden was the son of F.D. "Duke" Wieden, the former chairman of the Gerber agency in Portland, Oregon, a man greatly admired for his passion for advertising and for his craft as an ad man. The younger Wieden originally had intended to pursue a career in writing and attended the University of Oregon, earning a degree in journalism in 1967. After experimenting briefly with writing screenplays and short stories, however, he went to work at the McCann-Erickson advertising agency in Portland, Oregon.

Dan Wieden met David Kennedy in 1980 at McCann-Erickson. At the time, Kennedy's career in advertising was more extensive than Wieden's and included having worked for Leo Burnett and Young & Rubicam in Chicago. Like Wieden, Kennedy had a dislike for status quo advertising. He held a degree in fine art from the University of Colorado at Boulder and had "spent the '60s not telling anyone what [he] did for a living," according to a 1992 *Advertising Age* article. The pair began to work together at McCann on the NIKE account in 1980. Two years later, they left to create their own ad agency, taking with them their one client at McCann, NIKE. With a card table, borrowed typewriter, and pay phone, they opened Wieden + Kennedy in the basement of a Portland labor union hall.

Portland-based NIKE was still small and relatively unknown in the early 1980s. Company lore recounts that when Phil Knight met with Wieden and Kennedy for the first time, he told them, "I hate advertising." Wieden and Kennedy did not design NIKE's trademark "swoosh"; they did break new ground in advertising throughout the 1980s, however, by injecting irreverent humor, sophisticated film techniques, and hip cultural references into their ads for the shoe manufacturer. The firm put Lou Reed in a Honda commercial, used the Beatles' "Revolution" as an insurrectionist version of a jingle for NIKE in 1987, and introduced a cinematic, storytelling approach to print and television ads. Although NIKE moved most of its account to California-based Chiat/Day in 1983 in anticipation of the 1984 Olympics in Los Angeles, it returned to W + K in 1985. In 1988, Wieden coined the phrase, "Just Do It," which almost instantly won fame for both NIKE and W + K.

By 1990, Wieden + Kennedy had risen from obscurity to become one of the most acclaimed creative agencies in the United States. Its offices filled the former GranTree Rental Furniture building in downtown Portland. Wieden explained the company's unique approach to advertising in a 1990 *Advertising Age* article: "Philosophically, it's about having no formula for creativity—[W]e're not trained in the classical sense—we're not trained to produce ads. And one of the successes of our agency is to try to find out what it's all about. I'm not that interested in American advertising." In fact, Wieden and Kennedy referred to their work on numerous occasions not as

Company Perspectives:

*Wieden + Kennedy is an independent, creatively led adver-
tising agency that exists to create strong and provocative
relationships between good companies and their consumers.
Wieden + Kennedy was created to be a different type of
advertising agency: one where people come to do the best
work of their careers. After twenty years we are still true to
that mission and dream. That is why we have remained
independent, even as large corporations have gobbled up
our creative brethren around the globe. That is why we are
still run by creative people. That is also why we offer a
diversity of talent unequaled by any other agency.*

advertising but as communication. The work represented, according to Wieden in the 1990 *Advertising Age* piece, ''. . .
some honest, startling, refreshing communication with someone
we're talking to in whatever medium. This is not about one
brand or style. It's about a basic respect you have for the people
you're talking to.''

As the agency grew, Wieden and Kennedy spent less time on
the creative aspects of their business. From 1988 onward, the
team did not produce many ads, but instead oversaw the work of
staffers. For Wieden, the shift was welcome. ''I get very excited
about other people's work. I don't have a huge need to do
hands-on work,'' he said in 1990 in *Advertising Age*. The
change was harder for Kennedy. ''It's been extremely frustrat-
ing for me. I'm basically a creative type, but I found myself
sitting in more meetings than doing ads,'' he said in 1993 in
Advertising Age.

Growth continued for W + K throughout the early 1990s, but
that growth was not steady. In 1991, *Advertising Age* chose W +
K as its Agency of the Year, the same year W + K won a
substantial account with Subaru of America and opened an office
in Philadelphia to serve its new client. With the addition of
Subaru, the agency's billings rose 65 percent to $165 million. W
+ K did not fit easily into the Philadelphia community, however,
which was more staid than that of Portland. When in 1993 Subaru
fired the agency, W + K closed its Philadelphia office. Earlier
that same year, having experienced total losses of about $11
million in billings during a six-month period, it imposed austerity
measures on upper management and instituted layoffs for the first
time in its 11-year history, reducing its staff by about 15 people
and reducing its Portland staff by 10 percent.

1995–2000: A Period of Tremendous Change

David Kennedy's retirement at the end of 1995 inaugurated
another significant change at W + K in the day-to-day functions of the $200 million business. ''The way we worked,'' as
Wieden explained of his relationship with Kennedy in *Advertising Age* in 1993, ''was very much like an old married couple.
Instead of a division of labor, we were more two bodies with
one mind. We'd double up on most chores, such as reviewing
creative or dealing with financial issues.''

In fact, Kennedy's departure created a ripple effect throughout the agency. Prior to 1992, fewer than a dozen people had left

Wieden + Kennedy. But that changed in the second half of the
1990s; the agency began to experience turnover similar to that
of other advertising agencies, with some staffers moving on to
establish ad agencies of their own. In part this change was the
inevitable result of the company's growth, but former staffers
also described it as the product of W + K's cohesive, family-
like culture. As Wieden himself admitted to *Advertising Age* in
1992, ''It's pretty well known when you talk to headhunters that
we don't pay very well and we border on being a sweatshop.''
The company held on tightly to its workers and communicated a
sense of betrayal regarding those who left.

The second half of the 1990s was a time of steady growth for
Wieden + Kennedy despite the coming and going of some of
its more prominent clients. In 1996, the agency added additional
Microsoft products and Miller Genuine Draft to its roster and
billings rose to $624 million. Billings rose again to $877 million
in 1997, despite the fact that NIKE took more of its business to
Goodby, Silverstein & Partners in San Francisco that year. In
1998, Miller jumped ship, and NIKE returned again in 1999.
These events led to more layoffs, internal restructuring, and a
focus on recruiting new business.

Also in 1998, W + K opened a London office at least in part
as a way of winning NIKE's global business. The London office
eventually handled NIKE's U.K. work, as well as local projects
for Diet Coke, Virgin Interactive, and Flextech cable networks;
for the first six months of its existence, however, an agreement
with NIKE forbid the office from undertaking new business
efforts. As a result, W + K was perceived as being standoffish
in the London advertising community, and the office struggled
with high turnover. It went through three managing directors
and four creative directors during its first two and a half years.

At the same time, positive change was brewing at home in
the late 1990s. Part of Wieden's vision for W + K was to create
a company headquarters that would generate creativity and
nurture the staff's artistry. Although the GranTree Rental Furniture building in downtown Portland had been an adequate home
for the company in its early days, it had become a tight fit for the
agency's 250 employees and did not have enough of an innovative atmosphere to suit Wieden. Thus in 2000, with close to
$780 million in billings, W + K moved its headquarters to a
new space in Portland's trendy Pearl District, home to art
galleries, restaurants, shops, and upscale condos. Here Wieden
purchased a 22,000-square-foot cold-storage space and began to
realize his goal of building ''a creative institution, a synergistic
hub where business, art, and community [would thrive],'' as he
explained in a press release in 2001.

With the help of architects, Wieden cut out the building's
core, creating a naturally lit, open workspace with a six-story
atrium where everyone in the building could meet. The new
headquarters also housed a screening room, a 275-seat amphi-
theater, a penthouse floor with a café and reference library, and
a bona fide gymnasium. Instead of an awards case in the front
lobby, a totem pole and a wall covered with photos of employees shot by local photographer Peter Stone greeted visitors. The
building also housed the Portland Institute for Contemporary
Art, whose mission was to advance emerging ideas in new art in
Portland and in the international community and local artists-in-
residence so that staffers might draw inspiration from close

<table>
<tr><td colspan="2">Key Dates:</td></tr>
<tr><td>1982:</td><td>Dan Wieden and David Kennedy open Wieden + Kennedy.</td></tr>
<tr><td>1988:</td><td>The company's "Just Do It" campaign for NIKE wins international publicity.</td></tr>
<tr><td>1991:</td><td>Advertising Age chooses W + K as its Agency of the Year.</td></tr>
<tr><td>1992:</td><td>W + K opens an office in Amsterdam.</td></tr>
<tr><td>1994:</td><td>W + K opens an office in Tokyo.</td></tr>
<tr><td>1995:</td><td>David Kennedy retires.</td></tr>
<tr><td>1998:</td><td>The company opens an office in London.</td></tr>
<tr><td>2000:</td><td>W + K moves its headquarters to a new space in Portland.</td></tr>
<tr><td>2004:</td><td>The company opens an office in Shanghai.</td></tr>
</table>

contact with the arts. "I want people outside to think, 'Geez, that would be a cool place to work.' And I want the people already here to have a creative outlet—so they won't leave and go off to Hollywood," explained Wieden in an *Inc.com* magazine article in 2004. To that end, the company also encouraged and sometimes funded nonadvertising creative endeavors by staff, such as films, books, and stage plays.

From its new headquarters, W + K also began to pursue its goal of achieving "branded content"—advertising melded with other forms of entertainment, such as music, television, and film—and thereby extended the branded image into areas other than the 30-second television spot. The company created an in-house entertainment division to pursue projects funded by a client or produced by the agency itself. One such project produced by W + K was a book called *Cat Spelled Backwards Doesn't Spell God: The Dogs of Portland,* which hit bestseller lists overseas.

2000s: Continuing As a Leader and Trendsetter

Bad news came in 2001 when Coca-Cola pulled back much of its business from W + K and Microsoft cut its ties to the company completely. Both of these losses led to layoffs of a significant number of employees at W + K (despite the acquisition of Amazon.com as a new client). Notwithstanding the cutbacks, the company continued its experiments with branded content. New projects involved pairing clients with new media. For example, in 2001, NIKE worked with Radical Media to produce a documentary called *Road to Paris,* which followed Lance Armstrong on the Tour de France. Also in 2001, W + K debuted two-minute versions of NIKE commercials that were, in effect, music videos. The Tokyo office also began experimenting with music, commissioning original songs and music videos for NIKE advertisements. The success of NIKE music led NIKE and W + K to launch their own record label in the fall of 2003 and to start work on a production called "Ball: The Musical."

In 2004, W + K opened an office in Shanghai. This brought the company's number of overseas offices to four, with additional offices in London, Amsterdam, and Tokyo. W + K also had U.S. offices in New York and Portland. The company had billings of about $875 million and a staff of 523. Within W + K, a new generation of managers was being recruited as Wieden began to look toward retirement. Questions arose about the style of work W + K would produce without either Wieden or Kennedy, but one thing was certain: The contribution these two men had made to the field of advertising would continue to influence practitioners and agencies for years to come.

Further Reading

"America's 25 Most Fascinating Entrepreneurs," *Inc.,* April 1, 2004.

Cooper, Ann, "The Wieden Angle," *Advertising Age,* January 1, 1990, p. 14.

Cuneo, Alice, "Wieden's Horizons; New Architecture; Portland Shop Revamps Office and Future Outlook," *Advertising Age,* May 15, 2000, p. 20.

Horton, Cleveland, "Wieden & Kennedy: Keeping Ad Game Fresh," *Advertising Age,* April 13, 1992, p. S3.

——, "Wieden Minus Kennedy: Life Goes On," *Advertising Age,* June 7, 1993, p. 4.

LaBarre, Polly, "The Year of Learning Dangerously," *FastCompany,* December 2004, p. 34.

Lieber, Ron, "Creative Space," *FastCompany*, January 2001, p. 136.

Vagnoni, Anthony, "Wieden Scions Sprout Up As Execs at Far-Flung Shops," *Advertising Age,* October 25, 1999, p. 38.

Wentz, Laurel, "London Fog: A Tale of Two Agencies," *Advertising Age,* December 4, 2000, p. 16.

—Carrie Rothburd

Yeo Hiap Seng Malaysia Bhd.

7 Jalan Tandang
Petaling Jaya
46050
Malaysia
Telephone: + 60 3 7787 3888
Fax: + 60 3 7782 2730
Web site: http://www.yeos.com.my

Public Company
Founded: 1900
Employees: 1,700
Sales: MYR 373.24 million (2004)
Stock Exchanges: Kuala Lumpur
Ticker Symbol: YHMS
NAIC: 311611 Animal (Except Poultry) Slaughtering; 112990 All Other Animal Production; 311421 Fruit and Vegetable Canning; 311422 Specialty Canning; 311612 Meat Processed from Carcasses; 312111 Soft Drink Manufacturing

Yeo Hiap Seng Malaysia Bhd. is one of the leading food and beverages groups in the Malaysian and Singapore markets. The Petaling Jaya-based company produces a range of foods and carbonated and noncarbonated beverages under the brands Yeo's, Fizzi, Goodtaste, SoyRich, and Cintan. Core product areas include soy milk, tea, and instant noodles; the company holds the number one spot in its market for the first two, and has targeted the third category for future leadership as well. In addition, Yeo's product range includes canned goods, such as curries, coconut, and the like; sugarcane-based drinks and chrysanthemum tea; and other regional favorites. The company's logistics and distribution network gives it national reach. After a disastrous attempt to enter the U.S. market in the early 1990s (through the acquisition of Chinese food brand Chun King), Yeo has remained closer to home, focusing primarily on Malaysia and, through subsidiary YHS Beverage, Singapore. Nonetheless, the company also operates production and distribution joint ventures in China and Thailand. Yeo Malaysia has been listed on the Kuala Lumpur Stock Exchange

since 1975; the company is controlled at nearly 61 percent by Singapore's Yeo Hiap Seng, which has converted itself, in large part, into a real estate and property development holding company. In 2004, Yeo Hiap Seng Malaysia posted sales of more than MYR 375 million.

Early 20th-Century Soy Sauce Maker

Like many businesses in Malaysia and Singapore, Yeo Hiap Seng's origins lay in the vast ethnic Chinese community that helped transform much of the Southeast Asian region in the first half of the 20th century. The Chinese proved to be energetic entrepreneurs, often backed by strong support networks in their business endeavors. Over the course of the 20th century, the ethnic Chinese community, particularly in Singapore and Malaysia, developed into the region's strongest economic players. Although the Chinese avoided political involvement, and thus remained at the mercy of governmental will, they clearly controlled the regional economy.

Among the Chinese who arrived in Singapore in the years leading up to World War I was Yeo Keng Lian. Yeo had founded a soy sauce factory in Amoy, near Zhangzhou, in China's Fujian province, in 1900. Yet the Yeo family's greatest success came only after they immigrated to Singapore in 1935. By 1937, the family had incorporated its new business. The name chosen for the company, set up as a family-controlled partnership with a starting capital of just SGD 51,000, set the tone for the group. The Yeo family called their company Yeo Hiap Seng Sauce Factory (Yeo Hiap Seng literally translated as ''Yeo United to Succeed.'')

Success was indeed swift, as the city-state's large ethnic Chinese community embraced the Yeo family's soy sauce. By the early 1940s, the company's sauce also had begun developing a market in nearby Malaysia as well. Yeo Hiap Seng formally extended its sales reach to Malaysia in 1942. The manufacturing base of the company's operations remained limited to Singapore, however, into the 1950s.

The years following World War II saw a dramatic transformation of the region, as Singapore and Malaysia emerged from British colonial domination to set up their own independent

Company Perspectives:

Our Vision: To be the No. 1 Asian Food and Beverage Company in Malaysia. Current Achievements: No. 1 in Soy Milk Category; No. 1 in Tea Drink Category; No. 1 in Canned Meat Range. Targets: No. 1 in Instant Noodle Category; No. 1 in Canned Food Category.

governments. The Chinese community played an important role in creating a base of relative financial stability on which to build the new countries. As important partners for the country's emerging political elite, the Chinese community maintained their own economic prosperity.

For Yeo, the postwar period became a time of strong growth and expansion into new areas. By the late 1940s, the company had begun to prepare a diversification of its production, launching development of its first new product, a canned chicken curry, in 1950. In support of this effort, the company built a new and larger production facility in 1951. The following year, the company became the first in the region to market a canned chicken curry product.

That successful launch was soon followed by the company's expansion into the production and bottling of beverages, as well as the launch of a wider range of canned foods. Yeo also continued to produce its soy sauce. In the early 1950s, the company sought to leverage its expertise in soy products by experimenting with methods for bottling soy milk. Until then, consumers had to make their own soy drinks, boiling the soy over a fire for long periods. By 1955, however, Yeo had succeeded in developing a method for producing and bottling the soy milk. The launch of that product sparked a revolution of sorts in the region's beverage market. At the same time, the company recognized the potential for bottling another favorite regional beverage, chrysanthemum tea.

Yeo converted from its partnership status to that of a limited liability company in 1955. Two years later, with the declaration of Malaysia's independence, the company formalized its operation in that country as well, establishing a sales subsidiary there, Yeo Hiap Seng (Sarawak) Sdn. Bhd. Yet, with the new Malaysian government promoting the country's economic independence as well, Yeo quickly added a production component in that country. The new Yeo subsidiary, Yeo Hiap Seng Canning Factory (Malaya) Sdn. Bhd., opened in Petaling Jaya in 1959.

Canning and Bottling Innovator in the 1960s

Through the 1960s, Yeo continued expanding its range of products. By the early 1970s, the company had branched out into instant noodles, chili, and tomato and oyster sauces, among others. Yeo was also the first in Singapore and Malaysia to begin packaging a newly developed long-life UHT soy milk in disposable paper-based containers, starting in 1967. The popularity of the new packaging type led the company to launch a similar packaging for its chrysanthemum tea. In 1974, Yeo adopted the latest generation of paper-based packaging, the Tetrabrik. In support of its packaging conversion, the company acquired its own tetrabrik packaging machine in 1974. In the meantime, the com-

pany had begun to establish its brand name elsewhere in the world, launching exports of its canned curry in 1967.

Yeo went public on the Singapore Stock Exchange in 1969, at which time Alan Yeo, grandson of the company's founder, took over as CEO. The company by then also had gained the bottling franchise for Pepsi Cola in Singapore and Malaysia, boosting the company among the region's top beverage groups. Meanwhile, the determination for developing self-sufficiency by the Malaysian government led to the enactment of a new series of legislation governing the import sector. As a result, Yeo Malaysia built a new factory in Johor Baru in 1971, becoming a major Malaysian beverage and food producer in its own right. This led the company to go public in 1975, as Yeo Hiap Seng (Malaysia) Bhd. Yeo Hiap Seng maintained a controlling stake in its Malaysian counterpart, however, and the companies continued to evolve in parallel for some time. Gradually, however, the focus of the group's food and beverage manufacturing operations shifted to Malaysia, as the Yeo Hiap Seng group itself grew to include a range of diversified interests, especially real estate.

During the 1970s, Yeo launched a variety of new tetrapak beverages. In 1976, the company became the first to introduce herbal teas in tetrapaks. Yeo also unveiled its successful line of bottled sugarcane drinks in 1978. Into the 1980s, Yeo sought to expand its beverage offering. The company entered the carbonated beverage category in 1984 with the production of a range of "Fizzi" brand tropical fruit-flavored soft drinks. In that year, as well, Yeo became the first in Malaysia to offer a smaller format 100 percent juice for the childrens' market. The "Junior Juice" brand featured 125 ml tetrabriks.

By the end of the 1980s, Alan Yeo had developed the Yeo name into a major player in the food and beverage markets in Malaysia and Singapore. By 1987, Alan Yeo himself had earned recognition as Singapore's "Businessman of the Year."

Yet Yeo already faced dissension among the ranks of Yeo family members, many of whom remained active in the company's management. Tensions began to gather when Alan Yeo led the company on an attempt to enter the U.S. market in the late 1980s. Yeo accomplished this by buying the Chun King brand of Chinese food from Nabisco for $52 million.

The purchase proved to be a big mistake, and Alan Yeo's downfall. Nabisco had had the marketing clout to ensure Chun King a prominent place on supermarket shelves and in the minds of U.S. consumers. Yeo, however, lacked both experience in the U.S. market and sufficient funds to properly market the Chun King brand. Of importance, the success of the Chun King brand had come during a period when there were relatively few Chinese restaurants outside of the country's urban centers. By the early 1990s, however, Chinese restaurants had found their way throughout every segment of the American landscape. In this way, the Chun King brand lost its novelty, and sales began to slip.

The problems at Chun King quickly caught up with Yeo itself, and the company slipped into the red in the early 1990s. The Yeo family, whose shareholding interests in the company were bound together in a jointly owned private holding company, split into factions. One faction, led by Alan Yeo's nephew Charles, began calling for the ouster of Alan Yeo as head of the

Key Dates:

1900: Yeo Keng Lian begins producing soy sauce in Amoy, near Zhangzhou, in China's Fujian province.

1935: The Yeo family immigrates to Singapore and establishes Yeo Hiap Seng.

1942: The company establishes a sales operation in Malaysia.

1953: The company launches its first canned chicken curry; bottled soy milk and chrysanthemum tea are introduced.

1957: The Malaysian office is incorporated as Yeo Hiap Seng (Sarawak).

1959: The Malaysian branch begins food production in a facility in Petaling Jaya.

1969: Yeo Hiap Seng goes public on the Singapore Stock Exchange.

1975: Yeo Hiap Seng (Malaysia) goes public on the Kuala Lumpur Stock Exchange.

1984: The company launches the Fizzi brand of carbonated fruit-flavored beverages.

1989: The Chun King brand in the United States is acquired.

1990: The company launches production of soy milk under license in China.

1993: The company enters the Thai market through the WY Co. joint venture.

1995: The Ng family acquires control of the Yeo companies; noodle production begins in the Fujian province.

2001: The company establishes a Bahrain sales and distribution subsidiary.

2005: A sales and distribution alliance is formed with Hain Celestial, a U.S.-based organic foods and natural products company.

family. In response Alan Yeo won the right to break up the family holding company, which enabled him to sack Charles and other members of the dissenting group.

Yet Alan Yeo's victory was only temporary. The breakup of the holding company also enabled family members to sell off their stakes in the company. By 1995, the prominent Singaporean real estate family led by Ng Teng Fong had amassed 24.9 percent of Yeo, just below the threshold that would have triggered an automatic takeover offer. Yet during that year, Yeo, which owned some highly valuable properties, had found another suitor, Malaysian banker and industrialist Quek Leng Chan, head of the Dao Heng Bank in Hong Kong and the Hong Leong Group, among others. Quek was also cousin to the Singapore-based Kwek family, which controlled real estate and hotel group CDL. By the middle of 1995, Quek had quietly built up a stake of more than one-third of Yeo's shares, triggering a takeover battle with the Ng group.

Malaysia Base in the New Century

The Ng family ultimately emerged as victorious, with the Yeo family becoming the ultimate loser, removed from the company founded by their grandfather nearly a century before.

Under Chairman Robert Ng, Yeo increasingly split its Singapore and Malaysian operations, with the Singapore wing focusing on real estate development, and the Malaysian wing becoming the base for the company's continuing food and beverage operations. This transition was confirmed in 2001 when Yeo Hiap Seng in Singapore received permission to transfer control of its beverage business, YHS Beverage (International) Pte. to Yeo Malaysia in 2001. At the same time, the Ng family brought in France's Danone as a new major shareholder in Yeo Malaysia to assist in developing its food and beverage wing.

The arrival of Danone also played a part in Yeo's increasing interest in once again expanding beyond the Malaysian and Singapore markets. This process had begun in the early 1990s. Yet the company's new effort turned away from the U.S. market (the Chun King brand was sold) and focused instead on expanding Yeo's reach in Southeast Asia through the Yeo and other brands.

Joint ventures played a prominent part in the company's international expansion. In 1993, for example, the company formed a joint venture with World Grain Co. in Thailand to launch WY Co. Ltd., which launched a variety of teas, fruit juices, and other noncarbonated soft drinks under the Eliza brand. By then, the company had been manufacturing soy milk under license in mainland China. In 1994, the company launched the Rengo International holding company joint venture in Hong Kong, which then launched the manufacturing and sales of instant noodles on the mainland. The launch of Xiamen Rengo marked a return of the company to its roots, of sorts, as the company set up a production plant in the Fujian province. By the end of the decade, Yeo operated six food and beverage production facilities in China.

Yeo turned to the Persian Gulf region in the early 2000s, setting up a subsidiary in Bahrain. The new unit provided sales and marketing support for Yeo's effort to extend its brand reach into the West Asian region. At the same time the company continued to look for opportunities to expand its product range at home as well. This led to a marketing and distribution agreement with Hain Celestial Group, a U.S.-based maker of organic and natural foods, as well as personal care products. Yeo appeared to have set its sights on remaining a major Asian foods and beverage group for its second century in business.

Principal Subsidiaries

Bestcan Food Technological Industry Sdn. Bhd.; Esin Canning Industry Sdn. Bhd.; Leong Sin Nam Farms Bhd.; Rengo International Investment Ltd. (Hong Kong; 54.83%); Sarawak Coconut Enterprise Sdn. Bhd.; Senawang Edible Oil (Sendirian) Bhd.; WY Co. Ltd. (Thailand; 50%); Xiamen Rengo Food. Co. Ltd. (China; 54.83%); Yeo Hiap Seng (Middle East) Co. Ltd. (Bahrain); Yeo Hiap Seng (Perak) Sdn. Bhd.; Yeo Hiap Seng Trading Sdn. Bhd.; YHS Beverage (International) Pte. Ltd. (Singapore).

Principal Competitors

Nestlé S.A.; Procter & Gamble Co.; Unilever PLC; Japan Tobacco Inc.; Coca-Cola Co.; Philip Morris USA; Taian Taishan Brewery; Groupe Danone; Lamson Sugar Co.; Xiamen Cannery.

Further Reading

''The Hain Celestial Group Inc. Completed Its Asian Alliance with Yeo Hiap Seng Limited,'' *Food Institute Report,* September 12, 2005, p. 7.

''Hain Celestial Plans Expansion into Asia,'' *Nutraceuticals International,* September 2005.

Jin, Foo Eu, ''YHS Steps Up Efforts to Boost Brand Name,'' *Business Times (Malaysia),* June 9, 1999.

''Pyrrhic Victory: Yeo Hiap Seng Feud,'' *Asia Inc.,* October 1994.

''Tea for Two: Battle for a Great Name and Address,'' *Asiaweek,* July 28, 1995.

''Yeo Hiap Seng Looking at Double Digit Growth This Yr,'' *Bernama—the Malaysian National News Agency,* May 23, 2001.

''Yeo Hiap Seng Malaysia Aims to Be Leading Food & Beverage Co.,'' *AsiaPulse News,* May 1, 2001, p. 139.

''YHS Credits Better Cost Management for 28pc Rise in Profit,'' *Business Times (Malaysia),* February 16, 2004.

''YHS Gets Acquisition Go-Ahead,'' *Business Times (Malaysia),* January 30, 2001.

''YHS Incorporates Bahrain Unit,'' *Business Times,* May 22, 2001.

''YHSM Chairman Announces Retirement,'' *New Straits Times,* May 25, 2002.

Zuraidah, Omar, ''Eat, Drink and Multi-Task,'' *Graduan,* 2001.

—M.L. Cohen

INDEX TO COMPANIES ———————————————————

Index to Companies

Listings in this index are arranged in alphabetical order under the company name. Company names beginning with a letter or proper name such as Eli Lilly & Co. will be found under the first letter of the company name. Definite articles (The, Le, La) are ignored for alphabetical purposes as are forms of incorporation that precede the company name (AB, NV). Company names printed in bold type have full, historical essays on the page numbers appearing in bold. Updates to entries that appeared in earlier volumes are signified by the notation **(upd.)**. Company names in light type are references within an essay to that company, not full historical essays. This index is cumulative with volume numbers printed in bold type.

413

American Improved Cements. *See* Giant Cement Holding, Inc.

American Independent Oil Co. *See* Aminoil, Inc.

American Industrial Properties. *See* Developers Diversified Realty Corporation.

American Information Services, Inc., **11** 111

American Institute of Certified Public Accountants (AICPA), 44 27–30

American Institutional Products, Inc., **18** 246

American Instrument Co., **13** 233

American Insurance Group, Inc., **73** 351

American International Airways, Inc., **17** 318; **22** 311

American International Group, Inc., III 195–98; **15** 15–19 (upd.); **47** 13–19 (upd.)

American Isuzu Motors, Inc. *See* Isuzu Motors, Ltd.

American Italian Pasta Company, 27 38–40

American Janitor Service, **25** 15

American Jet Industries, **7** 205

American Ka-Ro, **8** 476

American Kennel Club, Inc., 74 17–19

American Knitting Mills of Miami, Inc., **22** 213

American La-France, **10** 296

American Land Cruiser Company. *See* Cruise America Inc.

American Lawyer Media Holdings, Inc., 32 34–37

American Learning Corporation, **7** 168

American Light and Traction. *See* MCN Corporation.

American Lightwave Systems, Inc., **10** 19

American Limousine Corp., **26** 62

American Linen Supply Company. *See* Steiner Corporation.

American Locker Group Incorporated, 34 19–21

American Lung Association, 48 11–14

American Machine and Foundry Co., **7** 211–13; **11** 397; **25** 197

American Machine and Metals, **9** 23

American Machine and Tool Co., Inc., **57** 160

American Machinery and Foundry, Inc., **57** 85

American Maize-Products Co., 14 17–20; **23** 464

American Management Systems, Inc., 11 18–20

American Materials & Technologies Corporation, **27** 117

American Media, Inc., 27 41–44

American Medical Association, 39 15–18

American Medical Disposal, Inc. *See* Stericycle, Inc.

American Medical Holdings, **55** 370

American Medical International, Inc., III 73–75, 79; **14** 232

American Medical Optics, **25** 55

American Medical Response, Inc., 39 19–22

American Medical Services, **II** 679–80; **14** 209

American Medicorp, Inc., **14** 432; **24** 230

American Melamine, **27** 317

American Merchandising Associates Inc., **14** 411

American Metal Climax, Inc. *See* AMAX.

American Metals and Alloys, Inc., **19** 432

American Metals Corporation. *See* Reliance Steel & Aluminum Company.

American Micro Devices, Inc., **16** 549

The American Mineral Spirits Company, **8** 99–100

American Modern Insurance Group. *See* The Midland Company.

American Motors Corp., I 135–37; 8 373; **10** 262, 264; **18** 493; **26** 403

American MSI Corporation. *See* Moldflow Corporation.

American Multi-Cinema. *See* AMC Entertainment Inc.

American National Bank, **13** 221–22

American National Can Co., **IV** 175

American National General Agencies Inc., **III** 221; **14** 109; **37** 85

American National Insurance Company, 8 27–29; **27** 45–48 (upd.); **39** 158

American Natural Resources Co., **13** 416

American Natural Snacks Inc., **29** 480

American Oil Co., **7** 101; **14** 22

American Olean Tile Company, **III** 424; **22** 48, 170

American Optical Co., **7** 436; **38** 363–64

American Overseas Airlines, **12** 380

American Pad & Paper Company, 20 18–21

American Paging, **9** 494–96

American Paper Box Company, **12** 376

American Patriot Insurance, **22** 15

American Payment Systems, Inc., **21** 514

American Petrofina, Inc., **7** 179–80; **19** 11

American Pfauter, **24** 186

American Pharmaceutical Partners, Inc., 69 20–22

American Phone Centers, Inc., **21** 135

American Pop Corn Company, 59 40–43

American Port Services (Amports), **45** 29

American Power & Light Co., **6** 545, 596–97; **12** 542; **49** 143

American Power Conversion Corporation, 24 29–31; **67** 18–20 (upd.)

American Premier Underwriters, Inc., 10 71–74; **48** 9

American Prepaid Professional Services, Inc. *See* CompDent Corporation.

American President Companies Ltd., 6 353–55; **54** 274. *See also* APL Limited.

American Printing House for the Blind, 26 13–15

American Prospecting Equipment Co., **49** 174

American Public Automotive Group, **37** 115

American Publishing Co., **24** 222; **62** 188

American Re Corporation, 10 75–77; **35** 34–37 (upd.); **46** 303; **63** 13–14, 411–12

American Recreation Company Holdings, Inc., **16** 53; **44** 53–54

American Red Cross, 40 26–29

American Refrigeration Products S.A, **7** 429

American Reprographics Company, 75 24–26

American Research and Development Corp., **19** 103

American Residential Mortgage Corporation, 8 30–31

American Residential Services, **33** 141

American Retirement Corporation, 42 9–12; **43** 46

American Rice, Inc., 17 161–62; **33** 30–33

American Rug Craftsmen, **19** 275

American Safety Razor Company, 20 22–24

American Salt Co., **12** 199

American Satellite Co., **15** 195

American Savings & Loan, **10** 117

American Savings Bank, **9** 276; **17** 528, 531

American Sealants Company. *See* Loctite Corporation.

American Seating Co., **I** 447; **21** 33

American Seaway Foods, Inc, **9** 451

American Securities Capital Partners, L.P., **59** 13; **69** 138–39

American Service Corporation, **19** 223

American Shipbuilding, **18** 318

American Ships Ltd., **50** 209

American Skiing Company, 28 18–21; **31** 67, 229

American Sky Broadcasting, **27** 305; **35** 156

American Smelting and Refining Co. *See* ASARCO.

American Society for the Prevention of Cruelty to Animals (ASPCA), 68 19–22

The American Society of Composers, Authors and Publishers (ASCAP), 29 21–24

American Software Inc., 22 214; **25** 20–22

American Southern Insurance Co., **17** 196

American Standard Companies Inc., III 663–65; **19** 455; **22** 4, 6; **28** 486; **30** 46–50 (upd.); **40** 452

American States Water Company, 46 27–30

American Steamship Company. *See* GATX.

American Steel & Wire Co., **13** 97–98; **40** 70, 72

American Steel Foundries, **7** 29–30

American Stock Exchange, **10** 416–17; **54** 242

American Stores Company, II 604–06; **12** 63, 333; **13** 395; **17** 559; **18** 89; **22** 37–40 (upd.); **25** 297; **27** 290–92; **30** 24, 26–27. *See also* Albertson's, Inc.

American Sugar Refining Company. *See* Domino Sugar Corporation.

American Sumatra Tobacco Corp., **15** 138

American Superconductor Corporation, **41** 141

American Surety Co., **26** 486

American Systems Technologies, Inc., **18** 5

American Teaching Aids Inc., **19** 405

American Technical Ceramics Corp., 67 21–23

American Technical Services Company. *See* American Building Maintenance Industries, Inc.; ABM Industries Incorporated.

American Telephone and Telegraph Company. *See* AT&T.

American Television and Communications Corp., **IV** 675; **7** 528–30; **18** 65

American Textile Co., **III** 571; **20** 362

American Thermos Bottle Company. *See* Thermos Company.

American Threshold, **50** 123

Bakers Square. *See* VICORP Restaurants, Inc.

Bakersfield Savings and Loan, **10** 339

Bakery Feeds Inc. *See* Griffin Industries, Inc.

Bal-Sam India Holdings Ltd., **64** 95

Balance Bar Company, **32 70–72**

Balatongáz Kft. (Ltd), **70** 195

Balchem Corporation, **42 21–23**

Balco, Inc., **7** 479–80; **27** 415

Balcor, Inc., **10** 62

Bald Eagle Corporation, **45** 126

Baldor Electric Company, **21 42–44**

Baldwin & Lyons, Inc., **51 37–39**

Baldwin-Ehret-Hill Inc., **28** 42

Baldwin Filters, Inc., **17** 104

Baldwin Hardware Manufacturing Co. *See* Masco Corporation.

Baldwin-Montrose Chemical Co., Inc., **31** 110

Baldwin Piano & Organ Company, **16** 201; **18 43–46**

Baldwin Rubber Industries, **13** 79

Baldwin Technology Company, Inc., **25 35–39**

Baldwin-United Corp., **III** 254, 293; **52** 243–44

Balfour Beatty Construction Ltd., **III** 433–34; **36 56–60 (upd.)**; **58** 156–57

Balfour Company, L.G., **19** 451–52

Ball & Young Adhesives, **9** 92

Ball Corporation, **I** 597–98; **10 129–31 (upd.)**; **13** 254, 256; **15** 129; **16** 123; **30** 38; **64** 86

The Ball Ground Reps, Inc., **26** 257

Ball Industries, Inc., **26** 539

Ball Stalker Inc., **14** 4

Ballantine Books, **13** 429; **31** 376–77, 379

Ballantyne of Omaha, Inc., **27 56–58**

Ballard Medical Products, **21 45–48**

Ballard Power Systems Inc., **73 49–52**

Ballast Nedam Group, **24** 87–88

Ballet Makers-Europe, Ltd., **62** 59

Balli Group plc, **26** 527, 530

Bally Entertainment Corp., **19** 205, 207

Bally Gaming International, **15** 539

Bally Manufacturing Corporation, **III** 430–32; **10** 375, 482; **12** 107; **15** 538–39; **17** 316–17, 443; **41** 214–15; **53** 364–65

Bally Total Fitness Holding Corp., **25 40–42**

Bâloise-Holding, **40 59–62**

Baltek Corporation, **34 59–61**

Baltic Cable, **15** 521

Baltic International USA, **71** 35

Baltica, **27** 54

Baltika Brewery Joint Stock Company, **65 63–66**

Baltimar Overseas Limited, **25** 469

Baltimore & Ohio Railroad. *See* CSX Corporation.

Baltimore Aircoil Company, Inc., **7** 30–31; **66 27–29**

Baltimore Gas and Electric Company, **V** 552–54; **11** 388; **25 43–46 (upd.)**

Baltimore Orioles L.P., **66 30–33**

Baltimore Paper Box Company, **8** 102

Baltimore Technologies Plc, **42 24–26**

Baltino Foods, **13** 383

Balzers Process Systems GmbH, **48** 30

Banamex. *See* Banco Nacional de Mexico; Grupo Financiero Banamex S.A.

Banana Boat Holding Corp., **15** 359

Banana Brothers, **31** 229

Banana Importers of Ireland, **38** 197

Banana Republic Inc., **25 47–49**; **31** 51–52

Banc Internacional d'Andorra-Banca Mora, **48** 51

Banc One Corporation, **9** 475; **10 132–34**; **11** 181. *See also* Bank One Corporation.

Banca Commerciale Italiana SpA, **II 191–93**, 242, 271, 278, 295, 319; **17** 324; **50** 410

BancA Corp., **11** 305

Banca del Salento, **65** 73

Banca di Roma S.p.A., **65** 86, 88

Banca Esperia, **65** 230–31

Banca Fideuram SpA, **63 52–54**

Banca Intesa SpA, **65** 27, 29, **67–70**

Banca Monte dei Paschi di Siena SpA, **65 71–73**

Banca Nazionale del Lavoro SpA, **72 19–21**

Banca Nazionale dell'Agricoltura, **II** 272

Banca Serfin. *See* Grupo Financiero Serfin, S.A.

Bancard Systems, **24** 395

BancBoston Capital, **48** 412

Bancen. *See* Banco del Centro S.A.

BancFinancial Services Corporation, **25** 187

BancMortgage Financial Corp., **25** 185, 187

Banco Alianca S.A., **19** 34

Banco Azteca, **19** 189

Banco Bilbao Vizcaya Argentaria S.A., **48 47–51 (upd.)**

Banco Bilbao Vizcaya, S.A., **II 194–96**

Banco Bradesco S.A., **13 69–71**; **19** 33

Banco Capitalizador de Monterrey, **19** 189

Banco Central, **II 197–98**; **56** 65. *See also* Banco Santander Central Hispano S.A.

Banco Central de Crédito. *See* Banco Itaú.

Banco Chemical (Portugal) S.A. *See* Chemical Banking Corp.

Banco Comercial, **19** 188

Banco Comercial de Puerto Rico, **41** 311

Banco Comercial Português, SA, **50 69–72**

Banco Credito y Ahorro Ponceno, **41** 312

Banco da América, **19** 34

Banco de Chile, **69 55–57**

Banco de Comercio, S.A. *See* Grupo Financiero BBVA Bancomer S.A.

Banco de Credito Local, **48** 51

Banco de Credito y Servicio, **51** 151

Banco de Galicia y Buenos Aires, S.A., **63** 178–80

Banco de Londres, Mexico y Sudamerica. *See* Grupo Financiero Serfin, S.A.

Banco de Madrid, **40** 147

Banco de Mexico, **19** 189

Banco de Ponce, **41** 313

Banco del Centro S.A., **51** 150

Banco del Norte, **19** 189

Banco di Roma, **II**, 257, 271

Banco di Santo Spirito, **I** 467

Banco di Sicilia S.p.A., **65** 86, 88

Banco do Brasil S.A., **II 199–200**

Banco Español de Credito, **II** 198

Banco Espírito Santo e Comercial de Lisboa S.A., **15 38–40**

Banco Federal de Crédito. *See* Banco Itaú.

Banco Frances y Brasiliero, **19** 34

Banco Industrial de Monterrey, **19** 189

Banco Itaú S.A., **19 33–35**

Banco Mercantil del Norte, S.A., **51** 149

Banco Nacional de Mexico, **9** 333; **19** 188, 193

Banco Opportunity, **57** 67, 69

Banco Pinto de Mahalhães, **19** 34

Banco Popolar. *See* Popular, Inc.

Banco Português do Brasil S.A., **19** 34

Banco Santander Central Hispano S.A., **36 61–64 (upd.)**; **42** 349; **63** 179

Banco Santander-Chile, **71** 143

Banco Serfin, **34** 82

Banco Sul Americano S.A., **19** 34

Banco União Comercial, **19** 34

BancOhio National Bank in Columbus, **9** 475

Bancomer S.A. *See* Grupo Financiero BBVA Bancomer S.A.

Bancorp Leasing, Inc., **14** 529

BancorpSouth, Inc., **14 40–41**

Bancrecer. *See* Banco de Credito y Servicio.

BancSystems Association Inc., **9** 475, 476

Bandag, Inc., **19 36–38**, 454–56

Bandai Co., Ltd., **23** 388; **25** 488; **38** 415; **55 44–48**; **61** 202; **67** 274

Bando McGlocklin Small Business Lending Corporation, **53** 222–24

Banesto. *See* Banco Español de Credito.

Banfi Products Corp., **36 65–67**

Banfield, The Pet Hospital. *See* Medical Management International, Inc.

Bang & Olufsen Holding A/S, **37 25–28**

Bangkok Airport Hotel. *See* Thai Airways International.

Bangkok Aviation Fuel Services Ltd. *See* Thai Airways International.

Bangladesh Krishi Bank, **31** 220

Bangor and Aroostook Railroad Company, **8** 33

Bangor Mills, **13** 169

Bangor Punta Alegre Sugar Corp., **30** 425

Banister Continental Corp. *See* BFC Construction Corporation.

Bank Austria AG, **23 37–39**; **59** 239

Bank Brussels Lambert, **II 201–03**, 295, 407

Bank Central Asia, **18** 181; **62** 96, 98

Bank du Louvre, **27** 423

Bank für Elektrische Unternehmungen. *See* Elektrowatt AG.

Bank Hapoalim B.M., **II 204–06**; **25** 266, 268; **54 33–37 (upd.)**

Bank Hofmann, **21** 146–47

Bank Leumi le-Israel B.M., **25** 268; **60 48–51**

Bank of America Corporation, **9** 50, 123–24, 333, 536; **12** 106, 466; **14** 170; **18** 516; **22** 542; **25** 432; **26** 486; **46 47–54 (upd.)**; **47** 37

The Bank of Bishop and Co., Ltd., **11** 114

Bank of Boston Corporation, **II 207–09**; **7** 114; **12** 31; **13** 467; **14** 90. *See also* FleetBoston Financial Corporation.

Bank of Brandywine Valley, **25** 542

Bank of Britain, **14 46–47**

Bank of China, **63 55–57**

Bank of Delaware, **25** 542

Bank of East Asia Ltd., **63 58–60**

Bank of England, **10** 8, 336; **14 45–46**; **47** 227

Bank of Hawaii Corporation, **73 53–56**

432 INDEX TO COMPANIES

Compañia Mexicana de Transportación Aérea, **20** 167
Compania Minera de Penoles. *See* Industrias Penoles, S.A. de C.V.
Compania Minera Las Torres, **22** 286
Compania Siderurgica Huachipato, **24** 209
Compañía Telefónica Nacional de España S.A. *See* Telefónica Nacional de España S.A.
Compaq Computer Corporation, III 124–25; 6 221–23 (upd.); 26 90–93 (upd.). *See also* Hewlett-Packard Company.
Comparex Holdings, **69** 127
Compart, **24** 341
Compass Airlines, **27** 475
Compass Bancshares, Inc., 73 92–94
Compass Design Automation, **16** 520
Compass Group PLC, 6 193; **24** 194; **27** 482; **34 121–24**
CompDent Corporation, 22 149–51
Compeda, Ltd., **10** 240
Competence ApS, **26** 240
Competrol Ltd., **22** 189
CompHealth Inc., 25 109–12
Complete Business Solutions, Inc., 31 130–33
Complete Post, **50** 126
Completion Bond Co., **26** 487
Components Agents Ltd., **10** 113; **50** 43
Composite Craft Inc., **I** 387
Composite Research & Management Co., **17** 528, 530
Comprehensive Care Corporation, 15 121–23
Compression Labs Inc., **10** 456; **16** 392, 394; **27** 365
Compressor Controls Corporation, **15** 404; **50** 394
Comptoir Général de la Photographie. *See* Gaumont SA.
Comptoir Métallurgique Luxembourgeois, **IV** 25
Comptoirs Modernes S.A., 19 97–99
Compton Foods, **II** 675
Compton's MultiMedia Publishing Group, Inc., **7** 165
Compton's New Media, Inc., **7** 168
Compu-Notes, Inc., **22** 413
CompuAdd Computer Corporation, 11 61–63
CompuChem Corporation, **11** 425
CompuCom Systems, Inc., 10 232–34, 474; **13** 176
CompuDyne Corporation, 51 78–81
Compumech Technologies, **19** 312
CompuPharm, Inc., **14** 210
CompUSA, Inc., 10 235–36; 35 116–18 (upd.)
Compuscript, Inc., **64** 27
CompuServe Incorporated, 9 268–70; 10 237–39; 12 562; **13** 147; **15** 265; **16** 467, 508; **26** 16; **29** 224, 226–27; **34** 361; **50** 329. *See also* America Online, Inc.
CompuServe Interactive Services, Inc., 27 106, **106–08 (upd.),** 301, 307; **57** 42. *See also* AOL Time Warner Inc.
Computer Associates International, Inc., 6 224–26; 10 394; **12** 62; **14** 392; **27** 492; **49 94–97 (upd.)**
Computer City, **12** 470; **36** 387
The Computer Company, **11** 112
Computer Consoles Inc., **III** 164

Computer Data Systems, Inc., 14 127–29
The Computer Department, Ltd., **10** 89
Computer Discount Corporation. *See* Comdisco, Inc.
Computer Discount Warehouse. *See* CDW Computer Centers, Inc.
Computer Engineering Associates, **25** 303
Computer Factory, Inc., **13** 176
Computer Learning Centers, Inc., 26 94–96
Computer Network Technology Corporation, **75** 256
Computer Peripheral Manufacturers Association, **13** 127
Computer Power, **6** 301
Computer Renaissance, Inc., **18** 207–8
Computer Resources Management, Inc., **26** 36
Computer Sciences Corporation, 6 25, **227–29; 13** 462; **15** 474; **18** 370
Computer Systems and Applications, **12** 442
Computer Systems Division (CDS), **13** 201
Computer Terminal Corporation, **11** 67–68
ComputerCity, **10** 235
ComputerCraft, **27** 163
Computerized Lodging Systems, Inc., **11** 275
Computerized Waste Systems, **46** 248
ComputerLand Corp., 13 174–76; 33 341–42
Computervision Corporation, 7 498; **10 240–42; 11** 275; **13** 201
Compuware Corporation, 10 243–45; 30 140–43 (upd.); 38 482; **66 60–64 (upd.)**
CompX International, Inc., **19** 466, 468
Comsat Corporation, 13 341; **23 133–36; 28** 241; **29** 42
Comshare Inc., 23 137–39
Comstock Canada, **9** 301
Comstock Resources, Inc., 47 85–87
Comtec Information Systems Inc., **53** 374
Comtech Telecommunications Corp., 75 103–05
Comtel Electronics, Inc., **22** 409
Comunicaciones Avanzados, S.A. de C.V., **39** 195
Comverse Technology, Inc., 15 124–26; 43 115–18 (upd.)
Comviq GSM AB, **26** 331–33
Con Ed. *See* Consolidated Edison, Inc.
Con-Ferro Paint and Varnish Company, **8** 553
ConAgra, Inc., II 493–95, 517, 585; **7** 432, 525; **8** 53, 499–500; **12 80–82 (upd.); 13** 138, 294, 350, 352; **14** 515; **17** 56, 240–41; **18** 247, 290; **21** 290; **23** 320; **25** 243, 278; **26** 172, 174; **36** 416; **42 90–94 (upd.); 50** 275, 295, 493; **55** 364–65; **64** 61
Conair Corporation, 16 539; **17 108–10; 24** 131; **25** 56; **69 104–08 (upd.)**
Concentra Inc., 71 117–19
Concept, Inc., **23** 154
Concepts Direct, Inc., 39 93–96
Concepts in Community Living, Inc., **43** 46
Concert Communications Company, **15** 69; **27** 304–05; **49** 72
Concesiones de Infraestructuras de Transportes, S.A., **40** 217
Concession Air, **16** 446
Concha y Toro. *See* Viña Concha y Toro S.A.

Concord Camera Corporation, 41 104–07
Concord EFS, Inc., 52 86–88
Concord Fabrics, Inc., 16 124–26
Concord Leasing, Inc., **51** 108
Concord Watch Company, S.A., **28** 291
Concorde Acceptance Corporation, **64** 20–21
Concorde Hotels & Resorts, **27** 421; **71** 176
Concrete Enterprises, Inc., **72** 233
Concrete Safety Systems, Inc., **56** 332
Concretos Apasco, S.A. de C.V., **51** 28–29
Concurrent Computer Corporation, 75 106–08
Condé Nast Publications, Inc., 13 177–81; 59 131–34 (upd.)
CONDEA Vista Company, **61** 113
Condor Systems Inc., **15** 530
Cone Communications, **25** 258
Cone Mills LLC, 8 120–22; 67 123–27 (upd.)
Conelectron, **13** 398
Conexant Systems, Inc., 36 121–25; 43 328
Confecciones Cuscatlecas, S.A. de C.V., **64** 142
Confectionaire, **25** 283
Confederacion Norte-Centromericana y del Caribe de Futbol, **27** 150
Confederacion Sudamericana de Futbol, **27** 150
Confederation Africaine de Football, **27** 150
Confederation Freezers, **21** 501
ConferencePlus, Inc., **57** 408–09
Confidata Corporation, **11** 111
Confiserie-Group Hofbauer, **27** 105
Confiseriefabrik Richterich & Co. Laufen. *See* Ricola Ltd.
Congas Engineering Canada Ltd., **6** 478
Congoleum Corp., 12 28; **16** 18; **18 116–19; 36** 77–78; **43** 19, 21; **63** 300
Congress Financial Corp., **13** 305–06; **19** 108; **27** 276
Congressional Information Services. *See* Reed Elsevier.
Conic, **9** 324
Conifer Records Ltd., **52** 429
Coniston Partners, **I** 130; **II** 680; **6** 130; **10** 302
Conn-Selmer, Inc., 55 111–14
Conn's, Inc., 67 128–30
CONNA Corp., **7** 113; **25** 125
Connect Group Corporation, **28** 242
Connecticut General Corporation. *See* CIGNA Corporation.
Connecticut Health Enterprises Network, **22** 425
Connecticut Light and Power Co., 13 182–84; 21 514; **48** 305
Connecticut Mutual Life Insurance Company, III 236–38, 254, 285
Connecticut National Bank, **13** 467
Connecticut River Banking Company, **13** 467
Connecticut Telephone Company. *See* Southern New England Telecommunications Corporation.
Connecticut Yankee Atomic Power Company, **21** 513
The Connection Group, Inc., **26** 257
Connective Therapeutics, Inc. *See* Connetics Corporation.

Franco-American Food Company. *See* Campbell Soup Company.
Francodex Laboratories, Inc., **74** 381
Frank & Pignard SA, **51** 35
Frank & Schulte GmbH, **8** 496
Frank Dry Goods Company, **9** 121
Frank H. Nott Inc., **14** 156
Frank Holton Company, **55** 149, 151
Frank J. Rooney, Inc., **8** 87
Frank J. Zamboni & Co., Inc., 34 173–76
Frank Russell Company, 45 316; **46 198–200**
Frank Schaffer Publications, **19** 405; **29** 470, 472
Frank W. Horner, Ltd., **38** 123
Frank's Nursery & Crafts, Inc., 12 178–79, 198–200
Frankel & Co., 39 166–69
Frankenberry, Laughlin & Constable, **9** 393
Frankford-Quaker Grocery Co., **II** 625
Frankfurter Allgemeine Zeitung GmbH, 66 121–24
Franklin Assurances, **III** 211
Franklin Brass Manufacturing Company, **20** 363
Franklin Coach, **56** 223
Franklin Container Corp., **IV** 312; **19** 267
Franklin Corp., **14** 130; **41** 388
Franklin Covey Company, 11 147–49; 37 149–52 (upd.)
Franklin Electric Company, Inc., 43 177–80
Franklin Electronic Publishers, Inc., 23 209–13
The Franklin Mint, **9** 428; **37** 337–38; **69 181–84**
Franklin Mutual Advisors LLC, **52** 119, 172
Franklin National Bank, **9** 536
Franklin Plastics, **19** 414
Franklin Research & Development, **11** 41
Franklin Resources, Inc., 9 239–40
Franklin Sports, Inc., **17** 243
Franklin Steamship Corp., **8** 346
Frans Maas Beheer BV, **14** 568
Franzia. *See* The Wine Group, Inc.
Frape Behr S.A. *See* Behr GmbH & Co. KG.
Fraser & Chalmers, **13** 16
Fraser & Neave Ltd., 54 116–18; 59 58–59
Fray Data International, **14** 319
Frazer & Jones, **48** 141
FRE Composites Inc., **69** 206
Fred Campbell Auto Supply, **26** 347
Fred Meyer Stores, Inc., II 669; **V 54–56; 18** 505; **20 222–25 (upd.); 35** 370; **50** 455; **64 135–39 (upd.)**
Fred Sammons Company of Chicago, **30** 77
Fred Schmid Appliance & T.V. Co., Inc., **10** 305; **18** 532
Fred Usinger Inc., 54 119–21
The Fred W. Albrecht Grocery Co., 13 236–38
Fred Weber, Inc., 61 100–02
Fred's, Inc., 23 214–16; 62 144–47 (upd.)
Freddie Mac, 54 122–25
Fredelle, **14** 295
Frederick & Nelson, **17** 462
Frederick Atkins Inc., 16 215–17
Frederick Bayer & Company, **22** 225

Frederick Gas Company, **19** 487
Frederick Manufacturing Corporation, **26** 119; **48** 59
Frederick's of Hollywood Inc., 16 218–20; 25 521; **59 190–93 (upd.)**
Fredrickson Motor Express, **57** 277
Free-lance Uitzendburo, **26** 240
Free People LLC. *See* Urban Outfitters, Inc.
Freeborn Farms, **13** 244
Freedom Communications, Inc., 36 222–25
Freedom Group Inc., **42** 10–11
Freedom Technology, **11** 486
Freeman Chemical Corporation, **61** 111–12
Freeman, Spogli & Co., **17** 366; **18** 90; **32** 12, 15; **35** 276; **36** 358–59; **47** 142–43; **57** 11, 242
Freemans. *See* Sears plc.
FreeMark Communications, **38** 269
Freeport-McMoRan Copper & Gold, Inc., IV 81–84; **7 185–89 (upd.); 16** 29; **23** 40; **57 145–50 (upd.)**
Freeport Power, **38** 448
Freezer Queen Foods, Inc., **21** 509
Freezer Shirt Corporation, **8** 406
Freight Car Services, Inc., **23** 306
Freight Outlet, **17** 297
Freixenet S.A., 71 162–64
Frejlack Ice Cream Co., **II** 646; **7** 317
Fremont Canning Company, **7** 196
Fremont Group, **21** 97
Fremont Investors, **30** 268
Fremont Partners, **24** 265
Fremont Savings Bank, **9** 474–75
French Connection Group plc, 41 167–69
French Fragrances, Inc., 22 213–15; 40 170. *See also* Elizabeth Arden, Inc.
French Kier, **I** 568
French Quarter Coffee Co., **27** 480–81
Frequency Electronics, Inc., 61 103–05
Frequency Sources Inc., **9** 324
Fresenius AG, 22 360; **49** 155–56; **56 138–42**
Fresh America Corporation, 20 226–28
Fresh Choice, Inc., 20 229–32
Fresh Enterprises, Inc., 66 125–27
Fresh Fields, **19** 501
Fresh Foods, Inc., 25 391; **29 201–03**
Fresh Start Bakeries, **26** 58
Freshbake Foods Group PLC, **II** 481; **7** 68; **25** 518; **26** 57
Fretter, Inc., 9 65; **10** 9–10, **304–06**, 502; **19** 124; **23** 52
Freudenberg & Co., 41 170–73
Friction Products Co., **59** 222
Frictiontech Inc., **11** 84
Friday's Front Row Sports Grill, **22** 128
Friden, Inc., **30** 418; **53** 237
Fried, Frank, Harris, Shriver & Jacobson, 35 183–86
Fried. Krupp GmbH, IV 85–89, 104, 128, 203, 206, 222, 234. *See also* Thyssen Krupp AG.
Friede Goldman Halter, **61** 43
Friedman, Billings, Ramsey Group, Inc., 53 134–37
Friedman's Inc., 29 204–06
Friedrich Grohe AG & Co. KG, 53 138–41
Friendly Hotels PLC, **14** 107
Friendly Ice Cream Corporation, 30 208–10; 72 141–44 (upd.)

Friesland Coberco Dairy Foods Holding N.V., 59 194–96
Frigidaire Home Products, 13 564; **19** 361; **22** 28, **216–18**, 349
Frigoscandia AB, **57** 300
Frimont S.p.A, **68** 136
Frisby P.M.C. Incorporated, **16** 475
Frisch's Restaurants, Inc., 35 187–89
Frisdranken Industries Winters B.V., **22** 515
Frisk Int. Nv, **72** 272
Frito-Lay North America, 32 205–10; **73 151–58 (upd.)**
Fritz Companies, Inc., 12 180–82
Fritz Gegauf AG. *See* Bernina Holding AG.
Fritz Schömer, **75** 56–57
Fritz W. Glitsch and Sons, Inc. *See* Glitsch International, Inc.
Frolich Intercon International, **57** 174
Fromagerie d'Illoud. *See* Bongrain SA.
La Fromagerie du Velay, **25** 85
Fromagerie Paul Renard, **25** 85
Fromageries Bel, 19 51; **23 217–19; 25 83–84**
Fromageries des Chaumes, **25** 84
Fromarsac, **25** 84
Frome Broken Hill Co., **IV** 59
Front Range Pipeline LLC, **60** 88
Frontec, **13** 132
Frontenac Co., **24** 45
Frontier Airlines, Inc., I 103, 118, 124, 129–30; **11** 298; **22 219–21; 25** 421; **26** 439–40; **39** 33
Frontier Communications, **32** 216, 218
Frontier Corp., 16 221–23; 18 164
Frontier Electronics, **19** 311
Frontier Expeditors, Inc., **12** 363
Frontier Pacific Insurance Company, **21** 263
Frontier Vision Partners L.P., **52** 9
FrontLine Capital Group, **47** 330–31
Frontline Ltd., 45 163–65
Frontstep Inc., **55** 258
Frosch Touristik, **27** 29
Frost & Sullivan, Inc., 53 142–44
Frost National Bank. *See* Cullen/Frost Bankers, Inc.
Frozen Food Express Industries, Inc., 20 233–35; 27 404
Fru-Con Holding Corporation, **I** 561; **55** 62
Fruehauf Corp., I 169–70, 480; **7** 259–60, 513–14; **27** 202–03, 251; **40** 432
Fruit of the Loom, Inc., 8 200–02; **16** 535; **25 164–67 (upd.); 54** 403
The Frustum Group Inc., **45** 280
Fruth Pharmacy, Inc., 66 128–30
Fry's Electronics, Inc., 68 168–70
Fry's Food Stores, **12** 112
Frye Copy Systems, **6** 599
Frymaster Corporation, 27 159–62
FSA Corporation, **25** 349
FSI International, Inc., 17 192–94. *See also* FlightSafety International, Inc.
FSP. *See* Frank Schaffer Publications.
FT Freeport Indonesia, **57** 145
FTD. *See* Florists Transworld Delivery, Inc.
F3 Software Corp., **15** 474
FTP Software, Inc., 20 236–38
Fubu, 29 207–09
Fuddruckers, **27** 480–82

INDEX TO INDUSTRIES ————————————————

Index to Industries

ACCOUNTING

ADVERTISING & OTHER BUSINESS SERVICES

CONSTRUCTION

ELECTRICAL & ELECTRONICS

ENGINEERING & MANAGEMENT SERVICES

ENTERTAINMENT & LEISURE

FOOD PRODUCTS

HOTELS

INFORMATION TECHNOLOGY

INSURANCE

MANUFACTURING

PERSONAL SERVICES

PETROLEUM

PUBLISHING & PRINTING

GEOGRAPHIC INDEX

Geographic Index

Ghana

Greece

United States

Vatican City

Venezuela

Vietnam

Virgin Islands

Wales

Zambia

NOTES ON CONTRIBUTORS ─────────────────────

Notes on Contributors

COHEN, M.L. Novelist and researcher living in Paris.

COVELL, Jeffrey L. Seattle-based writer.

CULLIGAN, Susan B. Minnesota-based writer.

DINGER, Ed. Writer and editor based in Bronx, New York.

HALASZ, Robert. Former editor in chief of *World Progress* and *Funk & Wagnalls New Encyclopedia Yearbook*; author, *The U.S. Marines* (Millbrook Press, 1993).

HEER-FORSBERG, Mary. Minneapolis-based researcher and writer.

INGRAM, Frederick C. Utah-based business writer who has contributed to *GSA Business, Appalachian Trailway News,* the *Encyclopedia of Business,* the *Encyclopedia of Global Industries,* the *Encyclopedia of Consumer Brands,* and other regional and trade publications.

PEIPPO, Kathleen. Minneapolis-based writer.

POGINY, Sara. Ohio-based writer.

RHODES, Nelson. Editor, writer, and consultant in the Chicago area.

ROTHBURD, Carrie. Writer and editor specializing in corporate profiles, academic texts, and academic journal articles.

SALAMIE, David E. Part-owner of InfoWorks Development Group, a reference publication development and editorial services company.

UHLE, Frank. Ann Arbor-based writer; movie projectionist, disc jockey, and staff member of *Psychotronic Video* magazine.